MUSICALS!

A Complete Selection Guide for Local Productions

second edition

RICHARD CHIGLEY LYNCH

W9-BON-423

AMERICAN LIBRARY ASSOCIATION
Chicago and London 1994

Managing Editor: Joan A. Grygel

Text designed by Dianne Rooney

Cover designed by Mark S. Hoover, Digital Graphics, Inc.

Composed by Digital Graphics, Inc. in Cheltenham, using TeX

Printed on 50-lb Springhill, a pH-neutral stock, and bound in 10-point C1S cover stock by Braun-Brumfield, Inc.

The paper used in this publication meets the minimum requirements of American National Standard for Information Sciences—Permanence of Paper for Printed Library Materials, ANSI Z39.48-1984. ∞

Library of Congress Cataloging-in-Publication Data

Lynch, Richard Chigley, 1932–
    Musicals! : a complete selection guide for local productions / Richard Chigley Lynch. — 2nd ed.
       p.   cm.
    Includes indexes.
    ISBN 0-8389-0627-3
     1. Musicals—Directories. I. Title.
    ML19.L9   1993
    782.1'4'02573—dc20   93-27387

Printed in the United States of America.

97 96 95 94   5 4 3 2 1

Contents

Introduction

Travelers to London have often noticed the popularity of American musicals there. But recently Budapest, Tokyo, and even Beijing have seen productions of *Sweeney Todd*, *Grand Hotel*, and *The Music Man*. On-Broadway revivals of *Guys and Dolls* and *The Most Happy Fella* appear alongside the newer entries. Off-Broadway frequently sees revivals of such properties as *Anyway Can Whistle* and *Jacques Brel Is Alive and Well*. . . . What does this mean? Only that the American musical is "alive and well" in the cities of the world.

The strongest evidence of the musical's continued appeal is found in the thousands of amateur theater companies that stage musicals throughout this country each year. By involving local citizens in all phases of a musical's production—including acting, directing, conducting, costuming, publicity, financing, and many other areas—the amateur theater company thus informs, entertains, and ultimately enriches the lives of its community members. As with the first edition, the purpose of this revision is to help the amateur company answer the question, "What musical shall we do next?"

A frequent question asked after the first edition was published was why certain shows were not included. There are many reasons why a certain property has not been licensed for production, the main one being that the owners of the property are not interested in having it performed. Even professional companies sometimes are unable to present a show they had advertised when the composer or author suddenly changes his mind about the advisability of allowing a new production. *Musicals!* offers a detailed compilation of almost 500 musical properties currently available for production. More than 100 new titles have been added. A few from the first edition have been deleted, either because they were not really musicals, or they have been dropped from the licensing agents' catalogs.

The entries have been expanded to include additional information, thus making this a handy reference guide to musicals. Listed in each entry are title, date of production, playwright, composer, lyricist, and a plot summary. A new feature of this edition is the addition of the original cast, the parts they played, and the songs they sang. If a production was revived, the revival cast may be listed and the songs are those in the revival. Not all song titles were available, and certain revues made up of nonoriginal songs or songs from other shows have not been included. Sound recordings were reviewed in order to designate the latest releases and casts. This book allows amateurs to sample shows by directing them to available sound recordings and librettos that might be used when the group gathers to discuss performances. The licensing agent for each musical was likewise reviewed in order to ensure its availability.

What musical to do next? Take your pick.

On Using This Book

Musicals! consists of an alphabetical listing, by title, of approximately 500 currently available musical properties. The reader will also find these properties entered by composer, lyricist, and librettist in the index at the end of the book.

The date following each entry indicates the first New York production. In those few cases where there was no New York production, the originating city is given.

Credits for writers, composers, lyricists, and source materials have been taken from programs, posters, and LP and CD recordings. The descriptive paragraph about each show has been drawn from published reviews, catalogs, album notes, and personal recollection. It is intended to give an idea of the musical's plot, locale, time period, audience suitability, and anything else that might be of interest to the theater amateur.

Unless otherwise identified, "original cast" means the New York production's cast. The characters they play and the songs they sing have been taken primarily from programs, although published scripts, reviews, and such sources as *Best Plays* have occasionally been used. Overtures, finales, and reprises by the same characters have been deleted.

For purposes of this directory, *piano-vocal score* refers to the complete score; *vocal selections* refers to the major songs. Occasionally, *music publisher* is indicated and refers to songbooks or individual songs. A great deal of the published material, including all LP recordings, is out of print but perhaps can be located through a library or a collector. In addition, a licensing agency normally will provide you with scripts, scores, and occasionally even a cassette recording of the score on request. Each entry provides the name of the licensing agent, and the list of agents in the appendix provides addresses of the nine agencies that control the rights to these musicals. A selected few titles not yet available have been included, as it is assumed they soon will be available and that there will be considerable amateur interest.

The reader should note that licensing agents and script availability change from time to time. A successful revival on Broadway, for example, may result in sudden restrictions on amateur productions. In any and all cases, amateur theater companies *must* obtain agency permission before beginning production on *any* musical.

Titles not included in the directory were not available for production at the time the book was being compiled. If you wish to stage a musical that is not listed here, first ask all the licensing agencies if they control it or if they know who does. If no one can help you, then you might seek out the copyright owners, or their estates, and make your own financial arrangements. If you have a script or score, contact first the publishers of the material. Other sources for help include:

Authors League of America, Inc. (for older or deceased writers)
    330 West 42nd Street
    New York, NY 10036
    (212) 564-8350

Dramatists Guild, Inc. (for current writers)
    234 West 44th Street
    New York 10036
    (212) 398-9366

American Society of Composers, Authors, and Publishers (ASCAP)
    One Lincoln Plaza
    New York, NY 10023
    (212) 595-3050

Broadway Music, Inc. (BMI)
    320 West 57th Street
    New York, NY 10019
    (212) 586-2000

In compiling *Musicals!* the most recent catalogs of the nine major licensing agents were examined. To obtain a list of published material, the following sources were used: the *Play Index,* published by H. W. Wilson; Books in Print, published by R. R. Bowker; and the *Dictionary Catalog of the Research Libraries of the New York Public Library* (including the music and theater collections), published by G. K. Hall. More current material was located by using the reader-friendly computers of both the research and branch libraries of the New York Public Library.

Musicals Available for Production

A . . . MY NAME IS ALICE (1984)

CONCEIVED BY: Joan Micklin Silver and Julianne Boyd; material from various contributors
PUBLISHED LIBRETTO: French, 1985
CONDENSATION: None
ANTHOLOGY: None
LICENSING AGENT: Samuel French
RECORDING: None
CAST: 5 F

In this revue about the problems and pleasures of being a woman, five song-and-dance women perform over two dozen songs and sketches. Subjects include an excursion into a male strip club, a competition to decide who is the most depressed, and a close analysis of sexual imagery in blues lyrics. This was most successful in an off-Broadway cabaret setting with simple staging and props. *A . . . My Name Is Still Alice*, a revised version of this show, was presented off-Broadway in 1992.

ORIGINAL CAST:

Roo Brown
Mary Gordon Murray
Charlaine Woodard
Randy Graff
Alaina Reed

SONGS:

Act I
All Girl Band (cast)
At My Age (Brown, Graff)
Trash (cast)
Good Thing I Learned to Dance (Woodard)
Welcome to Kindergarten (Murray, Brown)
I Sure Like the Boys (Graff)
The Portrait (Murray)
Bluer than You (Graff, Reed, Brown)

Act II
Pretty Young Men (Murray, Reed, Brown)
The French Song (Murray)
Pay Them No Mind (Reed)
Emily, the M.B.A. (Graff, Reed, Woodard, Murray)
Sisters (Brown)
Honey Pot (Graff, Reed)

THE ACT (1977)

BOOK BY: George Furth
MUSIC BY: John Kander
LYRICS BY: Fred Ebb
PUBLISHED LIBRETTO: French, 1987
CONDENSATION: None
ANTHOLOGY: None
VOCAL SELECTIONS: Chappell (Presser, 1987)
LICENSING AGENT: Samuel French
RECORDING: DRG 6101 CD (original cast)
CAST: 5 M; 2 F; plus male and female ensemble

Liza Minnelli starred in this musical as "Michelle Craig," an insecure movie star making her debut as a cabaret artist in a Las Vegas nightclub. All the numbers in this musical are performed by "Michelle" as part of her act, with occasional help from her backup group. In between the numbers there are flashbacks of her personal life with its troubles and triumphs. All the other cast members are speaking roles in these scenes. Brendan Gill wrote in the *New Yorker* of the "knock-your-eye-out-song-and-dance-numbers" so your production will require a dynamic female talent to carry this off.

ORIGINAL CAST:

Christopher Barrett (Lenny Kanter)
Arnold Soboloff (Nat Schreiber)
Roger Minami (Arthur)
Gayle Crofoot (Molly Connors)
Liza Minnelli (Michelle Craig)
Barry Nelson (Dan Connors)
Mark Goddard (Charley Pride)

SONGS:
Act I
Shine It On (Michelle, chorus)
It's the Strangest Thing (Michelle)
Bobo's (Michelle)
Turning (Shaker Hymn) (Michelle, chorus)
Little Do They Know (Michelle, Molly, chorus)
Arthur in the Afternoon (Michelle)
The Money Tree (Michelle)

Act II
City Lights (Michelle, chorus)

There When I Need Him (Michelle)
Hot Enough for You? (Michelle, chorus)
Little Do They Know (reprise) (chorus)
My Own Space (Michelle)
Walking Papers (Michelle, chorus)

AIN'T MISBEHAVIN' (1978)

MUSIC PRIMARILY BY: Thomas "Fats" Waller; based on an idea by Murray Horowitz and Richard Maltby, Jr.
PUBLISHED LIBRETTO: None
CONDENSATION: *Broadway Musicals Show by Show.* Stanley Green. Hal Leonard, 1985
ANTHOLOGY: None
VOCAL SELECTIONS: Big Three, 1978
LICENSING AGENT: Music Theatre International
RECORDING: RCA 2965-2-RC CD (original cast)
CAST: 2 M; 3 F

The small cast (variable), backed by a piano and small band, presents thirty songs composed or performed by Fats Waller. This is a musical revue with solos, group numbers, and some instrumentals presented in a simple cabaret setting with no dialogue. There was a later TV production. Some of the songs, performed in 1930s and 1940s Harlem style, include "Honeysuckle Rose," "Mean to Me," and "The Joint Is Jumpin'." Strong musical talents and personalities are required. This show made a star of Nell Carter.

Tony Award Winner (Best Musical)

ORIGINAL CAST:

Nell Carter
Armelia McQueen
Charlaine Woodard
Andre DeShields
Ken Page

This revue is made up of thirty songs divided into two acts.

ALICE IN CONCERT (1981)

BOOK, MUSIC, AND LYRICS BY: Elizabeth Swados;
  musical adaption based on *Alice in Wonderland*
  and *Through the Looking Glass* by Lewis Carroll
PUBLISHED LIBRETTO: French, 1985
CONDENSATION: None
ANTHOLOGY: None
LICENSING AGENT: Samuel French
RECORDING: None
CAST: 6 M; 6 F; 7-piece combo

Presented off-Broadway at the Public Theatre, this was a great success for Meryl Streep as "Alice." The following year she did it on television under the title "Alice at the Palace." While there was some critical comment that it had only a slight connection with its source material, most enjoyed the various rhythms (including calypso, county-western, and rock and roll) and the spirited cast. The musicians are on stage, and the production is choreographed beyond that of a concert. Costumes are basic, almost rehearsal clothes, with "Alice" in oversize coveralls. It is performed on a bare stage with only a few streamers for decor and a few basic props.

ORIGINAL CAST (IN A VARIETY OF ROLES):

Meryl Streep (Alice)

Stuart Baker-Bergen	Sheila Dabney
Betty Aberlin	Richard Cox
Rodney Hudson	Michael Jeter
Mark Linn-Baker	Amanda Plummer
Charles Lanyer	Kathryn Morath
Deborah Rush	

SONGS:
Act I
What There Is (Streep)
The Rabbit's Excuse (Linn-Baker, company)
Down Down Down (Streep, Aberlin, company)
Drink Me (Rush, Hudson, Jeter, Baker-Bergen, company)
Good-bye Feet (Streep, company)
The Rabbit's House (Jeter, Plummer, company)
Bill's Lament (Jeter, men)
Caterpillar's Advice (Cox, company)

Beautiful Songs (Streep)
Wow Wow Wow (Dabney, company)
Pretty Piggy (Streep, company)
Cheshire Puss (Hudson, company)
If You Knew Time (Aberlin, company)
No Room, No Room (Cox, Linn-Baker, Jeter, Streep, company)
Starting Out Again (Streep, company)
White Roses Red (Baker-Bergen, Jeter, Hudson, Rush)
Alphabet (company)
Red Queen (Rush, company)
Never Play Croquet (Streep, company)
Mock Turtle Lament (Linn-Baker, Rush, Streep)
The Lobster Quadrille (Cox, Aberlin, company)
Eating Mushrooms (Streep, company)
Act II
Child of Pure Unclouded Brow (Rush, Baker-Bergen)
Jabberwocky (Cox, company)
The Bird Song (Rush, Linn-Baker, Jeter)
Humpty Dumpty (Streep, company)
Tweedledum and Tweedledee (Jeter, Baker-Bergen)
The Walrus and the Carpenter (Lanyer, Plummer, company)
The White Queen (Streep)
The White Knight (Linn-Baker, Streep)
An Aged-Aged Man (Streep, Linn-Baker)
The Examination (Morath, Aberlin, Rush, Dabney)
The Lion and the Unicorn (Dabney)
Queen Alice (company)
What Is a Letter (Streep, Aberlin, company)

ALL AMERICAN (1962)

BOOK BY: Mel Brooks; based on *Professor Fodorski*
  by Robert Lewis Taylor
MUSIC BY: Charles Strouse
LYRICS BY: Lee Adams
PUBLISHED LIBRETTO: Dramatic, 1972
CONDENSATION: None
ANTHOLOGY: None
VOCAL SELECTIONS: Big Three, 1962

LICENSING AGENT: Dramatic
RECORDING: Sony SK 48216 CD (original cast)
CAST: 6 M; 6 F; flexible chorus

This college musical was described as an audience show and good clean fun. The plot revolves around a shy immigrant professor from Austria who goes to an American southern college to teach engineering and ends up as the football coach. The professor was originally played by Ray Bolger, so strong dancing skills are needed.

ORIGINAL CAST:

Ray Bolger (Professor Fodorski)
Eileen Herlie (Dean Hawkes-Bullock)
Ron Husmann (Ed Bricker)
Anita Gillette (Susan Johnson)
Fritz Weaver (Henderson)

SONGS:
Act I
Melt Us (Fodorski, chorus)
What a Country! (Fodorski, chorus)
Our Children (Fodorski, Hawkes-Bullock)
We Speak the Same Language (Bricker)
It's Fun to Think (chorus)
Once upon a Time (Fodorski,
    Hawkes-Bullock)
Nightlife (Johnson, chorus)
I've Just Seen Her (Bricker)
Physical Fitness (chorus)
The Fight Song (chorus)

Act II
I Couldn't Have Done It Alone (Bricker)
If I Were You (Fodorski, Hawkes-Bullock)
Have a Dream (Henderson)
I'm Fascinating (Fodorski)
The Real Me (Hawkes-Bullock, Bricker)
Which Way? (Fodorski)

ALL IN LOVE (1962)

BOOK AND LYRICS BY: Bruce Geller; based on *The
    Rivals* by William Sheridan
MUSIC BY: Jacques Urbont
PUBLISHED LIBRETTO: None
CONDENSATION: None
ANTHOLOGY: None

VOCAL SELECTIONS: Edwin B. Marks
LICENSING AGENT: Music Theatre International
RECORDING: Mercury OCS 6204 (original cast)
CAST: 9 M; 7 F

The famous Restoration comedy of eighteenth-century England has been transformed into a minuscule musical with rapid and involved period numbers and reminiscent tunes for operetta voices. The plot concerns an heiress infatuated with the "ideal lover" of romantic novels. There are incredible and mandatory complications before a finale of multiple marriages. Comedian Dom DeLuise was in the original off-Broadway production.

ORIGINAL CAST:

David Atkinson (Jack Absolute)
Lee Case (Sir Anthony Absolute)
Dom DeLuise (Bob Acres)
Mimi Randolph (Mrs. Malaprop)
Christina Gillespie (Lucy)
Gaylea Byrne (Lydia Languish)
Michael Davis (Sir Lucius O'Trigger)

SONGS:
Act I
Poor (Lydia, Jack)
What Can It Be? (Lucy, chorus)
Odds (Bob, Jack)
I Love a Fool (Jack)
A More than Ordinary Glorious Vocabulary
    (Mrs. Malaprop, Sir Anthony)
The Lady Was Made to Be Loved (Sir
    Anthony, Jack)
Honour (Sir Lucius, Bob)

Act II
I Found Him (Lucy)
Day Dreams (chorus)
Don't Ask Me (Jack)
Why Wives? (Sir Lucius, men)
All in Love (Sir Anthony, Jack, chorus)

THE ALL NIGHT STRUT (1979)

CONCEIVED BY: Fran Charnas
MUSIC AND LYRICS BY: Various
PUBLISHED LIBRETTO: None

CONDENSATION: None
ANTHOLOGY: None
LICENSING AGENT: Music Theatre International
RECORDING: Playhouse Square 1001 (Cleveland, Ohio, cast)
CAST: 2 M; 2 F

This entertainment began in 1975 in Cleveland, Ohio, and was performed in many locales before reaching New York. It is basically a cabaret revue that takes inspiration from the pop music of the 1930s and 1940s. Usually performed by a white couple and an African-American couple, it is primarily made up of four-part harmony, although each singer has a couple of solos. The choreography should accentuate the flavor of the period with plenty of pep. The music includes romantic ballads, waltzes, jazz, and blues from Fats Waller, Glenn Miller, World War II, and other familiar sources.

ORIGINAL CAST:

Andrea Danford   Tony Rich
Jess Richards   Juana Robbins

This revue is made up of thirty-seven musical sections with one intermission.

ALLEGRO (1947)

BOOK AND LYRICS BY: Oscar Hammerstein II
MUSIC BY: Richard Rodgers
PUBLISHED LIBRETTO: Knopf, 1948
CONDENSATION: *The Burns Mantle Best Plays of 1947–1948*. John Chapman, ed. Dodd, Mead, 1948; *Rodgers and Hammerstein*. Mordden, Ethan. Abrams, 1992
ANTHOLOGY: *Six Plays by Rodgers and Hammerstein*. Random House, 1955
PIANO-VOCAL SCORE: Williamson, 1948
LICENSING AGENT: Rodgers and Hammerstein Theatre Library
RECORDING: RCA LSO 1099(e) (original cast); RCA 52758 CD (original cast)
CAST: 25 M; 15 F

This show followed such Rodgers and Hammerstein hits as *Oklahoma!* and *Carousel* and was an attempt by the famous duo to do something different and original. It was called a drama with music, rather than a musical, and was a stylized production with a minimum of scenery. The story followed a small-town boy up to the age of thirty-five. One famous song from the score is "The Gentleman Is a Dope." *Allegro* has not been filmed and is not so well known as most other Rodgers and Hammerstein shows.

ORIGINAL CAST:

Annamary Dickey (Marjorie)
William Ching (Joe Sr.)
Muriel O'Malley (Grandma)
Roberta Jonay (Jennie)
Lisa Kirk (Emily)
John Battles (Joe Jr.)
Evelyn Taylor (Mabel)
John Conte (Charlie)
Harrison Muller (Georgie)
Gloria Wills (Beulah)

SONGS:
Act I
Joseph Taylor, Jr. (ensemble)
I Know It Can Happen Again (Grandma)
One Foot, Other Foot (chorus)
A Fella Needs a Girl (Joe Sr., Marjorie)
As They Imagine They Are (Mabel, Georgie)
A Darn Nice Campus (Joe Jr.)
The Purple and Brown (men)
So Far (Beulah)
You Are Never Away (Joe Jr., Jennie, chorus)
What a Lovely Day for the Wedding (ensemble)
It May Be a Good Idea for Joe (Charlie)
Wedding (chorus)

Act II
Money Isn't Everything (Jennie, girls)
Yatata, Yatata, Yatata (Charlie, ensemble)
The Gentleman Is a Dope (Emily)
Allegro (Emily, Charlie, Joe Jr., ensemble)
Come Home (Marjorie)

AMEN CORNER (1983)

BOOK BY: Philip Rose and Peter Udell; based on
  the play *The Amen Corner* by James Baldwin
MUSIC BY: Garry Sherman
LYRICS BY: Peter Udell
PUBLISHED LIBRETTO: None
CONDENSATION: None
ANTHOLOGY: None
LICENSING AGENT: Music Theatre International
RECORDING: None
CAST: 3 M; 4 F; singers, dancers

The time is the early 1960s and the scene is
a storefront church in New York's Harlem
and an adjoining apartment. The plot concerns a female preacher whose life is upset
by the return of her wayward husband, a
jazz musician. A rebellious son and muti-
nous congregation add to her problems.
The score is principally blues and gospel
and is performed by an all-black cast.

ORIGINAL CAST:

Rhetta Hughes (Margaret)
Ruth Brown (Odessa)
Helena-Joyce Wright (Sister Boxer)
Roger Robinson (Luke)
Jean Cheek (Sister Moore)
Keith Lorenzo Amos (David)
Chuck Cooper (Brother Boxer)

SONGS:
Act I
Amen Corner (Margaret)
That Woman Can't Play No Piano (David,
  friends)
In the Real World (Brother Boxer)
You Ain't Gonna Pick Up Where You Left Off
  (Margaret, Luke)
In the Real World (reprise) (Sister Boxer)
We Got a Good Thing Goin' (Luke, David)
In His Own Time (Sister Boxer, Brother Boxer,
  Sister Moore, Odessa, chorus)
Heat Sensation (Luke)
Everytime We Call It Quits (Luke)

Act II
Somewhere Close By (Odessa)

Leanin' on the Lord (Sister Moore, Brother
  Boxer, Sister Boxer, Odessa, chorus)
I'm Already Gone (David)
Love Dies Hard (Margaret)
Rise Up and Stand Again (Margaret)

ANASTASIA AFFAIRE (1965)

BOOK BY: Jerome Chodorov and Guy Bolton;
  based on *Anastasia* by Marcelle Maurette and
  Guy Bolton
LYRICS AND MUSICAL ADAPTION BY: Robert
  Wright and George Forrest; musical score based
  on themes from Sergei Rachmaninoff
PUBLISHED LIBRETTO: None
CONDENSATION: None
ANTHOLOGY: None
VOCAL SELECTIONS: Frank Music, 1965 (original
  version)
LICENSING AGENT: Music Theatre International
RECORDING: Bay Cities 3025 CD (studio cast)
CAST: Large mixed cast

This is a musical version of the play presented on Broadway in 1954 and later
filmed with Ingrid Bergman. It is Berlin in
1925 and a former cossack general is looking for a way to get at the impounded fortune of the Russian czars. He finds a young
woman in a sanatorium and attempts to
pass her off as a princess who survived the
massacre. Is she really the Princess Anastasia? This was a big operetta-style musical given a lavish production at New York's
Ziegfeld Theatre.

ORIGINAL CAST:

Constance Towers (Anna)
Michael Kermoyan (Bounine)
George S. Irving (Chernov)
Ed Steffe (Petrovsky)
John Michael King (Prince Paul)
Lillian Gish (Dowager Empress)

ADDITIONAL CAST AND CHARACTERS FROM THE
REVISED VERSION:

Walter Willison (Sergei)
Willi Burke (Sonia)

SONGS:

Act I

A Song from Somewhere (Anna, ensemble)
I Can See Her Now (Bounine, Sergei, Petrovsky, Chernov)
Homeward (Anna, Sonia, ensemble)
Born Aristocrat (Bounine, Prince Paul)
Drawn to You (Prince Paul)
My Kind of Love (Anna, Bounine)
Thanks to Her (Petrovsky, Chernov, Sergei)
That Song (Anna, ensemble)

Act II

Here Tonight, Tomorrow Where? (Chernov, Petrovsky, Bounine, Sergei)
The Anastasia Waltz (Bounine)
Lost and Found (Anna, Bounine, Prince Paul)
Think upon Something Beautiful (Anna, Empress)
Little Hands (Empress)
I Live Again (Anna)
If This Is Good-bye (Anna, Bounine)

AND THE WORLD GOES 'ROUND (1991)
The Songs of Kander and Ebb

MUSIC BY: John Kander
LYRICS BY: Fred Ebb
PUBLISHED LIBRETTO: None
CONDENSATION: None
ANTHOLOGY: None
PIANO-VOCAL SCORE: Fiddleback Music, 1991
LICENSING AGENT: Music Theatre International
RECORDING: RCA 09026-60904-2 CD (original cast)
CAST: 2 M; 3 F

The fabulous theater songs of Kander and Ebb were once again showcased in an off-Broadway production (see also *2 × 5*). The success of this particular revue was due not only to the quality of the material but also to the very talented cast. As before, very little scenery, props, and costumes are required. It will help if the cast can roller skate for the numbers from *The Rink*. *Cabaret*, *Zorba*, *Chicago*, and *Kiss of the Spider Woman* are some of the shows that contribute songs to this review.

ORIGINAL CAST:

Bob Cuccioli   Karen Mason
Brenda Pressley   Jim Walton
Karen Ziemba

This revue is made up of thirty-two songs divided into two acts.

ANGEL (1978)

BOOK BY: Ketti Frings and Peter Udell; based on the play *Look Homeward, Angel* by Ketti Frings, which was based on the novel by Thomas Wolfe
MUSIC BY: Gary Geld
LYRICS BY: Peter Udell
PUBLISHED LIBRETTO: French, 1979
CONDENSATION: None
ANTHOLOGY: None
VOCAL SELECTIONS: Udell-Geld Music
LICENSING AGENT: Samuel French
RECORDING: None
CAST: 10 M; 9 F

The original play won a Pulitzer Prize, but this musical adaption by the same author did not fare so well. The autobiographical Thomas Wolfe novel concerns a youth's formative years, his mother's pursuit of property and security, and his drunken stonecutter father. A lot of color and "calico" touches are evident in this family show set in North Carolina in 1916. A unit set with cyclorama is used.

ORIGINAL CAST:

Patti Allison (Mrs. Fatty Pert)
Patricia Englund (Madame Victoria)
Fred Gwynne (W. O. Gant)
Rex David Hayes (Joe Tarkington)
Joel Higgins (Ben Gant)
Carl Nicholas (Reed McKinney)
Leslie Ann Ray (Laura James)
Don Scardino (Eugene Gant)
Frances Sternhagen (Eliza Gant)
Norman Stotz (Tim Laughran)

SONGS:

Act I

All the Comforts of Home (chorus)
Like the Eagle Flies (Ben)
Make a Little Sunshine (Eliza, Eugene, Ben)
Fingers and Toes (W. O. Gant, Tim, Reed, Joe)
Fatty (Ben)
Astoria Gloria (Fatty, chorus)
Railbird (Eugene)
If I Ever Loved Him (Laura)
A Dime Ain't Worth a Nickel (Ben, Fatty)
I Got a Dream to Sleep On (Eugene)
Drifting (Eliza)

Act II

I Can't Believe It's You (W. O. Gant, Victoria)
Feelin' Loved (Eugene, Laura)
A Medley (Ben, Fatty, Eliza, Laura)
Tomorrow I'm Gonna Be Old (W. O. Gant)
How Do You Say Good-bye (Laura)
Gant's Waltz (W. O. Gant, Eliza)
Like the Eagles Fly (reprise) (Eugene)

ANGRY HOUSEWIVES (1986)

BOOK BY: A. M. Collins
MUSIC AND LYRICS BY: Chad Henry
PUBLISHED LIBRETTO: French, 1988
CONDENSATION: None
ANTHOLOGY: None
LICENSING AGENT: Samuel French
RECORDING: None
CAST: 4 M; 4 F

Often described as "a musical cartoon," this off-Broadway musical deals with four white middle-class suburban women in their middle thirties who decide to form a rock band. The score is modeled after the music of the late 1950s and early 1960s. The women's theme song is "Eat Your Friggin' Cornflakes!" Predictably, the men in their lives see the light and help the women solve their problems and finally come to support them. This show ran for some years in Seattle before it came to New York. It was not a big hit in New York, but it is the type of "audience show" that goes over well with regional audiences.

ORIGINAL CAST:

Michael Manasseri (Tim)
Carolyn Casanave (Bev)
Lorna Patterson (Wendy)
Vicki Lewis (Jetta)
Camille Saviola (Carol)
Nicholas Wyman (Larry)
Michael Lemback (Wallace)
Lee Wilkof (Lewd)

SONGS:

Act I

Think Positive (Bev)
It's Gonna Be Fun (Wendy, Bev, Carol, Jetta)
Generic Woman (Carol, Bev, Wendy, Jetta)
Not at Home (Jetta)
Betsy Moberly (Lewd, Wallace)
Cold Cruel Dark (company)

Act II

First Kid on the Block (Tim, Bev, Carol, Jetta, Wendy)
Love-O-Meter (Wallace, Wendy)
Trouble with Me (Wendy, Larry)
Stalling for Time (Lewd, Larry, Wallace, Tim)
Eat Your Friggin' Cornflakes! (Bev, Wendy, Jetta, Carol)

ANIMAL CRACKERS (1928)

BOOK BY: George S. Kaufman and Morrie Ryskind
MUSIC AND LYRICS BY: Bert Kalmar and Harry Ruby
PUBLISHED LIBRETTO: French, 1984
CONDENSATION: *New Complete Book of the American Musical Theater*. Ewen, David. Holt, 1970
ANTHOLOGY: None
MUSIC PUBLISHER: *The Kalmar-Ruby Song Book*, Random House, 1936
LICENSING AGENT: Samuel French
RECORDING: None
CAST: Large mixed cast

"Hooray for Captain Spalding," the theme of Groucho Marx, comes from this stage hit that was revived in 1982 by Washington's Arena Stage. "There are lots of atrocious puns and non sequiturs and sight gags which raise many, many laughs," reported a recent critic of that production. It was staged as a circus with the band up high. The choreography reminded some of Busby Berkeley. The finale is a costume ball with the Groucho character as Louis XVII. There was a Marx Brothers film version in 1930, but without most of the songs. There was a 1992 stage revival at the Goodspeed Opera House.

1982 ARENA STAGE CAST:

Peggy Hewett (Mrs. Rittenhouse)
Karen Jablons (Arabella)
J. Fred Shiffman (Jamison)
Stephen Mellor (Captain Spalding)
Charles Janasz (The Professor)
Richard Bauer (Hives)
Deborah Jean Templin (Mary)
Eric Weitz (Wally)
Donald Corren (Ravelli)
Bob Westenberg (John)

SONGS:
Act I
Opening/News (Hives, butlers)
Hooray for Captain Spaulding (company)
Three Little Words (Wally, Arabella)
Who's Been Listening to My Heart? (Mary, John)
Everyone Says I Love You (Ravelli, girls)
Keep Your Undershirt On (Captain Spaulding, Mrs Rittenhouse)
Why Am I So Romantic? (John, Mary)
Oh, by Jingo (Jamison, Captain Spaulding, Ravelli, Professor)

Act II
Long Island Low Down (Wally, Arabella, ensemble)
Show Me a Rose (Captain Spaulding)
Watching the Clouds Roll By (John, Mary, ensemble)
Musketeers (Jamison, Captain Spaulding, Ravelli, Professor)

ANNE OF GREEN GABLES (1971)

ADAPTION BY: Donald Harron; based on the novel by Lucy Maud Montgomery
MUSIC BY: Norman Campbell
LYRICS BY: Donald Harron and Norman Campbell
PUBLISHED LIBRETTO: French, 1972
CONDENSATION: None
ANTHOLOGY: None
VOCAL SELECTIONS: Chappell (Avonlea)
LICENSING AGENT: Samuel French
RECORDING: CBS 70053 (British—1969 London original cast)
CAST: 12 M; 17 F

This cheerfully old-fashioned Canadian musical was created for the Charlottetown Festival on Prince Edward Island. It was done at New York's City Center for the 1971 Christmas season. This is a real family show with folksy charms that is based on a Canadian children's classic story of an orphan at the end of the nineteenth century. It works well simply produced in a small, intimate theater. *Variety* reported, "It's good for a smile, a twinge of nostalgia and perhaps even an occasional sniffle."

ORIGINAL CAST:

Maude Whitmore (Rachel)
Grace Finley (Anne)
Elizabeth Mawson (Marilla)
Peter Mews (Matthew)
Flora MacKenzie (Mrs. Spencer)
Roma Hearn (Mrs. Blewett/Mrs. Stacy)
Jack Northmore (Mr. Philips)
Jeff Hyslop (Gilbert)
Cleone Duncan (Lucilla)
Barbara Barsky (Josie)
Kathryn Watt (Mrs. Pye)
Glenda Landry (Diana)

SONGS:
Act I
Great Workers for the Cause (Rachel, ladies)
Where Is Matthew Going? (chorus)
Gee I'm Glad I'm No One Else but Me (Anne)
We Clearly Requested (Marilla, Anne, Matthew)

The Facts (Anne, Mrs. Spencer, Mrs. Blewett, Marilla)
Where'd Marilla Come From? (chorus)
Humble Pie (Matthew, Anne)
Oh Mrs. Lynde! (Anne)
Avonlea We Love Thee (Philips, pupils)
Wonderin' (Gilbert)
Did You Hear? (Josie, Mrs. Pye, others)
Ice Cream (Diana, company)
The Picnic (company)

Act II
Where Did the Summer Go To? (pupils)
Kindred Spirits (Anne, Diana)
Open the Window! (Mrs. Stacy, pupils)
The Words (Matthew)
I'll Show Him (Anne, Gilbert)
General Store (Lucilla, Matthew, chorus)
Pageant Song (pupils)
If It Hadn't Been for Me (company)
Anne of Green Gables (Matthew)
The Words (reprise) (Marilla)

ANNIE (1977)

BOOK BY: Thomas Meehan; based on *Little Orphan Annie* by Harold Gray
MUSIC BY: Charles Strouse
LYRICS BY: Martin Charnin
PUBLISHED LIBRETTO: None
CONDENSATION: *The Best Plays of 1976–1977*. Otis L. Guernsey, Jr., ed. Dodd, Mead, 1977; *Ganzl's Book of the Musical Theatre*. Ganzl, Kurt. Schirmer (Macmillan), 1989
ANTHOLOGY: None
VOCAL SELECTIONS: Big Three, 1977
LICENSING AGENT: Music Theatre International
RECORDING: Columbia CK 34712 CD (original cast)
CAST: 8 M; 4 F; 6 orphans; chorus and 1 dog

Everyone knows the comic strip *Little Orphan Annie* as well as the successful Broadway musical and film based on it. This is a show for the whole family, and particularly for children. Costumes for both rich and poor are required; the setting is New York City in 1933. The production can be elaborate or moderate. Remember you need a dog for the role of "Sandy."

Tony Award Winner (Best Musical)

ORIGINAL CAST:
Laurie Beechman (Bonnie Boylan)
Edie Cowan (Mrs. Pugh/Connie Boylan)
Donald Craig (Bert Healy/others)
Barbara Erwin (Lily)
Sandy Faison (Grace Farrell)
Robert Fitch (Rooster)
Dorothy Loudon (Miss Hannigan)
Andrea McArdle (Annie)
Reid Shelton (Oliver Warbucks)
Raymond Thorne (Harry/FDR)
Penny Worth (Annette/Ronnie Boylan)

SONGS:
Act I
Maybe (Annie, girls)
It's the Hard-Knock Life (Annie, girls)
Tomorrow (Annie)
We'd Like to Thank You (chorus)
Little Girls (Miss Hannigan)
I Think I'm Gonna Like It Here (Grace, Annie, chorus)
N. Y. C. (Warbucks, Grace, Annie, girls)
Easy Street (Miss Hannigan, Rooster, Lily)
You Won't Be an Orphan for Long (Grace, chorus)

Act II
You're Never Fully Dressed without a Smile (Bert, Bonnie, Connie, Ronnie, girls)
Tomorrow (reprise) (Annie, Harry, Warbucks, men)
Something Was Missing (Warbucks)
I Don't Need Anything but You (Warbucks, Annie, Grace, chorus)
Annie (Grace, chorus)
A New Deal for Christmas (Annie, Warbucks, Grace, FDR, chorus)

ANNIE GET YOUR GUN (1946)

BOOK BY: Herbert and Dorothy Fields
MUSIC AND LYRICS BY: Irving Berlin
PUBLISHED LIBRETTO: Dramatic, 1946, 1952 (without songs)

CONDENSATION: *Ganzl's Book of the Musical Theatre*. Ganzl, Kurt. Schirmer (Macmillan), 1989
ANTHOLOGY: None
PIANO-VOCAL SCORE: Irving Berlin Music, 1947, 1967
VOCAL SELECTIONS: Irving Berlin Music, 1946
LICENSING AGENT: Rodgers and Hammerstein Theatre Library
RECORDINGS: MCA 10047 CD (original cast); RCA 1124 CD (1966 revival cast)
CAST: 20 M; 10 F; 7 children; singers, dancers

Surely everyone has seen this show, either on the stage, in the MGM movie version, or as a TV special. It is based on the exciting career of Annie Oakley, an expert sharpshooter who performed in the Buffalo Bill Wild West Show. It is full of simple, singable songs that the audience will know and love and nice homely humor.

1966 REVIVAL CAST:

Ethel Merman (Annie Oakley)
Bruce Yarnell (Frank Butler)
Ronn Carroll (Foster Wilson)
Jerry Orbach (Charlie Davenport)
Rufus Smith (Buffalo Bill)
Benay Venuta (Dolly Tate)

SONGS:
Act I
Colonel Buffalo Bill (Charlie, Dolly, chorus)
I'm a Bad, Bad Man (Frank, girls)
Doin' What Comes Natur'lly (Annie, Foster, children)
The Girl That I Marry (Frank)
You Can't Get a Man with a Gun (Annie)
There's No Business like Show Business (Annie, Frank, Buffalo Bill, Charlie)
They Say It's Wonderful (Annie, Frank)
Moonshine Lullaby (Annie, children)
My Defenses Are Down (Frank, boys)
I'm an Indian Too (Annie)

Act II
I Got Lost in His Arms (Annie, chorus)
I Got the Sun in the Morning (Annie, chorus)
An Old-Fashioned Wedding (Annie, Frank)
Anything You Can Do (Annie, Frank)

ANYONE CAN WHISTLE (1964)

BOOK BY: Arthur Laurents
MUSIC AND LYRICS BY: Stephen Sondheim
PUBLISHED LIBRETTO: Random House, 1965; Leon Amiel, 1976
CONDENSATION: *Sondheim and Co.* (2nd ed.) Zadan, Craig. Harper and Row, 1986
ANTHOLOGY: None
PIANO-VOCAL SCORE: Chappell, 1968
VOCAL SELECTIONS: Chappell, 1964
LICENSING AGENT: Music Theatre International
RECORDING: Columbia CK 2480 CD (original cast)
CAST: 5 M; 3 F; variable chorus, dancers

Initially this show was a failure, but over the years and with the subsequent career of Sondheim it has become more and more respected. It takes place in an imaginary township under the control of a corrupt mayor and her evil aides. A phony miracle is concocted to attract tourists to the area. There is also a subplot dealing with madness. Some of the staff at the local insane asylum become involved in the town's activities. This is an interesting and challenging property.

ORIGINAL CAST:

Gabriel Dell (Schub)
James Frawley (Magruder)
Harry Guardino (Hapgood)
Angela Lansbury (Cora)
Lee Remick (Fay)
Arnold Soboloff (Cooley)
Larry Roquemore (George)

SONGS:
Act I
I'm like the Bluebird (company)
Me and My Town (Cora, boys)
Miracle Song (Cora, Cooley, company)
Simple (Hapgood, company)

Act II
A-1 March (company)
Come Play wiz Me (Fay, Hapgood, boys)
Anyone Can Whistle (Fay)
A Parade in Town (Cora)
Everybody Says Don't (Hapgood)

ANYTHING GOES (1934)

BOOK BY: Guy Bolton and P. G. Wodehouse;
    revised by Howard Lindsay and Russel Crouse;
    1987 revised version by Timothy Crouse and
    John Weidman
MUSIC AND LYRICS BY: Cole Porter
PUBLISHED LIBRETTO: None
CONDENSATION: *Ganzl's Book of the Musical
    Theatre.* Ganzl, Kurt. Schirmer (Macmillan),
    1989
ANTHOLOGY: None
VOCAL SELECTIONS: Warner Bros. Music, 1983
LICENSING AGENT: Tams-Witmark
RECORDINGS: Smithsonian 2007 (original cast);
    Epic FLS 15100 CD (1962 revival cast); RCA
    7769-2 CD (1987 revival cast)
CAST: 12 M; 11 F

This is a great Cole Porter show that has been done many times on stage, screen, and television. It was a big hit at Lincoln Center during its 1987 revival and subsequently was performed in Britain, Australia, and other parts of the world. It's about a group of gangsters, nightclub performers, and English nobility at sea and bound for England in the mid-1930s. The songs are the attraction . . . such evergreens as "I Get a Kick out of You" and "Blow, Gabriel, Blow." This is sophisticated entertainment.

1987 REVIVAL CAST:

Patti LuPone (Reno Sweeney)
Howard McGillin (Billy Crocker)
Rex Everhart (Elisha Whitney)
Alec Timerman (Sailor)
Linda Hart (Erma)
Michele Pigliavento (Young Girl)
Anthony Heald (Lord Evelyn Oakleigh)
Kathleen Mahoney-Bennett (Hope Harcourt)
Bill McCutcheon (Moonface Martin)

SONGS:
Act I
I Get a Kick out of You (Reno)
No Cure Like Travel (Sailor, Girl, crew)
Bon Voyage (company)
You're the Top (Reno, Billy)
Easy to Love (Billy)
I Want to Row on the Crew (Whitney)
Lady Fair (four sailors)
Friendship (Reno, Moonface)
It's Delovely (Billy, Hope)
Anything Goes (Reno, company)

Act II
Public Enemy #1 (company)
Blow, Gabriel, Blow (Reno, company)
All through the Night (Hope)
Be like the Bluebird (Moonface)
All through the Night (reprise) (Billy, Hope, men)
The Gypsy in Me (Lord Evelyn)
Buddy, Beware (Erma, sailors)

APPLAUSE (1970)

BOOK BY: Betty Comden and Adolph Green; based
    on the film *All about Eve* and the original story
    by Mary Orr
MUSIC BY: Charles Strouse
LYRICS BY: Lee Adams
PUBLISHED LIBRETTO: Random House, 1971
CONDENSATION: *The Best Plays of 1969–1970.*
    Otis L. Guernsey, Jr., ed. Dodd, Mead, 1970;
    Ganzl's Book of the Musical Theatre. Ganzl, Kurt.
    Schirmer (Macmillan), 1989
ANTHOLOGY: *Great Musicals of the American Thea-
    tre*, vol. 2. Stanley Richards, ed. Chilton, 1976
PIANO-VOCAL SCORE: Morris, 1970 (MPL
    Communications)
VOCAL SELECTIONS: Big Three, 1970
LICENSING AGENT: Tams-Witmark
RECORDING: MCA 37100 (original cast)
CAST: 15 M; 6 F; singers, dancers

A musical about the theater—from the gypsies that make up the chorus to the superstars winning their awards. Due to the famous film, this show has much popular appeal. It has been updated to include disco rhythms. The plot centers on a female star (Margo Channing) who befriends and is betrayed by a young hopeful. A great deal of glamor is required for the part of Margo.

Tony Award Winner (Best Musical)

ORIGINAL CAST:

Lauren Bacall (Margo Channing)
Bonnie Franklin (Bonnie)
Len Cariou (Bill Sampson)
Penny Fuller (Eve Harrington)
Lee Roy Reams (Duane Fox)
Brandon Maggart (Buzz Richards)
Ann Williams (Karen Richards)
Robert Mandan (Howard Benedict)

SONGS:

Act I

Backstage Babble (company)
Think How It's Gonna Be (Bill)
But Alive (Margo, boys)
The Best Night of My Life (Eve)
Who's That Girl? (Margo)
Applause (Bonnie, chorus)
Hurry Back (Margo)
Fasten Your Seat Belts (Buzz, Karen, Howard, Duane, Bill, guests)
Welcome to the Theater (Margo)

Act II

Inner Thoughts (Karen, Buzz, Margo)
Good Friends (Margo, Karen, Buzz)
She's No Longer a Gypsy (Bonnie, Duane, chorus)
One of a Kind (Bill, Margo)
One Halloween (Eve)
Something Greater (Margo)

THE APPLE TREE (1966)

BOOK BY: Jerry Bock and Sheldon Harnick; based on "The Diary of Adam and Eve" by Mark Twain, "The Lady or the Tiger?" by Frank R. Stockton, and "Passionella" by Jules Feiffer; additional material by Jerome Coopersmith
MUSIC BY: Jerry Bock
LYRICS BY: Sheldon Harnick
PUBLISHED LIBRETTO: Random House, 1967
CONDENSATION: *The Best Plays of 1966–1967*. Otis L Guernsey, Jr., ed. Dodd, Mead, 1967
ANTHOLOGY: *The Best Short Comedies from Broadway and London*. Stanley Richards, ed. Random House, 1970
PIANO-VOCAL SCORE: Valando, 1968
LICENSING AGENT: Music Theatre International

RECORDING: Sony SK 48209 CD (original cast)
CAST: 5 M; 3 F; chorus

A trio of short stories has been transformed into a three-act musical. Usually each act is performed by the same cast, but this is not necessary. In fact, the three one-act musicals can be performed singly or as a trio. The first, naturally enough, is set in the Garden of Eden. The second is set in ancient Babylon, and the last in glamorous Hollywood. Even though there is not a lot of dancing, this is a challenging show to stage. Strong comic talents are required.

The Diary of Adam and Eve

ORIGINAL CAST:

Alan Alda (Adam)
Barbara Harris (Eve)
Larry Blyden (Snake)

SONGS:

Here in Eden (Eve)
Feelings (Eve)
Eve (Adam)
Friends (Eve)
The Apple Tree (Forbidden Fruit) (Snake)
Beautiful, Beautiful World (Adam)
It's a Fish (Adam)
Go to Sleep Whatever You Are (Eve)
What Makes Me Love Him (Eve)

The Lady or the Tiger?

ORIGINAL CAST:

Larry Blyden (Balladeer)
Marc Jordan (King Arik)
Barbara Harris (Princess Barbara)
Alan Alda (Captain Sanjar)

SONGS:

I'll Tell You a Truth (Balladeer)
Make Way (King Arik, court)
Forbidden Love (in Gaul) (Princess Barbara, Captain Sanjar)
The Apple Tree (reprise) (Balladeer)
I've Got What You Want (Princess Barbara)
Tiger, Tiger (Princess Barbara)
Which Door? (Captain Sanjar, Princess Barbara, King Arik, court)

Passionella

ORIGINAL CAST:

Larry Blyden (Narrator)
Barbara Harris (Ella and Passionella)
Robert Klein (Mr. Fallible)
Marc Jordan (Producer)
Alan Alda (Flip, The Prince Charming)

SONGS:
Oh, to Be a Movie Star (Ella)
Gorgeous (Passionella)
(Who, Who, Who, Who,) Who Is She?
    (company)
I Know (Passionella, company)
Wealth (Passionella)
You Are Not Real (Flip, company)
George L. (Ella, Flip)

---

archy and mehitabel (1957)

BOOK BY: Joe Darion and Mel Brooks; based on
    stories and vignettes by Don Marquis
MUSIC BY: George Kleinsinger
LYRICS BY: Joe Darion
PUBLISHED LIBRETTO: None
CONDENSATION: None
ANTHOLOGY: *The Best Short Plays of 1957–1958.*
    Margaret Mayorga, ed. Beacon, 1958
VOCAL SELECTIONS: Chappell, 1957
LICENSING AGENT: Music Theatre International
RECORDINGS: Columbia CPS AOL 4963 (1955
    studio cast); Sound of Broadway 300/1 (TV
    sound track and original cast)
CAST: 12 M; 8 F

This property started out as stories and
then was made into a "back-alley opera"
and recorded by Carol Channing and Eddie
Bracken. From this record came a Broadway musical retitled *Shinbone Alley*. It is
the wistful one-sided romance of a cockroach for an alley cat. These creatures sym-
bolize human emotions and frailties. It was
called novel and imaginative, with a happy
and jazzy score. The Broadway cast featured Bracken with Eartha Kitt, as well as
Jacques D'Amboise and Allegra Kent from
the New York City Ballet.

SHINBONE ALLEY ORIGINAL CAST:

Eddie Bracken (archy)
Eartha Kitt (mehitabel)
George S. Irving (Big Bill)
Ross Martin (Broadway)
Erik Rhodes (Tyrone)

SONGS:
Act I
What Do We Care? (mehitabel)
Toujours Gai (mehitabel)
Queer Little Insect (mehitabel, archy)
Big Bill (Big Bill, ladies)
True Romance (mehitabel, Big Bill)
The Lightning Bug Song (archy)
I Gotta Be (Broadway, archy)
Flotsam and Jetsam (archy, mehitabel)
Come to Mee-ow (Tyrone)
Suicide Song (archy)
Shinbone Alley (Big Bill, chorus)

Act II
The Moth Song (archy)
A Woman Wouldn't Be a Woman (mehitabel,
    chorus)
The Lullaby (mehitabel, girls)
What the Hell (mehitabel)
Pretty Kitty (girls)
Way Down Blues (mehitabel)
The Lady Bug Song (ensemble)
Be a Pussycat (mehitabel)
Quiet Street (archy)

AROUND THE WORLD IN 80 DAYS (1963)

BOOK BY: Sig Herzig; based on the motion picture
    and the story by Jules Verne
LYRICS BY: Harold Adamson
MUSIC BY: Sammy Fain and Victor Young
PUBLISHED LIBRETTO: None
CONDENSATION: None
ANTHOLOGY: None
MUSIC PUBLISHER: Chappell, 1957 (film score with
    no vocals)
LICENSING AGENT: Tams-Witmark
RECORDING: Everest LPBR 4001 (studio cast)
CAST: 20 M; 5 F; chorus

Michael Todd's gigantic 1956 film won five Academy Awards, including one to Victor Young for the musical score. After Todd's death his son had the property transformed into a stage production. He presented it successfully in 1963 at Jones Beach on Long Island, outside New York City. All Jones Beach productions were spectacular, but this can be produced on a reasonably modest scale.

ORIGINAL CAST:

Fritz Weaver (Phileas Fogg)
Robert Clary (Passpartout)
Dom DeLuise (Mr. Fix)
Laurie Franks (Gaby)
Elaine Malbin (Princess Aouda)
Edmund Lyndeck (M. Gasse)

SONGS:
Act I
March of the Grenadiers (ensemble)
Long Live the English Scene (ensemble)
Have You Heard about Phileas Fogg? (ensemble)
Hide Your Sister (Passpartout, singers)
I'm a Sleuth (Mr. Fix)
Sidewalks of Paris (Passpartout, ensemble)
I Hate to Travel (Fogg, M. Gasse)
Sky Symphony (ensemble)
Fiesta in Spain (dance)
Are We Talking about the Same Thing? (Fogg, Princess Aouda)
Lloyd's of London (ensemble)
His Little World (Princess Aouda)
One-Woman Man (Passpartout, girls)
Once I Wondered (Princess Aouda)
Dance of Sacrifice (ensemble)
Around the World (ensemble)

Act II
Hong Kong (ensemble)
Barbary Coast (ensemble)
Carry On (Fogg, Passpartout)
Way Out West (Fogg, singers)
India Raid (Princess Aouda, Fogg, Passpartout, Mr. Fix, ensemble)
Burning of the "Henrietta" (Fogg, Passpartout, ensemble)

ASPECTS OF LOVE (1990)

BOOK ADAPTION BY: Andrew Lloyd Webber; based on the novel by David Garnett
MUSIC BY: Andrew Lloyd Webber
LYRICS BY: Don Black and Charles Hart
PUBLISHED LIBRETTO: *The Complete Aspects of Love*. Ganzl, Kurt. Viking, 1990
CONDENSATION: *Andrew Lloyd Webber, His Life and Works*. Walsh, Michael. Abrams, 1989
ANTHOLOGY: None
VOCAL SELECTIONS: Hal Leonard, 1989
LICENSING AGENT: Not yet available; contact Music Theatre International
RECORDING: Polydor 841 126-2 CD (original London cast)
CAST: 5 M; 3 F; 2 young girls; chorus

Following a trend of the 1980s, this musical is "through sung," or like an opera, most of the dialog is sung rather than spoken. The cast includes a quintet of interrelated lovers in the south of France and England between the years 1947 and 1964. A seventeen-year-old boy is in love with an older actress who marries his uncle. This Lloyd Webber production does not depend on elaborate sets or complicated dances, but strong singing is required.

ORIGINAL CAST:

Michael Ball (Alex)
Ann Crumb (Rose)
Kevin Colson (George)
Kathleen Rowe McAllen (Giulietta)
Walter Charles (Marcel)
Danielle DuClos (Jenny)

SONGS:
Act I
Love Changes Everything (Alex)
Parlez-vous Français? (Rose, Alex, ensemble)
Seeing Is Believing (Alex, Rose)
A Memory of a Happy Moment (George, Giulietta)
Chanson d'enfance (Rose, Alex)
Everybody Loves a Hero (Barkers, ensemble)
She'd Be Far Better Off with You (Alex, George)
Stop. Wait, Please (Giulietta, George, ensemble)

Act II
Leading Lady (Marcel, ensemble)
Other Pleasures (George)
There Is More to Love (Giulietta, Rose)
Mermaid Song (Jenny, Alex)
The First Man You Remember (George,
　Jenny)
The Journey of a Lifetime (company)
Falling (George, Rose, Alex, Jenny)
Hand Me the Wine and the Dice (Giulietta,
　ensemble)
Anything but Love (Rose)

ASSASSINS (1990)

BOOK BY: John Weidman
MUSIC AND LYRICS BY: Stephen Sondheim
PUBLISHED LIBRETTO: Theatre Communications
　Group, 1991
CONDENSATION: None
ANTHOLOGY: None
PIANO-VOCAL SCORE: Warner Bros Music, 1991
VOCAL SELECTIONS: Warner Bros Music, 1992
LICENSING AGENT: Music Theatre International
RECORDING: RCA 60737-2 CD (original cast)
CAST: 12 M; 4 F

"Presidential assassins are hardly your
usual musical-theatre fare" warned the
New York Times. But Sondheim has always
dared to be different. This off-Broadway
show was presented for two months of
workshop performances in preparation for
a Broadway transfer, which never materi-
alized. The various musical numbers are
written in the style of folk music, barbershop quartets, spirituals, Sousa marches,
and national musical oratory. A strolling
balladeer brings unity to the mixing up
of time and characters—men and women
who have killed, or tried to kill, American
presidents. Described as somewhere between a book musical and an all-star revue,
this show was originally done on a small
stage with simple sets and a three-member
orchestra. This was done successfully in
London in 1992.

ORIGINAL CAST:

Jace Alexander (Lee Harvey Oswald)
Patrick Cassidy (Balladeer)
Victor Garber (Booth)
Marcus Olson (David Herold)
Eddie Korbich (Zangara)
Terrence Mann (Czolgosz)
Jonathan Hadary (Guiteau)
Deborah Monk (Moore)
Greg Germann (Hinckley)
Annie Golden (Fromme)
Lee Wilkof (Byck)

SONGS:
(performed without intermission)
Everybody's Got the Right (ensemble)
The Ballad of Booth (Balladeer, Booth,
　Herold)
How I Saved Roosevelt (Zangara, ensemble)
Gun Song (Czolgosz, Booth, Guiteau, Moore)
The Ballad of Czolgosz (Balladeer, ensemble)
Unworthy of Your Love (Hinckley, Fromme)
The Ballad of Guiteau (Guiteau, Balladeer)
Another National Anthem (Czolgosz, Booth,
　Hinckley, Fromme, Zangara, Guiteau,
　Moore, Byck, Balladeer)
November 22, 1963 (Booth, Oswald, Guiteau,
　Czolgosz, Byck, Hinckley, Fromme, Moore,
　Zangara)
You Can Close the New York Stock Exchange
　(Booth, Guiteau, Moore, Czolgosz,
　Fromme, Zangara, Hinckley, Byck)
Everybody's Got the Right (reprise)
　(ensemble)

BABES IN ARMS (1937)

BOOK BY: Richard Rodgers and Lorenz Hart
MUSIC BY: Richard Rodgers
LYRICS BY: Lorenz Hart
PUBLISHED LIBRETTO: None
CONDENSATION: *New Complete Book of the
　Americal Musical Theater*. Ewen, David. Holt,
　1970
ANTHOLOGY: None

PIANO-VOCAL SCORE: Chappell (1959 version), 1960
VOCAL SELECTIONS: Chappell, 1937
LICENSING AGENT: Rodgers and Hammerstein Theatre Library
RECORDING: New World NW 386-2 CD (1989 concert cast)
CAST: 11 M; 8 F; chorus

Often considered the archetypal "why-don't-us-kids-do-a-show-right-here-in-the-barn" musical, *Babes in Arms* opened in 1937 to reviews that called it "a musical of taste, smartness and delightful abandon." In the plot the children of vaudevillians find themselves about to be sent to a summer work camp on Long Island. To escape, the kids put on a show!

There's a lot of singing and dancing (including a dream ballet) by a young cast to some of the most famous Rodgers and Hart songs. This musical was presented outdoors at London's Regent's Park in 1988 and in a concert version at Lincoln Center in 1989.

ORIGINAL CAST:

Ray Heatherton (Val LaMar)
Mitzi Green (Billie Smith)
Alfred Drake (Marshall)
Grace MacDonald (Dolores)
Wynn Murray (Baby Rose)
Rolly Pickert (Gus)

SONGS:
Act I
Where or When (Billie, Val)
Babes in Arms (Billie, Val, Marshall, gang)
I Wish I Were in Love Again (Dolores, Gus)
Way Out West (Baby Rose, boys)
My Funny Valentine (Billie)
Johnny One-Note (Baby Rose, gang)

Act II
Imagine (Baby Rose, boys)
All at Once (Billie, Val)
The Lady Is a Tramp (Billie)
You Are So Fair (Dolores, Gus, chorus)

BABES IN THE WOOD (1964)

BOOK, MUSIC, AND LYRICS BY: Rick Besoyan; freely adapted from *A Midsummer Night's Dream* by William Shakespeare
PUBLISHED LIBRETTO: Broadway Play Publishing, 1983
CONDENSATION: None
ANTHOLOGY: None
LICENSING AGENT: Broadway Play Publishing
RECORDING: Cassette tape available from agent
CAST: 4 M; 4 F; 1 dancing extra

In this "extremely loose version" of Shakespeare we are mainly concerned with the mixed-up lovers lost in the enchanted woods of King Oberon. Titania and Bottom are other familiar characters. The show is full of pratfalls and cavorting, while the flowing, singable musical score is highlighted by some razzle-dazzle vaudeville turns, including an Al Jolson parody as Bottom sings "Mother." This was presented off-Broadway with a single forest set and a touch of "bellydance, barrelhouse, and striptease," according to James Davis in the *Daily News*.

ORIGINAL CAST:

Richard Charles Hoh (Oberon)
Carol Glade (Titania)
Ruth Buzzi (Helena)
Danny Carroll (Demetrius)
Kenneth McMillan (Bottom)
Elmarie Wendel (Robin Goodfellow)
Don Stewart (Lysander)
Joleen Fodor (Hermia)

SONGS:
Act I
This State of Affairs (Oberon, Goodfellow)
Titania's Philosophy (Titania)
A Lover Waits (Oberon)
The Gossip Song (Helena)
I'm Not for You (Demetrius)
Mother (Bottom)
Old-Fashioned Girl (Bottom, Goodfellow)
Love Is Lovely (Lysander, Hermia)
Babes in the Wood (Goodfellow)

Act II
Anyone Can Make a Mistake (Goodfellow)
Cavorting (Titania, Bottom)
There's a Girl (Oberon, Demetrius)
I'm Not for You (reprise) (Lysander)
Little Tear (Hermia)
Helena's Solution (Helena, Lysander,
    Demetrius)
Helena (Demetrius, Lysander)
Midsummer Night (Oberon, Lysander)
Moon Madness (Titania, Bottom)
The Alphabet Song (Titania, Hermia, Helena)

BABY (1983)

BOOK BY: Sybille Pearson; based on a story
    developed with Susan Yankowitz
MUSIC BY: David Shire
LYRICS BY: Richard Maltby, Jr.
PUBLISHED LIBRETTO: None
CONDENSATION: None
ANTHOLOGY: None
VOCAL SELECTIONS: Fiddleback Music, 1984
LICENSING AGENT: Music Theatre International
RECORDING: Polydor 821 593-2 CD (original cast)
CAST: 5 M; 3 F

Three couples in a college town are surprised to learn that they are expecting. For the young, unmarried students there are instant problems. For the married teachers who have wanted a family there is joy. But for the mature couple who have already raised three children there are doubts. These situations are resolved with both humor and compassion. For the Broadway production the small orchestra was on stage, and the basic set was a bed. Intricately swirling curtains served as various backgrounds. There were numerous film clips of pregnancies in progess, but these are not really necessary. The music has the sound of the 1980s—and there is a great deal of it. Very little dancing is required.

ORIGINAL CAST:

Liz Callaway (Lizzie Fields)
Todd Graff (Danny Hooper)

Beth Fowler (Arlene MacNally)
James Congdon (Alan MacNally)
Catherine Cox (Pam Sakarian)
Philip Hoffman (Mr. Weiss)
Dennis Warning (Dean Webber)
Martin Vidnovic (Nick Sakarian)

SONGS:
Act I
We Start Today (Danny, Lizzie, Alan, Arlene,
    Nick, Pam, chorus)
What Could Be Better? (Danny, Lizzie)
The Plaza Song (Alan, Arlene)
Baby, Baby, Baby (Nick, Pam, Alan, Arlene,
    Danny, Lizzie)
I Want It All (Pam, Lizzie, Arlene)
At Night She Comes Home to Me (Nick,
    Danny)
Fatherhood Blues (Danny, Alan, Nick, Mr.
    Weiss, Dean)
Romance (Nick, Pam)
I Chose Right (Danny)
The Story Goes On (Lizzie)

Act II
The Ladies Singin' Their Song (Lizzie,
    women)
Easier to Love (Alan)
Two People in Love (Danny, Lizzie)
With You (Nick, Pam)
And What if We Had Loved like That (Alan,
    Arlene)

BAJOUR (1964)

BOOK BY: Ernest Kinoy; based on the *New Yorker*
    stories by Joseph Mitchell
MUSIC AND LYRICS BY: Walter Marks
PUBLISHED LIBRETTO: Dramatic, 1976
CONDENSATION: None
ANTHOLOGY: None
VOCAL SELECTIONS: Morris, 1965 (MPL
    Communications)
LICENSING AGENT: Dramatic
RECORDINGS: Columbia KOS 2700 (original cast);
    Sony SK 48208 CD (original cast)
CAST: 7 M; 5 F; chorus

A "bajour" is a major caper that enriches a whole tribe of modern gypsies. While the gypsies are plotting and fighting among themselves, a female anthropologist arrives to live with and study them. She was played on Broadway by Nancy Dussault who stopped the show with her song "Where Is the Tribe for Me?" This show has a contemporary setting in and around New York City and features strong dancing.

ORIGINAL CAST:

Nancy Dussault (Emily)
Robert Burr (Lou)
Chita Rivera (Anyanka)
Gus Trikonis (Steve)
Mae Questel (Mrs. Kirsten)
Herschel Bernardi (Cockeye Johnny)
Herbert Edelman (King of Newark)

SONGS:
Act I
Move Over, New York (Johnny, chorus)
Where Is the Tribe for Me? (Emily)
The Haggle (Anyanka, Steve, men)
Love-Line (Anyanka)
Words, Words, Words (Emily, Johnny)
Mean (Anyanka)
Must It Be Love? (Emily)
Bajour (Anyanka, Emily, Johnny, chorus)

Act II
Soon (Anyanka, Steve, chorus)
I Can (Anyanka, Emily)
Living Simply (Lou, Emily, men)
Honest Man (Johnny, King of Newark)
Guarantees (Mrs. Kirsten)
Love Is a Chance (Emily)
The Sew-Up (Anyanka, Mrs. Kirsten, women)
Finale: Move Over, America (company)

BAKER STREET (1965)

BOOK BY: Jerome Coopersmith; adapted from the stories by Arthur Conan Doyle
MUSIC AND LYRICS BY: Marian Grudeff and Raymond Jessel
PUBLISHED LIBRETTO: Doubleday, 1966

CONDENSATION: *New Complete Book of the American Musical Theater.* Ewen, David. Holt, 1970
ANTHOLOGY: None
VOCAL SELECTIONS: Marks, 1964 (Belwin-Mills)
LICENSING AGENT: Tams-Witmark
RECORDING: MGM SE 7000 OC (original cast)
CAST: 16 M; 3 F; singers, dancers

A musical adventure with those old friends Sherlock Holmes and Doctor Watson. The plot deals with Irene Adler and Professor Moriarty. She is an American musical comedy star who is happy to be back in London, and he is out to steal the British crown jewels. Turn-of-the-century London lends itself to beautiful costumes and opulent sets. There is a tongue-in-cheek approach to all of this.

ORIGINAL CAST:

Fritz Weaver (Sherlock Holmes)
Peter Sallis (Dr. Watson)
Martin Gabel (Professor Moriarty)
Inga Swenson (Irene Adler)
Teddy Green (Wiggins)
Patrick Horgan (Captain Gregg)
Daniel Keyes (Inspector Lestrade)
Virginia Vestoff (Daisy)
Martin Wolfson (Baxter)

SONGS:
Act I
It's So Simple (Holmes, Watson, Gregg, Lestrade)
I'm in London Again (Adler)
Leave It to Us, Guv (Wiggins, men)
Letters (Adler)
Cold Clear World (Holmes)
Finding Words for Spring (Adler)
What a Night This Is Going to Be (Holmes, Adler, Watson, Daisy)
London Underworld (company)
I Shall Miss You (Moriarty)

Act II
Roof Space (Wiggins, men)
A Married Man (Watson)
I'd Do It Again (Adler)
Pursuit (Holmes)
Jewelry (Baxter, men)

THE BAKER'S WIFE (1976)

BOOK BY: Joseph Stein; based on the film *La Femme de Boulanger* by Marcel Pagnol and Jean Giono
MUSIC AND LYRICS BY: Stephen Schwartz
PUBLISHED LIBRETTO: None
CONDENSATION: *Broadway Bound.* Leonard, William Torbert. Scarecrow, 1983
ANTHOLOGY: None
VOCAL SELECTIONS: Warner Bros. Music, 1990
LICENSING AGENT: Music Theatre International
RECORDING: TER 21175 CD (1989 London cast)
CAST: 12 M; 7 F

In 1976 this musical starred Topol and was on a pre-Broadway tour when it closed out of town. It was presented off-Broadway in 1985 and then mounted in London in 1989. It is this London version that is available for production. The plot is of a small community in a crisis. Set in Concorde, France, the town's new baker loses his young wife to her lover, and the baker then is unable to bake. The townspeople, in order to have bread, endeavor to get the baker and his wife back together. Sheridan Morley wrote in the *Herald Tribune,* "a score of huge and magical delight" with French-flavored orchestrations. Two of the sets include the baker's lodging and a cafe. A sentimental show with old-fashioned oompah musical high jinks.

1989 LONDON CAST:

Jill Martin (Denise)
John Bennett (Teacher)
Neil McCaul (Priest)
James Villiers (Marquis)
Alun Armstrong (Aimable)
Sharon Lee Hill (Genevieve)
Drue Williams (Dominic)

SONGS:
Act I
Chanson (Denise)
If It Wasn't for You (Teacher, Priest, Marquis, ensemble)
Merci, Madame (Aimable, Genevieve)
Bread (ensemble)
Gifts of Love (Genevieve)
Plain and Simple (Aimable, Genevieve)
Proud Lady (Dominic)
Look for the Woman (Teacher, Marquis, ensemble)
Serenade (Dominic, Genevieve, Aimable)
Meadowlark (Genevieve)
Buzz-a-buzz (Aimable, Marquis, ensemble)

Act II
If It Wasn't for You (Priest, Teacher) reprise (Marquis, ensemble)
Any-Day-Now Day (Aimable, ensemble)
Endless Delights (Dominic, Genevieve)
The Luckiest Man in the World/Feminine Companionship (Marquis, ensemble)
If I Have to Live Alone (Aimable)
Romance (women)
Where Is the Warmth? (Genevieve)
Gifts of Love (reprise) (Genevieve, Aimable)

BALANCING ACT (1992)

BOOK, MUSIC, AND LYRICS BY: Dan Goggin
PUBLISHED LIBRETTO: French, 1993
CONDENSATION: None
ANTHOLOGY: None
LICENSING AGENT: Samuel French
RECORDING: DRG 19004 CD (original cast)
CAST: 2 M; 4 F

The action of this musical takes place in Hometown, U.S.A.; New York; and Hollywood. The time is the present. The plot concerns "one individual searching for identity," or more specifically, an actor looking for work. His search takes him to New York where he settles for work in commercials until he can obtain a TV series in Hollywood. The unusual angle to all this is that there are five sides, or aspects, to the main character, each played by a different actor or actress. The show is mostly sung through, and the off-Broadway set consisted of a multicolored assortment of steps.

ORIGINAL CAST:

Craig Wells (The Ambitious Side)
Diane Fratantoni (The Sensitive Side)
Christine Toy (The Optimistic Side)
J. B. Adams (The Skeptical Side)
Suzanne Hevner (The Humorous Side)
Nancy E. Carroll (Everybody Else including
    Maisie, Mr. Revere, Harriet, and Jane)

SONGS:
Act I
Life Is a Balancing Act (company)
Next Stop: New York City (ensemble)
Home Sweet Home (ensemble)
Play Away the Blues (Maisie)
My Bio Is a Blank (Maisie, ensemble)
A Tough Town (ensemble)
I Left You There (The Sensitive Side)
A Twist of Fate (ensemble)
A Casting Call (Mr. Revere, ensemble)
The Fifth from the Right (The Humorous
    Side)
You Heard It Here First (The Skeptical Side)
A Long, Long Way (The Optimistic Side)
The Woman of the Century (Jane, ensemble)
Act II
Welcome, Bienvenue (Maisie)
Where Is the Rainbow? (The Ambitious Side)
I Am Yours (ensemble)
That Kid's Gonna Make It (Harriet)
Chew Chewy Chow (Jane, ensemble)
Hollywood 'n' Vinyl (The Optimistic,
    Sensitive, and Humorous Sides)
California Suite (Mr. Revere, ensemble)
I Knew the Music (ensemble)

BALLROOM (1979)

BOOK BY: Jerome Kass; an adaption of "The
    Queen of the Stardust Ballroom," a TV musical
    special
MUSIC BY: Billy Goldenberg
LYRICS BY: Alan and Marilyn Bergman
PUBLISHED LIBRETTO: French, 1981
CONDENSATION: None
ANTHOLOGY: None
VOCAL SELECTIONS: Schirmer, 1979
LICENSING AGENT: Samuel French

RECORDINGS: Columbia 35762 (original cast); Sony
    SK 35762 CD (original cast)
CAST: 14 M; 17 F

A widow and a married man meet at a
public dance hall in this bittersweet romance originally done on television. The
Broadway production expanded the plot
and the score. A 1940s big-band orchestra
and many ballroom dancers are featured.

ORIGINAL CAST:

Dorothy Loudon (Bea Asher)
Vincent Gardenia (Alfred Rossi)
Bernie Knee (Nathan Bricker)
Lynn Roberts (Marlene)

SONGS:
(performed without intermission)
A Terrific Band and a Real Nice Crowd (Bea)
A Song for Dancing (Marlene, Nathan)
One by One (Marlene, Nathan)
Dreams (Marlene)
Somebody Did All Right for Herself (Bea)
I've Been Waiting All My Life (Nathan, Alfred)
How Can I Tell Her? (Alfred)
I Love to Dance (Bea, Alfred)
Good Night (Is Not Good-bye) (Marlene,
    Nathan)
More of the Same (Marlene, Nathan)
Fifty Percent (Bea)
I Wish You a Waltz (Bea)

BARNUM (1980)

BOOK BY: Mark Bramble
MUSIC BY: Cy Coleman
LYRICS BY: Michael Stewart
PUBLISHED LIBRETTO: Fireside Theatre Book Club,
    1982
CONDENSATION: *Ganzl's Book of the Musical
    Theatre*. Ganzl, Kurt. Schirmer (Macmillan),
    1989
ANTHOLOGY: None
VOCAL SELECTIONS: Notable Music, 1980;
    CPP/Belwin
LICENSING AGENT: Tams-Witmark
RECORDING: Columbia CK 36576 CD (original cast)
CAST: 11 M; 8 F

For this story of P. T. Barnum, the theater in New York was turned into a circus with the stage as the main ring. Not only did clowns and jugglers perform all over the auditorium but street performers were outside before the show. All this was clear in the British video version shown on PBS. The band was frequently on stage and marched in the aisles. The ringmaster announced high spots of Barnum's career, then P. T. proceeded to enact them. Although the action covers 1835 to 1880, Barnum never ages. The plot concerns Barnum and his levelheaded wife. It includes the possibility of Barnum's affair with Jenny Lind and his eventual merger with Bailey to form the "greatest show on earth." The highly praised score is made up of ballads, marches, and ragtime struts. A great deal of energy is required, from all concerned, in staging this show.

ORIGINAL CAST:

Jim Dale (Phineas Taylor Barnum)
Glenn Close (Chairy)
Terrence V. Mann (Lyman/Morrissey)
Terri White (Joice Heth/Blues Singer)
Leonard John Crofoot (Tom Thumb)
Karen Trott (Susan B. Anthony)
William C. Witter (Goldschmidt/Bailey)
Marianne Tatum (Jenny Lind)

SONGS:
Act I
There's a Sucker Born Ev'ry Minute (Barnum)
Thank God I'm Old (Joice Heth, players)
The Colors of My Life (Barnum, Chairy, waitresses)
One Brick at a Time (Chairy, bricklayers)
Museum Song (Barnum)
I Like Your Style (Barnum, Chairy)
Bigger Isn't Better (Tom Thumb)
Love Makes Such Fools of Us All (Jenny Lind)
Out There (Barnum)

Act II
Come Follow the Band (Barnum, company)

Black and White (Chairy, Barnum, Blues Singer, company)
The Prince of Humbug (Barnum)
Join the Circus (Barnum, Bailey, company)

BELLS ARE RINGING (1956)

BOOK AND LYRICS BY: Betty Comden and Adolph Green
MUSIC BY: Jule Styne
PUBLISHED LIBRETTO: Random House, 1957; *Theatre Arts* (magazine), April 1959
CONDENSATION: *Ganzl's Book of the Musical Theatre*. Ganzl, Kurt. Schirmer (Macmillan), 1989
ANTHOLOGY: *Comden and Green on Broadway*. Drama Book Specialists, 1981
PIANO-VOCAL SCORE: Chappell, 1967
VOCAL SELECTIONS: Hal Leonard
LICENSING AGENT: Tams-Witmark
RECORDING: Columbia CK 2006 CD (original cast)
CAST: 22 M; 6 F; chorus

Judy Holliday was the original telephone answering service operator taking a more than routine interest in her customers. This show was later made into a film, and some of the songs ("Just in Time") have become standards. This musical has fun and romance in a New York setting.

ORIGINAL CAST:

Judy Holliday (Ella)
Sydney Chaplin (Jeff)
Jean Stapleton (Sue)
Eddie Lawrence (Sandor)
Peter Gennaro (Carl)

SONGS:
Act I
Bells Are Ringing (girls' chorus)
It's a Perfect Relationship (Ella, men)
On My Own (Jeff)
It's a Simple Little System (Sandor, ensemble)
Is It a Crime? (Ella)
Hello, Hello There (Ella, Jeff, ensemble)
I Met a Girl (Jeff, ensemble)
Long before I Knew You (Ella, Jeff)

Act II
Mu-Cha-Cha (Ella, Carl, ensemble)
Just in Time (Ella, Jeff, ensemble)
Drop That Name (Ella, ensemble)
The Party's Over (Ella, ensemble)
Salzburg (Sue, Sandor)
The Midas Touch (ensemble)
I'm Going Back (Ella)

BEN FRANKLIN IN PARIS (1964)

BOOK AND LYRICS BY: Sidney Michaels
MUSIC BY: Mark Sandrich, Jr.
PUBLISHED LIBRETTO: Random House, 1965
CONDENSATION: None
ANTHOLOGY: None
VOCAL SELECTIONS: Morley Music Co., 1965
LICENSING AGENT: Samuel French
RECORDING: Capitol SVAS 2191 (original cast)
CAST: 18 M; 4 F; singers, dancers

The setting is Paris and the court of Louis XVI. Two of the delights include a love song sung in the gondola of a balloon and the monks singing "Hic Haec Hoc" as they go about their tasks in the vineyard. Ben goes to France to get aid for the American Revolution. He is helped by a countess who loves him and has strong influence with the French king. The subplot is a romance between Ben's grandson and a poor Parisienne.

ORIGINAL CAST:

Robert Preston (Ben Franklin)
Ulla Sallert (Diane)
Susan Watson (Janine)
Jack Fletcher (Pedro)
Sam Greene (Wickes)
Bob Kaliban (Pierre)
Franklin Kiser (Temple)
Jerry Schaefer (Bache)

SONGS:
Act I
We Sail the Seas (sailors)

I Invented Myself (Ben, company)
Too Charming (Ben, Diane)
Whatever Became of Old Temple (Temple)
Half the Battle (Ben, Bache, Temple, Pierre)
A Balloon Is Ascending (company)
To Be Alone with You (Ben, Diane, company)
You're in Paris (Janine, Temple, company)
How Laughable It Is (Diane)
Hic Haec Hoc (men)
God Bless the Human Elbow (Ben, Pedro, Pierre, men)

Act II
When I Dance with the Person I Love (Janine)
Diane Is (Ben)
Look for Small Pleasures (Ben, Diane)
I Love the Ladies (Ben, Wickes, Pierre, Temple, sailors)

BERLIN TO BROADWAY WITH KURT WEILL (1972)

MUSIC BY: Kurt Weill
TEXT AND FORMAT BY: Gene Lerner
LYRICS BY: Maxwell Anderson, Marc Blitzstein, Bertolt Brecht, Jacques Deval, Michael Feingold, Ira Gershwin, Paul Green, Langston Hughes, Alan Jay Lerner, Ogden Nash, George Tabori, and Arnold Weinstein
PUBLISHED LIBRETTO: None
CONDENSATION: None
ANTHOLOGY: None
MUSIC PUBLISHER: Chappell, 1975
LICENSING AGENT: Music Theatre International
RECORDING: Paramount PAS 4000 (original cast)
CAST: 2 M; 2 F; 1 narrator

This show is done as a selected biography of the composer with a narrator to bridge the songs. Slide projections were used in the original off-Broadway production. Featured are some of the truly great songs of the musical theater from *The Threepenny Opera* and *Lady in the Dark* to *Lost in the Stars*. Your cast will have to be up to this material!

ORIGINAL CAST:

Ken Kercheval (narrator)
Margery Cohen   Judy Lander
Jerry Lanning   Hal Watters

This revue is made up of thirty-nine songs divided into two acts.

BEST FOOT FORWARD (1941)

BOOK BY: John Cecil Holm
MUSIC AND LYRICS BY: Hugh Martin and Ralph
    Blane
PUBLISHED LIBRETTO: Dramatic, 1943
CONDENSATION: *New Complete Book of the
    American Musical Theater.* Ewen, David. Holt,
    1970
ANTHOLOGY: None
MUSIC PUBLISHER: Chappell, 1941
LICENSING AGENT: Tams-Witmark
RECORDING: DRG 15003 CD (1963 cast)
CAST: 12 M; 9 F

A fading film star agrees to appear at the annual prom at Winsocki and as a result causes confusion and pandemonium. This bright and appealing musical has a number of good songs: "Just a Little Joint with a Jukebox," "The Three Bs," and "Buckle Down, Winsocki." This was filmed by MGM with June Allyson. The off-Broadway revival introduced Liza Minnelli.

1963 REVIVAL CAST:

Liza Minnelli (Ethel Hofflinger)
Paul Charles (Fred Jones)
Paula Wayne (Gale Joy)
Kay Cole (Minerva Brooks)
Christopher Walken (Dutch Miller)
Edmund Gaynes (Hunk Hoyt)
Jack Irwin (Old Grad)
Gene Castle (Goofy Clarke)
Don Slaton (Satchel Moyer)
Grant Walden (Jack Haggerty)
Glenn Walken (Bud Hooper)
Renee Winters (Linda Ferguson)
Karin Wolfe (Helen Schlessinger)

SONGS:
Act I
Wish I May (ensemble)
Three Men on a Date (Dutch, Hunk, Bud)
The Old Hollywood Story (Gale, Jack)
Everytime (Helen)
Three Bs (Ethel, Minerva, Helen)
The Guy Who Brought Her (Gale, Dutch, Jack,
    Hunk, Bud)
Shady Lady-Bird (Helen, Hunk, Goofy, Satchel,
    Fred)

Act II
Buckle Down, Winsocki (Old Grad, Hunk,
    ensemble)
What Do You Think I Am? (Hunk, Ethel,
    Minerva, Dutch, ensemble)
Raving Beauty (Dutch, Minerva)
Just a Little Joint with a Jukebox (Ethel)
You Are for Loving (Ethel)

THE BEST LITTLE WHOREHOUSE IN TEXAS (1978)

BOOK BY: Larry L. King and Peter Masterson;
    based on an article by Larry L. King
MUSIC AND LYRICS BY: Carol Hall
PUBLISHED LIBRETTO: French, 1978
CONDENSATION: *The Best Plays of 1977–1978.*
    Otis L. Guernsey, Jr., ed. Dodd, Mead, 1978;
    Ganzl's Book of the Musical Theatre. Ganzl, Kurt.
    Schirmer (Macmillan), 1989
ANTHOLOGY: None
VOCAL SELECTIONS: MCA Music, 1979
LICENSING AGENT: Samuel French
RECORDING: MCA 3049 CD (original cast)
CAST: 13 M; 14 F; extras

This popular show and film take place in a brothel called "The Chicken Ranch" in a small Texas town. The plot revolves around a crusading TV moralist who is out to close down the ranch. It is very funny on a low, profane level. The original production was particularly praised for the direction and choreography of Tommy Tune.

ORIGINAL CAST:

Carlin Glynn (Mona)
Henderson Forsythe (Sheriff Ed Earl Dodd)
Clint Allmon (Melvin)
Lisa Brown (Imogene)
Paul Ukena, Jr. (Dogette)
Gerry Burkhardt (Shy Kid)
Jay Bursky (Dogette)
Michael Scott (Dogette)
Jay Garner (Governor)
Delores Hall (Jewel)
Susan Mansur (Doatsey Mae)

SONGS:
Act I
20 Fans (company)
A Lil Ole Bitty Pissant Country Place (Mona, girls)
Girl You're a Woman (Mona, girls)
Watch Dog Theme (Dogettes)
Texas Has a Whorehouse in It (Melvin, chorus)
Twenty-Four Hours of Lovin' (Jewel, girls)
Doatsey Mae (Doatsey)
The Angelette March (Imogene, girls)
The Aggie Song (men)
Bus from Amarillo (Mona)

Act II
The Sidestep (Governor, company)
No Lies (Mona, Jewel, girls)
Good Old Girl (Sheriff Ed, men)
Hard Candy Christmas (girls)

BIG RIVER (1985)

BOOK BY: William Hauptman; adapted from *The Adventures of Huckleberry Finn* by Mark Twain
MUSIC AND LYRICS BY: Roger Miller
PUBLISHED LIBRETTO: Grove Press, 1986
CONDENSATION: *Broadway Musicals Show by Show.* Green, Stanley. Hal Leonard Books, 1985
ANTHOLOGY: None
VOCAL SELECTIONS: Hal Leonard, 1986
LICENSING AGENT: Rodgers and Hammerstein Theatre Library
RECORDING: MCA 6147 CD (original cast)
CAST: 14 M; 7 F

The character of Mark Twain himself introduces this show to the audience and warns them not to look for a motive, a moral, or a plot. This award-winning version of his classic tale was deemed to be more a play with songs than a musical—but there are seventeen songs with a strong country-western flavor. The New York production featured sliding scenic props and a "spectacular riverscape" backdrop. The actors sometimes spilled over into the balcony boxes, and a runway around the orchestra pit was utilized. The sound effects included a chorus of crickets before the curtain went up. The runaway slave, Jim, requires a big voice for "Free at Last" and for his other numbers. The "Duke" and the "King" have a showstopping turn with "When the Sun Goes Down in the South." Costumed in the pre–Civil War period, there are forty-five scenes and sixty-five characters in this show. Most critics felt it preserved the heart of a great book and was distinctively American. For another musical based on this same material see *Downriver*.

Tony Award Winner (Best Musical)

ORIGINAL CAST:

Daniel Jenkins (Huck)
Ron Richardson (Jim)
Bob Gunton (The King)
Rene Auberjonois (The Duke)
Patti Cohenour (Mary Jane)
John Goodman (Pap)
Peggy Harmon (Susan)
Jennifer Leigh Warren (Alice's daughter)
Andi Henig (Joanna)
John Short (Tom)
William Youmans (A Young Fool)

SONGS:
Act I
Do You Want to Go to Heaven? (company)
The Boys (Tom, gang)
Waiting for the Light to Shine (Huck)
Guv'ment (Pap)
Hand for the Hog (Tom)
I, Huckleberry, Me (Huck)
Muddy Water (Jim, Huck)

Crossing Over (Slaves, Overseer)
River in the Rain (Huck, Jim)
When the Sun Goes Down in the South (Duke,
    King, Huck)

Act II
The Royal Nonesuch (Duke, company)
Worlds Apart (Jim, Huck)
Arkansas (Young Fool)
How Blest We Are (Alice's daughter,
    company)
You Ought to Be Here with Me (Mary Jane,
    Susan, Joanna)
Leaving's Not the Only Way to Go (Mary Jane,
    Jim, Huck)
Free at Last (Jim)

BILLION DOLLAR BABY (1945)

BOOK AND LYRICS BY: Betty Comden and Adolph
    Green
MUSIC BY: Morton Gould
PUBLISHED LIBRETTO: None
CONDENSATION: *New Complete Book of the
    American Musical Theater*. Ewen, David. Holt,
    1970
ANTHOLOGY: None
VOCAL SELECTIONS: Chappell
LICENSING AGENT: Tams-Witmark
RECORDING: Excerpt included on *Jerome Robbins'
    Broadway* RCA 60150-2 CD
CAST: 19 M; 12 F

A satire on the "terrific twenties," this show
takes place during the time of gangsters
and gangster funerals—of Texas Guinan
and her silly suckers—of beauty contests
and dance marathons—what John Chapman of the *New York Daily News* called "the
markhellinger era." There is a bit of satire in
the sets and costumes, and even in the production numbers. The "Charleston" number was featured in the 1989 *Jerome Robbins' Broadway*.

ORIGINAL CAST:

Joan McCracken (Maribelle)
Mitzi Green (Georgia)
David Burns (Dapper)

Don De Leo (Jerry)
David Thomas (Waiter)
Tony Cardell (Violin Player)
William Tabbert (Rocky)
Robert Chisholm (M. M. Montague)
Shirley Van (Esme)
Danny Daniels (Champ)

SONGS:
Act I
Who's Gonna Be the Winner (Maribelle, girls)
Dreams Come True (Maribelle, men)
Broadway Blossom (Georgia)
Speaking of Pals (Dapper, Jerry, Rocky,
    Waiter, Violin Player, ensemble)
There I'd Be (Georgia, M. M. Montague)
One-Track Mind (Esme, Champ)
Bad Timing (Rocky, Maribelle)
A Lovely Girl (Georgia, Maribelle)

Act II
Funeral Procession (the mob)
Havin' a Time (Georgia)
Faithless (M. M. Montague, Maribelle)
I'm Sure of Your Love (Rocky)
A Life with Rocky (Maribelle)

THE BIOGRAPH GIRL
(1980—London)

BOOK BY: Warner Brown
MUSIC BY: David Heneker
LYRICS BY: Warner Brown and David Heneker
PUBLISHED LIBRETTO: French, 1983
CONDENSATION: None
ANTHOLOGY: None
PIANO-VOCAL SCORE: Chappell (London), 1983
LICENSING AGENT: Samuel French
RECORDING: That's Entertainment Records
    (British) TER 1003 CD (London cast)
CAST: 6 M; 6 F

Lillian Gish, D. W. Griffith, and Mack Sennett
are some of the characters in this British
musical about early filmmaking, first in
New York and then in Hollywood. Mary
Pickford is "The Biograph Girl" and much of
the plot centers around her quest for fame

and fortune. The title song is a fast tap number for the company, and most critics mentioned the "Nineteen Twenty-Five" number that draws the silent film era to a close. This modest musical was particularly recommended for stock and community theaters by *Variety* when they reviewed it.

ORIGINAL LONDON CAST:

Sheila White (Mary Pickford)
Kate Revill (Lillian Gish)
Ron Berglas (Billy/Adolph)
Bruce Barry (D. W. Griffith)
Jane Hardy (Wally)
Guy Siner (Mack)

SONGS:
Act I
The Moving Picture Show (company)
Working in Flickers (Mary)
That's What I Get All Day (Wally, chorus)
The Moment I Close My Eyes (D. W. Griffith)
Diggin' Gold Dust (company)
Every Lady Needs a Master (Lillian)
I Just Wanted to Make Him Laugh (Mack, Lillian)
I Like to Be the Way I Am in My Own Front Parlor (Mary, company)
Beyond Babel (D. W. Griffith, company)

Act II
A David Griffith Show (company)
More than a Man (Lillian)
The Industry (company)
Gentle Fade (D. W. Griffith)
Nineteen Twenty-Five (company)
The Biograph Girl (company)
One of the Pioneers (D. W. Griffith)
Put It in the Tissue Paper (Mack, Mary, Lillian)

BIRDS OF PARADISE (1987)

BOOK BY: Winnie Holzman and David Evans
MUSIC BY: David Evans
LYRICS BY: Winnie Holzman
PUBLISHED LIBRETTO: French
CONDENSATION: None
ANTHOLOGY: None

LICENSING AGENT: Samuel French
RECORDING: TER 1196 CD (original cast)
CAST: 4 M; 4 F

The lives of a group of amateur players are changed by the visit of a professional actor as they prepare a musical version of Chekhov's *The Seagull*. As the opening approaches their lives begin to reflect their roles in the play in comic ways. Performed off-Broadway in New York.

ORIGINAL CAST:

Todd Graff (Homer)
Mary Beth Peil (Marjorie)
Barbara Walsh (Stella)
G. K. Simmons (Andy)
Donna Murphy (Hope)
Andrew Hill Newman (Dave)
Christa Moore (Julia)
John Cunningham (Wood)

SONGS:
Act I
So Many Nights (Homer, Marjorie, Stella, Andy, Hope, Dave)
Diva (Hope, Dave, Andy)
Every Dog's Night (Julia)
Somebody (Wood, company)
Coming True (Homer, Julia)
It's Only a Play (Homer, company)
She's Out There (Andy)
Birds of Paradise (Marjorie, Stella, Hope)
Imagining You (company)

Act II
Penguins Must Sing (Dave, Hope, Andy)
You're Mine (Marjorie)
Things I Can't Forget (Homer, Marjorie)
After Opening Night (Homer, Marjorie)
Chekhov (company)
Something New (company)

BITTER SWEET (1929)

BOOK, MUSIC, AND LYRICS BY: Noel Coward
PUBLISHED LIBRETTO: Doubleday, 1929
CONDENSATION: *Ganzl's Book of the Musical Theatre.* Ganzl, Kurt. Schirmer (Macmillan), 1989

ANTHOLOGY: *Play Parade*, vol. 1. Heinemann
(London), 1934
PIANO-VOCAL SCORE: Harms, 1929
LICENSING AGENT: Tams-Witmark
RECORDINGS: Angel S 35814 (studio cast); TER
1160 CD (British revival cast)
CAST: 22 M; 12 F

The time is the 1870s and the setting is Vienna. Sari has fallen in love with her music teacher and they have run away together; he leads the orchestra in a cafe and she works as a dance girl. This romantic operetta is called buoyant, light-hearted, and graciously amusing. Coward songs include "I'll See You Again" and "Zigeuner." Jeanette MacDonald and Nelson Eddy starred in the 1939 film.

ORIGINAL CAST:

Evelyn Laye (Sari/Sarah/Lady Shayne)
Gerald Nodin (Carl)
Zoe Gordon (Lotte)
Nancy Barnett (Freda)
Dorothy Debenham (Hansi)
Sylvia Leslie (Gussi)
Mireille (Manon)

SONGS:
Act I
The Call of Life (Lady Shayne, chorus)
If You Could Only Come with Me (Carl)
I'll See You Again (Sarah, Carl)
Tell Me What Love Is (Sarah, chorus)
The Last Dance (ensemble)

Act II
Ladies of the Town (Lotte, Freda, Hansi,
Gussi)
If Love Were All (Manon)
Evermore and a Day (Sari)
Little Cafe (Sari, Carl)
Tokay (Carl, chorus)
Bonne Nuit, Merci (Manon)
Kiss Me (Manon, chorus)

Act III
Ta-Ra-Ra Boom-De-Ay (ensemble)
Alas, the Time Is Past (girls)
Green Carnations (men)
Zigeuner (Sari)

BLOOMER GIRL (1944)

BOOK BY: Sig Herzig and Fred Saidy; based on the
play by Lilith and Dan James
MUSIC BY: Harold Arlen
LYRICS BY: E. Y. Harburg
PUBLISHED LIBRETTO: None
CONDENSATION: *New Complete Book of the
American Musical Theater.* Ewen, David. Holt,
1970
ANTHOLOGY: None
VOCAL SELECTIONS: Chappell, 1944
LICENSING AGENT: Tams-Witmark
RECORDING: MCA 10522 CD (original cast)
CAST: 18 M; 13 F; chorus

The original production was the biggest thing since *Oklahoma!* Dolly Bloomer, in rebellion against the suppression of women's rights, starts an anti-hoopskirt fashion. Hence the term bloomers. The time is 1861, so the Civil War figures in the plot. Ballets by Agnes de Mille were featured in the original production. There was a revival at Goodspeed in East Haddam, Connecticut, in 1981.

ORIGINAL CAST:

Celeste Holm (Evelina)
David Brooks (Jeff)
Mabel Taliaferro (Serena)
Matt Briggs (Horatio)
Dooley Wilson (Pompey)
Joan McCracken (Daisy)
Richard Huey (Alexander)
Joseph Florestano (Deputy)
Hubert Dilworth (Augustus)
Alan Gilbert (male soloist)

SONGS:
Act I
When the Boys Come Home (Serena,
daughters)
Evelina (Jeff, Evelina)
Welcome Hinges (Serena, Horatio, Evelina,
Jeff, daughters, sons-in-law)
Farmer's Daughter (sons-in-law)
It Was Good Enough for Grandma (Evelina,
girls)
The Eagle and Me (Pompey)

Right as the Rain (Jeff, Evelina)
T'morra' T'morra' (Daisy)
Rakish Young Man with the Whiskers
　(Evelina, Jeff)
Pretty as a Picture (male ensemble)

Act II
Sunday in Cicero Falls (company)
I Got a Song (Alexander, Augustus, Pompey)
Lullaby (Evelina)
Simon Legree (Deputy)
Liza Crossing the Ice (ensemble)
I Never Was Born (Daisy)
Man for Sale (male soloist)

BLUE PLATE SPECIAL (1983)

BOOK BY: Tom Edwards
MUSIC BY: Harris Wheeler
LYRICS BY: Mary L. Fisher
PUBLISHED LIBRETTO: Broadway Play Publishing,
　1985
CONDENSATION: None
ANTHOLOGY: None
LICENSING AGENT: Broadway Play Publishing
RECORDING: Cassette tape available from agent
CAST: 3 M; 3 F

Called a "country-music soap-opera spoof"
this musical is set in a diner in Morning Glory Mountain, Tennessee. Some of
the characters include the diner's owner,
whose vegetable stew comes from a garden
atop a nuclear waste dump, and a Nashville
country singer just out of jail. The music comes from an on-stage jukebox. A fun
show with some gentle messages.

ORIGINAL CAST:

Gretchen Cryer (Della)
Mary Gordon Murray (Connie Sue)
Tina Johnson (Ramona)
Gordon Paddison (Ronnie Frank)
Ron Holgate (Larry)

SONGS:
Act I
Morning Glory Mountain (Della, company)
At the Bottom Lookin' Up (Connie Sue)
Ramona's Lament (Ramona)

Never Say Never (Ramona, Ronnie Frank)
Halfway to Heaven (Connie Sue, Ramona,
　Della)
Satisfaction Guaranteed (Larry, Della,
　company)

Act II
Blue Plate Special (Della, company)
Twice as Nice (Della, Larry)
All-American Male (Ronnie Frank)
Side of Fries (Della, Connie Sue, Ramona)
Honky Tonk Queen (Connie Sue, Ramona)
I Ain't Looking Back (Connie Sue, company)
I'm Gonna Miss These Tennessee Nights (Della)

BLUES IN THE NIGHT (1982)

CONCEIVED BY: Sheldon Epps
MUSIC AND LYRICS BY: Various composers
PUBLISHED LIBRETTO: None
CONDENSATION: None
ANTHOLOGY: None
LICENSING AGENT: Music Theatre International
RECORDING: First Night Scene CD 9 CD (original
　London cast)
CAST: 1 M; 3 F

A unit set of a cheap hotel in 1938 Chicago
shows us three separate rooms occupied
by the three women. They sit in their
rooms, singing and talking. In the first act
they are dressing, presumably to go out.
In the second act they have returned and
are undressing. We never know who they
are, and they never acknowledge each
other. There is no dialogue, and a minimum of dancing. Done in a cabaret style,
the women take turns singing separately,
and sometimes together. Occasionally the
man sings. This was done in London and
returned to New York in an off-Broadway
theater.

ORIGINAL CAST:

Leslie Uggams (Woman #1)
Jean Du Shon (Woman #3)
Debbie Shapiro (Woman #2)
Charles Coleman (Saloon Singer)

SONGS:

Act I

Blue Blue (company)

Four Walls (and One Dirty Window) Blues
(Saloon Singer)

I've Got a Date with a Dream (Woman #1,
Woman #2)

These Foolish Things Remind Me of You
(Woman #1)

New Orleans Hop Scop Blues (Woman #3)

It Makes My Love Come Down (Women)

Copenhagen (Woman #2)

Wild Women Don't Have the Blues (Saloon
Singer)

Lover Man (Woman #1)

Take Me for a Buggy Ride (Woman #3)

Willow Weep for Me (Woman #2)

Kitchen Man (Woman #3)

Low (Woman #1)

Take It Right Back (Women)

Act II

Blues in the Night (Woman #1, Woman #2)

Dirty No-Gooder Blues (Woman #3)

When a Woman Loves a Man (Saloon Singer)

Am I Blue? (Women)

Rough and Ready Man (Woman #1)

Reckless Blues (Woman #2)

Wasted Life Blues (Woman #3)

Baby Doll (Saloon Singer)

Nobody Knows You When You're Down and
Out (Women)

I Gotta Right to Sing the Blues (Women)

This spoof of the boxing industry features
a wealthy young collegian boxer from Dart-
mouth who goes into professional fighting
and has various mishaps. This was a late
fifties show, so there is a rock-and-roll number by street kids in the Elvis Presley style.

ORIGINAL CAST:

Jack Warden (Dave)

Mindy Carson (Ann)

Mara Lynn (Gloria)

Barbara McNair (Marge)

William Hickey (Albert)

Lonnie Sattin (Harry)

Steve Forrest (Bob)

SONGS:

Act I

Where Are They? (Dave, chorus)

The Body Beautiful (Ann, men)

Pffft! (Bob, Albert)

Fair Warning (Marge, Harry, chorus)

Leave Well Enough Alone (Ann)

Blonde Blues (Dave)

Uh-Huh, Oh Yeah! (men)

All of These and More (Ann, Bob, chorus)

Nobility (men)

Act II

Summer Is (chorus)

The Honeymoon Is Over (Gloria, girls)

Just My Luck (Ann, kids)

All of These and More (reprise) (Marge,
Harry)

Art of Conversation (Albert, chorus)

Gloria (Dave, Gloria)

A Relatively Simple Affair (Ann, Marge)

THE BODY BEAUTIFUL (1958)

BOOK BY: Joseph Stein and Will Glickman

MUSIC BY: Jerry Bock

LYRICS BY: Sheldon Harnick

PUBLISHED LIBRETTO: French, 1959

CONDENSATION: None

ANTHOLOGY: None

VOCAL SELECTIONS: Valando, 1962

LICENSING AGENT: Samuel French

RECORDING: Blue Pear BP 1006 (original cast)

CAST: 20 M; 6 F; chorus

THE BOY FRIEND (1954)

BOOK, MUSIC, AND LYRICS BY: Sandy Wilson

PUBLISHED LIBRETTO: Dutton, 1955

CONDENSATION: *The Best Plays of 1954–1955.*
Louis Kronenberger, ed. Dodd, 1955; *Ganzl's
Book of the Musical Theatre.* Ganzl, Kurt.
Schirmer (Macmillan), 1989

ANTHOLOGY: None

PIANO-VOCAL SCORE: Chappell, 1960

VOCAL SELECTIONS: Chappell, 1954

LICENSING AGENT: Music Theatre International
RECORDING: RCA 60056 CD (original cast)
CAST: 12 M; 13 F

This musical comedy spoof of the 1920s has been consistently popular since 1954 and has been performed many times throughout the world. It has been called perfectly conceived and a classic. The plot is about a romance between a rich girl and a rich boy, each believing the other to be poor. But never mind the plot, concentrate on the 1926 sets of the Riviera, the flappers doing "Won't You Charleston with Me?" and all the clichés of twenties musicals! Julie Andrews was the first "Polly" on Broadway and Twiggy played the part in the 1971 film version.

ORIGINAL CAST:

Julie Andrews (Polly)
John Hewer (Tony)
Ruth Altman (Madame Dubonnet)
Ann Wakefield (Maisie)
Geoffrey Hibbert (Lord Brockhurst)
Eric Berry (Percival)
Paulette Girard (Hortense)
Dilys Lay (Dulcie)
Bob Scheerer (Bobby)

SONGS:
Act I
Perfect Young Ladies (Hortense, Maisie, Dulcie, girls)
The Boy Friend (Polly, Maisie, Dulcie, girls, boys)
Won't You Charleston with Me? (Maisie, Bobby)
Fancy Forgetting (Madame Dubonnet, Percival)
I Could Be Happy with You (Polly, Tony)

Act II
Sur La Plage (Maisie, Bobby, girls, boys)
A Room in Bloomsbury (Polly, Tony)
You Don't Want to Play with Me Blues (Madame Dubonnet, Percival, girls)
Safety in Numbers (Maisie, boys)

Act III
Riviera (Maisie, Bobby, girls, boys)

It's Never Too Late to Fall in Love (Lord Brockburst, Dulcie)
Poor Little Pierrette (Madame Dubonnet, Polly)

THE BOYS FROM SYRACUSE (1938)

BOOK BY: George Abbott; based on *The Comedy of Errors* by William Shakespeare
MUSIC BY: Richard Rodgers
LYRICS BY: Lorenz Hart
PUBLISHED LIBRETTO: None
CONDENSATION: *New Complete Book of the American Musical Theater.* Ewen, David. Holt, 1970
ANTHOLOGY: None
PIANO-VOCAL SCORE: Chappell, 1965
VOCAL SELECTIONS: Chappell, 1938
LICENSING AGENT: Rodgers and Hammerstein Theatre Library
RECORDINGS: Sony SK 53329 CD (studio cast); Capitol STAO 1933 (1963 revival cast); Angel ZDM 7 64695-2 CD (1963 revival cast)
CAST: 13 M; 7 F

Ephesus in ancient Greece is the scene for this tale of two sets of identical twins reunited through a wild series of improbable complications. Most critics agree that Rodgers and Hart were at their peak when they composed this famous score that includes "This Can't Be Love" and "Falling in Love with Love." There was a film version in 1940 with Martha Raye and Allan Jones.

ORIGINAL CAST:

Eddie Albert (Antipholus)
Jimmy Salvo (Dromio)
Muriel Angelus (Adriana)
Wynn Murray (Luce)
Ronald Graham (Antipholus of Ephesus)
Teddy Hart (Dromio of Ephesus)
Marcy Westcott (Luciana)
John O'Shaughnessey (Aegeon)
Bob Lawrence (Sergeant)
Carroll Ashburn (Duke)
John Clarke (Angelo)

SONGS:
(from 1963 revival)
Act I
I Had Twins (Aegeon, Sergeant, Duke, Angelo)
Dear Old Syracuse (Antipholus, Dromio)
What Can You Do with a Man (Luce, Dromio of Ephesus)
Falling in Love with Love (Adriana)
The Shortest Day of the Year (Antipholus of Ephesus)
This Can't Be Love (Antipholus, Luciana)

Act II
Ladies of the Evening (Sergeant, company)
He and She (Luce, Dromio)
You Have Cast Your Shadow on the Sea (Antipholus, Luciana)
Come with Me (Antipholus of Ephesus, Sergeant, Angelo, Duke, men)
Big Brother (Dromio of Ephesus)
Sing for Your Supper (Adriana, Luciana, Luce)
Oh Diogenes! (Luce, company)

BRIGADOON (1947)

BOOK AND LYRICS BY: Alan Jay Lerner
MUSIC BY: Frederick Loewe
PUBLISHED LIBRETTO: Coward, McCann, 1947; *Theatre Arts* (magazine), August 1952
CONDENSATION: *Burns Mantle Best Plays of 1946–1947.* Burns Mantle, ed. Dodd, Mead, 1947; *Ganzl's Book of the Musical Theatre.* Ganzl, Kurt. Schirmer (Macmillan), 1989
ANTHOLOGY: *Ten Great Musicals of the American Stage.* Stanley Richards, ed. Chilton, 1973
PIANO-VOCAL SCORE: Big Three
VOCAL SELECTIONS: Big Three; CPP/Belwin
LICENSING AGENT: Tams-Witmark
RECORDING: RCA 1001-2 CD (original cast)
CAST: 12 M; 5 F; extras

Brigadoon is a town in Scotland that comes awake for only one day in a century. Two Yanks stumble into the village and fall in love with two of the local girls. Some critics feel that this is the best Lerner and Loewe musical. Gene Kelly starred in the film. Recent revivals have emphasized the classical training of the dancers.

ORIGINAL CAST:
Marion Bell (Fiona)
David Brooks (Tommy)
Pamela Britton (Meg)
Lee Sullivan (Charlie)
Walter Scheff (Angus)
Elliott Sullivan (Archie)
Paul Anderson (Stuart)

SONGS:
Act I
Once in the Highlands (chorus)
Brigadoon (chorus)
Down on MacConnachy Square (Angus, Archie, Stuart, chorus)
Waitin' for My Dearie (Fiona, girls)
I'll Go Home with Bonnie Jean (Charlie, chorus)
The Heather on the Hill (Tommy, Fiona)
The Love of My Life (Meg)
Jeannie's Packin' Up (girls)
Come to Me, Bend to Me (Charlie)
Almost Like Being in Love (Tommy, Fiona)

Act II
There but for You Go I (Tommy)
My Mother's Weddin' Day (Meg, chorus)
From This Day On (Tommy, Fiona)

BRING BACK BIRDIE (1981)

BOOK BY: Michael Stewart
MUSIC BY: Charles Strouse
LYRICS BY: Lee Adams
PUBLISHED LIBRETTO: None
CONDENSATION: None
ANTHOLOGY: None
LICENSING AGENT: Tams-Witmark
RECORDING: Original Cast OC 8132 (original cast)
CAST: 11 M; 8 F; chorus

This is a sequel to *Bye Bye Birdie*. It is twenty years later and Albert and Rose set out to find Conrad Birdie so that he can appear on a special TV show saluting all-time great recording stars. Since Albert and Rose have teenage children, there is also an opportunity to satirize current music and mores.

ORIGINAL CAST:

Donald O'Connor (Albert)
Robin Morse (Jenny)
Chita Rivera (Rose)
Jeb Brown (Gary)
Maurice Hines (Mtobe)
Marcel Forestieri (Mayor Townsend/Conrad)
Frank DeSal (Reverend Sun)
Maria Karnilova (Mae/Dolores)

SONGS:
Act I
Twenty Happy Years (Rose, Albert)
Movin' Out (Jenny, Gary, kids)
Half of a Couple (Jenny, girl friends)
I Like What I Do (Rose)
Bring Back Birdie (Mtobe, company)
Baby, You Can Count on Me (Albert)
A Man Worth Fightin' For (Rose, cowboys)
You Can Never Go Back (Mayor Townsend)
Filth (rock group)
Back in Show Biz Again (Albert)

Act II
Middle Age Blues (Albert)
Inner Peace (Rose, Reverend Sun, group)
There's a Brand New Beat in Heaven (Mtobe, choir)
Well, I'm Not! (Rose)
When Will Grown-ups Grow Up? (kids)
Young (Albert)
I Love 'Em All (Dolores, men)
Bring Back Birdie (reprise) (Conrad, girls)

BROWNSTONE (1984)

BOOK BY: Josh Rubins, Peter Larson, and Andrew Cadiff
MUSIC BY: Peter Larson and Josh Rubins
LYRICS BY: Josh Rubins
PUBLISHED LIBRETTO: Broadway Play Publishing, 1987
CONDENSATION: None
ANTHOLOGY: None
LICENSING AGENT: Broadway Play Publishing
RECORDING: Demo cassette available from agent
CAST: 2 M; 3 F

Apartment living in Manhattan is the theme of this musical. The set will present a challenge for you, as you will need to show four apartments and one hallway. Your cast represents five diverse people, one married couple and three singles who live in the brownstone. The action takes place during the four seasons as the people move in, move out, tackle spring-cleaning, and otherwise go about the business of living. They read their mail, receive phone calls, repaint, repair, defrost, and take out the garbage. The dialogue is almost all sung.

1986 CAST:

Liz Callaway (Claudia)
Rex Smith (Stuart)
Kimberly Farr (Joan)
Ernestine Jackson (Mary)
Ben Harney (Howard)

SONGS:
Act I
Someone's Moving In (company)
Fiction Writer (Howard)
I Just Want to Know (Claudia)
There She Goes (Joan, Claudia)
We Should Talk (Mary, Howard)
Camouflage (company)
Thanks a Lot (Joan, Stuart, Claudia)
Neighbors Above, Neighbors Below (company)
I Wasn't Home for Christmas (Stuart)
What Do People Do? (Claudia)
Not Today (Joan, company)
You Still Don't Know (Mary)
Babies on the Brain (Howard, company)
Almost There (company)

Act II
Don't Tell Me Everything (Mary, Howard, Claudia, Stuart)
One of Them (Joan, Stuart)
Spring Cleaning (Claudia, Stuart)
Fiction Writer Duet (Howard, Mary)
He Didn't Leave It Here (Joan, Claudia)
It Isn't the End of the World (Mary, Howard)
See That Lady There (Stuart, Joan)
Since You Stayed Here (Claudia)

We Came Along Too Late (Joan, Stuart, Claudia)
Hi There, Joan (company)
It's a Funny Thing (Joan, Stuart)
Nevertheless (Mary, Howard)
Almost There (reprise) (Stuart, Claudia)
Someone's Moving Out (company)

BUBBLING BROWN SUGAR
(1976)

BOOK BY: Lofton Mitchell; based on a concept by Rosetta LeNoire
MUSIC AND LYRICS BY: Danny Holgate, Emme Kemp, Lillian Lopez, and others
PUBLISHED LIBRETTO: Broadway Play Publishing, 1985
CONDENSATION: None
ANTHOLOGY: None
VOCAL SELECTIONS: Chappell, 1976
LICENSING AGENT: Broadway Play Publishing
RECORDINGS: H & L Records 69011 (original cast); DRG 13106 CD (London cast)
CAST: 18 M; 11 F (minimum: 12 actors)

"Brown Sugar" is an affectionate term used to describe black chorus girls. A wisp of a plot concerns some contemporary tourists being taken on a tour back in time to Harlem in the 1920s, 1930s, and 1940s to hear some of the great music of Duke Ellington, Fats Waller, Eubie Blake, and other composers of Harlem's golden age. The primarily black cast sing and dance their way through production numbers and solos. Your set can be as lavish as you wish, and the costumes should dazzle.

ORIGINAL CAST:

Josephine Premice (Irene)
Vernon Washington (Bill)
Avon Long (John)
Barbara Rubenstein (Judy)
Alton Lathrop (Gene)
Carolyn Byrd (Carolyn)
Vivian Reed (Marsha)
Lonnie McNeil (Skip)

Newton Winters (Ray)
Chip Garnett (Jim)
Joseph Attles (Checkers)
Ethel Beatty (Ella)
Anthony Whitehouse (Dutch)
Barry Preston (Charlie)

SONGS:
Act I
Harlem '70 (company)
Bubbling Brown Sugar (company)
That's What Harlem Is to Me (Irene)
Bill Robinson Specialty (Bill)
Harlem Sweet Harlem (company)
Nobody (John)
Goin' Back in Time (Bill)
Some of These Days (Judy)
Movin' Uptown (Bill)
Strolling (Skip, ensemble)
I'm Gonna Tell God All My Troubles (Gene)
His Eve Is on the Sparrow/Swing Low Sweet Chariot (Carolyn, company)
Sweet Georgia Brown (Marsha, Skip, Ray)
Honeysuckle Rose (Irene, John)
Stormy Monday Blues (Carolyn)
Rosetta (Gene, Skip, Ray)
Sophisticated Lady (Jim, Bill)
In Honeysuckle Time (John, Checkers)
Solitude (Marsha, Gene, Skip, Ray)
C'mon Up to Jive Time (Bill)
Stompin' at the Savoy/Take the "A" Train (company)

Act II
Harlem-time (Bill)
Love Will Find a Way (Jim, Ella)
Dutch's Song (Dutch)
Brown Gal (John)
Pray for the Lights to Go Out (Checkers)
I Got It Bad (Ella)
Harlem Makes Me Feel (Charlie)
Jim, Jam, Jumpin' Jive (Bill, Skip, Ray)
There'll Be Some Changes Made (Irene)
God Bless the Child (Marsha)
It Don't Mean a Thing (Jim, Dutch, Irene, company)

BY HEX (1956)

BOOK BY: John Rengier; based on an idea
   suggested by Richard Gehman
MUSIC AND LYRICS BY: Howard Blankman;
   additional lyrics by Richard Gehman and John
   Rengier
PUBLISHED LIBRETTO: Dramatists Play Service,
   1956
CONDENSATION: None
ANTHOLOGY: None
PIANO-VOCAL SCORE: Dramatists Play Service
LICENSING AGENT: Dramatists Play Service
RECORDING: None
CAST: 9 M; 5 F; extras

A rebellious young Amish man named
Jonas wants to go modern with tractors,
television, and red suspenders. He ends
up getting himself "shunned." Jonas learns
his lesson and all ends well for him and
his sweetheart. This small-scale musical
with only one backdrop was first done
in Lancaster (Pennsylvania) and later off-
Broadway. A charming and easily presented score makes this an uncomplicated
show for family audiences.

ORIGINAL CAST:

Norman MacKay (Bishop)
Wynne Miller (Nancy)
Rita Shay (Lydia)
Tom Mixon (Eli)
Diane Griffith (Annie)
Ken Cantril (Jonas)

SONGS:
Act I
Market Day (Bishop, cast)
Shunned (Bishop)
Ferhuddled and Ferhexed (Nancy)
Wonderful Good (Lydia, Eli, company)
What Is Love? (Annie)
I Can Learn (Jonas, Nancy)
What Is Love? (reprise) (Nancy)
Only a Man (Bishop)

Act II
An Amishman (Eli, Lydia, others)
I Have Lived (Annie)

I Know My Love (Nancy)
The Trouble with Me (Jonas)
Something New (Jonas, Nancy)
It Takes Time (Bishop)

BY JUPITER (1942)

BOOK BY: Richard Rodgers and Lorenz Hart;
   based on the play *The Warrior's Husband* by
   Julian F. Thompson; additional material for the
   1967 production by Fred Ebb
MUSIC BY: Richard Rodgers
LYRICS BY: Lorenz Hart
PUBLISHED LIBRETTO: None
CONDENSATION: *New Complete Book of the
   American Musical Theater.* Ewen, David. Holt,
   1970
ANTHOLOGY: None
MUSIC PUBLISHER: Chappell, 1942
LICENSING AGENT: Rodgers and Hammerstein
   Theatre Library
RECORDING: RCA LSO 1137 (1967 cast recording)
CAST: 9 M; 8 F

Set in ancient Greece, this is the tale of
mighty Hercules, in a woman's world, who
sets out to wrest the girdle of domination from Hippolyta, Queen of the Ama-
zons. The original production was called
naughty and ribald; the songs include
"Ev'rything I've Got" and "Nobody's Heart."
This is a dancing show; Ray Bolger was the
original star.

ORIGINAL CAST:

Ray Bolger (Sapiens)
Constance Moore (Antiope)
Benay Venuta (Hippolyta)
Ronald Graham (Theseus)
Ralph Dumke (Hercules)
Bernie Gould (Homer)
Mark Dawson (Herald)
Jayne Manners (Buria)
Bertha Belmore (Pomposia)
Maidel Turner (Caustica)
Margaret Bannerman (Heroica)

SONGS:

(from 1967 revival)

Act I

For Jupiter and Greece (Hercules, Theseus, Homer, Herald, men)

Ride Amazon Ride (Buria, women)

Jupiter Forbid (Hippolyta, Pomposia, Caustica, Heroica, chorus)

Life with Father (Sapiens, men)

Nobody's Heart (Antiope)

In the Gateway of the Temple of Minerva (Theseus)

Here's a Hand (Theseus, Antiope)

Act II

Wait Till You See Her (Theseus, Homer, Herald, Hercules, men)

The Boy I Left Behind Me (Buria, women)

Nobody's Heart (reprise) (Sapiens)

Ev'rything I've Got (Hippolyta, Sapiens)

Bottoms Up (Hippolyta, Antiope, Herald, Homer, Caustica, Heroica, chorus)

Careless Rhapsody (Antiope, Theseus)

Now That I've Got My Strength (Sapiens, chorus)

BY STROUSE (1978)

MUSIC BY: Charles Strouse

LYRICS BY: Lee Adams, Martin Charnin, David Rogers, Charles Strouse, and Fred Tobias

PUBLISHED LIBRETTO: None

CONDENSATION: None

ANTHOLOGY: None

VOCAL SELECTIONS: None (see individual titles by Strouse)

LICENSING AGENT: Samuel French

RECORDING: None (see individual titles by Strouse)

CAST: 1 M; 3 F

This show includes thirty-five numbers— "I-feel-great-songs, I-feel-blue-songs, times-they-are-a-changing-songs," said Rex Reed of the *New York Daily News*—from a dozen different shows without dialogue or sets and with only a few props. Songs are from such Strouse shows as *Annie*, *Bye Bye Birdie*, and *Applause* and include the title song from the TV show *All in the Family*.

ORIGINAL CAST:

Gary Beach

Donna Marshall

Maureen Moore

Gail Nelson

This revue is made up of thirty-five songs performed without an intermission.

BY THE BEAUTIFUL SEA (1954)

BOOK BY: Herbert and Dorothy Fields

MUSIC BY: Arthur Schwartz

LYRICS BY: Dorothy Fields

PUBLISHED LIBRETTO: None

CONDENSATION: *New Complete Book of the American Musical Theater.* Ewen, David. Holt, 1970

ANTHOLOGY: None

VOCAL SELECTIONS: Edwin H. Morris

LICENSING AGENT: Music Theatre International

RECORDING: Angel 764889-2 CD (original cast)

CAST: 12 M; 7 F; chorus

The scene is Coney Island in the early 1900s. A boarding-house proprietor falls in love with a Shakespearean actor who is down on his luck and currently doing a vaudeville act. The sets include the Midway, the Old Mill, the Dreamland Casino, and the Brighton Beach Vaudeville Theater. This show was particularly praised for its star, Shirley Booth.

ORIGINAL CAST:

Shirley Booth (Lottie Gibson)

Richard France (Mickey Powers)

Robert Jennings (Half-Note)

Wilbur Evans (Dennis Emery)

Mae Barnes (Ruby Monk)

Eddie Roll (Sidney)

Larry Howard (Lenny)

Mary Harmon (Cora)

Cindy Robbins (Molly)

Gloria Smith (Lillian)

Thomas Gleason (Diabolo)

Larry Laurence (Burt)

SONGS:

Act I

Mona from Arizona (male quartet)
The Sea Song (Lottie, boarders, neighbors)
Old Enough to Love (Mickey)
Coney Island Boat (Lottie, Half-Note, visitors)
Alone Too Long (Dennis)
Happy Habit (Ruby)
Good Time Charlie (Mickey, Sidney, Lenny,
    Cora, Molly, Lillian)
I'd Rather Wake Up by Myself (Lottie)
Hooray for George the Third (Diabolo,
    visitors)

Act II

Hang Up (Ruby, boarders, visitors)
More Love than Your Love (Dennis)
Lottie Gibson Specialty (Lottie)
Throw the Anchor Away (Burt, Cora)

BYE BYE BIRDIE (1960)

BOOK BY: Michael Stewart
MUSIC BY: Charles Strouse
LYRICS BY: Lee Adams
PUBLISHED LIBRETTO: Drama Book Shop, 1962
CONDENSATION: *Broadway's Best, 1960.* John
    Chapman, ed. Doubleday, 1960; *Ganzl's Book
    of the Musical Theatre.* Ganzl, Kurt. Schirmer
    (Macmillan), 1989
ANTHOLOGY: None
PIANO-VOCAL SCORE: Big Three (Morris, 1962)
VOCAL SELECTIONS: Big Three (Morris, 1963)
LICENSING AGENT: Tams-Witmark
RECORDING: Columbia CK 2025 CD (original cast)
CAST: 22 M; 26 F

Conrad Birdie, a rock-and-roll singer, has
been drafted! This satire on the Elvis Presley incident was one of the earliest Broadway musicals to use rock-and-roll rhythms.
It first creeps into the "Telephone Hour"
number with all the teenagers in different
boxes. It was an amusing hit back then
and now has the added appeal of nostalgia. There is also an adult story with traditional show tunes. This was a popular film
with Ann-Margret in 1963.

Tony Award Winner (Best Musical)

ORIGINAL CAST:

Chita Rivera (Rose)
Dick Van Dyke (Albert)
Susan Watson (Kim)
Jessica Albright (Deborah)
Sharon Lerit (Alice)
Dick Gautier (Conrad)
Paul Lynde (Mr. MacAfee)
Marijane Maricle (Mrs. MacAfee)
Johnny Borden (Randolph)

SONGS:

Act I

An English Teacher (Rose, Albert)
The Telephone Hour (teenagers)
How Lovely to Be a Woman (Kim)
We Love You, Conrad! (teenagers)
Put on a Happy Face (Albert)
Normal American Boy (Rose, Albert, chorus)
One Boy (Kim, Deborah, Alice)
Reprise (Rose)
Honestly Sincere (Conrad, chorus)
Hymn for a Sunday Evening (Mr. MacAfee,
    Mrs. MacAfee, Kim, Randolph, chorus)
One Last Kiss (Conrad, company)

Act II

What Did I Ever See in Him? (Rose, Kim)
A Lot of Livin' to Do (Conrad, Kim, teenagers)
Kids (Mr. MacAfee, Mrs. MacAfee) Reprise
    (Randolph, ensemble)
Baby, Talk to Me (Albert, quartet)
Spanish Rose (Rose)
Rosie (Albert, Kim)

CABARET (1966)

BOOK BY: Joe Masteroff; based on the play *I Am
    a Camera* by John Van Druten and stories by
    Christopher Isherwood
MUSIC BY: John Kander
LYRICS BY: Fred Ebb
PUBLISHED LIBRETTO: Random House, 1967 (as
    "Harold Prince's Cabaret")
CONDENSATION: *The Best Plays of 1966–1967.*
    Otis L. Guernsey, Jr., ed. Dodd, Mead, 1967;
    Ganzl's Book of the Musical Theatre. Ganzl, Kurt.
    Schirmer (Macmillan), 1989

ANTHOLOGY: *Great Musicals of the American Theatre*, vol. 2. Stanley Richards, ed. Chilton, 1976

PIANO-VOCAL SCORE: Sunbeam Music (Valando), 1968

VOCAL SELECTIONS: New York Times Music, 1972

LICENSING AGENT: Tams-Witmark

RECORDING: Columbia CK 3040 CD (original cast)

CAST: 13 M; 15 F

The time is 1930 and the city is Berlin. There are several intertwined plots involving Sally, the young English girl who performs at the Kit Kat Club; Cliff, the American writer who lives at the same boarding house as Sally; and Fraulein Schneider, the landlady, and her romance with Herr Schultz. All these stories come together with the rise of Nazism. The role of the Master of Ceremonies is one of the most theatrical in modern musical comedy and made a star of Joel Grey. This is an extremely popular adult musical that was even more popular as a film with Liza Minnelli in 1972.

Tony Award Winner (Best Musical)

ORIGINAL CAST:

Joel Grey (Master of Ceremonies)
Bert Convy (Clifford Bradford)
Edward Winter (Ernst Ludwig)
Lotte Lenya (Fraulein Schneider)
Jack Gilford (Herr Schultz)
Peg Murray (Fraulein Kost)
Jill Haworth (Sally Bowles)
Jerry Admire (Bobby)

SONGS:

Act I

Willkommen (Emcee, company)
So What? (Fraulein Schneider)
Don't Tell Mama (Sally, girls)
Telephone Song (company)
Perfectly Marvelous (Cliff, Sally)
Two Ladies (Emcee, two ladies)
It Couldn't Please Me More (Fraulein Schneider, Herr Schultz)
Tomorrow Belongs to Me (Emcee, waiters)
Why Should I Wake Up? (Cliff)
The Money Song (Emcee, girls)

Married (Fraulein Schneider, Herr Schultz)
Meeskite (Herr Schultz)
Tomorrow Belongs to Me (reprise) (Fraulein Kost, Ernst, guests)

Act II

If You Could See Her (Emcee, girls) Reprise (Emcee, Bobby)
What Would You Do? (Fraulein Schneider)
Cabaret (Sally)

LA CAGE AUX FOLLES (1983)

BOOK BY: Harvey Fierstein; based on the play by Jean Poiret

MUSIC AND LYRICS BY: Jerry Herman

PUBLISHED LIBRETTO: French, 1984

CONDENSATION: *The Best Plays of 1983–1984.* Otis L. Guernsey, Jr., ed. Dodd, Mead, 1984; *Ganzl's Book of the Musical Theatre.* Ganzl, Kurt. Schirmer (Macmillan), 1989

ANTHOLOGY: None

PIANO-VOCAL SCORE: Hal Leonard, 1983

VOCAL SELECTIONS: Hal Leonard, 1983

LICENSING AGENT: Samuel French

RECORDING: RCA RCDI I4824 CD (original cast)

CAST: 7 M; 3 F; chorus

Set in St. Tropez on the French Riviera, this is the story of a homosexual love affair between Albin and Georges. Albin is the star of the transvestite floor show at the nightclub "La Cage aux Folles." Georges is the master of ceremonies. They have been living happily together for twenty years. Georges has a son (the result of an early indiscretion) who suddenly announces he is to wed the daughter of an antigay politician. As her parents are about to pay a visit, it seems expedient for Albin to disappear for a day. At the first act finale Albin, in full drag, defiantly sings "I Am What I Am." This was a lavish and popular Broadway musical with a transvestite chorus line doing a lot of dancing, including a can-can. A number of costumes and wigs are required. While not exactly a family show, there is a great deal of humor in this basically old-fashioned show, and it never offends. A popular song from the score is "The Best of Times."

Tony Award Winner (Best Musical)

ORIGINAL CAST:

George Hearn (Albin)
Gene Barry (Georges)
William Thomas, Jr. (Jacob)
Merle Louise (Marie)
Jay Garner (Edouard)
Elizabeth Parrish (Jacqueline)
John Weiner (Jean-Michel)

SONGS:
Act I

We Are What We Are (chorus)
A Little More Mascara (Albin, chorus)
With Anne on My Arm (Jean-Michel)
With You on My Arm (Georges, Albin)
The Promenade (chorus)
Song on the Sand (Georges)
La Cage aux Folles (Albin, chorus)
I Am What I Am (Albin)

Act II

Song on the Sand (reprise) (Georges, Albin)
Masculinity (Georges, Albin, chorus)
Look Over There (Georges)
Cocktail Counterpoint (Georges, Edouard, Marie, Jacob)
The Best of Times (Albin, Jacqueline, chorus)
Look Over There (reprise) (Jean-Michel)

CALAMITY JANE

BOOK: Adapted for the stage by Ronald Hammer and Phil Park; from the stage play by Charles K. Freeman after the 1953 screenplay by James O'Hanlon
MUSIC BY: Sammy Fain
LYRICS BY: Paul Francis Webster
PUBLISHED LIBRETTO: None
CONDENSATION: *The Book of 1,000 Plays.* Steve Fletcher, Norman Jopling, eds. Facts On File, 1989
ANTHOLOGY: None
VOCAL SELECTIONS: Harms-Witmark (London), 1962
LICENSING AGENT: Tams-Witmark

RECORDING: Columbia CL 6273 (film sound track)
CAST: 12 M; 4 F; chorus

This western musical's plot is about Calamity's offer to present the ravishing Adelaide Adams to Deadwood City, and her subsequent problems while doing so. Calamity was described as "a western shrew magnificently worth the taming." The musical score includes the 1953 Academy-Award-winning "Secret Love" and several new songs for a total of thirteen musical numbers. Doris Day was in the original film and Carol Burnett was Calamity on both regional stages and television.

1961 ST. LOUIS MUNICIPAL OPERA CAST:

Edith Adams (Calamity Jane)
Lou Wells, Jr. (Francis Fryer)
April Shawhan (Susan)
George Gaynes (Wild Bill Hickok)
Lila Gage (Adelaide)
Allyn Ann McLerie (Katie)

SONGS:
Act I

The Deadwood Stage (Calamity, ensemble)
Specialty: Careless with the Truth/Hive Full of Honey (Francis)
Everyone Complains about the Weather (Francis, Susan)
I Can Do without You (Calamity, Bill)
'Tis Harry I'm Planning to Marry (Adelaide, men)
Windy City (Calamity, ensemble)
Keep It under Your Hat (Katie)

Act II

Higher than a Hawk (Bill)
A Woman's Touch (Katie, Calamity)
Love You Dearly (Katie)
Black Hills of Dakota (Calamity, quartet)
Everyone Complains about the Weather (reprise) (Susan, Francis)
Secret Love (Calamity)
Take a Memo to the Moon Tonight (Susan, Francis)

CALL ME MADAM (1950)

BOOK BY: Howard Lindsay and Russel Crouse
MUSIC AND LYRICS BY: Irving Berlin
PUBLISHED LIBRETTO: None
CONDENSATION: *Ganzl's Book of the Musical Theatre*. Ganzl, Kurt. Schirmer (Macmillan), 1989
ANTHOLOGY: None
PIANO-VOCAL SCORE: Irving Berlin Music (London), 1952
LICENSING AGENT: Music Theatre International
RECORDINGS: RCA CBM 1-2032 (Dinah Shore and original cast); MCA 10521 CD (Ethel Merman and studio cast)
CAST: 15 M; 5 F; chorus

This fictional version of an incident in the career of Mrs. Perle Mesta, a famous Washington hostess and once Minister to Luxembourg, was devised specifically with Ethel Merman in mind for the leading role. She goes to "Lichtenburg" and falls in love with a diplomat. There is a secondary romance between a princess and a young man from the State Department. The well-known score includes "You're Just in Love." This musical was filmed with Ethel Merman and George Sanders in 1953.

ORIGINAL CAST:

Ethel Merman (Sally Adams)
Paul Lukas (Cosmo)
Russell Nype (Kenneth)
Galina Talva (Princess)
Pat Harrington (Wilkins)
Jay Velie (Brockbank)
Ralph Chambers (Gallagher)

SONGS:
Act I
Miss Sally Adams (company)
The Hostess with the Mostes' on the Ball (Sally, company)
The Washington Square Dance (Sally, company)
Lichtenburg (Cosmo, company)
Can You Use Any Money Today? (Sally)
Marrying for Love (Cosmo, Sally)
The Ocarina (Princess, company)
It's a Lovely Day Today (Kenneth, Princess)
The Best Thing for You (Sally)

Act II
Something to Dance About (Sally, company)
Once Upon a Time, Today (Kenneth)
They Like Ike (Wilkins, Brockbank, Gallagher)
You're Just in Love (Kenneth, Sally)

CAMELOT (1960)

BOOK AND LYRICS BY: Alan Jay Lerner; based on *The Once and Future King* by T. H. White
MUSIC BY: Frederick Loewe
PUBLISHED LIBRETTO: Random House, 1961
CONDENSATION: *Ganzl's Book of the Musical Theatre*. Ganzl, Kurt. Schirmer (Macmillan), 1989
ANTHOLOGY: *Great Musicals of the American Theatre*, vol. 2. Stanley Richards, ed. Chilton, 1976
PIANO-VOCAL SCORE: Chappell, 1962
LICENSING AGENT: Tams-Witmark
RECORDING: Columbia CK 32602 CD (original cast)
CAST: 14 M; 4 F; 1 dog; chorus

It is "a long time ago" at Camelot and the court of King Arthur and his Knights of the Round Table. His struggle to reconcile his difficult private life with his concepts of right and justice provides a moving and melancholy story. Beauty and pageantry are two terms frequently used to describe this show. The beauty may refer, at least in part, to the famous score, but it also refers to a show that lends itself to lavish sets and costumes. Richard Burton was the original King Arthur and Richard Harris starred in the film. Twenty years later Harris replaced Burton in the highly successful revival.

ORIGINAL CAST:

Richard Burton (King Arthur)
Julie Andrews (Queen Guenevere)
Robert Goulet (Lancelot)
Roddy McDowall (Mordred)
Mary Sue Berry (Nimue)

SONGS:

Act I

I Wonder What the King Is Doing Tonight?
(King Arthur)
The Simple Joys of Maidenhood (Guenevere)
Camelot (King Arthur, Guenevere)
Follow Me (Nimue)
C'est Moi (Lancelot)
The Lusty Month of May (Guenevere,
ensemble)
How to Handle a Woman (King Arthur)
The Jousts (King Arthur, Guenevere,
ensemble)
Before I Gaze at You Again (Guenevere)

Act II

If Ever I Would Leave You (Lancelot)
The Seven Deadly Virtues (Mordred)
What Do the Simple Folk Do? (Guenevere,
King Arthur)
Fie on Goodness (Mordred, men)
I Loved You Once in Silence (Guenevere)

CAN-CAN (1953)

BOOK BY: Abe Burrows
MUSIC AND LYRICS BY: Cole Porter
PUBLISHED LIBRETTO: None
CONDENSATION: *Ganzl's Book of the Musical
Theatre*. Ganzl, Kurt. Schirmer (Macmillan),
1989
ANTHOLOGY: None
PIANO-VOCAL SCORE: Chappell, 1954
LICENSING AGENT: Tams-Witmark
RECORDINGS: Capitol 92064 CD (original cast);
Monmouth Evergreen 7073E (London cast);
Angel ZDM 7 646642 CD (original cast)
CAST: 15 M; 7 F; chorus

Pistache is the proprietress of a Montmartre bistro in Paris during the Toulouse
Lautrec era in 1893. A young judge wants
to close down the "Bal du Paradis" as they
perform the forbidden can-can. The recent
Broadway revival was quite lavish. It featured ballets by Roland Petit, but this was
always a dancing show. Cole Porter's "I
Love Paris" and "C'est Magnifique" are two

of the jewels of the score. Frank Sinatra and
Maurice Chevalier were in the 1960 film.

ORIGINAL CAST:

Lilo (Pistache)
Peter Cookson (Aristide)
Gwen Verdon (Claudine)
Hans Conried (Boris)
Erik Rhodes (Jussac)

SONGS:

Act I

Maidens Typical of France (women)
Never Give Anything Away (Pistache)
C'est Magnifique (Pistache, Aristide)
Quadrille (Claudine, chorus)
Come Along with Me (Jussac, Boris)
Live and Let Live (Pistache)
I Am in Love (Aristide)
If You Loved Me Truly (Boris, Claudine,
others)
Montmart' (ensemble)
Allez-vous-en (Pistache)

Act II

Never, Never Be an Artist (Boris, others)
It's All Right with Me (Aristide)
Every Man Is a Stupid Man (Pistache)
I Love Paris (Aristide, Pistache)
Can-Can (Pistache, Claudine, ensemble)

CANDIDE (1956)

BOOK BY: Hugh Wheeler; based on Voltaire's
satire
MUSIC BY: Leonard Bernstein
LYRICS BY: Richard Wilbur; additional lyrics by
Stephen Sondheim and John Latouche
PUBLISHED LIBRETTO: Schirmer Books, 1976
CONDENSATION: *Ganzl's Book of the Musical
Theatre*. Ganzl, Kurt. Schirmer (Macmillan),
1989
VOCAL SELECTIONS: Schirmer, 1974
LICENSING AGENT: Music Theatre International
RECORDINGS: Columbia S2X 32923 (1973
production); New World NW 340/341 CD (1982
production); Sony 48017 CD (1956 production)
CAST: 11 M; 12 F

The original 1956 operetta by Lillian Hellman was considerably revised with a new book, but retained the Bernstein score, and was a smash hit in 1973. It is this 1973 version that is currently available. The classic plot concerns optimistic Dr. Pangloss sending Candide and his friends out into a cynical and predatory world. The Broadway revival production featured a complex set of platforms, drawbridges, trapdoors, and ramps. The New York City Opera staged *Candide* in 1982 in a production similar to the 1956 operetta and it was a sensational success.

ORIGINAL 1973 CAST:

Lewis J. Standlen (Voltaire/Pangloss/Spanish Governor)
Jim Corti (Coolie/Soldier/Priest)
Mark Baker (Candide)
David Horowitz (Huntsman/Officer/Sailor)
Deborah St. Darr (Paquette)
Maureen Breenan (Cunegonde)
Sam Freed (Maximillian)
Chip Garrett (Soldier/Agent/Pirate)
June Gable (Old Lady)
Robert Henderson (Servant/Don/Sailor)

SONGS:
(performed without intermission)
Life Is Happiness Indeed (Candide, Cunegonde, Maximillian, Paquette)
The Best of All Possible Worlds (Pangloss, Candide, Cunegonde, Maximillian, Paquette)
Oh Happy We (Candide, Cunegonde)
It Must Be So (Candide)
O Miserere (ensemble)
Glitter and Be Gay (Cunegonde)
Auto Da Fe (What a Day) (company)
This World (Candide)
You Were Dead, You Know (Candide, Cunegonde)
I Am Easily Assimilated (Old Lady, Candide, Cunegonde)
My Love (Spanish Governor, Maximillian)
Barcarolle (Upon a Ship at Sea) (Cunegonde)
Alleluia (company)
Sheep's Song (ensemble)

Bon Voyage (Spanish Governor, company)
Make Our Garden Grow (company)

CANTERBURY TALES (1969)

BOOK BY: Martin Starkie and Nevill Coghill; based on a translation from Chaucer by Nevill Coghill
MUSIC BY: Richard Hill and John Hawkins
LYRICS BY: Nevill Coghill
PUBLISHED LIBRETTO: None
CONDENSATION: *Ganzl's Book of the Musical Theatre*. Ganzl, Kurt. Schirmer (Macmillan), 1989
ANTHOLOGY: None
VOCAL SELECTIONS: Blackwood Music, 1969
LICENSING AGENT: Music Theatre International
RECORDING: Capitol SW 229 (original Broadway cast)
CAST: 12 M; 7 F; chorus

Four of Chaucer's famous tales have been musicalized. They are The Miller's, The Steward's, The Merchant's, and The Wife of Bath's. Some critics found these classic fourteenth-century tales bawdy and in doubtful taste in their reviews of the stories told by pilgrims to while away their time along the way to the shrine of Thomas à Becket. The music is a blend of modern and medieval rhythms. This can be staged very economically.

ORIGINAL CAST:

Edwin Steffe (Host)
Hermione Baddeley (Wife of Bath)
Bruce Hyde (Absalom/John/Young Knight)
Evelyn Page (Nun/Miller's Wife)
Suzan Sidney (Village Girl)
Roy Cooper (Miller/Pluto)
Ed Evanko (Squire/Nicholas/Alan/Damian)
Sandy Duncan (Alison/Molly/Mary)
Ann Gardner (Prioress/Proserpina)
George Rose (January)

SONGS:
Act I
Song of Welcome (Host, company)
Good Night Hymn (company)

Canterbury Day (company)
Pilgrim Riding Music (company)

The Miller's Tale
I Have a Noble Cock (Nicholas)
Darling, Let Me Teach You How to Kiss
   (Absalom)
There's the Moon (Nicholas, Alison)
It Depends on What You're At (Wife of Bath,
   Nun, company)
Love Will Conquer All (Prioress, Village Girl,
   company)

The Steward's Tale
Beer Is Best (Miller, Miller's Wife, Alan, John,
   Molly)

Act II
Come on and Marry Me, Honey (Wife of Bath,
   company)
Where Are the Girls of Yesterday? (Host,
   company)

The Merchant's Tale
Hymen, Hymen (company)
If She Had Never Loved Before (January)
I'll Give My Love a Ring (Damian, May)
Pear Tree Quintet (Damian, January, Pluto,
   Proserpina, May)
I Am All A-Blaze (Squire)

The Wife of Bath's Tale
What Do Women Want (Young Knight,
   ladies)
April Song (company)

CARNIVAL (1961)

BOOK BY: Michael Stewart; based on material by
   Helen Deutsch, the film *Lili*, and a short story
   by Paul Gallico
MUSIC AND LYRICS BY: Bob Merrill
PUBLISHED LIBRETTO: Drama Book Shop, 1968
CONDENSATION: *New Complete Book of the
   American Musical Theater.* Ewen, David. Holt,
   1970
ANTHOLOGY: None
VOCAL SELECTIONS: Big Three (Robbins Music,
   1961)
LICENSING AGENT: Tams-Witmark

RECORDING: Polydor 837 195-2 CD (original cast)
CAST: 13 M; 9 F

The orphan Lili comes to the circus seeking
a friend of her father's and with the hope of
finding a job. But the friend has gone and as
she is about to give up hope she gets a job
working with the puppet show. At first she
thinks she loves the magician but eventually realizes that the lame puppeteer is the
one for her. Some added attractions can include jugglers and other performers likely
to be found in a small European circus.

ORIGINAL CAST:
Pierre Olaf (Jacquot)
Henry Lascoe (Mr. Schiegel)
James Mitchell (Marco)
Kaye Ballard (Rosalie)
Anna Maria Alberghetti (Lili)
Jerry Orbach (Paul)

SONGS:
Act I
Direct from Vienna (Rosalie, Mr. Schiegel,
   chorus)
Mira (Can You Imagine That?) (Lili)
Sword, Rose, and Cape (Marco, men)
A Very Nice Man (Lili)
Fairyland (puppets)
I've Got to Find a Reason (Paul)
Humming (Rosalie, Mr. Schiegel)
Yes, My Heart (Lili, men)
Everybody Likes You (Paul)
Magic, Magic (Marco, Rosalie, Lili)
Tanz mit Mir (girls)
Love Makes the World Go Round (Lili,
   puppets)

Act II
Yum Ticky (Lili, puppets)
The Rich (Lili, puppets)
Beautiful Candy (Lili, chorus)
Her Face (Paul)
Grand Imperial Cirque de Paris (Jacquot,
   chorus)
I Hate Him (Lili)
Always Always You (Marco, Rosalie)
She's My Love (Paul)

CAROUSEL (1945)

BOOK AND LYRICS BY: Oscar Hammerstein II;
 based on *Liliom* by Ferenc Molnar
MUSIC BY: Richard Rodgers
PUBLISHED LIBRETTO: Knopf, 1946
CONDENSATION: *Ganzl's Book of the Musical
 Theatre*. Ganzl, Kurt. Schirmer (Macmillan),
 1989; *Rodgers and Hammerstein*. Mordden,
 Ethan. Abrams, 1992
ANTHOLOGY: *Six Plays by Rodgers and
 Hammerstein*. Random House, 1955; Modern
 Library, 1959
PIANO-VOCAL SCORE: Belwin-Mills
LICENSING AGENT: Rodgers and Hammerstein
 Theatre Library
RECORDINGS: MCA 10048 CD (original cast); RCA
 6395-2-RC CD (1965 Lincoln Center cast); MCA
 6209 CD (1987 studio cast)
CAST: 12 M; 7 F; chorus

The setting is a New England coastal town in 1873. Julie, a shy small-town girl, is attracted to Billy Bigalow, a barker in an amusement park. They marry and then he loses his job. In his famous "Soliloquy" Billy thinks about the child they soon will have. In this show the characters do not all live happily ever after. Agnes de Mille did the choreography for such famous numbers as "June Is Bustin' Out All Over," and everyone knows the beautiful "If I Loved You." There was a film in 1956.

ORIGINAL CAST:

John Raitt (Billy)
Jan Clayton (Julie)
Christine Johnson (Nettie)
Jean Darling (Carrie)
Murvyn Vye (Jigger)
Eric Mattson (Enoch Snow)
Connie Baxter (Arminy)

SONGS:
(from 1965 revival)
Act I
The Carousel Waltz (orchestra)
You're a Queer One, Julie Jordan (Carrie,
 Julie)
When I Marry Mr. Snow (Carrie)

If I Loved You (Billy, Julie)
June Is Bustin' Out All Over (Nettie, Carrie,
 ensemble)
When I Marry Mr. Snow (reprise) (Carrie,
 Enoch, girls)
When the Children Are Asleep (Enoch,
 Carrie)
Blow High, Blow Low (Jigger, Billy, male
 chorus)
Soliloquy (Billy)
Act II
This Was a Real Nice Clambake (Enoch,
 Carrie, Julie, Nettie, ensemble)
Geraniums in the Winder (Enoch)
There's Nothin' So Bad for a Woman (Jigger,
 ensemble)
What's the Use of Wond'rin' (Julie)
You'll Never Walk Alone (Nettie)
The Highest Judge of All (Billy)

THE CAT AND THE FIDDLE (1931)

BOOK AND LYRICS BY: Otto Harbach
MUSIC BY: Jerome Kern
PUBLISHED LIBRETTO: None
CONDENSATION: *Ganzl's Book of the Musical
 Theatre*. Ganzl, Kurt. Schirmer (Macmillan),
 1989
ANTHOLOGY: None
PIANO-VOCAL SCORE: Harms, 1932
LICENSING AGENT: Tams-Witmark
RECORDING: World Records SH 171 (*Jerome Kern
 in London*) (original London cast)
CAST: 9 M; 7 F; chorus

Victor is a serious-minded young gentleman who goes in for classical music. Shirley is not so serious and doesn't mind jazzing up a score Victor has written. Two famous Kern tunes are "The Night Was Made for Love" and "She Didn't Say Yes." Eddie Foy, Jr., who was in the original, stopped the show with "Ha! Cha! Cha!" There was a film version with Jeanette MacDonald in 1934.

ORIGINAL CAST:

George Meader (Pompineau)
Georges Metaxa (Victor)

Flora le Breton (Maizie)
Bettina Hall (Shirley)
Eddie Foy, Jr. (Alec)
Doris Carson (Angie)
Odette Myrtil (Odette)
Lucette Vaby (Claudine)
Margaret Adams (Constance)
Peter Chambers (Colbert)

SONGS:
Act I

The Night Was Made for Love (Pompineau)
The Breeze Kissed Your Hair (Victor)
The Love Parade (Pompineau, Maizie)
Try to Forget (Shirley, Alec, Angie)
Poor Pierrot (compere, commere)
The Passionate Pilgrim Episode (Odette,
	Claudine, Constance, Colbert)

Act II

She Didn't Say Yes (Shirley)
A New Love Is Old (Victor)
One Moment Alone (Shirley, Victor)
Ha! Cha! Cha! (Shirley, Alec, chorus)
Cafe Scene (Pompineau, Victor, Shirley)

CATS (1982)

BASED ON: *Old Possum's Book of Practical Cats*
	by T. S. Eliot with some additional material by
	Trevor Nunn and Richard Stilgoe
MUSIC BY: Andrew Lloyd Webber
PUBLISHED LIBRETTO: Harcourt, Brace, 1983
CONDENSATION: *Best Plays of 1982–1983*. Otis L.
	Guernsey Jr., ed. Dodd, Mead, 1983; *Ganzl's
	Book of the Musical Theatre*. Ganzl, Kurt.
	Schirmer (Macmillan), 1989
ANTHOLOGY: None
VOCAL SELECTIONS: Hal Leonard, 1981
LICENSING AGENT: Not yet available; contact
	Music Theatre International
RECORDING: Geffen 2031-2 CD (original Broadway
	cast)
CAST: Large mixed cast

One of the world's most popular shows
during the 1980s, this musical has been performed in many cities of the world. The plot
is minimal and takes place in the surreal
night world of London's alley cats. A feline
ball is being held in a junkyard, and one
cat will be selected by night's end to go
up to cat heaven. The setting is an enormous junkyard with outsized rubbish objects. Your audience will love your set as
well as the feline costumes. The show is
all songs, twenty in all, and "Memory" is
the big song hit. The music is a mixture of
various styles—from Broadway to operetta
to jazz to British music hall to rock! *Variety* mentioned the "gasp-inducing physical production, fiercely energetic dancing,
masterful staging and irresistibly insinuat-
ing music." This is a family show that the
New York Times called "theatrical magic."

Tony Award Winner (Best Musical)

ORIGINAL CAST:

Hector Jaime Mercado (Alonzo)
Stephen Hanan (Asparagus/Growltiger)
Donna King (Bombalurina)
Steven Gelfer (Carbucketty)
Rene Ceballos (Cassandra)
Wendy Edmead (Demeter)
Betty Buckley (Grizabella)
Cynthia Onrubia (Victoria)
Anna McNeely (Jennyanydots)
Timothy Scott (Mistoffelees)
Harry Groener (Munkustrap)
Ken Page (Old Deuteronomy)
Terrence V. Mann (Rum Tum Tugger)
Reed Jones (Skimbleshanks)
Janet L. Hubert (Tantomile)
Bonnie Simmons (Jellylorum/Griddlebone)

SONGS:
Act I

Jellicle Songs for Jellicle Cats (company)
The Naming of Cats (company)
The Invitation to the Jellicle Ball (Victoria,
	Mistoffelees, company)
The Old Gumbie Cat (Jennyanydots,
	Cassandra, Bombalurina, Jellylorum)
The Rum Tum Tugger (Rum Tum Tugger,
	company)
Grizabella, the Glamour Cat (Grizabella,
	Demeter, Bombalurina, company)
Bustopher Jones (Bustopher, Jennyanydots,
	Jellylorum, Bombalurina, company)

Mungojerrie and Rumpelteazer (Mistoffelees)
Old Deuteronomy (Munkustrap, Rum Tum
Tugger, Old Deuteronomy, company)
The Awefull Battle/Marching Songs
(Munkustrap, company)
The Jellicle Ball (company)
Memory (Grizabella)

Act II
The Moment of Happiness (Old
Deuteronomy)
Gus: The Theatre Cat (Jellylorum, Asparagus)
Growltiger's Last Stand (Growltiger,
Griddlebone, the crew)
Skimbleshanks (Skimbleshanks)
Macavity (Demeter, Bombalurina, Alonzo,
Macavity, Munkustrap)
Mr. Mistoffelees (Mistoffelees, Rum Tum
Tugger, company)
Memory (reprise) (Grizabella)
The Journey to the Heaviside Layer
(company)
The Ad-dressing of Cats (Old Deuteronomy)

CELEBRATION (1969)

BOOK AND LYRICS BY: Tom Jones
MUSIC BY: Harvey Schmidt
PUBLISHED LIBRETTO: None
ANTHOLOGY: *Fantasticks and Celebration*. Drama
Book Specialists, 1973
CONDENSATION: *The Best Plays of 1968–1969*. Otis
L. Guernsey, Jr., ed. Dodd, Mead, 1969
PIANO-VOCAL SCORE: Portfolio Music (Chappell),
1970
VOCAL SELECTIONS: Portfolio Music (Chappell),
1969
LICENSING AGENT: Music Theatre International
RECORDING: Bay Cities 3015 CD (original cast)
CAST: 3 M; 1 F; singers, dancers

It is the celebration of New Year's Eve, and
out of the masked crowds we meet a wistful, but hopeful, orphan. He becomes involved in a spiritual tug-of-war with a rich
old man. These are symbolic characters
who perform a parable of youth and age.
The other two characters are the narrator

and an angel (really a nightclub singer).
The original production was noted for its
costumes, particularly the masks, and the
staging. The scenery consisted of an arrangement of trestle-like platforms. Highly
original, the ritualistic morality play is a
celebration of life.

ORIGINAL CAST:

Keith Charles (Potemkin)
Michael Glenn-Smith (Orphan)
Susan Watson (Angel)
Ted Thurston (Rich)

SONGS:
Act I
Celebration (Potemkin, chorus)
Orphan in the Storm (Orphan, chorus)
Survive (Potemkin, chorus)
Somebody (Angel, chorus)
Bored (Rich)
My Garden (Orphan, chorus)
Where Did It Go? (Rich, chorus)
Love Song (Angel, Potemkin, Rich, Orphan,
chorus)
To the Garden (company)

Act II
I'm Glad to See You've Got What You Want
(Angel, Orphan)
It's You Who Makes Me Young (Rich, chorus)
Not My Problem (Potemkin, chorus)
Fifty Million Years Ago (Orphan)
The Beautician Ballet (Rich, chorus)
Saturnalia (Potemkin, chorus)
Under the Tree (Angel, chorus)
Winter and Summer (company)

CHARLIE AND ALGERNON (1980)

BOOK AND LYRICS BY: David Rogers; based on the
novel *Flowers for Algernon* by Daniel Keyes
MUSIC BY: Charles Strouse
PUBLISHED LIBRETTO: Dramatic, 1981
CONDENSATION: None
ANTHOLOGY: None
LICENSING AGENT: Dramatic

RECORDING: Original Cast OC 9221 CD (original London cast under the title *Flowers for Algernon*)
CAST: 5 M; 4 F; 1 child; 1 mouse (live or toy)

Charlie, a grown man with the mind of a child, is turned into a genius through a brain operation. Algernon is a mouse who also had the operation. Unfortunately the effects of the operation are not permanent. This was a popular (nonmusical) film with Cliff Robertson. The lead roles are a challenge, as are the scenes with the mouse.

ORIGINAL CAST:

P. J. Benjamin (Charlie)
Sandy Faison (Alice)
Edward Earle (Dr. Strauss)
Robert Sevra (Dr. Nemur)
Nancy Franklin (Mrs. Donner)
Loida Santos (Lita)
Patrick Jude (Frank)
Julienne Marie (Charlie's Mother)
Matthew Duda (Little Charlie)
Michael Vita (Charlie's Father)

SONGS:
(performed without intermission):
Have I the Right? (Alice, Dr. Nemur, Dr. Strauss)
I Got a Friend (Charlie)
I Got a Friend (reprise) (Charlie, Alice)
Some Bright Morning (Dr. Nemur, Charlie, Dr. Strauss, Alice)
Jelly Donuts and Chocolate Cake (Mrs. Donner, Lita, Frank)
Hey Look at Me (Charlie, Alice)
Reading (Charlie, Alice)
No Surprises (Alice)
Midnight Riding (Frank, Lita)
Dream Safe with Me (Charlie's Mother)
Not Another Day like This (Charlie's Mother and Father)
Somebody New (Mrs. Donner, Charlie)
I Can't Tell You (Charlie)
Now (Charlie, Alice)
Charlie and Algernon (Charlie)
The Maze (Charlie)
Whatever Time There Is (Alice, Charlie)

Everything Was Perfect (Dr. Strauss, Dr. Nemur)
Charlie (Charlie)
I Really Loved You (Charlie)

CHARLOTTE SWEET (1982)

LIBRETTO BY: Michael Colby
MUSIC BY: Gerald Jay Markoe
PUBLISHED LIBRETTO: French, 1983
CONDENSATION: None
ANTHOLOGY: None
VOCAL SELECTIONS: Hal Leonard
LICENSING AGENT: Samuel French
RECORDING: DRG 6300 CD (original cast)
CAST: 4 M; 4 F

Charlotte's father won't let her marry her beloved, so she joins a troupe of touring musicians and becomes "the incomparable" on the Victorian music-hall stage. When she begins to lose her high notes, the leader of the troupe puts her on helium, and she is soon addicted. There is no spoken dialogue in this music-hall pastiche. There are twenty-seven songs ranging from ballad to tango to march rhythm to patter song. The off-Broadway production was praised by the critic of the *New York Post* for its scenery with "flat surfaces and illusory depths of a pop-up valentine." The costumes were described as "slightly demented" versions of the authentic style. There is also a touch of Victorian melodrama, with the audience constantly hissing the villain.

ORIGINAL CAST:

Michael McCormick (Harry)
Nicholas Wyman (Bob/Patrick)
Mara Beckerman (Charlotte)
Christopher Seppe (Ludlow/Queen)
Sandra Wheeler (Katinka)
Alan Brasington (Barnaby)
Polly Pen (Skitzy)
Merle Louise (Cecily)

SONGS:

Act I

At the Music Hall (Harry, ensemble)

Charlotte Sweet (Bob, Charlotte, ensemble)

A Daughter of Valentine's Day (Charlotte, ensemble)

Forever (Ludlow, Charlotte)

Liverpool Sunset (ensemble)

Layers of Underwear (Bob, Katinka, Barnaby, Charlotte)

Quartet Agonistes (Katinka, Barnaby, Charlotte, Bob)

The Circus of Voices (Barnaby, Katinka, Skitzy, Cecily, Harry, Charlotte)

Keep It Low (Katinka, men)

Bubbles in Me Bonnet (Cecily)

Vegetable Reggie (Harry)

My Baby and Me (Skitzy)

A-Weaving (Charlotte, women)

Your High Note! (Charlotte, Barnaby, Katinka)

Katinka/The Darkness (Barnaby)

Act II

On It Goes (ensemble)

You See in Me a Bobby (Patrick, Barnaby, Katinka)

A Christmas Buche (Charlotte, Cecily, Skitzy, Harry)

The Letter (Me Charlotte Dear) (Ludlow)

Dover (Skitzy)

Good Things Come (Cecily)

It Could Only Happen in the Theatre (Harry, Patrick, Skitzy, Cecily)

Lonely Canary (Charlotte)

Queenly Comments (Queen, Barnaby, Katinka, Patrick, Charlotte)

Surprise! Surprise! (ensemble)

The Reckoning (ensemble)

Farewell to Auld Lang Syne (ensemble)

CHESS (1988)

BOOK BY: Richard Nelson

MUSIC BY: Benny Andersson and Bjorn Ulvaeus

LYRICS BY: Tim Rice

PUBLISHED LIBRETTO: French

CONDENSATION: *Ganzl's Book of the Musical Theatre.* Ganzl, Kurt. Schirmer (Macmillan), 1989

ANTHOLOGY: None

VOCAL SELECTIONS: MCA Music, 1986

LICENSING AGENT: Samuel French

RECORDING: RCA 7700-2-RC CD (original Broadway cast)

CAST: 9 M; 2 F; 1 female child, ensemble

The musical score for this production is by members of the rock group ABBA. The plot concerns two champion chess players— their rivalry not only at the game but for a girl as well. The chess players represent the U.S. and the USSR, and theirs is a politically and commercially exploited match that begins in Bangkok and continues to Budapest. Both the CIA and the KGB are involved in the intrigue. "One Night in Bangkok" was a popular song from the score. This show was a big hit in London before it opened on Broadway. It combines grandiose pop-rock with a traditional book musical.

ORIGINAL CAST:

David Carroll (Anatoly)

Judy Kuhn (Florence)

Philip Casnoff (Freddie)

Neal Ben-Ari (Gregor)

Harry Goz (Molokov)

Paul Harman (Arbiter)

Marcia Mitzman (Svetlana)

Dennis Parlato (Walter)

SONGS:

Act I

The Story of Chess (Gregor)

Where I Want to Be (Anatoly)

Quartet (A Model of Decorum and Tranquility) (Molokov, Florence, Arbiter, Anatoly)

Someone Else's Story (Florence)

One Night in Bangkok (Freddie, company)

Terrace Duet (Florence, Anatoly)

Nobody's Side (Florence)

Anthem (Anatoly)

Act II

Heaven Help My Heart (Florence)

No Contest (Freddie, Walter)

I Know Him So Well (Florence, Svetlana)
Pity the Child (Freddie)
Lullaby (Gregor, Florence)
Endgame (Anatoly, Freddie, company)
You and I (Anatoly, Florence)

CHICAGO (1975)

BOOK BY: Fred Ebb and Bob Fosse; based on the
    play *Chicago* by Maurine Dallas Watkins
MUSIC BY: John Kander
LYRICS BY: Fred Ebb
PUBLISHED LIBRETTO: French, 1976
CONDENSATION: *The Best Plays of 1975–1976.*
    Otis L. Guernsey, Jr., ed. Dodd, Mead, 1976;
    Ganzl's Book of the Musical Theatre. Ganzl, Kurt.
    Schirmer (Macmillan), 1989
ANTHOLOGY: None
VOCAL SELECTIONS: Chappell, 1975
LICENSING AGENT: Samuel French
RECORDING: Bay Cities BCD 3003 CD (original
    cast)
CAST: 9 M; 10 F; chorus, dancers

"Razzle Dazzle 'Em" goes the song, and
that's just what this show does. The tale
of Roxie Hart (a chorus girl who shoots a
lover but, due to her slick lawyer, beats the
rap) is told in the form of a 1920s vaudeville
show. This is a cynical but stylish and sophisticated show. Gwen Verdon and Liza
Minnelli both played "Roxie" on Broadway
with great success. The Bob Fosse choreography adds a great deal to the show's
lurid and sensational mood.

ORIGINAL CAST:

Chita Rivera (Velma Kelly)
Barney Martin (Amos Hart)
Jerry Orbach (Billy Flynn)
Graciela Daniele (Hunyak)
Michael Vita (Martin)
Gwen Verdon (Roxie Hart)
Mary McCarty (Mrs. Morton)
M. O'Haughey (Mary Sunshine)

Christopher Chadman (Fred Casely)
Pamela Sousa (Mona)

SONGS:
Act I
All That Jazz (Velma, company)
Funny Honey (Roxie)
Cell Block Tango (Velma, girls)
When You're Good to Mama (Mrs. Morton)
All I Care About (Billy, girls)
A Little Bit of Good (Mary)
We Both Reached for the Gun (Billy, Mary,
    Roxie, company)
Roxie (Roxie, boys)
I Can't Do It Alone (Velma)
My Own Best Friend (Roxie, Velma)

Act II
Me and My Baby (Roxie, boys)
Mr. Cellophane (Amos)
When Velma Takes the Stand (Velma, boys)
Razzle Dazzle (Billy, company)
Class (Velma, Mrs. Morton)
Nowadays (Roxie, Velma)

A CHORUS LINE (1975)

BOOK BY: James Kirkwood and Nicholas Dante
MUSIC BY: Marvin Hamlisch
LYRICS BY: Edward Kleban
PUBLISHED LIBRETTO: None
CONDENSATION: *Ganzl's Book of the Musical
    Theatre.* Ganzl, Kurt. Schirmer (Macmillan),
    1989
ANTHOLOGY: None
PIANO-VOCAL SCORE: E. H. Morris, 1977 (MPL
    Communications)
VOCAL SELECTIONS: E. H. Morris, 1975 (MPL
    Communications)
LICENSING AGENT: Tams-Witmark
RECORDING: Columbia CK 33581 CD (original cast)
CAST: 16 M; 16 F

A group of young hopefuls is auditioning for the chorus line of a Broadway
musical. The director asks them to tell
him about themselves, and through song
and dance we get to know them. This is
performed on a bare stage in rehearsal

costumes. As stated in the program, the characterizations are "for the most part, based upon the lives and experiences of Broadway dancers." After the selections are made the stage is transformed into a glittering mirrored setting for the finale with the chorus line in costume. Energetic Broadway/ballet dancing is required. The hit song from the score is "What I Did for Love." This extremely popular show closed in April 1990 after totaling 6,137 Broadway performances.

Tony Award Winner (Best Musical)

Pulitzer Prize

ORIGINAL CAST:

Renee Baughman (Kristine)
Carol Bishop (Sheila)
Pamela Blair (Val)
Wayne Cilento (Mike)
Kay Cole (Maggie)
Nancy Lane (Bebe)
Priscilla Lopez (Diana)
Donna McKechnie (Cassie)
Don Percassi (Alan)
Patricia Garland (Judy)
Thomas J. Walsh (Bobby)
Ronald Dennis (Richie)

SONGS:
(performed without intermission)
I Hope I Get It (company)
I Can Do That (Mike)
"And . . . " (Bobby, Richie, Val, Judy)
At the Ballet (Sheila, Bebe, Maggie)
Sing! (Kristine, Alan)
Hello Twelve, Hello Thirteen, Hello Love
　　(company)
Nothing (Diana)
Dance: Ten; Looks: Three (Val)
The Music and the Mirror (Cassie)
One (company)
The Tap Combination (company)
What I Did for Love (Diana, company)

CHRISTMAS IS COMIN' UPTOWN (1979)

(original Broadway title: *Comin' Uptown*)

BOOK BY: Philip Rose and Peter Udell; based on *A Christmas Carol* by Charles Dickens
MUSIC BY: Garry Sherman
LYRICS BY: Peter Udell
PUBLISHED LIBRETTO: French, 1982
CONDENSATION: None
ANTHOLOGY: None
LICENSING AGENT: Samuel French
RECORDING: None
CAST: 11 M; 8 F; chorus

Dickens' tale of London has been modernized and set in New York's Harlem. Scrooge is now a black slum landlord. The music has a modern beat with African ethnic and gospel touches. Gregory Hines was the Broadway star and received much praise for his singing and dancing, as did the elaborate, maneuverable settings.

ORIGINAL CAST:

Gregory Hines (Scrooge)
Tiger Haynes (Marley)
Larry Marshall (Christmas Past)
Kevin Babb (Tiny Tim)
Loretta Devine (Mary)
Robert Jackson (Christmas Future/Minister)
Saundra McClain (Christmas Present)
Esther Marrow (Gospel Singer)

SONGS:
Act I
Christmas Is Comin' Uptown (Scrooge, trio,
　　chorus)
Somebody's Gotta Be the Heavy (Scrooge)
Now I Lay Me Down to Sleep (Scrooge)
Get Your Act Together (Marley)
Lifeline (Christmas Past, trio)
What Better Time for Love (Scrooge, Mary)
It Won't Be Long (Gospel Singer, chorus)
What I'm Gonna Do for You (Scrooge)
Get Down Brother, Get Down (Christmas
　　Present, chorus)
Sing a Christmas Song (chorus)

What Better Time for Love (reprise) (Tiny Tim, family)
Have I Finally Found My Heart? (Scrooge)

Act II
Nobody Really Do (Christmas Future, trio)
Goin', Gone (Christmas Future)
One-Way Ticket to Hell (trio)
Born Again (Scrooge, company)

CINDERELLA (1993)

BOOK AND LYRICS BY: Oscar Hammerstein II;
    adapted for the stage by Donald Driver
MUSIC BY: Richard Rodgers
PUBLISHED LIBRETTO: None
CONDENSATION: *Rodgers and Hammerstein.*
    Mordden, Ethan. Abrams, 1992
ANTHOLOGY: None
PIANO-VOCAL SCORE: Williamson, 1962
VOCAL SELECTIONS: Williamson, 1957
LICENSING AGENT: Rodgers and Hammerstein
    Theatre Library
RECORDING: Columbia CK 2005 CD (original TV
    cast)
CAST: 10 M; 6 F; singing and dancing chorus

The classic tale of the prince and the glass slipper is followed in this production, with lavish costumes for the ball and a fairy tale atmosphere. There are no classic songs in the score, but any songs by Rodgers and Hammerstein are likely to please. Originally written as a TV musical in 1957, this has been done successfully on stage at the St. Louis Municipal Opera, in London, and in 1993 at New York's Lincoln Center.

ORIGINAL TV CAST:

Julie Andrews (Cinderella)
Jon Cypher (Prince)
Edith Adams (Godmother)
Kaye Ballard (Portia)
Dorothy Stickney (Queen)
Howard Lindsay (King)
Alice Ghostley (Joy)
Ilka Chase (Stepmother)
Bob Penn (Chancellor)

SONGS:
Act I
The Prince Is Giving a Ball (Chancellor,
    chorus)
A Very Special Day (Prince)
Ladies in Waiting (Joy, Portia)
In My Own Little Corner (Cinderella)
When You're Driving through the Moonlight
    (Prince, Cinderella)
A Lovely Night (Prince, Cinderella)
Impossible (Cinderella, Godmother)
Possible (Cinderella, Godmother, chorus)

Act II
Ten Minutes Ago (Prince, Cinderella)
Stepsisters' Lament (Joy, Portia)
Do I Love You Because You're Beautiful?
    (Prince, Cinderella)

CINDY (1964)

BOOK BY: Joe Sauter and Mike Sawyer
LYRICS AND MUSIC BY: Johnny Brandon
PUBLISHED LIBRETTO: None
CONDENSATION: None
ANTHOLOGY: None
LICENSING AGENT: Tams-Witmark
RECORDING: ABC S-OC-2 (original cast)
CAST: 6 M; 6 F

The leading lady's name is "Cindy Kreller"—say that aloud! A lively twentieth-century version of the classic Cinderella, this contemporary teen musical is set in a Jewish delicatessen. There is a lot of New York Lower East Side Jewish humor. In the original off-Broadway production the good fairy also played an insolent housemaid.

ORIGINAL CAST:

Jacqueline Mayro (Cindy Kreller)
Johnny Harmon (Lucky)
Dena Dietrich (Della)
Amelia Varney (Golda)
Frank Nastasi (Papa)
Mike Sawyer (David)
Sylvia Mann (Mama Kreller)

Lizbeth Pritchett (Ruth)
Joe Masiell (Chuck)
Thelma Oliver (Storyteller)
Tommy Karaty (Storyteller)
Mark Stone (Storyteller)

SONGS:
Act I
Once Upon a Time (Storytellers)
Let's Pretend (Cindy, Lucky)
Is There Something to What He Said? (Cindy)
Papa, Let's Do It Again (Mama Kreller, Papa)
A Genuine Feminine Girl (Cindy)
Cindy (Lucky)
Think Mink (Golda, Della)
Tonight's the Night (Storytellers)
Who Am I? (Cindy, Chuck)

Act II
If You've Got It, You've Got It (Della, Golda,
    Mama, Papa)
The Life That I Have Planned for Him (Ruth)
If It's Love (Chuck, Cindy)
Got the World in the Palm of My Hand
    (Chuck)
Call Me Lucky (Lucky)
Laugh It Up (Cindy)
What a Wedding (David, Ruth, Papa, Mama,
    Chuck, Della, Golda)

CITY OF ANGELS (1989)

BOOK BY: Larry Gelbart
MUSIC BY: Cy Coleman
LYRICS BY: David Zippel
PUBLISHED LIBRETTO: Applause, 1990
CONDENSATION: *The Theatre Year Book and The
    Best Plays of 1989–1990*. Otis L. Guernsey, Jr.,
    ed. Applause Books, 1990
ANTHOLOGY: None
VOCAL SELECTIONS: Notable Music, 1990
LICENSING AGENT: Tams-Witmark
RECORDING: CBS CK 46067 CD (original cast)
CAST: Large mixed cast

Set in Los Angeles in the late 1940s, this
comedy is a spoof of the "film noir" detective films of that period. Its original script

has been called "a writer's revenge on Hollywood." The plot revolves around the gimmick of having the writer, Stine, and his
fictional character, Stone, act out their adventures with the movie Stone in black
and white and the writer Stine and his real
world in color. The music is a jazzy pastiche
with a 1940s bebop quartet (Angel City 4)
frequently taking the spotlight. There is
very little dancing. This big production was
a big hit on Broadway.

Tony Award Winner (Best Musical)

ORIGINAL CAST:

James Naughton (Stone)
Dee Hoty (Alaura)
Rene Auberjonois (Buddy)
Gregg Edelman (Stine)
Kay McClelland (Gabby/Bobbi)
Randy Graff (Oolie/Donna)
Scott Waara (Jimmy Powers)
Rachel York (Mallory)
Shawn Elliott (Munoz)
Alvin Lum (Yamoto)

SONGS:
Act I
Theme from City of Angels (Angel City 4)
Double Talk (Stone, Alaura) Reprise (Buddy,
    Stine)
What You Don't Know about Women (Gabby,
    Oolie)
Ya Gotta Look Out for Yourself (Jimmy
    Powers, Angel City 4)
The Buddy System (Buddy, Donna)
With Every Breath I Take (Bobbi)
The Tennis Song (Stone, Alaura)
Ev'rybody's Gotta Be Somewhere (Stone,
    Angel City 4)
Lost and Found (Mallory)
All Ya Have to Do Is Wait (Munoz, Yamoto,
    others)
You're Nothing without Me (Stine, Stone)
Act II
Stay with Me (Jimmy Powers, Angel City 4)
You Can Always Count on Me (Oolie/Donna)
It Needs Work (Gabby)
With Every Breath I Take (reprise) (Stone,
    Bobbi)

Funny (Stine)
You're Nothing without Me (reprise) (Stone, Stine, Gabby)

CLOSER THAN EVER (1989)

CONCEIVED BY: Steven Scott Smith
MUSIC BY: David Shire
LYRICS BY: Richard Maltby, Jr.
PUBLISHED LIBRETTO: None
CONDENSATION: None
ANTHOLOGY: None
PIANO-VOCAL SCORE: Fiddleback Music, 1989
VOCAL SELECTIONS: Fiddleback Music, 1989
LICENSING AGENT: Music Theatre International
RECORDING: RCA 60399-2 RG CD (original cast)
CAST: 2 M; 2 F

The theme of love holds together this concert described as "a thoughtful, mildly bittersweet revue." Each song tells a story and is self-contained and complete. There is no in-between-the-numbers chatter. This is performed with four singers, a piano and a bass, and a nearly bare stage. Strong performers are required.

ORIGINAL CAST:

Brent Barrett   Sally Mayes
Richard Muenz   Lynne Wintersteller
Patrick Scott Brady (piano)
Robert Renino (bass)

SONGS:
Act I
Doors (company)
She Loves Me Not (Barrett, Wintersteller, Muenz)
You Want to Be My Friend? (Mayes, Muenz)
What Am I Doin'? (Barrett)
The Bear, the Tiger, the Hamster, and the Mole (Wintersteller)
Miss Byrd (Mayes)
The Sound of Muzak (company)
One of the Good Guys (Barrett)
There's Nothing Like It (company)
Life Story (Wintersteller)
Next Time (Muenz, company)
I Wouldn't Go Back (company)

Act II
Three Friends (Mayes, Wintersteller, Barrett)
Fandango (Wintersteller, Muenz)
There (Mayes, Brady)
Patterns (Wintersteller)
Another Wedding Song (Barrett, Mayes)
If I Sing (Muenz)
Back on Base (Mayes, Renino)
The March of Time (company)
Father of Fathers (Barrett, Brady, Muenz)
It's Never That Easy/I've Been Here Before (Wintersteller, Mayes)
Closer than Ever (Muenz, company)

THE CLUB (1976)

DEVISED BY: Eve Merriam; musical direction and arrangements by Alesandra Ivanoff
PUBLISHED LIBRETTO: French, 1977
CONDENSATION: None
ANTHOLOGY: None
LICENSING AGENT: Samuel French
RECORDING: None
CAST: 7 F

In the off-Broadway production of this show two platforms connected by a long, narrow ramp made up the acting area. It was here that the audience was introduced to the members of an all-male club, circa 1905. They talked and sang about their wives, alimony, card games, and the stock market. But they were all played by women disguised as men. They sang old songs (from the period 1894 to 1905) and exchanged antifeminist and sometimes smutty jokes. Merriam is deeply involved in the women's liberation movement and used this show as a vehicle of feminist protest.

Off-Broadway (OBIE) Award Winner

ORIGINAL CAST:

Marlene Dell (Johnny)
Gloria Hodes (Berrie)
Joanne Beretta (Algy)
Carole Monferdini (Freddie)

Julie J. Hafner (Bobby)
Memrie Innerarity (Maestro)
Terri White (Henry)

All the songs in *The Club* are from the period 1894–1905 and are performed without an intermission.

THE COCOANUTS (1925)

BOOK BY: George S. Kaufman
MUSIC AND LYRICS BY: Irving Berlin
PUBLISHED LIBRETTO: None
CONDENSATION: *New Complete Book of the American Musical Theater.* Ewen, David. Holt, 1970
ANTHOLOGY: None
LICENSING AGENT: Rodgers and Hammerstein Theatre Library
RECORDING: None
CAST: 5 M; 3 F; ensemble

The setting is the Cocoanuts Hotel, Cocoanut Beach, Florida. The time is 1925, during a Florida land boom. Groucho is attempting to auction off some apparently worthless land, while a subplot deals with a jewel theft. The 1988 Arena Stage revival in Washington, D.C., was described as full of awful/marvelous puns, "low comedy, verbal pyrotechnics and specialty numbers." You will need art deco sets and monkey costumes for "The Monkey Doodle-Do." Throughout it all the Marx Brothers' characters go their merry way in full cry. There was a film version in 1929.

1988 ARENA STAGE CAST:

Ralph Cosham (Jamison/Zeppo)
Bob Kirsh (Bob)
Deanna Wells (Polly)
Stephen Mellor (Schlemmer/Groucho)
Ronnie Farer (Penelope)
Charles Janasz (Silent Sam/Harpo)
Mitchell Greenberg (Willie/Chico)
Terrence Currier (Hennessey)

SONGS:
Act I
Florida by the Sea (Bob, Jamison, company)
The Bellhops (bellboys)
Family Reputation (Bob, Polly, company)
Lucky Boy (Jamison, Bob, boys)
Why Am I a Hit with the Ladies (Schlemmer, girls)
A Little Bungalow (Bob, Polly)
The Monkey Doodle-Do (Bob, Polly, company)

Act II
Five O'Clock Tea (company)
Everyone in the World Is Doing the Charleston (Penelope, company)
We Should Care (Bob, Polly, Silent Sam)
Tango Melody (Penelope, Schlemmer, company)
Piano Specialty (Willie)
The Tale of a Shirt (Hennessey, company)

COLE (1974—London)

DEVISED BY: Benny Green and Alan Strachan
LYRICS AND MUSIC BY: Cole Porter
PUBLISHED LIBRETTO: French, 1981
CONDENSATION: None
ANTHOLOGY: None
MUSIC PUBLISHER: *Music and Lyrics of Cole Porter*, 2 vols. Chappell, 1972–1975
LICENSING AGENT: Samuel French
RECORDING: RCA CRL 2-5054 (original London cast)
CAST: 5 M; 5 F

Today Cole Porter stands for great show tunes, sophistication, wit, and nostalgia. This revue was originally presented at the Mermaid Theatre in London. It takes us from 1916 to the mid-1950s with about fifty Porter songs. Although there are some biographical details in the first part, it is basically a song and dance show. It is performed in an art deco set that serves as an ocean liner, a Broadway stage, a bar, or in other words, the world of Cole Porter. Some slide projections were used in the original production.

ORIGINAL LONDON CAST:

Ray Cornell	Rod McLennan
Lucy Fenwick	Kenneth Nelson
Peter Gale	Elizabeth Power
Bill Kerr	Angela Richards
Julia McKenzie	Una Stubbs

Over fifty songs by Cole Porter are featured in this revue with one intermission.

COLETTE COLLAGE (1983)

BOOK AND LYRICS BY: Tom Jones
MUSIC BY: Harvey Schmidt
PUBLISHED LIBRETTO: None
CONDENSATION: None
ANTHOLOGY: None
LICENSING AGENT: Music Theatre International
RECORDING: None
CAST: 3 M; 2 F; chorus

This biographical musical about the famous French author went through several versions during a twenty-year period. In this final version Act I concerns a younger Colette married to an older man (Willy). Act II presents an older Colette married to a younger man (Maurice). The time period ranges from World War I to World War II. The simple but ingenuous sets include the French countryside and Parisian salons and music hall stages.

1991 REVIVAL CAST:

Betsy Joslyn (Colette)
Joanne Beretta (Sido)
Kenneth Kantor (Willy)
Ralston Hill (Jacques)
James J. Mellon (Maurice)

SONGS:
Act I
Joy (Colette, all)
Come to Life (Colette, Willy, all)
A Simple Country Wedding (all)
Do It for Willy (Willy, ensemble)

Willy Will Grow Cold (Jacques)
The Claudines (Colette, Willy, all)
Why Can't I Walk through That Door? (Colette)
The Music Hall (Jacques, ensemble)
Dream of Egypt (Jacques, Colette)
I Miss You (Sido)
La Vagabonde (Colette, women)
Love Is Not a Sentiment Worthy of Respect (Sido)
Now I Must Walk through That Door (Colette, all)

Act II
Autumn Afternoon (Colette, ensemble)
Riviera Nights (Jacques, all)
Ooh-La-La (Maurice, Colette)
Something for the Summer (Maurice, Colette, all)
Madame Colette (ensemble)
You Could Hurt Me (Colette)
Be My Lady (Maurice)
The Room Is Filled with You (Colette, women)
Growing Older (Colette)

COMPANY (1970)

BOOK BY: George Furth
MUSIC AND LYRICS BY: Stephen Sondheim
PUBLISHED LIBRETTO: Random House, 1970
CONDENSATION: *The Best Plays of 1969–1970.* Otis L. Guernsey, Jr., ed. Dodd, Mead, 1970; *Ganzl's Book of the Musical Theatre.* Ganzl, Kurt. Schirmer (Macmillan), 1989
ANTHOLOGY: *Ten Great Musicals of the American Stage.* Stanley Richards, ed. Chilton, 1973
PIANO-VOCAL SCORE: Valando, 1971
VOCAL SELECTIONS: Valando, 1970
LICENSING AGENT: Music Theatre International
RECORDING: Columbia CK 03550 CD (original cast)
CAST: 6 M; 8 F; small chorus

This musical takes a stinging look at the state of matrimony, particularly in a big city—New York. Various married couples try to convince a thirty-five-year-old bachelor that he should marry, but they do not present very good role models for marriage. This musical has been hailed as a landmark in American theater. The original set resembled a modern building skeleton with many different levels, stairs, and two elevators.

Tony Award Winner (Best Musical)

ORIGINAL CAST:

Dean Jones (Robert)
Barbara Barrie (Sarah)
Charles Kimbrough (Harry)
Merle Louise (Susan)
John Cunningham (Peter)
Teri Ralston (Jenny)
George Coe (David)
Beth Howland (Amy)
Steve Elmore (Paul)
Elaine Stritch (Joanne)
Charles Braswell (Larry)
Pamela Myers (Marta)
Donna McKechnie (Kathy)
Susan Browning (April)

SONGS:
Act I
Company (Robert, company)
The Little Things You Do Together (Joanne, company)
Sorry-Grateful (Harry, David, Larry)
You Could Drive a Person Crazy (Kathy, April, Marta)
Have I Got a Girl for You (Larry, Peter, Paul, David, Harry)
Someone Is Waiting (Robert)
Another Hundred People (Marta)
Getting Married Today (Amy, Paul, Jenny, company)

Act II
Side by Side by Side (Robert, company)
What Would We Do without You (Robert, company)
Poor Baby (Sarah, Jenny, Susan, Amy, Joanne)
Tick Tock (Kathy)
Barcelona (Robert, April)
The Ladies Who Lunch (Joanne)
Being Alive (Robert)

THE CONTRAST (1972)

BOOK ADAPTED BY: Anthony Stimac; based on the play *The Contrast* (the first American comedy, written in 1787) by Royall Tyler
MUSIC BY: Donald Pippin
LYRICS BY: Steve Brown
PUBLISHED LIBRETTO: French, 1972
CONDENSATION: None
ANTHOLOGY: None
LICENSING AGENT: Samuel French
RECORDING: None
CAST: 5 M; 5 F

This off-Broadway musical version of the first American comedy was described as being filled with satire and innuendo. For example, the cast also moves the props and scenery about, taking more and more elaborate bows after each shift. A sense of comic timing is required as the cast scurries about with split-second synchronization. The plot (and title) involves exaggerated European manners and the straightforwardness of Americans in the late eighteenth century. The score was described as a blend of everything from square dance to George M. Cohan, with a bit of rock thrown in.

ORIGINAL CAST:

Connie Danese (Charlotte)
Elaine Kerr (Letitia)
Patti Perkins (Maria)
Gene Kelton (Van Rough)
Philip MacKenzie (Jonathan)
Grady Clarkson (Jessamy)
Ty McConnell (Dimple)
Pamela Adams (Jenny)
Robert G. Denison (Manly)

SONGS:
Act I
A Woman Rarely Ever (Charlotte, Letitia)
A House Full of People (Maria)
Keep Your Little Eye upon the Main Chance, Mary (Van Rough)
So They Call It New York (Jonathan, Jessamy)

Dear Lord Chesterfield (Dimple) Reprise
(Jessamy)
A Sort of Courting Song (Jenny, Jonathan)
So Far (company)

Act II
She Can't Really Be (Dimple, Manly)
That Little Monosyllable (Charlotte, Maria)
It's Too Much (Dimple, Charlotte, Maria,
Manly, Letitia)
Wouldn't I (Maria, Manly)
A Hundred Thousand Ways (Jessamy,
Jonathan)
I Was in the Closet (company)

COTTON PATCH GOSPEL (1981)

BOOK BY: Tom Key and Russell Treyz; based on
The Cotton Patch Version of Matthew and John
by Clarence Jordan
MUSIC AND LYRICS BY: Harry Chapin
PUBLISHED LIBRETTO: Dramatic, 1982
CONDENSATION: None
ANTHOLOGY: None
LICENSING AGENT: Dramatic
RECORDING: Chapin Productions CP 101 (original
cast)
CAST: 1 M (plus backup group—may be done by
large cast)

Described as a down-home retelling of the
Christ story, this show asks the question,
"What if Jesus was born forty years ago
in Georgia?" The one actor/singer portrays
Matthew and thirty-three other characters.
The country band comments on the narrative through the songs. Politicians, the
moral majority, TV evangelists, the Ku Klux
Klan, and racial prejudice are just some
of the topics brought into the story. Jesus is born behind the Dixie Delight Motor
Lodge. Three scholars from the East give
him a gold American Express card, peach-
scented candles, and a bottle of Jade East!
The nineteen songs are described as rousing country and western songs and gospel
tunes. Simple to stage, the whole show
hinges on the music and the satire.

ORIGINAL CAST:
Tom Key (Matthew)
Scott Ainslie (Musician)
Michael Mark (Musician)
Pete Corum (Musician)
Jim Lauderdale (Musician)

SONGS:
Act I
Somethin's Brewin' in Gainesville (cast)
I Did It (Matthew, cast)
Mama Is Here (cast)
It Isn't Easy (cast)
Sho Nuff (Matthew, cast)
Turn It Around (Matthew, cast)
When I Look Up (cast)
There Ain't No Busy Signals (cast)
Spitball (cast)
We're Going to Atlanta (Matthew, cast)
What Does Atlanta Mean to Me? (cast)

Act II
Are We Ready? (cast)
You Are Still My Boy (cast)
We Got to Get Organized (Matthew, cast)
We're Gonna Love It (cast)
Jubilation (cast)
Jud (cast)
Agony Round (cast)
I Wonder (Matthew, cast)

COWARDY CUSTARD
(1972—London)

DEVISED BY: Gerald Frow, Alan Strachan, and
Wendy Toye
WORDS AND MUSIC BY: Noel Coward
PUBLISHED LIBRETTO: French, 1977
CONDENSATION: None
ANTHOLOGY: None
VOCAL SELECTIONS: *Noel Coward Songbook*. Simon
and Schuster, 1953
LICENSING AGENT: Samuel French
RECORDING: RCA LSO 6010 (original London cast)
CAST: 6 M; 6 F

In this revue the songs and sketches of
Noel Coward are bound together by au-

tobiographical material. This all takes us back to a smart era, with crisp, impertinent dialogue and familiar and witty songs. There are a London sequence ("London Pride"), a travel sequence ("Mad Dogs and Englishmen"), a party sequence ("I've Been to a Marvelous Party"), and excerpts from "Tonight at 8:30" and "Present Laughter." This material of Noel Coward, Gertrude Lawrence, and Bea Lillie calls for an extraordinary cast.

ORIGINAL LONDON CAST:

Olivia Breeze	Peter Gale
Geoffrey Burridge	John Moffatt
Jonathan Cecil	Patricia Routledge
Tudor Davies	Anna Sharkey
Elaine Delmar	Una Stubbs
Laurel Ford	Derek Waring

Over fifty songs by Noel Coward are featured in this revue with one intermission.

THE CRADLE WILL ROCK (1937)

A PLAY IN MUSIC BY: Marc Blitzstein
PUBLISHED LIBRETTO: Random House, 1938
CONDENSATION: *New Complete Book of the American Musical Theater.* Ewen, David. Holt, 1970
ANTHOLOGY: *The Best Short Plays of the Social Theatre.* William Kozlenko, ed. Random House, 1939
VOCAL SELECTIONS: Chappell, 1938
LICENSING AGENT: Tams-Witmark
RECORDINGS: American Legacy 1001 (original cast); Composers Recordings 2-CRI SD 266 (1964 cast); Polydor 827 973-1 Y-1 (1983 cast)
CAST: 10 M; 7 F

Subtitled "a worker's opera," this pro-labor union, anti-big business work features the "good guys" against the "bad guys" and moves in and out of court. Everyone is a caricature instead of a person. But never mind the dated social message. What's important now is the jazzy, mock-popular, and craggy musical score somewhat in the style of Kurt Weill. The songs are strung together by bits of dialogue. This is traditionally performed without scenery or costumes and usually with only a piano.

1983 REVIVAL CAST:
Patti LuPone (Moll/Sister Mister)
Henry Stam (Junior/Dick)
Brian Reddy (Harry Druggist)
Mary Lou Rosato (Mrs. Mister)
James Harper (Reverend Salvation)
David Schramm (Mr. Mister)
Tom Robbins (Editor Daily)
Daniel Corcoran (Steve)
Laura Hicks (Sadie)
Casey Biggs (Gus)
Gerald Gutierrez (Yasha)
Randle Mell (Dauber/Larry Foreman)
Michele-Denise Woods (Ella)

SONGS:
Act I
Moll's Song (Moll)
I'll Show You Guys (Moll, Dick)
Solicitin' (Moll, Harry Druggist)
Hard Times/The Sermon (Mrs. Mister, Reverend Salvation, congregation)
Croon Spoon (Sister Mister, Junior)
The Freedom of the Press (Mr. Mister, Editor Daily)
Let's Do Something (Sister Mister, Junior)
Honolulu (Editor Daily, Mr. Mister, Sister Mister, Junior)
Summer Weather (Harry Druggist, Steve)
Love Duet (Gus, Sadie)
Don't Let Me Keep You (Yasha, Dauber)
Ask Us Again (Mr. Mister, Yasha, Dauber)
Art for Art's Sake (Mrs. Mister, Yasha, Dauber)
Act II
The Nickel under Your Foot (Moll)
The Cradle Will Rock (Larry Foreman)
Joe Worker (Ella)

CRAZY FOR YOU (1992)

BOOK BY: Ken Ludwig; inspired by material by Guy Bolton and John McGowan
MUSIC BY: George Gershwin

LYRICS BY: Ira Gershwin
PUBLISHED LIBRETTO: None
CONDENSATION: *The Applause/Best Plays Theater Yearbook 1991–1992*. Otis L. Guernsey, Jr., and Jeffrey Sweet, eds. Applause, 1992
ANTHOLOGY: None
VOCAL SELECTIONS: Warner Bros. Music, 1992
LICENSING AGENT: Tams-Witmark
RECORDING: Angel 7 54618 2 CD (original cast)
CAST: Large mixed cast

Bobby Child, a playboy/banker, is sent from New York City to Deadrock, Nevada, to foreclose on a derelict theater. Naturally he falls in love with the daughter of the owner and decides to save the theater by putting on a show. To achieve this he masquerades as the famous musical producer Bela Zangler. Complications arise when the real Zangler arrives on the scene. Set in the 1930s, with the familiar plot line of an Easterner out West and with five songs from *Girl Crazy*, this show was billed as "the new Gershwin musical." It was the big hit of the 1991–1992 season and received much praise for its choreography, lavish sets and costumes, and "freshness and confidence." The marvelous score and the sensational production numbers made this show a real winner.

Tony Award Winner (Best Musical)

ORIGINAL CAST:

Harry Groener (Bobby)
Jodi Benson (Polly)
Beth Leavel (Tess)
Stacey Logan (Patsy)
Bruce Adler (Bela)
Michele Pawk (Irene)
John Hillner (Lank)
Stephen Temperley (Eugene)
Amelia White (Patricia)

SONGS:
Act I
K-ra-zy for You (Bobby)
I Can't Be Bothered Now (Bobby, girls)
Bidin' My Time (trio)
Things Are Looking Up (Bobby)
Could You Use Me? (Bobby, Polly)

Shall We Dance? (Bobby, Polly)
Someone to Watch over Me (Polly)
Slap That Bass (Bobby, Tess, Patsy, company)
Embraceable You (Polly, Bobby)
Tonight's the Night (company)
I Got Rhythm (Polly, Bobby, company)
Act II
The Real American Folk Song (Is a Rag) (trio)
What Causes That? (Bobby, Bela)
Naughty Baby (Irene, Lank)
Stiff Upper Lip (Bobby, Polly, Eugene, Patricia, company)
They Can't Take That Away from Me (Bobby)
But Not for Me (Polly)
Nice Work If You Can Get It (Bobby, girls)

CURLEY McDIMPLE (1967)

BOOK BY: Mary Boylan and Robert Dahdah
MUSIC AND LYRICS BY: Robert Dahdah
PUBLISHED LIBRETTO: French, 1967
CONDENSATION: None
ANTHOLOGY: None
VOCAL SELECTIONS: Chappell, 1968
LICENSING AGENT: Samuel French
RECORDING: Capitol 45-2116 (original cast—two songs)
CAST: 3 M; 3 F; 1 young girl

Two young song-and-dance vaudevillians are trying for success on Broadway. There's an Irish landlady and every other 1930s movie musical cliche you can imagine—plus an eight-year-old girl with Shirley Temple curls who must carry the bulk of the show all by herself. Curley has been left in a large laundry basket on the doorstep. Be prepared for lots of tap dancing. This show has simple sets and costumes, and the off-Broadway production used a combo of three musicians.

ORIGINAL CAST:

Paul Cahill (Jimmy)
Helen Blount (Sarah)
Bernadette Peters (Alice)
Bayn Johnson (Curley McDimple)
George Hillman (Bill)

Norma Bigtree (Miss Hamilton)
Gene Galvin (Mr. Gillingwater)

SONGS:
Act I
A Cup of Coffee (Jimmy)
I Try (Jimmy, Alice)
Curley McDimple (Curley, Jimmy, Sarah, Alice, Bill)
Love Is the Loveliest Love Song (Alice)
Are There Any More Rosie O'Gradys? (Sarah, Jimmy, Alice, Curley, Bill)
Dancing in the Rain (Curley, Bill, company)
At the Playland Jamboree (Curley, company)
I've Got a Little Secret (Jimmy, Curley)

Act II
Stars and Lovers (Alice, Jimmy, company)
The Meanest Man in Town (Alice, Jimmy, company)
Something Nice Is Going to Happen (Curley)
Swing-a-Ding-a-Ling (Curley)
Hi de hi de hi, Hi de hi de ho (Sarah, Alice, Jimmy, Bill, Mr. Gillingwater, Miss Hamilton)
Dwarfs' Song (Sarah, Alice, Jimmy, Bill, Mr. Gillingwater, Miss Hamilton)
Something Nice Is Going to Happen (reprise) (Miss Hamilton)
Love Is the Loveliest Love Song (reprise) (Jimmy, company)

DAMES AT SEA (1968)

BOOK AND LYRICS BY: George Haimsohn and Robin Miller
MUSIC BY: Jim Wise
PUBLISHED LIBRETTO: French, 1969
CONDENSATION: *New Complete Book of the American Musical Theater*. Ewen, David. Holt, 1970
ANTHOLOGY: None
VOCAL SELECTIONS: Big Three, 1969
LICENSING AGENT: Samuel French
RECORDING: Sony SK 42814 CD (original cast)
CAST: 4 M; 3 F

This spoof of elaborate movie musicals of the thirties started out in a coffee house in Greenwich Village. The production was staged "in the round" on a postage stamp-sized stage with only a piano. It went on to off-Broadway, London, and a television production with Ann Miller. It has the classic backstage plot of the young chorus girl going on at the last minute to save the show. The finale takes place on the deck of a battleship. All of the songs are meant to recall the famous movie musical songs, and the young lovers are appropriately named Dick and Ruby.

ORIGINAL CAST:

Tamara Long (Mona Kent)
Sally Stark (Joan)
Steve Elmore (Hennessey/Captain)
Bernadette Peters (Ruby)
David Christmas (Dick)
Joseph R. Sicari (Lucky)

SONGS:
Act I
Wall Street (Mona)
It's You (Dick, Ruby)
Broadway Baby (Dick)
That Mister Man of Mine (Mona, chorus)
Choo-Choo Honeymoon (Joan, Lucky)
The Sailor of My Dreams (Ruby)
Singapore Sue (Lucky, company)
Good Times Are Here to Stay (Joan, company)

Act II
Dames at Sea (company)
The Beguine (Mona, Captain)
Raining in My Heart (Ruby, chorus)
There's Something about You (Dick, Ruby)
The Echo Waltz (Mona, Joan, Ruby, company)
Star Tar (Ruby, chorus)
Let's Have a Simple Wedding (company)

DAMN YANKEES (1955)

BOOK BY: George Abbott and Douglas Wallop; based on the novel *The Year the Yankees Lost the Pennant* by Douglas Wallop
MUSIC AND LYRICS BY: Richard Adler and Jerry Ross

PUBLISHED LIBRETTO: Random House, 1956;
   Theatre Arts (magazine), November 1956
CONDENSATION: *Ganzl's Book of the Musical
   Theatre*. Ganzl, Kurt. Schirmer (Macmillan),
   1989
ANTHOLOGY: None
PIANO-VOCAL SCORE: Frank Music, 1957
VOCAL SELECTIONS: Frank Music, 1959
LICENSING AGENT: Music Theatre International
RECORDING: RCA 3948-2 CD (original cast)
CAST: 14 M; 7 F; chorus, children

In a slight twist of the *Faust* legend Joe
Hardy makes a deal with the Devil to re-
gain his youth and lead the Washington
Senators baseball team to victory. When
Joe shows signs of exercising his "escape
clause," the Devil sends in his helper, Lola,
to convince Joe. This is one of the very few
successful baseball musicals. It was filmed
in 1958 featuring the Broadway cast and
Bob Fosse choreography, plus Tab Hunter.
It was presented some years later at Jones
Beach with Joe Namath as "Joe Hardy."

Tony Award Winner (Best Musical)

ORIGINAL CAST:

Shannon Bolin (Meg)
Robert Shafer (Joe Boyd)
Ray Walston (Applegate)
Jean Stapleton (Sister)
Stephen Douglass (Joe Hardy)
Russ Brown (Van Buren)
Jimmie Komack (Rocky)
Rae Allen (Gloria)
Richard Bishop (Welch)
Gwen Verdon (Lola)
Albert Linville (Vernon)
Nathaniel Frey (Smokey)
Eddie Phillips (Sohovik)

SONGS:
Act I
Six Months Out of Every Year (Meg, Joe
   Boyd, company)
Good-bye, Old Girl (Joe Boyd, Joe Hardy)
(You've Got to Have) Heart (Van Buren,
   Rocky, Smokey, Vernon)
Shoeless Joe from Hannibal, Mo. (Gloria,
   men)

A Little Brains—a Little Talent (Lola)
A Man Doesn't Know (Joe Hardy, Meg)
Whatever Lola Wants (Lola)
(You've Got to Have) Heart (reprise) (Sister,
   three children)
Who's Got the Pain? (Lola, Sohovik)
Act II
The Game (Rocky, Smokey, men)
Near to You(Joe Hardy, Meg)
Those Were the Good Old Days (Applegate)
Two Lost Souls (Lola, Joe Hardy)
A Man Doesn't Know (reprise) (Meg, Joe
   Boyd)

A DAY IN HOLLYWOOD—A NIGHT IN THE UKRAINE (1980)

BOOK AND LYRICS BY: Dick Vosburgh; additional
   lyrics by Jerry Herman
MUSIC BY: Frank Lazarus; additional music by
   Jerry Herman
PUBLISHED LIBRETTO: French, 198–
CONDENSATION: *The Book of 1,000 Plays*. Steve
   Fletcher, Norman Jopling, eds. Facts On File,
   1989
ANTHOLOGY: None
VOCAL SELECTIONS: Big Three, 1980
LICENSING AGENT: Samuel French
RECORDING: DRG SBL 12580 CD (original cast)
CAST: 4 M; 4 F

Despite its title, this musical double feature started out in London before becoming a big hit on Broadway. The first half
is a spoof of Hollywood in the 1930s, with
reenactments of legendary anecdotes and
many popular songs of the era. Particularly praised was the "dancing feet" routine, as well as all the choreography of director Tommy Tune. Act II is a burlesque
of Chekhov's *The Bear* done in the style of
the Marx Brothers. An extremely versatile
cast is needed to handle both the musical
numbers and the Marx Brothers' parody.

ORIGINAL CAST (AND THE CHARACTERS THEY
PORTRAYED IN ACT II):

Kate Draper (Nina)
David Garrison (Serge B. Samovar)

Niki Harris (Marsha)
Frank Lazarus (Carlo)
Peggy Hewett (Mrs. Pavlenko)
Stephen James (Constantine)
Albert Stephenson (Sascha)
Priscilla Lopez (Gino)

SONGS:
Act I
Just Go to the Movies (company)
Famous Feet (James, Lopez, Garrison)
I Love a Film Cliche (Lazarus, company)
Nelson (Hewett)
The Best in the World (Lopez)
It All Comes Out of the Piano (Lazarus)
Richard Whiting Medley (company)
Thanks for the Memory (Draper, James)
Another Memory (Draper, James)
Doin' the Production Code (company)
A Night in the Ukraine (company)

Act II
Samovar the Lawyer (Garrison as "Samovar")
Just Like That (Draper as "Nina" and James
    as "Constantine")
Again (Draper as "Nina" and James as
    "Constantine")
A Duel! A Duel! (Hewett as "Mrs. Pavlenko"
    and Garrison as "Samovar")
Natasha (Garrison as "Samovar" and Hewett
    as "Mrs. Pavlenko")

DEAR WORLD (1969)

BOOK BY: Jerome Lawrence and Robert E. Lee;
    based on *The Madwoman of Chaillot* by Jean
    Giraudoux as adapted by Maurice Valency
MUSIC AND LYRICS BY: Jerry Herman
PUBLISHED LIBRETTO: None
CONDENSATION: None
ANTHOLOGY: None
VOCAL SELECTIONS: Morris, 1969
LICENSING AGENT: Tams-Witmark
RECORDING: Sony SK 48220 CD (original cast)
CAST: 14 M; 4 F; singers, dancers

This musical very closely follows the play
on which it is based. So we have the "Madwoman" in her clothes of yesteryear, various picturesque sets of Paris, and even a
trip to the sewers. The "Madwoman" and
her friends are out to save Paris from the
money-hungry capitalists who want to destroy the city by digging for oil. This is a real
tour de force for the leading lady (Countess Aurelia), with outlandish makeup, ec-
centric costumes, and big numbers with a
lot of singing.

ORIGINAL CAST:
Angela Lansbury (Countess Aurelia)
Kurt Peterson (Julian)
Pamela Hall (Nina)
Milo O'Shea (sewerman)
Jane Connell (Gabrielle)
Carmen Mathews (Constance)

SONGS:
Act I
The Spring of Next Year (chorus)
A Sensible Woman (Countess Aurelia)
Each Tomorrow Morning (Countess Aurelia,
    company)
I Don't Want to Know (Countess Aurelia)
I've Never Said I Love You (Nina)
Garbage (sewerman, Countess Aurelia,
    Gabrielle, Constance, company)
Dear World (Countess Aurelia, company)

Act II
I Like Me (Julian, company)
Memory (Constance)
Pearls (Countess Aurelia, Gabrielle)
Dickie (Gabrielle)
Voices (Constance)
Thoughts (Countess Aurelia)
And I Was Beautiful (Countess Aurelia)
Have a Little Pity on the Rich (sewerman, men)
Kiss Her Now (Countess Aurelia)

THE DECLINE AND FALL OF THE ENTIRE WORLD AS SEEN THROUGH THE EYES OF COLE PORTER (1965)

CONTINUITY BY: Ben Bagley and Bud McCreery
MUSIC AND LYRICS BY: Cole Porter
PUBLISHED LIBRETTO: None

CONDENSATION: None
ANTHOLOGY: None
LICENSING AGENT: Rodgers and Hammerstein
    Theatre Library
RECORDING: Painted Smiles 124 CD (original cast)
CAST: 2 M; 3 F

The outrageous and irrepressible Ben
Bagley started out producing revues before
he switched to record albums. This, his
most successful revue, was based on one
of his early albums of lesser-known Cole
Porter songs. He picked five very clever
performers for the show and later replaced
them with others of similar abilities. After a most successful off-Broadway run
the show toured for eight months and has
since been done in many small theater productions. Simple to stage in a cabaret setting, only a few basic props are required.
Costumes are minimal, with formal dress
required.

ORIGINAL CAST:

Carmen Alvarez   Kaye Ballard
William Hickey   Harold Lang
Elmarie Wendel

A revue of more than thirty Cole Porter
songs performed with one intermission.

THE DESERT SONG (1926)

BOOK AND LYRICS BY: Otto Harbach, Oscar
    Hammerstein II, and Frank Mandel
MUSIC BY: Sigmund Romberg
PUBLISHED LIBRETTO: French, 1932
CONDENSATION: *Ganzl's Book of the Musical
    Theatre.* Ganzl, Kurt. Schirmer (Macmillan),
    1989
ANTHOLOGY: None
PIANO-VOCAL SCORE: Harms (Warner Bros.
    Music), 1927
LICENSING AGENT: Samuel French; Tams-Witmark
    (professional and semiprofessional only)
RECORDINGS: Columbia CSP ACL 831; Angel 69052
    CD (studio casts)
CAST: 12 M; 6 F; singers, dancers

Pierre Birabeau, the lackluster son of a general, is in fact the "Red Shadow," a mysterious leader of the Riffs in French Morocco
during the 1920s. In this production there is
ample opportunity for fun and excitement
with the French Foreign Legion, Arabian
and Spanish dancing girls, and the romantic music that everybody knows. This is an
old-fashioned, vintage operetta and should
be staged accordingly; it certainly should
not be modernized or mocked. There were
several filmed versions—Dennis Morgan in
1944 and Gordon MacRae in 1953.

ORIGINAL CAST:

William O'Neal (Sid El Kar)
Robert Halliday (Red Shadow/Pierre)
Eddie Buzzell (Bennie)
Glen Dale (Captain Paul Fontaine)
Lyle Evans (Ali Ben Ali)
Nellie Breen (Susan)
Vivienne Segal (Margot)
Margaret Irving (Clementina)

SONGS:
Act I
Feasting Song (Sid, men)
The Riff Song (Red Shadow, Sid, men)
Margot (Paul, men)
Has Anyone Seen My Bennie? (Susan)
Why Did We Marry Soldiers? (women)
French Military Marching Song (Margot,
    chorus)
Romance (Margot, women)
Then You Will Know (Margot, Pierre, chorus)
I Want a Kiss (Margot, Pierre, Paul, chorus)
It (Bennie, Susan)
The Desert Song (Red Shadow, Margot)
Soft as a Pigeon (Sid, Paul, chorus)

Act II
Song of the Brass Key (Clementina, women)
One Good Boy Gone Wrong (Bennie,
    Clementina)
Let Love Go (Ali, men)
One Flower in Your Garden (Sid, men)
One Alone (Red Shadow, Sid, Ali, men)
The Sabre Song (Margot, Red Shadow)

DESTRY RIDES AGAIN (1959)

BOOK BY: Leonard Gershe; based on the story by
    Max Brand
MUSIC AND LYRICS BY: Harold Rome
PUBLISHED LIBRETTO: None
CONDENSATION: *New Complete Book of the
    American Musical Theater.* Ewen, David. Holt,
    1970
ANTHOLOGY: None
PIANO-VOCAL SCORE: Chappell, 1959
LICENSING AGENT: Tams-Witmark
RECORDING: Decca DL 79075 (original cast)
CAST: 14 M; 6 F; chorus

This lavish Broadway musical is a western melodrama with song and dance. The plot revolves around the town of Bottleneck, which is under the control of a tough gambler named Kent. Destry is brought in to maintain law and order. Frenchy is the star entertainer at the Last Chance Saloon. The choreography by Michael Kidd (particularly the "Whip Dance") was highly praised by the critics. The costumes were called flashy and fun, particularly those of the dance-hall girls. The score is in the traditional mood of cowboy music with some ragtime flourishes for the saloon festivities. A London production was done "in the round," and the bar used in the set was also used as a refreshment stand during the intermission.

ORIGINAL CAST:

Dolores Gray (Frenchy)
Andy Griffith (Destry)
Scott Brady (Kent)
Jack Prince (Wash)
Elizabeth Watts (Rose)

SONGS:
Act I
Bottleneck (chorus)
Ladies (Frenchy, girls)
Hoop-de-Dingle (Wash, chorus)
Ballad of the Gun (Destry, Wash)
The Social (chorus)
I Know Your Kind (Frenchy)
I Hate Him (Frenchy)

Paradise Alley (chorus)
Anyone Would Love You (Destry, Frenchy)
Once Knew a Fella (Destry, Wash, friends)
Every Once in a While (chorus)
Fair Warning (Frenchy)

Act II
Are You Ready, Gyp Watson? (chorus)
Not Guilty (the jury)
Only Time Will Tell (Destry)
Respectability (Rose, girls)
That Ring on the Finger (Frenchy, girls)
Once Knew a Fella (reprise) (Destry, Frenchy)
I Say Hello (Frenchy)

DIAMOND STUDS (1975)

BOOK BY: Jim Wann
ORIGINAL MUSIC AND LYRICS BY: Bland Simpson
    and Jim Wann
PUBLISHED LIBRETTO: French, 1976
CONDENSATION: None
ANTHOLOGY: None
LICENSING AGENT: Samuel French
RECORDING: Pasquotank 003 (original cast)
CAST: 12 M; 2 F

The off-Broadway production was an example of "environmental theater." The theater was transformed into a frontier saloon with dance-hall girls serving beer. Peanut shells were scattered on the floor. This show is primarily a concert of country music (both traditional and original) rather than a play. The story line concerns Jesse James and is told through narration and sketchy scenes. The performers are musicians first, actors second.

ORIGINAL CAST:

Jim Wann (Jesse James)
John Foley (Bob Ford)
Jan Davidson (Major Edwards)
Tommy Thompson (Zerelda/Cole)
Jim Watson (Jim Younger)
Bill Hicks (Bob Younger)
Mike Craver (Pappy)
Joyce Cohen (Zee James)

Rick Simpson (Frank James)
Madelyn Smoak (Belle Starr)

SONGS:

Act I

Jesse James Robbed This Train (Jesse,
  chorus)
These Southern States That I Love (Zerelda,
  Pappy, Frank, Jesse, company)
The Year of Jubilo (Cole, Bob Younger,
  Jim)
The Unreconstructed Rebel (Major Ed-
  wards)
Mama Fantastic (Jesse, Bob Younger, Frank,
  Jim, gang)
Steal Away (Jesse, gang)
I Don't Need a Man to Know I'm Good (Belle)
Northfield, Minnesota (Jesse, Frank, Cole, Bob
  Younger, Jim)
King Cole (Cole, chorus)
New Prisoner's Song (Jim, Cole)
K.C. Line (Jesse, Frank, Cole, Jim, Bob
  Younger, women)
Cakewalk into Kansas City (Jesse, chorus)

Act II

When I Was a Cowboy (Jim, chorus)
Pancho Villa (Jesse, Pancho)
Put It Where the Moon Don't Shine (Jesse,
  Bob Ford, chorus)
Sleepy Time Down South (Jesse, Zee)
Bright Morning Star (chorus)
When I Get the Call (Jesse)

DIAMONDS (1984)

BOOK BY: Ralph G. Allen, Jim Wann, John Lahr,
  Bud Abbott, others
MUSIC BY: Gerald Alessandrini, Craig Carnelia, Cy
  Coleman, Larry Grossman, John Kander, Doug
  Katsaros, Alan Menken, Jonathan Sheffer, Albert
  von Tilzer, Lynn Udall, and Jim Wann
LYRICS BY: Gerald Alessandrini, Howard Ashman,
  Craig Carnelia, Betty Comden, Fred Ebb, Ellen
  Fitzhugh, Adolph Green, Karl Kennett, Jack
  Norworth, Jim Wann, David Zippel
PUBLISHED LIBRETTO: French, 1985
CONDENSATION: None
ANTHOLOGY: None

LICENSING AGENT: Samuel French
RECORDING: None
CAST: 7 M; 3 F

The subject of this off-Broadway revue is
baseball. In New York it was staged "in the
round" in an environmental setting with the
audience seemingly on bleachers around
the sides. The cast added to the atmosphere by handing out bags of peanuts
and popcorn and nonalcoholic beverages.
There is no plot to this "good-natured celebration of the American national pastime."
Thirty-six writers, composers, and lyricists
contributed to the songs and sketches.
Some songs and sketches are new, while
others go back to the Abbott and Costello
"Who's on First?" routine and the popular song "Take Me Out to the Ball Game"
(here sung in French in the style of Maurice Chevalier). This show was noted for
its strength in its rapid-fire pacing and the
energy of the ensemble.

ORIGINAL CAST:

Loni Ackerman	Dwayne Markee
Susan Bigelow	Wade Raley
Jackee Harry	Larry Riley
Scott Holmes	Nestor Serrano
Dick Latessa	Chip Zien

SONGS:

Act I

Winter in New York (company)
In the Cards (Markee, Raley, Ackerman)
Favorite Sons (Harry, Riley, Serrano,
  Ackerman, Zien)
Song for a Pitch Hitter (Bigelow)
Vendors (cast)
What You'd Call a Dream (Holmes)
Escorte-moi (Take Me Out to the Ball Game)
  (Zien)
He Threw Out the Ball (Harry, company)
Hundreds of Hats (company)
1919 (Riley, Raley, Markee, Holmes)

Act II

Let's Play Ball (company)
The Boys of Summer (Bigelow)
Songs for a Hunter College Graduate
  (Ackerman)

Stay in Your Own Back Yard (Harry)
Ka-razy (company)
Diamonds Are Forever (company)

DIVORCE ME, DARLING! (1965—London)

BOOK, MUSIC, AND LYRICS BY: Sandy Wilson
PUBLISHED LIBRETTO: None
CONDENSATION: None
ANTHOLOGY: None
LICENSING AGENT: Music Theatre International
RECORDING: DRG DS 14009 (original London cast)
CAST: 18 M; 15 F

This is Wilson's sequel to his very popular *The Boy Friend*. Many of the same characters are used and are now ten years older. It's the 1930s and they are in Nice on holiday. They are all contemplating the possibility of being single again. Dance numbers are "a la Fred Astaire" and the music sometimes parodies Cole Porter. A Noel Coward terrace scene presents a golden opportunity for displaying high-fashion costumes of the period. This is very British and has never been done on Broadway.

ORIGINAL LONDON CAST:

Maria Charles (Dulcie Du Bois)
Vicky Clayton (Fay de la Falaise)
Philip Gilbert (Tony Brockhurst)
Irlin Hall (Hannah Van Husen)
Harry Haythorne (Alphonse Du Bois)
Joan Heal (Madame K.)
Geoffrey Hibbert (Lord Brockhurst)
Patricia Michael (Polly Brockhurst)
Robert Parvin (Monsieur Gaston)
Anna Sharkey (Maisie Van Husen)
Keith Smith (Sir Freddy)
Roy Sone (Marcel de la Falaise)
Jenny Wren (Nancy Lebrun)
Violetta (Hortense)
Charles Yates (Pierre Lebrun)
Cy Young (Bobby Van Husen)

SONGS:
Act I
Here We Are in Nice Again (Fay, Nancy, Dulcie, Hortense, Monsieur Gaston, ensemble)
Someone to Dance With (Bobby)
Whatever Happened to Love? (Polly, Fay, Nancy, Dulcie)
Lights! Music! (Madame K.)
On the Loose (Lord Brockhurst, Fay, Nancy, Dulcie)
Maisie (Marcel, Pierre, Alphonse)
Paradise Hotel (Hortense, Monsieur Gaston, ensemble)
No Harm Done (Bobby, Polly)
Together Again (Tony, Polly, Bobby, Maisie)

Act II
Divorce Me, Darling! (Polly, Bobby, Tony, Maisie, Fay, Nancy, Dulcie, Marcel, Pierre, Alphonse)
Here Am I (But Where's the Guy?) (Hannah)
Out of Step (Bobby, Maisie)
You're Absolutely Me (Hannah, Sir Freddy)
Back Where We Started (Polly, Tony) Reprise (Dulcie, Lord Brockhurst)
Blondes for Danger (Madame K.)
Swing-Time Is Here to Stay (Maisie, company)

DO BLACK PATENT LEATHER SHOES REALLY REFLECT UP? (1982)

BOOK BY: John R. Powers; based on his novel
MUSIC AND LYRICS BY: James Quinn and Alaric Jans
PUBLISHED LIBRETTO: French, 1988
CONDENSATION: None
ANTHOLOGY: None
LICENSING AGENT: Samuel French
RECORDING: Bay Cities 3033 CD (original cast)
CAST: 5 M; 9 F

This musical written and produced in Chicago enjoyed a healthy run there and in other cities before moving to New York. It takes a rather irreverent look at Roman Catholic education. The plot involves a group of children (played by adults) progressing through grade school and high school. Nuns and priests guide them in religious indoctrination, sex education, and other subjects that Catholic audiences are sure to enjoy. The score was described as "hummable" with a "snappy, bouncy beat." One dance number has the entire cast lie on their backs and wave their oversized shoes in the air. The sets were designed to look like cartoons.

ORIGINAL CAST:

Elizabeth Hansen (Sister Helen)
Maureen Moore (Becky)
Russ Thacker (Eddie)
Ellen Crawford (Sister Lee)
Robert Fitch (Father O'Reilly)
Karen Tamburrelli (Nancy)
Jason Graae (Louie)
Don Stitt (Felix)
Vicki Lewis (Virginia)

SONGS:
Act I
Get Ready, Eddie (company)
The Greatest Gift (Sister Helen, kids)
It's the Nuns (kids, nuns)
Little Fat Girls (Becky, Eddie)
Cookie Cutters (Sister Lee, Becky)
Patron Saints (Father O'Reilly, Eddie, kids, nuns)
How Far Is Too Far (Nancy, girls, boys)
Act II
Doo-Waa, Doo-Wee (Louie, company)
I Must Be in Love (Eddie)
Friends, the Best Of (Becky, Eddie)
Mad Bombers and Prom Queens (Felix, Virginia, kids)
Late Bloomer (Eddie, kids)
Thank God (company)

DO I HEAR A WALTZ? (1965)

BOOK BY: Arthur Laurents; based on his play *The Time of the Cuckoo*
MUSIC BY: Richard Rodgers
LYRICS BY: Stephen Sondheim

PUBLISHED LIBRETTO: Random House, 1966
CONDENSATION: *Ganzl's Book of the Musical Theatre*. Ganzl, Kurt. Schirmer (Macmillan), 1989
ANTHOLOGY: None
PIANO-VOCAL SCORE: Williamson, 1965
VOCAL SELECTIONS: Williamson, 1965
LICENSING AGENT: Rodgers and Hammerstein Theatre Library
RECORDINGS: Columbia CSP AKOS 2770 (original cast); Sony SK 48206 CD (original cast)
CAST: 6 M; 6 F; chorus

A vacationing spinster visits Venice, meets a handsome Italian, and falls in love. Before being turned into a musical, the original play was filmed as *Summertime* with Katharine Hepburn. The cast includes a young married couple, a worldly Italian landlady, and a young boy. This is a bittersweet love story that can be staged quite simply. Despite the title, there is little dancing. The critics of this show found Richard Rodgers a bit old-fashioned; but Stephen Sondheim was on his way up.

ORIGINAL CAST:

Elizabeth Allen (Leona)
Carol Bruce (Signora Fioria)
Stuart Damon (Eddie)
Julienne Marie (Jennifer)
Fleury D'Antonakis (Giovanna)
Sergio Franchi (Renato)
Madeline Sherwood (Mrs. McIlhenny)
Jack Manning (Mr. McIlhenny)
James Dybas (Vito)

SONGS:
Act I
Someone Woke Up (Leona)
This Week Americans (Fioria)
What Do We Do? We Fly! (Leona, Mr. and Mrs. McIlhenny, Eddie, Jennifer)
Someone Like You (Renato)
Bargaining (Renato)
Here We Are Again (Leona, Vito, ragazzi)
Thinking (Renato, Leona)
No Understand (Fioria, Eddie, Giovanna)
Take the Moment (Renato)

Act II

Moon in My Window (Jennifer, Fioria, Leona)
We're Gonna Be All Right (Eddie, Jennifer)
Do I Hear a Waltz? (Leona, company)
Stay (Renato)
Perfectly Lovely Couple (Leona, Renato,
    Mr. and Mrs. McIlhenny, Jennifer, Eddie,
    Giovanna, Fioria)
Thank You So Much (Renato, Leona)

DO RE MI (1961)

BOOK BY: Garson Kanin
MUSIC BY: Jule Styne
LYRICS BY: Betty Comden and Adolph Green
PUBLISHED LIBRETTO: None
CONDENSATION: *New Complete Book of the
    American Musical Theater.* Ewen, David. Holt,
    1970
ANTHOLOGY: None
PIANO-VOCAL SCORE: Chappell, 1961
VOCAL SELECTIONS: Hal Leonard, 1961
LICENSING AGENT: Tams-Witmark
RECORDING: RCA LSOD 2002 (original cast)
CAST: 8 M; 2 F; chorus; dancers

The original Broadway production had the benefit of two top comedians as stars: Phil Silvers and Nancy Walker. The plot concerns the world of jukebox rackets and deals with underworld characters in New York. There is a secondary pair of young lovers and they get to sing the score's big hit, "Make Someone Happy." The critics mentioned the extravagant production and the numerous scene changes. There are takeoffs on "The Late Late Show," Zen Buddhism, and other aspects of life in 1960.

ORIGINAL CAST:

Nancy Walker (Kay Cram)
Phil Silvers (Hubi)
John Reardon (John)
David Burns (Brains Berman)
Nancy Dussault (Tilda)
George Givot (Skin)
George Mathews (Fatso)

SONGS:

Act I

Waiting, Waiting (Kay)
All You Need Is a Quarter (chorus)
Take a Job (Hubie, Kay)
It's Legitimate (Hubie, Fatso, Brains, Skin,
    chorus)
I Know about Love (John)
Cry like the Wind (Tilda)
Ambition (Hubie, Tilda)
Fireworks (Tilda, John)
What's New at the Zoo (Tilda, girls)
Asking for You (John)
The Late Late Show (Hubie)

Act II

Adventure (Hubie, Kay)
Make Someone Happy (John, Tilda)
V. I. P. (Hubie, chorus)
All of My Life (Hubie)

DOCTOR SELAVY'S MAGIC THEATRE (1972)

CONCEIVED BY: Richard Foreman
MUSIC BY: Stanley Silverman
LYRICS BY: Tom Hendry
PUBLISHED LIBRETTO: None
CONDENSATION: None
ANTHOLOGY: None
LICENSING AGENT: Rodgers and Hammerstein
    Theatre Library
RECORDING: UA LA 196 G (original cast)
CAST: 4 M; 4 F; 1 girl

Originally subtitled "The Mental Cure," this one-hour entertainment is entirely sung and done in the tradition of the theater of the absurd. It concerns the experiences of a patient in a mental institution, and the theme is that the world is crazy and that gentle insanity is the best defense. Vaudeville tricks and dances are employed in a set described as "a large, live-in version of a Louise Nevelson sculpture." The pastiche score includes "soft Bach, hard rock and superfly soul," delivered through "a haze of irony and satire." This was a big off-Broadway hit.

ORIGINAL CAST:

Denise Delapenha (Fortune Teller)
Jessica Harper (Rock Singer)
Mary Delson (Pirate)
George McGrath (Selavy)
Steve Menken (Doctor)
Jackie Paris (Little Girl)
Rob Farber (Patient)
Robert Schlee (Short Doctor)
Amy Taubin (Female Doctor)

SONGS:
(performed without intermission)
I Live by My Wits (Patient)
Three Menu Songs (Pirate, Short Doctor)
Bankrupt Blues (Doctor)
Future for Sale (Fortune Teller)
Life on the Inside (Female Doctor)
Strawberry-Blueberry (Rock Singer, Doctor)
The More You Get (Patient)
Money in the Bank (Rock Singer, Patient)
If You're Proposing (Some Sort of Venture)
    (Selavy)
Life on the Inside (reprise) (Female Doctor,
    Short Doctor)
Long Live Free Enterprise (cast)
Doesn't It Bug You (Pirate, Female Doctor,
    Fortune Teller, Rock Singer)
Dusty Shadows (Doctor, Female Doctor)
Poor Boy (Patient, Fortune Teller, Short
    Doctor)
Dearest Man (Pirate)
Where You Been Hiding till Now (Fortune
    Teller, Doctor)
He Lived by His Wits (Doctor, Selavy, Short
    Doctor)
Fireman's Song (Patient)
What Are You Proposing? (Selavy, Short
    Doctor)
Doctors in the Chase Scene (Rock Singer,
    Doctor)
Requiem (Fortune Teller, Rock Singer, cast)
Let's Hear It for Daddy Moola (Fortune Teller,
    cast)
Life on the Inside (reprise) (Fortune Teller,
    Female Doctor, Rock Singer)

A DOLL'S LIFE (1982)

BOOK AND LYRICS BY: Betty Comden and Adolph
    Green
MUSIC BY: Larry Grossman
PUBLISHED LIBRETTO: French, 1982
CONDENSATION: None
ANTHOLOGY: None
VOCAL SELECTIONS: Fiddleback Music (Valando),
    1982
LICENSING AGENT: Samuel French
RECORDING: Bay Cities BCD 3031 (original cast)
CAST: Large mixed cast

The curtain goes up on a present-day rehearsal of Ibsen's *A Doll's House*. After Nora's final exit we are suddenly whisked back to Norway in 1879 to find out what happened to Nora after she left her husband and children. This is a serious work concerning women's rights and equality and was given a lavish Broadway production. The show's design in dark colors was based on the works of Edvard Munch. The score for this musical was described as quasi-operatic, or operetta-like, indicating a need for strong trained voices.

ORIGINAL CAST:

Betsy Joslyn (Nora)
Peter Gallagher (Otto)
Norman A. Large (Conductor/Gustafson)
Edmund Lyndeck (Eric)
George Hearn (Johan)
David Vosburgh (Berg)
Barbara Lang (Astrid)

SONGS:
Act I
A Woman Alone (Nora, Otto, Conductor,
    company)
Letter to the Children (Nora)
New Year's Eve (Eric, Johan, Berg, Gustafson)
Stay with Me, Nora (Otto, Nora)
Arrival (Astrid, company)
Loki and Baldur (Otto, singers)
You Interest Me (Johan)
Departure (Astrid, company)
Letter from Klemnacht (Astrid)
Learn to Be Lonely (Nora)

Rats and Mice and Fish (women)
Jailer. Jailer (Nora, women)
Rare Wines (Eric, Nora)

Act II
No More Mornings (Nora)
There She Is (Johan, Eric, Otto)
Power (Nora)
At Last (Johan)

DONNEYBROOK! (1961)

BOOK BY: Robert E. McEnroe; based on *The Quiet Man* by Maurice Walsh
MUSIC AND LYRICS BY: Johnny Burke
PUBLISHED LIBRETTO: None
CONDENSATION: None
ANTHOLOGY: None
LICENSING AGENT: Samuel French
RECORDING: Kapp KD 8500 S (original cast)
CAST: 9 M; 5 F; chorus

John Enright, a prizefighter who has killed an opponent in the ring, returns to Ireland seeking peace. Once there he falls in love with a vixenish colleen. Her bully-boy brother tries to get him to fight, and eventually we have an old-fashioned knock-down for the second act finale. This show was described as loud and lusty. The male dancers sometimes wear kilts.

ORIGINAL CAST:

Joan Fagan (Ellen)
Art Lund (Enright)
Eddie Foy (Flynn)
Susan Johnson (Kathy)
Charles C. Welch (Father Finucane)
Clarence Nordstrom (Toomey)
Sibyl Bowan (Sadie)
Grace Carney (Birdie)
Eddie Ericksen (An Irish Boy)

SONGS:
Act I
Sez I (Ellen, Toomey, men)
The Day the Snow Is Meltin' (An Irish Boy)
Sad Was the Day (Kathy, ensemble)
Donneybrook (ensemble)

Ellen Roe (Enright)
Sunday Morning (ensemble)
The Lovable Irish (Enright, Father Finucane)
I Wouldn't Bet One Penny (Kathy, Flynn)
He Makes Me Feel I'm Lovely (Ellen)
The Courting (ensemble)
I Have My Own Way (Enright, Ellen)
A Toast to the Bride (Toomey, ensemble)

Act II
Wisha Wurra (Flynn, Toomey, men)
A Quiet Life (Enright)
Mr. Flynn (Kathy, Sadie, Birdie)
Dee-lightful Is the Word (Flynn, Kathy)
For My Own (Ellen, Enright)

DON'T BOTHER ME, I CAN'T COPE (1972)

MUSIC BY: Micki Grant; conceived and directed by Vinnette Carroll
PUBLISHED LIBRETTO: French, 1972
CONDENSATION: *Broadway Musicals Show by Show.* Green, Stanley. Hal Leonard Books, 1985
ANTHOLOGY: None
VOCAL SELECTIONS: Fiddleback Music (Valando), 1973
LICENSING AGENT: Samuel French
RECORDING: Polydor PD 6013 (original cast)
CAST: 6 M; 6 F (may vary)

This black revue consists primarily of songs about being black and human and sensitive. There are also dancers and a gospel choir. There is no plot; this is a musical "happening," and it can be done in a simple setting.

ORIGINAL CAST:

Micki Grant   Charles Campbell
Alberta Bradford   Alex Bradford
Hope Clarke   Bobby Hill
Arnold Wilkerson

SONGS:
Act I
I Gotta Keep Movin' (Alberta Bradford, Alex Bradford, Campbell, Hill)
Lookin' Over from Your Side (Hill, company)
Don't Bother Me, I Can't Cope (company)

When I Feel Like Moving (Clarke)
Help (Clarke)
Fighting for Pharaoh (Alberta Bradford, Alex
    Bradford, Hill, Campbell)
Good Vibrations (Alex Bradford, company)
Love Power (Hill, Clarke, company)
They Keep Coming (company)
My Name Is Man (Wilkerson)

Act II
Questions (Grant)
It Takes a Whole Lot of Human Feeling
    (Grant)
You Think I Got Rhythm? (Wilkerson, Grant)
Time Brings about a Change (Grant,
    Wilkerson, company)
So Little Time (Grant)
Thank Heaven for You (Hill, Grant)
So Long Sammy (Hill, Clarke)
All I Need (Alberta Bradford, company)
I Gotta Keep Movin' (reprise) (Grant,
    company)

DOONESBURY (1983)

BOOK AND LYRICS BY: Garry Trudeau; based on
    his *Doonesbury* comic strip
MUSIC BY: Elizabeth Swados
PUBLISHED LIBRETTO: French, 1986; Holt,
    Reinhart, 1984
CONDENSATION: None
ANTHOLOGY: None
LICENSING AGENT: Samuel French
RECORDING: MCA 6129 (original cast)
CAST: 7 M; 4 F

Based on a popular comic strip known for
its social and political satire, this musical
features fourteen songs (mostly soft rock)
and some modest dance routines. The plot
concerns the Walden Puddle denizens on
the eve of college graduation. What will
Zonker do? Will his Uncle Duke turn the residence into a "vacation combo complex"?
Will Doonesbury marry J.J.? Will J.J. and
her mother be reconciled? In the course
of all this, Uncle Duke drives a bulldozer
through a wall, which will pose a problem
for your set designer. The sets are "cartoon-
like" pasteboard, and the small musical
group is offstage. There is a lot of Ronald
Reagan satire as well as satire about such
subjects as food stamps, unemployment,
feminism, and acid rain.

ORIGINAL CAST:
Reathel Bean (Roland)
Ralph Bruneau (Mike Doonesbury)
Mark Linn-Baker (Mark)
Laura Dean (Boopsie)
Albert Macklin (Zonker)
Keith Szarabajka (B.D.)
Gary Beach (Duke)
Lauren Tom (Honey)
Kate Burton (J.J.)
Barbara Andres (Joanie)
Peter Shawn (Provost)

SONGS:
Act I
Graduation (Roland, Mike, B.D., Boopsie,
    Mark, Zonker)
Just One Night (Mike)
I Came to Tan (Zonker, ensemble)
Guilty (Duke, ensemble)
I Can Have It All (Boopsie, ensemble)
Get Together (J.J., Mike)
Baby Boom Boogie Boy (Mark, Roland,
    ensemble)
Another Memorable Meal (Mike, B.D.,
    Boopsie, Mark, Zonker, J.J., Joanie)
Act II
Just a House (ensemble)
Complicated Man (Honey, Boopsie)
Real Estate (Duke, Zonker)
Mother (J.J., Joanie)
It's the Right Time to Be Rich (B.D., Roland)
Muffy and the Topsiders (Boopsie, Mike,
    Mark, Zonker)

DOWNRIVER (1975)

BOOK BY: Jeff Tambornino; based on *The
    Adventures of Huckleberry Finn* by Mark Twain
MUSIC AND LYRICS BY: John Braden
PUBLISHED LIBRETTO: None

CONDENSATION: None
ANTHOLOGY: None
LICENSING AGENT: Music Theatre International
RECORDING: Take Home Tunes THT 7811 (original cast)
CAST: 14 M; 7 F

This off-Broadway production was noted for its abstract settings, which utilized overhead projectors that gave an impressionistic atmosphere. The story is the familiar one about the misadventures of Huck and Jim, the freed slave (see also *Big River*). This bit of Americana can be simply staged for the whole family.

ORIGINAL CAST:

Richard Dunne (Huck)
Alvin Fields (Jim)
Donald Arrington (King)
Robert Price (Duke)
Marcia McLain (Mary Jane)
Michael Corbett (Tom)

SONGS:
Act I
Bound Away (Huck)
Till Our Good Luck Comes Along (Huck, Jim)
The Musicale (King)
Come Home, Runaway (Jim)
He's on His Way, Hallelujah! (chorus)

Act II
River Rats (King, Duke, Huck)
Just Like Love (Huck, Mary Jane)
What a Grand Day for an Auction Sell (King, chorus)
Downriver (Huck)
Tom and Huck's Argument (Tom, Huck)
Shine Down, Lord (Jim)
Finale (Huck)

DRAT! THE CAT! (1965)

BOOK AND LYRICS BY: Ira Levin
MUSIC BY: Milton Schafer
PUBLISHED LIBRETTO: None
CONDENSATION: None
ANTHOLOGY: None
VOCAL SELECTIONS: Morris, 1966

LICENSING AGENT: Samuel French
RECORDING: Blue Pear 1005 (original cast)
CAST: 9 M; 6 F; chorus

Around the turn of the century, a "cat burglar" has all of New York in a state of panic! "The Cat" turns out to be a millionaire's daughter who falls in love with a rookie cop (the son of a former detective chief). This high-spirited comedy is played somewhat in a "Keystone Cop" style. One popular song from the score is "She Touched Me." This was an elaborate Broadway musical with a Japanese Kabuki scene, a uniformed 1890s band on stage at one point, and a basement pipe that leaked real water.

ORIGINAL CAST:

Alfred Spindelman (The Mayor)
Charles Durning (Pincer)
Gene Varrone (Mallet)
David Gold (Roger Purefoy)
Lesley Ann Warren (Alice)
Elliott Gould (Bob)
Lu Leonard (Kate)
Jane Connell (Mrs. Van Guilder)
Jack Fletcher (Mr. Van Guilder)
Sandy Ellen (Emma)

SONGS:
Act I
Drat! The Cat! (The Mayor, Pincer, Mallet, chorus)
My Son, Uphold the Law (Roger, men)
Holmes and Watson (Alice, Bob)
She Touched Me (Bob)
Wild and Reckless (Alice)
She's Roses (Bob, Kate)
Dancing with Alice (Bob, Alice, Mr. and Mrs. Van Guilder, chorus)
Drat! The Cat! (reprise) (Mr. and Mrs. Van Guilder, chorus)
Purefoy's Lament (Bob)

Act II
A Pox upon the Traitor's Brow (Pincer, Mallet, Emma, men)
Deep in Your Heart (Bob)
Let's Go (Alice, Bob)
It's Your Fault (Mr. and Mrs. Van Guilder)
Wild and Reckless (reprise) (Bob)

Today Is a Day for a Band to Play (Pincer, Mallet, Emma, chorus)
She Touched Me (reprise) (Bob, Alice)
I Like Him (Alice)
Justice Triumphant (company)

DREAMGIRLS (1981)

BOOK BY: Tom Eyen
MUSIC BY: Henry Krieger
LYRICS BY: Tom Eyen
PUBLISHED LIBRETTO: None
CONDENSATION: *Broadway Musicals Show by Show.* Green, Stanley. Hal Leonard Books, 1985
ANTHOLOGY: None
PIANO-VOCAL SCORE: Warner Bros. Music, 1982
VOCAL SELECTIONS: Warner Bros. Music, 1982
LICENSING AGENT: Tams-Witmark
RECORDING: Geffen 2007-2 CD (original cast)
CAST: Large mixed cast

Starting out on the stage of the Apollo Theatre in Harlem in the early 1960s, this musical traces the rise of a black singing trio called "The Dreams." Although, as Frank Rich in the *New York Times* reported, "they bear more than a passing resemblence to 'The Supremes,'" composer Henry Krieger denies that his music is based on the Motown sound, but it does musically mirror the sixties. Effie, the group's best singer, is overweight and is replaced when the group needs a more glamorous appearance. In New York the sets had a high-tech look and consisted primarily of four towers of lights with occasional drop curtains and a staircase. The costumes for "The Dreams" become increasingly glamorous and exotic as their fortunes climb. Michael Bennett provided exciting (and occasionally satirical) choreography.

ORIGINAL CAST:

Deborah Burrell, Vanessa Bell, Tenita Jordan, Brenda Pressley (The Stepp Sisters)
Jennifer Holliday, Loretta Devine, Sheryl Lee Ralph (The Dreams)
Wellington Perkins (Little Albert)
Joe Lynn (Tiny Joe Dixon)

Cleavant Derricks (Jimmy Early)
Ben Harney (Curtis)
Obba Babatunde (C. C.)
Vondie Curtis-Hall (Marty)
Paul Binotto (Dave)
Tony Franklin (Wayne)
Sheryl Lee Ralph (Deena)
Loretta Devine (Lorrell)
Jennifer Holliday (Effie)
Deborah Burrell (Michelle)

SONGS:
Act I
I'm Looking for Something (Stepp Sisters)
Goin' Downtown (Little Albert, group)
Takin' the Long Way Home (Tiny Joe)
Move (Effie, Deena, Lorrell: The Dreams)
Fake Your Way to the Top (Jimmy Early, The Dreams)
Cadillac Car (Dave, company)
Steppin' to the Bad Side (Curtis, C. C., The Dreams, company)
Party, Party (company)
I Want You, Baby (Jimmy, The Dreams)
Family (C. C., Curtis, Jimmy, Deena, Lorrell)
Dream Girls (The Dreams)
Press Conference (company)
Only the Beginning (Curtis, Deena, Effie)
Heavy (The Dreams)
It's All Over (Curtis, Effie, Deena, Lorrell, C. C., Michelle, Jimmy)
And I Am Telling You I'm Not Going (Effie)
Love Love You, Baby (The Dreams)

Act II
"Dreams" Medley (Deena, The Dreams, company)
I Am Changing (Effie)
One More Picture Please (company)
When I First Saw You (Curtis, Deena)
Got to Be Good Times (group)
Ain't No Party (Lorrell, Jimmy)
I Meant You No Harm (Jimmy)
Quintette (Deena, Lorrell, Michelle)
The Rap (Jimmy, C. C., Curtis, Lorrell, company)
I Miss You Old Friend (Effie, Marty, C. C., group)
One Night Only (Effie, Deena, The Dreams, company)

I'm Somebody (Deena, The Dreams)
Faith in Myself (Effie)
Hard to Say Good-bye, My Love (Deena, The
Dreams)

DROOD (THE MYSTERY OF EDWIN) (1985)

BOOK, MUSIC, AND LYRICS BY: Rupert Holmes;
suggested by the unfinished novel by Charles
Dickens
PUBLISHED LIBRETTO: None
CONDENSATION: *The Best Plays of 1985–1986.* Otis
L. Guernsey, Jr., ed. Dodd, Mead, 1987
ANTHOLOGY: None
PIANO-VOCAL SCORE: Warner Bros. Music, 1986
VOCAL SELECTIONS: Warner Bros. Music, 1986
LICENSING AGENT: Tams-Witmark
RECORDING: Polydor 827 969-2 CD (original cast)
CAST: Large mixed cast

As a musical-within-a-musical, we begin at
a turn of the century amusement pier in
Dorping (England) where a theatrical troop
is presenting our mystery-musical. These
music-hall numbers should be done with
much enthusiasm. Since the Dickens novel
was unfinished, this musical has the unusual distinction of having several possible endings—the audience is allowed to
choose the solution to the crime! Note also
that famous actor George Spelvin is used to
conceal the identity of one character. Done
first outdoors in Central Park, this musical
is a real crowd pleaser.

Tony Award Winner (Best Musical)

ORIGINAL CAST:

George Rose (Chairman)
Howard McGillin (Jasper)
Betty Buckley (Drood)
Patti Cohenour (Rosa)
Jana Schneider (Helena)
Judy Kuhn (Alice)
Donna Murphy (Beatrice)
Cleo Laine (Puffer)
Nicholas Gunn (Shade of Jasper)
Brad Miskell (Shade of Drood)

John Herrera (Neville)
George N. Martin (Crisparkle)
Joe Grifasi (Bazzard)
George Spelvin (Dick Datchery)
Jerome Dempsey (Durdles)
Stephen Glavin (Deputy)

SONGS:
Act I
There You Are (Chairman, ensemble)
A Man Could Go Quite Mad (Jasper)
Two Kinsmen (Drood, Jasper)
Moonfall (Rosa) Reprise (Rosa, Helena, Alice,
Beatrice)
The Wages of Sin (Puffer)
Jasper's Vision (Shades of Jasper and Drood,
ensemble)
Ceylon (Drood, Rosa, Helena, Neville,
ensemble)
Both Sides of the Coin (Jasper, Chairman,
ensemble)
Perfect Strangers (Drood, Rosa)
No Good Can Come from Bad (Neville, Drood,
Rosa, Helena, Crisparkle, Jasper, Bazzard)
The Name of Love (Rosa, Jasper, ensemble)

Act II
Settling Up the Score (Datchery, Puffer,
ensemble)
Off to the Races (Chairman, Durdles, Deputy,
ensemble)
Don't Quit While You're Ahead (Puffer,
ensemble)
The Garden Path to Hell (Puffer)
The Solution (cast)

THE DRUNKARD (1970)

ADAPTATION BY: Bro Herrod; based on the
melodrama by W. H. S. Smith
MUSIC AND LYRICS BY: Barry Manilow for original
songs
PUBLISHED LIBRETTO: None
CONDENSATION: None
ANTHOLOGY: None
LICENSING AGENT: Music Theatre International
RECORDING: None
CAST: 4 M; 4 F

In this good old-fashioned "hiss-and-cheer" melodrama (with olio curtain) a young husband is ruined by drink and then rescued by last-minute faith. This show has been popular since 1844! "Do You Wanna Be Saved?" was a Salvation Army number most of the critics liked. The score is in traditional style. The off-Broadway production offered free beer (or root beer) and group singing between the acts. Simple to stage and it's good fun.

ORIGINAL CAST:

Susan Rush (Song Leader, Barmaid, Julia)
Lou Vitacco (Song Leader, Preacher, Barkeep)
Marie Santell (Mary)
Donna Sanders (Mrs. Wilson, Barmaid, Salvation Worker)
Christopher Cable (Cribbs)
Clay Johns (Edward Middleton)
Drew Murphy (William)
Joy Garrett (Agnes, Carry Nation, Old Man's Darling)

SONGS:
Act I
Something Good Will Happen Soon (Mary, Mrs. Wilson)
Whispering Hope (Mary, Mrs. Wilson)
Don't Swat Your Mother, Boys (Cribbs)
Strolling through the Park (Mary, Edward)
Good Is Good (William, Cribbs, Agnes)
Mrs. Mary Middleton (Preacher, William, Edward, Mrs. Wilson, Mary, Cribbs)

Act II
Have Another Drink (Barkeep, Edward, Carry Nation, Cribbs, Barmaids)
The Curse of an Aching Heart (Edward)
For When You're Dead (Cribbs)
A Cup of Coffee (Edward, Cribbs)

Act III
Garbage Can Blues (Edward)
Shall I Be an Old Man's Darling? (Old Man's Darling)
Julia's Song (Julia)
I'm Ready to Go (Edward)
Do You Wanna Be Saved? (cast)

DU BARRY WAS A LADY (1939)

BOOK BY: B. G. DeSylva and Herbert Fields
MUSIC AND LYRICS BY: Cole Porter
PUBLISHED LIBRETTO: None
CONDENSATION: *New Complete Book of the American Musical Theater*. Ewen, David. Holt, 1970
ANTHOLOGY: None
MUSIC PUBLISHER: *Music and Lyrics by Cole Porter*. 2 vols. Chappell, 1972–1975
LICENSING AGENT: Tams-Witmark
RECORDING: None
CAST: 12 M; 10 F; singers, dancers

The story begins at the Club Petite nightclub in New York City, circa 1939. The main characters are a former bathroom attendant, who has just come into a lot of money, and the female star of the floor show. He dreams they are at the Palace of Versailles and that he is Louis XV and she is Madame Du Barry. There is ample opportunity for elaborate costumes and powdered wigs. The show was described as rowdy and boisterous, almost a burlesque show. There was a film version in 1943 with Lucille Ball.

ORIGINAL CAST:

Ethel Merman (May/Du Barry)
Bert Lahr (Louis/Louis XV)
Ronald Graham (Alex/Alexandre)
Betty Grable (Alice/Alisande)
Charles Walters (Harry/Captain)
Benny Baker (Charley/Dauphin)
Jean Moorehead (Vi)

SONGS:
Act I
Ev'ry Day's a Holiday (Harry, Alice, ensemble)
It Ain't Etiquette (Louis, Vi)
When Love Beckoned (May, ensemble)
Come on In (May, starlets)
Dream Song (Charley)
Mesdames et Messieurs (chorus)
But in the Morning, No (Du Barry, Louis XV)
Do I Love You? (Alexandre, Du Barry)
Du Barry Was a Lady (Du Barry, company)

Act II
Give Him the Oo-La-La (May)
Well, Did You Evah? (Alisande, Captain)
Katie Went to Haiti (May, Harry, Alice,
     ensemble)
Friendship (May, Louis)

THE EDUCATION OF H*Y*M*A*N K*A*P*L*A*N (1968)

BOOK BY: Benjamin Bernard Zavin; based on
     stories by Leo Rosten
MUSIC AND LYRICS BY: Paul Nassau and Oscar
     Brand
PUBLISHED LIBRETTO: Dramatic, 1968
CONDENSATION: None
ANTHOLOGY: None
LICENSING AGENT: Dramatic
RECORDING: None
CAST: 9 M; 7 F

Mr. Kaplan is a Jewish immigrant who wants to become a United States citizen. The time is 1920 and the setting is New York City's Lower East Side. Mr. Kaplan attends night school and is threatened with deportation, but the story has a predictably happy ending. The critic at *Women's Wear Daily* summed it up as "singing . . . dancing . . . and other paraphernalia of the Lower East Side—Broadway style."

ORIGINAL CAST:

Gary Krawford (Parkhill)
Tom Bosley (Kaplan)
Beryl Towbin (Miss Vitale)
Dorothy Emmerson (Higby)
Barbara Minkus (Rose)
Mimi Sloan (Mrs. Mitnick)
Donna McKechnie (Kathy)
Dick Latessa (Pastora)
David Gold (Plonsky)
Nathaniel Frey (Pinsky)
Honey Sanders (Mrs. Moskowitz)
Maggie Task (Fanny)
Hal Linden (Fishbein)

SONGS:
Act I
Strange New World (Parkhill)
OOOO-EEEE (Kaplan, Rose, Parkhill, students)
A Dedicated Teacher (Higby, Miss Vitale,
     Parkhill)
Lieben Dich (Kaplan)
Loving You (Rose)
The Day I Met Your Father (Mrs. Mitnick)
Anything Is Possible (Kaplan, students)
Spring in the City (Kathy, Pastora, Plonsky,
     Pinsky, Mrs. Moskowitz, Fanny, chorus)

Act II
Old Fashioned Husband (Fishbein)
Julius Caesar (Kaplan)
I Never Felt Better in My Life (Kaplan,
     chorus)
When Will I Learn? (Rose)
All American (Pinsky, students)

ERNEST IN LOVE (1960)

BOOK AND LYRICS BY: Anne Croswell; based on
     The Importance of Being Earnest by Oscar Wilde
MUSIC BY: Lee Pockriss
PUBLISHED LIBRETTO: None
CONDENSATION: None
ANTHOLOGY: None
VOCAL SELECTIONS: Edwin H. Morris, 1960
LICENSING AGENT: Music Theatre International
RECORDING: Columbia OS 2027 (original cast)
CAST: 10 M; 6 F

This is an off-Broadway musical version of Wilde's classic comedy. While this production obviously did not improve on the original, most critics felt that it did not betray it, either. There was a small musical ensemble of five that was praised, and the overture was compared to chamber music. The small, jewel-like production was a very stylish show.

ORIGINAL CAST:

Leila Martin (Gwendolyn)
John Irving (Jack)
Gerrianne Raphael (Cecily)
Louis Edmonds (Algernon)

Sara Seegar (Lady Bracknell)
Margot Harley (Alice)
Lucy Landau (Miss Prism)
George Hall (Dr. Chasuble)
Christina Gillespie (Effie)
Alan Shayne (Lane)
George Hall (Perkins)

SONGS:

Act I

Come Raise Your Cup (servants, creditors)
How Do You Find the Words (Jack,
    Gwendolyn, Perkins, Alice)
The Hat (Jack, Gwendolyn, Perkins, Alice)
Mr. Bunbury (Algernon, Jack)
Perfection (Jack, Gwendolyn)
A Handbag Is Not a Proper Mother (Lady
    Bracknell, Jack)
A Wicked Man (Cecily)
Metaphorically Speaking (Miss Prism, Dr.
    Chasuble)
A Wicked Man (reprise) (Algernon)

Act II

You Can't Make Love (Effie, Lane)
Lost (Algernon, Cecily)
My Very First Impressions (Gwendolyn,
    Cecily)
The Muffin Song (Jack, Algernon)
My Eternal Devotion (Gwendolyn, Cecily,
    Algernon, Jack)
Ernest in Love (cast)

ESTHER (1988)

BOOK, MUSIC, AND LYRICS BY: Elizabeth Swados;
    based on Elie Wiesel's Purim lecture
PUBLISHED LIBRETTO: Broadway Play Publishing,
CONDENSATION: None
ANTHOLOGY: None
PIANO-VOCAL SCORE: Broadway Play Publishing,
    1988
LICENSING AGENT: Broadway Play Publishing
RECORDING: None
CAST: 3 M; 3 F; chorus

Originally presented by the American Jewish Theater in New York, this musical tells the Biblical story of Queen Esther, who saved the Jewish people from slaughter and who is celebrated in the Jewish holiday of Purim. The score combines reggae, rock, and traditional folk music. It was described as "a two hour carnival" complete with audience participation.

ORIGINAL CAST:

Peter Herber (Mordechai)
Laura Patinkin (Esther)
Louis Padilla (Haman)
Robert Ott Boyle (King Ahasuerous)
Nancy Ringham (Narrator—Ethyl)
Frederique S. Walker (Narrator—Lucy)

Musical numbers are not listed in the program.

EUBIE! (1978)

CONCEIVED BY: Julianne Boyd
MUSIC BY: Eubie Blake
LYRICS BY: Noble Sissle, Andy Razaf, others
PUBLISHED LIBRETTO: None
CONDENSATION: None
ANTHOLOGY: None
VOCAL SELECTIONS: Warner Bros. Music, 1979
LICENSING AGENT: Music Theatre International
RECORDING: Warner Bros. HS 3267 (original cast)
CAST: 5 M; 6 F (may vary)

This all-black musical revue features the music of Eubie Blake, whose popular show tunes of the 1920s and 1930s are perhaps exemplified by his hit show *Blackbirds of 1928*. His music, and the dazzling, dancing Hines brothers, were the primary reasons for this show's success. So you will need some tap dancers and period costumes to carry this off. Called a "guaranteed crowd pleaser," be prepared for some amusing, but adults only, lyrics to the songs.

ORIGINAL CAST:

Ethel Beatty   Terry Burrell
Leslie Dockery   Lynnie Godfrey
Gregory Hines   Maurice Hines
Mel Johnson, Jr.   Lonnie McNeil
Janet Powell   Marion Ramsey
Alaina Reed   Jeffrey V. Thompson

SONGS:
Act I
Shuffle Along (company)
In Honeysuckle Time (McNeil, Powell, company)
I'm Just Wild about Harry (M. Hines, Powell, Godfrey, Ramsey, Beatty)
Baltimore Buzz (McNeil, Thompson, Johnson, Powell, G. Hines, Dockery)
Daddy (Godfrey)
There's a Million Little Cupids in the Sky (M. Hines, G. Hines, McNeil, Beatty, Johnson, Thompson, Ramsey, Powell, Dockery, Reed)
I'm a Great Big Baby (Thompson)
My Handyman Ain't Handy Anymore (Reed, Johnson)
Low Down Blues (G. Hines)
Gee, I Wish I Had Someone to Rock Me in the Cradle of Love (Beatty)
I'm Just Simply Full of Jazz (company)
Act II
High Steppin' Days (company)
Dixie Moon (Johnson, G. Hines, M. Hines, company)
Weary (Burrell, company)
Roll Jordan (Reed, Burrell, Powell, company)
Memories of You (Beatty)
If You've Never Been Vamped (Ramsey, company)
You Got to Git the Gittin While the Gittin's Good (M. Hines)
Oriental Blues (Thompson, Beatty, Godfrey, Powell, Ramsey)
I'm Craving for That Kind of Love (Godfrey)
Hot Feet (G. Hines)
Good Night Angeline (Beatty, Johnson, McNeil, Powell)

EVITA (1979)

MUSIC BY: Andrew Lloyd Webber
LYRICS BY: Tim Rice
PUBLISHED LIBRETTO: MCA, 1979 (with vocal selections); Avon (New York), 1979
CONDENSATION: *Ganzl's Book of the Musical Theatre*. Ganzl, Kurt. Schirmer (Macmillan), 1989

ANTHOLOGY: None
VOCAL SELECTIONS: MCA Music, 1979
LICENSING AGENT: Music Theatre International
RECORDING: MCA MCAD 2-11007 CD (original New York cast)
CAST: Large mixed cast, including children

Completely sung, this "rock opera" began as a record album in England and then was very successful on the London stage before opening on Broadway. It begins and ends with Evita's bier surrounded by mourners. This is the story of an ambitious show girl who becomes the power behind a dictator and a legend in her own time, only to die of cancer at the age of thirty-three. Che Guevara is the narrator for the story of Juan and Eva Peron. The only other important roles are those of a male nightclub singer who discovers Evita and a young female who was Juan's mistress before Evita. Hal Prince, the original director, has said he feels the musical is more about the media than Evita. This was a lavish production (see photo on record album) with numerous slide projections and occasional film clips. The music was described as jagged and sweet as well as rock and latin. The most popular song from the score is "Don't Cry for Me Argentina."

Tony Award Winner (Best Musical)

ORIGINAL CAST:

Bob Gunton (Juan Peron)
Patti LuPone (Evita)
Mandy Patinkin (Che Guevara)
Mark Syers (Magaldi)
Jane Ohringer (Mistress)

SONGS:
Act I
Requiem for Evita (chorus)
Oh What a Circus (Che)
Don't Cry for Me Argentina (Evita, girls)
On This Night of a Thousand Stars (Che, Magaldi)
Eva and Magaldi (Evita, Magaldi, Che, chorus)
Buenos Aires (Evita, Che)
Good Night and Thank You (Che, Evita, Magaldi, men)

The Art of the Possible (Evita, men)
Charity Concert/I'd Be Surprisingly Good for
    You (Magaldi, Che, Evita, Juan)
Another Suitcase in Another Hall (Evita,
    Mistress, Che)
Peron's Latest Flame (Che, Evita, men)
A New Argentina (Juan, Evita, company)

Act II
On the Balcony of the Casa Rosada (Che,
    Juan, company)
High Flying, Adored (Che, Evita)
Rainbow High (Evita, chorus)
Rainbow Tour (Juan, Che, Evita, men)
The Actress Hasn't Learned (Evita, Che,
    company)
And the Money Keeps Rolling In (Che,
    company)
Santa Evita (Che, men, children)
Waltz for Eva and Che (Che, Evita)
She Is a Diamond (Che, Juan, men)
Dice Are Rolling (Juan, Evita)
Eva's Final Broadcast (Che, Evita)
Montage (Che, Magaldi, Evita, Juan,
    company)
Lament (Evita, Che, company)

FADE OUT FADE IN (1964)

BOOK AND LYRICS BY: Betty Comden and Adolph
    Green
MUSIC BY: Jule Styne
PUBLISHED LIBRETTO: Random House, 1965
CONDENSATION: *New Complete Book of the
    American Musical Theater.* Ewen, David. Holt,
    1970
ANTHOLOGY: None
VOCAL SELECTIONS: Stratford Music, 1964
LICENSING AGENT: Tams-Witmark
RECORDING: ABC OC 3 (original cast)
CAST: 26 M; 9 F

"Oh those Thirties" goes the opening number, and we go back to Hollywood in its
golden era. Hope Springfield, by mistake,
has been signed by a major studio to become a film star. Carol Burnett was "Hope"
on Broadway and this was a big musical.

The sets can be elaborate, and there is ample opportunity for dancing, spectacle, and
comedy. The original production even included a live seal!

ORIGINAL CAST:
Jack Cassidy (Bryon Prong)
Tiger Haynes (Lou Williams)
Carol Burnett (Hope Springfield)
Mitchell Jason (Ralph Governor)
Lou Jacobi (Lionel Z. Governor)
Dick Patterson (Rudolf Governor)
Tina Louise (Gloria)

SONGS:
Act I
The Thirties (Byron)
It's Good to Be Back Home (Hope, ensemble)
Fear (Rudolf, Ralph, men) Reprise (Byron, men)
Call Me Savage (Hope, Rudolf)
The Usher from the Mezzanine (Hope)
I'm with You (Hope, Byron, chorus)
My Fortune Is My Face (Byron)
Lila Tremaine (Hope)

Act II
Go Home Train (Hope)
Close Harmony (Lionel, Gloria, men)
You Mustn't Be Discouraged (Hope, Lou)
The Dangerous Age (Lionel)
The Fiddler and the Fighter (Byron,
    ensemble)
Fade Out—Fade In (Hope, Rudolf)

FALSETTOLAND (1990)

BOOK BY: William Finn and James Lapine
MUSIC AND LYRICS BY: William Finn
PUBLISHED LIBRETTO: French, 1990
CONDENSATION: *Applause Best Plays. Theater
    Year Book, 1990–1991.* Otis L. Guernsey, Jr.,
    and Jeffrey Sweet, eds. Applause Theater
    Books, 1992
ANTHOLOGY: *The Marvin Songs.* Fireside Theatre
    Publications
VOCAL SELECTIONS: Warner Bros. Music, 1991
LICENSING AGENT: Samuel French
RECORDING: DRG CDSBL 12601 CD (original cast)
CAST: 3 M; 3 F; 1 young boy

This is the third musical featuring the characters "Marvin" and "Whizzer." The other two are *In Trousers* and *March of the Falsettos*. Marvin and Whizzer are gay and in love. The time is 1981–1982, so when Whizzer becomes ill, AIDS is never named but is understood by the audience. Seventy-five minutes in length, it is possible to combine this with one of the other two musicals to provide a full evening's entertainment. And despite the subject, it is entertaining. A small on-stage band is utilized behind a scrim, and as with the others, minimal furniture is rolled onto the stage. Jason is Marvin's son, and it is time for his Bar Mitzvah, which is held in Whizzer's hospital room. Each character has at least one revealing song. Adult entertainment.

ORIGINAL CAST:

Lonny Price (Mendel)
Michael Rupert (Marvin)
Danny Gerard (Jason)
Stephen Bogardus (Whizzer)
Faith Prince (Trina)
Heather MacRae (Dr. Charlotte)
Janet Metz (Cordelia)

SONGS:
(performed without intermission)
Falsettoland (cast)
About Time (Marvin)
Year of the Child (Dr. Charlotte, Cordelia, Marvin, Trina, Mendel, Jason)
Miracle of Judaism (Jason)
The Baseball Game (cast)
A Day in Falsettoland (cast)
Planning the Bar Mitzvah (Jason, Trina, Mendel, Marvin)
Everybody Hates His Parents (Mendel, Jason)
What More Can I Say? (Marvin)
Something Bad Is Happening (Dr. Charlotte, Cordelia)
More Racquetball (Marvin, Whizzer)
Holding to the Ground (Trina)
Days Like This (Marvin, Whizzer, Cordelia, Trina, Mendel, Jason, Dr. Charlotte)
Canceling the Bar Mitzvah (Trina, Mendel, Jason)

Unlikely Lovers (Marvin, Whizzer, Cordelia, Dr. Charlotte)
Another Miracle of Judaism (Jason)
You Gotta Die Sometime (Whizzer)
Jason's Bar Mitzvah (Jason, Whizzer, Marvin, Trina, Mendel, Cordelia, Dr. Charlotte)
What Would I Do? (Marvin, Whizzer)

A FAMILY AFFAIR (1962)

BOOK, MUSIC, AND LYRICS BY: James Goldman, John Kander, and William Goldman
PUBLISHED LIBRETTO: None
CONDENSATION: None
ANTHOLOGY: None
VOCAL SELECTIONS: Valando, 1960
LICENSING AGENT: Music Theatre International
RECORDING: United Artists UAS 5099 (original cast)
CAST: 5 M; 9 F; chorus

Set in Chicago, the story begins with a proposal of marriage and ends with the wedding ceremony. In between are all the wedding preparations, with all the members of the bride's and groom's families trying to run the show. The families are Jewish, so there are a lot of Yiddish words and some ethnic humor. One critic called it a burlesque of a large Jewish wedding. The Broadway production included no elaborate sets or big production numbers.

ORIGINAL CAST:

Larry Kert (Gerry)
Rita Gardner (Sally)
Shelley Berman (Alfie)
Eileen Heckart (Tilly)
Beryl Towbin (Babs)
Jack De Lon (Mr. Weaver)
Morris Carnovsky (Morris)
Bibi Osterwald (Miss Lumpe)
Linda Lavin (Fifi)
Bill McDonald (Kenwood)
Alice Nunn (Mother)
Gino Conforti (Harry)

SONGS:

Act I

A Family Affair (chorus)
Anything for You (Gerry, Sally)
Beautiful (Alfie) Reprise (Tilly)
My Son the Lawyer (Tilly, chorus)
Every Girl Wants to Get Married (Sally, Babs)
Right Girls (Alfie, Mr. Weaver, men)
Kalua Bay (Tilly, Morris)
There's a Room in My House (Gerry, Sally)
Football Game (Babs, chorus)
Harmony (Miss Lumpe, Harry, Fifi, Mr. Weaver)

Act II

Now Morris (Morris, Tilly)
Wonderful Party (Gerry, Fifi, Kenwood)
Revenge (Alfie, Mother, chorus)
Summer Is Over (Tilly)
What I Say Goes (Gerry)
I'm Worse than Anybody (Alfie, Tilly, Morris)
The Wedding (company)

FANNY (1954)

BOOK BY: S. N. Behrman and Joshua Logan; based on the trilogy *Marius*, *Fanny*, and *Cesar* by Marcel Pagnol
MUSIC AND LYRICS BY: Harold Rome
PUBLISHED LIBRETTO: Random House, 1954
CONDENSATION: *Theatre '55*. John Chapman, ed. Random House, 1955
ANTHOLOGY: None
PIANO-VOCAL SCORE: Chappell, 1956
VOCAL SELECTIONS: Chappell, 1954
LICENSING AGENT: Tams-Witmark
RECORDING: RCA LSO 1015 E (original cast)
CAST: 10 M; 6 F; chorus, dancers

Cesar is the proprietor of a waterfront bistro in Marseilles "not so long ago" and Panisse is his lifelong friend. Panisse marries Cesar's daughter, Fanny, who really loves Marius. The original Broadway production was described as big, opulent, costly; the belly-dance number was called spectacular. The score was unusually rich (helped by voices like Ezio Pinza's) and the show was a big hit. It was subsequently filmed with the background music from Mr. Rome's score but with no songs!

ORIGINAL CAST:

William Tabbert (Marius)
Walter Slezak (Panisse)
Florence Henderson (Fanny)
Ezio Pinza (Cesar)
Edna Preston (Honorine)
Nejla Ates (Arab Dancing Girl)
Mohammed el Bakkar (Arab Singer)
Gerald Price (The Admiral)
Gary Wright (Cesario)

SONGS:

Act I

Octopus Song (The Admiral)
Restless Heart (Marius, male ensemble)
Never Too Late for Love (Panisse, ensemble)
Cold Cream Jar Song (Panisse)
Does He Know? (Fanny, Marius)
Why Be Afraid to Dance? (Cesar)
Never Too Late for Love (reprise) (Cesar, Panisse, Honorine)
Shika, Shika (Arab Dancing Girl, Arab Singer, ensemble)
Welcome Home (Cesar)
I Like You (Marius, Cesar)
I Have to Tell You (Fanny)
Fanny (Marius)
The Sailing (Fanny, Marius, Cesar, ensemble)
Oysters, Cockles, and Mussels (ensemble)
Panisse and Son (Panisse)

Act II

Birthday Song (Fanny, Honorine, ensemble)
To My Wife (Panisse)
The Thought of You (Marius, Fanny)
Love Is a Very Light Thing (Cesar)
Other Hands, Other Hearts (Fanny, Cesar, Marius)
Fanny (reprise) (Cesar, Fanny, Marius)
Be Kind to Your Parents (Fanny, Cesario)
Welcome Home (reprise) (Cesar, Panisse)

THE FANTASTICKS (1960)

BOOK AND LYRICS BY: Tom Jones; based on the
   play *Les Romanesques* by Edmond Rostand
MUSIC BY: Harvey Schmidt
PUBLISHED LIBRETTO: Drama Book Shop, 1964;
   Applause, 1990
CONDENSATION: *Ganzl's Book of the Musical
   Theatre*. Ganzl, Kurt. Schirmer (Macmillan),
   1989
ANTHOLOGY: *Fantasticks and Celebration*. Drama
   Book Specialists, 1973; *The Best American Plays*,
   6th series, 1963–67. John Gassner and Clive
   Barnes, eds. Crown, 1971
PIANO-VOCAL SCORE: Chappell, 1963
VOCAL SELECTIONS: Chappell, 1963
LICENSING AGENT: Music Theatre International
RECORDING: Polydor 821943-2 CD (original cast)
CAST: 8 M; 1 F; piano and harp

This is the ageless tale that love conquers
all. It is a harlequinade, a variation of the
Pierrot and Columbine theme. The girl and
boy have purposefully been kept apart by
their parents to foster a romance. The
first act takes place at night, and the parents have dreamed up a kidnapping of the
girl so the boy can rescue her. The sun
shines in the second act, and all ends well.
This simple off-Broadway musical ran more
than thirty years and broke all records for
longevity.

ORIGINAL CAST:

Jerry Orbach (The Narrator)
Rita Gardner (The Girl)
Kenneth Nelson (The Boy)
William Larsen (A Father)
Hugh Thomas (A Father)

SONGS:
Act I
Try to Remember (The Narrator)
Much More (The Girl)
Metaphor (The Boy, The Girl)
Never Say No (Fathers)
It Depends on What You Say (The Narrator,
   Fathers)
Soon It's Gonna Rain (The Boy, The Girl)
Rape Ballet (company)

Happy Ending (company)

Act II
This Plum Is Too Ripe (The Boy, The Girl,
   Fathers)
I Can See It (The Boy, The Narrator)
Plant a Radish (Fathers)
Round and Round (The Narrator, The Girl,
   company)
They Were You (The Boy, The Girl)

FASHION (1974)

BOOK ADAPTED BY: Anthony Stimac; based on
   the 1845 drama by Anna Cora Mowatt
MUSIC BY: Donald Pippin
LYRICS BY: Steve Brown
PUBLISHED LIBRETTO: French, 1974
CONDENSATION: None
ANTHOLOGY: None
VOCAL SELECTIONS: Edwin H. Morris, 1974
LICENSING AGENT: Samuel French
RECORDING: None
CAST: 1 M; 8 F

Using the play-within-a-play device, the authors present a production popular in 1845
that reflected American society and manners. But now it is a musical, done very
simply as a chamber-ensemble. The score
was described as having a rollicking charm
and the production was stylishly mounted.
The plot is a spoof about women who
turn their husbands' bank accounts into
clothes. Some of the women double as men
in the play they are rehearsing. This off-
Broadway production was also done on
PBS.

ORIGINAL CAST:

Mary Jo Catlett (Mrs. Tiffany)
Sandra Thornton (Seraphina)
Ty McConnell (Count Jolimaitre)
Joanne Gibson (Gertrude)
Jan Buttram (Mr. Tiffany)
Sydney Blake (Millinette)
Henrietta Valor (Mr. Trueman)

SONGS:

Act I

Rococo Rag (girls)

You See before You What Fashion Can Do
   (Jolimaitre, Mrs. Tiffany, Seraphina)

It Was for Fashion's Sake (Mr. Tiffany)

The Good Old American Way (Mr. Trueman,
   Mr. Tiffany)

What Kind of Man Is He? (Gertrude)

My Daughter, the Countess (Mrs. Tiffany)

Take Me (Jolimaitre, Seraphina)

Why Should They Know about Paris?
   (Jolimaitre, Millinette)

I Must Devise a Plan (company)

Act II

Meet Me Tonight (company)

My Title Song (Mrs. Tiffany, company)

A Life without Her (Mr. Trueman)

FESTIVAL (1979)

BOOK AND LYRICS BY: Stephen Downs and
   Randal Martin; additional material by Bruce
   Vilanch; based on the chantefable "Aucassin
   and Nicolette"

MUSIC BY: Stephen Downs

PUBLISHED LIBRETTO: French, 1979

CONDENSATION: None

ANTHOLOGY: None

LICENSING AGENT: Samuel French

RECORDING: Original Cast OC 7916 (original cast)

CAST: 5 M; 5 F

This zany musical begins with the pianist
dressed in tails, walking across the stage,
and unexpectedly doing a cartwheel! Members of the cast play multiple roles in modern dress in this fantasy with a carnival
setting. The story concerns young lovers,
their family quarrels, and their world-
hopping adventures before their final ful-
fillment. This show has a soft-rock musical score; it played successfully around
the United States before an off-Broadway
presentation.

ORIGINAL CAST:

Michael Rupert (Troubador)

Bill Hutton (Aucassin)

Maureen McNamara (Nicolette)

Tina Johnson (Shepherdess)

Michael Magnusen (Beaucaire)

Lindy Nisbet (Gypsy Queen)

Roxann Parker (Viscountess)

Leon Stewart (Oxherd)

Robin Taylor (Shepherdess)

John Windsor (Valence)

SONGS:

(performed without intermission)

Our Song (Troubador, company)

The Ballad of Oh (Troubador)

For the Love (Troubador, company)

Beata Biax (Beautiful, Beautiful) (Aucassin,
   company)

Just Like You (Beaucaire, Aucassin)

Special Day (Nicolette, Aucassin)

The Time Is Come (Troubador, Nicolette,
   Aucassin)

Roger the Ox (Oxherd)

When the Lady Passes (Aucassin,
   Shepherdesses, Valence, company)

Gifts to You (Nicolette, Aucassin, company)

The Escape (company)

The Pirates' Song (Troubador, company)

I Can't Remember (Valence, Oxherd,
   Troubador, Beaucaire, Nicolette)

One Step Further (Shepherdesses,
   Viscountess, Gypsy Queen, Nicolette)

Through Love's Eyes (Beaucaire, Aucassin)

Let Him Love You (Nicolette, Viscountess)

The Ceremony (Troubador, Nicolette,
   Aucassin, company)

I Speak of Love (Troubador)

FIDDLER ON THE ROOF (1964)

BOOK BY: Joseph Stein; based on Sholem
   Aleichem's stories

MUSIC BY: Jerry Bock

LYRICS BY: Sheldon Harnick

PUBLISHED LIBRETTO: Crown, 1964; Pocket Books
   (paperback), 1965

CONDENSATION: *The Best Plays of 1964–1965*.
Otis L. Guernsey, Jr., ed. Dodd, Mead, 1965;
Ganzl's Book of the Musical Theatre. Ganzl, Kurt.
Schirmer (Macmillan), 1989
ANTHOLOGY: *Ten Great Musicals of the American
Stage*. Stanley Richards, ed. Chilton, 1973; *The
Best American Plays*, 6th series, 1963–67. John
Gassner and Clive Barnes, eds. Crown, 1971;
Fifty Best Plays of the American Theatre, vol. 4.
Clive Barnes, ed. Crown, 1969
PIANO-VOCAL SCORE: Valando, 1965
VOCAL SELECTIONS: Times Square, 1964
LICENSING AGENT: Music Theatre International
RECORDING: RCA 7060 CD (original cast)
CAST: 12 M; 10 F; chorus, dancers

The time is 1905 and the place is Anatevka, a hamlet in Russia. The plot concerns Tevye and his daughters, and how their lives are changed by czarist repression of the Jews. This show is one of the most popular and long-running in the history of the musical theater. It has been performed all over the world. There was a film version in 1971.

Tony Award Winner (Best Musical)

ORIGINAL CAST:

Zero Mostel (Tevye)
Joanne Merlin (Tzeitel)
Julia Migenes (Hodel)
Tanya Everett (Chava)
Maria Karnilova (Golde)
Beatrice Arthur (Yente)
Michael Granger (Lazar)
Austin Pendleton (Motel)
Sue Babel (Grandma)
Carol Sawyer (Fruma-Sarah)
Bert Convy (Perchik)
Leonard Frey (Mendel)
Paul Lipson (Avram)

SONGS:
Act I
Tradition (Tevye, chorus)
Matchmaker, Matchmaker (Tzeitel, Hodel,
Chava)
If I Were a Rich Man (Tevye)
Sabbath Prayer (Tevye, Golde, chorus)
To Life (Tevye, Lazar, men)

Miracle of Miracles (Motel)
The Tailor, Motel Kamzoil (Tevye, Golde,
Grandma, Fruma-Sarah, chorus)
Sunrise, Sunset (Tevye, Golde, chorus)
Wedding Dance (chorus)

Act II
Now I Have Everything (Perchik, Hodel)
Do You Love Me? (Tevye, Golde)
I Just Heard (Yente, chorus)
Far from the Home I Love (Hodel)
Anatevka (Tevye, Golde, Yente, Lazar, Mendel,
Avram)

FINIAN'S RAINBOW (1947)

BOOK BY: E. Y. Harburg and Fred Saidy
MUSIC BY: Burton Lane
LYRICS BY: E. Y. Harburg
PUBLISHED LIBRETTO: Random House, 1947;
Theatre Arts (magazine), January 1949
CONDENSATION: *New Complete Book of the
American Musical Theater*. Ewen, David. Holt,
1970
ANTHOLOGY: None
PIANO-VOCAL SCORE: Chappell, 1968
VOCAL SELECTIONS: Chappell (DeSylva), 1946
LICENSING AGENT: Tams-Witmark
RECORDINGS: Col CK 4062 CD (original cast); RCA
1057-2 RG CD (1960 cast)
CAST: 23 M; 12 F; chorus

Finian has stolen the Glocca Morra pot of gold and is pursued by its guardian leprechaun to rural America. The book of this show contains a satiric plot line dealing with bigotry and politics that may seem a bit dated now; but the lovely score is not dated. It has been revived many times, and there was a film version in 1968 with Fred Astaire.

ORIGINAL CAST:

Donald Richards (Woody Mahoney)
David Wayne (Og)
Ella Logan (Sharon McLonergan)
Lorenzo Fuller (Second Passion Pilgrim
Gospeler)
Alan Gilbert (First Sharecropper)

Jerry Laws (First Passion Pilgrim Gospeler)
Delores Martin (Maude)
Lewis Sharp (Third Passion Pilgrim Gospeler)
Maud Simmons (Second Sharecropper)

SONGS:
Act I
This Time of Year (chorus)
How Are Things in Glocca Morra? (Sharon)
Look to the Rainbow (Sharon, Woody,
     chorus)
Old Devil Moon (Sharon, Woody)
Something Sort of Grandish (Sharon, Og)
If This Isn't Love (Sharon, Woody, chorus)
Necessity (Maude, Sharecroppers)
Great Come and Get It Day (Sharon, Woody,
     chorus)

Act II
When the Idle Poor Become the Idle Rich
     (Sharon, chorus)
The Begat (Passion Pilgrim Gospelers)
When I'm Not Near the Girl I Love (Og)

FIORELLO! (1959)

BOOK BY: Jerome Weidman and George Abbott
MUSIC BY: Jerry Bock
LYRICS BY: Sheldon Harnick
PUBLISHED LIBRETTO: Random House, 1960;
     Theatre Arts (magazine), November 1961
CONDENSATION: *Broadway's Best, 1960.* John
     Chapman, ed. Doubleday, 1960; *The Best Plays
     of 1959–1960.* Louis Kronenberger, ed. Dodd,
     Mead, 1960
ANTHOLOGY: *Great Musicals of the American
     Theatre*, vol. 2. Stanley Richards, ed. Chilton,
     1976
VOCAL SELECTIONS: New York Times Music, 1960;
     Warner Bros. Music
LICENSING AGENT: Tams-Witmark
RECORDING: Capitol 92052 CD (original cast)
CAST: Large mixed cast

This musicalized biography of the little Italian who became mayor of New York City covers the time from World War I to World War II. There is ample opportunity for period costumes and production numbers.

This is one of the few musical comedies to win the Pulitzer Prize.

Tony Award Winner (Best Musical)

Pulitzer Prize

ORIGINAL CAST:

Bob Holiday (Neil)
Nathaniel Frey (Morris)
Patricia Wilson (Marie)
Howard da Silva (Ben)
Tom Bosley (Fiorello)
Pat Stanley (Dora)
Mark Dawson (Floyd)
Ellen Hanley (Thea)
Eileen Rodgers (Mitzi)

SONGS:
Act I
On the Side of the Angels (Neil, Morris,
     Marie)
Politics and Poker (Ben, politicians)
Unfair (Fiorello, Marie, girls)
Marie's Law (Marie, Morris)
The Name's La Guardia (Fiorello, company)
The Bum Won (Ben, politicians)
I Love a Cop (Dora) Reprise (Dora, Floyd)
Till Tomorrow (Thea, company)
Home Again (company)

Act II
When Did I Fall in Love? (Thea)
Gentleman Jimmy (Mitzi, girls)
Little Tin Box (Ben, politicians)
The Very Next Man (Marie)

THE FIRST (1981)

BOOK BY: Joel Siegel with Martin Charnin
MUSIC BY: Bob Brush
LYRICS BY: Martin Charnin
PUBLISHED LIBRETTO: French, 1983
CONDENSATION: None
ANTHOLOGY: None
VOCAL SELECTIONS: Hal Leonard, 1981
LICENSING AGENT: Samuel French
RECORDING: None
CAST: Large mixed cast

Set during the postwar period (1945–1947), this is the story of how Jackie Robinson became the first black major league baseball player. Although there is very little dancing, there is considerable choreography required in staging the baseball game scenes. For the Broadway production the sets were particularly praised for their Brooklyn ambience and some abstract effects for Ebbets Field. Jackie's fans provide some needed humor. This is not an easy show to stage, but sports fans will enjoy it.

ORIGINAL CAST:

David Huddleston (Rickey)
Trey Wilson (Durocher)
Clent Bowers (Cool Minnie)
David Alan Grier (Jackie)
Luther Fontaine (Junkyard)
Lonette McKee (Rachel)
Court Miller (Higgins)
Ray Gill (Sukeforth)
George D. Wallace (Noonan)
Patricia Drylie (Eunice)
Jack Hallett (Huey)
Bill Buell (Frog)
Paul Forrest (Sorrentino)

SONGS:
Act I
Jack Roosevelt Robinson (Rickey, Durocher)
The National Pastime (Cool Minnie, Jackie, Junkyard, ensemble)
Will We Ever Know Each Other? (Jackie, Rachel)
The First (Jackie)
Bloat (Durocher, ensemble)
It Ain't Gonna Work (Higgins, Sukeforth, ensemble)
The Brooklyn Dodger Strike (Rickey, Durocher)
The First (reprise) (Rachel)

Act II
Is This Year Next Year? (Noonan, Eunice, Huey, Frog, Sorrentino)
You Do-Do-Do-Do-It Good! (Cool Minnie, Jackie, ensemble)
Is This Year Next Year? (reprise) (Rickey, ensemble)

There Are Days and There Are Days (Rachel)
It's a Beginning (Jackie, Rickey, Rachel)
The Opera Ain't Over (Noonan, ensemble)

FIRST IMPRESSIONS (1959)

BOOK BY: Abe Burrows; based on *Pride and Prejudice* by Jane Austen and the play by Helen Jerome
MUSIC AND LYRICS BY: Robert Goldman, Glenn Paxton, and George David Weiss
PUBLISHED LIBRETTO: French, 1962
CONDENSATION: None
ANTHOLOGY: None
VOCAL SELECTIONS: Stratford/Chappell, 1959
LICENSING AGENT: Samuel French
RECORDING: Columbia CSP AOS 2014 (original cast)
CAST: 12 M; 12 F; chorus

Set in England in the early 1800s, the story concerns a mother's desperate antics to marry off her five daughters. One daughter's first impression of her beau is that he is conceited and proud; he thinks she is prejudiced and distant. Many critics mentioned the massive sets and lavish gowns and called the production dazzling. The dancing includes gavottes, schottisches, and polkas. This is a charming and proper family show.

ORIGINAL CAST:

Hermione Gingold (Mrs. Bennet)
Polly Bergen (Elizabeth)
Farley Granger (Darcy)
Christopher Hewett (Collins)
Phyllis Newman (Jane)
Donald Madden (Charles Bingley)
Marti Stevens (Caroline)
Ellen Hanley (Charlotte)
James Mitchell (Wickham)
Lynn Ross (Lydia)

SONGS:
Act I
Five Daughters (Mrs. Bennet)
I'm Me (Elizabeth, sisters)

Have You Heard the News? (Mrs. Bennet,
  ensemble)
A Perfect Evening (Darcy, Elizabeth)
As Long As There's a Mother (Mrs. Bennet,
  daughters)
Love Will Find Out the Way (Elizabeth)
Gentlemen Don't Fall Wildly in Love (Darcy)
This Really Isn't Me (Elizabeth)
Fragrant Flower (Collins, Elizabeth)
I Feel Sorry for the Girl (Jane, Charles
  Bingley, ensemble)
I Suddenly Find You Agreeable (Elizabeth,
  Darcy)

Act II
Wasn't It a Simply Lovely Wedding?
  (Elizabeth, Mrs. Bennet, Charlotte, Collins,
  ensemble)
A House in Town (Mrs. Bennet)
The Heart Has Won the Game (Darcy)
Let's Fetch the Carriage (Elizabeth, Mrs.
  Bennet)
The Heart Has Won the Game (reprise)
  (Darcy, Elizabeth)

THE FIVE O'CLOCK GIRL (1927)

BOOK BY: Guy Bolton and Fred Thompson
MUSIC AND LYRICS BY: Bert Kalmar and Harry
  Ruby
PUBLISHED LIBRETTO: None
CONDENSATION: *New Complete Book of the
  American Musical Theater.* Ewen, David. Holt,
  1970
ANTHOLOGY: None
LICENSING AGENT: Tams-Witmark
RECORDING: None
CAST: 4 M; 4 F; singers, dancers

The hero of the story is a wealthy Beekman
Place playboy who loves a poor but honest laundry girl. She has been anonymously
telephoning him each afternoon at five. In
order to carry on the affair she poses as a
society girl. The recent Broadway revival
of this show was a Goodspeed Opera production, which means that there was careful attention to period costumes and decor.

There was also some outstanding choreography.

1981 REVIVAL CAST:
Sheila Smith (Madame Irene)
Lisby Larson (Pat)
Roger Rathburn (Gerry)
Barry Preston (Ronnie)
Timothy Wallace (Jasper)
Pat Stanley (Sue)
Ted Pugh (Hudgins)

SONGS:
(including some interpolated from other scores)
Act I
In the Old Neighborhood (Madame Irene,
  ensemble)
Keep Romance Alive (telephone girls)
Thinking of You (Pat, Gerry)
I'm One Little Party (Ronnie, female
  ensemble)
Up in the Clouds (Pat, Gerry, ensemble)
My Sunny Tennessee (Jasper, female
  ensemble)
Any Little Thing (Sue, Hudgins)
Manhattan Walk (Madame Irene, Ronnie,
  ensemble)

Act II
Long Island Low Down (Madame Irene,
  ensemble)
Who Did? You Did! (Pat, Gerry)
Nevertheless (Sue, Hudgins)
All Alone Monday (Gerry)
Dancing the Devil Away (Ronnie, ensemble)

FLORODORA (1899)

BOOK BY: Owen Hall
MUSIC BY: Leslie Stuart
LYRICS BY: E. Boyd Jones and Paul Rubens
PUBLISHED LIBRETTO: None
CONDENSATION: *Ganzl's Book of the Musical
  Theatre.* Ganzl, Kurt. Schirmer (Macmillan),
  1989
ANTHOLOGY: None
PIANO-VOCAL SCORE: Harms, 1899
LICENSING AGENT: Tams-Witmark

RECORDING: Opal 9835 CD (1900 recordings)
CAST: 10 M; 9 F

The setting for Act I is a mythical island in the Philippines. A wealthy American owns a factory there that manufactures perfume. There is some confusion about the actual ownership of the island, but our young heroine, Dolores, claims her right and is happily married in Wales in Act II. This show is remembered for its famous sextet of beauties, "The Florodora Girls," who flirted with the audience. A recent New York revival proved that this show still has an audience and that it can be simply staged.

1933 ST. LOUIS MUNICIPAL OPERA CAST:

Doris Patston (Lady Holyrood)
Nick Long (Donegal)
Helen Arnold (Angela)
Nancy McCord (Dolores)
Allan Jones (Abercold)
Leonard Ceeley (Gilfain)
George Hassell (Tweedlepunch)

SONGS:
Act I
The Credit's Due to Me (clerks, ladies)
Chorus of Welcome (company)
Come and See Our Land (company)
When I Leave Town (Lady Holyrood, girls)
Hello, People (Donegal, Angela, dancers)
Love Will Find You (Dolores, boys)
Somebody (Dolores, Abercold)
I Want to Marry a Man, I Do (Lady Holyrood, Gilfain, Tweedlepunch)
Phrenology (Tweedlepunch, company)
Shade of the Palm (Abercold)

Act II
Millionaire (Gilfain, ensemble)
Tact (Lady Holyrood, girls)
Tell Me, Pretty Maiden (ensemble)
Caramba (Dolores)
Queen of the Philippine Islands (Dolores)
Galloping (Angela, Donegal)
I Want to Be a Military Man (Abercold, company)
Come to St. George's (Donegal, Abercold, Lady Holyrood, company)

FLOWER DRUM SONG (1958)

BOOK BY: Oscar Hammerstein II and Joseph Fields; based on the novel by C. Y. Lee
MUSIC BY: Richard Rodgers
LYRICS BY: Oscar Hammerstein II
PUBLISHED LIBRETTO: Farrar, Straus, 1959
CONDENSATION: *Broadway's Best, 1959*. John Chapman, ed. Doubleday, 1959; *Rodgers and Hammerstein*. Mordden, Ethan. Abrams, 1992
ANTHOLOGY: None
PIANO-VOCAL SCORE: Williamson, 1959
LICENSING AGENT: Rodgers and Hammerstein Theatre Library
RECORDING: Columbia CK 2009 CD (original cast)
CAST: 11 M; 7 F; chorus

The new and old collide in this story of Chinese-Americans in San Francisco. Wang Ta is torn between two girls. Linda Low is a thoroughly Americanized nightclub entertainer, while Mei Li has just arrived from China. Although various others performed in the original Broadway production, the leading roles are supposed to be Chinese. The choreography by Carol Haney utilized paper lanterns and umbrellas and was particularly praised by critics. There was a film version in 1961.

ORIGINAL CAST:

Ed Kenney (Wang Ta)
Juanita Hall (Madame Liang)
Pat Suzuki (Linda Low)
Miyoshi Umeki (Mei Li)
Pat Adiarte (Wang San)
Larry Blyden (Sammy Fong)
Arabella Hong (Helen Chao)
Anita Ellis (Nightclub Singer)
Jack Soo (Frankie)
Keye Luke (Wang Chi Yang)

SONGS:
Act I
You Are Beautiful (Wang Ta, Madame Liang)
A Hundred Million Miracles (Mei Li, Wang Chi Yang, Madame Liang)
I Enjoy Being a Girl (Linda Low, dancers)
I Am Going to Like It Here (Mei Li)
Like a God (Wang Ta)

Chop Suey (Madame Liang, Wang San,
   ensemble)
Don't Marry Me (Sammy Fong, Mei Li)
Grant Avenue (Linda Low, ensemble)
Love Look Away (Helen Chao)
Fan Tan Fannie (Nightclub Singer, girls)
Gliding through My Memoree (Frankie, girls)

Act II

The Other Generation (Madame Liang, Wang
   Chi Yang)
Sunday (Linda Low, Sammy Fong)
The Other Generation (reprise) (Wang San,
   children)

FOLLIES (1971)

BOOK BY: James Goldman
MUSIC AND LYRICS BY: Stephen Sondheim
PUBLISHED LIBRETTO: Random House, 1971
CONDENSATION: *The Best Plays of 1970–71*. Otis L.
   Guernsey, Jr., ed. Dodd, Mead, 1971; *Ganzl's
   Book of the Musical Theatre*. Ganzl, Kurt.
   Schirmer (Macmillan), 1989
ANTHOLOGY: None
PIANO-VOCAL SCORE: Columbia Pictures (Hansen,
   1974)
VOCAL SELECTIONS: Valando, 1971
LICENSING AGENT: Music Theatre International
RECORDING: Angel ZDM 7-64666-2 CD (original
   cast)
CAST: Large mixed cast

Various cast members of the old Weis-
mann shows gather at a reunion just before the theater is to be torn down and
replaced with a parking lot. As they recall
their youth, we see them as young performers doing their numbers. We also find out
about their lives, as the title of the show
has a double meaning. For most of the action the set is the stage of a decrepit theater, but suddenly it is transformed into a
Ziegfeld Follies-type setting for the finale.
One appeal of the original Broadway (and
London) production was seeing old stars
return to the spotlight. Sondheim's score
has been described as "an incredible display of musical virtuosity."

ORIGINAL CAST:

Michael Bartlett (Roscoe)
Dorothy Collins (Sally)
John McMartin (Ben)
Gene Nelson (Buddy)
Alexis Smith (Phyllis)
Harvey Evans (Young Buddy)
Kurt Peterson (Young Ben)
Marcie Stringer (Emily Whitman)
Charles Welch (Theodore Whitman)
Virginia Sandifur (Young Phyllis)
Marti Rolph (Young Sally)
Fifi D'Orsay (Solange)
Ethel Shutta (Hattie)
Mary McCarty (Stella)
Yvonne De Carlo (Carlotta)
Justine Johnston (Heidi)
Victoria Mallory (Young Heidi)

SONGS:
(performed without intermission)
Beautiful Girls (Roscoe, company)
Don't Look at Me (Sally, Ben)
Waiting for the Girls Upstairs (Buddy, Ben,
   Phyllis, Sally, Young Buddy, Young Ben,
   Young Phyllis, Young Sally)
Rain on the Roof (Emily and Theodore
   Whitman)
Ah, Paris! (Solange)
Broadway Baby (Hattie)
The Road You Didn't Take (Ben)
In Buddy's Eyes (Sally)
Who's That Woman? (Stella, company)
I'm Still Here (Carlotta)
Too Many Mornings (Ben, Sally)
The Right Girl (Buddy)
One More Kiss (Heidi, Young Heidi)
Could I Leave You? (Phyllis)
Loveland (ensemble)
You're Gonna Love Tomorrow (Young Ben,
   Young Phyllis)
Love Will See Us Through (Young Buddy,
   Young Sally)
The God-Why-Don't-You-Love-Me-Blues
   (Buddy, girls)
Losing My Mind (Sally)
The Story of Lucy and Jessie (Phyllis)
Live, Laugh, Love (Ben)

FOREVER PLAID (1990)

WRITTEN, DIRECTED, AND STAGED BY: Stuart
   Ross
PUBLISHED LIBRETTO: None
CONDENSATION: None
ANTHOLOGY: None
LICENSING AGENT: Not yet available
RECORDING: RCA 60702-2-RC CD (original cast)
CAST: 4 M

Back in 1956 four high-school lads got together and formed a singing group called
"Forever Plaid." They worked and prac-
ticed until their first big break, singing at a
cocktail lounge in 1964. Unfortunately, on
the way to pick up their custom-made plaid
tuxedoes, they were killed in a traffic accident. This show has them returning from
Heaven to finally get to do their act, a highlight of which is a salute to the Ed Sullivan
Show. The original production was done in
a cabaret with only a small combo onstage
with the boys. A great deal of talent is required among your cast members; they not
only sing but also dance, play musical instruments, and require comic skills. A nostalgic score of songs is done in the style of
the Four Aces, the Four Lads, and so on.

ORIGINAL CAST:

Jason Graae (Sparky)
Stan Chandler (Jinx)
David Engel (Smudge)
Guy Stroman (Frankie)

SONGS:
Three Coins in the Fountain
Gotta Be This or That
Undecided
Moments to Remember
Crazy 'bout Ya Baby
No, Not Much
Perfidia
Cry
Sixteen Tons
Chain Gang
Anniversary Song
She Loves You
Dream Along with Me
Magic Moments
Temptation
Papa Loves Mambo
Sing to Me Mr. C
Catch a Falling Star
Day-O
Kingston Market
Jamaica Farewell
Matilda
Heart and Soul
Lady of Spain
Shangri-La
Rags to Riches
Theme from the Good, the Bad, and the Ugly
Love Is a Many-Splendored Thing

42nd STREET (1980)

BOOK BY: Michael Stewart and Mark Bramble;
   based on a novel by Bradford Ropes
MUSIC BY: Harry Warren
LYRICS BY: Al Dubin
PUBLISHED LIBRETTO: None
CONDENSATION: *Ganzl's Book of the Musical
   Theatre*. Ganzl, Kurt. Schirmer (Macmillan),
   1989; *The Best Plays of 1980–81*. Otis L.
   Guernsey, Jr., ed. Dodd, Mead, 1981
ANTHOLOGY: None
VOCAL SELECTIONS: Warner Bros. Music, 1980
LICENSING AGENT: Tams-Witmark
RECORDING: RCA RCD1 3891 CD (original cast)
CAST: Large mixed cast

Peggy Sawyer, a stage-struck chorus girl,
gets her big chance when Dorothy Brock,
the star of a new Broadway musical, breaks
her ankle during tryouts. All this is based
on the 1933 film starring Ruby Keeler. Numerous songs from other movie musicals
of the period have been added for a nostalgic treat. Set in 1933, a large cast of dancers,
beautiful costumes, and a touch of humor
are required. This was a big hit on Broadway, and in many other places as well.

Tony Award Winner (Best Musical)

ORIGINAL CAST:

Danny Carroll (Andy)
Lee Roy Reams (Billy)
Wanda Richert (Peggy)
Carole Cook (Maggie)
Tammy Grimes (Dorothy)
Karen Prunczik (Annie)
Ginny King (Lorraine)
Jeri Kansas (Phyllis)
James Congdon (Pat)
Joseph Bova (Bert)
Jerry Orbach (Julian Marsh)

SONGS:

Act I

Audition (Andy, ensemble)
Young and Healthy (Billy, Peggy)
Shadow Waltz (Maggie, Dorothy, girls)
Go into Your Dance (Maggie, Peggy, Annie,
    Andy, Lorraine, Phyllis)
You're Getting to Be a Habit with Me
    (Dorothy, Billy, Peggy, ensemble)
Getting Out of Town (Pat, Bert, Maggie,
    Annie, Dorothy, ensemble)
Dames (Billy, ensemble)
I Know Now (Dorothy)
I Know Now (reprise) (Billy, girls)
We're in the Money (Annie, Peggy, Lorraine,
    Phyllis, Billy, ensemble)

Act II

Sunny Side to Every Situation (Annie,
    ensemble)
Lullaby of Broadway (Julian, company)
About a Quarter to Nine (Dorothy, Peggy)
Shuffle Off to Buffalo (Annie, Bert, Maggie,
    girls)
42nd Street (Peggy, Billy, ensemble)
42nd Street (reprise) (Julian)

FRANK MERRIWELL (or Honor Challenged) (1971)

BOOK BY: Skip Redwine, Larry Frank, and
    Heywood Gould; based on *Frank Merriwell's
    School Days* by Burt L. Standish
MUSIC AND LYRICS BY: Skip Redwine and Larry
    Frank
PUBLISHED LIBRETTO: French, 1971

CONDENSATION: None
ANTHOLOGY: None
LICENSING AGENT: Samuel French
RECORDING: None
CAST: 7 M; 6 F; 1 boy

Frank Merriwell was a dime-novel hero
around the turn of the twentieth century.
He stood for courage, fair play, and hon-
esty. The plot of this gentle spoof concerns
Frank's adventures at college; he becomes
involved with a spy ring and saves the fair
Inza from a "death worse than fate." Although it was done on Broadway, this show
is ideally suited for a small production,
simply mounted. It is a wholesome, family
show.

ORIGINAL CAST:

Larry Ellis (Frank Merriwell)
Gary Keith Steven (Tad)
Liz Sheridan (Mrs. Snodd)
Neva Small (Belinda)
Linda Donovan (Inza)
Peter Shawn (Bart)
Thomas Ruisinger (Professor)
Bill Hinnant (Manuel)

SONGS:

Act I

There's No School like Our School (students,
    girls)
Howdy, Mr. Sunshine (Frank, Tad)
The Ladies Auxiliary Picnic Committee (Mrs.
    Snodd, Belinda)
Prim and Proper (students, girls)
Inza (Frank)
Only Our Love (Inza, Frank)
Look for the Happiness Ahead (Frank,
    company)
I'd Be Crazy to Be Crazy over You (Belinda,
    Bart)
Now It's Fall (students)
The Fallin'-Out-of-Love Rag (Belinda, Frank,
    students, girls)

Act II

Frank, Frank, Frank (company)
In Real Life (Frank)

The Broadway of My Heart (Professor, Mrs.
   Snodd)
Winter's Here (students)
The Pure in Heart (Frank, company)
Don't Turn His Picture to the Wall (Tad,
   students, girls)
Only Yesterday (Inza)
Manuel Your Friend (Manuel)

SONGS:
(performed without intermission)
Overture (ensemble)
Invocation and Instructions to the Audience
   (Dionysos, Zanthias, ensemble)
Travel (Dionysos, Zanthias, ensemble)
The Frogs (ensemble)
It's Only a Play (ensemble)
Fear No More (Shakespeare)
Exodus (ensemble)

THE FROGS (1974)

BOOK FREELY ADAPTED FOR TODAY BY:
   Burt Shevelove; based on the comedy by
   Aristophanes
MUSIC AND LYRICS BY: Stephen Sondheim
PUBLISHED LIBRETTO: Dramatic, 1975
CONDENSATION: None
ANTHOLOGY: None
LICENSING AGENT: Dramatic
RECORDING: RCA CBL 2-4745 Sondheim Evening
   (two selections)
CAST: 10 M; 2 F; large chorus, dancers, swimmers

The plot concerns the god Dionysos, dis-
satisfied with the current crop of playwrights, going down to Hades to bring back
George Bernard Shaw and restore him to
life. This ninety-minute farce was originally
staged at Yale around a swimming pool and
was later produced in New York City. Reviews indicate that there were various water ballets a la Busby Berkeley. There was
also dancing at the poolside, and the actors were sometimes in a rowboat in the
pool. The Yale production was quite spectacular with about 125 people involved in
the show.

YALE REPERTORY THEATER ORIGINAL CAST:

Larry Blyden (Dionysos)
Michael Vale (Zanthias)
Jeremy Geidt (Shakespeare)
Alvin Epstein (Aeakos)
Jerome Dempsey (Pluto)

FUNNY GIRL (1964)

BOOK BY: Isobel Lennart; from her original story
   based on the early life of Fanny Brice
MUSIC BY: Jule Styne
LYRICS BY: Bob Merrill
PUBLISHED LIBRETTO: Random House, 1964
CONDENSATION: Ganzl's Book of the Musical
   Theatre. Ganzl, Kurt. Schirmer (Macmillan),
   1989
ANTHOLOGY: None
PIANO-VOCAL SCORE: Chappell, 1964
VOCAL SELECTIONS: Chappell, 1968
LICENSING AGENT: Tams-Witmark
RECORDING: Angel ZDM7 64661-2 CD (original
   cast)
CAST: Large mixed cast

This musical comedy biography of Fanny
Brice made a superstar of Barbra Streisand.
She later starred in the film version. The
story begins with Fanny as a homely, gawky
girl on the Lower East Side. We follow her
career as a Ziegfeld star, and her romance
with gambler Nick Arnstein. The plot ends
there (and was later continued in the film
sequel, Funny Lady). There are numerous
musical numbers in the style of the period from 1914 to 1918. There are wonderful character parts, and a juicy one for
the lead. The Broadway production was described as sumptuous.

ORIGINAL CAST:

Barbra Streisand (Fanny)
Sydney Chaplin (Nick)
Danny Meehan (Eddie)
John Lankston (Ziegfeld Tenor)

Kay Medford (Mrs. Brice)
Jean Stapleton (Mrs. Strakosh)

SONGS:
Act I
If a Girl Isn't Pretty (Mrs. Strakosh, Mrs.
    Brice, Eddie, ensemble)
I'm the Greatest Star (Fanny)
Eddie's Fifth Encore (Eddie)
Coronet Man (Fanny)
Who Taught Her Everything? (Mrs. Brice,
    Eddie)
His Love Makes Me Beautiful (Ziegfeld Tenor,
    Fanny, ensemble)
I Want to Be Seen with You Tonight (Nick,
    Fanny)
Henry Street (ensemble)
People (Fanny)
You Are Woman (Eddie, Fanny)
Don't Rain on My Parade (Fanny)

Act II
Sadie, Sadie (Fanny, ensemble)
Find Yourself a Man (Eddie, Fanny, ensemble)
Rat-Tat-Tat-Tat (Eddie, Fanny, ensemble)
Who Are You Now? (Fanny)
The Music That Makes Me Dance (Fanny)

A FUNNY THING HAPPENED ON THE WAY TO THE FORUM (1962)

BOOK BY: Burt Shevelove and Larry Gelbart;
    based on the plays of Plautus
MUSIC AND LYRICS BY: Stephen Sondheim
PUBLISHED LIBRETTO: Dodd, Mead, 1963;
    Applause, 1991
CONDENSATION: *Ganzl's Book of the Musical
    Theatre*. Ganzl, Kurt. Schirmer (Macmillan),
    1989
ANTHOLOGY: None
PIANO-VOCAL SCORE: Chappell, 1964
LICENSING AGENT: Music Theatre International
RECORDING: Angel 64770 CD (original cast)
CAST: Large mixed cast

Hero, in love with a slave girl he cannot
afford to buy, turns over his problems to
a fast-talking slave, Pseudolus, who is the
real star of the show. After a good deal of
low comedy and confusion, all is straight-
ened out—lovers are united and Pseudolus
is set free. Zero Mostel starred on Broadway and in the film version, and Phil Silvers later starred in a revival. Set in ancient
Rome, this show is very funny and popular.
It is physical, energetic, unpretentious, and
for adults only! Audiences love it.

Tony Award Winner (Best Musical)

ORIGINAL CAST:
Zero Mostel (Pseudolus)
Brian Davies (Hero)
Jack Gilford (Hysterium)
David Burns (Senex)
John Carradine (Lycus)
Preshy Marker (Philia)
Ron Holgate (Miles)
Ruth Kobart (Domina)

SONGS:
Act I
Comedy Tonight (Pseudolus, company)
Love, I Hear (Hero)
Free (Pseudolus, Hero)
The House of Marcus Lycus (Lycus,
    Pseudolus, courtesans)
Lovely (Hero, Philia)
Pretty Little Picture (Pseudolus, Hero,
    Philia)
Everybody Ought to Have a Maid (Senex,
    Pseudolus, Hysterium, Lycus)
I'm Calm (Hysterium)
Impossible (Senex, Hero)
Bring Me My Bride (Miles, Pseudolus,
    ensemble)

Act II
That Dirty Old Man (Domina)
That'll Show Him (Philia)
Lovely (Pseudolus, Hysterium)
Funeral Sequence and Dance (Pseudolus,
    Miles, ensemble)

THE GAME OF LOVE

(based on the 1960 musical *Anatol*)

ADAPTION BY: Tom Jones; based on the plays of
  Arthur Schnitzler as translated by Lilly Lessing
MUSIC BY: Nancy Ford from themes of Jacques
  Offenbach
PUBLISHED LIBRETTO: None
CONDENSATION: None
ANTHOLOGY: None
LICENSING AGENT: Music Theatre International
RECORDING: None
CAST: 5 M; 5 F; other small parts

Set in turn-of-the-century Vienna, Anatol
drifts from one love affair to another and
shares his adventures with his philosoph-
ical friend and advisor Max. This material
first appeared in English in the "Dialogues
of Arthur Schnitzler" and was performed
in London in 1911. Since that time numerous versions had been staged, sometimes
as *The Affairs of Anatol*. For another musical version, see the entry in this directory
under *The High Life*.

ORIGINAL CAST (AT MCCARTER THEATRE,
PRINCETON):

William Larsen (Max)
Rosemary Harris (Gabrielle)
Richard Easton (Anatol)
Betty Hellman (Annette)
Keene Curtis (Franz)
Jacqueline Brooks (Illona)
Thayer David (Baron Dieble)
Eve Roberts (Cora)
Edward Grover (Flieder)
Joyce Ebert (Annie)

SONGS:
In Vienna
I Love to Be in Love
The Hypnotism Song
The Music of Bavaria
Finishing with an Affair
The Oyster Waltz
Come Buy a Trinket
There's a Room
Anatol's Last Night

Love Conquers All
Listen to the Rain
Seasons
It's for the Young
Menage-a-Trois
There's a Flower I Wear
The Game of Love

GEORGE M! (1968)

BOOK BY: Michael Stewart and John and Fran
  Pascal
MUSIC AND LYRICS BY: George M. Cohan; lyric
  and musical revisions by Mary Cohan
PUBLISHED LIBRETTO: None
CONDENSATION: *New Complete Book of the
  American Musical Theater*. Ewen, David. Holt,
  1970
ANTHOLOGY: None
VOCAL SELECTIONS: Cohan Music, 1968
LICENSING AGENT: Tams-Witmark
RECORDING: Col 03200 CD (original cast)
CAST: Large mixed cast

The life, career, loves, and songs of George
M. Cohan in this show provide a strong part
for a song-and-dance man; this was Joel
Grey's first starring role. The story line is
the usual backstage melodrama, with nostalgia and sentiment. The period is primarily around World War I and the staging and
dancing should reflect this spirit. Certainly
the famous Cohan songs will. This is a flag-
waving family show!

ORIGINAL CAST:

Jerry Dodge (Jerry Cohan)
Betty Ann Grove (Nellie Cohan)
Bernadette Peters (Josie Cohan)
Joel Grey (George M. Cohan)
Jamie Donnelly (Ethel Levey)
Jill O'Hara (Agnes Nolan)
Gene Castle (Willie)
Loni Ackerman (Rose)
Harvey Evans (Sam Harris)
Angela Martin (Ma Templeton)
Jacqueline Alloway (Fay Templeton)

SONGS:

Act I

Musical Moon (Jerry Cohan, Nellie Cohan)
Oh, You Wonderful Boy (Josie Cohan)
All Aboard for Broadway (Four Cohans)
Musical Comedy Man (Four Cohans, company)
I Was Born in Virginia (Ethel Levey)
Twentieth Century Love (Four Cohans, Ethel Levey)
My Town (George)
Billie (Agnes Nolan)
Push Me Along in My Pushcart (Ethel Levey, girls)
Ring to the Name of Rose (Josie Cohan, bell ringers)
Popularity (Willie, company)
Give My Regards to Broadway (George, company)

Act II

Forty-Five Minutes from Broadway (George, Rose)
So Long, Mary (George, Sam Harris, Rose, Ma Templeton)
Down by the Erie (company)
Mary (Fay Templeton)
All Our Friends (Sam Harris, company)
Yankee Doodle Dandy/Harrigan/Nellie Kelly I Love You/Over There/You're a Grand Old Flag (George, company)
The City (company)
I'd Rather Be Right (George, company)
Epilogue (company): Dancing Our Worries Away/The Great Easter Sunday Parade/Hannah's a Hummer/Barnum and Bailey Rag/The Belle of the Barber's Ball/The American Ragtime/All in the Wearing/I Want to Hear a Yankee Doodle Tune

THE GIFTS OF THE MAGI (1984)

BOOK BY: Mark St. Germain; based on stories of O. Henry
MUSIC BY: Randy Courts
LYRICS BY: Mark St. Germain and Randy Courts
PUBLISHED LIBRETTO: Dramatists Play Service, 1984

CONDENSATION: None
ANTHOLOGY: None
VOCAL SELECTIONS: Dramatists Play Service, 1984
LICENSING AGENT: Dramatists Play Service
RECORDING: CD available
CAST: 4 M; 2 F

This famous story of young lovers who cannot afford Christmas gifts was presented again in a recent musical version. Set in New York in 1905, the off-Broadway production was called "a singing and dancing Christmas card." Performed in one act on a near-bare stage, this is family entertainment directed more at the children. The *New York Times* reported "it should appeal to those with a hearty appetite for Holiday sweetness and light."

ORIGINAL CAST:

Brick Hartney (The City: Him)
Lynne Wintersteller (The City: Her)
Michael Brian (Willy)
Jeff McCarthy (Jim)
Leslie Hicks (Della)
Bert Michaels (Soapy)

SONGS:

(performed without intermission)

Star of the Night (Him, Her)
Gifts of the Magi (Willy, company)
Christmas to Blame (Willy, Him, Her)
How Much to Buy Me a Dream? (Jim)
The Restaurant (Soapy, Him, Her)
Once More (Jim, Della)
Bum Luck (Soapy, Jim)
Greed (company)
Pockets (Willy)
The Same Girl (Della)

GIGI (1973)

BOOK AND LYRICS BY: Alan Jay Lerner; based on the novel by Colette
MUSIC BY: Frederick Loewe
PUBLISHED LIBRETTO: None
CONDENSATION: None
ANTHOLOGY: None
PIANO-VOCAL SCORE: Chappell, 1975

VOCAL SELECTIONS: Chappell, 1974
LICENSING AGENT: Tams-Witmark
RECORDING: RCA ABL 1-0404 (original cast)
CAST: 14 M; 4 F; singers, dancers

Lerner and Loewe again struck pay dirt with the film *Gigi*, with Leslie Caron and Maurice Chevalier. When the film was made into a stage musical, a number of new songs were added to the score. Set in Paris at the turn of the century, this is a sentimental tale of a child in a family of courtesans who grows up rapidly and converts a playboy into an honest and adoring husband. The Broadway production was described as lavish with handsome costumes.

ORIGINAL CAST:

Alfred Drake (Honore)
Daniel Massey (Gaston)
Karin Wolfe (Gigi)
Truman Gaige (Manuel)
Agnes Moorehead (Aunt Alicia)
Maria Karnilova (Mamita)
Howard Chitjian (Duclos)
Richard Woods (Du Fresne)

SONGS:
Act I
Thank Heaven for Little Girls (Honore)
It's a Bore (Honore, Gaston)
The Earth and Other Minor Things (Gigi)
Paris Is Paris Again (Honore, ensemble)
She's Not Thinking of Me (Gaston)
It's a Bore (reprise) (Honore, Gaston, Manuel, Aunt Alicia)
The Night They Invented Champagne (Gigi, Gaston, Mamita)
I Remember It Well (Honore, Mamita)
I Never Want to Go Home Again (Gigi, ensemble)

Act II
Gigi (Gaston)
The Contract (Aunt Alicia, Mamita, Duclos, Du Fresne)
I'm Glad I'm Not Young Anymore (Honore)
In This Wide, Wide World (Gigi)

GIRL CRAZY (1930)

BOOK BY: Guy Bolton and John McGowan
MUSIC BY: George Gershwin
LYRICS BY: Ira Gershwin
PUBLISHED LIBRETTO: None
CONDENSATION: *New Complete Book of the American Musical Theater*. Ewen, David. Holt, 1970
ANTHOLOGY: None
PIANO-VOCAL SCORE: New World Music, 1954
LICENSING AGENT: Tams-Witmark
RECORDING: Elektra Nonesuch CD 9 79250-2 (studio cast)
CAST: 7 M; 6 F; male quartet, singers, dancers

This famous Gershwin show set in the Wild West introduced Ethel Merman to Broadway, although Ginger Rogers was the star of the show. Wealthy Danny Churchill arrives from the East for a two-year rest cure, opens a dude ranch, and imports Broadway talent. There have been several modernized revivals on Broadway, and a 1943 film version starred Mickey Rooney and Judy Garland.

ORIGINAL CAST:

Ethel Merman (Kate Fothergill)
Ginger Rogers (Molly Gray)
Willie Howard (Gieber Goldfarb)
William Kent (Slick Fothergill)
Allen Kearns (Danny Churchill)
Peggy O'Connor (Patsy)

SONGS:
(from 1990 studio recording)
Act I
Bidin' My Time (male quartet)
The Lonesome Cowboy (cowboys)
Could You Use Me? (Danny, Molly, male chorus)
Bronco Busters (ensemble)
Barbary Coast (Patsy, chorus)
Embraceable You (Danny, Molly)
Goldfarb! That's I'm! (Gieber, Slick, chorus)
Sam and Delilah (Kate, chorus)
I Got Rhythm (Kate, ensemble)

Act II
Land of the Gay Caballero (chorus)
But Not for Me (Molly)
But Not for Me (reprise) (Gieber, Molly)
Treat Me Rough (Slick)
Boy! What Love Has Done to Me! (Kate)
Cactus Time in Arizona (Molly, male chorus)

GOBLIN MARKET (1985)

BOOK AND LYRICS BY: Polly Pen and Peggy
    Harmon; adapted from the poem by Christina
    Rossetti
MUSIC BY: Polly Pen
PUBLISHED LIBRETTO: Dramatists Play Service,
    1985
CONDENSATION: *The Best Plays of 1985–1986*. Otis
    L. Guernsey, Jr., ed. Dodd, Mead, 1987
ANTHOLOGY: None
VOCAL SELECTIONS: Dramatists Play Service, 1985
LICENSING AGENT: Dramatists Play Service
RECORDING: TER 1144 CD (original cast)
CAST: 2 F

This memory play, called a "beguiling musical fairy tale for adults," concerns two Victorian-era sisters. They are dressed in mourning for the death of a parent as they return to their childhood nursery. They recall that when younger Laura was drawn out into the night to dance and feast with the goblins in the glen and Lizzie had to rescue her. Sexual awakenings are indicated in this adventure. The musical is seventy minutes long, with a Victorian nursery set and Victorian costumes. The musical score is made up of carols, baroque arias, Brechtian warnings, and nursery chants.

ORIGINAL CAST:

Terri Klausner (Laura)
Ann Morrison (Lizzie)

SONGS:
(performed without intermission)
Come Buy, Come Buy (Lizzie, Laura)
We Must Not Love (Laura, Lizzie)
Mouth So Charmful (Lizzie, Laura)
Do You Not Remember Jeanie? (Laura, Lizzie)

Sleep, Laura, Sleep (Lizzie)
The Sisters (Lizzie, Laura)
Some There Are Who Never Venture (Laura,
    Lizzie)
Mirage (Laura)
Passing Away (Laura, Lizzie)
Here They Come (Laura, Lizzie)
Like a Lily (Laura, Lizzie)
Lizzie, Lizzie, Have You Tasted? (Lizzie, Laura)
Two Doves (Lizzie, Laura)

GOD BLESS YOU, MR. ROSEWATER (1979)

BOOK AND LYRICS BY: Howard Ashman; based on
    the novel by Kurt Vonnegut, Jr.
MUSIC BY: Alan Menken
PUBLISHED LIBRETTO: French, 1980
CONDENSATION: None
ANTHOLOGY: None
VOCAL SELECTIONS: Warner Bros. Music, 1979
LICENSING AGENT: Samuel French
RECORDING: None
CAST: 10 M; 4 F; extras

Called "a satire on practically everything," this is the story of Eliot Rosewater, who controls an enormously wealthy charitable foundation, and of a greedy lawyer who wants to prove him insane. Unfortunately, Rosewater's do-gooding doesn't really do any good at all. Vonnegut's popular novel has been turned into an off-Broadway musical that was called "weird and wonderful fun."

ORIGINAL CAST:

Frederick Coffin (Eliot Rosewater)
Jonathan Hadary (Norman Mushari)
Pierre Epstein (Kilgore Trout)
Janie Sell (Sylvia Rosewater)
David Christmas (Charley)
Anne Desalvo (Mary/Jane)
Elizabeth Moore (Diana)
Charles C. Welch (Delbert)
Holly Villaire (Dawn/Caroline)
Alan David-Little (Jerome)
Peter J. Saputo (Fred)

SONGS:

Act I

The Rosewater Foundation (Eliot, chorus)

Dear Ophelia (Eliot)

Thank God for the Volunteer Fire Brigade
   (Eliot, firemen)

Mushari's Waltz (Norman)

Thirty Miles from the Banks of the Ohio/Look
   Who's Here (Eliot, chorus)

Cheese Nips (Sylvia, chorus)

The Rosewater Foundation (reprise) (Charley,
   Mary, Eliot)

Since You Came to This Town (Diana, Mary,
   Delbert, Dawn, Jerome, chorus)

Act II

A Poem by William Blake (Kilgore)

Rhode Island Tango (Fred, Caroline, Norman)

Eliot . . . Sylvia (Sylvia, Eliot)

Plain, Clean, Average Americans (Norman,
   Fred, Caroline, Jane, chorus)

A Firestorm Consuming Indianapolis (Eliot)

Dear Ophelia (reprise) (Sylvia)

I, Eliot Rosewater (Eliot, chorus)

GODSPELL (1971)

MUSIC AND NEW LYRICS BY: Stephen Schwartz;
   based on the gospel according to St. Matthew

PUBLISHED LIBRETTO: None

CONDENSATION: *Ganzl's Book of the Musical
   Theatre*. Ganzl, Kurt. Schirmer (Macmillan),
   1989

ANTHOLOGY: None

PIANO-VOCAL SCORE: Hansen, 1973

VOCAL SELECTIONS: Valando, 1971; Columbia
   Pictures, 1980

LICENSING AGENT: Theatre Maximus

RECORDING: Arista 8304 CD (original cast)

CAST: 5 M; 5 F

Described as a musical circus, *Godspell*
is a combination of vaudeville, clown and
minstrel show, and sweet-rock sounds. Ten
young performers dressed as clowns bring
the Bible to life. The performance includes
mime, magic, song and dance, charade,
clowning, and children's games. This was
one of the most popular shows of the

1970s and has been performed many times
all over the world. There was also a film
version.

ORIGINAL CAST:

David Haskell	Stephen Nathan
Robin Lamont	Gilmer McCormick
Joanna Jonas	Lamar Alford
Herb Simon	Peggy Gordon
Jeffrey Mylett	Sonia Manzano
Steve Reinhardt	Richard LaBonte
Jesse Cutler	

SONGS:

Act I

Prepare Ye the Way of the Lord (Haskell,
   company)

Save the People (Nathan, company)

Day by Day (Lamont, company)

Learn Your Lessons Well (McCormick)

Bless the Lord (Jonas, company)

All for the Best (Nathan, Haskell)

All Good Gifts (Alford, company)

Light of the World (Simon, Gordon, Mylett,
   Lamont, company)

Act II

Turn Back, O Man (Manzano)

Alas for You (Nathan)

By My Side (Gordon, McCormick, company)

We Beseech Thee (Mylett, company)

On the Willows (Reinhardt, LaBonte, Cutler)

GOING UP! (1917)

BOOK AND LYRICS BY: Otto Harbach; based on
   The Aviator by James Montgomery

MUSIC BY: Louis A. Hirsch

PUBLISHED LIBRETTO: None

CONDENSATION: *Ganzl's Book of the Musical
   Theatre*. Ganzl, Kurt. Schirmer (Macmillan),
   1989

ANTHOLOGY: None

PIANO-VOCAL SCORE: Witmark, 1918

LICENSING AGENT: Tams-Witmark

RECORDING: None

CAST: 11 M; 6 F

A young novelist writes a best-seller about flying and then becomes involved in a contest to win the girl he loves although he has never actually been in an airplane. This was revived on Broadway by the Goodspeed Opera from Connecticut and was noted for its high-spirited choreography. This is a period piece subtitled *An Uplifting Musical Comedy.*

1976 REVIVAL CAST:

Pat Lysinger (Miss Zonne)
Stephen Bray (Gordon)
Maureen Brennan (Madeline)
Walter Bobbie (Brown)
Kimberly Farr (Grace)
Brad Blaisdell (Street)
Noel Craig (Brooks)
Ronn Robinson (Robinson)
Michael Tartel (Gaillard)

SONGS:
(including interpolated numbers)
Act I
Paging Mr. Street (Miss Zonne, Gordon, ensemble)
I Want a Determined Boy (Madeline, Brown, men)
If You Look in Her Eyes (Grace, Street, Madeline)
Going Up (Street, company)
Hello Frisco (Miss Zonne, men)
Down, Up, Left, Right (Street, Brown, Brooks, Robinson)
Kiss Me (Grace, Gaillard)
The Tickle Toe (Grace, ensemble)

Act II
Brand New Hero (ensemble)
I'll Think of You (Grace, Street)
Do It for Me (Madeline, Brown)
My Sumurun Girl (Miss Zonne, Robinson)

THE GOLDEN APPLE (1954)

BOOK AND LYRICS BY: John Latouche; based on the Homeric legend of Ulysses
MUSIC BY: Jerome Moross
PUBLISHED LIBRETTO: Random House, 1954

CONDENSATION: *The Best Plays of 1953–54.* Louis Kronenberger, ed. Dodd, Mead, 1954; *Theatre '54.* John Chapman, ed. Random House, 1954
ANTHOLOGY: None
MUSIC PUBLISHER: Chappell, 1954
LICENSING AGENT: Tams-Witmark
RECORDINGS: RCA LOC 1014 (original cast); reissued as Elektra EKL 5000
CAST: 16 M; 6 F

This critically acclaimed musical was taken from the Greek and done entirely in song and dance. It has been transposed to America at the turn of the century. A New York revival was done with twin pianos and bright, simple sets. The principals and chorus should be musicians first and foremost. "Lazy Afternoon" is the most famous song from the score.

ORIGINAL CAST:

Priscilla Gillette (Penelope/Circe)
Stephen Douglass (Ulysses)
Kaye Ballard (Helen)
Jack Whiting (Hector)
Bibi Osterwald (Lovey Mars)
Jonathan Lucas (Paris)
Dean Michener (Menelaus)
Geraldine Viti (Mrs. Juniper)
Portia Nelson (Miss Minerva)
Nola Gay (Mother Hare)

SONGS:
Act I
Nothing Ever Happens in Angel's Roost (Helen, Lovey Mars, Mrs. Juniper, Miss Minerva)
Mother Hare's Séance (Mother Hare)
My Love Is on the Way (Penelope)
The Heroes Come Home (company)
It Was a Glad Adventure (Ulysses, men)
Come Along, Boys (men, ensemble)
It's the Going Home Together (Ulysses, Penelope)
Mother Hare's Prophecy (Mother Hare)
Helen Is Always Willing (men)
The Church Social (men, ensemble)
Introducin' Mr. Paris (Paris, ensemble)

The Judgment of Paris (Lovey Mars,
    Mrs. Juniper, Miss Minerva, Mother Hare,
    Paris)
Lazy Afternoon (Helen, Paris)
The Departure for Rhododendron (company)

Act II
My Picture in the Papers (Helen, Paris, men)
The Taking of Rhododendron (Ulysses,
    Hector, Paris)
Hector's Song (Hector)
Windflowers (Penelope)
Store-bought Suit (Ulysses)
Calypso (Mrs. Juniper)
Scylla and Charybdis (Menelaus, Hector)
Goona-Goona (Lovey Mars)
Doomed, Doomed, Doomed (Miss Minerva)
Circe, Circe (Circe, ensemble)
Ulysses' Soliloquy (Ulysses)
The Sewing Bee (Penelope, Helen, Miss
    Minerva, Mrs. Juniper, Lovey Mars,
    Ulysses)
The Tirade (Penelope)

GOLDEN BOY (1964)

BOOK BY: Clifford Odets and William Gibson;
    based on the play by Clifford Odets
MUSIC BY: Charles Strouse
LYRICS BY: Lee Adams
PUBLISHED LIBRETTO: Atheneum, 1965; French,
    1965
CONDENSATION: *New Complete Book of the
    American Musical Theater.* Ewen, David. Holt,
    1970
ANTHOLOGY: None
VOCAL SELECTIONS: Big Three (Morris, 1965)
LICENSING AGENT: Samuel French
RECORDING: Angel 65024 CD (original cast)
CAST: 9 M; 2 F; chorus

The famous 1937 Odets play was musicalized in the 1960s and changed to a
black boxer's resentment of racial prejudice and his desire for acceptance in the
white world. Along the way he has a romance with his manager's white secretary-
mistress. Sammy Davis starred on Broadway with a cast that included Billy Daniels

and Lola Falana. The settings were simple,
but projections on a back screen were used
to show Harlem and other locations.

ORIGINAL CAST:
Sammy Davis, Jr. (Joe)
Kenneth Tobey (Tom)
Paula Wayne (Lorna)
Terrin Miles (Terry)
Johnny Brown (Ronnie)
Ted Beniades (Roxy)
Billy Daniels (Eddie)
Charles Welch (Tokio)
Lola Falana (Lola)
Jaime Rogers (Lopez)

SONGS:
Act I
Workout (boxers)
Night Song (Joe)
Everything's Great (Tom, Lorna)
Gimme Some (Joe, Terry)
Stick Around (Joe)
Don't Forget 127th Street (Joe, Ronnie,
    company)
Lorna's Here (Lorna)
The Road Tour (Joe, Lorna, Tom, Roxy, Eddie,
    Tokio, company)
This Is the Life (Eddie, Joe, Lola, company)

Act II
Golden Boy (Lorna)
While the City Sleeps (Eddie)
Colorful (Joe)
I Want to Be with You (Joe, Lorna)
Can't You See It? (Joe)
No More (Joe, company)
The Fight (Joe, Lopez)

GOLDEN RAINBOW (1968)

BOOK BY: Ernest Kinoy; based on the play *A Hole
    in the Head* by Arnold Schulman
MUSIC AND LYRICS BY: Walter Marks
PUBLISHED LIBRETTO: None
CONDENSATION: None
ANTHOLOGY: None
VOCAL SELECTIONS: Damila Music, 1967
LICENSING AGENT: Samuel French

RECORDING: Calendar KOS 1001 (original cast)
CAST: 8 M; 4 F; 1 boy; chorus, show girls

A third-rate hotel in Las Vegas is about to go under. Larry Davis, its owner and a widower, is busy trying to concoct money-making schemes and leaves the management of the place to his ten-year-old son. But Larry's sister-in-law enters the picture and all ends happily. This show was tailored for the well-known husband-and-wife team of Steve Lawrence and Eydie Gorme. Their nightclub expertise was well used.

ORIGINAL CAST:

Steve Lawrence (Larry)
Scott Jacoby (Ally)
Eydie Gorme (Judy)
Joseph Sirola (Lou)

SONGS:
Act I
Golden Rainbow (chorus)
We Got Us (Larry, Ally)
He Needs Me Now (Judy)
Kid (Larry)
For Once in Your Life (Judy, Larry, boys)
Taking Care of You (Judy, Ally, friends)
I've Got to Be Me (Larry)

Act II
The Fall of Babylon (chorus)
Taste (Lou, friends)
Desert Moon (Larry, Judy)
All in Fun (Larry, Judy)
It's You Again (Judy)
How Could I Be So Wrong (Judy)
We Got Us (reprise) (Larry, Judy, Ally)

GOLDILOCKS (1958)

BOOK BY: Walter and Jean Kerr
MUSIC BY: Leroy Anderson
LYRICS BY: Joan Ford, Walter and Jean Kerr
PUBLISHED LIBRETTO: Doubleday, 1959; French, 1970
CONDENSATION: None
ANTHOLOGY: None
VOCAL SELECTIONS: Mills Music, 1958
LICENSING AGENT: Samuel French

RECORDING: Sony SK 48222 CD (original cast)
CAST: 8 M; 3 F; chorus

Featuring choreography by Agnes de Mille, this bouncy tale of early nickelodeon days around 1913 concerns a movie director and a Pearl White-like actress. She is about to leave a Broadway musical and marry a millionaire but eventually succumbs to both the movie director and the medium. Some of the musical numbers burlesque classic films like *Intolerance*, and the best numbers were "The Pussy Foot" and the dance number "Town House Maxixe." Some critics felt that the original production was overproduced, and mentioned excessively elaborate scenery. An off-Broadway revival was a much simpler affair.

ORIGINAL CAST:

Elaine Stritch (Maggie Harris)
Russell Nype (George)
Don Ameche (Max)
Pat Stanley (Lois)
Nathaniel Frey (Pete)
Margaret Hamilton (Bessie)
Richard Armbruster (Andy)
Gene Varrone (Assistant)

SONGS:
Act I
Lazy Moon (company)
Give the Little Lady (Maggie, company)
Save a Kiss (George, Maggie)
No One'll Ever Love You (Maggie, Max)
Who's Been Sitting in My Chair? (Maggie)
There Never Was a Woman (Max)
The Pussy Foot (Lois, company)

Act II
Lady in Waiting (Lois, George)
The Beast in You (Maggie)
Shall I Take My Heart and Go? (George)
I Can't Be in Love (Max)
Bad Companions (Pete, Bessie, Andy, Assistant)
I Never Know When (Maggie)
Two Years in the Making (Pete, Bessie, chorus)
Heart of Stone (company)

GOOD NEWS (1927)

BOOK BY: Laurence Schwab, B. G. DeSylva, and
    Frank Mandel
WORDS AND MUSIC BY: B. G. DeSylva, Lew Brown,
    and Ray Henderson
PUBLISHED LIBRETTO: French, 1932
CONDENSATION: *New Complete Book of the
    American Musical Theater.* Ewen, David. Holt,
    1970
ANTHOLOGY: None
VOCAL SELECTIONS: Chappell, 1974
LICENSING AGENT: Samuel French
RECORDING: None
CAST: 10 M; 5 F; chorus

The football coach at Tait College has a problem. His star player is temporarily ineligible to play in the big game because he's flunked his astronomy test. (In the 1947 film version with June Allyson, it was a French exam.) Energy and enthusiasm will be required from a youthful cast. The 1974 Broadway revival was described as being corny but fetching. The original 1927 version is the one that is available.

ORIGINAL CAST:

Don Tompkins (Sylvester)
Inez Courtney (Babe)
Ruth Mayon (Millie)
Wally Coyle (Windy)
John Price Jones (Tom)
Mary Lawlor (Connie)
Shirley Vernon (Patricia)
Zelma O'Neal (Flo)
Gus Shy (Bobby)
Jack Kennedy (Slats)

SONGS:
Act I
Opening Chorus (students)
A Ladies Man (Flo, students)
Flaming Youth (Babe, Millie, Windy, Flo,
    Slats)
Happy Days (Tom, trio)
Just Imagine (Connie, Patricia, Millie, girls)
The Best Things in Life Are Free (Tom,
    Connie)

On the Campus (Flo, Millie, Windy, Sylvester)
Varsity Drag (Flo, Millie, Windy, Sylvester,
    students)
Baby! What? (Babe, Bobby)
Tait Song (men)
Lucky in Love (Connie, Tom)

Act II
The Girl of the Phi Beta Phi (Patricia, girls)
Today's the Day (girls)
In the Meantime (Bobby, Babe)
Good News (Flo)

GOODTIME CHARLEY (1975)

BOOK BY: Sidney Michaels
MUSIC BY: Larry Grossman
LYRICS BY: Hal Hackady
PUBLISHED LIBRETTO: French, 1985
CONDENSATION: None
ANTHOLOGY: None
LICENSING AGENT: Samuel French
RECORDING: RCA ARL 1-1011 (original cast)
CAST: 15 M; 7 F; chorus

This musical presents the Dauphin of France as a weakling dominated by those surrounding him. When he comes into contact with Joan of Arc, she leads him on to drive the English out of France. The role of the Dauphin, played on Broadway by Joel Grey, is the starring one, rather than that of Joan. The original production was praised for its lavish costumes and medieval sets.

ORIGINAL CAST:

Brad Tyrrell (Henry V)
Hal Norman (Charles VI)
Grace Keagy (Isabella)
Rhoda Butler (Queen Kate)
Charles Rule (Phillip)
Peggy Cooper (Yolande)
Nancy Killmer (Marie)
Ed Becker (Pope)
Joel Grey (Charley)
Ann Reinking (Joan)
Susan Browning (Agnes)
Richard B. Shull (Minguet)

Louis Zorich (General)
Jay Garner (Archbishop)

SONGS:
Act I
History (Henry V, Charles VI, Isabella, Queen
    Kate, Phillip, Yolande, Marie, Pope,
    ensemble)
Goodtime Charley (Charley, ensemble)
Visions and Voices (Joan)
Bits and Pieces (Charley, Joan)
To Make the Boy a Man (Joan)
Why Can't We All Be Nice (Charley, Agnes)
Born Lover (Charley)
I Am Going to Love (the Man You're Going to
    Be) (Joan)
Castles of the Loire (Joan, soldiers)
Coronation (Charley, Joan, ensemble)

Act II
You Still Have a Long Way to Go (Joan,
    Charley)
Merci, Bon Dieu (Minguet, Agnes)
Confessional (General, Archbishop)
One Little Year (Joan)
I Leave the World (Charley)

GOREY STORIES (1978)

ADAPTION BY: Stephen Currens; based on
    illustrated stories by Edward Gorey
MUSIC BY: David Aldrich
PUBLISHED LIBRETTO: French, 1983
CONDENSATION: None
ANTHOLOGY: None
LICENSING AGENT: Samuel French
RECORDING: None
CAST: 5 M; 4 F

Gorey has written and illustrated many little volumes of mock-Gothic black-humor tales, sketches, rhymes, and limericks. He also designed the very successful revival of *Dracula* and the opening designs for the PBS series "Mystery." For this revue eighteen sketches are spoken, sung, and occasionally danced as deadpan spoofs. While this is all very sophisticated, it neverthe-

less appeals to young children and the innocent elderly. Martin Gottfried of *Saturday Review* described the music as "new classical music . . . a quirky score for a chamber group." The staging must be highly stylized. The two abstract sets represent a drawing room and a summer house. Costumes must be appropriately bizarre.

ORIGINAL CAST:

Sel Vitella (Harold)
Susan Marchand (Ortenzia/Rose)
John Michalski (Hamish)
June Squibb (Mary)
Leon Shaw (Earbrass)
Julie Kurnitz (Celia)
Gemze de Lappe (Mona)

SONGS:
Act I
The Wuggly Ump (company)
The Insect God (Harold, Ortenzia, Hamish,
    Mary, Earbrass, Celia, Mona)
Empty My Heart (Ortenzia)

Act II
The Osbick Bird (Harold)
The Eleventh Episode (Mary, Rose)
The Gashlycrumb Tines (company)

GRAND HOTEL (1989)

BOOK BY: Luther Davis; based on the novel by
    Vicki Baum
MUSIC AND LYRICS BY: Robert Wright and George
    Forrest; additional music and lyrics by Maury
    Yeston
PUBLISHED LIBRETTO: French, 1989
CONDENSATION: *The Theatre Year Book and Best
    Plays of 1989–1990.* Otis L. Guernsey, Jr., ed.
    Applause Books, 1990
ANTHOLOGY: None
VOCAL SELECTIONS: Hal Leonard, 1990
LICENSING AGENT: Samuel French
RECORDING: RCA 09026-61327-2 CD (original cast)
CAST: 5 M; 4 F; large ensemble

Vicki Baum's famous novel (and 1932 film starring Garbo) has been musicalized and was a great success on Broadway, due primarily to Tommy Tune's direction and choreography. In the Grand Hotel, "fortunes are made, jewels are stolen, hearts are won and lives are lost." The set, composed of 40 chairs, a revolving door, and four columns, provides "a suggestion of hotel spaces." Both the door and the chairs have metaphorical as well as functional purposes. Constantly changing, there are "superb kaleidoscopic effects." Five separate stories are intertwined in 1928 Berlin. Both the costumes and the dancing must refect the roaring twenties atmosphere. Glamorous costumes as well as hotel uniforms are required. Strong dancing abilities are necessary.

ORIGINAL CAST:

David Carroll (Baron)
John Wylie (Doctor)
Timothy Jerome (Preysing)
Jane Krakowski (Flaemmchen)
Karen Anders (Raffaela)
Liliane Montevecchi (Elizaveta)
David Jackson (Jimmy)
Danny Strayhorn (Jimmy)
Michael Jeter (Kringelein)

SONGS:
(performed without intermission)
The Grand Parade (company)
As It Should Be (Baron)
Some Have, Some Have Not (workers)
At the Grand Hotel (Kringelein)
Table with a View (Kringelein)
Maybe My Baby Loves Me (The Jimmys)
Fire and Ice (Elizaveta)
Twenty-Two Years (Raffaela)
Villa on a Hill (Raffaela)
I Want to Go to Hollywood (Flaemmchen, chorus)
The Crooked Path (Preysing, chorus)
Who Couldn't Dance with You? (Flaemmchen, Kringelein)
The Boston Merger (Preysing, men)
No Encore (Elizaveta)

Love Can't Happen (Elizaveta, Baron)
What She Needs (Raffaela)
Bonjour Amour (Elizaveta)
Happy (The Jimmys)
We'll Take a Glass Together (Kringelein, Baron, chorus)
I Waltz Alone (Doctor)
Roses at the Station (Baron)
How Can I Tell Her? (Raffaela)

THE GRAND TOUR (1979)

BOOK BY: Michael Stewart and Mark Bramble; based on the original play *Jacobowsky and the Colonel* by Franz Werfel and the American play based on the same by S. N. Behrman
MUSIC AND LYRICS BY: Jerry Herman
PUBLISHED LIBRETTO: French, 1980
CONDENSATION: None
ANTHOLOGY: None
VOCAL SELECTIONS: Schirmer, 1979
LICENSING AGENT: Samuel French
RECORDING: Columbia JS 35761 (original cast)
CAST: 29 roles; extras, singers, dancers

The theme is survival and the scene is France as the Germans begin their occupation during World War II. The hero is a Jew on the run. He joins a Polish colonel and they flee to the coast of France where they hope to get a boat to England. There are numerous scene changes—from crowded trains to a traveling circus. There is also a big Jewish wedding number. This was a big Broadway musical.

ORIGINAL CAST:

Joel Grey (Jacobowsky)
Grace Keagy (Mme Bouffier)
Ron Holgate (Colonel)
Florence Lacey (Marianne)
Stephen Vinovich (Szabuniewicz)
Gene Varrone (Bride's Father)
Travis Hudson (Mother Madeleine)

SONGS:
Act I
I'll Be Here Tomorrow (Jacobowsky)

Two Possibilities (Jacobowsky, Mme Bouffier, guests)
For Poland (Colonel, Mme Bouffier, chorus)
Marianne (Colonel)
We're Almost There (Marianne, Szabuniewicz, Jacobowsky, Colonel, chorus)
Having Someone There (Marianne)
Marianne (reprise) (Jacobowsky)
More and More/Less and Less (Marianne, Colonel)
One Extraordinary Thing (Jacobowsky, Marianne, Colonel, Szabuniewicz)

Act II

Mrs. S. L. Jacobowsky (Jacobowsky)
Wedding Conversation (Jacobowsky, Bride's Father)
Mazeltov (Bride's Father, guests)
I Think, I Think (Colonel)
For Poland (reprise) (Marianne, Mother Madeleine, sisters)
You I Like (Colonel, Jacobowsky)

EL GRANDE DE COCA COLA (1973)

WORDS AND MUSIC BY: Ron House and other cast members; based on an idea by Ron House and Diz White
PUBLISHED LIBRETTO: French, 1973
CONDENSATION: None
ANTHOLOGY: None
LICENSING AGENT: Samuel French
RECORDING: Bottle Cap 1001 (original cast)
CAST: 3 M; 2 F; piano and drum

Subtitled *A Refreshment*, this revue has an accent on comedy rather than music. Pepe Hernandez, a third-rate Honduran impresario, tries to pass off some of his relatives as an "International Parade of Stars" at a run-down nightclub in Trujillo. First of all, no English is spoken. The entire one-hour floor show is done in fractured Spanish, with German and other languages occasionally creeping in. This was a big success all over America and Europe. It is a simple show to produce, but a great deal of comic skill is required.

ORIGINAL CAST:

Ron House (Señor Don Pepe Hernandez)
Alan Shearman (Miguel Hernandez)
John Neville-Andrews (Juan Rodriguez)
Diz White (Consuela Hernandez)
Sally Willis (Maria Hernandez)

Performed without an intermission. Musical numbers are unlisted.

THE GRASS HARP (1971)

BOOK AND LYRICS BY: Kenward Elmslie; based on the novel by Truman Capote
MUSIC BY: Claibe Richardson
PUBLISHED LIBRETTO: French, 1971
CONDENSATION: None
ANTHOLOGY: None
VOCAL SELECTIONS: Thackaray Falls Music, 1971
LICENSING AGENT: Samuel French
RECORDING: Painted Smiles PSCD 102 CD (original cast)
CAST: 4 M; 5 F; small chorus

An important part of this musical is the set—a tree house. The original Broadway production filled the stage with a huge loop of swirling branches. The plot concerns a southern family, one of whom knows the secret recipe for their famous "dropsy cure." The older sister wants the secret so they can become rich. The big number is "Yellow Drum." Called charming, modest, tasteful, and unpretentious, this whimsical story is ideal for a family audience production.

ORIGINAL CAST:

Barbara Cook (Dolly)
Carol Brice (Catherine)
Russ Thacker (Collin)
Christine Stabile (Maude)
Max Showalter (Dr. Ritz)
Karen Morrow (Babylove)
Ruth Ford (Verena)

SONGS:

(performed without intermission)

Dropsy Cure Weather (Dolly, Catherine, Collin)

This One Day (Collin)

Think Big Rich (Dr. Ritz)

If There's Love Enough (Catherine)

Yellow Drum (Dolly, Catherine, Collin)

Marry with Me (Catherine)

I'll Always Be in Love (Chain of Love) (Dolly)

Floozies (Collin)

Call Me Babylove (Babylove)

Walk into Heaven (Babylove)

Hang a Little Moolah on the Washline (Babylove, chorus)

Talkin' in Tongues (Babylove)

Whooshin' through My Flesh (Babylove, Catherine, Dolly, Collin, company)

Something for Nothing (Dr. Ritz)

Indian Blues (Catherine, company)

Take a Little Sip (Collin, Dolly, Catherine, Maude, company)

What Do I Do Now? (Verena)

Pick Yourself a Flower (Babylove, company)

The Flower Fortune Dance (company)

Reach Out (Dolly, company)

GREASE (1972)

BOOK, MUSIC, AND LYRICS BY: Jim Jacobs and Warren Casey

PUBLISHED LIBRETTO: Winter House, 1972; Samuel French, 1972; Pocket Books, 1972

CONDENSATION: *Ganzl's Book of the Musical Theatre.* Ganzl, Kurt. Schirmer (Macmillan), 1989

ANTHOLOGY: *Great Rock Musicals.* Stanley Richards, ed. Stein and Day, 1979

PIANO-VOCAL SCORE: Warner Bros. Music, 1978; Hal Leonard, 1981

VOCAL SELECTIONS: Morris, 1972

LICENSING AGENT: Samuel French

RECORDING: Polydor 827 548-2 CD (original cast)

CAST: 9 M; 8 F

This musical hit followed the classic success story of starting off-Broadway, moving to Broadway for eight years, then being made into a hit movie, and finally having a movie sequel, *Grease II.* Described as a "loud, coarse, aggressively cheerful rock-and-roll parody" it is set in 1959 and clearly strikes a note of response in all of us. Stars from the 1950s, such as Elvis Presley, Sandra Dee, and James Dean, are all immortalized in this very popular musical.

ORIGINAL CAST:

Dorothy Leon (Miss Lynch)

Ilene Kristen (Patty)

Tom Harris (Eugene)

Carole Demas (Sandy)

Barry Bostwick (Danny)

James Canning (Doody)

Katie Hanley (Marty)

Garn Stephens (Jan)

Marya Small (Frenchy)

Adrienne Barbeau (Rizzo)

Timothy Meyers (Kenickie)

Walter Bobbie (Roger)

Alan Paul (Johnny Casino/Teen Angel)

SONGS:

Act I

Alma Mater (Miss Lynch, Patty, Eugene, ensemble)

Summer Nights (Sandy, Danny, ensemble)

Those Magic Changes (Doody, ensemble)

Freddy, My Love (Marty, Jan, Frenchy, Rizzo)

Greased Lightnin' (Kenickie, boys)

Mooning (Roger, Jan)

Look at Me, I'm Sandra Dee (Rizzo)

We Go Together (ensemble)

Act II

Shakin' at the High School Hop (company)

It's Raining on Prom Night (Sandy)

Born to Hand-Jive (Johnny Casino, company)

Beauty School Dropout (Teen Angel, Frenchy, choir)

Alone at a Drive-In Movie (Danny, boys)

Rock 'n' Roll Party Queen (Doody, Roger)

There Are Worse Things I Could Do (Rizzo)

Look at Me, I'm Sandra Dee (reprise) (Sandy)

All Choked Up (Sandy, Danny, company)

THE GREAT AMERICAN BACK-STAGE MUSICAL (1976)

BOOK BY: Bill Solly and Donald Ward
MUSIC AND LYRICS BY: Bill Solly
ADDITIONAL LYRICS BY: Dick Vosburgh
PUBLISHED LIBRETTO: French, 1979
CONDENSATION: None
ANTHOLOGY: None
LICENSING AGENT: Samuel French
RECORDING: AEI 1101 (original cast)
CAST: 3 M; 3 F

This is a good-humored spoof of Hollywood musicals before and during World War II. The story begins with a group of young-sters putting on a show in a New York cabaret. When the war begins they go to England with the U.S.O. This West Coast musical is small and simple to stage. This is the era of the jitterbug, the torch song, and Broadway vaudeville.

1982 GOODSPEED CAST:

Tom Burke (Johnny)
Jill Cook (Kelly)
Faith Prince (Sylvia)
Dennis Bailey (Banjo)
Ralph Burneau (Harry)
Nancy Callman (Constance)

SONGS:
Act I
Opening Number (Kelly, Johnny, Banjo, Sylvia, Harry)
I Got the What? (The Bug) (Banjo, Johnny, Kelly, Sylvia)
Crumbs in My Bed (Sylvia)
Cheerio (Johnny, Kelly, company)
You Should Be Made Love To (Constance)
The Star of the Show (Johnny)
When the Money Comes In (Kelly, company)

Act II
News of You (Constance, Harry)
I Could Fall in Love (Constance)
Ba-Boom (Johnny, Banjo)
I'll Wait for Joe (Sylvia)
The End (ensemble)

GREAT SCOT! (1965)

BOOK BY: Mark Conradt and Gregory Dawson
MUSIC BY: Don McAfee
LYRICS BY: Nancy Leeds
PUBLISHED LIBRETTO: Dramatists Play Service, 1969
CONDENSATION: None
ANTHOLOGY: None
VOCAL SELECTIONS: Valando, 1965
LICENSING AGENT: Dramatists Play Service
RECORDING: None
CAST: 8 M; 9 F

Set in eighteenth-century Edinburgh, this musical portrays the early life of poet Robert Burns. The plot revolves around his true love and how he finally returns to marry her after running off to sample the high life of the big city. There's plenty of dancing, including a balletic Highland game and an Edinburgh ball. Costumes should include lots of colorful tartans and tam-o-shanters. The off-Broadway produc-tion had an orchestra of four.

ORIGINAL CAST:

Allan Bruce (Robbie)
Joleen Fodor (Jean)
Charlotte Jones (Heather/Fishmonger)
Jack Eddleman (Creech)
Charles Hudson (Armour/Duffy)

SONGS:
Act I
You're the Only One (Robbie, fathers, ensemble)
Great Scott (Robbie, fathers, ensemble)
I'll Find a Dream Somewhere (Robbie)
He's Not for Me (Jean) Reprise (Robbie, Jean, ensemble)
That Special Day (Jean, Robbie, ensemble)
Brandy Is Your Champagne (Heather, Creech)
I'm Gonna Have a Baby (Robbie, ensemble)
Original Sin (Armour, elders)
I'll Still Love Jean (Robbie)
Where Is That Rainbow (Robbie, Jean)

Act II
Princes Street (ensemble)

Happy New Year (Robbie, court)
That Big-bellied Bottle (Duffy, Fishmonger, Robbie, ensemble)
He Knows Where to Find Me (Jean)
Where Does a Man Begin? (Robbie)
What a Shame (court)
I Left a Dream Somewhere (Robbie)
We're Gonna Have a Wedding (Robbie, Jean, ensemble)

THE GREAT WALTZ (1934)

BOOK BY: Moss Hart
MUSIC BY: Johann Strauss and his son, Johann Strauss, Jr.
LYRICS BY: Desmond Carter
PUBLISHED LIBRETTO: None
CONDENSATION: *New Complete Book of the American Musical Theater.* Ewen, David. Holt, 1970
ANTHOLOGY: None
VOCAL SELECTIONS: L. Feist, 1944 (from the 1934 film version)
LICENSING AGENT: Tams-Witmark
RECORDINGS: Capitol SVAS 2426 (1965 San Francisco production); Columbia SCX 6429 (1970 London production)
CAST: Large mixed cast

Called "the spectacle of the century," this play is the story of Johann Strauss and his jealousy of his son. Set in Vienna around 1850, the plot concerns a Russian countess and how she helps the son prove he has a talent of his own. The original New York production was lavish, and it has been revived many times. The recordings listed above are of revised versions by Jerome Chodorov, Robert Wright, and George Forrest. For the "Blue Danube" waltz the stage should be filled with suitably costumed dancers. This was filmed several times, most recently in 1972 with Mary Costa.

1965 SAN FRANCISCO CAST:

Wilbur Evans (Dommayer)
Anita Gillette (Resi)
Jean Fenn (Helene)
Frank Porretta (Schani)
Georgio Tozzi (J. Strauss)
Eric Brotherson (Hartkopf)
Leo Fuchs (Hirsh)

SONGS:
Act I
Two by Two (ensemble)
A Waltz with Wings (Dommayer, Resi)
I'm in Love with Vienna (Helene, ensemble)
Philosophy of Life (Strauss)
Love and Gingerbread (Schani, Resi)
Teeter-Totter Me (Schani, Helene)
The Birthday Song (Strauss, ensemble)
State of the Dance (Hirsh, Hartkopf, ensemble)
Of Men and Violins (Helene, Strauss)
An Artist's Life (Schani, Resi)

Act II
The Enchanted Wood (Strauss, Helene)
At Dommayer's (Dommayer, Hartkopf, ensemble)
The Gypsy Told Me (Resi, Schani)
No Two Ways (Strauss, Schani, Helene, Resi)
Music! (Hirsh, Dommayer, Hartkopf)
Finale: The Blue Danube (company)

GRIND (1985)

BOOK BY: Fay Kanin
MUSIC BY: Larry Grossman
LYRICS BY: Ellen Fitzhugh
PUBLISHED LIBRETTO: Broadway Play Publishing, 1985
CONDENSATION: None
ANTHOLOGY: None
VOCAL SELECTIONS: Fiddleback Music/New Start, 1985
LICENSING AGENT: Broadway Play Publishing
RECORDING: TER 1103 CD (original cast)
CAST: 9 M; 7 F; ensemble

Grind (as in "bump and grind") is set in a Chicago burlesque theater in 1933. The cast of the show is integrated. A black stripper is pursued by the black male star, but she falls in love with a white man. Things are compounded by a suicide and a race riot. American race relations and the Great Depression are the themes.

This show was praised for its elaborate set that shifted to include not only the theater's gaudy marquee but also the stage, wings, and dressing rooms. The costumes were described as "trashy—extravagant." The orchestra leader wore a bowler hat to add to the atmosphere. While many numbers are performed as "on stage," there is no nudity.

ORIGINAL CAST:

Joey Faye (Solly)
Stubby Kaye (Gus)
Sharon Murray (Romaine)
Leilani Jones (Satin)
Ben Vereen (Leroy)
Timothy Nolan (Doyle)
Carol Woods (Maybelle)

SONGS:
Act I
This Must Be the Place (company)
Cadava (Solly, Gus, Romaine)
A Sweet Thing like Me (Satin, girls)
I Get Myself Out (Gus)
My Daddy Always Taught Me to Share (Leroy)
All Things to One Man (Satin)
The Line (Leroy, girls)
Katie, My Love (Doyle)
The Grind (Gus, company)
Yes, Ma'am (Doyle)
Why, Mama, Why? (Satin, Leroy)
This Crazy Place (Leroy, company)

Act II
From the Ankles Down (Leroy, girls)
Who Is He? (Satin)
Never Put It in Writing (Gus)
I Talk, You Talk (Doyle)
Timing (Romaine, Solly)
These Eyes of Mine (Maybelle, company)
New Man (Leroy)
Down (Doyle)
A Century of Progress (Leroy, Satin, girls)

GUNMETAL BLUES (1992)

BOOK BY: Scott Wentworth
MUSIC AND LYRICS BY: Craig Bohmler and Marion Adler
PUBLISHED LIBRETTO: French, 1992
CONDENSATION: None
ANTHOLOGY: None
LICENSING AGENT: Samuel French
RECORDING: None
CAST: 3 M; 1 F

The setting for this private-eye murder-mystery musical is the Red Eye Lounge (one of those bars at one of those hotels near the airport). The time is tonight (pretty late). The ambience, however, is more late 1940s than that of today. For the off-Broadway production the multiuse set served not only as the lounge but also as the private eye's office, an apartment, and other locations. The score is in the style of vintage torch songs and jazz ballads. One critic said it had a "roadhouse quality." The excellent character development and film-noir/private-eye pastiche take precedence over the plot.

ORIGINAL CAST:

Daniel Marcus (Piano Player)
Michael Knowles (Barkeep)
Marion Adler (the Blondes)
Scott Wentworth (Private Eye)

SONGS:
Act I
Welcome to This Window
Don't Know What I Expected
Facts
The Well-to-Do Waltz
Spare Some Change
Mansion Hill
Shadowplay
Skeletons
The Blonde Song
Childhood Days
Take a Break

Act II
Not Available in Stores!
Gunmetal Blues
I'm the One That Got Away
Jenny
Put It on My Tab
The Virtuoso

GUYS AND DOLLS (1950)

BOOK BY: Jo Swerling and Abe Burrows; based on
   "The Idyll of Sarah Brown" and characters by
   Damon Runyon
MUSIC AND LYRICS BY: Frank Loesser
PUBLISHED LIBRETTO: None
CONDENSATION: *The Best Plays of 1950–1951.* John
   Chapman, ed. Dodd, Mead, 1951; *Ganzl's Book
   of the Musical Theatre.* Ganzl, Kurt. Schirmer
   (Macmillan), 1989
ANTHOLOGY: *The Modern Theatre*, vol. 4. Eric
   Bentley, ed. Doubleday, 1956
PIANO-VOCAL SCORE: Frank Music, 1953
VOCAL SELECTIONS: Frank Music, 1955
LICENSING AGENT: Music Theatre International
RECORDINGS: RCA 61317 CD (1992 revival cast);
   MCA D 10301 CD (1950 original cast)
CAST: 12 M; 5 F; chorus

There are two love stories involved in this
musical set in New York in the 1950s. One is
between Nathan Detroit, who runs a floating crap game, and Adelaide, a hoofer and
chanteuse. The other romance is between
big time gambler Sky Masterson and Sarah
Brown, a Salvation Army lass. It's all very
"Damon Runyon–New Yorkese," with several hit tunes. There is a Spanish interlude in Cuba. This was a big hit in 1982
at Britain's National Theatre and on Broadway in a 1992 revival. The film version
in 1955 starred Marlon Brando and Frank
Sinatra.

Tony Award Winner (Best Musical)

ORIGINAL CAST:

Stubby Kaye (Nicely)
Johnny Silver (Benny)
Douglas Deane (Rusty)
Isabel Bigley (Sarah)
Sam Levene (Nathan)
Robert Alda (Sky)
Vivian Blaine (Adelaide)
Pat Rooney (Arvide)

SONGS:
Act I
Runyonland (company)
Fugue for Tinhorns (Nicely, Benny, Rusty)
Follow the Fold (mission group)
The Oldest Established (Nathan, Nicely,
   Benny, ensemble)
I'll Know (Sarah, Sky)
A Bushel and a Peck (Adelaide, girls)
Adelaide's Lament (Adelaide)
Guys and Dolls (Nicely, Benny)
If I Were a Bell (Sarah)
My Time of Day (Sky)
I've Never Been in Love Before (Sky, Sarah)

Act II
Take Back Your Mink (Adelaide, girls)
More I Cannot Wish You (Arvide)
Luck Be a Lady (Sky, men)
Sue Me (Nathan, Adelaide)
Sit Down, You're Rocking the Boat (Nicely,
   ensemble)
Marry the Man Today (Adelaide, Sarah)

GYPSY (1959)

BOOK BY: Arthur Laurents; suggested by the
   memoirs of Gypsy Rose Lee
MUSIC BY: Jule Styne
LYRICS BY: Stephen Sondheim
PUBLISHED LIBRETTO: Random House, 1960;
   Theatre Arts (magazine), June 1962
CONDENSATION: *Broadway's Best, 1959.* John
   Chapman, ed. Doubleday, 1959; *Ganzl's Book
   of the Musical Theatre.* Ganzl, Kurt. Schirmer
   (Macmillan), 1989
ANTHOLOGY: *Ten Great Musicals of the American
   Stage.* Stanley Richards, ed. Chilton, 1973
PIANO-VOCAL SCORE: Chappell, 1960
VOCAL SELECTIONS: Chappell, 1959
LICENSING AGENT: Tams-Witmark

RECORDINGS: Columbia CK32607 CD (original cast); RCA 60571 CD (London cast); Elektra 79239-2 CD (1989 revival cast)
CAST: Large mixed cast

The plot of this musical has been called unpleasant because it deals with a demanding mother determined to make show biz stars of her children. It has also been said that it presents a romanticized version of the grubby world of burlesque. The original production was the climax of the brilliant career of Ethel Merman. It has since been revived with Angela Lansbury and Tyne Daly. The 1962 film starred Rosalind Russell. Costumes are late 1920s, and there's plenty of opportunity for children and adults to put over some great numbers.

ORIGINAL CAST:

Ethel Merman (Rose)
Jack Klugman (Herbie)
Sandra Church (Gypsy Rose Lee)
Lane Bradbury (June)
Faith Dane (Mazeppa)
Chotzi Foley (Electra)
Maria Karnilova (Tessie Tura)
Jacqueline Mayro (Baby June)
Karen Moore (Baby Louise)
Paul Wallace (Tulsa)

SONGS:
Act I
Let Me Entertain You (Baby June, Baby Louise)
Some People (Rose)
Small World (Rose, Herbie)
Baby June and Her Newsboys (Baby June, Baby Louise, boys)
Mr. Goldstone (Rose, Herbie, company)
Little Lamb (Gypsy)
You'll Never Get Away from Me (Rose, Herbie)
Dainty June and Her Farmboys (June, Gypsy, boys)
If Momma Was Married (Gypsy, June)
All I Need Is the Girl (Tulsa)
Everything's Coming Up Roses (Rose)

Act II
Toreadorables (Gypsy, girls)
Together (Rose, Herbie, Gypsy)
You Gotta Have a Gimmick (Mazeppa, Electra, Tessie Tura)
The Strip (Gypsy)
Rose's Turn (Rose)

THE HAGGADAH—A PASSOVER CANTATA (1980)

NARRATION ADAPTED FROM TEXTS BY: Elie Wiesel
MUSIC BY: Elizabeth Swados
PUBLISHED LIBRETTO: French, 1980
CONDENSATION: None
ANTHOLOGY: None
LICENSING AGENT: Samuel French
RECORDING: None
CAST: 10 M; 7 F; 3 children

The Haggadah is a book used in the structure of the Passover meal, at which the story of the Exodus is annually retold. This production is primarily made up of music, solos and choruses, and narrative and choral speaking. It incorporates Hebrew poetry as well as words and music from other cultures and times including blues and jazz. Off-Broadway it was performed on a long, narrow playing space with bleachers on each side for the audience. Masks and puppets were included in the dance and mime. There was a live telecast from the theater on PBS in 1981.

ORIGINAL CAST:

Roger Babb	Martha Plimpton
Suzanne Baxtresser	Martin Robinson
Shami Chaikin	Wes Sanders
Craig Chang	David Schechter
Victor Cook	Kate Schmitt
Keith David	Zvee Scooler
Patrick Jude	Ira Stiff
Aisha Kahlil	Kerry Stubbs
Esther Levy	Deborah Ann Wise
John S. Lewandowski	

SONGS:

(performed without intermission)

The Four Questions (Chang, Plimpton)

Prelude (Scooler)

Pesach Has Come to the Ghetto (Baxtresser, company)

Slave Chant (Levy, Scooler, company)

God of Faithful (Chaikin)

By the Waters of Babylon (David, Jude, company)

Shepherd Song (company)

The Burning Bush (company)

Pharaoh's Chant (Plimpton, Chang, Babb, Kahlil, Sanders, Lewandowski, company)

Why Hast Thou Done Evil to These People? (Kahlil, Chaikin, company)

The Plague (company)

Death of the Firstborn (Scooler, Plimpton, Chang, Sanders, Lewandowski, company)

Look at the Children (Chaikin)

We Are All Dead Men (Stiff)

The Puppet Rebbe (Schmitt, Stiff, Sanders, Baxtresser, Wise, Schechter, Babb, Jude)

Dayenu Chant (Levy, company)

Crossing the Red Sea (company)

Who Is Like Unto Thee? (Kahlil, company)

Three Midrash (Babb, Baxtresser, Schechter)

Country That Is Missing (company)

The Golden Calf (Schechter, Kahlil, Babb, company)

God of Mercy (Schechter, Jude, Baxtresser)

Ten Commandments (Scooler, company)

Hebrew Benediction (Stiff, company)

The Death of Moses (Chang, Chaikin)

A Blessing (Chaikin, company)

Elijah (Scooler, Chaikin)

Song of Songs (Cook, Stubbs, Plimpton, Chang)

HAIR (1967)

BOOK AND LYRICS BY: Gerome Ragni and James Rado

MUSIC BY: Galt MacDermot

PUBLISHED LIBRETTO: Pocket Books, 1969

CONDENSATION: *Ganzl's Book of the Musical Theatre*. Ganzl, Kurt. Schirmer (Macmillan), 1989

ANTHOLOGY: *Great Rock Musicals*. Stanley Richards, ed. Stein and Day, 1979

VOCAL SELECTIONS: United Artists Music, 1968

LICENSING AGENT: Tams-Witmark

RECORDING: RCA 1150-2 RC CD (original cast)

CAST: 12 M; 10 F

Called a "hippie rock-musical," this show sparked a long stream of theatrical productions reflecting new themes, new mores, and new music. But this is the one with "Aquarius" and "Frank Mills." There is a bit of a plot about a flower boy who is going to be drafted, but otherwise it's the songs and dances that make the show. Some brief nudity caused a sensation, but it was not included in the original production and is not necessary. It was filmed in 1979.

ORIGINAL CAST:

Marijane Maricle (Mom)

Ed Crowley (Dad)

Walker Daniels (Claude)

Gerome Ragni (Berger)

Steve Dean (Woof)

Arnold Wilkerson (Hud)

Sally Eaton (Jeannie)

Shelley Plimpton (Crissy)

Jonelle Allen (Dionne)

Jill O'Hara (Sheila)

Suzannah Evans (Suzannah)

Linda Compton (Linda)

Paul Jabara (Paul)

Susan Batson (Susan)

Alma Robinson (Alma)

SONGS:

Act I

Red, Blue, and White (Mom, Dad)

Ain't Got No (Claude, Berger, Woof, Hud, company)

I Got Life (Claude, Mom)

Air (Jeannie, Crissy, Dionne)

Going Down (Berger, company)

Hair (Claude, Berger, company)

Dead End (Sheila, company)

Frank Mills (Crissy)

Where Do I Go? (Claude, company)

Act II
Electric Blues (Suzannah, Linda, Paul)
Easy to Be Hard (Suzannah, Linda, Paul,
    company)
Manchester (Claude)
White Boys (Dionne, Susan, Alma)
Black Boys (Linda, Crissy, Suzannah)
Walking in Space (company)
Aquarius (company)
Good Morning Sunshine (Sheila, company)
Exanaplanetooch (Claude, Sheila)
Climax (Sheila)

HALF A SIXPENCE (1965)

BOOK BY: Beverley Cross; based on *Kipps* by H. G.
    Wells
MUSIC AND LYRICS BY: David Heneker
PUBLISHED LIBRETTO: Dramatic, 1967
CONDENSATION: *Ganzl's Book of the Musical
    Theatre.* Ganzl, Kurt. Schirmer (Macmillan),
    1989
ANTHOLOGY: None
PIANO-VOCAL SCORE: Chappell (London), 1967
VOCAL SELECTIONS: Chappell, 1965
LICENSING AGENT:Dramatic
RECORDING: RCA LSO 1110 (original cast); Deram
    820 589-2 CD (London cast)
CAST: 12 M; 11 F; chorus

This was a big English musical hit that
starred Tommy Steele; he later filmed it in
1968. Set around the turn of the century, a
poor but honest shop clerk inherits a fortune and travels to the seaside resort of
Folkstone for fun and romance. This musical is remembered for its spirited music,
bright dances, lovely costumes, and simple
but highly effective sets.

ORIGINAL CAST:

Tommy Steele (Kipps)
Will Mackenzie (Sid)
Norman Allen (Buggins)
Grover Dale (Pearce)
Eleonore Treiber (Laura)
Ann Shoemaker (Mrs. Walsingham)
Carrie Nye (Helen)

Polly James (Ann)
John Cleese (Walsingham)

SONGS:
Act I
All in the Cause of Economy (Kipps, Sid,
    Buggins, Pearce)
Half a Sixpence (Kipps, Ann)
Money to Burn (Kipps, Laura, men)
A Proper Gentleman (Kipps, Sid, Buggins,
    Pearce, shop girls)
She's Too Far Above Me (Kipps)
If the Rain's Got to Fall (Kipps, Pearce, Sid,
    Buggins, ensemble)
The Old Military Canal (ensemble)

Act II
A Proper Gentleman (reprise) (Kipps,
    Mrs. Walsingham, Helen, Walsingham,
    ensemble)
Long Ago (Kipps, Ann)
Flash Bang Wallop (Kipps, Ann, Sid, Buggins,
    Pearce, ensemble)
I Know What I Am (Ann)
The Party's on the House (Kipps, Pearce, Sid,
    Buggins, ensemble)

HALLELUJAH, BABY! (1967)

BOOK BY: Arthur Laurents
MUSIC BY: Jule Styne
LYRICS BY: Betty Comden and Adolph Green
PUBLISHED LIBRETTO: None
CONDENSATION: *New Complete Book of the
    American Musical Theater.* Ewen, David. Holt,
    1970
ANTHOLOGY: None
VOCAL SELECTIONS: Stratford Music, 1967
LICENSING AGENT: Music Theatre International
RECORDING: Sony SK 48218 CD (original cast)
CAST: Large mixed cast

This is a musical about racial problems in
the United States, starting in 1900 and continuing to the 1960s. The leading characters never age as we see blacks in transition
from servants to leaders. This allows a variety of styles in music, dancing, singing,
and costume. The production featured the
dancing of "Tip and Tap" and a very funny

Aunt Jemima-type parody. This was a big and brassy musical.

Tony Award Winner (Best Musical)

ORIGINAL CAST:

Leslie Uggams (Georgina)
Lillian Hayman (Momma)
Billy Dee Williams (Clem)
Lou Angel (Calhoun)
Michael Beirne (Captain Yankee)
Allen Case (Harvey)
Winston DeWitt Hemsley (Tip)
Alan Weeks (Tap)
Barbara Sharma (Mary)
Marilyn Cooper (Ethel)

SONGS:
Act I
Back in the Kitchen (Momma)
My Own Morning (Georgina)
The Slice (Clem, ensemble)
Farewell, Farewell (Calhoun, Captain Yankee, Georgina, Harvey)
Feet Do Yo' Stuff (Georgina, chorines, Tip, Tap)
Hey! (Georgina)
Smile, Smile (Clem, Georgina, Momma)
Witches' Brew (Georgina, Mary, Ethel, company)
Another Day (Harvey, Clem, Mary, Georgina)

Act II
Talking to Yourself (Georgina, Clem, Harvey)
Hallelujah, Baby! (Georgina, Tip, Tap)
Not Mine (Harvey)
I Don't Know Where She Got It (Momma, Clem, Harvey)
Now's the Time (Georgina, company)

HANS ANDERSEN (1974—London)

NEW BOOK BY: John Fearnley, Beverley Cross, and Tommy Steele; based on the Samuel Goldwyn film (1952) and the life of Hans Christian Andersen
MUSIC AND LYRICS BY: Frank Loesser; additional material by Marvin Laird
PUBLISHED LIBRETTO: None

CONDENSATION: *Ganzl's Book of the Musical Theatre*. Ganzl, Kurt. Schirmer (Macmillan), 1989
ANTHOLOGY: None
VOCAL SELECTIONS: Frank Music, 1952 (from the film)
LICENSING AGENT: Music Theatre International
RECORDING: Marble Arch 119 CD (original London cast)
CAST: 11 M; 5 F; singers, dancers, children

Back in 1952 Frank Loesser wrote a film musical for Danny Kaye. Some years later it was adapted for the stage and has been done several times in London with Tommy Steele and more recently in the U.S.A. with Michael Feinstein. Our hero sets off for "Wonderful Copenhagen" where he meets Jenny Lind. She helps him with his writing but rejects him as a suitor. Recent U.S.A. productions reverted to the original film plot. This is a family show with many happy songs.

ORIGINAL LONDON CAST:

Tommy Steele (Hans Andersen)
Bob Todd (Rector Meisling)
Milo O'Shea (Otto)
Colette Gleeson (Jenny Lind)

SONGS:
Act I
This Town (Hans)
Thumbelina (Hans, children)
Truly Loved (Jenny, company)
For Hans Tonight (Hans, Otto, company)
Jenny Kissed Me (Hans)
Inchworm (Hans, children)
Ecclesiasticus (Hans, Otto, company)
Anywhere I Wander (Hans)
Wonderful Copenhagen (company)

Act II
I'm Hans Christian Andersen (Hans, company)
Don't Talk to Me about Those Happy Days (Hans, Otto, company)
The Ugly Duckling (Hans)
No Two People (Hans, Jenny, company)
A Tune for Humming (Otto, dancers)
The King's New Clothes (Hans, company)

THE HAPPIEST GIRL IN THE WORLD (1961)

BOOK BY: Fred Saidy and Henry Myers; story
   by E. Y. Harburg; based on the Greek play
   Lysistrata by Aristophanes
MUSIC BY: Jacques Offenbach
LYRICS BY: E. Y. Harburg
PUBLISHED LIBRETTO: None
CONDENSATION: None
ANTHOLOGY: None
VOCAL SELECTIONS: Chappell, 1961
LICENSING AGENT: Tams-Witmark
RECORDING: Columbia KOS 2050 (original cast)
CAST: Large mixed cast

This is the familiar story of Lysistrata and how she gets the ladies of ancient Athens to go on a sex strike until the men stop making war. The Broadway production was noted for its wonderful music, sly antics, gorgeous settings, and pretty girls. Offenbach's music (particularly the "Barcarolle") was well liked in this adaption. The male lead plays nine roles, and the female lead should dance as well as sing. Back in the 1960s this show was considered racy!

ORIGINAL CAST:

Dran Seitz (Lysistrata)
Cyril Ritchard (Pluto)
Janice Rule (Diana)
Michael Kermoyan (Jupiter)
Bruce Yarnell (Kinesias)
Nancy Windsor (Sentinel)
Lu Leonard (Myrrhina)

SONGS:
Act I
The Glory That Is Greece (Pluto, Kinesias,
   ensemble)
The Happiest Girl in the World (Lysistrata,
   Kinesias)
The Greek Marine (Pluto, ensemble)
Shall We Say Farewell? (Lysistrata)
Never Be-Devil the Devil (Pluto)
Whatever That May Be (Diana, ensemble)
Eureka (Diana, ensemble)
The Oath (Lysistrata, ensemble)

Viva la Virtue (Pluto, Diana)
Adrift on a Star (Lysistrata, Kinesias)
Act II
That'll Be the Day (ensemble)
How Soon, Oh Moon? (Sentinel, Lysistrata,
   ensemble)
Love-Sick Serenade (Pluto, Myrrhina)
Five Minutes of Spring (Kinesias)
Never Trust a Virgin (Pluto, ensemble)
Entrance of the Courtesans (ensemble)

HAPPY END (1929)

BOOK AND LYRICS BY: Michael Feingold; based
   on the original German play by Elisabeth
   Hauptmann
MUSIC BY: Kurt Weill
LYRICS BY: Bertolt Brecht
PUBLISHED LIBRETTO: Methuen, 1982; French,
   1983
CONDENSATION: *Kurt Weill in Europe.* Kowalke,
   Kim H. UMI Research Press, 1979
ANTHOLOGY: None
PIANO-VOCAL SCORE: (in German) Universal
   Edition (Wein), 1958
LICENSING AGENT: Samuel French
RECORDING: Columbia CSP COS 2032 (German
   studio cast)
CAST: 9 M; 6 F, small chorus

In 1915 a group of second-rate Chicago gangsters is led by a mysterious lady called "The Fly." The Salvation Army enters the story and a humorous situation develops over the struggle for souls. This work is vintage Brecht–Weill—an animated cartoon of the 1920s with a message that is similar to the one in their more famous work, *The Threepenny Opera.* The songs are the most important part of this musical and will require a definite style and flair from the cast.

1977 NEW YORK REVIVAL CAST:

Meryl Streep (Lil)
Christopher Lloyd (Bill)
Tony Azito (The Governor)
Joe Grifasi (Hannibal)
Alexandra Borrie (Jane)

Benjamin Rayson (Sam)
Grayson Hall (The Fly)

SONGS:
Act I
The Bilbao Song (Bill, gang)
Lieutenants of the Lord (Lil, army)
March Ahead (army)
The Sailors' Tango (Lil)

Act II
Brother, Give Yourself a Shove (army,
    ensemble)
Song of the Big Shot (The Governor)
Don't Be Afraid (Jane, army, ensemble)
In Our Childhood's Bright Endeavor
    (Hannibal)
The Liquor Dealer's Dream (Hannibal, The
    Governor, Jane, army, ensemble)

Act III
The Mandalay Song (Sam, gang)
Surabaya Johnny (Lil)
Song of the Big Shot (reprise) (Bill)
Ballad of the Lily of Hell (The Fly)
Happy End Finale (company)

HAPPY HUNTING (1956)

BOOK BY: Howard Lindsay and Russel Crouse
MUSIC BY: Harold Karr
LYRICS BY: Matt Dubey
PUBLISHED LIBRETTO: Random House, 1957
CONDENSATION: *New Complete Book of the
    American Musical Theater.* Ewen, David. Holt,
    1970
ANTHOLOGY: None
VOCAL SELECTIONS: Chappell, 1957
LICENSING AGENT: Music Theatre International
RECORDING: RCA LOC 1026 (original cast)
CAST: Large mixed cast

For many years after this show closed,
Ethel Merman, its star, usually opened her
concert appearances with "Gee, But It's
Good to Be Here" from its score. This musical revolves around a big wedding in
Monaco with Merman playing the part of a
wealthy Philadelphia matron who was not
invited to the wedding. (Much of the humor referred to the then recent Grace Kelly
wedding.) She hopes to marry her daughter to the pretender to the Spanish throne,
but she ends up in love with him herself.
Scenes include not only the Riviera but the
Atlantic crossing and Philadelphia, as well.

ORIGINAL CAST:
Gordon Polk (Sandy)
Virginia Gibson (Beth)
Ethel Merman (Liz)
Fernando Lamas (The Duke)
Mary Finney (Maud)
Gene Wesson (Harry)
Seth Riggs (Jack)
Leon Belasco (Artufo)

SONGS:
Act I
Postage Stamp Principality (ensemble)
Don't Tell Me (Sandy, Beth)
Gee, But It's Good to Be Here (Liz,
    reporters)
Mutual Admiration Society (Liz, Beth)
For Love or Money (girls)
Bikini Dance (Beth)
It's Like a Beautiful Woman (The Duke)
Wedding-of-the-Year Blues (Maud, Harry, Jack,
    ensemble)
Mr. Livingstone (Liz)
If'n (Beth, Sandy, ensemble)
This Is What I Call Love (Liz)

Act II
A New-Fangled Tango (Liz, Beth, Arturo,
    guests)
She's Just Another Girl (Sandy)
The Game of Love (Liz)
Happy Hunting (Liz, The Duke, ensemble)
I'm a Funny Dame (Liz)
This Much I Know (The Duke)
Just Another Guy (Liz)
Everyone Who's "Who's Who" (Jack, Harry,
    ensemble)
Mutual Admiration Society (reprise) (Liz, The
    Duke)

HAPPY NEW YEAR (1980)

BOOK BY: Burt Shevelove; adapted from the play
   Holiday by Philip Barry
MUSIC AND LYRICS BY: Cole Porter; songs edited
   by Buster Davis
PUBLISHED LIBRETTO: French, 1982
CONDENSATION: None
ANTHOLOGY: None
VOCAL SELECTIONS: *Music and Lyrics by Cole
   Porter*, 2 vols. Chappell, 1972–1975
LICENSING AGENT: Samuel French
RECORDING: None
CAST: 14 M; 11 F

The plot of this musical is about a non-conformist young man who almost marries the conventional daughter of the country's richest banker. The time is the mid-1930s. The ladies' fashions were highly praised in the Broadway production. This is a Philip Barry play originally done in 1928; it has been refashioned into a musical with familiar Cole Porter songs. It is done as a "memory play" with an older man narrating the story. This is a chic, glamorous, nostalgic, and sophisticated show.

ORIGINAL CAST:

John McMartin (The Narrator)
Kimberly Farr (Julia)
Leslie Denniston (Linda)
Richard Bekins (Ned)
Michael Scott (Johnny)
J. Thomas Smith (Patrick)
Lara Teeter (Dixon)
Tim Flavin (Thompson)

SONGS:
Act I
At Long Last Love (Julia, Linda, Ned)
Ridin' High (Johnny, Julia)
Let's Be Buddies (Johnny, Linda)
Boy, Oh, Boy (Linda)
Easy to Love (men)
You Do Something to Me (Johnny)
Red, Hot, and Blue (Linda, Johnny, Patrick,
   ensemble)
Once Upon a Time (Ned, Linda)

Act II
Night and Day (The Narrator, Johnny)
Let's Make It a Night (Linda, Thompson, Dixon)
Ours (Julia)
After You, Who? (Johnny)
I Am Loved (Julia)
When Your Troubles Have Started (Linda, Ned)

THE HAPPY TIME (1968)

BOOK BY: N. Richard Nash; suggested by the
   characters in the stories by Robert L. Fontaine
MUSIC BY: John Kander
LYRICS BY: Fred Ebb
PUBLISHED LIBRETTO: Dramatic, 1969
CONDENSATION: *New Complete Book of the Ameri-
   can Musical Theater*. Ewen, David. Holt, 1970
ANTHOLOGY: None
VOCAL SELECTIONS: Valando, 1967
LICENSING AGENT: Dramatic
RECORDING: RCA 61016 CD (original cast)
CAST: Large mixed cast, including children

A well-traveled photographer returns to St. Pierre, his French-Canadian hometown. He considers taking his young nephew, Bibi, with him on his travels, but the wise old Grandpere convinces him otherwise. There is a love story between the photographer and the girl he left behind. The sets were not overly elaborate for this big Broadway musical, but slide projections were used.

ORIGINAL CAST:

Robert Goulet (Jacques)
David Wayne (Grandpere)
Michael Rupert (Bibi)
Julie Gregg (Laurie)

SONGS:
Act I
The Happy Time (Jacques, family)
He's Back (family)
Catch My Garter (girls)
Tomorrow Morning (Jacques, Grandpere,
   Bibi, girls)
Please Stay (Bibi, Jacques)
I Don't Remember You (Jacques)

St. Pierre (chorus)

I Don't Remember You (reprise) (Laurie, Jacques)

Without Me (Bibi, schoolmates)

Act II

Among My Yesterdays (Jacques)

The Life of the Party (Grandpere, girls, schoolboys)

Seeing Things (Jacques, Laurie)

A Certain Girl (Grandpere, Jacques, Bibi)

Being Alive (Jacques)

HARK! (1972)

MUSIC BY: Dan Goggin and Marvin Solley

LYRICS BY: Robert Lorick

PUBLISHED LIBRETTO: None

CONDENSATION: None

ANTHOLOGY: None

LICENSING AGENT: Samuel French

RECORDING: None

CAST: 4 M; 2 F

This is a lighthearted cabaret show that consists entirely of songs and a bit of dancing with no attempt at a story. Growing up in America is the theme. The cast starts as children and begins the life cycle. Overpopulation, pacifism, and funerals as big business are some of the universal subjects covered. The off-Broadway production used a circular, relatively bare playing area with changing lights and projections. The score was described as "melodious and literate in variety and scope."

ORIGINAL CAST:

Dan Goggin	Marvin Solley
Elaine Petricoff	Danny Guerrero
Sharon Miller	Jack Blackton

SONGS:

Act I

Hark! (company)

Take a Look (company)

George (company)

Hip Hooray for America (company)

Smart People (company)

Icarus (Solley, company)

Sun Down (Miller)

Conversation Piece (Petricoff, Blackton, Guerrero, Miller)

The Outstanding Member (Guerrero, company)

How Am I Doin', Dad? (company)

Molly (Goggin, Solley)

In a Hundred Years (company)

Act II

Coffee Morning (Blackton)

Suburbia Square Dance (Goggin, Solley, company)

I See the People (Blackton, Goggin, Solley)

Pretty Jack (Miller)

Big Day Tomorrow (Guerrero)

Lullaby (Petricoff)

Here's to You, Mrs. Rodriguez (Goggin, Solley)

Early Sunday (Blackton, company)

A Dying Business (Guerrero, company)

Waltz with Me, Lady (Solley)

Epilogue (company)

HARRIGAN 'N' HART (1985)

BOOK BY: Michael Stewart; based on material compiled by Nedda Harrigan Logan and *The Merry Partners* by E. J. Kahn, Jr.

MUSIC BY: Max Showalter

LYRICS BY: Peter Walker (songs of the period by Edward Harrigan and David Braham)

PUBLISHED LIBRETTO: French, 1985

CONDENSATION: None

ANTHOLOGY: None

LICENSING AGENT: Samuel French

RECORDING: None

CAST: 8 M; 7 F (multiple roles)

Edward Harrigan revolutionized nineteenth-century variety/vaudeville, integrating story, song, and dance into what would become the modern Broadway musical. In 1871 he met Tony Hart and they became a popular show team. Jealous misunderstandings brought an end to their partnership, and Hart died at an early age. This is their story, using both original songs and many of their famous numbers, including

"The Mulligan Guard." There are three main roles, Harrigan, Hart, and Hart's manipulative wife. The rest of the cast performs many roles in both onstage and offstage scenes. Many costumes are required, and many numbers are performed in dialect. A wooden clog dance was highly praised.

ORIGINAL CAST:

Mark Hamill (Tony Hart)
Harry Groener (Edward Harrigan)
Tudi Roche (Annie)
Clent Bowers (Sam)
Armelia McQueen (Mrs. Yeamons)
Christine Ebersole (Gerta)
Christopher Wells (Harry)
Mark Fotopoulos (Johnny)
Cleve Asbury (Billy)
Roxie Lucas (Ada)
Barbara Moroz (Elsie)
Amelia Marshall (Jennie)
Oliver Woodall (Martin)
Merilee Magnuson (Lily)

SONGS:
Act I
Put Me in My Little Bed (Tony Hart)
Dapper Dan McGee (Edward Harrigan, girls)
Wonderful Me (Edward Harrigan, Tony Hart)
The Mulligan Guard (Edward Harrigan, Tony Hart)
I Love to Follow a Band (Tony Hart, company)
Such an Education Has My Mary Ann (Edward Harrigan, Tony Hart, company)
Maggie Murphy's Home (Annie, Edward Harrigan, Sam, company)
McNally's Row of Flats (Mrs. Yeamons, company)
Something New, Something Different (Edward Harrigan, Tony Hart, company)
That's My Partner (Edward Harrigan, Tony Hart)
She's Our Gretel (Edward Harrigan, Tony Hart, Mrs. Yeamons, company)
What You Need Is a Woman (Gerta)
Knights of the Mystic Star (Mrs. Yeamons, company)
Girl of the Mystic Star (Gerta, men)

Act II
Skidmore Fancy Ball (Sam, Harry, Johnny, Billy)
Sweetest Love (Ada, Elsie)
The Old Barn Floor (Johnny, Jennie, Lily)
Silly Boy (Gerta, Billy, Harry)
We'll Be There (Edward Harrigan, Tony Hart, company)
Ada with the Golden Hair (Annie, Johnny, Billy)
That Old Featherbed (Harry, girls)
Sam Johnson's Colored Cakewalk (Sam, Jennie)
Dip Me in the Golden Sea (Edward Harrigan, Mrs. Yeamons, company)
I've Come Home to Stay (Tony Hart)
If I Could Trust Me (Tony Hart)
Maggie Murphy's Home (reprise) (Martin, Lily, Mrs. Yeamons, Ada)
I Need This One Chance (Gerta)
I Love to Follow a Band (reprise) (Annie, company)

HAZEL FLAGG (1953)

BOOK BY: Ben Hecht; based on a story by James Street and the film *Nothing Sacred*
MUSIC BY: Jule Styne
LYRICS BY: Bob Hilliard
PUBLISHED LIBRETTO: None
CONDENSATION: None
ANTHOLOGY: None
VOCAL SELECTIONS: Chappell, 1953
LICENSING AGENT: Tams-Witmark
RECORDING: RCA CBM 1-2207 (original cast)
CAST: Large mixed cast

A small-town girl in Vermont is diagnosed as dying from radium poisoning. An expense-paid trip to New York meant to boost the circulation of a magazine sets the stage for her sudden fame. She doesn't have radium poisoning, but she does manage to fall in love. This musical is set in the 1930s. The Dean Martin/Jerry Lewis film *Living It Up* was also based on this material and used some of the Broadway songs.

ORIGINAL CAST:
Benay Venuta (Laura)
John Howard (Wallace)
Helen Gallagher (Hazel)
John Brascia (Willie)
Jack Whiting (The Mayor)

SONGS:
Act I
A Little More Heart (Laura, Wallace, staff)
The World Is Beautiful Today (Hazel)
I'm Glad I'm Leaving (Hazel)
Hello, Hazel (Laura, ensemble)
Paris Gown (Hazel, men)
The World Is Beautiful Today (reprise)
   (Wallace, staff)
Every Street's a Boulevard in Old New York
   (The Mayor)
How Do You Speak to an Angel? (Wallace)
Autograph Chant (ensemble)
I Feel Like I'm Gonna Live Forever (Hazel)
You're Gonna Dance with Me, Willie (Hazel,
   Willie, company)

Act II
Who Is the Bravest? (glee club)
Salome (girls)
Everybody Loves to Take a Bow (Laura, The
   Mayor, men)
Laura De Maupassant (Hazel)

was particularly recommended for children during the Christmas season. It is rooted in commedia dell'arte with a plot about three charms in Punchinello's carpetbag, one of which is a hat that makes the wearer invisible.

ORIGINAL CAST:
John Cunningham (Punchinello)
Dennis Bailey (Harlequin)
Elizabeth Austin (Columbine)
Charles Michael Wright (Pierrot)
Gwyda Donhowe (Nurse)

SONGS:
Act I
New Loves for Old (Punchinello, lovers)
Perfection (Columbine, Nurse, Punchinello)
I'm in Love (Harlequin)
Aqua Vitae (Punchinello, Nurse)
Nowhere (Punchinello, Harlequin)
Finaletto (company)

Act II
Castles in the Sand (Columbine, Nurse)
As If (Columbine)
Could He Be You? (Punchinello, Nurse)
Lullabye to Myself (Pierrot)

HEAD OVER HEELS (1981)

BOOK BY: William S. Kilborne, Jr., and Albert T.
   Viola; based on the play *The Wonder Hat* by
   Kenneth Sawyer Goodman and Ben Hecht
MUSIC BY: Albert T. Viola
LYRICS BY: William S. Kilborne, Jr.
PUBLISHED LIBRETTO: Samuel French, 1981
CONDENSATION: None
ANTHOLOGY: None
LICENSING AGENT: Samuel French
RECORDING: None
CAST: 3 M; 2 F

Described by critics as a brief harlequinade about potions, spells, and suddenly requited love, this off-Broadway musical

HELLO, DOLLY! (1964)

BOOK BY: Michael Stewart; based on *The
   Matchmaker* by Thornton Wilder
MUSIC AND LYRICS BY: Jerry Herman
PUBLISHED LIBRETTO: Drama Book Shop, 1966
CONDENSATION: *The Best Plays of 1963–64*. Henry
   Hewes, ed. Dodd, Mead, 1964; *Ganzl's Book
   of the Musical Theatre*. Ganzl, Kurt. Schirmer
   (Macmillan), 1989
ANTHOLOGY: None
PIANO-VOCAL SCORE: Morris, 1964
VOCAL SELECTION: Big Three (Morris, 1964)
LICENSING AGENT: Tams-Witmark
RECORDINGS: RCA CD 3814 (original cast); RCA CD
   1147 (Pearl Bailey cast)
CAST: 8 M; 6 F; chorus

The widowed Dolly Gallagher Levi makes a precarious living as a matchmaker. Wealthy store owner Horace Vandergelder needs a wife and Dolly secretly sets out to marry him herself. Set in Yonkers and New York City around 1890, this show provides ample opportunity for lavish costumes, big production numbers, and a large cast. A staircase is needed for the big title number at the Harmonia Gardens Restaurant on 14th Street. This was filmed in 1969 with Barbra Streisand.

Tony Award Winner (Best Musical)

ORIGINAL CAST:

Carol Channing (Dolly)
David Burns (Horace)
Charles Nelson Reilly (Cornelius)
Jerry Dodge (Barnaby)
Eileen Brennan (Irene)
Sondra Lee (Minnie Fay)
Igors Gavon (Ambrose)
Alice Playten (Ermengarde)
David Hartman (Rudolph)

SONGS:
Act I
I Put My Hand In (Dolly, company)
It Takes a Woman (Horace, men)
Put on Your Sunday Clothes (Cornelius, Barnaby, Dolly, Ambrose, Ermengarde)
Ribbons Down My Back (Irene)
Motherhood (Dolly, Horace, Irene, Minnie Fay, Cornelius, Barnaby)
Dancing (Dolly, Cornelius, Barnaby, Minnie Fay, Irene, dancers)
Before the Parade Passes By (Dolly, Horace, company)

Act II
Elegance (Irene, Cornelius, Minnie Fay, Barnaby)
Hello, Dolly! (Dolly, Rudolph, waiters, chorus)
It Only Takes a Moment (Cornelius, Irene, chorus)
So Long Dearie (Dolly, Horace)
Hello, Dolly! (reprise) (Dolly, Horace)

HENRY, SWEET HENRY (1967)

BOOK BY: Nunnally Johnson; based on *The World of Henry Orient* by Nora Johnson
MUSIC AND LYRICS BY: Bob Merrill
PUBLISHED LIBRETTO: French, 1969
CONDENSATION: None
ANTHOLOGY: None
LICENSING AGENT: Samuel French
RECORDING: ABC S-OC-4 (original cast)
CAST: 8 M; 8 F; extras, chorus

Henry Orient is a small-time conductor. Valerie, a fourteen-year-old schoolgirl, has a crush on him. Valerie and her school chums shadow Henry just to be near him. This show featured choreography by Michael Bennett with a lot of young girls and a colorful set that was constantly in motion. The locale is New York City and the time is the 1960s. One dance number is a hippie event in Washington Square Park.

ORIGINAL CAST:

Robin Wilson (Valerie)
Alice Playten (Kafritz)
Don Ameche (Henry Orient)
Carol Bruce (Mrs Boyd)
Louise Lasser (Stella)
Neva Small (Marion Gilbert)

SONGS:
Act I
Academic Fugue (company)
In Some Little World (Valerie)
Pillar to Post (Henry Orient, Stella)
Here I Am (Valerie)
I Wonder How It Is to Dance with a Boy (Marion Gilbert, girls)
Nobody Steps on Kafritz (Kafritz)
Henry Sweet Henry (Valerie, Marion Gilbert)
Women in Love (Valerie, Marion Gilbert)
The People Watchers (company)

Act II
Weary Near to Dyin' (Valerie, ensemble)
Poor Little Person (Kafritz, ensemble)
I'm Blue Too (Valerie, Marion Gilbert)

To Be Artistic (Henry Orient, Mrs. Boyd)
Forever (Henry Orient)
Do You Ever Go to Boston? (Valerie)

HERE'S LOVE (1963)

BOOK, MUSIC, AND LYRICS BY: Meredith Willson;
    based on the film *The Miracle on 34th Street*,
    story by Valentine Davies, screenplay by
    George Seaton
PUBLISHED LIBRETTO: None
CONDENSATION: *New Complete Book of the*
    American Musical Theater. Ewen, David. Holt,
    1970
ANTHOLOGY: None
VOCAL SELECTIONS: Frank Music, 1963
LICENSING AGENT: Music Theatre International
RECORDINGS: Columbia KOS 2400 (original cast);
    Sony SK 48207 CD (original cast)
CAST: Large mixed cast

This contemporary New York show features the Macy's Thanksgiving Parade at the center of the plot. There is a love story between a professional woman who works for Macy's and an ex-Marine. There is also a charming old gentleman who is hired as Santa Claus, who then claims he really is Kris Kringle. Big production numbers (the parade, naturally), a good part for a young girl, and all the warmth of the Christmas season are features of this family show. Presented in 1991 at the Goodspeed Opera House.

ORIGINAL CAST:

Janis Paige (Doris)
Valerie Lee (Susan)
Laurence Naismith (Kris)
Craig Stevens (Fred)
Fred Gwynne (Shellhammer)
Kathy Cody (Hendrika)
Paul Reed (Macy)
Arthur Rubin (Tammany)

SONGS:
Act I
The Big Clown Balloons (ensemble)
Arm in Arm (Doris, Susan)

You Don't Know (Doris)
The Plastic Alligator (Shellhammer, clerks)
The Bugle (Kris, Hendrika)
Here's Love (Kris, Fred, Susan, ensemble)
My Wish (Fred, Susan)
Pine Cones and Holly Berries (Kris, Doris,
    Shellhammer)
Look, Little Girl (Fred) Reprise (Doris)
Expect Things to Happen (Kris)

Act II
She Hadda Go Back (Fred, marines)
That Man Over There (Macy)
My State (Doris, Macy, Shellhammer,
    Tammany, ensemble)
Nothing in Common (Doris)

HERRINGBONE (1982)

BOOK BY: Tom Cone
MUSIC BY: Skip Kennon
LYRICS BY: Ellen Fitzhugh
PUBLISHED LIBRETTO: None
CONDENSATION: None
ANTHOLOGY: *Plays from Playwrights Horizons.*
    Broadway Play Publishing, 1987
LICENSING AGENT: Broadway Play Publishing
RECORDING: Cassette tape available from agent
CAST: 1 M

A solo performer portrays a number of different roles—everything from a southern grandmother to a tap-dancing tot. The plot concerns a young boy from depression-era Georgia whose spirit is inhabited by a dancing midget who was murdered by his vaudeville partner. The actor in the New York production was praised for his breathtaking split-second changes of character. There is a music-hall setting, with the actor dipping into a trunk to flesh out his various guises, although there are no real sets or costumes required. An onstage pianist provides accompaniment.

ORIGINAL CAST:

David Rounds (Herringbone)
Skip Kennon (Thumbs Du Bois—on stage
    pianist)

SONGS:

(all performed by the actor portraying Herringbone)

Act I

Herringbone (Herringbone)

Not President, Please (George)

Uncle Billy (Arthur)

God Said (Arthur)

Finaletto: Little Mister Tippy Toes (George), George (Louise), The Cheap Exit (ensemble)

Act II

What's a Body to Do? (Herringbone)

The Chicken and the Frog (Lou)

Lily Pad Tango (Herringbone, Lou, George)

A Mother (Herringbone)

Lullabye (George)

Three Waltzes: Tulip Print Waltz (George, Dot, Lou), Ten Years (Lou), 3/4 for Three (Lou, George, Dot)

Herringbone (reprise) (Herringbone)

HIGH BUTTON SHOES (1947)

BOOK BY: Stephen Longstreet; based on his short stories

MUSIC BY: Jule Styne

LYRICS BY: Sammy Cahn

PUBLISHED LIBRETTO: None

CONDENSATION: *New Complete Book of the American Musical Theater.* Ewen, David. Holt, 1970

ANTHOLOGY: None

VOCAL SELECTIONS: Warner Bros. Music, 1989

LICENSING AGENT: Tams-Witmark

RECORDING: RCA LSO 1107(e) (original cast)

CAST: 10 M; 4 F; singers, dancers

This popular Broadway show originally starred Phil Silvers and has been successfully revived at the Goodspeed Opera in Connecticut. A big hit song from the score is "Papa, Won't You Dance with Me?" Set in 1913, the story involves a con man in New Brunswick (New Jersey), a Rutgers–Princeton football game, a "Keystone Comedy" sequence on the beach at Atlantic City, and various other old-fashioned musical activities. This is a wholesome family show.

ORIGINAL CAST:

Lois Lee (Fran)

Mark Dawson (Hubert)

Phil Silvers (Floy)

Nanette Fabray (Mama)

Jack McCauley (Papa)

Johnny Stewart (Stevie)

Joey Faye (Pontdue)

SONGS:

Act I

He Tried to Make a Dollar (Floy, Pontdue, ensemble)

Can't You Just See Yourself? (Fran, Hubert)

There's Nothing Like a Model T (company)

Next to Texas I Love You (Hubert, Fran, ladies)

On the Banks of the Old Raritan (Floy, gentlemen)

Security (Mama, ladies)

Bird-watchers Song (Mama, Fran, Floy, Pontdue, ladies)

Get Away for a Day in the Country (Papa, Stevie, company)

Papa, Won't You Dance with Me? (company)

Can't You Just See Yourself in Love with Me? (Fran, Floy)

Act II

On a Sunday by the Sea (ensemble)

You're My Girl (Hubert, Fran)

I Still Get Jealous (Mama, Papa)

You're My Boy (Floy, Pontdue)

Nobody Ever Died for Dear Old Rutgers (Floy, Pontdue, Hubert, men)

THE HIGH LIFE (1961)

(originally titled *THE GAY LIFE*)

BOOK BY: Fay and Garson Kanin; suggested by *Anatol* by Arthur Schnitzler

LYRICS AND MUSIC BY: Howard Dietz and Arthur Schwartz

PUBLISHED LIBRETTO: French

CONDENSATION: None

ANTHOLOGY: None
VOCAL SELECTIONS: Warner Bros. Music, 1988
LICENSING AGENT: Samuel French
RECORDING: Capitol SWAO 1560; Angel ZDM
    764763-2 CD (original cast; titled *The Gay Life*)
CAST: 21 M; 14 F (may double)

Turn-of-the-century Vienna is the setting for this witty and sophisticated musical. The fifteen scenes include apartments, halls, cafes, and the streets of Vienna. The costumes and sets for the New York production were described as opulent. The plot concerns a playboy hero who decides to marry and settle down. A plain but enchanting young maiden manages to win him over some competing enchantresses. The production was elaborate with spectacular dance numbers. One scene is set in the Paprikas Cafe with gypsy dancers and violins.

ORIGINAL CAST:

Jules Munshin (Max)
Barbara Cook (Liesl)
Walter Chiari (Anatol)
Jeanne Bal (Helene)
Lu Leonard (Frau Brandel)
Loring Smith (Herr Brandel)
Elizabeth Allen (Magda)

SONGS:
Act I
Bring Your Darling Daughter (Max, ensemble)
Now I'm Ready for a Frau (Anatol, Max)
You're Not the Type (Helene)
Magic Moment (Liesl)
Who Can? You Can (Anatol, Liesl)
Oh, Mein Liebchen (ensemble)
The Label on the Bottle (Liesl)
This Kind of Girl (Anatol, Liesl)
The Bloom Is Off the Rose (Max, male
    ensemble)

Act II
I'm Glad I'm Single (Max, male ensemble)
Something You Never Had Before (Liesl)
You Will Never Be Lonely (Frau Brandel, Herr
    Brandel, ensemble)
You're Not the Type (reprise) (Anatol, Liesl)
Come a-Wandering with Me (Magda)

I Never Had a Chance (Anatol)
I Wouldn't Marry You (Liesl)
For the First Time (Anatol)

HIGH SPIRITS (1964)

MUSIC, LYRICS, AND BOOK BY: Hugh Martin and
    Timothy Gray; based on *Blithe Spirit* by Noel
    Coward
PUBLISHED LIBRETTO: None
CONDENSATION: *New Complete Book of the
    American Musical Theater*. Ewen, David. Holt,
    1970
ANTHOLOGY: None
VOCAL SELECTIONS: Cromwell Music, 1964
LICENSING AGENT : Tams-Witmark
RECORDINGS: ABC S-OC-1; MCA 10767-CD (original
    cast)
CAST: 4 M; 6 F; singers, dancers

Noel Coward's very popular play was turned into a musical in 1964 and starred his old friend Beatrice Lillie as Madame Arcati. The plot concerns a happily married man who is haunted by the spirit of his first wife. The comedy begins when a medium arrives for a séance. This was a lavish Broadway and London musical that featured the spirit "flying" about the stage. This is a suave, sophisticated, drawing room comedy.

ORIGINAL CAST:

Edward Woodward (Charles)
Robert Lenn (Bob)
Louise Troy (Ruth)
Beth Howland (Beth)
Tammy Grimes (Elvira)
Beatrice Lillie (Madame Arcati)

SONGS:
Act I
Was She Prettier than I? (Ruth)
The Bicycle Song (Madame Arcati, ensemble)
You'd Better Love Me (Elvira)
Where Is the Man I Married? (Ruth, Charles)
The Sandwich Man (Bob, Beth)
Go into Your Trance (Madame Arcati,
    ensemble)

Forever and a Day (Charles, Elvira)
Something Tells Me (Elvira, ensemble)
I Know Your Heart (Charles, Elvira)
Faster than Sound (Elvira, ensemble)

Act II
If I Gave You (Charles, Ruth)
Talking to You (Madame Arcati)
Home Sweet Heaven (Elvira)
Madame Arcati's Tea Party (Madame Arcati, ensemble)
The Exorcism (Madame Arcati, ensemble)
What in the World Did You Want? (Charles, Elvira, Ruth)

SONGS INCLUDE:

Love's Old Sweet Song
Home Sweet Home
Captain Jinks of the Horse Marines
Will You Love Me in December as You Do in May?
Last Rose of Summer
Beautiful Dreamer
Silver Threads among the Gold
Good-bye, My Lady Love
Wait Till the Sun Shines, Nellie

HIJINKS! (1980)

BOOK BY: Robert Kalfin, Steve Brown, and John McKinney; adapted from *Captain Jinks of the Horse Marines* by Clyde Fitch
PUBLISHED LIBRETTO: French, 1980
CONDENSATION: None
ANTHOLOGY: None
LICENSING AGENT: Samuel French
RECORDING: None
CAST: 9 M; 6 F

The setting is New York City in the era of gaslit streets and the music of Stephen Foster. Our hero is Jinks, a man-about-town, who makes a wager with his pals about which of them can first have a flirtation with a beautiful opera singer. The recent off-Broadway production featured familiar songs of the period and the audience was encouraged to sing along in some of the numbers. The sets were described as flexible and resembling lithographs. The show is simple to stage and is for the entire family.

ORIGINAL CAST:

Jeannine Taylor (Madame Trentoni/Aurelia Johnson)
Joseph Kolinski (Captain Jinks)
Michael Connelly (Clyde Fitch)
Christopher Farr (Peter)
Evalyn Baron (Fraulein Hochspits)
Marian Primont (Mrs. Jinks)

A HISTORY OF AMERICAN FILM (1978)

BOOK AND LYRICS BY: Christopher Durang
MUSIC BY: Mel Marvin
PUBLISHED LIBRETTO: French, 1978; Avon (paperback), 1978
CONDENSATION: None
ANTHOLOGY: None
LICENSING AGENT: Samuel French
RECORDING: None
CAST: 9 M; 6 F

Called a social history of America during the past seventy years, the premise of Durang's musical is that it is often difficult to separate life on the silver screen from real life. The show begins in a theater with the cast as the audience watching the screen. Then they step forward and become the characters they are watching. They are thrown into situations we instantly recognize, and then they progress into absurd variations. Characters include Loretta, Bette, Hank, and a host of others as the small cast play many different parts. The songs and dancing take second place to the comedy and the content of the show.

ORIGINAL CAST:

Gary Bayer (Jimmy)
Swoosie Kurtz (Bette)
April Shawhan (Loretta)
Brent Spiner (Hank)

Eric Weitz (Eric)
Joan Pape (Eve)
Mary Catherine Wright (Clara)
Kate McGregor-Stewart (Singing WAC)
David Garrison (David)

SONGS:
Act I
Minstrel Song (ensemble)
Shanty Town Romance (Jimmy, Loretta)
They Can't Prohibit Love (Bette)
We're in a Salad (Hank, Loretta, Bette, Eve,
    ensemble)
Euphemism (Loretta)
Ostende Nobis Tosca (Bette, Hank, David,
    Eric)
The Red, the White, and the Blue (Eve,
    company)
Act II
Pretty Pinup (Eve, Loretta, Bette, Clara)
Apple Blossom Victory (Bette, Eve, Singing
    WAC)
Isn't It Fun to Be in the Movies? (David, Eric)
Search for Wisdom (Jimmy, Loretta,
    company)

HIT THE DECK (1927)

BOOK BY: Herbert Fields; adapted from the play
    Shore Leave by Hubert Osborne
MUSIC BY: Vincent Youmans
LYRICS BY: Leo Robin and Clifford Grey
PUBLISHED LIBRETTO: None
CONDENSATION: *Ganzl's Book of the Musical Thea-
    tre.* Ganzl, Kurt. Schirmer (Macmillan), 1989
ANTHOLOGY: None
PIANO-VOCAL SCORE: Harms, 1925
LICENSING AGENT: Tams-Witmark
RECORDING: World SH 176 (original London cast)
CAST: 14 M; 5 F; chorus

Looloo is a coffeehouse manager who falls
in love with a sailor and follows him around
the world until she gets him. This has been
a popular show for many years. It was lavishly mounted at Jones Beach and was also
filmed in 1930 and 1955. There's a lot of
"hoofing" by the sailors, and a good time is
had by all.

1942 SAN FRANCISCO CAST:
Joan Roberts (Looloo)
Robert Stanford (Alan)
Joan Woodbury (Charlotte)
Frank Albertson (Bilge)
June Preisser (Toddy)
Ruby Dandridge (Lavinia)
Eddie Foy, Jr. (Bunny)
Jack Durant (Matt)
Tom Kennedy (Bat)

SONGS:
Act I
Join the Navy (Looloo, ensemble)
Nothing Could Be Sweeter (Alan, Charlotte,
    girls)
The Harbor of My Heart (Looloo, Bilge)
Shore Leave (Toddy, Bunny, ensemble)
Join the Navy (reprise) (Alan, ensemble)
Looloo (Looloo, sailors)
Sometimes I'm Happy (Looloo, Bilge)
Act II
Hallelujah! (Lavinia, ensemble)
More than You Know (Looloo, Lavinia)
Why, Oh Why? (ensemble)

HOT GROG (1977)

BOOK BY: Jim Wann
MUSIC AND LYRICS BY: Bland Simpson and Jim
    Wann
PUBLISHED LIBRETTO: French, 1977
CONDENSATION: None
ANTHOLOGY: None
LICENSING AGENT: Samuel French
RECORDING: None
CAST: 7 M; 4 F

The plot of this rock/pirate musical concerns a southern belle who signs on in dis-
guise as a cabin boy on a pirate ship. All
this takes place off the Carolina coast in
1718. Some of the characters include Edward (Blackbeard) Teach and Anne Bon-
ney. The authors have used this idea to
make a statement regarding both capital
punishment and women's lib. For the off-
Broadway production the set was a mul-

tipurpose wooden scaffolding. The music was provided by a small rock band.

ORIGINAL CAST:

Terry O'Quinn (Calico)
Mimi Kennedy (Anne)
Mary Bracken Phillips (Read)
Roger Howell (Rhett)
Timothy Meyers (Blackbeard)
Homer Foil (Stede)
John McCurry (Caesar)
Patrick Hines (Governor)

SONGS:
Act I

Seizure to Roam (Calico, company)
Got a Notion (Anne, Calico)
Hot Grog (company)
The Pirate's Life (Anne, company)
The Difference Is Me (Read)
Change in Direction (Read, Anne, company)

Act II

Heaven Must Have Been Smiling (Anne, Calico, company)
Hack 'Em (Rhett)
Treasure to Bury/One of Us (Blackbeard, Read, Stede, Caesar, Calico)
Sea Breeze (Anne, Governor)
The Chase (the band)
Skye Boat Song (Anne, Read, Stede)
Marooned (Calico, Anne, Read, Stede)
The Sword Fight (the band)
The Head Song (Blackbeard, Caesar, men)
Drinking Fool (Calico, company)
Bound Away (Anne, company)

HOW NOW, DOW JONES (1967)

BOOK BY: Max Shulman; based on an original idea by Carolyn Leigh
MUSIC BY: Elmer Bernstein
LYRICS BY: Carolyn Leigh
PUBLISHED LIBRETTO: French, 1968
CONDENSATION: None
ANTHOLOGY: None
VOCAL SELECTIONS: United Artists Music (Carwin, 1968)

LICENSING AGENT: Samuel French
RECORDING: RCA LSO 1142 (original cast)
CAST: 14 M; 9 F; singers, dancers

This is a musical about the New York Stock Exchange. Kate reads the Dow-Jones quotations over the radio each day. She is loved by two gentlemen, one of whom promises to marry her when the Dow-Jones average hits a certain high. There is also a secondary romance between an absentminded tycoon and a stock exchange guide. The snappy score is by the Hollywood composer Elmer Bernstein. The sets are offices and Wall Street environs in this contemporary musical.

ORIGINAL CAST:

Brenda Vaccaro (Cynthia)
Marlyn Mason (Kate)
Tony Roberts (Charley)
Hiram Sherman (Wingate)
Barnard Hughes (McFetridge)
Sammy Smith (Gilman; Sammy)
Fran Stevens (Mrs. Klein)
Tommy Tune (Virgil)
Yanco Inone (Amigo)

SONGS:
Act I

A-B-C (Cynthia, ensemble)
They Don't Make 'em Like That Anymore (Kate, Cynthia)
Live a Little (Charley, Kate, ensemble)
A Little Investigation (Wingate, McFetridge, men)
Walk Away (Kate)
Music to Their Ears (Charley, men)
Step to the Rear (Charley, ensemble)
Shakespeare Lied (Kate, Cynthia, Gilman)
Big Trouble (Kate)

Act II

Credo (Gilman, Mrs Klein, ensemble)
One of Those Moments (Kate)
Big Trouble (reprise) (Wingate, men)
He's Here! (Cynthia)
We'll Stand and Cheer (Kate, Sammy, Virgil, Amigo)
Where You Are (Charley, Kate)
Panic (Gilman, ensemble)

HOW TO SUCCEED IN BUSINESS WITHOUT REALLY TRYING (1961)

BOOK BY: Abe Burrows, Jack Weinstock, and
   Willie Gilbert; based on the novel by Shepherd
   Mead
MUSIC AND LYRICS BY: Frank Loesser
PUBLISHED LIBRETTO: None
CONDENSATION: *The Best Plays of 1961–1962.*
   Henry Hewes, ed. Dodd, Mead, 1962; *Ganzl's
   Book of the Musical Theatre.* Ganzl, Kurt.
   Schirmer (Macmillan), 1989
ANTHOLOGY: None
PIANO-VOCAL SCORE: Frank Music, 1962
VOCAL SELECTIONS: Frank Music, 1961
LICENSING AGENT: Music Theatre International
RECORDING: RCA 60352 CD (original cast)
CAST: Large mixed cast

This is the story of how ruthless but charming J. Pierpont Finch works his way to the top of the World Wide Wicket Company. A 1972 off-Broadway revival was noted for its use of a few doors, sparse furniture, and some sliding elevator panels to simulate offices and lobbies. This contemporary story set in New York's business world is a jovial lampoon of a business office in operation. Stars Robert Morse and Rudy Vallee also appeared in the 1967 film version.

Tony Award Winner (Best Musical)

Pulitzer Prize

ORIGINAL CAST:

Robert Morse (Finch)
Bonnie Scott (Rosemary)
Charles Nelson Reilly (Frump)
Claudette Sutherland (Smitty)
Sammy Smith (Twimble/Womper)
Paul Reed (Bratt)
Rudy Vallee (Biggley)
Virginia Martin (Hedy)
Ruth Kobart (Miss Jones)

SONGS:
Act I
How To (Finch)
Happy to Keep His Dinner Warm (Rosemary)
Coffee Break (Frump, Smitty, ensemble)

The Company Way (Finch, Twimble, Bratt,
   ensemble)
Been a Long Day (Finch, Rosemary, Smitty,
   Biggley, Hedy, Frump)
Grand Old Ivy (Finch, Biggley)
Paris Original (Rosemary, Smitty, Miss Jones,
   secretaries)
Rosemary (Finch, Rosemary)
Finaletto (Finch, Rosemary, Frump)

Act II
Cinderella, Darling (Rosemary, Smitty,
   secretaries)
Love from a Heart of Gold (Biggley, Hedy)
I Believe in You (Finch, Frump, Bratt,
   ensemble)
The Yo Ho Ho (ensemble)
Brotherhood of Man (Finch, Biggley, Frump,
   Bratt, Womper, Miss Jones, ensemble)

THE HUMAN COMEDY (1984)

LIBRETTO BY: William Dumaresq; from the novel
   by William Saroyan
MUSIC BY: Galt MacDermot
PUBLISHED LIBRETTO: French, 1984
CONDENSATION: None
ANTHOLOGY: None
LICENSING AGENT: Samuel French
RECORDING: None
CAST: Large mixed cast

Described as an "oratorio" or "folk opera," this show is entirely sung. The musical styles include gospel, country, and blues. It is based on a 1943 nonmusical film script that was later published as a novel. The setting is a small California town during World War II. The warm and sentimental plot concerns a family and their young son who delivers telegrams, including those that contain "killed in action." There is no set and only chairs, tables, and minimal props are used. The cast members sit upstage, join in the choruses, and step forward as characters when required by the plot. The homey costumes should convey the "Norman Rockwell look" of the period. For the Broadway production, slides were used as backgrounds. Clive Barnes in the *New York Post* said it would make you "want to go out and buy War Bonds."

ORIGINAL CAST:

David Johnson (Trainman)
Josh Blake (Ulysses)
Bonnie Koloc (Mrs. Macauley)
Stephen Geoffreys (Homer)
Mary Elizabeth Mastrantonio (Bess)
Anne Marie Bobby (Helen)
Laurie Franks (Miss Hicks)
Rex Smith (Spangler)
Gordon Connell (Mr. Grogan)
Delores Hall (Beautiful Music)
Caroline Peyton (Mary)
Olga Merediz (Mexican Woman)
Don Kehr (Matthew/Marcus)
Christopher Edmonds (Thief)
Joe Kilinski (Toby)
Leata Galloway (Diana)

SONGS:
Act I
In a Little Town in California (company)
Hi Ya, Kid (Trainman, Ulysses)
We're a Little Family (Mrs. Macauley, Homer, Ulysses, Bess)
The Assyrians (Helen, Miss Hicks)
Noses (Homer)
You're a Little Young for the Job (Spangler, Homer)
I Can Carry a Tune (Homer)
Happy Birthday (Homer)
Happy Anniversary (Homer, Spangler, Mr. Grogan)
I Think the Kid Will Do (Mr. Grogan, Spangler)
Beautiful Music (Beautiful Music, company)
Coconut Cream Pie (Mr. Grogan, Spangler)
When I Am Lost (Homer, Beautiful Music, company)
I Said, Oh No (Bess, Mary, Mexican Woman)
Daddy Will Not Come Walking through the Door (Mrs. Macauley)
The Birds in the Sky (Bess)
Remember Always to Give (Mrs. Macauley)
Long Past Sunset (Matthew)

Don't Tell Me (Mary, Marcus, family, company)
The Fourth Telegram (Spangler, Mr. Grogan)
Give Me All the Money (Thief, Spangler)
Everything Is Changed (Homer, Mrs. Macauley)
The World Is Full of Loneliness (Mrs. Macauley)
Act II
How I Love Your Thingamajig (soldiers)
Everlasting (Toby)
An Orphan I Am (Toby)
I'll Tell You about My Family (Marcus)
I Wish I Were a Man (Mary)
Marcus, My Friend (Toby)
My Sister Bess (Marcus)
I've Known a Lot of Guys (Diana)
Diana (Spangler)
Dear Brother (Homer, Marcus)
The Birds in the Trees/A Lot of Men (Diana, Spangler)
Parting (Mrs. Macauley, company)
Mr. Grogan, Wake Up (Homer)
Hello, Doc (Spangler)
What Am I Supposed to Do? (Homer, Spangler)
Long Past Sunset (Mrs. Macauley, company)
I'm Home (Toby)
Somewhere, Someone (Bess)
I'll Always Love You (Mary, company)
Fathers and Mothers (and You and Me) (company)

I CAN GET IT FOR YOU WHOLESALE (1962)

BOOK BY: Jerome Weidman; based on his novel
MUSIC AND LYRICS BY: Harold Rome
PUBLISHED LIBRETTO: Random House, 1962
CONDENSATION: *New Complete Book of the American Musical Theater.* Ewen, David. Holt, 1970
ANTHOLOGY: None
PIANO-VOCAL SCORE: Chappell, 1963
LICENSING AGENT: Tams-Witmark
RECORDING: Columbia CSP AKOS 2180 (original cast)
CAST: 18 M; 13 F; singers, dancers

The time is 1937 in New York City. Harry quickly rises in the Seventh Avenue garment business by brashness, ruthlessness, and chicanery. His mother, who lives in the Bronx, helps him charm his friends. There are also a couple of girlfriends and an office secretary (a part that launched Barbra Streisand). The scenes include showrooms, a nightclub, homes, and offices. This was successfully revived in 1991 with a small cast and done in the round with almost no scenery or props. There is a bit of ethnic color, including a Bar Mitzvah at the beginning of Act II. One critic called this show "a semi-serious song-and-dancer."

ORIGINAL CAST:

Jack Kruschen (Pulvermacher)
Barbra Streisand (Miss Marmelstein)
Elliott Gould (Harry)
Marilyn Cooper (Ruthie)
Lillian Roth (Mrs. Bogen)
Sheree North (Martha)
Harold Lang (Teddy)
Ken Le Roy (Meyer)
Bambi Linn (Blanche)

SONGS:
Act I
I'm Not a Well Man (Pulvermacher, Miss Marmelstein)
The Way Things Are (Harry)
When Gemini Meets Capricorn (Harry, Ruthie)
Momma, Momma! (Harry, Mrs. Bogen)
The Sound of Money (Harry, Martha)
The Family Way (Mrs. Bogen, Ruthie, Blanche, Harry, Teddy, Meyer)
Too Soon (Mrs. Bogen)
Who Knows? (Ruthie, Harry)
Have I Told You Lately? (Meyer, Blanche)
Ballad of the Garment Trade (Miss Marmelstein, Mrs. Bogen, Ruthie, Blanche, Harry, Meyer, Teddy)

Act II
A Gift Today (company)
Miss Marmelstein (Miss Marmelstein)
The Sound of Money (reprise) (Harry, Meyer)
A Funny Thing Happened (Ruthie, Harry)

What's in It for Me? (Martha, Teddy)
What Are They Doing to Us Now? (Miss Marmelstein, company)
Eat a Little Something (Mrs. Bogen)

I CAN'T KEEP RUNNING IN PLACE (1981)

BOOK, MUSIC, AND LYRICS BY: Barbara Schottenfeld
PUBLISHED LIBRETTO: French, 1982
CONDENSATION: None
ANTHOLOGY: None
LICENSING AGENT: Samuel French
RECORDING: Painted Smiles PSCD 132 (original cast)
CAST: 7 F

Set in a loft in New York's Soho district, this is a feminist play with music. The theme is woman's need to change. Six contemporary women and a psychologist go through six sessions of a woman's assertiveness training workshop. Each of the women acts out a personal problem, including the psychologist who is going through the breakup of her marriage. There are some brief dance routines and twelve songs. For the off-Broadway production the small band was onstage (behind some potted plants).

ORIGINAL CAST:

Evalyn Baron (Alice)
Mary Donnet (Mandy)
Joy Franz (Eileen)
Bev Larson (Sherry)
Jennie Ventriss (Gwen)
Helen Gallagher (Beth)
Marcia Rodd (Michelle)

SONGS:
Act I
I'm Glad I'm Here (company)
Don't Say Yes If You Want to Say No (Michelle, company)
I Can't Keep Running in Place (Eileen)
I'm on My Own (Michelle)
More of Me to Love (Gwen, Alice)

I Live Alone (Beth)
I Can Count on You (Alice, company)

Act II
Penis Envy (Michelle, company)
Get the Answer Now (Sherry, company)
What If We— (Michelle)
Almosts, Maybes, and Perhapses (Beth)
Where Will I Be Next Wednesday Night?
  (company)

I DO! I DO! (1966)

BOOK AND LYRICS BY: Tom Jones; based on *The Fourposter* by Jan de Hartog
MUSIC BY: Harvey Schmidt
PUBLISHED LIBRETTO: None
CONDENSATION: *New Complete Book of the American Musical Theater.* Ewen, David. Holt, 1970
ANTHOLOGY: None
PIANO-VOCAL SCORE: Portfolio Music (Chappell), 1968
VOCAL SELECTIONS: Portfolio Music (Chappell), 1966
LICENSING AGENT: Music Theatre International
RECORDING: RCA 1128 CD (original cast)
CAST: 1 M; 1 F

The show, with a cast of two, begins with a wedding (and the bride tossing her bouquet to the audience). We then follow the couple through fifty years of matrimony as they raise their family, despite an occasional roving eye. The Broadway set consisted of a bed in center stage and a few graceful screens for walls. A few props and simple costumes carry the audience along through the years. There are nineteen songs including some vaudeville turns as well as some tender moments.

ORIGINAL CAST:

Mary Martin (Agnes)
Robert Preston (Michael)

SONGS:
Act I
All the Dearly Beloved (both)
Together Forever (both)
I Do! I Do! (both)

Good Night (both)
I Love My Wife (Michael)
Something Has Happened (Agnes)
My Cup Runneth Over (both)
Love Isn't Everything (both)
Nobody's Perfect (both)
A Well-Known Fact (Michael)
Flaming Agnes (Agnes)
The Honeymoon Is Over (both)

Act II
Where Are the Snows? (both)
When the Kids Get Married (both)
The Father of the Bride (Michael)
What Is a Woman? (Agnes)
Someone Needs Me (Agnes)
Roll Up the Ribbons (both)
This House (both)

I LOVE MY WIFE (1977)

BOOK AND LYRICS BY: Michael Stewart; from the play *Viens Chez Moi* by Luis Rego
MUSIC BY: Cy Coleman
PUBLISHED LIBRETTO: French, 1980
CONDENSATION: *Broadway Musicals Show by Show.* Green, Stanley. Hal Leonard Books, 1985
ANTHOLOGY: None
VOCAL SELECTIONS: Big Three (Notable Music), 1977
LICENSING AGENT: Samuel French
RECORDING: DRG CDRG 6109 CD (original cast)
CAST: 6 M; 2 F

The plot of this very contemporary musical set in Trenton, New Jersey, involves wife-swapping. But never fear, the group sex is mostly talk and each person winds up with his or her proper mate. In addition to the two couples, there are four musicians onstage. The musicians change costumes and occasionally play small parts, in addition to providing the music. This mildly sexy musical was quite popular and was one of several Broadway shows that switched to an all-black cast at one point in its run.

ORIGINAL CAST:

Lenny Baker (Alvin)
Joanna Gleason (Monica)
James Naughton (Wally)
John Miller (Harvey)
Ilene Graff (Cleo)
Joe Saulter (Quentin)
Ken Bichel (Norman)
Michael Mark (Stanley)
Michael Mark, Ken Bichel, John Miller, Joe
    Saulter (The Four Guys)

SONGS:
Act I
We're Still Friends (company)
Monica (Alvin, Monica, The Four Guys)
By Threes (Wally, Alvin, Harvey)
A Mover's Life (Alvin, The Four Guys)
Love Revolution (Cleo)
Someone Wonderful I Missed (Monica,
    Cleo)
Sexually Free (Alvin, Cleo, Wally)

Act II
Hey There, Good Times (Harvey, Stanley,
    Quentin, Norman)
Lovers on Christmas Eve (Monica, Wally,
    Norman)
Scream (Harvey, Stanley, Quentin, Norman)
Everybody Today Is Turning On (Alvin, Wally)
Married Couple Seeks Married Couple (Alvin,
    Cleo, Wally, Monica)
I Love My Wife (Alvin, Wally)

I MARRIED AN ANGEL (1938)

BOOK BY: Richard Rodgers and Lorenz Hart;
    adapted from the play by John Vaszary
MUSIC BY: Richard Rodgers
LYRICS BY: Lorenz Hart
PUBLISHED LIBRETTO: None
CONDENSATION: *New Complete Book of the
    American Musical Theater.* Ewen, David. Holt,
    1970
ANTHOLOGY: None
VOCAL SELECTIONS: *The Best of Rodgers and Hart.*
    Chappell, 1974
LICENSING AGENT: Rodgers and Hammerstein
    Theatre Library

RECORDING: AEI 002 CD (original cast)
CAST: Large mixed cast

An angel comes down to console an ideal-
istic Budapest banker, marries him, loses
her wings, and almost ruins his banking
business. Vera Zorina originally played the
angel and the original choreography was
by George Balanchine. The show features
some great Rodgers and Hart songs, including "At the Roxy Music Hall" and the title
tune. This show was described as "an imaginative, opulent and tuneful frolic." There
was a 1942 film version with Jeanette Mac-
Donald.

1986 NEW YORK CONCERT CAST:

Kurt Peterson (Willy)
Phyllis Newman (Peggy)
Lee Lobenhofer (Peter)
Virginia Seidel (Angel)
David Wasson (Harry)
Karen Ziemba (Anna)

SONGS:
Act I
Did You Ever Get Stung? (Willy, Peggy, Peter)
I Married an Angel (Willy, Angel)
The Modiste (Willy, Angel, ensemble)
I'll Tell the Man in the Street (Peggy, Harry)
How to Win Friends and Influence People
    (Anna, Peter, ensemble)

Act II
Spring Is Here (Willy, Peggy)
Angel without Wings (Angel, female
    ensemble)
A Twinkle in Your Eyes (Peggy, Angel)
At the Roxy Music Hall (Anna, ensemble)

I REMEMBER MAMA (1979)

BOOK BY: Thomas Meehan; based on the play by
    John Van Druten and stories by Kathryn Forbes
MUSIC BY: Richard Rodgers
LYRICS BY: Martin Charnin and Raymond Jessel
PUBLISHED LIBRETTO: None
CONDENSATION: None
ANTHOLOGY: None
VOCAL SELECTIONS: Remembra (MCA Music)

LICENSING AGENT: Rodgers and Hammerstein
   Theatre Library
RECORDINGS: Polydor 827 336-2 CD (studio cast);
   Musical Heritage Society MHS 512418H CD
   (studio cast)
CAST: Large mixed cast, including children

This well-remembered play, film, and TV series was Richard Rodgers' final Broadway
musical. The period is just before World
War I. The plot concerns a Norwegian immigrant in San Francisco who is married to
a ship's carpenter and is having a hard time
keeping her family fed and clothed. This
was a big, expensive, old-fashioned family
show that was upbeat and cheerful.

ORIGINAL CAST:

Liv Ullmann (Mama)
George Hearn (Papa)
Maureen Silliman (Katrin)
George S. Irving (Uncle Chris)
Armin Shimerman (Thorkelson)
Myvanwy Jenn (Dame Sybil)
Elizabeth Hubbard (Aunt Trina)
Dolores Wilson (Aunt Jenny)
Betty Ann Grove (Aunt Sigrid)

SONGS:
Act I
I Remember Mama (Katrin)
A Little Bit More (Mama, Papa, children)
A Writer Writes at Night (Mama, Katrin)
Where We Came From (company)
Ev'ry Day (Comes Something Beautiful)
   (Mama, company)
You Could Not Please Me More (Papa, Mama)
Uncle Chris (the aunts, Uncle Chris,
   Thorkelson)
Easy Come, Easy Go (Uncle Chris, ensemble)
It Is Not the End of the World (Mama, Papa,
   children)

Act II
Mama Always Makes It Better (children)
Lars, Lars (Mama)
Fair Trade (Dame Sybil, Mama, ensemble)
It's Going to Be Good to Be Gone (Uncle
   Chris)
I Don't Know How (Thorkelson, Aunt Trina)
Time (Mama)

I'D RATHER BE RIGHT (1937)

BOOK BY: George S. Kaufman and Moss Hart
MUSIC BY: Richard Rodgers
LYRICS BY: Lorenz Hart
PUBLISHED LIBRETTO: Random House, 1937
CONDENSATION: *New Complete Book of the
   American Musical Theater*. Ewen, David. Holt,
   1970
ANTHOLOGY: None
LICENSING AGENT: Rodgers and Hammerstein
   Theatre Library
RECORDING: None
CAST: 19 M; 6 F

Described as a daring and brilliant satire
on Roosevelt and the New Deal, the plot of
this musical concerns a young couple who
can't marry until the country's budget is
balanced! (The bridegroom's boss is beset
by taxation.) They meet the President of
the United States in Central Park, who finally decides he needs a third term to solve
the crisis. The only setting is in the park,
with the paths, benches, bridges, and the
New York skyline in the background.

ORIGINAL CAST:

Joy Hodges (Peggy)
Austin Marshall (Phil)
Mary Jane Walsh (Judge's Girl)
Joseph Macauley (Federal Theater Director)
George M. Cohan (President of the United
   States)
Georgie Tapps (Social Security Messenger)
Florenz Ames (James B. Maxwell)
Taylor Holmes (Secretary of the Treasury)

SONGS:
Act I
A Homogeneous Cabinet (ensemble)
Have You Met Miss Jones? (Peggy, Phil)
Take and Take and Take (Judge's girl,
   ensemble)
Spring in Milwaukee (Federal Theater
   Director)
A Little Bit of Constitutional Fun (Judge's Girl,
   ensemble)
Sweet Sixty-Five (Peggy, Phil)

We're Going to Balance the Budget
(President, company)

Act II

What It's All About (Social Security
Messenger, ensemble)
Labor Is the Thing (James B. Maxwell)
I'd Rather Be Right (Peggy, Phil, Judge's Girl,
President, ensemble)
Off the Record (President)
A Baby Bond (Secretary of the Treasury)

ILLYA DARLING (1967)

BOOK BY: Jules Dassin; based on the film *Never
on Sunday*
MUSIC BY: Manos Hadjidakis
LYRICS BY: Joe Darion
PUBLISHED LIBRETTO: None
CONDENSATION: *New Complete Book of the
American Musical Theater.* Ewen, David. Holt,
1970
ANTHOLOGY: None
LICENSING AGENT: Tams-Witmark
RECORDING: United Artists UAS 9901 (original
cast)
CAST: Large mixed cast

This musical was a vehicle for Melina Mercouri, who had starred in the original film
version. An American tourist in Greece
learns all about life from a wild assortment
of locals, and in particular a strumpet from
the seaport of Piraeus. The show features
energetic male folk dances and bouzouki
music. The very popular "Never on Sunday" theme from the film is included. This
is a big, Greek-flavored musical.

ORIGINAL CAST:

Orson Bean (Homer)
Nikos Kourkoulos (Tonio)
Titos Vandis (Yorgo)
Melina Mercouri (Illya)
Despo (Despo)
Rudy Bond (Captain)
Joe E. Marks (Vassily)
Harold Gary (Waiter)

SONGS:
Act I
Po, Po, Po (Homer, Tonio)
Zebekiko (Yorgo)
Piraeus, My Love (Illya, men)
Golden Land (Homer, ensemble)
Love, Love, Love (Illya)
I Think She Needs Me (Homer)
I'll Never Lay Down Any More (Despo)
After Love (Tonio)
Birthday Song (Tonio, Captain, men)
Medea Tango (Illya, men)
Illya Darling (Illya, Yorgo, ensemble)

Act II
Dear Mr. Schubert (Illya)
The Lesson (Illya, Homer)
Never on Sunday (Illya, ensemble)
Medea Tango (reprise) (Tonio)
Heaven Help the Sailors on a Night Like This
(ensemble)
Dance (Illya, Homer, Yorgo, Tonio, Captain,
Vassily, Waiter, ensemble)
Ya Chara (company)

I'M GETTING MY ACT TOGETHER AND TAKING IT ON THE ROAD (1978)

BOOK AND LYRICS BY: Gretchen Cryer
MUSIC BY: Nancy Ford
PUBLISHED LIBRETTO: French, 1980
CONDENSATION: *Broadway Musicals Show by Show.*
Green, Stanley. Hal Leonard Books, 1985
ANTHOLOGY: None
PIANO-VOCAL SCORE: Fiddleback Music, 1978
LICENSING AGENT: Samuel French
RECORDING: Columbia CSP S14885 (original cast)
CAST: 6 M; 4 F

This musical deals with complex feminist questions. The central plot concerns
Heather, a thirty-nine-year-old performer
and songwriter who is launching her comeback act. Her manager wants her to continue in her old image, but Heather has
more progressive ideas. It all takes place
as she rehearses in a club. This is a show

of the 1970s and was a very popular off-Broadway hit. The score was variously described as one of pleasant tunes and sweet rock music.

ORIGINAL CAST:

Gretchen Cryer (Heather)
Margot Rose (Alice)
Betty Aberlin (Cheryl)
James Mellon (Jake)

SONGS:
(performed without intermission)
Natural High (Heather, Alice, Cheryl, band)
Smile (Heather, Jake, Cheryl, Alice, band)
In a Simple Way I Love You (Heather, band)
Miss America (Heather, Alice, Cheryl)
Strong Woman Number (Alice, Heather, Cheryl)
Dear Tom (Heather)
Old Friend (Heather)
In a Simple Way I Love You (reprise) (Jake)
Put in a Package and Sold (Heather, Alice, Cheryl)
If Only Things Were Different (Jake)
Feel the Love (company)
Lonely Lady (Heather)
Happy Birthday (Heather, band)

IN TROUSERS (1979)

MUSIC AND LYRICS BY: William Finn
PUBLISHED LIBRETTO: French
ANTHOLOGY: *The Marvin Songs.* Fireside Theatre Publications
CONDENSATION: None
LICENSING AGENT: Samuel French
RECORDING: Original Cast OC 7915 (original cast)
CAST: 1 M; 3 F

In the first of the Marvin trilogy of musicals, we see Marvin as a married man on the verge of poking his head out of the closet. Whenever things get too hot for the older Marvin, he reverts back to himself at age fourteen. There are a series of numbers that demonstrate Marvin's most embarrassing moments with girls. His high-

school sweetheart, his teacher, and his wife are all involved in his struggle to find his sexual self. As with *March of the Falsettos* and *Falsettoland*, this is staged simply and is nonstop musically.

ORIGINAL CAST:

Chip Zien (Marvin)
Alison Fraser (Wife)
Joanna Green (High-School Sweetheart)
Mary Testa (Miss Goldberg)

SONGS
(performed without intermission)
Marvin's Giddy Seizures (Marvin, ladies)
How the Body Falls Apart (ladies)
Your Lips and Me (Wife)
My High-School Sweetheart (cast)
Set Those Sails (Miss Goldberg, ladies)
My Chance to Survive the Night (Marvin)
I Am Wearing a Hat (cast)
How Marvin Eats His Breakfast (Marvin, ladies)
A Breakfast Over Sugar (Marvin, Wife)
Whizzer Going Down (Marvin, ladies)
High School Ladies at 5 o'Clock (High-School Sweetheart, ladies)
The Rape of Miss Goldberg by Marvin (Marvin, Miss Goldberg)
The Nausea before the Game (Marvin, ladies)
Love Me for What I Am (Wife)
How America Got Its Name (Marvin)
Marvin Takes a Victory Shower (cast)
Another Sleepless Night (cast)
In Trousers (Marvin, ladies)

INTO THE WOODS (1987)

BOOK BY: James Lapine
MUSIC AND LYRICS BY: Stephen Sondheim
PUBLISHED LIBRETTO: Theatre Communications Group/Crown, 1987
CONDENSATION: *The Theatre Year Book and Best Plays of 1987–1988.* Otis L. Guernsey, Jr., ed. Applause Books, 1988
ANTHOLOGY: None
PIANO-VOCAL SCORE: Warner Bros. Music, 1989
VOCAL SELECTIONS: Warner Bros. Music, 1988

LICENSING AGENT: Music Theatre International
RECORDING: RCA 6796-2 RC CD (original cast)
CAST: 7 M; 10 F

Called an adult morality tale for the modern era, this musical explores what happened to various fairy-tale characters after they "lived happily ever after." Act I concerns Little Red Riding Hood, Cinderella, and Jack (of the beanstalk) solving their problems. Act II carries on as everything seems to go wrong because that happy ending was achieved by lying, cheating, and murder. "All fairy tales are steps to maturity," says Sondheim. Complicated sets, costumes, and, most of all, the Sondheim songs make this a difficult show to stage.

ORIGINAL CAST:

Robert Westenberg (Wolf/Cinderella's Prince)
Danielle Ferland (Little Red Riding Hood)
Ben Wright (Jack)
Joanna Gleason (Baker's Wife)
Chuck Wagner (Rapunzel's Prince)
Chip Zien (Baker)
Bernadette Peters (Witch)
Merle Louise (Cinderella's Mother)
Kim Crosby (Cinderella)
Tom Aldredge (Narrator/Mysterious Man)

SONGS:
Act I
Into the Woods (company)
Hello, Little Girl (Wolf, Little Red Riding Hood)
I Guess This Is Good-bye (Jack)
Maybe They're Magic (Baker's Wife)
I Know Things Now (Little Red Riding Hood)
First Midnight (company)
Giants in the Sky (Jack)
Agony (Cinderella's Prince, Rapunzel's Prince)
It Takes Two (Baker, Baker's Wife)
Second Midnight (company)
Stay with Me (Witch)
On the Steps of the Palace (Cinderella)
So Happy (Cinderella, Cinderella's Prince, Baker's Wife, Cinderella's Mother)
Ever After (Narrator, company)

Act II
Lament (Witch)
Any Moment (Cinderella's Prince, Baker's Wife)
Moments in the Woods (Baker's Wife)
Your Fault (Jack, Baker, Witch, Cinderella, Little Red Riding Hood)
Boom Crunch! (Witch)
No More (Baker, Mysterious Man)
No One Is Alone (Cinderella, Little Red Riding Hood, Baker, Jack)

IRENE (1919)

BOOK BY: Hugh Wheeler and Joseph Stein; from an adaption by Harry Rigby; based on the play by James Montgomery
MUSIC BY: Harry Tierney
LYRICS BY: Joseph McCarthy; additional lyrics and music by Charles Gaynor and Otis Clements
PUBLISHED LIBRETTO: None
CONDENSATION: *Ganzl's Book of the Musical Theatre.* Ganzl, Kurt. Schirmer (Macmillan), 1989
ANTHOLOGY: None
VOCAL SELECTIONS: Big Three, 1973
LICENSING AGENT: Tams-Witmark
RECORDING: Sony SK 32266 CD (1973 revival cast)
CAST: Large mixed cast

The original musical was considerably revised for its 1973 Broadway revival with Debbie Reynolds. Irene is a piano tuner. At a wealthy home where she is working, she is spotted by a clothes designer who asks her to become a model. Naturally she falls in love with the heir to a Long Island fortune. The designer ends up with Irene's Irish mother. This is a big musical set in 1919 with lavish costumes and a large cast. The dances include tango, tap, soft-shoe, and an Irish jig. This is a family show.

1973 REVIVAL CAST:

Debbie Reynolds (Irene)
Ruth Warrick (Mrs. Marshall)
George S. Irving (Madame Lucy)
Carmen Alvarez (Helen)

Janie Sell (Jane)
Patsy Kelly (Mrs. O'Dare)
Ted Pugh (Ozzie)
Monte Markham (Donald)

SONGS:
(including some interpolated numbers)
Act I
The World Must Be Bigger than an Avenue
    (Irene)
The Family Tree (Mrs. Marshall, debutantes)
Alice Blue Gown (Irene)
They Go Wild, Simply Wild, over Me (Madame
    Lucy, debutantes)
An Irish Girl (Irene, company)
Stepping on Butterflies (Madame Lucy, Irene,
    Helen, Jane)
Mother Angel Darling (Irene, Mrs. O'Dare)
The Riviera Rage (Irene, company)

Act II
The Last Part of Every Party (company)
We're Getting Away with It (Madame Lucy,
    Helen, Jane, Ozzie)
Irene (Irene, company)
The Great Lover Tango (Donald, Helen,
    Jane)
You Made Me Love You (Irene, Donald)
    Reprise (Madame Lucy, Mrs. O'Dare)

IRMA LA DOUCE (1960)

ORIGINAL BOOK AND LYRICS BY: Alexandre
    Breffort; English book and lyrics by Julian
    More, David Heneker, and Monty Norman
MUSIC BY: Marguerite Monnot
PUBLISHED LIBRETTO: None
CONDENSATION: *Ganzl's Book of the Musical
    Theatre.* Ganzl, Kurt. Schirmer (Macmillan),
    1989
ANTHOLOGY: None
LICENSING AGENT: Tams-Witmark
RECORDING: Sony SK 48018 CD (original cast)
CAST: 15 M; 1 F; singers, dancers

Irma is a streetwalker in modern-day Paris.
A young law student falls in love with her

and, to keep other men away, masquerades as an elderly gentleman who pays her
10,000 francs a day. This show started out
in Paris (the music is by the composer who
wrote many of Edith Piaf's hits) and then
became a long-run success in London before coming to Broadway. *Irma la Douce* is a
dancing show with accordion music part of
the atmosphere. There was a film version
with the background music from the score,
but no vocals! One critic claims that this
tale of French prostitution could offend no
one, but another critic warned it was not
for the prudish.

ORIGINAL CAST:

Clive Revill (Bob)
Elizabeth Seal (Irma)
Keith Michell (Nestor)
George S. Irving (Police Inspector)
Fred Gwynne (Polyte)
Rudy Tronto (Tax Inspector)
George Del Monte (Bougne)

SONGS:
Act I
Valse Milieu (Bob)
Sons of France (Polyte, Police Inspector,
    men)
The Bridge of Caulaincourt (Irma, Nestor)
Our Language of Love (Irma, Nestor)
She's Got the Lot (Police Inspector, men)
Dis-donc (Irma)
Le Grisbi Is le Root of le Evil in Men (Bob,
    Nestor, men)
Wreck of a Mec (Nestor)
That's a Crime (Bob, Nestor, men)

Act II
From a Prison Cell (Nestor, men)
Irma-la-Douce (Irma)
There Is Only One Paris for That (Nestor,
    company)
The Freedom of the Seas (Nestor, company)
But (Nestor, Police Inspector, Tax Inspector,
    Bougne, Polyte)
Christmas Child (company)

IS THERE LIFE AFTER HIGH SCHOOL? (1982)

BOOK BY: Jeffrey Kindley; suggested by the book
    by Ralph Keyes
MUSIC AND LYRICS BY: Craig Carnelia
PUBLISHED LIBRETTO: French
CONDENSATION: None
ANTHOLOGY: None
LICENSING AGENT: Samuel French
RECORDING: Original Cast OC 902 CD (original
    cast)
CAST: 5 M; 4 F

Described as gentle and low-key, this musical concerns high-school days as we remember them—how high school affected us and is still with us. It is not really a play, but a revue of song, anecdotes, monologues, and vignettes. The cast not only portrays the characters as they were in high school but as they are today. The set for the New York production was multilevel and functioned as the gym, locker rooms, and other school areas. The costumes were primarily street clothes with a suggestion of band uniforms and other high-school modes. For an added touch of nostalgia ring a bell when intermission time is over.

ORIGINAL CAST:

Raymond Baker	Cynthia Carle
Alma Cuervo	Sandy Faison
Harry Groener	Philip Hoffman
David Patrick Kelly	Maureen Silliman
James Widdoes	

SONGS:
Act I
The Kid Inside (company)
Things I Learned in High School
    (Groener)
Second Thoughts (Baker, Faison, Kelly,
    Silliman, Widdoes)
Nothing Really Happened (Cuervo)
Beer (Baker, Groener, Kelly)

For Them (Hoffman, company)
Diary of a Homecoming Queen (Silliman)

Act II
Thousands of Trumpets (Widdoes, company)
Reunion (company)
High School All Over Again (Kelly)
Fran and Janie (Faison, Silliman)
I'm Glad You Didn't Know Me (Carle,
    Hoffman)

IT'S A BIRD IT'S A PLANE IT'S SUPERMAN (1966)

BOOK BY: David Newman and Robert Benton;
    based on the comic strip *Superman*
MUSIC BY: Charles Strouse
LYRICS BY: Lee Adams
PUBLISHED LIBRETTO: None
CONDENSATION: *The Best Plays of 1965–1966*. Otis
    L. Guernsey, Jr., ed. Dodd, Mead, 1966
ANTHOLOGY: None
VOCAL SELECTIONS: Big Three (Morris, 1966)
LICENSING AGENT: Tams-Witmark
RECORDING: Sony SK 48207 CD (original cast)
CAST: Large mixed cast

Superman is the familiar hero of this tale. Other characters include reporter Lois Lane and the mad atomic scientist Abner Sedgwick, who is out to put an end to Superman. There are also a miserable newspaper gossip columnist named Max Mencken and some villainous Chinese acrobats. This big musical was done in a "pop art" style that was fashionable in the 1960s. Superman flies about the stage a la Peter Pan. There are no messages, just comic-strip adventure. The whole show is a parody with energetic dances and some spectacular effects.

ORIGINAL CAST:

Bob Holiday (Superman/Clark Kent)
Jack Cassidy (Max)
Patricia Marand (Lois)
Don Chastain (Jim)

Michael O'Sullivan (Abner)
Linda Lavin (Sydney)

SONGS:
Act I
Doing Good (Superman)
We Need Him (Max, Lois, Clark,
    company)
It's Superman (Lois)
We Don't Matter at All (Jim, Lois)
Revenge (Abner)
The Woman for the Man (Max)
You've Got Possibilities (Sydney)
What I've Always Wanted (Lois)
Everything's Easy When You Know How
    (Chinese acrobats)
It's Super Nice (company)

Act II
So Long, Big Guy (Max)
The Strongest Man in the World
   (Superman)
Ooh, Do You Love You! (Sydney)
You've Got What I Need (Max, Abner)
I'm Not Finished Yet (Lois)
Pow! Bam! Zonk! (Superman, Chinese
    acrobats)

IT'S SO NICE TO BE CIVILIZED
(1980)

BOOK, MUSIC, AND LYRICS BY: Micki Grant
PUBLISHED LIBRETTO: French, 1982
CONDENSATION: None
ANTHOLOGY: None
LICENSING AGENT: Samuel French
RECORDING: None
CAST: 4 M; 6 F; singers, dancers

Various vignettes of life with a message
of brotherhood in a poor urban neighborhood on "Sweetbitter Street" make up the
plot of this musical. The cast is primarily black. Some of the characters include a
cardshark who sometimes serves as a narrator, an elderly matriarch who still likes
to kick up her heels, a disco owner, and
a white social worker who is trying to
get the street kids to paint a mural. For
the Broadway production slide projections
of cityscapes were the primary scenery.
The music is contemporary and includes
gospel.

ORIGINAL CAST:

Obba Babatunde (Sharky)
Vivian Reed (Mollie)
Larry Stewart (Larry)
Vickie D. Chappell (Sissy)
Carol Lynn Maillard (Luanne)
Mabel King (Grandma)
Stephen Pender (Mr. Anderson)
Dan Strayhorn (Blade)
Eugene Edwards (Reverend Williams)

SONGS:
Act I
Step into My World (ensemble)
Keep Your Eye on the Red (Sharky)
Wake-Up, Sun (Sharky, Mollie)
Subway Rider (ensemble)
God Help Us (Larry, Luanne)
Who's Going to Teach the Children?
    (Grandma)
Out on the Street (ensemble)
Welcome, Mr. Anderson (Blade, gang)
Why Can't Me and You? (Mr. Anderson)
    Reprise (Sissy, Mr. Anderson)
When I Rise (Reverend Williams)
The World Keeps Going Round (Mollie,
    ensemble)

Act II
Antiquity (ensemble)
I've Still Got My Bite (Grandma)
Look at Us (Larry, Luanne)
The American Dream (Mr. Anderson)
Bright Lights (Mollie)
Step into My World (reprise) (Sharky,
    Mollie)
It's So Nice to Be Civilized (Mr. Anderson,
    Sissy, gang)
Like a Lady (Mollie)
Pass a Little Love Around (ensemble)

JACQUES BREL IS ALIVE AND WELL AND LIVING IN PARIS (1968)

MUSIC BY: Jacques Brel
PRODUCTION, CONCEPTION, ENGLISH LYRICS, AND ADDITIONAL MATERIAL BY: Eric Blau and Mort Shuman; based on lyrics and commentary by Jacques Brel
PUBLISHED LIBRETTO: Dutton, 1971
CONDENSATION: None
ANTHOLOGY: None
VOCAL SELECTIONS: Big Three, 1972
LICENSING AGENT: Music Theatre International
RECORDING: Columbia CGK 40817 CD (original cast)
CAST: 3 M; 1 F

This very popular show is made up of twenty-four songs sung by four performers. The songs are by the late Belgian composer and performer and have been translated into English. There are no sets. This cabaret show has proved extremely popular over the years and was elaborately filmed in 1975. The songs describe and celebrate the struggles of Paris lowlife and the bustle of the streets. They have a lot to do with death, but they are mainly about love. Dramatic interpretations are essential.

ORIGINAL CAST:

Shawn Elliott   Mort Shuman
Elly Stone   Alice Whitfield

SONGS:
Act I
Marathon (company)
Alone (Elliott)
Madeleine (company)
I Loved (Stone)
Mathilde (Shuman)
Bachelor's Dance (Elliott)
Timid Frieda (Whitfield, company)
My Death (Stone, company)
Jackie (Shuman)
Girls and Dogs (Elliott, Whitfield)
Desperate Ones (company)
Sons of . . . (Stone)
Amsterdam (Shuman, company)

Act II
The Bulls (Elliott, company)
Old Folks (Stone, company)
Marieke (Stone, company)
Brussels (Whitfield, company)
Fanette (Elliott)
Funeral Tango (Shuman)
Middle Class (Shuman, Elliott)
You're Not Alone (Stone)
Next (Shuman, company)
Carousel (Stone, company)
If We Only Have Love (company)

JAMAICA (1957)

BOOK AND LYRICS BY: E. Y. Harburg
MUSIC BY: Harold Arlen
PUBLISHED LIBRETTO: None
CONDENSATION: *New Complete Book of the American Musical Theater.* Ewen, David. Holt, 1970
ANTHOLOGY: None
VOCAL SELECTIONS: Morris, 1963
LICENSING AGENT: Tams-Witmark
RECORDING: RCA LOC 1036 (original cast) .
CAST: 11 M; 6 F; chorus

The plot revolves around Savannah, a Caribbean island girl who wants to go to New York. "Push de Button" is how she describes life there, and that song is still sung by this show's star, Lena Horne. But her fisherman fiance doesn't want her to go. This big, lush Broadway musical has lots of tropical song and dance costumed in the hot colors of the Caribbean. This show was described as buoyant, spirited, and wholesome.

ORIGINAL CAST:

Ricardo Montalban (Koli)
Augustine Rios (Quico)
Lena Horne (Savannah)
Adelaide Hall (Grandma Obeah)
Josephine Premice (Ginger)
Ossie Davis (Cicero)
Hugh Dilworth (Hucklebuck)
Joe Adams (Joe)

SONGS:

Act I

Savannah (Koli, men)

Savannah's Wedding Day (Joe, Hucklebuck, Grandma Obeah, Quico, chorus)

Pretty to Walk With (Savannah, chorus)

Push de Button (Savannah, chorus)

Incompatibility (Koli, Quico, Joe, Hucklebuck, chorus)

Little Biscuit (Cicero, Ginger)

Cocoanut Sweet (Savannah)

Pity the Sunset (Savannah, Koli)

Yankee Dollar (Ginger, chorus)

What Good Does It Do? (Koli, Cicero, Quico)

Monkey in the Mango Tree (Koli, men)

Take It Slow, Joe (Savannah)

Ain't It the Truth (Savannah)

Act II

Leave the Atom Alone (Ginger, women)

For Every Fish (Grandma Obeah, chorus)

I Don't Think I'll End It All Today (Savannah, Koli, chorus)

Napoleon (Savannah)

JELLY'S LAST JAM (1992)

BOOK BY: George C. Wolfe
MUSIC BY: Jelly Roll Morton
LYRICS BY: Susan Birkenhead
PUBLISHED LIBRETTO: None
CONDENSATION: None
ANTHOLOGY: None
LICENSING AGENT: Not yet available
RECORDING: Mercury 314-510846-2 CD (original cast)
CAST: Large mixed cast

The legendary jazz composer Jelly Roll Morton was born in the Creole gentry of New Orleans in 1891. His music integrated the sounds of ragtime, blues, African rhythms, and French opera. While this musical follows his life story, song hits, and love life until his death in 1941, it is also an attempt to show what it was like to be black during this time. There is a lot of strong language and song and dance from the primarily black cast, with sensational tap-dancing routines by the star.

ORIGINAL CAST:

Gregory Hines (Jelly)

Savion Glover (Young Jelly)

Mary Bond Davis (Miss Mamie)

Ruben Santiago-Hudson (Buddy)

Ann Duquesnay (Gran Mimi)

Stanley Warner Mathis (Jack)

Keith David (Chimney Man)

Tonya Pinkins (Anita)

SONGS:

Act I

Jelly's Jam (ensemble)

In My Day (Jelly, ensemble)

The Creole Way (Young Jelly, ensemble)

The Whole World's Waitin' to Sing Your Song (Jelly, Young Jelly, ensemble)

Michigan Water (Miss Mamie, Buddy, ensemble)

The Banishment (Gran Mimi, Young Jelly, Jelly)

Somethin' More (Jack, Jelly, Chimney Man, ensemble)

That's How You Jazz (Jelly, ensemble)

The Chicago Strut (Chimney Man)

Play the Music for Me (Anita)

Lovin' Is a Lowdown Blues (girls)

Dr. Jazz (Jelly, ensemble)

Act II

Good Ole New York (Chimney Man, Jelly, ensemble)

Too Late, Daddy (Jelly, ensemble)

That's the Way We Do Things in New York (Jelly, ensemble)

The Last Chance Blues (Anita, Jelly)

Boy Pretty Boy (Gran Mimi)

Creole Boy (Jelly)

JERRY'S GIRLS (1981)

MUSIC AND LYRICS BY: Jerry Herman; based on a concept by Jerry Herman and Larry Alford
PUBLISHED LIBRETTO: French
CONDENSATION: None
ANTHOLOGY: None

PIANO-VOCAL SCORE: Hal Leonard, 1982
LICENSING AGENT: Samuel French
RECORDING: Polydor 820 207-2 CD (studio cast)
CAST: 3 F; female chorus (or cabaret version with
4 F)

This is a revue made up of the songs of
Jerry Herman. The cast of four females
in the original New York cabaret production was accompanied by a female three-
piece combo. But this is not a feminist revue, just Broadway show tunes arranged
as medleys (optimist, vaudeville, movies,
etc.) and sung singularly. The songs come
from *Mame, Hello, Dolly!, Milk and Honey,
Mack and Mabel, The Grand Tour, Dear
World, Hollywood/Ukraine, La Cage*, and *Parade*. This can be simply staged with only
suggestions of costume change.

ORIGINAL CAST:

Dorothy Loudon   Leslie Uggams
Chita Rivera

This revue is made up of thirty-seven musical selections sung with one intermission.

JESUS CHRIST SUPERSTAR (1971)

MUSIC BY: Andrew Lloyd Webber
LYRICS BY: Tim Rice
PUBLISHED LIBRETTO: (see VOCAL SELECTIONS
listed below)
CONDENSATION: *Ganzl's Book of the Musical
Theatre*. Ganzl, Kurt. Schirmer (Macmillan),
1989
ANTHOLOGY: *Great Rock Musicals*. Stanley
Richards, ed. Stein and Day, 1979
VOCAL SELECTIONS: Leeds Music, 1973 (MCA
Music); includes libretto
LICENSING AGENT: Music Theatre International
RECORDINGS: MCA 7-1503 (original cast); RCA
09026 61435-2 CD (1992 London cast)
CAST: Large mixed cast

The last seven days in the life of Jesus are
portrayed in this musical. Passion plays
have been around since the Middle Ages,
and this is simply a contemporary, or "rock

opera," version. This was originally a lavish Broadway musical that later returned
in a scaled-down version after touring most
major cities. The critics found it a serious
work with sincere intentions told entirely
in song, the most familiar one being "I Don't
Know How to Love Him." The show was
staged on a basically bare, raked stage with
drapes and platform sets lowered from the
flies. There was also a film version.

ORIGINAL CAST:

Ben Vereen (Judas)
Jeff Fenholt (Jesus)
Yvonne Elliman (Mary)
Bob Bingham (Caiaphas)
Phil Jethro (Annas)
Barry Dennen (Pilate)
Michael Jason (Peter)
Paul Ainsley (Herod)
Peter Schlosser (Old Man)
Linda Rios (Maid)
Dennis Buckley (Simon)

SONGS:
Act I
Heaven on Their Minds (Judas)
What's the Buzz? (Jesus, Mary, ensemble)
Strange Thing Mystifying (Judas, Jesus,
ensemble)
Everything's Alright (Mary, Judas, Jesus,
ensemble)
This Jesus Must Die (Caiaphas, Annas,
ensemble)
Hosanna (Caiaphas, Jesus, company)
Simon Zealotes (Simon, company)
Poor Jerusalem (Jesus)
Pilate's Dream (Pilate)
The Temple (Jesus, company)
I Don't Know How to Love Him (Mary, Jesus)
Damned for All Times (Judas, Annas,
Caiaphas, priests)

Act II
The Last Supper (Jesus, Judas, ensemble)
Gethsemane (Jesus)
The Arrest (Peter, Jesus, Caiaphas, Annas,
ensemble)
Peter's Denial (Maid, Peter, Mary, Old Man)
Pilate and Christ (Pilate, Jesus, company)

King Herod's Song (Herod)
Could We Start Again, Please? (Mary, Peter)
Judas' Death (Judas, Annas, Caiaphas)
Trial before Pilate (Pilate, Jesus, Caiaphas, ensemble)
Superstar (Judas, company)
The Crucifixion (Jesus, company)

JO (1964)

BOOK AND LYRICS BY: Don Parks and William Dyer; based on *Little Women* by Louisa May Alcott
MUSIC BY: William Dyer
PUBLISHED LIBRETTO: Dramatists Play Service, 1964
CONDENSATION: None
ANTHOLOGY: None
VOCAL SELECTIONS: Sunbeam (Valando)
LICENSING AGENT: Dramatists Play Service
RECORDING: None
CAST: 10M; 12F (including 3 girls)

This is the famous story of four girls growing up in Harmony, Massachusetts, during the Civil War. The off-Broadway production was noted for its picture-book sets edged in red velvet and gilt frames. The costumes were described as valentines made of ribbons and lace. This was considered an ideal family show and extra matinee performances were given for children. Twin pianos provided the accompaniment.

ORIGINAL CAST:

Karin Wolfe (Jo)
Susan Browning (Meg)
Judith McCauley (Beth)
April Shawhan (Amy)
Joy Hodges (Marmee)
Don Stewart (Laurie)
Lowell Harris (John)
Joyce Lynn (Hannah)
Paul Blake (Freddie)
Bernard F. Wurger (Professor)
Mimi Randolph (Aunt Marsh)

SONGS:
Act I
Harmony, Mass. (ensemble)
Deep in the Bosom of the Family (Jo, Meg, Beth, Amy)
Hurry Home (Marmee, Meg, Jo, Beth, Amy)
Let's Be Elegant or Die! (Meg, Jo, Beth, Amy)
Castles in the Air (Laurie)
Friendly Polka (Jo, Laurie, guests)
Time Will Be (John)
What a Long Cold Winter! (Amy, Beth, Hannah)
Moods (Jo, Laurie)
Afraid to Fall in love (Jo)
A Wedding! A Wedding! (Beth, Amy, Meg, ensemble)
I Like (Laurie)

Act II
Genius Burns (Jo, Freddie)
If You Find a True Love (Professor, children)
Nice as Any Man Can Be (Jo)
More than Friends (Laurie)
Taking the Cure (Amy, Aunt March, Laurie, ensemble)

JOHNNY JOHNSON (1936)

BOOK AND LYRICS BY: Paul Green
MUSIC BY: Kurt Weill
PUBLISHED LIBRETTO (REVISED AND REWRITTEN): French, 1971
CONDENSATION: *New Complete Book of the American Musical Theater*. Ewen, David. Holt, 1970
ANTHOLOGY: *Twenty Best Plays of the Modern American Theatre*. John Gassner, ed. Crown, 1939
MUSIC PUBLISHER: Chappell
LICENSING AGENT: Samuel French
RECORDING: Polydor 831 384-2 CD (studio cast)
CAST: Large mixed cast

Despite the doubling up by the male cast members, this was one of the most expensive undertakings of the Group Theatre in the 1930s. At the original production, handbills proclaiming "this is a play with songs, not a musical show" were handed out, so afraid were they that it would be considered light and frivolous. The plot concerns a young southern boy who enlists during World War I to end all wars. He is wounded in France, sent back home to a mental hospital, and eventually becomes a peddler of toys. Pacifist viewpoints are expressed in satire and song. The Kurt Weill score was described as haunting. The later off-Broadway production used slides as projected backgrounds.

1956 REVIVAL CAST:

Sidney Armus (Mayor/Commander-in-Chief)
Rosemary O'Reilly (Minny Belle)
Maurice Edwards (Grandpa Joe)
James Broderick (Johnny)
Alice Winston (Aggie)
Logan Ramsey (Captain Valentine)
Betty Kent (The Goddess)
Robert Minford (British Sergeant)
Gerald Garrigan (Private Harwood)
Elizabeth Parrish (French Nurse)
Gene Saks (Dr. Mahodan)

SONGS:
Act I
Over in Europe (Mayor, ensemble)
Democracy's Call (Minny Belle, ensemble)
The Battle of San Juan Hill (Grandpa Joe,
   ensemble)
Aggie's Song (Aggie)
Oh Heart of Love (Minny Belle)
Captain Valentine's Song (Captain Valentine)
The Song of the Goddess (The Goddess)
The Tea Song (British Sergeant, men)
The Rio Grande (Private Harwood)
Song of the Guns (ensemble)

Act II
Mon Ami, My Friend (French Nurse)
The Allied High Command
   (Commander-in-Chief, staff)
The Laughing Generals (ensemble)
Psychiatry Song (Dr. Mahodan)
The Asylum Chorus (ensemble)
A Hymn to Peace (ensemble)
Johnny's Song (Johnny)

JOSEPH AND THE AMAZING TECHNICOLOR DREAMCOAT (1982)

MUSIC BY: Andrew Lloyd Webber
LYRICS BY: Tim Rice; from the biblical story of
   Joseph and his brethren
PUBLISHED LIBRETTO: Holt, Rinehart and Winston,
   1982
CONDENSATION: *Ganzl's Book of the Musical Thea-
   tre*. Ganzl, Kurt. Schirmer (Macmillan), 1989
ANTHOLOGY: None
PIANO-VOCAL SCORE: Sevenoaks, Kent, Novello,
   1975
VOCAL SELECTIONS: Theodore Presser (Novello,
   1982); Hal Leonard
LICENSING AGENT: Music Theatre International
RECORDING: Chrysalis F2 21387 CD (original
   Broadway cast)
CAST: Large mixed cast

This musical version of the biblical story predates the hit show *Jesus Christ Superstar. Joseph* . . . is the first show Webber and Rice composed back in 1967. It is perhaps the most performed musical in schools and universities although it was not performed on Broadway until 1982 when it transferred from off-Broadway. The latest version runs ninety minutes—entirely sung. Some numbers are done in country-western style, while Pharaoh's number is strictly Elvis style. This musical appeals to young people.

ORIGINAL CAST:

Cleavon Little (Narrator)
Tony Hoty (Jacob)
David Carroll (Joseph)
Stuart Pankin (Reuben)
Terry Eno (Potiphar)
Virginia Martin (Mrs. Potiphar)
Kurt Yahjian (Baker)
David Patrick Kelly (Butler)
Jesse Pearson (Pharaoh)

SONGS:
Act I
Jacob and Sons/Joseph's Coat (Narrator,
   Jacob, Joseph, choir)

Joseph's Dreams (Narrator, Joseph, brothers)
Poor, Poor Joseph (Narrator, brothers, choir)
One More Angel in Heaven (Narrator,
   brothers, girl)
Potiphar (Narrator, Joseph, Potiphar, Mrs.
   Potiphar, chorus)
Close Every Door (Joseph, choir)
Go, Go, Go, Joseph (Narrator, Butler, Baker,
   Joseph, chorus)

Act II
Pharaoh's Story (Narrator, choir)
Poor Poor Pharaoh/Song of the King
   (Narrator, Pharaoh, chorus)
Pharaoh's Dreams Explained (Joseph, chorus)
Stone the Crows (Narrator, Pharaoh, Joseph,
   chorus)
Those Canaan Days (Reuben, brothers)
The Brothers Came to Egypt/Grovel, Grovel
   (Narrator, Joseph, brothers, chorus)
Who's the Thief? (Joseph, brothers, choir)
Benjamin Calypso (brothers)
Joseph All the Time (Narrator, Joseph,
   brothers, choir)
Jacob in Egypt (Narrator, choir, chorus)
Any Dream Will Do (Joseph, choir, chorus)

JUST SO (1985)

BOOK BY: Mark S. Germain; based on *Just So
   Stories* by Rudyard Kipling
MUSIC BY: Doug Katsaros
LYRICS BY: David Zippel
PUBLISHED LIBRETTO: French
CONDENSATION: None
ANTHOLOGY: None
LICENSING AGENT: Samuel French
RECORDING: None
CAST: 5 M; 2 F

Some of the characters in this family show
include a bespectacled giraffe, a haughty
and lazy camel, a practical-joking leopard,
and a humble primate. What is going on?
It is all about the world's first day. In a colorful jungle setting the "Eldest Magician"
assembles certain creatures that have not
yet acquired their distinctive characteristics and a human who is unsure of his role.

The costumes of the animals are suggested,
rather than realistic, in this show children
will surely enjoy.

ORIGINAL CAST:
Andre de Shields (Eldest Magician/
   Djinn/Parsee man/Kolokolo Bird)
Keith Curran (Giraffe)
Teresa Burrell (Camel)
Tom Robbins (Rhino)
Tina Johnson (Elephant Child)
Tico Wells (Leopard)
Jason Graae (Man)

SONGS:
Act I
Just So (Eldest Magician, animals)
The Whole World Revolves around You
   (Eldest Magician, animals, Man)
Arm in Arm in Harmony (Man, animals)
Chill Out! (Djinn, Man)
Camel's Blues (Camel)
Eat, Eat, Eat (Rhino, Man, animals)
Desert Dessert (Parsee man, Man,
   animals)
Itch, Itch, Itch (Rhino)
Everything under the Sun (Man)
The Gospel According to the Leopard
   (Leopard, Man, animals)

Act II
My First Mistake (Eldest Magician)
Shadowy Forest of Garadufi Dance (Leopard,
   animals)
Giraffe's Reprise (Giraffe)
The Answer Song (Kolokolo Bird, Elephant
   Child)
I've Got to Know (Elephant Child)
I Have Changed (Eldest Magician, animals)
Lullaby (Eldest Magician)

THE KING AND I (1951)

BOOK AND LYRICS BY: Oscar Hammerstein
   II; based on *Anna and the King of Siam* by
   Margaret Landon
MUSIC BY: Richard Rodgers
PUBLISHED LIBRETTO: Random House, 1951

CONDENSATION: *Ganzl's Book of the Musical Theatre*. Ganzl, Kurt. Schirmer (Macmillan), 1989; *Rodgers and Hammerstein*. Mordden, Ethan. Abrams, 1992

ANTHOLOGY: *Six Plays by Rodgers and Hammerstein*. Random House, 1955; Modern Library, 1959

PIANO-VOCAL SCORE: Williamson, 1951

VOCAL SELECTIONS: Williamson, 1951

LICENSING AGENT: Rodgers and Hammerstein Theatre Library

RECORDING: MCA D-18849 CD (original cast)

CAST: 9 M; 4 F; children, singers, dancers

One of the most popular Rodgers and Hammerstein shows, this has been presented many times all over the Western world and was beautifully filmed in 1956. The story is about an English teacher who goes to Siam in the 1860s to instruct the royal children, and all her confrontations with the customs and the king of the land. There is a good deal of Siamese color and decor required and some exotic dancing. But the famous score is sure to please. This is most effective if given a lavish production.

Tony Award Winner (Best Musical)

ORIGINAL CAST:

Gertrude Lawrence (Anna)
Yul Brynner (King)
Sandy Kennedy (Louis)
Doretta Morrow (Tuptim)
Dorothy Sarnoff (Lady Thiang)
Larry Douglas (Lun Tha)
Ronnie Lee (Prince Chulalongkorn)

SONGS:

Act I

I Whistle a Happy Tune (Anna, Louis)
My Lord and Master (Tuptim)
Hello, Young Lovers! (Anna)
A Puzzlement (King)
The Royal Bangkok Academy (Anna, pupils)
Getting to Know You (Anna, wives, children)
We Kiss in a Shadow (Tuptim, Lun Tha)
A Puzzlement (reprise) (Prince Chulalongkorn, Louis)
Shall I Tell You What I Think of You? (Anna)
Something Wonderful (Lady Thiang)

Act II

Western People Funny (Lady Thiang, wives)
I Have Dreamed (Tuptim, Lun Tha)
Ballet Narrator: The Small House of Uncle Thomas (Tuptim)
Shall We Dance? (Anna, King)

KISMET (1953)

BOOK BY: Charles Lederer and Luther Davis; based on the play by Edward Knoblock

MUSIC AND LYRICS BY: Robert Wright and George Forrest; from themes of Alexander Borodin

PUBLISHED LIBRETTO: Random House, 1954

CONDENSATION: *Ganzl's Book of the Musical Theatre*. Ganzl, Kurt. Schirmer (Macmillan), 1989

ANTHOLOGY: None

PIANO-VOCAL SCORE: Frank Music, 1955

LICENSING AGENT: Music Theatre International .

RECORDING: Columbia CK 32605 CD (original cast)

CAST: Large mixed cast

This is a popular story of a king of beggars who pretends to be a visiting nobleman to the court of the Caliph of ancient Baghdad. This Arabian Nights fantasy fills the stage with colorful sets, costumes, and dancing girls. It has been produced as a straight play and film and then in a musical version filmed in 1955 with Howard Keel. A lavish production will certainly be expected. This story seems to lend itself to ethnic adaptions; it was performed by the Puerto Rican Traveling Theater and a recent black version was called *Timbuktu!*

Tony Award Winner (Best Musical)

ORIGINAL CAST:

Richard Oneto (Imam)
Alfred Drake (Hajj)
Doretta Morrow (Marsinah)
Joan Diener (Lalume)
Richard Kiley (Caliph)
Henry Calvin (Wazir)
Lucy Andonian (Ayah to Zubbediya)

SONGS:

Act I

Sands of Time (Imam, chorus)

Rhymes Have I (Hajj, Marsinah)

Fate (Hajj)

Bazaar of the Caravans (chorus)

Not Since Ninevah (Lalume, chorus)

Baubles, Bangles, and Beads (Marsinah, Caliph, chorus)

Stranger in Paradise (Marsinah, Caliph)

Gesticulate (Hajj, Wazir, Lalume, ensemble)

Act II

Night of My Nights (Caliph, chorus)

Was I Wazir? (Wazir, ensemble)

The Olive Tree (Hajj)

Rahadlakum (Lalume, Hajj, harem girls)

And This Is My Beloved (Marsinah, Caliph, Hajj, Wazir)

Zubbediya (Ayah to Zubbediya)

KISS ME, KATE (1948)

BOOK BY: Bella and Samuel Spewack; Shakespeare's *The Taming of the Shrew* is the play-within-the-play

MUSIC AND LYRICS BY: Cole Porter

PUBLISHED LIBRETTO: Knopf, 1953; *Theatre Arts* (magazine), January 1955

CONDENSATION: *Ganzl's Book of the Musical Theatre.* Ganzl, Kurt. Schirmer (Macmillan), 1989

ANTHOLOGY: *Ten Great Musicals of the American Stage.* Stanley Richards, ed. Chilton, 1973

PIANO-VOCAL SCORE: Harms (Chappell), 1967

LICENSING AGENT: Tams-Witmark

RECORDING: Columbia CK 4140 CD (original cast)

CAST: 17 M; 5 F; chorus

A production of *The Taming of the Shrew* is overshadowed by the on- and offstage battles of the stars, plus the secondary plot of a dancer in trouble with some gangsters. Some of the musical numbers are done in Shakespearean costume and style, while others are offstage and backstage. The score is considered the best of Cole Porter. This sophisticated Broadway show

was a big hit all over the world, and it was filmed in 1953.

Tony Award Winner (Best Musical)

ORIGINAL CAST:

Alfred Drake (Fred/Petruchio)

Patricia Morison (Lilli/Kate)

Harold Lang (Bill/Lucentio)

Lisa Kirk (Lois/Bianca)

Annabelle Hill (Hattie)

Harry Clay (Ben/Hortensio)

Charles Wood (Chas/Gremio)

Lorenzo Fuller (Paul)

Harry Clark (Gangster)

Jack Diamond (Gangster)

SONGS:

Act I

Another Op'nin', Another Show (Hattie, chorus)

Why Can't You Behave? (Lois, Bill)

Wunderbar (Lilli, Fred)

So in Love (Lilli)

We Open in Venice (Kate, Petruchio, Bianca, Lucentio, chorus)

Tom, Dick, or Harry (Bianca, Lucentio, Hortensio, Gremio)

I've Come to Wive It Wealthily in Padua (Petruchio, men)

I Hate Men (Kate)

Were Thine That Special Face (Petruchio)

I Sing of Love (Bianca, Lucentio, chorus)

Kiss Me, Kate (Kate, Petruchio, company)

Act II

Too Darn Hot (Paul, boys)

Where Is the Life That Late I Led? (Petruchio)

Always True to You (in My Fashion) (Lois)

Bianca (Lucentio, girls)

Brush up Your Shakespeare (Gangsters)

I Am Ashamed That Women Are So Simple (Kate)

KNICKERBOCKER HOLIDAY (1938)

BOOK AND LYRICS BY: Maxwell Anderson; suggested by *Father Knickerbocker's History of New York* by Washington Irving

MUSIC BY: Kurt Weill

PUBLISHED LIBRETTO: Anderson House, 1938
CONDENSATION: *New Complete Book of the
    American Musical Theater.* Ewen, David. Holt,
    1970
ANTHOLOGY: None
PIANO-VOCAL SCORE: Crawford Music, 1951
LICENSING AGENT: Rodgers and Hammerstein
    Theatre Library
RECORDING: Joey 7243 (radio version)
CAST: 14 M; 6 F; soldiers, citizens, Indians

The setting is New Amsterdam (old New
York) in 1647. Tyrannical Peter Stuyvesant
with a peg leg sings the show's famous
"September Song." The story includes
Washington Irving as a narrator, a pair of
young lovers, and a chorus of Dutch beauties. There is a message about tyranny and
democracy. This has been done on a lavish
scale and also in a concert version without
costumes or sets. There was a film version
(minus much of the score) in 1944 with Nelson Eddy.

1977 NEW YORK CONCERT CAST:

Kurt Peterson (Washington Irving)
Gene Varrone (Roosevelt)
Edward Evanko (Brom)
Clay Causey (Tenpin)
Maureen Brennan (Tina)
Richard Kiley (Peter Stuyvesant)
Eric Brotherson (Tienhoven)

SONGS:
Act I
Introduction/Washington Irving Song
    (Washington Irving)
Clickety-Clack (girls)
Entrance of the Council (Washington Irving)
Hush Hush (Roosevelt, council)
There's Nowhere to Go but Up! (Brom,
    Tenpin, company)
It Never Was You (Brom, Tina)
How Can You Tell an American? (Washington
    Irving, Brom)
Will You Remember Me? (Tina, Brom)
Stuyvesant's Entrance (company)
One Touch of Alchemy (Stuyvesant,
    company)

The One Indispensable Man (Stuyvesant,
    Tienhoven)
Young People Think about Love (Tina, Brom,
    company)
September Song (Stuyvesant)
All Hail the Political Honeymoon (Stuyvesant,
    company)

Act II
Ballad of the Robbers (Washington Irving)
Sitting in Jail (Stuyvesant)
We Are Cut in Twain (Tina, Brom, company)
The Army of New Amsterdam (ensemble)
To War! (ensemble)
Our Ancient Liberties (ensemble)
May and January (ensemble)
The Scars (Stuyvesant, company)
Dirge for a Soldier (company)
No, Ve Vouldn't Gonto Do It (ensemble)

KNIGHTS OF SONG (1938)

BOOK BY: Glendon Allvine and Adele Gutman
    Nathan
MUSIC BY: Arthur Sullivan
LYRICS BY: W. S. Gilbert
PUBLISHED LIBRETTO: None
CONDENSATION: None
ANTHOLOGY: None
LICENSING AGENT: Tams-Witmark
RECORDING: None
CAST: 11 M; 3 F; chorus

Subtitled *A Musical Romance about Gilbert
and Sullivan*, the book presents some biographical incidents from the lives of the
famous team of composers. It begins with
a rehearsal of *Pinafore* and ends after the
death of Sullivan. Some of the characters
include D'Oyly Carte, Oscar Wilde, George
Bernard Shaw, and Queen Victoria. But it
is really the musical excerpts the audience
will be waiting to hear. This is a show for
all good Savoyards.

ORIGINAL CAST:

Nigel Bruce (W. S. Gilbert)
Natalie Hall (Cynthia Bradley)

John Moore (Arthur Sullivan)
Robert Chrisholm (Oscar Wilde)
Reginald Bach (D'Oyly Carte)
Monty Woolley (Prince of Wales)
Molly Pearson (Queen Victoria)
Winston O'Keefe (George Bernard Shaw)

The musical numbers consist of selections from Gilbert and Sullivan, including *HMS Pinafore*, *The Pirates of Penzance*, *The Mikado*, and *Patience*.

KUNI-LEML or The Mismatch (1984)

BOOK BY: Nahma Sandrow; based on *The Fanatic, or the Two Kuni-Lemls* by Avrom Goldfadn
MUSIC BY: Raphael Crystal
LYRICS BY: Richard Engquist
PUBLISHED LIBRETTO: French, 1986
CONDENSATION: None
ANTHOLOGY: None
LICENSING AGENT: Samuel French
RECORDING: None
CAST: 6 M; 2 F

This farce of mistaken identity is set in Odessa in the Ukraine during the reign of Czar Alexander II. It is based on a Yiddish Theater classic that was popular in Kharkov, Russia, in 1880. The story concerns a daughter's battle against her arranged marriage to a Yeshiva student who is a lame, nearsighted stutterer. She would rather marry her tutor. Her struggle concerns secular and religious Judaism as much as her personal life. But the creators insist this is not essentially a Jewish show, that it actually deals with universals. There are fourteen musical numbers and a finale for each act. The *New York Times* found it "has bounce and brio—and it is as contemporary as it is old."

ORIGINAL CAST:

Stuart Zagnit (Kuni-Leml)
Susan Friedman (Libe)

Scott Wentworth (Max)
Gene Varrone (Kalmen)
Barbara McCulloh (Carolina)
Mark Zeller (Pinkhos)
Adam Heller (Yankl/Yasha)
Steve Sterner (Simkhe/Sasha)

SONGS:
Act I
Celebrate! (Simkhe, Yankl, Pinkhos, Carolina)
The Boy Is Perfect (Kalmen)
Carolina's Lament (Carolina)
The World Is Getting Better (Sasha, Yasha, Max)
Cuckoo (Max, Carolina)
The Matchmaker's Daughter (Libe)
A Meeting of the Minds (Pinkhos, Carolina)

Act II
A Little Learning (Pinkhos)
Nothing Counts but Love (Max, Carolina)
What's My Name? (Kuni-Leml)
Purim Song (Sasha, Yasha, Kalmen)
Do Horses Talk to Horses? (Libe, Kuni-Leml)
Lovesongs and Lullabies (Libe, Carolina)
Be Fruitful and Multiply (Simkhe, Yankl)

LADY AUDLEY'S SECRET (1972)

BOOK BY: Douglas Seale; based on the novel by Mary Elizabeth Braddon
MUSIC BY: George Goehing
LYRICS BY: John B. Kuntz
PUBLISHED LIBRETTO: None
CONDENSATION: None
ANTHOLOGY: None
LICENSING AGENT: Music Theatre International
RECORDING: None
CAST: 8 M; 6 F

Based on a famous Victorian novel, this off-Broadway musical was praised for its postcard scenery, lively dances, and attractive costumes. Lady Audley, a former governess, has wed an elderly nobleman. When a previous husband reappears, she "does him in" and then is set upon by blackmailers. This was presented in a melodramatic fashion, with cliches, leers, and asides to the audience. The score is made up of ballads in a Victorian manner and British music-hall-type songs. There was a single piano for accompaniment.

ORIGINAL CAST:

LuAnn Post (Phoebe)
Donna Curtis (Lady Audley)
Douglas Seale (Sir Michael)
Richard Curnock (George)
Russell Nype (Robert)
June Gable (Alicia)
Danny Sewell (Luke)

SONGS:
Act I
A Mother's Wish Is a Daughter's Duty
   (Phoebe)
The English Country Life (chorus)
The Winter Rose (Lady Audley, Sir Michael)
That Lady in Eng-a-land (George, Robert)
Civilized (Lady Audley, Robert, Alicia)
Dead Men Tell No Tales (Lady Audley)

Act II
An Old Maid (Alicia)
Repose (Lady Audley)
The Audley Family Honor (Lady Audley,
   Robert)
La-De-Da-Da (Lady Audley, Alicia, Sir Michael)
A Man's Home Is His Castle (Luke, chorus)
I Wait for Him (Phoebe)
How-What-Why (Robert, Lady Audley,
   Phoebe)
Fireman's Quartet (men)
Forgive Her, Forgive Her (George, Robert,
   Alicia, Lady Audley, chorus)

LADY BE GOOD! (1924)

BOOK BY: Guy Bolton and Fred Thompson
MUSIC BY: George Gershwin
LYRICS BY: Ira Gershwin
PUBLISHED LIBRETTO: None
CONDENSATION: *Ganzl's Book of the Musical
   Theatre*. Ganzl, Kurt. Schirmer (Macmillan),
   1989
VOCAL SELECTIONS: Warner Bros. Music

LICENSING AGENT: Tams-Witmark
RECORDINGS: Smithsonian Collection R008
   (original London cast); Elektra 79308-2 CD
   (1992 studio cast)
CAST: Large mixed cast

In the original production Adele Astaire played a poor girl who impersonates a Spanish heiress to collect four million dollars. Her brother, Fred, played the brother she tries to keep out of a bad marriage. Cliff (Ukelele Ike) Edwards participated and stopped the show. The Gershwin score (even then) was hailed as brilliant. The Astaires seem to have swept all the critics right into their pockets—particularly Adele, who charmed them all. A London revival changed the period to the glamorous thirties but retained the famous songs.

ORIGINAL CAST:

Fred Astaire (Dick)
Adele Astaire (Susie)
Walter Catlett (Watty)
Bill Bailey (Bill)
Alan Edwards (Jack)
Kathlene Martyn (Shirley)
Gerald Oliver Smith (Bertie)
Barney Barnum (Jeff)

SONGS:
Act I
Hang on to Me (Dick, Susie, company)
A Wonderful Party (ensemble)
The End of a String (ensemble)
We're Here Because (Dick, Bertie, ensemble)
Fascinating Rhythm (Dick, Susie, Bill, Jeff)
So Am I (Susie, Jack)
Oh, Lady Be Good! (Watty, company)

Act II
Linger in the Lobby (ensemble)
The Half of It, Dearie Blues (Dick, Shirley)
Juanita (Susie)
Leave It to Love (ensemble)
Little Jazz Bird (Jeff, Susie, Dick)
Carnival Time (ensemble)
Swiss Miss (Dick, Susie)

LADY DAY AT EMERSON'S BAR AND GRILL (1986)

BOOK BY: Lanie Robinson
MUSIC AND LYRICS: Various
PUBLISHED LIBRETTO: French, 1983
CONDENSATION: None
ANTHOLOGY: None
LICENSING AGENT: Samuel French
RECORDING: None
CAST: 1 M (who also plays piano); 1 F; other
    musicians

Billie Holiday, the great black blues and jazz singer, drank and drugged herself to death at the age of forty-four. This production is set in a seedy south Philadelphia joint in 1959, shortly before her death. The talented singer tells us her life story, and along the way she sings a number of songs. The biographical material is weaved through the songs by means of club-act patter, temper tantrums, and other devices as she remembers her life and hard times. The pianist has a small but crucial dramatic role. Since this is essentially a one-woman show, you will need a very talented actress who can also sing "Strange Fruit" and "God Bless the Child."

ORIGINAL CAST:

Lonette McKee (Billie Holiday)
Danny Holgate (pianist)

SONGS:
(performed without intermission)
Baby Doll
Crazy He Calls Me
Deep Song
Easy Livin'
Foolin' Myself
Gimme a Pigfoot
God Bless the Child
I Wonder Where Our Love Has Gone
Strange Fruit
'Taint Nobody's Biz-ness If I Do
Them There Eyes
What a Little Moonlight Can Do

When a Woman Loves a Man
Don't Explain
Somebody's on My Mind

LADY IN THE DARK (1941)

BOOK BY: Moss Hart
MUSIC BY: Kurt Weill
LYRICS BY: Ira Gershwin
PUBLISHED LIBRETTO: Random House, 1941;
    Dramatists Play Service, 1941
CONDENSATION: *The Best Plays of 1940–1941.*
    Burns Mantle, ed. Dodd, Mead, 1941; *Ganzl's
    Book of the Musical Theatre.* Ganzl, Kurt.
    Schirmer (Macmillan), 1989
ANTHOLOGY: *Great Musicals of the American
    Theatre*, vol. 2. Stanley Richards, ed. Chilton,
    1976
PIANO-VOCAL SCORE: Chappell, 1941
LICENSING AGENT: Rodgers and Hammerstein
    Theatre Library
RECORDING: AEI 003 CD (radio version)
CAST: 9 M; 11 F; chorus

This famous show is officially billed as a "musical play." The plot concerns psychoanalysis and the editor of a fashion magazine who cannot make up her mind. This was a lavish production with revolving stages and a large cast. The production numbers are fantasies, including the circus one with the famous "Saga of Jenny" number. Gertrude Lawrence was the star, and Danny Kaye became one. There was a film version in 1944 with Ginger Rogers, and Angela Lansbury appeared in a concert version in 1969 at Lincoln Center.

ORIGINAL CAST:

Gertrude Lawrence (Liza)
Victor Mature (Randy)
MacDonald Carey (Charley)
Danny Kaye (Russell/Ringmaster)

SONGS:
Act I
O Fabulous One (men)
The World's Inamorata (Liza, maid)
One Life to Live (Liza, chauffeur)

Girl of the Moment (ensemble)
It Looks Like Liza (company)
This Is New (Randy, Liza)
The Princess of Pure Delight (Liza, children)
This Woman at the Altar (company)

Act II
The Greatest Show on Earth (Ringmaster, ensemble)
The Best Years of His Life (Charley, Randy)
Tschaikowsky (Ringmaster, ensemble)
The Saga of Jenny (Liza, jury, ensemble)
My Ship (Liza)

THE LAST SWEET DAYS OF ISAAC (1970)

BOOK AND LYRICS BY: Gretchen Cryer
MUSIC BY: Nancy Ford
PUBLISHED LIBRETTO: None
CONDENSATION: *New Complete Book of the American Musical Theater*. Ewen, David. Holt, 1970
ANTHOLOGY: None
LICENSING AGENT: Samuel French
RECORDING: RCA LSO 1169 (original cast)
CAST: 1 M; 1 F; chorus

This 1970 show is, in fact, two one-act musicals (an Isaac character is in both). The first involves a couple trapped in an elevator. The second takes place in jail with two people who have been arrested. Isaac believes that a person's whole life can be taped, recorded, photographed, and preserved so that future generations can relive his experiences. This is a spoof on "the age of technology has arrived." Some names that popped up in most reviews were Marshall McLuhan and Woody Allen, although neither was in any way involved in the production. This can be simply staged with a cast of two and a small backup group. The rock score was described as loud but agreeable.

Off-Broadway (OBIE) Award Winner

ORIGINAL CAST:
Austin Pendleton (Isaac)
Fredricka Weber (Ingrid)

SONGS:
Act I (The Elevator)
Opening (ensemble)
The Last Sweet Days of Isaac (Isaac)
A Transparent Crystal Moment (Isaac)
My Most Important Moments Go By (Ingrid)
Love You Came to Me (Ingrid, Isaac)

Act II (I Want to Walk to San Francisco)
I Want to Walk to San Francisco (ensemble)
Touching Your Hand Is Like Touching Your Mind (ensemble)
Yes, I Know That I'm Alive (Ingrid, Isaac, ensemble)
I Want to Walk to San Francisco (reprise) (Isaac, Ingrid, ensemble)

LEADER OF THE PACK (1985)

BOOK BY: Anne Beatts
MUSIC AND LYRICS BY: Ellie Greenwich and friends
PUBLISHED LIBRETTO: French, 1985
CONDENSATION: None
ANTHOLOGY: None
LICENSING AGENT: Samuel French
RECORDING: Elektra 960409-1-Q (original cast)
CAST: 4 M; 10 F; extras

Ellie Greenwich's music was primarily for "girl groups" and is reprised in this show for nostalgic American children of the 1960s. The Broadway production used a unit set suggesting giant 45 rpm records. There was a "disarming tackiness" to the costumes and "campy beehive wigs." The show ran a bit over ninety minutes without an intermission and featured twenty-four songs. The musical staging was called "hypercharged" and the dancing was energetic. There is also a backstage story about Ellie, her marriage to Jeff Barry and a breakup. The title number should be staged with prop motorcycle handlebars and goggles that light up.

ORIGINAL CAST:

Annie Golden (Annie)
Darlene Love (Darlene)
Dinah Manoff (Young Ellie)
Barbara Yeager (Shelley)
Jasmine Guy (Mickey)
Patrick Cassidy (Jeff)
Pattie Darcy (Lounge Singer/Pattie)
Gina Taylor (Gina)
Ellie Greenwich (Ellie)

SONGS:

(performed without intermission)
Be My Baby (Annie, girls)
Wait 'Til My Bobby Gets Home (Darlene, company)
A . . . My Name Is Ellie (Young Ellie)
Jivette Boogie Beat (Young Ellie, Shelley, Mickey)
Why Do Lovers Break Each Others' Hearts (Darlene, company)
Today I Met the Boy I'm Gonna Marry (Darlene, company)
I Want to Love Him So Bad (Young Ellie, girls)
Do Wah Diddy (Jeff)
And Then He Kissed Me (Young Ellie, girls)
Hanky Panky (Jeff, guys)
Not Too Young (to Get Married) (Darlene, girls)
Chapel of Love (company)
Baby I Love You (Annie, girls)
Leader of the Pack (Annie, company)
Look of Love (Lounge Singer)
Christmas—Baby Please Come Home (Darlene, girls)
I Can Hear Music (Jeff, Annie, Pattie)
Rock of Rages (Young Ellie)
Keep It Confidential (Gina)
Da Doo Ron Ron (Ellie, company)
What a Guy (Ellie, company)
Maybe I Know (Ellie, Darlene, Annie, girls)
River Deep, Mountain High (Darlene, company)
We're Gonna Make It (After All) (Ellie, Darlene, Annie, company)

LEAVE IT TO JANE (1917)

BOOK AND LYRICS BY: Guy Bolton and P. G. Wodehouse; based on the play *The College Widow* by George Ade
MUSIC BY: Jerome Kern
PUBLISHED LIBRETTO: None
CONDENSATION: *Ganzl's Book of the Musical Theatre*. Ganzl, Kurt. Schirmer (Macmillan), 1989
ANTHOLOGY: None
VOCAL SELECTIONS: Harms, 1961
LICENSING AGENT: Tams-Witmark
RECORDING: DRG 15017 CD (1959 cast recording)
CAST: 9 M; 3 F; chorus

This musical is considered a landmark in musical comedy history as it uses purely American characters, locale, and spirit, rather than the traditions of European operetta. It is the story of how a college professor's daughter manages to lure a football player away from a rival institution. The off-Broadway revival retained the pre–World War I setting and the music was provided by a piano, saxophone-clarinet, banjo, and drums. The critics found the show a nostalgic antique but all enjoyed the Jerome Kern score. This can be simply staged with a relatively small cast, and for maximum charm should not be spoofed.

1985 NEW YORK CONCERT CAST:

Jason Graae (Ollie)
George Dvorsky (Stub)
Judy Kaye (Bessie)
Jeanne Lehman (Jane)
Alix Korey (Flora)
Ray Gill (McGowan)
Michael Maguire (Billy)
Deborah Rhodes (Sally)
Lara Teeter (Bub)

SONGS:
Act I
Atwater Song (Ollie, students)
Peach of a Life (Stub, Bessie)
Wait Till Tomorrow (Jane, boys)
Just You Watch My Step (Stub, Bessie, girls)
Leave It to Jane (Bessie, Stub, Jane, girls)

The Crickets Are Calling (Jane, Billy)
The Siren's Song (Bessie, Jane, girls)
There It Is Again (Sally, Billy, girls)
Cleopatterer (Flora)
What I'm Longing to Say (Jane, Billy)

Act II
Football Song (Bessie, ensemble)
Sir Galahad (Flora, Bub, Stub)
The Sun Shines Brighter (Stub, Bessie)
I'm Going to Find a Girl (Stub, Bub, Ollie)

LEND AN EAR (1948)

SKETCHES, MUSIC, AND LYRICS BY: Charles
   Gaynor
PUBLISHED LIBRETTO: French, 1971
CONDENSATION: *New Complete Book of the
   American Musical Theater.* Ewen, David. Holt,
   1970
ANTHOLOGY: None
LICENSING AGENT: Samuel French
RECORDING: None
CAST: 19 M; 11 F

This is a revue, and revues generally do
not stand the test of time for revivals.
But in this case the author wisely avoided
topical material, so this show has been
brought back twice off-Broadway. There
are skits about travel, psychiatry, school,
operas, and other timeless subjects. The
original cast included Carol Channing, and
she recorded some of her "Gladiola Girl"
routine on one of her albums (Vanguard
VRS 9056).

ORIGINAL CAST:

Yvonne Adair   Anne Renee Anderson
Dorothy Babbs   Carol Channing
Robert Dixon   William Eythe
Gloria Hamilton   Arthur Maxwell
Bob Scheerer   Lee Stacy

SONGS:
Act I
After Hours (chorus)
Give Your Heart a Chance (Babbs, men)
I'm Not in Love (Maxwell, Adair)
Friday Dancing Class (company)

Ballade (Anderson)
When Someone You Love Loves You
   (Hamilton, Dixon)
The Gladiola Girl (Adair, Channing, Eythe,
   Hamilton, company)

Act II
I'm on the Lookout (Hamilton)
Three Little Queens of the Silver Screen
   (Stacy, Anderson, Channing)
Molly O'Reilly (Scheerer, Babbs)
Who Hit Me? (Adair)

LET 'EM EAT CAKE (1933)

BOOK BY: George S. Kaufman and Morrie Ryskind
MUSIC BY: George Gershwin
LYRICS BY: Ira Gershwin
PUBLISHED LIBRETTO: Knopf, 1933
CONDENSATION: *New Complete Book of the
   American Musical Theater.* Ewen, David. Holt,
   1970
ANTHOLOGY: None
PIANO-VOCAL SCORE: New World Music, 1933
LICENSING AGENT: Music Theatre International
RECORDING: CBS M2K 42522 CD (1987 concert
   version)
CAST: 13 M; 7 F; chorus

According to the licensing agent's catalog,
this property is currently available as either a single-concert presentation or combined with *Of Thee I Sing* in duo-concert
format. The cast of this musical includes
some characters from *Of Thee I Sing.* President Wintergreen is defeated by Tweedledee and returns to New York with Mary
to manufacture blue shirts. He organizes a
blue-shirt revolution and almost ends up
on the guillotine. Mary stages a fashion
show at the last moment that rallies the
female population.

1987 CONCERT VERSION CAST:

Paige O'Hara (Trixie)
Larry Kert (Wintergreen)
George Dvorsky (Speaker)
Maureen McGovern (Mary)

Casper Roos (Chief Justice)
Jack Dabdoub (General)
Jack Gilford (Throttlebottom)
David Garrison (Kruger)

SONGS:
Act I
Tweedledee for President (chorus)
Union Square (Kruger, chorus)
Shirts for the Millions (chorus)
Comes the Revolution (Throttlebottom, chorus)
Mine (Wintergreen, Mary, chorus)
Climb up the Social Ladder (Mary, chorus)
The Union League (chorus)
On and On and On (General, Wintergreen, chorus)
Mothers of the Nation (Mary, chorus)
Let 'em Eat Cake (Wintergreen, chorus)

Act II
Blue, Blue, Blue (chorus)
Who's the Greatest? (Wintergreen, chorus)
The League of Nations (Speaker, Mary, Wintergreen, chorus)
No Comprenez, No Capish, No Versteh! (Kruger, Wintergreen, chorus)
When Nations Get Together (Wintergreen, Mary, chorus)
Why Speak of Money (chorus)
The Trial of Throttlebottom (Kruger, Wintergreen, Throttlebottom, chorus)
The Trial of Wintergreen (Wintergreen, Kruger, Mary, chorus)
First Lady and First Gent (Trixie, Kruger)
Hanging Throttlebottom in the Morning (chorus)
Fashion Show (Mary, Trixie, Kruger, chorus)
Of Thee I Sing (chorus)

LIES AND LEGENDS (1985)

ORIGINAL CONCEPT BY: Joseph Stern
MUSIC AND LYRICS BY: Harry Chapin
PUBLISHED LIBRETTO: None
CONDENSATION: None
ANTHOLOGY: None
MUSIC PUBLISHER: Cherry Lane Music

LICENSING AGENT: Rodgers and Hammerstein Theatre Library
RECORDING: Titanic T-0184 (studio cast)
CAST: 3 M; 2 F

The popular songwriter Harry Chapin was a storyteller who took the frustrations, joys, dreams, and fantasies of the common folk and turned them into musical portraits. This off-Broadway "unpretentious musical revue" is almost 100 percent music. It was presented in a straightforward manner without elaborate settings or choreography. It is a cabaret-type entertainment with the New York production utilizing a multilevel staging with a five-piece onstage band.

ORIGINAL CAST:

Mark Fotopoulos   Joanna Glushak
Terri Klausner   Ron Orbach
Martin Vidnovic

SONGS:
Act I
Circle/Story of a Life (company)
Corey's Coming (Fotopoulos, company)
Salt and Pepper (Klausner, Orbach, company)
Mr. Tanner (Glushak, Vidnovic, company)
The Rock (Orbach, company)
Old College Avenue (Klausner)
Taxi (Fotopoulos)
Winter Song (Glushak, boys)
Bananas (Vidnovic)
Get on with It (Glushak, Orbach)
Shooting Star (Klausner)
Sniper (Vidnovic, Fotopoulos, company)

Act II
Dance Band on the Titanic (company)
W*O*L*D (Fotopoulos)
Dogtown (Klausner, company)
Mail Order Annie (Fotopoulos, Glushak)
Odd-Job Man (Orbach, company)
Dreams Go By (Fotopoulos, Glushak)
Tangled up Puppet (Klausner)
Cat's in the Cradle (Vidnovic)
Halfway to Heaven (Orbach)
Better Place to Be (Klausner, Vidnovic)
You Are the Only Song/Circle (company)

LI'L ABNER (1956)

BOOK BY: Norman Panama and Melvin Frank; based on comic-strip characters created by Al Capp
MUSIC BY: Gene de Paul
LYRICS BY: Johnny Mercer
PUBLISHED LIBRETTO: None
CONDENSATION: *New Complete Book of the American Musical Theater*. Ewen, David. Holt, 1970
ANTHOLOGY: None
VOCAL SELECTIONS: Commander, 1959 (Twentieth Century Music)
LICENSING AGENT: Tams-Witmark
RECORDING: Sony A 5150 CD (original cast)
CAST: Large mixed cast

This big Broadway musical is based on the popular comic-strip characters and was filmed with members of the original cast in 1959. There is a complicated plot and some political satire. The sets are usually done in cartoon style, and there are lots of regional/hoedown dances. A collection of barnyard animals will add to the fun. There is a big "Sadie Hawkins Day" ballet. This show has been popular with high schools all over the country.

ORIGINAL CAST:

Peter Palmer (Li'l Abner)
Edith Adams (Daisy Mae)
Stubby Kaye (Marryin' Sam)
Howard St. John (General Bullmoose)

SONGS:
Act I
A Typical Day (ensemble)
If I Had My Druthers (Li'l Abner, ensemble) Reprise (Daisy)
Jubilation T. Cornpone (Marryin' Sam, ensemble)
Rag Offen the Bush (ensemble)
Namely You (Daisy Mae, Li'l Abner)
Unnecessary Town (Li'l Abner, Daisy Mae, ensemble)
What's Good for General Bullmoose (female ensemble)

The Country's in the Very Best of Hands (Li'l Abner, Marryin' Sam)

Act II
Oh Happy Day (male ensemble)
I'm Past My Prime (Daisy Mae, Marryin' Sam)
Love in a Home (Li'l Abner, Daisy Mae)
Progress Is the Root of All Evil (General Bullmoose)
Put 'em Back (female ensemble)
The Matrimonial Stomp (Marryin' Sam, ensemble)

LITTLE JOHNNY JONES (1904)

BOOK, MUSIC, AND LYRICS BY: George M. Cohan; 1982 version adapted by Alfred Uhry
PUBLISHED LIBRETTO: None
CONDENSATION: *Ganzl's Book of the Musical Theatre*. Ganzl, Kurt. Schirmer (Macmillan), 1989
ANTHOLOGY: None
VOCAL SELECTIONS: Cohan (G. M.) Publishing Company
LICENSING AGENT: Tams-Witmark
RECORDING: None
CAST: 8 M; 3 F; singers, dancers

Johnny Jones, "the most sought-after jockey in the world," is pursued to England and back by young heiress Goldie Gates. Some of the other characters include her dowager aunt, a fortune hunter, and a society reporter. The 1982 revival was done at the Goodspeed Opera in Connecticut and toured successfully before reaching Broadway. The score includes a number of Cohan songs interpolated from other scores. The sets and costumes reflected the nostalgic appeal of this early American show.

1982 CAST:

Donny Osmond (Johnny Jones)
Maureen Brennan (Goldie Gates)
Peter Van Norden (Anthony Anstey)
Jane Galloway (Florabelle Fly)
Anna McNeely (Mrs. Kenworth)
Tom Rolfing (Timothy McGee)
Jack Bittner (Captain/Starter)

SONGS:
Act I
The Cecil in London (Starter, ensemble)
Then I'd Be Satisfied with Life (Anthony
   Anstey)
Yankee Doodle Boy (Johnny Jones, ensemble)
Oh, You Wonderful Boy (Goldie Gates,
   Florabelle Fly, female ensemble)
The Voice in My Heart (Mrs. Kenworth,
   ensemble)
Finaletto (company)

Act II
Captain of a Ten-Day Boat (Captain,
   ensemble)
Good-bye Flo (Florabelle Fly, sailors)
Life's a Funny Proposition (Johnny Jones)
Let's You and I Just Say Good-bye (Goldie
   Gates)
Give My Regards to Broadway (Johnny jones,
   ensemble)
Extra! Extra! (newsboys)
American Ragtime (Florabelle Fly, Timothy
   McGee, Johnny Jones, ensemble)

LITTLE MARY SUNSHINE (1959)

BOOK, MUSIC, AND LYRICS BY: Rick Besoyan.
PUBLISHED LIBRETTO: French, 1960; *Theatre Arts*
   (magazine), December 1960
CONDENSATION: *New Complete Book of the
   American Musical Theater.* Ewen, David. Holt,
   1970
ANTHOLOGY: None
PIANO-VOCAL SCORE: Sunbeam (Valando), 1965
VOCAL SELECTIONS: New York Times Music, 1962
LICENSING AGENT: Samuel French
RECORDING: Angel 64774 CD (original cast)
CAST: 13 M; 10 F

This is a musical spoof of the operettas
of the 1920s. Echoes of the most famous
shows are either seen or heard in this
very popular off-Broadway show. Set in Colorado "early in this century," little Mary (an
orphan found by the last of the Kadota Indians) runs a mountain inn. Some of the
guests include a group of finishing-school
girls and a visiting opera star. There is also

a troop of handsome forest rangers nearby.
(Yes, there is a "Colorado Love Call.") This
can be done very simply with a small cast
and twin pianos. Some of the critical comments referred to the show as sidesplitting
and wonderful fun.

ORIGINAL CAST:
Eileen Brennan (Mary)
William Graham (Captain Jim)
Elizabeth Parrish (Madame Ernestine)
John McMartin (Billy)
Elmarie Wendel (Nancy)
Mario Siletti (Oscar)
Ray James (Yellow Feather)

SONGS:
Act I
The Forest Rangers (Captain Jim, men)
Little Mary Sunshine (Mary, men)
Look for a Sky of Blue (Mary, men)
You're the Fairest Flower (Captain Jim)
In Izzenschooken (Madame Ernestine)
Playing Croquet and Swinging (ladies)
How Do You Do? (men, ladies)
Tell a Handsome Stranger (sextette)
Once in a Blue Moon (Billy, Nancy)
Colorado Love Call (Captain Jim, Mary)
Every Little Nothing (Madame Ernestine,
   Mary)
Finale—What Has Happened? (company)

Act II
Such a Merry Party (Nancy, men, ladies)
Say, "Uncle" (Oscar, ladies)
Me, a Big Heap Indian (Billy)
Naughty, Naughty Nancy (Mary, ladies)
Mata Hari (Nancy, ladies)
Do You Ever Dream of Vienna? (Madame
   Ernestine, Oscar)
A "Shell Game" (Billy, Yellow Feather, Nancy)
Coo Coo (Mary)

LITTLE ME (1962)

BOOK BY: Neil Simon; based on a novel by Patrick
   Dennis
MUSIC BY: Cy Coleman
LYRICS BY: Carolyn Leigh

PUBLISHED LIBRETTO: None
CONDENSATION: *Ganzl's Book of the Musical Theatre*. Ganzl, Kurt. Schirmer (Macmillan), 1989
ANTHOLOGY: *The Collected Plays of Neil Simon*, vol. II. Random House, 1979
VOCAL SELECTIONS: Morris (Hansen), 1962
LICENSING AGENT: Tams-Witmark
RECORDING: RCA 61462 CD (original cast)
CAST: Large mixed cast

In the original production Sid Caesar played a number of different roles, but in the revival the parts were divided among several different men. This is a wild farce told in flashbacks about the career of Belle Poitrine. She is a vaudeville entertainer, a gangster's moll, a film star, and a passenger on the *Titanic*. The time is around World War I and there are some scenes with the American soldiers in France. This is a big musical requiring a number of sets and costumes and with involved dance numbers. The leading roles present a challenge to the cast.

ORIGINAL CAST:

Nancy Andrews (Miss Poitrine)
Peter Turgeon (Patrick)
Virginia Martin (Belle)
Sid Caesar (Noble/Mr. Pinchley/Val Du Val/Fred/Prince Cherney)
Mickey Deems (Pinchley, Jr./Yulnick)
Joey Faye (Bernie)
Mort Marshall (Bennie)
Swen Swenson (George)

SONGS:
Act I
The Truth (Miss Poitrine, Patrick, servants)
The Other Side of the Tracks (Belle)
Birthday Party (ensemble)
I Love You (Noble, Belle)
Deep Down Inside (Pinchley; Belle; Pinchley, Jr.; ensemble)
Be a Performer! (Bennie, Bernie)
Dimples (Belle, men)
Boom—Boom (Val Du Val, girls)
I've Got Your Number (George, Belle)

Real Live Girl (Fred, men)
Boom—Boom (reprise) (Belle)

Act II
Poor Little Hollywood Star (Belle)
Little Me (Miss Poitrine, Belle)
The Prince's Farewell (Cherney, Yulnick, ensemble)
Here's to Us (Miss Poitrine, ensemble)

LITTLE NELLIE KELLY (1922)

BOOK, MUSIC, AND LYRICS BY: George M. Cohan
PUBLISHED LIBRETTO: None
CONDENSATION: None
ANTHOLOGY: None
LICENSING AGENT: Tams-Witmark
RECORDING: None
CAST: Large mixed cast

The original production was described as the snappiest, liveliest, danciest, cleanest, and most wholesome show that had been presented in some time. The last act was particularly praised for its gorgeous set and costumes. The plot concerns the loss of a pearl necklace and how Nellie saves the day and finds her true love. This was meant to be a satire of popular mystery plays of the day. "Till My Luck Comes Rolling Along" was a hit number in the show. There was a Judy Garland film version that barely used the original plot and only one song from the score.

ORIGINAL CAST:

Barrett Greenwood (Jack)
Elizabeth Hines (Nellie)
Robert Pitkin (DeVere)
Frank Otto (Sidney)
Marion Saki (Marie)
Charles King (Jerry)
Harold Vizard (Wellesby)
Edna Whistler (Matilda)
Dorothy Newell (Jean)
Arthur Deagon (Kelly)

SONGS:

Act I

Over the Phone (Jack, ensemble)
All in the Weaving (Nellie, ensemble)
Girls from DeVere's (DeVere, girls)
Dancing My Worries Away (Sidney, Marie)
Nellie Kelly, I Love You (Jerry, ensemble)
When You Do the Hinky Dee (Jerry, Nellie, Sidney, Marie, ensemble)
Something's Got to Be Done (Wellesby, Matilda, Jean, DeVere)
The Name of Kelly (Kelly, ensemble)

Act II

The Busy Bees of DeVere's (ensemble)
The Dancing Detective (girls)
They're All My Boys (Nellie, ensemble)
You Remind Me of My Mother (Jerry, Nellie)
The Great New York Police (Kelly, ensemble)
The Mystery Play (girls)
The Voice in My Heart (Nellie)
Till My Luck Comes Rolling Along (Jerry, Nellie, company)

A LITTLE NIGHT MUSIC (1973)

BOOK BY: Hugh Wheeler; suggested by a film by Ingmar Bergman
MUSIC AND LYRICS BY: Stephen Sondheim
PUBLISHED LIBRETTO: Dodd, Mead, 1974; Applause Books, 1991
CONDENSATION: *The Best Plays of 1972–1973.* Otis L. Guernsey, Jr., ed. Dodd, Mead, 1973; *Ganzl's Book of the Musical Theatre.* Ganzl, Kurt. Schirmer (Macmillan), 1989
ANTHOLOGY: *Great Musicals of the American Theatre*, vol. 2. Stanley Richards, ed. Chilton, 1976; *Best American Plays*, 8th series. Clive Barnes, ed. Crown, 1983
PIANO-VOCAL SCORE: Revelation Music, 1974
VOCAL SELECTIONS: Revelation Music, 1973
LICENSING AGENT: Music Theatre International
RECORDING: Columbia CK 32263 CD (original cast)
CAST: Large mixed cast

Called a musical with elegance, this show is set in Sweden at the turn of the century.
The central character is a middle-aged actress, and the plot concerns her family and loves. Most of the music is in three-quarter time, and there is almost no dancing. This show was highly praised for its style and imagination and for its combination of humor and sadness. The big song is "Send in the Clowns." There was a film version in 1977 with Elizabeth Taylor. In 1990 it was presented at Lincoln Center by the New York City Opera.

Tony Award Winner (Best Musical)

ORIGINAL CAST:

Mark Lambert (Henrik)
Victoria Mallory (Anne)
Len Cariou (Fredrik)
Judy Kahan (Fredrika)
Hermione Gingold (Madame Armfeldt)
Glynis Johns (Desiree)
Despo (Malla)
Laurence Guittard (Carl-Magnus)
Patricia Elliott (Charlotte)
D. Jamin-Bartlett (Petra)

SONGS:

Act I

Overture (ensemble)
Night Waltz (company)
Later (Henrik)
Now (Fredrik)
Soon (Anne, Henrik, Fredrik)
The Glamorous Life (Fredrika, Desiree, Malla, Madame Armfeldt, ensemble)
Remember? (ensemble)
You Must Meet My Wife (Desiree, Fredrik)
Liaisons (Madame Armfeldt)
In Praise of Women (Carl-Magnus)
Every Day a Little Death (Charlotte, Anne)
A Weekend in the Country (company)

Act II

The Sun Won't Set (ensemble)
It Would Have Been Wonderful (Fredrik, Carl-Magnus)
Perpetual Anticipation (female ensemble)
Send in the Clowns (Desiree)
The Miller's Son (Petra)

LITTLE SHOP OF HORRORS
(1982)

BOOK BY: Howard Ashman; based on the film by
Roger Corman
MUSIC BY: Alan Menken
LYRICS BY: Howard Ashman
PUBLISHED LIBRETTO: French, 1982
CONDENSATION: *Ganzl's Book of the Musical
Theatre*. Ganzl, Kurt. Schirmer (Macmillan),
1989
ANTHOLOGY: None
PIANO-VOCAL SCORE: Menken Music/Warner Bros.
Music, 1983
VOCAL SELECTIONS: Warner Bros. Music, 1983
LICENSING AGENT: Samuel French
RECORDING: Geffen GEFD 2020 CD (original cast)
CAST: 4 M; 4 F; 1 strong offstage voice

Based on a low budget horror film that
has since become a cult classic, this
musical spoofs not only that type of
film but the popular music of the early
1960s as well. The young hero of this
tale works in a "God and customer for-
saken" flower shop in a skid row section of a large city. He finds an exotic
plant that requires a diet of human blood.
The plant becomes a tourist attraction
that continues to grow as cast members disappear! This off-Broadway show
has a small cast and is relatively simple to stage, except for the plant. As it
grows you will need a crew to manipu-
late it—by the finale it engulfs the entire
stage and threatens to consume the audience. Steve Martin starred in the 1986 film
version.

ORIGINAL CAST:

Leilani Jones (Chiffon)
Jennifer Leigh Warren (Crystal)
Sheila Kay Davis (Ronnette)
Lee Wilkof (Seymour)
Michael Vale (Mushnik)
Ellen Greene (Audrey)
Franc Luz (Orin)
Ron Taylor (Audrey II voice)

SONGS:
Act I
Little Shop of Horrors (Chiffon, Crystal,
Ronnette)
Skid Row (Downtown) (company)
Grow for Me (Seymour)
Don't It Go to Show Ya Never Know
(Mushnik, Chiffon, Crystal, Ronnette,
Seymour)
Somewhere That's Green (Audrey)
Closed for Renovations (Seymour, Audrey,
Mushnik)
Dentist! (Orin, Chiffon, Crystal, Ronnette)
Mushnik and Son (Mushnik, Seymour)
Git It! (Seymour, Audrey II)
Now (It's Just the Gas) (Seymour, Orin)

Act II
Call Back in the Morning (Seymour, Audrey)
Suddenly, Seymour (Seymour, Audrey)
Suppertime (Audrey II)
The Meek Shall Inherit (company)
Finale: Don't Feed the Plants (company)

LOCK UP YOUR DAUGHTERS
(1959—London)

ADAPTION BY: Bernard Miles; based on the
comedy *Rape upon Rape* by Henry Fielding
MUSIC BY: Laurie Johnson
LYRICS BY: Lionel Bart
PUBLISHED LIBRETTO: French, 1967
CONDENSATION: *Ganzl's Book of the Musical Thea-
tre*. Ganzl, Kurt. Schirmer (Macmillan), 1989
ANTHOLOGY: None
PIANO-VOCAL SCORE: Maurice Music (London),
1960
LICENSING AGENT: Samuel French
RECORDING: London 5766/TER 1047 (original
London cast)
CAST: 15 M; 4 F

The plot of this musical is about a villainous British magistrate who extorts money
from those whom he judges. In this farce
some of his victims plan revenge. This
musical was a hit in London at the Mermaid Theatre in 1959 but closed "out of
town" when it tried for Broadway. It has

been successfully staged at the Goodspeed Opera in Connecticut. The London setting in 1730 requires various streets, taverns, and courtrooms, as well as wigs, breeches, and dresses of the period. The plot is somewhat bawdy.

ORIGINAL LONDON CAST:

Robin Wentworth (Staff)
Stephanie Voss (Hilaret)
Madeline Newbury (Cloris)
John Sharp (Politic)
Brendan Barry (Dabble)
Frederick Jaeger (Ramble)
Keith Marsh (Sotmore)
Hy Hazell (Mrs. Squeezum)
Richard Wordsworth (Squeezum)
Terence Cooper (Constant)

SONGS:
Act I
All's Well (Staff)
A Proper Man (Hilaret, Cloris)
It Must Be True (Politic, Dabble)
Red Wine (Ramble, Sotmore)
On the Side (Squeezum)
When Does the Ravishing Begin? (Mrs. Squeezum)
Lovely Lover (Hilaret, Constant)
Lock Up Your Daughters (Ramble, Constant, Sotmore)
There's a Plot Afoot (company)

Act II
Mr. Jones (Squeezum)
On a Sunny Morning (Hilaret, Squeezum)
If I'd Known You (Sotmore)
'Tis Plain to See (Hilaret, Ramble, chorus)
Kind Fate (Hilaret, Constant, chorus)
I'll Be There (Mrs. Squeezum, company)
Lock Up Your Daughters (reprise) (Hilaret, company)

LORELEI (1974)

NEW BOOK BY: Kenny Solms and Gall Parent; from *Gentlemen Prefer Blondes* by Anita Loos
MUSIC BY: Jule Styne

LYRICS BY: Leo Robin; additional lyrics by Betty Comden and Adolph Green
PUBLISHED LIBRETTO: None
CONDENSATION: *Ganzl's Book of the Musical Theatre.* Ganzl, Kurt. Schirmer (Macmillan), 1989
ANTHOLOGY: None
VOCAL SELECTIONS: Consolidated Music, 1974
LICENSING AGENT: Tams-Witmark
RECORDINGS: MGM M3G 55; Verve MV 5097 (original cast)
CAST: Large mixed cast

Lorelei Lee is the most famous gold digger of this century. This often reworked Anita Loos story has Lorelei sailing for Europe in the roaring twenties. This is a revision of a 1949 musical, *Gentlemen Prefer Blondes*, that was filmed in 1953 with Marilyn Monroe. Carol Channing, however, starred in both stage versions and "Diamonds Are a Girl's Best Friend" became her signature song. Careful attention should be given to costume, set design, and choreography (tap, Charleston). The music is bouncy and fun. This is a real "audience show" and needs a strong Lorelei.

ORIGINAL CAST:

Carol Channing (Lorelei)
Peter Palmer (Gus)
Tamara Long (Dorothy)
Dody Goodman (Mrs. Spofford)
Jack Fletcher (Lord Francis)
Lee Roy Reams (Henry)
Bob Fitch (Robert)
Ian Tucker (Louis)
Brandon Maggart (Gage)

SONGS:
Act I
Looking Back (Lorelei)
Bye, Bye, Baby (Gus, Lorelei, ensemble)
High Time (Dorothy, Mrs. Spofford, ensemble)
A Little Girl from Little Rock (Lorelei)
I Love What I'm Doing (Dorothy)
It's Delightful Down in Chile (Lorelei, Lord Francis, men)
I Won't Let You Get Away (Henry, Dorothy)

Keeping Cool with Coolidge (Henry, Dorothy,
    Mrs. Spofford, ensemble)
Men (Lorelei)

Act II
Coquette (Dorothy, Lorelei, girls)
Mamie Is Mimi (Lorelei, Robert, Louis)
Diamonds Are a Girl's Best Friend (Lorelei)
Homesick (Lorelei, Gus)
Miss Lorelei Lee (Henry, Dorothy, Mrs
    Spofford, Gage, Robert, Louis, ensemble)
Button Up with Esmond (Lorelei, girls)
Lorelei (Lorelei, company)

LOST IN THE STARS (1949)

BOOK AND LYRICS BY: Maxwell Anderson; based
    on the novel *Cry, the Beloved Country* by Alan
    Paton
MUSIC BY: Kurt Weill
PUBLISHED LIBRETTO: Sloan (Anderson House),
    1950; *Theatre Arts* (magazine), December 1950
CONDENSATION: *The Burns Mantle Best Plays of
    1949–1950*. John Chapman, ed. Dodd, Mead,
    1950
ANTHOLOGY: *Great Musicals of the American
    Theatre*, vol. 2. Stanley Richards, ed. Chilton,
    1976; *Famous American Plays of the 1940s*.
    Henry Hewes, ed. Laurel, 1988
PIANO-VOCAL SCORE: Chappell, 1950
LICENSING AGENT: Rodgers and Hammerstein
    Theatre Library
RECORDING: MCA 10302 CD (original cast)
CAST: Large mixed cast, primarily black

This is a serious look at South Africa and
its apartheid system in the 1940s. Absalom, a young black man from a rural area,
comes to Johannesburg. He becomes involved in a robbery and is sentenced to
be hanged. For the 1972 revival the stage
was a circular platform with bleachers on
each side and overhead screens for projected images. African flavor is expected in
the costumes and choreography. The cast
is primarily black, including a young boy
who sings "Big Mole." Clive Barnes of the
New York Times called the Kurt Weill score
(his last) a "considerable piece of musical

theater." There was a film version in 1974
with Melba Moore.

1972 REVIVAL CAST:
Rod Perry (Leader)
Lee Hooper (Answerer)
Brock Peters (Stephen)
Gilbert Price (Absalom)
Margaret Cowie (Irina)
Giancarlo Esposito (Alex)

SONGS:
Act I
The Hills of Ixopo (Leader, Answerer,
    ensemble)
Thousands of Miles (Stephen)
Train to Johannesburg (Leader, ensemble)
The Search (Stephen, Leader, ensemble)
The Little Grey House (Stephen, ensemble)
Stay Well (Absalom)
Trouble Man (Irina)
Murder in Parkwold (ensemble)
Fear (ensemble)
Lost in the Stars (Stephen, ensemble)

Act II
The Wild Justice (Leader, ensemble)
O Tixo, Tixo, Help Me (Stephen)
Cry, the Beloved Country (Leader, singers)
Big Mole (Alex)
Thousands of Miles (reprise) (ensemble)

LOVELY LADIES, KIND GENTLEMEN (1970)

BOOK BY: John Patrick; based on *The Teahouse
    of the August Moon* by Vern J. Sneider and the
    play by John Patrick
MUSIC AND LYRICS BY: Stan Freeman and Franklin
    Underwood
PUBLISHED LIBRETTO: French, 1971
CONDENSATION: None
ANTHOLOGY: None
VOCAL SELECTIONS: Ruxton Music and Eastgate
    Music, 1971
LICENSING AGENT: Samuel French
RECORDING: None
CAST: Large mixed cast

Since this musical is set in 1946 on Okinawa (Japan) an Oriental cast will help but is not required. A goat is required for the part of "Lady Astor." Most people are probably familiar with the plot of the American forces of occupation knee-deep in black-market operations and home brew. Sakini, the narrator and con-man extraordinary, was once played by Marlon Brando in a nonmusical film version of the play. A captain is sent to westernize a native village, but instead of building a school the villagers end up building a teahouse. The sets and costumes of the Broadway production were praised for their Oriental beauty. The musical style is both exotic and boogie-woogie.

ORIGINAL CAST:

Kenneth Nelson (Sakini)
David Burns (Purdy)
Ron Husmann (Fisby)
David Thomas (Oshira)
Lori Chinn (Higa Jiga)
Eleanor Calbes (Lotus Blossom)
Remak Ramsay (McLean)
Lou Wills (Gregovich)

SONGS:

Act I
With a Snap of My Finger (Sakini, ensemble)
Right-Hand Man (Purdy, Sakini, Fisby, ensemble)
Find Your Own Cricket (Sakini, Oshira, Higa Jiga, ensemble)
One Side of World (Sakini)
Geisha (Lotus Blossom)
You Say—They Say (Sakini, ensemble)
This Time (Fisby)
Simple Word (Lotus Blossom)
Garden Guaracha (McLean)
If It's Good Enough for Lady Astor (Fisby, McLean, Sakini, ensemble)

Act II
Chaya (Sakini, ensemble)
Call Me Back (Fisby, McLean, Sakini)
Lovely Ladies, Kind Gentlemen (Sakini)
You've Broken a Fine Woman's Heart (Purdy)
One More for the Last One (Sakini, Gregovich, ensemble)

MACK AND MABEL (1974)

BOOK BY: Michael Stewart; based on an idea by Leonard Spigelgass
MUSIC AND LYRICS BY: Jerry Herman
PUBLISHED LIBRETTO: Samuel French, 1976
CONDENSATION: *The Book of 1,000 Plays.* Steve Fletcher, Norman Jopling, eds. Facts On File, 1989
ANTHOLOGY: None
VOCAL SELECTIONS: Hal Leonard, 1974
LICENSING AGENT: Samuel French
RECORDING: MCA 10523 CD (original cast)
CAST: 10 M; 5 F; singers, dancers

Mabel Normand was working in a Brooklyn delicatessen back in 1911 when she was discovered by Mack Sennett. The plot follows them to California and the big days of silent films. There are bathing beauties, Keystone Kops, the unsolved murder of William Desmond Taylor, the coming of sound, and drugs. This was a spectacular Broadway production of the tragic lives of some real Hollywood personalities.

ORIGINAL CAST:

Robert Preston (Mack)
Bernadette Peters (Mabel)
Lisa Kirk (Lottie Ames)
Robert Fitch (Wally)
Christopher Murney (Charlie)
Jerry Dodge (Frank)

SONGS:

Act I
Movies Were Movies (Mack)
Look What Happened to Mabel (Mabel, Wally, Charlie, Frank, men)
Big Time (Lottie, family)
I Won't Send Roses (Mack) Reprise (Mabel)
I Wanna Make the World Laugh (Mack, company)
Wherever He Ain't (Mabel, men)
Hundreds of Girls (Mack, girls)

Act II
When Mabel Comes in the Room (company)
My Heart Leaps Up (Mack)

Time Heals Everything (Mabel)
Tap Your Troubles Away (Lottie, girls)
I Promise You a Happy Ending (Mack)

THE MAD SHOW (1966)

BOOK BY: Larry Siegel and Stan Hart; based on
    Mad (magazine)
MUSIC BY: Mary Rodgers
LYRICS BY: Marshall Barer, Larry Siegel, Steven
    Vinaver, and Esteban Ria Nido (Stephen
    Sondheim)
PUBLISHED LIBRETTO: French, 1973
CONDENSATION: None
ANTHOLOGY: None
LICENSING AGENT: Samuel French
RECORDING: Columbia OS 2930 (original cast)
CAST: 3 M; 2 F; extras

This musical revue's basis was a popular
comic book, and it was staged in a "pop
art" comic-book style. The various skits are
directed at baby-sitters, children's television programs, the bossa nova, Bob Dy-
lan, and Christmas gifts. Curiously, there is
very little political satire. This can be simply staged and will appeal to the college
crowd. A talented and funny cast is needed.

ORIGINAL CAST:

MacIntyre Dixon   Dick Libertini
Linda Lavin   Paul Sand
Jo Anne Worley

SONGS:
Act I
Opening (company)
You Never Can Tell (Lavin, Dixon, Worley)
Eccch (company)
The Real Thing (Sand)
Well It Ain't (Libertini)
Misery Is (Lavin, Dixon, Sand)
Hate Song (company)

Act II
Looking for Someone (Lavin, Sand, Worley)
The Gift of Maggie (and others) (Worley)
The Boy From . . . (Lavin)

MLLE MODISTE (1905)

BOOK AND LYRICS BY: Henry Blossom
MUSIC BY: Victor Herbert
PUBLISHED LIBRETTO: None
CONDENSATION: *Ganzl's Book of the Musical
    Theatre.* Ganzl, Kurt. Schirmer (Macmillan),
    1989
ANTHOLOGY: None
PIANO-VOCAL SCORE: Witmark, 1905
VOCAL SELECTIONS: *The Music of Victor Herbert.*
    Warner Bros. Music, 1976
LICENSING AGENT: Tams-Witmark
RECORDING: Readers Digest RD 40-N1 (studio cast)
CAST: Large mixed cast

Fifi is employed at Madame Cecelie's hat
shop on the Rue de la Paix in turn-of-
the-century Paris. She loves Etienne, who
is forbidden to marry beneath his social
level. Through the help of an American
millionaire, Fifi becomes a famous singer
and eventually weds Etienne. The role of
Fifi was written for opera star Fritzi Scheff,
and she introduced "Kiss Me Again," which
is considered one of the great American
songs. Although this was originally a big
Broadway production with a cast of eighty-
five, it was later simply staged by the Light
Opera of Manhattan. The 1930 film version
was called *The Toast of the Legion.*

1930 REVIVAL CAST:

Fritzi Scheff (Fifi)
Edith Artley (Fanchette)
Florence Cazelle (Nanette)
Flavia Arcaro (Mme Cecelie)
Nathaniel Wagner (Etienne)
Robert Rhodes (Gaston)
Detmar Poppen (Comte de St. Mar)
Rowan Tudor (René)
Sarah Edwards (Mrs. Bent)

SONGS:
Act I
When the Cat's Away, the Mice Will Play
    (Fanchette, Nanette, Mine Cecelie)
The Time, the Place, and the Girl (Etienne,
    ensemble)
If I Were on the Stage (Fifi)

Kiss Me Again (Fifi)
Love Me, Love My Dog (Gaston)

Act II

I Want What I Want, When I Want It (Comte de St. Mar)
The English Language (Gaston)
The Mascot of the Troop (Fifi, men)
The Dear Little Girl Who Is Good (René, girls)
The Keokuk Culture Club (Mrs. Bent, ensemble)
The Nightingale and the Star (Fifi)

MAGDALENA (1948)

BOOK BY: Frederick Hazlitt Brennan and Homer Curran
MUSIC BY: Heitor Villa-Lobos
LYRICS BY: Robert Wright and George Forrest
PUBLISHED LIBRETTO: None
CONDENSATION: None
ANTHOLOGY: None
PIANO-VOCAL SCORE: Villa-Lobos Music Corp. (Robbins), 1948
VOCAL SELECTIONS: Villa-Lobos Music Corp. (Robbins), 1948
LICENSING AGENT: Music Theatre International
RECORDING: CBS MK 44945 CD (1987 concert cast)
CAST: Large mixed cast

A strike by the native workers brings home from Paris the absent landlords to Colombia in 1912. A big festival welcomes them. Pedro steals the statue of the Madonna from the shrine that Maria is responsible for keeping safe. The strike ends, Pedro returns the statue and is reunited with Maria. This "musical adventure" was performed in a concert version in 1987 that was recorded and has reintroduced this lovely—if exotic—score to the world. The original production was lavish, but this can be done on a more modest scale. A colorful production, however, is required.

1987 CONCERT CAST:

Charles Damsel (Padre Jose)
Faith Esham (Maria)
Kevin Gray (Pedro)
Keith Curran (Major Blanco)
Charles Repole (Zoggie)
George Rose (General Carabana)
Judy Kaye (Teresa)
John Raitt (Tribal Elder)

SONGS:
Act I
The Jungle Chapel (Padre Jose, indians)
The Omen Bird (Maria, women)
My Bus and I (Pedro, ensemble)
The Emerald (Pedro, Maria)
The Civilized People (Zoggie, General Carabana, ensemble)
Food for Thought (Teresa, ensemble)
Colombia Calls (Major Blanco, General Carabana, Zoggie, Teresa, ensemble)
Magdalena (Tribal Elder)
Festival of the River (Maria, ensemble)
The Forbidden Orchid (Maria, Pedro)

Act II
The Singing Tree (Pedro, Maria, Indians)
Lost (Maria, Pedro)
Freedom! (Pedro, Indians)
In the Kitchen (Teresa, General Carabana)
Piece de Resistance (Teresa, General Carabana, ensemble)
The Seed of God (Padre Jose, Maria, Pedro, ensemble)

MAGGIE FLYNN (1968)

BOOK, MUSIC, AND LYRICS BY: Hugo Peretti, Luigi Creatore, and George David Weiss; book in collaboration with Morton Da Costa; based on an idea by John Flaxman
PUBLISHED LIBRETTO: French, 1968
CONDENSATION: None
ANTHOLOGY: None
VOCAL SELECTIONS: Valando, 1968
LICENSING AGENT: Samuel French
RECORDING: RCA LSOD 2009 (original cast)
CAST: 12 M; 6 F; chorus, children

The heroine of this musical is a girl in charge of a Negro orphanage in New York City in 1863. The plot involves her husband, an actor, and a colonel in the U.S.

Army. Race riots and draft dodgers are major plot elements, and there are obvious comparisons with the 1960s and the Vietnam War, as noted by the critics. But this is basically an old-fashioned musical and a family show. It includes a big circus parade and provides an opportunity for colorful period costumes and sets.

ORIGINAL CAST:

William James (Timmy)
Shirley Jones (Maggie)
Jack Cassidy (Phineas)
Jennifer Darling (Mary)
Robert Kaye (Colonel Farraday)
Sibyl Bowan (Mrs. Vanderhoff)
Austin Colyer (Donnelly)
Stanley Simmonds (O'Brian)

SONGS:
Act I
Never Gonna Make Me Fight (Timmy,
　　soldiers, men)
It's a Nice Cold Morning (Maggie, children)
I Wouldn't Have You Any Other Way (Maggie,
　　men)
Learn How to Laugh (Phineas, ensemble)
Maggie Flynn (Phineas)
The Thank You Song (Maggie, Mary, children)
Look around Your Little World (Colonel
　　Farraday, Phineas)
Maggie Flynn (reprise) (Phineas, Maggie,
　　children, men)
I Won't Let It Happen Again (Maggie)
How about a Ball? (Phineas, Maggie, Mrs.
　　Vanderhoff, ladies)
Pitter Patter (Phineas)

Act II
Never Gonna Make Me Fight (reprise)
　　(Timmy, Donnelly, O'Brian, men)
Why Can't I Walk Away? (Phineas)
The Game of War (children)
Mr. Clown (Phineas, Maggie, children,
　　ensemble)
Pitter Patter (reprise) (Maggie)
Don't You Think It's Very Nice? (Maggie,
　　Phineas, children)

MAIL (1988)

BOOK AND LYRICS BY: Jerry Colker
MUSIC BY: Michael Rupert
PUBLISHED LIBRETTO: French
CONDENSATION: None
ANTHOLOGY: None
LICENSING AGENT: Samuel French
RECORDING: None
CAST: 9 M; 6 F

A young novelist returns home after four months to find a huge pile of mail. It is both personal and junk mail and comes to life as he reads it. So we have visits from utility men, his best friend, magazine executives, political delegates, IRS auditors, and on and on. For the Broadway production they popped up in and out of mirrors, desks, windows, the refrigerator, etc. The score was described as a mixture of soft rock, country-western, soft-shoe, and show music.

ORIGINAL CAST:

Michael Rupert (Alex)
Mary Bond Davis (Radio Singer)
Mary Getz (Dana)
Brian Mitchell (Franklin)
Antonia Ellis (Sandi)
Robert Mandan (Max)

SONGS:
Act I
Monolithic Madness (Alex)
Gone So Long (Radio Singer)
Hit the Ground Running (Dana, Alex)
It's Your Life (ensemble)
Cookin' with Steam (Franklin)
It's Just a Question of Technique (Sandi,
　　Alex)
It's None of My Business (Max)
Crazy World (Dana)
Ambivalent Rag (Alex)
You Better Get Out of Town (ensemble)
We're Gonna Turn Off Your Juice (ensemble)
The World Set on Fire by a Black and a Jew
　　(Franklin, Alex)
Where Are You/Where Am I? (Dana)

Family Ties (Max)
Our Lost Weekend (Sandi, Alex, Dana)
Junk Mail/Disconnected (ensemble)
Helplessness at Midnight (Radio Singer)
What Have You Been Doing for the Past Ten
    Years (Alex, ensemble)
A Blank Piece of Paper (Alex)

Act II
Sweepstakes (Alex, ensemble)
It's Getting Harder to Love You (Dana,
    ensemble)
Publish Your Book (Sandi, Alex, ensemble)
Pages of My Diary (Dana, Alex, ensemble)
One Step at a Time (Alex, ensemble)
Don't Count on It (Sandi, Alex)
Friends for Life (Franklin, Alex)
Twenty-Nine Years Ago (Max, Alex)
Crazy World (reprise) (Alex, Dana)

MAME (1966)

BOOK BY: Jerome Lawrence and Robert E. Lee;
    based on the novel *Auntie Mame* by Patrick
    Dennis and the play *Auntie Mame* by Lawrence
    and Lee
MUSIC AND LYRICS BY: Jerry Herman
PUBLISHED LIBRETTO: Random House, 1967
CONDENSATION: *New Complete Book of the
    American Musical Theater.* Ewen, David. Holt,
    1970
ANTHOLOGY: None
PIANO-VOCAL SCORE: Big Three (Morris, 1967)
LICENSING AGENT: Tams-Witmark
RECORDING: Columbia CK 3000 CD (original cast)
CAST: Large mixed cast

Everyone knows "Auntie Mame." She was
introduced in a novel, then returned in a
play, in this musical version, and finally in
a film musical. She is the madcap aunt of
Patrick Dennis who loses her fortune in the
1929 stock-market crash, meets wealthy
Beauregard while clerking in a department
store, and goes to the South to meet his
aristocratic family. It is a funny book with
some sensational songs. This is a big musical with 1920s and 1930s ambience for the
whole family.

ORIGINAL CAST:
Angela Lansbury (Mame)
Frankie Michaels (Patrick, age 10)
Jerry Lanning (Patrick, age 19–29)
Jane Connell (Agnes)
Beatrice Arthur (Vera)
Charles Braswell (Beauregard)
Sab Shimono (Ito)

SONGS:
Act I
St. Bridget (Agnes; Patrick, age 10)
It's Today (Mame, ensemble)
Open a New Window (Mame, ensemble)
The Man in the Moon (Vera, ensemble)
My Best Girl (Patrick, age 10; Mame)
We Need a Little Christmas (Mame; Agnes;
    Ito; Beauregard; Patrick, age 10)
The Fox Hunt (ensemble)
Mame (Beauregard, ensemble)

Act II
Mame (reprise) (Patrick)
My Best Girl (reprise) (Patrick)
Bosom Buddies (Mame, Vera)
Gooch's Song (Agnes)
That's How Young I Feel (Mame, ensemble)
If He Walked into My Life (Mame)

MAN OF LA MANCHA (1965)

BOOK BY: David Wasserman; suggested by the life
    and works of Miguel de Cervantes y Saavedra
MUSIC BY: Mitch Leigh
LYRICS BY: Joe Darion
PUBLISHED LIBRETTO: Random House, 1966
CONDENSATION: *The Best Plays of 1965–1966.*
    Otis L. Guernsey, Jr., ed. Dodd, Mead, 1966;
    Ganzl's Book of the Musical Theatre. Ganzl, Kurt.
    Schirmer (Macmillan), 1989
ANTHOLOGY: *Great Musicals of the American Thea-
    tre*, vol. 2. Stanley Richards, ed. Chilton, 1976
PIANO-VOCAL SCORE: Cherry Lane Music (S. Fox),
    1968
VOCAL SELECTIONS: Cherry Lane Music (S. Fox),
    1965
LICENSING AGENT: Tams-Witmark
RECORDING: MCA 1672 CD (original cast)
CAST: Large mixed cast

This musical play about Cervantes and his "Don Quixote" had a long initial run of over 2,000 performances. It has returned to Broadway several times, most recently with Raul Julia, has been performed all over the world, and was filmed in 1972 with Peter O'Toole. The setting is Spain at the end of the sixteenth century. It was originally presented on a thrust stage without intermission. The show is an old-fashioned, sentimental extravaganza that was called a "ten handkerchief" play. Audiences love it.

Tony Award Winner (Best Musical)

ORIGINAL CAST:

Richard Kiley (Don Quixote/Cervantes)
Irving Jacobson (Sancho)
Joan Diener (Aldonza)
Mimi Turque (Antonia)
Ray Middleton (Innkeeper)
Robert Rounseville (Padre)
Eleanore Knapp (Housekeeper)
Jon Cypher (Dr. Carrasco)
Harry Theyard (Anselmo)
Gino Conforti (Barber)

SONGS:
(performed without intermission)
Man of La Mancha (Don Quixote, Sancho, ensemble)
It's All the Same (Aldonza, ensemble)
Dulcinea (Don Quixote)
I'm Only Thinking of Him (Padre, Antonia, Housekeeper, Carrasco)
I Really Like Him (Sancho)
What Does He Want with Me? (Aldonza)
Little Bird, Little Bird (Anselmo, ensemble)
Barber's Song (Barber)
Golden Helmet (Don Quixote, Sancho, Barber, ensemble)
To Each His Dulcinea (To Every Man His Dream) (Padre)
The Quest (The Impossible Dream) (Don Quixote)
The Combat (Don Quixote, Aldonza, Sancho, ensemble)
The Dubbing (Innkeeper, Aldonza, Sancho)
The Abduction (Aldonza, ensemble)
Aldonza (Aldonza)

The Knight of the Mirrors (ensemble)
A Little Gossip (Sancho)
The Psalm (Padre)

MAN WITH A LOAD OF MISCHIEF (1966)

BOOK BY: Ben Tarver; adapted from the play by Ashley Dukes
MUSIC BY: John Clifton
LYRICS BY: John Clifton and Ben Tarver
PUBLISHED LIBRETTO: None
CONDENSATION: None
ANTHOLOGY: None
LICENSING AGENT: Samuel French
RECORDING: Kapp KRS 5508 (original cast)
CAST: 3 M; 3 F

This off-Broadway musical was almost an operetta, with much charm and appeal. It is based on an English play and the title is the name of a roadside inn in the early nineteenth century. The plot is simply about a lord who makes love to a maid, and a servant who makes love to a lady. A revival used a four-piece ensemble for accompaniment and a set that swung around from the inn to a garden. The score was described as lovely and enchanting.

ORIGINAL CAST:

Tom Noel (Innkeeper)
Lesslie Nicol (His Wife)
Raymond Thorne (Lord)
Reid Shelton (Man)
Virginia Vestoff (Lady)
Alice Cannon (Maid)

SONGS:
Act I
Wayside Inn (Innkeeper)
The Rescue (Wife)
Entrance Polonaise (company)
Good-bye, My Sweet (Lady)
Romance! (Innkeeper, Wife, Lord, Maid)
Lover Lost (Lady)
Once You've Had a Little Taste (Maid)
Hulla-Baloo-Balay (Man)

Dinner Minuet (company)
You'd Be Amazed (Lord, Lady, Man)
A Friend Like You (Lady, Lord)
Masquerade (Man)
Man with a Load of Mischief (Lady)

Act II
What Style! (Innkeeper)
A Wonder (Lady)
Make Way for My Lady (Man)
Forget (Lord)
Any Other Way (Wife, Innkeeper)
Little Rag Doll (Maid)
Romance (reprise) (Lady)
Sextet (company)
Make Way for My Lady (reprise) (Man, Lady)

MARCH OF THE FALSETTOS
(1981)

MUSIC AND LYRICS BY: William Finn
PUBLISHED LIBRETTO: French, 1981
CONDENSATION: None
ANTHOLOGY: *The Marvin Songs*. Fireside Theatre
  Publications; *Plays from Playwrights Horizon*.
  Broadway Play Publishing, 1987
LICENSING AGENT: Samuel French
RECORDING: DRG 12581 CD (original cast)
CAST: 3 M; 1 F; 1 young boy

This is a mini-opera-like musical (and part of a trilogy) that is entirely sung and performed for about one hour without an intermission. The hero is Marvin, who is Jewish, married, and has a young son. The plot finds Marvin leaving his family for a male lover, while his psychiatrist takes up with Marvin's wife. The *New York Daily News* described the music as soft rock with "cascading melodies, intricate harmonies, complex arrangements and show-stopping deliveries." This is a simple show to stage (the scenery consists of chairs and tables) but is demanding, adult entertainment. *In Trousers* and *Falsettoland* are the other parts of the trilogy.

ORIGINAL CAST:

Michael Rupert (Marvin)
Alison Fraser (Trina)
James Kushner (Jason, young boy)
Stephen Bogardus (Whizzer)
Chip Zien (Mendel)

SONGS:
(performed without intermission)
Four Jews in a Room Bitching (cast)
A Tight-Knit Family (Marvin)
Love Is Blind (Trina, Mendel, cast)
The Thrill of First Love (Marvin, Whizzer)
Marvin at the Psychiatrist (Marvin, Mendel, Jason)
My Father's a Homo (Jason)
Everyone Tells Jason to See a Psychiatrist (cast)
This Had Better Come to a Stop (cast)
Please Come to My House (Trina, Mendel, Jason)
Jason's Therapy (Jason, Mendel, cast)
A Marriage Proposal (Mendel)
A Tight-Knit Family (reprise) (Marvin, Mendel)
Trina's Song (Trina)
March of the Falsettos (men)
The Chess Game (Marvin, Whizzer)
Making a Home (Trina, Mendel, Whizzer)
The Games I Play (Whizzer)
Marvin Hits Trina (cast)
I Never Wanted to Love You (cast)
Father to Son (Marvin, Jason)

MARRY ME A LITTLE (1980)

CONCEIVED AND DEVELOPED BY: Craig Lucas and
  Norman René
MUSIC AND LYRICS BY: Stephen Sondheim
PUBLISHED LIBRETTO: None (lyrics included with
  LP recording)
CONDENSATION: None
ANTHOLOGY: None
MUSIC PUBLISHER: Revelation Music
LICENSING AGENT: Music Theatre International
RECORDING: RCA 7142 CD (original cast)
CAST: 1 M; 1 F

A one-hour musical (without intermission) made up of bits and pieces of Sondheim scores dropped from other shows. The set is a run-down studio apartment and the cast of two are both onstage, although they are both meant to be alone in their own apartments. There is no spoken dialogue. Through the songs we learn of their lives and loneliness. The sixteen Sondheim songs are the main reason for this show. It can be simply staged with only a piano accompaniment.

ORIGINAL CAST:

Suzanne Henry (She)
Craig Lucas (He)

SONGS:
(performed without intermission)
Two Fairy Tales (both)
Saturday Night (both)
Can That Boy Foxtrot (She)
All Things Bright and Beautiful (both)
Bang! (both)
The Girls of Summer (She)
Uptown, Downtown (He)
So Many People (both)
Your Eyes Are Blue (both)
A Moment with You (both)
Marry Me a Little (She)
Happily Ever After (He)
Pour le Sport (both)
Silly People (He)
There Won't Be Trumpets (She)
It Wasn't Meant to Happen (both)

MAYOR (1985)

BOOK BY: Warren Leight; based on *Mayor* by
   Edward I. Koch
MUSIC AND LYRICS BY: Charles Strouse
PUBLISHED LIBRETTO: French, 1987
CONDENSATION: None
ANTHOLOGY: None
VOCAL SELECTIONS: Big Three (Columbia
   Pictures), 1985
LICENSING AGENT: Samuel French

RECORDING: New York Music NYM 21 CD (original
   cast)
CAST: 4 M; 4 F

Although called "the musical," this is actually a musical revue based on the autobiography of the (then) Mayor of New York City. It is, however, as much about the city as the man. One slight plot thread concerns the redevelopment of Times Square as a theme park ("Manhabitat"). The show has been designed to entertain; it does not attempt a serious analysis of the Mayor and skirts political issues. John Beaufort, in the *Christian Science Monitor*, wrote, "If Ed Koch is the quintessential New Yorker, *Mayor* is essentially New York-y." The cast members (except for the Mayor) all play multiple roles on a bare stage.

ORIGINAL CAST:

Lenny Wolpe (Mayor)
Douglas Bernstein
Marion J. Caffey
Keith Curran
Nancy Giles
Ken Jennings
Ilene Kristen
Kathryn McAteer

SONGS:
Act I
Mayor (Wolpe)
You Can Be a New Yorker Too! (Curran,
   Bernstein, company)
You're Not the Mayor (McAteer, Caffey,
   Jennings)
March of the Yuppies (Giles, Curran,
   Bernstein, company)
Hootspa (Wolpe, Curran, Jennings)
What You See Is What You Get (Giles, Wolpe)
Ballad (Kristen, Curran)
I Want to Be the Mayor (Bernstein)
The Last "I Love New York" Song (company)

Act II
Good Times (Kristen, Giles, Curran, Jennings,
   Bernstein, Wolpe)
I'll Never Leave You (Caffey, McAteer, Kristen,
   Curran)

How'm I Doin'? (Wolpe, Jennings, company)
Finale (Wolpe, company)
My City (company)

ME AND JULIET (1953)

BOOK AND LYRICS BY: Oscar Hammerstein II
MUSIC BY: Richard Rodgers
PUBLISHED LIBRETTO: Random House, 1953
CONDENSATION: *Rodgers and Hammerstein.*
    Mordden, Ethan. Abrams, 1992
ANTHOLOGY: *Six Plays by Rodgers and*
    Hammerstein. Random House, 1955; Modern
    Library, 1959
PIANO-VOCAL SCORE: Williamson, 1953
LICENSING AGENT: Rodgers and Hammerstein
    Theatre Library
RECORDING: RCA 61480 CD (original cast)
CAST: 17 M; 13 F; chorus

This is a musical about backstage show business—a show-within-a-show. There are two romances: one is between a dancer and a stage manager, and the other is between an understudy and a young staff assistant. The sets for the original production were praised for their ingenious way of showing the stage, the wings, and even the lobby during intermission. A revival was called a spoof of 1950s-style musicals. Rodgers and Hammerstein musicals are always good family entertainment.

ORIGINAL CAST:

Isabel Bigley (Jeanie)
Arthur Maxwell (Charlie)
Helena Scott (Lily)
Mark Dawson (Bob)
Bob Fortier (Jim)
Bill Hayes (Larry)
Joan McCracken (Betty)
Jackie Kelk (Herbie)

SONGS:
Act I
A Very Special Day (Jeanie, trio)
That's the Way It Happens (Jeanie, trio)
Marriage Type Love (Charlie, Lily, ensemble)
Keep It Gay (Bob, Jim, chorus)

The Big Black Giant (Larry)
No Other Love (Jeanie, Larry)
It's Me (Betty, Jeanie)

Act II
Intermission Talk (Herbie, ensemble)
It Feels Good (Bob)
The Baby You Love (Lily, dancers)
We Deserve Each Other (Betty, Jim, chorus)
I'm Your Girl (Jeanie, Larry)

ME AND MY GIRL (1986)

BOOK AND LYRICS BY: L. Arthur Rose and
    Douglas Furber; revised by Stephen Fry
MUSIC BY: Noel Gay
PUBLISHED LIBRETTO: French, 1990
CONDENSATION: *Ganzl's Book of the Musical*
    Theatre. Ganzl, Kurt. Schirmer (Macmillan),
    1989
ANTHOLOGY: None
VOCAL SELECTIONS: Hal Leonard, 1984
LICENSING AGENT: Samuel French
RECORDING: MCA 6169 CD (1986 New York cast)
CAST: Large mixed cast

A young cockney lad is discovered as the long lost Earl of Hareford. But in order to take over his title and estate, he must learn how to behave in society. Along with a lot of slapstick humor and awful-but-funny puns, he must decide between his cockney girlfriend and a gold-digging society girl. Originally a big hit in London in 1937, this show has been revised and revived as a big hit in both London and New York. The score has a "music-hall melodiousness" and the Lambeth Walk will take the entire cast down into the audience.

ORIGINAL CAST:

Jane Summerhays (Lady Jaquie)
George S. Irving (Sir John)
Jane Connell (Duchess)
Nick Ullett (Gerald)
Timothy Jerome (Parkchester)
Thomas Toner (Heathersett)
Robert Lindsay (Bill)
Maryann Plunkett (Sally)

SONGS:

Act I

A Weekend at Hareford (ensemble)

Thinking of No-One but Me (Lady Jaquie, Gerald)

The Family Solicitor (Parkchester, family)

Me and My Girl (Bill, Sally)

An English Gentleman (Heathersett, staff)

You Would If You Could (Lady Jaquie, Bill)

Hold My Hand (Bill, Sally, ensemble)

Once You Lose Your Heart (Sally)

Preparation Fugue (company)

The Lambeth Walk (Bill, Sally, company)

Act II

The Sun Has Got His Hat On (Gerald, Lady Jaquie, ensemble)

Take It on the Chin (Sally)

Song of Hareford (Duchess, Bill, ensemble)

Love Makes the World Go 'Round (Bill, Sir John)

Leaning on a Lamppost (Bill, ensemble)

THE ME NOBODY KNOWS (1970)

BASED ON THE BOOK EDITED BY: Stephen M. Joseph

MUSIC BY: Gary William Friedman

LYRICS BY: Will Holt

PUBLISHED LIBRETTO: None

CONDENSATION: None

ANTHOLOGY: None

VOCAL SELECTIONS: New York Times Music, 1970

LICENSING AGENT: Samuel French

RECORDING: Atlantic SD 1566 (original cast)

CAST: 6 M; 6 F

"These are children's voices from the ghetto. In their struggle lies their hope, and ours. They are the voices of change" (program note). There is no story line in the usual sense in this show; it is based on writings from school classes of ghetto children. The off-Broadway cast (which later moved to Broadway) was composed of twelve children, eight black and four white. Their lives are surrounded by poverty, drugs, and oppression. They recite poems and prose reflections, sing songs, and perform simple

dance routines. Some of this is poignant, sad, happy, and humorous. The Broadway production used projected photographs and paintings, while the set was basically a dim alleyway in a slum area of a big city.

Off Broadway (OBIE) Award Winner

ORIGINAL CAST:

Melanie Henderson (Rhoda)

Gerri Dean (Melba)

Kevin Lindsay (William)

Beverly Ann Bremers (Catherine)

Jose Fernandez (Carlos)

Laura Michaels (Lillian)

Northern Calloway (Lloyd)

Hattie Winston (Nell)

Douglas Grant (Benjamin)

Carl Thoma (Clorox)

Irene Cara (Lillie Mae)

SONGS:

Act I

Introduction (Rhoda)

Dream Babies (Melba)

Light Sings (William, company)

This World (company)

How I Feel (Catherine, Carlos)

The White House (Lloyd)

If I Had a Million Dollars (company)

Act II

Fugue for Four Girls (Lillie Mae, Catherine, Lillian, Nell)

Sounds (Nell, Catherine)

The Tree (Carlos)

Something Beautiful (Rhoda)

Black (Benjamin, Clorox, Lillie Mae, Lloyd, Melba, Nell, Rhoda, William)

War Babies (Lloyd)

Let Me Come In (company)

MEET ME IN ST. LOUIS (1989)

BOOK BY: Sally Benson; based on her *Kensington Stories* and the 1944 MGM film; 1989 production book revisions by Hugh Wheeler

MUSIC AND LYRICS BY: Hugh Martin and Ralph Blane

PUBLISHED LIBRETTO: None

CONDENSATION: None
ANTHOLOGY: None
MUSIC PUBLISHER: CPP/Belwin
LICENSING AGENT: Tams-Witmark
RECORDING: DRG 19002 CD (original cast)
CAST: Large mixed cast

This is the story of the Smith family in St. Louis. The four daughters in the family are all excited about the World's Fair to be held there in the summer of 1904. For a time it looks like they will be leaving St. Louis before the fair opens, but all works out well. The 1944 film was adapted for the stage and was presented successfully all over the country; however, it was almost forty-five years before it was finally presented on Broadway. Judy Garland was the original film star, and Jane Powell played the part in a 1959 TV version. This homespun, turn-of-the-century show is certainly family entertainment.

ORIGINAL CAST:

Milo O'Shea (Grandpa)
Courtney Peldon (Tootie)
Donna Kane (Esther)
Rachael Graham (Agnes)
Juliet Lambert (Rose)
Michael O'Steen (Lon)
Betty Garrett (Katie)
Charlotte Moore (Mrs. Smith)
George Hearn (Mr. Smith)
Peter Reardon (Warren)
Gregg Whitney (Douglas)
Jason Workman (John)

SONGS:
Act I
Meet Me in St. Louis (ensemble) Reprise (Grandpa, Tootie)
The Boy Next Door (Esther)
Be Anything But a Girl (Grandpa, Agnes, Tootie)
Skip to My Lou (Rose, Esther, Lon, Douglas, John, Warren, company)
Under the Bamboo Tree (Esther, Tootie)
Banjos (Lon, company)
Ghosties and Ghoulies (Katie, Agnes, Tootie, children)

Wasn't It Fun? (Mr. Smith, Mrs. Smith)
The Trolley Song (Esther, company)
Act II
Ice (Rose, Warren, Douglas, company)
Raving Beauty (Warren, Douglas, Rose)
A Touch of the Irish (Katie, Esther, Rose)
You Are for Loving (John, Esther)
A Day in New York (Mr. Smith, family)
The Ball (Grandpa, company)
Diamonds in the Starlight (John, Esther)
Have Yourself a Merry Little Christmas (Esther)
Paging Mr. Sousa (Mr. Smith, company)

MERRILY WE ROLL ALONG (1981)

BOOK BY: George Furth; based on the play by George S. Kaufman and Moss Hart
MUSIC AND LYRICS BY: Stephen Sondheim
PUBLISHED LIBRETTO: Dodd, Mead, 1982
CONDENSATION: None
ANTHOLOGY: None
VOCAL SELECTIONS: Revelation Music (Valando), 1981
LICENSING AGENT: Music Theatre International
RECORDING: RCA 5840 CD (original cast)
CAST: A young cast of 27

Based on a 1934 play, this musical tells the story of some young hopefuls (songwriters and a novelist) and their careers over a twenty-five-year period. An unusual technique of going backward in time is used. The story begins when one of the leads returns to address the graduating class at his old high school; the plot continues in reverse until he is graduating. The Broadway set was high-tech bleachers with skyline projections. Members of the young cast wore T-shirts with their names or titles on them. Since its original production, several revised versions have been done in both the United States and England.

ORIGINAL CAST:

Jim Walton (Frank)
Terry Finn (Gussie)
Ann Morrison (Mary)

Lonny Price (Charley)
Sally Klein (Beth)
Jason Alexander (Joe)
David Loud (Ted)

SONGS:
Act I
The Hills of Tomorrow (company)
Merrily We Roll Along (company)
Rich and Happy (Frank, guests)
Old Friends (Mary, Charley)
Like It Was (Mary)
Franklin Shepard, Inc. (Charley)
Not a Day Goes By (Frank)
Now You Know (Mary, company)

Act II
It's a Hit! (Frank, Mary, Charley, Joe, Beth)
Good Thing Going (Charley, Frank, company)
Bobby and Jackie and Jack (Charley, Beth,
    Frank, Ted)
Not a Day Goes By (reprise) (Frank, Beth)
Opening Doors (Frank, Charley, Mary, Joe,
    Beth, Ted, company)
Our Time (Frank, Charley, Mary, company)

THE MERRY WIDOW (1907)

BOOK AND LYRICS BY: Charles George
MUSIC BY: Franz Lehar
PUBLISHED LIBRETTO: French
CONDENSATION: *Ganzl's Book of the Musical
    Theatre.* Ganzl, Kurt. Schirmer (Macmillan),
    1989; *The Complete Book of Light Operas.*
    Lubbock, Mark. Putnam (London), 1962
VOCAL SELECTIONS: Chappell, 1977 (lyrics by
    Sheldon Harnick)
LICENSING AGENTS: Tams-Witmark; Samuel French
RECORDING: TER 1111 CD (1986 Sadler's Wells
    production)
CAST: Large mixed cast

Perhaps the most famous of all Viennese operettas, this show has been revived and filmed many times. The reviewer for an opulent 1943 production at the Majestic Theater in New York felt the show would have been buried years ago except for the lilting Lehar music. The plot involves the very wealthy widow whose millions draw suitors like flies. But she marries the heir to the throne of an impoverished little kingdom just because she loves him. Set in turn-of-the-century Paris, costumes and sets can be lavish. The third act is set at the famous Maxim's restaurant. Everyone will exit the theater humming the beautiful "Merry Widow Waltz." This is frequently presented by the New York City Opera at Lincoln Center.

1951 DALLAS STATE FAIR CAST:
Dorothy Kirsten (Sonia)
John Tyers (Danilo)
Vera Brynner (Natalie)
Lloyd Thomas Leech (Camille)
Hiram Sherman (Popoff)
Arny Freeman (Nish)

SONGS:
Act I
A Dutiful Wife (Natalie, Camille)
In Marsovia (Sonia, men)
Maxim's (Danilo)

Act II
Vilia (Sonia)
Women (Danilo, Popoff, Nish, ensemble)
The Merry Widow Waltz (Sonia, Danilo)
Love in My Heart (Natalie, Camille)

Act III
The Girls at Maxim's (ensemble)
Can-Can (dance)
I Love You So (The Merry Widow Waltz)
    (Sonia, Danilo)

THE MIDDLE OF NOWHERE (1988)

BOOK BY: Tracy Friedman
MUSIC AND LYRICS BY: Randy Newman
PUBLISHED LIBRETTO: None
CONDENSATION: None
ANTHOLOGY: None
LICENSING AGENT: Rodgers and Hammerstein
    Theatre Library
RECORDING: None
CAST: 4 M; 1 F

The songs of popular singer and songwriter Randy Newman have been fashioned into a contemporary minstrel show. The show begins in a Louisiana bus station where five strangers find themselves stranded all night. The bus station is transformed into a theater and the five strangers become song-and-dance performers singing Newman's "mordant, ironic, witty songs." Some of the songs include "Sail Away," "Lonely at the Top," and "I Think It's Gonna Rain Today." Critics found the songs to have an odd aftertaste and called the evening "diverting, but disturbing." Minstrel show conventions are used, but no blackface. The show runs ninety minutes and utilizes a five-piece band.

ORIGINAL CAST:

Diana Castle (Girl)
Michael Arkin (Salesman)
Vondie Curtis-Hall (G.I.)
Tony Hoylen (Redneck)
Roger Robinson (Joe)

This revue contains twenty-five songs performed without intermission.

MILK AND HONEY (1961)

BOOK BY: Don Appell
MUSIC AND LYRICS BY: Jerry Herman
PUBLISHED LIBRETTO: None
CONDENSATION: *New Complete Book of the American Musical Theater.* Ewen, David. Holt, 1970
ANTHOLOGY: None
PIANO-VOCAL SCORE: Big Three, 1963
VOCAL SELECTIONS: *Jerry Herman Songbook.* Morris, 1974
LICENSING AGENT: Tams-Witmark
RECORDING: RCA LSO 1065 (original cast)
CAST: Large mixed cast

Modern-day Israel is the setting for this musical that involves Sabras (native-born Israelis) and American tourists. The dance numbers include the hora and the big number celebrates Israeli Independence Day. The settings include a street in Jerusalem, a cafe in Tel Aviv, and a kibbutz. Besides the expected costumes, there is a Yemenite wedding scene with three gorgeously clad couples married in parallel ceremonies. For humor there is the American widow in search of a new mate. This was Jerry Herman's first Broadway score.

ORIGINAL CAST:

Robert Weede (Phil)
George Zima (Shepherd Boy)
Mimi Benzell (Ruth)
Tommy Rall (David)
Juki Arkin (Adi)
Molly Picon (Mrs. Weiss)

SONGS:
Act I
Shepherd's Song (Shepherd Boy, Phil)
Shalom (Phil, Ruth)
Independence Day Hora (company)
Milk and Honey (David, Adi, company)
There's No Reason in the World (Phil)
Chin Up, Ladies (Mrs. Weiss, widows)
That Was Yesterday (Ruth, Phil, David, Adi, company)
Let's Not Waste a Moment (Phil)
The Wedding (Ruth, Phil, company)

Act II
Like a Young Man (Phil)
I Will Follow You (David)
Hymn to Hymie (Mrs. Weiss)
There's No Reason in the World (reprise) (Ruth)
As Simple as That (Ruth, Phil)

MINNIE'S BOYS (1970)

BOOK BY: Arthur Marx and Robert Fisher; based on the lives of the Marx Brothers
MUSIC BY: Larry Grossman
LYRICS BY: Hal Hackady
PUBLISHED LIBRETTO: French
CONDENSATION: *New Complete Book of the American Musical Theater.* Ewen, David. Holt, 1970
ANTHOLOGY: None

VOCAL SELECTIONS: New York Times Music, 1970
LICENSING AGENT: Samuel French
RECORDING: Project 3 SPRD 6002 CD (original
cast)
CAST: 18 M; 2 F; chorus

The setting is New York City from the early twentieth century to the 1920s. Minnie Marx has five sons. They are lazy, stealing trouble-makers. Minnie comes from a show-business background, so she decides to put her sons on the stage. We follow their misadventures in vaudeville until the "Marx Brothers" begin to take shape. The critics particularly liked the actors cast as the brothers and the re-creation of some of their routines with Margaret Dumont. The production needs the usual backstage and vaudeville sets of the period. Minnie Marx also sings and dances, and she performs with the boys in one number dressed as a giant rabbit.

ORIGINAL CAST:

Shelley Winters (Minnie)
Mort Marshall (Al)
Lewis J. Stadlen (Julie "Groucho")
Alvin Kupperman (Herbie "Zeppo")
Daniel Fortus (Adolph "Harpo")
Arny Freeman (Frenchie)
Gary Raucher (Milton)
Irwin Pearl (Leonard "Chico")
David Vaughan (Production Singer)
Richard B. Shull (Maxie)
Julie Kurnitz (Mrs. Rittenhouse)

SONGS:
Act I
Five Growing Boys (Minnie, ensemble)
Rich Is (Al, Marx family)
More Precious Far (Julie, Herbie, Adolph,
Minnie, Frenchie)
Empty (Frenchie, Minnie, Milton)
The Four Nightingales (Julie, Herbie, Adolph)
Underneath It All (Julie, Herbie, Adolph,
Leonard, Maxie, girls)
Mama a Rainbow (Adolph, Minnie)
You Don't Have to Do It for Me (Minnie, Julie,
Herbie, Adolph, Leonard)

If You Wind Me Up (Minnie, Julie, Herbie,
Adolph, Leonard)
Rich Is (reprise) (Julie, Herbie, Adolph,
Leonard)
Be Happy (Minnie)

Act II
Guess Where I'm Going (Production Singer,
ensemble)
Where Was I When They Passed Out the
Luck? (Julie, Herbie, Adolph, Leonard)
Minnie's Boys (Minnie)
You Remind Me of You (Julie, Mrs.
Rittenhouse)
The Act (Marx Brothers, ensemble)

LES MISERABLES (1987)

BOOK BY: Alain Boublil and Claude-Michel
Schonberg; based on the novel by Victor Hugo
MUSIC BY: Claude-Michel Schonberg
LYRICS BY: Herbert Kretzmer
PUBLISHED LIBRETTO: *The Complete Book of Les
Miserables*. Arcade, 1990
CONDENSATION: *Ganzl's Book of the Musical
Theatre*. Ganzl, Kurt. Schirmer (Macmillan),
1989; *The Best Plays of 1986–1987*. Otis L.
Guernsey, Jr., ed. Dodd, Mead, 1987
ANTHOLOGY: None
VOCAL SELECTIONS: Hal Leonard, 1986
LICENSING AGENT: Not yet available; contact
Cameron Mackintosh, Inc., 226 West 47th
Street, New York, NY 10036; (212) 921-9290
RECORDING: Geffen 9-24151-2 CD (original cast)
CAST: Large mixed cast

A sensational hit in many cities of the world, this all-singing "pop opera" is over three hours long and requires strong voices and an elaborate production. The plot is distilled from the novel but does not slavishly adhere to all the details. Police Inspector Javert searches for the unjustly hounded Jean Valjean and the lovers Marius and Cosette are tearful while the revolutionary students mount the barricades in 1832 Paris. Your barricade must be large and strong enough to support a number of cast members. The original production used a large turntable, but probably you can bring this off without one. But this will be a real challenge.

Tony Award Winner (Best Musical)

ORIGINAL CAST:

Randy Graff (Fantine)
Colm Wilkinson (Jean Valjean)
Terrence Mann (Javert)
Judy Kuhn (Cosette)
Leo Burmester (Thenardier)
Jennifer Butt (Mme Thenardier)
Michael Maguire (Enjolras)
Braden Danner (Gavroche)
David Bryant (Marius)
Frances Ruffelle (Eponine)
Anthony Crivello (Grantaire)

SONGS:
Act I
At the End of the Day (ensemble)
I Dreamed a Dream (Fantine)
Lovely Ladies (ensemble)
Who Am I? (Valjean)
Come to Me (Fantine, Valjean)
Confrontation (Javert, Valjean)
Castle on a Cloud (Cosette)
Master of the House (Thenardiers, ensemble)
Thenardier Waltz (Thenardiers, Valjean)
Look Down (Gavroche, men)
Stars (Javert)
Red and Black (Enjolras, Marius, students)
Do You Hear the People Sing? (Enjolras, ensemble)
In My Life (Cosette, Valjean, Marius, Eponine)
A Heart Full of Love (Cosette, Marius, Eponine)
One Day More (company)

Act II
On My Own (Eponine)
Javert at the Barricade/Little People (Javert, Enjolras, Gavroche)
The First Attack (Enjolras, students)
A Little Fall of Rain (Eponine, Marius)
Drink with Me (Grantaire, ensemble)
Bring Him Home (Valjean)
Dog Eats Dog (Thenardier)
Javert's Suicide (Javert)

Turning (women)
Empty Chairs and Empty Tables (Marius)
Beggars at the Feast (Thenardiers, ensemble)

MISS LIBERTY (1949)

BOOK BY: Robert E. Sherwood
MUSIC AND LYRICS BY: Irving Berlin
PUBLISHED LIBRETTO: French, 1949
CONDENSATION: *New Complete Book of the American Musical Theater.* Ewen, David. Holt, 1970
ANTHOLOGY: None
VOCAL SELECTIONS: Hal Leonard, 1990
LICENSING AGENT: Rodgers and Hammerstein Theatre Library
RECORDING: Sony 48015 CD (original cast)
CAST: Large mixed cast

Set in New York and Paris in 1885, the plot deals with the adventures of a young French girl who is alleged to be the model for the Statue of Liberty. There is also a circulation war going on between Joseph Pulitzer, publisher of the *New York World*, and James Gordon Bennett, publisher of the *New York Herald*. Irving Berlin's famous score includes several popular songs of a few years ago. The New York production was particularly praised for the lively and imaginative dance routines, including the Irish dancing at the Policeman's Ball. There was a revival of this show at the Goodspeed Opera House in Connecticut in 1983.

ORIGINAL CAST:

Mary McCarty (Maisie)
Eddie Albert (Horace)
Philip Bourneuf (Pulitzer)
Charles Dingle (Bennett)
Donald McClelland (Mayor)
Allyn McLerie (Monique)
Johnny Thompson (Lamplighter)
Ethel Griffies (The Countess)
Tommy Rall (The Dandy)

SONGS:

Act I

Extra, Extra (newsboys, ensemble)

What Do I Have to Do to Get My Picture Took? (Maisie, Horace, ensemble)

The Most Expensive Statue in the World (Pulitzer, Bennett, Mayor, ensemble)

A Little Fish in a Big Pond (Horace, Maisie, ensemble)

Let's Take an Old-Fashioned Walk (Horace, Monique, ensemble)

Homework (Maisie)

Paris Wakes Up and Smiles (Lamplighter, Monique, ensemble)

Only for Americans (The Countess, Horace, ensemble)

Just One Way to Say I Love You (Horace, Monique)

Act II

Miss Liberty (company)

The Train (Monique, ensemble)

You Can Have Him (Maisie, Monique)

The Policeman's Ball (Maisie, The Dandy, ensemble)

Follow the Leader Jig (ensemble)

Me an' My Bundle (Horace, Monique, ensemble)

Falling Out of Love Can Be Fun (Maisie)

Give Me Your Tired, Your Poor (Monique, ensemble)

MISS SAIGON (1991)

BOOK BY: Alain Boublil and Claude-Michel Schonberg

MUSIC BY: Claude-Michel Schonberg

LYRICS BY: Richard Maltby, Jr., and Alain Boublil

PUBLISHED LIBRETTO: None (lyrics with LP recording)

CONDENSATION: *The Story of Miss Saigon*. Behr, Edward, and Steyn, Mark. Arcade, 1991; *Applause Best Plays. Theater Year Book, 1990–1991*. Guernsey, Otis L., Jr., and Sweet, Jeffrey, eds. Applause Theater Books, 1992

ANTHOLOGY: None

PIANO-VOCAL SCORE: Hal Leonard, 1990

VOCAL SELECTIONS: Hal Leonard, 1990

LICENSING AGENT: Not yet available; contact Cameron Mackintosh, Inc., 226 West 47th Street, New York, NY 10036; (212) 921-9290

RECORDING: Geffen 24271 CD (original London cast)

CAST: Large mixed cast

The basic plot comes from *Madame Butterfly*. The authors were inspired to write their version after seeing some photographs of the Vietnam War. Chris, an American marine in Saigon, falls in love with Kim, a bar girl, but is separated from her during the evacuation, not knowing she is pregnant. Some years later he and his American wife search for her in Bangkok. The leading role of the "engineer" has the big "American Dream" number. Frank Rich, in the *New York Times*, wrote that this musical was "gripping entertainment of the old school," referring to the East-meets-West themes of some Rodgers and Hammerstein musicals, as well as offering some lush melodies and a good cry. This musical also comes from the more recent trend in musicals with spectacular effects (a helicopter, for instance) and a large cast (including a large number of Orientals). Scenes include the sleazy bars of Saigon and Bangkok, as well as military offices and Vietnamese interiors.

ORIGINAL CAST:

Jonathan Pryce (Engineer)

Marina Chapa (Gigi)

Lea Salonga (Kim)

Hinton Battle (John)

Willy Falk (Chris)

Barry K. Bernal (Thuy)

Liz Callaway (Ellen)

SONGS:

Act I

The Heat Is on in Saigon (Engineer, ensemble)

The Movie in My Mind (Gigi, Kim, girls)

The Transaction (John, Engineer, Chris, company)

Why God Why? (Chris)

Sun and Moon (Kim, Chris)

The Telephone (John, Chris, Engineer)

The Ceremony (Kim, Chris, girls)
The Last Night of the World (Kim, Chris)
The Morning of the Dragon (Thuy, Engineer,
    company)
I Still Believe (Kim, Ellen)
Back in Town (Kim, Engineer, Thuy)
You Will Not Touch Him (Kim, Thuy)
If You Want to Die in Bed (Engineer)
I'd Give My Life for You (Kim, company)

Act II
Bui-Doi (John, company)
What a Waste (Engineer, company)
Please (John, Kim)
The Guilt Inside Your Head (Thuy, Kim, Chris,
    John, company)
Room 317 (Ellen, Kim)
Now That I've Seen Her (Ellen)
The Confrontation (Ellen, Chris, John)
The American Dream (Engineer, company)
Little God of My Heart (Kim)

MR. PRESIDENT (1962)

BOOK BY: Howard Lindsay and Russel Crouse
MUSIC AND LYRICS BY: Irving Berlin
PUBLISHED LIBRETTO: None
CONDENSATION: *New Complete Book of the
    American Musical Theater.* Ewen, David. Holt,
    1970
ANTHOLOGY: None
VOCAL SELECTIONS: Irving Berlin Music
LICENSING AGENT: Music Theatre International
RECORDING: Sony SK 48212 CD (original cast)
CAST: Large mixed cast

Irving Berlin's last Broadway musical dealt with the First Family (people wondered if it was based on the Kennedys). The first act is about their home life while in office; the second concerns retirement after two terms in office. President Henderson is unbelievably noble and blessed with courage in his confrontations with the Russians. This is basically a flag-waving comedy with a First Lady who yearns for her hometown supermarket, a son who likes fast cars and belly dancers, and a daughter

about to marry a Middle Eastern wheeler-dealer. This big musical features a formal White House ball among the production numbers.

ORIGINAL CAST:
Robert Ryan (Steve)
Nanette Fabray (Nell)
Jack Haskell (Pat)
Stanley Grover (Charley)
Anita Gillette (Leslie)
Jack Washburn (Youssein)
Jerry Strickler (Larry)
Wisa D'Orso (Princess Kyra)

SONGS:
Act I
Let's Go Back to the Waltz (Nell, ensemble)
In Our Hide-Away (Nell, Steve)
The First Lady (Nell)
Meat and Potatoes (Pat, Charley)
I've Got to Be Around (Pat)
The Secret Service (Leslie)
It Gets Lonely in the White House (Steve)
Is He the Only Man in the World? (Nell,
    Leslie)
They Love Me (Nell)
Pigtails and Freckles (Pat, Leslie)
Don't Be Afraid of Romance (Youssein)
Laugh It Up (Nell, Steve, Leslie, Larry)
Empty Pockets Filled with Love (Pat, Leslie)

Act II
Glad to Be Home (Nell, ensemble)
You Need a Hobby (Nell, Steve)
The Washington Twist (Leslie, ensemble)
The Only Dance I Know (Princess Kyra)
I'm Gonna Get Him (Nell, Leslie)
This Is a Great Country (Steve, ensemble)

MR. WONDERFUL (1956)

BOOK BY: Joseph Stein and Will Glickman
MUSIC AND LYRICS BY: Jerry Bock, Larry
    Holofcener, and George David Weiss
PUBLISHED LIBRETTO: None
CONDENSATION: *New Complete Book of the
    American Musical Theater.* Ewen, David. Holt,
    1970

ANTHOLOGY: None
VOCAL SELECTIONS: Warner Bros. Music
LICENSING AGENT: Music Theatre International
RECORDING: MCA 10303 CD (original cast)
CAST: Large mixed cast

Sammy Davis, Jr., was "Mr. Wonderful" and this show was tailored for him. In fact, at one point the show stopped and Sammy and the Will Mastin Trio entertained with his songs and impressions. This show could be considered for a nightclub entertainer who wants to try a book show. The thread of a plot is about a young performer who lacks self-confidence. The locales include New York City; Union City, New Jersey; and Miami, Florida. Some of the songs were quite popular. Wolcott Gibbs, however, started off his review by asking, "Mr. Who?"

ORIGINAL CAST:

Chita Rivera (Rita)
Hal Loman (Hal)
Jack Carter (Fred)
Pat Marshall (Lil)
Sammy Davis, Jr. (Charlie)
Will Mastin (Uncle)
Sammy Davis, Sr. (Dad)
Olga James (Ethel)

SONGS:
Act I
1617 Broadway (Rita, Hal, ensemble)
Without You, I'm Nothing (Fred, Lil)
Jacques D'Iraq (Charlie, Uncle, Dad, ensemble)
Ethel, Baby (Ethel, Charlie)
Mr. Wonderful (Ethel)
Charlie Welch (Fred)
Talk to Him (Lil, Ethel)
Too Close for Comfort (Charlie)
Without You, I'm Nothing (reprise) (Fred, Charlie)

Act II
There (Charlie)
Miami (Lil, ensemble)
I've Been Too Busy (Ethel, Fred, Lil, Charlie)
The Act (Charlie, Uncle, Dad)

THE MOONY SHAPIRO SONGBOOK (1981)

BOOK BY: Monty Norman and Julian More
MUSIC BY: Monty Norman
LYRICS BY: Julian More
PUBLISHED LIBRETTO: French
CONDENSATION: None
ANTHOLOGY: None
LICENSING AGENT: Samuel French
RECORDING: Pye NSPL 18609 (original London cast, titled *Songbook*)
CAST: 3 M; 2 F; backup singers

Done originally in London as *Songbook*, this musical chronicles the career of a fictional songwriter and includes pastiche versions of popular songs of the thirties and onward. The five cast members play a total of about ninety different roles. The show is a retrospective of the life and career of Moony and is a mild spoof of the recent "side by side" type of shows devoted to a composer's work. The spoof extends to film, television, Broadway, and Hollywood and to numerous composers and performers. The New York production used a blue set with a white piano and projected backgrounds.

ORIGINAL CAST (all play multiple roles):

Jeff Goldblum   Judy Kaye
Timothy Jerome   Annie McGreevey
Gary Beach

SONGS:
Act I
Songbook (company)
East River Rhapsody (Beach, company)
Talking Picture Show (Goldblum, Kaye, McGreevey, Beach)
Meg (Jerome)
Mister Destiny (Kaye)
Your Time Is Different to Mine (Kaye)
Pretty Face (Beach, McGreevey, Kaye)
Je Vous Aime, Milady (Goldblum)
Les Halles (McGreevey)
Olympics '36 (company)
Nazi Party Pooper (Jerome)

I'm Gonna Take Her Home to Momma
(McGreevey, Kaye, Goldblum, Beach)
Bumpity-Bump (McGreevey)
The Girl in the Window (Kaye)
Victory (company)
April in Wisconsin (Beach)
It's Only a Show (Beach)
Bring Back Tomorrow (Beach)

Act II
Happy Hickory (McGreevey)
When a Brother Is a Mother to His Sister
(Jerome)
Climbin' (McGreevey)
Don't Play That Lovesong Any More (Jerome)
Happy Hickory (company)
Lovely Sunday Mornin' (McGreevey, Beach)
Rusty's Dream Ballet (Kaye, Goldblum)
A Storm in My Heart (Beach, McGreevey,
Goldblum, Kaye)
The Pokenhatchit Public Protest Committee
(company)
I Accuse (McGreevey, Kaye)
Messages I (Goldblum)
Messages II (Beach)
I Found Love (McGreevey, Kaye, Goldblum,
Beach)
Golden Oldie (Jerome)
Climbin' (reprise) (McGreevey, Beach,
Goldblum, Kaye, Jerome)
Nostalgia (Goldblum)

THE MOST HAPPY FELLA (1956)

BOOK, MUSIC, AND LYRICS BY: Frank Loesser;
based on the play *They Knew What They
Wanted* by Sidney Howard
PUBLISHED LIBRETTO: *Theatre Arts* (magazine),
October 1958
CONDENSATION: *Ganzl's Book of the Musical
Theatre.* Ganzl, Kurt. Schirmer (Macmillan),
1989; *Theatre '56.* John Chapman, ed. Random
House, 1956
ANTHOLOGY: None
PIANO-VOCAL SCORE: Frank Music, 1957
VOCAL SELECTIONS: Frank Music, 1956
LICENSING AGENT: Music Theatre International
RECORDING: Sony 48010 CD (original cast)
CAST: Large mixed cast

This musical version of the famous play is
about a middle-aged Italian wine grower in
California who sends a photograph of his
young, handsome foreman to get a mail-
order bride for himself. This is almost an
opera, and it has been successfully revived
many times not only at the New York City
Opera but also on Broadway. There are
thirty-three musical numbers that require
genuine singing ability. There are three acts
with colorful sets and costumes.

ORIGINAL CAST:
Robert Weede (Tony)
Susan Johnson (Cleo)
Jo Sullivan (Rosabella)
Lee Cass (Cashier/Postman)
Mona Paulee (Marie)
Shorty Long (Herman)
Art Lund (Joe)
Rico Froehlich (Pasquale)
Arthur Rubin (Giuseppe)
Alan Gilbert (Clem)
John Henson (Ciccio/Jake)
Keith Kaldenberg (Doctor)
Roy Lazarus (Al)

SONGS:
Act I
Ooh, My Feet (Cleo)
I Know How It Is (Cleo, Rosabella)
Seven Million Crumbs (Cleo)
The Letter (Rosabella)
Somebody Somewhere (Rosabella)
The Most Happy Fella (Tony, ensemble)
Standing on the Corner (Herman, Clem, Jake,
Al)
The Letter Theme (Tony, Marie)
Joey, Joey, Joey (Joe)
Soon You Gonna Leave Me, Joe (Tony)
Rosabella (Tony)
Abbondanza (Giuseppe, Pasquale, Ciccio)
Sposalizio (ensemble)
Special Delivery! (Postman)
Benvenuta (Giuseppe, Pasquale, Ciccio, Joe)
Don't Cry (Joe, Rosabella)

Act II
Fresno Beauties (Cold and Dead) (Rosabella,
Joe, ensemble)

Love and Kindness (Doctor)
Happy to Make Your Acquaintance
    (Rosabella, Tony, Cleo)
I Don't Like This Dame (Marie, Cleo)
Big "D" (Cleo, Herman, ensemble)
How Beautiful the Days (Tony, Rosabella,
    Marie, Joe)
Young People (Marie, Tony, ensemble)
Warm All Over (Rosabella)
Old People (Tony)
I Like Everybody (Herman, Cleo)
I Know How It Is (Cleo)
I Love Him (Rosabella)
Like a Woman in Love (Rosabella)
My Heart Is So Full of You (Tony, Rosabella)
Hoedown (Tony, Rosabella, ensemble)
Mama, Mama (Tony)

Act III
Goodbye, Darlin' (Cleo, Herman)
Song of a Summer Night (Doctor, ensemble)
Please Let Me Tell You (Rosabella)
Tony's Thoughts (Tony)
She's Gonna Come Home with Me (Tony,
    Marie, Cleo)
I Made a Fist (Herman, Cleo)

MUSIC IN THE AIR (1932)

BOOK AND LYRICS BY: Oscar Hammerstein II
MUSIC BY: Jerome Kern
PUBLISHED LIBRETTO: None
CONDENSATION: *Ganzl's Book of the Musical
    Theatre*. Ganzl, Kurt. Schirmer (Macmillan),
    1989
ANTHOLOGY: None
PIANO-VOCAL SCORE: Harms 1933
LICENSING AGENT: Tams-Witmark
RECORDING: RCA LK 1025 (1951 studio cast)
CAST: Large mixed cast

An elderly, genial music teacher in rural Bavaria has written a pleasant tune,
and the local schoolteacher has composed
some lyrics for it. They set off for Mu-
nich with a walking club to see about getting the song published. The plot thickens
when they meet the prima donna of a forth-
coming show. This is an old-fashioned,
sentimental, and nostalgic show. The sets
should be the colorful never-never world
of European operetta (the program for the
1951 Broadway revival stated, "the present
time"). The Jerome Kern score contains
several well-remembered songs. There was
a 1934 film version with Gloria Swanson.

1985 CONCERT VERSION CAST:

Christopher Wells (Karl)
Rebecca Luker (Sieglinde)
Kurt Peterson (Cornelius)
John Reardon (Bruno)
Patrice Munsel (Frieda)
Edmund Lyndeck (Ernst)
Louis Beachner (Walther)
Muriel Costa-Greenspon (Lilli)

SONGS:
Act I
Melodies of May (ensemble)
I've Told Every Little Star (Karl)
There's a Hill Beyond a Hill (Karl, Sieglinde,
    ensemble)
And Love Was Born (Cornelius)
I've Told Every Little Star (reprise) (Karl,
    Sieglinde)
I'm Coming Home (Bruno)
I'm Alone (Frieda)
I Am So Eager (Bruno, Frieda, ensemble)
Finaletto (Ernst, Walther)

Act II
One More Dance (Bruno)
Night Flies By (Frieda)
Egern on the Tegern See (Lilli)
When the Spring Is in the Air (Sieglinde,
    ensemble)
The Song Is You (Bruno)
We Belong Together (ensemble)

THE MUSIC MAN (1957)

BOOK, MUSIC, AND LYRICS BY: Meredith Willson;
    story by Meredith Willson and Franklin Lacey
PUBLISHED LIBRETTO: Putnam, 1958
CONDENSATION: *Ganzl's Book of the Musical
    Theatre*. Ganzl, Kurt. Schirmer (Macmillan),

1989; *Broadway's Best.* John Chapman, ed.
  Doubleday, 1958
ANTHOLOGY: None
PIANO-VOCAL SCORE: Frank Music, 1958
LICENSING AGENT: Music Theatre International
RECORDINGS: Capitol CDP 46633 CD (original
  cast); Angel ZDM 64663-2 CD (original cast)
CAST: Large mixed cast

This show needs a fast-talking, high-stepping song-and-dance man. He plays a confidence man in the pre–World War I Midwest. Along the way he falls in love with a librarian. Robert Preston created the part of Professor Harold Hill and also played the role in the 1962 film version. The score includes a number of popular songs. This family show is a big slice of Americana, with a barbershop quartet, lots of kids (including one sizable role for a lisping boy), flashy costumes, and production numbers.

Tony Award Winner (Best Musical)

ORIGINAL CAST:

Robert Preston (Harold)
Paul Reed (Charlie)
Barbara Cook (Marian)
Pert Kelton (Mrs. Paroo)
Marilyn Siegel (Amaryllis)
Iggie Wolfington (Marcellus)
Eddie Hodges (Winthrop)
Danny Carroll (Tommy)
Dusty Worrall (Zaneeta)

SONGS:
Act I
Rock Island (Charlie, ensemble)
Iowa Stubborn (ensemble)
Trouble (Harold, ensemble)
Piano Lesson (Marian, Mrs. Paroo, Amaryllis)
Goodnight My Someone (Marian)
Seventy-Six Trombones (Harold, ensemble)
Sincere (quartet)
The Sadder-but-Wiser Girl (Harold, Marcellus)
Pickalittle (ladies)
Good Night Ladies (quartet)
Marian the Librarian (Harold, ensemble)
My White Knight (Marian)
Wells Fargo Wagon (Winthrop, ensemble)

Act II
It's You (quartet, ensemble)
Shipoopi (Marcellus, Harold, Marian, Tommy,
  Zaneeta, ensemble)
Lida Rose (quartet)
Will I Ever Tell You (Marian)
Gary, Indiana (Winthrop)
Till There Was You (Marian, Harold)

MUSICAL CHAIRS (1980)

BOOK BY: Barry Berg, Ken Donnelly, and Tom
  Savage; based on an original story concept by
  Larry J. Pontillo
MUSIC AND LYRICS BY: Tom Savage
PUBLISHED LIBRETTO: French, 1982
CONDENSATION: None
ANTHOLOGY: None
LICENSING AGENT: Samuel French
RECORDING: Original Cast OC 8024 (original cast)
CAST: 8 M; 8 F

It is opening night for a new play. The author is a Pulitzer Prize and Tony Award winner who hasn't done so well recently and is trying a comeback. The cast of this musical plays the audience, which includes ex-wives, lovers, and the critics. The cast of the New York production sat in chairs on a steeply raked stage and looked out at the audience. Each cast member has a number to explain his or her problem or predicament.

ORIGINAL CAST:

Ron Holgate (Joe)
Leslie-Anne Wolfe (Miranda)
Brandon Maggart (Harold)
Joy Franz (Janet)
Rick Emery (Tuxedo)
Scott Ellis (Sally's Boyfriend)
Patti Karr (Lillian)
Tom Breslin (Blue Suit)
Edward Earle (Brown Suit)
Jess Richards (Gary)
Grace Keagy (Roberta)
Enid Blaymore (Millie)

Randall Esterbrook (Brad)
Lee Meredith (Valerie)

SONGS:
Act I
Tonight's the Night (ensemble)
My Time (Joe)
Who's Who (ensemble)
If I Could Be Beautiful (Miranda, boys)
What I Could Have Done Tonight (Harold,
    Janet)
There You Are (Tuxedo)
Sally (Sally's Boyfriend, ensemble)
Other People (Janet)
Hit the Ladies (Lillian, ladies)

Act II
Musical Chairs (Tuxedo, Blue Suit, Brown
    Suit)
Suddenly, Love (Gary)
Better than Broadway (Millie, Roberta)
Everytime the Music Starts (Brad, ensemble)
There You Are (reprise) (Tuxedo, Joe,
    Valerie)

MY FAIR LADY (1956)

BOOK AND LYRICS BY: Alan Jay Lerner; adapted
    from the play *Pygmalion* by George Bernard
    Shaw
MUSIC BY: Frederick Loewe
PUBLISHED LIBRETTO: Coward-McCann, 1956; New
    American Library, 1956
CONDENSATION: *The Best Plays of 1955–1956.*
    Louis Kronenberger, ed. Dodd, Mead, 1956;
    Ganzl's Book of the Musical Theatre. Ganzl, Kurt.
    Schirmer (Macmillan), 1989
ANTHOLOGY: None
PIANO-VOCAL SCORE: Chappell, 1969
VOCAL SELECTIONS: *The Best of Lerner and Loewe.*
    Chappell, 1974
LICENSING AGENT: Tams-Witmark
RECORDING: Columbia CK 5090 CD (original cast)
CAST: Large mixed cast

Henry Higgins, an expert on dialects,
makes a wager with his friend, Colonel
Pickering, that he can give a cockney girl
speech instruction and pass her off as a
lady. The place is London in 1912. The
scenes include a Covent Garden flower
market, Ascot, an embassy ballroom, and
Higgins' study. Rex Harrison was the
original Higgins and starred in the 1964
film. This show has everything: wonderful
songs, excellent roles, a classic book, endless opportunities for elegant and colorful
sets and costumes, and several big dance
numbers.

Tony Award Winner (Best Musical)

ORIGINAL CAST:
Rex Harrison (Higgins)
Julie Andrews (Eliza)
John Michael King (Freddy)
Robert Coote (Pickering)
Philippa Bevans (Mrs. Pearce)
Rod McLennan (Jamie)
Stanley Holloway (Doolittle)
Gordon Dilworth (Harry)

SONGS:
Act I
Why Can't the English? (Higgins)
Wouldn't It Be Loverly (Eliza, ensemble)
With a Little Bit of Luck (Doolittle, Harry,
    Jamie)
I'm an Ordinary Man (Higgins)
Just You Wait (Eliza)
The Rain in Spain (Higgins, Eliza, Pickering)
I Could Have Danced All Night (Eliza, Mrs.
    Pearce, maids)
Ascot Gavotte (ensemble)
On the Street Where You Live (Freddy)
The Embassy Waltz (Higgins, Eliza,
    ensemble)

Act II
You Did It (Higgins, Pickering, Mrs. Pearce,
    servants)
Show Me (Eliza, Freddy)
Get Me to the Church on Time (Doolittle,
    Harry, Jamie, ensemble)
A Hymn to Him (Higgins)
Without You (Eliza, Higgins)
I've Grown Accustomed to Her Face
    (Higgins)

MY OLD FRIENDS (1979)

BOOK, MUSIC, AND LYRICS BY: Mel Mandel and
  Norman Sachs
PUBLISHED LIBRETTO: French, 1980
CONDENSATION: None
ANTHOLOGY: None
LICENSING AGENT: Samuel French
RECORDING: None
CAST: 7 M; 4 F

A new "inmate" in an old people's home
and hotel resists the tendency to succumb
to the mood of the place. The title of the
show refers to the pills and medicines he
must take. Eventually he has enough and
leaves to again take up his life as a carpenter. This is a show for a mature cast and an
audience that will appreciate its humor and
messages. It is performed without intermission, with sets consisting of a few chairs
and painted flats. There are fourteen musical numbers. The New York production
used only a piano and bass.

ORIGINAL CAST:

Peter Walker (Pete)
Robert Weil (Slocum)
Norberto Kerner (Arias)
Allen Swift (Catlan)
Leslie Barrett (Fineberg)
Sylvia Davis (Heloise)
Maxine Sullivan (Mrs. Cooper)

SONGS:
(performed without intermission)
I'm Not Old (ensemble)
My Old Friends (Pete)
For Two Minutes (Slocum, Arias, Catlan,
  Fineberg)
What We Need Around Here (Pete, Heloise)
Oh, My Rose (Pete)
I Bought a Bicycle (Fineberg, ensemble)
The Battle at Eagle Rock (Heloise, ensemble)
Dear Jane (ensemble)
The One Place for Me (ensemble)
I Work with Wood (Pete, Slocum)
Mambo '52 (Arias, Mrs. Cooper)

A Little Starch Left (Mrs. Cooper)
Our Time Together (Heloise)
You've Got to Keep Building (Pete)

MY ONE AND ONLY (1983)

BOOK BY: Peter Stone and Timothy S. Mayer
MUSIC BY: George Gershwin
LYRICS BY: Ira Gershwin
PUBLISHED LIBRETTO: None
CONDENSATION: The Best Plays of 1982–83. Otis L.
  Guernsey, Jr., ed. Dodd, Mead, 1983
ANTHOLOGY: None
VOCAL SELECTIONS: Warner Bros. Music, 1983
LICENSING AGENT: Tams-Witmark
RECORDING: Atlantic 80110-2 CD (original cast)
CAST: Large mixed cast

It is 1927 and Captain Billy Buck Chandler,
an aviator from Texas, is in a hurry to be
the first person to fly solo across the Atlantic. But he meets Miss Edith Herbert,
an English Channel swimmer in New York
with an aquacade. Their hectic romance involves government agents, Russian spies,
and even a trip to Morocco before it all
ends well. The many set changes can be
merely suggested in bright-colored drops.
You should try to have a shallow trough
of water, however, for the beach scene. But
most of all, be prepared for a lot of tap dancing. The Gershwin score is from Funny Face
and several other sources, but the book is
"a wholly new invention."

ORIGINAL CAST:

Tommy Tune (Billy)
Twiggy (Edith)
Bruce McGill (Prince Nikki)
Denny Dillon (Mickey)
Charles "Honi" Coles (Magix)
Roscoe Lee Brown (Montgomery)

SONGS:
Act I
I Can't Be Bothered Now (Billy, Edith, Prince
  Nikki, Mickey, ensemble)
Blah, Blah, Blah (Billy)
Boy Wanted (Edith)

Soon (Billy)

High Hat/Sweet and Low-Down (Magix, Billy, ensemble)

Blah, Blah, Blah (reprise) (Edith)

He Loves and She Loves (Billy, Edith)

'S Wonderful (Billy, Edith)

Strike Up the Band (Billy)

Act II

In the Swim/What Are We Here For? (Prince Nikki, ensemble)

Nice Work if You Can Get It (Edith)

My One and Only (Magix, Billy)

Funny Face (Mickey, Prince Nikki)

Kickin' the Clouds Away (Montgomery, ensemble)

How Long Has This Been Going On? (Edith, Billy)

NAUGHTY MARIETTA (1910)

BOOK AND LYRICS BY: Rida Johnson Young
MUSIC BY: Victor Herbert
PUBLISHED LIBRETTO: None
CONDENSATION: *Ganzl's Book of the Musical Theatre*. Ganzl, Kurt. Schirmer (Macmillan), 1989
ANTHOLOGY: None
VOCAL SELECTIONS: *The Music of Victor Herbert*. Warner Bros. Music, 1976
LICENSING AGENT: Tams-Witmark
RECORDING: Smithsonian N 026 (studio cast)
CAST: Large mixed cast

Jeanette MacDonald and Nelson Eddy are remembered for their roles in the 1935 film, but this operetta is frequently revived and was recently presented by the New York City Opera. The time is "about 1870" and the place is old New Orleans. A shipload of "casket girls" arrives from France seeking husbands. Hidden among them is the runaway Contesse Marietta. This romantic operetta has been staged simply "in the round" and elaborately at Jones Beach (New York). This family show ends happily to the strains of "Ah, Sweet Mystery of Life."

1978 NEW YORK CITY OPERA CAST:

Elizabeth Hynes (Marietta)
Howard Hensel (Captain Dick)
Susanne Marsee (Adah)
Charles Roe (Etienne)
Harlan Foss (Rudolfo)
Russ Thacker (Silas)
James Billings (Grandet)

SONGS:
Act I
Prologue (Marietta)
It Never, Never Can Be Love (Marietta, Captain Dick)
This Brave New Land (Adah, Etienne)
Tramp, Tramp, Tramp (Captain Dick, men)
Taisez-vous (ensemble)
All I Crave Is More of Life (Marietta)
Italian Street Song (Marietta, ensemble)
Opening Music (Marietta, Rudolfo)
Naughty Marietta (Marietta)
If I Were Anybody Else but Me (Silas, Marietta)

Act II
New Orleans Jeunesse Doree (male ensemble)
You Marry a Marionette (Etienne, men)
'Neath a Southern Moon (Adah)
Loves of New Orleans (ensemble)
It's Pretty Soft for Silas (Silas)
Live for Today (Marietta, Adah, Captain Dick, Etienne, ensemble)
The Sweet By and By (Grandet)
I'm Falling in Love with Someone (Captain Dick)
Ah, Sweet Mystery of Life (Marietta, Captain Dick, ensemble)

NEW GIRL IN TOWN (1957)

BOOK BY: George Abbott; based on the play *Anna Christie* by Eugene O'Neill
MUSIC AND LYRICS BY: Bob Merrill
PUBLISHED LIBRETTO: Random House, 1958
CONDENSATION: *New Complete Book of the American Musical Theater*. Ewen, David. Holt, 1970
ANTHOLOGY: None
VOCAL SELECTIONS: Chappell, 1957

LICENSING AGENT: Music Theatre International
RECORDING: RCA LSO 1027 (original cast)
CAST: Large mixed cast

The time is the early 1900s. Anna, a prostitute, arrives on the New York waterfront to join her father, a barge captain she hasn't seen in many years. She meets and falls in love with a sailor and is redeemed by true love. The New York production was a big, colorful dancing show with Bob Fosse doing the choreography and Gwen Verdon as the star. Most reviews mentioned a dream-ballet sequence. They all praised Thelma Ritter in the meaty role of "Marthy." The sets and costumes were called eye-smacking.

ORIGINAL CAST:

Lulu Bates (Lily)
Cameron Prud'homme (Chris)
H. F. Green (Seaman)
Thelma Ritter (Marthy)
Del Anderson (Oscar)
Eddie Phillips (Pete)
Mark Dawson (Bartender)
Gwen Verdon (Anna)
Mara Landi (Pearl)
George Wallace (Mat)

SONGS:
Act I
Roll Yer Socks Up (Seaman, ensemble)
Anna Lilla (Chris)
Sunshine Girl (Oscar, Pete, Bartender)
On the Farm (Anna)
Flings (Marthy, Lily, Pearl)
It's Good to Be Alive (Anna)
Look at 'er (Mat)
It's Good to Be Alive (reprise) (Mat)
Yer My Friend Ain'tcha? (Marthy, Chris)
Did You Close Your Eyes? (Anna, Mat)

Act II
At the Check Apron Ball (ensemble)
There Ain't No Flies on Me (ensemble)
Ven I Valse (Anna, Chris, ensemble)
If That Was Love (Anna)
Chess and Checkers (Marthy, ensemble)

THE NEW MOON (1928)

BOOK AND LYRICS BY: Oscar Hammerstein II, Frank Mandel, and Lawrence Schwab
MUSIC BY: Sigmund Romberg
PUBLISHED LIBRETTO: None
CONDENSATION: *Ganzl's Book of the Musical Theatre*. Ganzl, Kurt. Schirmer (Macmillan), 1989
ANTHOLOGY: None
PIANO-VOCAL SCORE: Harms, 1928
VOCAL SELECTIONS: *The Music of Sigmund Romberg*. Warner Bros. Music, 1977
LICENSING AGENT: Tams-Witmark
RECORDING: Columbia CSP P 13878 (studio cast)
CAST: Large mixed cast

The plot deals with the adventures of Robert Mission and is set in New Orleans in 1791. He is a French nobleman and political refugee who is indentured to the wealthy Monsieur Beaunoir. Mission is in love with Beaunoir's daughter, Marianne. They sail on the ship *The New Moon*, go through a mutiny, and end up in Florida. The show was filmed in 1930 with Grace Moore and in 1940 with Jeanette MacDonald and Nelson Eddy. Fully staged productions require elaborate costumes and wigs. It was most recently done by the New York City Opera and telecast on PBS.

1986 NEW YORK CITY OPERA CAST:

Richard White (Robert)
Leigh Munro (Marianne)
Joseph McKee (Duval)
Michael Cousins (Philippe)
Joyce Campana (Julie)
Muriel Costa-Greenspon (Clotilde)
Gerald Isaac (Alexander)

SONGS:
Act I
Dainty Wisps of Thistledown (ladies)
Servant of the King (ensemble)
Marianne (Robert) Reprise (Marianne, men)
The Girl on the Prow (Marianne, ensemble)
Interrupted Trio (Marianne, Duval, Robert)
Softly as in a Morning Sunrise (Philippe, ensemble)

Stouthearted Men (Robert, Philippe, men)
Gorgeous Alexander (Julie, Clotilde, Alexander)
One Kiss (Marianne, ladies)
Gentle Airs, Courtly Manners (ensemble)
Wanting You (Robert, Marianne, ensemble)

Act II
Lover, Come Back to Me (Marianne, Robert)
Try Her Out at Dances (Alexander, Julie, ensemble)

NIGHTCLUB CANTATA (1977)

CONCEIVED, COMPOSED, AND DIRECTED BY: Elizabeth Swados
PUBLISHED LIBRETTO: None
CONDENSATION: None
ANTHOLOGY: None
VOCAL SELECTIONS: Dramatists Play Service
LICENSING AGENT: Dramatists Play Service
RECORDING: None
CAST: 4 M; 4 F

This musical entertainment was originally performed in a cabaret setting. It lasts a bit over an hour and was described as all-singing, all-dancing, all-acting. There are some mild gymnastic feats performed by the men. The twenty numbers are primarily by Swados, but the works of Sylvia Plath, Frank O'Hara, Carson McCullers, and others are also utilized. The sets, lighting, and costumes were minimal and unobtrusive. The accompaniment consisted of piano, percussion, and Swados on guitar. Some critical comment referred to the show as avant-garde and as "bohemian vaudeville."

ORIGINAL CAST:

Karen Evans	Shelley Plimpton
Rocky Greenberg	David Schechter
Paul Kander	Elizabeth Swados
JoAnna Peled	Mark Zagaeski

SONGS:
(performed without intermission)
Things I Didn't Know I Loved (company)
Bestiario (company)

Bird Chorus (company)
Bird Lament (Swados)
Ventriloquist and Dummy (Schechter, Evans, Zagaeski, Plimpton)
The Applicant (Evans)
To the Harbormaster (Greenberg, Zagaeski)
Adolescents (Greenberg, Evans)
Indecision (company)
Dibarti (Peled, Zagaeski)
In Dreams Begin Responsibilities (company)
Are You with Me? (Plimpton)
Raga (Schechter, company)
Waking This Morning (Plimpton, Evans, Swados, Peled)
Pastrami Brothers (Zagaeski, Greenberg, Schechter, Kander)
The Ballad of the Sad Cafe (Peled, Evans)
Isabella (Peled, company)
Waiting (Greenberg, Evans, Schechter, Peled)
The Dance (Peled, company)
On Living (company)

NINE (1982)

BOOK BY: Arthur Kopit; adaption from the Italian by Mario Fratti
MUSIC AND LYRICS BY: Maury Yeston
PUBLISHED LIBRETTO: French, 1983
CONDENSATION: *The Best Plays of 1981–1982*. Otis L. Guernsey, Jr., ed. Dodd, Mead, 1982
ANTHOLOGY: None
VOCAL SELECTIONS: Belwin-Mills, 1983
LICENSING AGENT: Samuel French
RECORDINGS: CBS CK 38325 CD (original cast); RCA 09026-61433 CD (1992 London cast)
CAST: 1 M; 22 F; 4 boys *or* 10 M; 13 F; 4 boys

The scene is an Italian spa near Venice. For the New York production the unit set was designed as a white-tiled Roman bath with tiered boxes scattered about. Guido is an Italian film director suffering from a midlife crisis. He is unable to come up with an idea for his next film, and his relationships with his wife, his mistress, and his favorite leading lady are all in jeopardy.

Most of the play takes place in Guido's mind, so the styles range from the 1930s to the 1980s. Everyone is in black at the beginning, but gradually color is introduced. The score includes romantic ballads, the can-can, tarantellas, and even operatic passages. This musical was praised for its intelligence, wit, sophistication, chic, and European elegance. It was "unofficially" based on the Fellini film $8\frac{1}{2}$.

Tony Award Winner (Best Musical)

ORIGINAL CAST:

Raul Julia (Guido)
Camille Saviola (Chief)
Anita Morris (Carla)
Liliane Montevecchi (Liliane Le Fleur)
Taina Elg (Guido's Mother)
Karen Akers (Luisa)
Kathi Moss (Saraghina)
Shelly Burch (Claudia)
Cameron Johann (Young Guido)

SONGS:
(performed without intermission)
Overture Delle Donne (company)
Guido's Song (Guido)
Coda di Guido (company)
The Germans at the Spa (Chief, ensemble)
A Call from the Vatican (Carla)
Only with You (Guido)
Folies Bergere (Liliane, company)
Nine (Guido's Mother, company)
My Husband Makes Movies (Luisa)
Ti Voglio Bene/Be Italian (Saraghina, boys, company)
The Bells of St. Sebastian (Guido, boys, company)
A Man Like You/Unusual Way/Duet (Claudia, Guido)
The Grand Canal (Guido, company)
Simple (Carla)
Be on Your Own (Luisa)
I Can't Make This Movie (Guido)
Getting Tall (Young Guido)
My Husband Makes Movies/Nine (reprise) (Guido, Luisa)

THE 1940S RADIO HOUR (1979)

WRITTEN BY: Walton Jones
MUSIC AND LYRICS BY: Various
PUBLISHED LIBRETTO: French, 1981
CONDENSATION: None
ANTHOLOGY: None
LICENSING AGENT: Samuel French
RECORDING: None
CAST: 10 M; 5 F

Performed without intermission, this is actually a play about a group preparing a radio broadcast on December 21, 1942, from the Astor Hotel in New York City. When the show actually goes on the air, a number of familiar songs are spiritedly performed by the cast along with some hilarious commercials. When the show is over, they all pack up and go home. There are some threads of plots involving the various performers. This can be simply staged and costumed, and all nostalgia buffs will have a great time.

ORIGINAL CAST:

Kathy Andrini (Connie Miller)
Dee Dee Bridgewater (Geneva Lee Browne)
John Doolittle (Biff Baker)
Merwin Goldsmith (Lou Cohn)
Joe Grifasi (Neal Tilden)
Mary-Cleere Haran (Ann Collier)
Stephen James (B. J. Gibson)
Jeff Keller (Johnny Cantone)
Crissy Wilzak (Ginger Brooks)

SONGS:
(performed without intermission)
Chattanooga Choo Choo
How about You?
Blue Moon
Have Yourself a Merry Little Christmas
I Got It Bad and That Ain't Good
Little Brown Jug
At Last
I'll Be Seeing You
Love Is Here to Stay
You, You're Driving Me Crazy
Boogie Woogie Bugle Boy from Company B
I'll Never Smile Again

Rose of the Rio Grande
Ain't She Sweet
Strike Up the Band
Daddy
That Old Black Magic
The Mutual Manhattan Variety Cavalcade
Chiquita Banana

NO, NO, NANETTE (1925)

BOOK BY: Otto Harbach and Frank Mandel
MUSIC BY: Vincent Youmans
LYRICS BY: Irving Caesar and Otto Harbach
PUBLISHED LIBRETTO: None
CONDENSATION: *Ganzl's Book of the Musical Theatre*. Ganzl, Kurt. Schirmer (Macmillan), 1989
ANTHOLOGY: None
PIANO-VOCAL SCORE: Warner Bros. Music, 1972
VOCAL SELECTIONS: Warner Bros. Music, 197–
LICENSING AGENT: Tams-Witmark
RECORDING: Columbia CK 30563 CD (1971 revival cast)
CAST: Large mixed cast

Back in New York City in 1925, bible publisher Jimmy Smith and his wife have taken a schoolgirl ward, Nanette, to raise as a lady. Nanette wants to go to Atlantic City with her friends for the weekend, but the Smiths say "no." Through a series of misunderstandings, everyone turns up in Atlantic City for Act II. The 1971 revival was a lavish Busby Berkeley production. The cast LP recording album includes a number of color photographs of the sets and costumes, excellent notes, and, of course, the score.

1971 REVIVAL CAST:

Helen Gallagher (Lucille)
Ruby Keeler (Sue)
Jack Gilford (Jimmy)
Susan Watson (Nanette)
Roger Rathburn (Tom)
Bobby Van (Billy)
Patsy Kelly (Pauline)

SONGS:
Act I
Too Many Rings Around Rosie (Lucille, ensemble)
Only a Moment Ago (Sue, Jimmy)
I've Confessed to the Breeze (Nanette, Tom)
Call of the Sea (Billy, girls)
I Want to Be Happy (Jimmy, Nanette, Sue, ensemble)
No, No, Nanette (Nanette, Tom)

Act II
Peach on the Beach (Nanette, ensemble)
Tea for Two (Nanette, Tom, ensemble)
You Can Dance with Any Girl (Lucille, Billy)

Act III
Telephone Girlie (Billy, girls)
"Where-Has-My-Hubby-Gone" Blues (Lucille, boys)
Waiting for You (Nanette, Tom)
Take a Little One-Step (Sue, Billy, Lucille, Pauline, ensemble)

NO STRINGS (1962)

BOOK BY: Samuel Taylor
MUSIC AND LYRICS BY: Richard Rodgers
PUBLISHED LIBRETTO: Random House, 1962
CONDENSATION: *New Complete Book of the American Musical Theater*. Ewen, David. Holt, 1970
ANTHOLOGY: None
PIANO-VOCAL SCORE: Williamson, 1962
LICENSING AGENT: Rodgers and Hammerstein Theatre Library
RECORDINGS: Capitol SO 1695 (original cast); Angel ZDM 764694-2 CD (original cast)
CAST: 5 M; 5 F

This is Richard Rodgers' only solo musical. Set in contemporary Paris, it is about a black fashion model and a white writer on the skids. There is no mention of the racial situation until the very end. In the Broadway production the orchestra (without any strings!) was located onstage and musicians wandered on and off as the situation warranted. The sets were highly stylized. This bittersweet romance with very stylish people and places doesn't end happily. It has an excellent score, although there are no standards.

ORIGINAL CAST:

Diahann Carroll (Barbara)
Richard Kiley (David)
Mitchell Gregg (Louis)
Bernice Massi (Comfort)
Don Chastain (Mike)
Alvin Epstein (Luc)
Ann Hodges (Gabrielle)
Noelle Adam (Jeanette)
Polly Rowles (Mollie)

SONGS:
Act I
The Sweetest Sounds (Barbara, David)
How Sad (David)
Loads of Love (Barbara)
The Man Who Has Everything (Louis)
Be My Host (David, Comfort, Mike, Luc,
    Gabrielle, ensemble)
La La La (Jeanette, Luc)
You Don't Tell Me (Barbara)
Love Makes the World Go (Mollie, Comfort,
    ensemble)
Nobody Told Me (David, Barbara)

Act II
Look No Further (David, Barbara)
Maine (David, Barbara)
An Orthodox Fool (Barbara)
Eager Beaver (Comfort, Mike, ensemble)
No Strings (David, Barbara)

NOBODY'S EARNEST (1973)

ADAPTED BY: Arnold Sundgaard; from *The
    Importance of Being Earnest* by Oscar Wilde
MUSIC BY: Alec Wilder
LYRICS BY: Ethan Ayer
PUBLISHED LIBRETTO: French, 1978
CONDENSATION: None
ANTHOLOGY: None
LICENSING AGENT: Samuel French
RECORDING: None
CAST: 5 M; 4 F

Following the original play closely, this is more a play with songs than a full musical. There are no big dance numbers and no chorus. The Victorian flavor is evident in the musical arrangements. This show was first presented by the Williamstown (Massachusetts) Theater and has not been done in New York City. Alec Wilder is well known for a number of popular songs he composed and for his book *American Popular Song*.

WILLIAMSTOWN ORIGINAL CAST:

Kent Stephens (Lane)
John Cunningham (Algernon)
Clifford David (Jack)
Elizabeth Parrish (Lady Bracknell)
Marian Mercer (Gwendolen)
Henrietta Valor (Cecily)
Emery Battis (Dr. Chasuble)
Glenn Mure (Merriman)
June Gable (Miss Prism)

SONGS:
Act I
In This Delicious World (Algernon, Lane)
Jack in the Country (Jack, Algernon)
Pray Don't Talk about the Weather
    (Gwendolen)
Miss Fairfax, Ever Since I Met You (Jack,
    Gwendolen)
A Girl Brought Up with the Upmost Care
    (Lady Bracknell)
Ernest, Beware (Gwendolen)

Act II
I Worship the Lily (Cecily)
On the Day I Lost My Novel (Miss Prism)
Cecily (Algernon, Cecily)
How Wonderfully Blue Your Eyes (Algernon,
    Cecily)

Act III
Well, to Speak with Perfect Candor
    (Gwendolen, Cecily)
The Most Important Thing (Algernon, Cecily,
    Jack, Gwendolen)
Guardians of the Nation (Lady Bracknell, Dr.
    Chasuble, Miss Prism, Merriman)
At Last (company)

NOEL AND GERTIE (1982)

DEVISED BY: Sheridan Morley
MUSIC AND LYRICS BY: Noel Coward
PUBLISHED LIBRETTO: None
CONDENSATION: None
ANTHOLOGY: None
VOCAL SELECTIONS: *Noel Coward Songbook*. Simon
    and Schuster, 1953; *Sir Noel Coward, His Words
    and Music*. Chappell, 1973
LICENSING AGENT: Samuel French
RECORDING: TER 1117 (original London cast)
CAST: 1 M; 1 F

This affectionate re-creation in words and
music of the highlights of the careers of
Noel Coward and Gertrude Lawrence was
first presented on Broadway for one performance only as a charity benefit in 1982.
It has since been revised and staged off-
Broadway in 1992. "Sophisticated, sentimental, witty" is how critics described this
look at the friendship of two British stage
stars. They perform excerpts from *Red Peppers*, *Private Lives*, *Still Life*, and other Coward plays. They sing many of his songs,
which were described as "just as potent as
cheap music could ever be" in a play on a
famous line from *Private Lives*. Performed
in an elegant black-and-chrome set, your
cast need not attempt impersonations of
the stars.

ORIGINAL LONDON CAST:

Lewis Fiander (Noel)
Patricia Hodge (Gertie)

This entertainment includes twenty musical numbers divided into two acts.

THE NO-FRILLS REVUE (1987)

CONCEIVED BY: Martin Charnin
MUSIC AND LYRICS: Various
PUBLISHED LIBRETTO: None
CONDENSATION: None
ANTHOLOGY: None
LICENSING AGENT: Music Theatre International

RECORDING: None
CAST: 3 M; 3 to 6 F

Called "a fast-paced, bare-bones show,"
this revue contains songs, sketches, skits,
and lampoons, going out of its way not
to be too topical or to offend. It was performed on a bare stage with just a few
stools and basic costuming. Critics liked
best the show-business sections, particularly the "lost" compositions of various top
composers.

ORIGINAL CAST:

Adinah Alexander   Eddie Korbich
Sasha Charnin   Andre Montgomery
Clare Fields   Lynn Paynter
Stephani Hardy   Justin Ross
Sarah Knapp   Bob Stillman

SONGS:
(performed without intermission)
The No-Frills Revue (cast)
Stools (cast)
Being with Me (Knapp)
A Brand New Hammer (Stillman, Paynter,
    Korbich, Ross)
I Know Where the Bodies Are Buried
    (Alexander)
Pax de Don't (Ross, Fields, Korbich)
A Vicious Cycle (Charnin)
We Know Why You're Here! (cast)
I Luv You (cast)
Runnin' with the Brat Pack (Charnin, Paynter,
    Fields, Alexander, Montgomery)
In the Quiet of Your Arms (Stillman, ladies)
Yes! We Have the Manuscripts! (Charnin,
    Montgomery, Alexander, Ross, Knapp,
    Stillman, Korbich, company)
It Hasn't Been Easy (cast)

NOW IS THE TIME FOR ALL GOOD MEN (1967)

BOOK AND LYRICS BY: Gretchen Cryer
MUSIC BY: Nancy Ford
PUBLISHED LIBRETTO: French, 1969
CONDENSATION: None
ANTHOLOGY: None

LICENSING AGENT: Samuel French
RECORDING: Columbia OS 3130 (original cast)
CAST: 6 M; 6 F

A young man has been court-martialed out of the U.S. Army for refusing to do battle. He gets a job as a schoolteacher in a small town, where he teaches his students to question established values, causes one boy to refuse the draft, and becomes involved with the music teacher. This is a look at middle America during the Vietnam crisis and does not have a happy ending. This was the first musical by these composers; they have gone on to write several others, always with something relevant to say. This was simply staged off-Broadway with no dances and with only a piano, bass, and percussion for accompaniment.

ORIGINAL CAST:

Art Wallace (Herbert)
David Sabin (Albert)
Regina Lynn (Esther)
David Cryer (Mike)
Margot Hanson (Betty)
Gretchen Cryer (Sarah)
Murray Olson (Jasper)
John Long (Miller)
Donna Curtis (Tooney)
Judy Frank (Eugenie)
Anne Kaye (Ramona)
Steve Skiles (Tommy)

SONGS:
Act I
We Shall Meet in the Great Hereafter
   (company)
Keep 'em Busy, Keep 'em Quiet (Miller,
   Albert, Esther, Mike, Betty, Sarah, Jasper,
   Herbert)
What's in the Air (Mike)
Tea in the Rain (Sarah)
What's a Guy Like You Doin' in a Place Like
   This? (Eugenie)
Halloween Hayride (Betty, Tooney, Esther,
   Miller, Jasper, Tommy, Ramona)
Campfire Songs (Betty, Miller, Esther, Jasper,
   Tooney, Tommy, Ramona)
See Everything New (Mike, Sarah)

All Alone (Mike)
He Could Show Me (Sarah)
Washed Up (Tooney, Esther, Albert, Sarah,
   Herbert, Jasper, Miller, Tommy, Ramona,
   Betty)
Stuck-Up (Eugenie)
My Holiday (Sarah, Mike)
On My Own (Tommy, Ramona) Reprise
   (Tommy, Mike)

Act II
It Was Good Enough for Grandpa (company)
A Simple Life (Albert, Sarah)
A Star on the Monument (Herbert, Miller,
   Jasper, Tommy)
Rain Your Love on Me (Mike, Sarah)
There's Goin' to Be a Wedding (Herbert,
   Tooney, Tommy, Ramona, Betty, Miller,
   Esther, Jasper)

NUNSENSE (1985)

BOOK, MUSIC, AND LYRICS BY: Dan Goggin
PUBLISHED LIBRETTO: French
CONDENSATION: *The Book of 1,000 Plays.* Steve
   Fletcher, Norman Jopling, eds. Facts On File,
   1989
ANTHOLOGY: None
VOCAL SELECTIONS: Warner Bros. Music
LICENSING AGENT: Samuel French
RECORDING: DRG 12539 CD (original cast)
CAST: 5 F

It seems that a case of botulism has decimated the order of the Little Sisters of Hoboken. To make matters worse, an impulsive purchase of a videotape recorder has left them without funds to bury four sisters (on ice temporarily in the convent freezer). So the five remaining sisters decide to put on a talent show to raise funds. You will need a variety of talents in your cast, as the nuns sing, tap-dance, do stand-up comic routines, conduct an audience quiz, clown, and even engage in a bit of toe dancing and ventriloquism. The small band for the original production wore monk's robes to add to the fun. This family show (occasionally a bit risque) will appeal to both Catholic and non-Catholic audiences.

ORIGINAL CAST:

Marilyn Farina (Sister Mary Cardelia)
Edwina Lewis (Sister Mary Hubert)
Christine Anderson (Sister Robert Anne)
Semina de Laurentis (Sister Mary Amnesia)
Suzi Winson (Sister Mary Leo)

SONGS:
Act I
Nunsense Is Habit-Forming (cast)
A Difficult Transition (cast)
Benedicite (Sr. Mary Leo)
The Biggest Ain't the Best (Srs. Mary Hubert, Mary Leo)
Playing Second Fiddle (Sr. Robert Anne)
So You Want to Be a Nun (Sr. Mary Amnesia)
Turn Up the Spotlight (Sr. Mary Cardelia)
Lilacs Bring Back Memories (Srs. Mary Cardelia, Mary Hubert, Mary Leo, Mary Amnesia)
Tackle That Temptation with a Time Step (cast)

Act II
Growing Up Catholic (Srs. Robert Anne, Mary Leo, Mary Hubert, Mary Amnesia)
We've Got to Clean Out the Freezer (cast)
Just a Coupl'a Sisters (Srs. Mary Cardelia, Mary Hubert)
Soup's On (The Dying Nun Ballet) (Sr. Mary Leo)
I Just Want to Be a Star (Sr. Robert Anne)
The Drive In (Srs. Robert Anne, Mary Amnesia, Mary Leo)
I Could've Gone to Nashville (Sr. Mary Amnesia)
Gloria in Excelsis Deo (cast)
Holier than Thou (Sr. Mary Hubert, cast)

OF THEE I SING (1931)

BOOK BY: George S. Kaufman and Morrie Ryskind
MUSIC BY: George Gershwin
LYRICS BY: Ira Gershwin
PUBLISHED LIBRETTO: Knopf, 1932; French, 1959

CONDENSATION: *Ganzl's Book of the Musical Theatre.* Ganzl, Kurt. Schirmer (Macmillan), 1989
ANTHOLOGY: *The Pulitzer Prize Plays.* Kathryn Coe and William Cordell, eds. Random House, 1940; *Ten Great Musicals of the American Stage.* Stanley Richards, ed. Chilton, 1973
PIANO-VOCAL SCORE: New World Music, 1932
LICENSING AGENT: Samuel French (amateur); Music Theatre International (professional)
RECORDING: CBS M2K 42522 CD (1987 concert version)
CAST: 14 M; 5 F; extras

John P. Wintergreen is elected president of the United States on a platform of love. This is a satire on presidential campaigns that is well remembered for its Gershwin score. It is a big musical and dressy costumes and snappy dance routines are necessary. There have been Broadway and TV revivals, and a big concert version was recently performed and recorded. Most critics seem to feel that this should be done as a 1930s period show.

Pulitzer Prize

1987 CONCERT VERSION CAST:

Paige O'Hara (Diana)
Larry Kert (Wintergreen)
George Dvorsky (Jenkins)
Louise Edeiken (Miss Benson)
Maureen McGovern (Mary)
Casper Roos (Chief Justice)
Jack Dabdoub (French Ambassador)
Jack Gilford (Throttlebottom)

SONGS:
Act I
Wintergreen for President (chorus)
Who Is the Lucky Girl to Be? (Diana, chorus)
The Dimple on My Knee (Diana, chorus)
Because, Because (chorus)
Never Was There a Girl So Fair (Diana, Wintergreen, ensemble)
Some Girls Can Bake a Pie (Wintergreen, Diana, ensemble)
Love Is Sweeping the Country (Jenkins, Miss Benson, chorus)
Of Thee I Sing (Wintergreen, Mary, chorus)

Supreme Court Judges (Chief Justice,
Wintergreen, chorus)
A Kiss for Cinderella (Wintergreen, chorus)

Act II
Hello, Good Morning (Jenkins, Miss Benson,
chorus)
Who Cares? (Wintergreen, Mary, chorus)
The Illegitimate Daughter (French
Ambassador, Wintergreen, ensemble)
Because, Because (reprise) (Diana, Mary,
Wintergreen, French Ambassador, chorus)
The Senator from Minnesota (Throttlebottom,
chorus)
The Senate (Jenkins, Throttlebottom,
ensemble)
Jilted (Diana, Throttlebottom, chorus)
I'm about to Be a Mother (Mary, chorus)
Posterity Is Just around the Corner
(Wintergreen, Mary, chorus)
Trumpeter Blow Your Golden Horn
(ensemble)

OH! BOY! (1917)

BOOK AND LYRICS BY: Guy Bolton and P. G.
Wodehouse
MUSIC BY: Jerome Kern
PUBLISHED LIBRETTO: None
CONDENSATION: *Ganzl's Book of the Musical
Theatre*. Ganzl, Kurt. Schirmer (Macmillan),
1989
ANTHOLOGY: None
LICENSING AGENT: Tams-Witmark
RECORDING: None
CAST: 9 M; 8 F

The 1979 off-Broadway production of this
Jerome Kern musical featured a score (piano and cello accompaniment) that included "Till the Clouds Roll By." The time
is 1917. The plot, which was compared to
that of a French farce, concerns a secretly
married bachelor. During a party given by
his best friend, an actress chased by the police comes in through an open window. Misunderstandings abound. The second act is
set at the country club, and all ends well.

This is one of the "Princess" musicals (originally performed at the Princess Theater)
and was intended as an intimate production with no big numbers and only a small
chorus.

1985 CARNEGIE HALL CONCERT CAST:
Michael Maguire (Jim)
Cris Groenendaal (George)
Jeanne Lehman (Lou Ellen)
Paige O'Hara (Jacky)
Suzanne Briar (Polly/Jane)
Dillon Evans (Judge Carter)

SONGS:
Act I
Let's Make a Night of It (ensemble)
Ain't It a Grand and a Glorious Feeling (Jim,
ensemble)
I Never Knew about You (George, Lou Ellen)
A Package of Seeds (Jim, girls)
An Old-Fashioned Wife (Lou Ellen, girls)
A Pal Like You (Jacky, Jim)
The Letter Song (George)
Till the Clouds Roll By (George, Jacky)
That's the Kind of Man I'd Like to Be (George,
girls)
A Little Bit of Ribbon (Jane, girls)
The First Day of May (George, Jim, Jacky)
Act II
The Land Where Good Songs Go (Jim,
ensemble)
Rolled into One (Jacky)
Oh, Daddy, Please (Lou Ellen, George, Judge
Carter)
Nesting Time in Flatbush (Jim, Jacky)
Words Are Not Needed (Lou Ellen, boys)
Flubby Dub, the Caveman (George, Jim,
Jacky)

OH! BROTHER! (1981)

BOOK AND LYRICS BY: Donald Driver; based on
works by Shakespeare and Plautus
MUSIC BY: Michael Valenti
PUBLISHED LIBRETTO: French, 1982
CONDENSATION: None
ANTHOLOGY: None

MUSIC PUBLISHER: Mac Music (Schirmer), 1982
LICENSING AGENT: Samuel French
RECORDING: Original Cast OC 915 CD (original
      cast)
CAST: 7 M; 3 F; chorus

The place is the Persian Gulf and the time
is "today" (meaning 1981 with Arab-Israeli-
Iranian-energy problems). This is another
musical version of *A Comedy of Errors*
about the identical twins who were separated at birth and not quite meeting (until
the end of the show) but causing a great
deal of confusion and hilarity. This show
has a lot of topical humor (including the
Ayatollah), some exotic dancers, and a nice
score. It is played in one basic set of sand
dunes. Critics called it mindless fun.

ORIGINAL CAST:

Larry Marshall (Revolutionary Leader)
Harry Groener (Western Mousada)
David Carroll (Eastern Mousada)
Alan Weeks (Western Habim)
Joe Morton (Eastern Habim)
Mary Mastrantonio (Musica)
Judy Kaye (Saroyana)
Alyson Reed (Fatatatatatima)

SONGS:
(performed without intermission):
We Love an Old Story (Revolutionary Leader,
      ensemble)
I to the World (Mousadas and Habims)
How Do You Want Me? (Saroyana)
That's Him (Musica, ensemble)
Everybody Calls Me by My Name (Western
      Mousada, ensemble)
O.P.E.C. Maiden (Western Mousada,
      ensemble)
A Man (Eastern Mousada)
Tell Sweet Saroyana (Eastern Mousada,
      Western Habim, ensemble)
What Do I Tell People This Time? (Saroyana)
O.P.E.C. Maiden (reprise) (Musica, women)
A Loud and Funny Song (Saroyana, Musica,
      Fatatatatatima)
The Chase (company)
Oh, Brother (company)

OH CAPTAIN! (1958)

BOOK BY: Al Morgan and Jose Ferrer; based on
      the screenplay *The Captain's Paradise* by Alec
      Coppel
MUSIC AND LYRICS BY: Jay Livingston and Ray
      Evans
PUBLISHED LIBRETTO: None
CONDENSATION: None
ANTHOLOGY: None
VOCAL SELECTIONS: Chappell
LICENSING AGENT: Tams-Witmark
RECORDING: Columbia CSP AOS 2002 (original
      cast)
CAST: Large mixed cast

This is the musical tale of a British freighter
captain with a wife at home and a mistress
in Paris. Unexpectedly, the wife visits Paris,
meets the mistress, and together they con-
nive to teach the captain a lesson. The
contemporary settings include a town near
London, on shipboard, and then in Paris.
This big Broadway musical had sets that
moved on treadmills, but it can be simply
staged. Atmosphere is important.

ORIGINAL CAST:

Tony Randall (Henry)
Jacquelyn McKeever (Maud)
Edward Platt (Manzoni)
Alexandra Danilova (Lisa)
Abbe Lane (Bobo)
Paul Valentine (Spaniard)
Susan Johnson (Mae)

SONGS:
Act I
A Very Proper Town (Henry, company)
Life Does a Man a Favor (Maud, Henry)
A Very Proper Week (ensemble)
Life Does a Man a Favor (reprise) (Henry,
      Manzoni, ensemble)
Captain Henry St. James (ensemble)
Three Paradises (Henry)
Surprise (Maud, ensemble)
Hey Madame (Henry, Lisa)
Femininity (Bobo)
It's Never Quite the Same (Maud, Manzoni,
      ensemble)

We're Not Children (Maud, Spaniard)
Give It All You Got (Mae, ladies)
Keep It Simple (Bobo, ensemble)

Act II
The Morning Music of Montmartre (Mae, ensemble)
You Don't Know Him (Bobo, Maud)
I've Been There and I'm Back (Manzoni, Henry)
Double Standard (Bobo, Maud)
All the Time (Henry)
You're So Right for Me (Manzoni, Bobo)
All the Time (reprise) (Maud)

OH COWARD! (1972)

MUSIC AND LYRICS BY: Noel Coward; production devised by Roderick Cook
PUBLISHED LIBRETTO: Doubleday, 1974
CONDENSATION: None
ANTHOLOGY: None
VOCAL SELECTIONS: *Noel Coward Songbook.* Simon and Schuster, 1953; *Sir Noel Coward, His Words and Music.* Chappell, 1973
LICENSING AGENT: Music Theatre International
RECORDING: Bell 9001 (original cast)
CAST: 2 M; 1 F

This revue is made up of songs and witty observations by Noel Coward and performed by a cast of three. It is organized into a biographical outline of the famous writer/actor/composer/wit. The show begins with "the boy actor" and proceeds through sections on "music hall," "travel," "theater," "love," and so on. The off-Broadway production used only twin pianos and percussion. The setting can be a very simple Victorian proscenium with a few props and formal attire. This is a sophisticated adult entertainment. Your cast should primarily be actors who are able to carry off the outrageous and sentimental moments.

ORIGINAL CAST:

Barbara Cason   Roderick Cook
Jamie Ross

Over fifty songs by Noel Coward (and one by Cole Porter) are featured in this revue presented in two acts.

OH! KAY! (1926)

BOOK BY: Guy Bolton and P. G. Wodehouse
MUSIC BY: George Gershwin
LYRICS BY: Ira Gershwin
PUBLISHED LIBRETTO: None
CONDENSATION: *Ganzl's Book of the Musical Theatre.* Ganzl, Kurt. Schirmer (Macmillan), 1989
ANTHOLOGY: None
VOCAL SELECTIONS: Harms, 1926
LICENSING AGENT: Tams-Witmark
RECORDING: DRG 15017 CD (1960 revival cast)
CAST: 8 M; 8 F

The story is about a titled Englishman and his sister who get mixed up with prohibition and bootleggers on Long Island in 1926. The original Broadway production featured Gertrude Lawrence singing "Someone to Watch Over Me." The off-Broadway revival was an attempt to re-create the style and atmosphere on a less grand scale. One critic declared that no Gershwin song ever gets old. There was a 1990 all-black Broadway revival reset in Harlem.

1990 REVIVAL CAST:

Kyme (Dolly)
Gregg Burge (Billy)
Stanley Wayne Mathis (Duke)
Helmar Augustus Cooper (Shorty)
Brian Mitchell (Jimmy)
Angela Teek (Kay)
Kevin Ramsey (Potter)

SONGS:
(including augmented numbers)
Act I
New York Serenade (Dolly, ensemble)
Slap That Bass (ensemble)
When Our Ship Comes Sailing In (Duke, Shorty, ensemble)
Dear Little Girl (Jimmy, Shorty)

Maybe (Jimmy, Kay)
You Got What Gets Me (Billy, Dolly)
Do, Do, Do (Jimmy, Kay)
Clap Yo' Hands (Potter, ensemble)
Someone to Watch Over Me (Kay)

Act II
Oh, Kay! (Billy, Kay, ensemble)
Ask Me Again (Jimmy)
Fidgety Feet (Duke, ensemble)
Someone to Watch Over Me (reprise) (Jimmy)
Somehow It Seldom Comes True (Shorty)
Where's the Boy? Where's the Girl? (Kay)
Heaven on Earth (Potter, Duke, Billy)
Show Me the Town (Kay, Billy, Dolly, Potter,
    Duke, ensemble)

OH! LADY! LADY!! (1918)

BOOK AND LYRICS BY: Guy Bolton and
    P. G. Wodehouse
MUSIC BY: Jerome Kern
PUBLISHED LIBRETTO: None
CONDENSATION: *New Complete Book of the
    American Musical Theater*. Ewen, David. Holt,
    1970
ANTHOLOGY: None
PIANO-VOCAL SCORE: Harms, 1918
LICENSING AGENT: Tams-Witmark
RECORDING: None
CAST: 10 M; 10 F; ensemble

This is a Jerome Kern "Princess" musical
from 1918. The "Princess" refers to the theater where it was originally done and indicates a small, intimate production. The
most famous song from the score is "Bill,"
although it was dropped and later used in
Show Boat. The plot deals with a mix-up between a young man and his fiancée. There
are two sets. One is the heroine's Long Island home and the other is the terrace of
a Greenwich Village penthouse. There are
some jewel thieves, and it is all giddy, obvious, and fun. There was a concert version
done at Carnegie Hall in 1985.

1985 CONCERT VERSION CAST:
Jeanne Lehman (Molly)
George Dvorsky (Willoughby)
Ron Raines (Hale)
David Garrison (Spike)
Paige O'Hara (Fanny)
Judy Kaye (May)
Roderick Cook (Twombley)

SONGS:
Act I
The Wedding We Have Come to See
    (ensemble)
I'm to Be Married Today (Molly, ensemble)
Bill (Molly)
Not Yet (Willoughby, Molly)
Do It Now (Willoughby, Hale, Spike)
Our Little Nest (Spike, Fanny)
Do Look at Him (Molly, girls)
Oh, Lady! Lady!! (Willoughby, girls)
I Found You and You Found Me (Hale, May)

Act II
Moon Song (Hale)
Waiting 'Round the Corner (May, boys)
Dear Old Prison Days (Spike, Fanny)
When the Ships Come Home (Molly, girls)
Before I Met You (Willoughby, Molly)
Greenwich Village (Willoughby, Spike, Fanny)
Wheatless Days (Hale, May)
It's a Hard, Hard World (Willoughby, Hale,
    Twombley)

OH WHAT A LOVELY WAR (1964)

BOOK BY: The Theatre Workshop, Charles Chilton,
    and members of the cast
MUSICAL NUMBERS: Consist of traditional World
    War I songs
PUBLISHED LIBRETTO: Methuen (London), 1965
CONDENSATION: *The Book of 1,000 Plays*. Steve
    Fletcher, Norman Jopling, eds. Facts On File,
    1989
ANTHOLOGY: None
LICENSING AGENT: Carole Christensen Love, 923
    Coachway, Annapolis, Md.
RECORDING: London 25906 (original London cast)
CAST: 12 M; 5 F (may vary)

Beginning as a British seaside Pierrot show in 1914, the cast is costumed in black and white Pierrot costumes. They change characters by using different hats, additions of capes, scarves, and so forth. Performing on a basically bare stage, they mix music, song, dance, and mime in an elaboration of British Music Hall techniques. They follow the events of World War I in what has been called one of the most effective theatrical indictments against war. Nothing sung or spoken was written outside the period 1914–1918. One character serves as a master of ceremonies and chats casually with the audience, tells poor jokes, and breezily bridges the various events. The songs are what the public thought war was like, while statistics projected on a screen behind the players show what it was actually like. There was an all-star film version in 1969.

ORIGINAL CAST (known as the Pierrots and playing various roles):

Fanny Carby	Myvanwy Jenn
Colin Kemball	Murray Melvin
Brian Murphy	Ian Paterson
Marcia Rodd	Victor Spinetti
Valerie Walsh	Barbara Windsor

SONGS:
Act I
Row Row Row (ensemble)
We Don't Want to Lose You (the ladies)
Belgium Put the Kibosh on the Kaiser (Valerie Walsh)
Medley: Are We Downhearted/It's a Long Way to Tipperary/Hold Your Hand Out Naughty Boy (the men)
I'll Make a Man of You (Barbara Windsor)
Pack Up Your Troubles (the men)
Hitchykoo (Fanny Carby)
Heilige Nacht (Silent Night) (Colin Kemball)
Christmas Day in the Cookhouse (Brian Murphy)
Good-bye–ee (Victor Spinetti)

Act II
Oh What a Lovely War (ensemble)
Gassed Last Night (the men)

Roses of Picardy (Marcia Rodd, Ian Paterson)
Hush Here Comes a Whizzbang (the men)
There's a Long, Long Trail (Ian Paterson)
I Don't Want to Be a Soldier (the men)
Kaiser Bill (the men)
They Were Only Playing Leapfrog (the men)
Old Soldiers Never Die (Murray Melvin)
If You Want the Old Battalion (the men)
Far Far from Wipers (Colin Kemball)
If the Sergeant Steals Your Rum (the men)
I Wore a Tunic (Ian Paterson)
Forward Joe Soap's Army (the men)
Fred Karno's Army (the men)
When This Lousy War Is Over (Colin Kemball)
Wash Me in the Water (the men)
I Want to Go Home (the men)
The Bells of Hell (the men)
Keep the Home Fires Burning (Myvanwy Jenn)
Sister Susie's Sewing Shirts (Barbara Windsor)
Finale: Chanson de Craonne/I Don't Want to Be a Soldier/They'll Never Believe Me (ensemble)

OIL CITY SYMPHONY (1987)

BOOK, MUSIC, AND LYRICS BY: Mike Craver, Mark Hardwick, Debra Monk, Mary Murfitt, and others
PUBLISHED LIBRETTO: None
CONDENSATION: None
ANTHOLOGY: None
LICENSING AGENT: Music Theatre International
RECORDING: DRG 12594 CD (original cast)
CAST: 2 M; 2 F

The scene is a high-school gymnasium in Oil City set in the mid-1950s. Four former band members have gathered to honor their music teacher. You will need four talented musicians (who must play various instruments) to perform as four *untalented* musicians. The humor of this musical lies in its satire of the untalented. As one critic wrote, "City folk just love to laugh at bumpkins making fools of themselves!"

The show is about eighty minutes long and has some audience participation. The cast serves punch and cookies to one and all after the show.

ORIGINAL CAST:

Mike Craver	Mark Hardwick
Michelle Horman	Mary Murfitt

SONGS:

Act I

Count Your Blessings (company)
Czardas (Murfitt, Hardwick)
This Afternoon (Horman)
Baby It's Cold Outside (company)
Beaver Ball at the Bug Club
    (company)
Beehive Polka (Murfitt, company)

Act II

Dizzy Fingers (Hardwick, Craver)
Iris (Craver)
The End of the World (Horman,
    Murfitt)
Coaxing the Ivories (company)
Bus Ride (company)
In the Sweet By and By (company)
My Old Kentucky Rock and Roll Home
    (Hardwick, company)

OKLAHOMA! (1943)

BOOK AND LYRICS BY: Oscar Hammerstein II;
    based on *Green Grow the Lilacs* by Lynn Riggs
MUSIC BY: Richard Rodgers
PUBLISHED LIBRETTO: Random House, 1943
CONDENSATION: *Burns Mantle Best Plays*
    1942–1943. Burns Mantle, ed. Dodd, Mead, 1944;
    Ganzl's Book of the Musical Theatre. Ganzl,
    Kurt. Schirmer (Macmillan), 1989; *Rodgers and*
    Hammerstein. Mordden, Ethan. Abrams, 1992
ANTHOLOGY: *Six Plays by Rodgers and*
    Hammerstein. Random House, 1955; Modern
    Library, 1959
PIANO-VOCAL SCORE: Williamson, 1943
LICENSING AGENT: Rodgers and Hammerstein
    Theatre Library

RECORDING: MCA 10046 CD (original cast)
CAST: Large mixed cast

The action takes place in the Indian Territory (now Oklahoma) just after the turn of the century. This show changed the form and direction of musical theater; plot, music, and dancing were all integrated. The plot really amounts to a box social, and whether Curly or Jud will escort Laurey. There is also a reference to the rivalry between the farmers and cattlemen. The dances were Agnes de Mille ballets. There are numerous well-known songs from the score. The popular film version in 1955 starred Gordon MacRae. The title song was made the state's official song. A real family show.

ORIGINAL CAST:

Alfred Drake (Curly)
Joan Roberts (Laurey)
Howard Da Silva (Jud)
Betty Garde (Aunt Eller)
Lee Dixon (Will)
Celeste Holm (Ado Annie)
Joseph Buloff (Ali)

SONGS:

Act I

Oh, What a Beautiful Mornin' (Curly)
The Surrey with the Fringe on Top (Curly,
    Laurey, Aunt Eller)
Kansas City (Will, Aunt Eller, boys)
I Cain't Say No (Ado Annie)
Many a New Day (Laurey, girls)
It's a Scandal (Ali, boys)
People Will Say We're in Love (Curly,
    Laurey)
Poor Jud (Curly, Jud)
Lonely Room (Jud)
Out of My Dreams (Laurey, girls)

Act II

The Farmer and the Cowman (Aunt Eller,
    ensemble)
All 'Er Nothin' (Ado Annie, Will)
Oklahoma! (Curly, Laurey, Aunt Eller,
    ensemble)

OLIVER! (1963)

BOOK, MUSIC, AND LYRICS BY: Lionel Bart; freely
adapted from *Oliver Twist* by Charles Dickens
PUBLISHED LIBRETTO: None
CONDENSATION: *Ganzl's Book of the Musical
Theatre.* Ganzl, Kurt. Schirmer (Macmillan),
1989
ANTHOLOGY: None
PIANO-VOCAL SCORE: Hollis Music, 1960
VOCAL SELECTIONS: Hollis Music, 1968 (motion
picture edition)
LICENSING AGENT: Tams-Witmark
RECORDING: RCA 4113 CD (original cast)
CAST: Large mixed cast

This British musical is about a young boy
adrift in London around 1850 who falls in
with the "Artful Dodger" and Fagin's gang
of thieves. The plot includes the adult story
of Nancy and Bill Sikes. This show was revived several times in London, had a very
successful New York run, and was filmed in
1968. It was a lavish production with some
elaborate sets, but it can be staged on a
simple scale. Costumes need to be Dicken-
sian. A number of young boys are required
for the cast.

ORIGINAL CAST:

Willoughby Goddard (Mr. Bumble)
Hope Jackman (Widow Corney)
Bruce Prochnik (Oliver)
Robin Ramsay (Mr. Sowerberry)
Helena Carroll (Mrs. Sowerberry)
David Jones (Artful Dodger)
Clive Revill (Fagin)
Georgia Brown (Nancy)
Alice Playten (Bet)
Danny Sewell (Bill)
Dortha Duckworth (Mrs. Bedwin)

SONGS:
Act I
Food, Glorious Food (boys)
Oliver! (Mr Bumble, Widow Corney, Oliver,
boys)
I Shall Scream (Widow Corney, Mr. Bumble)
Boy for Sale (Mr. Bumble)

That's Your Funeral (Mr. Sowerberry, Mr.
Bumble, Mrs. Sowerberry)
Where Is Love? (Oliver)
Consider Yourself (Artful Dodger, Oliver,
ensemble)
You've Got to Pick a Pocket or Two (Fagin,
boys)
It's a Fine Life (Nancy, Bet)
I'd Do Anything (Artful Dodger, Nancy, Oliver,
Bet, Fagin)
Be Back Soon (Fagin, Artful Dodger, Oliver,
boys)
Act II
Oom-Pah-Pah (Nancy, company)
My Name (Bill)
As Long as He Needs Me (Nancy)
Where Is Love? (reprise) (Mrs. Bedwin)
Who Will Buy? (Oliver, chorus)
It's a Fine Life (reprise) (Bill, Nancy, Fagin,
Artful Dodger)
Reviewing the Situation (Fagin)
Oliver! (reprise) (Mr. Bumble, Widow Corney)
Food, Glorious Food (reprise) (boys)

OLYMPUS ON MY MIND (1986)

BOOK AND LYRICS BY: Barry Harman; suggested
by *Amphitryon* by Heinrich Von Kleist
MUSIC BY: Grant Sturiale
PUBLISHED LIBRETTO: French, 1986; Fireside
Theatre Book Club
CONDENSATION: None
ANTHOLOGY: None
LICENSING AGENT: Samuel French
RECORDING: TER 1131 (original cast)
CAST: 3 M; 3 F; male chorus

The familiar plot of this musical concerns
the Greek god Jupiter impersonating the
virile, mortal warrior Amphitryon in order
to seduce Amphitryon's beautiful wife, Alcmene. It has been done in many versions,
including Cole Porter's *Out of This World.*
An added subplot concerns a chorus girl
who got her job through the friendship of
one of the backers of the show ("Murray
the Furrier"). Consequently she wears several fur coats throughout the show, even

though the rest of the cast wears ancient Grecian costumes. The "bubbly score" contains not only sophisticated patter songs but pop-rock ballads as well. "It percolates with an old-fashioned sense of naughty musical comedy fun," wrote Stephen Holden in the *New York Times*.

ORIGINAL CAST:

Ron Raines (Jupiter/Amphitryon)
Emily Zacharias (Alcmene)
Faith Prince (Delores)
Jason Graae (Mercury)
Lewis J. Stadlen (Sosia)
Peggy Hewett (Charis)

SONGS:

Act I
Welcome to Greece (chorus)
Heaven on Earth (Jupiter, Alcmene, chorus)
The Gods on Tap (Delores, Jupiter, Mercury, chorus)
Surprise! (Sosia)
Wait 'Til It Dawns (Mercury)
I Know My Wife (Amphitryon)
It Was Me (Sosia)
Back So Soon? (Amphitryon, Sosia, chorus)
Wonderful (Alcmene)
At Liberty in Thebes (Charis, chorus)
Jupiter Slept Here (company)

Act II
Back to the Play (chorus)
Don't Bring Her Flowers (Mercury)
Generals' Pandemonium (Amphitryon, Jupiter, Sosia, chorus)
Heaven on Earth (reprise) (Sosia, Charis)
Olympus Is a Lonely Town (Jupiter)
A Star Is Born (Delores, company)
Final Sequence (Amphitryon, Alcmene, Mercury, Jupiter, Charis, Sosia, chorus)

ON A CLEAR DAY YOU CAN SEE FOREVER (1965)

BOOK AND LYRICS BY: Alan Jay Lerner
MUSIC BY: Burton Lane
PUBLISHED LIBRETTO: Random House, 1966

CONDENSATION: *New Complete Book of the American Musical Theater*. Even, David. Holt, 1970
ANTHOLOGY: None
PIANO-VOCAL SCORE: Chappell, 1967
VOCAL SELECTIONS: Chappell, 1970
LICENSING AGENT: Tams-Witmark
RECORDING: RCA 60820 CD (original cast)
CAST: 14 M; 7 F; chorus

A young college student tries hypnosis to stop smoking. She turns out to have a subconscious memory of an earlier life. Thus the time and place shift back and forth from present-day New York to eighteenth-century London. The critics liked the score, calling it one of the loveliest heard in years, and the beautiful sets and costumes. There is a great deal of humor in the book, although some critics wondered if it was basically a comedy. The film version in 1970 starred Barbra Streisand.

ORIGINAL CAST:

Barbara Harris (Daisy)
John Cullum (Mark)
Byron Webster (Hubert)
Gordon Dilworth (Samuel)
Blanche Collins (Mrs. Welles)
Barbara Monte (Muriel)
William Reilly (Preston)
Gerald M. Teijelo, Jr. (Millard)
Clifford David (Edward)
William Daniels (Warren)
Titos Vandis (Kriakos)

SONGS:

Act I
Hurry! It's Lovely up Here (Daisy)
Ring Out the Bells (Samuel, Mrs. Welles, Hubert, ensemble)
Tosy and Cosh (Daisy)
On a Clear Day You Can See Forever (Mark)
On the SS *Bernard Cohn* (Daisy, Muriel, Preston, Millard)
At the Hellrakers' (ensemble)
Don't Tamper with My Sister (Edward, Hubert, ensemble)
She Wasn't You (Edward)
Melinda (Mark)

Act II

When I'm Being Born Again (Kriakos)
What Did I Have That I Don't Have (Daisy)
Wait 'Til We're Sixty-Five (Warren, Daisy)
Come Back to Me (Mark)

ON THE TOWN (1944)

BOOK AND LYRICS BY: Betty Comden and Adolph
   Green; based on the ballet *Fancy Free* by
   Jerome Robbins
MUSIC BY: Leonard Bernstein
PUBLISHED LIBRETTO: None
CONDENSATION: *Ganzl's Book of the Musical
   Theatre*. Ganzl, Kurt. Schirmer (Macmillan),
   1989
ANTHOLOGY: *Comden and Green on Broadway*.
   Drama Book Specialists, 1981
VOCAL SELECTIONS: Warner Bros. Music
MUSIC FOR DANCE EPISODES: Schirmer, 1945
LICENSING AGENT: Tams-Witmark
RECORDINGS: MCA 10280 CD (original cast);
   Columbia CK 2038 CD (1960 recording)
CAST: Large mixed cast

The adventures of three sailors on twenty-
four hours' leave in New York City are featured in this popular musical. It was filmed
in 1949 with Gene Kelly and Frank Sinatra.
There was a recent revival on Broadway
with Bernadette Peters. Called a classic
musical, this show requires a lot of dancing. Sets are numerous from museums to
taxis to streets to subways to apartments.
The 1944 ambience should include zoot
suits and wedgies.

1971 REVIVAL CAST:

Jess Richards (Chip)
Remak Ramsay (Ozzie)
Ron Husmann (Gabey)
Donna McKechnie (Ivy)
Bernadette Peters (Hildy)
Phyllis Newman (Claire)
Fran Stevens (Madame Dilly)
Sandra Dorsey (Diana Dream)
Laura Kenyon (Señorita Dolores)
Carol Petri (Flossie)

SONGS:
Act I
I Feel Like I'm Not out of Bed Yet (men)
New York, New York (Chip, Ozzie, Gabey)
Come up to My Place (Hildy, Chip)
Carried Away (Claire, Ozzie)
Lonely Town (Gabey, ensemble)
Do-Do-Re-Do (Ivy, Madame Dilly, ensemble)
I Can Cook Too (Hildy, Chip)
Lucky to Be Me (Gabey, ensemble)

Act II
Nightclub Song (Diana Dream), in Spanish
   (Señorita Dolores)
You Got Me (Claire, Ozzie, Hildy, Chip)
Some Other Time (Claire, Hildy, Chip, Ozzie)
Coney Island Hep Cats (Flossie, ensemble)

ON THE TWENTIETH CENTURY (1978)

BOOK AND LYRICS BY: Betty Comden and
   Adolph Green; based on *Twentieth Century* by
   Ben Hecht and Charles MacArthur and *The
   Napoleon of Broadway* by Bruce Millholland
MUSIC BY: Cy Coleman
PUBLISHED LIBRETTO: Drama Book Specialists,
   1981; Samuel French
CONDENSATION: *Ganzl's Book of the Musical
   Theatre*. Ganzl, Kurt. Schirmer (Macmillan),
   1989
ANTHOLOGY: None
MUSIC PUBLISHER: Notable Music, 1978
LICENSING AGENT: Samuel French (specify musical
   version)
RECORDING: Sony 35330 CD (original cast)
CAST: Large mixed cast

Based on the play *Twentieth Century*, this is
a wild, madcap train ride from Chicago to
New York. The main characters are theater
impresario Oscar Jaffee and Lily Garland,
a Hollywood star. Jaffee needs Garland for
a play. This show is set in the early 1930s,
and critics praised the art deco designs of
the sets and costumes. There are a number
of flamboyant parts and some tap-dancing
train porters. The music is unusually challenging with several large production num-

bers. A New York critic called it "a real musical comedy, and a truly grand one at that."

ORIGINAL CAST:

Charles Rule (Bishop)
Hal Norman (Actor)
Imogene Coca (Letitia)
Tom Batten (Conductor)
Stanley Simmonds (Rogers)
John Cullum (Oscar)
George Coe (Owen)
Dean Dittman (Oliver)
Madeline Kahn (Lily Garland/Mildred Plotka)
Willi Burke (Imelda)
Kevin Kline (Bruce)
George Lee Andrews (Max)

SONGS:
Act I
Stranded Again (Bishop, Actor, ensemble)
On the Twentieth Century (Letitia, Conductor, Rogers, ensemble)
I Rise Again (Oscar, Owen, Oliver)
Indian Maiden's Lament (Imelda, Mildred)
Veronique (Lily, male ensemble)
I Have Written a Play (Conductor)
Together (Oscar, ensemble)
Never (Lily, Owen, Oliver)
Our Private World (Lily, Oscar)
Repent (Letitia)
Mine (Oscar, Bruce)
I've Got It All (Lily, Oscar)

Act II
Five Zeros (Owen, Oliver, Letitia, Oscar)
Sextet (Owen, Oliver, Oscar, Letitia, Lily, Bruce)
She's a Nut (company)
Max Jacobs (Max)
Babbette (Lily)
The Legacy (Oscar)
Lily, Oscar (Lily, Oscar)

ON YOUR TOES (1936)

BOOK BY: Richard Rodgers, Lorenz Hart, and George Abbott
MUSIC BY: Richard Rodgers

LYRICS BY: Lorenz Hart
PUBLISHED LIBRETTO: None
CONDENSATION: *Ganzl's Book of the Musical Theatre*. Ganzl, Kurt. Schirmer (Macmillan), 1989
ANTHOLOGY: None
VOCAL SELECTIONS: Hal Leonard
LICENSING AGENT: Rodgers and Hammerstein Theatre Library
RECORDING: Polydor 813 667-2 CD (1983 revival cast)
CAST: Large mixed cast

This was the first musical to make important use of ballet. Two major ballet numbers are required, plus one big tap number to the title tune. In the plot of this famous musical, Junior has once danced in vaudeville with his parents but has now settled down to teaching music. It is the mid-1930s and a famous Russian ballet is soon to perform at the Cosmopolitan Opera House. Junior is torn between his love for one of his students and for the tempestuous ballerina Vera Baronova. The 1983 revival on Broadway was a big hit. There was a 1939 film version with Vera Zorina.

1983 REVIVAL CAST:

Eugene J. Anthony (Phil II)
Philip Arthur Ross (Phil III)
Betty Ann Grove (Lil)
Lara Teeter (Junior)
Christine Andreas (Frankie)
George S. Irving (Sergei)
Dina Merrill (Peggy)
Natalia Makarova (Vera)
Michael Vita (Hank)

SONGS:
Act I
Two a Day for Keith (Phil II, Phil III, Lil)
Questions and Answers (The Three Bs) (Junior, ensemble)
It's Got to Be Love (Frankie, Junior, ensemble)
Too Good for the Average Man (Sergei, Peggy)
The Seduction (Vera, Junior)

There's a Small Hotel (Frankie, Junior)
Princess Zenobia (ballet)

Act II
The Heart Is Quicker than the Eye (Peggy,
   Junior)
Glad to Be Unhappy (Frankie)
Quiet Night (Hank, students)
On Your Toes (Frankie, ensemble)
Quiet Night (reprise) (Sergei)
Slaughter on Tenth Avenue (ballet)

ONCE ON THIS ISLAND (1990)

BOOK AND LYRICS BY: Lynn Ahrens; based on the
   novel *My Love, My Love* by Rosa Guy
MUSIC BY: Stephen Flaherty
PUBLISHED LIBRETTO: None
CONDENSATION: *The Theatre Year Book and Best
   Plays of 1989–1990.* Otis L. Guernsey, Jr., ed.
   Applause Books, 1990
ANTHOLOGY: None
VOCAL SELECTIONS: Warner Bros. Music, 1990
LICENSING AGENT: Music Theatre International
RECORDING: RCA 60595-2 CD (original cast)
CAST: 5 M; 6 F

Set in the French Antilles, the stage is
alive with bright colors, reminding some of
Haitian folk art. The music has a Caribbean
beat with ethnic choreography somewhat
like that of Katherine Dunham. The plot
concerns a powerful landowner's light-
skinned son who is injured in a car crash.
He is nursed back to health by a dark-
skinned peasant girl, and they fall in love.
He ultimately returns to the light-skinned
girl he was originally engaged to wed. Critics were divided over this ninety-minute
intermission-less musical. Some felt it was
too slight for Broadway, while another
wrote that "its simplicity arrives like a
refreshing tropical breeze to blow away
the stale spectacles of London and New
York."

ORIGINAL CAST:

Jerry Dixon (Daniel)
Andrea Frierson (Erzulie)
Sheila Gibbs (Euralie)
Ellis E. Williams (Tonton)
Afi McClendon (Little Ti Moune)
Kecia Lewis-Evans (Asaka)
Milton Craig Nealy (Agwe)
Eric Riley (Papa Ge)
Nikki Rene (Andrea)
La Chanze (Ti Moune)
Gerry McIntyre (Armand)

SONGS:
(performed without intermission):
We Dance (ensemble)
One Small Girl (Euralie, Tonton, Little Ti
   Moune, ensemble)
Waiting for Life (Ti Moune, ensemble)
And the Gods Heard Her Prayer (Asaka,
   Agwe, Papa Ge, Erzulie)
Rain (Agwe, ensemble)
Pray (Ti Moune, Tonton, Euralie, ensemble)
Forever Yours (Ti Moune, Daniel, Papa Ge)
The Sad Tale of the Beauxhommes (Armand,
   ensemble)
Ti Moune (Euralie, Tonton, Ti Moune)
Mama Will Provide (Asaka, ensemble)
Some Say (ensemble)
The Human Heart (Erzulie, ensemble)
Some Girls (Daniel)
The Ball (Andrea, Daniel, Ti Moune,
   ensemble)
Forever Yours (reprise) (Papa Ge, Ti Moune,
   Erzulie, ensemble)
A Part of Us (Euralie, Little Ti Moune, Tonton,
   ensemble)
Why We Tell the Story (ensemble)

ONCE UPON A MATTRESS (1959)

BOOK BY: Jay Thompson, Marshall Barer, and
   Dean Fuller; based on "The Princess and the
   Pea"
MUSIC BY: Mary Rodgers
LYRICS BY: Marshall Barer
PUBLISHED LIBRETTO: *Theatre Arts* (magazine),
   July 1960
CONDENSATION: *Ganzl's Book of the Musical
   Theatre.* Ganzl, Kurt. Schirmer (Macmillan),
   1989

ANTHOLOGY: None
PIANO-VOCAL SCORE: Chappell, 1967
VOCAL SELECTIONS: Chappell, 1960
LICENSING AGENT: Rodgers and Hammerstein
   Theatre Library
RECORDING: MCA 10768 CD (original cast)
CAST: Large mixed cast

Carol Burnett starred in this musical, first off-Broadway, then on Broadway, and twice (in 1964 and 1972) on television. The plot of this family musical is based on the fairy tale about the princess being put to a test to see if she can feel a pea through twenty mattresses. Costumed in the never-never medieval land of fairy tales, this tongue-in-cheek farce includes a court wizard who longs for the good old days of vaudeville and a Harpo Marx-type mute King. There is sophistication for the adults, and fun for the children.

ORIGINAL CAST:

Harry Snow (Minstrel)
Joe Bova (Prince Dauntless)
Anne Jones (Lady Larken)
Alan Case (Sir Harry)
Carol Burnett (Winnifred)
Jane White (Queen)
Robert Weil (Wizard)
Jack Gilford (King)
Matt Mattox (Jester)
Gina Viglione (Nightingale)

SONGS:
Act I
Many Moons Ago (Minstrel, ensemble)
An Opening for a Princess (Prince Dauntless, Lady Larken, ensemble)
In a Little While (Lady Larken, Sir Harry)
Shy (Winnifred, ensemble)
The Minstrel, the Jester, and I (King, Minstrel, Jester)
Sensitivity (Queen, Wizard)
Swamps of Home (Winnifred, Prince Dauntless, ladies)
Normandy (Minstrel, Jester, King, Lady Larken)
Spanish Panic (Jester, Queen, Winnifred, Prince Dauntless, ensemble)

Song of Love (Prince Dauntless, Winnifred, ensemble)
Act II
Quiet (Jester, ensemble)
Happily Ever After (Winnifred)
Man to Man Talk (King, Prince Dauntless)
Very Soft Shoes (Jester, ensemble)
Yesterday I Loved You (Sir Harry, Lady Larken)
Lullaby (Nightingale)

---

110 IN THE SHADE (1963)

BOOK BY: N. Richard Nash; based on his play *The Rainmaker*
MUSIC BY: Harvey Schmidt
LYRICS BY: Tom Jones
PUBLISHED LIBRETTO: None
CONDENSATION: *New Complete Book of the American Musical Theater*. Ewen, David. Holt, 1970
ANTHOLOGY: None
PIANO-VOCAL SCORE: Chappell, 1964
VOCAL SELECTIONS: *The Best of Schmidt and Jones*. Chappell, 1975
LICENSING AGENT: Tams-Witmark
RECORDING: RCA 1085 CD (original cast)
CAST: 8 M; 8 F; children, townspeople

A handsome confidence man collects $100 on the premise that he will make it rain within twenty-four hours. He also convinces the ugly-duckling daughter of a wealthy rancher that she is really beautiful. Settings should create the atmosphere of the great Southwest around 1900 with parched land, small towns, and colorful western costumes. Some numbers suggest a revival meeting. The dancing is hoedown style. This was revived by the New York City Opera at Lincoln Center in 1992.

ORIGINAL CAST:

Stephen Douglass (File)
Will Geer (H. C.)
Steve Roland (Noah)
Scooter Teague (Jimmie)
Inga Svenson (Lizzie)

Robert Horton (Starbuck)
George Church (Toby)
Lesley Warren (Snookie)

SONGS:
Act I
Another Hot Day (File, ensemble)
Lizzie's Coming Home (H. C., Noah, Jimmie)
Love, Don't Turn Away (Lizzie)
Poker Polka (File, H. C., Noah)
Hungry Men (ensemble)
The Rain Song (Starbuck, ensemble)
You're Not Foolin' Me (Lizzie, Starbuck)
Raunchy (Lizzie, H. C.)
A Man and a Woman (Lizzie, File)
Old Maid (Lizzie)

Act II
Everything Beautiful Happens at Night (Toby,
    Jimmie, Snookie, ensemble)
Melisande (Starbuck)
Simple Little Things (Lizzie)
Little Red Hat (Snookie, Jimmie)
Is It Really Me? (Lizzie, Starbuck)
Wonderful Music (File, Starbuck, Lizzie)

ONE MO' TIME (1979)

CONCEIVED BY: Vernel Bagneris
MUSIC AND LYRICS BY: Various
PUBLISHED LIBRETTO: French
CONDENSATION: None
ANTHOLOGY: None
LICENSING AGENT: Samuel French
RECORDING: Warner Bros. HS 3454 (original cast)
CAST: 2 M; 3 F

Set in New Orleans in 1926, the plot of this
show concerns a troupe of black vaudeville
performers appearing at the Lyric Theater.
The one white actor portrays the theater
owner who is "pulling a flim-flam" with their
salaries. Professional rivalries abound, and
there is lots of tough talk. All this action
takes place in a crowded dressing room,
but the real show is onstage with one sensational number after another. There are lots
of double entendres performed in tacky period costumes. You will need talented performers and a good Dixieland band.

ORIGINAL CAST:
Sylvia "Kuumba" Williams (Bertha)
Thais Clark (Ma Reed)
Topsy Chapman (Thelma)
Vernel Bagneris (Papa Du)

SONGS:
Act I
Down in Honky Tonk Town (Papa Du, Ma
    Reed, Thelma)
Kiss Me Sweet (Papa Du, Thelma)
Don't Turn Your Back on Me (Bertha)
Jenny's Ball (Ma Reed, Papa Du)
Cake Walkin' Babies from Home (Bertha, Papa
    Du, Thelma)
I've Got What It Takes (Thelma)
C. C. Rider (Ma Reed)
He's in the Jailhouse Now (Papa Du)
He's Funny That Way (Thelma)
Kitchen Man (Bertha)
Charleston (Papa Du, Ma Reed, Thelma)

Act II
Black Bottom (Ma Reed, Papa Du, Thelma)
The Party (Bertha, Papa Du, Thelma)
New Orleans Hop Scop Blues (Papa Du)
Exotic Dance: Hindustan (Ma Reed)
What It Takes to Bring You Back (Bertha,
    Papa Du)
Everybody Loves My Baby (Thelma)
The Right Key but the Wrong Keyhole
    (Bertha)
After You've Gone (Ma Reed)
My Man Blues (Thelma, Bertha)
Papa De Da Da (Papa Du, Ma Reed, Thelma)
Muddy Waters (Bertha)
Hot Time in the Old Town (company)

ONE TOUCH OF VENUS (1944)

BOOK BY: S. J. Perelman and Ogden Nash
MUSIC BY: Kurt Weill
LYRICS BY: Ogden Nash
PUBLISHED LIBRETTO: Little, 1944
CONDENSATION: *Ganzl's Book of the Musical
    Theatre.* Ganzl, Kurt. Schirmer (Macmillan),
    1989
ANTHOLOGY: *Ten Great Musicals of the American
    Stage.* Stanley Richards, ed. Chilton, 1973

LICENSING AGENT: Rodgers and Hammerstein
   Theatre Library
RECORDING: Decca DL 79122 (original cast)
CAST: Large mixed cast

This story concerns a priceless statue of
Venus that suddenly vanishes from a New
York museum. It seems that while the museum owner was admiring his new treasure he was also having his morning shave.
When he was called from the room for a
moment, the barber put his sweetheart's
engagement ring on the statue. The statue
came to life! There were several ballets by
Agnes de Mille. There was a film version
with Ava Gardner in 1948 but without most
of the songs.

ORIGINAL CAST:

Kenny Baker (Rodney)
Mary Martin (Venus)
John Boles (Savory)
Paula Laurence (Molly)
Adelaide Klein (Mrs. Kramer)
Ruth Bond (Gloria)

SONGS:
Act I
New Art Is True Art (Savory, chorus)
One Touch of Venus (Molly, girls)
How Much I Love You (Rodney)
I'm a Stranger Here Myself (Venus)
Forty Minutes for Lunch (ballet)
West Wind (Savory)
Way Out West in Jersey (Mrs. Kramer, Gloria,
   Rodney)
Foolish Heart (Venus)
The Trouble with Women (Rodney, Savory)
Speak Low (Venus, Rodney)
Dr. Crippen (Savory, chorus)

Act II
Who Am I? (Savory)
Very, Very, Very (Molly)

Catch Hatch (Savory, Molly, ensemble)
That's Him (Venus)
Wooden Wedding (Rodney)
Venus in Ozone Heights (ballet)

OUT OF THIS WORLD (1950)

BOOK BY: Dwight Taylor and Reginald Lawrence;
   freely adapted from the Amphitryon myth
MUSIC AND LYRICS BY: Cole Porter
PUBLISHED LIBRETTO: None
CONDENSATION: None
ANTHOLOGY: None
LICENSING AGENT: Tams-Witmark
RECORDING: Sony SK 48223 CD (original cast)
CAST: Large mixed cast

A young couple are on their honeymoon in
Greece. The young man is also looking for
information for a news story about a gangster. From high above on Mount Olympus,
Jupiter, the king of the gods, sees the young
bride and takes a fancy to her. So the new-
lyweds are involved with Greek gods and
gangsters in this opulent Broadway musical. Cole Porter's songs are even more sophisticated than usual, thus making this
bawdy farce adult entertainment. Modestly
staged versions of this musical have been
done off-Broadway.

ORIGINAL CAST:

George Jongeyans (Jupiter)
William Redfield (Mercury)
Priscilla Gillette (Helen)
Peggy Rea (Vulcania)
Charlotte Greenwood (Juno)
Barbara Ashley (Chloe)
David Burns (Niki)

SONGS:
Act I
I Jupiter, I Rex (Jupiter, ensemble)

Use Your Imagination (Mercury, Helen)
Hail, Hail, Hail (Vulcania, Mercury, ensemble)
I Got Beauty (Juno, ensemble)
Maiden Fair (ensemble)
Where, Oh, Where (Chloe)
I Am Loved (Helen)
They Couldn't Compare to You (Mercury, ensemble)
What Do You Think about Men? (Helen, Chloe, Juno)
I Sleep Easier Now (Juno)

Act II
Climb Up the Mountain (Juno, Niki, company)
No Lover for Me (Helen)
Cherry Pies Ought to Be You (Mercury, Chloe, Juno, Niki)
Hark to the Song of the Night (Jupiter)
Nobody's Chasing Me (Juno)

OVER HERE! (1974)

BOOK BY: Will Holt
MUSIC AND LYRICS BY: Richard M. Sherman and Robert B. Sherman
PUBLISHED LIBRETTO: French, 1979
CONDENSATION: None
ANTHOLOGY: None
VOCAL SELECTIONS: New York Times Music, 1974
LICENSING AGENT: Samuel French
RECORDING: Sony SK 32961 CD (original cast)
CAST: 10 M; 8 F; chorus

With this musical Broadway took a nostalgic look at World War II "B" movies. The plot involves a sister act that entertains the boys at camps. The Andrews Sisters did just that and also made movies about it. Two of the Andrews Sisters returned to the limelight to star in this show. There is an attractive German spy who sings with the girls and adds to the plot. While the score is original, it sounds like the popular big-band music of the era. On Broadway the Andrews Sisters also sang a medley of their biggest hits. Costumes and sets (including a cross-country railroad trip) should be in keeping with the period.

ORIGINAL CAST:

Maxine Andrews (Pauline)
Patty Andrews (Paulette)
April Shawhan (June)
Ann Reinking (Maggie)
John Mineo (Lucky)
Douglass Watson (Norwin)
William Griffis (Rankin)
MacIntyre Dixon (Father)
John Travolta (Misfit)
Jim Weston (Make-out)
John Driver (Bill)
Janie Sell (Mitzi)
Samuel E. Wright (Sam)

SONGS:
Act I
The Beat Begins (company)
Since You're Not Around (Make-out, company)
Over Here (Paulette, Pauline)
Buy a Victory Bond (company)
My Dream for Tomorrow (June, soldiers)
Charlie's Place (Pauline, Maggie, Lucky, company)
Hey Yvette/The Grass Grows Greener (Norwin, Rankin, Father)
My Dream for Tomorrow (reprise) (June, Bill)
The V. D. Polka (Paulette, company)
Wait for Me Marlena (Mitzi, company)
We Got It (Paulette, Pauline, Mitzi, company)

Act II
Wartime Wedding (Paulette, Pauline, company)
Don't Shoot the Hooey to Me, Louie (Sam)
Where Did the Good Times Go? (Paulette)
Dream Drummin'/Soft Music (Misfit, company)
The Big Beat (Paulette, Pauline, Mitzi)
No Goodbyes (Paulette, Pauline, company)

PACIFIC OVERTURES (1976)

BOOK BY: John Weidman, additional book material
   by Hugh Wheeler
MUSIC AND LYRICS BY: Stephen Sondheim
PUBLISHED LIBRETTO: Dodd, Mead, 1977
CONDENSATION: *The Best Plays of 1975–1976*. Otis
   L. Guernsey, Jr., ed. Dodd, Mead, 1976
ANTHOLOGY: None
PIANO-VOCAL SCORE: Revelation Music, 1977
LICENSING AGENT: Music Theatre International
RECORDING: RCA RCD-1 4407 CD (original cast)
CAST: Large male cast

Performed in the style of the Japanese
Kabuki theater, this is the story of Commodore Perry's "opening up" of Japan in
1853. The original production (with an all-
male cast, some in female roles) was highly
praised for its costumes and sets. The
Sondheim score commands a great deal
of attention. A jump at the finale brings
the story to the present. This is a real
challenge.

ORIGINAL CAST:

Mako (Reciter)
Soon-Teck Oh (Tamate)
Jae Woo Lee (Fisherman)
Mark Hsu Syers (Thief)
Alvin Ing (Shogun's Mother)
Freda Foh Shen (Shogun's Wife)
Freddy Mao (Kayama)
Sab Shimoda (Manjiro)
Ernest Harada (Madam)
James Dybas (Old Man)
Gedde Watanabe (Boy)
Haruki Fujimoto (Commodore Perry)
Yuki Shimoda (Abe)

SONGS:
Act I
The Advantages of Floating in the Middle of
   the Sea (Reciter, company)
There Is No Other Way (Tamate, ensemble)
Four Black Dragons (Fisherman, Thief,
   Reciter, ensemble)
Chrysanthemum Tea (Reciter, Shogun's
   Mother, Shogun's Wife, ensemble)
Poems (Kayama, Manjiro)

Welcome to Kanagawa (Madam, girls)
Someone in a Tree (Old Man, Reciter, Boy)
Lion Dance (Commodore Perry)

Act II
Please Hello (Abe, Reciter, ensemble)
A Bowler Hat (Kayama, Manjiro)
Pretty Lady (sailors)
Next (Reciter, company)

PAINT YOUR WAGON (1951)

BOOK AND LYRICS BY: Alan Jay Lerner
MUSIC BY: Fredrick Loewe
PUBLISHED LIBRETTO: Coward-McCann, 1952;
   Theatre Arts (magazine), December 1952
CONDENSATION: *Ganzl's Book of the Musical
   Theatre.* Ganzl, Kurt. Schirmer (Macmillan),
   1989
ANTHOLOGY: None
PIANO-VOCAL SCORE: Chappell, 1951
LICENSING AGENT: Tams-Witmark
RECORDING: RCA 60243 CD (original cast)
CAST: 8 M; 6 F; chorus

Ben Rumson and his daughter are in California panning for gold in 1853. She finds a
nugget, and the rush is on. When she falls in
love with one of the miners, Ben sends her
back East to school. Agnes de Mille staged
the dances for the original production and
they were called explosive and sensational,
particularly the one involving the "fancy
ladies" that come into town. Clint East-
wood starred in the 1969 film. This musical was a 1992 attraction at the Goodspeed
Opera House in East Haddam, Connecticut.

ORIGINAL CAST:

James Barton (Ben)
Olga San Juan (Jennifer)
Tony Bavaar (Julio)
Rufus Smith (Steve)
Marijane Maricle (Elizabeth)
Robert Penn (Jake)

SONGS:

Act I

I'm on My Way (Steve, Jake, male ensemble)
What's Going on Here? (Jennifer)
I Talk to the Trees (Julio, Jennifer)
They Call the Wind Maria (Steve, male
  ensemble)
I Still See Elisa (Ben)
How Can I Wait? (Jennifer)
Whoop-Ti-Ay! (Ben, Elizabeth, male ensemble)
Carino Mio (Julio, Jennifer)
There's a Coach Comin' In (male ensemble)

Act II

Hand Me Down That Can o' Beans (male
  ensemble)
Another Autumn (Julio)
Movin' (ensemble)
All for Him (Jennifer)
Wand'rin' Star (Ben)

THE PAJAMA GAME (1954)

BOOK BY: George Abbott and Richard Bissell;
  based on $7\frac{1}{2}$ Cents by Richard Bissell
MUSIC AND LYRICS BY: Richard Adler and Jerry
  Ross
PUBLISHED LIBRETTO: Random House, 1954;
  Theatre Arts (magazine), September 1955
CONDENSATION: *Ganzl's Book of the Musical
  Theatre.* Ganzl, Kurt. Schirmer (Macmillan),
  1989
ANTHOLOGY: None
PIANO-VOCAL SCORE: Frank Music, 1955
VOCAL SELECTIONS: Frank Music, 1954
LICENSING AGENT: Music Theatre International
RECORDING: Columbia CK 32606 CD (original cast)
CAST: 12 M; 6 F; chorus

With a contemporary setting in Iowa, the
plot concerns a new superintendent at the
Sleep-Tite Pajama Factory and his problems with the workers' union. Along the
way he falls in love with the chief of the
grievance committee. There are many wonderful numbers, and the original Bob Fosse
choreography required considerable dancing talent. There was a faithful film version
with Doris Day and the original cast in 1957.

The New York City Opera presented a big
revival in 1989.

Tony Award Winner (Best Musical)

ORIGINAL CAST:

Eddie Foy (Hines)
Stanley Prager (Prez)
Carol Haney (Gladys)
John Raitt (Sid)
Reta Shaw (Mabel)
Janis Paige (Babe)

SONGS:

Act I

The Pajama Game (Hines)
Racing with the Clock (ensemble)
A New Town Is a Blue Town (Sid)
I'm Not at All in Love (Babe, girls)
I'll Never Be Jealous Again (Hines, Mabel)
Hey There (Sid)
Her Is (Prez, Gladys)
Sleep-Tite (Babe, ensemble)
Once a Year Day (Sid, Babe, company)
Small Talk (Sid, Babe)
There Once Was a Man (Sid, Babe)

Act II

Steam Heat (Gladys, boys)
Hey There (reprise) (Babe)
Think of the Time I Save (Hines, girls)
Hernando's Hideaway (Sid, Gladys, company)
$7\frac{1}{2}$ Cents (Babe, Prez, ensemble)

PAL JOEY (1940)

BOOK BY: John O'Hara
MUSIC BY: Richard Rodgers
LYRICS BY: Lorenz Hart
PUBLISHED LIBRETTO: Random House, 1952
CONDENSATION: *Ganzl's Book of the Musical
  Theatre.* Ganzl, Kurt. Schirmer (Macmillan),
  1989
ANTHOLOGY: None
PIANO-VOCAL SCORE: Chappell, 1962
LICENSING AGENT: Rodgers and Hammerstein
  Theatre Library
RECORDINGS: Columbia CK 4364 CD (studio cast);
  Angel ZDM 7 64696-2 CD (1952 revival cast)
CAST: 10 M; 15 F; chorus

Joey is a nightclub performer and a heel. He would like to own his own club and becomes friendly with the older and wealthy Vera when she agrees to finance him. But it's just a fling for her and he loses in the end. This realistic, unpleasant story helped change the direction of American musicals. Joey is basically a dancing role and there are several tacky nightclub numbers. This is a sophisticated, adult musical. The 1959 film with Frank Sinatra changed the plot and score considerably.

1952 REVIVAL CAST:

Harold Lang (Joey)
Helen Gallagher (Gladys)
Patricia Northrop (Linda)
Vivienne Segal (Vera)
Robert Fortier (Victor)
Helen Wood (Kid)
Lewis Bolyard (Louis)
George Martin (Waiter)
Elaine Stritch (Melba)

SONGS:
Act I
You Mustn't Kick It Around (Joey, Gladys, ensemble)
I Could Write a Book (Joey, Linda)
Chicago (girls)
That Terrific Rainbow (Gladys, Victor, ensemble)
What Is a Man (Vera)
Happy Hunting Horn (Joey, Kid, Victor, ensemble)
Bewitched, Bothered, and Bewildered (Vera)
Pal Joey (Joey)
Joey Looks to the Future (ballet)

Act II
The Flower Garden of My Heart (Louis, Gladys, Waiter, ensemble)
Zip (Melba)
Plant You Now, Dig You Later (Gladys, Waiter, ensemble)
In Our Little Den (Vera, Joey)
Do It the Hard Way (Joey)
Take Him (Linda, Vera)

PANAMA HATTIE (1940)

BOOK BY: Herbert Fields and B. G. DeSylva
MUSIC AND LYRICS BY: Cole Porter
PUBLISHED LIBRETTO: None
CONDENSATION: *New Complete Book of the American Musical Theater*. Ewen, David. Holt, 1970
ANTHOLOGY: None
MUSIC PUBLISHER: *Music and Lyrics by Cole Porter*. 2 vols. Chappell, 1972–1975
LICENSING AGENT: Tams-Witmark
RECORDING: MCA 10521 CD (original cast)
CAST: Large mixed cast

Hattie is a dance-hall hostess with a heart of gold. A widower with an eight-year-old daughter is in love with her. He is employed in the operations of the Panama Canal. There are three sailors "on the town" who detect some spies trying to sabotage the canal. All this is just at the beginning of World War II. The original production was described as rowdy and replete with sex and sumptuous sets. Ethel Merman was Hattie and repeated her role on television in 1954. There was also a film version in 1942 with Ann Sothern.

ORIGINAL CAST:

Ethel Merman (Hattie)
Pat Harrington (Skat)
Frank Hyers (Windy)
Rags Ragland (Woozy)
James Dunn (Nick)
Betty Hutton (Florrie)
Joan Carroll (Jerry)
Arthur Treacher (Budd)

SONGS:
Act I
Join It Right Away (Woozy, Skat, Windy)
Visit Panama (Hattie, ensemble)
My Mother Would Love You (Hattie, Nick)
I've Still Got My Health (Hattie, ensemble)
Fresh as a Daisy (Florrie, Skat, Windy)
Let's Be Buddies (Hattie, Jerry)
They Ain't Done Right by Our Nell (Florrie, Budd)

I'm Throwing a Ball Tonight (Hattie,
  ensemble)

Act II
I Detest a Fiesta (ensemble)
Make It Another Old-Fashioned, Please
  (Hattie)
All I've Got to Get Now Is My Man (Florrie,
  ensemble)
You Said It (Hattie, Budd, Woozy, Windy, Skat)
God Bless the Women (Woozy, Windy, Skat)

PARK (1970)

BOOK AND LYRICS BY: Paul Cherry
MUSIC BY: Lance Mulcahy
PUBLISHED LIBRETTO: French, 1970
CONDENSATION: None
ANTHOLOGY: None
LICENSING AGENT: Samuel French
RECORDING: None
CAST: 2 M; 2 F

Four strangers meet near a bandstand in
a park and proceed to tell each other their
secrets and indulge in a form of group therapy. It turns out they are a family—mother,
father, son, and daughter trying to work
out problems of communication within the
family. The Broadway production used a
simple set and a small rock band. There
was very little dancing. It was called an intimate "minimusical."

ORIGINAL CAST:

Don Scardino (Young Man)
Joan Hackett (Young Woman)
David Brooks (Man)
Julie Wilson (Woman)

SONGS:
Act I
All the Little Things in the World Are Waiting
  (Young Man)
Hello Is the Way Things Are (Young Woman)
Bein' a Kid (Young Man, Young Woman)
Elizabeth (Man)
He Talks to Me (Woman, Man)
Tomorrow Will Be the Same (all)

One Man (Woman)
A Park Is for People (Young Man)
Act II
I Want It Just to Happen (Young Woman)
I Can See (Woman)
Compromise (Young Man)
Jamie (Young Man, Man)
I'd Marry You Again (Woman, Man)
Bein' a Kid (reprise) (all)
A Park Is for Kids (reprise) (all)

PEACE (1969)

BOOK AND LYRICS BY: Tim Reynolds; based on
  the play *Peace* by Aristophanes
MUSIC BY AND LYRICS ADAPTED BY: Al Carmines
PUBLISHED LIBRETTO: None
CONDENSATION: None
ANTHOLOGY: None
VOCAL SELECTIONS: CAAZ Music (Chappell), 1969
LICENSING AGENT: Samuel French
RECORDING: Metromedia MP 33001 (original cast)
CAST: 8 M; 9 F

During the 1960s and 1970s a Greenwich Village assistant church minister
composed a number of rollicking off-
Broadway musicals. They were entertainments with messages. This adaption from
Aristophanes is about a "heedless monster" who is about to push a panic button
and explode the world. Tygaeus decides
to fly up to heaven on the back of a giant
green beetle to see what the gods are going to do about the situation. Described as
a blend of humor, satire, and bawdiness,
this avant-garde minstrel musical is perhaps most suitable for adult audiences.

ORIGINAL CAST:

Julie Kurnitz (Mother)
Reathel Bean (Tygaeus)
George McGrath (Father)
Essie Borden (Daughter)
Ann Dunbar (Daughter)
David Vaughn (Hermes)
David Pursley (War)
David Tice (Disorder)
Margaret Wright (Prosperity)

Lee Crespi (Abundance)
Arlene Rothlein (Peace)

SONGS:
Act I
Through Excessive Concern (Mother)
Oh God (Tygaeus, Mother)
Trio (Father, Mother, Tygaeus)
Oh Daddy Dear (Daughters)
The Gods Have Gone Away (Hermes,
   Tygaeus)
Plumbing (War, Disorder)
Peace Medley (ensemble)
Things Starting to Grow Again (Prosperity,
   Abundance, ensemble)

Act II
Muse, Darling (Prosperity, ensemble)
Up in Heaven (ensemble)
My Name's Abundance (Abundance,
   ensemble)
You've Got Yourself a Bunch of Women
   (Prosperity, ensemble)
All the Dark Is Changed to Sunshine
   (ensemble)
Poor Mortals (Peace, ensemble)
Just Sit Around (Mother, Father, ensemble)
Summer's Nice (Mother, ensemble)
America the Beautiful (Prosperity, ensemble)

PERFECTLY FRANK (1980)

BOOK BY: Kenny Solms
MUSIC AND LYRICS BY: Frank Loesser; additional
   music and lyrics by various collaborators
PUBLISHED LIBRETTO: None
CONDENSATION: None
ANTHOLOGY: None
VOCAL SELECTIONS: *The Frank Loesser Songbook.*
   Simon and Schuster, 1971 (see also various
   show titles)
LICENSING AGENT: Music Theatre International
RECORDING: None
CAST: 5 M; 5 F

Frank Loesser wrote songs for over sixty
Hollywood films and five Broadway shows.
The numbers in this show are arranged into

his Hollywood studio period, World War
II, Broadway, and such categories as "marriage" and "blues" and are joined together
by mini-skits and narrative material. The
costumes were described as functional and
casual. The Broadway set was an arrangement of platforms and arches. *Guys and
Dolls*, *Hans Christian Andersen*, *The Most
Happy Fella*, and *Where's Charley?* are just
some of the shows that are included.

ORIGINAL CAST:

Andra Akers	David Ruprecht
Wayne Cilento	Virginia Sandifur
Jill Cook	Debbie Shapiro
Don Correia	Jo Sullivan
David Holliday	Jim Walton

This revue is made up of fifty-five songs divided into two acts.

PERSONALS (1985)

BOOK AND LYRICS BY: David Crane, Seth
   Friedman, and Marta Kauffman
MUSIC BY: William Dreskin, Joel Phillip Friedman,
   Seth Friedman, Alan Menken, Stephen Schwartz,
   and Michael Skloff
PUBLISHED LIBRETTO: French, 1987
CONDENSATION: None
ANTHOLOGY: None
LICENSING AGENT: Samuel French
RECORDING: None
CAST: 3 M; 3 F

The authors worked on this revue for
several years before its New York off-
Broadway production, even including a
U.S.O. tour near the former East German
border. It is described as "an intimate musical look at modern New York life from the
classified pages of your favorite newspapers." Some of the material is about the
ads themselves—a sex-starved teenager's
open call for his "first time" or a bisexual's search for her Mr. or Mrs. Right. The

themes of the show include looking for happiness in the big city, making connections, and finding the right soul mate. One critic recommended it "for anyone who has ever been single—or would like to be again." Stephen Schwartz (of *Godspell*) and Alan Menken (of *Little Shop of Horrors*) contributed to the "catchy, effective, successful" score.

ORIGINAL CAST:

Jason Alexander	Laura Dean
Dee Hoty	Jeff Keller
Nancy Opel	Trey Wilson

SONGS:
Act I
Nothing to Do with Love (company)
After School Special (Alexander, company)
Mama's Boys (Hoty, Dean, Wilson, company)
A Night Alone (Keller, Alexander, Wilson, company)
I Think You Should Know (Keller, Dean)
Second Grade (Keller, Alexander, Wilson, company)
Imagine My Surprise (Hoty)
I'd Rather Dance Alone (company)

Act II
Moving in with Linda (Keller, company)
A Little Happiness (Wilson)
I Could Always Go with You (Hoty, Opel)
The Guy I Love (Opel, Alexander)
Michael (Dean)
Picking Up the Pieces (Alexander, Wilson)
Some Things Don't Eat (company)

PETER PAN (1954)

MUSIC BY: Moose Charlap; additional music by Jule Styne; based on the play by James M. Barrie
LYRICS BY: Carolyn Leigh; additional lyrics by Betty Comden and Adolph Green
PUBLISHED LIBRETTO: None
CONDENSATION: *Broadway Musicals Show by Show.* Green, Stanley. Hal Leonard Books, 1985
ANTHOLOGY: None
VOCAL SELECTIONS: Big Three (Morris, 1974)
LICENSING AGENT: Samuel French
RECORDING: RCA 3762-2-RG CD (original cast)
CAST: Large mixed cast, including children

The charm of Barrie and of Peter, Tinker Bell, the children, and the pirates in "Never Never Land" are all rolled up in this musical version. The audience will expect Peter to "fly" with the children, so this will present a staging challenge for you. Mary Martin was the original Peter Pan and she also performed the role on television, a videocassette of which is available. Sandy Duncan and Cathy Rigby have played the role on Broadway recently. This is a magical show that children love.

ORIGINAL CAST:

Mary Martin (Peter Pan)
Margalo Gillmore (Mrs. Darling)
Kathy Nolan (Wendy)
Robert Harrington (John)
Joseph Stafford (Michael)
Cyril Ritchard (Captain Hook)
Sondra Lee (Tiger Lily)

SONGS:
Act I
Tender Shepherd (Mrs. Darling, Wendy, John, Michael)
I've Got to Crow (Peter)
Neverland (Peter)
I'm Flying (Peter, Wendy, John, Michael)

Act II
Morning in Neverland (ensemble)
Pirate Song (pirates)
A Princely Scheme (Captain Hook, pirates)
Indians! (Tiger Lily, Indians)
Wendy (Peter, ensemble)
Another Princely Scheme (Captain Hook, pirates)
I Won't Grow Up (Peter, ensemble)
Mysterious Lady (Peter, Captain Hook, ensemble)
Ugg-a-Wugg (Peter, Tiger Lily, ensemble)
Distant Melody (Wendy)

Act III
Hook's Waltz (Captain Hook, pirates)
The Battle (Peter, Captain Hook)
I've Got to Crow (reprise) (Peter, ensemble)

I Won't Grow Up (reprise) (Darling Family,
   ensemble)
Neverland (reprise) (Peter)

PETTICOAT LANE (1979)

BOOK, MUSIC, AND LYRICS BY: Judd Woldin;
   based on *King of Schnorrers* by Israel Zangwill
PUBLISHED LIBRETTO: French, 1981
CONDENSATION: None
ANTHOLOGY: None
LICENSING AGENT: Samuel French
RECORDING: None
CAST: 5 M; 2 F; chorus

This was done off-Broadway as *King of
Schnorrers*. "Schnorrer" is a Yiddish term
for moocher or beggar who is able to get
something for free while making you feel
he has done you a favor. This musical is
set in the Jewish quarter of London around
1790. There are rival sects of Jews, and the
son of one falls in love with the daughter
of another. For the New York production
multipanel curtains strung on wires were
used, along with occasional chairs and tables to suggest different locales. The costumes were brightly hued. This production
was directed by a dancer, and the cast was
described as nimble. This show is particularly appealing to those interested in Jewish culture and tradition.

ORIGINAL CAST:

Lloyd Battista (Da Costa, the King)
Thomas Lee Sinclair (Rodriguez)
Sophie Schwab (Deborah)
John Dossett (David)
Ralph Bruneau (Tinker)
Ed Dixon (Belasco)
Jerry Mayer (Furtado)
Paul Binotto (Flower Seller)

SONGS:
Act I
Hail to the King (Da Costa, Rodriguez,
   ensemble)
Chutzpah (Da Costa, Rodriguez, quartet)

I'm Only a Woman (Deborah)
Just for Me (David, Tinker)
I Have Not Lived in Vain (Belasco)
The Fine Art of Schnorring (Da Costa)
Tell Me (Deborah)
What Do You Do? (David)
It's Over (ensemble)

Act II
Murder (Tinker, ensemble)
Dead (David, Furtado)
Guided by Love (Deborah)
Tell Me (reprise) (Deborah, David)
Sephardic Lullaby (Flower Seller)
Each of Us (company)

THE PHANTOM OF THE OPERA (1988)

BOOK BY: Richard Stilgoe and Andrew Lloyd
   Webber; from the novel by Gaston Leroux
MUSIC BY: Andrew Lloyd Webber
LYRICS BY: Charles Hart
PUBLISHED LIBRETTO: *The Complete Phantom of
   the Opera*. Holt, 1988
CONDENSATION: *Ganzl's Book of the Musical
   Theatre*. Ganzl, Kurt. Schirmer (Macmillan),
   1989; *The Theatre Year Book and Best Plays of
   1987–1988*. Otis L. Guernsey, Jr., ed. Applause
   Books, 1988
ANTHOLOGY: None
VOCAL SELECTIONS: Hal Leonard, 1987
PIANO-VOCAL SCORE: Hal Leonard, 1987
LICENSING AGENT: Not yet available; contact
   Music Theatre International
RECORDING: Polydor 831 273-2 CD (original
   London cast)
CAST: Large mixed cast

The Paris Opera House in 1881 is the setting for this musical phenomenon of the
1980s. The Phantom, a disfigured and frus-
trated composer, resides in the bowels of
the opera house. He is enamoured of Christine and determined that she will star in
his new opera. This musical was one of
the most popular of its time, not only in
London and New York but in many other

cities of the world. The staging was spectacular, including a chandelier that crashed down onto the audience (in fact the front of the stage) for an exciting climax. There are several opera sequences requiring a large company and elaborate costumes, as well as various backstage locales. The famous lake underneath the opera house was accomplished by mist over the stage floor. Strong voices are required as the show is sung throughout.

Tony Award Winner (Best Musical)

ORIGINAL CAST:

Michael Crawford (Phantom)
Sarah Brightman (Christine)
Judy Kaye (Carlotta)
Steve Barton (Raoul)
Elisa Heinsohn (Meg)
Philip Steele (Buquet)
Leila Martin (Madame Giry)
Nicholas Wyman (Firmin)
Cris Groenendaal (Andre)
David Romano (Piangi)

SONGS:
Act I
Think of Me (Carlotta, Christine, Raoul)
Angel of Music (Christine, Meg)
Little Lotte/The Mirror (Raoul, Christine, Phantom)
The Phantom of the Opera (Phantom, Christine)
The Music of the Night (Phantom)
I Remember/Stranger than You Dreamt It (Christine, Phantom)
Magical Lasso (Buquet, Meg, Madame Giry, girls)
Notes/Prima Donna (Firmin, Andre, Raoul, Carlotta, Madame Giry, Meg, Phantom)
Poor Fool, He Makes Me Laugh (Carlotta, company)
Why Have You Brought Me Here?/Raoul, I've Been There (Raoul, Christine)
All I Ask of You (Raoul, Christine) Reprise (Phantom)

Act II
Masquerade/Why So Silent? (company)

Notes/Twisted Every Way (Andre, Firmin, Carlotta, Piangi, Raoul, Christine, Madame Giry, Phantom)
What I'd Give to Have You Here Again (Christine)
Wandering Child/Bravo, Bravo (Phantom, Christine, Raoul)
The Point of No Return (Phantom, Christine)
Down Once More/Track Down the Murderer (company)

PHILEMON (1975)

BOOK AND LYRICS BY: Tom Jones
MUSIC BY: Harvey Schmidt
PUBLISHED LIBRETTO: None
CONDENSATION: None
ANTHOLOGY: None
LICENSING AGENT: Music Theatre International
RECORDING: Gallery OC-1 (original cast)
CAST: 4 M; 3 F

This story is based on an incident that took place in the Roman city of Antioch in A.D. 287. A cheap street clown is arrested and forced to impersonate Philemon, a great Christian leader. There is some humor, but the story is essentially a tragic one. This was very simply staged off-Broadway with piano and percussion for accompaniment. The emphasis is on the music and words, rather than the scenery (some scaffolding) and costumes (leotards and capes). This musical is for adults as well as young people. There was a TV production in 1976.

ORIGINAL CAST:

Michael Glenn-Smith (Andos)
Virginia Gregory (Marsyas)
Charles Lane (Servillus)
Dick Latessa (Cockian)
Leila Martin (Wife)
Howard Ross (Commander)
Kathrin King Segal (Kiki)

SONGS:

Act I

Within This Empty Space (all)

The Streets of Antioch Stink (Cockian, Commander)

Don't Kiki Me (Kiki, Cockian)

I'd Do Almost Anything to Get out of Here and Go Home (Cockian, Commander)

He's Coming/Antioch Prison (ensemble)

Name: Cockian (Cockian, all)

Act II

I Love Order (Commander, all)

My Secret Dream (Andos, Cockian, ensemble)

I Love His Face (Marsyas, Cockian)

Sometimes (Cockian, ensemble)

The Greatest of These (Wife)

The Confrontation (Cockian, Commander, all)

The Vision (all)

PIAF (1981)

BOOK BY: Pam Gems

MUSIC BY: Various composers

PUBLISHED LIBRETTO: French

CONDENSATION: *The Book of 1,000 Plays.* Steve Fletcher, Norman Jopling, eds. Facts On File, 1989

ANTHOLOGY: None

LICENSING AGENT: Samuel French

RECORDING: None

CAST: 9 M; 5 F

The life of the famous French chanteuse Edith Piaf was neither happy nor wholesome. She started out as a streetwalker, sang on street corners and in cafes, and eventually became an international star. Along the way she had numerous affairs, automobile accidents, drug problems, and cancer. When she died at age forty-seven, she was penniless. All this is graphically portrayed with occasional songs from the Piaf repertoire. The London and Broadway productions used a raked platform stage for the acting area with the cast, costumes, and props all around the sides and back. The cast double up on small parts and only

assume their characterizations while in the acting area. This is a sensational part for the star, but it is strictly adult entertainment. This was shown on cable TV in 1982. Jane Lapotaire portrayed Piaf in both London and New York and sang a number of songs from the Piaf repertoire.

PIANO BAR (1978)

MUSIC BY: Rob Fremont

STORY BY: Doris Willens and Rob Fremont

LYRICS BY: Doris Willens

PUBLISHED LIBRETTO: French, 1978

CONDENSATION: None

ANTHOLOGY: None

LICENSING AGENT: Samuel French

RECORDING: Original Cast OC 7812 (original cast)

CAST: 4 M; 2 F

The contemporary setting is Sweet Sue's Piano Bar in Manhattan. It is a rainy night and four customers meet and unload their problems. The other two characters are the piano player and a silent bartender. The show is just one song after another with very few spoken lines. Eventually the four customers pair off and leave. The off-Broadway production was a simple one. The critics found the score pleasant and enjoyed the tango and the inebriated waltz.

ORIGINAL CAST:

Joel Silberman (Prince, the piano player)

Jim McMahon (Bartender)

Richard Ryder (Walt)

Kelly Bishop (Julie)

Karen DeVito (Debbie)

Steve Elmore (Ned)

SONGS:

Act I

Introduction (Prince)

Sweet Sue's Piano Bar (Prince, ensemble)

Pigeonhole Time (Ned, Walt, Debbie)

Congratulations (Debbie)

Believe Me (Walt, Julie)

Tango (Julie, Walt)

Everywhere I Go (Debbie)

Dinner at the Mirklines (Ned)
Scenes from Some Marriages (Prince, ensemble)
Personals (Prince)
Nobody's Perfect (company)

Act II
One, Two, Three (Prince, ensemble)
Greenspons (Debbie, Julie)
Moms and Dads (Prince, ensemble)
Meanwhile Back in Yonkers (Julie)
Alas, Alack (Walt, Ned)
New York Cliche (Ned, Debbie)
Tomorrow Night (Prince)
Closing (Prince, company)

PIPE DREAM (1955)

BOOK AND LYRICS BY: Oscar Hammerstein II, based on *Sweet Thursday* by John Steinbeck
MUSIC BY: Richard Rodgers
PUBLISHED LIBRETTO: Viking, 1956
CONDENSATION: *Rodgers and Hammerstein.* Mordden, Ethan. Abrams, 1992
ANTHOLOGY: None
PIANO-VOCAL SCORE: Williamson, 1956
LICENSING AGENT: Rodgers and Hammerstein Theatre Library
RECORDING: RCA 61481 CD (original cast)
CAST: 17 M; 10 F

Set on the California coast in Monterey County, Steinbeck's tale concerns a waterfront bohemian who gathers and sells marine specimens, a young homeless girl, and a bordello madam. There is a large assortment of vagrants, waterfront denizens, and prostitutes to liven up the evening. There are a costume party and opportunities for colorful locales. While the score is far better than most musicals can offer, the critics found it "minor key" and there are no standard songs.

ORIGINAL CAST:

William Johnson (Doc)
Mike Kellin (Hazel)
G. D. Wallace (Mac)
Judy Tyler (Suzy)
Helen Traubel (Fauna)
Steve Roland (Esteban)
Stokely Gray (Jim)

SONGS:
Act I
All Kinds of People (Doc, Hazel)
The Tide Pool (Doc, Hazel, Mac)
All Kinds of People (reprise) (Jim)
Everybody's Got a Home but Me (Suzy)
A Lopsided Bus (Mac, Hazel, ensemble)
The Man I Used to Be (Doc)
Sweet Thursday (Fauna)
Suzy Is a Good Thing (Fauna, Suzy)
All at Once You Love Her (Doc, Suzy, Esteban)

Act II
The Happiest House on the Block (Fauna, girls)
The Party That We're Gonna Have Tomorrow Night (Mac, ensemble)
The Party Gets Going (ensemble)
I Am a Witch (Fauna, girls)
Will You Marry Me? (Suzy, Fauna, Doc)
Thinkin' (Hazel)
All at Once You Love Her (reprise) (Fauna)
How Long? (Fauna, Doc, ensemble)
The Next Time It Happens (Suzy, Doc)

PIPPIN (1972)

BOOK BY: Roger O. Hirson
MUSIC AND LYRICS BY: Stephen Schwartz
PUBLISHED LIBRETTO: Drama Book Specialists, 1975; Bard (paperback), 1977
CONDENSATION: *Broadway Musicals Show by Show.* Green, Stanley. Hal Leonard Books, 1985
ANTHOLOGY: None
VOCAL SELECTIONS: Belwin-Mills, 1972
LICENSING AGENT: Music Theatre International
RECORDING: Motown MOTD 06186 CD (original cast)
CAST: 11 M; 3 F; chorus

The year is A.D. 780. Pippin is the oldest son of Charlemagne and heir to the Holy Roman Empire. "Magic to Do" is the famous opening number performed by Ben Vereen in the original Broadway production. "No

Time at All" is a show-stopping number performed by Pippin's grandmother. The critics liked the style of the production—a commedia dell'arte atmosphere with sensational choreography by Bob Fosse. This stylized rock musical has been extremely popular with young audiences and has been done on cable television.

ORIGINAL CAST:

Ben Vereen (Leading Player)
John Rubinstein (Pippin)
Eric Berry (Charles)
Irene Ryan (Berthe)
Jill Clayburgh (Catherine)
Leland Palmer (Fastrada)

SONGS:
(performed without intermission)
Magic to Do (the players)
Corner of the Sky (Pippin)
Welcome Home (Charles, Pippin)
War Is a Science (Charles, Pippin)
Glory (Leading Player)
Simple Joys (Leading Player)
No Time at All (Berthe, boys)
With You (Pippin, girls)
Spread a Little Sunshine (Fastrada)
Morning Glow (Pippin)
On the Right Track (Leading Player, Pippin)
Kind of Woman (Catherine, girls)
Extraordinary (Pippin)
Love Song (Pippin, Catherine)

THE PIRATES OF PENZANCE
(1980)

LYRICS BY: W. S. Gilbert
MUSIC BY: Arthur Sullivan
CONTEMPORARY ADAPTION BY: William Elliott
PUBLISHED LIBRETTO: None
CONDENSATION: *Ganzl's Book of the Musical Theatre*. Ganzl, Kurt. Schirmer (Macmillan), 1989
ANTHOLOGY: None for this adaption
PIANO-VOCAL SCORE: None for this adaption
LICENSING AGENT: Music Theatre International

RECORDING: Elektra VE 601 (original cast)
CAST: Large mixed cast

This popular version of Gilbert and Sullivan's operetta was first presented in Central Park as part of the New York Shakespeare Festival and then moved to Broadway for a long and prosperous run. One review mentions a "Mack Sennett wackiness" that has been interjected into the tale of Frederic, the unwilling pirate apprentice. Still, certain traditional expertise is required to pull off the difficult "Modern Major-General" and other numbers. The Broadway scenery was described as "twopence-coloured" cutouts. The modern musical arrangements were called amiably sacrilegious by some, but overwhelmingly successful by all. Costumes are Victorian in the traditional Gilbert and Sullivan fashion. The film version featured Angela Lansbury and the original cast.

ORIGINAL CAST:

Rex Smith (Frederic)
Marcie Shaw (Kate)
George Rose (Major-General)
Linda Ronstadt (Mabel)
Patricia Routledge (Ruth)
Kevin Kline (Pirate King)
Stephen Hanan (Samuel)
Tony Azito (Sergeant)
Alice Playten (Edith)

SONGS:
Act I
Pour, O Pour the Pirate Sherry (Pirate King, Samuel, Frederic, pirates)
When Frederic Was a Little Lad (Ruth)
Oh, Better Far to Live and Die (Pirate King, pirates)
Oh, False One, You Have Deceived Me! (Ruth, Frederic)
Climbing over Rocky Mountains (daughters)
Stop, Ladies, Pray! (Frederic, daughters)
Oh, Is There Not One Maiden Breast? (Frederic, daughters)
Poor Wandering One (Mabel, daughters)

What Ought We to Do? (Kate, Edith,
daughters)

How Beautifully Blue the Sky (Mabel,
Frederic, daughters)

Stay, We Must Not Lose Our Senses (Frederic,
daughters, pirates)

Hold, Monsters! (Mabel, Samuel,
Major-General, daughters, pirates)

I Am the Very Model of a Modern
Major-General (Major-General, ensemble)

Oh, Men of Dark and Dismal Fate (ensemble)

Act II

Oh, Dry the Glistening Tear (Mabel,
daughters)

Then Frederic (Major-General, Frederic)

When the Foeman Bares His Steel (Sergeant,
Mabel, ensemble)

Now for the Pirate Lair! (Frederic, Pirate King,
Ruth)

When You Had Left Our Pirate Fold (Ruth,
Frederic, Pirate King)

My Eyes Are Fully Open (Frederic, Ruth,
Pirate King)

Away, Away! My Heart's on Fire (Ruth, Pirate
King, Frederic)

All Is Prepared (Mabel, Frederic)

Stay, Frederic, Stay! (Mabel, Frederic)

Sorry Her Lot (Mabel)

No, I Am Brave (Mabel, Sergeant, police)

When a Felon's Not Engaged in His
Employment (Sergeant, police)

A Rollicking Band of Pirates We (pirates,
Sergeant, police)

With Cat-Like Tread, upon Our Prey We Steal
(pirates, police, Samuel)

Hush, Hush! Not a Word (Frederic, pirates,
police, Major-General)

Sighing Softly to the River (Major-General,
ensemble)

PLAIN AND FANCY (1955)

BOOK BY: Joseph Stein and Will Glickman
MUSIC BY: Albert Hague
LYRICS BY: Arnold B. Horwitt
PUBLISHED LIBRETTO: Random House, 1955;
French, 1956; *Theatre Arts* (magazine), July 1956

CONDENSATION: *New Complete Book of the
American Musical Theater.* Ewen, David. Holt,
1970

ANTHOLOGY: None

PIANO-VOCAL SCORE: Chappell, 1956

LICENSING AGENT: Samuel French

RECORDING: Angel ZDM 764762-2 CD (original
cast)

CAST: Large mixed cast

This contemporary musical is set in an
Amish community in Pennsylvania. The
plot deals with a young New York couple
who arrive in the area for a real estate deal
and become involved in the romantic problems of two young brothers. All ends happily, with lots of song and dance in rustic
American style. There is a barn-raising sequence with onstage construction. Amish
costumes need to be reasonably authentic.

ORIGINAL CAST:

Richard Derr (Dan)
Shirl Conway (Ruth)
Gloria Marlowe (Katie)
Douglas Fletcher Rodgers (Ezra)
Elaine Lynn (Young Miller)
David Daniels (Peter)
Barbara Cook (Hilda)
Stefan Schnabel (Papa)
Nancy Andrews (Emma)

SONGS:

Act I

You Can't Miss It (Dan, Ruth, ensemble)

It Wonders Me (Katie)

Plenty of Pennsylvania (Emma, Ezra, Young
Miller, ensemble)

Young and Foolish (Peter, Katie)

Why Not Katie? (Ezra, men)

It's a Helluva Way to Run a Love Affair (Ruth)

This Is All Very New to Me (Hilda, ensemble)

Plain We Live (Papa, men)

Act II

How Do You Raise a Barn? (company)

Follow Your Heart (Peter, Katie, Hilda)

City Mouse, Country Mouse (Emma, women)

I'll Show Him (Hilda)

Take Your Time and Take Your Pick (Hilda,
Dan, Ruth)

PORGY AND BESS (1935)

BOOK BY: DuBose Heyward; based on the play
    Porgy by Dorothy and DuBose Heyward
MUSIC BY: George Gershwin
LYRICS BY: Ira Gershwin
PUBLISHED LIBRETTO: None
CONDENSATION: *New Complete Book of the*
    American Musical Theater. Ewen, David. Holt,
    1970
ANTHOLOGY: *Ten Great Musicals of the American*
    Stage. Stanley Richards, ed. Chilton, 1973
PIANO-VOCAL SCORE: Chappell, 1935
VOCAL SELECTIONS: Chappell, 1935
LICENSING AGENT: Tams-Witmark
RECORDING: RCA 2109 CD (1976 revival cast)
CAST: Large mixed cast

Walter Kerr says that this is an opera. But
it's a Gershwin opera that has graced the
stages of several Broadway houses. The
score is legendary. Set in a Negro slum in
Charleston, South Carolina, it takes place
around 1935. Porgy is a crippled beggar in
love with Bess. She stays with him briefly
but then leaves for New York City. He sets
out after her as the final curtain falls. The
leading roles are called grueling and a
strong cast is needed. The score is vocally
demanding. There was a 1959 film version
with Sidney Poitier, but his singing voice
was dubbed.

1983 RADIO CITY MUSIC HALL CAST:

Luvenia Garner (Clara)
Alexander Smalls (Jake)
Mervin Bertel Wallace (Peter)
Robert Mosley, Jr. (Porgy)
Shirley Baines (Serena)
Priscilla Baskerville (Bess)
Loretta Holkmann (Maria)
Larry Marshall (Sportin' Life)
Gregg Baker (Crown)
Y. Yvonne Matthews (Lily)

SONGS:
Act I
Summertime (Clara)
A Woman Is a Sometime Thing (Jake, men)
Here Come De Honey Man (Peter)

They Pass by Singin' (Porgy)
Oh Little Stars (Porgy)
Gone, Gone, Gone (ensemble)
Overflow (ensemble)
My Man's Gone Now (Serena)
Leavin' for the Promise' Lan' (Bess,
    ensemble)
It Takes a Long Pull to Get There (Jake, men)
I Got Plenty o' Nuttin' (Porgy, ensemble)
Struttin' Style (Maria)
Buzzard Song (Porgy, ensemble)
Bess, You Is My Woman Now (Porgy, Bess)
Oh, I Can't Sit Down (ensemble)
I Ain't Got No Shame (ensemble)
It Ain't Necessarily So (Sportin' Life,
    ensemble)
What You Want Wid Bess? (Bess, Crown)

Act II
Oh, Doctor Jesus (Serena, Maria, Peter, Lily,
    Porgy)
I Loves You, Porgy (Porgy, Bess)
Oh, He'venly Father (ensemble)
Oh, De Lawd Shake De Heavens (ensemble)
Oh, Dere's Somebody Knockin' at De Do'
    (ensemble)
A Red-Headed Woman (Crown, ensemble)
Clara, Clara (ensemble)
There's a Boat Dat's Leavin' Soon for New
    York (Sportin' Life, Bess)
Good Mornin', Sistuh! (ensemble)
Oh Bess, Oh Where's My Bess (Porgy, Serena,
    Maria)
Oh Lawd, I'm on My Way (Porgy, ensemble)

PREPPIES (1983)

BOOK BY: David Taylor with Carlos Davis
MUSIC AND LYRICS BY: Gary Portnoy and Judy
    Hart Angelo
PUBLISHED LIBRETTO: French, 1983
CONDENSATION: None
ANTHOLOGY: None
LICENSING AGENT: Samuel French
RECORDING: Alchemy Records AL 1001 (original
    cast)
CAST: 7 M; 5 F

Does the environment make the Preppy—or must people be born Preppies? What exactly is a Preppy? This parody of WASP life-styles shows the privileged classes enjoying their privileges. Set on Long Island, the plot concerns the son of a maid who is adopted by a dying millionaire, his growing up and going to prep school, and so on for a twenty-one-year time span. All the critics liked the costumes, which made "amusing hay of the Preppy predilection for pastels." The musical score included some vaudeville-type song-and-dance numbers, one done on a beach with the cast wearing flippers.

ORIGINAL CAST:

David Sabin (Mr. Endicott)
Michael Ingrain (Joe)
Beth Fowler (Marie)
Tom Hafner (Jinks)
Bob Walton (Cotty)
Kathleen Rowe McAllen (Muffy)
Dennis Bailey (Bugsy)

SONGS:
Act I
People Like Us (company)
Chance of a Lifetime (Mr. Endicott, Joe,
    Marie, Jinks)
One Step Away (Marie)
Summertime (company)
Fairy Tales (Cotty, Muffy, Bugsy,
    company)
Parents' Farewell (company)
Bells (company)
Moving On (company)

Act II
Summertime (reprise) (boys)
We've Got Each Other (Joe, Marie)
Gonna Run (Cotty)
No Big Deal (company)
Worlds Apart (Cotty, Muffy)
Loot (Bugsy, company)

PRETZELS (1974)

MUSIC AND LYRICS BY: John Forster
BOOK BY: Jane Curtin, Fred Grandy, and Judy
    Kahan
PUBLISHED LIBRETTO: French, 1975
CONDENSATION: None
ANTHOLOGY: None
LICENSING AGENT: Samuel French
RECORDING: None
CAST: 2 M; 2 F

Called sparkling and urbane, this little show carries on that endangered species—the revue—with satiric sketches and catchy songs. The critics found it more personal than political and recommended it for the college crowd. Some highlights were a foreign actress applying for unemployment, "The Cockroach Song," a class reunion, and a section called "Classical Music" performed by the pianist. A performance was taped and shown on cable television.

ORIGINAL CAST:

Jane Curtin   John Forster
Timothy Jerome   Judy Kahan

SONGS:
Act I
Pretzels (company)
Unemployment (Curtin, Jerome, Kahan)
Take Me Back (Jerome)
Cosmetology (Kahan, Curtin)
Sing and Dance (Kahan, Curtin)
Wild Strawberries (Curtin, Jerome)
Jane's Song (Curtin)
The Waitress (Kahan, Jerome)
The Cockroach Song (Forster, Jerome, Kahan)

Act II
Richie and Theresa (Curtin, Jerome)
Classical Music (Forster)
Monologue (Kahan)
Tim Vander Beek (Curtin, Jerome, Kahan)
Loehmann's (Curtin, Kahan)
The Reunion (company)

PRIVATES ON PARADE (1989)

BOOK AND LYRICS BY: Peter Nichols
MUSIC BY: Dennis King
PUBLISHED LIBRETTO: French, 1977
CONDENSATION: None
ANTHOLOGY: None
LICENSING AGENT: Samuel French
RECORDING: EMI (British) EMC 3233 (original 1977
    London cast)
CAST: 10 M; 1 F

This spoof on British colonial. army life in and around Singapore in 1948 was a big hit when performed by the Royal Shakespeare Company in London. It was finally done off-Broadway in 1989. The plot involves a group of soldiers, some of whom are homosexual, putting on a camp show for the boys. Some female impersonation is required. This is actually a comedy with music. It was called boisterous and outrageous and perhaps a "bit too English." The costumes are British (tropical) military and female 1940s attire. The sets are simple. An onstage quartet provides the music. There was a 1982 film version with members of the original British cast.

1989 OFF-BROADWAY CAST:

Jim Fyfe (Steven)
Gregory Jbara (Kevin)
Jim Dale (Terri)
John Curry (Charles)
Ross Bickell (Len)
Edward Hibbert (Eric)
Donna Murphy (Sylvia)

SONGS:
Act I
S.A.D.U.S.E.A. (company)
Les Girls (Steven, Kevin)
Danke Schon (Terri, Charles, Len, Eric, Kevin)
Western Approach Ballet (Sylvia, Terri, Charles, Kevin)
The Little Things We Used to Do (Terri, Eric, Kevin, Charles, Len, Steven)
Black Velvet (Charles, Kevin, Eric, Len)
The Prince of Peace (company)

Act II
Could You Please Inform Us (Terri)
Privates on Parade (company)
The Latin American Way (Terri, Kevin, Eric)
Sunnyside Lane (Charles, Len)

THE PRODIGAL SISTER (1974)

BOOK BY: J. E. Franklin
MUSIC BY: Micki Grant
LYRICS BY: J. E. Franklin and Micki Grant
PUBLISHED LIBRETTO: French, 1974
CONDENSATION: None
ANTHOLOGY: None
LICENSING AGENT: Samuel French
RECORDING: None
CAST: 15 M; 20 F (may double)

This contemporary retelling of the prodigal son parable concerns a black teenage girl who is disowned by her family when she finds herself pregnant. She goes to a big city and becomes involved with prostitutes, a fast-talking pimp, and the police. She eventually goes back home, a sadder but wiser young lady. It is both comic and touching. An all-black cast performed this off-Broadway. The dialogue is in rhyme. Clive Barnes in the New York Times found the music "an easy-on-the-ear mixture of rhythm with blues." The characters are exaggerated, cartoon-like stereotypes. They are costumed to look like cardboard cutout dolls. It is performed in a simple set with some dancing required.

ORIGINAL CAST:

Paula Desmond (Jackie)
Frances Salisbury (Mother)
Esther Brown (Mrs. Johnson)
Ethel Beatty (Sissie)
Kirk Kirksey (Slick)
Victor Willis (Caesar)
Saundra McClain (Lucille)
Frank Carey (Reverend)

SONGS:

(performed without intermission)

Slip Away (Jackie, ensemble)

Talk, Talk, Talk (Mother, Mrs. Johnson, ensemble)

Ain't Marryin' Nobody (Jackie, ensemble)

If You Know What's Good for You (Jackie)

First Born (Mother, Sissie)

Woman Child (Mother, Jackie)

Sister Love (Slick)

Remember Caesar (Caesar)

Superwoman (Lucille)

Look at Me (Sissie)

I Been up in Hell (Jackie, company)

Thank You Lord (Reverend, company)

Remember (Jackie)

Celebration (company)

The Prodigal Has Returned (company)

PROM QUEENS UNCHAINED (1991)

BOOK BY: Stephen Witkin
MUSIC BY: Keith Herrmann
LYRICS BY: Larry Goodsight
PUBLISHED LIBRETTO: French
CONDENSATION: None
ANTHOLOGY: None
LICENSING AGENT: Samuel French
RECORDING: None
CAST: 8 M; 8 F

For this spoof of high-school life and activities circa 1959, you can decorate your theater to be part of the school (cafeteria, gym, classroom, etc.) as the action will sometimes overflow into the audience area. The slight plot concerns the competition for prom queen, with a ruthless cheerleader, a pregnant beatnik, and a plain-looking "good" girl as candidates. The music has a 1950s rock-and-roll flavor, and costumes include beaded cardigans, head scarfs, and saddle shoes.

ORIGINAL CAST:

Don Crosby (Kelty)

Mark Traxler (Richie)

Dana Ertischer (Cindy)

Natasha Baron (Venulia)

David Phillips (Switch)

Kathy Morath (Bunny)

Susan Levine (Carla)

Mark Edgar Stephens (Minka)

Connie Ogden (Sherry)

Sandra Purpuro (Louise)

SONGS:

Act I

Down the Hall (students)

That Special Night (students)

Dustbane: the Ballad of Minka (Kelty, ensemble)

Eat the Lunch (company)

Most Likely (Richie, Cindy, glee club)

The Venulia/Seeing Red (Venulia, Switch, students)

Act II

Corsage (Bunny, Cindy)

Squeeze Me in the Rain (Carla, Minka, ensemble)

Going All the Way (Cindy, Carla, Sherry, Louise)

Alaska, Our Frozen Friend (company)

Give Your Love (company)

PROMENADE (1969)

BOOK AND LYRICS BY: Maria Irene Fornes
MUSIC BY: Al Carmines
PUBLISHED LIBRETTO: None
CONDENSATION: *New Complete Book of the American Musical Theater*. Ewen, David. Holt, 1970
ANTHOLOGIES: *Great Rock Musicals*. Stanley Richards, ed. Stein and Day, 1979; *Promenade and Other Plays*. Fornes, Maria Irene. Winter House, 1971
VOCAL SELECTIONS: CAAZ Music (Chappell), 1970
LICENSING AGENT: Samuel French
RECORDING: RCA LSO 1161 (original cast)
CAST: 10 M; 5 F

Two prisoners escape from jail and promenade through life, illuminating the comic lunacy of attitudes toward sex, war, fashion, nudity, and wealth. There are satiric jabs at modern society, which is depicted as an Alice-in-Wonderland world of cynicism and cruelty. The score is the thing, ranging in style from the tango to a plaintive tune, reminding the critics of Weill and Brecht. The costumes were described as everything from Elinor Glyn to Carnaby Street. The set included a collage of bicycle wheels. The show includes thirty-one songs and very little dancing.

ORIGINAL CAST:

Ty McConnell (105)
Gilbert Price (106)
Margot Albert (Miss I)
Carrie Wilson (Miss O)
Alice Playten (Miss U)
Marc Allen III (Mr. R)
Glenn Kezer (Mr. S)
Michael Davis (Mr. T)
Madeline Kahn (Servant)
Edmund Gaynes (Waiter)
Art Ostrin (Dishwasher)
Florence Tarlow (Rosita)
George S. Irving (Mayor)
Pierre Epstein (Jailer)
Shannon Bolin (Mother)

SONGS:
Act I
Dig, Dig, Dig (105, 106)
Unrequited Love (Misses I, O, U; Messrs. R, S, T; Servant; Waiter; 105; 106)
Isn't That Clear? (Mr. S, ensemble)
Don't Eat It (ensemble)
Four (ensemble)
Chicken Is He (Rosita)
A Flower (Miss I)
Rosita Rodriquez: Serenade (Mayor)
Apres Vous I (105, 106, Jailer)
Bliss (Servant, 105, 106, ensemble)
The Moment Has Passed (Miss O)
Thank You (Dishwasher)
The Clothes Make the Man (Servant, 105, 106)
The Cigarette Song (Servant, 105, 106)
Two Little Angels (Mother, 105, 106)
The Passing of Time (105, 106)
Capricious and Fickle (Miss U)
Crown Me (Servant, 105, 106)

Act II
Mr. Phelps (Waiter)
Madeline (Waiter)
Spring Beauties (ensemble)
A Poor Man (105, 106)
Why Not? (Dishwasher, Servant, Mother, Waiter, 105, 106)
The Finger Song (Mr. R, ensemble)
Little Fool (Mr. T, ensemble)
Czardas (Servant, Miss I)
The Laughing Song (ensemble)
A Mother's Love (Mother)
Listen, I Feel (Servant)
I Saw a Man (Mother)
All Is Well in the City (105, 106, ensemble)

PROMISES, PROMISES (1968)

BOOK BY: Neil Simon; based on the screenplay *The Apartment* by Billy Wilder and I. A. L. Diamond
MUSIC BY: Burt Bacharach
LYRICS BY: Hal David
PUBLISHED LIBRETTO: Random House, 1969
CONDENSATION: *Ganzl's Book of the Musical Theatre*. Ganzl, Kurt. Schirmer (Macmillan), 1989
ANTHOLOGY: *The Comedy of Neil Simon*. Random House, 1971
PIANO-VOCAL SCORE: Morris, 1969
VOCAL SELECTIONS: Warner Bros. Music
LICENSING AGENT: Tams-Witmark
RECORDING: UA UAS 9902 (original cast)
CAST: 11 M; 9 F; chorus

A young insurance employee lends his apartment to company executives so they can use it for illicit sex. The cast includes a number of business stereotypes, from the contemptible boss to the understanding secretary. The office setting has been used successfully in many plays and musicals. This show has the added advantage of Neil Simon dialogue and a catchy Burt Bacharach score. The modern, Manhattan-style sets include offices, the apartment, and a crowded saloon called "The Grapes of Roth." This was presented at Goodspeed

Opera House, East Haddam, Connecticut, in 1993.

ORIGINAL CAST:

Jerry Orbach (Chuck)
Jill O'Hara (Fran)
Edward Winter (Sheldrake)
Paul Reed (Dobitch)
Norman Shelly (Kirkeby)
Vince O'Brien (Eichelberger)
Dick O'Neill (Vanderhof)
Donna McKechnie (Vivien)
Margo Sappington (Miss Polansky)
Baayork Lee (Miss Wong)
Marian Mercer (Marge)
A. Larry Haines (Dr. Dreyfuss)

SONGS:
Act I

Half as Big as Life (Chuck)
Upstairs (Chuck)
You'll Think of Something (Fran, Chuck)
Our Little Secret (Chuck, Sheldrake)
She Likes Basketball (Chuck)
Knowing When to Leave (Fran)
Where Can You Take a Girl? (Dobitch,
    Kirkeby, Eichelberger, Vanderhof)
Wanting Things (Sheldrake)
Turkey Lurkey Time (Vivien, Miss Polansky,
    Miss Wong)

Act II

A Fact Can Be a Beautiful Thing (Chuck,
    Marge, ensemble)
Whoever You Are (Fran)
A Young Pretty Girl Like You (Chuck, Dr.
    Dreyfuss)
I'll Never Fall in Love Again (Fran, Chuck)
Promises, Promises (Chuck)

PUMP BOYS AND DINETTES
(1981)

BOOK BY: John Foley, Mark Hardwick, Margaret
    LaMee, Debra Monk, Malcolm Ruhl, and John
    Schimmel
MUSIC AND LYRICS BY: Jim Wann
PUBLISHED LIBRETTO: French

CONDENSATION: None
ANTHOLOGY: None
LICENSING AGENT: Samuel French
RECORDING: CBS MK 37790 CD (original cast)
CAST: 4 M; 2 F

Called "an idyll of rural innocence" by a critic with the *Village Voice*, this is a revue of nineteen country and western songs tied together by a bit of dialogue. The men are filling-station attendants along a North Carolina highway and the women wait tables in a nearby diner. This show was described as a theatrical concert and the setting merely an accessory. The subjects covered in song include love, fishing, drinking beer, and the nearby shopping mall. The mood ranges from the sentimental to the comic. This is folksy, family fun.

ORIGINAL CAST:

John Foley (Jim)
Mark Hardwick (L. M.)
Debra Monk (Prudie)
John Schimmel (Eddie)
Cass Morgan (Rhetta)
Jim Wann (Jackson)

SONGS:
Act I

Highway 57 (all)
Taking It Slow (pump boys)
Serve Yourself (L. M.)
Menu Song (dinettes)
The Best Man (Prudie)
Fisherman's Prayer (pump boys)
Catfish (pump boys)
Mamaw (Jim)
Be Good or Be Gone (Rhetta)
Drinkin' Shoes (all)

Act II

Pump Boys (pump boys)
Mona (Jackson)
T N D P W A M (L. M.)
Tips (dinettes)
Sister (dinettes)
Vacation (all)
No Holds Barred (all)
Farmer Tan (L. M., dinettes)
Closing Time (all)

PURLIE (1970)

BOOK BY: Ossie Davis, Philip Rose, and Peter
    Udell; based on the play *Purlie Victorious* by
    Ossie Davis
MUSIC BY: Gary Geld
LYRICS BY: Peter Udell
PUBLISHED LIBRETTO: French, 1971
CONDENSATION: *New Complete Book of the
    American Musical Theater*. Ewen, David. Holt,
    1970
ANTHOLOGY: None
VOCAL SELECTIONS: Mourbar Music, 1970
LICENSING AGENT: Samuel French
RECORDING: RCA 60229 CD (original cast)
CAST: Large mixed cast

Purlie is a self-taught black preacher who
returns home to reopen an abandoned
church. Set in the deep South, the show features characters that are caricatures. The
story line involves $500 that belonged to a
deceased servant and which "evil ol' Cap'n
Cotchipee" won't give up. Melba Moore became a star as "Lutiebelle" singing the title song. The sets and costumes depict a
run-down Southern plantation. The music
frequently has the intensity of a church revival meeting. The dancing should be sensational. There was a TV version in 1981.

ORIGINAL CAST:

Cleavon Little (Purlie)
Sherman Hemsley (Gitlow)
Linda Hopkins (Church Soloist)
Melba Moore (Lutiebelle)
C. David Colson (Charlie)
John Heffernan (Ol' Cap'n)
Novella Nelson (Missy)

SONGS:
Act I
Walk Him up the Stairs (company)
New Fangled Preacher Man (Purlie)
Skinnin' a Cat (Gitlow, field hands)
Purlie (Lutiebelle)
The Harder They Fall (Purlie, Lutiebelle)
Charlie's Songs (Charlie)
Big Fish, Little Fish (Ol' Cap'n, Charlie)
I Got Love (Lutiebelle)

Great White Father (field hands)
Skinnin' a Cat (reprise) (Gitlow, Charlie)
Down Home (Purlie, Missy)
Act II
First Thing Monday Mornin' (field hands)
He Can Do It (Missy, Lutiebelle)
The Harder They Fall (reprise) (Gitlow,
    Lutiebelle, Missy)
The World Is Comin' to a Start (Charlie,
    company)

QUILTERS (1984)

BOOK BY: Molly Newman and Barbara Damashek;
    based on *The Quilters* by Patricia Cooper and
    Norma Bradley Allen
MUSIC AND LYRICS BY: Barbara Damashek
PUBLISHED LIBRETTO: Dramatists Play Service,
    1986
CONDENSATION: None
ANTHOLOGY: None
PIANO-VOCAL SCORE: Dramatists Play Service,
    1986
LICENSING AGENT: Dramatists Play Service
RECORDING: None
CAST: 7 F; musicians

Quilting was both a necessity and a means
of expression for pioneer women. Song,
dance, and monologue are used in retelling
the joys and sorrows of life for American women on the prairies. Staged as a
series of vignettes, the cast consists of
seven women in homespun costumes and
also has five musicians. Simple props are
used with mime to convey the idea of covered wagons, streams, and fires. One critic
noted the "down home, salt of the earth
philosophy" bares the roots of current-
day feminists. Throughout the play, as the
women spin their tales, the corresponding quilt blocks are sewn together. By the
last scene the audience beholds a finished
quilt composed of the bits and pieces of
the women's lives.

ORIGINAL CAST:

Lenka Peterson (Sarah)
Evalyn Baron

Marjorie Berman
Alma Cuervo
Lynn Lobban
Rosemary McNamara
Jennifer Parsons

SONGS:
Act I
Pieces of Lives
Rocky Road
Little Babes That Sleep All Night
Thread the Needle
Cornelia
The Windmill Song
Are You Washed in the Blood of the Lamb?
The Butterfly
Green, Green, Green
The Needle's Eye

Act II
Hoedown
Quiltin' and Dreamin'
Every Log in My House
Land Where We'll Never Grow Old
Who Will Count the Stitches?
The Lord Don't Rain Down Manna
Dandelion
Everything Has a Time
Hands Around

RAGS (1986)

BOOK BY: Joseph Stein
MUSIC BY: Charles Strouse
LYRICS BY: Stephen Schwartz
PUBLISHED LIBRETTO: None
CONDENSATION: None
ANTHOLOGY: None
VOCAL SELECTIONS: CPP/Belwin, 1992
LICENSING AGENT: Rodgers and Hammerstein
   Theatre Library
RECORDING: Sony SK 42657 CD (original cast)
CAST: Large mixed cast (can be cut down)

Although the original New York production was a big, lavish Broadway musical, a subsequent off-Broadway revival was done with a cast of nine and almost no scenery. The setting is en route to and in New York City around 1910. Rebecca and her son arrive in the new world expecting to be met by her husband. He is an opportunist on the political make and is not there. She is ultimately disenchanted with him and determines to rise above the sweatshop squalor of the Lower East Side of New York City. The original production was called a "gigantic patchwork" with too many subplots, but Frank Rich in the *New York Times* wrote, "this musical has its share of first rate show tunes."

ORIGINAL CAST:

Andy Gale (Homesick Immigrant)
Teresa Stratas (Rebecca)
Josh Blake (David)
Dick Latessa (Avram)
Terrence Mann (Saul)
Peter Samuel (Hamlet)
Michael Cone (Frankie/Irish Tenor)
Michael Davis (Mike)
Rex Everhart (Big Tim)
Larry Kert (Harris)
Lonny Price (Ben)
Judy Kuhn (Bella)
Marcia Lewis (Rachel)

SONGS:
Act I
I Remember (Homesick Immigrant)
Greenhorns (ensemble)
Brand New World (Rebecca, David)
Children of the Wind (Rebecca, Avram, David)
Penny a Tune (Rachel, ensemble)
Easy for You (Saul, Rebecca, David)
Hard to Be a Prince (Hamlet, ensemble)
Blame It on the Summer Night (Rebecca)
What's Wrong with That (Frankie, Mike, Big Tim, Harris)
For My Mary (Irish Tenor, Ben)
Rags (Bella, Avram)
On the Fourth of July (ensemble)
To America (Rebecca, Harris)

Act II
Yankee Boy (Harris, ensemble)
Uptown (Harris, Rebecca)
Wanting (Rebecca, Saul)

Three Sunny Rooms (Rachel, Avram)
The Sound of Love (Ben, David, ensemble)
For My Mary (reprise) (Bella, Ben)
Democratic Club Dance (Rebecca, Big Tim, Harris, ensemble)
Bread and Freedom (Rebecca, ensemble)
Dancing with the Fools (Rebecca, Harris, ensemble)

RAISIN (1973)

BOOK BY: Robert Nemiroff and Charlotte Zaltzberg; based on *A Raisin in the Sun* by Lorraine Hansberry
MUSIC BY: Judd Woldin
LYRICS BY: Robert Brittan
PUBLISHED LIBRETTO: French, 1978
CONDENSATION: *Broadway Musicals Show by Show.* Green, Stanley. Hal Leonard Books, 1985
ANTHOLOGY: None
VOCAL SELECTIONS: Blackwood Music, 1974
LICENSING AGENT: Samuel French
RECORDING: Sony SK 32754 CD (original cast)
CAST: 9 M; 6 F; chorus

With a theme of "black identity," this musical takes place in a black Chicago slum. The plot concerns a proud black matriarch and her family's ambitions to escape their run-down tenement life. She wants to move to a nice (white) suburb. When they receive a $10,000 insurance check, conflicts arise. The set consists of the apartment and fire escapes; the furniture and costumes are simple and worn. Called a picture of a family fighting for life, this show offers a wide range of good parts, from the mother to her grown son, his wife and little boy, and a Nigerian student.

Tony Award Winner (Best Musical)

ORIGINAL CAST:

Joe Morton (Walter Lee)
Ernestine Jackson (Ruth)
Virginia Capers (Mama)
Elaine Beener (Bar Girl)
Walter P. Brown (Willie)
Ted Ross (Bobo)

Robert Jackson (Asagai)
Deborah Allen (Beneatha)
Herb Downer (Pastor)
Marenda Perry (Pastor's Wife)
Helen Martin (Mrs. Johnson)
Ralph Carter (Travis)

SONGS:
Act I
Man Say (Walter Lee)
Whose Little Angry Man (Ruth)
Runnin' to Meet the Man (Walter Lee, company)
A Whole Lotta Sunlight (Mama)
Booze (Bar Girl, Willie, Bobo, Walter Lee, company)
Alaiyo (Asagai, Beneatha)
African Dance (Beneatha, company)
Sweet Time (Ruth, Walter Lee)
You Done Right (Walter Lee)

Act II
He Come Down This Morning (Mama, Pastor, Pastor's Wife, Mrs. Johnson, Ruth, Travis, company)
It's a Deal (Walter Lee)
Sidewalk Tree (Travis)
Not Anymore (Walter Lee, Ruth, Beneatha)
Measure the Valleys (Mama)

RAP MASTER RONNIE (1984)

BOOK AND LYRICS BY: Garry Trudeau
MUSIC BY: Elizabeth Swados
PUBLISHED LIBRETTO: (in manuscript) Broadway Play Publishing
CONDENSATION: None
ANTHOLOGY: None
LICENSING AGENT: Broadway Play Publishing
RECORDING: Silver Screen SSR-115 (original cast)
CAST: Small mixed cast

A Partisan satiric revue by the author of the *Doonesbury* comic strip, it was originally presented off-Broadway in Greenwich Village at the Top of the Gate in 1984. It has since been done in various parts of the country with updated material. It is mostly songs, with no real spoken dialogue.

The music ranges from highly sophisticated to country-western. Poverty, the environment, bureaucrats, nuclear war, and many other subjects are covered. The leading character, the "Ronnie" of the title, is Ronald Reagan.

ORIGINAL CAST:

Reathel Bean	Catherine Cox
Ernestine Jackson	Mel Johnson, Jr.
Richard Ryder	

SONGS:

(performed without intermission)

The Assistant Undersecretary of State for
    Human Rights (Cox)
The Class of 1984 (Bean, Cox, Johnson,
    Ryder)
Cheese (Johnson)
The Empire Strikes First (company)
Facts (Cox)
The Majority (company)
New Years in Beirut, 1983 (Ryder)
Nine to Twelve (Bean, Johnson, Ryder)
O, Grenada (Jackson, Johnson)
One More Study (Cox, Jackson)
Rap Master Ronnie (company)
The Round Up (Bean, Johnson)
Self-Made Man (Ryder, company)
Something for Nothing (company)
Take That Smile off Your Face (Jackson)
Thinking the Unthinkable (company)
You're Not Ready (Bean, Cox)

This is a musical about children to be performed by children. Rosie lives in Brooklyn. She entertains herself and her friends by acting out her show biz dreams, which include directing and starring in a film and winning an Oscar. Other than a few offstage voices, there are no adult roles. The basis for this hour-long musical is six Sendak books. The show was originally an animated cartoon TV special. For in-depth information, see Bill Powers' *Behind the Scenes of a Broadway Musical* (Crown, 1982).

ORIGINAL CAST:

Tisha Campbell (Rosie)
April Lerman (Kathy)
Joe La Benz IV (Alligator)
Wade Raley (Johnny)
B. J. Barie (Pierre)

SONGS:

(performed without intermission)

Really Rosie (Rosie)
Simple Humble Neighborhood (Rosie)
Alligators All Around (Alligator, company)
One Was Johnny (Johnny)
Pierre (Pierre, company)
Screaming and Yelling (Rosie, company)
The Awful Truth (Kathy, Johnny, Alligator,
    Pierre)
Very Far Away (company)
Avenue P (Rosie)
Chicken Soup with Rice (company)

REALLY ROSIE (1980)

BOOK AND LYRICS BY: Maurice Sendak
MUSIC BY: Carole King
PUBLISHED LIBRETTO: French
CONDENSATION: None
ANTHOLOGY: None
VOCAL SELECTIONS: Columbia Pictures, 1975
LICENSING AGENT: Samuel French
RECORDING: Caedmon TRS 368 (original cast)
CAST: 4 M; 3 F; extras (all children)

THE RED MILL (1906)

ORIGINAL BOOK AND LYRICS BY: Henry Blossom
NEW BOOK BY: Milton Lazarus
ADDITIONAL LYRICS BY: Forman Brown
MUSIC BY: Victor Herbert
PUBLISHED LIBRETTO: None
CONDENSATION: *Ganzl's Book of the Musical
    Theatre.* Ganzl, Kurt. Schirmer (Macmillan),
    1989
ANTHOLOGY: None
PIANO-VOCAL SCORE: Witmark, 1906

VOCAL SELECTIONS: *The Music of Victor Herbert.*
    Warner Bros. Music, 1976
LICENSING AGENT: Tams-Witmark
RECORDING: Turnabout 34766 (studio cast)
CAST: Large mixed cast

Two Americans are stranded in Europe in the Dutch port of Katwyk-ann-Zee. They manage to rescue the Burgomaster's daughter from a loveless marriage. This is a very old-fashioned operetta with plenty of opportunity for low comedy and pretty girls. The time is around 1900 and the scenes include the Inn at the Red Mill and a neighborhood street. There was a silent film version with Marion Davies in 1927 and a TV version in 1958.

1945 REVIVAL CAST:

Dorothy Stone (Tina)
Michael O'Shea (Con)
Eddie Foy, Jr. (Kid)
Ann Andre (Gretchen)
Robert Hughes (Hendrik)
Charles Collins (Gaston)
Odette Myrtil (Madame)
Billy Griffith (Pennyfeather)
Frank Jaquet (Burgomaster)
Lorna Byron (Juliana)
Edward Dew (Governor)

SONGS:
Act I
Mignonette (Tina, ensemble)
Whistle It (Con, Kid, Tina)
Isle of Our Dreams (Gretchen, Hendrik)
The Dancing Lesson (Gaston, ensemble)
In Old New York (Con, Kid, ensemble)
When You're Pretty and the World Is Fair
    (Madame, Pennyfeather, ensemble)
Moonbeams (Gretchen, Hendrik, Tina,
    Gaston, Burgomaster, ensemble)

Act II
Why the Silence? (ensemble)
Legend of the Mill (Juliana, ensemble)
Every Day Is Ladies' Day with Me (Governor,
    ensemble)
I Want You to Marry Me (Gretchen, Hendrik)
Al Fresco (Tina, Gaston)

Because You're You (Governor, Juliana,
    ensemble)
Romanza? (Kid, Madame)
Wedding Bells (Governor, Madame, Juliana,
    Burgomaster, Gretchen, Hendrik)

REDHEAD (1959)

BOOK BY: Herbert and Dorothy Fields, Sidney
    Shelton, and David Shaw
MUSIC BY: Albert Hague
LYRICS BY: Dorothy Fields
PUBLISHED LIBRETTO: None
CONDENSATION: *New Complete Book of the
    American Musical Theater.* Ewen, David. Holt,
    1970
ANTHOLOGY: None
PIANO-VOCAL SCORE: Chappell, 1960
LICENSING AGENT: Music Theatre International
RECORDING: RCA LSO 1104 (original cast)
CAST: Large mixed cast

Essie Whimple makes wax figures for a museum operated by her aunts, the Simpson Sisters. It is turn-of-the-century London and this musical "whodunit" is about a fiend who has strangled a chorus girl. This show was tailored for the talents of Gwen Verdon, with choreography by Bob Fosse. It was described as a mixture of old-time melodrama and British music hall. The hero is an American, but British accents predominate. The sets include a theater, a pub, and the wax museum. This was a big, handsome musical with lavish costumes. Critics called it funny, fast, opulent, and refreshing.

Tony Award Winner (Best Musical)

ORIGINAL CAST:

Gwen Verdon (Essie)
Richard Kiley (Tom)
Leonard Stone (George)
Cynthia Latham (Maude)
Doris Rich (Sarah)
Joy Nichols (May)
Pat Ferrier (Tilly)
Buzz Miller (Jailer)

SONGS:

Act I

The Simpson Sisters (ensemble)
The Right Finger on My Left Hand (Essie)
Just for Once (Essie, Tom, George)
Merely Marvelous (Essie)
The Uncle Sam Rag (George, ensemble)
Erbie Fitch's Twitch (Essie)
She's Not Enough Woman for Me (Tom, George)
Behave Yourself (Essie, Maude, Sarah, Tom)
Look Who's in Love (Essie, Tom)
My Girl Is Just Enough Woman for Me (Tom, ensemble)
Two Faces in the Dark (Essie, ensemble)

Act II

I'm Back in Circulation (Tom)
We Loves Ya, Jimey (Essie, May, Tilly, ensemble)
Pick-Pocket Tango (Essie, Jailer)
I'll Try (Essie, Tom)

THE RINK (1984)

BOOK BY: Terence McNally
MUSIC BY: John Kander
LYRICS BY: Fred Ebb
PUBLISHED LIBRETTO: French, 1985
CONDENSATION: None
ANTHOLOGY: None
PIANO-VOCAL SCORE: Fiddleback Music, 1983
VOCAL SELECTIONS: Fiddleback Music, 1983
LICENSING AGENT: Samuel French
RECORDING: Polydor 823 125-2 CD (original cast)
CAST: 6 M; 2 F; 1 young girl

The place is a roller rink somewhere on the Eastern seaboard and the time is the 1970s. Anna has sold the rink and is just leaving for a vacation in Italy when her thirty-year-old daughter, Angel, appears at the door. It has been seven years since they have seen each other, and relationships become even more tense because Angel does not want to give up the rink. Most of this musical consists of brief memories of Anna's courtship and Angel's childhood. The six males make up the wrecking crew and they have several numbers including the title tune done on roller skates. On Broadway they also doubled as various other characters, but this is not necessary should you wish to use a larger cast. There is considerable dancing in the role of Anna, which won Chita Rivera a Tony.

ORIGINAL CAST:

Angel (Liza Minnelli)
Anna (Chita Rivera)
Scott Holmes (Dino)
Scott Ellis (Danny/Sugar)
Mel Johnson, Jr. (Hiram/Mrs. Jackson)
Frank Mastrocola (Tom)
Jason Alexander (Lenny)
Ronn Carroll (Dino's Father/Mrs. Silverman)

SONGS:

Act I

Colored Lights (Angel)
Chief Cook and Bottle Washer (Anna)
Don't Ah Ma Me (Anna, Angel)
Blue Crystal (Dino)
Under the Roller Coaster (Angel)
Not Enough Magic (Dino, Angel, Anna, Sugar, Hiram, Tom, Lenny, Dino's Father)
We Can Make It (Anna)
After All These Years (men)
Angel's Rink and Social Center (Angel, men)
What Happened to the Old Days? (Anna, Mrs. Silverman, Mrs. Jackson)

Act II

The Apple Doesn't Fall (Anna, Angel)
Marry Me (Lenny)
Mrs. A (Anna, Angel, Lenny, men)
The Rink (men)
Wallflower (Anna, Angel)
All the Children in a Row (Angel, Danny)

RIO RITA (1927)

MUSIC BY: Harry Tierney
WORDS BY: Joseph McCarthy
BOOK BY: Guy Bolton and Fred Thompson
PUBLISHED LIBRETTO: French, 1926

CONDENSATION: *New Complete Book of the American Musical Theater.* Ewen, David. Holt, 1970
ANTHOLOGY: None
PIANO-VOCAL SCORE: L. Feist
LICENSING AGENT: Tams-Witmark
RECORDING: Monmouth-Evergreen MES 7058 (1930 London cast)
CAST: Large mixed cast

Set in the early part of the twentieth century, this romantic story is about the love of a Texas Ranger for a Mexican girl. The show includes all kinds of intrigue, a Mexican bandit, and a few weddings. This was a lavish Ziegfeld musical and some critics were disappointed that revival productions were not up to his standards. Brooks Atkinson of the *New York Times* wrote that you should have "pretty cabaret girls, beautiful dancing girls, South American troubadours and a Marimba band!" This was filmed in 1929 and 1942. There was a TV version in 1950.

1941 SAN FRANCISCO CAST:

Joe E. Brown (Lovett)
Suzanne Sten (Rita)
Mary Healy (Dolly)
Peter Lind Hayes (Chuck)
Walter Cassel (Jim)

SONGS:
Act I
The Best Little Lover in Town (Lovett, girls)
Sweetheart (Rita)
River Song (Rita, ensemble)
Are You There? (Dolly, Chuck)
Rio Rita (Rita, Jim)
Song of the Rangers (Jim, men)
The Kinkajou (Dolly, girls)
If You're in Love, You'll Waltz (Rita, Jim)
Out on the Loose (Chuck)

Act II
Yo Ho and a Bottle of Rum (ensemble)
I Can Speak Español (Dolly, Lovett)
Following the Sun Around (Jim)
Reverie of Love (Rita)

THE RISE OF DAVID LEVINSKY (1987)

BOOK AND LYRICS BY: Isaiah Sheffer; based on the novel by Abraham Cahan
MUSIC BY: Bobby Paul
PUBLISHED LIBRETTO: French
CONDENSATION: None
ANTHOLOGY: None
LICENSING AGENT: Samuel French
RECORDING: None
CAST: 21 M; 15 F (9 M; 6 F possible)

Told as a first-person flashback, the character of David is played by a younger as well as an older actor. Occasionally they share the stage at the same time. This tale of the Jewish immigration experience around 1900 features music with a more European than American flavor. There is almost no choreography. The ambience of New York's Lower East side is among the various settings required.

ORIGINAL CAST:

Larry Kert (Levinsky)
Avi Hoffman (David)
Jean Kauffman (Matilda/Rosie)
Jack Kenny (Naphtali/Little Getzel)
Larry Raiken (Reb/Max)
Bruce Adler (Gitelson)
Judith Cohen (Mrs. Deinstog/Mrs. Noodleman)
David Vosburgh (Barber/Muttel/Moscowitz)
Arthur Howard (Shlankie)
Eleanor Reissa (Dora)

SONGS:
Act I
Who Is This Man? (Levinsky)
Five Hundred Pages (David)
Grand Street (Matilda, Naphtali, Reb, David)
In America (Gitelson, ensemble)
The Boarder (Mrs. Dienstog)
The Transformation (David, Barber, ensemble)
Sharp (Max, Shlankie, Muttel, Getzel)
Two of a Kind (Dora)
Little Did I Know (Levinsky)
Hard Times (David, Levinsky)

Credit Face (Levinsky, David)
Five Hundred Garments (David, Levinsky)

Act II
The Garment Trade (Levinsky, ensemble)
Some Incredible Guy (Gitelson, ensemble)
Just . . . Like . . . Me (Max, Dora, Levinsky)
Be Flexible (David)
A Married Man (Mrs. Noodleman, Max,
    Moscowitz, Levinsky, girls)
Little Did We Know (Levinsky, Dora)
Bittersweet (Dora, Levinsky)
Survival of the Fittest (Levinsky)
A View from the Top (David, Levinsky)
In America (reprise) (Levinsky, David,
    ensemble)

RIVERWIND (1962)

BOOK, MUSIC, AND LYRICS BY: John Jennings
PUBLISHED LIBRETTO: None
CONDENSATION: None
ANTHOLOGY: None
LICENSING AGENT: Music Theatre International
RECORDING: London AMS 78001 (original cast)
CAST: 3 M; 4 F

Reviews of an off-Broadway revival called this show simple, non-neurotic, and old-fashioned. The dialogue is clever and contains homespun philosophy. The setting is a run-down motel in Indiana. The cast includes the widow who owns and runs the motel, her daughter, a young local boy in love with the daughter, and two visiting couples (one married, one not). The various stages and ages of love are all settled by the final curtain. The set is divided into a guest-house bedroom, the yard, and a corner of the main house.

ORIGINAL CAST:

Lovelady Powell (Virginia)
Brooks Morton (Burt)
Elizabeth Parrish (Louise)
Martin J. Cassidy (John)
Dawn Nickerson (Jenny)
Lawrence Brooks (Fred)
Helon Blount (Mrs. Farrell)

SONGS:
Act I
I Cannot Tell Her So (John)
I Want a Surprise (Jenny)
Riverwind (Louise)
American Family Plan (Virginia, Burt)
Wishing Song (Fred, Jenny, John, Louise)
Pardon Me While I Dance (Fred, Jenny)
Sew the Buttons On (Mrs. Farrell, Jenny)
Riverwind (reprise) (Louise)

Act II
Almost, but Not Quite (Virginia, Burt)
A Woman Must Think of These Things
    (Louise)
I Love Your Laughing Face (Mrs. Farrell, John)
A Woman Must Never Grow Old (Mrs. Farrell,
    Louise)
I'd Forgotten How Beautiful She Could Be
    (Fred, Jenny)
Sew the Buttons On (reprise) (company)

THE ROAR OF THE GREASEPAINT—THE SMELL OF THE CROWD (1965)

BOOK, MUSIC, AND LYRICS BY: Leslie Bricusse and
    Anthony Newley
PUBLISHED LIBRETTO: None
CONDENSATION: *Broadway Musicals Show by Show.*
    Green, Stanley. Hal Leonard Books, 1985
VOCAL SELECTIONS: Musical Comedy Productions
    (TRO), 1965
LICENSING AGENT: Tams-Witmark
RECORDING: RCA 60351 CD (original cast)
CAST: 4 M; 2 F; chorus

The theme of this musical is playing the game of life. The little man is "Cocky" and "Sir" is the maker of the rules. Sir always gets, and Cocky is always bested. These two characters carry the bulk of the show, with topics covering religion, hunger, work, success, and so on. The cast includes an assortment of urchins, a girl, a bully, and a black. For the Broadway production the set was a series of platforms with a central playing area. In that production a great deal of mime was used by the star,

Anthony Newley, and he reminded many of Chaplin. Most critics did not feel this show had anything new to say but found it most entertaining.

ORIGINAL CAST:

Cyril Ritchard (Sir)
Anthony Newley (Cocky)
Sally Smith (The Kid)
Joyce Jillson (The Girl)
Gilbert Price (The Negro)

SONGS:

Act I

The Beautiful Land (urchins)
A Wonderful Day Like Today (Sir, Cocky, urchins)
It Isn't Enough (Cocky, urchins)
Things to Remember (Sir, The Kid, urchins)
Put It in the Book (The Kid, urchins)
This Dream (Cocky)
Where Would You Be without Me? (Sir, Cocky, The Kid)
Look at That Face (Sir, The Kid, urchins)
My First Love Song (Cocky, The Girl)
The Joker (Cocky)
Who Can I Turn To (When Nobody Needs Me) (Cocky)

Act II

That's What It Is to Be Young (urchins)
What a Man! (Cocky, Sir, The Kid, urchins)
Feeling Good (The Negro, urchins)
Nothing Can Stop Me Now (Cocky, urchins)
My Way (Cocky, Sir)
Sweet Beginning (Cocky, Sir)

THE ROBBER BRIDEGROOM
(1975)

BOOK AND LYRICS BY: Alfred Uhry; based on the novella by Eudora Welty
MUSIC BY: Robert Waldman
PUBLISHED LIBRETTO: Drama Book Specialists, 1978
CONDENSATION: None
ANTHOLOGY: None
VOCAL SELECTIONS: Schirmer, 1976
LICENSING AGENT: Music Theatre International

RECORDING: Columbia CSP P 14589 (original cast)
CAST: Large mixed cast

This is a country-western musical that combines backwoods legends and fairy tales. Set in Mississippi, the story deals with a girl in love with a bandit. They do not know that the marriages being arranged for them are with each other. A square dance is going on when the folks begin to tell the tale of "The Robber Bridegroom." The production includes an onstage fiddler, a small country band, hoedown costumes and dancing, and very simple sets. The Broadway production included some nudity and earthy dialogue.

ORIGINAL CAST:

Lawrence John Moss (Little Harp)
Ernie Sabella (Big Harp)
Barry Bostwick (Jamie)
Rhonda Coullet (Rosamund)
Barbara Lang (Salome)
Stephen Vinovich (Clemment)
Trip Plymale (Goat)

SONGS:

(performed without intermission)

Once upon the Natchez Trace (company)
Two Heads (Big Harp, Little Harp)
Steal with Style (Jamie)
Rosamund's Dream (Rosamund)
The Pricklepear Bloom (Salome)
Nothin' Up (Rosamund)
Deeper in the Woods (company)
Riches (Clemment, Jamie, Salome, Rosamund)
Love Stolen (Jamie)
Poor Tied Up Darlin' (Little Harp, Goat)
Good-bye Salome (company)
Sleepy Man (Jamie)
Where Oh Where (Jamie, Clemment, Rosamund)

ROBERTA (1933)

BOOK AND LYRICS BY: Otto Harbach; adapted from *Gowns by Roberta* by Alice Duer Miller
MUSIC BY: Jerome Kern
PUBLISHED LIBRETTO: None

CONDENSATION: *New Complete Book of the American Musical Theater*. Ewen, David. Holt, 1970
ANTHOLOGY: None
PIANO-VOCAL SCORE: Harms, 1933, 1950
LICENSING AGENT: Tams-Witmark
RECORDING: Sony A 7030 CD (studio cast)
CAST: Large mixed cast

A young American football player inherits a famous Parisian fashion salon. He falls in love with one of the employees who is a Russian princess in exile. This was filmed twice (in 1935 with Fred Astaire and Ginger Rogers and in 1952 with Gower Champion and Ann Miller) and done as a TV special in 1969. A big fashion show is a necessity for this production, even if the 1930s script is updated. This musical has been particularly successful in lavish summer productions in such locations as Jones Beach (New York), St. Louis, and Dallas.

1984 NEW YORK CONCERT VERSION CAST:

Russ Thacker (Huck)
David Carroll (John)
Paula Laurence (Aunt Minnie)
Judith Blazer (Stephanie)
Loni Ackerman (Scharwenka)
Jeff Keller (Ladislaw)

SONGS:
Act I
Let's Begin (Huck)
Alpha, Beta, Pi (Huck, John, quartet)
You're Devastating (John)
Yesterdays (Aunt Minnie)
You're Devastating (reprise) (Stephanie)
Something's Got to Happen (Scharwenka)
The Touch of Your Hand (Stephanie, Ladislaw)
Yesterdays (reprise) (Stephanie)
I'll Be Hard to Handle (Scharwenka)

Act II
Hot Spot (Scharwenka)
Smoke Gets in Your Eyes (Stephanie)
Let's Begin (reprise) (Huck, Stephanie)
Don't Ask Me Not to Sing (ensemble)
Clementina (quartet)
I Won't Dance (Scharwenka, Huck)

THE ROCKY HORROR SHOW (1975)

BOOK, MUSIC, AND LYRICS BY: Richard O'Brien
PUBLISHED LIBRETTO: French, 1983
CONDENSATION: *Ganzl's Book of the Musical Theatre*. Ganzl, Kurt. Schirmer (Macmillan), 1989
ANTHOLOGY: None
VOCAL SELECTIONS: Columbia Pictures, 1974
LICENSING AGENT: Samuel French
RECORDING: Ode 9009 CD (Tim Curry and the original Roxy cast)
CAST: 7 M; 3 F

The title of this British musical refers to horror films, which it ridicules, and rock music. This was not particularly successful on Broadway, but the 1975 film version has become a cult favorite. The grotesque cast includes Dr. Frank N. Furter (a bisexual drag queen), a humpback dwarf, and some groupies. A straight young American couple turn up to take refuge at the castle. This show runs about ninety minutes without an intermission. While this is not a family show, adolescents love it.

ORIGINAL CAST:

Jamie Donnelly (Trixie/Magenta)
Bill Miller (Brad)
Abigale Haness (Janet)
Tim Curry (Frank)
Boni Enten (Columbia)
Ritz O'Brien (Riff-Raff)
William Newman (Narrator)
Kim Milford (Rocky)
Meat Loaf (Eddie/Dr. Scott)

SONGS:
(performed without intermission)
Science Fiction (Trixie)
Wedding Song (Brad, Janet)
Over at the Frankenstein Place (Brad, Janet)
Dammit Janet (Janet, Brad)
Sweet Transvestite (Frank)
Time Warp (Magenta, Columbia, Riff-Raff, Narrator)
The Sword of Damocles (Rocky)
Charles Atlas Song (Frank)

What Ever Happened to Saturday Night
(Eddie)
Eddie's Teddy (Dr. Scott, Columbia, company)
Once in a While (Brad)
Planet Shmanet Janet (Frank)
It Was Great When It All Began (company)
Super Heroes (company)

RODGERS AND HART (1975)

MUSIC BY: Richard Rodgers
LYRICS BY: Lorenz Hart
CONCEPT BY: Richard Lewine and John Fearnley
PUBLISHED LIBRETTO: None
CONDENSATION: None
ANTHOLOGY: None
MUSIC PUBLISHERS: *The Best of Rodgers and Hart.*
Chappell, 1974; The *Rodgers and Hart Songbook.*
Simon and Schuster, 1951
LICENSING AGENT: Rodgers and Hammerstein
Theatre Library
RECORDING: None
CAST: 5 M; 7 F (or less)

This salute to the great musical stage collaborators features fifty-nine of their songs. "Manhattan," "My Heart Stood Still," and "Lover" are just a few of them. There is no master of ceremonies and almost no dialogue. There are a few brief dance numbers. The Broadway stage setting was a simple arrangement of platforms and steps. The costumes were modern and informal. This is one of many salutes to composers that take songs from a career and put them into what is really a nonstop concert. The material is top class. A talented and energetic cast is needed for this show.

ORIGINAL CAST:

Barbara Andres   Mary Sue Finnerty
Jimmy Brennan   Laurence Guittard
Wayne Bryan   Stephen Lehew
David Carroll   Jim Litten
Jamie Donnelly   Virginia Sandifur
Tovah Feldshuh   Rebecca York

This revue is made up of fifty-nine songs divided into two acts.

ROMANCE ROMANCE (1988)

BOOK AND LYRICS BY: Barry Harman; Act I based
on the short story by Arthur Schnitzler; Act II
based on the play *Pain de Menage* by Jules
Renard
MUSIC BY: Keith Herrmann
PUBLISHED LIBRETTO: Fireside Theatre, 1989;
French, 1989
CONDENSATION: None
ANTHOLOGY: None
VOCAL SELECTIONS: Warner Bros. Music, 1988
LICENSING AGENT: Samuel French
RECORDING: MCA MCAD 6252 CD (original cast)
CAST: 2 M; 2 F

A cast of four carry off two separate but related one-act musicals about people searching for romance, not those who have it. The first act is set in Vienna at the turn of the century. The second concerns some yuppies at the beach on New York's Long Island. The first act has two singing parts, with the second couple waltzing in the background. All four participate in the second act. The music for Act I has a fin de siecle lilt, while Act II has a more pop-rock beat. Simple to stage, this musical was praised for its modesty and taste. There was a TV version in 1993.

ORIGINAL CAST:

Scott Bakula (Alfred/Sam)
Alison Fraser (Josefine/Monica)
Robert Hoshour (Lenny)
Deborah Graham (Barb)

SONGS:
Act I The Little Comedy
The Little Comedy (Alfred, Josefine)
Good-bye, Emil (Josefine)
It's Not Too Late (Alfred, Josefine)
Great News (Alfred, Josefine)
Oh, What a Performance! (Alfred, Josefine)
I'll Always Remember the Song (Alfred,
Josefine)
Happy, Happy, Happy (Alfred)
Women of Vienna (Alfred)
Yes, It's Love (Josefine)

A Rustic Country Inn (Alfred, Josefine)
The Night It Had to End (Josefine)

Act II Summer Share
Summer Share (all)
Think of the Odds (Barb, Lenny)
It's Not Too Late (reprise) (Sam,
   Monica)
Plans A & B (Monica, Lenny)
Let's Not Talk about It (Sam, Barb)
So Glad I Married Her (all)
Small Craft Warnings (Barb, Lenny)
How Did I End Up Here? (Monica)
Words He Didn't Say (Sam)
My Love for You (Lenny, Barb)
Moonlight Passing through a Window
   (Sam)
Now (Monica)
Romantic Notions (all)

ROSALIE (1928)

BOOK BY: William Anthony McGuire and Guy
   Bolton
LYRICS BY: P. G. Wodehouse and Ira Gershwin
MUSIC BY: Sigmund Romberg and George
   Gershwin
PUBLISHED LIBRETTO: None
CONDENSATION: *New Complete Book of the
   American Musical Theater.* Ewen, David. Holt,
   1970
ANTHOLOGY: None
LICENSING AGENT: Tams-Witmark
RECORDING: None
CAST: Large mixed cast

The original plot deals with a princess from the mythical kingdom of Romanza who falls in love with an American flyer. It was a lavish Ziegfeld production with Marilyn Miller. A later production staged outdoors in Central Park was not lavish but was entertaining. One of the Gershwin songs featured is "Oh Gee! Oh Joy!" The 1937 film version featured a different score by Cole Porter, and some songs from it are sometimes interpolated into revival productions.

1983 NEW YORK CONCERT VERSION CAST:
Alexandra Korey (Mary)
Marianne Tatum (Rosalie)
Richard Muenz (Dick)
Russ Thacker (Delroy)
George S. Irving (King)

SONGS:
Act I
Here They Are (ensemble)
Show Me the Town (Mary, ensemble)
Entrance of the Hussars (ensemble)
Hussar March (Rosalie, ensemble)
Beautiful Gypsy (Rosalie, Dick)
New York Serenade (Mary)
West Point Bugle (Dick, ensemble)
Say So (Rosalie, Dick)
Oh Gee! Oh Joy! (Rosalie, Delroy)
Kingdom of Dreams (Rosalie)

Act II
The King Can Do No Wrong (King)
Everybody Knows I Love Somebody (Mary,
   Delroy)
Follow the Drum (Rosalie)
How Long Has This Been Going On? (Mary)
Setting-up Exercises (Rosalie, Delroy)

ROSE-MARIE (1924)

BOOK AND LYRICS BY: Otto Harbach and Oscar
   Hammerstein II
MUSIC BY: Rudolf Friml and Herbert Stothart
PUBLISHED LIBRETTO: None
CONDENSATION: *Ganzl's Book of the Musical
   Theatre.* Ganzl, Kurt. Schirmer (Macmillan),
   1989
ANTHOLOGY: None
MUSIC PUBLISHER: Harms, 1924
LICENSING AGENT: Tams-Witmark
RECORDING: RCA LSO 1001 (studio cast)
CAST: 7 M; 4 F; chorus

The time is 1924 and the setting is Canada. Rose-Marie is a favorite of both the Mounties and the trappers in Saskatchewan, but she really loves Jim, who is accused of murder. But virtue is triumphant and evil is destroyed! There have been several film versions (featuring Jeanette MacDonald in 1936 and Howard Keel in 1954). This is a costume show; in addition to the famous red uniforms of the Mounties, the trappers, and flappers, there are lots of Indians for the elaborate "Totem Tom-Tom" number. The show includes an elaborate fashion show, a formal ball at the Chateau Frontenac, and a big wedding scene. The score is full of familiar tunes, and most of the audience will exit happily singing the "Indian Love Call."

ORIGINAL CAST:

Mary Ellis (Rose-Marie)
Dennis King (Jim)
Edward Ciannelli (Emile)
Pearl Regay (Wanda)
William Kent (Herman)
Arthur Ludwig (Black Eagle)
Dorothy Mackaye (Lady Jane)
Arthur Deagon (Malone)
Frank Greene (Hawley)
Lela Bliss (Ethel)

SONGS:

Act I

Vive La Canadienne (Emile, Wanda, Black Eagle, ensemble)
Hard-Boiled Herman (Herman, Lady Jane, ladies)
Rose-Marie (Jim, Malone)
The Mounties (Malone, men)
"Lak Jeem" (Rose-Marie, men)
Rose-Marie (reprise) (Malone, Rose-Marie, Emile, Hawley, men)
Indian Love Call (Rose-Marie, Jim)
Campfire Impression (men)
Pretty Things (Rose-Marie, ensemble)
Why Shouldn't We? (Herman, Lady Jane)
Totem Tom-Tom (Wanda, ensemble)

Act II

Pretty Things (reprise) (Ethel, ladies)
Only a Kiss (Herman, Lady Jane, Malone, ensemble)
The Minuet of the Minute (Rose-Marie, Herman, ensemble)
Wanda Waltz (Wanda)

The Door of My Dreams (Rose-Marie, ensemble)
Bridal Finale (Emile, Wanda, Malone, Rose-Marie, ensemble)

THE ROTHSCHILDS (1970)

BOOK BY: Sherman Yellen; based on *The Rothschilds* by Frederic Morton
MUSIC BY: Jerry Bock
LYRICS BY: Sheldon Harnick
PUBLISHED LIBRETTO: None
CONDENSATION: *Broadway Musicals Show by Show*. Green, Stanley. Hal Leonard Books, 1985
ANTHOLOGY: None
VOCAL SELECTIONS: Valando, 1970
LICENSING AGENT: Rodgers and Hammerstein Theatre Library
RECORDING: Sony SK 30337 CD (original cast)
CAST: 29 M; 4 F; chorus

This is the musical story of the founding and growth of the House of Rothschild, with a strong Jewish theme of the indomitable character of an oppressed people. The Broadway production was called an opulent one with sets ranging from the ghetto to stately palaces. The staging and choreography were described as discreet. A recent and highly successful off-Broadway revival was done with a small cast and almost no sets. The story begins in Germany in 1772 and proceeds to 1818. This is a musical about wealth and should have an elegant, stylish production.

ORIGINAL CAST:

Keene Curtis (Prince William/Fouche/Herries/Metternich)
Hal Linden (Mayer)
Leila Martin (Mama)
Chris Sarandon (Jacob)
Paul Hecht (Nathan)
David Garfield (Solomon)
Allan Gruet (Kalman)
Timothy Jerome (Amshel)
Paul Tracey (Sceptic)
Jill Clayburgh (Hannah)

SONGS:
Act I
Pleasure and Privilege (Prince William,
    ensemble)
Jew, Do Your Duty (ensemble)
One Room (Mayer, Mama)
He Tossed a Coin (Mayer, ensemble)
Sons (Mayer, Mama, boys)
Everything (Nathan, Mama, Solomon, Kalman,
    Amshel, Jacob)
Rothschild and Sons (Mayer, Nathan,
    Solomon, Kalman, Amshel, Jacob)
Allons (Fouche)

Act II
Give England Strength (Herries, ensemble)
This Amazing London Town (Nathan)
They Say (Sceptic, ensemble)
I'm in Love! I'm in Love! (Nathan, Hannah)
In My Own Lifetime (Mayer)
Have You Ever Seen a Prettier Little
    Congress? (Metternich, ensemble)
Stability (Metternich, ensemble)
Bonds (Metternich, Nathan, Jacob, Solomon,
    Kalman, Amshel, ensemble)

RUNAWAYS (1978)

BOOK, MUSIC, AND LYRICS BY: Elizabeth Swados
PUBLISHED LIBRETTO: French, 1980; Bantam
    Books, 1979
CONDENSATION: None
ANTHOLOGY: None
LICENSING AGENT: Samuel French
RECORDING: Columbia JS 35410 (original cast)
CAST: 11 M; 9 F

Called a musical collage in two acts, this
show is about runaway children. The cast
in New York was primarily made up of non-
professionals between the ages of eleven
and twenty-four with diverse ethnic and financial backgrounds. The show has no actual plot and consists of songs and monologues dealing with runaway experiences.
The music is a combination of rock, blues,
salsa, country, and western. The themes
of abandonment, anger, and bewilderment

are intertwined with those of bravery, humor, and opportunism.

ORIGINAL CAST:
Bruce Hlibok (Hubbell)
Lorie Robinson (Interpreter)
Rachael Kelly (Jackie)
Nan-Lynn Nelson (Nikki)
Jossie De Guzman (Lidia)
Randy Ruiz (Manny)
Jon Matthews (Eddie)
Carlo Imperato (A. J.)
Bernie Allison (Sundar)
Venustra K. Robinson (Roby)
Ray Contreras (Luis)
David Schechter (Lazar)
Evan H. Miranda (Eric)
Jonathan Feig (Iggy)
Kate Schellenbach (Jane)
Leonard D. Brown (EZ)
Mark Anthony Butler (Mex-Mongo)
Karen Evans (Diedre)

SONGS:
(and speeches)
Act I
You Don't Understand (Hubbell, Interpreter)
I Had to Go (A. J.)
Parent/Kid Dance (company)
Appendectomy (Jackie)
Where Do People Go (company)
Footstep (Nikki, Lidia, Manny)
Once upon a Time (Lidia, company)
Current Events (Eddie)
Every Now and Then (A. J., Sundar, company)
Out on the Street (Hubbell, Interpreter)
Minnesota Strip (Roby)
Song of a Child Prostitute (Jackie, Lidia,
    Manny, Luis)
Christmas Puppies (Nikki)
Lazar's Heroes (Lazar)
Find Me a Hero (Lazar, company)
Scrynatchkielooaw (Nikki)
The Undiscovered Son (Eric)
I Went Back Home (Iggy, Jane)
This Is What I Do When I'm Angry (A. J.,
    Nikki)
The Basketball Song (EZ, company)
Spoons (Manny)

Lullaby for Luis (Lidia, Luis, company)
We Are Not Strangers (Eric, company)

Act II
In the Sleeping Line (company)
Lullaby from Baby to Baby (Hubbell, Diedre)
Tra Gog Vo In Dein Whole/I Will Not Tell a
    Soul (Lazar, Hubbell)
Revenge Song (company)
Enterprise (Diedre, Nikki, Roby, company)
Sometimes (Roby, Lazar, company)
Clothes (Iggy)
We Are Not Strangers (reprise) (EZ,
    company)
Mr. Graffiti (Mex-Mongo)
The Untrue Pigeon (Nikki)
Señoras de la Noche (Lidia, Manny, Nikki)
We Have to Die? (Diedre)
Where Are Those People Who Did *Hair*?
    (Lazar, Diedre, company)
Appendectomy II (Jackie)
Let Me Be a Kid (company)
To the Dead of Family Wars (Diedre)
Problem after Problem (Hubbell, Interpreter)
Lonesome of the Road (Luis, company)

RUTHLESS! (1992)

BOOK AND LYRICS BY: Joel Paley
MUSIC BY: Marvin Laird
PUBLISHED LIBRETTO: None
CONDENSATION: None
ANTHOLOGY: None
LICENSING AGENT: Not yet available
RECORDING: None
CAST: 5 F; 1 young girl

A very funny satiric look at child actors,
stage mothers, and show business in general. Act I is in the present time in "Small
Town, U.S.A." and is set in the living room
of the Denmark family. Act II is four years
later in New York City—set in the same
room. This is explained as the family has
moved all their furniture to the big city so
they would not forget their roots. Eight-
year-old Tina wants desperately to play
the lead in a school play—so desperately

that she kills the star, and as the star's understudy, takes over the role. But Tina is
exposed and locked up for four years. In
Act II she is released and finds her mother
has become a Broadway star. For the off-
Broadway production the cast doubled up
on some of the roles, and two pianos provided the accompaniment. Sophisticated
adults will find this just as much fun as
young children.

ORIGINAL CAST:

Donna English (Judy)
Laura Bundy (Tina, aged eight)
Joel Vig (Sylvia)
Susan Mansur (Myrna)
Joanne Baum (Louise/Eave)
Denise Lor (Lita)

SONGS:
Act I
Tina's Mother (Judy)
Born to Entertain (Tina)
Talent (Sylvia)
To Play This Part (Tina)
Third Grade (Myrna)
The Lippy Song (Louise)
Where Tina Gets It From (Judy)
Kisses and Hugs (Judy, Tina)
Tina, My Darling (Judy)
I Hate Musicals (Lita)

Act II
Eave's Song (Eave)
Look at Me (Sylvia)
Ruthless! (Judy) Reprise (Judy, Tina, Sylvia)

SAIL AWAY (1961)

BOOK, MUSIC, AND LYRICS BY: Noel Coward
PUBLISHED LIBRETTO: Dramatic
CONDENSATION: None
ANTHOLOGY: None
VOCAL SELECTIONS: Chappell
LICENSING AGENT: Dramatic
RECORDING: Angel 64759 CD (original cast)
CAST: 4 M; 7 F; chorus, children

Noel Coward first conceived this musical while observing tourists on foreign soils. It concerns a luxury cruise from New York to Europe, the passengers, and the tour hostess (Mimi) who falls in love with one of them (Johnny). In addition to the shipboard sets, there are several excursions ashore to exotic Tangiers and Naples for a large Italian wedding. The score is both sentimental and satiric.

ORIGINAL CAST:

Elaine Stritch (Mimi)
James Hurst (Johnny)
Patricia Harty (Nancy)
Grover Dale (Barnaby)
Charles Braswell (Joe/Ali)
Paul O'Keefe (Alvin)

SONGS:
Act I
Come to Me (Mimi, men)
Sail Away (Johnny)
Where Shall I Find Him? (Nancy)
Beatnick Love Affair (Barnaby)
Later than Spring (Johnny)
The Passenger's Always Right (Joe, men)
Useful Phrases (Mimi)
Where Shall I Find Her? (reprise) (Barnaby)
You're a Long, Long Way from America (Mimi, company)

Act II
The Customer's Always Right (Ali, men)
Something Very Strange (Mimi)
Go Slow, Johnny (Johnny)
The Little Ones' ABC (Mimi, Alvin, children)
Don't Turn Away from Love (Johnny)
When You Want Me (Barnaby, Nancy)
Why Do the Wrong People Travel? (Mimi)

SALAD DAYS (1958)

BOOK AND LYRICS BY: Dorothy Reynolds and Julian Slade
MUSIC BY: Julian Slade
PUBLISHED LIBRETTO: French, 1961

CONDENSATION: *Ganzl's Book of the Musical Theatre*. Ganzl, Kurt. Schirmer (Macmillan), 1989
ANTHOLOGY: None
VOCAL SELECTIONS: Francis, Day, and Hunter (London), 1954
LICENSING AGENT: Tams-Witmark
RECORDING: TER 1018 CD (London revival cast)
CAST: 6 M; 6 F

This 1954 British musical was a favorite of Princess Margaret and had a long run in London. A Canadian cast presented it off-Broadway in 1958. The plot involves a tramp with a piano in a park. The piano has magical powers and brings happiness to everyone. Members of the small cast portray approximately forty characters, in the manner of British revue or repertory. Some critics found the puns and the odd walks just a bit too slapstick, but they also found it imaginative, fanciful, and youthful. This is a family show that can be simply staged.

NEW YORK CAST:

Richard Easton (Timothy)
Barbara Franklin (Jane)
Jack Creley (Uncle Clam)
Tom Kneebone (Nigel/Zed/Manager/Fosdyke)
Gillie Fenwick (Mrs. Dawes)
Norma Renault (Asphinxia/Lady Raeburn)

SONGS:
Act I
The Dons' Chorus (company)
We Said We Wouldn't Look Back (Timothy, Jane)
Find Yourself Something to Do (family)
I Sit in the Sun (Jane)
Look at Me! (Timothy, Jane)
Hush-Hush (Uncle Clam, Fosdyke, Timothy)
Out of Breath (company)

Act II
Cleopatra (Manager)
Sand in My Eyes (Asphinxia)
It's Easy to Sing (Jane, Timothy, Nigel)
Let's Take a Stroll through London (ensemble)
We're Looking for a Piano (company)
The Time of My Life (Jane)

The Saucer Song (Zed, Timothy, Jane)
We Don't Understand Our Children (Mrs.
     Dawes, Lady Raeburn)

SALLY (1920)

BOOK BY: Guy Bolton
MUSIC BY: Jerome Kern; ballet music by Victor
     Herbert
LYRICS BY: Clifford Grey and B. G. DeSylva
PUBLISHED LIBRETTO: None
CONDENSATION: *Ganzl's Book of the Musical
     Theatre*. Ganzl, Kurt. Schirmer (Macmillan),
     1989
ANTHOLOGY: None
MUSIC PUBLISHER: Harms
LICENSING AGENT: Tams-Witmark
RECORDING: Monmouth-Evergreen 7053 (original
     London cast)
CAST: 7 M; 7 F; chorus

Sally is an orphan who goes to work as a
dishwasher in a cafe. At the cafe she meets
and falls in love with Blair. Through a series
of misunderstandings she masquerades as
a famous singer at a party, is unmasked,
and ends up a Ziegfeld star! In a 1982 New
York revival this was done without any sets
and only a suggestion of costume. Yet the
audience was charmed and thoroughly enjoyed the seldom-heard Kern score. There
was a film version in 1929 and a London
revival in 1942 under the title *Wild Rose*.

1988 NEW YORK CONCERT VERSION CAST:

Alan Sues (Otis)
Louisa Flaningam (Rosie)
Christina Saffran (Sally)
Don Correia (Blair)
Jack Dabdoub (Connie)

SONGS:
Act I
In the Night Time (ensemble)
On with the Dance (Otis, Rosie, girls)
Joan of Arc (Sally)
Look for the Silver Lining (Sally, Blair,
     ensemble)
Sally (Blair, ensemble)

Act II
The Social Game (ensemble)
A Wild, Wild Rose (Sally, men)
The Schnitza Komiski (Connie)
Whip-Poor-Will (Sally, Blair)
The Lorelei (Rosie, Otis, Connie)
The Church around the Corner (Rosie, Otis)
The Nockerova Ballet (Sally, ensemble)

SALVATION (1969)

BOOK, MUSIC, AND LYRICS BY: Peter Link and
     C. C. Courtney
PUBLISHED LIBRETTO: None
CONDENSATION: *New Complete Book of the
     American Musical Theater*. Ewen, David. Holt,
     1970
ANTHOLOGY: None
VOCAL SELECTIONS: Chappell, 1969
LICENSING AGENT: Music Theatre International
RECORDING: Capitol SO 337 (original cast)
CAST: 4 M; 4 F; rock band

The New York critics liked the music and
the cast better than the theme of this 1960s
rock musical. The idea is that organized religion no longer meets the needs of the individual. There was some nudity and sex
with appropriate biblical quotations. The
plot involves a southern evangelist who
attempts to turn a group of young people away from their evil ways. Psychedelic
slides were used in the New York production. The critic of the *Chelsea Clinton
News* suggested, "Keep your Bible-quoting
maiden aunt away."

ORIGINAL CAST:

Yolande Bavan (Ranee)
Peter Link (Farley)
C. C. Courtney (Monday)
Joe Morton (Mark)
Boni Enten (Boo)
Annie Rachel (Dierdre)
Marta Heflin (Betty Lou)
Chapman Roberts (Le Roy)

SONGS:

(performed without intermission)

Salvation (Monday, Ranee, Dierdre, Le Roy, Mark, Betty Lou)

Honest Confession Is Good for the Soul (Monday, Boo, Farley, company)

Ballin' (company)

Let the Moment Slip By (Dierdre)

Gina (Mark, Farley, company)

Stockhausen Potpourri (company)

If You Let Me Make Love to You Then Why Can't I Touch You (company)

There Ain't No Flies on Jesus (company)

Daedalus (Ranee)

Deuteronomy XVII Verse 2 (Mark, Betty Lou, girls)

For Ever (Le Roy, Mark, girls)

Footloose, Youth, and Fancy Free (Boo, Le Roy)

Schwartz (company)

Let's Get Lost in Now (Mark, company)

Back to Genesis (company)

Tomorrow Is the First Day of the Rest of My Life (Farley, company)

SAY, DARLING (1958)

BOOK BY: Richard Bissell, Abe Burrows, and Marian Bissell; based on the novel by Richard Bissell

MUSIC BY: Jule Styne

LYRICS BY: Betty Comden and Adolph Green

PUBLISHED LIBRETTO: None

CONDENSATION: None

ANTHOLOGY: None

LICENSING AGENT: Tams-Witmark

RECORDING: RCA LOC 1045 (original cast)

CAST: Large mixed cast

A writer from the Midwest becomes involved with show biz when his novel is turned into a musical comedy. Some of the other leading parts include a beautiful but slipping Hollywood star trying to go "legit" and a young (and not so sincere) producer. This is actually a satire on the author's experiences when his first novel became *The*

Pajama Game. It is a comedy about a musical with many of the numbers and the main dance routines presented as part of the show being rehearsed. The Broadway production used only two pianos although the cast recording features a full orchestra.

ORIGINAL CAST:

David Wayne (Jack Jordan)

Vivian Blaine (Irene Lovelle)

Johnny Desmond (Rudy Lorraine)

Mitchell Gregg (Rex Dexter)

SONGS:

Act I

Try to Love Me (Irene)

It's Doom (Rudy)

The Husking Bee (Rudy, company)

Act II

It's the Second Time You Meet That Matters (Rudy)

Chief of Love (Irene)

Say, Darling (Rudy)

The Carnival Song (Jack, Irene)

Act III

Try to Love Me (Rudy)

Dance Only with Me (Irene, Rex)

Something's Always Happening on the River (Jack, company)

SCRAMBLED FEET (1979)

BOOK, MUSIC, AND LYRICS BY: John Driver and Jeffrey Haddow

PUBLISHED LIBRETTO: French

CONDENSATION: None

ANTHOLOGY: None

LICENSING AGENT: Samuel French

RECORDING: DRG 6105 CD (original cast)

CAST: 3 M; 1 F; 1 duck

This revue was done at New York's Village Gate nightclub on a small proscenium stage fringed by tiny light bulbs. The cast of four (and Hermione, the duck) go through twenty-two numbers about various aspects of the theater—mostly spoofs but with a couple of serious moments. Two skits include auditioning for a Latin American road company of *Annie* and an "Avant-Garde Playwriting Kit." The show is structured around getting to the theater, what we see, and ending with perhaps an insincere curtain call. The only onstage prop is a grand piano.

ORIGINAL CAST:

Evalyn Baron   John Driver
Jeffrey Haddow   Roger Neil

SONGS:
Act I
Haven't We Met? (ensemble)
Going to the Theater (ensemble)
Makin' the Rounds (ensemble)
Composer Tango (Neil, Baron)
Huns/British (Haddow, Baron, Driver)
Could Have Been (Driver, Baron, Neil)
Theater-Party-Ladies (ensemble)

Act II
Love in the Wings (Baron, Neil)
Good Connections (ensemble)
Have You Ever Been on Stage? (Baron, Driver)
Advice to Producers (ensemble)
Happy Family (ensemble)

THE SECRET GARDEN (1991)

BOOK AND LYRICS BY: Marsha Norman; based on
    the novel by Frances Hodgson Burnett
MUSIC BY: Lucy Simon
PUBLISHED LIBRETTO: French, 1992; Theatre
    Communications Group, 1992
CONDENSATION: None
ANTHOLOGY: None
VOCAL SELECTIONS: Warner Bros. Music, 1992
LICENSING AGENT: Samuel French
RECORDING: Columbia CK 48817 CD (original cast)
CAST: 12 M; 10 F

The childhood classic, set around 1906, has been transformed into a lavish musical fantasy. Young Mary Lenox, orphaned in India, is sent to a bleak manor house in England. Here she and her bedridden cousin, Colin, share the secret of the garden. The score was described as "olde England" with various madrigals, jigs, rounds, and folk songs. The Broadway production was designed as a nineteenth-century toy theater with a Victorian valentine prettiness. You will need Edwardian gothic settings and costumes. The role of Mary is an award-winning one for your young actress.

ORIGINAL CAST:

Rebecca Luker (Lily)
Peter Marinos (Fakir)
Daisy Eagan (Mary)
Mandy Patinkin (Archibald)
Alison Fraser (Martha)
Tom Toner (Ben)
John Cameron Mitchell (Dickon)
John Babcock (Colin)
Kay Walbye (Rose)
Robert Westenberg (Neville)
Michael De Vries (Albert)

SONGS:
Act I
Opening Dream (Lily, Fakir, Mary, company)
There's a Girl (company)
The House upon the Hill (company)
I Heard Someone Crying (Mary, Archibald,
    Lily, company)
A Fine White Horse (Martha)
A Girl in the Valley (Lily, Archibald, dancers)
It's a Maze (Ben, Mary, Dickon)
Winter's on the Wing (Dickon)
Show Me the Key (Mary, Dickon)
A Bit of Earth (Archibald)
Storm I (company)
Lily's Eyes (Archibald, Neville)
Storm II (Mary, company)
Round-Shouldered Man (Colin)
Final Storm (company)

Act II
The Girl I Mean to Be (Mary, company)
Quartet (Archibald, Neville, Rose, Lily)
Race You to the Top of the Morning
    (Archibald)
Wick (Dickon, Mary)
Come to My Garden (Lily, Colin)
Come Spirit, Come Charm (Mary, Martha,
    Dickon, Lily, Fakir, company)

A Bit of Earth (reprise) (Lily, Rose, Albert)
Disappear (Neville)
Hold On (Martha)
Letter Song (Mary, Martha)
Where in the World (Archibald)
How Could I Ever Know (Lily, Archibald)

THE SECRET LIFE OF WALTER MITTY (1964)

BOOK BY: Joe Manchester; based on the story by
  James Thurber
MUSIC BY: Leon Carr
LYRICS BY: Earl Shuman
PUBLISHED LIBRETTO: French, 1968
CONDENSATION: None
ANTHOLOGY: None
LICENSING AGENT: Samuel French
RECORDING: Columbia OS 2720 (original cast)
CAST: 5 M; 6 F

Walter Mitty is America's everyman. As he approaches his fortieth birthday, nagged by his wife and bullied by his boss, he finds escape in his daydreams. So we have Mitty as a surgeon, an astronaut, and even producing the "Folies de Mitty" in Paris. This off-Broadway musical can be economically staged and offers several good parts, including Mitty's ten-year-old daughter. The critics liked the score, made up of marches, hymns, jazzy little waltzes, and ballads.

ORIGINAL CAST:

Marc London (Walter)
Christopher Norris (Peninnah)
Lorraine Serabian (Agnes)
Cathryn Damon (Willa)
Eugene Roche (Gorman)
Rudy Tronto (Harry)
Charles Rydell (Irving)
Rue McClanahan (Hazel)
Lette Rehnolds (Ruthie)

SONGS:
Act I
The Secret Life (company)
The Walter Mitty March (company)
By the Time I'm Forty (Walter)

Walking with Peninnah (Walter, Peninnah)
Drip, Drop Tapoketa (company)
Aggie (Walter)
Don't Forget (Walter, Agnes)
Marriage Is for Old Folks (Willa)
Hello, I Love You (Gorman, Walter, Harry)
Willa (Irving)
Confidence (Harry, Walter, Willa, company)

Act II
Fan the Flame (Willa)
Two Little Pussycats (Hazel, Ruthie)
She's Talking Out (company)
By the Time I'm Forty (reprise)(Walter, Willa,
  Harry, company)
You're Not (Walter, Agnes)
Aggie (reprise) (Agnes)
Lonely Ones (Walter, Willa, Gorman, Harry,
  Irving)

SEESAW (1973)

BOOK BY: Michael Bennett; based on the play *Two
  for the Seesaw* by William Gibson
MUSIC BY: Cy Coleman
LYRICS BY: Dorothy Fields
PUBLISHED LIBRETTO: French, 1975
CONDENSATION: None
ANTHOLOGY: None
VOCAL SELECTIONS: Notable Music (Big Three,
  1973)
LICENSING AGENT: Samuel French
RECORDING: DRG 6108 CD (original cast)
CAST: 4 M; 4 F; chorus, dancers

A fancy-free lawyer from Nebraska is in New York making a new start. He meets and has an affair with a dancer from the Bronx. The bittersweet ending has him going back home to Nebraska and his wife. A secondary part had Tommy Tune as a choreographer; he always stopped the show with his balloon dance. There is also a good part for a young Spanish boy with a big voice. "The essence of *Seesaw* is its very New Yorkishness," wrote John Beaufort of the *Christian Science Monitor*. It's a big, brassy show with big numbers and a good score.

ORIGINAL CAST:

Michele Lee (Gittel)
Ken Howard (Jerry)
Giancarlo Esposito (Julio)
Joshie Jo Armstead (Sophie)
Tommy Tune (David)
LaMonte des Fontaines (Sparkle)

SONGS:
Act I
Seesaw (company)
My City (Jerry, ensemble)
Nobody Does It Like Me (Gittel)
In Tune (Gittel, Jerry)
Spanglish (Julio, Gittel, Jerry, Sophie,
    company)
Welcome to Holiday Inn (Gittel)
You're a Lovable Lunatic (Jerry)
He's Good for Me (Gittel)
Ride Out the Storm (Sparkle, Sophie,
    company)

Act II
We've Got It (Jerry)
Poor Everybody Else (Gittel)
Chapter 54, Number 1909 (David, Jerry, Gittel,
    ensemble)
The Concert (Gittel, ensemble)
It's Not Where You Start (David, company)
I'm Way Ahead/Seesaw (reprise) (Gittel)

SEVEN BRIDES FOR SEVEN BROTHERS (1982)

BOOK BY: Lawrence Kasha and David Landay;
    based on the 1954 film and *The Sobbin' Women*
    by Stephen Vincent Benét
MUSIC BY: Gene de Paul; new songs by Al Kasha
    and Joel Hirschhorn
LYRICS BY: Johnny Mercer
PUBLISHED LIBRETTO: None
CONDENSATION: None
ANTHOLOGY: None
VOCAL SELECTIONS: Belwin
LICENSING AGENT: Music Theatre International
RECORDING: First Night CD8 CD (1986 London
    cast)
CAST: Large mixed cast

The setting is the Pacific Northwest in the 1850s. Adam desperately needs a wife to take care of him and his six brothers. Milly marries him without knowing about the brothers, so she sets out to find brides for all of them. This was a popular film in 1954 with Jane Powell and Howard Keel, although this stage version retains only four songs from the film. The Broadway production featured elaborate sets and athletic dances.

ORIGINAL CAST:

David Carroll (Adam)
Debby Boone (Milly)
Craig Peralta (Gideon)

SONGS:
Act I
Bless Your Beautiful Hide (Adam)
Wonderful, Wonderful Day (Milly, brides,
    townspeople)
One Man (Milly)
Goin' Courting (Milly, brothers)
Social Dance (Milly, Adam, brides, brothers,
    suitors, townspeople)
Love Never Goes Away (Adam, Milly, Gideon)
Sobbin' Women (Adam, brothers)

Act II
The Townsfolk's Lament (suitors,
    townspeople)
A Woman Ought to Know Her Place (Adam)
We Gotta Make It through the Winter (Milly,
    brides, brothers)
Spring Dance (brides, brothers)
A Woman Ought to Know Her Place (reprise)
    (Adam, Gideon)
Glad That You Were Born (Milly, brides,
    brothers)
Wedding Dance (Milly, Adam, company)

SEVENTEEN (1951)

BOOK BY: Sally Benson; based on the novel by
    Booth Tarkington
MUSIC BY: Walter Kent
LYRICS BY: Kim Gannon
PUBLISHED LIBRETTO: French, 1954

CONDENSATION: None
ANTHOLOGY: None
PIANO-VOCAL SCORE: French, 1954
LICENSING AGENT: Samuel French
RECORDING: RCA CBM 1-2034 (original cast)
CAST: 13 M; 12 F; extras

The famous summertime "puppy love" story set in Indiana in 1907 was musicalized for Broadway. The plot concerns Lola Pratt visiting for the summer and causing all sorts of problems with the local teenagers and their parents. Called by Brooks Atkinson in the *New York Times* a "touching and uproarious portrait of the torture of adolescence," it is a show for the entire family. The sets and costumes need to suggest the pre–World War I period, and the whole show should have charm, style, and innocence.

ORIGINAL CAST:

Kenneth Nelson (Willie Baxter)
Ann Crowley (Lola Pratt)
Ellen McCown (May)
Helen Wood (Emmie)
Joan Bowman (Nan)
Bonnie Brae (Madge)
Carol Cole (Ida)
Sherry McCutcheon (Jenny)
Elizabeth Pacetti (Sue)
Richard France (Lester)
Doris Dalton (Mrs. Baxter)
Frank Albertson (Mr. Baxter)
Harrison Muller (George)
Maurice Ellis (Genesis)
Alonzo Bosan (Mr. Genesis)
Dick Kallman (Joe)

SONGS:
Act I
Weatherbee's Drug Store (ensemble)
This Was Just Another Day (Lola Pratt, Willie Baxter)
Things Are Gonna Hum This Summer (Lola Pratt, May, Emmie, Joe, Madge, ensemble)
How Do You Do, Miss Pratt? (Willie Baxter)
Summertime Is Summertime. (Emmie, May, Lester, Joe, ensemble)
Reciprocity (Lola Pratt, Lester, ensemble)

Ode to Lola (May, Emmie, Nan, Madge, Ida, Jenny, Sue)
Headache and Heartache (Mr. Baxter, Mrs. Baxter)
OO-OOOO-OOO, What You Do to Me (George)
Act II
The Hoosier Way (George, Emmie, Lester, Ida, ensemble)
I Could Get Married Today (Willie Baxter, Genesis, Mr. Genesis)
After All, It's Spring (May, Joe, ensemble)
If We Only Could Stop the Old Town Clock (Lola Pratt, Willie Baxter, George, Joe, May, Emmie, ensemble)

1776 (1969)

BOOK BY: Peter Stone
MUSIC AND LYRICS BY: Sherman Edwards
PUBLISHED LIBRETTO: Viking, 1970
CONDENSATION: *The Best Plays of 1968–1969.* Otis L. Guernsey, Jr., ed. Dodd, Mead, 1969; *Ganzl's Book of the Musical Theatre.* Ganzl, Kurt. Schirmer (Macmillan), 1989
ANTHOLOGIES: *Ten Great Musicals of the American Stage.* Stanley Richards, ed. Chilton, 1973; *Best American Plays*, 7th series. Clive Barnes, ed. Crown, 1975
VOCAL SELECTIONS: Schirmer, 1969
LICENSING AGENT: Music Theatre International
RECORDING: Sony SK 48215 CD (original cast)
CAST: 25 M; 2 F

All the delegates are there—John Adams, John Hancock, Ben Franklin—the object is to get the Second Continental Congress to draft and adopt the Declaration of Independence. At the final curtain the group freezes in the pose of the familiar Trumbull painting of the event. The two women in the cast are Abigail Adams and Martha Jefferson. The script was described as "touching, funny, endearing, frank and truthful." There is no chorus and only an impromptu waltz for choreography. There was a film version in 1972. Even the most jaded sophisticate cannot help but be touched and inspired by this show.

Tony Award Winner (Best Musical)

ORIGINAL CAST:

William Daniels (Adams)
Virginia Vestoff (Abigail Adams)
Ronald Holgate (Lee)
Howard Da Silva (Franklin)
Ken Howard (Jefferson)
David Vosburgh (Sherman)
Betty Buckley (Martha Jefferson)
Henry Le Clair (Livingston)
Paul Hecht (Dickinson)
Scott Jarvis (Courier)
Clifford David (Rutledge)

SONGS:

(performed without intermission)
Sit Down, John (Adams, congress)
Piddle, Twiddle, and Resolve (Adams)
Till Then (Adams, Abigail Adams)
The Lees of Old Virginia (Lee, Franklin,
    Adams)
But, Mr. Adams (Adams, Franklin, Jefferson,
    Sherman, Livingston)
Yours, Yours, Yours (Adams, Abigail Adams)
He Plays the Violin (Martha Jefferson,
    Franklin, Adams)
Cool, Cool, Considerate Men (Dickinson,
    ensemble)
Momma Look Sharp (Courier, ensemble)
The Egg (Franklin, Adams, Jefferson)
Molasses to Rum (Rutledge)
Yours, Yours, Yours (reprise) (Abigail Adams)
Is Anybody There? (Adams)

70, GIRLS, 70 (1971)

BOOK BY: Fred Ebb and Norman L Martin; based
    on the play *Breath of Spring* by Peter Coke
MUSIC BY: John Kander
LYRICS BY: Fred Ebb
PUBLISHED LIBRETTO: None
CONDENSATION: None
ANTHOLOGY: None
VOCAL SELECTIONS: Valando, 1971
LICENSING AGENT: Samuel French
RECORDING: Sony SK 30589 CD (original cast)
CAST: 11 M; 13 F

The girls in the title are all in the vicinity
of seventy years old and live in a seedy retirement hotel on New York's upper West
Side. They decide to fix things up a bit
by shoplifting and specialize in stores that
stock expensive furs. Occasionally, the actors step out of their roles and speak to the
audience. In the New York production the
orchestra wore colorful jerseys and the piano player ("Hit It, Lorraine") was onstage.
There are banjo and other vaudeville-type
numbers. The only young person in the
cast is the bellhop. There was a major revival in London in 1991.

ORIGINAL CAST:

Mildred Natwick (Ida)
Hans Conried (Harry)
Lillian Roth (Gert)
Gil Lamb (Walter)
Lillian Hayman (Melba)
Lucie Lancaster (Eunice)
Goldye Shaw (Fritzi)
Dorothea Freitag (Lorraine)
Joey Faye (Callahan)
Henrietta Jacobson (Grandmother)
Coley Worth (Kowalski)
Tommy Breslin (Eddie)

SONGS:
Act I
Old Folks (company)
Home (Ida, Gert, Eunice, Walter, Harry, Melba,
    Fritzi)
Broadway My Street (Melba, Fritzi, Callahan,
    Grandmother, ensemble)
The Caper (Harry)
Coffee in a Cardboard Cup (Melba, Fritzi)
You and I, Love (ensemble)
Do We? (Eunice, Walter)
Hit It, Lorraine (Ida, Harry, Gert, Eunice,
    Lorraine)
See the Light (Gert, Callahan, ensemble)

Act II
Boom Ditty Boom (Ida, Harry, Gert, Walter,
    Melba, Eunice, Fritzi)
Believe (Melba, Ida, Harry, Gert, Walter,
    Eunice, Fritzi)
Go Visit (Eddie, Grandmother)

70, Girls, 70 (company)
The Elephant Song (Ida, Melba, Fritzi)
Yes (Ida, company)

SHE LOVES ME (1963)

BOOK BY: Joe Masteroff; based on the play
   Parfumerie by Miklos Laszlo
MUSIC BY: Jerry Bock
LYRICS BY: Sheldon Harnick
PUBLISHED LIBRETTO: Dodd, Mead, 1964
CONDENSATION: *The Best Plays of 1962–1963.*
   Henry Hewes, ed. Dodd, Mead, 1963
ANTHOLOGY: None
VOCAL SELECTIONS: Valando/Hal Leonard, 1963;
   Warner Bros. Music
LICENSING AGENT: Tams-Witmark
RECORDING: Polydor 831 968-2 CD (original cast)
CAST: 13 M; 8 F

This charming musical is set in Budapest
in the 1930s. A young clerk who works in a
shop carries on a romance by mail with a
girl he doesn't know. By chance, she comes
to work in the same shop and complications develop. This show and the recording have reached a cult status. It has been
revived several times and done on PBS in
a slightly abridged version.

ORIGINAL CAST:

Ralph Williams (Arpad)
Nathaniel Frey (Sipos)
Barbara Baxley (Ilona)
Jack Cassidy (Kodaly)
Ludwig Donath (Maraczek)
Barbara Cook (Amalia)
Daniel Massey (Georg)
Gino Conforti (Waiter)

SONGS:
Act I
Good Morning, Good Day (Arpad, Sipos,
   Ilona, Kodaly, Georg)
Sounds While Selling (Georg, Sipos, Kodaly,
   customers)
Thank You, Madame (clerks)
Days Gone By (Maraczek)
No More Candy (Amalia)

Three Letters (Amalia, Georg)
Tonight at Eight (Georg)
I Don't Know His Name (Amalia, Ilona)
Perspective (Sipos)
Good-bye, Georg (ensemble)
Will He Like Me? (Amalia)
Ilona (Kodaly, Sipos, Arpad)
I Resolve (Ilona)
A Romantic Atmosphere (Waiter, patrons)
Tango Tragique (Georg)
Dear Friend (Amalia)

Act II
Try Me (Arpad)
Where's My Shoe? (Amalia, Georg)
Ice Cream (Amalia)
She Loves Me (Georg)
A Trip to the Library (Ilona)
Grand Knowing You (Kodaly)
Twelve Days to Christmas (ensemble)

SHELTER (1973)

BOOK AND LYRICS BY: Gretchen Cryer
MUSIC BY: Nancy Ford
PUBLISHED LIBRETTO: French, 1973
CONDENSATION: None
ANTHOLOGY: None
MUSIC PUBLISHER: Belwin-Mills, 1973
LICENSING AGENT: Samuel French
RECORDING: None
CAST: 3 M; 3 F; offstage voices

A television writer and a model meet in a
TV studio and spend the night there. He
prefers the TV sets to his own home, and
through the use of the equipment he can
provide a sky of stars, crickets chirping,
or whatever mood he wants. There is also
a talking computer. This shelter from the
real world is a psychological metaphor and
the themes involved include time and reality. The sets should include a convincing studio with excellent projections for
the required effects. Critics described the
show as an intimate musical with a soft-
rock score.

ORIGINAL CAST:

Marcia Rodd (Maud)
Terry Kiser (Michael)
Tony Wells (Arthur—offstage voice)
Susan Browning (Wednesday)

SONGS:

Act I

Overture (Arthur)
Changing (Maud, Arthur)
Welcome to a New World (Michael, Arthur)
It's Hard to Care (Michael, Arthur, Maud)
Woke Up Today (Maud, Arthur)
Mary Margaret's House in the Country (Maud, Arthur)
Sleep, My Baby, Sleep (Arthur, Michael)
Woman on the Run (Arthur)
Don't Tell Me It's Forever (Maud, Michael, Arthur)

Act II

I Bring Him Seashells (Wednesday)
She's My Girl (Michael, Maud, Arthur)
Comfort (Maud, Michael, Arthur, Wednesday)
Too Many Women in My Life (Michael)
He's a Fool (Wednesday, Maud)
Goin' Home with My Children (Maud, Arthur)

SHENANDOAH (1975)

BOOK BY: James Lee Barrett, Peter Udell, and
 Philip Rose; based on the 1965 film; original
 screenplay by James Lee Barrett
MUSIC BY: Gary Geld
LYRICS BY: Peter Udell
PUBLISHED LIBRETTO: French, 1975
CONDENSATION: None
ANTHOLOGY: None
PIANO-VOCAL SCORE: Morris, 1977
VOCAL SELECTIONS: Morris, 1975 (Hal Leonard)
LICENSING AGENT: Samuel French
RECORDING: RCA 3763-2-RG CD (original cast)
CAST: 11 M; 3 F; children, chorus

Charlie Anderson, a widower with six sons
and a daughter, lives with his family on
a Virginia farm in the Shenandoah Valley.
When the Civil War begins, Charlie does not
let his sons enlist; he believes the war vi-
olates the will of God. Then his youngest
son is kidnapped by Yankee soldiers. This
musical (based on the 1965 film with Jimmy
Stewart) was described as traditional and
old-fashioned. Most critics compared it to
the works of Rodgers and Hammerstein. A
prologue includes a ballet in which the opposing soldiers face each other in a military
drill. The New York sets were described as
semiabstract. The score includes country
tunes, love songs, hymns, and lullabies.

ORIGINAL CAST:

John Cullum (Charlie)
Joseph Shapiro (Boy)
Chip Ford (Gabriel)
Penelope Milford (Jenny)
Donna Theodore (Anne)
Gary Harger (Corporal)
Gordon Halliday (Sam)
Joel Higgins (James)

SONGS:

Act I

Raise the Flag of Dixie (ensemble)
I've Heard It All Before (Charlie)
Pass the Cross to Me (ensemble)
Why Am I Me? (Boy, Gabriel)
Next to Lovin' (I Like Fightin') (sons)
Over the Hill (Jenny)
The Pickers Are Comin' (Charlie)
Next to Lovin' (reprise) (Jenny, sons)
Meditation (Charlie)
We Make a Beautiful Pair (Anne, Jenny)
Violets and Silverbells (Jenny, Sam, ensemble)
It's a Boy (Charlie)

Act II

Freedom (Anne, Gabriel)
Violets and Silverbells (reprise) (James, Anne)
Papa's Gonna Make It Alright (Charlie)
The Only Home I Know (Corporal, soldiers)
Papa's Gonna Make It Alright (reprise) (Jenny)

SHOW BOAT (1927)

BOOK AND LYRICS BY: Oscar Hammerstein II;
based on the novel by Edna Ferber
MUSIC BY: Jerome Kern
PUBLISHED LIBRETTO: None
CONDENSATION: *Ganzl's Book of the Musical
Theatre*. Ganzl, Kurt. Schirmer (Macmillan),
1989
ANTHOLOGY: None
PIANO-VOCAL SCORE: Harms, 1927 (Cherry Lane
Music)
LICENSING AGENT: Rodgers and Hammerstein
Theatre Library
RECORDING: Angel CDS 749108 2 CD (1988 studio
cast)
CAST: 14 M; 19 F; singers, dancers

This world-famous musical begins in Natchez, Mississippi, on the Mississippi River, around 1880. The following scenes include the Chicago World's Fair in 1893, New Year's Eve at the Trocadero in 1905, and back to the showboat in 1927. The plot concerns Magnolia, who sings on the showboat, and her unfortunate marriage to Gaylord Ravenal. This musical has frequently been presented in outdoor summer theaters, usually on a lavish scale. More recently there have been a number of revivals on Broadway and in England. The Lincoln Center production had a showboat that moved out onto the stage! The most recent film version was in 1951 with Howard Keel and Kathryn Grayson.

1983 REVIVAL CAST:

Donald O'Connor (Cap'n Andy)
Ron Raines (Ravenal)
Dale Kristien (Magnolia)
Bruce Hubbard (Joe)
Lonette McKee (Julie)
Karla Burns (Queenie)
Avril Gentles (Parthy)
Paige O'Hara (Ellie)
Paul Keith (Frank)

SONGS:
Act I
Cotton Blossom (ensemble)

Show People Parade and Ballyhoo (Cap'n
Andy, ensemble)
Only Make Believe (Ravenal, Magnolia)
Ol' Man River (Joe, men)
Can't Help Lovin' Dat Man (Julie, Queenie,
Magnolia, Joe, ensemble)
Life upon the Wicked Stage (Ellie, ensemble)
I Might Fall Back on You (Frank, Ellie)
Queenie's Ballyhoo (Queenie, Cap'n Andy,
ensemble)
You Are Love (Magnolia, Ravenal)
Act II
At the Fair (ensemble)
Why Do I Love You? (Magnolia, Ravenal,
Cap'n Andy, Parthy, ensemble)
Bill (Julie)
Good-bye My Lady Love (Frank, Ellie)
After the Ball (Magnolia, ensemble)
Hey, Feller (Queenie, ensemble)

SHOW ME WHERE THE GOOD TIMES ARE (1970)

BOOK BY: Lee Thuna; suggested by *The Imaginary
Invalid* by Moliere
MUSIC BY: Kenneth Jacobson
LYRICS BY: Rhoda Roberts
PUBLISHED LIBRETTO: French, 1970
CONDENSATION: None
ANTHOLOGY: None
VOCAL SELECTIONS: Valando
LICENSING AGENT: Samuel French
RECORDING: None
CAST: 6 M; 4 F; extras

Moliere's play has been transformed into a Jewish musical comedy. It is spring 1913 on New York's Lower East Side. Aaron is the imaginary invalid (reminding many critics of Groucho Marx) and Bella is his scheming wife, anxious for him to die and leave her his fortune. Annette is their daughter who doesn't want to marry the doctor's son. There is a touch of ragtime in the score that evokes the early 1900s and was performed by a seven-piece orchestra in the off-Broadway production. For one number the audience was encouraged to sing along.

The lively choreography and colorful period costumes were noted in the reviews.

ORIGINAL CAST:

Arnold Soboloff (Aaron)
Gloria LeRoy (Rachael)
Neva Small (Annette)
Cathryn Damon (Bella)
John Bennett Perry (Maurice)
Christopher Hewitt (Kolinsky)
Mitchell Jason (Dr. Perlman)
Michael Berkson (Thomas)

SONGS:
Act I
How Do I Feel? (Aaron, Rachael, Annette, Bella)
He's Wonderful (Annette, Rachael)
Look Up (Annette, Rachael, Bella, Maurice, company)
Show Me Where the Good Times Are (Bella, company)
You're My Happiness (Aaron, Bella)
Cafe Royale Ragtime (company)
Staying Alive (Kolinsky, Rachael, company)
One Big Happy Family (Aaron, Maurice, Bella, Annette, Rachael, Kolinsky, Dr. Perlman, Thomas)

Act II
Follow Your Heart (Bella, ladies)
Look Who's Throwing a Party (Aaron, guests)
When Tomorrow Comes (Maurice)
One Big Happy Family (reprise) (Maurice)
The Test (Aaron, Rachael, Kolinsky)
I'm Not Getting Any Younger (Bella, men)
Who'd Believe? (Aaron)

SIDE BY SIDE BY SONDHEIM (1977)

MUSIC AND LYRICS BY: Stephen Sondheim (with additional music by various collaborators); continuity by Ned Sherrin
PUBLISHED LIBRETTO: None
CONDENSATION: None
ANTHOLOGY: None

MUSIC PUBLISHER: *The Hansen Treasury of Stephen Sondheim Songs.* Hansen, 1974
LICENSING AGENT: Music Theatre International
RECORDING: RCA 1851 CD (original cast)
CAST: 2 M; 2 F

This revue was conceived and first presented in Great Britain. It was a great success on Broadway, however, and has been presented in many locations since that time. There is a cast of four—three singers with a "wry narration" and perhaps a song by the fourth. According to director and star Ned Sherrin, "We wanted to explore three propositions. Sondheim as the best lyric writer, . . . the most adventurous composer of musicals, and the most considerable musical dramatist." *Company, Follies,* and *Anyone Can Whistle* are the main sources of material, although such obscure titles as *The Seven Percent Solution* and *Evening Primrose* are included. A simple set with stools and two pianos is all that is required.

ORIGINAL CAST:

David Kernan
Julia McKenzie
Millicent Martin
Ned Sherrin (Narrator)

This revue is made up of thirty-one songs divided into two acts.

SILK STOCKINGS (1955)

BOOK BY: George S. Kaufman, Leueen MacGrath, and Abe Burrows; suggested by *Ninotchka* by Melchior Lengyel
MUSIC AND LYRICS BY: Cole Porter
PUBLISHED LIBRETTO: None
CONDENSATION: *New Complete Book of the American Musical Theater.* Ewen, David. Holt, 1970
ANTHOLOGY: None
VOCAL SELECTIONS: Chappell, 1954
LICENSING AGENT: Tams-Witmark

RECORDING: RCA 1102 CD (original cast)

CAST: Large mixed cast

This 1930s film comedy was updated to the 1950s for a Broadway musical. Three Russian agents are sent to Paris to bring back a leading, and defecting, Soviet composer. When the three agents do not return, Ninotchka is sent to bring them all home. But once in Paris she meets Hollywood agent Canfield and falls in love. There is also a subplot about a Hollywood swimming star making a film version of *War and Peace*. Some of the Cole Porter score has become familiar to all. An off-Broadway production used a simple rotating staircase as the set. There was a film version with Fred Astaire in 1957.

ORIGINAL CAST:

Henry Lascoe (Ivanov)

Leon Belasco (Brankov)

David Opatoshu (Bibinski)

Don Ameche (Canfield)

Hildegarde Neff (Ninotchka)

Gretchen Wyler (Janice)

SONGS:

Act I

Too Bad (Ivanov, Brankov, Bibinski, ensemble)

Paris Loves Lovers (Canfield, Ninotchka)

Stereophonic Sound (Janice)

It's a Chemical Reaction, That's All (Ninotchka)

All of You (Canfield)

Satin and Silk (Janice)

Without Love (Ninotchka)

Act II

Hail, Bibinski (Iranov, Brankov, Bibinski, ensemble)

As on through the Seasons We Sail (Canfield, Ninotchka)

Josephine (Janice, chorus)

Siberia (Ivanov, Brankov, Bibinski)

Silk Stockings (Canfield)

The Red Blues (ensemble)

SIMPLY HEAVENLY (1957)

BOOK AND LYRICS BY: Langston Hughes; based on the "Simple" stories by Langston Hughes

MUSIC BY: David Martin

PUBLISHED LIBRETTO: Dramatists Play Service, 1959

CONDENSATION: None

ANTHOLOGY: *Five Plays by Langston Hughes*. Webster Smalley, ed. Indiana University Press, 1963

VOCAL SELECTIONS: Dramatists Play Service

LICENSING AGENT: Dramatists Play Service

RECORDING: Columbia OL 5240 (original cast)

CAST: 11 M; 8 F

In Harlem, Jess Simple is trying to raise enough money to divorce a wife he doesn't love in order to remarry. The set is two rooms divided by Paddy's Bar. Simple is described as a comical and lovable barroom philosopher with many things to say about the Negro in American life. Langston Hughes presents Harlem and the New York Negro as they really were and as no outsider would see them. This is family entertainment. The score includes blues, calypso, and early rock and roll. The cast album also includes some of Simple's monologues.

ORIGINAL CAST:

Melvin Stewart (Simple)

Marilyn Berry (Joyce)

Anna English (Zarita)

Brownie McGhee (Gitfiddle)

John Bouie (Melon)

Claudia McNeil (Mamie)

SONGS:

Act I

Love Is Simply Heavenly (Joyce)

Let Me Take You for a Ride (Zarita, Simple)

Broken String Blues (Gitfiddle)

Did You Ever Hear the Blues? (Mamie, Melon, ensemble)

I'm Gonna Be John Henry (Simple)

Act II

When I'm in a Quiet Mood (Mamie, Melon)

Look for the Morning Star (Zarita)
Let's Ball Awhile (Zarita, ensemble)
The Men in My Life (Zarita)
I'm a Good Old Girl (Mamie)

SING OUT, SWEET LAND! (1944)

BOOK BY: Walter Kerr
MUSIC COMPOSED AND ARRANGED BY: Ellie
    Siegmeister
PUBLISHED LIBRETTO: Baker, 1949
CONDENSATION: None
ANTHOLOGY: None
LICENSING AGENT: Baker's Plays
RECORDING: AEI 1137 (original cast)
CAST: Large mixed cast

Called a saga of American folk and popular
music, this show starred Alfred Drake and
Burl Ives when the Theatre Guild presented
it on Broadway. Some songs were composed for the show and others are by such
well-known composers as W. C. Handy, but
the majority of the songs are those whose
origins and authors are unknown. There is
a slight plot line about Barnaby Goodlove,
condemned to go through the ages singing
and dancing. The original production had
choreography by Charles Weidman and
Doris Humphrey. The cast can double up
on the parts, and a simple piano could work
as well as a full orchestra.

ORIGINAL CAST:

Alfred Drake (Barnaby)
Bibi Osterwald (Farm Woman/Mrs. Casey
    Jones/Maxie)
Burl Ives (Fiddler/Bonaforte/First Sol-
    dier/Jolly Tramp/Petty Officer)
Adrienne Gray (Farm Girl)
Ted Tiller (Bill/Jack)
Juanita Hall (Watermelon Woman)
Alma Kaye (Mohee/Frankie/Daisy)
Jack McCauley (Johnny/Gentleman Tramp)
Ellen Love (Frankie's Mother)
Christine Karner (Nellie Bly)
Morty Halpern (Old Timer)
James Westerfield (Yard Boss)
Ruth Tyler (Blues Singer)

SONGS:
Act I
Who Is the Man? (ensemble)
As I Was Going Along (Barnaby)
Way Down the Ohio (Barnaby)
When I Was Single (Farm Woman)
Foggy, Foggy Dew (Fiddler)
Hardly Think I Will (Farm Girl, Bill)
The Devil and the Farmer's Wife (Barnaby,
    ensemble)
Little Mohee (Barnaby, Mohee)
Oh Susannah (ensemble)
Springfield Mountain (Barnaby)
Watermelon Cry (Watermelon Woman)
Hammer Ring (ensemble)
You Better Mind (ensemble)
Didn't My Lord Deliver Daniel?
    (ensemble)
The Roaring Gambler (Johnny, Frankie,
    Frankie's Mother)
Louisiana Gals/Camptown Races (ensemble)
Frankie and Johnnie (Bonaforte, Frankie,
    Johnny, Nellie Bly)
Polly Wolly Doodle (ensemble)

Act II
Cap'n Jinks (male ensemble)
Blue Tail Fly (First Soldier)
Marching down the Road (Barnaby, First
    Soldier)
Casey Jones (Mrs. Casey Jones, Yard Boss,
    Old Timer)
Rock Candy Mountain (Jolly Tramp)
I Have Been a Good Boy (Gentleman Tramp)
Wanderin' (Barnaby)
Hallelujah, I'm a Bum (Barnaby)
While Strolling through the Park
    (ensemble)
Bicycle Built for Two (Daisy, Jack)
Heaven Will Protect the Working Girl (Daisy,
    Jack)
Trouble, Trouble (Blues Singer)
Basement Blues/Some of These Men (Blues
    Singer, ensemble)
At Sundown/My Blue Heaven (Barnaby)
Yes Sir, She's My Baby (Maxie)
Sea Chanty (Petty Officer)
Where (Barnaby)
More than These (Barnaby, company)

SINGIN' IN THE RAIN (1985)

SCREENPLAY AND ADAPTION BY: Betty Comden
   and Adolph Green
MUSIC BY: Nacio Herb Brown, others
LYRICS BY: Arthur Freed, others
PUBLISHED LIBRETTO: Viking Press, 1972
   (screenplay)
CONDENSATION: *Ganzl's Book of the Musical
   Theatre*. Ganzl, Kurt. Schirmer (Macmillan),
   1989
ANTHOLOGY: None
VOCAL SELECTIONS: IMP (British), 1983
LICENSING AGENT: Music Theatre International
RECORDING: Safari RAIN 1 (original London cast)
CAST: 4 M; 4 F; chorus

The 1952 classic film musical used actual songs from early sound musicals. Thirty-four years later the property was adapted for the stage and has been popular in London, Budapest, and other cities as well as New York. Your biggest production challenge will be the title number. The licensing agent has several suggestions to help you achieve the rain effect. Production numbers should be as lavish as possible with costumes of the late 1920s. This is a dancing show.

ORIGINAL CAST:

Don Correia (Don)
Peter Slutsker (Cosmo)
Mary D'Arcy (Kathy)

SONGS:
Act I
Fit as a Fiddle (Don, Cosmo)
I've Got a Feelin' You're Foolin' (Kathy, ensemble)
Make 'em Laugh (Cosmo)
Hub Bub (ensemble)
Wedding of the Painted Doll/Sunshowers/Rag Doll/Temptation/Takin' Miss Mary to the Ball/Love Is Where You Find It (ensemble)
You Are My Lucky Star (Don, Kathy)
Moses Supposes (Don, Cosmo)

Act II
Good Mornin' (Don, Kathy, Cosmo)
Singin' in the Rain (Don)
Would You? (Kathy)
Broadway Rhythm (company)
Blue Prelude (company)
You Are My Lucky Star (Don, Kathy, company)

SKYSCRAPER (1965)

BOOK BY: Peter Stone; based on *Dream Girl* by
   Elmer Rice
MUSIC BY: James van Heusen
LYRICS BY: Sammy Cahn
PUBLISHED LIBRETTO: French, 1967
CONDENSATION: *New Complete Book of the
   American Musical Theater*. Ewen, David. Holt,
   1970
ANTHOLOGY: None
VOCAL SELECTIONS: Harms, 1965
LICENSING AGENT: Samuel French
RECORDING: Capitol SVAS 2422 (original cast)
CAST: 11 M; 5 F; chorus

This musical about New York was praised for capturing the personality of the city. The title refers to the building Timothy Bushman would construct if only Georgina Allerton would sell her brownstone. Georgina is dedicated to preserving old New York. Georgina also daydreams, so the show includes her numerous fantasies—cavaliers fighting over her, she as Scarlett O'Hara, and so on. This is a big musical and the fantasies require special costuming. Some of the Michael Kidd dances involve construction workers with jackhammers and a foreman beating out the rhythm on a large oil drum. Another number depicts the typical New York delicatessen during the lunch hour rush. The New York production also included a filmed sequence satirizing Italian movies.

ORIGINAL CAST:

Julie Harris (Georgina)
Peter Marshall (Tim)
Dick O'Neill (Bert)

Rex Everhart (Stanley)
Charles Nelson Reilly (Roger)
Nancy Cushman (Mrs. Allerton)
Lesley Stewart (Charlotte)

SONGS:
Act I
Occasional Flight of Fancy (Georgina, ensemble)
Run for Your Life (Tim, Bert)
Local 403 (Stanley, ensemble)
Opposites (Georgina, Tim)
Run for Your Life (reprise) (Tim)
Just the Crush (Roger, Bert)
Everybody Has a Right to Be Wrong (Georgina, Tim)
Wrong! (Georgina, Mrs. Allerton, Charlotte, ensemble)
The Auction (ensemble)

Act II
The Gaiety (ensemble)
More than One Way (Tim, ensemble)
Don't Worry (Roger, Bert)
I'll Only Miss Her When I Think of Her (Tim)

SMILE (1986)

BOOK BY: Howard Ashman; based on the screenplay by Jerry Belson
MUSIC BY: Marvin Hamlisch
LYRICS BY: Howard Ashman
PUBLISHED LIBRETTO: French
CONDENSATION: None
ANTHOLOGY: None
LICENSING AGENT: Samuel French
RECORDING: None
CAST: 6 M; 7 F; ensemble

A California beauty pageant for high school girls is the setting for this tale of competition and the drive to win among the young. The various contestants all have their stories to tell as the jaded choreographer tries to turn high-school students into Las Vegas show girls. The score is by the composer of *A Chorus Line*, and the lyricist also wrote *Little Shop of Horrors* and *Beauty and the Beast*.

ORIGINAL CAST:
Anne Marie Bobby (Robin)
Marsha Waterbury (Brenda)
Jodi Benson (Doria)
Michael O'Gorman (Tommy)
Jeff McCarthy (Big Bob)
Dick Patterson (Ted)

SONGS:
Act I
Orientation/Postcard #1 (Brenda, Robin, contestants)
Disneyland (Doria)
Shine (Tommy, Brenda, contestants)
Postcard #2 (Robin)
Nerves (contestants)
Young and American (Preliminary Night) (contestants)
Until Tomorrow Night (Brenda, Big Bob, contestants)

Act II
Postcard #3/Dressing Room Scene (Robin, Doria, Ted, contestants)
Smile (Ted, contestants)
In Our Hands (contestants)
Pretty as a Picture (Ted, Big Bob, Robin, contestants)

SMITH (1973)

BOOK BY: Dean Fuller, Tony Hendra, and Matt Dubey
MUSIC AND LYRICS BY: Matt Dubey and Dean Fuller
PUBLISHED LIBRETTO: French, 1972
CONDENSATION: None
ANTHOLOGY: None
LICENSING AGENT: Samuel French
RECORDING: None
CAST: 6 M; 4 F; chorus

This is the story of a man whose life assumes the form of a musical comedy! Smith is a staid young botanist who, after firing a lab assistant, finds a musical-comedy script about his life. This comedy takes him to the South Seas. The New York production included an erupting volcano. The costumes include not only chic New York but grass skirts for the islanders. The action is interrupted by stagehands moving the sets and prompting forgetful actors. Some critics felt that this was all a satire on the big musicals of the 1950s.

ORIGINAL CAST:

Mort Marshall (Baggett)
Don Murray (Smith)
Carol Morley (Mrs. Smith)
Bonnie Walker (Melody)
Michael Tartel (Jacques)
Louis Criscuolo (Ralph)
Don Prieur (Herbie)
David Vosburgh (Bruce)
William James (Ernie)
Ted Thurston (Firestone)

SONGS:
Act I
Boy Meets Girl (ensemble)
There's a Big Job Waiting for You (Baggett, ensemble) Reprise (Mrs. Smith)
To the Ends of the Earth (Melody, ensemble)
Balinasia (ensemble)
Onh-Honh-Honh! (Jacques)
Police Song (men)
You Need a Song (Ralph, Smith, Herhie, Bruce, Ernie)
How Beautiful It Was (Melody, Smith, ensemble)
Island Ritual (ensemble)
People Don't Do That (Smith)

Act II
You're in New York (ensemble)
It Must Be Love (Smith, Melody, ensemble)
Song of the Frog (Firestone, Smith, Baggett)
G'bye (Melody)
Melody (Smith, company)

SNOOPY (1982)

BOOK BY: Charles M. Schulz; based on his comic strip *Peanuts*
MUSIC BY: Larry Grossman
LYRICS BY: Hal Hackady
PUBLISHED LIBRETTO: None

CONDENSATION: None
ANTHOLOGY: None
VOCAL SELECTIONS: Chappell, 1984
LICENSING AGENT: Tams-Witmark
RECORDINGS: DRG 6103 CD (San Francisco cast); Polydor 820-247-2 CD (London cast)
CAST: 5 M; 2 F

After the great success of *You're a Good Man, Charlie Brown* it was decided to develop another musical revue from the *Peanuts* material and concentrate on the dog Snoopy. This new show started out in San Francisco in 1976. After much traveling and changing it finally opened off-Broadway in 1982. The format is merely quick bits and tunes, briskly and simply staged. The dialogue is carefully based on the comic strip. Some of the characters are a bit more cynical than in the earlier show. This will appeal to adults as well as to children.

ORIGINAL CAST:

Terry Kirwin (Charlie Brown)
Stephen Fenning (Linus)
Deborah Graham (Sally)
Kay Cole (Lucy)
Vicki Lewis (Peppermint Patty)
David Garrison (Snoopy)

SONGS:
Act I
The World According to Snoopy (ensemble)
Snoopy's Song (Snoopy, ensemble)
Edgar Allan Poe (Peppermint Patty, Lucy, Sally, Charlie, Linus)
Mother's Day (Snoopy)
I Know Now (Lucy, Sally, Peppermint Patty)
Vigil (Linus)
Clouds (ensemble)
Where Did That Little Dog Go? (Charlie Brown)
Dime a Dozen (Lucy, Peppermint Patty, Sally, Snoopy)
Daisy Hill (Snoopy)

Act II
Bunnies (Snoopy)
The Great Writer (Snoopy)
Poor Sweet Baby (Peppermint Patty)

Don't Be Anything Less than Everything You Can Be (Charlie, Linus, Sally, Peppermint Patty)
The Big Bow-Wow (Snoopy)
Just One Person (ensemble)

SOME ENCHANTED EVENING— THE SONGS OF RODGERS AND HAMMERSTEIN (1983)

CONCEPT BY: Jeffrey B. Moss
MUSIC BY: Richard Rodgers
LYRICS BY: Oscar Hammerstein II
PUBLISHED LIBRETTO: None
CONDENSATION: None
ANTHOLOGY: None
MUSIC PUBLISHER: Williamson
LICENSING AGENT: Rodgers and Hammerstein Theatre Library
RECORDING: None (see individual show recordings)
CAST: 2 M; 3 F

This was originally one of several revues celebrating the Golden Age of Broadway performed at the St. Regis Hotel in New York City. Your cast should be formally attired and present a sophisticated appearance and style. The songs are drawn from *State Fair, Carousel, Oklahoma!, South Pacific,* and other popular shows by the famous songwriter team.

ORIGINAL CAST:

Laurie Beechman
Lisby Larson
Martin Vidnovic
Ernestine Jackson
Russ Thacker

This revue is made up of thirty-four songs and medleys performed in two acts.

SOMETHING'S AFOOT (1976)

BOOK, MUSIC, AND LYRICS BY: James McDonald, David Vos, and Robert Gerlach; additional music by Ed Linderman
PUBLISHED LIBRETTO: French, 1975
CONDENSATION: None

ANTHOLOGY: None
VOCAL SELECTIONS: Hansen, 1976
LICENSING AGENT: Samuel French
RECORDING: None
CAST: 6 M; 4 F

The plot of this musical farce is a tribute to the British "whodunit," particularly the works of Agatha Christie. In an isolated mansion with a missing host, a strange assortment of guests are successively bumped off. A chandelier even falls on one victim! The setting is a country estate in the English Lake District in 1935, and the musical numbers spoof musicals of the thirties. *New York Magazine* described the production as full of "manic movement, scenery-climbing and eyeball rolling" and considered it an audience show. Someone like Tessie O'Shea would be a good choice for the Miss Marple-type character.

ORIGINAL CAST:

Neva Small (Lettie)
Marc Jordan (Flint)
Sel Vitella (Clive)
Barbara Heuman (Hope)
Jack Schmidt (Dr. Grayburn)
Gary Beach (Nigel)
Liz Sheridan (Lady Grace)
Gary Gage (Colonel Gillweather)
Tessie O'Shea (Miss Tweed)
Willard Beckham (Geoffrey)

SONGS:
Act I
A Marvelous Weekend (Miss Tweed, Colonel Gillweather, Dr. Grayburn, Hope, Lady Grace, Nigel, Clive, Flint, Lettie)
Something's Afoot (Miss Tweed, Lettie, Dr. Grayburn, Nigel, ensemble)
Carry On (Miss Tweed, Lady Grace, Lettie, Hope, ensemble)
I Don't Know Why I Trust You (but I Do) (Hope, Geoffrey)
The Man with the Ginger Moustache (Lady Grace)
Suspicious (Miss Tweed, ensemble)

Act II
The Legal Heir (Nigel)
You Fell out of the Sky (Hope)
Dinghy (Flint, Lettie)
I Owe It All (Miss Tweed, Hope, Geoffrey)
New Day (Geoffrey, Hope)

SONG AND DANCE (1985)

MUSIC BY: Andrew Lloyd Webber
LYRICS BY: Don Black
PUBLISHED LIBRETTO: None
CONDENSATION: *Andrew Lloyd Webber, His Life and Work*. Walsh, Michael. Abrams, 1989
ANTHOLOGY: None
PIANO-VOCAL SCORE: Hal Leonard, 1985
VOCAL SELECTIONS: Hal Leonard, 1985
LICENSING AGENT: Rodgers and Hammerstein Theatre Library
RECORDING: Polydor PODV 4 CD (original London cast)
CAST: Tell Me on a Sunday: 1 F; offstage female singers
VARIATIONS: 9 dancers, or as desired

This unusual attraction was presented on Broadway in 1985, but it is the original London version that is offered for license. It is made up of two separate attractions that may be presented individually. Act I is a one-woman musical, entirely sung. Act II is entirely danced, except for one song sung by a chorus late in the act. Act I was originally done on British television under the title *Tell Me on a Sunday* and concerns a British girl living in New York and her romantic adventures and disappointments. Act II, entitled *Variations*, is loosely related to Act I in that it concerns one of the young men in her life. The staging of this attraction should not present a problem, but the singing and dancing roles are most demanding.

ORIGINAL LONDON CAST:
Marti Webb (The Girl)
Wayne Sleep (The Man)

SONGS:
Act I
Tell Me on a Sunday (all sung by the girl)
Take That Look off Your Face
It's Not the End of the World
Letter Home
Sheldon Bloom
Capped Teeth and Caesar Salad
You Made Me Think You Were in Love
Second Letter Home
The Last Man in My Life
Come Back with the Same Look in Your Eyes
Let's Talk about You
Tell Me on a Sunday
I Love New York
Married Man
Third Letter Home
Nothing Like You've Ever Known
Let Me Finish

Act II
Variations (all danced, except for one number)
When You Want to Fall in Love (chorus)

SONG OF NORWAY (1944)

BOOK BY: Milton Lazarus; from a play by Homer Curran
MUSIC BY: Edvard Grieg
LYRICS AND MUSICAL ADAPTION BY: Robert Wright and George Forrest
PUBLISHED LIBRETTO: None
CONDENSATION: *Ganzl's Book of the Musical Theatre*. Ganzl, Kurt. Schirmer (Macmillan), 1989
ANTHOLOGY: None
PIANO-VOCAL SCORE: Chappell, 1951
LICENSING AGENT: Tams-Witmark
RECORDING: TER 2-1173 CD (studio cast)
CAST: Large mixed cast

Based on incidents in the life of Edvard Grieg, the story begins in Troldhaugen on

Midsummer's Eve in 1860. Grieg and his friend Rikard share the dream of making Norway more important in the world of music and literature. But Grieg is attracted to the Countess Louisa, a tempestuous opera star, and follows her to Rome. This lavish musical was presented outdoors at Jones Beach with Viking ships and icebergs, as well as by the New York City Opera with choreography by Eliot Feld. The musical score, not an easy one to sing, includes the popular "Strange Music." There are dancing villagers in folk costumes and a Peer Gynt ballet. This family show was filmed in 1970.

ORIGINAL CAST:

Robert Shafer (Rikard)
Helena Bliss (Nina)
Lawrence Brooks (Edvard)
Irra Petina (Louisa)
Walter Kingsford (Father Grieg)
Frederic Franklin (Freddy)
Ivy Scott (Mother Grieg)
Sig Arno (Peppi)

SONGS:
Act I
The Legend (Rikard)
Hill of Dreams (Nina, Edvard, Rikard)
Freddy and His Fiddle (Freddy, ensemble)
Now (Louisa, ensemble)
Strange Music (Edvard, Nina)
Midsummer's Eve (Rikard, Louisa)
March of the Trolgers (Nina, Louisa, Edvard, ensemble)
Hymn of Betrothal (Mother Grieg, Rikard, ensemble)

Act II
Bon Vivant (Peppi, Edvard, ensemble)
Three Loves (Louisa, Edvard)
Waltz Eternal (ensemble)
Peer Gynt Ballet (Louisa, ensemble)
I Love You (Nina)
At Christmastime (Father Grieg, Mother Grieg, Nina, ensemble)
Reminiscence (Edvard, Nina)

SONG OF SINGAPORE (1991)

BOOK BY: Allan Katz, Erik Frandsen, Robert Hipkens, Michael Garin, and Paula Lockheart
MUSIC AND LYRICS BY: Erik Frandsen, Robert Hipkens, Michael Garin, and Paula Lockheart
PUBLISHED LIBRETTO: French, 1992
CONDENSATION: None
ANTHOLOGY: None
LICENSING AGENT: Samuel French
RECORDING: DRG 19003 CD (original cast)
CAST: 8 M; 2 F

Set in Singapore in December 1941, this musical takes place entirely in a nightclub. The melodramatic highjinks, including a murdered customer and stolen jewels, take place as the enemy troops are massing at the border. "The Malayan Melody Makers" are the nightclub band and serve as both the cast and the accompaniment for the show. Rose, the vocalist for the band, suffers from amnesia. Two other characters are "Chah Li," an Oriental lady of mystery, and "Inspector Kurland" of the local constabulary. This property is ideal for dinner theaters; your cafe can serve food and drink and the customers can dance. Your theater should be decorated with paper lanterns, screens, fans, and all the other orientalia you can manage to find. The audience may even be called on to join in a conga line!

ORIGINAL CAST:

Erik Frandsen (Spike)
Michael Garin (Freddy)
Robert Hipkens (Hans)
Donna Murphy (Rose)
Cathy Fox (Chah Li)
Francis Kane (Inspector)

SONGS:
Act I
Song of Singapore (band)
Inexpensive Tango (Spike)
I Miss My Home in Haarlem (Hans)
You Gotta Do What You Gotta Do (Rose)
The Rose of Rangoon (Spike)
Necrology (band)

Sunrise (Rose)
Never Pay Musicians What They're Worth
   (Freddy)
Harbour of Love (Inspector)
I Can't Remember (Rose)
I Want to Get Offa This Island (Inspector,
   band)

Act II
Foolish Geese (Chah Li)
Serve It Up (Rose)
Fly Away Rose (Hans, Freddy, Spike)
I Remember (Rose, band)
Shake, Shake, Shake (Freddy, band)
We're Rich (band)

SOPHISTICATED LADIES (1981)

CONCEPT BY: Donald McKayle
MUSIC AND LYRIC BY: Duke Ellington and others
PUBLISHED LIBRETTO: None
CONDENSATION: *Broadway Musicals Show by Show.*
   Green, Stanley. Hal Leonard Books, 1985
ANTHOLOGY: None
VOCAL SELECTIONS: Belwin, 1981
LICENSING AGENT: Rodgers and Hammerstein
   Theatre Library
RECORDING: RCA 6208-2-RC CD (original cast)
CAST: 4 M; 5 F; chorus

This is a nonstop musical revue with no story, no sketches, and very few lines of dialogue. The New York production was in an art deco design with a lot of neon lights. The orchestra was onstage, steeply terraced behind a space used for the performers. There was a staircase designed to look like piano keys. This is primarily a dance presentation, sung with great style, and danced with galvanizing energy and enthusiasm.

ORIGINAL CAST:

Gregory Hines	Judith Jamison
Phyllis Hyman	Gregg Burge
Mercedes Ellington	Hinton Battle
Terri Klausner	P. J. Benjamin
Priscilla Baskerville	

This revue is made up of thirty-seven songs divided into two acts.

THE SOUND OF MUSIC (1959)

BOOK BY: Howard Lindsay and Russel Crouse;
   suggested by *The Trapp Family Singers* by
   Maria Augusta Trapp
MUSIC BY: Richard Rodgers
LYRICS BY: Oscar Hammerstein II
PUBLISHED LIBRETTO: Random House, 1960
CONDENSATION: *Ganzl's Book of the Musical
   Theatre.* Ganzl, Kurt. Schirmer (Macmillan),
   1989; *Rodgers and Hammerstein.* Mordden,
   Ethan. Abrams, 1992
ANTHOLOGY: None
PIANO-VOCAL SCORE: Williamson, 1960
VOCAL SELECTIONS: Williamson, 1960
LICENSING AGENT: Rodgers and Hammerstein
   Theatre Library
RECORDING: Columbia CK 32601 CD (original cast)
CAST: 9 M (2 boys); 15 F (4 girls); chorus

Set in Austria during the months immediately preceding the outbreak of World War II, this is the story of Maria Rainer, a postulant not ready to take her final vows. She is sent to the home of widower Captain von Trapp as a governess to his seven children. Maria falls in love with Captain von Trapp and they marry as the Nazi menace threatens. Some critics were irritated by the sentimentality of this tale, but that same quality has endeared it to the masses. It has become one of the select giants of the musical stage. Although revivals tend to be lavish, an off-Broadway production proved that the music and the children will carry the most simple production. Many people know all the songs and remember the Julie Andrews 1965 film version.

Tony Award Winner (Best Musical)

ORIGINAL CAST:

Mary Martin (Maria Rainer)
Patricia Neway (Mother Abbess)
Lauri Peters (Liesl)
Brian Davies (Rolf)

Kurt Kasznar (Max)
Theodore Bikel (Captain)
Marion Marlowe (Elsa)

SONGS:
Act I
The Sound of Music (Maria)
Maria (Mother Abbess, sisters)
My Favorite Things (Maria, Mother Abbess)
Do Re Mi (Maria, children)
You Are Sixteen (Liesl, Rolf)
The Lonely Goatherd (Maria, children)
How Can Love Survive? (Elsa, Captain, Max)
The Sound of Music (Maria, Captain,
    children)
So Long, Farewell (children)
Climb Every Mountain (Mother Abbess)

Act II
No Way to Stop It (Captain, Max, Elsa)
Ordinary Couple (Maria, Captain)
Processional (ensemble)
You Are Sixteen (reprise) (Maria, Liesl)
Do Re Mi (reprise) (Maria, Captain, children)
Edelweiss (Captain, Maria, children)
So Long, Farewell (reprise) (Maria, Captain,
    children)

SOUTH PACIFIC (1949)

BOOK BY: Oscar Hammerstein II and Joshua
    Logan; adapted from *Tales of the South Pacific*
    by James A. Michener
MUSIC BY: Richard Rodgers
LYRICS BY: Oscar Hammerstein II
PUBLISHED LIBRETTO: Random House, 1949
ANTHOLOGIES: *Six Plays by Rodgers and
    Hammerstein*. Random House, 1955; Modern
    Library, 1959; *Representative American Plays*.
    7th ed. Arthur H. Quinn, ed. Appleton, 1953
CONDENSATION: *Ganzl's Book of the Musical
    Theatre*. Ganzl, Kurt. Schirmer (Macmillan),
    1989; *Rodgers and Hammerstein*. Mordden,
    Ethan. Abrams, 1992
PIANO-VOCAL SCORE: Williamson, 1949
LICENSING AGENT: Rodgers and Hammerstein
    Theatre Library

RECORDING: Columbia CK 32604 CD (original cast)
CAST: 22 M; 15 F; 2 children; islanders, sailors

Set on a tropical isle during World War
II, the plot revolves around two love affairs that offer a lesson in human toler-
ance and understanding. Nellie Forbush,
the nurse from Arkansas, falls in love
with Emile de Becque, a mature expatriate
French planter. Meanwhile, young Seabee
Lieutenant Joe Cable falls in love with
Liat, a lovely native girl. Nellie traditionally
washes her hair onstage as she sings one of
the many famous songs. *Variety* called this
"one of the great shows of legit history." A
two-piano arrangement is available. There
was a film version in 1958.

Tony Award Winner (Best Musical)

Pulitzer Prize

ORIGINAL CAST:

Mary Martin (Nellie Forbush)
Ezio Pinza (Emile de Becque)
Juanita Hall (Bloody Mary)
Barbara Luna (Ngana)
Michael de Leon (Jerome)
William Tabbert (Joe)
Myron McCormick (Billis)

SONGS:
Act I
Dites-Moi Pourquoi (Ngana, Jerome)
A Cockeyed Optimist (Nellie)
Twin Soliloquies (Nellie, Emile)
Some Enchanted Evening (Emile)
Bloody Mary Is the Girl I Love (ensemble)
There Is Nothing Like a Dame (Billis, men)
Bali Ha'i (Bloody Mary)
I'm Gonna Wash That Man Right Outa My
    Hair (Nellie, nurses)
I'm in Love with a Wonderful Guy (Nellie,
    nurses)
Younger than Springtime (Joe)

Act II
Happy Talk (Bloody Mary, Joe)
You've Got to Be Taught (Joe)
Honey Bun (Nellie, Billis)
This Nearly Was Mine (Emile)
Some Enchanted Evening (reprise) (Nellie)

SPOKESONG or THE COMMON WHEEL (1979)

BOOK AND LYRICS BY: Stewart Parker
MUSIC BY: Jimmy Kennedy
PUBLISHED LIBRETTO: French, 1980
CONDENSATION: None
ANTHOLOGY: None
VOCAL SELECTIONS: None (some new songs
    included in published libretto)
LICENSING AGENT: Samuel French
RECORDING: None
CAST: 4 M; 2 F

This musical is set in and around a bicycle shop in Belfast, Northern Ireland. The shop is used as a metaphor to point out the problems of Northern Ireland and, in fact, of modern civilization. This folk comedy is really a play with songs, rather than a musical. The off-Broadway production featured a one-man band and fine cycling by the entire cast. In addition to the new songs, "A Bicycle Built for Two" is also used. The other numbers were described as music-hall types. The "loose-jointed" form of this show includes flashbacks to the hero's grandparents and a mustached man on a unicycle who rides in and out while singing and commenting on the action.

ORIGINAL CAST:

Joseph Maher (Trick Cyclist)
John Lithgow (Frank)
Virginia Vestoff (Daisy)
Josef Sommer (Francis)
Maria Tucci (Kitty)
John Horton (Julian)

SONGS:

Act I
A Bicycle Built for Two (Trick Cyclist, cast)
Daisy Bell (Frank)
The Parlour Song (Francis)
Cocktail Song (Trick Cyclist)
Cowboy Song (Trick Cyclist)

Act II
Music-Hall Song (Trick Cyclist, Frank)
Spokesong (Trick Cyclist)

Army Song (Trick Cyclist)
The Maiden with Her Wheel (Frank)
The Anthem (Kitty, Francis, Daisy)

STARLIGHT EXPRESS (1987)

MUSIC BY: Andrew Lloyd Webber
LYRICS BY: Richard Stilgoe
PUBLISHED LIBRETTO: None
CONDENSATION: *Ganzl's Book of the Musical
    Theatre.* Ganzl, Kurt. Schirmer (Macmillan),
    1989
ANTHOLOGY: None
VOCAL SELECTIONS: Hal Leonard, 198–
LICENSING AGENT: Not yet available; contact
    Music Theatre International
RECORDING: Polydor 821 597 2 CD (original
    London cast)
CAST: Large mixed cast

Set in the sci-fi future, the plot of this musical concerns a great train race to determine the fastest locomotive in the world. The various trains are portrayed by humans, with such names as "Rusty" (a steam train), "Electra" (an electric train), and "Greaseball" (a diesel). The set is high tech, costumes are robotic, and the music has a rock beat. The unusual feature of this musical is that the cast is on roller skates. In the London production they skated all around the audience, but in New York they kept the skating to the stage and around the orchestra pit. This is a very popular show with youngsters and should be as elaborate as you can manage.

ORIGINAL CAST:

Richard Torti (Greaseball)
Greg Mowry (Rusty)
Reva Rice (Pearl)
Jane Krakowski (Dinah)
Andrea McArdle (Ashley)
Jamie Beth Chandler (Buffy)
Janet Williams Adderley (Belle)
Ken Ard (Electra)
Joey McKneely (Krupp)

Christina Youngman (Wrench)
Nicole Picard (Joule)
Mary Ann Lamb (Volta)
Michael-Demby Cain (Purse)
Michael Berglund (Weltschaft)
William Christopher Frey (Turnov)
Barry K. Bernal (Red Caboose)
Steve Fowler (Poppa)
A. A. Ciulla (Bobo)

SONGS:
Act I
Rolling Stock (Greaseball, gang)
Engine of Love (Rusty, Pearl, Dinah, Ashley, Buffy)
Lotta Locomotion (Dinah, Ashley, Buffy, Rusty)
Freight (company)
AC/DC (Electra, Krupp, Wrench, Joule, Volta, Purse, company)
Pumping Iron (Greaseball, Pearl, Ashley, Dinah, Buffy, Joule, Volta, Wrench)
Make Up My Heart (Pearl)
Race One (Greaseball, Dinah, Weltschaft, Turnov, Red Caboose, ensemble)
There's Me (Red Caboose, Dinah)
Poppa's Blues (Poppa, ensemble)
Belle (Belle, Poppa, ensemble)
Race Two (Bobo, Buffy, ensemble)
Laughing Stock (company)
Starlight Express (Rusty)

Act II
Silver Dollar (company)
U.N.C.O.U.P.L.E.D. (Dinah, Ashley, Buffy)
Rolling Stock (reprise) (Dinah, Ashley, Buffy)
Wide Smile, High Style, That's Me (Red Caboose, Electra, Krupp, ensemble)
First Final (Greaseball, Pearl, ensemble)
Right Place, Right Time (ensemble)
I Am the Starlight (Rusty, Poppa)
Final Selection (Rusty, Dinah, Greaseball, ensemble)
Only You (Pearl, Rusty)
Chase (company)
One Rock and Roll Too Many (Greaseball, Electra, Red Caboose)
Light at the End of the Tunnel (company)

STARMITES (1989)

BOOK BY: Stuart Ross and Barry Keating
MUSIC AND LYRICS BY: Barry Keating
PUBLISHED LIBRETTO: French, 1990
CONDENSATION: None
ANTHOLOGY: None
LICENSING AGENT: Samuel French
RECORDING: None
CAST: 7 M; 7 F

A gawky teenage girl who loves her comic books becomes, in her fantasy world, Milady, Queen of Inner Space. In her attempt to save Inner Space and Earth from the villain "Shak Graa," she comes up against Diva and a quartet of banshees. This sci-fi rock musical has numerous galactic confrontations featuring zappings (with powder flashes), lightnings, fake steam, and electronic sound effects. The sets were described as colorful, imaginative, and simple. The costumes evoked comic-book characters.

ORIGINAL CAST:

Liz Larson (Eleanor/Bizarbara)
Sharon McNight (Mother/Diva)
Ariel Grabber (Shak Graa)
Brian Lane Green (Spacepunk)
Gabriel Barre (Trinkulus)

SONGS:
Act I
Superhero Girl (Eleanor)
Starmites (Spacepunk, ensemble)
Trink's Narration (Trinkulus, ensemble)
Afraid of the Dark (Spacepunk, Eleanor, Trinkulus, ensemble)
Little Hero (Eleanor)
Attack of the Banshees (ensemble)
Hard to Be a Diva (Diva, ensemble)
Love Duet (Spacepunk, Eleanor)
The Dance of Spousal Arousal (Bizarbara, ensemble)
Finaletto (company)

Act II
Bizarbara's Wedding (Bizarbara, ensemble)
Milady (Spacepunk, ensemble)

Beauty Within (Diva, Bizarbara)
The Cruelty Stomp (Trinkulus, ensemble)
Reach Right Down (Diva, ensemble)
Immolation (Eleanor, Shak Graa, Spacepunk)

STARTING HERE, STARTING NOW (1977)

LYRICS BY: Richard Maltby, Jr.
MUSIC BY: David Shire
PUBLISHED LIBRETTO: None
CONDENSATION: None
ANTHOLOGY: None
VOCAL SELECTIONS: Fiddleback Music, 1978
LICENSING AGENT: Music Theatre International
RECORDING: RCA 2360-2-RG CD (original cast)
CAST: 1 M; 2 F (some productions have enlarged casts)

Presented off-Broadway in a theater-restaurant, this is a cabaret revue of songs composed by Maltby and Shire. One cast member described it as a show about how people cope with life. A critic thought it was about love, lost and found. In any case, it has no plot or dialogue but consists of twenty-five numbers done as solos, duets, and big production numbers. Some numbers were written for this show, but others were written earlier. Barbra Streisand sang the title song on her TV special "Color Me Barbra." Musical support can be a piano and a bass (sometimes switching to a guitar).

ORIGINAL CAST:

Loni Ackerman   Margery Cohen
George Lee Andrews

This revue is made up of twenty-five songs divided into two acts.

STOP THE WORLD—I WANT TO GET OFF (1962)

BOOK, MUSIC, AND LYRICS BY: Leslie Bricusse and Anthony Newley
PUBLISHED LIBRETTO: None

CONDENSATIONS: *The Best Plays of 1962–1963.* Henry Hewes, ed. Dodd, Mead, 1963; *Ganzl's Book of the Musical Theatre.* Ganzl, Kurt. Schirmer (Macmillan), 1989
ANTHOLOGY: None
VOCAL SELECTIONS: Ludlow Music, 1961; *The Songs of Leslie Bricusse.* Chappell, 1976
LICENSING AGENT: Tams-Witmark
RECORDING: Polydor 820 261-2 CD (original cast)
CAST: 1 M; 10 F; 2 boys

This musical combines British music-hall style with commedia dell'arte as it uses clown-show acts to tell the story of Littlechap. He is the only male in the cast (except for the children) and the women in his life are all played by the same female. The chorus is composed of assorted beautiful girls. There are three popular songs from the score. In the original production the costumes were leotards and clown outfits, although a Sammy Davis revival featured more conventional street wear. An off-Broadway production was noted for its elegant and effective set, a raised ring in the center of the stage that provided focus for the implied circus atmosphere. The original production employed a great deal of pantomime in the style of Marcel Marceau. A 1966 film version preserved the original costumes and style of this show. This show was revived in 1989 in London with Anthony Newley.

ORIGINAL CAST:

Anthony Newley (Littlechap)
Anna Quayle (Women in Littlechap's life)
Jennifer Baker (Daughter)
Susan Baker (Daughter)

SONGS:
Act I
The A. B. C. Song (ensemble)
I Wanna Be Rich (Littlechap)
Typically English (Woman)
A Special Announcement (Littlechap)
I've Been Lumbered (Littlechap)
Welcome to Sludgepool (ensemble)
Gonna Build a Mountain (Littlechap)
Glorious Russian (Woman)

Meilinki Meilchick (Littlechap, woman)
Family Fugue (Littlechap, Woman, Daughters)
Typically Deutsche (Woman)
Nag! Nag! Nag! (ensemble)

Act II
All American (Woman)
Once in a Lifetime (Littlechap)
Mumbo Jumbo (Littlechap)
Welcome to Sunvale (ensemble)
Someone Nice Like You (Littlechap, Woman)
What Kind of Fool Am I? (Littlechap)

STREET DREAMS (1972)

(performed on Broadway as *Inner City*)

BASED ON THE BOOK: *The Inner City Mother Goose*
    by Eve Merriam
MUSIC BY: Helen Miller
LYRICS BY: Eve Merriam
PUBLISHED LIBRETTO: None
CONDENSATION: None
ANTHOLOGY: None
LICENSING AGENT: Samuel French
RECORDING: RCA LSO 1171 (original cast as *Inner
    City*)
CAST: 4 M; 5 F

Members of the small cast play a wide variety of roles—all types that would be found in an inner-city ghetto. This cynical revue has almost no dialogue and is billed as a "street cantata" with no overall plot. The show is about such subjects as muggers, corrupt cops, garbage disposal, overpopulation, and prostitution. Some critics were taken with the setting—a pyramid of gorgeous junk: bedsprings, car mufflers, garbage cans, stove pipes, and so on. The rock musical score should be performed with great spirit and liveliness by an integrated company.

ORIGINAL CAST:

Joy Garrett   Carl Hall
Delores Hall   Fluffer Hirsch
Linda Hopkins   Paulette Ellen Jones
Larry Marshall   Allan Nicholls
Florence Tarlow

SONGS:
Act I
Fee Fi Fo Fum (Hopkins)
Now I Lay Me (C. Hall, D. Hall, Nicholls)
Hushabye Baby/My Mother Said (Jones)
Ding Dong Bell (C. Hall, cast)
The Nub of the Nation (cast)
Mary, Mary (cast)
City Life (Tarlow)
One Misty Moisty Morning (Marshall)
If Wishes Were Horses (D. Hall)
One Man/Deep in the Night (Hopkins)
Christmas Is Coming (Hirsch)
Jeremiah Obadiah (Marshall)
Riddle Song (cast)
Shadow of the Sun (cast)

Act II
Boys and Girls Come out to Play (cast)
Lucy Locket (Hirsch)
Wisdom (Marshall)
The Hooker (Garrett)
Law and Order (D. Hall, cast)
Kindness (Nicholls, cast)
As I Went Over (Nicholls)
There Was a Little Man (cast)
Who Killed Nobody (cast)
It's My Belief (Hopkins)
Street Sermon (C. Hall)
The Great If (C. Hall, cast)
On This Rock (cast)

STREET SCENE (1947)

BOOK BY: Elmer Rice; based on his Pulitzer
    Prize-winning play
MUSIC BY: Kurt Weill
LYRICS BY: Langston Hughes
PUBLISHED LIBRETTO: None
CONDENSATION: *New Complete Book of the
    American Musical Theater*. Ewen, David. Holt,
    1970
ANTHOLOGY: None
PIANO-VOCAL SCORE: Chappell, 1948
LICENSING AGENT: Rodgers and Hammerstein
    Theatre Library
RECORDING: CBS MK 44668 CD (original cast)
CAST: 18 M; 15 F; extras

The romantic tragedy of urban alienation was turned into an American opera by Kurt Weill in 1947. The single setting is a tenement street in New York City. The plot follows both the murder of an adulterous woman and her lover and the romance of her daughter with a young Jewish intellectual. Originally done on Broadway, this was later done by the New York City Opera and was telecast in 1979. The challenging score contains some American jazz phrases.

ORIGINAL CAST:

Polyna Stoska (Anna Maurrant)
Norman Cordon (Frank Maurrant)
Anne Jeffreys (Rose Maurrant)
Brian Sullivan (Sam Kaplan)
Creighton Thompson (Henry Davis)
Don Saxon (Harry Easter)

SONGS:
Act I
Ain't It Awful the Heat (ensemble)
I Got a Marble and a Star (Henry Davis)
Get a Load of That (women)
When a Woman Has a Baby (Anna Maurrant, women)
Somehow I Never Could Believe (Anna Maurrant)
Wrapped in a Ribbon and Tied with a Bow (young girls)
Lonely House (Sam Kaplan)
Wouldn't You Like to Be on Broadway? (Harry Easter)
What Good Would the Moon Be? (Rose Maurrant)
Remember That I Care (Sam Kaplan, Rose Maurrant)

Act II
Catch Me If You Can (children)
A Boy Like You (Anna Maurrant)
We'll Go Away Together (Sam Kaplan, Rose Maurrant)
The Woman Who Lived up There (ensemble)
Lullaby (nursemaids)
I Loved Her Too (Frank Maurrant, Rose Maurrant, ensemble)
Don't Forget the Lilac Bush (Sam Kaplan, Anna Maurrant)

THE STREETS OF NEW YORK (1963)

BOOK AND LYRICS BY: Barry Alan Grael; based on the play by Dion Boucicault
MUSIC BY: Richard B. Chodosh
PUBLISHED LIBRETTO: French, 1965
CONDENSATION: None
ANTHOLOGY: None
LICENSING AGENT: Samuel French
RECORDING: None
CAST: 8 M; 6 F; chorus

Based on a "hearts-and-flowers" nineteenth-century play, this musical is set in New York City around 1880 and is about a hard-hearted banker and his scheming daughter. She wants to marry a young aristocrat whose fortune has been stolen by the banker. The off-Broadway production was noted for its handsome production, colorful costumes, and the excellent voices of the entire cast. The scenery was described as simple and smart. The score contains a hint of Gilbert and Sullivan, as well as a Mexican ballad, Christmas carols, and madrigals. This is a family musical melodrama of incorruptible virtue and "hissable" villainy. A two-piano accompaniment is used.

ORIGINAL CAST:

Ralston Hill (Bloodgood)
Ian Brown (Fairweather)
Barry Alan Grael (Badger)
Don Phelps (Puffy)
Barbara Williams (Alida)
Gail Johnston (Lucy)
Joan Kroschell (Bridget)
Ann Clements (Kathleen)
Nina Miller (Moira)
David Cryer (Mark)
Margot Hand (Mrs. Fairweather)
Janet Raymond (Mrs. Puffy)
Fred Cline (Edwards)

SONGS:
Act I
Prologue (Bloodgood, Badger, Fairweather, ensemble)

Tourist Madrigal (Bloodgood, Puffy,
ensemble)
He'll Come to Me Crawling (Alida)
If I May (Lucy, Bridget, Kathleen, Moira)
Reprise (Mark)
Aren't You Warm? (Lucy, Mark, Mrs.
Fairweather)
Where Can the Rich and Poor Be Friends?
(Mrs. Fairweather, Puffy, Mrs. Puffy, Mark,
Lucy, Bloodgood, ensemble)
California (Badger, Bloodgood, ensemble)

Act II

Christmas Carol (Puffy, Mrs. Puffy, Mark,
Badger, Bloodgood, ensemble)
Laugh after Laugh (Alida, ensemble)
Arms for the Love of Me (Lucy)
Close Your Eyes (Lucy, Mrs. Fairweather,
Badger)
Love Wins Again (Lucy, Mark)

STRIDER (1979)

BOOK BY: Mark Rozovsky; adapted from a story
by Leo Tolstoy; English stage version by Robert
Kalfin and Steve Brown
MUSIC BY: M. Rosovsky and S. Vetkin
PUBLISHED LIBRETTO: French, 1981
CONDENSATION: None
ANTHOLOGY: None
VOCAL SELECTIONS: Schirmer, 1980
LICENSING AGENT: Samuel French
RECORDING: None
CAST: 12 M; 7 F; 4 musicians (some doubling)

Tolstoy's allegory of a century ago has
been musicalized. It is the story of a beaten
and abused horse who, like the Russian
peasant he represents, is indefatigable.
There are two challenges in the staging of
this show. The first challenge is that the actors must portray horses—nuzzle, twitch
tails, and whinny through skillful use of
mime. The title role is a real challenge.
The second challenge is locating a small
onstage gypsy ensemble to provide atmosphere and accompaniment for the songs
and lively folk dances. There are people in
the story, including the prince who owns

Strider and the ballerina he loves. A number of critics mentioned that while this is
an unusual attraction, children will love it.

ORIGINAL CAST:

Gerald Hiken (Strider)
Gordon Gould (Serpuhofsky)
Pamela Burrell (Viazapurikha)
Benjamin Hendrickson (Bobrinsky)

SONGS:
(unlisted in program)
Oh, Mortal
Song of the Herd
Duet (Warm and Tender)
Darling, Romance
Serpuhofsky's Song
Troika
Serpuhofsky's Romance
Live Long Enough

STRIKE UP THE BAND (1927)

BOOK BY: George S. Kaufman
MUSIC BY: George Gershwin
LYRICS BY: Ira Gershwin
PUBLISHED LIBRETTO: None
CONDENSATION: *New Complete Book of the
American Musical Theater.* Ewen, David. Holt,
1970
ANTHOLOGY: None
PIANO-VOCAL SCORE: New World Music, 1930
VOCAL SELECTIONS: Warner Bros. Music, 1984
LICENSING AGENT: Music Theatre International
(1927 version)
RECORDING: Elektra Nonesuch 79273-2 CD (1991
studio cast)
CAST: 7 M; 3 F; chorus

The satiric plot of this musical concerns
a war between the U.S. and Switzer-
land over cheese. It offers sharp crit-
icism of the relationships between big
business and government and of the
public's susceptibility to war fever. The
U.S. eventually entraps the Swiss army
with a yodeling trick! The absurdist book
was considered too strong for Broad-

way, and a highly revised version finally opened in 1930. The American Musical Theatre Festival in Philadelphia successfully revived this original 1927 version in 1984. This is available for concert performance, as well as in a fully staged version.

ORIGINAL CAST:

Max Hoffman, Jr. (Timothy)
Robert Bentley (Sloane)
Herbert Corthell (Fletcher)
Dorothea James (Anne)
Roger Pryor (Jim)
Vivian Hart (Joan)
Edna Mae Oliver (Mrs. Draper)
Jimmy Savo (Spelvin)
Lew Hearn (Holmes)

SONGS:
(1927 version)
Act I

Fletcher's American Cheese Choral Society (Timothy, Sloane, Fletcher, chorus)
17 and 21 (Timothy, Anne)
Typical Self-Made American (Fletcher, Jim, men)
Meadow Serenade (Jim, Joan)
Unofficial Spokesman (Fletcher, Holmes, chorus)
Patriotic Rally (chorus)
The Man I Love (Joan, Jim)
Yankee Doodle Rhythm (Spelvin, chorus)
Strike Up the Band (Timothy, chorus)

Act II

Oh This Is Such a Lovely War (ensemble)
Hoping That Someday You'd Care (Jim, Joan)
Military Dancing Drill (Timothy, Anne, chorus)
How about a Man? (Mrs. Draper, Holmes, Fletcher)
Homeward Bound (men)

SONGS:
(from the 1930 version)
I Mean to Say (Anne, Timothy)
Soon (Jim, Joan)
If I Became the President (Mrs. Draper, Holmes)
Hangin' around with You (Anne, Timothy)

Mademoiselle in New Rochelle (Holmes, Gideon, girls)
I've Got a Crush on You (Timothy, Anne)

THE STUDENT GYPSY, OR THE PRINCE OF LIEDERKRANZ (1963)

BOOK, MUSIC, AND LYRICS BY: Rick Besoyan
PUBLISHED LIBRETTO: None
CONDENSATION: None
ANTHOLOGY: None
VOCAL SELECTIONS: Valando
LICENSING AGENT: Samuel French
RECORDING: None
CAST: Large mixed cast

Described by the critic of *Variety* as "a large, ornate imitation antique," this is a spoof of the light operas of the 1920s. The wildly convoluted plot is meant to be ridiculous; it concerns the adopted daughter of the monarch of a mythical kingdom and a prince disguised as a soldier. In this never-never land the "painted trees should look like painted trees" and bright-eyed maidens dance "in their beruffled and beflowered peasant dresses." There are the soldiers, the gypsies, and the royal court to be costumed, as well. The musical score is richly melodic, with amusing love songs, drinking songs, bell songs (the cast should include a bell ringer), and a "seventh heaven waltz." A full orchestra or two pianos can be used.

ORIGINAL CAST:

Allen Swift (Papa Johann)
Eileen Brennan (Merry May)
Don Stewart (Rudolph)
Dom DeLuise (Muffin)
Shannon Bolin (Zampa)
Dick Hoh (Blunderbuss)
Mitzi Welch (Ginger)
Bill Fletcher (Gryphon)
Edward Miller (Humperdinck)
Donald Babcock (Osgood)

SONGS:

Act I

Welcome Home Anthem (girls)

Singspielia (Papa Johann, girls)

Romance (Merry May, girls)

Somewhere (Rudolph)

It's a Wonderful Day to Do Nothing (Muffin)

The Gypsy Life (Zampa, Muffin, Merry May)

The Grenadiers' Marching Song (Blunderbuss, men)

Greetings (men)

Kiss Me (ensemble)

Ting-a-Ling-Dearie (Ginger, Blunderbuss)

Merry May (Muffin, Merry May)

Seventh Heaven Waltz (Merry May, Rudolph)

A Gypsy Dance (Zampa, Muffin, Gryphon)

The Gypsy Violin and I (Zampa, men)

Hail to the Lad (all)

Act II

A Whistle Works (Humperdinck)

Wake Up Singing (Blunderbuss, men)

Gypsy of Love (Rudolph)

Our Love Has Flown Away (Merry May)

A Woman Is a Woman Is a Woman (Blunderbuss, Rudolph, Muffin)

Schtine, Schtine (Sleep, Sleep) (Papa Johann, Osgood)

Very Much in Love (Ginger, girls)

My Love Is Yours (Rudolph, Merry May)

There's Life in the Old Folks Yet (Papa Johann, Zampa, Osgood)

The Drinking Song (Merry May, Muffin, Ginger, Blunderbuss)

Walk On! (Zampa)

THE STUDENT PRINCE (1924)

BOOK AND LYRICS BY: Dorothy Donnelly; based on the play *Old Heidelberg* by Wilhelm Meyer-Forster

MUSIC BY: Sigmund Romberg

PUBLISHED LIBRETTO: None

CONDENSATION: *Ganzl's Book of the Musical Theatre*. Ganzl, Kurt. Schirmer (Macmillan), 1989

ANTHOLOGY: None

PIANO-VOCAL SCORE: Chappell, 1932; Harms, 1932

VOCAL SELECTIONS: *The Music of Sigmund Romberg*. Warner Bros. Music, 1977

LICENSING AGENT: Tams-Witmark

RECORDING: TER 1005 CD (1991 studio cast)

CAST: Large mixed cast

This musical romance set in 1860 relates the sentimental story of the love of a prince for a waitress at a students' inn. Unfortunately, duty calls and he gives her up in favor of a wedding with a princess from a neighboring country. It's not possible to modernize a story like this one, so the production must have the colorful peasant costumes, the student drinking songs, and the schmaltz. The required settings are the garden of the Inn of the Three Golden Apples, the prince's sitting room at the inn, and a state room at the royal palace. There have been several film versions, including one in 1954 with the voice of Mario Lanza. A perennial favorite, this show was performed in 1993 by the New York City Opera.

ORIGINAL CAST:

Howard Marsh (Prince)

Greek Evans (Engel)

Raymond Marlowe (Detleff)

Ilsa Marvenga (Kathie)

Roberta Beatty (Princess)

John Coast (Tarnitz)

Charles Williams (Hubert)

Violet Carson (Gretchen)

SONGS:

Act I

Golden Days (Prince, Engel)

Garlands Bright (girls)

To the Inn We're Marching (students)

Drinking Song (Detleff, students)

Come Boys (Kathie, chorus)

Heidelberg Fair (Kathie, Prince, Engel, girls)

Deep in My Heart, Dear (Kathie, Prince)

Serenade (Prince, chorus)

Act II

Student Life (Prince, Kathie, students)

Parting Scene (Prince, Kathie, Engel)

By Our Bearings So Sedate (ensemble)

Just We Two (Princess, Tarnitz, male chorus)
Vision Scene (Prince)
I Like You More and More (Hubert, Gretchen)
Do You Love Me? (Prince)

SUGAR (1972)

BOOK BY: Peter Stone; based on the screenplay
   Some Like It Hot by Billy Wilder and I. A. L.
   Diamond; from a story by Robert Thoeren
MUSIC BY: Jule Styne
LYRICS BY: Bob Merrill
PUBLISHED LIBRETTO: None
CONDENSATION: *Broadway Musicals Show by Show*.
   Green, Stanley. Hal Leonard Books, 1985
ANTHOLOGY: None
LICENSING AGENT: Tams-Witmark
RECORDINGS: United Artists UAS 9905 (original
   cast); First Night Cast CD 28 (1992 London
   version entitled *Some Like It Hot*)
CAST: Large mixed cast

This story begins in Chicago in 1931 as a couple of musicians witness the St. Valentine's Day massacre. In their efforts to escape being rubbed out themselves, they masquerade as women and join a women's orchestra traveling to Florida. There's a lot of humor in this "theatrical drag" show. Other major roles are Sugar (the band's singer), Sweet Sue (the bandleader), a naughty old millionaire, and a tap-dancing gangster. This is an old-style Broadway musical staged and choreographed by Gower Champion. It was recently revived in London under the title *Some Like It Hot*. If done with good taste, this is plain popular theater with lots of laughs.

ORIGINAL CAST:

Sheila Smith (Sweet Sue)
Tony Roberts (Joe)
Robert Morse (Jerry)
Steve Condos (Spats)
Elaine Joyce (Sugar)
Alan Kass (Bienstock)
Cyril Ritchard (Osgood)

SONGS:
Act I
Windy City Marmalade (Sweet Sue, band)
Penniless Bums (Jerry, Joe, ensemble)
Tear the Town Apart (Spats, ensemble)
The Beauty That Drives Men Mad (Jerry, Joe)
We Could Be Close (Jerry, Sugar)
Sun on My Face (Jerry, Joe, Sugar, Sweet Sue,
   Bienstock, ensemble)
November Song (Osgood, ensemble)
Sugar (Jerry, Joe)

Act II
Hey, Why Not! (Sugar, ensemble)
Beautiful Through and Through (Osgood,
   Jerry)
What Do You Give to a Man Who's Had
   Everything? (Joe, Sugar)
Magic Nights (Jerry)
It's Always Love (Joe)
When You Meet a Man in Chicago (Jerry, Joe,
   Sugar, Sweet Sue, ensemble)

SUGAR BABIES (1979)

BOOK BY: Ralph G. Allen; based on traditional
   burlesque material
MUSIC BY: Jimmy McHugh
LYRICS BY: Dorothy Fields and Al Dubin
PUBLISHED LIBRETTO: French
CONDENSATION: *Broadway Musicals Show by Show*.
   Green, Stanley. Hal Leonard Books, 1985
ANTHOLOGY: None
VOCAL SELECTIONS: Jimmy McHugh Music
LICENSING AGENT: Samuel French
RECORDING: IBR Classics CD1BR 9012 CD (original
   cast)
CAST: 8 M; 2 F; chorus girls, extras

Described by Julius Novick in the *Village Voice* as "somewhere between recollection and parody," this is a tribute to the burlesque show of yesteryear. There is a great deal of humor in the gags, the pitchman selling postcards down in front of the house, the chorus girls, and the specialty acts. The original New York production featured a hilarious dog act, later replaced by a comic juggler, so its possible to interpolate. The songs are mostly standards. There are affectionate salutes to Sally Rand and her fan dance and other burlesque "greats." There's plenty of corn, risqué one-liners, slapstick, cute chorines, and a patriotic red-white-and-blue finale.

ORIGINAL CAST:

Mickey Rooney	Peter Leeds
Jack Fletcher	Anita Morris
Jimmy Mathews	Scot Stewart
Ann Miller	Sid Stone

SONGS:
Act I
A Good Old Burlesque Show (Rooney, ensemble)
Let Me Be Your Sugar Baby (Leeds, Fletcher, girls)
I Want a Girl (Mathews, Stewart, Leeds, Rooney, Morris, ensemble)
In Louisiana/I Feel a Song Comin' On/Goin' Back to New Orleans (Miller, ensemble)
Sally (Stewart, ensemble)
Immigration Rose (Rooney, quartet)
Don't Blame Me (Miller)
The Sugar Baby Bounce (Anita, ensemble)
Down at the Gaiety Burlesque/Mr. Banjo Man (Miller, Rooney, girls)

Act II
Candy Butcher (Stone, girls)
I'm Keeping Myself Available for You/Exactly Like You (Morris, girls)
Warm and Willing (Morris)
Cuban Love Song (Stewart, ensemble)
Jimmy McHugh Medley (Rooney, Miller)
You Can't Blame Your Uncle Sammy (company)

SUNDAY IN THE PARK WITH GEORGE (1984)

BOOK BY: James Lapine
MUSIC AND LYRICS BY: Stephen Sondheim
PUBLISHED LIBRETTO: Applause Books, 1991; Dodd, Mead, 1986

CONDENSATION: *The Best Plays of 1983–1984*. Otis L. Guernsey, Jr., ed. Dodd, Mead, 1984
ANTHOLOGY: *Famous American Plays of the 1980s*. Robert Marx, ed. Laurel, 1988
PIANO-VOCAL SCORE: Revelation Music, 1984
VOCAL SELECTIONS: Revelation Music, 1987
LICENSING AGENT: Music Theatre International
RECORDING: RCA 5042 CD (original cast)
CAST: 7 M; 8 F (one child)

Act I is set in 1884 on the island of La Grande Jatte just outside Paris as Georges Seurat creates his masterpiece. Act II is one-hundred years later as George (a descendent of Seurat) is unveiling his abstract sculptural object, complete with smoke, lasers, music, and projections. (A laser package to create the Chromolume is available for rental from the licensing agent.) For Act I you must duplicate the painting, "tableaux vivants" fashion, as at the end of the act the work is finished. Act II is both an American art museum and a return to the island, now crowded with modern buildings. The actors in Act I will also appear as modern characters in Act II. A challenging musical score, with no dancing, this musical was done in London at the National Theatre in 1990.

Pulitzer Prize

ORIGINAL CAST:

Mandy Patinkin (George)
Bernadette Peters (Dot/Marie)
Charles Kimbrough (Jules)
Dana Ivey (Yvonne)
Barbara Bryne (Old Lady)
Judith Moore (Nurse)
Brent Spiner (Franz)
Nancy Opel (Frieda)
Cris Groenendaal (Louis)

SONGS:
Act I
Sunday in the Park with George (Dot)
No Life (Jules, Yvonne)
Color and Light (Dot, George)
Gossip (Nurse, Old Lady, Jules, Yvonne, ensemble)

The Day Off (George, Nurse, Franz, Frieda,
   Jules, Louis, ensemble)
Everybody Loves Louis (Dot)
Finishing the Hat (George)
We Do Not Belong Together (Dot, George)
Beautiful (Old Lady, George)
Sunday (company)

Act II
It's Hot up Here (company)
Chromolume #7 (George, Marie)
Putting It Together (George, company)
Move On (George, Dot)

SUNNY (1925)

BOOK AND LYRICS BY: Otto Harbach and Oscar
   Hammerstein II
MUSIC BY: Jerome Kern
PUBLISHED LIBRETTO: None
CONDENSATION: *New Complete Book of the
   American Musical Theater.* Ewen, David. Holt,
   1970
ANTHOLOGY: None
PIANO-VOCAL SCORE: Chappell, 1925, 1934
LICENSING AGENT: Tams-Witmark
RECORDING: Stanyan SR 10035 (1926 London cast)
CAST: Large mixed cast

The settings for this 1920s musical include
a circus in England, aboard the SS *Triumphant,* and finally in Florida. The big
song from the score is "Who?" (which was
done by Judy Garland in a circus setting
in the film *Till the Clouds Roll By*). A group
of American ex-soldiers have been revisit-
ing the French battlefields of World War I.
While in England and on their way home,
they notice that a circus bareback rider is
"Sunny," the little entertainer for their out-
fit in France. She decides to see them off
and ends up as a stowaway. This was originally a lavish production, and in England
it was described as a spectacular revue.
A 1972 Goodspeed Opera revival in Connecticut reproduced *Sunny* without conde-
scension or kidding, with a succession of
songs, and dancing of all varieties from acrobatic to soft-shoe to tap. Marilyn Miller

was the original "Sunny" and starred in a
1930 film version. There was another film
in 1941 with Anna Neagle.

ORIGINAL CAST:
Paul Frawley (Tom)
Marilyn Miller (Sunny)
Mary Hay (Weenie)
Jack Donahue (Jim)
Esther Howard (Sue)
Clifton Webb (Wendell)

SONGS:
Act I
Here We Are Together Tonight (ensemble)
Sunny (Tom, ensemble)
Who? (Sunny, Tom, ensemble)
Let's Say Good Night (Weenie, Jim)
Do You Love Me? (Sunny, ensemble)
The Wedding Knell (Sunny, men)

Act II
We're Gymnastic (Sue, girls)
Two Little Bluebirds (Weenie, Wendell)
I Might Grow Fond of You (Weenie, Wendell)
The Chase (Sunny, Tom, ensemble)

SUSAN B! (1981)

BOOK BY: Jules Tasca
LYRICS BY: Ted Drachman
MUSIC BY: Thomas Tierney
PUBLISHED LIBRETTO: Dramatic
CONDENSATION: None
ANTHOLOGY: None
LICENSING AGENT: Dramatic
RECORDING: None
CAST: 3 M; 3 F

The off-Broadway production of this one-
act musical featured a cast of six in multiple roles (a larger cast can be used) and
recorded music for accompaniment. The
plot concerns Susan B. Anthony and her
fight for women's rights. It is presented
through a series of biographical vignettes
with Horace Greeley as a narrator.

ORIGINAL CAST:

Lillian Byrd (Susan)
Frank Groseclose (Greeley/Daniel)
Julianne Ross (Guelma)
Kathleen McGrath (Lucy/Elizabeth)
Greg Gunning (Aaron/Tasche)
Larry Cahn (Parker)

Musical numbers are not listed in the program.

SWEENEY TODD THE DEMON BARBER OF FLEET STREET (1979)

BOOK BY: Hugh Wheeler; based on a version of
  Sweeney Todd by Christopher Bond
MUSIC AND LYRICS BY: Stephen Sondheim
PUBLISHED LIBRETTO: Dodd, Mead, 1979;
  Applause Books, 1991
CONDENSATION: *The Best Plays of 1978–1979.*
  Otis L. Guernsey, Jr., ed. Dodd, Mead, 1979;
  Ganzl's Book of the Musical Theatre. Ganzl, Kurt.
  Schirmer (Macmillan), 1989
ANTHOLOGY: None
PIANO-VOCAL SCORE: Revelation Music, 1981
VOCAL SELECTIONS: Revelation Music, 1979
LICENSING AGENT: Music Theatre International
RECORDING: RCA 3379-2-RC CD (original cast)
CAST: Large mixed cast (can be reduced)

A cutthroat barber practices above a pie shop supplying it with cheap and easy meat! Todd is an escaped convict who was unjustly sentenced so that the Judge could have Mrs. Todd. He returns to find his wife a suicide and his daughter the ward of the Judge. Victorian London is presented as a plague spot—a dark grotesque underworld. This needs to be awesome, staggering, epic, monumental—a huge factory signifying the Industrial Revolution covers the stage, and center stage becomes the pie shop, a lunatic asylum, the wharf, the basement furnace, the barber shop, and the street. There is no choreography. It is almost completely sung. This is one of the more challenging shows to produce; it is also a challenge vocally. There was a cable telecast in 1982, and a very successful small version was done in New York in 1989.

Tony Award Winner (Best Musical)

ORIGINAL CAST:

Cris Groenendaal (Anthony)
Len Cariou (Sweeney)
Merle Louise (Beggar Woman)
Angela Lansbury (Mrs. Lovett)
Betsy Joslyn (Johanna)
Jen Jennings (Tobias)
Joaquin Romaguera (Pirelli)
Edmund Lyndeck (Judge)
Jack Eric Williams (Beadle)

SONGS:
Act I
The Ballad of Sweeney Todd (company)
No Place Like London (Anthony, Sweeney,
  Beggar Woman)
The Worst Pies in London (Mrs. Lovett)
Poor Thing (Mrs. Lovett, company)
My Friends (Sweeney, Mrs. Lovett)
Green Finch and Linnet Bird (Johanna)
Ah, Miss (Anthony, Johanna, Beggar Woman)
Johanna (Anthony)
Pirelli's Miracle Elixir (Tobias, Sweeney, Mrs.
  Lovett, company)
The Contest (Pirelli)
Johanna (reprise) (Judge)
Wait (Mrs. Lovett, Beggar Woman)
Kiss Me (Johanna, Anthony)
Ladies in Their Sensitivities (Beadle, Judge)
Pretty Women (Judge, Sweeney)
Epiphany (Sweeney, Mrs. Lovett)
A Little Priest (Mrs. Lovett, Sweeney)
Act II
God, That's Good (Tobias, Mrs. Lovett,
  Sweeney, Beggar Woman, company)
Johanna (reprise) (Anthony, Sweeney,
  Johanna, Beggar Woman)
By the Sea (Mrs. Lovett, Sweeney)
Wigmaker Sequence (Sweeney, Anthony,
  quintet)
Not While I'm Around (Tobias, Mrs. Lovett)
Parlour Songs (Beadle, Mrs. Lovett, Tobias)
City on Fire (company)
The Judge's Return (Sweeney, Judge)

SWEET CHARITY (1966)

BOOK BY: Neil Simon; based on the film *The Nights of Cabiria* by Frederico Fellini, Tullio Pinelli, and Ennio Flaiano
MUSIC BY: Cy Coleman
LYRICS BY: Dorothy Fields
PUBLISHED LIBRETTO: Random House, 1966
CONDENSATION: *Ganzl's Book of the Musical Theatre*. Ganzl, Kurt. Schirmer (Macmillan), 1989
ANTHOLOGY: *The Collected Plays of Neil Simon*, vol. III. Random House, 1991
VOCAL SELECTIONS: Notable Music, 1969
LICENSING AGENT: Tams-Witmark
RECORDING: Columbia CK 2900 CD (original cast)
CAST: 22 M; 12 F; extras

This sensational dancing show starred Gwen Verdon (and later Debbie Allen) as a Times Square dance-hall hostess. The honky-tonk atmosphere should be shown in both the sets and costumes. Charity, our luckless heroine, has several unfortunate encounters with men. All she wants is to be loved for herself. Bob Fosse did the very stylish choreography and the Broadway production had the "gut thrill of big time Broadway" (Martin Gottfried, *Women's Wear Daily*). Shirley MacLaine starred in the 1969 film.

1986 REVIVAL CAST:

Debbie Allen (Charity)
David Warren Gibson (Dark Glasses)
Bebe Neuwirth (Nickie)
Allison Williams (Helene)
Mark Jacoby (Vittorio)
Michael Rupert (Oscar)
Irving Allen Lee (Daddy Johann)
Lee Wilkof (Herman)

SONGS:
Act I
You Should See Yourself (Charity, Dark Glasses)
The Rescue (ensemble)
Big Spender (Nickie, Helene, girls)
Rich Man's Frug (ensemble)
If My Friends Could See Me Now (Charity)
Too Many Tomorrows (Vittorio)
There's Gotta Be Something Better than This (Charity, Nickie, Helene)
I'm the Bravest Individual (Charity, Oscar)
Act II
Rhythm of Life (Daddy Johann, ensemble)
Baby Dream Your Dream (Nickie, Helene)
Sweet Charity (Oscar)
Where Am I Going? (Charity)
I'm a Brass Band (Charity, ensemble)
I Love to Cry at Weddings (Herman, Nickie, Helene, ensemble)

SWEETHEARTS (1913)

BOOK BY: Harry B. Smith and Fred De Gresac
MUSIC BY: Victor Herbert
LYRICS BY: Robert B. Smith
PUBLISHED LIBRETTO: None
CONDENSATION: *Ganzl's Book of the Musical Theatre*. Ganzl, Kurt. Schirmer (Macmillan), 1989
ANTHOLOGY: None
PIANO-VOCAL SCORE: Chappell, 1913
MUSIC PUBLISHER: *The Music of Victor Herbert*. Warner Bros. Music, 1976
LICENSING AGENT: Tams-Witmark
RECORDING: Moss Music Group MMG 1129 (1981 studio cast)
CAST: 9 M; 9 F; chorus, dancers

Considered to be one of Herbert's most ambitious scores, this is very close to being an opera. (Tams-Witmark has a simplified version suitable for high schools.) The locale is the city of Bruges, Belgium, around the turn of the century. A woman finds an abandoned infant in a tulip garden. The baby grows into a beautiful young lady. Prince Franz, about to ascend the throne of Zilania, meets and falls in love with her, not knowing that she is the long-lost crown princess. Bobby Clark, Gil Lamb, and other comedians have starred in revivals of this operetta. A rollicking wooden-shoe episode is one of the show's highlights. The 1938 film version with Jeanette

MacDonald and Nelson Eddy has a modern setting.

1983 NEW YORK CONCERT VERSION CAST:

Cris Groenendaal (Karl)
SuEllen Estey (Liane)
Judy Kaye (Sylvia)
Brent Barrett (Franz)
Herndon Lackey (Von Tromp)
Dale Radunz (Caniche)
Christopher Hewett (Mikel)
Elaine Bonazzi (Paula)
Roderick Cook (Slingsby)

SONGS:
Act I
On Parade (Karl, ensemble)
There Is Magic in a Smile (Liane, ensemble)
Sweethearts (Sylvia, ensemble)
Every Lover Must Meet His Fate (Franz, ensemble)
Mother Goose (Sylvia, ensemble)
The Angelus (Sylvia, Franz, ensemble)
Jeanette and Her Wooden Shoes (Liane, Von Tromp, Caniche)

Act II
Pretty as a Picture (Mikel)
Welcoming the Bride (ensemble)
In the Convent They Never Taught Me That (Sylvia, ensemble)
The Game of Love (Karl, ensemble)
I Don't Know How I Do It, but I Do (Slingsby)
The Cricket on the Hearth (Sylvia, Franz)
The Pilgrims of Love (Slingsby, Mikel, Caniche, Von Tromp)

TAKE ME ALONG (1959)

BOOK BY: Joseph Stein and Robert Russell; based on the play *Ah, Wilderness* by Eugene O'Neill
MUSIC AND LYRICS BY: Bob Merrill
PUBLISHED LIBRETTO: None
CONDENSATION: *New Complete Book of the American Musical Theater.* Ewen, David. Holt, 1970
ANTHOLOGY: None

LICENSING AGENT: Tams-Witmark
RECORDING: RCA LSO 1050 (original cast)
CAST: Large mixed cast

The setting is Centerville, Connecticut, around the Fourth of July in 1906. A brother-in-law who drinks a bit too much visits his relatives for the holiday. Another important character is the family's sixteen-year-old son who has his first taste of liquor and women. Based on O'Neill's only comedy, this was described as bright, warm-hearted, and likable. There are some rousing numbers, but overall this is a quiet, nostalgic musical. Jackie Gleason and Walter Pidgeon did a soft-shoe to the title tune.

ORIGINAL CAST:

Walter Pidgeon (Nat)
Una Merkel (Essie)
Eileen Herlie (Lily)
Susan Luckey (Muriel)
Robert Morse (Richard)
Jackie Gleason (Sid)
Peter Conlow (Wint)

SONGS:
Act I
The Parade (Nat, ensemble)
Oh, Please (Nat, Essie, Lily, family)
I Would Die (Muriel, Richard)
Sid, Ol' Kid (Sid, ensemble)
Staying Young (Nat)
I Get Embarrassed (Sid, Lily)
We're Home (Lily)
Take Me Along (Sid, Nat)
For Sweet Charity (Sid, Nat, ensemble)
Pleasant Beach House (Wint)
That's How It Starts (Richard)

Act II
The Beardsley Ballet (Richard, Muriel, ensemble)
Promise Me a Rose (Lily, Sid)
Little Green Snake (Sid)
Nine o'Clock (Richard)
But Yours (Sid, Lily)
Take Me Along (reprise) (Lily, Sid, ensemble)

TAKING MY TURN (1983)

BOOK BY: Robert H. Livingston
MUSIC BY: Gary William Friedman
LYRICS BY: Will Holt
PUBLISHED LIBRETTO: French
CONDENSATION: None
ANTHOLOGY: None
VOCAL SELECTIONS: Hampshire House, 1984
LICENSING AGENT: Samuel French
RECORDING: Columbia Special Products CSP BLR
 1001 (original cast)
CAST: 4 M; 4 F

Called "the musical that celebrates the joys of living a long life," this show is ideal for senior citizens. The cast of eight portrays specific characters, even though the show has no plot. The entire cast is always onstage, and through speech and song they interact and reflect on the pleasures of growing and being old. There are eighteen songs, some brief dancing, and a small combo may be used for accompaniment. Mel Gussow in the *New York Times* reported it "deals sensitively with a serious subject." For the off-Broadway production one basic set designed in a series of overlapping levels was used with effective dramatic lighting. The action takes place during the course of one year—this year. Costumes are variations of normal street wear. This was performed on PBS by the original cast and a videotape is available.

ORIGINAL CAST:

Mace Barrett (Eric)
Marni Nixon (Edna)
Victor Griffin (John)
Cissy Houston (Helen)
Tiger Haynes (Charles)
Margaret Whiting (Dorothy)
Ted Thurston (Benjamin)
Sheila Smith (Janet)

SONGS:
Act I
This Is My Song (company)
Somebody Else (company)

Fine for the Shape I'm In (Dorothy, Edna, Helen)
Two of Me (Janet)
Janet, Get Up (company)
I Like It (company)
I Never Made Money from Music (Charles)
Vivaldi (Edna, company)
Do You Remember? (Ben, company)
In April (Dorothy)
Pick More Daisies (company)

Act II
Taking Our Turn (company)
Sweet Longings (Janet, company)
I Am Not Old (Helen)
The Kite (John)
Good Luck to You (Eric, company)
In the House (Eric)
It Still Isn't Over (Ben, Dorothy)

THE TAP-DANCE KID (1983)

BOOK BY: Charles Blackwell; based on the novel
 Nobody's Family Is Going to Change by Louise
 Fitzhugh
MUSIC BY: Henry Krieger
LYRICS BY: Robert Lorick
PUBLISHED LIBRETTO: French
CONDENSATION: *Broadway Musicals Show by Show.*
 Green, Stanley. Hal Leonard Books, 1985
ANTHOLOGY: None
VOCAL SELECTIONS: Hal Leonard, 1984
LICENSING AGENT: Samuel French
RECORDING: Polydor 820 210-2 CD (original cast)
CAST: 5 M; 5 F; chorus, dancers

Willie (aged ten) has decided he wants to be a dancer. He is from a black upper-middle-class family and his father, a lawyer, opposes the idea. "We didn't get off the plantation until we stopped dancing and started doing," he says. Willie, however, is encouraged by his uncle (a dancer) who still hopes for a Broadway show. In this musical "nobody loses, everybody wins, and virtuosity triumphs." The sets include their apartment, a waterside bench, a loft, and the rehearsal hall. Critics liked the collage impressions of Manhattan. The score was described as "mostly traditional show music." Both Willie and his uncle must be accomplished tap dancers.

ORIGINAL CAST:

Alfonso Ribeiro (Willie)
Hattie Winston (Ginnie)
Barbara Montgomery (Dulcie)
Martine Allard (Emma)
Hinton Battle (Dipsey)
Alan Weeks (Daddy Bates)
Jackie Lowe (Carole)
Samuel E. Wright (William)

SONGS:
Act I
Another Day (Ginnie, Emma, Dulcie)
Four Strikes against Me (Emma)
Class Act (Ginnie, Dipsey, Daddy Bates)
They Never Hear What I Say (Emma, Willie)
Dancing Is Everything (Willie)
Crosstown (Willie, ensemble)
Fabulous Feet (Dipsey, Carole, ensemble)
I Could Get Used to Him (Carole, ensemble)
Man in the Moon (Dipsey)

Act II
Like Him (Ginnie, Emma)
My Luck Is Changing (Dipsey)
I Remember How It Was (Ginnie)
Someday (Emma, Willie)
Lullaby (Ginnie)
Tap Tap (Daddy Bates, Willie, Dipsey)
Dance if It Makes You Happy (Willie, Dipsey, Daddy Bates, Carole, ensemble)
William's Song (William)

TEDDY AND ALICE (1987)

BOOK BY: Jerome Alden
MUSIC BY: John Philip Sousa; adaptions and original music by Richard Kapp
LYRICS BY: Hal Hackady
PUBLISHED LIBRETTO: None
CONDENSATION: None
ANTHOLOGY: None
LICENSING AGENT: Music Theatre International

RECORDING: ESS.A.Y. 1003 CD ("Sousa for Orchestra" contains some selections by the original cast)
CAST: 5 M; 3 F; 5 children; chorus

Called "an extravagant treatment of the life of our 26th president," the plot of this show primarily deals with Teddy trying to prevent his daughter, Alice, from marrying Congressman Longworth. Your "Teddy" must have charm, bustle, and high spirits. The sets include White House interiors, exteriors, and the Rose Garden. One critic confessed he loved Sousa's music and thrilled to its theatricality and the "flag-waving finales."

ORIGINAL CAST:

Len Cariou (Teddy Roosevelt)
Nancy Hume (Alice)
Michael McCarty (Taft)
Gordon Stanley (Root)
Raymond Thorne (Lodge)
Nancy Opel (Eleanor)
Beth Fowler (Edith)
Ron Raines (Nick)

SONGS:
Act I
This House (Teddy, ensemble)
But Not Right Now (Alice)
She's Got to Go (Taft, Root, Lodge)
The Fourth of July (Alice, Eleanor)
Charge (Teddy, Edith, children)
Battlelines (Edith)
The Coming-Out Party Dance (Teddy, Alice, Nick, Edith, ensemble)
Leg-O'-Mutton (Alice, Nick, ensemble)
Not Love (Nick, Taft, Root, Lodge)
Her Father's Daughter (Teddy)
Perfect for Each Other (Nick)
He's Got to Go (Taft, Root, Lodge, Nick)
Wave the Flag (Teddy, Edith, Eleanor, ensemble)

Act II
The Fourth of July (reprise) (Teddy, ladies)
Nothing to Lose (Nick, Alice)
Election Eve (Taft, Root, Lodge, ensemble)
Perfect for Each Other (reprise) (Alice)
Can I Let Her Go? (Teddy)

Private Thoughts (Taft, Root, Lodge, Edith, ensemble)
This House (reprise) (Teddy, Edith, ensemble)

TEN PERCENT REVUE (1988)

BOOK, MUSIC, AND LYRICS BY: Tom Wilson Weinberg
PUBLISHED LIBRETTO: New Music Theatre Library, 1989
CONDENSATION: None
ANTHOLOGY: None
LICENSING AGENT: Broadway Play Publishing
RECORDING: Cassette tape available from agent
CAST: 2 M; 3 F

The title of this revue comes from the estimate of the number of gays in the U.S. population. The theme of the revue is gay pride—"affirmative without being polemical." The multistyled score was presented off-Broadway in a three-sided playing area, keeping the staging tight. There were few props and costume changes and only one backdrop. It was described as "lively, funny, and sometimes bittersweet."

ORIGINAL CAST:

Lisa Bernstein (vocals and piano)
Valerie Hill
Trish Kane
Robert Tate
Timothy Williams

SONGS:
Act I
Flaunting It (company)
Best Years of My Life (company)
Threesome (Bernstein, Hill, Kane)
Wedding Song (company)
If I Were/I'd Like to Be (Hill, Tate)
Gay Name Game (company)
Home (Kane)
Not Allowed (Tate, Williams)
Personals (company)
Safe Sex Slut (company)

Act II
Homo Haven Fight Song (company)
Turkey Baster Baby (Hill, Kane)
High Risk for Afraids (company)
Obituary (Williams)
And the Supremes (Kane, company)
Before Stonewall (company)
Write a Letter (Tate, company)
We're Everywhere (company)

TENDERLOIN (1960)

BOOK BY: George Abbott and Jerome Weidman; based on the novel by Samuel Hopkins Adams
MUSIC BY: Jerry Bock
LYRICS BY: Sheldon Harnick
PUBLISHED LIBRETTO: Random House, 1961
CONDENSATION: *New Complete Book of the American Musical Theater.* Ewen, David. Holt, 1970
ANTHOLOGY: None
VOCAL SELECTIONS: Valando, 1957
LICENSING AGENT: Tams-Witmark
RECORDING: Angel 65022 CD (original cast)
CAST: 15 M; 12 F; chorus

The minister of a New York church in the 1890s decides to close down the nearby red-light district. He is joined by a young reporter for a scandal sheet who also warns the crooked politicians who run the "Tenderloin." Maurice Evans was the minister. The off-Broadway revival featured a cast of twenty-five, two pianos and a drum, and simple but appropriate sets.

ORIGINAL CAST:

Ron Husmann (Tommy)
Eileen Rodgers (Nita)
Maurice Evans (Brock)
Lee Becker (Gertie)
Wynne Miller (Laura)
Margery Gray (Margie)
Irene Kane (Jessica)

SONGS:
Act I
Bless This Land (choir)
Little Old New York (Nita, Gertie, company)

Dr. Brock (Brock)
Artificial Flowers (Tommy)
What's in It for You? (Brock, Tommy)
Reform (Gertie, ensemble)
Tommy, Tommy (Laura)
Artificial Flowers (reprise) (Margie)
The Picture of Happiness (Tommy)
Dear Friend (Brock, Laura, Jessica)
The Army of the Just (Brock, ensemble)
How the Money Changes Hands (Brock, Nita, company)

Act II
Good Clean Fun (Brock, company)
My Miss Mary (Tommy, Laura, ensemble)
My Gentle Young Johnny (Nita)
The Trial (company)
The Tenderloin Celebration (ensemble)

THEY'RE PLAYING OUR SONG (1979)

BOOK BY: Neil Simon
MUSIC BY: Marvin Hamlisch
LYRICS BY: Carole Bayer Sager
PUBLISHED LIBRETTO: Random House, 1980; French, 1980
CONDENSATION: *Ganzl's Book of the Musical Theatre.* Ganzl, Kurt. Schirmer (Macmillan), 1989
ANTHOLOGY: *The Collected Plays of Neil Simon*, vol. III. Random House, 1991
VOCAL SELECTIONS: Chappell, 1979
LICENSING AGENT: Samuel French
RECORDING: Casablanca 826 249-2 CD (original cast)
CAST: 1 M; 1 F; backup group of 6; offstage voice

He is an established pop composer. She is a younger aspiring lyricist. As they work together, they fall in love. Can an older man open himself to a younger woman? These two are backed up by their "voices"—alter egos that appear in costumes appropriate to the plot situation. The critics all liked Lucie Arnaz—a kook from 18th Street wearing costumes left over from various shows—and Robert Klein—a neurotic, demanding egomaniac. The show, like the music, is lively and modern. The two leads should have both talent and charm.

ORIGINAL CAST:
Robert Klein (Vernon)
Lucie Arnaz (Sonia)

SONGS:
Act I
Fallin' (Vernon)
Workin' It Out (Vernon, Sonia, ensemble)
If He Really Knew Me (Sonia, Vernon)
They're Playing Our Song (Vernon, Sonia)
Right (Vernon, Sonia, ensemble)
Just for Tonight (Sonia)

Act II
When You're in My Arms (Vernon, Sonia, ensemble)
I Still Believe in Love (Sonia)
Fill in the Words (Vernon, ensemble)

THIRTEEN DAUGHTERS (1961)

BOOK, MUSIC, AND LYRICS BY: Eaton Magoon, Jr.; additional book material by Leon Tokatyan
PUBLISHED LIBRETTO: None
CONDENSATION: None
ANTHOLOGY: None
VOCAL SELECTIONS: Hill and Range
LICENSING AGENT: Music Theatre International
RECORDING: Mahalo M 3003 (original Hawaiian cast)
CAST: 14 M; 11 W; 6 children; chorus

The action takes place in Hawaii in the late nineteenth century. The composer of this musical was born and raised in Hawaii where this show was first presented. Don Ameche and Sylvia Syms starred in the Broadway production. In the plot a young Chinese merchant marries a Hawaiian princess. The natives resent him as a foreigner and predict that he will have thirteen daughters, but no sons. Described as a lush and ornate musical with energetic, rousing dances, this provides the opportunity for Polynesian atmosphere and the hula. The critic for the *New York Daily News* described the music as having "more of Hawaii than Tin Pan Alley—which is high praise!" In New York on the opening night, the orchestra conductor sported a lei around his neck.

ORIGINAL CAST:

Don Ameche (Chun)
Sylvia Syms (Kinau)
Ed Kinney (Mana)
Diana Corto (Malia)
Honey Sanders (Kamakia)
Richard Tone (Jacques)
Monica Boyar (Emmaloa)
Gina Viglione (Isabel)
Stanley Grover (Willoughby)
Isabelle Farrell (Cecelia)

SONGS:
Act I
Kuli Kuli (Kinau, company)
House on the Hill (Chun)
Thirteen Daughters (Chun, daughters)
Let-a-Go Your Heart (Mana, Malia)
Alphabet Song (children)
Throw a Petal (Malia)
When You Hear the Wind (Mana)
Ka Wahine Akamai (Smart Woman) (Kinau, Kamakia, Emmaloa, ensemble)
You Set My Heart to Music (Emmaloa, Chun, Isabel)
The Cotillion (company)

Act II
Thirteen Old Maids (daughters)
Oriental Plan (Chun)
Hoomalimali (Kinau)
My Pleasure (Willoughby, Isabel)
Puka Puka Pants (Cecelia, Jacques)
My Hawaii (Mana)
Hiiaka E (Emmaloa, ensemble)

THREE GUYS NAKED FROM THE WAIST DOWN (1985)

BOOK AND LYRICS BY: Jerry Colker
MUSIC BY: Michael Rupert
PUBLISHED LIBRETTO: French, 1985
CONDENSATION: None
ANTHOLOGY: None

LICENSING AGENT: Samuel French
RECORDING: Polydor 820 244-2 CD (original cast)
CAST: 3 M

Three stand-up comics get together in a New York club, form an act, and go on to stardom on television. But all does not end happily with their "mindless pursuit of success." The title refers to the idea that doing stand-up routines is like being naked in front of an audience. The songs are primarily rock, and all three cast members must sing and dance as well as put over comic routines. The off-Broadway production utilized locale projections in an all-purpose nightclub setting. There are many costume changes. One critic found this "a rare and unusual musical which has some serious things to say about funny people."

ORIGINAL CAST:

Scott Bakula (Ted)
John Kassir (Kenny)
Jerry Colker (Phil)

SONGS:
Act I
Promise of Greatness (Ted)
Angry Guy/Lovely Day (Phil)
Don't Wanna Be No Superstar (Ted, Phil)
Operator (Kenny)
Screaming Clocks (The Dummies Song) (cast)
Don't Wanna Be No Superstar (reprise) (cast)
The History of Stand-Up Comedy (cast)
Dreams of Heaven (Kenny)
Kamikaze Kabaret (cast)

Act II
The American Dream (cast)
What a Ride (cast)
"Hello Fellas" Theme/TV Special World Tour (cast)
A Father Now (Phil)
Three Guys Naked from the Waist Down Theme (cast)

THE THREE MUSKETEERS (1928)

BOOK BY: William Anthony McGuire; adapted from
the novel by Alexandre Dumas
MUSIC BY: Rudolf Friml
LYRICS BY: P. G. Wodehouse and Clifford Grey
PUBLISHED LIBRETTO: None
CONDENSATION: *New Complete Book of the
American Musical Theater.* Ewen, David. Holt,
1970
ANTHOLOGY: None
PIANO-VOCAL SCORE: Chappell, 1932; Harms, 1932
LICENSING AGENT: Tams-Witmark
RECORDING: Monmouth Evergreen MES 7050 (1930
London cast)
CAST: Large mixed cast

A review of the original Ziegfeld production indicates that this musical retains
most of the original Dumas plot. Naturally
it was a lavish production with a good,
rambunctious score. Dennis King and Vivienne Segal were the stars. There are twelve
scenes with locales including the garden
of the Tuileries, Cardinal Richelieu's chambers, and the Duke of Buckingham's palace
in England. The score does not contain
any Friml standards, although some people may recognize "Ma Belle." In addition
to the ornate fifteenth-century court costumes, the production should include a
certain amount of onstage sword play.

1984 REVIVAL CAST:

Michael Praed (D'Artagnan)
Joseph Kolinski (Buckingham)
Liz Callaway (Constance)
J. P. Dougherty (Innkeeper)
Darlene Anders (Queen Anne)
Marianne Tatum (Milady)
Raymond Patterson (Jussac)
Ed Dixon (Cardinal)
Michael Dantuono (Rochefort)
Roy Brocksmith (King)
Chuck Wagner (Athos)
Brent Spiner (Aramis)
Ron Taylor (Porthos)

SONGS:
(including interpolations from other scores)
Act I
Gascony Bred (D'Artagnan, Innkeeper, company)
All for One (Three Musketeers)
Only a Rose (D'Artagnan, Constance)
My Sword and I (D'Artagnan, company)
Carnival of Fools (company)
L'Amour Toujours L'Amour (Buckingham,
Queen Anne)
Come to Us (Milady, Jussac)
March of the Musketeers (Three Musketeers,
D'Artagnan, company)
Bless My Soul (Cardinal, Milady, Rochefort)
Act II
Vive La France (King, company)
The Actor's Life (Three Musketeers,
D'Artagnan)
Ma Belle (D'Artagnan, Constance)
The Chase (company)
Dreams (Buckingham)
Gossip (Three Musketeers, D'Artagnan,
Milady, Jussac, Cardinal, Constance, King,
Queen, company)

THREE POSTCARDS (1987)

BOOK BY: Craig Lucas
MUSIC AND LYRICS BY: Craig Carnelia
PUBLISHED LIBRETTO: Dramatists Play Service
CONDENSATION: None
ANTHOLOGY: None
PIANO-VOCAL SCORE: Dramatists Play Service
LICENSING AGENT: Dramatists Play Service
RECORDING: None
CAST: 2 M; 3 F

Three women are having dinner in a Manhattan restaurant. We hear what they are
thinking, as well as what they are saying, as their lives, dreams, and fears are
revealed to us. The two men portray a
variety of roles, including the waiter, a
piano player, husbands, a shrink, and a
teacher. This ninety-minute entertainment
was staged on a steeply raked stage with
a high-tech design. It is performed without
an intermission.

ORIGINAL CAST:

Craig Carnelia (Bill)
Brad O'Hare (Walter)
Jane Galloway (Big Jane)
Maureen Silliman (Little Jane)
Karen Trott (K. C.)

Song titles are not listed.

THREE WISHES FOR JAMIE (1952)

BOOK BY: Charles O'Neal and Abe Burrows; based
    on the novel by Charles O'Neal
MUSIC AND LYRICS BY: Ralph Blane
PUBLISHED LIBRETTO: None
CONDENSATION: None
ANTHOLOGY: None
VOCAL SELECTIONS: Chappell
LICENSING AGENT: Samuel French
RECORDING: Angel 764888-2 CD (original cast)
CAST: 12 M; 5 F; 1 boy; chorus

This musical version of a Christopher
Award novel concerns Jamie McRuin who
is granted three wishes. The first is to
travel, the second is to marry the girl of
his dreams, and the third is to have a
son who can speak the old Gaelic tongue.
So he leaves Ireland and turns up at a
horse traders' camp in Georgia in 1896.
The Broadway production was applauded
for its colorful settings and handsome costumes. The "Trottin' to the Fair" number
was one of the highlights of the production, being both vigorous and imaginative.
There is also a comic ballet depicting the
agony of expectant fatherhood. The production had plenty of Irish wit and humor.

ORIGINAL CAST:

Robert Halliday (Tim)
Charlotte Rae (Tirsa)
Bert Wheeler (Tavish)
John Raitt (Jamie)
Anne Jeffreys (Maeve)
Peter Conlow (Dennis)

SONGS:
Act I
The Wake (Tim, Tirsa, Tavish, ensemble)
The Girl That I Court in My Mind (Jamie)
My Home's a Highway (Maeve, ensemble)
We're for Love (Tavish, ensemble)
My Heart's Darlin' (Jamie)
Goin' on a Hayride (Jamie, Maeve, ensemble)
Love Has Nothing to Do with Looks (Tirsa,
    Tim, Tavish)
I'll Sing You a Song (Tirsa, Tim, Dennis,
    Tavish, ensemble)
It Must Be Spring (Maeve, female ensemble)
Wedding March (company)

Act II
The Army Mule Song (Jamie, ensemble)
What Do I Know? (Maeve)
It's a Wishing World (Maeve, Jamie)
Trottin' to the Fair (Jamie, Tim, Dennis,
    ensemble)
Love Has Nothing to Do with Looks (reprise)
    (Tirsa, Dennis)
April Face (Tavish, Maeve, Jamie)

THE THREEPENNY OPERA (1933)

BOOK BY: Bertolt Brecht; English adaption of book
    and lyrics by Marc Blitzstein; based on *The
    Beggar's Opera* by John Gay
MUSIC BY: Kurt Weill
PUBLISHED LIBRETTO: Vintage Books, 1976
CONDENSATION: *The Best Plays of 1975–1976.*
    Otis L. Guernsey, Jr., ed. Dodd, Mead, 1976;
    Ganzl's Book of the Musical Theatre. Ganzl, Kurt.
    Schirmer (Macmillan), 1989
ANTHOLOGY: *Brecht, Bertolt. Collected Plays*, vol. 2.
    Vintage, 1977
PIANO-VOCAL SCORE: Universal Edition (Wein),
    1928 (German)
VOCAL SELECTIONS: Warner Bros. Music
LICENSING AGENT: Rodgers and Hammerstein
    Theatre Library
RECORDING: Polydor 820260-2 CD (1955 original
    cast)
CAST: 12 M; 8 F

Revived many times and in different translations, this particular version was first presented off-Broadway in 1955 with Lotte Lenya, and it was a sensation. The original premiere was in Berlin in 1928 and the first Broadway production was in 1933. The setting is London's Soho before and during the coronation of Queen Victoria. The master criminal Macheath marries Polly Peachum, and his old flame, Jenny, turns him in to the police. The cast is largely made up of criminals, beggars, and tarts. Brecht is interested in exposing the corrupt officials of a sad and vicious society. But the Kurt Weill score is actually what has made this show a classic. Everyone knows "Mack the Knife."

1955 NEW YORK REVIVAL CAST:

Tige Andrews (Streetsinger)
Frederic Downs (Peachum)
Jane Connell (Mrs. Peachum)
Jo Sullivan (Polly)
Scott Merrill (Macheath)
Richard Verney (Tiger Brown)
Lotte Lenya (Jenny)
Beatrice Arthur (Lucy)

SONGS:
Act I
Mack the Knife (Streetsinger)
Morning Anthem (Peachum)
Instead-of Song (Peachum, Mrs. Peachum)
The Bide-a-Wee in Soho (Polly)
Wedding Song (ensemble)
Army Song (Macheath, Tiger Brown, ensemble)
Love Song (Polly, Macheath)
Ballad of Dependency (Mrs. Peachum)
The World Is Mean (Polly, Mrs. Peachum, Peachum)

Act II
Polly's Song (Polly, Macheath)
Pirate Jenny (Jenny)
Tango-Ballad (Jenny, Macheath)
Ballad of the Easy Life (Macheath)
Barbara-Song (Lucy)
Jealousy Duet (Lucy, Polly)

How to Survive (Macheath, Mrs. Peachum, ensemble)

Act III
Useless Song (Peachum, ensemble)
Solomon Song (Jenny)
Call from the Grave (Macheath)
Death Message (Macheath)/The Mounted Messenger (company)

NOTE: A new production of this show was presented on Broadway in 1989 starring Maureen McGovern, Sting, Alvin Epstein, and Georgia Brown. The translation was by Michael Feingold and it is now available for production from: European American Music Corporation, P. O. Box 850, Valley Forge, PA 19482; (215) 648-0506.

TIMBUKTU! (1978)

BOOK BY: Luther Davis; based on the musical *Kismet* by Charles Lederer and Luther Davis; from the play by Edward Knoblock
MUSIC AND LYRICS BY: Robert Wright and George Forrest; from themes of Alexander Borodin and African folk music
PUBLISHED LIBRETTO: None
CONDENSATION: None
ANTHOLOGY: None
VOCAL SELECTIONS: Blackwood Music, 1978
LICENSING AGENT: Music Theatre International
RECORDING: None
CAST: Large mixed cast

Once upon a time in the 1950s, the team of Wright and Forrest took some themes from Borodin and turned an old play into a smash musical called *Kismet*. It was an Arabian adventure. Now it has been reset in fourteenth-century Africa for an all-black cast. The plot is basically the same. A beggar-poet's beautiful daughter meets the Prince and they fall in love. This is an opportunity for exotic costuming, ethnic-based choreography, big voices, and "Baubles, Bangles, and Beads."

ORIGINAL CAST:

Ira Hawkins (Hadji)
Melba Moore (Marsinah)
Eartha Kitt (Sahleem-La-Lume)
Gilbert Price (Mansa)
George Bell (Wazir)
Bruce Hubbard (Chief of Police)

SONGS:

Act I

Rhymes Have I (Hadji, Marsinah, ensemble)
Fate (Hadji)
In the Beginning, Women (Sahleem-La-Lume)
Baubles, Bangles, and Beads (Marsinah,
    ensemble)
Stranger in Paradise (Mansa, Marsinah)
Gesticulate (Hadji)
Night of My Nights (Mansa, company)

Act II

The Mansa Marries Tonight (company)
My Magic Lamp (Marsinah)
Rahadlakum (Sahleem-La-Lume, harem girls)
And This Is My Beloved (Hadji, Marsinah,
    Mansa, Wazir)
Golden Land, Golden Life (Chief of Police,
    company)
Night of My Nights (reprise) (Mansa,
    Marsinah, Hadji, company)
Sands of Time (Hadji, Sahleem-La-Lume)

TINTYPES (1980)

CONCEIVED BY: Mary Kyte with Mel Marvin and
    Gary Pearle
PUBLISHED LIBRETTO: None
CONDENSATION: None
ANTHOLOGY: None
LICENSING AGENT: Music Theatre International
RECORDING: DRG CDXP 5196 CD (original cast)
CAST: 2 M; 3 F

This revue comprises various character
types who span the period from 1890
to 1920, showing an image of American
history through approximately more than
forty songs of the period. On Broadway this
was performed on an almost bare stage
with just a few props and some glorious

costumes. Accompaniment was provided
by an onstage upright piano. The show has
some dialogue, but no book or plot. The
various characters include a Jewish immigrant, a black maid, a Broadway star, a U.S.
president, and a poor-but-honest working
girl. There was a television version in 1983.

ORIGINAL CAST:

Carolyn Mignini   Lynne Thigpen
Trey Wilson   Mary Catherine Wright
Jerry Zaks

SONGS:

Act I

Ragtime Nightingale (piano)
The Yankee Doodle Boy (Zaks, company)
Ta-Ra-Ra Boom-De-Ay! (company)
I Don't Care (company)
Come Take a Trip in My Airship (company)
Kentucky Babe (company)
A Hot Time in the Old Town Tonight
    (Thigpen, company)
Stars and Stripes Forever (company)
Electricity (company)
El Capitan (Wilson, company)
Pastime Rag (piano)
Meet Me in St. Louis (Mignini)
Waltz Me around Again, Willie (Mignini,
    company)
Wabash Cannonball (company)
In My Merry Oldsmobile (company)
Wayfaring Stranger (Thigpen)
Sometimes I Feel Like a Motherless Child
    (Thigpen)
Aye, Lye, Lyu Lye (Mignini)
I'll Take You Home Again, Kathleen (Wilson)
America, the Beautiful (Thigpen, company)
Wait for the Wagon (company)
What It Takes to Make Me Love You (Wilson,
    Wright)
The Maiden with the Dreamy Eyes (company)
Kiss Me Again (Mignini)
Shortnin' Bread (company)
Nobody (Thigpen)
Elite Syncopations (piano)
I'm Going to Live Anyhow, 'Til I Die (Thigpen,
    company)

Act II
The Ragtime Dance (Thigpen, company)
I Want What I Want When I Want It (Wilson)
It's Delightful to Be Married (Mignini)
Fifty-Fifty (Thigpen, Wright, Mignini)
Then I'll Be Satisfied with Life (Zaks)
Jonah Man (Wright)
When It's All Goin' Out (Wilson, Mignini, company)
We Shall Not Be Moved (company)
Hello, Ma Baby (company)
Teddy Da Roose (Wilson)
Bill Bailey, Won't You Please Come Home? (Thigpen)
She's Gettin' More Like the White Folks (Zaks, company)
You're a Grand Old Flag (company)
Toyland (Mignini)
Smiles (Zaks, Wright, company)

TIP-TOES (1925)

BOOK BY: Guy Bolton and Fred Thompson
MUSIC BY: George Gershwin
LYRICS BY: Ira Gershwin
PUBLISHED LIBRETTO: None
CONDENSATION: *New Complete Book of the American Musical Theater*. Ewen, David. Holt, 1970
ANTHOLOGY: None
LICENSING AGENT: Tams-Witmark
RECORDING: Monmouth-Evergreen 7052E (original London cast)
CAST: 13 M; 8 F

"When Do We Dance?" they sing at the Surf Club in Palm Beach, Florida, in those golden musical-comedy days of the 1920s. Other settings include the deck of Steve's yacht and the lobby of the Everglades Inn. The Three Kayes are in Florida for a dancing engagement. Tip-Toes falls in love with a millionaire and pretends to be of high position herself. The Goodspeed Opera revival in Brooklyn was noted for its choreography, with tap, soft-shoe, Charleston, and Peabody routines. There are also some very corny routines done by the other two

Kayes. But the wonderful Gershwin score makes up for everything. There was a silent film version in 1928!

1979 NEW YORK REVIVAL CAST:
Jana Robbins (Sylvia)
Bob Gunton (Rollo)
Georgia Engels (Tip-Toes)
Russ Thacker (Steve)
Sally O'Donnell (Binnie)
Nicole Barth (Denise)
Michael Hirsch (Al)
Haskell Gordon (Hen)
Susan Danielle (Lucille)
Ronn Robinson (Hodge)

SONGS:
Act I
Waiting for the Train (ensemble)
Nice Baby (Sylvia, Rollo, ensemble)
Looking for a Boy (Tip-Toes)
Lady Luck (ensemble)
When Do We Dance? (Steve, Binnie, Denise, Sylvia, ensemble)
These Charming People (Tip-Toes, Al, Hen)
That Certain Feeling (Tip-Toes, Steve)
Sweet and Low-Down (Al, Tip-Toes, Binnie, Denise, Lucille, Hodge, ensemble)

Act II
Our Little Captain (Tip-Toes, men)
Looking for a Boy (reprise) (Tip-Toes, Steve)
It's a Great Little World (Steve, girls)
Why Do I Love You? (Sylvia, Rollo)
Nightie-Night (Tip-Toes, Steve)
Tip-Toes (Tip-Toes, company)

TOMFOOLERY (1981)

WORDS, MUSIC, AND LYRICS BY: Tom Lehrer; adapted from the recording *Songs of Tom Lehrer* by Cameron Mackintosh and Robin Ray
PUBLISHED LIBRETTO: French, 1986
CONDENSATION: None
ANTHOLOGY: None
VOCAL SELECTIONS: *Too Many Songs by Tom Lehrer*. Pantheon Books, 1981
LICENSING AGENT: Samuel French

RECORDINGS: Monza Records MONMT 102
   (original London cast); Reprise 6216 (Songs
   by Tom Lehrer)
CAST: 3 M; 1 F

In the 1950s Tom Lehrer was a Harvard grad student who also taught mathematics. To amuse himself he wrote "wickedly iconoclastic ditties" and occasionally performed them in clubs. He also made some recordings and, although he has long since given it all up, is warmly remembered. This revue, which started in London and then moved off-Broadway to the Village Gate, somewhat updates his material but retains its black humor. There is a brief innocuous narration bridging the twenty-eight numbers. There are numerous costume changes, and Glenn Loney writing in *Other Stages* remarked on the "deft use of props and a set that continually unfolds visual surprises." *Variety* called it a "smartly staged revue of good nasty fun." The production utilizes a five-piece combo.

ORIGINAL CAST:

Donald Corren   MacIntyre Dixon
Joy Franz   Jonathan Hadary

SONGS:
Act I
Be Prepared (company)
Poisoning Pigeons (Franz, Corren)
I Wanna Go Back to Dixie (Dixon, company)
My Home Town (Corren)
Pollution (Franz, Dixon, company)
Bright College Days (Hadary, Corren)
Fight Fiercely, Harvard (Hadary, Dixon,
   Corren)
The Elements (Hadary)
The Folk Song Army (company)
In Old Mexico (Franz, company)
She's My Girl (Corren)
When You Are Old and Grey (company)
Wernher von Braun (Dixon)
Who's Next? (company)
I Got It from Agnes (Hadary)
National Brotherhood Week (company)

Act II
So Long, Mom (Corren, Hadary)
Send the Marines (company)
Hunting Song (Dixon)
Irish Ballad (Franz, company)
New Math (Corren, Dixon)
Silent E (company)
Oedipus Rex (Franz, company)
I Hold Your Hand in Mine (Corren)
Masochism Tango (Dixon)
The Old Dope Peddler (Hadary)
The Vatican Rag (company)
We Will All Go Together (company)

TOO MANY GIRLS (1939)

BOOK BY: George Marion, Jr.
MUSIC BY: Richard Rodgers
LYRICS BY: Lorenz Hart
PUBLISHED LIBRETTO: Dramatists Play Service,
   1940
CONDENSATION: None
ANTHOLOGY: None
LICENSING AGENT: Rodgers and Hammerstein
   Theatre Library
RECORDING: Painted Smiles PSCD 104 CD (studio
   cast)
CAST: Large mixed cast

This musical is all about undergraduates, football, and sex in the days before World War II. Four eastern football players go to Pottawatomie (a college in Stop Gap, New Mexico) as secret bodyguards to protect a wealthy Easterner's daughter. Critics found almost every song a delight and praised the colorful southwestern setting and costumes. There was a film version in 1940 with a new song ("You're Nearer") that is usually interpolated into stage revivals. This show will appeal to young audiences.

ORIGINAL CAST:

Desi Arnaz (Manuelito)
Richard Kollmar (Clint)
Eddie Bracken (Jojo)
Hal LeRoy (Al)
Hans Robert (Mr. Lister)
Marcy Wescott (Consuelo)

Mary Jane Walsh (Eileen)
Diosa Costello (Pepe)
Clyde Fillmore (Harvey)

SONGS:
Act I
Heroes in the Fall (ensemble)
Tempt Me Not (Manuelito, Jojo, ensemble)
My Prince (Consuelo)
Pottawatomie (Harvey, Mr Lister, ensemble)
'Cause We Got Cake (Eileen)
Love Never Went to College (Consuelo, Clint)
Spic and Spanish (Pepe)
I Like to Recognize the Tune (Jojo, Consuelo,
    Eileen, Clint, Al)
Look Out (Eileen, ensemble)

Act II
The Sweethearts of the Team (Eileen,
    ensemble)
She Could Shake the Maracas (Pepe,
    Manuelito)
I Didn't Know What Time It Was (Consuelo,
    Clint)
Too Many Girls (Manuelito)
Give It Back to the Indians (Eileen)

TOP BANANA (1951)

BOOK BY: Hy Kraft
MUSIC AND LYRICS BY: Johnny Mercer
PUBLISHED LIBRETTO: None
CONDENSATION: None
ANTHOLOGY: None
LICENSING AGENT: Tams-Witmark
RECORDING: Angel 764772-2 CD (original cast)
CAST: Large mixed cast

The plot of this musical features a burlesque comic who has a popular TV show,
suggesting perhaps Milton Berle in the
early 1950s. He runs into problems with
his soap sponsor when he inadvertantly
marries off the leading lady to his male
singer. This has been revived in Las Vegas.
The show should have some pretty girls
for the "Burlesk Kuties" and comics who
can handle the campy routines. Your "top
banana" will need a brash, hearty, forceful
style and good timing. There are also some

secondary roles for good singers. There
was a 1954 film featuring Phil Silvers and
most of the original cast.

ORIGINAL CAST:
Phil Silvers (Jerry)
Eddie Hanley (Danny)
Danny Scholl (Cliff)
Herbie Faye (Moe)
Joey Faye (Pinky)
Judy Lynn (Sally)
Rose Marie (Betty)
Jack Albertson (Vic)
Bill Callahan (Tommy)
Zachary A. Charles (Russ)
Bradford Hatton (Parker)

SONGS:
Act I
The Man of the Year This Week (ensemble)
You're So Beautiful That— (Cliff)
Top Banana (Jerry, Vic, Cliff, Pinky, Moe)
Elevator Song (ensemble)
Hail to MacCracken's (ensemble)
Only if You're in Love (Cliff, Sally)
My Home Is in My Shoes (Tommy, ensemble)
I Fought Every Step of the Way (Betty)
OK for TV (Jerry, Vic, Sally, Pinky, Moe,
    Danny, Russ)
Slogan Song (Jerry, Betty, Vic, Sally, Cliff,
    Tommy, Pinky, Moe, Danny, Russ, Parker)
Meet Miss Blendo (company)

Act II
Sans Souci (Betty, ensemble)
A Dog Is a Man's Best Friend (Jerry,
    ensemble)
Be My Guest (Cliff, Sally, ensemble)
A Word a Day (Jerry, Betty)

A TREE GROWS IN BROOKLYN
(1951)

BOOK BY: Betty Smith and George Abbott; based
    on the novel by Betty Smith
MUSIC BY: Arthur Schwartz
LYRICS BY: Dorothy Fields
PUBLISHED LIBRETTO: Harper, 1951

CONDENSATION: *New Complete Book of the American Musical Theater.* Ewen, David. Holt, 1970
ANTHOLOGY: None
VOCAL SELECTIONS: Chappell
LICENSING AGENT: Samuel French
RECORDING: Sony SK 48014 CD (original cast)
CAST: 17 M; 12 F; chorus

If you remember the novel or the 1945 film, you probably expect this to be the story of a young girl, Francie, growing up in Brooklyn in the early 1900s. But the plot emphasis has been shifted to her parents and Aunt Cissy, who collects "husbands." The original Broadway production was a large one requiring turn-of-the-century costumes. The songs were described as alternately humorous and sentimental. The dancing includes beer garden vaudeville style to a "nightmare" ballet.

ORIGINAL CAST:

Johnny Johnston (Johnny Nolan)
Marcia Van Dyke (Katie)
Shirley Booth (Cissy)
Nomi Mitty (Francie)
Albert Linville (Harry)

SONGS:
Act I
Payday (company)
Mine 'Til Monday (Johnny, company)
Make the Man Love Me (Katie, Johnny)
I'm Like a New Broom (Johnny, company)
Look Who's Dancing (Katie, Cissy, company)
Love Is the Reason (Cissy)
If You Haven't Got a Sweetheart (company)
I'll Buy You a Star (Johnny, company)

Act II
That's How It Goes (company)
He Had Refinement (Cissy)
Growing Pains (Johnny, Francie)
Is That My Prince? (Cissy, Harry)
Don't Be Afraid (Johnny)

TREEMONISHA (1975)

LYRICS AND MUSIC BY: Scott Joplin
PUBLISHED LIBRETTO: Included with LP recording
CONDENSATION: None
ANTHOLOGY: None
VOCAL SELECTIONS: Chappell, 1975
LICENSING AGENT: Dramatic
RECORDING: Deutsche Grammophon 2707 083 (Houston Grand Opera Production)
CAST: 8 M; 3 F; chorus

Treemonisha is found abandoned under a tree just after the Civil War and is adopted by a former slave couple. She grows up and tries to educate her people. There is a "conjur" man who thrives on their superstitions and opposes her. Described as authentic musical Americana, this all-black story set on an Arkansas plantation is sung, rather than spoken. It is called an opera and is much more than just ragtime music. Written in 1907, it is a mixture of nineteenth-century music hall and operetta. There is some exciting dancing, including a rousing cakewalk. There was a TV production in 1985.

1975 NEW YORK CAST:

Ben Harvey (Zodzetrick)
Willard White (Ned)
Betty Allen (Monisha)
Carmen Balthrop (Treemonisha)
Curtis Rayam (Remus)
Kenneth Hicks (Andy)
Cora Johnson (Lucy)
Clark Morgan (Parson Alltalk)
Raymond Bazemore (Simon)
Dwight Ransom (Cephus)
Dorceal Duckins (Luddud)

SONGS:
Act I
The Bag of Luck (Treemonisha, Monisha, Remus, Ned, Zodzetrick)
The Cornhuskers (Treemonisha, chorus)
We're Goin' Around (Treemonisha, Monisha, Lucy, Remus, Ned, ensemble)
The Wreath (Treemonisha, Monisha, Lucy)
The Sacred Tree (Monisha)

reemonisha)

la's Bringing Up (Treemonisha, Monisha)

Good Advice (Parson Alltalk, ensemble)

Confusion (Monisha, Lucy, Remus, Ned)

Superstition (Simon, Cephus)

Treemonisha in Peril (Zodzetrick, Simon, Luddud, Cephus)

The Wasp Nest (Simon, Cephus)

The Rescue (Treemonisha, Remus)

We Will Rest Awhile (quartet)

Going Home (Treemonisha, Remus)

Aunt Dinah Has Blowed de Horn (ensemble)

Act II

I Want to See My Child (Monisha, Ned)

Treemonisha's Return (Treemonisha, Monisha, Remus, Ned, Andy)

Wrong Is Never Right (Remus, ensemble)

Abuse (Treemonisha, Andy)

When Villains Ramble Far and Near (Ned)

Conjuror's Forgiven (Treemonisha, Andy)

We Will Trust You As Our Leader (ensemble)

A Real Slow Drag (company)

TRICKS (1973)

BOOK BY: Jon Jory; based on the play *Scapin* by Moliere

MUSIC BY: Jerry Blatt

LYRICS BY: Lonnie Burstein

PUBLISHED LIBRETTO: French, 1971

CONDENSATION: None

ANTHOLOGY: None

VOCAL SELECTIONS: Chappell, 1972

LICENSING AGENT: Samuel French

RECORDING: None

CAST: 6 M; 3 F; 4 musicians, 3 dancers

The action of this story is set in and around Venice during the Renaissance. The style is a cross between commedia dell'arte and vaudeville with juggling, puppetry, acrobatic tumbling, and slapstick. The plot concerns the servant Scapin, a twin set of lovers, and two masters being outwitted. The Broadway costumes were described as bright and vivid. The rock score includes some pop-soul. This production, which came to Broadway by way of regional theater, was designed for a small cast, limited facilities, and a small budget.

ORIGINAL CAST:

Walter Bobbie (Octave)

Rene Auberjonois (Scapin)

Christopher Murney (Sylvestre)

Carolyn Mignini (Hyacinthe)

Mitchell Jason (Argante)

Tom Toner (Geronte)

Joe Morton (Arlecchino)

June Helmers (Zerbinetta)

SONGS:

Act I

Love or Money (ensemble)

Who Was I? (Octave, ensemble)

Trouble's a Ruler (Scapin, Sylvestre, Octave)

Enter Hyacinthe (Octave, ensemble)

Believe Me (Octave, Hyacinthe, ensemble)

Tricks (Scapin, Sylvestre)

A Man of Spirit (ensemble)

Where Is Respect? (Argante, Geronte)

Somebody's Doin' Somebody All the Time (Scapin, ensemble)

A Sporting Man (Scapin, ensemble)

Act II

Scapin (Arlecchino)

Anything Is Possible (Scapin, Sylvestre)

How Sweetly Simple (Hyacinthe, Zerbinetta)

Gypsy Girl (Zerbinetta, ensemble)

Life Can Be Funny (ensemble)

TRIXIE TRUE, TEEN DETECTIVE (1980)

BOOK, MUSIC, AND LYRICS BY: Kelly Hamilton

PUBLISHED LIBRETTO: French, 1981

CONDENSATION: None

ANTHOLOGY: None

LICENSING AGENT: Samuel French

RECORDING: None

CAST: 4 M; 4 F

Two different kinds of entertainment are spoofed in the off-Broadway musical. First of all, there is the "Nancy Drew" type of juvenile mystery, and second, a far more sophisticated takeoff on the style of Hollywood films in the 1940s. The action switches from publishing offices to a mythical town as the author of the stories dreams up Trixie's adventures. The plot of "The Secret of the Tapping Shoes" is played out for us with some doubling up of the cast. The author wants to "kill off" Trixie, so Trixie has him as well as the Nazis to worry about! The sets may be simply suggested and music can be provided by a quintet alongside the stage.

ORIGINAL CAST:

Gene Lindsey (Joe)
Marilyn Sokol (Miss Snood/Olga)
Kathy Andrini (Trixie)
Keith Rice (Dick)
Alison Bevan (LaVerne)
Marianna Allen (Maxine)
Jay Logan (Al/Wilhelm)
Keith Caldwell (Radio Singer/Rick)

SONGS:
(performed without intermission):
Trixie's on the Case (Joe, Trixie, ensemble)
Lucky Day (Trixie, Radio Singer)
Most Popular (Dick, ensemble)
Mr. and Mrs. Dick Dickerson (Dick, Trixie, Radio Singer)
Juvenile Fiction (Miss Snood)
Sleuthing (Trixie, Maxine, LaVerne, ensemble)
Katzenjammer Kinda Song (Olga, Wilhelm)
Haven't Got Time for Love (Dick, Trixie)
Good-bye Helen Hathway (Joe, Trixie)
Mystery of the Moon (Trixie, Rick)
Secret of the Tapping Shoes (Trixie, Radio Singer, ensemble)
Joe's Lucky Day (Joe, ensemble)
Rita from Argentina (Miss Snood, Joe)
Rescue (company)

2 × 5 (1976)

MUSIC BY: John Kander
LYRICS BY: Fred Ebb
PUBLISHED LIBRETTO: None
CONDENSATION: None
ANTHOLOGY: None
LICENSING AGENT: Samuel French
RECORDING: None
CAST: 2 M; 3 F; 1 pianist

Approximately thirty songs from the shows of Kander and Ebb have been put together in a cabaret-style revue that was originally presented off-Broadway in Greenwich Village. Some of the things the critics liked include the use of flashlights in the dark to light up each face from below for the song "Money" from *Cabaret*; the funny "Class" duet from *Chicago*; all the numbers from *Flora the Red Menace*; and the movie song "New York, New York." The set was simply a pair of stairs, a few chairs and tables, and some portable props. These tuneful and intelligent songs are about the best Broadway has to offer. (See also *And the World Goes 'Round*.)

ORIGINAL CAST:

D'Jamin Bartlett   Kay Cummings
Danny Fortus   Shirley Lemmon
Scott Stevensen

This revue is made up of thirty songs divided into two acts.

TWO BY TWO (1970)

BOOK BY: Peter Stone; based on *The Flowering Peach* by Clifford Odets
MUSIC BY: Richard Rodgers
LYRICS BY: Martin Charnin
PUBLISHED LIBRETTO: None
CONDENSATION: None
ANTHOLOGY: None
PIANO-VOCAL SCORE: Williamson, 1971
VOCAL SELECTIONS: Williamson, 1971

LICENSING AGENT: Rodgers and Hammerstein
    Music Library
RECORDINGS: Columbia S 30338 (original cast);
    Sony SK 30338 CD (original cast)
CAST: 4 M; 4 F

The time is before, during, and after the biblical flood. The locales are in and around Noah's home, the ark, and atop Mt. Ararat. The Broadway sets were simple with projections on a white backdrop. This is a humorous telling of the biblical story with "clean dirty jokes and cautiously blasphemous God gags" (John Simon, *New York Magazine*). Noah is an old sot with a dismal wife and three dismal sons. Danny Kaye played Noah, besieged with dreary domestic problems until the flood (which occurs during the intermission). The attractive Richard Rodgers score has not yet produced any standards. There is no dancing or chorus.

ORIGINAL CAST:

Danny Kaye (Noah)
Harry Goz (Shem)
Michael Karm (Ham)
Marilyn Cooper (Leah)
Walter Willison (Japheth)
Joan Copeland (Esther)
Tricia O'Neil (Rachel)
Madeline Kahn (Goldie)

SONGS:
Act I
Why Me? (Noah)
Put Him Away (Shem, Ham, Leah)
The Gitka's Song (Noah, unidentified offstage
    voice)
Something, Somewhere (Japheth, family)
You Have Got to Have a Rudder on the Ark
    (Noah, Shem, Ham, Japheth)
Something Doesn't Happen (Rachel, Esther)
An Old Man (Esther)
Ninety Again! (Noah)
Two by Two (Noah, family)
I Do Not Know a Day I Did Not Love You
    (Japheth)
Something, Somewhere (reprise) (Noah)

Act II
When It Dries (Noah, family)
Two by Two (reprise) (Noah, Esther)
The Golden Ram (Goldie)
Poppa Knows Best (Noah, Japheth)
I Do Not Know a Day I Did Not Love You
    (reprise) (Rachel, Japheth)
As Far As I'm Concerned (Shem, Leah)
Hey, Goldie (Noah)
The Covenant (Noah)

TWO GENTLEMEN OF VERONA (1971)

BOOK ADAPTED BY: John Guare and Mel Shapiro;
    based on the play by Shakespeare
MUSIC BY: Galt MacDermot
LYRICS BY: John Guare
PUBLISHED LIBRETTO: Holt, 1973
CONDENSATION: *Broadway Musicals Show by Show.*
    Green, Stanley. Hal Leonard Books, 1985
ANTHOLOGY: *Great Rock Musicals.* Stanley
    Richards, ed. Stein and Day, 1979
PIANO-VOCAL SCORE: Chappell, 1973
VOCAL SELECTIONS: Chappell, 1972
LICENSING AGENT: Tams-Witmark
RECORDING: ABC BCSY 1001 (original cast)
CAST: 10 M; 3 F; extras

This popular rock show started off in New York's Central Park as part of the Shakespeare Festival and then moved to Broadway for a successful run of over 600 performances. It is a love story—Valentine loves Silvia. Valentine's friend Proteus, who loves Julia, also decides to love Silvia. This story was considerably modernized and had ethnic actors in the leads. The dialogue is a mixture of Shakespeare and modern passages. The score was described by Julius Novick in the *Village Voice* as "soft-rock-pop-quasi-Latin-semi-soul" and is by the composer of *Hair.* The scenery was "scaffoldy" and costuming "hippie-Renaissance" (see record album photos). The finale features soap bubbles, Frisbees, and yo-yos.

Tony Award Winner (Best Musical)

ORIGINAL CAST:

Clifton Davis (Valentine)
Raul Julia (Proteus)
Diana Davila (Julia)
Frank O'Brien (Thurio)
John Bottoms (Launce)
Georgyn Geetlein (citizen)
Alix Elias (Lucetta)
Jose Perez (Speed)
Norman Matlock (Duke of Milan)
Jonelle Allen (Silvia)
Alvin Lum (Eglamour)

SONGS:

(performed without intermission)
Summer, Summer (I Love My Father)
(ensemble)
That's an Interesting Question (Valentine,
Proteus)
I'd Like to Be a Rose (Valentine, Proteus,
ensemble)
Thou Hast Metamorphosed Me (Proteus)
Reprise (Julia)
Symphony (Proteus, ensemble)
I Am Not Interested in Love (Julia)
Love Is That You? (Thurio, citizen)
What Does a Lover Pack? (Proteus, Julia,
ensemble)
Pearls (Launce)
I Love My Father (Proteus)
Two Gentlemen of Verona (Julia, Lucetta,
ensemble)
Follow the Rainbow (Valentine, Proteus, Julia,
Lucetta, Launce, Speed)
Where's North? (ensemble)
Bring All the Boys Back Home (Duke of Milan,
ensemble)
Love's Revenge (Valentine)
To Whom It May Concern Me (Silvia,
Valentine)
Night Letter (Silvia, Valentine)
Calla Lily Lady (Proteus)
Land of Betrayal (Lucetta)
Thurio's Samba (Thurio, Duke of Milan,
ensemble)
Hot Lover (Speed, Launce)
What a Nice Idea (Julia)
Who Is Silvia? (Proteus, ensemble)
Love Me (Silvia)

Eglamour (Eglamour, Silvia)
The Lovers Have Been Sighted (Duke of
Milan, Proteus, ensemble)
Mansion (Valentine)
What's a Nice Girl Like Her? (Proteus)
Don't Have the Baby (Lucetta, Speed, Julia,
Launce)
Milkmaid (Launce, citizen)
Love Has Driven Me Sane (company)

THE UNSINKABLE MOLLY BROWN (1960)

BOOK BY: Richard Morris
MUSIC AND LYRICS BY: Meredith Willson
PUBLISHED LIBRETTO: Putnam, 1961; *Theatre Arts*
(magazine), February 1963
CONDENSATION: *New Complete Book of the*
American Musical Theater. Ewen, David. Holt,
1970
ANTHOLOGY: None
PIANO-VOCAL SCORE: Frank Music, 1962
VOCAL SELECTIONS: Frank Music, 1964
LICENSING AGENT: Music Theatre International
RECORDING: Angel ZDM 764761-2 CD (original
cast)
CAST: 28 M; 9 F

Turn-of-the-century Denver and the Rocky
Mountain area are the settings for this
musical, although Europe and even the
sinking of the *Titanic* get into the act.
Molly, the "hillbilly heroine," marries into
unexpected wealth and is determined to
crash society. There is a bouncy score with
opportunities for several energetic dance
numbers. Costuming style is both "back-
hills" and "high society." This big Broadway musical was a triumph for Tammy
Grimes, and it was filmed in 1964 with Debbie Reynolds.

ORIGINAL CAST:

Tammy Grimes (Molly)
Joseph Sirola (Christmas)
Harve Presnell (Johnny)
Woody Hurst (Charlie)
Tom Larson (Burt)
Joe Pronto (Gitter)

Jack Harrold (Monsignor)
Mony Dalmes (Princess DeLong)
Mitchell Gregg (Prince DeLong)

SONGS:
Act I
I Ain't Down Yet (Molly, brothers)
Belly Up to the Bar, Boys (Molly, Christmas,
    ensemble)
I've A'ready Started In (Johnny, Christmas,
    Charlie, Burt, Gitter)
I'll Never Say No (Johnny)
My Own Brass Bed (Molly)
The Denver Police (ensemble)
Beautiful People of Denver (Molly)
Are You Sure? (Molly, Monsignor, ensemble)
I Ain't Down Yet (reprise) (Molly, Johnny)

Act II
Happy Birthday, Mrs. J. J. Brown (Princess
    DeLong, Prince DeLong, ensemble)
Bon Jour (The Language Song) (Molly, Prince
    DeLong, ensemble)
If I Knew (Johnny)
Chick-a-Pen (Molly, Johnny)
Keep-a-Hoppin' (Johnny, ensemble)
Leadville Johnny Brown (Soliloquy) (Johnny)
Dolce Far Niente (Prince DeLong, Molly)
Colorado, My Home (Johnny, Molly,
    ensemble)

UNSUNG COLE (AND CLASSICS TOO) (1977)

CONCEIVED AND ARRANGED BY: Norman L.
    Berman
MUSIC AND LYRICS BY: Cole Porter
PUBLISHED LIBRETTO: French, 1981
CONDENSATION: None
ANTHOLOGY: None
MUSIC PUBLISHER: *Music and Lyrics of Cole Porter*.
    2 vols. Chappell, 1972–75
LICENSING AGENT: Samuel French
RECORDING: None
CAST: 2 M; 3 F

The seldom heard songs of Cole Porter are featured in this cabaret-style revue. This was performed off-Broadway in a simple but elegant setting with twin pianos for accompaniment. Called a musical entertainment, there is no plot and only a bit of spoken dialogue. Some of the songs are from shows like *Mexican Hayride* while other songs were dropped from such shows as *Kiss Me, Kate*. Scattered throughout the evening are the amusing verses from "Nobody's Chasing Me Now" from *Out of This World*. There are familiar songs as well, and "Friendship" makes a happy finale.

ORIGINAL CAST:

Gene Lindsey   Mary Louise
Maureen Moore   Anita Morris
John Sloman

This revue consists of thirty-three songs presented in two acts.

UP FROM PARADISE (1983)

BOOK AND LYRICS BY: Arthur Miller; based on
    his play *The Creation of the World and Other
    Business*
MUSIC BY: Stanley Silverman
PUBLISHED LIBRETTO: French, 1985
CONDENSATION: None
ANTHOLOGY: None
LICENSING AGENT: Samuel French
RECORDING: None
CAST: 9 M; 1 F

Described as casual and warm-spirited, the first part of this musical concerns Adam and Eve and their expulsion from paradise. The second part moves on to Cain and Abel. The off-Broadway production was more a staged concert performance, in contemporary dress, on a bare platform, and with few props. Len Cariou was highly praised playing God as a sophisticated but vain personage who likes to hear himself praised and enjoys an occasional glass of wine. The musical score is made up of blues, gospel, ragtime, and jazz. This was recommended for amateur church and synagogue theater groups.

ORIGINAL CAST:

Len Cariou (God)
Austin Pendleton (Adam)
Alice Playten (Eve)
Lonny Price (Abel)
Paul Ukena, Jr. (Cain)
Walter Bobbie (Lucifer)

SONGS:

Act I

The Lord Is a Hammer of Light (ensemble)
How Fine It Is (Adam, God, ensemble)
When Night Starts to Fall (Adam)
Bone of Thy Bones (God)
Hallelujah (ensemble)
The Center of Your Mind (God, Adam, Eve, ensemble)
It's Just Like I Was You (Adam, Eve)
Recitative (God)
But If Something Leads to Good (Lucifer)
I'm Me—We're Us (Adam, Eve)
Curses (God)
Lonely Quartet (Adam, Eve, Lucifer, God)
How Lovely Is Eve (Lucifer)
I Am the River and Waltz (Eve)

Act II

All of That Made for Me (ensemble)
As Good As Paradise (Adam, Eve, Cain, Abel)
It Was So Peaceful before There Was Man (God).
It Comes to Me (Abel)
I Don't Know What Is Happening to Me (Cain, Abel)
All Love (Eve, Adam, Abel, ensemble)
Nothing's Left of God (Lucifer)
Passion (God)
I Know He Wants Us to Praise His Mornings (Adam, Eve, ensemble)

UP IN THE AIR, BOYS (1974)

BOOK BY: Robert Dahdah and Mary Boylan
MUSIC AND LYRICS BY: Robert Dahdah
PUBLISHED LIBRETTO: None
CONDENSATION: None

ANTHOLOGY: None
LICENSING AGENT: Samuel French
RECORDING: None
CAST: 5 M; 5 F

If you know your movie musicals, the character names of the cast of this off-Broadway musical tell it all. If not, this is a spoof of all those Fred and Ginger musicals, with a typical show biz tale about a pair of demobilized pilots and two aspiring young show girls and how they all get together and put on a show. This was modestly staged in New York but had lots of tap dancing.

ORIGINAL CAST:

Tom Offt (Fred)
Peggylee Brennan (Ginger)
Margaret Benczak (Irene)
Gail Cook (Lucille)
Denis Deal (Eddie)
Lisa Marina Passero (Fifi)
Jack Weaver (Randy)

SONGS:

Act I

Up in the Air, Boys (company)
You Never Change (Fred, Ginger)
Top Spot (Fred, men)
Dreams Don't Mean a Thing (Irene)
Don't Make Me Dance (Fred, Ginger)
Laughing Daffodil (Lucille, Eddie, company)
Musical Me (Fred, Ginger)
When Marie Antoinette Learned How to Pet (Fifi, company)

Act II

Voodoo Night in Hotchkiss Corners (Fred, company)
How Could I Forget? (Fred, Ginger)
Apache Dance (Fifi, Fred, Randy)
Reach (Lucille, Irene, ensemble)
Do the Heavenenthal (Fifi, Fred, Ginger, company)

THE UTTER GLORY OF MORRISSEY HALL (1979)

BOOK BY: Clark Gesner and Nagle Jackson
MUSIC AND LYRICS BY: Clark Gesner

PUBLISHED LIBRETTO: French, 1982
CONDENSATION: None
ANTHOLOGY: None
LICENSING AGENT: Samuel French
RECORDING: Original Cast OC 7918 (original cast)
CAST: 4 M; 18 F (includes 12 schoolgirls)

The setting is a girl's school somewhere in the English countryside. The atmosphere is reminiscent of the St. Trinian movies. There are all sorts of problems that the headmistress must resolve; the climax is an all-out war between the students, using arrows, bombs, and even a cannon! The set is a large Victorian-Gothic mansion converted into a school; it includes offices, closets, and two upstairs rooms. The score has a hint of Gilbert and Sullivan. Most of the adults are a bit off balance, and the girls are malevolent!

ORIGINAL CAST:

Celeste Holm (Headmistress)
Patricia Falkenhain (Studley)
Marilyn Caskey (Elizabeth)
Taina Elg (Mrs. Delmonde)
Becky McSpadden (Helen—student)
John Gallogly (Charles)
Willard Beckham (Richard)
Laurie Franks (Winkle)
Mary Saunders (Carswell—student)

SONGS:
Act I
Promenade (company)
Proud, Erstwhile, Upright, Fair (Headmistress, Studley, Elizabeth)
Elizabeth's Song (Elizabeth)
Way Back When (Headmistress, Studley)
Lost (students)
Morning (Mrs. Delmonde, students)
The Letter (Helen, Charles, company)
Oh Sun (Helen, Mrs. Delmonde, students)
Give Me That Key (Headmistress, Helen, Elizabeth)
Duet (Elizabeth, Richard, company)
Act II
Interlude and Gallop (students)
You Will Know When the Time Has Arrived (Winkle, Carswell, students)

You Would Say (Helen, Charles, students)
See the Blue (Headmistress, students)
Dance of Resignation (Mrs. Delmonde)
Reflection (Headmistress)
The War (company)

THE VAGABOND KING (1925)

BOOK AND LYRICS BY: Brian Hooker and W. H. Post; based on *If I Were King* by Justin Huntley McCarthy
MUSIC BY: Rudolf Friml
PUBLISHED LIBRETTO: French, 1929, 1956
CONDENSATION: *Ganzl's Book of the Musical Theatre*. Ganzl, Kurt. Schirmer (Macmillan), 1989
ANTHOLOGY: None
PIANO-VOCAL SCORE: Famous Music, 1926
LICENSING AGENT: Tams-Witmark (for professional productions); Samuel French (for amateur productions)
RECORDING: Monmouth-Evergreen MES 7050 (original London cast)
CAST: 18 M; 11 F; chorus

Set in fifteenth-century France, this is the tale of a poet-thief and his adventures with royalty, prostitutes with hearts of gold, and comedians. The hero assumes the kingship of France for a day and repels a Burgundian invasion. This popular show has had several lavish Broadway productions and has also been produced around the country and in the British Isles. There have also been numerous simple versions with unpretentious costumes and limited props. It is described as a colorful, exciting family entertainment with ample opportunity for swordplay. It was filmed in 1930 with Jeanette MacDonald and again in 1956 with Kathryn Grayson.

ORIGINAL CAST:

Robert Craik (René)
Jane Carroll (Huguette)
Herbert Corthell (Tabarie)
Dennis King (Villon)
Carolyn Thomson (Katherine)
Marion Alta (Lady Suzanne)

Herbert Delmore (Noel)
Julian Winter (Oliver)
Olga Treskoff (Lady Mary)
G. L. Mortimer (Bishop)

SONGS:
Act I
Opening Chorus (René, ensemble)
Love for Sale (Huguette, ensemble)
Drinking Song (Tabarie, men)
Song of the Vagabonds (Villon, ensemble)
Some Day (Katherine)
Only a Rose (Katherine, Villon)
Hunting (Noel, ensemble)
Scottish Archers Song (ensemble)
Tomorrow (Villon, Katherine)

Act II
Nocturne (Noel, Lady Suzanne, ensemble)
Serenade (Tabarie, Oliver, Lady Mary)
The Huguette Waltz (Huguette)
Love Me Tonight (Katherine, Villon)
Te Deum (Bishop, ensemble)
Victory March (ensemble)

VARIETY OBIT (1973)

BOOK BY: Ron Whyte
MUSIC BY: Mel Marvin
LYRICS BY: Ron Whyte and Bob Satuloff
PUBLISHED LIBRETTO: French, 1973
CONDENSATION: None
ANTHOLOGY: None
LICENSING AGENT: Samuel French
RECORDING: None
CAST: 2 M; 1 F

The title of this one-act musical refers to the obituaries of show biz personalities that appear in *Variety*. It begins with a blowup of the *Variety* obit of Danny Jefferson, the last member of an obscure show business family. We then have the family history done in song and dance. There are just two performers and a narrator. It is simply staged with a piano and drum. The off-Broadway production used a number of slide projections.

ORIGINAL CAST:
Andrea Marcovicci (Girl)
Richard Cox (Boy)
David Clennon (Narrator)

SONGS:
(performed without intermission)
Central Park, 1917 (Boy, Girl)
The Wolves of Kultur on a Bright and Silent
    Saturday (Girl)
Ellesburg, Ohio (company)
Song for Sunday (Boy, Girl)
Carnival (Girl, Boy)

VERY GOOD EDDIE (1915)

BOOK BY: Guy Bolton; based on the farce by
    Phillip Bartholomae
MUSIC BY: Jerome Kern
LYRICS BY: Schuyler Greene
PUBLISHED LIBRETTO: None
CONDENSATION: *New Complete Book of the
    American Musical Theater.* Ewen, David. Holt,
    1970
ANTHOLOGY: None
PIANO-VOCAL SCORE: Harms, 1915
LICENSING AGENT: Tams-Witmark
RECORDING: DRG 6100 CD (1975 revival cast)
CAST: 11 M; 7 F

The plot of this musical concerns two honeymooning couples who take a boat to Poughkeepsie and are separated. The right bride ends up with the wrong groom at Honeymoon Inn. The time is circa 1915. This is another Kern "Princess" musical that was revived and brought to Broadway by the Goodspeed Opera House. The first act is aboard the Hudson River boat and the second act is in the lobby of the hotel. The critics found it dated, if innocent. The score of eighteen songs is tuneful but will probably not be familiar to the audience. Lively choreography and simple period costumes and sets will make this a popular, nostalgic attraction.

1975 NEW YORK CAST:

Cynthia Wells (Lilly)
David Christmas (Dick)
Charles Repole (Eddie)
Virginia Seidel (Elsie)
Nicholas Wyman (Percy)
Spring Fairbank (Georgina)
Joel Craig (M. de Rougemont)
Travis Hudson (Mme Matroppo)

SONGS:
(including some interpolated numbers)
Act I
We're on Our Way (ensemble)
Some Sort of Somebody (Lilly, Dick)
Thirteen Collar (Eddie)
Bungalow in Quogue (Elsie, Percy)
Isn't It Great to Be Married? (Elsie, Georgina,
    Eddie, Percy)
Good Night Boat (ensemble)
Left All Alone Again Blues (Elsie)
Hot Dog! (ensemble)
If You're a Friend of Mine (Elsie, Eddie)
Wedding Bells Are Calling Me (ensemble)

Act II
Honeymoon Inn (Lilly, ensemble)
I've Got to Dance (M. de Rougemont,
    ensemble)
Moon of Love (Mme Matroppo, ensemble)
Old Boy Neutral (Lilly, Dick)
Babes in the Wood (Elsie, Eddie)
Katy-did (Mme Matroppo)
Nodding Roses (Lilly, Dick)

VIA GALACTICA (1972)

BOOK BY: Christopher Gore and Judith Ross
MUSIC BY: Galt MacDermot
LYRICS BY: Christopher Gore
PUBLISHED LIBRETTO: None
CONDENSATION: None
ANTHOLOGY: None
LICENSING AGENT: Samuel French
RECORDING: None
CAST: 16 M; 11 F; 2 children

Described as a space-age musical, this story is set 1,000 years in the future. Most Earthlings are without feeling—they do not love or hate, and they commit suicide at the age of fifty-five. But there is one tiny outpost, a small asteroid called Ithaca, made up of some nonconformists. The production in New York was extremely elaborate with trampolines used to simulate weightlessness, a flying garbage truck, a lot of moving scenery, and blinking lights. The almost nonstop score (all the lines are sung) was described by critics as agreeable and pleasant. A note to the makeup department: all Earthlings have blue skin!

ORIGINAL CAST:

Irene Cara (Storyteller)
Raul Julia (Gabriel)
Damon Evans (Hels)
Edloe (April)
Virginia Vestoff (Omaha)
Keene Curtis (Dr. Isaacs)
Bill Starr (Provo)

SONGS:
Act I
We Are One (ensemble)
Helen of Troy (Gabriel)
Oysters (Hels, April)
The Other Side of the Sky (Hels)
Children of the Sun (Omaha)
Different (April, company)
Take Your Hat Off (Omaha, company)
Ilmar's Tomb (Gabriel)
Shall We Friend? (Gabriel)
The Lady Isn't Looking (Omaha)
Hush (Gabriel)
Cross on Over (Dr. Isaacs, Omaha, company)
The Gospel of Gabriel Finn (Gabriel)

Act II
Terre Haute High (April)
Life Wins (Omaha)
The Worm Germ (Provo)
Isaacs' Equation (Dr. Isaacs)
Dance the Dark Away (Storyteller, company)
Four Hundred Girls Ago (Gabriel)
All My Good Mornings (Omaha)
New Jerusalem (company)

WALKING HAPPY (1966)

BOOK BY: Roger O. Hirson and Ketti Frings;
    based on the play *Hobson's Choice* by Harold
    Brighouse
MUSIC BY: James van Heusen
LYRICS BY: Sammy Cahn
PUBLISHED LIBRETTO: French, 1967
CONDENSATION: None
ANTHOLOGY: None
VOCAL SELECTIONS: Shapiro, Bernstein, 1966
LICENSING AGENT: Samuel French
RECORDING: Capitol SVAS 2631 (original cast)
CAST: 14 M; 7 F

Hobson is a widowed merchant with three daughters. The original title stems from his choice and their choices for their husbands. Maggie, the oldest, is set on Will Mossop, a bootmaker. This is set in the North Country of England in the 1870s, so there is a music-hall flavor to the numbers. There was an excellent clog dance, which much later was re-created on Broadway by the American Dance Machine. The Broadway production was praised for its ingenious motor-driven scenery of skyline, chimney pots, and neighborhood pubs. This is a family show.

ORIGINAL CAST:

George Rose (Hobson)
Ed Bakey (Beenstock)
Louise Troy (Maggie)
Norman Wisdom (Will)
Gordon Dilworth (Tubby)
Lucille Benson (Mrs. Figgins)
Jane Laughlin (Ada)
Gretchen Van Aken (Vickie)
Sharon Dierking (Alice)

SONGS:
Act I
Think of Something Else (Hobson, Beenstock, ensemble)
Where Was I? (Maggie)
How D'ya Talk to a Girl? (Will, Tubby)
Clog and Grog (ensemble)
If I Be Your Best Chance (Will)

A Joyful Thing (Will, Mrs. Figgins, Ada, ensemble)
What Makes It Happen? (Will)
Use Your Noggin (Maggie, Vickie, Alice)
Act II
You're Right, You're Right (Maggie)
I'll Make a Man of the Man (Maggie)
Walking Happy (Will, Maggie, ensemble)
I Don't Think I'm in Love (Will, Maggie)
Such a Sociable Sort (Hobson, ensemble)
It Might as Well Be Her (Will, Tubby)
People Who Are Nice (Hobson)
You're Right, You're Right (reprise) (Will, Maggie, Hobson)
I Don't Think I'm in Love (reprise) (Will)

WEST SIDE STORY (1957)

BOOK BY: Arthur Laurents; based on a concept by
    Jerome Robbins
MUSIC BY: Leonard Bernstein
LYRICS BY: Stephen Sondheim
PUBLISHED LIBRETTO: Random House, 1958;
    Theatre Arts (magazine), October 1959
CONDENSATION: *Broadway's Best, 1958*. John
    Chapman, ed. Doubleday, 1958; *Ganzl's Book
    of the Musical Theatre*. Ganzl, Kurt. Schirmer
    (Macmillan), 1989
ANTHOLOGY: *Ten Great Musicals of the American
    Stage*. Stanley Richards, ed. Chilton, 1973
PIANO-VOCAL SCORE: Schirmer and Chappell, 1959
VOCAL SELECTIONS: Schirmer and Chappell, 1957
LICENSING AGENT: Music Theatre International
RECORDINGS: Columbia CK 32603 CD (original
    cast); Sony CK 53152 CD (original cast)
CAST: 16–22 M; 11–15 F

This famous musical concerns rival teenage gangs in New York City in the late 1950s. It is a retelling of the *Romeo and Juliet* story with a tragic love affair between Tony and Maria. By now it has become a classic landmark of the American musical theater. The Bernstein score includes many familiar songs. Both the stage and the 1961 film versions are noted for their vigorous and athletic choreography. The settings are back streets, alleys, and fire escapes of lower-class Manhattan white and Puerto Rican neighborhoods. This is a great singing show and a great dancing show.

ORIGINAL CAST:

Mickey Calin (Riff)
David Winters (Baby John)
Grover Dale (Snowboy)
Larry Kert (Tony)
Carol Lawrence (Maria)
Chita Rivera (Anita)
Marilyn Cooper (Rosalia)
Lynn Ross (Estella)
Reri Grist (Consuelo)
Eddie Roll (Action)

SONGS:
Act I
Jet Song (Riff, Baby John, Snowboy, ensemble)
Something's Coming (Tony)
Maria (Tony)
Tonight (Tony, Maria)
America (Anita, Rosalia, girls)
Cool (Riff, ensemble)
One Hand, One Heart (Tony, Maria)
The Rumble (ensemble)

Act II
I Feel Pretty (Maria, Estella, Rosalia, Consuelo)
Somewhere (Consuelo)
Gee, Officer Krupke (Action, Snowboy, ensemble)
A Boy Like That (Anita, Maria)
I Have a Love (Anita, Maria)
Taunting (Anita, ensemble)

WHAT ABOUT LUV? (1984)

(original New York production title: *Love*)

BOOK BY: Jeffrey Sweet; based on the play *Luv* by Murray Schisgal
MUSIC BY: Howard Marren
LYRICS BY: Susan Birkenhead
PUBLISHED LIBRETTO: None
CONDENSATION: None
ANTHOLOGY: None

LICENSING AGENT: Music Theatre International
RECORDING: TER 1171 CD (studio cast)
CAST: 2 M; 1 F

The action takes place entirely on a New York bridge with a one year lapse between Act I and Act II. Two college buddies meet again by accident; one contemplates suicide and the other wants to get rid of his wife. The wife appears and agrees to leave her husband for the other man. But when we meet them again, one year later, all is changed. Costumes and props are minimal. The music is not simple, so trained voices are recommended. In describing this musical farce the adjectives most used were wacky, zany, nutty, kookie, and absurd. There was a film version of the play in 1967.

1991 NEW YORK REVIVAL CAST:

David Green (Milt)
Judy Kaye (Ellen)
Austin Pendleton (Harry)

SONGS:
Act I
Harry's Letter (Harry)
Reunion/Polyart U (Milt, Harry)
Paradise (Milt, Harry)
Carnival Ride (Milt, Harry)
The Chart (Harry, Milt, Ellen)
Harry Meets Ellen (Milt, Harry, Ellen)
Starlight/Lesbian (Harry, Ellen)
Paradise II/Election Stats (Ellen, Harry)
I Believe in Marriage (Ellen)
Somebody (Harry, Ellen)
The Test/Yes, Yes I Love You (Ellen, Harry)

Act II
How Beautiful the Night Is (Ellen)
What a Life (Milt, Ellen)
Lady (Milt, Ellen)
If Harry Weren't Here (Milt, Ellen)
My Brown Paper Bag (Harry, Ellen, Milt)
Yes, Yes I Love You (reprise) (Ellen, Milt)
Do I Love Him? (Ellen, Harry)
Harry's Resolution (Harry, Milt, Ellen)
What about Love? (Ellen, Milt, Harry)

WHAT MAKES SAMMY RUN? (1964)

BOOK BY: Budd and Stuart Schulberg; based on
  the novel by Budd Schulberg
MUSIC AND LYRICS BY: Ervin Drake
PUBLISHED LIBRETTO: Random House, 1965
CONDENSATION: *New Complete Book of the
  American Musical Theater*. Ewen, David. Holt,
  1970
ANTHOLOGY: None
VOCAL SELECTIONS: Harms, 1964
LICENSING AGENT: Tams-Witmark
RECORDING: Columbia COS 2440 (original cast)
CAST: Large mixed cast

This is a big musical set in Hollywood and New York in the 1930s. In addition to Grauman's Chinese Theater, studios, and offices, there are biblical and South Sea production numbers (for films being made), elegant clothes, and energetic choreography. Sammy is a fast-talking Lower East Side kid who becomes a big Hollywood producer after taking advantage of almost everybody along the way. Since Schulberg grew up in Hollywood, there may be more fact than fiction to this. Steve Lawrence was very successful in his Broadway debut as Sammy.

ORIGINAL CAST:

Steve Lawrence (Sammy)
Robert Alda (Al)
Barry Newman (Sheik)
Sally Ann Howes (Kit)
Graciela Daniele (Rita)
Richard France (Tracy)
Bernice Massi (Laurette)

SONGS:
Act I
A New Pair of Shoes (Sammy, Al, ensemble)
You Help Me (Sammy, Al)
A Tender Spot (Kit)
Lites—Camera—Platitude (Sammy, Kit, Al)
My Hometown (Sammy)
Monsoon (Rita, Tracy, ensemble)
I See Something (Laurette, Sammy)
Maybe Some Other Time (Kit, Al)
You Can Trust Me (Sammy)

A Room without Windows (Kit, Sammy)
Kiss Me No Kisses (Kit, Sammy)

Act II
I Feel Humble (Sammy, Sheik, ensemble)
Something to Live For (Kit)
Paint a Rainbow (Rita, Tracy, ensemble)
You're No Good (Laurette, Sammy)
Something to Live For (reprise) (Al)
The Friendliest Thing (Laurette)
Wedding of the Year (ensemble)
Some Days Everything Goes Wrong (Sammy)

WHAT'S A NICE COUNTRY LIKE YOU DOING IN A STATE LIKE THIS? (1984)

MUSIC BY: Cary Hoffman; based on an original
  concept by Ira Gasman, Cary Hoffman, and
  Bernie Travis
LYRICS BY: Ira Gasman
PUBLISHED LIBRETTO: French
CONDENSATION: None
ANTHOLOGY: None
LICENSING AGENT: Samuel French
RECORDING: Galaxy GAL 6004 (original London
  cast)
CAST: 3 M; 2 F

"It's a Political-Satirical Revue" is the opening number in this show. There are no sketches—just songs or song scenes. This was called "soft-core" political satire rather than real political cabaret. Some of the subjects covered include liberals, women's liberation, political scandal, life in New York, and changing sex styles. This is simple to stage but requires talented performers.

ORIGINAL CAST:

Missy Baldino   Patty Granau
Steve Mulch   Hugh Panaro
Rob Resnick

SONGS:
Act I
Get Out of Here (company)
Church and State (Mulch, Resnick)
What the Hell (Granau)
I'm in Love with . . . (Baldino)

Terrorist Trio (Panaro, Resnick, Mulch)
Hard to Be a Liberal (Panaro)
Male Chauvinist Pig of Myself (Panaro)
Liberation Tango (Granau)
Changing Partners (Baldino, Mulch,
    Granau)
The Last One of the Boys (Mulch)
Runaway Suite (company)
Update (Resnick)
I Just Pressed Button A (Resnick)
Nuclear Winter (Baldino, Panaro)
New York Suite (company)

Act II
Why Do I Keep Coming to the Theater?
    (company)
Carlos, Juan, and Miguel (Mulch, Panaro,
    Resnick)
Nicaragua (Granau)
I'm Not Myself Anymore (Resnick)
Keeping the Peace (company)
America, You're Looking Good (Panaro)
They Aren't There (Baldino, Mulch)
Farewell (company)
Fill-er Up (Baldino)
Porcupine Suite (company)
Everybody Ought to Have a Gun (Resnick,
    company)
Hallelujah (Mulch, company)
Johannesburg (Mulch)
Take Us Back, King George (Granau, Panaro,
    Resnick, Mulch)
Come on, Daisy (Baldino, company)

WHERE'S CHARLEY? (1948)

BOOK BY: George Abbott; based on *Charley's Aunt*
    by Brandon Thomas
MUSIC AND LYRICS BY: Frank Loesser
PUBLISHED LIBRETTO: None
CONDENSATION: *New Complete Book of the
    American Musical Theater.* Ewen, David. Holt,
    1970
ANTHOLOGY: None
MUSIC PUBLISHER: Frank Music, 1964
LICENSING AGENT: Music Theatre International

RECORDING: Monmouth-Evergreen ME 5-7029
    (original London cast)
CAST: Large mixed cast

The plot of this musical is much the same
as the famous play. A young Oxford student is forced to masquerade as his aunt
from Brazil and various complications develop. This farce is set in Victorian England.
This was performed in the round at New
York's Circle in the Square. *Charley's Aunt*
is a family show that has been a success
in any revival or reincarnation. Ray Bolger
starred on Broadway and in the 1952 film
version.

1974 REVIVAL CAST:

Louis Beachner (Brassett)
Marcia McClain (Amy)
Carol Jo Lugenbeal (Kitty)
Raul Julia (Charley)
Jerry Lanning (Jack)
Peter Walker (Sir Francis)
Tom Aldredge (Mr. Spettigue)
Taina Elg (Donna Lucia)

SONGS:
Act I
Where's Charley? (Brassett, ensemble)
The Years Before Us (ensemble)
Better Get Out of Here (Amy, Kitty, Charley,
    Jack)
The New Ashmolean Marching Society and
    Students Conservatory Band (Jack, Amy,
    Kitty, Charley, Sir Francis, Mr. Spettigue,
    Brassett, ensemble)
My Darling, My Darling (Kitty, Jack)
Make a Miracle (Charley, Amy)
Serenade with Asides (Mr. Spettigue)
Lovelier than Ever (Donna Lucia, Sir Francis,
    ensemble)
The Woman in His Room (Amy)
Pernambuco (Charley, company)

Act II
Where's Charley? (reprise) (Amy)
Once in Love with Amy (Charley)
The Gossips (ladies)
At the Red Rose Cotillion (ensemble)

WHISPERS ON THE WIND (1970)

BOOK AND LYRICS BY: John B. Kuntz
MUSIC BY: Lor Crane
PUBLISHED LIBRETTO: French, 1971
CONDENSATION: None
ANTHOLOGY: None
LICENSING AGENT: Samuel French
RECORDING: None
CAST: 3 M; 2 F

This off-Broadway musical is about growing up, leaving home, and falling in love in the big city. The time is the present and the city is New York. The costumes were described as modish and the setting as handsome ramps and screens. The music was called "plastic rock" and there is very little dancing. The cast of five assume a variety of roles.

ORIGINAL CAST:

Nancy Dussault (First Woman)
David Cryer (Narrator)
Mary Louise Wilson (Second Woman)
R. G. Brown (Second Man)
Patrick Fox (First Man)

SONGS:
Act I
Whispers on the Wind (company)
Welcome Little One (company)
Midwestern Summer (First Man, company)
Why and Because (Narrator)
Children's Games (company)
Miss Cadwallader (First Woman)
Upstairs-Downstairs (Narrator, First Man)
Strawberries (company)

Act II
Is There a City? (company)
Carmen Viscenzo (Second Man, company)
Neighbors (Second Woman)
Apples and Raisins (company)
Things Are Going Nicely (First Woman, company)
It Won't Be Long (company)
Prove I'm Really Here (First Woman)

WHITE HORSE INN (1936)

BOOK BY: Hans Mueller
MUSIC BY: Ralph Benatzky
LYRICS BY: Robert Gilbert
PUBLISHED LIBRETTO: French (London), 1957
CONDENSATION: *Ganzl's Book of the Musical Theatre*. Ganzl, Kurt. Schirmer (Macmillan), 1989
ANTHOLOGY: None
PIANO-VOCAL SCORE: Chappell, 1931
LICENSING AGENT: Samuel French
RECORDING: Angel S 35815 (English studio cast)
CAST: 16 M; 6 F; chorus

There really is a White Horse Inn in Austria, and this lavish spectacle set there began in Europe and has since been a popular favorite around the world. New York first saw it at Rockefeller Center in 1936 with Kitty Carlisle. There is very little to the plot. A headwaiter is in love with the lady who operates the inn. There are Tyrolean dancers, mountain crags, lakes, village streets, and wine gardens. The New York version utilized three revolving stages, numerous settings, and hundreds of performers. In 1954 there was a production on ice at Empress Hall in London. There was also a German language film version in 1956.

ORIGINAL CAST:

Kitty Carlisle (Katarina)
William Gaxton (Leopold)
Robert Halliday (Hutton)
Ann Barrie (Natalie)
Buster West (Sylvester)
Melissa Mason (Gretel)
Albert Mahler (Serenader)

SONGS:
Act I
Arrival of Tourists (children, ensemble)
Leave It to Katarina (Katarina, ensemble)
I Cannot Live without Your Love (Leopold, Katarina)
Arrival of Steamboat (ensemble)
The White Horse Inn (Katarina, Hutton, ensemble)
Cowshed Rhapsody (ensemble)

Blue Eyes (Hutton, Natalie, ensemble)
Rain Finale (company)

Act II

Market Day in the Village (Katarina, Leopold,
    ensemble)
Good-bye, Au Revoir, Auf Wiedersehn
    (Leopold, men)
High up on the Hills (Katarina, ensemble)
I Would Love to Have You Love Me (Sylvester,
    Gretel, ensemble)
Alpine Symphony (ensemble)
Welcome on the Landing Stage (ensemble)

Act III

Serenade to the Emperor (ensemble)
We Prize Most the Things We Miss (Katarina)
The Waltz of Love (Hutton, Natalie,
    Serenader, ensemble)

WHOOPEE (1928)

BOOK BY: William Anthony McGuire; based on *The
    Nervous Wreck* by Owen Davis
MUSIC BY: Walter Donaldson
LYRICS BY: Gus Kahn
PUBLISHED LIBRETTO: None
CONDENSATION: *New Complete Book of the
    American Musical Theater.* Ewen, David. Holt,
    1970
ANTHOLOGY: None
VOCAL SELECTIONS: Macmillan, 1979
LICENSING AGENT: Tams-Witmark
RECORDING: Smithsonian R 012 (original cast)
CAST: Large mixed cast

Eddie Cantor starred in this show for
Ziegfeld and then made the film version
for Goldwyn in 1930. "Makin' Whoopee!"
became his theme song. A hypochon-
driac vacationer at a dude ranch becomes involved with cowboys and Indians
and a lovelorn ingenue named Sally. The
Goodspeed Opera revived this show and
brought it back to Broadway in 1979. There
are cardboard auto chases, tap-dancing Indians, and a canoe ride. This is an old-
fashioned musical that should be done in
period and style.

1979 NEW YORK CAST:

Charles Repole (Henry)
Franc Luz (Wanenis)
J. Kevin Scannell (Sheriff)
Beth Austin (Sally)
Carol Swarbrick (Mary)
Catherine Cox (Harriet)

SONGS:
(including interpolations)
Act I

Let's All Make Whoopee Tonight (ensemble)
Makin' Whoopee (Henry, ladies)
I'm Bringing a Red, Red Rose (Wanenis)
Go Get 'Im (Sheriff, ensemble)
Until You Get Somebody Else (Henry, Sally)
Love Me or Leave Me (Mary, Henry)
I'm Bringing a Red, Red Rose (reprise)
    (Wanenis, Sally)
My Baby Just Cares for Me (Henry, ensemble)

Act II

Out of the Dawn (Wanenis, Sally)
The Tapahoe Tap (ensemble)
Reaching for Someone (Sheriff)
You (Harriet)
Yes, Sir, That's My Baby (Henry, ensemble)

WILDCAT (1960)

BOOK BY: N. Richard Nash
MUSIC BY: Cy Coleman
LYRICS BY: Carolyn Leigh
PUBLISHED LIBRETTO: None
CONDENSATION: *New Complete Book of the
    American Musical Theater.* Ewen, David. Holt,
    1970
ANTHOLOGY: None
PIANO-VOCAL SCORE: Morris, 1964
LICENSING AGENT: Tams-Witmark
RECORDING: RCA 60353 CD (original cast)
CAST: 14 M; 5 F; chorus

In 1912 an oil prospector arrives at a southwestern border town called Centavo City,
where she hopes to strike it rich to provide for her lame sister. Romance blossoms
with a drilling-gang foreman. There is also
a romantic subplot between the lame sister and a young Mexican. Most critics liked

the sombrero dance with choreography by Michael Kidd. A working rig is assembled onstage during the "Corduroy Road" number.

ORIGINAL CAST:

Lucille Ball (Wildy)
Paula Stewart (Jane)
Keith Andes (Joe)
Don Tomkins (Sookie)
Bill Walker (Tattoo)
Swen Swenson (Oney)
Ray Mason (Sandy)
Charles Braswell (Matt)
Clifford David (Hank)
Al Lanti (Cisco)
Edith King (Countess)

SONGS:
Act I
I Hear (ensemble)
Hey Look Me Over (Wildy, Jane)
Wildcat (Wildy, ensemble)
You've Come Home (Joe)
That's What I Want for Janie (Wildy)
What Takes My Fancy (Wildy, Sookie)
You're a Liar (Wildy, Joe)
One Day We Dance (Hank, Jane)
Give a Little Whistle and I'll Be There
    (Wildy, Joe, ensemble)
Tall Hopes (Tattoo, Oney, Sandy, Matt,
    ensemble)

Act II
Tippy Tippy Toes (Wildy, Countess)
El Sombrero (Wildy, Cisco, Oney,
    ensemble)
Corduroy Road (Joe, ensemble)

THE WILL ROGERS FOLLIES
(1991)

BOOK BY: Peter Stone
MUSIC BY: Cy Coleman
LYRICS BY: Betty Comden and Adolph Green
PUBLISHED LIBRETTO: None

CONDENSATION: None
ANTHOLOGY: None
PIANO-VOCAL SCORE: Warner Bros. Music, 1991
VOCAL SELECTIONS: Warner Bros. Music, 1991
LICENSING AGENT: Not yet available
RECORDING: Columbia CK 48606 CD (original cast)
CAST: Large mixed cast

Show girls, staircases, and lavish costumes return to the musical stage in this supposedly brand-new edition of the Ziegfeld Follies in which Will Rogers comes down from Heaven to guide his chronological biography. His life is played out in Follies acts, which include tableaux vivants, dog acts, a stage-wide staircase, and lots of precision dancing by beautiful girls. There are also serious moments, including a real-life Depression speech by Will that has contemporary meanings.

Tony Award Winner (Best Musical)

ORIGINAL CAST:

Cady Huffman (Ziegfeld's Favorite)
Keith Carradine (Will)
Dick Latessa (Clem)
Dee Hoty (Betty)

SONGS:
Act I
Will-a-Mania (Ziegfeld's Favorite,
    ensemble)
Give a Man Enough Rope (Will, ensemble)
It's a Boy! (Clem)
Giddyap, Whoa (Will)
My Unknown Someone (Betty)
The Big Time (Will, Betty, children)
My Big Mistake (Betty)
Once in a While (Betty)
Without You (Will)

Act II
Favorite Son (Will, ensemble)
No Man Left for Me (Betty)
Presents for Mrs. Rogers (Will, ensemble)
Just a Coupla Indian Boys (Will, Clem)
Without You (reprise) (Betty)
Never Met a Man I Didn't Like (Will,
    company)

WISH YOU WERE HERE (1952)

BOOK BY: Arthur Kober and Joshua Logan; based
  on the play *Having Wonderful Time* by Arthur
  Kober
MUSIC AND LYRICS BY: Harold Rome
PUBLISHED LIBRETTO: None
CONDENSATION: *Theatre '53*. John Chapman, ed.
  Random House, 1953
ANTHOLOGY: None
PIANO-VOCAL SCORE: Chappell, 1955
LICENSING AGENT: Music Theatre International
RECORDINGS: RCA LSO 1108 (original cast); Stet
  DS 15015 (London cast)
CAST: 5 M; 2 F; chorus

Fun, frolic, and romance are the main attractions at Camp Karefree in the Catskills.
Although the original play was set in the
1930s, this musical version has been updated. The plot concerns a young secretary spending her two weeks' vacation in
the pursuit of romance. Among other activities there is a beauty contest alongside the
swimming pool. The twenty-foot pool used
in the New York production generated a lot
of publicity, as did the athletic cast prac-
ticing basketball and swimming. The title
song was very popular in the 1950s.

ORIGINAL CAST:

Patricia Marand (Teddy)
Jack Cassidy (Chick)
Sammy Smith (Kandel)
Sheila Bond (Fay)
Sidney Armus (Itchy)
Paul Valentine (Pinky)

SONGS:
Act I
Camp Karefree (Kandel, ensemble)
Good-bye Love (Teddy, Fay, girls)
Social Director (Itchy, ensemble)
Shopping Around (Fay)
Bright College Days (ensemble)
Mix and Mingle (Chick, ensemble)
Could Be (Teddy, girls)
Tripping the Light Fantastic (ensemble)
Where Did the Night Go? (Chick, Teddy,
  ensemble)

Certain Individuals (Fay, ensemble)
They Won't Know Me (Chick)
Summer Afternoon (Pinky, ensemble)

Act II
Don Jose (Itchy, ensemble)
Everybody Loves Everybody (Fay, ensemble)
Wish You Were Here (Chick, ensemble)
Relax (Pinky, Teddy)
Flattery (Teddy, Fay, Itchy)

THE WIZ (1975)

BOOK BY: William F. Brown; based on *The
  Wonderful Wizard of Oz* by L. Frank Baum
MUSIC AND LYRICS BY: Charlie Smalls
PUBLISHED LIBRETTO: French, 1979
CONDENSATION: *Broadway Musicals Show by Show.*
  Green, Stanley. Hal Leonard Books, 1985
ANTHOLOGY: *Great Rock Musicals*. Stanley
  Richards, ed. Stein and Day, 1979
VOCAL SELECTIONS: Fox Fan-Fare, 1975; Columbia
  Pictures, 1975
LICENSING AGENT: Samuel French
RECORDING: Atlantic 18137-2 CD (original cast)
CAST: 11 principals; singers, dancers

The music is rock, soul, gospel, and rhythm
and blues in this black spoof of *The Wizard of Oz*. Called flamboyant and imaginative, the Broadway production was noted
for its stylish design and kaleidoscopic
dances. The elaborate costumes include
blue mushroom-cap munchkins and funky
monkeys. A dog is needed for "Toto." There
was a film version in 1978 with Diana Ross.

Tony Award Winner (Best Musical)

ORIGINAL CAST:

Tasha Thomas (Aunt Em)
Clarice Taylor (Addaperle)
Stephanie Mills (Dorothy)
Hinton Battle (Scarecrow)
Tiger Haynes (Tinman)
Ted Ross (Lion)
Andre De Shields (The Wiz)
Mabel King (Evillene)
Dee Dee Bridgewater (Glinda)

SONGS:

Act I

The Feeling We Once Had (Aunt Em)

Tornado Ballet (company)

He's the Wizard (Addaperle, ensemble)

Soon as I Get Home (Dorothy)

I Was Born on the Day before Yesterday
(Scarecrow, ensemble)

Ease on Down the Road (Dorothy, Scarecrow,
ensemble)

Slide Some Oil to Me (Tinman, Dorothy,
Scarecrow)

Mean Ole Lion (Lion)

Kalidah Battle (ensemble)

Be a Lion (Dorothy, Lion)

Lion's Dream (Lion, ensemble)

Emerald City Ballet (company)

So You Want to Meet the Wizard (The Wiz)

To Be Able to Feel (Tinman)

Act II

No Bad News (Evillene)

Funky Monkeys (ensemble)

Everybody Rejoice (ensemble)

Who Do You Think You Are? (ensemble)

Believe in Yourself (The Wiz)

Y'all Got It! (The Wiz)

A Rested Body Is a Rested Mind (Glinda)

Believe in Yourself (reprise) (Glinda)

Home (Dorothy)

THE WIZARD OF OZ

ADAPTION BY: Frank Gabrielson; from the 1939
MGM film and the stories of L. Frank Baum

MUSIC BY: Harold Arlen

LYRICS BY: E. Y. Harburg

PUBLISHED LIBRETTO: None

CONDENSATION: *The Book of 1,000 Plays*. Steve
Fletcher, Norman Jopling, eds. Facts On File,
1989

ANTHOLOGY: None

VOCAL SELECTIONS: Big Three, 1968 (film)

LICENSING AGENT: Tams-Witmark

RECORDING: London 838 350 CD (1989 London
production)

CAST: Large mixed cast

There have been numerous stage versions of this popular fantasy, but none is so popular as the Judy Garland film version that is shown regularly on television. This is a stage adaption of that film with all the famous songs. It is billed as suitable for youngsters from six to sixty! Young people can be cast as munchkins. Costuming of the lion, the scarecrow, and the tin woodman will be a challenge. A dog is needed to play "Toto." A popular Christmas attraction, it was recently presented in London by the Royal Shakespeare Company with "Miss Gulch" and "The Wicked Witch" played by a man.

1989 LONDON CAST:

Imelda Staunton (Dorothy)

Dilys Laye (Glinda)

Paul Greenwood (Scarecrow)

John Bowe (Tinman)

Jim Carter (Lion)

David Glover (Guard)

SONGS:

Act I

Over the Rainbow (Dorothy)

The Twister (company)

Munchkinland (Glinda, Dorothy, ensemble)

Ding, Dong, the Witch Is Dead (ensemble)

Follow the Yellow Brick Road (ensemble)

Off to See the Wizard (ensemble)

If I Only Had a Brain (Scarecrow, Dorothy,
ensemble)

If I Only Had a Heart (Tinman, Dorothy,
Scarecrow, ensemble)

If I Only Had the Nerve (Lion, Dorothy,
Scarecrow, Tinman)

Off to See the Wizard (reprise) (Lion,
Dorothy, Scarecrow, Tinman)

Poppies (company)

Optimistic Voices (Glinda, company)

Act II

The Merry Old Land of Oz (Dorothy,
Scarecrow, Tinman, Lion, Guard, company)

If I Were King of the Forest (Lion, Dorothy,
Scarecrow, Tinman)

Winkies March (ensemble)

The Jitterbug (Dorothy, Scarecrow, Tinman,
Lion, ensemble)
Ding, Dong, the Witch Is Dead (reprise)
(Dorothy, ensemble)

WOMAN OF THE YEAR (1981)

BOOK BY: Peter Stone; based on the MGM film by
Ring Lardner, Jr., and Michael Kanin
MUSIC BY: John Kander
LYRICS BY: Fred Ebb
PUBLISHED LIBRETTO: French, 1981
CONDENSATION: *Broadway Musicals Show by Show.*
Green, Stanley. Hal Leonard Books, 1985
ANTHOLOGY: None
VOCAL SELECTIONS: Fiddleback Music, 1981
LICENSING AGENT: Samuel French
RECORDING: Bay Cities BCD 3008 CD (original
cast)
CAST: 11 M; 6 F; chorus

Lauren Bacall was the Broadway star of this
big, splashy musical with elaborate sets
and lively dances. Your glamorous star will
portray a female television commentator
and the plot concerns her romance with
a cartoonist. The Broadway production
used some screen animation for "Katz,"
the hero's cartoon character that serves
as a cynical everyman's cat/sociologist.
(Samuel French has an address where
you can rent this film for your production.) Sumptuous, sassy, witty, sophisticated, and drily romantic are some of the
terms used to describe this show, with
Brendan Gill commenting in the *New Yorker*
that it has "unfailingly clever songs."

ORIGINAL CAST:

Marilyn Cooper (Jan)
Lauren Bacall (Tess)
Harry Guardino (Sam)
Roderick Cook (Gerald)
Rex Everhart (Maury)
Daren Kelly (Chip)
Grace Keagy (Helga)
Eivind Harum (Alexi)

SONGS:
Act I
Woman of the Year (Tess, women)
The Poker Game (Sam, ensemble)
See You in the Funny Papers (Sam)
When You're Right, You're Right (Tess,
Gerald)
Shut Up, Gerald (Tess, Sam, Gerald)
So What Else Is New? (Sam, with recorded
voice)
One of the Boys (Tess, Maury, ensemble)
Table Talk (Tess, Sam)
The Two of Us (Tess, Sam)
It Isn't Working (Chip, Helga, Gerald,
ensemble)
I Told You So (Gerald, Helga)

Act II
I Wrote the Book (Tess, women)
Happy in the Morning (Alexi, Tess, ensemble)
Sometimes a Day Goes By (Sam)
The Grass Is Always Greener (Tess, Jan)
We're Gonna Work It Out (Tess, Sam)

THE WONDER YEARS (1985)

BOOK BY: David Levy, David Hodgrive, Steve
Liebman, and Terry LaBolt
MUSIC AND LYRICS BY: David Levy
PUBLISHED LIBRETTO: None
CONDENSATION: None
ANTHOLOGY: None
LICENSING AGENT: Broadway Play Publishing
RECORDING: None
CAST: 3 M; 3 F

The theme of this revue is the experiences
of five baby boomers (those born after
World War II who grew up in the 1950s). The
eras covered include the sixties of the hip-
pies, the "me" seventies, and the eighties
when we made money. This was presented
in New York in a cabaret setting.

ORIGINAL CAST:

Kathy Morath (Patty)
Peter Boynton (Ken)
Marilyn Pasekoff (Carol)
Stuart Zagnit (Scott)

Nona Waldeck (Lynnie)
Stephen Berger (Skippy)

SONGS:
Act I
Baby Boom Babies (company)
Thru You (Scott, Carol)
Another Elementary School (company)
First Love (company)
The Monarch Notes (Lynnie)
Teach Me How to Fast Dance (Patty, Carol, Lynnie)
Skippy a Go-Go (Skippy, company)

Act II
The Wonder Years (Carol, company)
Flowers from the Sixties (Ken, company)
The "Me" Suite (company)
Pushing Thirty (Patty)

Act III
Takin' Him Home to Meet Mom (Scott)
Baby Boom Babies (reprise) (Skippy)
The Girl Most Likely (Carol)

WONDERFUL TOWN (1953)

BOOK BY: Joseph Fields and Jerome Chodorov; based on their play *My Sister Eileen* and the stories of Ruth McKenney
MUSIC BY: Leonard Bernstein
LYRICS BY: Betty Comden and Adolph Green
PUBLISHED LIBRETTO: Random House, 1953
CONDENSATION: *The Best Plays of 1952–1953*. Louis Kronenberger, ed. Dodd, Mead, 1953; *Ganzl's Book of the Musical Theatre*. Ganzl, Kurt. Schirmer (Macmillan), 1989
ANTHOLOGY: *Great Musicals of the American Theatre*, vol. 2. Stanley Richards, ed. Chilton, 1976; *Comden and Green on Broadway*. Drama Book Specialists, 1981
VOCAL SELECTIONS: Chappell, 1953
LICENSING AGENT: Tams-Witmark
RECORDINGS: MCA 10050 CD (original cast); Sony 48021 CD (TV cast)
CAST: Large mixed cast

Two sisters from Ohio arrive in New York's Greenwich Village in the late 1930s hoping to make their fortunes. Ruth wants to write, and her sister Eileen wants to be an actress. Their adventures have been told several times, including this musical version that starred Rosalind Russell. It was recently revived in London. A dancing highlight is the famous conga number with some Brazilian sailors.

Tony Award Winner (Best Musical)

ORIGINAL CAST:
Warren Galjour (Guide)
Rosalind Russell (Ruth)
Edith Adams (Eileen)
George Gaynes (Robert)
Jordan Bentley (Wreck)
Cris Alexander (Lippencott)
Dort Clark (Chick)

SONGS:
Act I
Christopher Street (Guide, ensemble)
Ohio (Ruth, Eileen)
Conquering New York (Ruth, Eileen, ensemble)
One Hundred Ways to Lose a Man (Ruth)
What a Waste (Robert, Ruth, ensemble)
A Little Bit in Love (Eileen)
Pass That Football (Wreck, ensemble)
Conversation Piece (Ruth, Eileen, Robert, Lippencott, Chick)
Quiet Girl (Robert)
Conga (Ruth, ensemble)

Act II
Darling Eileen (Eileen, ensemble)
Swing (Ruth, ensemble)
It's Love (Robert, Eileen)
Village Vortex Blues (ensemble)
Wrong Note Rag (Ruth, Eileen, company)
It's Love (reprise) (Eileen, Robert, Ruth, company)

WORKING (1978)

ADAPTED BY: Stephen Schwartz and Nina Faso; from the book by Studs Terkel
SONGS BY: Craig Carnelia, Micki Grant, Mary Rodgers, Susan Birkenhead, Stephen Schwartz, and James Taylor

PUBLISHED LIBRETTO: None
CONDENSATION: None
ANTHOLOGY: None
VOCAL SELECTIONS: Valando, 198–
LICENSING AGENT: Music Theatre International
RECORDING: Columbia JS 35411 (original cast)
CAST: 8 M; 6 F (may vary)

This musical was described as being concerned with the longings and frustrations of the working class. The set can be a simple scaffold with the cast moving in and out as they portray many different workers from cleaning women to firemen to parking lot attendants. There is no plot or story line, just the thematic link. Taken from actual interviews, this show tells you a lot about America. There are songs, sketches, and some dancing. The Broadway production was elaborate with sliding floor panels, projections, and elevators. There was a TV adaption in 1982.

ORIGINAL CAST:

David Langston Smyrl (Al/Mr. Robinson)
Matthew McGrath (John/Newsboy)
Bobo Lewis (Rose)
Joe Mantegna (Emilio/Dave)
Susan Bigelow (Kate)
Arny Freeman (Joe)
Lenora Nemetz (Delores)
Bob Gunton (Frank/Father)
David Patrick Kelly (Matt/Mason)
Lynne Thigpen (Mrs. Robinson/Maggie)
John Rushton (Newsboy)
Robin Lamont (Mill Worker)

SONGS:
Act I
All the Livelong Day (company)
Lovin' Al (Al, company)
The Mason (Mason)
Neat to Be a Newsboy (Newsboy)
Nobody Tells Me How (Rose)
Treasure Island Trio (dance trio)
Un Mejor Dia Vendra (Emilio,
    ensemble)
Just a Housewife (Kate, women)
Millwork (Mill worker)
Nightskate (dance)

Joe (Joe)
If I Could've Been (company)
Act II
It's an Art (Delores, ensemble)
Brother Trucker (Dave, Frank, men)
Husbands and Wives (Mr. Robinson, Mrs.
    Robinson, ensemble)
Fathers and Sons (Father)
Cleanin' Women (Maggie)
Something to Point To (company)

THE YEARLING (1965)

BOOK BY: Herbert Martin and Lore Noto; based
    on the novel by Marjorie Kinnan Rawlings
MUSIC BY: Michael Leonard
LYRICS BY: Herbert Martin
PUBLISHED LIBRETTO: Dramatic, 1973
CONDENSATION: None
ANTHOLOGY: None
VOCAL SELECTIONS: Morris, 1966
LICENSING AGENT: Dramatic
RECORDING: None
CAST: 14 M; 8 F; extras

Anyone who has read the novel will be concerned about the live deer. While the licensing agent assures would-be producers that the deer need not appear, one was used in the Broadway production (along with a dog and a raccoon). The plot concerns a Florida backwoods boy who brings home a fawn. In the 1946 nonmusical film Gregory Peck and Jane Wyman played his parents. The music reminded some of Aaron Copland's folk themes. There are Christmas festivities and a bit of country dancing. This is a family show that children will particularly enjoy.

ORIGINAL CAST:

David Wayne (Penny)
Dolores Wilson (Ora)
Steve Sanders (Jody)
Peter Falzone (Fodder-Wing)
Carmen Mathews (Mrs. Hutto)
Carmen Alvarez (Twink)
David Hartman (Oliver)

Gordon B. Clarke (Doc)
Allan Louw (Buck)
Tom Fleetwood (Millwheel)

SONGS:
Act I
Let Him Kick Up His Heels (Penny, Ora)
Boy Talk (Jody, Fodder-Wing)
Bear Hunt (Penny, Jody, ensemble)
Some Day I'm Gonna Fly (Jody, Fodder-Wing,
    ensemble)
Lonely Clearing (Penny)
Everything in the World I Love (Jody, Mrs.
    Hutto)
I'm All Smiles (Twink) Reprise (Oliver)
The Kind of Man a Woman Needs (Ora)
What a Happy Day (Ora, Jody, Doc, Buck,
    Millwheel)

Act II
Ain't He a Joy? (Penny, Jody)
Why Did I Choose You? (Penny, Ora)
One Promise (Ora)
Nothing More (Penny, Jody)
Everything Beautiful (Ora)

YOU NEVER KNOW (1938)

BOOK BY: Rowland Leigh; based on the play *By
    Candlelight* by Siegfried Geyer and Karl Farkas
MUSIC BY: Cole Porter and Robert Katscher
LYRICS BY: Cole Porter, Rowland Leigh, and Edwin
    Gilbert
PUBLISHED LIBRETTO: French
CONDENSATION: None
ANTHOLOGY: None
MUSIC PUBLISHER: *Music and Lyrics by Cole Porter.*
    2 vols. Chappell, 1972–75
LICENSING AGENT: Samuel French
RECORDING: Blue Pear 1015 (1973 recording)
CAST: 3 M; 3 F; 1 extra

The time is 1938 and the place is Paris. The
plot involves a valet and his master who
change positions to fool two young ladies.
Of course, the young ladies are maid and
mistress who have also changed positions.
There are a number of Cole Porter songs

that may be familiar. Revival productions
usually interpolate other Porter songs. The
silver-and-white 1930 set was praised in an
off-Broadway revival that included an onstage pianist.

1991 LOS ANGELES REVIVAL CAST:
Harry Groener (Baron)
David Garrison (Gaston)
Megan Mullally (Maria)
Donna McKechnie (Mme Baltin)
Angela Teek (Ida)

SONGS:
(including interpolations)
Act I
By Candlelight (Baron, Gaston)
You Never Know (Baron)
Let's Not Talk about Love (Gaston)
I'm Going in for Love (Maria)
I'm Back in Circulation (Ida)
From Alpha to Omega (Gaston, Maria)

Act II
What Shall I Do? (Maria, Gaston, Baron)
Let's Misbehave (Gaston, Maria)
I Happen to Be in Love (Gaston, Baron)
From Alpha to Omega (reprise) (Baron,
    Maria)

Act III
You Never Know (Mme Baltin)
What Is That Tune? (Baron, Mme Baltin)
At Long Last Love (Baron)
Ridin' High (Gaston, Maria)

YOUR OWN THING (1968)

BOOK BY: Donald Driver; based on *Twelfth Night*
    by William Shakespeare
MUSIC AND LYRICS BY: Hal Hester and Danny
    Apolinar
PUBLISHED LIBRETTO: Dell, 1970
CONDENSATION: *The Best Plays of 1967–1968.* Otis
    L. Guernsey, Jr., ed. Dodd, Mead, 1968
ANTHOLOGY: *All the World's a Stage.* Lowell
    Swortzell, ed. Delacorte, 1972; *Great Rock
    Musicals.* Stanley Richards, ed. Stein and Day,
    1979

VOCAL SELECTIONS: National General/Shayne, 1968
LICENSING AGENT: Tams-Witmark
RECORDING: RCA LSO 1148 (original cast)
CAST: 6 M; 3 F

The Shakespearean love tangle involving Orsino, Viola, Olivia, and Sebastian is retold here in the rock style of the late 1960s. Illyria is now "fun city" and a discotheque is part of the action. The show is about one and one-half hours long and is performed without intermission. Called "a show about crazy music and clothes and lightshows," the original off-Broadway production used fourteen projectors, films, slides, and tapes to create a multimedia experience. The actual voices of well-known personalities were used, with references to Vietnam, the draft, and the generation gap. This show was very popular, with productions presented all over the world.

ORIGINAL CAST:

Rusty Thacker (Sebastian)
Leland Palmer (Viola)
Marian Mercer (Olivia)
Tom Ligon (Orson)

SONGS:
(performed without intermission)
No One's Perfect, Dear (Sebastian, Viola)
The Flowers (Viola)
I'm Me! (I'm Not Afraid) (ensemble)
Baby! Baby! (Viola, ensemble)
Come Away, Death (Sebastian)
I'm on My Way to the Top (Sebastian)
Let It Be (Olivia)
She Never Told Her Love (Viola)
Be Gentle (Viola, Orson)
What Do I Know? (Viola, company)
The Now Generation (Viola, ensemble)
The Middle Years (Sebastian, Olivia)
When You're Young and in Love (Orson)
Hunca Munca (ensemble)
Don't Leave Me (Olivia, Sebastian)
Do Your Own Thing (ensemble)

YOU'RE A GOOD MAN, CHARLIE BROWN (1967)

BOOK BY: John Gordon; based on the comic strip *Peanuts* by Charles M. Schulz
MUSIC AND LYRICS BY: Clark Gesner
PUBLISHED LIBRETTO: Random House, 1967
CONDENSATION: *The Best Plays of 1966–1967*. Otis L. Guernsey, Jr., ed. Dodd, Mead, 1967
ANTHOLOGY: None
PIANO-VOCAL SCORE: Jeremy Music, 1972
VOCAL SELECTIONS: Jeremy Music, 1967
LICENSING AGENT: Tams-Witmark
RECORDING: Polydor 820 262-2 CD (original cast)
CAST: 4 M; 2 F

This musical revue was a surprise hit off-Broadway where it ran for almost 1,600 performances. The simple staging consists of a bare stage littered with several oversize building blocks, which serve as the doghouse or whatever is needed. Charlie Brown, Lucy, and the others go through a disastrous baseball game, book reports on *Peter Rabbit*, a glee club rehearsal, and other hilarious episodes. Snoopy is concerned with shooting down the Red Baron! A small combo provides the musical accompaniment. This family show was performed on TV in 1973. For another show on this same material, see *Snoopy*.

ORIGINAL CAST:

Reva Rose (Lucy)
Skip Hinnant (Schroeder)
Gary Burghoff (Charlie Brown)
Bob Balaban (Linus)
Bill Hinnant (Snoopy)

SONGS:
Act I
You're a Good Man, Charlie Brown (company)
Schroeder (Lucy, Schroeder)
Snoopy (Snoopy, Charlie Brown)
My Blanket and Me (Linus)
Kite (Charlie Brown)
Dr. Lucy (the Doctor Is In) (Lucy, Charlie Brown)
Book Report (Charlie Brown, Lucy, Linus, Schroeder)

Act II
The Red Baron (Snoopy)
T E A M (the Baseball Game) (company)
Glee Club Rehearsal (company)
Little Known Facts (Lucy, Linus, Charlie
  Brown)
Suppertime (Snoopy)
Happiness (company)

YOU'RE GONNA LOVE TOMORROW (1983)

CONTINUITY BY: Paul Lazarus
MUSIC AND LYRICS BY: Stephen Sondheim
PUBLISHED LIBRETTO: None
CONDENSATION: None
ANTHOLOGY: None
LICENSING AGENT: Music Theatre International
RECORDING: RCA CBL2-4745 (original cast as
  A Stephen Sondheim Evening)
CAST: 4 M; 3 F

This collection of songs was first presented in concert style in New York City
in 1983. The purpose was to make a
recording of some Sondheim songs (including some previously unrecorded material)
with some leading show tune interpreters
of the day. John Wilson in the *New York
Times* review pointed out that the cast set
the scene and established the characters
for the songs with such skill that it made
this much more than just a concert. He also
wrote that it was "a varied, provocative,
demanding and rewarding program" that
no other composer of his type would have
been able to achieve.

ORIGINAL CAST:

Liz Callaway	Judy Kaye
Cris Groenendaal	Angela Lansbury
Bob Gunton	Victoria Mallory
George Hearn	Stephen Sondheim
Steven Jacob	

This revue is made up of twenty-two songs
performed without intermission.

YOURS, ANNE (1985)

LIBRETTO BY: Enid Futterman; based on *Anne
  Frank: The Diary of a Young Girl* and the play
  by Frances Goodrich and Albert Hackett
MUSIC BY: Michael Cohen
PUBLISHED LIBRETTO: None
CONDENSATION: None
ANTHOLOGY: None
LICENSING AGENT: Rodgers and Hammerstein
  Theatre Library
RECORDING: TER 1118 (original cast)
CAST: 4 M; 4 F

Based on the famous diary and play, this is
the true story of a Jewish girl whose family hid in an attic in Amsterdam during the
Nazi occupation. The prologue is the only
time the characters are seen outside the
walls of their attic, making this a one-set
play. The music was described as more operatic than popular, and your "Anne" must
carry the bulk of the show. A concert version is also available for presentation.

ORIGINAL CAST:

Trini Alvardo (Anne)
Ann Talman (Margot)
Dana Zeller-Alexis (Mrs. Frank)
George Guidall (Mr. Frank)
David Cady (Peter)
Hal Robinson (Dussel)
Merwin Goldsmith (Mr. Van Daan)

SONGS:
Act I
Dear Kitty: I Am Thirteen Years Old (Anne)
Dear Kitty: It's a Dangerous Adventure (Anne)
An Ordinary Day (company)
Schlaf (Mrs. Frank)
She Doesn't Understand Me (Mrs. Frank,
  Anne)
Dear Kitty: In the Night (Anne)
They Don't Have To (company)
Hollywood (Anne)
Dear Kitty: I Have a Nicer Side (Anne)
We Live with Fear (company)
A Writer (Mrs. Frank, Anne)
I'm Not a Jew (Peter, Anne)
The First Chanukah Night (company)

Act II

Dear Kitty: It's a New Year/We're Here (Anne, company)

Dear Kitty: My Sweet Secret (Anne)

My Wife (Mr. Van Daan, Mrs. Frank, Dussel)

Dear Kitty: I Am Longing (Anne)

I Remember (company)

I Think Myself Out (Anne, Peter)

Nightmare (Anne)

For the Children (Mr. Frank, Mrs. Frank)

Something to Get Up For (Margot)

Dear Kitty: I Am a Woman (Anne)

When We Are Free (company)

Dear Kitty: I Still Believe (Anne)

ZORBA (1968)

BOOK BY: Joseph Stein; adapted from *Zorba the Greek* by Nikos Kazantzakis

MUSIC BY: John Kander

LYRICS BY: Fred Ebb

PUBLISHED LIBRETTO: Random House, 1969

CONDENSATION: *New Complete Book of the American Musical Theater*. Ewen, David. Holt, 1970

ANTHOLOGY: None

VOCAL SELECTIONS: New York Times Music, 1968

LICENSING AGENT: Samuel French

RECORDINGS: Capitol 92053 CD (original cast); Angel ZDM 64665 2 CD (original cast)

CAST: Large mixed cast

The setting of the story is Piraeus, Greece, and the island of Crete in 1924. The curtain rises on a bouzouki circle. Nikos arrives in Piraeus, Greece. Zorba (an aging Lothario, philosopher, and confidence man) goes with him to Crete to reopen an abandoned mine Nikos has inherited. They both experience brief and tragic love affairs and then leave when the mine proves to be worthless. Despite some moments of humor, this is a serious musical drama. The Broadway production included an onstage bouzouki musical group, and dances were described as a series of Greek celebrations. A Greek chorus, all dressed in black, was particularly praised, as was the earthy performance of Herschel Bernardi in the title role. Anthony Quinn played the original movie role and appeared on Broadway in a revival production.

ORIGINAL CAST:

Lorraine Serabian (Leader)

Herschel Bernardi (Zorba)

Maria Karnilova (Hortense)

John Cunningham (Nikos)

Carmen Alvarez (Widow)

SONGS:

Act I

Life Is (Leader, company)

The First Time (Zorba)

The Top of the Hill (Leader, ensemble)

No Boom Boom (Hortense, Zorba, Nikos, ensemble)

Vive La Difference (ensemble)

The Butterfly (Nikos, Leader, Widow, ensemble)

Goodbye, Canavaro (Hortense, Zorba, Nikos)

Grandpapa (Zorba)

Only Love (Hortense)

The Bend of the Road (Leader, ensemble)

Only Love (reprise) (Leader)

Act II

Y'assou (Zorba, Hortense, Nikos, Leader, company)

Why Can't I Speak? (Widow)

The Crow (Leader, women)

Happy Birthday (Hortense)

I Am Free (Zorba)

THE ZULU AND THE ZAYDA (1965)

BOOK BY: Howard Da Silva and Felix Leon; based on a story by Dan Jacobson

MUSIC AND LYRICS BY: Harold Rome

PUBLISHED LIBRETTO: Dramatists Play Service, 1966

CONDENSATION: None

ANTHOLOGY: None

VOCAL SELECTIONS: Chappell, 1966

LICENSING AGENT: Dramatists Play Service
RECORDING: Columbia KOS 2880 (original cast)
CAST: 17 M; 4 F

A Zayda (a Jewish grandfather) is living in present-day (1965) Johannesburg with his son and grandchildren. He likes to go walking about the city, so his son hires a Zulu to keep track of him. This play with music is really about their friendship overcoming their racial and language problems. For the Broadway production the program included a glossary of the Zulu and the Yiddish phrases used in the play. The musical numbers were a blend of African Yiddish. "You don't have to be Jewish . . . ," a popular New York advertising slogan, applies to the enjoyment of this racially mixed entertainment.

ORIGINAL CAST:

Ossie Davis (Johannes)
Menasha Skulnik (Zayda)
Louis Gossett (Paulus)
Peter DeAnda (Peter)
Christine Spencer (Joan)

SONGS:

Act I

Tkambuza (Johannes)
Crocodile Wife (Johannes)
Good to Be Alive (Zayda, Paulus)
The Water Wears Down the Stone (Johannes)
Rivers of Tears (Zayda)
Like the Breeze Blows (Peter, Joan, ensemble)
Oisgetzaychnet (Zayda, ensemble)

Act II

Some Things (ensemble)
Zulu Love Song (Paulus)
L'Chayim (Zayda)
Cold, Cold Room (Johannes)

Appendix A

Licensing Agents

All of the titles listed in this directory are available from one of the following companies. Permission *must* be obtained and fees and royalties paid before production can begin. These agents will provide scripts and scores.

Baker's Plays
100 Chauncey St.
Boston, MA 02111-1783
(617) 482-1280
Fax (617) 482-7613

Broadway Play Publishing Co.
357 W. Twentieth St.
New York, NY 10011
(212) 627-1055
(800) 752-9782
Fax (212) 627-1057

Dramatic Publishing Co.
311 Washington St.
P.O. Box 129
Woodstock, IL 60098
(815) 338-7170
Fax (800) 334-5302

Dramatists Play Service, Inc.
440 Park Ave. South
New York, NY 10016
(212) 683-8960
Fax (212) 213-1539

Music Theatre International
545 Eighth Ave.
New York, NY 10018
(212) 868-6668
Fax (212) 643-8465

Rodgers and Hammerstein Theatre Library
1633 Broadway, Ste. 3801
New York, NY 10019
(212) 541-6900
Fax (212) 586-6155

Samuel French, Inc.
45 W. Twenty-Fifth St.
New York, NY 10010
(212) 206-8990
Fax (212) 206-1429

Tams-Witmark Music Library
560 Lexington Ave.
New York, NY 10022
(212) 688-2525
Fax (212) 688-3232

Theatre Maximus
1650 Broadway
New York, NY 10019
(212) 765-5913

Appendix B

Music Publishers

Many of the vocal selections and piano-vocal scores in this directory are out of print. The major current publishers are listed here if you wish to try and obtain something currently available. Once you have made a selection, the licensing agent should be able to provide you with both script and score.

If you and your music dealer are unable to locate a particular publication, you may get some help from:

National Music Publishers Association, Inc.
205 E. Forty-Second St.
New York, NY 10017
(212) 370-5330

This organization also publishes a "Sales Agency List" that is most helpful in locating various publishers.

Belwin-Mills Publishing Corp.
3808 Riverside Dr., Ste. 408
Burbank, CA 91505

Big Three Music Corp.
See: CPP/Belwin

Berlin, Irving, Music Corp.
1633 Broadway
New York, NY 10019
(212) 262-1800

Blackwood Music, Inc.
1290 Avenue of the Americas
New York, NY 10020
(212) 492-1200

CPP/Belwin Music
15800 N.W. Forty-Eighth Ave.
Miami, FL 33014
(305) 620-1500
Fax (305) 621-4869

Chappell Music Co. (Warner Chappell Music)
1290 Avenue of the Americas
New York, NY 10019
(212) 399-6910

Cherry Lane Music Co.
10 Midland Ave.
Port Chester, NY
(914) 973-8601
Fax (914) 973-0614

Cohan Music
See: Leonard, Hal

Columbia Pictures Publications
Columbia Plaza E.
Burbank, CA 91505

Consolidated Music
24 E. Twenty-Second St.
New York, NY 10011
(212) 254-2100

Cromwell Music, Inc.
11 W. Nineteenth St.
New York, NY 10011
(212) 627-4646

Famous Music
15 Columbus Cir.
New York, NY 10023
(212) 373-7433

Fiddleback Music Publishing Co., Inc.
1270 Avenue of the Americas
New York, NY 10019
(212) 489-9696

Frank Music Corp.
39 W. Fifty-Fourth St.
New York, NY 10019
(212) 246-5757

Hansen House
1804 West Ave.
Miami, FL 33139
(305) 532-5461

Harms, T. B., Music
See: Warner/Chappell

Herald Square Music
See: Leonard, Hal

Hollis Music, Inc.
11 W. Nineteenth St.
New York, NY 10011
(212) 627-4646

Jeremy Music, Inc.
16 Ervilla Dr.
Larchmont, NY 10538
(914) 834-0598

Leeds Music
See: Plymouth Music Co.

Leonard, Hal, Publishing Co.
7777 W. Bluemound Rd.
Milwaukee, WI 53213
(414) 774-3630
Fax (414) 774-3259

Ludlow Music, Inc.
11 W. Nineteenth St.
New York, NY 10011
(212) 627-4646

MCA Music
1755 Broadway
New York, NY 10019
(212) 841-8000

McHugh, Jimmy, Music
See: Plymouth Music Co.

Mills Music
See: CPP/Belwin Music

Morley Music
See: Leonard, Hal

Morris, Edwin H., and Co.
See: Leonard, Hal

MPL Communications, Inc.
39 W. Fifty-Fourth St.
New York, NY 10019
(212) 246-5757
Fax (212) 977-8408

Musical Comedy Productions
11 W. Nineteenth St.
New York, NY 10011
(212) 627-4646

New World Music Corp.
See: Warner Bros. Music Publications

Notable Music Co., Inc.
161 W. Fifty-Fourth St.
New York, NY 10019
(212) 757-9547

Plymouth Music Co.
170 N.E. Thirty-Third St.
Fort Lauderdale, FL 33334
(305) 563-1844
Fax (305) 563-9006

Presser, Theodore, Co.
Presser Place
Bryn Mawr, PA 19010

Revelation Music Publishing Corp.
1270 Avenue of the Americas
New York, NY 10019
(212) 489-9696

Robbins
See: CPP/Belwin Music

Schirmer Music
61 W. Sixty-Second St.
New York, NY 10022
(212) 541-6236

Shapiro, Bernstein and Co., Inc.
10 E. Fifty-Third St.
New York, NY 10022
(212) 751-3395

Times Square Music Publications
See: Leonard, Hal

Udell-Geld Music
See: Plymouth Music Co.

United Artists Music Corp.
See: CPP/Belwin Music

Valando Music Publishing Group, Inc.
1270 Avenue of the Americas
New York, NY 10019
(212) 489-9696

Warner Bros. Music Publications
265 Secaucus Rd.
Secaucus, NJ 07096
(201) 348-0700
Fax (201) 348-0301

Warner/Chappell Music, Inc.
1290 Avenue of the Americas
New York, NY 10019
(212) 399-6910

Williamson Music, Inc.
1633 Broadway
New York, NY 10019
(212) 541-6968

Witmark Music
See: Warner/Chappell Music

Composers, Lyricists, and Librettists

Song Index

Richard Chigley Lynch is a retired librarian who has compiled three discographies of show recordings and contributes regularly to *Show Music: The Musical Theatre Magazine.*

INSIGHT ⊙ GUIDES

LAOS & CAMBODIA

www.insightguides.com/Laos

⊙ Walking Eye App

YOUR FREE DESTINATION CONTENT AND EBOOK AVAILABLE THROUGH THE WALKING EYE APP

Your guide now includes a free eBook and destination content for your chosen destination, all for the same great price as before. Simply download the Walking Eye App from the App Store or Google Play to access your free eBook and destination content.

HOW THE WALKING EYE APP WORKS

Through the Walking Eye App, you can purchase a range of eBooks and destination content. However, when you buy this book, you can download the corresponding eBook and destination content for free. Just see below in the grey panels where to find your free content and then scan the QR code at the bottom of this page.

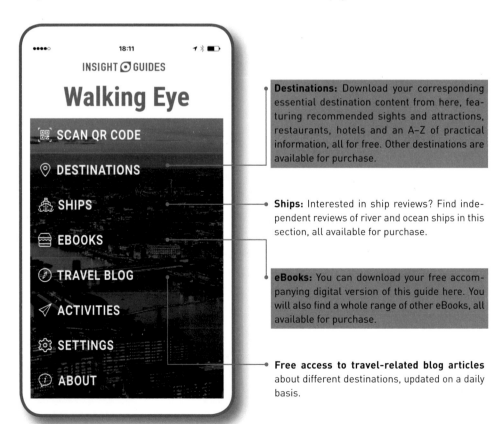

Destinations: Download your corresponding essential destination content from here, featuring recommended sights and attractions, restaurants, hotels and an A–Z of practical information, all for free. Other destinations are available for purchase.

Ships: Interested in ship reviews? Find independent reviews of river and ocean ships in this section, all available for purchase.

eBooks: You can download your free accompanying digital version of this guide here. You will also find a whole range of other eBooks, all available for purchase.

Free access to travel-related blog articles about different destinations, updated on a daily basis.

HOW THE DESTINATION CONTENT WORKS

Each destination includes a short introduction, an A–Z of practical information and recommended points of interest, split into 4 different categories:

- Highlights
- Accommodation
- Eating out
- What to do

You can view the location of every point of interest and save it by adding it to your Favourites. In the 'Around Me' section you can view all the points of interest within 5km.

HOW THE EBOOKS WORK

The eBooks are provided in EPUB file format. Please note that you will need an eBook reader installed on your device to open the file. Many devices come with this as standard, but you may still need to install one manually from Google Play.

The eBook content is identical to the content in the printed guide.

HOW TO DOWNLOAD THE WALKING EYE APP

1. Download the Walking Eye App from the App Store or Google Play.
2. Open the app and select the scanning function from the main menu.
3. Scan the QR code on this page – you will then be asked a security question to verify ownership of the book.
4. Once this has been verified, you will see your eBook and destination content in the purchased ebook and destination sections, where you will be able to download them.

Other destination apps and eBooks are available for purchase separately or are free with the purchase of the Insight Guide book.

Contents

THE BEST OF LAOS & CAMBODIA: TOP ATTRACTIONS

A selection of the top sights of the two countries, from the haunting Plain of Jars to romantic Luang Prabang, vibrant Phnom Penh and the unmatched splendour of Angkor.

△ **Phnom Penh**. Cambodia's animated capital is a city that has rediscovered itself. Wonderful restaurants, lots to see and a pleasant riverside setting. See page 263.

△ **Angkor**. Indochina's top attraction dates from almost 900 years ago, the golden years of the Khmer civilisation. The sprawling site is a unique repository of incredible craftsmanship on a staggering scale. The towers at Angkor Wat, the most famous site of all, appear otherworldly at sunset as they are flanked by hordes of flying foxes. See page 285

◁ **Luang Prabang**. This beautiful royal capital is the religious centre of Laos. The old stupas and temples give the city a unique ambience, populated in part by hundreds of saffron-robed monks. See page 127.

△ **Vientiane**. A smaller and more unassuming capital city would be hard to imagine. French-flavoured Vientiane extends languidly along the Mekong – walk along the river banks at sunset and enjoy a Beer Lao. See page 105.

△ **Tonlé Sap**. Cambodia's extraordinary river system reverses its flow during the rainy season, making the Tonlé Sap lake – the region's largest – a perfect breeding ground for fish and rare birdlife. See page 282.

△ **French colonial architecture**. The French left more than baguettes and coffee. Numerous elegant villas, shops and administrative buildings remain throughout Indochina, and are well represented in cities like Vientiane, Luang Prabang, Savannakhet and Phnom Penh. See page 114.

△ **The Plain of Jars**. These mysterious giant stone vats are a highlight of any trip to Laos. Their origins are obscure, though one legend suggests they were built by giants to store rice wine. See pages 138 and 144.

△ **Si Phan Don**. These numerous Mekong islands in southern Laos make a wonderful antidote to the stresses of modern life. See page 177.

▽ **The Mekong River**. This mighty waterway is a thread that weaves its way through China, Burma, Thailand, Laos, Cambodia and Vietnam. It is one of the planet's top areas of biodiversity and the 11th-longest river in the world. See page 166.

▽ **Cambodian islands**. For snorkelling, diving, camping and lounging on tropical beaches, there's no better place than the islands off Sihanoukville. See page 317.

THE BEST OF LAOS & CAMBODIA: EDITOR'S CHOICE

Unique cultural attractions, glittering temples and ancient sites, colourful markets, wildlife-rich forests, mountains and the Mekong River... here at a glance are our recommendations on what to prioritise to make the most of your trip.

Market stall.

ONLY IN LAOS AND CAMBODIA

Khmer Classical Dance. This highly stylised art flourished in the royal court and continues to be performed regularly. See pages 237, 242.

Shadow Puppets. Often mixed with live performance and accompanied by an orchestra. See page 238.

Secret Caves. Remote caves around Vieng Xai in northeastern Laos provided shelter for communist guerrillas. See page 142.

Pristine Forests. Laos offers some of the best-preserved jungles in Asia. See page 42.

The Tai Lu minority of northern Laos. Weave some of the finest textiles available in Southeast Asia and have their own distinctive temple architecture. See page 152.

Traditional dance school, Phnom Penh.

TEMPLES AND RELIGIOUS COMPLEXES

Angkor Wat. Built in the early 12th century, this amazing temple-city in the jungle has long been a symbol of Cambodia. See page 288.

Banteay Srei. The "Citadel of Women", an exquisite, pink sandstone temple dating from the 10th century. See page 296.

Preah Vihear. Enjoy grand vistas across from Thailand at this wonderful temple. See page 308.

Wat Phu, Champasak. The only noteworthy Angkorean temple in Laos is a highlight of any visit. See page 174.

Wat Xieng Thong. Luang Prabang's most impressive and historically significant temple sits at the confluence of the Khan and Mekong rivers. See page 130.

That Luang. Built in 1566, Vientiane's iconic stupa is a monument to both Lao independence and national Buddhism. See page 112.

Jayavarman VII figure at Angkor.

Wat Phu.

CULTURAL EXPERIENCES

Phare Ponleu Selpak. Acrobats blend French and Khmer artistry to tell contemporary Cambodian stories accompanied by a traditional orchestra. See page 283.

Monks in Alms. Every morning monks gather rice for their daily meal. Luang Prabang is the most popular place to observe the sai baat procession. See page 133.

Hill Tribe Villages. Northern Laos harbours a treasure trove of minority culture. See pages 80, 135, 147.

Bamboo Train. Battambang's unique railway utilises a great deal of creative ingenuity. See page 283.

Royal Ballet. Witness this refined art form in Phnom Penh. See pages 237, 242.

BEST MARKETS AND SHOPPING

Central Market, Phnom Penh. You can find almost anything in the country's largest market. See page 267.

Angkor Silk Farm, Siem Reap. Observe the entire silk-manufacturing process, from worm to weaving, then purchase some of the finest silk in Indochina. See page 281.

Talaat Sao, Vientiane. Modern supermarket and department stores meet traditional outdoor markets at the largest

shopping venue in Laos. See page 112.

Old Market (Psar Chas) and Pithnou Street, Siem Reap. Find local handicrafts and everyday items in the traditional market, or head up the adjoining Pithnou Street for higher-quality items sold in trendy boutiques. See page 281.

Handicraft Night Market, Luang Prabang. Countless clothes, shoes, jewellery, minority handicrafts and souvenirs. See page 130.

OUTDOOR ACTIVITIES

Koh Kong Conservation Corridor. At the southwest coastal corner of Cambodia, this matrix of protected forests, national forests, wildlife sanctuary and offshore islands is only now being properly explored. See page 319.

Ream National Park. One of Cambodia's most accessible National Parks sits just east of Sihanoukville and offers hiking, boating and wildlife. See page 315.

Vang Vieng. Indochina's adventure capital offers a full round of activities, including spelunking, rock climbing, trekking, mountain biking, abseiling, kayaking, rafting and tubing. See page 123.

The Mekong River. Enjoy a boat ride to watch Irrawaddy dolphins in Cambodia, or a leisurely meal at a riverside café in Luang Prabang to take in the ambiance of the river. See pages 127, 159, 166, 177, 303.

Bolaven Plateau. Dramatic waterfalls cut through lush scenery and rich coffee plantations in southern Laos. See page 179.

Phu Khao Khuai National Park. Easily accessed from Vientiane, this protected forest shelters endangered wildlife and offers chances to visit plunging waterfalls and treks to minority villages. See page 120.

Khon Phapheng falls.

Water-throwing as part of New Year festivities, Luang Prabang.

FESTIVALS AND EVENTS

Boun Pi Mai Lao, Luang Prabang. A gentler version of the water-throwing New Year festival in Chiang Mai, held in April. See pages 133, 307.

Bon Om Tuk, Phnom Penh. Unique October/November celebration of the reversal of the Tonle Sap River. See page 306.

Boun Awk Phansa, Vientiane. Boat racing on the Mekong and traditional Lao games at the end of Buddhist Lent. See page 306.

Boun Pha That Luang, Vientiane. In October/November, this is a three-day Buddhist festival at the Lao national symbol, with candle-lit procession.

ROYAL PALACES

Royal Palace, Phnom Penh. Classic architecture in beautiful grounds in the heart of the Cambodian capital. See page 263.

Royal Palace Museum, Luang Prabang. The former palace of the kings of Luang Prabang now restored and housing royal regalia, art and paintings. See page 128.

Palace Hotel, Champasak. The

elaborate residence built for Chao Boun Oum that has now been converted into an iconic hotel. See page 171.

King's Terraces, Angkor Thom. The Elephant Terrace and the Terrace of the Leper King used by the kings of Angkor in its prime to watch military reviews and other entertainments. See page 288.

FOOD AND CUISINE

Amok. Cambodia's signature dish is a delicate fish curry steamed in a banana leaf with lemon grass, galangal, turmeric, fish paste and coconut milk. See page 247.

Khao Jii with fresh coffee. This may be common enough in France, but not elsewhere in Southeast Asia. Lao or Cambodian baguettes make a really welcome breakfast served with scrambled eggs or pâté. See page 88.

Mango, Mangosteen and Rambutan. The range and quality of truly delicious exotic fruit in both Laos and Cambodia has to be seen and tasted to be believed. See pages 90, 247.

Pho noodle soup. A gift to both Laos and Cambodia from neighbouring Vietnam, but popular enough to count as indigenous. A broth of rice noodles topped with beef, fresh herbs, bean sprouts and a squeeze of lime makes a popular breakfast dish or anytime snack. See page 248.

Royal Palace Museum, Luang Prabang.

Cambodian amok.

MUSEUMS AND GALLERIES

National Museum, Phnom Penh. Purpose-built in Khmer style and opened in 1917, this houses one of the finest collections of Khmer artistic and cultural artefacts anywhere in the world – as well as an invisible but noisy community of bats. See page 266.
Haw Pha Kaew. The former royal temple of the Lao monarchy in Vientiane, now used as a museum and including many old Buddha images. See page 110.

S21 Tuol Sleng Genocide Museum, Phnom Penh. With its instruments of torture and its poignant photographs of the victims, the former prison where, during the Pol Pot years, thousands were interrogated and murdered makes for a harrowing visit. See page 270.
21 Khmer heritage houses, Battambang. Outside the city, two of these old wooden stilt-houses are open to visitors, of which Khor Song is the more popular. See page 283.

Jade Buddha statue at Haw Pha Kaew temple, Vientiane.

MONEY-SAVING TIPS

Cambodia
When visiting Angkor – unless you are only planning on a day trip – buy a seven- or three-day pass, a substantial saving on a single-day pass.

For smaller purchases like street snacks or cold drinks, pay in the local currency, not the universally preferred US$ dollar. You will only get change from a dollar in riel or kip, and outside Cambodia and Laos, the local currency is worthless.

Cutting back on beer, which carries a substantial government tax, will save a surprising amount of money.

Laos
Try a local baguette with pâté or cheese for breakfast, accompanied by a strong Lao coffee. The quality is excellent, and a street café is much cheaper than a hotel restaurant.

Like Cambodia, Laos is a poor country, but souvenir vendors will certainly have factored bargaining into their first asking price: bargain for at least 20 percent off these items.

If you're entering Laos from Thailand, stock up on toiletries beforehand as these may cost double the Thai price in Laos.

Haw Pha Bang Buddhist temple and the Luang Prabang night market.

LAOS AND CAMBODIA

Ignored for decades, these two countries have emerged as two of the most exciting travel destinations in Southeast Asia

Baguettes in Vientiane.

Together, Laos and Cambodia form the little-known hinterland of Indochina. In the colonial period they were considered backwaters by the French, who concentrated on exploiting the resources of Vietnam – the third and dominant country in French Indochina. During the turbulent years that followed independence, the United States waged a viciously destructive "Secret War" against the North Vietnamese Army and its Lao allies, the Pathet Lao, while Cambodia, having been illegally carpet-bombed by the US Air Force, was then "liberated" by the genocidal Khmer Rouge. Both countries experienced impoverishment and isolation from the outside world.

Nowadays both have put this brutal period behind them, although it has been a long and tortuous process for Cambodia. Opening their doors to the international community and to overseas visitors, the governments in Vientiane and Phnom Penh perceive tourism as a way to increase national development and assure a more prosperous future.

There are good reasons for linking Laos and Cambodia in a single guidebook. Both countries have a long tradition of Indic culture, as well as being closely related through Theravada Buddhism (northern parts of Laos are rather different in this respect, however) and long years of interaction with neighbouring Thailand and Vietnam. Each

Fisherman casting his nets.

is startlingly beautiful and relatively undeveloped, populated by generous and friendly people, and home to some unforgettable sights. Their dependence on the mighty Mekong River and a shared colonial past further bind them, with both having benefited from the French culinary tradition – as Cambodia's King Sihanouk once put it: "I am an anti-colonialist, but if one must be colonised it is better to be colonised by gourmets." Today both countries are members of ASEAN, are developing and are increasingly prosperous. There has never been a better time to visit them.

SPIRITUAL PEOPLES

Both Laos and Cambodia have a strong spiritual base. Buddhism is the major religion, but a significant number of people adhere to other faiths.

The dominant religion in both Laos and Cambodia is Buddhism – its followers account for around 65 percent of the population of Laos and 90 percent of the population of Cambodia, although other religions – Islam, Christianity and spirit cults – also flourish. As in Thailand, Burma and Sri Lanka, the Buddhists are followers of the Theravada system, or "Way of the Elders". In contrast, the Buddhism practised in neighbouring Vietnam (and among the Vietnamese population of Laos), as in China, Korea and Japan, is of the Mahayana school.

Buddhism in Laos and Cambodia

Buddhism is thought to have been introduced to Luang Prabang in the late 13th or early 14th century. The first ruler of the Lao Kingdom of Lan Xang, Fa Ngum, declared Buddhism the state religion, but it took centuries for the faith to spread throughout the lowland Lao inhabitants of the region – indeed, to this day pre-Buddhist spirit cults remain widespread.

While the Communist government in Laos made some effort to circumscribe or eliminate Buddhism in the first years after its seizure of power in 1975, such attempts met with the overt hostility of the population and were soon abandoned. Today the lowland Lao – that is, mainly, the people of the Mekong and other major river valleys – are overwhelmingly Buddhist and generally quite devout. The women are, perhaps, more pious than the men, but it is commonplace throughout the country to see lines of both men and women offering alms to the saffron-clad monks early each morning.

Buddhism had an earlier impact in Cambodia, gradually spreading throughout the country from the 10th century onwards and receiving a significant boost during the reign of

Monks visit the Pak Ou caves near Luang Prabang.

the Buddhist monarch Jayavarman VII (1181–1219). In time it replaced Hinduism as the state religion – although some residual respect for Vishnu and Shiva may still be encountered. Like other religions, it suffered terribly under the Khmer Rouge (see page 215), but in Cambodia today it has made a major comeback.

Theravada and Mahayana Buddhism

The religious face of both Laos and Cambodia most immediately apparent to the visitor is Theravada Buddhist. Saffron- and orange-robed monks, white-robed nuns, richly ornamented temples with characteristic *chao-fa* "sky hook" eaves reaching to the heavens, alms bowls, *chedis* and *naga* serpents all epitomise the essence of Theravada Buddhism – closely paralleling the Theravada establishments in Thailand, Burma (Myanmar) and Sri Lanka.

Yet not far from the surface, in the dragon-ornamented temples of Vientiane's Chinatown, or behind a shopfront in Phnom Penh or Battambang, a parallel Buddhist tradition, the Mahayana, also exists. This is best seen in the Chinese and Vietnamese temples, where the Mahayana Buddhist traditions of Central Asia merge and mingle with Chinese Confucianism, Daoism and the archaic spirit worship that is

accruing good *karma* and minimising bad *karma*: in short, by being and doing good.

The Mahayanist ideal, on the other hand, is that of the *bodhisattva* – one who has perfected the virtues of generosity, morality, patience, vigour, concentration and wisdom, but elects voluntarily to stay in this world and help others, rather than entering directly into Nirvana.

The Mahayana school of Buddhism considers that Gautama, "the Enlightened One", is just one of many manifestations of the Buddha. They believe that there are countless Buddhas and *bodhisattvas*. Together with an equally

Xieng Khuan Buddha Park, near Vientiane.

indigenous to the civilisations of mainland Southeast Asia (see page 23).

The main difference between Mahayana and Theravada lies in subtle issues of emphasis and interpretation. Theravadins stress the importance of personal salvation – that is, the temporary renunciation of personal salvation in order to help humanity achieve enlightenment. A Theravadin strives to become a worthy one, an *arhat*, ready to attain Nirvana ("self-extinction"). In essence this means an end to corporeal existence and the endless cycle of rebirth. Not many people seriously aspire to become an *arhat* or achieve extinction in this life – that is usually seen as many lifetimes away. Instead, most Theravada Buddhists aim to achieve a better rebirth, which can be realised by

large number of Daoist divinities, these have combined to form a pantheon of deities and demi-gods whose aid and advice can be sought on any issue through invocations and offerings.

Despite Buddhism's division into two main sects, its central tenets are common to both – specifically, the principles contained in the Four Noble Truths and the Eightfold Path, the laws of *karma* and the goal of Nirvana.

Theravada is also known as the "Way of the Elders" variant of Buddhism, so called because of its great antiquity – it has existed for around 2,400 years, or as long as Buddhism itself. The Mahayana, by contrast, is regarded as a relative newcomer, having developed in South India a mere 1,900 years ago.

Spirit cults

Although frowned upon by both the Theravada Buddhist establishment and the Communist government, spirit cults have many adherents throughout Laos and remain the dominant non-Buddhist belief system in the country. Essentially, most Lao believe in the existence of spirits or *phii*. These are often associated with trees, rocks, waterfalls, and other natural elements or phenomena.

Spirits should be treated with proper caution and respect. Sometimes they need appeasing. Of special importance are the 32 *khwan*

Phnom Penh's Catholic cathedral was totally demolished by the Khmer Rouge in 1975. For the radicals, Catholicism represented both the former French colonial power and the despised Vietnamese.

good, bad and indifferent character are widely believed in and revered right across the country. Animism in Cambodia is generally limited to upland minority peoples – Khmer Loeu – such as the Kuy, Mnong, Brao and Jarai of

Phnom Penh street scene.

or guardian spirits necessary for good health and mental equilibrium. A common Lao spirit practice is the *basi* ceremony, which ensures that the 32 *khwan* are all present in a person's body. Respected elders tie loose loops of string around the wrists of those undergoing the ceremony; the *khwan* are implored to return to the body, and when they do equanimity is restored. Belief in spirits is very prevalent among the upland peoples of Laos, notably the Black Tai, while animism and shamanism play central roles in the rites and religious beliefs of the Hmong, Akha and Mien minorities.

The spirit world is also very real to the people of Cambodia. Spirit houses are frequently found in Khmer homes, and tutelary spirits of

RULES FOR A GOOD REBIRTH

Simple ways of achieving a good rebirth are: not taking life, refraining from alcohol, gambling and sexual promiscuity, keeping calm, not getting angry and honouring elderly people. Merit can be gained by giving donations to temples and monks, perhaps by regilding a *stupa* or donating a handful of rice to an itinerant monk. Above all, honour and respect should be paid to the *triratana*, or "Three Jewels": the Buddha, *sangha* (order of monks) and *dhamma* (sacred teachings). Most men will join the *sangha* and become monks at least once in their lives. Women may also be ordained as nuns, but this decision is often delayed until child-raising is complete.

northeastern Mondolkiri and Rattanakiri, and the Pear and Saoch of the southwestern Cardamom and Elephant Mountains.

Ancestor worship, known in Vietnamese as *hieu*, or the ritual expression of filial piety, is also very important and widely practised in the Vietnamese immigrant community, alongside other belief systems. Yet even this truly heterogeneous mixture of beliefs is not enough to satisfy the spiritual needs of the eclectic Vietnamese. It may be that the Triple Religion of Buddhism, Daoism and Confucianism is just too Chinese for Viet tastes.

The former French Roman Catholic Cathedral still stands in Vientiane, but these days it is attended by relatively few worshippers.

In Cambodia, too, Christianity is more associated with Viet Kieu – expat Vietnamese – than with Europeans or Khmers. This is probably why the Khmer Rouge, who sought to exterminate the Vietnamese, went to the trouble of completely destroying Phnom Penh Cathedral so that not one brick remained. Today Christian missionaries are once more openly preaching the Gospel, although indigenous Christians – including Vietnamese residents of Cambodia

Ruins of a 19th-century French Catholic church at Bokor National Park, Cambodia.

After all, Vietnam's long relationship with the Middle Kingdom has been essentially a love–hate relationship, with greater emphasis on the latter emotion. The Vietnamese, Sinicised though their civilisation maybe, are still a Southeast Asian people, so locality spirits, too, must be appeased.

Christianity

Christianity, introduced to Indochina by the French, never made much headway among the Buddhist Lao or Khmers. In Laos, Vietnamese converts to Christianity migrated to the large cities, and because of this, Christianity in Laos is more closely associated with Vietnamese expats than with Europeans or indigenous Lao.

– do not constitute more than 1 to 2 percent of the population.

Vietnamese and Chinese religions

Although the Vietnamese are associated with Catholicism, the majority of the ethnic Vietnamese in Laos are in fact Mahayana Buddhists. There are two practising *chua* or Vietnamese temples in Vientiane. The larger of these, Chua Ban Long, is located in a small Vietnamese enclave to the west of Khun Boulom Road and is well worth a visit.

With about 1 million people, the ethnic Vietnamese constitute the largest ethnic minority in Cambodia, and, as in Laos, most are Buddhists, of the Mahayana school. The distinction between Theravada and Mahayana Buddhism reinforces already deep cultural and social differences between the Khmer and Viet peoples.

Furthering the divide, the Vietnamese minority – made up of a wide cross section of Viet society – includes representatives of all Vietnamese religious persuasions: as well as Buddhists, Confucians and Christians there are followers of such exclusively Vietnamese faiths as Cao Dai and Hoa Hao Buddhism (a kind of Buddhist cult, Hoa Hao is puritanical, opposed to established Buddhist clerical influence, and very patriotic to the Vietnamese state). The

made up of South Asian migrants of Punjabi and Tamil origin. More recently Cham Muslim refugees from Cambodia, victims of the Khmer Rouge reign of terror, have settled in Laos, while small numbers of Muslim Yunnanese or Chin Haw may be found in the north of the country. There are two mosques in Vientiane; one – the Jama' Masjid – is very central, close to Fountain Circle.

Perhaps surprisingly, Islam is Cambodia's second religion. Nearly all Cambodia's Muslims are ethnic Chams – at around 500,000 people they are the country's largest minority after

Cambodian Muslims, ethnic Chams, at the window of a mosque.

Inside Vientiane's Jamia Mosque.

Holy See of the Cao Dai is in the Vietnamese province of Tay Ninh, close to the Cambodian frontier, and this extraordinary syncretic religion – which counts Victor Hugo, Laozi and Jesus among its saints – has in some cases bridged the wide Viet–Khmer divide to win Khmer converts.

The Chinese population of Laos comprises mostly urban-dwellers, whose temples are readily visible in the towns. They practise a mixture of Confucianism, Daoism, Mahayana Buddhism and ancestor worship.

Islam

There are almost no ethnic Lao Muslims, but the country does have a small Muslim minority

THE TRIPLE RELIGION

For ethnic Chinese and Vietnamese believers, the "Great Vehicle" of Mahayana Buddhism is closely associated with *Khong Giao*, or Confucianism, an ethical system which originated in China and was based on the teachings of the great moral philosopher Confucius (551–479 BC).

Similarly linked is Daoism, or Lao Giao, founded in China during the 6th century BC by Laozi as a system of speculative philosophy centring on the concept of man's oneness with the universe. As the basic tenets of the three teachings are not in conflict they have practically fused, and are known as *Tam Giao*, or the Triple Religion.

the Vietnamese. Originally refugees from 18th-century Vietnam, the Chams practise a rather lax form of Sunni Islam: fasting one day a week during the month of Ramadan, abstaining from pork but often drinking alcohol.

Since the time of the Khmer Rouge, when Islam suffered particularly severely, aid in the form of money, assistance in building new mosques, and the provision of books and educational help from Malaysia and the Middle East is gradually resulting in the establishment of a more orthodox Sunni Muslim tradition.

Monks collect alms during the daily procession, or sai baat.

Buddhism and the Khmer Rouge

Traditionally Cambodia was considered the most Buddhist country in Southeast Asia. To be a Khmer meant being a Buddhist. The three jewels – the Buddha, *sangha*, *dhamma* – were everywhere honoured, if not always followed, and the national religion was omnipresent. From the smallest upcountry village to the heart of Phnom Penh the country was studded with Theravada Buddhist temples and stupas. Everywhere, too, were spirit houses – those less orthodox but enduringly popular ancillary manifestations of Southeast Asian Buddhism.

Before the Khmer Rouge seized power in 1975, Cambodia had almost 3,000 registered temples, and most Khmer men became monks

for at least some part of their lives. For example, in the mid-1930s the young Pol Pot spent several months as a novice at Wat Botum Vaddei, a monastery near the Royal Palace in Phnom Penh. Buddhism provided a spiritual explanation for existence, a moral code for living and a retreat from mundane concerns when this proved necessary or desirable. Disgraced politicians, or those who had fallen from power, often took refuge in the saffron robe.

All this changed with astonishing swiftness after the Khmer Rouge seized power. In the new society that Democratic Kampuchea (DK) was building there was no room for any spiritual or moral authority other than that of the Party. Angkar – the Organisation – would brook no rival in its bid to establish total control over the hearts and minds of the Cambodian people, and this alone would have been enough to seal the fate of Buddhism in Democratic Kampuchea.

Yet apart from the issue of control, there were ideological reasons for the Khmer Rouge leadership's determination to stamp out Buddhism. The driving force behind the ideology of the DK leadership – ideologues like Pol Pot and Ieng Sary – was nothing less than the complete transformation of Cambodian society. This goal was to be achieved by blending elements of China's Cultural Revolution with North Korea's *Juche*, or "self-reliance", but taking both processes further, and from an exclusively Khmer base.

Pol Pot and his comrades scorned ideas of a simple "great leap forward" and transitional stages to building socialism. Democratic Kampuchea would achieve Communism in a single bound, and that bound would be a "super great leap forward", trebling agricultural production at a stroke.

How could monks possibly fit into such a society? Monks were wandering mendicants, begging for their food and thus permitting others to improve their *karma* through the act of giving. They were prohibited by *dhamma* from working in the fields in case they harmed any living creature – even an insect – which might be crushed underfoot.

Worse still, from a Khmer Rouge viewpoint, monks preached the transience of mundane objectives (such as tripling the harvest, for example), and held the achievement of Nirvana, or self-extinction, as the ultimate purpose of existence. Clearly these views, aims and objectives were at a variance with those of DK political leaders like Pol Pot and military commanders like Ta Mok. To the Khmer Rouge, therefore, monks were nothing more than worthless parasites who – rather like townspeople, only more so – lived free of cost, depending on the labour of the peasantry, contributing nothing to society other than a negative, non-productive superstition. Quite simply, they had to go. And go they did.

Nor did the spirits fare better – there are accounts of Khmer Rouge militiamen spraying

Khmer Rouge propaganda and slogans from this period provide a telling record of DK attitudes towards Buddhism and the Buddhist establishment. Pol Pot wished to establish a militarised, fiercely nationalistic state, which would be capable of taking back the Mekong Delta from Vietnam and the Khmer-speaking border regions of Surin and Buriram from the Thais. Buddhism abhorred violence, therefore, according to the Khmer Rouge: "The Buddhist religion is the cause of our country's weakness." During a little more than three years of DK rule, between April 1975 and December 1978 – the terrible time

At Don Khong, Siphandon, boy monks apply themselves to the study of scripture.

spirit houses with machine-gun fire to prove to the superstitious peasantry that a new force was in charge, and one that would brook no interference, even from the spirit world.

Monks in the Killing Fields

From 1975 – even earlier in those areas that had been under Khmer Rouge control during the civil war – Buddhism was proscribed: it was not merely discouraged, or simply prohibited, but physically expunged. Temples were closed (and sometimes torn down), while resident monks were ordered to take off their robes, don black peasant garb and go to work in the fields. Those who refused were unceremoniously killed.

POL POT AND THE PARASITES

Pol Pot wished to build a controlled society based primarily on agriculture, in which everyone worked. As monks were forbidden to work in the fields, they were parasites. "The monks are bloodsuckers, they oppress the people, they are imperialists," it was claimed. "Begging for charity... maintains the workers in a down-trodden condition." The people were forbidden to support the *sangha*: "It is forbidden to give anything to those shaven-arses, it would be pure waste"; and, more chillingly: "If any worker takes rice to the monks, we shall set him to planting cabbages. If the cabbages are not fully grown in three days, he will dig his own grave."

called the "zero years" – the Khmer Rouge set out to disestablish Buddhism completely. Worship, prayer, meditation and religious festivals were forbidden. All Buddha figures, scriptures and other holy objects and relics were desecrated by fire or water, or simply smashed to pieces.

Pali, the theological language of Theravada Buddhism, was banned. Most temples were turned into storehouses or factories; some were destroyed, others were converted into prisons and execution centres. Only symbols of past Khmer greatness, such as Angkor Wat, were actively preserved, although many temple buildings in

Slaughter of the Buddhists

Before the Khmer Rouge seizure of power, Cambodia supported an estimated 60,000 Buddhist monks. After 44 months of DK rule, in January 1979, fewer than 1,000 remained alive to return to their former monasteries. The rest had died – many murdered outright by the Khmer Rouge, but still more as a result of brutality, starvation and disease.

Only at Wat Ko, the birthplace of Nuon Chea, Pol Pot's shadowy right-hand man and DK's "Brother No. 2", was a monastery permitted to remain open. Here four monks – almost certainly

Prayer offerings at Phnom Bakheng temple, Siem Reap.

Phnom Penh and the other main cities survived the DK period in varying states of disrepair.

At the same time the brotherhood of monks was forcibly disbanded and almost completely destroyed. The most prominent, most senior and most popular monks, including the abbots of many temples, were simply taken outside and killed – on occasion the DK cadres responsible for such executions would display the saffron robes of the murdered monk on nearby trees for the people to see. Monks who agreed to abandon their robes were forced, against all their principles, to marry. Angkar needed a growing population to fight the more numerous Vietnamese, so celibacy ran counter to the interests of the revolution.

the only practising monks left in the whole of Democratic Kampuchea – received alms from Nuon Chea's mother on an almost daily basis. She disapproved of DK anticlericalism, and clearly wasn't taking any notice of her doting son.

With the destruction of the DK regime and the expulsion of the Khmer Rouge from Phnom Penh in 1978, a concerted and increasingly successful attempt was made by the new Cambodian authorities to restore the national culture. At the forefront of this movement has been the return of organised religion. Monasteries have gradually reopened, prohibitions on making offerings and holding festivals have been lifted, and Cambodian Buddhism has made a rapid and lasting recovery from the Khmer Rouge onslaughts.

The stupa at Udong, near Phnom Penh.

*View from Mount Phu Si,
Luang Prabang.*

The ruins at Wat Phu.

The daily market at Luang Prabang.

LAOS

Laos is a fascinating and rewarding country to visit. Definitively off the beaten track, it has retained its culture and charm, traditional village life, wild forests and beautiful countryside.

Rice is the main Laotian crop.

One of Southeast Asia's least-known countries, Laos is an ancient land with a surprisingly sophisticated culture; at the same time, it is easy-going and a great deal of fun to visit. From the 14th century to the 16th century, when the Kingdom of Lan Xang or "One Million Elephants" was at its peak, this was one of the most important states in Southeast Asia, and many of the country's religious and cultural traditions date from this period. Subsequently Lan Xang went into decline, and the Lao people found themselves dominated by their more powerful neighbours, Thailand and Vietnam.

Throughout the centuries it remained distinctively Lao, however – a society dominated by lowland, wet-rice growing Buddhists closely related to the neighbouring Thai. Yet in the mountains almost 50 percent of the population is still made up of widely varying minority groups, each with its own distinctive and colourful traditions, clothing and world-view.

A visit to Laos is, in many ways, a trip back into the past. Cultural links with neighbouring Thailand are immediately apparent in the saffron robes of the Buddhist monks, the similarities in temple architecture and the speech of the people – yet Laos is more like the Thailand of 30 years ago. Although it has opened up to tourism in the past decade, there is still little of the rampant commercialism and vibrant entertainment industry which characterise its neighbour. The waters of the Mekong River which forms the boundary between the two countries may flow past both Lao and Thai banks at the same rate, but the flow of life in the two countries proceeds at two entirely different speeds.

The most important temple in Laos, Pha That Luang.

There is another side to Laos, too, which distinguishes the country from Thailand and further enriches an already sophisticated culture. At least in terms of architecture and cuisine, Laos has benefited from its long association with its other neighbours and from French influences. Lao food is delicious, but one is also able to eat in Chinese and Vietnamese restaurants, as well as enjoy excellent coffee, fresh baguettes, croissants and French haute cuisine.

Gathering rice on the Bolaven Plateau, a highland region known for its relatively cool climate.

THE LAY OF THE LAND

Laos is a mountainous country, cut through and bounded to the west by the Mekong River. Some 40 percent remains forested, a sanctuary for many rare and endangered species.

S et firmly within tropical Southeast Asia between latitudes 14°N and 23°N, the Lao People's Democratic Republic, as it has been known officially since 1975, covers just over 236,800 sq km (91,400 sq miles). It shares borders with China and Burma (Myanmar) in the north and northwest, Thailand in the west, Cambodia in the south and Vietnam in the east. The familiarity of the alliterative cliché "land-locked Laos" perhaps disguises the significance of the republic's geographical insularity. It is the only country in Southeast Asia, an area traditionally heavily involved in maritime trade, which doesn't have a coastline. What Laos does have in abundance are mountains and rivers. Over 90 percent of the country lies more than 180 metres (585ft) above sea level, and around 70 percent comprises mountains and plateaux.

There are no extensive areas of flatland anywhere in the country – the largest being around the capital, Vientiane, and the southern city of Savannakhet, although the northern region is more consistently mountainous than the south, and is characterised by rugged ranges cut through by narrow river valleys. Most of these rivers eventually flow into the Mekong (Mae Nam Khong in Lao), which forms Laos's border with Burma before sweeping east towards Luang Prabang and then swinging south to Vientiane to form much of the country's border with Thailand before entering Cambodia. Rivers in the far east drain through Vietnam into the Gulf of Tonkin and the South China Sea.

Mountains and plateaux

The country's highest mountains are found in Xieng Khuang province in the central

Ferrying traffic across the Mekong to Don Khong.

northeast. The landscape is typified by jagged limestone peaks, often severely eroded to form serrated ridges and ranges. Many of the mountains exceed 2,000 metres (6,500ft) in height, the highest being Phu Bia, which reaches 2,820 metres (9,165ft). Behind that peak is the extensive Xieng Khuang Plateau, the largest such feature in the country, which is principally rolling grasslands rather than a flat plain. Prehistoric stone jar-shaped vessels dot some of the plateau, lending it its popular name, the Plain of Jars (see page 138). Most of southern Laos is at a lower elevation than the north, except for the Annamite Cordillera, the principal mountain range, which runs northwest to southeast for some 1,100km (690 miles) – half the length of the country – comprising much of its border with Vietnam and forming the watershed between the Mekong and the South China Sea. Geologically the range is a complex mix of rock formations. Ancient lava flows have

It is difficult to overestimate the importance of the Mekong to the Lao people and their country. In addition to depositing fertile alluvial silt, the river is a major artery of trade and travel and source of fish.

The limestone landscapes of Laos are riddled with caves.

formed several notable plateaux within central and southern Laos: the Khammuan Plateau, in the cordillera's central stretch, is an area of karst peaks, steep valleys and grottoes. Further south the beautiful Bolaven Plateau extends for 10,000 sq km (3,860 sq miles).

The mighty Mekong

The mountainous terrain of Laos makes much of the country relatively inaccessible and unsuitable for high-yield or commercial agriculture. It is no surprise, then, that the main population centres are found in the Mekong Valley, particularly in the southern flood plains. The two biggest cities – the capital, Vientiane, and Savannakhet, which are also the administrative centres of Laos's most populous provinces – are on the Mekong.

The transport infrastructure in Laos has improved, and the river remains a practical means of moving goods and people effectively and efficiently. The central stretch of the Mekong, from Luang Prabang to slightly north of the Khemmarat rapids in Savannakhet province, remains navigable all year round, but, despite the fact that the river swells to widths of almost 15km (9 miles) in the south (around the Si Phan Don area), the upper stretches beyond Luang Prabang can be treacherous and shallow in the dry months, impassable to most vessels. There are plans to blast these areas to afford the river year-round navigability and increase its potential as an international trade route, but there is opposition to such schemes, both in Laos and in neighbouring countries, especially Thailand and Cambodia.

CONSERVATION IN LAOS

Timber is an important source of revenue, although at great cost to the environment. Areas which 30 years ago were covered in forest, today have but a few trees left after irresponsible logging. Efforts have been made to curb the deforestation, including setting up 17 National Biodiversity Conservation Areas (NBCAS), covering just over 10 percent of the land area, but logging continues. Even within the NBCAS concessions are granted, and elsewhere the military runs its own concerns, in breach of all agreements and laws. The revenues are too high for laws to have much effect.

Despite such justifiable worries about logging in various parts of the country, Laos still has one of the most unspoilt environments in Southeast Asia and retains much of its wildlife. However, with few controls on hunting, trapping and exporting endangered species, and little public awareness of the value of maintaining biodiversity, conservation measures seem unlikely. Laos has been slow to ratify the Convention on International Trade in Endangered Species (CITES), although how much difference this would make is questionable. Much of the Lao population beyond the few large cities still relies on "bush meat" to supplement its diet, and this is particularly true of the upland people such as the Hmong, who have hunted small game and birds for centuries, and see little reason to stop now.

Blasting is only one of a number of Mekong projects that have been discussed, most revolving around damming the river to provide irrigation and hydroelectric power. Upstream, China has already built six dams, the most recent of which opened in 2016. A major dam on the Nam Ngum River was constructed in 1975, flooding an area of 250 sq km (96 sq miles) and forming the Ang Nam Ngum Reservoir, 90km (55 miles) north of Vientiane. A hydroelectric power station here generates much of the capital city's power, and the excess is sold to Thailand. The Lao authorities commissioned such ventures. While supporters argue that dams provide a stable and sustainable source of foreign exchange for a poor country such as Laos, opponents claim that new dams will have profoundly adverse effects on the environment and economy, and that much of the projected income will be needed to pay off foreign debt, while local people are rarely, if ever, properly compensated.

Climate and farming

The tropical climate of Laos revolves around the annual monsoon cycle, which produces three distinct seasons. The southwest mon-

Lodges at Si Phan Don.

Dusk falls on the Mekong River.

the Name Theun II dam on the Nam Theun River in the Nakai district of Khammuan province in 2010; the completed dam is 50 metres (165ft) high and, at a cost of flooding 450 sq km (175 sq miles), provides 1,070MW of power for development and export.

At present, at least 11 possible future sites have been identified as other locations for new dams projected to be built by 2020 and to raise the country's power-generating capacity by at least 5,000MW. This would make hydroelectric power – already a key element in the Lao economy – a truly major contributor to the annual GDP, though understandably environmentalists worry about both the long-term effects of damming and the logging concessions that are invariably part of

soon arrives between May and July and continues until November, bringing most of the year's rainfall. From November to March the country is almost completely dry and relatively cool, catching breezes from the tail end of the northeast monsoon; from March to May temperatures edge higher, and with little rain the countryside becomes ever drier and dustier. Through the year as a whole, the low-lying Mekong Valley is warmer and more humid than the more mountainous areas. The provinces of Vientiane and Savannakhet get more rainfall than the north-central provinces of Xieng Khuang and Luang Prabang but substantially less than the southern areas of the Annamite Cordillera.

The great majority of the Lao people still live and work in rural areas; for example, Vientiane – by some margin the largest city – has a population of less than 250,000 (although the metropolitan area is around three times that). Traditionally the lowland river valleys are inhabited by those who are ethnically Lao – about 50 percent of the population – and they are involved in subsistence wet-rice cultivation, which still accounts for most of the use of valley land. Upland areas are inhabited by other ethnic groups, who cultivate dry rice as well as practising slash-and-burn agriculture, and

Lao woman from the Lantan tribe harvesting corn near Luang Namtha, in Northern Laos.

hunting and gathering. Agriculture, albeit at subsistence level, occupies most of the population, although less than 10 percent of the land is suitable for cultivation. Apart from rice, crops include tobacco, wheat, corn, soybeans, fruits, nuts and vegetables in the lowlands, and tobacco, tea, coffee, maize and, still of significant economic importance, opium in the hills.

Flora and fauna

Laos has emerged as an ecotourism destination in recent years, with visitors attracted by some of the most pristine natural environments in Southeast Asia – and the wildlife that these environments sustain. Some 40 percent of the

During the late 20th century, scientists discovered a previously unknown mammal in the Annamite Cordillera, the spindlehorn or Vu Quang's ox, called nyang in Lao and also known as the saola.

country remains forested (down from around 70 percent in the 1960s), with the largest surviving tracts of woodland in Indochina. Around 21 percent of the land is protected, although illegal hunting and poaching is a problem. The forests largely consist of tall thin dipterocarps, often reaching 30 metres (100ft), and valuable hardwood trees including teak and rosewood. Along river valleys bamboos are particularly prolific. A few regions have slightly different forest cover, including evergreen and tropical pine. On the plateaux of the Annamite Cordillera, forests give way to savannah.

These forests and grasslands support a diverse array of wildlife, some of which have been hunted to extinction in neighbouring countries. Among mammal species are the Asiatic black bear, the Malayan sun bear, the Asiatic jackal, red panda, concolor gibbon and giant barking deer. There are still a few hundred wild elephants, and over 1,000 more are used for logging and transport. A small number of rhinoceros *sondaicus* survive on the Bolaven Plateau, and elsewhere in the south there have been sightings of kouprey, a rare species of wild cattle. Other mammals that may be seen with luck and patience include the gibbon (of which there are five species in Laos), the douc langur, banteng, Fea's muntjac, Indian muntjac, marbled cat, leopard cat – perhaps even an extremely rare Indochinese tiger. The freshwater Irrawaddy dolphin can sometimes be seen in the Mekong around the Si Phan Don area in southern Laos.

Non-mammalian species include snakes, of which six are venomous (two types of cobra, three species of viper, and the banded krait), while the large Tokay gecko is a highly audible presence in villages throughout the country. There are many colourful birds, indigenous and migratory. Birdwatchers are rewarded with a huge variety, from the sub-Himalayan species found in the northern forests to spectacular birds such as the giant ibis and sarus cranes in the Mekong Valley – itself an important migration route.

Khon Phapheng falls in Southern Laos.

Wat Xieng Thong, Luang Prabang.

DECISIVE DATES

3000 BC–AD 1000
Laos is settled by Austro-Tai-speaking peoples.

The Kingdom of One Million Elephants

1353
Fa Ngum founds the Kingdom of Lan Xang. He makes Theravada Buddhism the state religion.

1421–1520
Lan Xang suffers 100 years of petty wars and rivalries.

1520
King Phothisarat comes to the throne and reunifies the kingdom. Forty years later his son Setthathirat moves the capital from Luang Prabang to Vientiane.

1637–94
King Sulinya Vongse presides over the Golden Age of Lan Xang from his capital at Vientiane.

1700
After the death of Sulinya Vongse, Lan Xang begins to break up.

Fragmentation and Decline

1775–1800
The Siamese absorb southern Laos.

1826–8
Chao Anuvong of Vientiane attempts to re-establish Lao independence but is unsuccessful. In 1828, Vientiane is comprehensively sacked by the invading Siamese.

1870s–1880s
Laos, as far south as Vientiane, is plundered by bands of Yunnanese Chinese known as Haw in the Haw Wars.

The Colonial Interlude

1893–1907
Unequal colonial treaties forced on Siam lead to French control over all Lao territories east of the Mekong.

1900–39
French colonial policy continues traditional Vietnamese policies east of the Mekong. In Laos, as in Cambodia, Vietnamese settlement is encouraged. Laos remains a colonial backwater, of little economic value.

1939–45
World War II ends in Laos with a brief Japanese-inspired declaration of independence, followed by the return of the French.

The flag of French Laos.

1949
Laos is recognised as an "Independent Associate State" under French tutelage.

1950–1
The United States and the United Kingdom recognise Laos as part of the French Union. The pro-Communist Pathet Lao rejects this development and forms a government of national resistance.

Laos and the Indochina Wars

1952
The Pathet Lao begins a low-scale insurgency in the northeast of the country.

1953
France withdraws, leaving an independent Laos divided between royalist forces in Vientiane and the leftist Pathet Lao.

1955
Laos is admitted to the United Nations.

The Second Indochina War, otherwise known as the Vietnam War.

1957
Prince Souvanna Phouma leads a coalition government in Vientiane.

1963
The Communist government of North Vietnam begins extensive use of the Ho Chi Minh Trail in Laos. Covert US military activities begin.

1973
US troops withdraw from Vietnam, and the CIA "Secret War" in Laos is wound down.

1975
After the Communist victory in Vietnam, the Lao People's Democratic Republic is established.

The Development of Modern Laos

1975–89
Rigid socialist policies introduced; most of the country's intelligentsia and urban middle classes flee. Communist attempts to weaken the popularity of Buddhism do not work. Former King Savang Vatthana and other members

of the royal family die in prison camps. Disaffection grows as poverty increases.

1977
Treaty of friendship and cooperation signed between Laos and Vietnam.

1989–90
Collapse of the Soviet Union.

1993
A slow start is made in restoring individual liberties;

The Prime Minister of Laos, Bounnhang Vorachith, and his Russian counterpart, Dmitry Medvedev, shaking hands in 2016.

the country begins opening up to tourism.

1994
The Friendship Bridge opens across the Mekong, linking Laos and Thailand.

1997
Laos is admitted to the Association of Southeast Asian Nations (ASEAN).

1998
Khamtay Siphandone becomes president.

1999
Laos moves cautiously closer to Thailand as Vietnamese influence diminishes.

2003
Gradual transition to market economy continues.

2006
Choummaly Sayasone becomes president in June.

2009
Rail link with Thailand opened over the Mekong at Nong Kai.

2011
A new stock market opens in Vientiane. Choummaly Sayasone elected for a further five-year term by parliament.

2012
Viet-Lao Solidarity and Friendship Year marks 50 years of diplomatic ties and 35 years of the Vietnam–Laos Friendship Agreement.

2016
Bounnhang Vorachith elected president and General Secretary of the Lao People's Revolutionary Party; Thongloun Sisoulith elected prime minister.

THE KINGDOM OF LAN XANG

The early development of Laos was initiated by the southward migration of Tai-speaking peoples, leading to the rise of the kingdom of Lan Xang. The many internal conflicts remained largely unresolved until the 17th-century reign of King Sulinya Vongse.

The Lao people – both the lowland Lao and the various Tai minorities of northern Laos, together with the Thais – are part of the Tai-speaking ethnic group who are thought to have moved south into Indochina around 1,200 years ago. Academic opinion differs as to their origins. Many historians have associated the southward migration with the disintegration of the supposed Tai Kingdom of Nan Chao in southern China; other opinions suggest that pressure from Mongol hordes drove them southwards into the fertile ricelands of mainland Southeast Asia. A more radical school of thought – fascinating, though largely discredited – has the Tai moving northwards and inland from an original home in the Pacific.

It is never easy to be precise about the early history of any people: their origins, early movements and way of life are lost in the mists of time. It is now generally accepted, however, that the first Tai peoples lived in southern China, where they had established small statelets, often no larger than a single valley, called *muang*. From around AD 800 these hardy, independent agriculturalists gradually expanded southwards, not in a wave of conquest of already settled land but into hills and valleys as yet unsettled, or only partially so, by peoples such as the Mon and the Khmer.

Founding two kingdoms

By about 1200, various larger Tai-speaking *muang* were beginning to emerge across a broad belt of land, from the Shan state of Burma (Myanmar) in the west, through the region which is now northern Thailand, to the forest-clad riverine valleys of upper Laos.

The most significant of these "super" *muang* – which can really be classified as kingdoms – were located in the northern part of mainland

Illustration of two early indigenous Tai men.

Southeast Asia. In the east, in an area rather larger than present-day Laos, the Kingdom of Lan Xang ("One Million Elephants") was established in 1353 by King Fa Ngum. Meanwhile to the west, approximately within the frontiers of present-day northern Thailand, King Mangrai had founded the Kingdom of Lan Na ("One Million Rice Fields") in the late 13th century.

These first major Tai *muang* were destined to be overshadowed by more powerful southern neighbours – Sukhothai, Ayutthaya and eventually Bangkok. This does not detract from the grandeur of their achievement, however, and although Lan Na eventually became part of Siam (Thailand), the Kingdom of Lan Xang – albeit battered and bruised by a series of more

> *Fa Ngum made Theravada Buddhism the religion of the new state. The Pha Bang, a golden image of the Buddha from his Khmer neighbours installed at the new capital, Luang Prabang, became the national symbol of the Lao.*

powerful neighbours – survives to this day in its modern Lao incarnation.

Very little is known about the early history of Laos before the rise of Lan Na and Lan Xang.

(literally "City of Sandalwood") with the assistance of 10,000 Khmer troops.

Having grown up in exile at Angkor under the protection of King Jayavarman Paramesvara, Fa Ngum married one of Jayavarman's daughters, before leading mixed forces of Lao and Khmer northwards to conquer not just Vientiane but also the region around the Plain of Jars, parts of northeast Thailand, and finally Luang Prabang.

Having completed these conquests, Chao Fa Ngum felt able to declare himself the first king of Lan Xang, one of the largest kingdoms

Boat races on the Mekong River.

Indeed, it seems likely that the various Lao *muang* were little more than a series of vassal states of the powerful but declining Khmer Empire further to the south. Boundaries were inevitably less rigid than they are today, and at the height of its power in the 14th century Lan Na included the Lao *muang* of Luang Prabang within its borders. However, times changed and, as Lan Na found itself increasingly pressured by the growing power of Burma, so Lan Xang (Laos) found itself presented with the opportunity to expand as the Khmer Empire retracted.

Brave new conqueror

In 1353 a Lao warlord, Chao Fa Ngum, captured the important Lao town of Vientiane

in mainland Southeast Asia, with its capital at Luang Prabang. (The role played by Khmer mercenary troops in Chao Fa Ngum's empire building should be noted, however. It has been suggested that the first Lao kingdom was, in essence, a Khmer state.)

Chao Fa Ngum constantly strove to expand the frontiers of his new state. Within a few years his armies had reached the natural barrier of the Annamite Cordillera, which cut Laos off from Vietnam to the north and the Champa kingdom to the south.

Lan Xang was not a state in the modern sense of the word. The king directly ruled and taxed only Vientiane and its immediate area, while the rulers of nearby smaller dependent *muang* raised their own taxes and generally ruled as they saw fit. Their duties to the king were to pay an annual tribute, attend the royal court for major ceremonies, and raise forces to support the king when he waged war. Thus Lan Xang can be thought of more as a loose federation rather than a centralised kingdom with clear boundaries.

Building up a state

Fa Ngum was succeeded by his eldest son, who took the title Phaya Samsenthai ("Lord of Three Hundred Thousand Tai"), who underscored the

least the kingdom survived – although by the time of the death of King Wisunalat in 1520, Burma, which was already coming to dominate neighbouring Lan Na, was also knocking at the western gateway of Lan Xang.

Rulers and hill people

King Phothisarat, who took the throne in 1520, was a different character from his predecessors. By the 1540s he had subdued Lan Na and placed his son Setthathirat on the throne there.

In 1548 Setthathirat inherited the throne of Lan Xang, bringing with him the prestigious

The Pak Ou caves, discovered, it is said, by King Setthathirat in the 16th century.

ties of blood and culture within the various Tai *muang* by marrying a Lan Na princess from Chiang Mai and a Siamese princess from Ayutthaya. He then devoted himself to reorganising and strengthening the state administration of Lan Xang, basing it largely on principles already established at Ayutthaya. He built temples and schools, discouraged foreign military adventures and devoted himself to building up Lan Xang as a trading nation. In this he was largely successful.

Following his death in 1421 at the age of 60, less competent hands took control. Over the next century no fewer than 12 rulers succeeded to the throne of Lan Xang. None has left remarkable records or monuments, but at

Pha Kaew (Emerald Buddha). He ordered the building of Wat Pha Kaew to house the new national symbol, and also gave orders for the construction of That Luang, the country's largest and most distinctive stupa (see page 112). Still, apart from these successes, times were dangerous; Lan Xang's control of all but the broad riverine valleys was tenuous, and many of the hill people were still free, proud men who recognised no lowland authority. In 1560 Setthathirat moved the capital from Luang Prabang south to Vientiane, although in reality the two towns functioned almost as joint capitals, with Luang Prabang as the "royal" capital and Vientiane as the "administrative" capital.

In 1571 King Setthathirat's death began another downward cycle for Lan Xang. For 60 years no leader of merit emerged, and this led to long periods of internecine strife and intervention by the forces of Burma. Only in 1637 did a Lao king worthy of the name once more ascend the throne. His name was Sulinya Vongse, and his 57-year rule – the longest of any Lao monarch – is generally considered the Golden Age of the kingdom.

Under King Sulinya Vongse, Vientiane was endowed with many palaces and temples, becoming a great centre of Buddhist scholarship, with monks coming from Siam and Cambodia to train in its seminaries.

The Golden Age

There is no doubt that Sulinya Vongse (1637–94) was a wise ruler. A good deal is known about this period of Lao history, largely as a result of the peaceful conditions and relative prosperity that distinguished it. Spared the long years of warfare with Burma and courtly struggles with

An early print of That Luang in Vientiane, the most important national monument in Laos.

WESTERN VIEWS OF LAN XANG

Perhaps the most interesting account of Lan Xang at the time of Sulinya Vongse comes from Giovanni Maria Leria, an Italian Jesuit missionary abroad in the region in the 1640s. Leria notes: "The royal palace, of which the structure and symmetry are admirable, can be seen from afar. Truly it is of a prodigious extent, and so large that one would take it for a town, both with respect to its situation and the infinite number of people who live there. The apartment of the king, which is adorned with a superb and magnificent gateway, and a quantity of fine rooms together with a great hall, are all made of incorruptible timber and adorned outside and in with excellent bas-reliefs, so delicately gilded that they seem to be plated with gold rather than covered with gold leaf."

Another view of King Sulinya Vongse is afforded by Gerrit van Wuysthoff, a merchant of the Dutch East India Company. Van Wuysthoff travelled to Vientiane in 1641. After a warm welcome he followed a royal procession from the royal palace to the grounds of That Luang, the most important Buddhist edifice in the city. He reported: "The king is a young man, about 23 years old. Before him marched about 300 soldiers with spears and guns; behind him elephants carried armed men, followed by some groups of musicians. They were followed in turn by 200 soldiers and by 16 elephants carrying the king's five wives (and their ladies in waiting)."

Ayutthaya, the king was able to spend lavishly on temples and Buddhist endowments and on generally embellishing the capital. As a consequence Vientiane acquired a reputation as a centre of Buddhist learning, attracting novices and devotees from as far afield as Burma, Cambodia and northern Thailand.

An invaluable source of information about Sulinya Vongse's capital is the extensive diaries and mission reports of Western visitors (see panel), who sought to take advantage of the peaceful conditions for once prevailing in the Middle Mekong. Most of the visiting businessmen were Dutch Protestants. A steady flow of Portuguese Catholic missionaries also provided written accounts of the area.

Sulinya Vongse was an absolute monarch who appears to have ruled justly and wisely, despite his remoteness from his people. Certainly his lengthy reign ensured that Laos enjoyed peace and prosperity for most of the 17th century. He established cordial relations with the Siamese King Narai at Ayutthaya, and this alliance was strong enough to ward off the Burmese and the Vietnamese for many years.

Nevertheless, two unfortunate developments combined to weaken Lan Xang; one of these can be blamed on the king, while the other was effectively beyond his control.

Adultery and isolation

Sulinya Vongse may have had many wives, but he had only one son – Chao Rachabut. This royal heir was essential to the continuity of Sulinya Vongse's line, but when Chao Rachabut was found guilty of adultery with the wife of a palace servant the irascible and unbending old king ordered his son's execution.

The second adverse development was the growing power and influence of neighbouring states such as Burma, Vietnam and, above all, Siam – all of which had the distinct advantage of a coastline. Lan Xang remained an isolated inland entity, wishing and indeed eager to trade with the advancing Western powers but increasingly cut off by its more powerful neighbours, who effectively limited Vientiane's access to foreign trade. The inevitable results were poverty and backwardness.

King Sulinya Vongse eventually died in 1694, leaving two young prospective heirs, the children of the son he had executed. In an all-too-familiar pattern, no regency was established;

the throne was usurped by a powerful minister, who was in turn overthrown six months later. After more than half a century of peace and stability, Lan Xang was fast descending into factionalism and chaos.

Powerful neighbours

On this occasion, however, things were worse than usual. To the east, Vietnam had expanded hugely in terms of both power and territory. To the west and south, an even more formidable rival had developed in the Siamese Kingdom of Ayutthaya. To the north, albeit more remote

That Luang today.

from Vientiane, lay the still-powerful Qing Empire of the Chinese.

In these circumstances, factionalism at the Lao court was damaging. For instance, if one faction seized power with tacit Siamese support, its rivals would turn to Vietnam for backing. Both Siam and Vietnam encouraged these manoeuvrings. Siam eyed all Lao territories west of the Mekong and considered itself the rightful ruler of Luang Prabang and Vientiane, while Vietnam coveted the Xieng Khuang region around the Plain of Jars, to which it gave a Vietnamese name, Tranh Ninh, to justify its attentions. To use an antiquated but entirely appropriate Thai phrase, Laos without Sulinya Vongse had become "a bird with two heads"

– a weak power paying tribute to two masters, while trying to play one off against the other. This was a bad time for Laos: the ordinary people mired in poverty, the court divided by petty squabbles, and Siam and Vietnam competing for land, people and tax.

Overall, and for obvious geographical reasons, it was the Siamese who tended to be the more powerful of the two overlords. By the beginning of the 18th century Ayutthaya had intervened in the politics of Laos to divide the former Lan Xang into three petty fiefdoms, centred on Luang Prabang in the

A depiction of rural life at Wat Xieng Thong, Luang Prabang, which was built in 1560.

north, Vientiane in the centre and Champasak in the south. Meanwhile, the inhabitants of Xieng Khuang continued to be effectively dominated by the Vietnamese. By contrast, in the far north, the various *panna* (small states) of Sipsongpanna, territory far removed from even Luang Prabang, paid tribute to China; the question of their partial incorporation into modern Laos would not arise until the advent of French colonialism at the end of the 19th century.

Laos was, however, saved briefly from the growing weight of Siamese power as Ayutthaya itself came under attack from Burma. Unfortunately for Laos, the Siamese made a truly remarkable recovery. Between about 1775 and 1800 King Taksin and then King Rama I established a Siamese hegemony throughout Siam and Laos as well as the greater part of Cambodia. The Burmese had to fall back on their own devices, and the Vietnamese, at least temporar-

> Both animism and Hinduism were present in Laos before the ascendancy of Buddhism in the 16th century, and traces of these earlier beliefs remain clearly apparent in Laos today.

ily, were emasculated. Siamese armies occupied both Vientiane and Champasak in 1779, and a few months later King Surinyavong of Luang Prabang opened the gates of the city to their advancing forces.

Nor was it just historical Laos that fell so completely under Siamese hegemony – the various Lao-speaking *muang* of the northeast, which now make up the Thai region of Isaan, were brought fully under Siamese rule for the first time. Henceforth cities such as Si Saket, Ubon Ratchathani, Surin, Roi Et, Mukdahan, Nong Khai and Udon Thani became definitively Siamese, and not Lao, in their political fealty.

Yet, badly defeated though Laos had been, worse was to come. By the beginning of the 19th century three separate Lao kingdoms continued to exist, albeit much curtailed. Separate Lao kings ruled, always under Siamese suzerainty, at Luang Prabang, Champasak and Vientiane. Of these, the first two had lost much of their territory, particularly on the west bank of the Mekong. Vientiane, by contrast, remained a substantial territory. Its major dependencies included Xieng Khuang, Nakhon Phanom, Udon Thani and Mukdahan, the last three extending over much of the Khorat Plateau in present-day Thailand. Vientiane retained political aspirations, too. The last representative of the once great kingdom of Lan Xang did not intend to go quietly.

Vientiane revolt

The first signs of Vientiane's ambitions occurred in 1792. King Nanthasen reinforced his suzerainty over Xieng Khuang by seizing the Phuan prince and putting him under house arrest in Vientiane. He was only released on promising to pay an annual tribute to Vientiane similar to that already paid to Vietnam. Shortly thereafter Nanthasen's forces surrounded Luang Prabang, eventually taking the town by guile.

Next, in 1796, word reached Bangkok of a plot between Nanthasen and the governor of Nakhon Phanom to throw off Siamese rule. King Rama I, a forceful and active man, moved immediately: Nanthasen and the governor were arrested and escorted to Bangkok.

Bangkok thought – mistakenly – that the Vientiane problem had been nipped in the bud, and appointed two new rulers to govern the troublesome province. Rama's choice fell on two of Nanthasen's younger brothers – Inthavong to reign as first king and Anuvong to reign as *uparat*, or second king, in the Siamese fashion – but he soon found that his decision had been unwise.

Inthavong's reign was uneventful, but following his death in 1804 Anuvong took over: the new king was well known at the Siamese court, and trusted by Rama I and Rama II. For the first 20 years of his reign he seems to have had no serious problems with Bangkok. He began his reign in the expected way, by con-

An early painting of Wat Mai Suwannaphumaham at Luang Prabang.

THE STORY OF KHUNYING MO

A popular story recounts how the population of Khorat was rounded up by Anuvong's men and sent towards Vientiane. Male prisoners were kept in close captivity, but the women were instructed to act as menials, serving the Lao soldiers their meals and generally "attending to their needs at night". One of the captive women, Khunying Mo, encouraged the soldiers in drunken revelry. When the festivities were at their height she slipped away and released the male prisoners, who made short work of their drunken foes. Two thousand of the invaders were reportedly slain. Mo is still revered by the people of Khorat, with a statue erected in her honour.

structing a new palace as well as numerous monasteries, restoring That Luang and generally observing Lao and Buddhist customs. On the other hand – a possible sign of future ambition – Anuvong was quick to recognise Gia Long, the first Nguyen emperor at Hue, by sending tribute.

Things changed in 1825, however, after the death of Rama II. Relations between Anuvong and Rama III seem to have been poor from the start. Anuvong is said to have felt slighted because Rama III treated King Manthathurat of Luang Prabang with more respect than he received himself, and he also resented the Siamese king's widespread use of unpaid Lao labour.

War with Siam

Whatever really happened, Anuvong appears to have returned to Vientiane a changed man, determined to throw off Bangkok's authority and re-establish the glories of the former Lao kingdom. He lost no time erecting new defensive works, and called a general council of senior Lao leaders to plan his revolt. It appears that Anuvong felt that Bangkok's power was in decline and the time was right for action. Alas, from a Lao point of view, he was quite wrong. One ally who might have helped him, Vietnam, was not kept fully informed of his plans; another potential ally, Burma, was preoccupied in a war with Britain. Not even Luang Prabang could be counted on. The Lao states remained disunited to the end.

Anuvong's plan was to send four armies across the Khorat Plateau to seize Khorat (Nakhon Ratchasima), Ubon Ratchathani and Suvannaphum, gather up the entire population and take everyone back to Vientiane, leaving an unpopulated wilderness between Bangkok and himself. Perhaps he believed that undecided *muang* such as Luang Prabang and even Chiang Mai would join his cause.

Inhabitants of the Xieng Tong and Xieng Hong kingdoms, as observed by Louis Delaporte during a 1895 exploration.

TAX BANDS

An inventive method of distributing tax revenues was introduced in Laos during the 18th century: if people lived in stilt houses, ate sticky rice with their fingers and decorated their temples with images of *naga* (like the Siamese), then they were obliged to pay tax to the representatives of Ayutthaya in Siam; if, on the other hand, they lived at ground level, ate long-grain rice with chopsticks and decorated their temples with dragons (like the Vietnamese), they had to pay tax to the representatives of Hue. This was a complex, if logical, recognition of the age-old fault line between the Indic and Sinitic traditions along which Laos lies.

The campaign began in December 1826, but from the beginning it was apparent that the Siamese were both more numerous and better armed. Despite initial successes – Khorat was seized, as well as numerous smaller towns – the offensive became bogged down, and the Siamese began a swift-moving counterattack.

The defeat of Anuvong

Anuvong, meanwhile, had fled back across the Mekong but, realising there would be no security in Vientiane from the Siamese armies, he left with his family to seek asylum in Vietnam. Within five days Vientiane was in Siamese hands. Palaces and other buildings were burnt and Buddha images were carried off, although monasteries were, by and large, left untouched. Some months later Anuvong returned from Vietnam, apparently in the hope of restoring the status quo, but he was betrayed to the Siamese by Chao Noi, the ruler of Xieng Khuang, whom he had held for four years under house arrest in Vientiane. He was then taken to Bangkok, where he was condemned to a lingering death, exposed in an iron cage over the waters of the Chao Phraya River. The palladium of the Vientiane Kingdom, the Emerald Buddha, was also

With the death of Anuvong the dream of a renewed Lan Xang ended, and a new stamp was put on Siamese–Lao relations which has lasted to the present day, although things now seem to be improving. Siam inherited dominance over most of the Tai-speaking world, Laos was relegated to an impoverished and greatly reduced state, and much bitterness was generated. It is not without reason that the present-day government of the Lao PDR refers to the war of 1826–8 as Chao Anuvong's War for Independence, but the official Thai view remains that Anuvong was a rebel troublemaker.

A wat mural depicting water carriers.

King Chao Anouvong statue, Vientiane.

taken to Bangkok, where it remains to this day.

Thereafter Siamese puppet rulers occupied the Lao throne. Many leading Lao families were deported and forcibly resettled in Siamese lands. The southern Lao Kingdom of Champassak was also brought under Siamese control, although some of the smaller Lao statelets in the eastern uplands continued to be tributary to the Vietnamese court at Hue. In 1792 the Siamese occupied Luang Prabang, but the ancient capital was treated more kindly than Vientiane had been. It was not looted, it was permitted to keep its palladium, the Phra Bang, and the king kept his throne after due submission to Siam.

STEALING THE PEOPLE

A significant part of the logistics of and motivation for pre-modern warfare in mainland Southeast Asia rested on the acquisition of people rather than territories. This concept, alien to the Europeans, is based on the effect of warfare on a defeated nation. If Siamese armies penetrated into the traditional territory of Lan Xang – as they often did – they were more likely to withdraw with spoils, including much of the population, than to establish permanent bases. Lao prisoners were, in fact, very much in demand. They were seen as a brother people, obedient, and good farmers. This added to the weakness of Lan Xang, plunging it deeper into despair.

PAUL DARCY

1 Fr. 25
LE VOLUME

no = 2

BÂH-MIANG
LE TIGRE DU LAOS

A. FAYARD & Cie ÉDITEURS PA

COLONIALISM AND INDEPENDENCE

Complex power struggles between foreign nations during the early part of the 20th century eventually led to the formation of the Lao PDR in 1975.

In the half-century following their conquest of Vientiane in 1827–8 the Siamese continued to expand their influence over the Tai and Lao *muang*, from Sipsongpanna in Yunnan to the remote Hua Phan region of Laos, and even to Sipsongchuthai, which today constitutes the westernmost part of northern Vietnam. For their part, the Vietnamese responded by occupying Xieng Khuang, executing Chao Noi for allegedly betraying Chao Anuvong to the Siamese (see page 56), and incorporating the region into Vietnam as the prefecture of Tranh Ninh, under direct Vietnamese rule. As a consequence of the Siamese–Vietnamese struggle for the spoils of the former Lan Xang, the Lao territories east of the Mekong River suffered serious depopulation through forced resettlement in Siam (Thailand). Xieng Khuang eventually emerged as a joint tributary statelet, though for many years Vietnam continued to hold the upper hand.

Colonial-style homes in Luang Prabang.

The French arrive

And there it might have ended, with Laos effectively partitioned between Siam and Vietnam, but for the arrival of the French in Indochina. French adventurers and priests had been targeting Vietnam and the Indochinese hinterlands since the late 17th century. By the mid-1800s, driven to seek new colonies by their continuing rivalry with the more successful British, imperialist advocates in Paris had determined to establish a colony in the region. The process of colonisation began in 1858 when the French seized the Vietnamese port of Da Nang, which was to become their major naval base in Indochina.

By 1862 France occupied most of southern Vietnam; in 1863 protectorate status was imposed on Cambodia, and in 1867 Siam was obliged to accept the new status quo in exchange for the former Cambodian provinces of Battambang and Siem Reap. It was the era of high imperialism and mercantile adventure, and having secured control of the lower Mekong, France now sought a "river route" to China – a route which led through the very heart of Lan Xang.

A solitary French explorer, Henri Mouhot, had penetrated Laos from Siam as far as Luang Prabang, where he died in 1861. In 1863 his young compatriot Francis Garnier proposed the idea of a voyage up the Mekong, and in 1865 official approval came from Paris. The expedition, led by Doudart de Lagrée and accompanied by Garnier, set out from Saigon on 5 June

1866. It returned just over two years later, having navigated its way up the Mekong, marched through Yunnan and sailed down the Yangtze to Shanghai. From a commercial point of view the mission was a total failure – the "river route" to China was completely blocked by the great Khone Falls on the Lao–Cambodian border – but Garnier did bring back to Europe the first detailed information on Laos since the 17th century, which he published in 1873 in an extraordinary two-volume publication, complete with paintings and engravings, entitled *Voyage d'Exploration en Indochine*.

Lao prince on his way to the temple (c.1910).

This remarkable work makes clear the extent of the devastation which 50 years of war had wrought on Laos. Vientiane, in particular, lay mainly in ruins, semi-deserted by its population, with many buildings overgrown by jungle. In the interests of French imperialism, however, Garnier emphasised the desirability of the region, based on potential mineral and agricultural wealth rather than the disproved possibility of riverine trade. The French, almost without knowing it, were taking a Vietnamese perspective on Indochina.

The Haw Wars

However, a further three decades were to pass before the French inherited the Vietnamese "forward imperative" in Laos as well as Cambodia. In the meantime Laos would have to endure a terrible period of invasion and looting known as the Haw Wars.

"Haw" is a generic name given by the Tai-speaking peoples to the Chinese of Yunnan and southern China. In the mid-19th century this region was torn apart by the Taiping and Yunnan Muslim rebellions. As the Chinese Qing Empire slowly struggled to reassert itself, defeated rebels fleeing Qing reprisals crossed the borders into Laos and northern Vietnam in ever increasing numbers. Armed, ruthless, with nothing to lose, they banded together in so-called "Flag Gangs", which looted and killed at will. In Vietnam the "Black Flags" emerged as an anti-French force, and so enjoyed some rather dubious political legitimacy. In Laos, by contrast, the "Red Flags", "Yellow Flags" and "Striped Flags" were bandits pure and simple.

BENIGN NEGLECT

The laissez-faire spirit of the former French administration in Laos has been described by Martin Stuart-Fox: "Apart from constructing 5,000km (3,000 miles) of mediocre roads with *corvée* labour, France did virtually nothing either to encourage economic development or to improve social welfare... Ninety percent of the population remained subsistence farmers; there was no industry and a small tin-mining venture benefited only the French and Vietnamese... Health care failed to decrease child mortality... Primary education was left to the Buddhist pagoda schools... Secondary education in French was confined to a tiny minority... French policy in Laos was limited to administering the colony at minimal

cost." No doubt a major part of this easy occupation lay in the fact that the Lao rather welcomed the French, not as liberators, but because they provided an invaluable counterbalance to the external threat of both the Vietnamese and the Siamese. Largely as a result of this there was virtually no opposition to French rule until after the Battle of Dien Bien Phu (in Vietnam) in 1954.

Back in France Laos became famous as a land of lotus-eaters, the easiest and reputedly the most dissolute posting east of Suez. However, at no time did Laos account for more than 1 percent of the exports of French Indochina, and by far the most important part of this was opium, which France made a state monopoly.

With years of fighting experience behind them, they swept aside local Lao and Vietnamese forces, easily reaching as far south as Tha Khaek. Luang Prabang was threatened, Vietnamese forces were driven from Xieng Khuang, and most seriously, from a Siamese perspective, Vientiane was taken. Everywhere Buddhist temples were sacked.

For Bangkok this situation was intolerable, but defeating the Haw was not going to prove easy. In 1886, angered by the continuing failure of his forces to dislodge their foes, and alarmed by French advances in Indochina, King Chulalongkorn ordered a third, more ambitious expedition to the region. On this occasion the objective was not merely to defeat the Haw but also to annex to Siam all regions formerly subject to Luang Prabang, together with as much of Sipsongchuthai as possible.

This time the Siamese army, together with troops levied from the Lao, at last succeeded in dispersing the Haw. Chulalongkorn's first territorial objective, Xieng Khuang, was seized, and its rulers were escorted to Bangkok to prevent their appealing to Hue – or, even worse, France – for assistance. Next the Siamese turned their attention to Sipsongchuthai, threatened from the east by a major French expeditionary force which had invaded Tonkin in 1883. Muang Thaeng (better known today by its Vietnamese name, Dien Bien Phu) was taken, and three princes of the Sipsongchuthai ruling family were seized and sent to Luang Prabang as hostages in a bid to ensure the submission of their brother, the White Tai chieftain Kham Hum.

This was the high point of Siam's control in the region. Had Chulalongkorn's bold move succeeded, not only Laos but also a sizeable portion of northern Vietnam might have been incorporated within Siam. Kham Hum, however, chose not to submit and, allied with Haw bands, advanced on Luang Prabang, which had been left largely undefended. On 7 June 1887 the Lao royal capital was seized and sacked; the elderly ruler, King Unkham, barely escaped with his life. As luck would have it, he was accompanied by the French vice-consul, Auguste Pavie, from whom he requested formal protection. Six years later, in 1893, this appeal would be used as legal justification for the French annexation of Laos, resulting in Siam's permanent loss of control over the region.

Land of the lotus-eaters

Through a succession of treaties essentially forced on Bangkok by Paris using military strength, or the threat of it, between 1893 and 1907, Siam gradually relinquished control of all territories east of the Mekong, the islands in

> *Vientiane's symbol of nationhood, the gilded spire of That Luang, was thrown to the ground in a frenzied search for gold by the Haw invaders.*

French and local authorities in Luang Prabang.

the great river, and the territories of Sainyabuli and part of Champasak on the west bank. The French Indochinese administration united all former Lao principalities within a single colonial territory which they called "Laos". The word was, in fact, a misnomer which has stuck, since in the Lao language both country and people were, and remain, simply "Lao".

In 1900 France chose Vientiane as the administrative capital of this newly created entity, and began the establishment of a simple colonial administration. By 1904 a mere 75 French officials were administering the whole of Laos, and by 1940 no more than 600 French citizens were resident there. Most administrative officials under the new regime were Vietnamese.

In fact, the brief French presence in Laos may be seen as a fleeting interruption of the social and political relationship between the Lao and the Vietnamese, with France representing traditional Vietnamese interests. Initially there were plans for a railway from Da Nang to Tha Khaek, and for extensive Vietnamese migration to farm the underpopulated lands of the eastern Mekong Valley. Had these come to fruition, Laos might eventually have become entirely absorbed within Vietnam. But the railway was not built, and the many Vietnamese who settled in Laos chose to do so not as farmers but as city-dwellers: members of the civil service, jewellers, tailors, hairdressers, restaurateurs and so on. By 1945, as a result of this immigration, Viet Kieu (migrant Vietnamese) communities dominated all the major Lao towns except Luang Prabang, accounting for more than 50 percent of the inhabitants of the capital, Vientiane, and as much as 85 percent of the second city, Tha Kaek.

The lowland Lao mostly accepted the status quo, though they chafed under the pressure of rising Viet immigration, French taxation and French-imposed *corvée* (unpaid labour). What

French troops on patrol in Laos.

THE RED PRINCE

Souphanouvong, a member of the royal house of Luang Prabang, revolutionary nationalist and founding member of the Lao Communist movement, was born in 1912, one of 23 children sired by the Luang Prabang viceroy, or second king, Boun Khong. Due to his privileged birth, Souphanouvong automatically acquired the status of a royal prince. He and his three elder half-brothers would go on to play important roles in the government of post-1953 independent Laos.

As a young man, Souphanouvong studied in Hanoi and France, later marrying a Vietnamese and becoming involved in the anti-colonial movement. Under the guidance of Ho Chi Minh, he set up the Pathet Lao (Lao People's Liberation Army) in 1951. With his half-brothers serving in the French-supported Royal Lao government in the years 1953–75, Souphanouvong took to the jungle in pursuit of the revolutionary goals which earned him the sobriquet "the Red Prince".

He did not return to Vientiane until 1974, by which time the Communist victory in Indochina was assured. The people of Laos met his return with great enthusiasm, and after the establishment of the Lao PDR in 1975 he was appointed president, a post he held until the Fourth Party Congress in 1986, when he retired because of ill health. Until his death in 1995, Souphanouvong remained popular with ordinary Lao people.

nationalist opposition there was to French rule came mainly from the highlanders and the Vietnamese of the cities, although the concern of the latter was almost exclusively for their homeland, of which they saw both Laos and Cambodia as future appendages. Only a few lowlanders paid any attention to the rise of Vietnamese nationalism, and these were almost exclusively children of the Lao elite studying in Hanoi or Saigon. Communist ideals, similarly, took no root in Laos, Marxists being limited to Viet Kieu followers of Ho Chi Minh who were constantly harassed by French security police. The Indo-

on the west bank of the Mekong. Though the struggle was indecisive on land (the Thais suffered defeat at sea), Japan intervened and imposed an armistice. As a result of this agreement France ceded all Lao west-bank territories to Thailand. The French, though humiliated, were to retain nominal power in Indochina for a further four years, but on 9 March 1945 the Japanese, sensing defeat by the Allied forces, staged a coup against the Vichy administration and forced the pro-French Lao monarch, King Sisavang Vong, to declare independence. Despite this confidence, within months Japan had sur-

Left to right, Pathet Lao's Prince Souphanouvong; Prime Minister Souvanna Phouma and right-wing General Phoumi Nasavan.

chinese Communist Party was formed, under Vietnamese auspices, but only one ethnic Lao is known to have joined before World War II.

Japan intervenes

The period of "lotus-eating" came to an abrupt end in 1940 with the German defeat of the French in World War II, the establishment of the collaborationist Vichy regime in France, and increasing Japanese interference in Indochina, where the colonial administration supported Vichy.

In 1941, under the military ruler Phibun Songkhram, Thai forces fought a series of battles with French Indochinese troops for control of the Lao territories of Champasak and Sainyabuli

rendered, and the first French paratroopers had landed in southern Laos.

Free Lao movement

The French were opposed by Prince Phetsarath, the wartime prime minister, and by the small Lao Issara ("Free Lao") underground movement which had grown up in protest against both French and Japanese rule. For six months, from October 1945 to April 1946, a Lao Issara government, backed by the Viet Minh government of Ho Chi Minh, attempted to set up a functioning administration. A small defence force was set up under Phetsarath's half-brother, Prince Souphanouvong (who later became famous as "the Red Prince" – see panel), and negotiations were entered into with the French, but to no avail. In March 1946 French forces moved north. Lao Issara forces, supported by resident Viet Kieu, attempted to make a stand at Tha Khaek but were roundly defeated.

Although Laos was back in French hands by the end of May, within months the restored colonial authority indicated a willingness to concede autonomy. This offer caused the Lao Issara to become hopelessly split. One faction, led by Prince Phetsarath, set up a government in exile in Bangkok; a second faction, led by Prince Souphanouvong, favoured an alliance with Ho Chi Minh and the Vietnamese Communists; while a third faction, led by Prince Souvanna Phouma, another half-brother, favoured a deal with the French. As a consequence, France proceeded without Lao Issara cooperation, and in 1949 recognised Laos as an "Independent Associate State" of the French Union. This unilateral move caused the break-up of the Lao Issara movement, but in 1951 Prince Souphanouvong announced the formation of the Neo Lao Issara, or "Free Lao Front" – a pro-Communist organisation later known as the Pathet Lao, or "Land of the Lao".

At the time of the 1957 coalition the Communists controlled a mere two of the country's 13 provinces; by 1973 this equation had been almost precisely reversed.

Map of Communist-controlled Laos.

MOUNTAIN WARRIORS

The Hmong have long been celebrated – and feared – warriors in Laos. As the main ally of the USA in the CIA's "Secret War", many refused to surrender when the Communists seized power in 1975 and took to the remote mountain tops, where they harassed the Communist authorities in a low-key but long-running insurgency, supported financially and politically by Hmong refugees who had resettled in the United States. In 2004, two Swiss tourists were killed when they ran into an exchange of hostilities, but after a large group of insurgents surrendered in 2006, the Hmong military struggle seems all but to have ended, and the roads safe for travel.

Independence and Communism

Souphanouvong was given the full backing of the Viet Minh authorities in Hanoi. The consequence would be some 25 years of armed struggle, during which Laos would become inextricably bound up with the war in Vietnam, culminating in the establishment of the Lao People's Democratic Republic (Lao PDR) in 1975. For the moment, however, the Pathet Lao remained a tiny force, with their Viet Minh allies doing most of the fighting against France on Lao soil.

France, being fully caught up in its punishing war of attrition with the Viet Minh, continued largely to ignore Laos. As a consequence, in 1953, with the decisive battle of Dien Bien Phu looming, Laos was granted full sovereignty and independence as a constitutional monarchy known as the Kingdom of Laos.

Following the French withdrawal from Indochina in 1954 the United States, anxious to counter rising Communist influence in Laos, began to fill the coffers of the Royal Lao government in Vientiane. During the same period the Pathet Lao established secure bases in the northeastern provinces of Hua Phan and Phongsali, within easy supply distance of Hanoi. There followed years of complex political and military manoeuvring, with a royalist-Pathet Lao coalition in 1957–60, followed by a series of neutralist and royalist coups and counter-coups until 1964.

The most violent episode was the so-called battle of Vientiane, which took place in December 1960 between neutralist and "rightist" forces. The "leftist" Pathet Lao delegation swiftly left town to avoid becoming caught up in the fighting, and Pathet Lao forces stationed at Na Khang, some 60km (37 miles) to the north, did not intervene. A massive display of firepower by the rightist forces resulted in the deaths of 400 to 500 civilians in the town, mostly Vietnamese residents, and the wounding of another 1,000 to 1,500 civilians. The neutralist troops only lost 17 killed. Rightist armour rolled into town and the victorious commander, Phoumi, installed a royalist, Prince Boun Oum, as premier in the new administration. The Boun Oum administration survived until 1962, and was then replaced by the royalist government of Prince Souvanna Phouma. After the Communist seizure of power in 1975, Phoumi Nosavan fled to Bangkok, where he died in 1985. Boun Oum died in France in 1980. From the time of the battle in 1960, the Pathet Lao refused to participate in any negotiations, believing correctly that it would eventually seize power through military means.

Between 1964 and 1973 the Pathet Lao areas of Laos suffered massive bombing by the United States (see page 67) but nevertheless continued inexorably to expand. In 1973, when the US eventually negotiated its way out of direct military involvement in Vietnam, a ceasefire was negotiated in Laos. This time the Pathet Lao was clearly the dominant party. In 1975 first Phnom Penh, then Saigon, fell to the Communists. The writing was on the wall in Vientiane, and a mass exodus of royalist ministers and generals across the Mekong to Thailand began. The subsequent takeover was bloodless, with the Lao PDR formally established on 2 December 1975.

For the next five years Communist policy was extremely harsh, particularly by the usually relaxed standards of the Lao people. Buddhism was curtailed, links with Thailand were practically cut, and a vicious campaign was mounted against the Hmong minority, many of whom had refused to accept the Lao PDR or to lay down their arms. Tens of thousands of people were arrested and sent for "re-education" to camps known as *samana* in the remote northeast. These arrests covered all levels of society, from the prostitutes and pickpockets

of Vientiane through small businessmen and landholders to members of the former ruling elite. In 1977 King Savang Vatthana, who had abdicated, joined this group, together with his

> Unexploded Ordnance (UXO) remains a major problem in Laos and, despite the best efforts of international de-mining groups, will continue to do so. Most populated areas are safe, but in the uplands along the Vietnamese border, much UXO still remains lethally concealed.

King Savang Vatthana reigned for 17 years from 1959–76 before being ousted by the Pathet Lao.

family; they reportedly died of malnutrition in a remote part of Hua Phan.

New Thinking

By 1979 these policies had aroused fierce resentment among the Lao peasantry, the traditional power base of the Pathet Lao. It was also becoming painfully apparent that Communist economic policies were failing to deliver positive results as Laos slumped far behind its rich Thai neighbour. This resulted in perhaps as many as 400,000 people (about 12 percent of the population) taking the relatively easy option of crossing the Mekong to Thailand, where many simply blended in with their fellow ethnic Lao.

Laos was losing many of its brightest and best-qualified citizens.

As a result, younger, less hardline party members, together with non-party members, increased pressure on the old, pro-Vietnamese leadership of the Lao PDR – particularly since Communist economic policies in Vietnam were manifestly failing too. Eventually, in 1989, this led to the introduction of *jintanakan mai*, or "New Thinking", an economic and political liberalisation which in some ways closely paralleled the process of *perestroika* in the former Soviet Union, and went beyond the supposedly

Hmongs in Laos.

parallel process of *doi moi* in Vietnam. During the 1990s this process continued, particularly after the death of the Lao PDR president and the Communist hardliner Kaysone Phomvihane in 1992. Restrictions on individual liberties were slowly lifted, Lao émigrés (especially businessmen) were encouraged to return home, and the country was gradually opened to tourism. Relations with Thailand improved dramatically, symbolised by the opening of the "Friendship Bridge" in 1994 and the official visit of then-President Nouhak Phoumsavanh to Thailand in 1995. As a direct result of these reforms, the Lao PDR joined ASEAN in 1997.

Unfortunately, in the same year, the Asian economic crisis brought about the collapse of the Thai baht, dragging down the value of the Lao kip. The government reintroduced currency controls in an effort to control the situation, but it would be four years before the kip stabilised again.

This state of relative stability was still occasionally disturbed. In 2000, for example, a series of minor bombings took place in Vientiane, Savannakhet and Pakse involving hand grenades and small handmade explosives. The bombings were suspected to be the work of a group called the Underground Government in Exile. There was an additional bombing incident in October 2003. Today, however, the process of reform is so far advanced that it would be impossible to turn back the clock, and the Lao people continue to enjoy peace and an improving standard of living.

In March 2006, Choummaly Sayasone took over from Siphandone as leader of the ruling Communist Party. He also officially replaced Siphandone as president in June that year. In December 2006, a group of 400 ethnic Hmong insurgents who had been waging a low-level insurgency against the Lao authorities since 1975 surrendered. Subsequently, in June 2007, US prosecutors charged nine US residents – including the former royalist Hmong general Vang Pao – with planning a coup against the Lao authorities. These events, taken with the country's application to become a full member of the World Trade Organization (WTO) in January 2008, seem indicative of improving ethnic relations within Laos and the adoption of a generally less authoritarian attitude by the Lao authorities. Links with outside nations other than Vietnam continued to improve, too, with the construction of a fully sealed road between Xhiang Khong in Thailand and Boten on the Chinese frontier, as well as the opening of a rail link across the Friendship Bridge between Thailand and Laos in 2009. In January 2011, former general Vang Pao died in California, bringing a symbolic closure to the CIA "Secret War". In June of the same year, Choummaly Sayasone was confirmed in office as President of the Lao PDR for a further five-year term, strengthening the reform process under way in the country.

In January 2016, Bounnhang Vorachith was elected General Secretary of the Lao People's Revolutionary Party and in April of the same year, he succeeded Choummaly Sayasone as President of Laos. Thongloun Sisoulith was also elected prime minister in April 2016.

The Secret War

Caught up in the global struggle between Communism and the USA, strategically located Laos was the setting for a covert war in the 1970s.

For more than 10 years, between 1963 and 1973, Laos was the hidden arena for a "Secret War" that most of the world knew little or nothing about. Under the Geneva Accord of 1962 Laos was officially recognised as a neutral state in which no foreign military personnel might be stationed, but in practice this was ignored by all sides. The greatest violator of Lao neutrality was North Vietnam. The Communists had used northeastern Laos as a springboard for attacks on the French during the First Indochina War and never subsequently withdrew. By 1970 an entire North Vietnamese division – the 316th – was deployed in Laos, fielding a total of more than 75,000 troops. Other areas of eastern Laos, too, were crisscrossed with a network of hidden tracks comprising the notorious "Ho Chi Minh Trail" (see page 165) for resupplying Communist units in Cambodia and South Vietnam.

Communist China, too, maintained an area of special interest in the far northwest of Laos at this time, arming and supplying leftist opponents of the Royal Lao government in Vientiane, not least to offset the predominance of Vietnamese influence over their Pathet Lao allies. This policy reached its zenith during the 1960s and early 1970s, when the People's Liberation Army built a network of roads throughout Phongsali and Luang Nam Tha, reaching as far south as Pakbeng in Udomxai province. This road-building programme owed its origins to an agreement reached between Chou En-lai and the Lao premier, Prince Souvanna Phouma, at Beijing in January 1962. By the mid-1960s, however, Vientiane could only watch helplessly as the Chinese, without consultation, built roads throughout the far northwest. At the height of the programme as many as 10,000 labourers toiled under the protection of Chinese armed sentries and anti-aircraft units.

Meanwhile the USA was equally active. Although it was legally prohibited from intervening in support of the royalist forces, US "technicians" appeared in Laos as early as 1959, when they began training the Royal Lao army and building up a Hmong hill-tribe army under the leadership of Vang Pao. By 1962 this US-equipped secret army had reached a strength of around 10,000, centred on Vang Pao's

headquarters at Long Tien in the Plain of Jars. So secret was this US involvement that the name Laos was never used in official communications – the country was known simply as "The Other Theatre", and Long Tien as "Alternate".

Civil war

Meanwhile, as Laos was torn apart by civil war, involving Vietnamese, Chinese and US-backed forces, the USA resorted increasingly to air power in an attempt to defeat the leftist forces. By 1973 nearly 600,000 sorties had been flown over the country, dropping an average of one planeload of

Sitting on a bomb dropped by a US B-52.

bombs every eight minutes, 24 hours a day, for nine years. In the end, almost 2 million tonnes of bombs had been dropped on Laos – about half a tonne of explosives for every person in the country. And every year, around 300 people are killed or maimed by the lethally hidden remaining bombs.

And yet it was to no avail. The Hmong secret army and Royal Lao forces were consistently out-manoeuvred by the North Vietnamese and their Pathet Lao surrogates. The single most expensive covert paramilitary operation ever conducted by the USA ended in failure with the Communist takeover of Vientiane in December 1975. And yet, despite the bombing, bloodshed and years of brutality on both sides, the US Embassy was shut for a total of just one day.

*Monks at Wat Nam Kaew Luang,
Luang Nam Tha.*

Hmong mother and baby.

POPULATION, SOCIETY AND ECONOMY

The population of Laos is a broad ethnic mix, the product of an uneasy history, but past hostilities are giving way to mutual cooperation.

With around 6.9 million inhabitants, Laos has one of the lowest population densities in Asia – just over 22 people per sq km (9 per sq mile). Outside a handful of relatively large towns in the Mekong Valley, most Lao – around 85 percent – live in rural areas and lead agricultural lives.

In fact, only around 50 percent of the country's population is ethnically Lao, the rest being divided between numerous tribal groups, although the methods of classification for these are varied and frequently contradictory.

The Lao government divides the population into three main ethnic categories, ostensibly according to the altitude at which they live: Lao Soung (higher mountain), Lao Theung (lower mountain) and Lao Loum (lowland). Some 50–60 percent of the population are Lao Loum, 20–30 percent are Lao Theung and 10–20 percent are Lao Soung. This is, however, a somewhat arbitrary categorisation, as there are at least 49 different ethnic groups in Laos, each with its own linguistic, religious and culinary traditions.

A resident of Phongsali.

Lao Loum

In general, the Lao Loum live in the Mekong River Valley, subsist on wet-rice cultivation and practise Theravada Buddhism. These are the people of the Mekong Valley lowlands who predominate in the provinces of Luang Prabang, Vientiane, Tha Kaek, Savannakhet and Pakse, and who have traditionally controlled Lao government and society. The Lao Loum are closely related to the Lao-speaking inhabitants of neighbouring northeastern Thailand and, slightly more distantly, to the central Thai or Siamese. The distinction between Lao and Thai is rather indistinct and something of a new (and politically motivated) phenomenon. Certainly the two groups are part of the same family, something both sides will happily accept – yet the Lao can be irritated by the rather arrogant and frequently stated Thai contention that the Lao are their "little brothers".

Lao Theung and Lao Soung

Next there are the Lao Theung, or "approaching the top of the mountain Lao", a loose affiliation of mostly Mon-Khmer-speaking people who live at moderate altitudes and are generally animists rather than Buddhists. Formerly known to the ruling Lao Loum by the pejorative term *kha*, or slave, this group constitutes a further

15–20 percent of the population, and makes up by far the most economically disadvantaged section of Lao society.

Finally, on the distant mountain tops live – as might be expected – the Lao Soung, or

> *It's common in Laos for shows to be put on of Lao Loum, Lao Theung and Lao Soung women dancing together in harmony in their diverse ethnic clothing. In reality, all the dancers are usually Lao Loum lowlanders.*

"High Lao", people whose communities are at altitudes of more than 1,000 metres (3,200ft) above sea level. Representatives of this group are also to be found in northern Thailand, northwestern Vietnam and southern China, and include Hmong and Mien, together with smaller numbers of Akha, Lisu and Lahu. The Lao Soung have traditionally relied on the cultivation of dry rice and opium. An estimated 20 percent of these upland dwellers comprise Tai-speaking minority groups such as the Tai Dam (Black Tai), Tai Daeng (Red Tai) and Tai Khao (White Tai), all ethnic

Laos has a small Muslim community.

Out and about in Vientiane.

THE MUSLIMS OF LAOS

Chinese Muslims from China's southwestern province of Yunnan once carried on much of the traditional trade in the mountains of Laos. Known to the Lao and Thais as Chin Haw, these pioneering caravaneers drove their mule trains south to Luang Prabang and beyond. In the 19th-century Haw Wars (see page 60) outlaw bands of Haw sacked Vientiane, where they tore the spire off That Luang in search of buried gold. Some Haw Muslims still live in the mountains, where they act as middlemen in the trade between lowlanders and hill people.

There is also a small South Asian Muslim community in Vientiane, centred on the Jamia Masjid behind the central Nam Phu fountain. Signs inside the mosque are written in five languages – Tamil, Urdu, Arabic, Lao and English. This unexpected Tamil influence derives from Pondicherry, France's former Tamil toehold on the southeastern coast of India, which sent many Chulia or Tamil Muslim businessmen to Indochina during the period of French rule. Most of Vientiane's South Asian Muslims are businessmen, involved in the manufacturing of textiles, in various branches of import-export, or in serving their community as butchers and restaurateurs.

There is also a minuscule Cham Muslim community in Vientiane, with its own mosque. Refugees fleeing Pol Pot's Cambodia arrived in the 1970s, to be joined over the years by small numbers of relatives.

Tai sub-groups. All these groups are closely related to the Lao Loum.

Laos is also home to sizeable and very significant ethnic Vietnamese (Viet Kieu) and ethnic Chinese (Hua Jiao) communities. In the past decade Hua Jiao have increased markedly, as overland Chinese from Yunnan and Guangdong have migrated to Vientiane and other cities, where they are overwhelmingly engaged in business. Viets also make up an influential portion of the traders and small business owners in Laos – not to mention the continuing Vietnamese military presence in some prov-

Relations between Lao and Viet have not always run smoothly. In terms of their traditions the two peoples live on opposite sides of the great cultural fault line that divides mainland Southeast Asia into Indic and Sinitic zones. In geographical terms, too, they are largely divided by the mountainous Annamite Cordillera, which separates the two countries along the ridges of a shared 1,950km (1,220-mile) border. A number of folk aphorisms exist which supposedly sum up the ethnocentric views which the two peoples have of each other. "Lao and Viet, Cat and Dog" is an old

A time for prayer and reflection at Wat Phu, Champasak.

The European expat community in Laos remains small (less than 3,000), and is mostly made up of employees of international aid organisations in Vientiane, as well as hoteliers and restaurateurs, especially from France.

inces. Both groups are largely urban-based, the Chinese more in the north of the country and in Vientiane, the ethnic Viets in the Mekong Valley towns like Tha Khaek and Savannakhet. The Vietnamese, in particular, settled in Laos during colonial times, and were employed by the French authorities as teachers and civil servants and at lower levels of administration.

Lao proverb which indicates the difficulties of mutual co-existence, while another old saying claims: "The Viets plant the rice, the Khmers watch them planting, but the Lao listen to the rice grow."

Today a small but flourishing Viet Kieu element survives in Vientiane, although it is rapidly being outnumbered by incoming Thai entrepreneurs and Chinese business people. In the last decade, the sheer numbers of the incoming Chinese, coupled with their relative wealth and political influence, have made the local population suspicious of, and even hostile to, further Chinese immigration.

The hostility of the Lao to the Vietnamese on an ethnic basis has perhaps dulled over the years, yet the failure of Vietnam's socialist economic system has inevitably affected Lao thinking; Thailand, whose economy for decades far outperformed that of Vietnam, is now generally regarded as a better model for economic (but not social) development for the Lao PDR, even though Vietnam is now catching up fast.

Thai migration

One other important immigrant community is the Thai – though it's difficult to know quite where new Thai migration begins and old Lao re-immigration ends. This is because of the almost identical linguistic and ethnic character of the lowland Lao and the people of northeastern Thailand (also known as Isaan), who also quite happily call themselves "Lao". They are, in fact, one and the same people. Thai immigrants from Bangkok are easier to identify, as they speak Central Thai rather than Lao. They, too, are appearing in increasing numbers, especially in the main towns of Laos, where their longer acquaintance with capitalism, business savvy and access to financial capital combines to give them a distinct business advantage. As with the ethnic Chinese, this

Ethnic Vietnamese (Viet Kieu).

TOURISM'S INFLUENCE ON LAOS

Tourism is, inevitably, having an increasing impact on Lao society – and not all of it good. The Lao leadership looks askance at some aspects of the impact of tourism on Thailand, especially concerning issues of morality. Vientiane wants the revenue that international tourism brings, but not the debauchery. Vang Vieng, once a sleepy village, slowly built up a reputation as a hedonistic haven, drawing increasing levels of negative attention. This culminated in a series of tragic deaths in 2011 and 2012, which forced the Lao authorities to crack down on the sale of drugs and alcohol. Thankfully, Vang Vieng is now well on the road to recovery (see page 123).

leads to a degree of suspicion and even envy on the part of the Lao – but the fact remains that Lao and Thai are ethnic and cultural kin, speaking almost identical languages, and both devout Theravada Buddhists. This means that hostility levels to the Thai incomers is substantially less than towards the Han Chinese. The former may be seen as "city slickers" and "wide boys", but the latter are considered to pose a more significant threat to the Lao identity in the long term.

The economy

Laos remains one of the world's poorer countries, its economy heavily propped up by extensive foreign aid, which currently accounts for

25–30 percent of the annual budget, down from around 50 percent in the late 1990s. Important exports include wood, wood products and electricity. Laos is rich in minerals; tin and gypsum are the most important, but copper, gold, iron and zinc are also present. As yet these natural resources remain largely untapped, although several companies are engaged in oil exploration. Secondary manufacturing industry is slowly developing, with some clothing now being exported, but investment is needed in education to increase the skills of the workforce before more sophisticated manufacturing concerns move in. Some basic products are already produced in local factories, helping to keep imports low.

When the current government took control in 1975 it implemented a brief, disastrous programme of nationalisation and collectivisation of agriculture. In 1979 it abruptly reversed course and embarked on a process of reform in agriculture, monetary policy and commodity pricing that still continues today. The economies of urban centres like Vientiane have been transformed since the mid-1980s, when restrictions on private enterprise and ownership of private property began to be lifted, and the economy is now "socialist" in name only.

Laos now has a liberal foreign investment which allows 100 percent foreign ownership for government-approved projects. Thailand, the USA and Australia now top the list of foreign investors.

However, Laos remains one of the poorest nations in Asia. Eighty-five percent of the population work in agriculture, fishing and forestry, and 10 percent in the armed forces or the civil service. Industry is almost non-existent, and the economy is overwhelmingly dependent on foreign aid from bodies like the UN and the World Bank. Annual per capita income hovers just over US$1,000. The Asian economic crisis of the late 1990s, particularly the currency woes in Thailand, sent the kip on a free-fall. Civil service salaries did not keep pace with the resulting inflation, and were rendered almost worthless. Today the authorities in Vientiane are watching the current world recession anxiously, fearful of another Asian financial meltdown.

The currency, while not convertible outside the country, has been allowed to float according to market forces, largely eliminating a once-thriving black market in the kip. In a sign of continuing economic and fiscal weakness, however, the US dollar and also the Thai baht are generally preferred to the local currency.

Still deeply suspicious of outside influences, authorities restrict marriages between Lao nationals and overseas visitors. Foreigners require special permission, and a reference from their embassy, before they can wed a Lao citizen.

Relations between Laos and Vietnam have not always been harmonious.

The best hope for future economic growth seems to lie in the many hydroelectric projects under discussion or development – despite the environmental concerns surrounding them, as well as the forestry and mining potential. Thai, American, French and Australian as well as Lao companies have poured money into these developments, secure in the knowledge that the regional market for electricity, particularly in Thailand and Vietnam, will continue to grow rapidly. A possible by-product of hydroelectric projects is the fish which can be farmed in the new lakes, for which there is a ready market both in Laos and in neighbouring countries.

Several international companies, Non-Governmental Organisations and local government offices have been upgrading the road network throughout the country in order to provide a more workable infrastructure for economic development and tourism. New highways and bridges linking Laos to its neighbours and putting it at an economic crossroads have been – or are being – built. With improved communications, investors are looking to develop southern towns, especially those on the Thai border and the cross-country routes to Vietnam. China, too, is very active in the transport development

stakes, and a new bridge across the Mekong between Huay Xay in Laos and Chiang Khong in Thailand, jointly financed by China and Thailand, was opened in December 2013. This project linked China with Thailand by road across northern Laos; a future rail link is also planned.

Education

Public education in Laos involves five years of primary school, three of middle school and three of high school. The National University in Vientiane provides what is really the only opportunity for higher education inside the

Body-building contest in Vientiane.

THE GOVERNMENT

The Lao People's Democratic Republic (Lao PDR) was formed on 2 December 1975, when the Communist Lao People's Revolutionary Party (LPRP) took over from the Royal Lao government. Today, the LPRP remains the primary ruling institution in Lao; power within the LPRP lies in the 11-member Politburo, the 59-member Central Committee and the Permanent Secretariat. The Secretary General of all three bodies was President Khamtay Siphandone until 2006, when Choummaly Sayasone took over as the head of the LPRP and succeeded Siphandone as president. In 2016, Bounnhang Vorachith succeeded Sayasone as the head of the LPRP and the President of Laos.

State administration is made up of the Council of Ministers, which includes the 15 ministries, the Office of the Prime Minister and the National Planning Committee. Since April 2016, the Council of Minsters has been headed by Thongloun Sisoulith, who is the Prime Minister of Laos. The National Assembly is the nation's sole legislative body. Representatives, almost all of whom are party members, are elected by the public and meet once a year to rubber-stamp Central Committee decisions and prime ministerial declarations.

Laos is divided into 17 different provinces and one municipality, Vientiane. Each province is further divided into district, subdistrict and village levels.

country. Most rural Lao complete less than three years of formal education. Public-school teachers are notoriously under-educated and underpaid, and educational facilities throughout the country are still extremely poor. The

Laos is still considered a francophone nation by the French – but not by anyone else. As in neighbouring Vietnam and Cambodia, English is popular as a second language, taught in schools as the international tongue.

elementary schools were opened in Vientiane and Luang Prabang. Children of the Lao upper classes would study at French *lycées* in the country's urban centres, while royalty were sent off to study in France. Today, however, French-speaking Lao are few in number and increasingly elderly.

After the revolution in 1975 there was a marked decline in the quality of public education. While the number of schools expanded rapidly, the limited facilities served as little more than centres for political indoctrination. Lack of funding for buildings and

Many Lao schoolchildren – here in a classroom in Champasak – must attend school on a shift basis.

government has upgraded existing schools, built new ones and expanded adult education, but it still cannot afford to pay teachers or to provide textbooks. School buildings are inadequate both in facilities and numbers, and most Lao children (as in neighbouring Vietnam) are obliged to attend school on a shift basis – one group in the morning, another in the afternoon.

Almost all Lao men spend at least a part of their youth studying at the local wat, or Buddhist temple; for Lao boys in rural areas, the wat might offer the only chance to obtain an education and to work their way up in society.

Public education was introduced into Laos under the French in 1902, when the first public

books, and a serious lack of qualified teachers (most of the educated population fled after 1975), plague the system to this day. The country still loses around 35 percent of its educated youth to migration.

During the Cold War, Laos's best students completed their education abroad, usually in Eastern Bloc countries. Most of these Lao later struggled to replace whatever largely irrelevant language they learnt overseas with English. Today, however, very little English is spoken except in tourist areas and aspiring Lao students want to learn English and Chinese. The second language will remain Thai, however, especially in urban areas – an indication of the power and influence of Thai TV and radio.

Neighbourly Relations?

Throughout its history, Laos has been hugely influenced by its three powerful neighbours – Vietnam, China and Thailand.

Traditional antagonisms between Lao and Viet are rooted in their disparate cultural godfathers, India and China, and the widely divergent Brahmin and Mandarin world-views – but they

Pathet Lao forces take power, 1975.

have also been sharpened by practical realities. To begin with, and most importantly, there are a great many more Vietnamese than there are Lao, making the former of necessity an expansionist people. Fortunately for the Lao, their homeland is protected by the jagged mountains of the Annamite Cordillera, so they have escaped the full weight of Vietnamese expansion.

Instead, the territorial imperative of the Viets has been channelled south, to the former Kingdom of Champa, the Mekong Delta and Cambodia. For this reason anti-Vietnamese feeling is much stronger in Cambodia than in Laos. Still, an inherent suspicion of their serious, hard-working and disturbingly numerous Viet neighbours runs deep in the psyche of most Lao.

During the half-century which elapsed between France's acquisition of Laos in 1893 and the subjugation of Indochina by the Japanese, the French actively encouraged the migration of Vietnamese to Laos. These immigrants, who totalled more than 50,000 people by the outbreak of World War II, included technicians, artisans, lower-ranking officials, schoolteachers, doctors, dentists and other professionals. By 1939 the public services of Laos were all largely staffed by Vietnamese, and the urban population, too, was predominantly Viet Kieu (migrant Vietnamese settlers).

When Laos eventually achieved independence from France in 1953, the traditional ethnic balance of the country had changed almost beyond recognition. Viet Kieu made up 7 percent of the total population, and ethnic Chinese (primarily from Fujian and Guangdong) a further 2–3 percent. In urban terms the contrast was startling: between them the two non-indigenous peoples dominated urban Laos, constituting 57 percent of the population of Vientiane, 89 percent of that of Tha Kaek and 85 percent of that of Pakse.

During the Indochina Wars which followed France's withdrawal, much of the hostility of the Royal Lao government and the general urban populace towards the Vietnamese stemmed from this colonial experience. By contrast the Chinese, who were involved almost exclusively in trade and had eschewed government service under the French, were generally accepted by the Lao.

Political links with Vietnam

Meanwhile, in the mountain fastnesses of Sam Neua and Phongsali in the far north, opponents of the Royal Lao regime – dissident Lao, who enjoyed strong links with Vietnam – set up the Lao Issara, or Free Lao, which subsequently became known as the Pathet Lao. Given the special links between the Pathet Lao leadership and the Viet Minh, strengthened by 30 years of mutually supportive armed struggle, it was widely expected that, following the Pathet Lao victory and the establishment of the Lao PDR in 1975, Vietnamese migration to Laos would resume in a big way. This did not prove to be the case, however. During this time the special relationship between the governments of Laos and Vietnam was described by the Lao as "closer than the lips and the teeth" and by the Viets as "deeper than the Mekong River".

After 1975 the relationship between the Lao PDR and the Socialist Republic of Vietnam was marked more by continuing military cooperation, and the presence in Laos of Vietnamese advisers and specialists at all levels, than by the return of Viet Kieu settlers. For example, at the height of the Sino-Vietnamese hostilities of the early 1980s, following China's "lesson" to Vietnam, between 50,000 and 80,000 Vietnamese troops were moved into northern Laos to deter further Chinese attack. Yet as tension declined these troop levels were reduced.

Some migration – or re-migration – of Vietnamese people to Laos took place during the late 1980s and the early 1990s, but this was at a time when both Thai and Western influences were clearly on the increase in the Lao PDR. A census of the Vientiane population found 15,000 Vietnamese living illegally in the capital. Most of themwere promptly deported back to Vietnam.

China

Following the fall of Saigon in April 1975, and the establishment of Communist rule over Laos in December of the same year, the new Lao authorities did their best to keep on good terms with both Hanoi and Beijing. Vietnam was undoubtedly the dominant power in Indochina, but China was invited to stay on and to continue road-building and other developmental aid in the northwest of the country as far south as Luang Prabang.

During the early 1980s, however, relations between Laos and China deteriorated. The Lao Communist leader Kaysone Phomvihane publicly accused Beijing of "dark and extremely cruel schemes against Laos", and Beijing responded with a warning that "criminal Vietnamese schemes to intensify their control over Laos will only invite stronger opposition from the Lao people". Many ethnic Chinese residents fled Laos during this period, and were eventually resettled on Hainan Island.

However, during the mid-1980s, the conflict between Vietnam and China gradually began to die down and Laos wasted absoloutley no time in discreetly re-establishing amicable relations with Beijing. Since that time Beijing has hardly looked back; today, China's political and economic influence over northwestern Laos is paramount.

In time, no doubt, the people of northwestern Laos will benefit substantially from political and economic developments. Certainly standards of living are already rising for the residents of Luang Nam Tha and Bokeo, strategically located between the fast-expanding economies of China and Thailand, as they begin to feel the benefits of free trade. In economic terms the area is rapidly becoming more closely tied to China than it has been at any time since the French annexation in 1896.

Thailand

Meanwhile the third and culturally closest of Laos's big neighbours, Thailand, is making a sig-

Bridging the gap to Thailand.

nificant comeback in the friendship stakes. Thai cultural influences permeate Laos, and Thai television and radio – readily comprehended by most Lao in a way that simply doesn't hold true for either Vietnamese or Chinese programming – are watched avidly throughout the country. This suggests that, at long last, the legacy of the Lao suspicion of its brasher, larger and stronger neighbour to the west of the Mekong is finally begining to disappear. Road – and now rail – bridges are springing up fast, and many Lao, both in government positions and ordinary citizens, now see Thailand as a useful counterweight to their Vietnamese and Chinese neighbours, as well as an economic role model to follow in the future.

ETHNIC MINORITIES

Highland areas in both Laos and Cambodia are home to a rich assortment of ethnic-minority peoples.

Laos is ethnically very diverse. The majority Lao – **Lao Loum**, or "Lowland Lao" – constitute around half of the population, while the remainder is made up of various "hill peoples", as well as urban-dwelling Viets and Chinese.

In all, there are 49 officially recognised nationalities. The **Lao Theung** ("Approaching the top of the mountain Lao") traditionally live at moderate altitudes and include the **Khamu** and the **Htin**. They are largely descended from Mon-Khmer groups living in the region before the southward migration of the Lao from the 8th century. These ethnic groups no longer wear particularly distinctive costumes – the "Lao Theung" dancers you will see at cultural shows in Vientiane and Luang Prabang are generally lowland Lao wearing idealised costumes.

The most distinct minorities are found in the north. The **Lao Tai**, the Tai-speaking groups, including the **Tai Dam** (Black Tai). They form part of the **Lao Soung** ("Highland Lao") and include the **Hmong**, **Akha**, **Lanten** and **Mien** (Yao).

Cambodia is much more ethnically homogeneous than Laos, though the government's claim that ethnic **Khmer** make up around 95 percent of the population is certainly on the high side. Aside from the ethnic Chinese and Vietnamese, Cambodia's most distinctive and accessible minority are the lowland-dwelling **Cham Muslims**. Other **Khmer Loeu** or "Upland Khmer" minorities live much further off the beaten track, chiefly in the northeastern provinces of Rattanakiri and Mondolkiri (the **Tompuon**, **Pnong**, **Kreung**, **Brau** and **Jarai**), whose women tend to wear heavy jewellery, especially earrings, and to smoke pipes, as well as the truly remote Pear and Saoch of the Cardamom Mountains in southwestern Cambodia, whose costume is – well, very little clothing at all.

A village elder smokes a waterpipe in Longloa.

The Lowland Lao are the traditional rice farmers of the Mekong Valley. They first arrived in the region as part of a larger migration of Tai-speaking peoples from southern China in the 8th century and are now a majority in much of northeastern Thailand.

The Akha, a distinctive Lao Soung (highland) group.

Lanten woman and child.

MINORITY POLITICS

The Lao authorities are very keen both to promote good inter-ethnic relations and to portray the Lao PDR as a happy family of equal nationalities. In fact, power tends to lie with the Lowland Lao population, as it has done for centuries. To be fair to the Lao government, however, it must be said that the position of minority groups has probably never been better, both in terms of representation and standard of living. One continuing problem for the government have been the Hmong. The authorities wish to see the Hmong settled, with schools teaching their children Lao. Some Hmong, however, would prefer to stay on their distant mountain tops, remote from government authority.

Cambodian government policy towards minorities is less clear-cut and less legally codified. In theory, all nationalities living in Cambodia are equal, though the Khmer majority is clearly predominant. The Cham and the ethnic Chinese are generally well treated, as are – in a rather paternalistic manner – such indigenous groups as the Brau, Jarai, Pnong, Pear and other minorities. A major exception are the ethnic Vietnamese, thought to be the largest minority group in Cambodia, but generally mistrusted by most Khmers, whether urban elite or rural peasantry. Cambodia's ethnic Vietnamese, generally readily distinguishable by the all-but-ubiquitous *non la* conical hat worn by the women, continue to suffer widespread de facto discrimination.

...mong children; the Hmong have been persecuted in Laos due ...their links with the US during the Vietnam War years.

...Lao Theung woman gathers firewood in Udomxai province. ...e various Lao Theung groups have been historically ...isparaged as backward by the lowland Lao majority.

A colourfully clad Mien woman in northwestern Laos. The Lao Soung highland peoples are relatively recent arrivals, having only migrated into the region (mostly from China) in the past 200–300 years.

CULTURE, ART AND ARCHITECTURE

Lao culture, like that of neighbouring Cambodia,
suffered under the Communists; but traditional art
forms have survived and are re-emerging into daily life.

The traditional art and culture of Laos are closely related to those of neighbouring Thailand, and especially to those of Thailand's Lao-speaking northeastern provinces. The very close relationship between Lao and Thai culture is immediately apparent to anyone crossing the Mekong River between the two countries.

Yet the 15 years of rigid Communist domination and isolation behind the "bamboo curtain" between 1975 and 1990 have had a lasting impact which, given the slow-moving pace of Laos, is unlikely to disappear completely for some years to come. Some of the most interesting aspects of contemporary Lao cultural arts are directly related to the brief period of Communist ascendancy.

Literature

The most popular and enduring epic in Lao literature is the *Pha Lak Pha Lam*, the Lao version of the Hindu *Ramayana* (see page 235). This classic is thought to have come to Laos about 1,000 years ago, when the southern part of the country was dominated by the Hindu Khmer Empire. Also derived from Indian tradition are the *jataka*, the stories of the life cycle of the Buddha, called *saa-tok* in Lao. Traditionally, religious texts and other literature were written by hand on palm leaves.

Music and dance

Traditional Lao music is much less complex than that of Vietnam and Cambodia. When sung it is always memorised, and improvisation is popular.

The main Lao instrument is the flute-like *khene*, which is made of bamboo. There are two types of orchestra, the *seb gnai* which uses large drums and wind instruments to play religious

The khene, a traditional flute made from bamboo.

State-sponsored dances in both Laos and Cambodia generally feature smiling minorities dancing in unison with the dominant Lao or Khmer ethnic group. It's likely that few of the performers are really from minority ethnic groups.

music, and the *seb noi* which employs *khene*, flutes called *khuy*, a two-stringed instrument called the *so*, and the *nangnat*, which is a form of xylophone. To this is generally added the music of the *khong vong*, a semicircular instrument made from cane which carries 16 cymbals around its periphery.

Modern popular Lao music is often based on *khene* music. However, most Lao living in the Mekong Valley tend to tune in to Thai radio stations and watch Thai TV programmes, and in Thailand's Isaan provinces the influence of Thai popular music culture is predictably great.

Lamvong, the Lao equivalent of Thai *ram-wong* dancing, is extremely popular. At its best this is performed by graceful female dancers who use their arms and hands to relate stories from the *Ramayana* and other epics. In general, though, *lamvong* may be performed by anyone of either gender, spontaneously at parties and festivals.

Contemporary Lao socialist art

With Social Realism established as the sole legitimate art form in both the Soviet Union and Communist China, it followed naturally that the genre was introduced throughout Vietnam following the Communist victory in 1975. The Lao Communists, always strongly influenced by their Vietnamese "elder brothers", had long applied Social Realist standards in their northeastern base in the provinces of Hua Phan and Phongsali. Following the establishment of the Lao PDR in December 1975, the highly formalised style was extended to the rest of the country as a matter of course – as usual, brooking no rivalry.

In easy-going non-industrialised Buddhist Laos the results of this policy seemed particularly incongruous. Images of heroic peasants shooting down marauding US planes with AK47 assault rifles alternated with images of massively muscled Lao "shock workers" building steel mills for the socialist society. Other unlikely images included, for example, Lao hill tribes demonstrating their unshakeable solidarity with Cuban forces in Angola.

In Eastern Europe and the Soviet Union, following the collapse of Communist power, Social Realism was abandoned almost overnight as people celebrated their new-found cultural freedom. Some countries of the former Soviet Bloc even established museums to house especially lurid examples of totalitarian kitsch. In cautious, sleepy Laos, by contrast, change has been rather more gradual.

Today, militant images celebrating the anti-imperialist struggle have all but disappeared – except from the walls of the People's Museum of the Lao Army, which is, in any case, generally closed to visitors. By contrast, hoardings

celebrating the more pacific side of Communist aspirations – mass inoculation campaigns, the construction of heavy industry, and the "bumper harvest" – still survive. A revealing change around the start of the new millennium was the introduction of two previously uncelebrated elements of Lao society: the monk and the businessman. In downtown Vientiane these formerly shunned figures have joined those stalwarts of Lao Social Realism, the peasant, the soldier and the worker, in hoardings celebrating the achievements of the government. In the Lao PDR the writing is, literally, on the wall

Communist Party propaganda.

FOLK THEATRE

Maw lam khuu is a traditional music drama during which a man courts a woman by singing love songs. The songs involve question-and-answer "dialogues". By contrast, *maw lam dio* is a popular form of folk theatre sometimes used as a propaganda vehicle for government doctrines, although in the past – and, increasingly, again today – it was used to teach or promote religious concepts. It is always performed by a single person. *Maw lam luang* is a popular and more light-hearted form of Lao musical drama, while *maw lam chot* is a form of folk theatre where two performers of the same sex will either discuss or argue about a particular subject.

– Buddhism and private enterprise are both back in style.

Architecture

Laos is blessed with a surprisingly rich range of temple styles, with most traditional Lao architecture relating directly to Theravada Buddhism. A Lao wat complex will typically consist of several structures including a *sim*, or building where *phra* – that is, monks – are ordained; a *haw tai*, or library; *kuti*, or monks' dwelling places; *that*, or stupas; and generally a *haw kawng*, or drum tower.

The classic temple style of Vientiane and the lower Mekong differs from that of the north. The *sim* is generally narrower and higher than in the north of the country, with heavy columns and much steeper eaves, and is often distinguished by an elaborately carved wooden screen over the front entrance porch. Figures in such carvings may represent the Buddha or be mythical figures such as the *garuda* (a fierce half-bird, half-human creature from Hindu and Buddhist mythology) or the *kinnari* (a female creature with a human upper torso but the wings and legs of a bird). The main part of the

Traditional Lao textiles.

TEXTILES AND JEWELLERY

Weaving is an ancient and honoured craft throughout Laos, but especially among the lowland ethnic Lao. Both silk and cotton fabrics are woven, generally as a cottage craft beneath the stilt houses of villagers by the banks of the Mekong River and along its tributary valleys. Patterns comprise repeated geometric shapes, or feature animals and flowers. The most common item manufactured is the traditional *phaa nung*, or tube-skirt, which forms part of the Lao female national dress. Weaving is also practised among upland peoples and among the Mon-Khmer minorities of the southern uplands.

Gold, jewellery and silverware are all manufactured to a high standard in Laos and are for sale, notably at Vientiane's *talaat sao* (morning market). The highest standards of craftsmanship are attained by the Lao silversmiths, whose intricate belts complete the traditional costume of Lao women. Fine handbags and other decorative items are also manufactured, as well as equally fine rings, bracelets, necklaces and various vessels. Lao silverware is closely related to that of Chiang Mai in Thailand; this probably dates from the time when the two independent kingdoms of Lan Na and Lan Xang were neighbours, and their respective courts exchanged cultural gifts and skilled artisans.

sim is generally made of brick and stucco. Roofs are high-peaked and culminate in characteristic *jao faa* or upward-sweeping hooks. The architectural school in evidence here is Rattanakosin, from Bangkok in central Thailand, and quite different to the various northern schools – it's grander, certainly, but less intimate.

Luang Prabang temples differ quite markedly in style from those of Vientiane. The north of the country shares cultural and artistic links with the ancient northern Tai Kingdom of Lan Na, now the region around Chiang Mai, as well as the Thai Lu principalities of Sipsongpanna,

the Luang Prabang temple style but with single rather than tiered roofs. Unfortunately the unrestrained bombing of the Plain of Jars during the Vietnam War resulted in the total destruction of all Xieng Khuang temples in their native Phuan region. Fortunately, however, a few still survive in Luang Prabang, adding to the richness of the architectural heritage of the northern capital – Wat Sop on Thanon Xieng Thong is the best such example.

The pre-eminent religious building in the country is That Luang in Vientiane – effectively the symbol of Lao nationhood (see

Wat Xieng Thong typifies the Luang Prabang temple style.

now at the heart of China's Xishuangbanna Dai Autonomous Region. Part of the sophisticated Tai Lu architectural heritage lies in Laos, notably at Muang Singh in the far northwest.

The temples of Luang Prabang are lower and broader than those of Vientiane, with sweeping, multi-tiered roofs and "eyebrow" pelmets, the *sim* being reached by a narrow flight of *naga* (river snake spirit) -lined stone steps. Wat Xieng Thong, with its spectacular roofs and liberal use of gold, is probably the best example of this style (see page 130).

There was once a third Lao temple style, that of the ancient Phuan Kingdom centred on the Plain of Jars. This style – known as Xieng Khuang after the old Phuan capital – resembled

page 112). It is part of a distinctive style associated with Vientiane and the northeast, distinguished by tall, gilded *chedi (that)*, reliquaries for venerated Buddha relics. That Phanom, just across the Mekong in Thailand, is similarly impressive and is sacred to the Lao people of northeastern Thailand.

There are other religious traditions present in Vientiane and the central Mekong Valley – French colonial-period churches and chapels, and even a tiny mosque in central Vientiane – while the architectural treasures of southern Laos are in fact Cambodian, and are best represented by Wat Phu in Champasak (see page 174), which was founded in pre-Angkorean times, but also has later Angkor-era structures.

Lemongrass stalks stuffed with ground pork and shallots, a dish locally known as oua si khai.

LAO FOOD

Lao cuisine is similar to that of Thailand and has grown in popularity, though the country dishes of raw meat may not appeal to all.

Lao cuisine, although distinctively and unmistakably "Lao", is by no means confined to Laos. Just across the Mekong River in northeastern Thailand (known as Isaan) there are perhaps six times as many ethnic Lao as there are in Laos itself, while the number of Lao-speaking inhabitants flocking to Bangkok means that there are now far more ethnic Lao in the Thai capital than in any other city, Vientiane included. As a consequence, Lao cuisine has gained in fame and popularity, being enjoyed throughout Thailand and even having a chain of fast-food restaurants developed to serve it called "Isaan Classic".

Lao cuisine may be seen as the cooking tradition and style of the entire Lao ethnic group and is based on the consumption of sticky rice as a staple. Other essential ingredients include *kha*, or galangal (a ginger-like rhizome with a peppery flavour), and *nam paa* (fish sauce). Lao cuisine has numerous regional variations, but that of Vientiane, the capital, is generally considered the most sophisticated.

Staple diet

In common with neighbouring Southeast Asian countries, the Lao diet is based on rice. This isn't the long-grain rice that Viets, Central Thai and most Westerners are used to eating, however, but *khao niaw*, or glutinous "sticky rice", deftly rolled into a neat, small ball and eaten with the hand. In Vientiane, as indeed in all other large towns, long-grain rice, or *khao jao*, is readily available, but *khao niaw* remains the basic staple of the Lao people and is the single most distinctive feature of the cuisine. Along with it there is another vital ingredient, *paa daek*, a highly pungent fermented fish

Transplanting rice.

paste. On the back veranda of virtually every Lao peasant's house you will find an earthenware jar of *paa daek*.

Sticky rice is generally accompanied by a selection of dips, parboiled vegetables, salads, soups and various curried meat or fish dishes. The rice is usually served in a simple but attractive woven bamboo container called a *tip khao*. It's considered bad luck not to replace the lid on top of the *tip khao* at the end of the meal. When Lao go off to work in the fields or elsewhere you will often see hanging at their sides small woven baskets in which they carry supplies of sticky rice and perhaps small amounts of fish or meat which will serve as their midday meal. While sticky rice is eaten by hand, long-grain rice is always eaten with a spoon and fork. Chopsticks are reserved for Chinese-style noodle dishes or for use in Chinese and Vietnamese restaurants.

Dishes are generally cooked with fresh ingredients that include vegetables, poultry

> Soup is considered a necessary part of any Lao meal. Visitors should look out for kaeng no may, fresh bamboo-shoot soup, and kaeng het bot, made with a variety of fresh mushrooms.

The galangal root and other seasonings.

(chicken, duck), pork, beef and water buffalo. Fish and prawns are readily available but, with Laos being a landlocked country, are nearly always of the freshwater variety. Mutton is not eaten except by the country's small South Asian Muslim population, nearly all of whom live in Vientiane.

Upcountry, particularly in the north, jungle foods and game are more in evidence. Besides wild boar and deer these include such unlikely animals as pangolin, monitor lizard, civet, wild dog and field rat.

Popular dishes

Popular Lao dishes include *tam som* – the equivalent of Thai *som tam* – a spicy salad made of sliced green papaya mixed with chilli peppers, garlic, tomatoes, ground peanuts, crab, lime juice and fish sauce. This is often eaten with sticky rice and *ping kai* (grilled chicken). Another standby is *laap*, a spicy dish of minced meat, poultry or fish mixed with lime juice, garlic, chilli pepper, onion and mint. Meats and innards used in *laap* are finely chopped and spiced with onion, chillies and other herbs such as mint. Lao *laap* is generally cooked, unlike *laap dip* in northern Thailand, but can be raw. If you are concerned about this, ask for *laap suk* (cooked *laap*). Many rural Lao prefer *laap seua*, or "tiger *laap*", which is raw chopped meat. Visitors will usually be served cooked *laap*, especially in restaurants.

Other dishes include *tom khaa kai* (chicken soup with galangal and coconut milk), *kaeng jeut* (mild soup with minced pork and bitter gourd), and *khao laat kaeng*, or curry, served on a bed of *khao jao* long-grain rice – all virtually identical to Thai dishes of the same name served on the other side of the Mekong. Then there is rice vermicelli, or *khao poun*. This is served cold with a variety of raw chopped vegetables, on top of which is placed coconut-milk sauce flavoured with meat and chillies. This is considered an auspicious dish at weddings and other celebrations, and is usually a favourite with foreigners. A popular regional dish is *or lam* from Luang Prabang. Lemon grass, dried buffalo meat and skin, chillies and aubergine along with *paa daek* are slowly stewed together, then eaten with crisp-fried pork skin and sweet basil.

Other popular cuisines available include Italian and French (especially in Vientiane and Luang Prabang), and South Asian (in Vientiane). Laos is an excellent place for breakfast, chiefly because of the French colonial legacy. French bread or *khao jii* is freshly baked each day and served with pâté, fried eggs and omelette. Good coffee, grown in the hills of southern Laos, is also available; you can start the day with coffee and croissants in the major urban centres, though upcountry the croissants may have to be replaced with *pah thawng ko*, or deep-fried Chinese dough sticks.

Also popular at breakfast, or as a snack at any time, is Vietnamese *pho* (noodle soup) and *yaw jeun*, deep-fried spring rolls. For a variant try *yaw dip* or fresh spring rolls. Vietnamese food is good and plentiful, especially in Vientiane and the larger cities. The same is true of Chinese food, which is generally Cantonese or Hokkienese, though some Yunnanese food is sold in Vientiane.

Country cuisine

Travelling upcountry away from the "big cities" is a rather different experience, and not necessarily to every visitor's liking food-wise. Upcountry Lao cuisine is very definitely an acquired taste. Raw meat is common, served

long been absent from most Lao dining tables. As Laos increases in prosperity, and as tourist demand rises, this distinguished form of cooking is making a return. Fortunately its secrets have been kept alive in a book published in Lao and English called *Traditional Recipes of Laos*. The author, Chaleunsilp Phia Sing, was born at Luang Prabang in 1898. According to Alan Davidson, a former British Ambassador to Laos, Phia Sing was both the master chef at the royal palace in Luang Prabang and the Royal Master of Ceremonies. Davidson describes him as a "sort of Lao Leonardo da

Waffles stacked high at the Km 52 market, near Vientiane.

Watermelon makes a juicy snack.

with a salad of chopped jungle leaves and herbs, usually washed down with fiery home-made rice whisky. Many people live near to forests where hunting and gathering of food remain a way of life. When a deer is shot it is carried back to the village; there the whole animal is prepared for *laap*, to be eaten at once (partly because there are very few refrigerators in these areas), and so the family's friends and neighbours come to join in the feasting and drinking.

Haute cuisine

The haute cuisine once served at the royal court of Luang Prabang is worlds away from the "peasant food" described above, and it has

LAO DINING STYLE

In traditional Lao society, eating is communal and an important social occasion. Diners, whether members of the same family or neighbours, will sit together at floor level on reed mats surrounding a raised rattan platform called a *kantoke*. Each *kantoke* will bear several communal dishes of laap, or curry, as well as small woven baskets of sticky rice – the essential wherewithal, without which Lao people often feel that they have not eaten. Traditionally, as in northern Thailand, sticky rice and curries are eaten by hand. Spoons are used for soup and for long-grain rice, but only noodles, a Chinese cultural and culinary import, are eaten with chopsticks.

Vinci… at a court of many and beautiful ceremonies, a physician, architect, choreographer, sculptor, painter and poet". His last years were devoted to compiling a detailed account of his experiences as a royal chef, listing 114 recipes in all. They have since been painstakingly translated and annotated.

Fruit and drinks

There is plenty of fruit in Laos, although – as with food in general – the range and quality is much better in the Mekong Valley than upcountry and in the hills. In the appropriate seasons, and especially towards the end of the hot season in May, local markets overflow with a wide variety of exotic fruits including mango, papaya, coconut, rambutan, durian, custard apple, guava, mangosteen, starfruit, pineapple, watermelon, jackfruit and bananas.

It is always advisable to drink bottled water in Laos. Beware of ice that may have a dubious origin, particularly upcountry or at street stalls, as it is often made from unsafe tap water that can cause stomach upsets. Soft drinks are available everywhere, as is canned

A glutinous dessert.

LAO DINING ETIQUETTE

Lao meals typically consist of a soup dish, a grilled dish, a sauce, greens and a stew. The greens are usually fresh raw greens, herbs and other vegetables, though depending on the dish they accompany, they could also be steamed or, more typically, parboiled, and are therefore very healthy. Dishes are not eaten one after the other, but at the same time; the soup is sipped throughout the meal. When guests are present, the meal should always be a feast, with food made in quantities sufficient for twice the number of diners. For a host, not having an abundance of food for the guests would be considered excruciatingly embarrassing.

and bottled beer. The real treat to look out for is the excellent and cheap local product, Beer Lao, which comes both bottled and draught. Imported wine – a reminder of Laos's colonial past – is available in major towns.

Caution should be exercised when purchasing fresh fruit juices and sugar-cane juice, but cartons and cans of fruit juice, milk and drinking yoghurt are available in supermarkets in Vientiane and Luang Prabang.

Good coffee and tea are a cornerstone of life in Laos and are generally available throughout the country. Chinese tea is often served as a free accompaniment to meals or with the thick strong Lao coffee.

The Plain of Jars.

Along the banks of the Mekong River, near Vientiane.

Street food in Vientiane.

LAOS: PLACES

A detailed guide to the entire country, with principal
sites clearly cross-referenced by number to the maps.

Wat Phu, near Champasak.

Laos is often described as a tiny, landlocked country. It is true that the population of around 6.9 million is not large, especially set against those of nearby China and Vietnam, but at 236,800 sq km (91,400 sq miles) Laos is almost exactly the same size as the United Kingdom, and has many spectacular rivers and mountain ranges for the visitor to explore.

The outstanding destination in this little-known Southeast Asian backwater must be the ancient royal capital of Luang Prabang, set amid beautiful scenery on a bend of the mighty Mekong River. Now a World Heritage Site, it is the most perfectly preserved traditional capital in Southeast Asia. It is difficult to exaggerate the tranquillity of the atmosphere and the exquisite distinction of the architecture in this elegant little town. Further down the Mekong there is the capital, Vientiane, the region's smallest and quietest, a hybrid, French-influenced city which combines the best of both Lao and French architectural traditions, as well as Sino-Vietnamese temples and shophouses.

That Ing Hang Stupa, near Savannakhet.

Winding through the country from north to south, the Mekong serves as a source of nutrition in the form of plentiful fish and provides irrigation for the surrounding rice paddies. It is also a major commercial highway, linking Luang Prabang with Vientiane and the cities of the south – Tha Kaek, Savannakhet, Pakse and Champasak. Just a few kilometres from the last are the outstanding remains of Wat Phu, a magnificent Angkor-period Khmer temple in a spectacular mountain setting. The nearby islands of the Si Phan Don, the beautiful Bolavan Plateau and the mighty Khone Falls are other southern attractions.

Laos has long been isolated from the outside world by poor communications and an inward-looking, rather secretive government. Things are changing, however. Three new highways are set to link southwestern China with Thailand and Vietnam, putting Laos at a crucial crossroads. A high-speed rail link between China and Thailand running across northern Laos is also being considered. Yet, for now at least, this Buddhist country remains a sleepy anachronism, offering a tantalising glimpse of a fast-disappearing world.

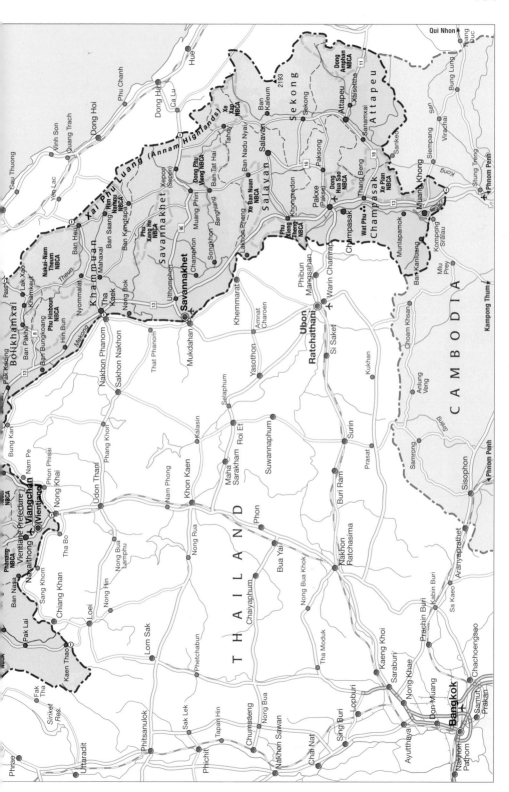

Scenery near Vang Vieng.

A tuk-tuk hits the streets.

VIENTIANE

This small city on the Mekong is lethargic in comparison with other Asian capitals, and its air of decaying charm adds to this relaxed ambience.

"**V**ientiane is exceptional, but inconvenient," wrote Paul Theroux in 1975. "The brothels are cleaner than the hotels, marijuana is cheaper than pipe tobacco, and opium easier to find than a cold glass of beer." Though much has changed in Laos since Theroux's romp through Southeast Asia, after almost 40 years of Communist rule Vientiane still retains a bit of its old frontier-town spirit: a city where almost anything goes, but not quite everything works. For a capital city, it is remarkably quiet, laid-back and, above all, petite – the population of the entire metropolitan area is less than 790,000 (although it is still comfortably the largest city in Laos).

Sometimes spelled Vieng Chan, Viengchan or Viangchan (the name "Vientiane" is a French romanised version), the city has been controlled at various times by the Vietnamese, the Siamese, the Burmese and the Khmers – and, more recently, the French. A positive result of all this outside intervention is that the streets are a compelling mélange of Lao, Thai, Chinese, Vietnamese, French and even Russian influences in architecture, cuisine and culture. It is home to a little over 10 percent of the country's population, but a far larger share of its wealth.

As a result of rapid modernisation in recent years, today's Vientiane is a far cry from the time immediately after the Second Indochina War, when the author Norman Lewis found that light bulbs only worked occasionally – and never at night. Today not only is electricity reliable but there is also ready access to the internet and, in more expensive hotels, to BBC and CNN news networks.

Downtown Vientiane

Vientiane owed its early prosperity to its founding on the fertile alluvial plains on the banks of the Mekong River – as good a place as any to begin

Main Attractions
Mekong River
Nam Phu
Haw Pha Kaew
Colonial Architecture
Wat Si Muang
Patuxai
That Luang

Vegetables for sale at Talaat Sao's morning market.

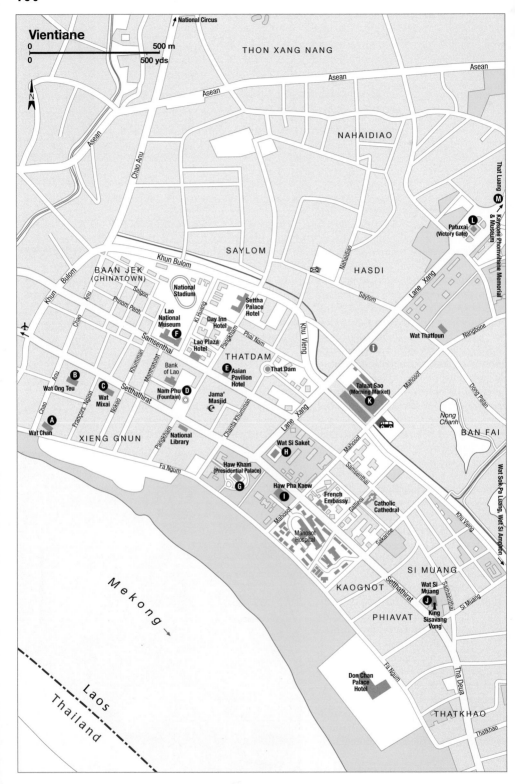

your exploration of the city. Named after the founder of the Kingdom of Lan Xang, **Fa Ngum Road** is a pleasant riverfront boulevard that runs right along the Mekong at the southern edge of the town. Head for the path on top of the reinforced dyke – actually the site of the old town wall, built as a line of defence against invading armies and overflowing waters – for a pleasant stroll with a view across the river to Thailand. Many outdoor cafés and small restaurants line the riverfront, offering food, fruit shakes and beer.

A few small streets run through the neighbourhoods between Fa Ngum Road and **Setthathirat Road**, named after the king who consolidated the move of the capital of Lan Xang from Luang Prabang to Vientiane in 1560. **Chao Anu Road** is a reminder of Chao Anuvong, the ruler of the Kingdom of Vientiane from 1805 until 1828. In 1826 Anuvong launched an ill-fated attack on neighbouring Siam which prompted a fierce response, resulting in the partial destruction of the city in 1828. The Siamese resettled large numbers of local residents in northeastern Thailand (even today there are around six times more ethnic Lao living in Thailand than in Laos), and captured Anuvong, bringing him to Bangkok, where he was executed.

This area of the town is dotted with temples that were restored after their abandonment following the 1828 Siamese invasion. The *sim* of **Wat Chan** Ⓐ (daily; free/voluntary donation), located at the intersection of Chao Anu and Fa Ngum roads, houses a large bronze seated Buddha that survived the destruction, in addition to a series of beautifully carved wooden panels. **Wat Ong Teu** Ⓑ (daily; free/voluntary donation), a short distance to the north on Setthathirat Road, is named after the large 16th-century "Heavy Buddha" found at the rear of the *sim*. Home to the Buddhist Institute, a school for monks who come from all over Laos to study here, Wat Ong Teu is one of the most important religious centres in the country. **Wat Mixai** Ⓒ (daily; free/voluntary donation), east of Wat Ong Teu on Setthathirat Road, is built in the Bangkok style with a surrounding veranda.

Wat Mixai.

Jumbos or tuk-tuks are a good way to get about town, but agree the fare before you start your journey.

Lamvong traditional dance enacts scenes from the Ramayana.

Two guardian giants stand to attention outside the heavy gates.

Continuing east on Setthathirat Road you will see **Nam Phu** , the central fountain at the heart of Vientiane's downtown area, built in the late 1960s on the site of an old roofed market. Across the street from Nam Phu, and lined with a row of beautiful frangipani trees (*dok champa*, Laos's national flower), is the **National Library** (www.nationallibraryoflaos.org; daily 8–11.30am and 2–4.30pm, closed on the 29th of every month), built by the French as a police headquarters. Just to the east is the **Vientiane Jama' Masjid** (closed to non-Muslims during prayer times; free), the hub of the city for the small Tamil Muslim community (see page 25). The even smaller Cham Muslim community uses the Azhar Mosque in the north of the city. These are the only two mosques in the entire country.

Lao and Chinese commerce

North of the Nam Phu fountain is **Samsenthai Road**, the main route through Vientiane's prosperous commercial district. As recently as the mid-1990s this area was something of a ghost town: most of the shops were shut, as the government had yet to initiate economic reform or to open up Vientiane to foreign investment. Things have changed a good deal since then, and the imposing Thai-owned **Lao Plaza Hotel** is a monument to the city's recent economic growth. The nearby **Asian Pavilion Hotel** was popular with the press corps during the Second Indochina War, when it was known as the Hotel Constellation; journalists sat out the 1960 battle of Vientiane in the lobby while, outside, 500 people died during the fighting that followed a coup by the neutralist general Kong Le.

Just to the northeast, off Samsenthai Road, is **That Dam**, the Black Stupa, which dates to the early Lan Xang period. According to local legend, it is home to a seven-headed dragon that came to life and protected Vientiane residents during the 1828 Siamese invasion. Nearby is the sprawling **US Embassy** complex, once one of the largest in the world (now far outstripped by the US Embassy in Baghdad); the

CITY OF SANDALWOOD

According to the Lao interpretation of the Indian *Ramayana*, the *Phra Lak Phra Lam*, Vientiane – which means "City of Sandalwood" in Lao – was founded by the legendary Prince Thattaradtha in the mists of time. Most historians, however, take a rather more prosaic view, considering the embryonic city on the Mekong to have developed as an early Khmer settlement clustered about a Hindu temple. The Phra That Luang stupa would eventually replace the temple as the focus of the city as Buddhism became the state religion. After 1354, when King Fa Ngum established the Kingdom of Lan Xang, Vientiane became the main administrative centre of Laos and most important city in the realm, a position traded with Luang Prabang over the centuries but re-established in the present day.

embassy remained open even at the height of the Indochina Wars and after a two-day closure, following the Communist takeover.

West on Samsenthai Road, adjacent to the **National Stadium**, is the **Lao National Museum** ❶ (daily 8am–noon and 1–4pm). Built in 1925, this elegant structure was once the French governor's residence, and was used by the Lao government as an administrative building before being converted into a museum in 1985. The permanent exhibition provides a selective history of Laos's struggle for independence, leaving out major details like the heavy Vietnamese involvement in the "revolution". But it is filled with interesting artefacts from the war, particularly the weapons, clothing and supplies of key revolutionary figures.

Continuing west on Samsenthai you will enter **Baan Jek**, Vientiane's **Chinatown** district, home to the city's growing ethnic Chinese population and one of the capital's most vibrant areas. North of Chinatown, at the corner of Thong Khan Kham Road (Chao Anu) and Dong Miang Road (Asean), is **Thong Khan Kham Market**, the largest produce market in Vientiane, selling just about everything. It is also one of the best places in the town to buy traditional Lao baskets and pottery. Laos's **National Circus**, built by the Soviet Union at the height of the Cold War, is located nearby. The national circus troupe offers irregular performances, and occasional pop and classical music performances also take place here.

Royal and Buddhist headquarters

Heading east from Nam Phu fountain on Setthathirat Road, past a series of restored French colonial villas, you soon arrive at the **Presidential Palace** ❼ (Haw Kham), originally built as the French colonial governor's residence. The French took control of Laos in 1893 and administered the territory directly through the *résident supérieur* in Vientiane. After independence, King Sisavang Vong and, later, his son Savang Vatthana used the palace as a residence when visiting Vientiane from the royal seat in Luang Prabang. It is now used for hosting foreign guests of the Lao

The Presidential Palace.

Wat Si Saket, probably the oldest original temple in Vientiane.

Prayers at the main city mosque.

government and for meetings of the presidential cabinet – the president himself does not live here. The building is not open to the public.

Across the street from the Presidential Palace is **Wat Si Saket** ⊕ (daily 8am–noon and 1–4pm), built in 1818 by Chao Anuvong. The temple was designed in the early Bangkok style, which possibly explains why it was left relatively untouched when the Siamese destroyed the city in 1828. Wat Si Saket is probably the oldest original temple in Vientiane – all the others were either constructed after this one or were rebuilt after the invasion.

The interior walls of the cloister surrounding the central *sim* of Wat Si Saket are filled with small niches containing more than 2,000 miniature silver and ceramic Buddha images, most of them made in Vientiane between the 16th and 19th centuries. On the western side of the cloister is a pile of broken and melted-down images, relics of the 1828 war and intended as a reminder of past Thai aggression. Behind the *sim* is a long wooden trough resembling a *naga*, or river-snake spirit, used during the Lao New Year celebrations to pour cleansing water over the temple's Buddha images. To the left of the *sim* is a raised Burmese-style structure that was once a library containing Buddhist scriptures, which are now housed in Bangkok. Today Wat Si Saket is home to the head of the Lao *sangha*, the order of Buddhist monks.

Home of the Emerald Buddha

Haw Pha Kaew ❶ (daily 8am–noon and 1–4pm), the former royal temple of the Lao monarchy, is next door to the Presidential Palace and just across the street from Wat Si Saket. King Setthathirat built the original in 1565 to house the Emerald Buddha which he brought with him when he moved to Vientiane from Lan Na (the former Kingdom of Chiang Mai) following the death of his father, King Phothisarat. During the Siamese invasion of 1779, Vientiane was looted, and a host of sacred images was carried off to Bangkok along with members of the Lao royal family; today the Emerald Buddha sits in Bangkok's own Wat Phra Kaew.

The current structure is the result of a 1937–40 restoration under the supervision of Prince Souvanna Phouma, a Paris-educated engineer and, later, prime minister of an independent Laos. While Haw Pha Kaew is no longer used as a temple, bus-loads of Thai tourists often visit here. The museum contains a gilded throne, Khmer Buddhist stelae, and bronze frog drums of the royal family. The two main doors contain the only remnants of the original temple – sculptured wooden panels with images of the Buddha in nature, while the garden, a peaceful retreat from the dust and heat of Vientiane, contains a small jar from the Plain of Jars in Xieng Khuang province.

The surrounding area was once the administrative centre of French colonial rule, and in this neighbourhood are the spectacular **French Embassy** and residential complex, the Roman

Catholic **Cathedral**, built by the French in 1928 and still offering daily services, and a number of administrative and residential buildings. Considering it was the capital of a colony that ran at a financial loss – the French made up for Laos with profits from operations in Cambodia and Vietnam – Vientiane experienced a fair amount of construction under French rule.

The lucky temple

Wat Si Muang ➊ (daily; free), one of the most active temples in Vientiane, is located to the southeast of the French Embassy on Setthathirat Road. After the temple site was selected in 1563 by a group of King Setthathirat's advisers, a large hole was dug to receive the *lak muang*, or city pillar, which contains the city's protective deity. Legend has it that, on the day the temple was dedicated, the *lak muang* was suspended over the hole with ropes as the authorities waited for a volunteer to jump in. A pregnant woman (or a virgin, depending on whom you ask) finally did, and the ropes were severed, the woman's sacrifice bringing good luck

to the new capital. The *sim* was constructed around the *lak muang*, which is wrapped in sacred cloth. However this did not prevent Wat Si Muang from being destroyed by the Siamese in 1828. It was reconstructed in 1915.

The temple is filled with Buddha images, at least one of which dates from before the 1828 invasion; partially damaged, it sits on a pillow in front and to the left of the main altar. Worshippers believe that the image has the power to grant wishes and answer important questions about the future. The platters of fruit and flowers scattered throughout the *sim* are evidence of the popularity of this belief (offerings are brought to the temple when a wish is granted), as are the votive flowers, candles and other offerings sold at the small market across the street.

Just to the south is a small public park surrounding a statue of **King Sisavang Vong**, a somewhat unlikely prewar gift from the Soviet Union. In his outstretched hand the king holds a palm-leaf manuscript of the country's first legal code.

FACT

The museum at Haw Pha Kaew houses some excellent examples of the three Buddhist sculpture types common in Laos: "calling for rain", with hands straight at the sides; "offering protection", with palms stretched out in front; and "contemplating the Tree of Enlightenment", with hands crossed at the wrist in front.

A Buddhist monk prays with a couple at Wat Si Muang.

Ancient Buddha statue in Wat Si Saket, whose cloister wall niches reveal a multitude of miniature Buddhas.

The Patuxai, which means Gate of Triumph in Sanskrit.

North to Patuxai

Arrowing northeast from the Presidential Palace is **Lane Xang Avenue** ("Avenue de France" under the French), which runs past the **Talaat Sao** Ⓚ (Morning Market). The market, despite its name, is open daily from 7am to 5pm and is a maze of individually owned stalls selling everything from antique textiles and carvings to household appliances. You will probably see stalls selling tickets for the immensely popular National Lottery, which is a central preoccupation of Vientiane residents, many of whom will consult monks or nuns before choosing a lucky number. Next to the old market is the air-conditioned Talaat Sao Shopping Mall (www.talatsaomall.com), the only one of its kind in Laos.

Lane Xang Avenue ends at a traffic circle resembling the Etoile in Paris, at the centre of which stands **Patuxai** Ⓛ, Vientiane's own Arc de Triomphe. Patuxai (Victory Gate) was completed in 1969 in memory of the Lao killed in wars before the Communist revolution. It is also known as the "vertical runway", as the project was finished with cement paid for by the Americans and intended to be used for the construction of a new airport in Vientiane. Despite the French inspiration, uniquely Lao elements are evident: Buddhist imagery is present in the Lao-style mouldings, and the frescoes under the arches represent scenes from the *Ramayana*. Climb the winding staircase to the top of the monument for a panoramic view of the low-rise city (Mon–Fri 8am–4.30pm, Sat–Sun until 5pm).

That Luang – symbol of Laos

Around 2km (1.2 miles) northeast of Patuxai is the shining, 45-metre (146ft) **That Luang** Ⓜ (daily), the Great Sacred Stupa. It is a striking sight, and of great spiritual significance for the Lao people, considered the symbol of Lao independence and sovereignty ever since it was built in the mid-16th century. It is a strange and exotic structure, combining the features of a Buddhist temple with the mundane requirements of a fortress.

According to legend, That Luang was first established in the 4th century BC,

when five Lao monks who had been studying in India returned home bearing the breastbone of the Buddha, and a stupa was duly built over the sacred relic. It is commonly believed that this, the earliest stupa at That Luang, is enclosed within the present structure.

The second historic establishment of That Luang was undertaken by King Setthathirat the Great, who consolidated the move of the Lao capital from Luang Prabang to Vientiane begun by his father, King Phothisarat. Construction of the great stupa began in 1566, on the site of the former Khmer temple, and in subsequent years four smaller temples were built at the cardinal points around the central *that*.

Today the great edifice still retains a very fortress-like appearance. It is surrounded by a high-walled cloister, which is pierced by tiny windows, and access is by way of finely gilded red-lacquer doors which add to the impression of a medieval keep. Close up, however, the sacred character of the structure is unmistakable because of the abundant religious imagery. Naga serpents – those characteristic insignia of Theravada Buddhism – compete for space with gilded figurines of the Buddha and stylised lotus flowers. The cloister's tiny windows were added by Chao Anuvong as a defence against attack, but they were of little use during the Siamese, Burmese and Chinese invasions of the 18th and 19th centuries, which left That Luang in ruins. Serious restoration work didn't begin until the French initiated a project in the 1930s.

That Luang originally faced east, with its back to Vientiane (Buddhism divides the world between East, the sphere of illumination, and West, the sphere of inauspiciousness), but the restoration authorities failed to respect this orientation, so the temple now faces west. The surface of the stupa was regilded in 1995, the 20th anniversary of the founding of the Lao People's Democratic Republic.

Of the four temples that King Setthathirat originally had built to surround That Luang, only two remain: **Wat That Luang Neua** to the north and **Wat That Luang Tai** to the south; both are open daily (free).

Northern suburbs

Further north from That Luang is the **National Assembly** building, and beyond, on Phon Kheng Road, the **Unknown Soldiers Memorial**. This white stupa-like monument is dedicated to Pathet Lao soldiers who died during the Second Indochina War.

Phon Kheng Road takes you northeast from Patuxai to the **Kaysone Phomvihane Memorial and Museum** (Tue–Sun 8am–noon and 1–4pm), at Km 6. The exhibits detail Kaysone's childhood in Savannakhet province, his role in the Communist revolution, and his leadership of Lao PDR from 1975 until his death in 1992. Certainly the most interesting portion of the museum is the tour of Kaysone's private living quarters, a small house among a series of identical structures inside the compound, reminiscent of post-war suburban America (the museum is on the site of the former USAID/CIA compound).

That Luang, Vientiane's golden icon.

FRANCE ON THE MIDDLE MEKONG

The Gallic lifestyle influenced the Lao urban elite throughout the French colonial period, and has left its mark to this day.

One of the most pleasant surprises awaiting the visitor to Vientiane is the French cultural influence surviving in the city. It is a pleasure to enjoy a breakfast of croissants and *café au lait*. Lunch may well comprise freshly baked baguettes and pâté accompanied by a carafe of wine. In the evening, excellent French cuisine is available at upmarket restaurants, following years of socialist austerity.

This agreeable ambience aside, Vientiane's most notable memorial to the French influence must be its architecture. There are numerous small residences, and not a few mansions, built in the style of the former colonial power. Many of these may be found in the older part of the town, along the riverside appropriately designated Quai Fa Ngum. Here, as by the shaded boulevards in the vicinity of That Dam and along Lane Xang Avenue, the "Champs Élysées" of Vientiane, may be found fine examples of colonial French architecture, complete with shutters and red-tiled roofs, which would not be out of place in a French provincial city, such as Dijon or Tours. A decade or so ago, many of these former private residences were in stages of advanced decay, and some were clearly beyond saving. In recent years, however, many have been painstakingly restored – clearly, as the authorities came to realise the potential value to tourism of this unique architectural legacy, not to mention the inherent charm of the Lao capital, preservation rather than demolition became the order of the day.

Baguettes on sale in Vientiane – and across most of the country – are one of the most visible reminders of the French influence. Stock usually runs out by lunchtime.

The restored facade of the National Library in Vientiane, originally built in the colonial era as a police station.

French still appears alongside Lao on local letterboxes.

Le petit déjeuner – watch the world go by and start the day the French way with a (Lao) coffee and croissant at a Vientiane café.

THE FACE OF FRANCE IN LAOS

Born in France in 1847, Auguste Pavie was a French explorer and diplomat who almost single-handedly brought Laos under French control. Pavie had a gift for languages and learned to speak Vietnamese, Khmer, Thai and Lao. In 1886, he became the first French vice-consul in Luang Prabang, the Lao capital. During the next five years he travelled throughout northern Laos and gained the friendship of local rulers for France, frustrating Bangkok's attempts to bring the region fully under Siamese control. Arguing that the Lao states had been vassals of Vietnam and that France had succeeded to Vietnam's rights in Laos, Pavie justified regional military movements, provoking a crisis that resulted in Laos becoming a French protectorate in 1893.

...ne of the less attractive aspects of French colonisation: Lao ...rvée (unpaid) workers on road construction duties.

...familiar name for a tailor shop in Vientiane.

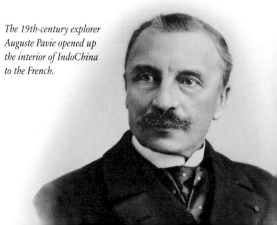

The 19th-century explorer Auguste Pavie opened up the interior of IndoChina to the French.

Bridge across the Nam Song at Vang Vieng.

VIENTIANE ENVIRONS

Beautiful river and lake scenery and a national park are some of the attractions within easy reach of the capital. Further north are the stunning landscapes and adventure sports of Vang Vieng.

Most visitors to Laos end up staying in **Vientiane (Viang-chan)** ❶ for only a few days, and relatively few visitors take time to explore the area around the city. This is a pity, as there is a great deal to see in the districts surrounding the capital; you don't have to go far from the capital to find beautiful natural areas and simple village life. Most of the attractions surrounding Vientiane lie along a loop just to its north; we will follow Route 13 northwards as far as Ang Nam Ngum, and then return to Vientiane in a southerly direction via Route 10. The final section of this chapter highlights the attractions of Vang Vieng on Route 13 north towards Luang Prabang. Vang Vieng is known for its beautiful scenery, "tubing" on the Nam Song River, and increasingly wild party life.

North to Ang Nam Ngum

About 25km (16 miles) north of Vientiane, just off the main road to Luang Prabang (Route 13), lies the **Nam Tok Tat Son** ❷ waterfall. Created by the construction of a dam in the 1970s, the "waterfall" is really a series of modest rapids. A recreational area with restaurants, picnic facilities and caged animals surrounds the falls. Walk away from the rest area for about 200 metres/ yds and you'll find a peaceful rock upon which sits a simple altar with primitive Buddhist statues; the shaded spot overlooks the surrounding forest.

More rewarding is the area near an incomplete temple, **Wat Lansoun** (free), 2km (1.2 miles) beyond Nam Tok Tat Son at the end of a dirt road. Too isolated to have resident monks, the temple sits upon a hill among age-ing Buddha images and caves. Some of the imposing rock formations are marked by Buddhist stele inscriptions. The panoramic view of the valley below is one of the most breathtaking in central Laos.

Main Attractions
Nam Tok Tat Son waterfall
Ang Nam Ngum lake
Phu Khao Khuai
Vang Vieng

Watering crops on the banks of the Mekong.

Continuing along Route 13 will bring you to the **Talaat Lak Haa-Sip Sawng** (Km 52 Market) in the village of Ban Lak Haa-Sip Sawng, a large daily market offering wild foods (including some rare and endangered species, much to the chagrin of environmental organisations working in Vientiane) and minority handicrafts, frequented by Hmong and other local ethnic minorities.

Further north, near the town of Phonsavang, is **Vang Sang** ❸ (free), or "Elephant Palace", a supposedly Mon sanctuary featuring 10 sculptures of the Buddha on cliffs. The site dates as far back as the 11th century, and may have been a stopover for Buddhist worshippers heading north from Mon-Khmer city-states in today's southern Laos. The name refers to an elephant graveyard that was once found nearby. Another small cluster of images can be found about 20km (13 miles) away from the main site.

Ang Nam Ngum ❹, about 90km (55 miles) from Vientiane, is a large reservoir created in 1972 when the Nam Ngum was dammed and the entire area flooded. The dam remains a symbol of development, generating enough electricity both for Vientiane and for export to Thailand. When the lake was created, 250 sq km (100 sq miles) of forest were submerged, although some areas of higher land remain visible as hundreds of small islands. Prostitutes, drug addicts and petty criminals were sent to the islands following the Communist takeover in 1975, and two – one for women and the other for men – are still used as prisons to this day.

To reach the reservoir, turn off Route 13 at the town of Phon Hong and head east to **Thalat**, where the central market – as at the Km 52 Market mentioned above – specialises in deer, rats and assorted insects for local consumption.

An easily arranged boat cruise from the main pier in **Na Keun**, beyond Thalat, will allow you to explore the lake and to view the beautiful scenery. Waterfront restaurants offer tasty lunches featuring fresh fish from the lake: grilled fish,

Logging trucks.

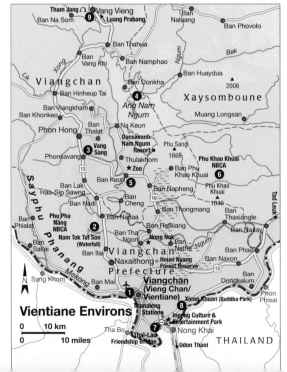

Vientiane Environs

fish *laap*, fish soup – all the dishes are generally excellent.

Most visitors come to Ang Nam Ngum on day trips, but there are a few guesthouses in the villages at the northern end, such as in Ban Thahua, which is on the main Route 13 north. There is also a resort – the **Dansavanh Nam Ngum Resort** (www.dansavanh.net; tel: 20-5827 6666) – on the southern shore of the lake for those with a larger budget. Built by Malaysian developers, this US$200 million casino and lakeside resort on Ang Nam Ngum offers hang-gliding, powerboat cruises, an "island floating shopping network", a golf course, a disco and, unusually, an insect museum. The Gaming Centre offers gamblers roulette, baccarat and blackjack as well as the usual slot machines. Most customers are from Thailand, China, Vietnam, Taiwan and Malaysia; Lao citizens are forbidden by law to gamble and may only enter the casino to work there. The resort can be reached by boat in about 20 minutes from the lakeside at Na Keun, but is more usually accessed by a small side road north of Highway 10 just beyond Ban Keun and Thulakhom Zoo.

Around Ang Nam Ngum Lake

Heading back southwards towards Vientiane from the reservoir on Route 10, you will soon come to **Ban Keun** ❺, a bustling town on the banks of the Nam Ngum, which means Silver Water. The remaining French colonial buildings and riverfront scenery are worth a short stroll, as is a visit to the local market place, which is quite different to the larger markets of Vientiane. Here you can see rural Laos at its most picturesque, though be warned that you may well see local "bush meat" for sale – wild animals such as deer, squirrel and pangolin are brought here to be sold as food.

Just beyond Ban Keun, about 60km (40 miles) from Vientiane, lies the **Thulakhom Inter Zoo**, a complex of animals kept in surprisingly humane conditions. The zoo, also known as the Vientiane Zoological Gardens or the national Lao Zoo, features tigers,

Sunset on the Nam Song River, Vang Vieng.

THE WINDING ROAD

It's a long and rather tortuous 168km (105-mile) journey between Vang Vieng and Luang Prabang. Closed for many years due to the insurgency from the Hmong rebels, the road is extremely winding, and if you suffer from car sickness it's best to stock up on motion-sickness pills. This area is the very heart of mountain Laos, with switchback roads leading over and past spectacular karst outcrops. There are many minority villages in the area, but few are as yet developed in any way, and there are few or no facilities for overnight stays. The small town of **Kasi**, 55km (35 miles) north of Vang Vieng, is certainly the best place to break for a lunch stop en route to Luang Prabang, but accommodation is basic at best, and it's best to press on to your destination.

An Indochinese tiger surveys his domain from the water.

Statue at Xieng Khuan.

sun bears, a white elephant, emus and camels. The zoo is currently being transformed – in partnership with the Laos Wildlife Friends Foundation of Thailand – into an animal rescue and education centre. Further along Route 10 is the beautiful **Nong Nok** (bird lake) at Ban Sivilay village. A seasonally flooded wetland, it is home to a great variety of birds – including the Chinese pond heron, black crowned night heron, common kingfisher, cattle egret and little egret. In the latter stages of the dry season more than 1,200 whistling teal roost in the wetland. The lake is used by the villagers for commercial fish-breeding; fish are released annually during the wet season, and then from February to April they are caught and sold to nearby communities and in Vientiane. Nong Nok is a good example of a community-managed ecosystem, and the villagers work to maintain an ecological balance: regular guards ensure that birds are not killed and fish are not poached. Income from fish is evenly distributed in the village, which now has more than 225 shareholding householders.

At the moment there are very limited tourist facilities at Nong Nok, but the Lao government has plans, dependent on outside funding, to improve transportation to the lake and to develop the area as an ecotourism site. The plans involve building birdwatching hides, a guard facility and a parking area. It's already possible to camp at a government-approved site by the lake.

Mountain reserve

Further south along Route 10 is the turning for the conservation area of **Phu Khao Khuai** (Water Buffalo Mountain) ❻, a pine-forested plateau surrounded by 2,000-metre (6,500ft) peaks. One of the country's National Biodiversity Conservation Areas (NBCA), the 2,000-sq-km (770-sq-mile) Phu Khao Khuai is rich in wildlife, with elephants, black bears, tigers and clouded leopards. Seventeen NBCAs, totalling 24,600 sq km (9,500 sq miles), or about 10 percent of the country, were designated by the Lao government in 1993. While this marked a positive step forward for

environmental protection in Laos, the familiar story of corruption, lax enforcement and inadequate planning and management have combined to plague the NBCA initiative.

Inside the reserve there is a pleasant picnic area by the Nam Ngum from which you can take short nature walks, while a telecommunications centre on the top of the mountain provides a good view of Vientiane and the surrounding districts. In the years following the Communist victory in 1975, foreigners were not allowed into this area as it contained a military base – the old airstrip is still visible today. Phu Khao Khuai offers a cool retreat from the heat of Vientiane during the hot season; at other times of the year it can be cold and misty, so it is a good idea to bring extra clothing with you for the evenings. Visitor facilities are lacking, so it is also advisable to bring food with you.

Back on Route 10, you will cross a small toll bridge at the village of **Tha Ngon**. Just under the bridge are a number of floating restaurants where you can sit and watch the Nam Ngum flow past as you eat some of the freshest fish and stickiest rice in the area.

One of the best-kept secrets in the vicinity of Vientiane is the **Houei Nyang** forest reserve, just off Route 10 about 20km (12 miles) from the centre of the city. The field centre was built with funding from the Swedish government, and offers an English-language guide to the Mai Te Kha nature trail. The nature walk lasts about two hours, leading you past numbered points of interest described in the trail guide. You won't find any large animals in Houei Nyang, but smaller species such as mouse deer, porcupines and wild cats thrive here (although they are difficult to see). A variety of birds and beautiful butterflies can easily be seen, however (and, in the case of the former, heard). The reserve is probably of greatest interest to plant-lovers – the forest has experienced considerable disturbance from agriculture and other human involvement over the years, and thus provides opportunities for a good look at the stages in the development of an old-growth forest.

Go for a guided jungle trek on Phu Khao Khuai for a chance to spot wildlife such as the rare clouded leopard.

Containers for the ubiquitous Lao sticky rice are fashioned from bamboo.

Along the Mekong

If you are only in Vientiane for a short while, it is still possible to make afternoon or day trips just outside the city to other attractions. South of the city centre, Tha Deua Road runs alongside the Mekong and leads to the **Inpeng Culture & Entertainment Park** (daily 8am–5pm), at Km 18 (about 2km/1.2 miles before the Friendship Bridge). This large water park has swimming pools, restaurants, cafes and souvenir shops, as well as a museum and the Ethnic Cultural Park, featuring mock houses in the style of the Lao Loum, Lao Theung and Lao Soung ethnic groups. The concrete structures are not at all authentic, but the place gives you some idea of the way in which the current government is attempting to combine the diverse ethnic groups of Laos into a unified Lao people.

Beyond the Inpeng Culture and Entertainment Park, still on Tha Deua Road, is the **Thai–Lao Friendship Bridge ❼**. Completed in 1994 at a cost of about US$30 million, the project was funded by the Australian government. Some 1,240 metres (0.7 miles) long, it connects Nong Khai in Thailand to Vientiane, and is symbolic of the opening of Laos to outside (especially Thai) influences. A railway line across the bridge ends at Thanaleng Railway Station, Dongphosy Village, just 20km (12.5 miles) east of Vientiane. Plans to extend the line to Vientiane were abandoned in 2010.

Prior to 1994 there were no bridges across the Mekong between Laos and Thailand; a second bridge was built near Savannakhet in 2006, and a third opened between Thakek and Nakhon Phanom some 100km (60 miles) further north in 2011. A fourth Thai–Lao Friendship Bridge between Chiang Khong in Thailand's northernmost Chiang Rai Province and Ban Houaxay in Laos was opened in late 2013 and provides a direct road link across Laos between Thailand and China via the border crossing at Boten.

Still further along Tha Deua Road, 3km (2 miles) east of the bridge, is the odd yet interesting **Xieng Khuan ❽**, or Buddha Park (daily 8am–5pm), which features a Tim Burton-esque

More outsize creations at Xieng Khuan.

collection of Buddhist and Hindu sculptures built in 1958. The park was constructed by Bunleua Sulitat, a priest-shaman who merged Hindu and Buddhist traditions to develop quite a following in Laos and northeastern Thailand; he left Vientiane in 1975 and moved across the river to Nong Khai, where he built a second Buddha Park. The oversized concrete statues – images of Shiva, Vishnu, Buddha and even a few secular Lao figures – give the place an air of fantasy which is emphasised by the massive pumpkin-shaped structure that dominates the park. This has three levels, representing hell, earth and heaven, and there is a good view from the very top, which is reached by a spiral staircase. Xieng Khuan is now a popular public park, complete with riverfront food stalls, and the whole place makes an enjoyable half-day out of town, though the atmosphere is more kitsch than religious to most visitors.

Vang Vieng

Located close to the midway point between Vientiane (156km/116 miles south) and Luang Prabang (168km/ 105 miles north), the tiny settlement of **Vang Vieng** ❾ is a convenient place to break the journey between these two towns in either direction. Set by the banks of the Nam Song, amidst a startlingly beautiful natural terrain of limestone karsts, Vang Vieng was once a little backpacker haven; a relatively inexpensive, relaxed destination, with all the usual budget travel-ler restaurants and bars. Over time, Vang Vieng emerged as Laos's most popular, most accessible and most reasonably priced adventure destination, with tubing and kayaking on the river, caving in the surrounding hills, and climbing on the precipitous limestone karst faces. Other popular activities include mountain biking, trekking, rafting and freshwater swimming in the Nam Song River.

As a result of its popularity, Vang Vieng gradually attracted an increasing number of backpacker-oriented restaurants and bars, serving all the usual budget travel dishes, from banana pancakes and fruit smoothies to Mexican chilli con carne

TIP

Head out west on a hire bike or motorbike to Ban Na Som and several other tiny villages in the heart of the karst country. It's just a half-day's excursion from Vang Vieng, and you can be back in town for *laap*, pizza or burritos by dusk.

The forests and grasslands of Laos are home to dozens of species of butterfly, with new species being discovered each year.

– in addition to hallucinogenic magic mushrooms and marijuana-laced pizzas. Unfortunately, this led to the Vang Vieng becoming a hotspot for drugs, drink and debauchery. Foreign embassies begun recognising it as an increasingly dangerous place, with a disturbing number of drunk or high young visitors diving into the river, only to hit the rocks or drown. Following a series of tragic deaths during 2011 and 2012, and the public outcry that followed, the Lao government finally began to act, shutting down the riverside rave bars, strictly enforcing the drug laws and removing the most dangerous river slides.

Over the next couple of years, the rave scene almost entirely dried up and Vang Vieng's tarnished reputation slowly began to recover. New bungalows and boutique hotels have been constructed, encouraging many families and cultured visitors, including many Koreans, Chinese and outdoor pursuit enthusiasts to visit the town. The new-look, new-feel Vang Vieng is well worth a visit for its natural beauty alone.

The many caves around Vang Vieng are spectacular, vast and filled with wildlife of all kinds, from swiftlets and bats to centipedes and blind fish. At the same time they remain largely unexplored, often slippery, dank, dark – and dangerous. It's better to explore these caverns in a group, preferably with a guide, and definitely carrying a flashlight.

For those not interested in caving or kayaking, Vang Vieng also has its share of cultural attractions too. There are three small temples in the town which are worth visiting, as well as two Hmong villages, the resettled inhabitants of which provide a colourful addition to Vang Vieng market.

About 40km (25 miles) north of Kasi on the road between Vang Vieng and Luang Prabang, **Muang Phu Khoun** is a rather melancholy reminder of the former French presence in colonial Laos. Today there is little to see beyond a few shophouses and a small hotel – but in times past this was an isolated but important French garrison on the key route between the administrative and royal capitals.

Hanging out near Vang Vieng.

Cycling in Laos

Laos has plenty to draw the cyclist, from world-famous heritage sites to its caves and jungles. Its quiet roads and friendly welcome make Laos an exciting destination for cycle touring.

Cyclists in Laos have many options open to them; there are the hills and mountains of north Laos or the laid-back charms of the flat south. The main transport spine, Route 13, runs north to south and covers the full length of the country.

A major draw for cyclists to Laos is the amount of accommodation that has become available in recent years. Every small town now has a guesthouse, making it easier for cyclists to negotiate the roads of Laos without heavy camping equipment. Where accommodation is not available, cyclists have found local homestays and temples are very happy to put up a weary traveller, thus enhancing the cultural experience.

Cyclists will find the north challenging for its topology, while the south will be more challenging for the distance covered between towns (and accommodation), and the country in general will be challenging on account of its heat. Laos is a popular place to cycle because of its variety and its relative freedom.

When cyclists come to Laos, there are two major starting points, and a whole host of minor ones. Most begin their journeys in Vientiane or Luang Prabang. Vientiane is situated close to Thailand and its transport network, allowing easy access to Laos and its mysterious tourist delights. Many cyclists fly into Bangkok and catch the train up to Nong Khai and enter Laos over the Friendship Bridge. There is a simple 20km (12.5-mile) cycle into the heart of Vientiane and the gateway to the north and south of Laos. For Luang Prabang, cyclists can either choose to fly in or take the boat down the Mekong from the Chiang Khong/Huay Xai border point.

Popular routes

To cycle all the roads and see all the sights of Laos would potentially take the cycle tourist many months; however, most cyclists choose to see as much as possible in a few weeks or a month. There are a number of main routes to choose from that can be taken to see the major highlights on offer.

Probably the most popular route and one of the shorter journeys in Laos is the road between Luang Prabang and Vientiane. This is a short trip of between 4 and 5 days; however, it does offer some of the best combinations of delights that Laos has to offer the cyclist. From the UN-sponsored religious chic of Luang Prabang's old town and the hills of Northern Laos, to the flat plains and quiet charms of Vientiane and its surroundings, this route dominates as a classic. This route is principally responsible for the explosion in the numbers of cyclists over the last 10 years.

Other popular routes in the country include the east-to-west route through Northern Laos. The starting point is usually Vietnam and there is a choice of roads through some of the most glorious hills that Southeast Asia has to offer. Additionally, this route offers the wonder of Phonsavan and the Plain of Jars, the caves at Vieng Xai and the trekking delights of the far north in Pongsali.

The final main route is the ride through the south. Leaving from Vientiane, cyclists head down Route 13 alongside the Mekong, taking in the flat plains of Southern Laos and the pleasures of the Bolaven Plateau, eventually ending up at the Laos/ Cambodia border.

A tour group of mountain bikers cycle along a dirt road beside the Mekong River.

Monks pay a visit to the Pak Ou caves.

LUANG PRABANG

The temples and culture of Luang Prabang,
capital of Laos and seat of the monarchy until
the 16th century, have been so well preserved
that the city is now a World Heritage Site.

With its splendid natural setting amid forested hills at the confluence of the Mekong and Nam Khan rivers, and a long, illustrious history as a royal capital, **Luang Prabang** ❶ (Louangphabang) is one of the most intriguing, magical and romantic cities in Asia. Added to Unesco's World Heritage List in 1995, the city is filled with fine old temples, and its quiet streets are lined with handsome colonial buildings.

For centuries before the city was founded, the area around played host to various Thai–Lao principalities in the valleys of the Mekong, Khan, Ou and Xuang rivers. In 1353 King Fa Ngum consolidated the first Lao Kingdom, Lan Xang (see page 49), on the site of present-day Luang Prabang. At the time the city was known as Xawa, possibly a local form of Java, but it was soon renamed Meuang Xieng Thong (Gold City District). A little later, Fa Ngum received from the Khmer sovereign the gift of a Sinhalese Buddha image called Pha Bang, from which the city's modern name derives.

Two centuries later, King Phothisarat moved the capital of Lan Xang to Vientiane, but Luang Prabang nonetheless remained the royal heart of the kingdom. After the collapse of Lan Xang in 1694 an independent kingdom was established in Luang Prabang, which co-existed with kingdoms based in Vientiane and Champasak further south. Kings ruled Luang Prabang until the monarchy was officially dissolved by the Pathet Lao in 1975, though they were at various times forced to pay tribute to the Siamese and the Vietnamese and, later, to submit authority to the French. The last king and queen were imprisoned in a cave in the northeast of the country, where they died in the early 1980s.

Main Attractions

Royal Palace Museum
Mount Phu Si
Wat Xieng Thong
Mekong waterside
    restaurants and bars
Wat Paa Phon Phao
Pak Ou caves

That Makmo stupa.

The Royal Palace Museum

In the centre of the city, between Mount Phu Si and the Mekong, is the **Royal Palace Museum**  (Haw Kham; Thanon Sisavangvong; Wed–Mon 8–11am and 1.30–4pm), which offers an insight into the history of the region. The palace was constructed from 1904 as the residence of King Sisavang Vong, and is a pleasing mix of classical Lao and French styles, cruciform in layout and mounted on a multi-tiered platform. In a room at the front of the building is the museum's prize, the famed Pha Bang Buddha image after which the city is named. The 83cm (32-inch) -tall image, in the attitude of Abhayamudra, or "dispelling fear", is almost pure gold. Legend says that it originated in Sri Lanka in the 1st century AD; it was presented to the Khmers, who gave it to King Fa Ngum. The image was twice seized by the Siamese before finally being returned to Laos in 1867.

The Pha Bang Buddha shares a room with several beautifully embroidered silk screens and engraved

Lavish detail on the facade of the Royal Palace Museum.

Family posing on top of Mount Phu Si.

elephant tusks, while the rest of the museum houses a fairly substantial collection of regalia, portraits, diplomatic gifts and art treasures, friezes, murals and mosaics.

In the southeastern area of the same compound is the **Royal Ballet Theatre**, formerly a palace building. Performances by local dancers are scheduled every Monday, Wednesday, Friday and Saturday at 6pm, and include a traditional ballet performance of an extract from *Phra Lak Phra Ram* (the Lao version of the Indian epic *Ramayana*). Tickets are available at the door on the evenings of the performances.

To the southwest of the Royal Palace is **Wat Mai Suwannaphumaham** ❸ (Thanon Sisavangvong; daily 8am–5pm). Dating from the early 19th century, this temple was once the residence of the Sangkhalat, the supreme patriarch of Buddhism in Laos. The *sim* is wooden, with a five-tiered roof in classic Luang Prabang style (see page 85). The main attraction is the gilded walls of the front veranda, the designs of which recount scenes from the *Ramayana* and the Buddha's penultimate incarnation. For the first half of the 20th century the Pha Bang was housed inside, and it is still put on display here during the Lao New Year celebrations. Within the compound are two longboats, kept in their own shelter, which play a part in the celebrations at New Year.

Mount Phu Si

On the other side of Thanon Sisavangvong rises **Mount Phu Si**, the rocky 100-metre (330ft) hill that dominates the centre of Luang Prabang. At its foot stands **Wat Paa Huak** ❻ (daily 8am–5pm), which features well-preserved 19th-century murals showing Mekong scenes. From this temple 328 steps wind up the forested slopes to the 24-metre (79ft) **That Chom Si** on the summit, which has an impressive gilded stupa in classical Lao form,

as well as a rusting anti-aircraft gun. There are magnificent views across the ancient city, best at sunset, with the Mekong and Nam Khan rivers encircling the historic Unesco-protected peninsula that lies at the heart of old Luang Prabang.

The path continues down the other side of Phu Si to **Wat Tham Phu Si**, a cave shrine housing a Buddha image of wide girth, in the style known locally as *Pha Kachai*. Close by the main road is **Wat Pha Phutthabaat** ❶ (free), a temple containing a 3-metre (10ft) Buddha footprint dating from the late 14th century.

Along the peninsula

Heading northeast along Thanon Sisavangvong from the foot of Phu Si towards the confluence of the Nam Khan and the Mekong you pass a string of glittering temples, interspersed with evocative colonial buildings. **Wat Paa Phai** (Bamboo Forest Temple; daily; free) on the left is noteworthy for its 100-year-old fresco and carved wooden facade depicting secular Lao scenes. Further along the street, also on the left, is **Wat Saen** ❸ (One Hundred Thousand Temple; daily; free), whose name refers to the value of the donation with which it was constructed. This temple is different in style from most others in Luang Prabang, and the trained eye will immediately identify it as central Thai in style. The *sim* was originally constructed in 1718 but was restored twice in the 20th century.

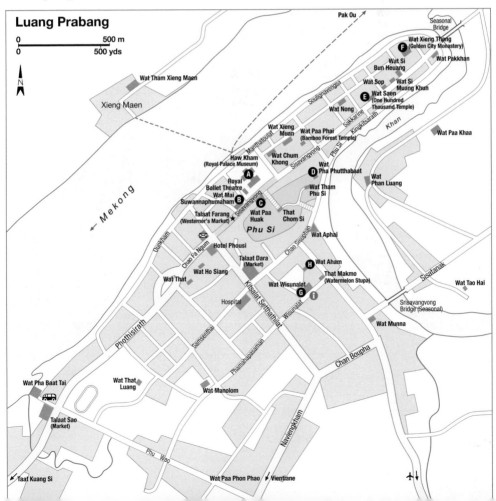

SHOP

Every afternoon and evening, between about 4pm and 10.30pm, the southwest part of Sisavangvong Road and its extension towards Chao Fa Ngum set up shop as Luang Prabang's "night market", also styled Talaat Farang or the "Westerners' Market" by the locals. This is *the* place to go to buy local handicrafts of all kinds, from Hmong woven clothing, through Lao lanterns and paintings, to just about anything. Iluminated by street lights and gas lanterns, this is a quiet and conservative market, but you should still expect to bargain hard.

Shopfront in Luang Prabang.

Wat Xieng Thong

Close to the tip of the peninsula, on the banks of the Mekong, reminding the visitor of the importance of river transport in Laos, is Luang Prabang's most renowned temple, **Wat Xieng Thong** ➏ (Golden City Monastery; Thanon Sakkarine; daily 8am–5pm). This temple, with its low sweeping roofs epitomising the classic Luang Prabang style, was built in 1560 by King Setthathirat (1548–71) and was patronised by the monarchy right up until 1975. Inside the *sim* the eight thick supporting pillars, richly stencilled in gold, guide the eye to the serene golden Buddha images at the rear, and upwards to the roof, which is covered in *dhamma* wheels. On the outside of the *sim*, at the back, is an elaborate mosaic of the Tree of Life set against a deep red background. Throughout, the combination of splendid gold and deep red gives this temple a captivatingly regal atmosphere.

Adjacent to the *sim* is a smaller building, dubbed by the French *La Chapelle Rouge*, containing a unique reclining Buddha figure. What makes the image so unusual is the Lao proportions, especially the robe curling outwards at the ankles, and the graceful position of the hand supporting the head. This figure was displayed at the Paris Exhibition in 1931, but happily returned to Luang Prabang in 1964 after several decades in Vientiane. The chapel itself is exquisitely decorated. On the outside of the rear wall is a mosaic showing rural Lao village life, executed in the 1950s in celebration of two and a half millennia since the Buddha's attainment of Nirvana.

Also in the Xieng Thong compound are various monks' quarters, reliquary stupas and a boat shelter. Close to the east gate is a building housing the royal funeral carriage; the interior decoration is only half-finished, as work ceased after the Communist victory in 1975.

It is a very pleasant stroll back towards the Royal Palace along the Mekong. Nothing appears to have changed in the past 30 years, nor is it likely to under the present Unesco

regulations. Boutique restaurants have largely replaced the scruffy old sticky-rice places, while the colonial-style buildings have been painstakingly restored or rebuilt.

Southeast of Phu Si

Back in the vicinity of Mount Phu Si, another temple of note is **Wat Wisunalat G** (Wat Vixoun; Thanon Wisunalat; daily 8am–5pm; voluntary donation). Built by King Wisunalat (1501–20) between 1512 and 1513, this is the oldest temple in the city still in use. The *sim*, rebuilt a decade after the original wooden structure was destroyed by fire in 1887, is unique in style, with a front roof sloping down over the terrace. Sketches by Louis Delaporte of the original building exist from the 1860s, and confirm what a later visitor wrote: "[Wat] Visunalat is shaped like a boat, the same shape that Orientals give to their coffins. The wooden walls are sculpted with extreme refinement and delicacy." Though the wood has gone, the builders who performed the

restoration attempted to capture the shapes of the original wood in the stucco work. Inside is an impressive collection of Buddhist sculpture.

In the temple grounds is That Pathum, or Lotus Stupa, which is affectionately referred to as That Makmo, or Watermelon Stupa, and which is just as distinctive as the temple itself. The stupa is over 30 metres (100ft) high, and was constructed in 1503–4, at which time it was filled with small, precious Buddha images. Many of these were stolen by Chin Haw marauders from Yunnan in the 19th century – the rest are now safely on display in the Royal Palace Museum.

Next to Wat Wisunalat is the peaceful **Wat Aham H** (daily 8am–5pm; voluntary donation), formerly – before Wat Mai took the honour – the residence of the supreme patriarch of Buddhism in Laos. The temple's red facade combines with striking green *yak* temple guardians and mildewed stupas to create an atmosphere of extreme tranquillity. The temple rarely has many visitors, other than those

Mosaic detail in the Red Chapel of Wat Xieng Thong.

Inside the Wat Xieng Thong compound.

quietly making offerings at an important shrine at the base of the two large old pipal trees.

Outside town

Across the Mekong from Luang Prabang, in Xieng Maen district, are no fewer than four more temples set in beautiful surroundings. Boats depart from the pier behind the Royal Palace, or you can charter a vessel from the pier 500 metres (yards) further north. **Wat Tham Xieng Maen** ❷ is situated in a 100-metre (330ft) -deep cave. This is generally kept locked, but the keys are held at nearby Wat Long Khun, the former retreat of kings awaiting their coronation. A small donation is requested for access to the cave temple.

Close to the southern edge of the city is a forest retreat, **Wat Paa Phon Phao** ❸, comprising a three-floor pagoda (daily 8–10am and 1–4.30pm; voluntary donation), complete with an external terrace near the top which affords excellent views of the surrounding countryside. The *chedi* is a popular destination for locals and visitors alike.

One of the royal guardian deities, or devata luang, of Luang Prabang.

Further out, about 4km (2.5 miles) beyond the airport, is the Tai Lü village of **Ban Phanom** ❹, renowned as a silk- and cotton-weaving village. At weekends a small market is set up for those interested in seeing the full range of fabrics produced. There are also a number of well-stocked shops that open on a daily basis. All weaving and dyeing is done by hand using traditional techniques, a fascinating process to watch. In the vicinity, a few kilometres along the river, is the tomb of Henri Mouhot, the French explorer who took the credit for "discovering" Angkor Wat in 1860. He died of malaria in Luang Prabang in 1861, though his tomb was not rediscovered until 1990.

A two-hour (by long-tail boat), 25km (15-mile) journey upriver from Luang Prabang is the confluence of the Mekong and the Nam Ou. Opposite the mouth of the Nam Ou, in the side of a large limestone cliff, are the **Pak Ou caves** ❺ (daily). Legend maintains that King Setthathirat discovered these two caves in the 16th century, and they

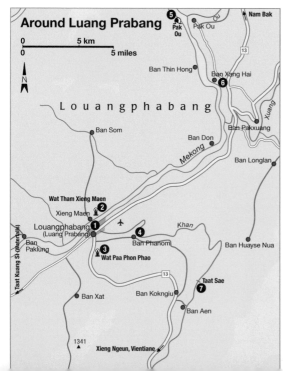

Around Luang Prabang

0   5 km
0   5 miles
N

❺ Pak Ou   Pak Ou   Nam Bak
13
Ban Thin Hong   Ban Xang Hai ❻

L o u a n g p h a b a n g

Ban Som   Ban Pakxuang
Ban Don
Mekong   Ban Longlan

Wat Tham Xieng Maen
Xieng Maen ❷
Louangphabang ❶
(Luang Prabang)   Khan
Ban Paklung   Ban Phanom ❹   Ban Huayse Nua
❸ Wat Paa Phon Phao
Taat Kuang Si (Waterfalls)
13   Taat Sae ❼
Ban Xat   Ban Kokngiu
Ban Aen
1341 ▲   Xieng Ngeun, Vientiane

have been venerated ever since. Both caves are full of Buddha images, some of venerable age. The lower of the two caves, Tham Ting, is easily accessible from the river. The upper cave, Tham Phum, is reached by a staircase, and is considerably deeper, requiring a torch for full exploration. There is a pleasant shelter between the two caves, an ideal spot for a picnic lunch.

On the way to Pak Ou, boats will stop by request at **Ban Xang Hai** ❻ (Jar-Maker Village), named after the village's former main industry. Jars still abound, but they are made elsewhere, and the village devotes itself to producing *lao-lao*, the local moonshine rice spirit. Archaeologists digging around the village have unearthed jars dating back more than 2,000 years. Opposite, at Ban Thin Hong, close to Pak Ou village, recent excavations have uncovered even earlier artefacts – tools, pottery and fabrics – around 8,000 years old. As yet the site hasn't been developed as a tourist attraction.

Several waterfalls are in the vicinity of Luang Prabang which can make for attractive half-day or day excursions, perhaps combined with stops in some rural villages along the way. About 30km (20 miles) south of the town are the multi-tiered **Kuang Si Waterfalls**, replete with beguiling limestone formations and crystal-clear pools. Food vendors keep most of the local visitors at the lower level of the falls, which can be very crowded during holidays. Up a trail to the left of the lower cascade is a second fall with a pool which makes for good swimming and is generally quieter. The trail continues to the top of the falls, though after rain it can be dangerously slippery.

Taat Sae ❼, also south of town, is closer to the city (15km/9 miles away), and hence more crowded at weekends. The falls here have more pools and shorter drops. They can be reached by boat from the delightful village of Ban Aen on the Nam Khan.

Festivals in Luang Prabang

Because of Luang Prabang's long status as the chief royal city of Laos – a status surpassing that of the less princely cities of Vientiane and Champasak – it is richly associated with festivals. The re-emergence of festivals in recent years, after a period of decline, is both a result of Unesco World Heritage Site status, and because the Lao authorities are keenly aware of the potential appeal such traditions can bring to the expanding tourist market. It is also explained by the simple fact that the Lao people delight in festivals and festivities.

The most exciting event is the **Lao New Year** (Boun Pi Mai), celebrated each April full moon to mark the beginning of the agricultural year. In times past, celebrations lasted for around three weeks as the entire population of the city indulged in an apparently endless round of ceremonies, rituals, games and processions. These days the New Year is celebrated with great vigour all over Laos, but most extensively at Luang Prabang. Boat races are held on the Mekong, and much water is thrown and poured over the celebrants.

Perhaps the most remarkable sight to be seen in Luang Prabang is the early morning sai baat, when devout citizens (and foreign photographers) gather at dawn to greet lines of saffron-clad monks receiving their alms. Lines of as many as 400 monks wend their way around the narrow streets on a daily basis.

Tthe multi-tiered Kuang Si Waterfalls.

Pedal power.

NORTHEASTERN LAOS

One of the most memorable sights in Laos, the ancient Plain of Jars, brings tourists to the far-flung northeast of the country. Other highlights include the secret caves of Vieng Xai.

The northeastern provinces of Xieng Khuang and Hua Phan owe much of their history and character to their proximity to Laos's eastern neighbour, Vietnam; indeed, both of these provinces have existed more often as independent statelets, or vassal states, of Vietnam than as part of a Lao political entity. In the post-colonial era the Pathet Lao forces chose the area as their headquarters for its close strategic position to their North Vietnamese allies. This attracted the attention of the Americans, who pounded both provinces from their B-52s during the Vietnam War, obliterating dozens of towns and villages and forcing the population, both military and civilian, to make their homes in the region's plentiful caves. It should be noted that the North Vietnamese also took part in the destruction, attacking areas under control of the royalist forces with heavy artillery.

Although the scars of war remain, northeastern Laos has much to offer the visitor. The local people have put the past behind them and bear no ill will to foreigners. Fascinating – and as yet not fully explained – archaeological sites, rugged mountainous terrain (particularly in Hua Phan province), a relatively benign climate and a plethora of ethnic minorities

make this remote, sparsely populated region well worth a visit.

Exploring the northeast

The following pages take the reader from Phonsavan, the capital of Xieng Khuang province, to Sam Neua, the capital of Hua Phan province, and to the limestone mountains and caves beyond.

Lao Airlines operate regular flights between Vientiane and Xieng Khuang, and sometimes schedule flights between Luang Prabang and Xieng Khuang as well, especially during the

Main Attractions

Plain of Jars
Muang Khun
Nam Ngum River springs
Suan Hin
Sam Neua market
Vieng Xai caves

Bomb cases from the war are scattered throughout the region.

high seasons. Their flight schedule changes frequently, so it is necessary to check prior to travelling (www.laoairlines.com). Travel by land to Xieng Khuang is also possible via Route 13 and the now-sealed Route 7. Daily buses from Vientiane take around 11 hours to reach Phonsavan, while buses from Luang Prabang take about 10 hours. Vang Vieng is 6 hours away. Sam Neua is a further 8–10 hours from Phonsavan.

Those with less time and/or less inclination to endure long journeys on bone-shaking buses should take one of the flights that operate most days from Vientiane or Luang Prabang to Phonsavan, travel by land from there to Hua Phan province, enjoying the various sights en route, and return to Vientiane by air. For the hardy, and those not wishing to double back to Vientiane, fly into Sam Neua, then travel by land to Phonsavan.

Xieng Khuang province

Home to a proud and independent people, Xieng Khuang province has often been something of a battleground. This was possibly due to its strategic location equidistant between the Lao and Vietnamese capital cities, or to its agriculturally fertile, temperate plain. Attempts to exist as an independent state have largely failed, and although it was only briefly subsumed into the Lao Kingdom of Lan Xang (see page 49), the region has spent long periods under Siamese and Vietnamese control. Indeed, during the 1830s it was formally a part of Vietnam, and the local inhabitants were forced to dress and behave according to Vietnamese custom.

In the centre of the province, the present-day provincial hub, **Phonsavan ❶**, was established after the former capital (which was called Xieng Khuang), located to the southeast, was obliterated during the Vietnam War (it has now been rebuilt and renamed Muang Khun). With a large number of bland modern buildings housing

FACT

Travellers who wish to break their journey between Vientiane or Luang Prabang and the northeast can do so at Muang Phu Khoun, the town at the point where Route 7 turns off from the main north–south Route 13. Muang Phu Khoun is the site of a former French garrison and its strategic location was constantly fought over during the Second Indochina War. Alternatively, for those coming from Vientiane, the backpacker centre of Vang Vieng makes a good stopover

The origin of the huge jars on the Plain of Jars remains a subject of debate among archaeologists.

At Muang Khun, the ravages of war are plain to see.

a rapidly expanding population (now exceeding 37,000), it is not the most attractive place in Laos; nonetheless, there are some reasonable hotels, and its proximity to some of the Plain of Jars sites makes it a good base for exploring the region.

A large market in the middle of town offers tribal handicrafts as well as the standard range of goods that sustains the local population. Other handicraft shops on the main street of Phonsavan offer interesting local textiles and silver wares. Recently, due to increased trade with nearby Vietnam, Vietnamese ceramics, woodcarvings, reproduction opium pipes and even *non la* conical hats have also appeared for sale.

The Plain of Jars

The **Plain of Jars** ❷ is Xieng Khuang's major attraction. Huge stone jar-shaped vessels are scattered over a dozen locations on the lonely plateau around Phonsavan, fascinating and mysterious. Key questions remain unanswered. What exactly are these ancient megaliths? Who

constructed them? When did they build them, and why?

Three major sites are easily accessible from Phonsavan, and have been cleared of unexploded American bombs (UXO), although it's still best to stay on the main paths. **Site 1** or **Thong Hai Hin** (Stone Jar Plain) is located 15km (9 miles) southwest of Phonsavan (open daily). This site has the biggest collection of jars, numbering over 250, and also the largest jar, which according to local lore is the victory cup of the legendary Lao king Khun Jeuam, who is said to have liberated the local people from an oppressive ruler. On nearby hillsides are odd bottle-shaped excavations; the locals use these as bird traps. Although the site is impressive, the presence of a nearby Lao air force base and some buildings erected for the visit of Thailand's crown prince a decade or so back detract from the overall atmosphere.

Another jar site, known locally as **Hai Hin Phu Salato** (open daily), or **Site 2**, is located 25km (16 miles) south of Phonsavan. Here about 100

jars are spread across two adjacent hillsides. The view from the top is worth the short climb.

The most attractive site is a further 10km (6 miles) south from Site 2, and is called **Hai Hin Laat Khai** (open daily), or **Site 3**. Here about 150 jars are located on top of a small hill from which one can enjoy great views not only of the surrounding plains, but also of the relatively prosperous farming community of Ban Sieng Dee, set on an adjacent hillside. This Lao village, another 2km (1.2-mile) walk from the jar site, has a small Buddhist temple and visitors are welcome. (For more information on the Plain of Jars, see page 144.)

Time permitting, you could also visit old Xieng Khuang, now known as **Muang Khun ❸**, located 30km (18 miles) southeast of Phonsavan, about 10km (6 miles) beyond Site 3. This town was once a royal capital, the centre of the Phuan Kingdom. This period ended when Vietnamese invaders abducted the king, Chao Noi Muang Phuan, in the mid-19th century. The town was heavily bombed during the war and its once beautiful temples pulverised (see panel). The palace of the French legation, though badly damaged by the bombs, still stands. The authorities' decision to relocate the provincial capital, and leave the destruction visible, makes Muang Khun a memorable but painful place to visit.

East to the Vietnam border

The comparatively well-surfaced Route 7 runs east from Phonsavan to the market town of **Nong Haet** and the border with Vietnam, where the crossing is open to international travellers. En route you can visit a variety of local attractions, each of which, in its own way, offers an insight into the history and everyday life of the Xieng Khuang region.

About 25km (15 miles) east of Phonsavan, the Nam Ngum River begins its journey south to the Ang Nam Ngum (see page 118). Known as **Nong Pet**, this tranquil spring is a pleasant picnic or swimming spot. A few kilometres further, on the south side of Route 7, is **Baw Noi**, a hot mineral spring which

TIP

If you plan to visit only Site 1 on the Plain of Jars, a jumbo (motorised trishaw) chartered in Phonsavan will suffice, but for visiting all three sites hardier transport, for example a jeep, is recommended. Any of the hotels or travel agencies in Phonsavan can make the necessary arrangements. Hmong villages are located in the vicinity of Phonsavan and can be included in the itinerary.

Overgrown temple ruins at Muang Khun.

THE LOST TEMPLES

Before the destructive bombing of the Vietnam War, the northeastern region boasted its own unique and beautiful temple architecture, generally called the "Xieng Khuang style". Xieng Khuang temples had sweeping, low-eaved, single-tiered roofs with gracefully curved pediments. Unfortunately, almost every temple in the region was destroyed during the aerial onslaught, along with just about all of the secular buildings in Xieng Khuang town (now Muang Khun). Fortunately a few examples of Xieng Khuang temple style have managed to survive, most notably at Wat Xieng Muang in Luang Prabang, as well as in French colonial photographs and architectural drawings. Hopefully in future, as both Laos and Xieng Khuang develop, some of these lost temples can be recreated from these examples.

The ubiquitous two-stroke motorbike, the main form of transport throughout the length and breadth of Laos.

Children supervising a grazing buffalo.

makes another pleasant spot for a dip – especially when the weather is cool. A further 5km (3 miles) brings you to the turn-off for **Baw Yai ④** (open daily), another mineral spring, larger than Baw Noi, which has now been developed as a resort, with bungalows and bathing facilities. The resort was originally open only to the Party elite, but is now open to the public.

At **Muang Kham,** 50km (30 miles) and a two-hour drive from Phonsavan, the road forks. The left fork becomes Route 6, heading north into Hua Phan province, while the right continues to the Vietnamese border.

Muang Kham itself is no more than a crossroads trading village, but there are guides who will take you to nearby **jar sites** or on to **Tham Piu ⑤**, a cave a few kilometres northeast of town. Tham Piu is another Vietnam War site, where in 1969 a single rocket fired from a royalist (or American, depending on the version you choose) aircraft caused the death of hundreds of people who had taken refuge in the cave. Controversy still exists about whether these were Lao locals or, in

fact, Vietnamese who had set up a makeshift hospital in the cave.

For those who might wish to avoid another reminder of the region's troubled past, it is still worth making the trip to Tham Piu to enjoy the beautiful scenery and the tribal villages in the vicinity. Another cave, **Tham Piu Song,** which was spared the bombing, can also be visited. Although the caves are only a few kilometres from the main Route 7, a guide is recommended, as the trails are not clearly marked and, as always in this area, the risks posed by UXO remain real. It is best to hire guides in Phonsavan, where you can arrange an itinerary to include a visit to the mineral springs as well as the caves and a minority village.

Hua Phan province

Lying northeast of Xieng Khuang province, Hua Phan province shares a similar history. It has, for the past several hundred years, been alternately a vassal state of Vietnam, known as Ai Lao, owing to its position close to Hanoi, or an independent

kingdom. Even more remote than Xieng Khuang from the traditional Lao capitals of Luang Prabang and Vientiane, it was in fact only fully incorporated into the Lao polity during the French colonial period.

Hua Phan currently has a population of approximately 280, 000 people. More mountainous than Xieng Khuang, it is home to over 20 ethnic minorities, most of whom are Tai-speaking. The weather up here can become quite cold during winter, especially for those accustomed to the adjacent lower-lying tropical regions.

To reach Hua Phan from Xieng Khuang province, travel northeast to Muang Kham via Route 7, bear left onto Route 6, and continue to Nam Noen, which is about a four-hour trip in total. Past Nam Noen the road is well graded but ceases to be paved, and starts to climb through beautiful mountain scenery with many tribal villages in evidence. About 20km (12 miles) beyond Nam Noen is the village of Hua Muang, where, unless you already have a guide, it is possible to obtain directions to **Suan Hin ❻**,

literally meaning "Stone Garden" in Lao. This site is an earlier manifestation of the civilisation that built the jars of Xieng Khuang. Here, rather than jars, one sees several groupings of upright stone pillars, ranging in height from 1–3 metres (3–10ft).

Adjacent to the pillars are small underground chambers, believed to be burial crypts. This site was also researched in the 1930s by the French archaeologist Madeleine Colani (see page 144). It was inhabited before the Plain of Jars, as witnessed by the fact that only stone and not iron cutting tools were used to produce these pillars, which Colani called "menhirs". The site calls to mind a miniature Stonehenge, and Colani also hypothesised the existence of a sun cult among the prehistoric inhabitants of the region.

The menhirs of Suan Hin are several kilometres off the main Route 6, but are now accessible by vehicle. An American government opium-suppression project built a road to some nearby Hmong villages, hoping to give the inhabitants access to local markets

FACT

The indigenous Lao people of Xieng Khuang are known as the Lao Phuan. During 19th-century wars with Siam, many were carried off and resettled in Thailand. Today substantial communities that still call themselves Phuan live in Thailand, notably at Suphanburi just to the north of Bangkok.

The menhir-strewn landscape of Suan Hin.

Sets of cutlery for sale around Sam Neua may or may not have been made from shot-down aircraft. On balance, it seems unlikely, not least because Lao people generally eat with their fingers! But evidence of recycled UXO, especially bomb cases, is not hard to find. They are used for everything from temple gongs and school bells, through planting pots, to stilts to hold up houses.

Returning from the maize fields.

with the produce they were to grow instead of opium. Unfortunately, the road passes dangerously close to the main grouping of stelae, and this has caused some to collapse. Local villagers have carted the smaller pillars away to use as tables. Nonetheless, the menhirs of Suan Hin are an impressive and mysterious sight, spread over several adjacent hillsides. Constructed of stone containing silica-like chips, they sparkle in the afternoon sun.

Sam Neua 7, the capital of Hua Phan, is 45km (28 miles) northeast of the Suan Hin site. Its setting in a verdant valley at an altitude of 1,200 metres (3,900ft) is more attractive than the town itself, although Sam Neua's **market** is thriving as the largest in the region, and is a good spot to observe the many ethnic minorities, including Hmong, Tai Daeng and Tai Lü, who come here for supplies. Sam Neua's famous handwoven textiles, as well as handmade silver jewellery, are sold in some of the small shops and market stalls. Cutlery said to be made from downed aeroplanes can also be found, as well as ceramics and other cheap

souvenirs imported from nearby Vietnam (Sam Neua is only 150km/90 miles from Hanoi by road, although there are no buses between the two).

Although Sam Neua remains one of the least visited towns in the country, basic accommodation is readily available. Two kilometres (1.2 miles) from Sam Neua's market is **Wat Pho Xai**, a tiny monastery with only five monks in residence. A 1979 independence monument, mounted on a red star, is situated on a hill on the outskirts and has views over the town.

Vieng Xai and the Pathet Lao caves

The heart of Hua Phan's significance is the district of **Vieng Xai 8** (a recent appellation meaning "City of Victory"), some 30km (20 miles) east of Sam Neua close to the Vietnam border. It was here that the Pathet Lao leadership established its headquarters during the 20-year struggle for supremacy in the Second Indochina War. The area was chosen for its proximity to Vietnam and also for the abundance of caves which afforded

shelter from American bombs. Not coincidentally, this is a wild, remote area, and the karst and jungle scenery is spellbinding. Combined with the historical significance, it all adds up to make a visit to this inaccessible corner of Indochina a memorable experience.

The authorities have an ambivalent attitude towards allowing foreigners to visit these sites. On the one hand, they are proud of their tenacious struggle and resourcefulness in surviving in these conditions; on the other hand, they still consider the area to be a high-security military zone. An explanation for their reticence to allow visitors free access to the area is no doubt the legacy of *samana*, the re-education camps of the Pathet Lao gulag.

After the Pathet Lao victory in 1975 thousands of Lao were sent to camps for lengthy "re-education" under extremely harsh conditions, including isolation, forced labour and political indoctrination. Many did not survive. The camps that held the higher officials (including the Lao royal family and former ministers) were located in Vieng Xai and nearby Sop Hao. Most camps were closed by 1989, but there is a belief that at least one camp still exists.

The caves of the Pathet Lao leaders, of which there are estimated to be about 100, are within walking distance of Vieng Xai. Located in an impressively steep and narrow limestone valley, the caves are treated as a serious historical monument by the military "guides" who must accompany all visitors. Tours take in three or four caves and last a couple of hours. The first cave, which one must visit to register, pay a nominal fee and be assigned a guide/guard, is **Tham Thaan Souphanouvong**. This was the home and office of the famous "Red Prince", Souphanouvong, a member of the Lao royal family who sided with the revolutionaries (see page 62). Befitting his royal background, this cave is well appointed, with wooden walls

and floors dividing it into different working areas. A comfortable house was constructed for the Red Prince outside the mouth of the cave after the 1973 Paris accords brought an end to the American bombing.

Tham Thaan Kaysone was the cave residence and headquarters of the Pathet Lao supremo and first president of the Lao People's Democratic Republic, Kaysone Phomvihane. Larger and more office-like than the Red Prince's cave, it extends down to a depth of around 150 metres (490ft), including a meeting room and library, and has an exit at the back which leads to an outdoor meeting area and a kitchen. An attractive house stands in front of the cave. One of the deepest caves, **Tham Xieng Muang**, was used as a temporary military hospital.

The remote border crossing on Route 6B east of Vieng Xai is open to travellers, although there are no buses either side of the border, only *songthaews* (pick-up trucks) and motorbikes. A visa on arrival has been available at this border crossing for a number of years.

One of the many caves used to shelter the Pathet Lao forces from US bombing.

Several of the cave sites in the hills around Vieng Xai are open to visitors.

MYSTERIOUS JARS

Strewn across the rolling plateau around Phonsavan are clusters of large stone jars of obscure origin. The remote setting and sense of mystery make for a memorable experience.

One of the best-known sights in Laos, the jars of Xieng Khuang province are ranged across three separate sites (see page 138) in the vicinity of Phonsavan.

A French archaeologist, Madeleine Colani, undertook a comprehensive study of the jars during the 1930s. Colani spent three years in the region, travelling mainly by elephant. Her work, *Mégalithes du Haut-Laos*, published in Paris in 1935, details the history of both the jars and the upright stone pillars found in Hua Phan province. Colani conclusively linked the two sets of monuments to a single civilisation which she believed flourished in the area between 300 BC and AD 300, postulating that both the jars and what she called the "menhirs" of Hua Phan were funerary monuments.

Other artefacts found in and around the jars included beads from China, bronze figurines from Vietnam and ornaments associated with Tai culture. This allowed Colani to conclude that the civilisation that produced these monuments was highly developed and had trading links throughout the region. She drew no direct conclusions as to the origins of the civilisation, but more recent researchers have attempted to trace them alternatively to the Cham of Vietnam or to some of the Lao Theung groups which now inhabit Attapeu province in southeastern Laos. No researcher has yet offered a convincing explanation for the civilisation's demise.

The traditional local explanation for the jars is that a Lao king, Khun Jeaum, deposed the sadistic local chief of the region in the 6th century. To mark his conquest, he ordered a huge quantity of rice wine to be made and the casting of thousands of stone jars in which to store it.

The largest jars weigh several tonnes. Some are made from granite, others from limestone, but the majority from a sandstone-like conglomerate called molasse. Each jar is thought to have been cut from an individual boulder.

Celebrating the ancient Rocket Festival (Boun Bang Fai) at Site 1.

This small Buddha statue was excavated at Site 3 and is on view at the Unesco office in Phonsavan.

A bomb-clearance operation uses coloured sticks to mark unexploded ordnance. Although the tourist sites have been largely cleared of explosives from the Vietnam War, other areas remain dangerous – stick to the paths.

BUT WHAT WERE THEY FOR?

The jars of Xieng Khuang average about 1.5 metres (5ft) in both diameter and height, although some are considerably larger. The largest weighs an estimated 15 tonnes. Most were carved from the local sandstone, using iron implements. Madeleine Colani established her hypothesis that the jars were funerary monuments by recovering charred human bone fragments from them, and she also discovered what appears to be a central crematorium at the village of Ban Ang on the Xieng Khuang Plateau. The round discs which are now scattered in the vicinity of the jars were not lids, as one might logically suppose, but were placed, decorative side down, over ritual objects such as stone axes. It is sometimes suggested, especially by her detractors, that the jars were in fact used for storing rice wine (this is the traditional Lao story). The obvious problem here is that bamboo, wooden or ceramic rice containers would have been far cheaper to produce and, crucially, portable. The counter-argument is that they may have been used for storing these foodstuffs for ritual offerings.

of the jars are uncovered, but there is disagreement about ther they were originally built with stone lids. The disc-ped objects alongside a few of the jars do appear to be lids, are generally believed to have had a different function ted to ritual objects. Many of the smaller jars, being more ly moved, have long since been carted off, but several dred remain – Site 1 alone has around 250.

The plateau is home to a large Hmong minority.

NORTHWESTERN LAOS

The remote northwestern districts of Laos are where
the borders of China, Thailand and Burma converge.
The scattered towns and villages give a glimpse into
the lives of the numerous ethnic minorities.

Laos's wild and mountainous northwest shares frontiers with Thailand, China and Burma. The region has long been a natural path of migration, generally from north to south, for a wide variety of peoples; many of them – intentionally or otherwise – ended their peregrination in these hills. The cultural and ethnic ancestors of the Lao people, the Tai, originated just to the north in the area of China's Yunnan province known as Sipsongpanna (Xishuangbanna in Chinese), while the greatest of the Lao kingdoms, Lan Xang, traces its origins to the early *muang* (city-states) which originated here (see page 49).

In addition to the Tai, northwestern Laos is home to a large number of colourful Tibeto-Burmese peoples, such as the Yao, Hmong and Akha. The Lao government now collectively refers to these groups as Lao Soung or "High Lao", a reference to the mountain tops that they have historically chosen to inhabit. In Luang Nam Tha province these "ethnic minorities" are in fact a majority, outnumbering the Lao by two to one.

Malefactors and opium

Being a frontier region is not without dangers, and the area's history is characterised by periods of violence. The depredations of the Haw, "Overland Chinese" freebooters, accompanied

by Vietnamese mercenaries and French deserters who terrorised Laos at the end of the 19th century, were particularly brutal here. More recently the area has become known as part of the infamous "Golden Triangle", where an ever-changing parade of malefactors of various nationalities has chosen to profit from one of the local people's traditional crops, opium. Although it was spared the heavy American bombing which devastated northeastern Laos during the 1970s, the northwest was heavily

Main Attractions

Nam Ou boat trips
Nong Khiaw
Phongsali
Luang Nam Tha
Muang Sing
Gibbon Experience

Floating down the Nam Ou.

Loading up the riverboats.

involved in the strife, largely because the Hmong, supported by the American CIA, resisted the Communist Pathet Lao forces which had major bases in Luang Nam Tha province. Air America, the CIA airline, based many "training forces" here, and once again the lure of opium as a source of financing military activities raised its ugly but profitable head.

Towards the end of the Vietnam War the northwest was "liberated", and the Chinese allies built a network of paved roads connecting Mengla in China with Udomxai, Nong Khiaw on the Nam Ou and Pakbeng on the Mekong. Currently undergoing widespread and thorough upgrading, these roads continue to provide the major land thoroughfares of the region. With the rapid reopening of Chinese borders in recent years, road-building soldiers have been replaced by a variety of traders and skilled labourers from the neighbouring provinces of China. Sometimes trading only in Laos, sometimes en route to and from Thailand, they add another interesting dimension to this

multifaceted cultural environment. This ethnic pot-pourri, combined with the mountainous geography and possibility of river travel, makes this region well worth the sometimes arduous conditions.

Along the Nam Ou

Indeed it is travel by river, not only the mighty Mekong but also large tributaries such as the Nam Ou, which offers the visitor a truly Lao experience. Nonetheless, with the roads improving, slow riverboats are becoming a less cost-effective way for the Lao to travel and their future is uncertain. Since for most villages the river is the focus of many daily activities, social and domestic, travel on a riverboat will, for now at least, provide glimpses of Lao rural life that you simply cannot get from road travel.

The Nam Ou, a major tributary of the Mekong, flows south from the mountains of China's Yunnan province through the Lao provinces of Phongsali and Luang Prabang before reaching the Mekong 20km (12 miles) upstream from Luang Prabang. It is

possible to travel along the Ou by boat from its confluence with the Mekong way up north to within a few kilometres of the mountain-top town of Phongsali (see page 151).

One can negotiate directly with the boatmen for a charter from Luang Prabang as far as Nong Khiaw or points further north. Since the completion of the road (Route 13) north to Pakmong (and on to the Chinese border), the locals have understandably chosen to forgo the river in favour of the usually faster (journey time around four hours) and cheaper buses, so there are no regular ferries and travellers must rely on charters. Rates vary according to water level and demand, but US$100 should secure a worthy craft. These boats can take up to 10 passengers, so sharing with others makes the cost quite reasonable. Water levels are low from January to June, and at times may be low enough to prevent boats (particularly speedboats) sailing up the river. Journey times vary, but four to six hours is typical. Speedboats can do it in two hours when the water levels

are high. These noisy, high-powered vessels now begin their journey at **Ban Don**, a small village on the Mekong some 10km (6 miles) north of Luang Prabang.

The trip north to Nong Khiaw passes through splendid mountainous scenery, with small villages clustered around every bend in the river. Soon after embarking at the confluence of the Ou and the Mekong, you reach the Pak Ou caves (see page 132). If you charter a boat, be sure to ask the boatman to make brief stops at one of the picturesque villages en route.

You will eventually arrive in **Nong Khiaw ⑨** a large village set amid glorious karst scenery, which seems to owe its existence to a bridge that crosses the river here. A further 10km (6 miles) upriver lies another attractive settlement, Muang Ngoi Neua – boats travel between the two, taking around one hour. Both places have basic accommodation available and, if you don't mind roughing it a bit, either town makes a wonderfully picturesque base in which to immerse yourself in the backwaters of Laos.

A small cargo boat hoisted onto stilts and used as a home.

Limestone cliffs at the confluence of the Nam Ou and the Mekong near Luang Prabang.

Most slow boats have covered areas to protect passengers from the sun or, depending on the season, rain. Yet these areas are often packed with people, and many foreign visitors choose to travel, for much of the time, on the deck or even the roof. Be warned – serious sunburn is a real possibility: bring a hat, sun lotion, sunglasses and an umbrella, and avoid shorts and T-shirts.

The cool mountain setting of Phongsali.

The aforementioned bridge is an important link in the Chinese-built Route 1, which travels from Luang Nam Tha province in the west to Xieng Khuang province in the east, so if you choose not to travel further north on the Ou it is possible to secure public transport either towards Udomxai in the west (about three hours by bus) or to Sam Neua in the east, via Vieng Kham (7–8 hours in all), or through to Phonsavan in Xieng Khuang in the southeast (about 10–12 hours).

Travelling by boat up the Nam Ou is still an effective way to continue north from Nong Khiaw, at least when the waters are sufficiently deep – this can be an issue in the dry season between February and June. (If there are no boats, there are always daily buses from Luang Prabang, taking eight hours.) A wider variety of craft ply the river from here on up, catering to locals and making intermediate stops at villages totally unreachable by road. In addition to the ubiquitous speedboats, a slower variety of riverboat leaves Nong Khiaw for Muang

Khua on a regular basis. What these craft forfeit in speed they gain in comfort. Unlike the speedboats, they have covered cabins which give shelter from the sun.

The boat trip to Muang Khua takes anything between four and 12 hours depending on the season and, because of constant local demand for the service, prices are reasonable. The boat ride also offers a glimpse into the life of the people who have dwelt for centuries along the banks of the Ou. If you have chartered your own riverboat you should ask to stop in some of these villages. Although contact with the outside world is limited, the fertile land and river sustain the local inhabitants with abundant food and building supplies. The people, though not prosperous in a Western sense, are certainly contented. Visitors are welcomed.

Muang Khua to Phongsali

The village of **Muang Khua** ⑩ is, like Nong Khiaw, located next to a bridge that crosses the Ou. Road access is via Route 4, which runs from Udomxai in

the west (3–4 hours) and goes east to the Vietnamese border at Sop Houn (Dien Bien Phu is just 35km/22 miles further). It is possible to cross the border into Vietnam here, and this is fortunate as Dien Bien Phu is the site of the battle that doomed the French presence in Indochina. Muang Khua offers a wider choice of accommodation than Nong Khiaw or Muang Ngoi Neua, which is also fortunate, since if you are coming from Luang Prabang this will be about as much travel as can be comfortably accomplished in a day. Muang Khua itself is a tranquil and friendly town, with many people from the local ethnic minorities visiting the town for trade or transport.

Proceeding upriver from Muang Khua into the heart of Phongsali province, your next destination is **Hat Sa**. Again, in season, there is a choice between a powerful speedboat and a placid "slow boat", as the Lao name translates. The trip takes two hours by speedboat, six hours by slow boat. This section of the river is even more spectacular than the Nong Khiaw to Muang Khua sections, with thick primary forest cover and a never-ending parade of pristine villages. The mountains looming in the distance are of substantial elevations. The air is cool regardless of the time of year, and particularly pleasant after the often torrid plains. The village of Hat Sa is the northern terminus of river traffic on the Ou, although little but its remoteness and the variety of ethnic groups who visit it distinguish the place.

From here one can board a jeep or similar four-wheel-drive vehicle to travel the remaining 20km (12 miles) to Phongsali. The fact that this short passage requires up to two hours indicates the condition of the road.

Phongsali ⓫ (population 25,000), capital of the province of the same name, is located along the lower slopes of Phu Fa (Sky Mountain). Its 1,400-metre (4,550ft) elevation guarantees a year-round temperate climate

and cold winter nights. No doubt as a result of its strategic location, sandwiched between China and Vietnam, the French took an interest in the area and established a garrison. A few traces of French architecture remain, but this is being quickly overshadowed by the utilitarian Chinese style of construction that characterises most towns near the frontier of Laos's immense neighbour. The French wrested Phongsali from Chinese control by a treaty in 1895. Prior to this time it was affiliated with the Tai Lü statelet of Sipsongpanna, and under Chinese suzerainty.

The province of Phongsali is ethnically one of the most diverse in Laos. In addition to the well-known Hmong, Akha and Yao there are several branches of Tai tribal groups, Vietnamese and Chinese, both longterm residents and recent immigrants. The Lao government, with its penchant for "unity in diversity", lists about 28 ethnic groups, although anthropologists would probably dispute this number. Phongsali's market is a good place to see the great variety

The ethnically diverse residents of Phongsali gather to watch a communal video screening.

Barber at Phongsali.

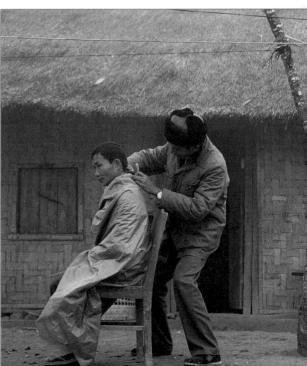

Many of the roads in northwestern Laos are still dirt tracks, but thanks to foreign investment, paved roads are gradually taking their place.

In full swing – the morning market at Luang Nam Tha.

of peoples who call the province home, although traditional costume is becoming far less visible these days. The oddly named Viphaphone Hotel offers reasonable accommodation.

South to Udomxai

From Phongsali, you have the option of journeying south on a relatively improved but still partially unpaved road towards Udomxai. After a steep descent, the road eventually joins Route 4 which runs from Udomxai to the Vietnamese border. Travel time is 6–7 hours, and the scenery is not as spectacular as that previously seen along the Nam Ou. In addition, the provincial capital of **Udomxai** ⑫ (also known as Muang Xay), although the key crossroads in the north, is not particularly attractive.

In the 1970s, Udomxai was the centre of Chinese support for the Pathet Lao forces in northern Laos. As payment for their road-building efforts, the Chinese were given carte blanche to log the Udomxai Valley, and the resultant deforestation makes for a somewhat dusty and bleak environment. The town still has a notably strong Chinese influence, but this is now more commercial than political. In the centre, across the street from the bus station, a **Kaysone Monument** is located in the middle of a run-down park. As a backdrop the government has constructed a large stupa or *that* on a hilltop southeast of the town. Udomxai has a lively market, located in the centre of the town across from the tourist office.

Another, recently rediscovered, attraction, is the Chom Ong caves. The cave system is located 45km (28 miles) from the town near the village of Khmu Lu. The caves rank as the longest cave system in Northern Laos, spanning some 13.5km (8.5 miles) and containinh a variety of fossils. The Nam Kaang River flows through the lower stretches. The tourist office in town can help with trips to the cave system.

Luang Nam Tha

Winding its way northwest towards Luang Nam Tha, the Chinese-built Route 1 enters some spectacular

THE TAI LÜ

The Tai Lü are the original inhabitants of the former Tai principality of Sipsong-panna or "Twelve Thousand Rice Fields", most of which lies in southern China's Yunnan province (where it is known as Xishuangbanna). The French detached two of the 12 administrative districts, including Muang Sing, at the end of the 19th century, and incorporated them within Laos. There are also substantial numbers of Tai Lü living across the Mekong in neighbouring Thailand and in northwestern Vietnam. A sophisticated and cultured people, they are generally very conscious of their shared roots. Their language, which is close to northern Thai, is spoken by some 700,000 people across the region, including about 300,000 in China, 200,000 in Burma, 150,000 in Thailand, perhaps 50,000 in Laos and 10,000 in Vietnam.

mountain scenery, although some sections have been heavily deforested, both by logging and the slash-and-burn agricultural techniques used by local farmers. The area is home to sizeable populations of Akha, Hmong and Yao. At the village of **Na Toei**, about 90km (55 miles) from Udomxai, the road forks, with the right-hand route leading to **Boten**, a Lao village at the Chinese border. With a Chinese visa (obtainable in Vientiane) you can cross into China's Yunnan province from here.

If you bear left at Na Toei you will find yourself at the pleasant town of **Luang Nam Tha** ⓭ within the hour. During the Vietnam War, this area witnessed fierce fighting between the Pathet Lao forces and the CIA-backed tribal (largely Hmong) guerrillas, and after the war the devastated town was relocated about 7km (4 miles) north of its former site. It now boasts wide avenues (usually empty of traffic) and a pleasant location on the Nam Tha River. Wander down to the footbridge east of the town's main road at sunrise. The **morning market**, south of the "bus station" (in fact a large vacant field), is full of local products and people. Handicraft shops in this area offer interesting local Tai Lü and other textiles as well as woven bamboo artefacts. About 2km (1.2 miles) out of town on the road to Muang Sing, a European Union-funded project, the **Hat Yao Village Handicrafts Cooperative**, helps villagers get their handmade products to the market.

The former site of Luang Nam Tha, south of the "new town", is still home to a large market, a Buddhist temple, the airport and a boat landing. As the road south to the Thai border at Huay Xai is greatly improved (once an insecure track, now a safe but still slow 5–7 hours by bus), the boat traffic on the Nam Tha is diminishing. A good way to enjoy the scenery would be to negotiate a two-hour round-trip cruise. This is possible only after the summer monsoon rains have raised the waters to a navigable level.

Muang Sing

Continuing northwest on Route 3, a 60km (37-mile) two-hour trip leads through steep mountains and along raging rivers to the town of **Muang Sing** ⓮. Located on a fertile plain surrounded by mountains and irrigated by the waters of the Nam Yuan and Nam Ma, this town of 25,000 is a centre of Tai Lü culture and has a rich history. Muang Sing has existed as a small but important urban centre for hundreds of years as a result of its strategic location and agricultural wealth. At times it was under the rule of various northern Siamese principalities, but mainly of China. The British, and later the French, laid claim to it, the latter building a garrison which still exists today.

The predominant Lü people are a branch of the Tai ethno-linguistic family, who also inhabit the southern part of China's Yunnan province (the border lies just 10km (6 miles) from Muang Sing). They are arguably the

FACT

The Chinese People's Liberation Army built many of the roads in northwestern Laos during the Vietnam War, secure in the knowledge that the United States Air Force would not risk bombing them and bringing them directly into the war. Yet they did so not so much to help their purported Vietnamese Communist allies, as to keep the latter out of the area which they considered a traditional Chinese fiefdom.

Young monk at Wat Nam Kaew Luang.

TIP

The Tai Lü villages surrounding Muang Sing are interesting, and bicycles for hire in restaurants and guesthouses are an ideal way to explore. Just head north towards the village of Udomsin and take any side road that looks promising.

most ethnically and culturally homogeneous of the many sub-groups of Tai outside their ancestral homeland (see panel).

Lü society is matrilineal: the women have strong influence in family decision-making, and are keen upholders of the group's traditions. A people known for their grace and physical beauty, they are Buddhists but also have a rich oral tradition of various mythical heroes and spirits. Among these tales is one that relates how they were taught to build their distinctive sloping roofed, stilted houses by a divine swan, and they still refer to their traditional style of dwellings as *heuan hong* ("swan houses").

A Tai Lü-style Buddhist temple, **Wat Luang Baan Xieng Jai** (free), located just west of the town's main street, near the river, shows the characteristic small windows and red lacquered pillars which typify Tai Lü temple architecture. In the centre of town, behind yet another Kaysone memorial, you can see the **former French garrison**, which is now a Lao army base, and a colourful market is located across the

The morning rush at Muang Sing's morning market.

main street from the memorial. If you go south for about 1km (0.6 miles), another Buddhist temple, **Wat Nam Kaew Luang** (free), is housed in an agreeable tree-filled compound. In addition to the Tai Lü, Muang Sing is also home to a large population of Yao, Akha and Lanten tribal peoples whose villages are located in the surrounding hills. Local guides can arrange trekking tours to these areas. At present the Lao government still "strongly discourages" visitors from staying overnight in tribal villages, more to protect the villagers from the visitors than the other way round.

Muang Sing is also noted for its **annual festival**, the Boun That Muang Sing. The festival's date varies according to the lunar calendar, but it is always towards the end of October or beginning of November, at the full moon. The festival occurs at a Buddhist stupa or *that* on a hill south of town. Since it is a Buddhist religious rite, the presentation of incense and candles at the stupa and the offering of alms to the monks who converge on the site for this event are central

to the festival, but it is also an important social and commercial gathering. The crowds dance to live bands in the evenings, with tasty snacks for the children and home-distilled spirits for the adults adding to the fun. Although not Buddhists, the local hill-tribe population would not dream of missing the fun, and attend in full regalia. Muang Sing is also an excellent venue for participating in the festivities associated with Lao New Year in April, or the rocket festivals that call for rain during the dry season – all festivals that are celebrated in neighbouring Thailand and Xishuangbanna in China.

Although the Chinese border is only a few kilometres northeast of Muang Sing, for the present only Lao and Chinese nationals are permitted to cross at this point.

From Muang Sing it is possible to double back to Luang Nam Tha and reach the Thai border at Huay Xai by road, but a much more interesting route is via **Xieng Kok**, a small village on the Mekong 75km (47 miles) west of Muang Sing. The road has been improved, and the trip takes two to three hours, passing through beautiful scenery along the Nam Ma. Across the Mekong from Xieng Kok is Burma, although only Lao and Burmese nationals are permitted to cross. With little to detain you in Xieng Kok (there is a guesthouse should necessity require), you can board a speedboat for the four-hour trip downriver to Huay Xai, river levels permitting. All boats stop at **Ban Muam**, which could be considered a centre of the Golden Triangle since the borders of Laos, Burma and Thailand converge here. Truck-buses leave Muang Sing for Xieng Kok early in the morning, so it's possible to reach Huay Xai the same day, although, as with all travel in Laos, be prepared for surprises.

Huay Xai and the Mekong River

Huay Xai ⓯, the Lao town across the Mekong from Chiang Khong in Thailand, is a popular entry point for visitors wishing to cross from Thailand. It is possible to get a 30-day Lao visa on arrival in Huay Xai.

A colourful minority shopper at Muang Sing's morning market.

The northwestern region – Muang Sin in particular – may be historically linked to the poppy trade, but opium remains illegal in Laos.

THE OPIUM TRADE

It would be remiss to discuss northwestern Laos without mentioning something that will certainly confront any visitor: the use of opium – even though it is notably less prevalent than it was just a few years ago. Muang Sing has historically been a centre of poppy production; during their period of rule the French sanctioned and monopolised the trade. Traditionally used as a medicine and by the elderly, opium is now discreetly proffered to foreign tourists on the streets of Muang Sing by emaciated local addicts, who use the profits from sales at inflated prices to finance their habits. Opium is *not* legal in Laos. The government does not appreciate Muang Sing's reputation, and unpleasant encounters between the police and foreigners using opium have been reported.

TIP

There is a certain amount of un-Laos-like hustle in Huay Xai. Travellers arriving from Thailand are likely to be accosted by vendors selling boat trips downriver to Luang Prabang or up to Luang Nam Tha. It's best to ignore them as tickets are likely to be cheaper when purchased directly from the boat operators at their respective jetties, or from agents in town.

Villagers watch as an elephant drags an old deactivated bomb across a tributary of the Mekong.

Alternatively, you can apply for a visa from any Lao Embassy or Consulate abroad. Since becoming a legal port of entry, it has experienced a mini-boom, with new hotels, shops and even some palatial private homes in evidence. The fourth Thai–Lao Friendship Bridge between Huay Xai and Chiang Khong was opened in December 2013 and now, with the recently upgraded Huay Xai–Luang Nam Tha road, vehicular travel can proceed relatively easily between Bangkok and China, and vice versa. Predictably, the Thais and Chinese have been most enthusiastic.

Huay Xai itself is a pleasant little town ranged around the low hills that descend to the banks of the river. A Buddhist temple, **Wat Jom Khao Manilat** (free), can be reached by a long staircase with serpentine *naga* balustrades. Built in the late 19th century, the temple affords good views of the town and the river below. Nearby, **Fort Carnot**, built by the French, is visible from the outside, but is off limits to visitors since it is now a Lao military installation. Travel agents in town

offer trips to the nearby **sapphire mine** (the province's name, Bokeo, means "gem mine" in Lao), but the site is not particularly attractive, and the uninitiated who purchase the stones on offer will not be getting a bargain.

A three-hour ride northeast of Huay Xai, off Route 3, brings you to the **Gibbon Experience** (tel: 084-212 021; www.gibbonexperience.org), an exciting (but expensive) opportunity to see these long-limbed apes thanks to a system of zip-lines strategically hung below the jungle canopy. Two days are required. The Gibbon Experience has an office in Huay Xai.

Mekong transport

From Huay Xai there are several forms of river transport. The ubiquitous speedboats leave from about 2km (1.2 miles) south of town. These six-passenger craft can reach Luang Prabang in six to seven hours, or the town of Pakbeng in about half that time. Helmets and life jackets are supplied and obligatory by Lao law. Even so, not everyone enjoys the speedboat trip down the Mekong. The vast expanses

of smooth water, unlike the Nam Ou that reaches north from Luang Prabang, allow the speedboat jockeys to propel their light but powerful craft at high speeds: exhilarating or nerve-racking, depending on your perspective, but certainly dangerous. Seven hours of this would rattle even the most steely nerved, so consider breaking the trip up with a night in Pakbeng. The fare per passenger to Luang Prabang is approximately US$50, and that to Pakbeng is about US$20. Hiring the whole boat will cost four to six times more than the individual fare.

A more placid alternative to the speedboats is the 40-person passenger ferries. Called *heua saa* (slow boats) by the Lao, they live up to their name. Reaching Luang Prabang requires spending one night en route at Pakbeng, arriving at Luang Prabang in the afternoon on the second day. The boats leave in the early mornings from a terminal just north of the Lao immigration checkpoint in Huay Xai. Prices for the ferries are about US$40 from Huay Xai to Luang Prabang. Be sure to bring your own food, water, sunglasses and hat or umbrella.

A third travel alternative will appeal to those wishing to make this trip in style: if you have the budget, opt for Asian Oasis's (www.asian-oasis.com) comfortable cruise on a luxurious modern vessel, the *Luang Say*, which offers onboard refreshments and washrooms. The *Luang Say* leaves Huay Xai twice a week, stopping to visit scenic spots on the way to Pakbeng, where passengers spend the night at the Luangsay Lodge, located just outside the town. It then sets out the following morning to reach Luang Prabang in the afternoon. The price includes all meals, guides and accommodation.

Some travellers choose a mixture of passenger ferry and speedboat travel by breaking the trip in Pakbeng. Obviously the slower boats give you a better chance of taking in the attractive scenery: mountains on both sides

border this stretch of the Mekong, and the forest cover is often pristine. You may even see (domesticated) elephants bathing in the shallows.

Pakbeng to Luang Prabang

Pakbeng ⑯ is a pleasant small town at the confluence of the Mekong and Beng rivers. Built on steep slopes, it has several adequate guesthouses and restaurants, and many hill-tribe villagers visit its market. An interesting Buddhist temple, **Wat Sin Jong Jaeng** (free), just north of the town, has an exterior mural of the *sim* depicting earlier moustached Caucasian visitors. For those who do not wish to continue downriver to Luang Prabang, the improved road north from Pakbeng, Route 2, leads to Udomxai (150km/93 miles). The trip takes about 3–4 hours.

If you continue on to Luang Prabang by passenger ferry or the *Luang Say* you will arrive at the old city. Those travelling by speedboat will be deposited a few kilometres upstream at Ban Don, from where songthaews complete the journey.

Backpackers on the Mekong River boat between Pakbeng and Luang Prabang.

Fishing in the Mekong near Tha Kaek.

THE MEKONG VALLEY

Journey along the Mekong to visit the three pleasantly laid-back provincial capitals. This is the most developed part of the country, but still timeless, and temples and historic buildings abound.

For much of its length from a point west of Vientiane, the Mekong River marks the political divide between Laos and Thailand. From Vientiane all the way to Champasak, however, the two banks of the Mekong are closely related linguistically, culturally and ethnically – this rich, well-watered river valley is the very heartland of the lowland Lao, both in Laos and in Thailand's much larger, ethnically Lao northeast. Over the past two decades once-difficult relations between the two neighbours have improved beyond all recognition, and today new bridges are being built, both figuratively and literally, across the Mekong Valley.

The eastern bank of the Mekong is dominated by Laos's second- and third-largest urban centres after the capital, Vientiane. These are Tha Kaek (population 85,000) and Savannakhet (population 120,000). By no means large cities, they are both respectively linked and influenced by the neighbouring Thai towns, just across the Mekong, of Nakhon Phanom and Mukdahan.

Following the opening of the first Thai–Lao Friendship Bridge between Vientiane and Nong Khai in 1994, a second bridge was opened between Savannakhet and Mukdahan in 2007, and a third between Tha Kaek and

Nakhon Phanom was opened in 2011. A fourth Thai–Lao Friendship Bridge further to the north, between Huay Xai and Chiang Khong, was opened in December 2013. The Savannakhet–Mukdahan bridge is part of an "East–West Corridor" linking Vietnam with Thailand via Laos. This greatly improved communications network represents both the increasing economic importance of the Mekong Valley and the strengthening cultural and political links between Laos and Thailand.

Main Attractions

Tha Kaek
Limestone caves
Savannakhet
Heuan Hin Khmer temple

Mekong Valley transport.

Southern Laos

0   50 km
0   50 miles

Inset (top right)

Champasak · Don San · Pakxe
LAOS
Don Khong · Muang Khong · Hat Xai Khun
Ban Huay
Ban Hang Khong · Ban Hat · Ban Xot
Ban Som · Don Loppadi · Don Som · Don Det · Taat Khon Phapheng (Falls)
CAMBODIA · Nakasang · Don Khon
Taat Li Phi (Somphamit Falls) · Ban Khon · Don Khon
Irrawaddy Dolphins

0   5 km
0   5 miles

Main map labels

Bolikhamxai · Kaew Nua Pass · Duc Tho
Ban Nachia · Lak Xao (Sao)
Ban Pakha · Khamkeut · Cau Thuong
Theun · Ban Napung · Phu Laoko 2288 · Ky Anh
Saiphu Ak · Nakai-Nam Theum NBCA · Thanh Lang Xa
Vientiane · Phu Hin Bun NBCA · Nakai · Ngan Sau · Vinh Son · Quang Trach
Hinboun · Ban Vieng Kham · Nyommalat · Ban Xiangdao · Mu Gia Pass · Don Bai Dinh · Cha Noi · Minh Hoa · Ly Nhon Bac
Ban Hatkham · Khammuan · Tham Pha Pa · Ban Nuan · Ban Heu · Dong Hoi
Friendship Bridge No 3 · Tha Kaek · Ban Naden · Ban Saang
Nakhon Phanom · Wat Pha That Sikhotabong · Mahaxai · Him Namnu NBCA · Ban Bungnyalao
Bua La Pha · Ban Panam Mai · Ban Chala · Phu Sala 1268
Nong Bok · Xai Bua Thong · Ban Kengtapa · BIEN DONG
Ban Naxoy · Ban Sopxe · Ban Nanyon · Phu Xang He NBCA · Ban Kengkhup · Dong Ha
That Phanom · Ban Sikhai · Ban Ngonsai · Xepon (Sepon) · Quang Tri
Ban Pong · Xaibuli · Atsaphangthong · Ban Nabo · Cam Lo · Ca Lu
Uthomphon · That Ing Hang · Ban Dong · Lao Bao · Phong Dien
Friendship Bridge No 2 · Savannakhet · Ban Xethamuak · Muang Phin · Ban Samuay · Hue
Mukdahan · Ban Pha · Champhon · Savannakhet · Ban Salang · Nong · Ban Sala
Don Tan · Ban Naphan · Xonbuli · Ban Lamvay · Dong Phu Vieng NBCA · Xe Xap NBCA · A Luoi
Loeng Nok Tha · Heuan Hin · Songkhon · Banghiang · Ban Tat Hai · Tahoy · Ban Tapung · 2066
Chanuman · Ban Pakxong · Dong Sithuan · Ban Lanong · Ban Adeut
Khemmarat · Ban Xenuan · Toumlan · Kong · Ai Yin Young
Ban Naxuak · Xe Ban Nuan NBCA · Ban Nadu Nyai
Lakhon Pheng · Ban Taleo
Amnat Charoen · Salavan · Ban Kaleum · 2193
Rai Khi · Vapi · Ban Bungxai · Salavan · Ban Kathang · Sekong
Ban Samrong · Ban Napong · Ban Beng · Ban Songkhon · Muang Dak Cheung
Trakan Phutphon · Khongxedon · Taat Lo · Tha Teng · Sekong · Ban Palong Nyai
Muang Sam Slip · Phu Xieng Thong NBCA · Lao Ngam · Phuphadeng · Taat Hua Khon
THAILAND · Sanasombun · Bachiang · Bolaven · Ban Donchan
Ubon Ratchathani · Khong Chiam · Ban Bungkha · Pakxe (Pakse) · Paksong · Nam Tók Katamtok (Waterfall) · Kaman
Phibun Mangsahan · Phonthong · Taat Fan · Ban Huaxe · Dong Hua Sao NBCA · Ban Pongkham · Ban Sok · Dong Amphan NBCA
Warin Chamrap · Sirinthorn Res. · Champasak (Ban Wat Thong) · Bolaven Plateau · Pa'am
Det Udom · Wat Phu · Ban Muang · Um Muang · Attapeu (Muang Samakhi Xai) · Xaisettha · Ban Antum
Buntharik · Thang Beng · Sanamxai · Ban Uk · Attapeu · Plei Kan
Kantharalak · Sukhuma · Champasak · Ban Phonsaat · Ban Sompoy
Saiphu Damlek · Xe Pian NBCA · Sankeo
Preah Vihéar · Ban Huayxai
Chôâm Khsan · Ban Kadian · Munlapamok · Ban Phonsaat · CAMBODIA
Ban Vin Tai · Don Khong · Muang Khong · Siêmpang · Phlevleu
Ban Taseun · Ban Kanluang · Ban Xot · Virachai · San
Trapeăng Pring · Kâmpóng Srâlau · Si Phan Don · Krâcheh

Provinces: Khammuan · Savannakhet · Salavan · Sekong · Champasak · Attapeu

Tha Kaek and environs

Located directly across the Mekong from Nakhon Phanom in Thailand, **Tha Kaek ❶** is Lao for "guest landing", a reference to its former function as a boat landing for foreign traders. This pleasant town, located 350km (220 miles) southeast of Vientiane via Route 13 (buses take around six hours), still greets its foreign visitors as its name suggests. Although shortly after the revolution it was renamed Muang Khammuan, the name Tha Kaek appearing to have sounded insufficiently nationalistic to the current regime, the only place one sees this appellation used is on government maps.

Historians have concluded that the area just to the south of the present-day city was settled by the Funan and Chen La Khmer kingdoms around the 5th century AD and was known as Sri Gotabura. The current site was chosen by the French, and building began in 1910. Little remains of Tha Kaek's distant past, but the French era is still evident, not only in architecture but in the central *place de la ville* and fountain.

The most atmospheric section of Tha Kaek is the pleasant tree-lined esplanade along the river, extending from the old fountain (at the end of the central city square) north to the ferry landing. Directly west of the fountain is the former colonial-era **customs house**, now housing the Tourist Police office. As you go north along riverside Setthathirat Road, a few tables shaded by large trees are good for a cold drink. On the right side of the street, after the large blue-painted four-storey **Mekong Khammuan Hotel** (tel: 51-250 777), lies **Wat Nabo** (daily; free), a tree-filled temple which also houses a school and a large banyan tree. Adjacent to Wat Nabo, the **Sooksomboon Hotel** (tel: 51-212 225) is worth a visit. This used to be a police station. It was built in the 1930s in an unusual blend of Art Deco and neo-rococo styles. Further north is the **passenger ferry landing** to Nakhon Phanom: ferries leave throughout the day. Back on the other (south) side of the fountain square, a boat restaurant called **Smile Barge Restaurant** (tel: 51-212 150), serving fresh fish dishes, is berthed on the Mekong.

To the east of town, across the road from the Lao Development Bank, the large **Km 2 Market** consists of two sections – the outer "dry" section, whose vendors sell every daily necessity you can think of, and the inner "wet" area, where a fascinating array of fresh produce is sold.

Wat Pha That Sikhotabong (daily 8am–6pm) is an active Buddhist temple on the riverside about 6km (4 miles) south of Tha Kaek. The complex includes an impressive *stupa*, a worship hall and Buddha images. The *stupa* was built during the reign of King Setthathirat, the Lao monarch who ruled in the mid-16th century. The name of the temple is the Lao spelling of Sri Gotabura, the 5th-century Khmer settlement, and local lore relates that the site has been sacred since antiquity.

Other side trips worth making from Tha Kaek are to the various **limestone caves** about 10–20km (6–12 miles) east of the town on the

Many Lao women are pipe-smokers.

unpaved Route 12. They are all located down side roads without signposts, so engaging the services of a local jumbo (motorised trishaw) driver to serve as a guide is necessary. One popular cave, **Tham Nang Aen** (daily) – *tham* is Lao for cave – unfortunately suffers from the presence of multicoloured fluorescent lights that have been installed to "enhance the atmosphere". As recently as 2004 a major new cave, **Tham Pha Pa** (daily 8am–noon and 1–4pm), was discovered by a local man, featuring over 200 bronze Buddhas thought to be several hundred years old. An attractive cave closer to the town is **Tham Xiengliab**, through which a stream flows.

For more information, contact the Provincial Tourist Office (tel: 51-212 512), or call **Thakhek Travel Lodge** (tel: 030-530 0145). The lodge provides useful travel details and helps make arrangements for tour options in the area, including "The Loop", which is a popular three-day circuit by a combination of motorbike and boat through the remote areas of Khammuan and Bolikhamxai provinces, to explore caves

Meander through an underground landscape at Tham Nang Aen.

and swimming spots and enjoy stunning views along the way.

Northeast of Tha Kaek, about 90km (55 miles) on Route 13 and another 130km (80 miles) east on Route 8, is the town of **Lak Sao ❷** (Lak Xao). The headquarters of the military-controlled Mountainous Areas Development Company (MADC), the town, which had a population of 24 in 1984, is now home to almost 30,000 people. The government is now promoting Lak Sao as a tourist destination, emphasising the attractive limestone karst formations, the forest cover and the tribal villages. The hype is justified – this is a wonderfully scenic area. Route 8 continues on to the Vietnam border 33km (21 miles) away, and border crossings are permitted in either direction.

Savannakhet

The 125km (78 miles) of main road between Tha Kaek and **Savannakhet ❸**, the second-largest urban centre in Laos, takes around 2.5–3 hours by bus (or around 8 hours direct from Vientiane). Also known (again, only officially) as Muang Khanthabuli and

(unofficially) as "Savan", it is not without interest, and is one of the best places in Laos to catch a glimpse of the old French ambience (decaying old buildings along the Mekong, baguette vendors and coffee), but lacks the small-town charm of Tha Kaek. Located across the Mekong from the Thai city of Mukdahan, this growing city is a major transit point for trade between Thailand and Vietnam, even more so since the 2007 opening of a second Friendship Bridge across the Mekong just to the north of town. Route 9, one of the best roads in Laos, runs east to the Vietnamese border and has long been the main overland crossing point into Laos for travellers coming from Vietnam.

As in Tha Kaek, the most appealing part of Savannakhet is the street running parallel to the river, Tha He Road. Towards its northern end is **Wat Sainyaphum** (daily; free), an active temple complex housing a school building constructed in an interesting mixture of French colonial and Buddhist architectural styles, a *sim* (ordination hall) with fantastic stucco bas-reliefs of camels and rhinoceros on the exterior walls, and French tiled floors. The southern gate of the temple is an exceptionally well-executed example of Theravada Buddhist temple architecture. A drum tower and many trees add to the atmosphere of this temple, the oldest (founded 1896) and largest in Savannakhet.

Across the street on the river embankment, more arcane deities are worshipped at a **Chinese temple** called San Jao Suttano. A pantheon of varied spirits – derived from the *san jiao* or "three religions" of Mahayana Buddhism, Daoism and Confucianism – are venerated here, with Kuan Yin, the Goddess of Mercy, notable among them. The raised pavilion is small, but rich with incense smoke and mystical imagery.

A range of stalls and small cafés next to Wat Sainyaphum offers a variety of Lao dishes as well as the ubiquitous Beer Lao, served at open-air tables. Housed in a colonial-era villa on the riverfront nearby, the Hotel Mekong offers live music in the adjacent nightclub, which caters mainly to visiting Vietnamese businessmen.

A few blocks away from the river on Sutthanu Road is a historically

Colonial relics in Savannakhet.

Wat Sainyaphum.

significant **statue of Than Kou Voravong** (1914–54), a hero in the resistance against the Japanese and Minister of Defence under the royalist regime. The elegant statue, depicting him clad in the upper-class *sompot* (men's collarless shirt), was cast after Voravong's assassination, but changing political winds did not allow this allegory of the vicissitudes of Lao politics to be erected until 1995.

A couple of blocks north from the statue, the **Dinosaur Museum** (Kanthabuli Road; daily 8–11.30am and 1.30–4.30pm) displays Jurassic-era bone samples that have been unearthed at five different sites in Savannakhet province.

Further south along the waterfront is the **passenger ferry terminal**, and around 300 metres beyond that is the Savannakhet Provincial Museum (Mon–Fri 8.30–11.30am and 1.30–4pm). Housed in an old colonial pile, it showcases war memorabilia and has a great deal of information on Kaysone Phomvihane, president until 1992.

Turning away from the river at the passenger ferry terminal onto Si Muang Road, you pass through the old commercial town centre, where the colonial ambience still prevails. A few hundred metres further in this direction, **St Teresa's Catholic Church** (daily) attends to the spiritual needs of Savannakhet's Christian community, most of whom are Vietnamese.

About two blocks northeast of the church, **Wat Rattanalangsi** (daily; free) is a large but modern temple whose claims to fame are its glazed windows and a large reclining Buddha image.

To explore further in Savannakhet you'll need to hire a jumbo or taxi. Two kilometres (1.2 miles) east of the river, along Sisavangvong Road, is the **Talaat Savan Xay**, a large covered building with stores offering an eclectic mixture of jewellery, upmarket goods and basic commodities. The vendors and their customers can be as interesting as the goods on sale, with Lao, Thai, Vietnamese, Chinese and other ethnic-minority people all present. Outside the building, a motley crowd of makeshift stalls sells fresh produce and other daily necessities: come before noon if you wish to witness the hustle and bustle of a local market, as these stalls are all cleared out by lunchtime.

East and south from Savannakhet

Continuing a further 10km (6 miles) east on Route 13 and then 3km (2 miles) down a secondary road to the right, you come to **That Ing Hang ④** (daily 8am–6pm); the Lao word *that* refers to any shrine said to contain a relic of the Lord Buddha. This is a site of great religious significance to the Lao. Both the site and the lower part of the structure itself date to later Khmer times (9th century AD), as indicated by the Hindu erotic art on the doorways. As with many Khmer religious sites in the region, That Ing Hang was restored and converted to a Buddhist place of worship during the time of the kingdom of Lan Xang – in this case, during the 16th century. The French, during their rule in Laos, again restored the *that*. In spite of this mixture of cultural influences, the 25-metre (80ft) -high stupa, which stands on top of a hollow chamber containing Buddha images (entry allowed only to men), retains an elegant and powerful presence.

For those with either a thirst for adventure or a profound interest in Khmer civilisation, a trip to **Heuan Hin ⑤** (literally, stone house) could be worthwhile. Located on the Mekong, 75km (47 miles) south of Savannakhet, this Khmer temple, which dates from the 6th century, is set in a small grove of plumeria trees. The ruins remain unrestored, and most of the bas-relief stone carvings which once decorated the site have been removed. Nonetheless, it's a pleasant three-hour cruise downriver from Savannakhet.

Some 160km (100 miles) east of Savannakhet via Route 9 – the main transport artery into Vietnam – lies Xepon (also spelled Sepon), one of the closest towns to what was once the Ho Chi Minh Trail (see panel). Old Xepon was destroyed during the war and rebuilt 5km (3 miles) to the west; the battle-scarred old town is littered with destroyed and damaged military detritus, half-covered by the jungle. The area is still rife with unexploded ordnance (UXO), so it is essential to keep to the marked paths.

Buddha images at the That Ing Hang stupa.

Supplies being carried along the Ho Chi Minh Trail in 1969.

THE HO CHI MINH TRAIL

The Ho Chi Minh Trail was less an actual route than a frequently shifting and complex network of jungle trails, concealed from the air by heavy foliage, along which the Communist North Vietnamese sent men and supplies to their southern compatriots, the National Liberation Front, better known as the Viet Cong. Crossing the Vietnamese Cordillera south and west of the port of Vinh, the trail entered Laos in the vicinity of present-day Route 8 and followed the spiny, jungle-covered Truong Son, or "Long Mountains", south through Lao territory to Cambodia and southern Vietnam. Far removed from the Pathet Lao base areas further north (see page 142), the trail had little to do with Laos – except that, of course, it ran across Lao territory.

In their attempts to cut this vital communications artery, the US Air Force bombed the entire region between Bolikhamxai in the north and Attapeu in the south, a territorial violation that the Lao could do nothing about, and one which was kept secret from Congress. At the end of the war, in 1975, the local peoples and the newly installed Lao PDR government were left to pick up the pieces. This is a process which continues today, and may do so for decades to come, as the amount of ordnance dropped on Laos during the war made it the most bombed country, per capita, in the history of modern warfare.

THE MEKONG RIVER

The world's 11th-longest river is a vital transport artery for both Laos and Cambodia, while its relatively unpolluted waters are an important source of fish.

The Mekong is truly a mighty river, rising on a distant Himalayan plateau in China and flowing south and east for 4,350km (2,700 miles); en route, it passes through Burma, Laos, Thailand, Cambodia and Vietnam before flowing into the South China Sea just south of Saigon. It is the seventh-longest river in Asia, and the 11th-longest in the world. By the time it reaches its nine-branched delta in Vietnam, its flow is so great that the silt it carries extends the surrounding shoreline out to sea by more than 1 metre (3ft) each year.

For much of its passage through Laos, the Mekong remains relatively narrow, surging between sharp rocky outcrops and limestone cliffs, through largely uninhabited forest, as well as past all the country's major towns, linking Huay Xai in the north with Luang Prabang, Vientiane, Tha Kaek, Savannakhet and Pakse. Still largely undeveloped, in its remote reaches it provides a refuge for wildlife of all kinds (see opposite page). In southernmost Laos it surges over the Khon Phapheng Falls, which, although only 21 metres (69ft) high, stretch for more than 10km (6 miles) and are quite impassable to navigation.

Surging southwards into Cambodia, the Mekong broadens to majestic proportions, so that at the Chatomuk near Phnom Penh, where it joins with the Sap and Bassac rivers, it is almost too broad to see across. In contrast to its rapid passage through Laos, in Cambodia the river flows languidly through flat and fertile lowlands, cutting a deep channel between rice paddies and rubber plantations, and providing the major source of water for the great Tonlé Sap lake, Cambodia's "riverine lung" and an all but inexhaustible source of fish.

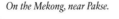

On the Mekong, near Pakse.

Building materials are ferried to Silk Island near Phnom Penh. The Mekong is a vital transport link throughout the region, although marked seasonal variations in flow and the presence of numerous rapids restrict river traffic to small vessels.

A fisherman casts his net in the lower reaches of the Mekong around Si Phan Don. River fish include various species of catfish and carp, some of which grow extremely large.

A rural scene near Kratie.

A RICH HABITAT

Despite concerns over damming projects and other environmental woes (see pages 41 and 195), the Mekong is still relatively unpolluted and rich in wildlife. Some 1,250 species of fish have been discovered in its waters, with new species being identified on a regular basis and more large fish than any river on the planet. Many of the villages along the river banks in Laos and Cambodia depend on fishing for their livelihood, with fishermen landing various species of catfish and carp. In the lower reaches, especially, some of these can grow extremely large: the giant river carp can reach a length of 1.5 metres (5ft) and weigh up to 70kg (150lb), while the Mekong giant catfish is the world's largest freshwater fish at up to 3 metres (10ft) and 315kg (650lb).

Aquatic mammals include the Irrawaddy dolphin, also known as the Mekong dolphin, which was once widespread but is now increasingly rare, with fewer than 100 surviving individuals in total; there are small populations around the Si Phan Don islands of southern Laos and around Kratie in Cambodia. A few endangered Siamese crocodiles also survive but, sadly, their days appear to be numbered, while the river dugong is also in serious decline. Semi-aquatic mammals include the smooth-coated otter and fishing cat, and the Mekong Valley is also an important migration route for birds.

Dolphin-viewing trip near Kratie. Small populations of Irrawaddy dolphins survive in southern Laos and Cambodia.

Khon Phapheng Falls close to the Laos–Cambodia border.

A back road in Champasak.

SOUTHERN LAOS

Ancient temples, idyllic waterfalls, ethnic villages and captivating landscapes are just some of the attractions of the southern Lao regions, reached by scenic boat trips along the Mekong.

Southern Laos offers a great diversity of attractions in close proximity. Travellers seeking insights into ancient history and culture will want to linger at the Khmer temple of **Wat Phu**, while the **Si Phan Don** (Four Thousand Islands) region in the far south will appeal to anyone who appreciates scenic beauty and tranquil rural life. Of the main urban centres, Pakse still has sufficient Vietnamese and Chinese residents to feel distinctly Indochinese, while Champasak still carries the unexpected air of a former tiny Lao royal principality. The temperate **Bolaven Plateau** is home to a number of Mon-Khmer minorities and offers superlative natural beauty, but still bears some scars from the Vietnam War. Attapeu is, literally, the end of the road in southern Laos – but this is precisely its appeal.

Pakse and environs

The town of **Pakse** (Pakxe) ❻, unlike Tha Kaek and Savannakhet, can lay no claim to having been home to ancient civilisations. The French founded it in 1905, possibly to offset the influence of nearby Champasak (Ban Wat Thong, the "settlement of the golden temple"), which traces its lineage back to pre-Khmer inhabitants. Pakse (literally meaning "river mouth") is located at the confluence of the Don and Mekong rivers, some 200km (125 miles) southeast of Savannakhet; frequent buses take three or four hours.

The population of about 88,000 is notable for its diversity and vivacity – Pakse is home to many ethnic Chinese and Vietnamese, and one senses a less restrained ambience here. The town is constructed on a grid of intersecting roads, so orientation is not difficult and the principal sights can be covered on foot within a day.

A walking tour should begin at the confluence of the two rivers; have coffee at one of the small **outdoor food stalls**

Main Attractions

Pakse
Champasak Historical
 Heritage Museum
Champasak
Wat Phu
Um Muang
Si Phan Don
Khon Phapheng waterfalls
Bolaven Plateau
Attapeu

Wat Luang, Pakse.

A small wall-mounted figure in a Pakse wat.

Watering the crops using a home-made system, Pakse.

just above the road leading down to the river ferry. Walking down the ferry road and bearing left, you will find small long-tail boats for hire. An interesting excursion is to cross the Don River and visit **San Jao Suk Se** (daily; free). Located on the northern bank of the Don where it meets the Mekong, this quiet and idyllic temple serves local devotees of the various deities of Mahayana Buddhism, Daoism and Confucianism. Statues of a wide variety of wise men and minor gods line the walls of the incense-clouded temple.

Various other shrines dot the grounds, and the view of the Mekong and of Pakse is excellent. The best time to visit is morning, when the mainly elderly devotees come with offerings of food and drink for the gods and linger to chat among themselves. Be sure to negotiate a round trip with your boatman; the boat service to the temple is irregular.

Returning to Pakse proper, walk along the bank of the Don and turn right at any of the main roads, all of which lead to the **Central Market**. The covered building housing the vendors here is a new structure – the former was completely razed to the ground in a 1997 fire, and for a few years, vendors simply operated around the old site, even though a vast **New Market** was built near the Lao-Japanese Bridge after the blaze. Next to the central market building is the more upmarket **Champasak Plaza Shopping Centre**. Long-distance buses to Vientiane depart from here.

A fine example of French colonial architecture, just north of the cloth shops, now houses the **Pakse Chinese Association**. As you return towards the main road that parallels the Don River, the impressive compound of **Wat Luang** (daily; free) is hard to miss. Surrounded by large funerary urns, often shaped like *stupas*, this temple, which was built in 1935, contains the remains of many of the former Champasak royal family, including Katay Don Sasorith, a staunch anti-Communist and prime minister during the royalist period. The Communist regime removed his statue which once stood in front of the temple, but wisely stopped short of disturbing

his remains. The temple also houses a large school for monks, located in a beautiful wooden building behind the temple on the banks of the Don.

Champasak Palace Hotel

From Wat Luang, you could be forgiven for hailing a jumbo to the next point of interest, the **Champasak Palace Hotel** about 500 metres east on busy Route 13. Construction of this edifice began in 1968; it was to serve as the residence of the last Prince of Champasak, Chao Boun Oum na Champasak. Boun Oum is remembered as a voluble and corpulent oriental potentate, renowned more for his *joie de vivre* than his political prowess.

He served as prime minister of Laos from 1960 to 1962. As the tides of war turned against his faction he fled the country in 1974, dying in Paris a few years later and fated never to occupy his pleasure palace that commands lovely views of the Don River and the Bolaven Plateau. After the revolution the building was completed and served as a venue for Communist

Party congresses and accommodation for visiting dignitaries. In 1995 a Thai company succeeded in its negotiations with the Lao government and, after renovating the palace, converted it into a hotel. Although the hotel is highly recommended as *the* place to stay in Pakse, it is worth a visit even if you are based elsewhere. The foyer uses gilt woodcarvings to set an oriental tone, but the meeting hall behind it, with its murals showing happily cooperating lowland Lao and hill tribes gathering the bountiful harvest, still recalls the building's days as a meeting place for the Party elite.

The atmosphere is relaxed, so it is not hard to wander to the upper floors – though it is better to ask – where you can experience the effect that the building's intended inhabitant had planned. Huge pavilions (now hotel suites) are surrounded by private balconies, beneath which spread tiled terraces. The two top floors contain increasingly intimate reception rooms which command panoramic views of the entire region. Note the area just beneath the eaves on the upper floors

Men and women of the southern minorities smoke long pipes.

of the building: as the Communists completed the building they added bas-reliefs of the new national symbol of Laos, which included the obligatory hammer and sickle. Not content with merely painting over such images of the past, the new proprietors have placed bad luck-deflecting *feng shui* mirrors over the slogan that extols the virtues of socialism. Without ever intending to be so, the Champasak Palace Hotel is now a living historical museum.

Celebrating past and present

Directly east of the Champasak Palace Hotel lies **Wat Tham Fai** (daily; free), which, because of its sprawling grounds, is the site of many temple fairs. Should you be fortunate enough to be in Pakse when such an event is taking place (usually timed to coincide with major Buddhist holidays), be sure not to miss it; otherwise the temple has little to recommend it to the casual visitor.

Another 200 metres east on Route 13, a small **Chinese temple** (daily; free) offers pleasant respite from the heat. Housed on two levels, it contains the garish images of the gods venerated by local Vietnamese and Chinese Mahayana Buddhists.

A further 400 metres/yds east on Route 13 (it may be easier to hail another jumbo rather than walk) lies the **Champasak Historical Heritage Museum** (daily 8.30–11.30am and 1.30–4pm). Currently something of a cultural mishmash, the museum nevertheless has some beautiful pieces on the ground floor, including carved sandstone 7th-century Khmer lintels from Um Muang (see page 177) and some less interesting photographs of Communist Party officials greeting visiting dignitaries. Unfortunately many of the exhibits are labelled only in Lao or French, while the friendly guides speak limited English. The first floor is more interesting, focusing on the various ethnic minorities who inhabit the region, including their jewellery and textiles.

After this admittedly lengthy day trip around Pakse (which, if you have the time, could be divided into two forays), a return to the starting point

Wat Phu, Champasak.

to watch the sunset at the confluence of the Don and Mekong rivers will provide an excellent perspective to reflect (over a chilled Beer Lao) on this varied and vibrant southern terminus of the Mekong Valley.

Downriver from Pakse

Travelling south from Pakse, you leave a Laos bustling towards modernity and re-enter a more rural past. There are regular buses and songthaews heading south to **Champasak** on the western bank of the Mekong River, the starting point for a visit to Wat Phu and nearby sights of historical interest. Alternatively, you can take a boat: depending upon your budget – and your pain threshold – there is a variety of options available for the 30km (20-mile) cruise down the Mekong. From the Pakse ferry terminal, located on the Se Don about 200 metres upstream from its confluence with the Mekong, covered public boats leave throughout the morning. Each vessel carries around 50 passengers, plus cargo. Choice of seating is either under or on the roof, although both

chivalry and Lao custom require that women do not ride on the roof. Boats take 2–3 hours to reach Champasak, crisscrossing the river to deposit or collect passengers at various riverside villages en route. The fare is minimal. A faster, more comfortable and obviously more expensive alternative is to charter a smaller craft either from the same terminal or on the Mekong, just south of the confluence of the two rivers. These vessels carry 10–20 passengers (avoid the smaller, uncovered long-tail boats) and take just over an hour to reach Champasak.

A final option is to travel in style on the *Vat Phou*, a steel-hulled, air-conditioned cruiser with private bathrooms and 12 state rooms. The company operating this vessel offers guided tours of the Wat Phu and Si Phan Don regions lasting three days and two nights, with both Lao and French cuisine served on board. Bookings can be arranged through the many travel agencies in Pakse. Prices vary according to season, but are never cheap. Check www.vatphou.com for more information.

Ornate woodcarvings in a doorway at Wat Luang.

The extensive Wat Phu complex.

FACT

Champasak was the smallest and least influential of the three Lao kingdoms that emerged after the break-up of Lan Xang, always over-shadowed by the larger and more prestigious kingdoms of Luang Prabang and Vientiane. Between 1713 and 1904 it was ruled by a succession of 11 kings, before becoming a reduced-status princedom under the French. The last royal prince, Boun Oum, renounced his rights in favour of King Sisa-vangvong of Luang Prabang in 1946.

A Champasak classroom.

Champasak

Prior to the establishment of Pakse by the French in 1905, sleepy **Champasak** ❼ served as the administrative centre for the Champasak region, and the residence of Champasak's royal family when it was an independent kingdom. All that is left of this sumptuous past today are two former colonial-era royal residences, now both guesthouses, located just south of the fountain circle that marks the centre of town.

While in Champasak, stroll along the tree-lined lanes and visit **Wat Thong** (daily; free), also known as Wat Nyutthitham, located on the road directly west of the royal residences. Formerly the temple of the local royal family, it is now the final resting place of many of its members, and captures the essence of this city which time has eclipsed.

Faded grandeur notwithstanding, Champasak has a very agreeable ambience. With comfortable accommodation available in the Sala Wat Phou, a restored colonial hotel, the town serves as an excellent base from which to explore ancient Wat Phu.

Wat Phu

Ancient and magnificent, the complex of **Wat Phu** ❽ (www.vatphou-champasak.com; daily site 8am–6pm, museum 8am–4.30pm) – literally "Mountain Temple" – is located on a site which has been sacred to at least three cultures. The Chen La Kingdom venerated the site from the 6th to the 8th centuries AD (reportedly placating the spirits with human sacrifices), and was followed by a pre-Angkor Khmer civilisation which built most of the present edifices, beginning around the 9th century. Lastly, the Theravada Buddhist Kingdom of Lan Xang converted the Hindu temples into Buddhist shrines.

What appears to have attracted the attention of all of these civilisations is an unusually shaped mountain behind the temple, Phu Pasak. The summit juts skywards to a narrow precipice, which to the Hindu Khmers seemingly called to mind the holy Shiva *lingam*, or phallus. Locals still refer to the mountain, colloquially if somewhat irreverently, as Phu Kuay (Mount Penis). This geological formation also brings to mind a

Buddhist *stupa*, which enhances its mystical significance. Adding to the symbolic power of the site, an underground spring flows from the mouth of a cave near the top of the temple complex. Although it lacks the grandeur of Angkor, Wat Phu nonetheless exudes a presence that even those not impressed by its architectural significance will find palpable.

Located 9km (5.5 miles) south of Champasak, Wat Phu begins at river level and rises three levels to reach the foot of the mountain. Outside the complex is a large reservoir which in times past was the site of boat races and ritual bathing. The bathing (and fishing) continue, somewhat less ritualistically.

As you enter the complex you can see the remains of palaces built by Champasak royalty, towards the end of their dynasty, from which they viewed the annual festivities held on the full moon of the third lunar month. An east–west axial promenade passes between two rectangular *baray* or bathing ponds and leads to the base of the middle level. At the top of a flight of irregular stone stairs two large quadrangular pavilions

flank the central promenade. Some have suggested, from the deities carved into the stone, that the right-hand pavilion was used by male worshippers and the left by women, though scholars tend to dismiss this as a local myth. Currently only the former is open to visitors. As you climb through the small access door you can see Hindu bas-reliefs on the lintels. Most of the free-standing statuary has been removed or damaged.

Returning to the central promenade, you will pass some pavilions whose function remains uncertain, owing to their state of disrepair. About 10 metres (30ft) to the right of the central passageway is a stone *yoni*, the stylised Hindu female fertility symbol. This artefact is constantly covered with offerings of flowers and incense, illustrating the continuing power of the ancient Hindu symbols among today's Buddhist Lao.

The third level of the temple, which contains the main sanctuary, is approached by a steep flight of stairs flanked by frangipani trees (*dok champa* in Lao, the national flower).

Prayer flags at Wat Phuang Kaew.

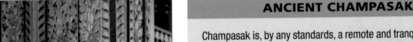

ANCIENT CHAMPASAK

Champasak is, by any standards, a remote and tranquil rural retreat town, yet about 1,600 years ago it was an important Khmer centre called Shrestapura or Kuruksestra, which is thought to have been the northern capital of the ancient Chen La Kingdom which dominated Cambodia and southern Laos between the 6th and 8th centuries AD. Today Shrestapura – known locally as Muang Kao, or "Old Town" – is little more than a barely discernible rectangular twin earthen rampart on the right (west) bank of the Mekong about 40km (25 milles) south of modern Champasak town, astride the dirt road leading to Wat Phu. Except from the air, it's difficult to detect the outlines of the ancient city, which measure about 2,300 metres by 1,800 metres (1.5 by 1 mile) and are protected on the east by the Mekong River itself. The Chinese seem to have known of its existence, however, Tang annals naming two kings, Shrutavarman and Shreshtavarman, who ruled there before the Khmer capital was transferred to Sambor Prei Kuk, near Kompong Thom in Cambodia, during the 7th century.

Today ancient Shrestapura is best known, at least among archaeologists of Southeast Asia, as being the site where the region's oldest inscribed stone stele was found. The stele, dating from the 5th century AD, records the founding of Shrestapura by King Devanika.

TIP

One of the more unusual attractions of remote Don Khong is an abandoned and rusting locomotive that survives there, dating from French colonial times. Check this relic out by all means, but be aware that it stands amid patches of a kind of local "poison ivy" which produces painful swelling and irritating itching among those liable to allergies.

The third full moon heralds the Wat Phu Festival.

Large trees and the remains of statues surround the sanctuary, which is in a good state of preservation, as are the bas-reliefs on the lintels. When this was a Hindu site of worship, a stone Shiva *lingam* occupied the central place of veneration, bathed by spring water piped in from the cave; now large Buddha images take pride of place.

The mountain spring is still venerated by the Lao: bottles of the water are collected, and heads are held beneath the pipe emitting the spring water for both physical and spiritual refreshment. In the small cave behind the spring, worshippers have collected a variety of Buddhist and Hindu religious statuary, including what appears to be a stone Shiva *lingam*. Behind and to the right of the sanctuary, a stone carving depicts the Hindu trinity of Shiva, Vishnu and Brahma. Also to the right is a wooden Buddhist temple. A winding path leading from behind the temple (a small fee will secure the services of any of the young guides) leads to two interesting carvings of a crocodile and an elephant, the former thought to date from the early Angkor

period, the latter from the 18th or 19th century.

Wat Phu is famous for its *boun* (festival), which attracts visitors from throughout Laos and beyond. The precise dates vary according to the lunar calendar, but in most years it falls in February. During the three-day event Wat Phu is filled with pilgrims, who make offerings at various sites of the temple complex, particularly the sacred *yoni* and the elephant and crocodile carvings. On the final day of the festival monks accept alms from the pilgrims, and in the evening a candlelight procession circles the pavilions at the lower level of the complex. Far from being a purely solemn event, the festival is also characterised by a myriad of more worldly diversions such as boat races, cock fighting and kick-boxing competitions. In the evenings popular music and drinking add to the revelry.

Um Muang

Across the river on the east bank from Wat Phu, located in a forest about 1km (0.6 miles) north of the nearest village,

EMERGING SI PHAN DON

Southern Laos's "Four Thousand Islands" have remained remote and undeveloped throughout history. In the past decade or so, however, they have emerged as an increasingly important tourist destination, initially for backpackers and budget travellers, but now attracting a more upmarket clientele as well. Despite its name and the plethora of small islands that are scattered across the Mekong at this point, only three main islands have developed, so far, as tourist centres. These are Don Det, Don Khon and Don Khong. The most developed islands are Don Khon, with the best accommodation and – if things are working properly – 24-hour electricity, and Don Khong, which has the only surfaced road. In southern Laos times are changing, however, and Si Phan Don looks sure to become an important tourist destination.

Ban Tomo, is another Khmer ruin, **Um Muang** (also known as Um Tomo; free). This is thought to have been built in the 10th century, and to have been dedicated to Parvati, also known as Uma, the consort of the god Shiva. This temple is in a much greater state of disrepair than Wat Phu, but what remains is still mysterious and evocative of Champasak's distant past. The most interesting relic is a stone pillar carved with faces of an as yet unidentified deity who may, perhaps, be Shiva. There are also a few lintels still *in situ*, though others have been removed to museums for safe keeping.

The easiest and most direct way to visit Um Muang is from Champasak by long-tail boat, a return journey of about two hours, depending on the season. Make sure to hire the boat for the return trip, or you risk getting stranded at Ban Tomo, which is not regularly served by river traffic.

Si Phan Don and Don Khong

After the historical and cultural focus of Wat Phu, the islands of **Si Phan Don** are a natural attraction, offering scenic beauty and a glimpse into the life of Laos's more remote rural population. The Mekong River is at its widest in Laos here, close to the Cambodian border: during the rainy season it is up to 12km (7.5 miles) across, and when the waters recede many small islands emerge. It is from this phenomenon that the Si Phan Don region takes its name, meaning "Four Thousand Islands".

One of the larger and permanently inhabited islands – 6km (4 miles) at it widest, 12km (7.5 miles) north to south – is **Don Khong ❾**, located about 120km (75 miles) downstream from Wat Phu. Taking the public passenger ferry is for the hardy; depending on the passenger and cargo load, as well as the number of intermediate stops, the trip from Champasak can take 6–8 hours, but services are irregular these days. Alternatively,

charters can be arranged from either Pakse or Champasak. The journey can also be made by road, along Route 13 on the east bank of the Mekong; it takes about 2–3 hours in a public bus from Ban Muang across the river ("Lot 13") from Champasak. Direct buses from Pakse also reach Hat Xai Khun, a village east of Don Khong.

Don Khong offers no sites of historical significance, but compensates by giving the visitor a glimpse of southern Lao river life. Being the largest and most "developed" island, it has decent accommodation in restored French villas from the colonial era, in the main town, **Muang Khong**, and a small choice of bucolic restaurants accessible by motorcycle or bicycle. The island can be explored by either; a reasonable dirt road goes right round its circumference, and there are several interesting villages dotted along it. Since all overnight visitors will stay in Muang Khong, an exploration logically begins here. **Wat Phuang Kaew** (daily; free), located behind the Auberge Sala Don Khong, greets

TIP

Don Det, in Si Phan Don, is a very laid-back place. Yet it has also started to attract a rather drug-orientated clientele, as well as a reputation for indolence, indulgence and easy morality among its visitors. This is well known to the local Lao police.

The islands of Si Phan Don are said to number 4,000.

Cycling to school. Bikes are the standard form of transport for the young people of rural Laos.

The Taat Lo falls: the chalets here make it a good base for exploring the Bolaven Plateau.

visitors with a massive and gaudy stucco Buddha image.

Heading north, you will find the oldest temple on the island, **Wat Jawm Thong** (daily; free), which has recently undergone restoration work. Interesting village temples can also be found at the southern tip of the island in Ban Huay and Ban Hang Khong, where a small temple, **Wat Hang Khong** (daily; free), is especially peaceful and attractive. Apart from the temples, Muang Khong is best enjoyed for its pleasant atmosphere and as a staging post en route to the islands further south.

Li Phi and Khon Phapheng waterfalls

Located just 15km (9 miles) by river south of Muang Khong, a one-hour trip which passes through a maze of small islands, **Don Khon** is the site of the **Li Phi Falls** ❿ (open daily), also known as Taat Somphamit. Also to be visited here are the remains of a 12km (7.5-mile) railway built by the French to allow cargo transfer without having to circumvent the rapids and

waterfalls that abound on this section of the Mekong. During low-water-level periods larger boats can reach only to **Don Det**, the island north of Don Khon, and a smaller long-tail boat navigates the channel between Don Det and Don Khon. Only basic accommodation is available in this area, and there is no electricity, so it is best explored on a day trip from Don Khong. Any of the Don Khong lodges can arrange such trips.

Disembarking on Don Khon, you can pause for refreshment at one of the riverside restaurants. Across the road is a former French hospital. Turning right on the road in front of the hotel, you pass through the village of **Ban Khon**, where a few colonial villas are shaded by trees. If you bear right where the road forks in the village you will reach the remains of a railway bridge built by the French. Passing beneath the bridge and turning left, you come to the remains of an old steam locomotive which once plied the only railway ever constructed in Laos, in the early part of the 20th century. The hospital, villas and defunct

railway all combine to epitomise the audacity and futility of the grand ambitions of *la mission civilisatrice*.

About 1km (0.6 miles) further down what becomes more of a path than a road, the Li Phi Falls rage over ragged boulders. Although the drop is only a few metres, their volume and power are impressive. A second set of falls is located about 500 metres/yds further downstream. Fishermen use traps and nets in the pools at the base of the falls.

A unique attraction of Don Khon is the endangered **Irrawaddy dolphin**, which can be seen off the southern tip of the island. This mammal can survive in both fresh and salt water, but it is now mainly indigenous to the lower reaches of large Asian rivers, such as the Mekong and Irrawaddy. Boats can be chartered at Kong Ngay beach, about 3km (2 miles) from Ban Khon.

The **Khon Phapheng** (Phapheng Falls; open daily) are the largest series of waterfalls on the lower Mekong. What they lack in height they make up for in sheer volume. Several of the cascades are visible from the east bank of the Mekong, about 10km (6 miles) south of the village of Ban Nakasang. From Don Khon or Don Det you must travel by boat to Ban Nakasang, and proceed south by land. The falls are a very impressive sight, and are best viewed from a pavilion located above them – three separate cascades merge at this spot. Fishermen clamber precariously across the raging torrents on bamboo ladders to lay lines, while birds dive through the spray seeking smaller fry. Phapeng has its share of vendors of roasted chicken and other local delicacies, and plenty of cold beer: it's a lovely spot for a picnic and a great conclusion to this tiring but certainly rewarding journey through a unique part of southern Laos.

The Bolaven Plateau

The lush **Bolaven Plateau** is known for its temperate climate and Mon-Khmer minority peoples; indeed, the name Bolaven means "place of the Laven", once the predominant ethnic group in the region. Other attractions include waterfalls, boat cruises and, for those so inclined, visits to the

Quiet meditation at Khon Phapheng.

FACT

The French colonialists were the first to recognise the agricultural possibilities of the temperate Bolaven Plateau, introducing coffee, rubber and banana as cash crops in the early 20th century. The region also produces a wide variety of fruit, vegetables and spices, including cardamom – yet today coffee remains king, yielding a valuable harvest of 15,000 to 20,000 tonnes a year.

Ho Chi Minh Trail (see page 165). Hotels and travel agencies in Pakse offer a variety of guided tours to the region, ranging from day trips to three- to four-day itineraries.

The plateau spreads over Salavan, Sekong, Champasak and Attapeu provinces, and with an average altitude of 1,200 metres (4,000ft) the area is suitable for the cultivation of temperate crops. The French introduced the production of coffee, high-quality stock of both arabica and robusta strains; production declined during the Vietnam War but is now experiencing a major renaissance.

In addition to the Laven minority, other groups include the Katu, Alak, Tahoy and Suay. All of these peoples have animist beliefs. The Laven in particular are famed for their handwoven cloth, with patterns of beads woven into the fabric. Foot looms are used to produce this cloth which, while not as fine as the work found in the north, certainly has a distinct style, more Khmer- than Thai-influenced.

A good starting point for an exploration of the region is the **Taat Lo** (Lo Waterfall), 94km (58 miles) northeast of Pakse. The road is paved throughout, and the journey time is no more than two hours; Laven villages can be visited en route. The falls drop only a few metres, but are wide and surrounded by lush vegetation. Taat Lo Lodge (tel: 034-211 889) offers attractive chalets overlooking the falls. Alak, Katu and Suay villages can be found near the resort, which also arranges elephant day treks. Alternatively, contact **Tim's Guesthouse and Restaurant** (tel: 034-211 885) for information on Taat Lo and for trips in Salavan Province. Further south, Taat Fan (see page 181) to the east of Pakse in Champasak province is another popular base for travellers wishing to explore the Bolaven Plateau.

The town of **Salavan** is located 40km (25 miles) northeast of Taat Lo. Devastated during the Vietnam War, it has been rebuilt and its only charm lies in its splendid isolation. Those interested in investigating the customs of the local Mon-Khmer ethnic minorities might consider a visit.

A more interesting itinerary upon leaving the Taat Lo area would be to take the turn-off to **Sekong** ⓫ (Route 16), just east of the Taat Lo road. This two-hour journey passes through verdant coffee plantations with views of the mountains rising above the plateau to the southwest. Sekong town, like Salavan, has been rebuilt since the war, and has a continuing military presence. **Sekong Souksamlane Hotel** across from the market has an adjacent restaurant, and a good selection of minority handicrafts on sale. Otherwise the main reason to visit Sekong is to arrange a boat trip down the scenic Kong River to Attapeu, which takes about 4–7 hours.

Attapeu and environs

Arriving in **Attapeu** ⓬ (now officially known as Muang Samakhi Xai, a Communist-era designation meaning "Victorious Harmony" that has failed to enter into local use), you see why

The Sekong River at Attapeu.

the Lao call this their "garden city". All the houses seem to be surrounded by trees and shrubbery, both ornamental and agricultural. But, although strong on rural atmosphere, the town is without any specific attractions.

East of Attapeu, however, you can reach the **Ho Chi Minh Trail**. In the **Sansai** district you can see abandoned and damaged war equipment, and, near the village of **Pa'am**, a long-defunct Russian surface-to-air missile and launcher, looking sad and incongruous in this rural setting. Although villages have been rebuilt, you can still see the crumbling foundations of temples destroyed by the bombing, and the defoliants used have left mainly scrub forests. Overall, the experience is unsettling but worthwhile. Those undertaking this trip should be particularly careful not to leave marked paths, since the concentration of unexploded ordnance (UXO) here is among the highest in Laos.

Attapeu is literally the end of the line in terms of vehicular travel, so you must double back about 50km (30 miles) north towards Sekong in order to return to Pakse. Around halfway between Attapeu and Sekong, a road built to service a large hydroelectric project leads westwards back to the Bolaven Plateau. About 30km (19 miles) along it is **Nam Tok Katamtok** (Katamtok Waterfall). After you have become accustomed to the short but wide waterfalls of southern Laos, this cascade is spectacular in its 100-metre (320ft) drop. A small pavilion provides a good viewing point, but no trails to the base are discernible, and the route would be precipitous and also hazardous due to the possibility of UXO. About 2km (1.2 miles) beyond the waterfall the road crosses a bridge, and to the right another small waterfall makes a pleasant picnic stop.

As you leave the more mountainous regions and descend to the lower-lying Bolaven Plateau, you will come to prosperous-looking **Alak villages**. These settlements are accustomed to visitors, and offer handicrafts for sale. **Paksong** ⑬ serves as a major market town where the region's farmers sell their crops, notably coffee, to middlemen from Pakse. The morning market is quite animated and filled with interesting minority groups who have descended from their home villages.

Beyond Paksong, on the way to Pakse, another spectacular series of waterfalls, **Taat Fan**, tumbles 120 metres (390ft) – believed to be the highest waterfalls in Laos. The **Tad Fane Resort** (Ban Lak 38; www.tadfaneresort.com; tel: 020-566 93366), with its wooden bungalows overlooking the spectacular falls and the dense forests of the Dong Hua Sao NPA, is a good place to base yourself. The resort can arrange guided treks into the area, which take one through coffee plantations to the top of the Taat Fan waterfalls and to two other sets of waterfalls in the area (a small charge is payable at each waterfall). The trek will also take you through minority villages and across the temperate Dan Sin Xay plain.

Reminders of the war years are visible all over the region. These American bombs stand outside a house in Attapeu.

Men sip rice alcohol through straws to celebrate the Lao New Year.

Rural scene on the banks of the Mekong River, near Kompong Cham.

Khmer sculpture at Wat Nokor,
Kompong Cham.

CAMBODIA

After its brutal recent past, Cambodia is now emerging as a beguiling destination. The magnificent ruins of Angkor are without equal, while the buzzing capital city, coastal resorts and untrammelled backwoods complete the picture.

Monks test out the waters at Kep.

A visit to Cambodia is truly a unique experience. Once the greatest city in the world, with over 1 million inhabitants, Angkor dominates the country's past and present, and is now making an invaluable commercial contribution to its future. Even after several visits one struggles to come to terms with the immensity of its scale; it is as though all the treasures of the Valley of the Nile were assembled in a single place. There is nowhere else like it on the face of the earth.

Of course Cambodia is more than just Angkor. There is Phnom Penh, once an exquisite hybrid of Cambodian and French architecture and – despite the destruction of the war years and depopulation by the Khmer Rouge – destined to become so again. Like Laos, Cambodia has retained many of the beneficial aspects of French colonialism, and there can be few more romantic settings in which to sample French haute cuisine and sip a glass of wine than by the Chatomuk, or Quatre Bras, where the Mekong, Bassac and Sap rivers come together.

There are also many wonderful temples, hundreds of years old and still buried in the forests, waiting to be discovered. Some are not yet accessible, but each year clearance and restoration work is pressed forward, so that in the not-too-distant future Cambodia is destined to become one of the region's major tourist destinations.

Finally, there is the Cambodian coast, once the weekend retreat of French colonial officials and the Cambodian elite, but which suffered badly

Part of the 7km (4-mile) stretch of Kep beach.

under the puritanical Khmer Rouge regime. Now the coastal resort of Kep is being rebuilt, while the beaches of Sihanoukville are being developed into a tourist playground. Offshore, the warm waters of the Gulf of Thailand are studded with some entrancingly beautiful tropical islands. Meanwhile, in the remote and inaccessible Cardamom Mountains and elsewhere, national parks are being established, so Cambodia also looks set to develop as a major wildlife destination in the years to come.

Traditional farming methods persist.

AN ENVIRONMENT UNDER THREAT

Dominated by the Mekong River and the great
lake of Tonlé Sap, Cambodia is finding it hard to
reconcile ecological and economic priorities.

In contrast to the rugged terrain of Laos,
Cambodia is a relatively flat, low-lying land.
Situated at the heart of Indochina, it has a
total area of slightly over 180,000 sq km (70,000
sq miles), and shares land borders with Laos to
the northeast, Vietnam to the east and southeast, and Thailand to the north and west. In
addition, Cambodia has a 443km (277-mile)
coastline on the Gulf of Thailand in the southwest. For administrative purposes, Cambodia is
divided into 24 provinces and the municipality of Phnom Penh. The capital, Phnom Penh
(population 2 million), is in the southeast.

The lay of the land

Two water features dominate the landscape: the
Mekong River and the great lake of Tonlé Sap.
The Mekong enters from Laos and flows for
around 500km (300 miles) through Cambodia,
up to 5km (3 miles) wide in places, before passing into Vietnam bound for the South China
Sea. The river splits in two at Phnom Penh,
the first major division of its large delta, where
the broader, northern branch retains the name
Mekong, while the southern branch is known
as the Bassac. Tonlé Sap lake, vital to the Cambodian economy, dominates the centre of the
country (see page 195).

Beyond the Mekong-Tonlé Sap Basin, low-
lying plains extend across much of central and
northern Cambodia. Towards the periphery
of the country, however, are several mountain
ranges; the northern border with Thailand is
marked by the Dongrak Mountains, a 350km
(220-mile) range of south-facing sheer sandstone cliffs rising 180–550 metres (585–1,800ft)
above the plain. In the southwest, covering
much of the region between the Tonlé Sap
and the Gulf of Thailand, two separate ranges,

Female workers planting rice.

the Kravanh (Cardamom Mountains) and the
Damrei (Elephant Mountains), form a remote
upland area. It is here that Cambodia's highest peak, Mount Aoral (1,813 metres/5,892ft),
is found. Beyond these ranges, on the coast, is a
narrow lowland strip, cut off from the central
plains and sparsely populated. In the northeast
of the country, occupying the remote provinces
of Rattanakiri and Mondolkiri, rise the eastern
highlands. This region of thickly forested hills
and plateaus, which extends east across the border into Vietnam and north into Laos, is wild
and remote, but is becoming deforested at an
alarming rate.

Cambodia also has many islands off its
southern coast in the Gulf of Thailand. Koh

Kompong Som lie to the west of Sihanouk-ville within a half-day boat trip. The Koh Ream Archipelago is scattered to the east towards the fishing village of Phsar Ream. Koh Tang is further out to sea, between four and eight hours' journey from Sihanoukville by boat.

Most of Cambodia's 16 million inhabitants live in small villages in the Mekong-Tonlé Sap Basin and practise subsistence wet-rice cultivation or fishing. Phnom Penh, emptied by the Khmer Rouge regime between 1975 and 1979, is now bursting at the seams, and many poorer

The various mountain ranges in the country support several different forest types. Large areas of the Cardamom and Elephant mountains in the southwest are covered in virgin rainforest, where the upper canopy often reaches 50 metres (160ft). Elsewhere in these mountains, at the highest elevations, are subtropical pine forests. The eastern mountain ranges bordering Vietnam and Laos are covered with deciduous forests and thick grasslands.

Among Cambodia's larger animals are small populations of tigers, leopards, rhinoceros and elephants. Present in somewhat

A disabled child serves as a potent reminder of the misery wreaked by landmines.

people are being driven out by speculation and high land prices. Set against this, the government is distributing free land to poor farmers in undeveloped areas, such as around Bang Melea in Siem Reap province.

Flora and fauna

Cambodia plays host to a diversity of natural environments. The central lowland plains are largely agricultural; but outside the cultivated fields of rice, maize and tobacco and, in some places, rubber plantations, they are thinly forested, with scrub-like areas of reeds and grasses covering large areas. Around the periphery, the transitional plains are covered with savannah grasses and small bushes.

greater numbers are various species of bear, deer and wild cattle. There are also numerous smaller mammals, including monkeys, squirrels, voles and rats. The country is rich in birdlife: notable species include those found in wetland and grassland ecosystems such as cranes, herons, pelicans, cormorants, ducks and grouse.

Much of the wildlife is threatened, notably the rare Irrawaddy dolphins in the Mekong near Kratie (see page 302); on the other hand, genuine efforts are being made to establish national parks and nature reserves such as the bird reserve at Prek Toal (see box), and as these begin to generate income from tourism, so local people are learning to appreciate their value. Cambodia's first national parks were established as recently as 1993. Today there are seven – Kirirom, Preah Monivong, Kep, Ream, Botum Sakor, Phnom Koulen and Virachey.

Prek Toal Biosphere on the northwestern shore of Tonlé Sap is sometimes billed as the premier birdwatching destination in all Southeast Asia. It is home to a plethora of rare species, and is easily accessible by boat from Siem Reap.

The driest months are January and February, when often there is no rainfall, and the wettest usually September and October. Rainfall varies quite considerably from year to year and region to region. The southwestern highlands, with their seaward-facing slopes, can exceed 5,000mm (200 inches) a year, while the central plains generally average only 1,400mm (55 inches). Greater problems arise when the southwest monsoon fails. This can cause severe food shortages for the many Cambodians dependent on the Tonlé Sap and its surrounding fertile soils for their sustenance. Droughts are not

Fields given over to wet-rice cultivation.

There are also 10 designated wildlife sanctuaries across the country.

Climate

Cambodia's climate is governed by the annual monsoon cycle. From May to October the southwest monsoon carries heavy daily rainfall. The northwest monsoon, between November and March, brings slightly lower temperatures and less precipitation. In between are transitional periods, with changeable cloud cover and rainfall, but consistently high temperatures. The coolest months are between November and January, though even then temperatures rarely fall below 20°C (68°F): Cambodia is generally a few degrees hotter than Laos.

uncommon, and, despite the fact that historical evidence suggests they have always been a problem in the region, many blame irresponsible loggers in the more northerly countries on the Mekong for exacerbating the situation.

Environmental issues

Over the past four decades large-scale logging has continued unabated throughout much of Cambodia; estimates put the reduction in forest cover at around one-third since 1970. While the Khmer Rouge started the exploitation of the forests, subsequent governments have helped to accelerate it. With international demand for timber high, and stricter controls on logging and the export of wood continually being imposed in surrounding countries, Cambodia has not hesitated to cash in on its forests. Logging concessions have been sold to foreign nations, particularly Malaysia and Indonesia, bringing much-needed cash to the ailing economy, but with little thought for the future. Several times the government in Phnom Penh has rescinded concessions, but so far greed has proved too powerful, and new concessions continue to be sold.

Loss of forest cover and encroachment on previously uninhabited forests, together with many years of war, also continue to pose a seri-

southwestern mountains and the Gulf of Thailand. The delicate ecology here is threatened by commercial shrimp farming, largely the province of Thai entrepreneurs. To raise the profitable tiger-shrimps, mangroves must be cleared to make ponds. Fertilisers are added, and waste water is pumped out, an extremely destructive process which makes a farm useless within four years. As elsewhere in the region, offshore coral reefs are at risk from dynamite fishing.

Inevitably, the economic possibilities of the Mekong River have not gone unnoticed. As

Mine warning at Preah Vihear, northern Cambodia.

Khmer woman chopping firewood in Kratie.

ous threat to the country's wildlife. As in neighbouring Laos, animal conservation still remains at best a minor concern. Many people still hunt – though, happily, the country is no longer a major game-hunting destination – and there is little education regarding the importance of maintaining a balanced ecosystem. Quite simply, most people are concerned only with finding their next meal. On the other hand, large areas of the country are still only lightly populated, and little-visited by locals or foreigners, so – with the exception of logging – environmental pressures are reduced.

Another habitat at risk is the salt marshes and mangroves which make up the narrow strip of land on the coast between the

in other countries on the Mekong, various proposals have been made, mainly revolving around the establishment of hydroelectric facilities. So far little has come of these proposals, but they have brought to light the serious risks posed by similar projects upstream in Laos and China. Because Cambodia is so dependent on the annual rise in the waters of the Mekong and the Tonlé Sap for the fertile deposits this brings, any change in the flow of the river could have disastrous effects on agriculture. The possibility of a decline in fish is a concern. Furthermore, future developments upriver could severely affect the performance of hydroelectric stations and dams within Cambodia.

Tonlé Sap

Cambodia's great lake, swelling and shrinking with the seasons, sustains the country with its fertile sediment and abundance of fish.

The vast freshwater lake known as Tonlé Sap is truly a remarkable phenomenon. The very heart of Cambodia's rich agricultural and fishing economies, it is the riverine "lung" on which much of the country's prosperity depends. During the annual monsoon rains it swells greatly in size, becoming a natural reservoir which then gradually releases its accumulated waters during the long, hot months of the dry season. It also provides the surrounding plains with a never-ending supply of rich silt for farming, and is an equally reliable source of nutrition in the form of fish, snails, snakes, frogs and all manner of aquatic wildlife.

The lake, which is surrounded by a fertile rice-growing plain, dominates Cambodia's central northwest. During the dry season, approximately between November and May, the lake is at its smallest, though it still covers 2,500–3,000 sq km (950–1,160 sq miles). The Sap River runs from its southeastern corner to join the Mekong and Bassac rivers at Phnom Penh, some 100km (60 miles) distant.

The reversal of the Sap River

The confluence of these rivers, known in Khmer as Chatomuk or "Four Faces", and in French as Quatre Bras or "Four Arms", is remarkable for a unique phenomenon, the reversal of the Sap River. From May to October, during the annual monsoon rains, the hugely increased volume of the Mekong forces the Sap River to back up, and finally reverse its course, flowing northwards to flood the Tonlé Sap with vast quantities of fresh water and rich sediment. During this period the Tonlé Sap almost trebles in size, from 3,000 sq km (1,160 sq miles) to as much as 8,000 sq km (3,100 sq miles). At its lowest level, most of the lake is less than 2 metres (6.5ft) deep and is like a marsh with crisscrossing navigable channels; at its fullest the lake is as much as 14 metres (45ft) deep, and it can gain 70km (44 miles) in width.

Then, in mid-October, as the cool, dry winds begin to blow from the north and the level of the Mekong diminishes, the flow of the Sap is again reversed, carrying the surplus waters of the Tonlé Sap southwards to the Mekong and Bassac deltas. The annual flooding of the Tonlé Sap makes the lake an incredibly rich source of fish, while the farmland around it benefits from an annual deluge of rich sediment.

The Tonlé Sap is mainly fished by Muslim Chams and migrant communities of Vietnamese. These peoples are less concerned about taking life than the Theravada Buddhist Khmers who till the nearby fields – not that the latter show any concern at all about eating the fish once it has been caught and killed by someone else. There are few dinner tables anywhere in Cambodia that are without a supply of

Out on the waters of Tonlé Sap.

prahok – fermented fish paste from the great lake – and fish is a national staple.

The time of the October reversal of the waters is celebrated as Bon Om Tuk, one of Cambodia's most important festivals. For three days an estimated 250,000 revellers join in the festivities, which include longboat races, music, dancing, fireworks and a great deal of eating and drinking. Teams compete in the traditional boat racing, which is said to celebrate an event in 1177, when Angkor was invaded and sacked by a fleet of Cham warships which sailed up the Sap River and across the Tonlé Sap. The Chams were then defeated by the country's most illustrious monarch, Jayavarman VII. Bas-reliefs in the Bayon at Angkor commemorate the great victory.

The southern gateway to Angkor Thom.

DECISIVE DATES

A stone image at Bayon, Angkor Thom.

Earliest Times

100 BC–AD 500
Establishment of a flourishing trading state called Funan in the Mekong Delta.

500–700
A proto-Khmer state, known as Chen La, is established inland from Funan near the confluence of the Mekong and Sap rivers.

The Greatness of Angkor

802–50
Reign of Jayavarman II, who proclaims himself a god-king and begins the great work of moving the capital to Roluos near Angkor.

889–908
Yasovarman I moves the capital to Angkor.

1113–50
Surayavarman II begins the construction of Angkor Wat.

1177
The Chams sack Angkor.

1181–1220
Jayavarman VII constructs the Bayon at Angkor Thom.

1352–1430
The Siamese Kingdom of Ayutthaya sacks and pillages Angkor four times, taking away the court regalia and many prisoners.

Division and Decline

1432
King Ponhea Yat abandons Angkor. Subsequently Lovek, to the north of Phnom Penh, becomes the capital.

1618–1866
The capital is moved to Udong, north of Phnom Penh.

The French in Cambodia

1863
The French force King Norodom to sign a treaty making Cambodia a French protectorate.

1866
A new capital is established at Phnom Penh.

1904
King Norodom dies and is succeeded by King Sisowath, who reigns until 1927.

1941
Thailand invades northwestern Cambodia.

1942
Norodom Sihanouk becomes king.

Independence and the Indochina Wars

1945
King Sihanouk declares Cambodian independence from France, with Japanese support.

1953
Cambodia gains full independence from France under King Sihanouk.

1954
At the Geneva Conference, France formally confirms its withdrawal from Cambodia.

1955
Sihanouk abdicates but retains real power for himself.

1965
Vietnam War escalates; Communist forces begin to seek sanctuary in eastern Cambodia.

1967
Pol Pot's group of Cambodian Communists – dubbed "Khmer Rouge" by Sihanouk – launches an insurgency in the northwest.

1969
US B-52 bombardment of Vietnamese sanctuaries in Cambodia begins.

1970
A coup is launched by right-wing General Lon Nol. Sihanouk takes refuge in Beijing.

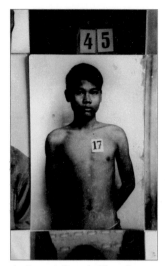

A grim reminder at the Khmer Rouge prison, Tuol Sleng.

The Zero Years

1975
Khmer Rouge take Phnom Penh on 17 April; cities are immediately evacuated, and the country is cut off from the outside world. Brutal persecution of Buddhism and other religions.

1976
Large-scale starvation occurs in the northwest of the country as hundreds of thousands of urban-dwellers are deported there.

1978
Refusal to negotiate with Vietnam over burgeoning border war.

1979
Vietnamese troops invade and overthrow Pol Pot regime. People's Republic of Cambodia established.

Cambodia Reborn

1979–88
Up to 100,000 Vietnamese forces are stationed in Cambodia to prevent a DK resurgence.

1989
Vietnamese forces start to withdraw.

1991
Prince Sihanouk returns to Phnom Penh.

1993
General elections are held, supervised by the United Nations. Coalition government of Prince Norodom Ranariddh's FUNCINPEC Party and Hun Sen's People's Party.

1996
Khmer Rouge forces split; Ieng Sary defects to the government in return for an amnesty.

1998
Pol Pot dies in mysterious circumstances and the Khmer Rouge finally disintegrates.

1999
Cambodia joins ASEAN.

2004
Hun Sen is re-elected by parliament. King Sihanouk abdicates on account of ill health and Norodom Sihamoni is elected to succeed him.

2007
UN-backed genocide trials of surviving Khmer Rouge leaders begin.

2008
Hun Sen's ruling Cambodian People's Party retains power in elections.

2009
Former S21 commander Comrade Duch is the first former Khmer Rouge leader to stand trial; tensions flare with Thailand over the border dispute at Preah Vihear.

2012
Comrade Duch is sentenced to life imprisonment for genocide and crimes against humanity.

2014
Khmer Rouge leaders Nuon Chea and Khieu Samphan are sentenced to life imprisonment.

2015
Hun Sen celebrates 30 years as prime minister.

2016
In July, Kem Ley, a political commentator, activist and critic of Hun Sen is shot dead in Phnom Penh.

Welcoming Norodom Sihanouk back to Cambodia after years in exile, 1991.

Carving at Sambor Prei Kuk.

THE RISE AND FALL OF THE KHMER

Cambodia's history has been a story of rise and fall. The early days of Funan and Chen La were followed by the emergence of the powerful empire of Angkor, and in turn by a long period of decline ending in the loss of independence.

As with the Lao, there is some controversy surrounding the origins of the Cambodian people. Some suggest that they originated from the south, in present-day Malaysia and Indonesia, while others point to the southwards territorial expansion from what is now mainland China, which would indicate a Tai or Sinitic link. What is clear is that at least 4,000 years ago the fertile flood plains of the lower Mekong and Bassac rivers, as well as the Tonlé Sap (Great Lake of Cambodia), were inhabited by a people of indeterminate origins, although logic dictates that they are at least partly ancestors of today's Cambodians.

Not a great deal is known about these early inhabitants, but they certainly baked earthenware pots to hold water and fermented toddy palm, or to store the fish in which the region has always abounded. It was a forested area which flooded frequently, so it should be no surprise that they lived in stilt houses, just as most rural Cambodians do today.

Conditions for settled agriculture were unusually rich. The waters teemed with fish, rice could be grown with little effort in the fertile soil around the Great Lake, and primitive boats were built to travel from stilt house to stilt house and from village to village. The region, moreover, was close to the South China Sea, within easy access of the developing trade routes between China, South Asia and the Middle East. All the prerequisites existed for the development of a potentially rich and advanced civilisation, which began to coalesce around the 1st century AD.

The first kingdom

The first civilisation to appear was the Kingdom of Funan (1st–6th centuries AD), almost

Ayutthaya; the Thai kingdom often influenced Cambodian affairs.

nothing of which survives today beyond the ruins of the supposed capital, Oc Eo, deep in the south Vietnamese delta province of An Giang. Oc Eo was a trading port which is thought to have flourished between about AD 100 and 400, after which it became submerged; it was discovered in the 1940s. Excavations reveal evidence of trade links, however tenuous, with Southeast Asia, China, India, the Middle East and even as far as the Mediterranean and Rome. In other words, Funan made up part of the flourishing coastal trade network which girdled Asia at that time, from the region of Canton to the Red Sea.

The rise of the Khmer people

By 500 Funan appears to have been in decline, although the reason is unclear. Meanwhile, a new proto-Khmer state was developing further inland, near the confluence of the Mekong and Sap rivers, in the region of present-day Phnom Penh. The inhabitants of this state, known to the Chinese annals as Chen La, spoke a Mon-Khmer language and were strongly influenced by Indian religious traditions (see page 204). They may be regarded as the progenitors of the first authentically Cambodian state.

The first dated Khmer-language inscription known to history dates from 611, while the earliest known Sanskrit inscription from the region dates from just two years later. The historian David Chandler employs these and other, later, inscriptions to deduce that early Cambodian society was divided, in general terms, into two classes – those who understood both Sanskrit and Khmer, and those who only knew and spoke the latter.

The division between the two classes was not merely linguistic; it was also between those who grew rice and those who did not.

Khmer inscription at Lolei, Roluos.

SANSKRIT AND KHMER

Sanskrit was the language of the gods and the priestly classes, and of matters of philosophic and esoteric concern. The records recount the genealogies of rulers, actions of the elite and meritorious deeds. They are all in highly polished verse. Khmer, by contrast, was the language of the *nak ta*, or "ancestor people", the indigenous, ordinary Cambodians. Inscriptions in Khmer are all in prose and record more mundane matters, such as temple administration, landholdings, tax and secular law. In this distinction between Sanskrit and Khmer lies much of the dichotomy which has distinguished Cambodian society to the present day.

"It was everyone's ambition to be 'rescued from the mud', but very few succeeded," Chandler explains. It was the destiny of almost all Khmers to work the land and to plant and harvest rice. All else rested on this fundamental, immutable fact. When sufficient surplus had been accumulated the "greater ones" – those "rescued from the mud" – could be maintained, and in turn they could devote their energies to maintaining the complex administration which would be required to build Angkor (see page 205).

Life in Chen La

By around 800 the nascent Khmer state known to the Chinese as Chen La had developed into a fully-fledged kingdom, with its capital at Isanapura (modern-day Sambor Prei Kuk, near Kompong Thom). At the time Isanapura was, according to one contemporary commentator, "the most extensive complex of stone buildings in all Southeast Asia, built a century ahead of similar constructions in Java".

For several centuries, and certainly from the middle of the 3rd century AD, irregular tribute missions had been sent from the Lower Mekong Valley to China, and adventurous Chinese traders and other travellers had visited Funan and later Chen La. There is some confusion between descriptions of "Water Chen La", which may have been a Mekong Delta successor to Funan, with its capital at Vyadhapura (Angkor Borei, near Phnom Penh), and "Land Chen La", which lay further inland.

Around the middle of the 6th century, moreover, tribute missions seem to have stopped, perhaps at about the time that Funan was eclipsed by Chen La. Therefore very little is known of Chen La, or of why and how it developed.

The move inland

By the 7th century "Land Chen La" seems to have eclipsed "Water Chen La" in importance as the centre of the kingdom moved northwestwards, beyond Isanapura and towards the region which would eventually become Angkor. At the same time the state seems to have acquired a new cohesiveness, though precisely why remains uncertain. Chandler suggests that this may have resulted from increasing population density, improved wet-rice-farming techniques and victories in local, unrecorded wars, the last perhaps resulting in a protracted period of peace.

It is clear that by the 8th century "Land Chen La" was developing into an increasingly wealthy and centralised kingdom. Moreover, as the centre moved inland, away from the sea, it relied less on subsistence agriculture and trade, and more on organised manpower, irrigation technology and intensive rice production. In this way the foundations were gradually laid for the establishment of the Khmer Empire which would develop in the region of Angkor.

The empire of Angkor

The Angkorean period of Cambodian history is generally considered to have extended from AD 802 to 1431, although these dates

should not be interpreted too literally – there were Khmers in the Angkor region before it became the capital, and Angkor was not completely deserted when the capital returned eastwards. Still, the six centuries between these two dates mark the peak of Cambodia's power and influence in Southeast Asia, as well as the pinnacle of Khmer artistic and cultural achievement.

The foundation of Angkor (meaning "city", from a Khmer variant of the Sanskrit *nagara*) is generally attributed to Jayavarman II. Little is known of him, but inscriptions dating from the

Bust of Jayavarman VII, Royal Palace, Phnom Penh.

11th century – two centuries after the events in question – suggest that, as a young man, Jayavarman visited Java, returning in the late 8th century. He then travelled throughout the country from the Phnom Penh region, through the old capital at Sambor Prei Kuk, before settling in the region of Aninditapura, to the northeast of the Tonlé Sap.

Here he proclaimed himself a *devaraja*, or "god-king", creating a type of universal kingship clearly associating the ruler with the Hindu god Shiva. Although the records are few, it is clear that Jayavarman must have been a man of royal rank by birth and one who had already distinguished himself in various ways, not least in battle. Certainly his subsequent career involved numerous military campaigns, though the power he accrued also rested on a careful series of alliances, marriages and grants of land.

Jayavarman was undoubtedly successful: one inscription describes his realm as extending to "China, Champa, the ocean, and the land of cardamom and mangoes" (the last is probably central Thailand). An exaggeration, certainly – even at its height the Khmer Empire never reached as far north as China. Nonetheless, it is probable that Jayavarman's influence extended over all of present-day Cambodia as well as to neighbouring territories which

Vishnu statue, Angkor Wat.

today constitute parts of eastern and central Thailand, southern Laos and the Mekong Delta region of Vietnam.

As a consequence of his successes, Jayavarman II is remembered as the founder of the first unified Cambodian state. He made his capital at Hariharalaya, an area today marked by the Roluos complex of monuments about 13km (8 miles) southeast of Siem Reap, the oldest temple group in the Angkor region.

Triad monarchs

Jayavarman was followed by a line of more than 30 monarchs who ruled from the Angkor region. Many of these incorporate the word *varman* (Sanskrit for "armour") in their titles. Not all are well known, nor did they all achieve greatness. Some, however, were clearly remarkable men, whose achievements, writ large in stone, retain the power to surprise and impress even today.

King Indravarman I (877–89) was one such, who during his rule established a "triadic" pattern that would be followed by many subsequent monarchs. Firstly, he busied himself with major irrigation works to increase both the agricultural production of the state and his power. Next, he commissioned statues of his parents and other relatives and ancestors shown as various gods. Statues of Jayavarman II and his queen, for example, depict them as Shiva and his consort, and were made for the temple complex of Preah Ko, near Roluos.

The third stage of Indravarman's rule was characterised by the construction of a temple-mountain, made in the form of a

INDIA'S PERVADING INFLUENCE

It is not clear when Indian traders first arrived in Southeast Asia, but commercial and cultural contacts are believed to extend back as far as 4,000 years. It is thought that these early Indian visitors sought wealth in the form of gold, tin, precious woods and spices, rather than conquest.

The region proved a rich source of valuable goods, as well as a fertile and receptive ground for the dissemination of Indian culture. So rich was Southeast Asia that the Indians named the region Suvarnabhumi, "Golden Land" in Sanskrit. In fact, Suvarnabhumi was more of a cultural and trading network than a single unitary state, encompassing

the coastal regions of Southeast Asia from Malaya and Sumatra, through Java and Bali to Cambodia and Champa. It is true that Chinese influence, too, was felt, particularly via Chen La in the Mekong Delta, but – with the exception of Vietnam – Indian influence remained dominant, with Tamil and other South Indians visiting, trading, settling, and converting the indigenous population to Hinduism. As a result, by the 5th century AD all of mainland Southeast Asia except Vietnam, as well as most of the neighbouring Malay region, was dominated by a number of closely related Hindu-Buddhist kingdoms ruled by semi-divine Maharajas or "Great Kings".

stepped pyramid and dedicated to him. It was designed to serve as both his tomb and a lasting monument to the glory of his rule. Known as the Bakong, the temple-mountain was the first great Khmer religious edifice to

> An inscription at Preah Ko tells of Indravarman as a monarch victorious in war: "In battle, which is like a difficult ocean to cross, he raised a pathway, made up of the heads of his arrogant enemies."

be made from stone rather than brick, and it still survives at Roluos.

Indravarman was succeeded in 899 by his son, Yasovarman, who ruled until about 908 and was the monarch who began the move to Angkor, known as Yasodharapura in honour of its founder – the name Angkor did not come into general use until the 14th century.

Yasovarman's decision to move to Angkor was probably influenced by the presence in the region of a small hill on which he determined to build his own temple-mountain. In fact he built three, all symbolic representations of Mount Meru (the mythical Buddhist axis of the world; Buddhism was emerging as a new religion in the Khmer world at this time) and all still surviving.

The largest, Phnom Kandal or "Central Mountain", lies near the heart of the Angkor complex.

Building Angkor

To construct Angkor, Yasovarman needed to be both a ruler of vision and a great builder. He ordered the construction of a vast reservoir, the Yasodharatataka, along the southern shore of which he erected temples to honour Shiva, Vishnu and the Buddha, for by this time Buddhism had already started to make a significant impact on Khmer customs and religious beliefs. He also ordered the construction of numerous

A close up of the intricate carvings at Angkor Wat's eastern lintel.

temples on hills throughout his domains. The most noteworthy of these is the great Preah Vihear, set high on an all but inaccessible ridge of the Phnom Dangrek mountain range which separates Cambodia from northeastern Thailand.

Over the next century Angkor continued to expand, despite the construction of an elaborate rival city at Koh Ker, about 85km (53 miles) to the north, by a usurper king. By the time of Jayavarman V (968–1001), Angkor had grown considerably, and the ruler clearly commanded the loyalty of many thousands of field workers, stonemasons and soldiers. Jayavarman V was a Shivaist but was notably tolerant of Buddhism, which continued to exert an increasing influence at the royal court. One of the most beautiful temples at Angkor, Banteay Srei or "Citadel of Women", dates from this time.

Inevitably a great city like Angkor attracted trade and foreign businessmen, although it seems that most international commerce was in the hands of the Chams, Chinese and Vietnamese rather than the Khmers. Goods traded included porcelain, cloth and textiles, forest produce, rice, buffalo and slaves. Unfortunately, little information regarding such matters survives, but some can be gleaned from the complex and detailed bas-reliefs on the pediments of some Angkorean monuments, especially the Bayon.

Jayavarman V's patronage of Buddhism was continued by his successor, Surayavarman I (1002–50). However, Utyadityavarman II, who ruled between 1050 and 1086, was a devotee of Shiva, and he built a great temple-mountain, the famed Baphuon, to house the Shiva *lingam* (phallus) associated with his reign.

Military power and diplomacy

By the late 11th century the line of kings ruling at Angkor was in decline, with two or even three rivals competing for the position of "universal monarch". At the beginning of the 12th

A stone carving in the South Gallery at Angkor Wat showing Surayavarman II surrounded by followers.

A CENTRALISED STATE

Jayavarman V's successor, Surayavarman I (1002–50), emerged as a patron of Buddhism. He also expanded the Khmer territories, conquering the Theravada Buddhist Kingdom of Louvo, which was centred on the town of Lopburi in present-day Thailand. Great hydraulic systems were built, and there is evidence of tight control over the people, who were obliged to live in close proximity in communities called *pura*. To meet the demands of his bureaucracy and the cost of running his kingdom, Surayavarman obliged the peasantry to work all year, utilising the reservoirs and irrigation canals to produce two harvests annually.

century, however, a new dynasty was founded by Jayavarman VI (1080–1107), which was to rule the Khmer Empire for more than 100 years.

Little is known about the first two kings in this dynastic line, but the third, Surayavarman II (1112–52), was a powerful ruler who presided over a unified kingdom. As soon as he had ascended to the throne he began to act with vigour and speed to expand the territory and manpower under his control. His armies campaigned in the east, attacking both Vietnam and Champa. He employed mercenary troops drawn mainly from tributary regions in the west; it is likely that these included Siamese, who appear in the bas-reliefs at Angkor wearing grass skirts, carrying spears and marching out of step, in contrast to the serried ranks of Khmer soldiers.

Surayavarman II also established diplomatic relations with China – the first Angkorean monarch to do so, and possibly the first Khmer ruler since the days of "Water Chen La" to send missions to the Middle Kingdom. Unusually for a Khmer ruler, Surayavarman II was neither a partisan of Shiva nor a patron of Buddhism; rather, he was a devotee of the Hindu god Vishnu, and to the glory of this deity (and himself) he commissioned the largest and most magnificent of all the monuments at Angkor, the great temple

As a young man Jayavarman VII (1181–1219) studied the doctrines of Mahayana Buddhism, the "Greater Vehicle" variant of the doctrine found in Vietnam, China and Northeast Asia, rather than Theravada Buddhism, "The Way of the Elders", more generally associated with Southeast Asia and Sri Lanka. This devotion to Mahayana Buddhism was to become a major feature of Jayavarman VII's reign, as he strove to associate traditional features of Khmer kingship – the *devaraja* concept of a universal god-king – with the teachings of Buddhism. This was at variance with the concept of divine Khmer

A 19th-century engraving of Angkor Wat.

complex of Angkor Wat (see page 288). Construction of this monumental building was begun early in his reign, and was not completed until after his death in about 1152.

Kingship and religion

There is little information about the three decades between Surayavarman II's death and the coronation of Jayavarman VII in 1181 – only one inscription survives from this period – but the latter's assumption of power represents a high point in Angkorean history. By this time the population of Angkor's great city complex, Angkor Thom, is thought to have been over 1 million, making it the largest city in the world at the time.

kingship, which generally associated the ruler with Shiva or, less often, Vishnu, or, on occasion, with Hari-Hara, a composite of the two. The Khmer kings employed this association to emphasise their grandeur, while in the minds of their subjects it had much to do with rice production, irrigation and adequate rainfall.

The new *bodhisattva*-kingship instituted and promoted by Jayavarman VII differed from the forms which had gone before in that the king no longer sought to be represented as the devotee of a divinity, or as a *devaraja* drawn up to divinity in death. Rather, through a combination of meritorious acts, he sought to redeem both himself and his kingdom in the time-honoured Buddhist way.

Cham invasion

The French historians Paul Mus and Jean Boiselier identify the central event of Jayavarman VII's reign as the Cham invasion of 1177. The Chams (see page 227) had a powerful, marine-orientated kingdom in central and southern Indochina and controlled all of what is now central Vietnam between the 2nd and 12th centuries.

Jayavarman VII seems to have had some strong links with the Court of Champa and its capital at My Son, near present-day Da Nang in Vietnam. In the 1160s he seems to have spent some time there as either a guest or an exile, or per-

this point on, the Cham threat diminished – although this was largely due to Vietnamese expansion rather than the rise of Angkor.

On assuming his crown in 1181, Jayavarman VII found Angkor "plunged into a sea of misfortune and heavy with crimes". As a Buddhist – instead of a Hindu – monarch, he believed he owed little to his predecessors, and so over the next three decades he sought to stamp his authority on the Khmer Empire.

Once securely in power, Jayavarman VII put in place a major series of road-building and other public works programmes. He also built

Bas-relief of Chams fighting Khmers at the Bayon.

haps leading a military campaign – as ever, the sources are sparse and imprecise. In 1177–8 the Chams invaded, first by water, and then by land. Their chief objectives seem to have been booty, prisoners of war and possibly revenge for earlier assaults against their own kingdom, especially by Surayavarman II. In 1178 they took the great city of Yasodharapura by surprise and pillaged it. According to a Cambodian stele, the Cham King Jaya Indravarman IV "put the king to death, without listening to any proposal for peace".

Jayavarman, still three years away from his coronation, responded in kind. He defeated the Chams in a naval battle on the Tonlé Sap, while another Khmer prince killed the Cham king "with a hundred million arrows". From

numerous public resthouses and reservoirs. He expanded the frontiers of his kingdom, bringing much of what is now central Thailand, southern Laos and southern Vietnam under his control. Jayavarman was also a temple builder *par excellence*. In 1186 he erected the Ta Prohm complex in honour of his parents; this was followed by Preah Khan ("Sacred Sword") in 1191, and finally the famous Bayon, with its hundreds of enigmatic faces, each representing a *bodhisattva*-like image of himself.

A new belief system

In many ways Jayavarman VII's reign can be seen as seminal for the development of Buddhism in Cambodia – not that he was anything but a syncretist: facilities and cells for Vishnuist and Shivaist devotees and for temple Brahmans were included in his major works. Nevertheless, it was from this time that Buddhism began to supersede Hinduism as the main belief system of the Cambodian people.

Yet the gradual conversion of the great majority of people to Theravada Buddhism during the 13th century is not solely attributable to Jayavarman's personal belief system – which was, in any case, Mahayanist. Equally important were his conquests to the west, where the south-moving Tai peoples and the long-established Mon population were already Theravada Buddhist. Wandering Sri Lankan monks may also have played a part in the conversion process.

The abandonment of Angkor
Following the reign of Indravarman III (1295–1308), the Kingdom of Angkor entered a period of slow but terminal decline of which we know relatively little. Few inscribed stelae survive – if, indeed, they were ever created, as the old Hindu-orientated elite gradually embraced Theravada Buddhism. Our knowledge of the period, such as it is, rests on Chinese records, one Cham inscription and a few Tai ones, the evidence of archaeology and the uncertain process of logical deduction. As a result, historians tend to disagree about the progress of events in Cambodia in the two centuries between about 1350 and 1550.

Return to the coast
What is clear is that the country's political and economic centre of gravity began a long but inexorable shift back from "Land Chen La" – that is, the Roluos-Angkor region at the head of the Tonlé Sap – to "Water Chen La" – the region around Phnom Penh, Lovek and Udong – in the mid-14th century.

Some historians argue that this striking reversal of the Cambodian historical imperative was due to the rise of the Thai kingdoms (and especially that of the Kingdom of Ayutthaya) to the west and north of Angkor; others contend that the shift back to the southeast was more probably linked to the rapid expansion of maritime trade between China and Southeast Asia which took place during the late Mongol and early Ming dynasties in the 13th to 15th centuries. Proponents of the first school of thought tend to represent this as a period of Angkorean "decline", while those of the second, more recent,

school, see it as a period of Cambodian "change". As is usual in such dialogues, there is doubtless an element of truth in both hypotheses.

The most reliable references we have, as well as the most numerous, are Chinese. According to the historian David Chandler, more than a dozen tributary missions were sent from the Khmer Empire to China between 1371 and 1419 – more than during the entire Angkorean period. The Chinese clearly valued these contacts which, as usual, were as much commercial as tributary missions, and afforded the visiting Cambodian delegates appropriate dignity and respect.

Hindu religious symbols, such as this nandi bull, declined with the 13th-century rise of Buddhism.

> Angkor Wat remains the largest religious monument ever built. Based on a model of the Hindu universe centred on Mount Meru, it required as much stone as the great pyramid in Egypt – yet is also exquisitely carved with bas-reliefs.

But what actually happened "on the ground"? Viewed from an Angkorean perspective, the great temple complexes dedicated to Hindu deities such as Shiva and Vishnu may have declined in significance as Buddhism became the predominant religion of the state.

The Siamese threat

Then there was the unsettling question of the Siamese. Once a tributary people who had served as mercenaries in the Angkorean armies, these relative newcomers to the region grew rapidly both in numbers and in strength, posing an increasing threat to the Kingdom of Angkor. This threat became palpable with the establishment, in 1350, of the Siamese Kingdom of Ayutthaya, centred on the Lower Chao Phraya River Basin, within easy striking distance of Angkor.

Wars soon broke out, with the Siamese generally, though not always, gaining the upper

Maritime trade

Viewed, on the other hand, from a Phnom Penh perspective, the rich and expanding possibilities of maritime trade with China and elsewhere in Southeast Asia must have appeared tremendously attractive. As the Angkor region came under repeated Siamese attack, this commercial alternative to an apparently endless cycle of war, temple-building and intensive rice cultivation must have become appealing. Accordingly, historians suggest that while one portion of Angkor's population departed westwards in a slow

Crude figures near a stupa in Udong.

hand. Angkor was captured and sacked on several occasions, most notably in 1431. In sparsely populated Southeast Asia the "spoils of war" usually meant seizing people rather than land (see page 57), and these Siamese victories would have meant the large-scale transfer of captured Cambodian prisoners to the west, which deprived Angkor of much of the massed labour necessary for the maintenance of its great irrigation systems, not to mention skilled stonemasons and other temple builders.

On a more mundane level, the first- and second-quality sandstone used in temple construction had begun to run out, and the builders were increasingly obliged to use poorer-quality laterite. The time had come to move elsewhere.

haemorrhage of power as prisoners of the Siamese, another portion – perhaps a trickle, not a stream – migrated southeast, to the vicinity of Phnom Penh, in search of a more prosperous and more secure existence.

Significantly, this latter group of migrants would probably have included many of Angkor's richer and better-educated classes – clerks, merchants, overseas businessmen such as the influential Chinese community, and perhaps even private slave-owners and landholders.

Reasons for choosing the Phnom Penh region for a new capital were plentiful and logical. To begin with, there seems to have been the well-established tradition of royal rule from the Lower Mekong region dating back to "Water Chen La" and even Funan. In a way the Khmers were merely retracing their steps.

Beyond this there was the question of geographical location. Far from Ayutthaya and therefore (for some time, at least) safe from Siamese attack, the Phnom Penh region was strategically centred on the confluence of three rivers, the Mekong, Sap and Bassac, at a region known in Khmer as Chatomuk, or "Four Faces", subsequently known to the French as Quatre Bras, or "Four Arms" (see page 195).

court in Ayutthaya, sometimes emerging victorious, but more often on the losing side. Meanwhile, Vietnamese migrants began to move into the still predominantly Khmer region of the Mekong Delta until, by the 18th century, the new arrivals outnumbered the original Khmers by as many as 10 times.

A direct result of Cambodia's gradual shrinkage, caught between the Vietnamese hammer and the Siamese anvil, was a commensurate growth in both Siamese and Viet interference in Cambodian affairs. Relations with the Siamese court were better than those with the Vietnamese; a

18th-century map of Siam (Thailand), Laos and the Khmer Empire (Cambodia).

Depiction of a Cambodian village scene, c. 1888.

15th–19th centuries: a shrinking nation

The final move from Angkor seems to have taken place sometime after 1432. Successive capitals were established, first at Lovek and then at Udong in the 15th and 17th centuries, both slightly to the north of Phnom Penh, and finally at Phnom Penh itself. Though smaller and less magnificent than Angkor, these new centres prospered, with international trade burgeoning, and distinct trading communities of Chinese, Malays, Portuguese, Spanish, Japanese and Arabs established in the area.

During these years the Khmer Empire frequently found itself at war with the Siamese

shared Indic perception of the world and many other similar values made the courts of Ayutthaya and Phnom Penh at least mutually comprehensible to each other. There was little understanding for or sympathy with the Vietnamese court, however, particularly as the Nguyen rulers of central Vietnam began a sustained effort to "Vietnamise" Cambodian society, encouraging the wearing of Vietnamese clothes while also isolating Phnom Penh from direct contact with the outside world. The Cambodians were thought of contemptuously as the "little brothers" of the Vietnamese.

From this point onwards, anti-Vietnamese sentiment became established throughout Cambodian society – a theme that would continue into the present day.

Sobering exhibits at Phnom Penh's Tuol Sleng Genocide Museum include thousands of photos of prisoners, alive and dead.

FROM COLONIALISM TO THE KILLING FIELDS AND BEYOND

The modern history of Cambodia is one of tragedy: it is estimated that nearly a fifth of the population was killed in the brutal Khmer Rouge years.

By the mid-19th century the once-mighty Khmer Empire had been reduced to a weakened rump state, dominated in the east by Vietnam and in the west by Siam. This disastrous situation, which would almost certainly have resulted in the loss of Cambodian independence and the division of all remaining Cambodian territories between these powerful neighbours, was brought to an end in 1863 when King Norodom was persuaded to accept the establishment of a French protectorate over Cambodia. As a consequence Cambodia became a rather sleepy backwater under French protection – a colony, true, but still a definable nation.

French rule

Until 1941 all seemed to run smoothly in Cambodia. Most Cambodians accepted the French almost with relief as a welcome alternative to the expansionist Vietnamese, while the French helped transform the country into a regional rice bowl. Beyond this – starting with the adventurer Henri Mouhot (1826–61) – the colonials "rediscovered" the glories of Angkor, and contributed greatly to the establishment of two immensely significant truths which now form a central part of the Cambodian national psyche: firstly, that the Cambodians built Angkor; and, secondly, that French intervention saved most of Cambodia from division between Siam and Vietnam.

Not everyone agreed, of course. And in the vanguard of the anti-colonialist elements, predictably, were the nationalists of the Indochinese Communist Party (ICP). Here, without descending too far into the racial maelstrom of Cambodian politics, a problem arose. Perhaps inevitably, the larger and more sophisticated

King Sisowath, pictured in 1922.

Vietnamese element in the ICP dominated the lesser Lao and Cambodian contingents, leading to fears that "Big Brother" Vietnam might seek to replace the French as masters of a unified Indochina. Such, at least, were the fears of some Lao and, especially, a group of ultra-nationalist Cambodians for whom hostility towards and fear of Vietnam was second nature.

The events which followed resulted in a bitter civil war and, after Democratic Kampuchea's seizure of power in 1975, the deaths of 2–3 million Cambodians – Khmers, Cham Muslims, ethnic Chinese, Thais, Vietnamese, Lao, Shan and various minority hill peoples.

How did this tragedy come about? Cambodian resistance to the French was of a very limited nature, but events elsewhere, in Europe and East Asia, were to intervene. In 1940 France fell to Nazi Germany. The colonial authorities in Indochina responded by supporting the pro-Nazi Vichy regime, and in 1941, with French backing, Norodom Sihanouk became King of Cambodia. On 9 March 1945 the Japanese armed forces moved to oust the Vichy administration, and on 13 March, in response to a direct request from Japan, King Sihanouk proclaimed Cambodia independent and changed the official name from Cambodge to Kampuchea. Within a few short

Lon Nol.

weeks, however, the French were back in an ultimately doomed attempt to restore their colonial presence in Indochina.

The Indochina Wars

What followed, tragically, were three consecutive Indochina Wars. The main protagonists were the Vietnamese Communists, who took on and defeated first the French, then the United States, and finally an unlikely alliance of fellow "Socialists" from China and Cambodia.

At first it appeared as though Cambodia might avoid serious involvement in Vietnam's long and vicious war with the French. Certainly most anti-colonialist fighting went on further to the north, culminating in the French debacle

at Dien Bien Phu in 1954. Inevitably, however, as Ho Chi Minh's Hanoi-based government (The Democratic Republic of Vietnam) sought to take on and destabilise the Franco-American regime in Saigon (The Republic of Vietnam),

> General Lon Nol was something of an enigma to the Americans. A senior military source once said "the only thing we know about Lon Nol is that if you spell his name backwards it is still Lon Nol".

Cambodia, together with neighbouring Laos, was drawn into the fray. Tentacles of the "Ho Chi Minh Trail" crossed and recrossed each other throughout Laos and into the remote northeastern Cambodian provinces of Rattanakiri and Mondolkiri.

In 1969, without Congressional approval, the USA began a series of massive air strikes against Viet Cong and NVA (North Vietnamese Army) bases in Cambodia. Huge areas of the eastern part of Cambodia were carpet-bombed by B-52 bombers flying out of Thailand and Guam, devastating much of the country and driving the surviving Khmer peasantry to despair. They responded in one of three ways – massacring ethnic Vietnamese by way of "revenge"; flooding into an already bursting Phnom Penh; or joining the nascent Khmer Communist insurgency, dubbed by Sihanouk the "Khmer Rouge" (KR). Indeed, had not Kissinger's "sideshow" in Cambodia taken place it is doubtful whether the few hundred Khmer Communists hiding in remote Mondolkiri could have ever seized power.

As it was, a tragedy was played out. In March 1970, while on a visit to Beijing, Sihanouk was overthrown in a coup d'état by the Cambodian military headed by General Lon Nol, who was anti-Communist and hostile to the Vietnamese, and the coup was tacitly supported by the USA. Lon Nol then sent two military columns northwards into Communist territory. However, though grandiosely named Chen La 1 and Chen La 2, they were comprised mainly of ill-trained and poorly armed boys, who were cut to pieces by the insurgents.

Meanwhile, as territories under the control of the Lon Nol regime shrank, Sihanouk took up residence in Beijing and allied himself with his erstwhile Communist enemies, the Khmer Rouge. Embittered by its casualties and the failure of its strategy, the USA withdrew most of its combat troops from Vietnam by 1973, leaving the Army of the Republic of Vietnam (ARVN) to fight the NVA with just US intelligence help and occasional air power.

The Khmer Rouge

Cambodia remained a sideshow – but word had spread amongst correspondents based in Phnom Penh that the Khmer Rouge were

last over, and were prepared to give the victorious Communist guerrillas a courteous if careful welcome. Instead they watched with mounting dismay as groups of sullen-faced, often openly hostile child-soldiers swarmed into the city.

Almost the first order broadcast by the new regime, which called itself Democratic Kampuchea (DK), was the expulsion of the entire population of Phnom Penh on the pretext that a bombing raid was to be launched by the USAF. In fact, KR policy was the complete ruralisation of Cambodian society – all

Lon Nol's troops at the southern front.

strangely different from the Viet Cong, the NVA and the Communist Pathet Lao. While they fought just as well, they were said to be quite merciless, and to be emptying small cities and towns of people as they fell under their control. Moreover, they were increasingly hostile to their supposed Vietnamese "mentors" – by no means the puppet army of Hanoi that had been imagined by the USA.

The true nature of Cambodian Communism as interpreted by the Khmer Rouge leadership began to become clear on 17 April 1975, when Phnom Penh fell to the KR fully two weeks before the NVA rolled into Saigon. Most residents of the Cambodian capital were openly delighted the war was at

ROYAL ALLIES CAST ASIDE

After the Khmer Rouge took power the former king, Sihanouk – the KR's erstwhile ally – was flown back to Phnom Penh from Beijing, where he was held under de facto house arrest in the Royal Palace. He was then forcibly retired; a statue was to be built in his honour, and he was to receive a pension of US$8,000 a year, but neither of these ever materialised. During the Zero Years around 20 of Sihanouk's family were murdered by the Khmer Rouge; it is more than likely that he too would have become a victim had it not been for direct appeals on his behalf from such Communist luminaries as Mao Tse-tung, Chou En-lai and Kim Il-sung.

cities, towns and major villages were to be emptied, and the population sent to work in the fields. This policy was implemented with extraordinary ruthlessness – even patients in operating theatres were turned out onto the street to fend for themselves. Those who could not do so or who argued were shot or beaten to death. Meanwhile, a search was instituted for all members of the former Lon Nol army, who were marked for execution. A similar fate awaited all "intellectuals", from university professors and doctors to anybody who spoke a foreign language.

Norodom Sihanouk, the former King of Cambodia, speaks at the United Nations.

Meanwhile, KR's shadowy elite, who would control the fate of DK, installed themselves in some considerable comfort in the administrative centre of Phnom Penh. The core group included, besides Pol Pot and Ieng Sary, the former schoolteacher Khieu Samphan, Thai-educated Nuon Chea – who would emerge as "Brother No. 2", and Vorn Vet. Also of considerable importance were two sisters, Khieu Ponnary and Khieu Thirith, the former married to Pol Pot, the latter to Ieng Sary.

Once in power, the new elite began building a "new society" through what they called a "Super Great Leap to Socialism" – clearly designed to surpass China's disastrous "Great Leap Forward". Society at all levels was divided and then subdivided into different groups. The "Old People" – those who had lived under KR rule before the fall of Phnom Penh – were most favoured, while the former city-dwellers, or "New People", were without any rights at all. In between were "Depositees": potential supporters of the revolution. A chilling but common threat made against New People in DK was "destroying you is no loss; keeping you is no gain". Tens of thousands were either bludgeoned to death, forced to labour on massive construction sites or sent to develop "new frontiers" in the malarial Elephant and Cardamom mountains.

Frontiers were sealed. All religion was banned, the Buddhist supreme patriarch murdered, temples were turned into rice barns and mosques into pigsties. Pol Pot announced that feeding monks was a crime punishable by death, but his associate Nuon Chea kept one temple with four monks open for his pious old mother. Pol Pot and his immediate henchmen saw traitors and Vietnamese agents everywhere they looked, and even as mad instructions were given for the country to be turned into a precise chequerboard of identically shaped rice fields, the dreaded *santebal* or secret police began a witch-hunt for opponents of the regime, real or imagined.

The Killing Fields

The interrogation and torture centre known as S21 or Tuol Sleng, a special prison under the direction of a high-ranking KR official called Kang Kek Iew, known as Comrade Duch, became the nerve centre of this operation. During 1975 and the first part of 1976 the majority of the victims of KR brutality were ordinary people, but as time passed so *Angkar* – the organisation – began to consume more and more of its own. Pol Pot particularly distrusted the khaki-clad troops of the Eastern Zone who had not been under his direct command during the civil war, denouncing them as "Khmer bodies with Vietnamese minds". In 1976–7 he unleashed his most loyal and most feared military commander, the one-legged General Ta Mok, against them.

Ta Mok and his dreaded *nirdei*, Southeast Zone soldiers, gradually extended their control

– and thereby that of their master, Pol Pot – across the entire country. Communist cadres and party members arrested and taken to Tuol Sleng were forced, under the most barbarous tortures, to confess to ridiculous conspiracies. Old revolutionaries like Hu Nim and even Vorn Vet were beaten and electrocuted until they signed statements saying that they worked for the CIA, Vietnam, the KGB or an unlikely combination of all three. Most were then taken to the nearby Killing Fields of Choeung Ek just south of Phnom Penh and executed with axe-handles or hoes "to avoid wasting bullets".

Attacks on Vietnam

It is now known that the DK regime systematically starved its population both as a method of political control and to raise rice exports to China and North Korea in exchange for armaments. But why did the KR need all this new weaponry? The war with Lon Nol and the USA was over and won, the people were incapable of rebellion, but by 1977 relations with Hanoi had reached an all-time low. Vietnam, the old enemy, was the new target.

Pol Pot openly announced his intention of recovering "Kampuchea Krom", or

The "Map of Skulls" at Phnom Penh's Tuol Sleng Museum of Genocidal Crime was taken down in 2002 - it was deemed too disturbing.

HARD LABOUR AND ABSTINENCE

The barbarism of the Killing Fields apart, other nightmare Khmer Rouge policies made people miserable throughout the country, and the regime was increasingly despised. After the introduction of compulsory collectivised eating, in 1976, even the once-favoured "Old People" began to turn against the KR – though nobody questioned the regime directly and survived.

Orders were given to the effect that rice production should be increased threefold, and people laboured long into the night. They returned home to eat a thin gruel of rice chaff and morning glory vines, followed by long sessions of political propaganda, before being allowed a few hours' sleep. Marriage was permitted only with the permission of *Angkar* (the Organisation). Extra-marital sex was punishable by death. Women were obliged to cut their hair short and wear identical clothing.

Medical treatment was basic in the extreme because most doctors had been killed, and those who had not were obliged to hide their identities to survive. KR "hospitals" were generally dirty shacks where illiterate teenagers administered injections of coconut juice.

Schools were closed, money was banned and any form of trading was made illegal. Even "foraging" for food such as lizards and insects after work was made a capital offence, so the entire population was kept in a state of perpetual hunger.

Pol Pot

Born into a relatively prosperous family, the man who was to become one of the most reviled in history remains something of an enigma.

The Khmer Rouge leader Pol Pot, known to his followers as "Brother No. 1", was born in 1928 in the village of Prek Sbauv, near the provincial capital of Kompong Thom, some 140km (88 miles) north of

Pol Pot, a "lovely child" who was to become a monster.

Phnom Penh. He was the eighth of nine children of well-to-do farmers and was named Saloth Sar. In common with most revolutionary Communist leaders, Saloth Sar was neither a peasant nor a proletarian; his family enjoyed close relations with the royal court in Phnom Penh.

In 1934 Saloth Sar was sent to live with his relatives at court. During this time he spent several months as a novice monk at Wat Bottum Vaddei, a monastery near the palace which was favoured by the royal family, and studied the Buddhist scriptures and Khmer language. Later he learnt French and studied at Russei Keo Technical College in Phnom Penh. Although not an outstanding student, he was chosen as one of a group sent for further education in Paris. Here he came into contact with

Cambodian nationalists, including Ieng Sary, who would become one of his key associates.

In 1952, having returned to Cambodia without any qualifications but with a newly acquired and keen sense of nationalism, he joined the Indochinese Communist Party, which was dominated by the Vietnamese. Although secretly nurturing an intense hatred for all things Vietnamese, Saloth Sar rose steadily through the ranks and became General Secretary of the (still clandestine) Cambodian Communist Party in 1962.

Soon after that Saloth Sar and his close colleagues disappeared into the jungled hills of Rattanakiri province, where they began building the Communist guerrilla faction which King Sihanouk dubbed the "Khmer Rouge". During the subsequent years of civil war Saloth Sar used his increasingly powerful position to eliminate Hanoi-trained or pro-Vietnamese cadres – building, in essence, a movement which, though nominally internationalist, was deeply xenophobic, anti-urban and, above all, hostile to Vietnam.

In 1975 – Year Zero – the Khmer Rouge seized power and established the Democratic Kampuchea regime, but still Saloth Sar, now hiding behind the pseudonym "Pol Pot", remained out of the limelight. Between 1975 and his overthrow in 1979 he gradually eliminated all those whom he saw as a potential threat to his personal power – not to mention more than 2 million ordinary Cambodians who were murdered, worked to death or died of starvation.

Overthrown by the Vietnamese in 1979, Pol Pot and his followers took to the jungles where, for almost 20 years, their numbers dwindled through desertion, disease and military attrition. Pol Pot was eventually arrested by his few remaining comrades in 1998. In retrospect it is difficult to see what inner demons drove Saloth Sar to develop into the paranoid political monster Pol Pot. Certainly his elder brother, Loth Suong, who survived the Zero Years, was unable to explain it, commenting with obvious bewilderment that Pol Pot was "a lovely child".

Pol Pot didn't live to face judicial justice and died in 1998; nor did his chief military commander Ta Mok, who died in prison in Phnom Penh in 2006. However, a handful of the aged Khmer Rouge leadership, including Brother No. 2 Nuon Chea, Ieng Sary, Khieu Samphan and Comrade Duch, survived long enough to go on trial before a UN-backed Genocide Tribunal, which began proceedings in February 2009. Comrade Duch was sentenced to life imprisonment in 2012, as were Nuon Chea and Khieu Samphan in 2014. Ieng Sary died from ill health in 2013.

the Mekong Delta, from Vietnam (similar Khmer-speaking areas around Surin in northeastern Thailand would be recovered later). Vicious cross-border attacks resulting in brutal rapes and massacres were launched around the Parrot's Beak area of Vietnam. Vietnam responded by launching warning counterattacks across the border, sometimes pushing 30km (20 miles) into Cambodia before withdrawing. The once-formidable KR soldiers offered weak opposition to the Vietnamese. Many of them were purged and demoralised, sick of killing their own people and far from loyal to the regime in Phnom Penh.

As the Vietnamese withdrew, so thousands of Khmers fled with them, taking refuge across the frontier in Vietnam. Among those who deserted at this time was a young Khmer Rouge commander called Hun Sen. Subsequently, in collaboration with the Vietnamese, he began to build a Cambodian liberation army with the aim of overthrowing Pol Pot and establishing a regime friendly to Vietnam in Phnom Penh.

The end of the Khmer Rouge

By the end of 1978 Khmer Rouge provocations had driven the Vietnamese to the brink of open warfare, and Hanoi took a decision to seize the eastern part of Cambodia as far as the Mekong River to create a *cordon sanitaire* (quarantine line) between its territory and the Democratic Kampuchea regime. This was not an easy decision to make, as Vietnam was war-weary and the leadership in Hanoi fully appreciated that such an attack would infuriate Cambodia's powerful ally China.

Vietnamese troops moved suddenly across the frontier on 25 December 1978. The Khmer Rouge put up little resistance, and the Vietnamese decided not just to occupy the eastern part of the country, but to seize Phnom Penh and overthrow the regime entirely. The discredited Khmer Rouge leadership fled in disarray to the Thai frontier, and a pro-Vietnamese administration, the People's Republic of Kampuchea, was set up in Phnom Penh on 8 January 1979.

Just one month later, on 17 February, China responded by invading Vietnam to "teach the Vietnamese a lesson". China's plan was to force Vietnam to withdraw its troops from Cambodia and send them instead to the Chinese frontier, but in the event this failed as the Vietnamese held the Chinese in the north with locally based troops and militia, holding back their main force for defending Hanoi, and declining to withdraw any troops from Cambodia. The Chinese invasion of Vietnam was immensely costly and destructive to the Vietnamese, but China withdrew its forces in March 1979, without breaking Vietnam's will and without achieving any of its strategic targets.

There followed a decade of guerrilla

Tuol Sleng torture cell, in what was formerly a high-school building.

warfare in Cambodia as Vietnam and its Cambodian allies in Phnom Penh fought a debilitating struggle against Khmer Rouge remnants – these guerrilla remnants backed by an unlikely collection of international forces. This period is characterised by particularly cynical realpolitik in which Vietnam was condemned for occupying Cambodia even though just about everyone – China excluded – recognised that Vietnam had in fact done Cambodia a considerable service in overthrowing the Pol Pot regime.

Unfortunately for Vietnam, the continuing war in Cambodia was less about destroying the Khmer Rouge guerrillas than about bringing down the Soviet Union and ending the Cold War. A decision was taken by the UK and US governments of Mrs Thatcher and Ronald Reagan to bleed the Soviet regime economically by backing the Khmer Rouge. They were enthusiastically supported in this endeavour both by China, at this time bitterly anti-Soviet, and by Thailand, which stood to profit from the resupplying of the Khmer Rouge guerrillas.

Despite the shocking evidence of Khmer Rouge brutality that was exposed by the Vietnamese invasion, "Democratic Kampuchea"

the austere and doctrinaire government of Le Duan, was also on the verge of economic collapse and starvation.

By the late 1980s it was clear to Hanoi that it would have to reach a compromise over Cambodia and withdraw its troops. In 1986 Le Duan died and was replaced by the more flexible Nguyen Van Linh. In 1989 the USSR withdrew its last forces from Afghanistan and, faced with imminent bankruptcy, began to disintegrate. By 1991 the Soviet Union had ceased to exist, and Vietnam had lost its main ally and chief military and financial backer.

Vietnamese troops arrive in Ho Chi Minh City, Vietnam, after withdrawal from Cambodia (28 September 1989).

retained its seat at the United Nations and was regularly supported by the United States, the United Kingdom and other Western governments, as well as by China. The Khmer Rouge fighting inside Cambodia were armed and financed by China, while – astonishingly – the British government went so far as to provide covert military training to Khmer Rouge forces.

Cynical though this strategy was, it worked all too well. The Soviet Union, already fighting a losing battle in Afghanistan which it occupied between 1979 and 1989, was rapidly running out of money and could not afford to lavish unlimited military supplies on its Vietnamese allies. Meanwhile Vietnam, under

In fact, the writing had been on the wall since the death of Le Duan in 1986, and Vietnam had already begun to wind down its operations in Cambodia. Meanwhile the implosion of the Soviet Union and the approaching end of the Cold War meant that Western backing for the Khmer Rouge guerrillas was no longer politically necessary for the West, though China would continue to back its Khmer Rouge protégés well into the 1990s. After a decade of fighting, it was now possible for a compromise to be reached in Cambodia, while Vietnam – now embarked on a series of economic reforms collectively known as *doi moi* or "renovation" – was desperately anxious to exit the Cambodian quagmire and avoid the fate of its erstwhile Soviet ally.

Crimes against humanity

In September 1989 Vietnam finally withdrew its forces from Cambodia, handing over control to the United Nations Transitional Authority in Cambodia (UNTAC). In May 1993, following UN-organised elections, Cambodia officially became a constitutional monarchy with King Sihanouk as head of state. The KR opted out of the elections, however, and this led to five more years of intermittent warfare during which the KR was gradually worn down. The KR leader, Pol Pot, died in 1998, while the last KR diehard,

In 2005, a war crimes tribunal to try surviving KR leaders finally received long-awaited UN approval. Even so, political infighting and fear of just what such a trial might expose delayed the legal process until 2009, when Kang Kek Iew, better known as Comrade Duch, the former commandant of S21 interrogation centre, became the first KR leader to go on trial. He was convicted of genocide and crimes against humanity in 2012 and sentenced to life imprisonment. In 2014, former Brother No 2, Nuon Chea, was also sentenced to life imprisonment. Brother

military leader Ta Mok, was captured near Anlong Veng in the north of Cambodia and taken to trial in Phnom Penh in early 1999. As a consequence, the power of the once greatly feared KR was broken for ever.

In 1999, Cambodia finally became a member of the Association of Southeast Asian Nations (ASEAN). Five years later, Sihanouk abdicated from the throne due to ill health. His second son, Norodom Sihamoni, was elected by a hastily assembled nine-member Throne Council to succeed him as king. Sihanouk retained the position of "King-Father" and spent much of his time in Beijing, returning to Cambodia for brief periods on an annual basis, before dying of a heart attack in 2012 in.

No 4, Ieng Sary, died in 2013, before a verdict could be reached; his wife, Ieng Thirith, the only Cambodian woman indicted for crimes against humanity, also died before being sentenced, in 2015. Meanwhile prime minister Hun Sen remains in undisputed power, ruling for over 30 years now, with a very firm hand amid suggestions and accusations of corruption.

Nevertheless, in today's Cambodia personal freedoms are greater, the press is more independent and there is more evidence of increasing prosperity now than at any time in the past 50 years. After their experience of unparalleled suffering in the preceding quarter-century, most Cambodians remain relatively satisfied with the current order.

Children from a Vietnamese floating village near Phnom Penh head for school.

Khmer man from a village near Kompong Cham.

POPULATION, SOCIETY AND ECONOMY

Ethnic Khmers dominate, but Cambodia is also home to a significant number of minority groups. All have benefited from a strong recovery of the economy.

Ethnic Khmer, Cambodia's predominant indigenous people, make up more than 90 percent of the country's 16-million-strong population. The Khmers are a predominantly agricultural people, subsisting on a diet of rice and fish, and living in wooden stilted houses in villages of several hundred people.

Khmers tend to think of themselves as a single people, the dominant ethnic group of Cambodia, the founders of the Khmer Empire and builders of Angkor Wat. This is by and large correct, but it is also something of a simplification, constructed on a nationalist desire to emphasise Khmer unity in the face of external challenges, particularly from Vietnam. Certainly the Khmer can be considered a single entity, but they may also be further subdivided into Cambodian Khmer, the Khmer Krom or "Lower Khmer" of "Lower Cambodia" – that is, the Mekong Delta which now forms part of Vietnam, and the Khon Suay or Surin Khmers of Thailand, especially in Sisaket, Surin and Buriram provinces, all former outliers of the Cambodian Empire which are now part of Thailand.

The Khmers are among the longest-established of settled agricultural peoples in Southeast Asia, all speaking variants or dialects of the same Khmer language, which is a part of the larger Mon-Khmer linguistic group that includes Vietnamese and extends from the Kasi in eastern India, through the Nicobar Islands in the southern Bay of Bengal and the Mon in Burma, to the Senoi in Malaysia and the Bugan in China. It is one of the oldest language groups in Southeast Asia, linked by linguistic specialists with the larger Austroasiatic family, and it predates both Sino-Tai and Sino-Tibetan languages (such as Burmese) in the region.

Woman wearing a krama.

Despite – indeed because of – the early migration of Khmer-speaking people into mainland Southeast Asia, little is known of the precise origins of the Khmers. It is thought that they arrived at least 3,000 years ago, probably from the north, at about the same time as ethnic Malays were migrating south from Taiwan to the Malay-Indonesian Archipelago. Why the Khmers migrated south remains unclear – it is possible that they may have been pushed south by expanding waves of Sino-Tibetan and Sino-Tai peoples, themselves under pressure from the expanding Han Chinese population to the north. The Khmer are related to the nearby Mon people of lower Burma and west-central Thailand who established the Mon Kingdom of Dvaravati which flourished between approximately AD 600 and 1100.

In recent decades, as elsewhere in the developing world, there has been a marked degree of urbanisation as Khmers move to cities such as Phnom Penh, Battambang, Sihanoukville (Kompong Som) and Kompong Cham. They remain the dominant political and cultural force of the Cambodian population, although their economic influence is far less, on a per capita basis, than that of the ethnic Chinese and Vietnamese. Most Khmers are Theravada Buddhists, although Christianity made a small number of converts during the 20th century.

> *A citizen of Cambodia is generally referred to as a "Cambodian" regardless of ethnicity or linguistic background. This includes ethnic Vietnamese, Chinese or Thai immigrants. To be a Khmer, however, is something else again.*

The Vietnamese

The largest national minority in Cambodia is the Viet Kieu or migrant Vietnamese, gener-

Street-food vendor, Phnom Penh.

THE KINGDOM OF CHAMPA

The earliest records of the Kingdom of Champa are Chinese, dating from AD 192. In these the Chams are described as having "dark skin, deep-set eyes, turned-up noses and frizzy hair", characteristics which are often still recognisable in the modern descendants of the Chams. The annals record that the Chams dressed, like the Malays, "in a single piece of cotton or silk wrapped about the body. They wear their hair in a bun on the top of their head, and they pierce their ears in order to wear small metal rings. They are very clean. They wash themselves several times each day, wear perfume, and rub their bodies with a lotion made of camphor and musk."

ally known in Cambodian as Youn. Because traditionally little love has been lost between Khmer and Viet, there is a tendency on the part of the Cambodian authorities to underestimate the number of Vietnamese in the country. According to figures published by the Cambodian government in 2003, there were just 100,000 Vietnamese residents, but independent estimates suggest there are now between 1.5 and 2.5 million. They tend to live in the big cities, where they work as restaurateurs or in other small businesses, or make a living as fishermen along the Mekong and Sap rivers. Ethnic Vietnamese also make a disproportionately large contribution to Cambodia's sex industry.

Relations between Cambodia's dominant Khmer population and the Cambodian Vietnamese go back hundreds of years but have rarely been good. To compound the settlement and eventual seizure of former Cambodian territory in southern Vietnam – still called "Lower Cambodia" by the Khmers – the French imported large numbers of ethnic Vietnamese to work on the rubber plantations and to staff the Franco-Cambodian bureaucracy. This inevitably engendered jealousy and added to old antipathies.

After independence the unilateral military actions of both North Vietnam and South citizenship laws effectively deny rights of citizenship to ethnic Vietnamese. To make matters worse, ethnic Vietnamese are readily identifiable, especially in rural areas, by their trademark mollusc hats or non la. Even today they are at risk of violent attack, especially at election times. It remains difficult to see the situation improving in the foreseeable future.

The Cham

A second distinctive minority in Cambodian society is the Cham Muslims, one of the oldest, but nowadays least considered, peoples of Indo-

New Year celebrations.

Vietnam compounded this issue. During the Sihanouk era the Cambodian Vietnamese were regarded as foreign residents and not Cambodian nationals. Under the Lon Nol regime, between 1969 and 1975, anti-Vietnamese pogroms killed thousands and caused perhaps 150,000 to flee to the relative security of Vietnam. Under the Khmer Rouge all Vietnamese were seen as foreign agents and killed or expelled.

Today the ethnic Vietnamese remain the most vulnerable of Cambodia's ethnic minorities. Khmer hostility and suspicion remains visceral, and while Khmers will intermarry readily with Chinese, intermarriage with Viets remains rare. Cambodian state schools provide no instruction in Vietnamese, and current Cambodian china. There are some 400,000–500,000 Chams in Cambodia, despite their having been particularly targeted for extermination by the Khmer Rouge in the 1970s. Gifted silversmiths, they also make a living by fishing and by butchering animals for their more fastidious Buddhist neighbours.

Chams are inheritors of a proud tradition that stretches back some 2,000 years: Champa was the first Indianised kingdom in Indochina, its founding predating both Chen La (6th century AD) and the first major expansion of the Vietnamese south from Tonkin (mid-10th century). At the peak of their power, about 12 centuries ago, the Chams controlled rich and fertile lands stretching from north of Hue, in central Annam, to the Mekong Delta in Cochin China;

yet today Vietnamese cities like Nha Trang and Da Nang dominate these regions. Only mysterious brick temples, known as "Cham towers", dot the skyline around Thap Cham and Po Nagar, while in Cambodia the name of an eastern province and its capital, Kompong Cham, remain as testimony to the lost kingdom.

The Chams are an Austronesian people, more closely linked, in ethnic terms, with the islands of the Malay-Indonesian world and the Philippines than with the mainland. We can only surmise that at some distant time they migrated from the Indonesian archipelago and settled in what is now southern Vietnam, and what we know of early Cham society seems to bear this out. Unlike their Viet and Khmer neighbours, whose society is based on intensive rice cultivation, the Chams had little time for agriculture. Their prosperity was based on maritime trade – and more than likely on a certain amount of piracy.

In 1471 the Chams suffered a terrible defeat at the hands of the Vietnamese. Champa was reduced to a thin sliver of territory in the region of Nha Trang, which survived until 1820, when the king and many subjects fled to Cambodia rather than submit to the Vietnamese. The

Removing wheat husks.

THE KRAMA, CAMBODIA'S TRADITIONAL CHEQUERED SCARF

Perhaps no garment is as distinctively Khmer as the Cambodian *krama*. Worn by men, women and children of just about every social class across the country, it is unique to Cambodia and the Khmer people.

It's not clear why the *krama* should be so uniquely Cambodian, though it has been speculated that it may be a link with the country's ancient Indic past, since turbans are more generally associated with South Asia than with Southeast Asia. Not that the *krama* is simply a turban – it can be used as one, and often is, but it has many more uses.

Generally chequered, and made of cotton or silk, *krama* are generally brightly coloured in red and white or blue and white, although more expensive silk ones may be multi-coloured and interwoven with gold thread. They are worn wrapped around the head to provide protection from wind, rains and especially Cambodia's blistering summer heat, or around the the shoulder or waist. Besides functioning as a protection against the weather, they are used for carrying fruit, vegetables and even small children, as well as substituting for pillows, shopping bags and even sarongs – and of course they make excellent towels for washing or drying the face, as well as providing modesty when bathing in a stream or pond. And of course, from a visitor's point of view, they make cheap, attractive and unusual souvenirs.

Cham diaspora dates from this period, and the diverse Cham communities later established in Cambodia, Thailand and Laos trace their common origin to this event.

Most Chams moved up the Mekong, into territories that now constitute the Cambodian heartland. They settled along the banks of the great river north and east of Phnom Penh, notably in the province and town of Kompong Cham, but also along the shores of the Tonlé Sap, Cambodia's great lake. Here they became well known and relatively prosperous through their skills as fishermen, settling into the ebb and flow of

such as the ethnic Vietnamese, Chinese and Thai were marked for expulsion or death. By contrast, indigenous minorities, although mistreated by Cambodian rulers for centuries, were spared the worst of the Khmer Rouge excesses.

The one major exception to this policy was

> Unusually, the Cambodian Chams are called to prayer by drum beats as well as the azaan – the call of the muezzin to the faithful – so familiar in Muslim lands.

Elderly woman wearing a krama, Battambang.

Cambodian life, and acquiring a widespread reputation for their abilities as practitioners of traditional medicine. During the 18th and 19th centuries Sunni Islam spread widely among the Cambodian Chams, while their fellows in Vietnam remained only partly Islamicised.

In 1975, when the Khmer Rouge seized power, nearly 400,000 Chams were living peacefully along the Mekong north and east of Phnom Penh. They followed the faith of their fathers in over 100 mosques, caught fish, grew rice and tried to stay neutral in the war which was destroying Cambodia. Even before Pol Pot's seizure of power in 1975 the Khmer Rouge had begun implementing special policies towards Cambodia's various minority peoples. "Recent migrants"

the Cham community, which was picked out for especially harsh treatment, probably because its members spoke a private community language unintelligible to the Khmer Rouge, read Arabic, wore distinctive clothing and followed an "alien" religion. Whatever the logic behind the decision, after the Khmer Rouge seizure of power in April 1975, anti-Cham policies were ruthlessly implemented.

During the ensuing three and a half years of terror, Cambodia's Chams were systematically victimised. All mosques – traditionally the spiritual and social centres of Cham community life – were either demolished or turned over to secular purposes for use as ammunition stores and Khmer Rouge barracks. Like their Khmer compatriots, only proportionately in much higher numbers, tens of thousands of Chams were murdered by the Khmer Rouge. By the time Vietnamese armed forces swept across the frontier in December 1978, between a half and two-thirds of the Cham community had been murdered, starved to death or driven out of the country.

The ethnic Chinese

Most of Cambodia's Hua Chiao, or Overseas Chinese, trace their origins to the southern coastal provinces of Hainan, Guangdong and Fujian. Authorities suggest that as many as 60 percent of Cambodia's ethnic Chinese belong to the Guangdong Teochiu group, followed by 20 percent "Cantonese" from Guangdong, 7 percent Hokkien, 4 percent Hakka from Fujian and 4 percent Hailam from Hainan Island. Estimates of their overall numbers vary from 500,000 to 1,200,000. In recent years a new wave of Chinese migration to Cambodia has got under way, and the presence of both Taiwanese and Malaysian Chinese in business circles is marked. The Chinese are almost exclusively urban, and, since they intermarry readily with urban Khmers, are not Muslim like the

Preparing fruit for sale in a Phnom Penh market.

AN INSPIRATIONAL PEOPLE

According to the historian David Chandler, after the Khmer Rouge victory of 17 April 1975 Pol Pot claimed to have derived revolutionary inspiration from the Khmer Loeu upland hill tribes – "people who had no private property, no markets and no money. Their way of life corresponded to the primitive communist phase of social evolution in Marxist thinking." In 1971, after eight years in the jungle, the Ieng Sary commented that the movement's tribal followers "may be naked, but they have never been colonised". At a lecture in Phnom Penh in 1976, he characterised the tribespeople as "faithful to the revolution... and possessing class hatred".

Chams, and are not disliked and feared like the Vietnamese, Chinese ethnicity is more readily subsumed within Khmer society. It is also interesting to note that fully 80 percent of the top Khmer Rouge leadership, including Pol Pot and Nuon Chea, were Sino-Khmers. Intermarriage between Khmers and Chinese is common and widespread, especially in urban areas. In this case, the Chinese often assimilate into Khmer society over two or three generations, though few if any forget their Chinese ancestry.

The Khmer Loeu

Other minorities include the Khmer Loeu or Upland Khmer – hill tribes of Mondolkiri and Rattanakiri, such as the Kuy, Mnong, Brao,

Tapuon and Jarai, as well as th e Pear and Saoch of the southwest. Strangely, several of these groups fared comparatively well under the Khmer Rouge – ruthless in their treatment of "outsider" minorities – because they were seen as "pure", unpolluted by capitalism and an urban environment, even models of primitive communism (see panel). Collectively they probably number around 500,000.

In 1968, shortly after the Khmer Rouge took the decision to embark on an armed struggle, its leadership began operations in regions inhabited by non-Khmer upland minorities such as the Brao, the Tapuon and the Jarai. These people, traditionally looked down on by the Khmer and known by the derogatory term *phnong*, "savages", were of great interest to the KR's largely urban leadership for their knowledge of the jungle, survival skills and prowess as hunters. They were also "poor and blank": in Maoist terms, ideal vessels for indoctrination. Finally, they are said to have shown great obedience to authority.

Because of this belief in "the noble savage", and in sharp contrast to the KR treatment of national minorities such as the Vietnamese, who were systematically persecuted and subjected to policies amounting to genocide, the Khmer Loeu were generally well treated and absorbed, wherever possible, into the ranks of the revolution.

Even before the KR seizure of power in 1975, many upland tribal people already served the KR leadership as special cadres, messengers and bodyguards.

Some indication of the position of trust attained by these tribal minorities – and of the culture shock caused to ordinary Khmers on seeing people they traditionally perceived as "savages" bearing AK47s in the midst of the victorious Communist forces – can be gleaned from contemporary accounts of the KR seizure of power. Peang Sophi, a factory worker in Battambang, recalls that the peasant soldiers who occupied his city were "real country people, from very far away. Many of them had never seen a city or printed words. They held Cambodian texts upside down, pretending to puzzle them out." Still more telling is an account by Dith Pran (who became widely known in the West through the film *The Killing Fields*), who comments on KR troops entering his village in Siem Reap: "They didn't even look like Cambodians; they seemed to be from the jungle, or a different world."

Other minorities

Three smaller groups who fared less well than the Khmer Loeu under the Khmer Rouge were the Thai, Lao and Shan. Faced with vicious discrimination in 1976–9, those Thais who were not

The Khmer Krom or "Lower Khmer" are essentially the ethnic Khmer inhabitants of the Mekong Delta who were left residing in the area after the Vietnamese conquest in the 18th and 19th centuries.

Miniature banana-leaf boats sail on the Mekong River during the New Year celebrations.

killed fled to neighbouring Thailand. Surviving Lao also fled in droves. The Shan – a few thousand were long-term residents of Pailin, where they worked as gem miners – were even less fortunate, and seem to have been wiped out entirely.

Finally, mention should be made of the South Asians, a few hundred of whom live in the larger cities like Phnom Penh and Battambang, working chiefly as small businessmen and traders. In the late 1960s several thousand South Asians, mainly identified as "Pakistanis" because of their Sindhi or Pathan origins, lived in the countryside around Battambang, Poipet and Siem Reap, where they specialised as cattle-breeders and milk-producers. But they, too, fell foul of the Khmer Rouge – simply because of their ethnicity – and those not lucky enough to flee the country were killed en masse.

Economy and industry

The Cambodian economy was virtually destroyed twice in recent decades, first when the Khmer Rouge entered Phnom Penh in 1975, and again with the 1989 withdrawal of the Vietnamese and the collapse of the Soviet Union, a major source of aid. Today, with Phnom Penh's move away from Communist ideology to market economics, the situation has improved, but the long-term development of the economy still remains a huge challenge, and prospects are not helped by the fact that corruption is so well entrenched. Cambodia became a member of ASEAN in 1999, and opened itself up to global markets in 2005 when it joined the WTO.

By far the largest sources of foreign revenue are wood exports and foreign aid, neither of which is sustainable in the long term. Another significant area of revenue, also of dubious long-term soundness, derives from the shipment of gold and cigarettes from other Asian countries to Vietnam, where tariffs are significantly

Garment factory workers get a lift to work.

BORDER DISPUTES WITH THAILAND

Traditionally, Cambodians regard both their Vietnamese neighbours to the east and their Thai neighbours to the west with suspicion and even hostility. Despite their partially shared Mon-Khmer linguistic routes, the ethnic Khmer particularly distrust the Vietnamese, whom they accuse of detaching and absorbing "Kampuchea Krom" – that is, "Lower Cambodia", or the area now comprising Saigon and the Mekong Delta. Relations with neighbouring Thailand are better than with Vietnam, but still far from good. As far as Khmer nationalists are concerned, Thailand occupies three northern Khmer provinces, identified with Sisaket, Surin and Buriram. More significantly, Cambodians as a whole dislike Thailand's sometime claims to Angkor Wat, the spiritual heart of the Cambodian nation. Another ongoing bone of contention is the status of Preah Vihear (see page 308), the Khmer temple occupying an inaccessible clifftop on the very fringes of Thailand's northeastern plateau, overlooking the Cambodian plains below. It was awarded to Cambodia by the International Court of Justice in 1962, but this decision was only ever grudgingly accepted by Thailand. Tempers flared up in 2011, when several soldiers from either side were killed and the temple was temporarily closed. In 2013, the International Court of Justice ruled that the land to the east and the west of the temple belongs to Cambodia.

higher. Other than timber and gemstones, also a source of income, Cambodia has few natural resources. Rubber used to be a major export, with the Soviet Union purchasing almost the

> For thirty years, Cambodia's brutal Khmer Rouge past was known to its younger citizens through word of mouth only. The history of Pol Pot and Democratic Kampuchea was not included in the Cambodian school curriculum until as recently as 2009.

The Cambodian government continues to work with bilateral and multilateral donors, including the World Bank and IMF, to resolve the country's many pressing needs. The major challenge in the short to medium term is to adapt the economic environment to the country's demographic imbalance – more than 50 percent of the population is 20 years or younger. Cambodia is attracting increased Foreign Direct Investment (FDI) – mainly Chinese, Taiwanese, Vietnamese, Thai and Malaysian – in the services sector. With the tourist industry growing stronger by the year

En route to market.

entire annual production, but has become less important in recent years. The garment industry, however, is robust and continues to expand.

Various proposals have been made, mainly for the establishment of hydroelectric facilities. So far nothing has come of these proposals, but they have brought to light the serious risks to Cambodia posed by similar projects upstream in Laos and China. As Cambodia is so dependent on the annual rise in the waters of the Mekong and Tonlé Sap and the fertile deposits this brings, any change in the flow of the river could potentially have disastrous effects on agriculture. The possibility of a decline in numbers and species of fish in the lake and river is also of concern.

(foreign arrivals rose from 2 million in 2007 to 4.7 million in 2015), there is potential for major expansion. This unprecedented growth has made tourism the nation's second-largest source of foreign exchange after textiles, and has transformed Siem Reap from a sleepy village 15 years ago to a fast-expanding tourism metropolis.

As in neighbouring Laos, new investment in education, basic infrastructure and telecommunications is making Cambodia increasingly attractive to foreign investors.

For the foreseeable future, tourism may be Cambodia's greatest chance of securing sustainable foreign exchange, with Angkor being one of the travel world's most marketable assets.

CULTURE, ART AND ARCHITECTURE

Despite attempts by the Khmer Rouge regime to destroy many of the traditional arts, Cambodian culture has managed to survive in all its forms.

Defining the "cultural arts of Cambodia" is no simple matter. The main problem is deciding just where the "Cambodian" element starts and ends. To begin with, Khmer culture – together with that of the Mon and the Chams – is about the earliest known indigenous high culture in the region, yet even in the distant days of Chen La and early Angkor it drew heavily on Indian cultural, religious and artistic influences – so heavily, indeed, that Cambodian culture is generally defined as "Indic". The Khmers in turn went on to influence their neighbours, particularly the Lao and the Thais. Thai writing, for example, is derived from Khmer, as is much of Thai court language.

But who gave what to whom? Indicisation may have started with the Khmer Empire, but at times of Cambodian weakness and Siamese strength the flow was often reversed. An interesting if little-known example of this, through the unlikely medium of French colonialism, was the re-establishment of traditional court dance in the royal palace at Phnom Penh in the early 20th century. Standards had fallen so far in Phnom Penh that the French invited classical dance masters from the court of Bangkok to reinvigorate the tradition in Cambodia. Thus it is difficult to draw clear dividing lines between the Indic cultures of Southeast Asia. Much of what is Cambodian is also, with minor variations, Thai or Lao or, at one remove, Burmese or even Javanese.

The Ramayana

Perhaps the paramount example of this is the great Hindu epic, the *Ramayana*, which has influenced both Cambodian and Lao culture (music, dance, literature, painting) to a considerable extent. Known as *Reamker* in Khmer, it is

Khmer sculpture, Wat Nokor, Kampong Cham.

a story as old as time and – at least in the Indian subcontinent and across much of Southeast Asia – of unparalleled popularity. More than 2,300 years ago, at about the same time as Alexander the Great invaded northwestern India, in another, less troubled part of that vast country the scholar-poet Valmiki sat down to write his definitive epic of love and war.

The poem Valmiki composed is in Sanskrit; its title means "Romance of Rama". The shorter of India's two great epic poems – the other being the *Mahabharata*, or "Great Epic of the Bharata Dynasty" – the *Ramayana* is, nevertheless, of considerable length. In its present form the Sanskrit version consists of some 24,000 couplets divided into seven books. It's astonishing, then, to think that people have memorised the entire work, and that since its initial composition it has enjoyed continual passionate recitation somewhere in Asia. Today it remains as vital as ever, though television, film and radio have brought it to a wider audience than Valmiki could ever have imagined – and its appeal continues to grow.

The story it tells, considered by scholars as more of a romance than an epic, begins with the birth of Prince Rama in the Kingdom of Ayodhya in northern India. Rama's youth is spent in the royal palace, under the tutelage of the sage Vishvamitra, from whom he learns patience, wisdom and insight, the qualities for a just and perfect king.

As a young man Rama wins the contest for the hand of Sita, the beautiful daughter of King Janaka. The couple marry, and for some time all is well – but then Rama falls victim to intrigue at the royal court, loses his position as heir, and withdraws to the forest for 14 years. Sita accompanies Rama into exile, as does his half-brother, the loyal Lakshmana.

Word of Rama's exile then reaches Ravana, demon-king of the island of Lanka. Ravana lusts

Sections of a Ramayana mural in the Silver Pagoda, Phnom Penh.

WORLDWIDE INFLUENCE

The *Ramayana* quickly became popular in India, where its recitation is considered an act of great merit. It was translated from the original Sanskrit into numerous vernacular versions, often works of great literary merit themselves, including the Tamil version *Kampan*, the Bengali *Krttibas* and the popular Hindi version, the *Ramcaritmanas* of Tulsidas. Other celebrations of the poem which continue to flourish in India today include the annual Ram-Lila pageant of northern India, and the Kathkali dance-drama of Kerala. So powerful was the *Ramayana* that it soon spread throughout the Hindu-Buddhist world, including Laos and Cambodia.

after Sita and, having sent a magical golden deer to lead Rama and Lakshmana off hunting, he seizes Sita and takes her to his palace in Lanka. Sita resists all his advances, while Rama and Lakshmana, realising they have been tricked, organise her rescue. Enlisting the help of the noble monkey-god Hanuman, among others, to invade Lanka and defeat Ravana and his devilish cohorts, Rama eventually manages to rescue Sita.

At this point in the story a darker side of Rama becomes apparent, as he accuses Sita of infidelity and requires her to undergo an ordeal by fire to prove her innocence. Rama seems satisfied, but on returning to Ayodhya he learns that the people still question Sita's virtue, and he banishes her to the forest. In exile, Sita meets the sage Valmiki and at his hermitage gives birth to Rama's two sons. The family is reunited when the sons come of age, but Sita, once again protesting her innocence, asks to be received by the earth, which swallows her up.

> A burgeoning contemporary art scene is now developing, especially in Phnom Penh and at Siem Reap. A number of younger artists have combined traditional Khmer art with Western modernism, creating an array of styles.

Bangkok and Phnom Penh were close, and the *Ramayana* – in Thai, *Ramakien* – murals came to the notice of visiting Cambodian nobles. In 1866 Cambodia's King Norodom began building a new royal palace in Phnom Penh, using French and Cambodian architects but drawing much of his inspiration directly from the Chakri royal complex in Bangkok.

Some 30 years later, following the completion of the Silver Pagoda at the Royal Palace in Phnom Penh, a decision was taken to tell the story of the *Ramayana* in murals along the inner face of the wall surrounding the complex.

Sections of a Ramayana mural in the Silver Pagoda, Phnom Penh.

The impact of the *Ramayana* on Lao and Cambodian culture can scarcely be overstated. The love of Rama for Sita, the loyalty of Lakshmana and the heroism of Hanuman have left an indelible mark on many aspects of traditional drama, literature and dance.

The Phnom Penh murals

In 1831 King Rama III of Siam ordered master-painters to begin the great task of painting the *Ramayana* in murals at Wat Phra Kaew in Bangkok. Over several years the story of Rama, Sita, Ravana and Hanuman unfolded over hundreds of square metres of cloister wall, shaded from the sun by long roofs of orange tiles. At the time relations between the royal courts of

The resulting mural, which was not completed until the reign of King Sisowath, is protected by cloister-like arcades, and has been restored on a number of occasions.

King Norodom's decision to order the painting of the murals, together with the style and technique, was clearly influenced by the *Ramakien* murals at Bangkok, yet they have a charm and distinction which are their own, and in some sections are better preserved than their Bangkok counterparts.

Dance

The beauty and elegance of the Cambodian Royal Ballet has to be seen to be believed. The writer Somerset Maugham was fortunate enough to witness a performance at Angkor in the 1920s, and enthused: "The beauty of these dances against the dark mystery of the temple made it the most beautiful and unearthly sight imaginable. It was certainly more than worthwhile to have travelled thousands of miles for this." The dancers had an even greater impact on Auguste Rodin, who exclaimed on seeing a performance in Paris in 1906: "These Cambodian women have given us everything antiquity could hold. It's impossible to see human nature reaching such perfection. There is only this and the Greeks."

As with other art forms, the ballet suffered badly in the terror of the Khmer Rouge period. Under Pol Pot – who had relatives in the Royal Ballet and spent some time with them in his youth – an attempt was made to destroy the ballet. Instruments were smashed, costumes and books burnt, while musicians and dancers were systematically killed.

Fortunately one or two dancers survived, among them Princess Bupphadevi, a favourite daughter of King Sihanouk, who was in exile in France. Today there are several *apsara* (celestial dancer) dance centres spreading the

Learning music at school.

SHADOW PUPPETRY

In common with the inhabitants of the Malay world and southern Thailand, the Cambodians have a strong tradition of shadow puppetry, which they call *nang sbaek thom*, or "shadow plays". Generally performed during festivals, weddings and funerals, the plays are narrated by actors concealed beneath the puppet screen. A light behind the screen casts images of the puppets onto the screen for the audience to watch. The puppets are usually made of cow or buffalo hide, and can be very intricate in their design. Siem Reap in the northwest of the country (see page 280) is considered by many to be the original home of this art form.

skills of Cambodian Royal Ballet, most notably at the Choreographic Arts Faculty at the Royal University of Fine Arts in Phnom Penh. Performances are regularly given at other locations.

Classical Khmer dance *(lamthon)* as performed by the Royal Ballet bears a striking resemblance to that of the Thai royal court, and indeed the two traditions influenced each other in turn and have now become practically a shared art form. Training takes many years, and elaborate costumes and headdresses are worn. It is a real spectacle that should not be missed. Cambodian masked theatre, known as *khaul*, is very similar to the Thai *khon*. Classical dances depicting incidents from the Buddha life-cycle stories, the *Jataka*, are often performed.

Music

Music has long flourished in Cambodia in both court and village settings, some kinds associated with specific functions, others with entertainment. In villages weddings are celebrated with *kar* music, communication with spirits is accompanied by *arakk* music, and entertainments include *ayai* repartee singing, *chrieng chapey* narrative, and *yike* and *basakk* theatres. At court, dance, masked and shadow plays and religious ceremonies are accompanied by *pinn peat* ensembles and entertainment by *mohori* ensembles. Temples often possess a *pinn peat* ensemble and a *korng skor* ensemble for funerals.

Traditional Cambodian music probably reached its zenith during the Angkor period. Carved on the walls of the great temples of Angkor and the vicinity are the *apsara* figures along with musical instruments: the *pinn* (angular harp), *korng vung* (circular frame gongs), *skor yol* (suspended barrel drum), *chhing* (small cymbals) and *sralai* (quadruple-reed flute). These are believed to have developed into the *pinn peat* ensemble.

Sometime around the year 1431 Angkor was looted by Siamese armies; the king and his musicians fled, and the city was abandoned and overrun by vegetation. Subsequently the capital was moved to Lovek, which itself was sacked by the Siamese in 1594. Khmer music and its functions were deeply affected by these events, and a new melancholic and emotional style is said to have emerged.

The period 1796–1859 represented a renaissance for the Khmer cultural arts. King Ang Duong, the greatest of the monarchs of this period, ascended the throne in 1841 in the then capital, Udong, and under his rule Cambodian music and other art forms were revived and began to flourish again. During the French colonial period Cambodian classical dance and music were truly appreciated by a small circle of French intellectuals and academics, but on the whole Cambodian classical music made little impression on the average *colon*.

These days, foreign influences play a large part in Cambodian music. Cambodian and Thai musical tastes and traditions are close, and Thai ramwong (popular dance), luk-tung (peasant songs from the countryside) and popular music alike have swept Cambodia and are to be heard everywhere, from taxis to hotel foyers. As with traditional ballet, there is a movement to re-establish traditional Cambodian

In the 1950s and 60s Cambodia was home to a lively local film scene. King Sihanouk was a rather self-indulgent movie fan and in the 1960s began making films which he wrote, directed and often starred in.

Dancer from the Cambodian Royal Ballet.

music, and King Sihanouk's classically minded, ballet-dancing daughter Princess Bupha Devi has stated that "classical music is in the Khmer national soul". Even so, there are relatively few traditional orchestras to be heard except at religious shrines – notably at Tonlé Bati, as well as at Preah Khan and Neak Pean in Angkor.

There are two types of traditional orchestra in Cambodia, the all-male *pip hat* and the all-female *mohori*. Both comprise 11 traditional instruments, including flutes, gongs, xylophones and three-stringed guitars. Music is sometimes accompanied by song, either improvised ballads or court chants. At some festivals an orchestra known as *phleng pinpeat* will perform court music. Another type of orchestra is the *phleng khmer*, which performs at weddings. Popular music has been recently influenced by the Thais and Chinese.

Architecture

Cambodia is home to possibly the greatest and certainly the oldest high civilisation in mainland Southeast Asia, and the country is studded with outstandingly beautiful temple complexes, both Hindu and Buddhist, dating from the 6th to the 15th centuries. The early Khmer architectural tradition – dating from around AD 500 to around 1350 – is unsurpassed, and several struc-

Ta Prohm temple, Angkor.

Angkor Wat has appeared on the flags of Cambodian regimes of all political persuasions, including the Khmer Rouge. The great temple complex is a potent image of national identity which has always transcended politics.

tures, including Preah Khan (see page 292), Ta Prohm (see page 294), the matchless Bayon (see page 286) and, of course, Angkor Wat (see page 288), remain the chief cultural reason for visiting the country.

The temple architecture of ancient Khmer civilisation, both Hindu and Buddhist, is readily identifiable. Building materials include laterite surmounted by structures of sandstone and/or stucco-covered brick. Elaborately carved sandstone lintels feature scenes from the Hindu pantheon, commonly the churning of the primeval ocean of milk or Vishnu reclining on a lotus flower. Scenes from the *Ramayana* and, from around 1200 on, the Buddhist *Jataka*, illuminate bas-reliefs of extraordinary quality. Everywhere, too, there are figures of *apsara* with jewellery and headdresses (see page 298).

The glory of this Khmer architecture makes it all the more surprising that post-Angkorean temples, whether Udong or Phnom Penh period, are really quite undistinguished by comparison, and lack a distinctly Cambodian style other than the extensive use of unadorned cement and now, increasingly, reinforced concrete.

There are Rattanakosin-style Buddhist temples in Phnom Penh and Battambang, among other cities, reflecting former Thai colonial rule and continuing Thai cultural influence, and artistic merit is not always lacking. The influence of Siam is dominant, though few if any contemporary Cambodian temples can match up to their Thai counterparts. The Royal Palace is based on the court in Bangkok, and was constructed under the supervision of French architects (see page 263). Other buildings of note in the capital include the National Museum and a plethora of early 20th-century French colonial architecture. Similar architecture can be found in Siem Reap, Kompong Cham, Battambang and Kampot.

The presence of Cham Muslims in many towns means that mosques and minarets also form part of the Cambodian skyline. They are mostly unremarkable imitations of Middle Eastern Islamic architecture, but to the north of Phnom Penh some interesting mosques, painted in the Cham colour of pale blue in contrast to the traditional Islamic green, have been erected in the wake of Khmer Rouge persecution.

Between 1975 and 1979, the Khmer Rouge destroyed the Roman Catholic Cathedral at Phnom Penh, and temples and mosques were turned into storage barns or pigsties. Fortunately there were limits to this vandalism – Angkor and other wonders of ancient Khmer civilisation were either protected or ignored and left to the encroaching jungle.

Banteay Kdei, Angkor.

THE ROYAL BALLET OF CAMBODIA

The elegant and sophisticated tradition of the Cambodian Royal Ballet is thought to date back to the times of the kings of Angkor.

The tradition of royal dancing in Cambodia is at least 1,000 years old. Inscriptions indicate that the kings of Angkor maintained hundreds of dancers at their royal courts. The celebrated temple of Ta Prohm, endowed by Jayavarman VII in 1186, maintained no fewer than 615 dancers. The origins of Cambodian dance are not hard to discern – like so much in Khmer culture, they are rooted in Indic tradition, especially that of the *Ramayana*, though a great deal of cultural exchange has also taken place between the royal courts of Phnom Penh and Bangkok.

The Royal Ballet suffered particularly badly during the vicious years of Khmer Rouge rule, when Pol Pot – who had relatives who danced in the company – attempted to crush the tradition completely. Fortunately a handful of dancers survived, either in hiding in Cambodia or in exile in France, and today the ancient tradition is being carefully revived. There are currently around 50 teachers of classical dance and between 300 and 400 students at the Royal University of Fine Arts in Phnom Penh, and another school called the Music and Art School has recently been established at Siem Reap near Angkor.

Two Royal Ballet dancers, c. 1955.

Classical Khmer dance continues to be taught at the School of Fine Arts in Phnom Penh.

Dancers depict scenes from the Ramayana. Great emphasis is placed on symbolic and graceful hand movements.

Wall carvings depict apsara celestial dancers at the Chan Chaya Pavilion in Phnom Penh's Royal Palace.

CELESTIAL DANCERS

Cambodian mythology and, more particularly, Cambodian temples are both richly endowed with bas-reliefs and murals of *apsara* or celestial dancing girls. These nymphs are graceful, sensuous females who dance to please the gods and to keep the cosmos moving in an orderly fashion. In technical parlance, the term *apsara* refers to celestial females who dance or fly, while their sisters who merely stand, albeit with amazing grace, are called *devata* or "angels". Almost every temple has its quota of *apsara*, but it is generally agreed that the finest examples are to be found in the bas-reliefs at Angkor, and that the best *apsara* are in the "Churning of the Ocean of Milk" in Angkor Wat's East Gallery. In this epic scene from the *Bhagavad-Gita*, gods are encouraged in their creative endeavours by beautiful *apsara* flying above them.

troupe of dancers from the Royal Ballet performing at the Chatomuk Theatre in Phnom Penh.

Most dancers in the Royal Ballet are women, but they may play male roles. Male and female roles are defined by elaborate costume.

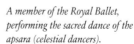

A member of the Royal Ballet, performing the sacred dance of the apsara (celestial dancers).

Street vendor preparing food in Phnom Penh.

CAMBODIAN FOOD

Like many things in the country in the aftermath of the Khmer Rouge period, Cambodian cuisine is experiencing a renaissance.

Khmer cuisine is often said to be like Thai food, but less spicy. This is partially true. Cambodian cuisine developed more than 1,000 years ago, before the local introduction of the chilli pepper by the Portuguese, or the founding of the first Thai kingdom in the 13th century. Unlike their neighbours to the west, the Khmer cooks kept chilli to the side, as a condiment rather than a central ingredient. Later Thai cooks derived many of their dishes from older Cambodian cuisine, adding chilli and other spices to create new national dishes. Of course other cultures have, in turn, strongly influenced Cambodia's food. Central in the nation's cuisine are soups and fish sauce from the Vietnamese and the Chams; Indian curries; stir-fries, fried rice and sweet and sour dishes from the Chinese; pastries, baguettes and coffee from the French; spices from the Far East, and fruit and vegetables from the Americas.

Baguettes, a culinary reminder of Cambodia's colonial past, for sale in Phnom Penh.

> Traditionally the Cambodians ate with their hands. The Thais and French introduced forks and spoons, while the Chinese and Vietnamese lent chopsticks to the dinner table.

Even so, Khmer cuisine has combined these elements with a distinct set of flavours and ingredients to form a unique taste. Below is a list of the key ingredients found in every Khmer cook's palette:

Galangal is a light-coloured root that resembles ginger, although the flavour is much milder. It is often ground into a paste before being added to a dish.

Kaffir lime is native to Indonesia and Malaysia. Its rind and leaves are ground and added to curries, soups and salads, lending a pungent, lemony flavour and deep green colour.

Lemon grass has a distinctive balmy, lemon flavour.

Palm sugar is reduced from palmyra or sugar palms. It has a richer, earthier flavour than cane sugar. It comes in solid, golden blocks or packed in jars, and can easily be crumbled or melted.

Prahok is a grey, fermented fish paste, with a pungent, salty flavour. It is used as a seasoning, condiment, or even primary ingredient.

Star anise is native to China and is used in caramelised meats. It is also used medicinally as an aid to digestion.

Tamarind is a dark, sticky fruit native to tropical Africa. It hangs from the tree in long pods, with a thin layer of sour fruit surrounding a string of hard, black seeds. It was brought to Indochina by Indian traders long ago, and is commonly used to darken or sour soups and sauces.

Turmeric is a rhizome that is ground and added to curries to give a rich, orange colour. It has a faint, bitter flavour and a distinctive, mustard-like smell.

Despite their Buddhist faith, the majority of Cambodians do not adhere to strict vegetarianism. "Vegetarian" dishes will often be cooked with fish sauce and incorporate animal fat or broth.

Finally, **kroeung**, or curry paste, forms the base of many Cambodian dishes, including the famous *amok*. It comes in green or red (*cham pour* seeds are added to give the red colour). The mix typically includes kaffir lime, galangal, turmeric, prahok shrimp paste, shallots and garlic.

Street food in Phnom Penh.

UNUSUAL DELICACIES

Cambodians are adventurous eaters, perhaps even more so than their neighbours. In any village market you may find whole fried snake, barbecued field rat, grilled dog meat, fried baby frogs, fried giant water bugs and beetles – as well as more mundane offerings like marinated chicken feet, fried mole crickets and grasshoppers. *Pong tea kon* is a fertilised duck egg containing an embryo, and is a favourite roadside snack to accompany a beer. Certain towns are famous for particular items. The small town of Skuon, for example, on the main route between Phnom Penh and Kompong Cham, specialises in deep-fried tarantulas and "tarantula wine".

The national diet

Cambodia's central staple is rice. Interestingly, the Khmer word for "to eat" is *nam bai*, which directly translates as "eat rice". A meal without rice is regarded as merely a snack. Other important starches include manioc (also known as cassava), taro and sweet potatoes.

Fish and other seafood are the top protein on the menu, thanks to the abundance of life in the rivers, the Tonlé Sap lake and offshore. Beef, pork, chicken, duck and other poultry are widely available but more expensive than fish dishes. Other less common sources of protein include locusts, water insects, various snakes and land crabs.

The national dish

Amok, a fish curry steamed in banana leaves, is Cambodia's best-known dish. *Amok chouk* is another version made with snails steamed in their shells. The curry sauce *(kroeung)* is steamed until solid, but smooth and moist. Less traditional variations may use chicken or seafood, and be served as a thinner, creamy soup contained in coconut husks.

Soups

Samlor, or traditional Cambodian soup, is served as an accompaniment to almost all main courses. Some of the better-known varieties include *samlor machou* (a tangy soup combining shrimp, tomatoes and fried garlic, garnished with fresh mint), *samlor machou banle* (sour fish soup), *samlor machou bangkang* (sour and spicy prawn soup, akin to Thai *tom yam gung*), *samlor chapek* (pork soup with ginger), *s'ngao moan* (shredded chicken breast simmered with lemon grass, holy basil, scallions and fresh lime), *b'baw moan* (a "hearty rice soup" with chicken, coriander, bean sprouts and fried garlic) and *kuy tieu* (rice-noodles cooked with sliced pork, bean sprouts, red onions and fish sauce). Additionally, *bobor* is rice porridge, and one of the cheapest meals you'll find, served with ginger and fish or poultry.

Salads

Cambodian salads are similar in form to Thai and Vietnamese salads, and thus very different from the concept of salads in the West. Typically sweet and tangy, they incorporate shredded meats and vegetables, mint and other herbs, banana flowers, and sour, shredded fruits like green mango and papaya. They are usually mixed with a fish-sauce dressing, not unlike Vietnam's *nuoc cham*. Salads are light and usually the first course or appetiser in a meal.

Eaten with rice

Well-known dishes eaten with rice include *saich moan chha khnhei* (stir-fried chicken with ginger), *an sam jruk* (sticky rice wrap with pork and mung beans), *nataing* (ground pork simmered in coconut milk, sliced garlic, peanuts and chilli peppers), *leah chah* (green mussels cooked with garlic, holy basil, red onions, chilli peppers and lime), *mee siem* (rice noodles sautéed with shredded chicken, soybeans,

chives, red peppers, bean sprouts and fried egg), *cha'ung cha'ni jruk ang* (spare ribs marinated with mushrooms, soy sauce, garlic and black pepper, served with pickled cabbage), *trey aing k'nyei* (grilled catfish served with a sauce of ginger, salted soybeans and coconut milk), *moan dhomrei* (sliced chicken sautéed with holy basil, bamboo shoots, pineapple and kaffir lime leaves) and, finally, *chau haun* (mixed chicken, beef and shrimp cooked in a sauce of garlic, shallots, ginger, lemon grass and peanuts). Many of these dishes are available at restaurants in Phnom Penh and Siem

Limes and chillies.

Reap, but if you fancy trying one and it is not on the menu, just ask.

Desserts

A lot of great sweets are readily available in covered markets and on street corners. Puddings and sweet soups (much like Vietnamese *che*) made with tapioca, coconut milk, beans, corn and fruit are a popular and inexpensive snack typically available in the evening. Sticky rice with coconut and mango, as well as a large range of custards, are also very popular.

Fruit

Cambodia has a large variety of tropical fruits that are common throughout Southeast Asia.

Everyone will recognise the many varieties of *chek* (bananas), *svay* (mangoes), *l'howng* (papaya), *duong* (coconuts) and *menoa* (pineapples). More unusual fruits include the stinky *tourain* (durian), enormous *khnau* (jackfruit), creamy *tiep* (milk fruit), hairy *sao mao* (rambutan) and purple *mongkut* (mangosteen). The last was the focus of a health-food craze in the West, due to its high levels of antioxidants and other nutritional qualities. One tasty fruit to watch for is the *salacca*, or snake fruit, which is not normally available in neighbouring Laos or Vietnam. Its rough, red outer covering looks

Collecting fruit from the top of the tree.

like snake skin, and the orange fruit inside looks dry but is surprisingly juicy and delicious, if a bit tangy.

Drinks

Chinese tea and Vietnamese coffee are the drinks of choice in Cambodia, although beer and local rice wines are a close second. Sugar palm wine is a strong but tasty home-made concoction sold from open bamboo containers, carried on the backs of motorbikes.

Teuk kalohk are fruit shakes, made with the fruit of your choice and ample amounts of sugar and condensed milk. Commonly sold at evening roadside stands, they are an enjoyable way to get your daily serving of fruit.

Vietnamese dishes

Vietnamese cuisine is widely available throughout the country. As in Cambodian restaurants, dishes are served all at the same time rather than by course, and are eaten with long-grain rice, *nuoc cham* (fish sauce) and a range of herbs and vegetables, generally with chopsticks.

Some of the more popular Vietnamese dishes include *cha gio*, small spring rolls of minced pork, prawn, crabmeat, mushrooms and vegetables wrapped in rice paper and then deep-fried. The spring rolls are frequently rolled in a lettuce leaf with fresh mint and other herbs and then dipped in a sweet fish sauce. Another dish eaten in a similar fashion is *cuon diep*: shrimp, noodles, coriander and pork wrapped in lettuce leaves.

Vietnamese soups are popular too. *Mien ga* is a noodle soup blending chicken, coriander, fish sauce and spring onions; *canh chua*, a sour soup served with fish, is a blend of tomato, pineapple, star fruit, bean sprouts, okra and coriander; and finally *pho*, often eaten for breakfast or as a late-night snack, is a broth of rice noodles topped with beef or chicken, fresh herbs and bean sprouts. Egg yolk is often added to *pho*, along with lime juice, chilli peppers and sweet bean sauce. *Pho* is generally served with *quay* – fried flour dough.

Other foreign foods

Chinese food (predominantly Cantonese) is widely available in the larger towns. In the west of the country, notably at Poipet, Sisophon, Battambang and Siem Reap, Thai cuisine is widespread. Siem Reap and Sihanoukville have a broad selection of foreign restaurants, while in Phnom Penh there are French, Mexican, Italian, Greek, Turkish, North Indian, South Indian, Sri Lankan, Malay and – increasingly – fast-food restaurants. The Sorya shopping centre is the best place in the country to find Western fast-food franchises.

Where to eat

The cheapest eats are found in street-side and market stalls, and the noodle shops where locals congregate. Markets are a great place to buy items for picnic lunches and snacks, although you may find that bargaining for individual components is overall more expensive than ordering meals-to-order at local eateries. It can be difficult for foreigners to haggle down to the low prices that locals pay, even when they know the price already.

The Independence Monument,
Phnom Penh.

Prasat Thom temple, Koh Ker.

CAMBODIA: PLACES

A detailed guide to the entire country, with principal
sites clearly cross-referenced by number to the maps.

Fun in the water.

Like Laos, Cambodia is often described as a small place.
True, at 181,000 sq km (69,900 sq miles) it's not large
– about the same size as Missouri and roughly three-
quarters as large as Laos. However, it has more historic
sites per square kilometre than almost anywhere else on
earth. The Khmers were master-builders, and the product
of more than a millennium of magnificent temple construction awaits the visitor.

Of course, the most important site in the country, if not
in all of Southeast Asia, is the great temple-city of Angkor,
which must not be missed. Other great temples, too, are now open to
visitors – Ta Prohm and Phnom Chisor near Phnom Penh; the spectacular mountain-top sanctuary of Preah Vihear, though, is
periodically out of bounds due to a long-running border dispute with Thailand.

Cambodia is geographically unique. Tonlé Sap, the
great lake which dominates the west of the country,
expands and shrinks with the rainy and dry seasons,
providing a vast natural reservoir for the waters of the
Mekong River. One way to visit Angkor is to take the
boat from Phnom Penh, the country's shabbily elegant
capital, across the Tonlé Sap to Siem Reap. En route it is
possible to see something of the lifestyle of Cham and
Vietnamese fisherfolk, many of whom spend all their
lives on the water. The river port of Kompong Chang,

Stilt house at Tonlé Sap.

located on the south side of the Sap River, is a quiet
and attractive stopover for travellers to Tonlé Sap. Raised on astonishingly high stilts, the houses and shops at Kompong Chang are at water
level during the rainy season, but stand many metres above the Sap River
during the dry season, giving an indication of how the level of the Tonlé
Sap rises and falls.

Finally, Cambodia has at least one thing that neighbouring Laos lacks
– a coastline. Although dilapidated by years of neglect and deliberate
destruction by the Khmer Rouge, Cambodia's "Riviera" is fast coming
back into fashion. The port city of Sihanoukville offers beaches and some
fine seafood, while the old resort town of Kep is being rebuilt and refur-
bished. Idyllic tropical islands such as Koh Kong, now developing resort
facilities, complete the picture.

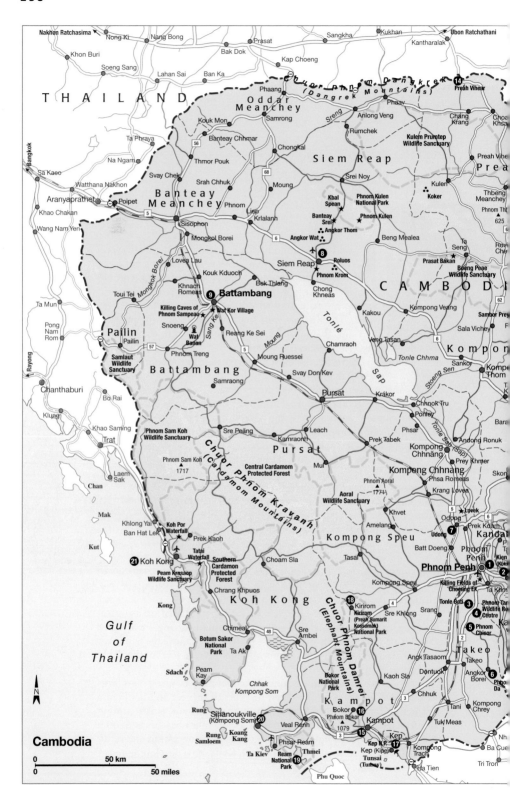

Cambodia

0   50 km

0   50 miles

The timeless charm of rural
Cambodia.

Khmer fish seller.

PHNOM PENH

Phnom Penh's fortunes have risen and fallen with Cambodia's turbulent history, but the future looks bright as new skyscrapers, hotels, restaurants and shops move in with the booming economy.

Phnom Penh **❶**, the Cambodian capital, is an attractive riverside city of broad boulevards and numerous sights to please the visitor. Until recently rather shabby and run-down owing to the long years of war and four years of Khmer Rouge abandonment, the future now looks bright, with new shopping centres, luxury residence complexes, enormous hotels, and fine-dining restaurants opening often. Most of the important attractions for the tourist are located beside or within walking distance of the Phnom Penh riverside, and this area also contains many of the best restaurants and cafés.

Once a Funan-era settlement, the city was re-founded in the 1430s, with the decline of Angkor and the shift of power eastwards (see page 209). The legend relates how a woman named Penh found four images of the Buddha on the shores of the Mekong River, and subsequently built a temple on the tallest hill in the area in which to keep them. The city that later grew up around the hill became known as Phnom Penh, or "Penh's Hill".

In 1772, now a major centre of commerce, Phnom Penh was completely destroyed by the Thais. The city was soon rebuilt but grew little until 1863, when the French took control. A relatively prosperous period ensued. Growth continued until the

Khmer Rouge arrived in 1975, forcing the urban dwellers into the countryside and leaving the city virtually abandoned.

The Royal Palace

A good place to start a tour of Phnom Penh, the extensive grounds of the **Royal Palace ❹** (daily 8–11am and 2–5pm) are off Sothearos Boulevard, immediately to the south of the National Museum. The palace was built in Khmer style with French assistance in 1866. It functioned as the

Main Attractions

Royal Palace and Silver Pagoda
National Museum
Central Market
Wat Phnom
Psar Tuol Tom Pong (Russian Market)
Tuol Sleng Genocide Museum (S21)

City street scene.

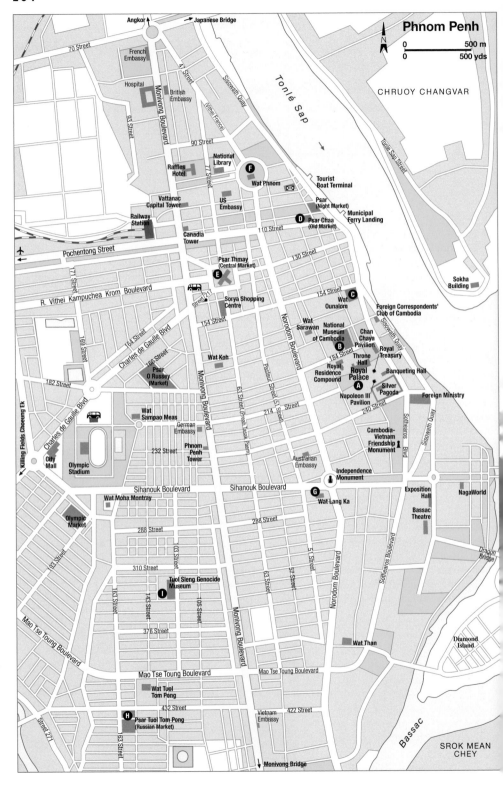

Angkor ↑ → Japanese Bridge

Phnom Penh

N

| 0 | | 500 m |
| 0 | | 500 yds |

Tonlé Sap

CHRUOY CHANGVAR

70 Street

French Embassy

Hospital

British Embassy

47 Street

Sisowath Quay

(Vithei France)

90 Street

Monivong Boulevard

333 Street

National Library

Raffles Hotel

77 Street

F

Wat Phnom ✉

Tourist Boat Terminal

Vattanac Capital Tower

US Embassy

Psar (Night Market)

Municipal Ferry Landing

Railway Station

Canadia Tower

110 Street

D Psar Chaa (Old Market)

Pochentong Street

Psar Thmay (Central Market)

130 Street

E

Sokha Building

771 Street

R. Vithei Kampuchea Krom Boulevard

154 Street

Street 217

154 Street

Sorya Shopping Centre

Wat Ounalom

C

Foreign Correspondents' Club of Cambodia

169 Street

154 Street

Charles de Gaulle Blvd

166 Street

Wat Sarawan

Norodom Boulevard

National Museum of Cambodia

Chan Chaya Pavilion

B

Royal Treasury

Wat Koh

Pasteur Street 51

184 Street

Throne Hall

Royal Residence Compound

Royal Palace

Banqueting Hall

Psar O Russey (Market)

182 Street

63 Street (Preah Sihanouk)

51 Street

A

Napoleon III Pavilion

Silver Pagoda

Foreign Ministry

Killing Fields Choeung Ek

Charles de Gaulle Blvd

Wat Sampao Meas

German Embassy

214 Street

240 Street

Sothearos

Cambodia-Vietnam Friendship Monument

City Mall

Olympic Stadium

232 Street

Phnom Penh Tower

Australian Embassy

Independence Monument

Exposition Hall

NagaWorld

Sihanouk Boulevard

Sihanouk Boulevard

G

Wat Lang Ka

Bassac Theatre

Olympic Market

Wat Moha Montray

288 Street

288 Street

Sothearos Boulevard

Dragon Bridge

333 Street

288 Street

103 Street

310 Street

63 Street

57 Street

5 Street

Norodom Boulevard

163 Street

143 Street

Tuol Sleng Genocide Museum

I

105 Street

376 Street

Wat Than

Diamond Island

Mao Tse Toung Boulevard

Mao Tse Toung Boulevard

Mao Tse Toung Boulevard

Wat Tuol Tom Pong

432 Street

422 Street

Bassac

H Psar Tuol Tom Pong (Russian Market)

Vietnam Embassy

SROK MEAN CHEY

Street 271

163 Street

Monivong Boulevard

↓ Monivong Bridge

official residence of King Norodom Sihanouk from the time of his return to the capital in 1991, followed by his son, King Norodom Sihamoni, who ascended to the throne in 2004.

The public entrance to the palace is opposite the now-closed, colonial-style Renakse Hotel, to the east of the palace grounds. Certain areas within the complex, including the king's residential quarters, are not open to the general public, but much of the rest of the site is accessible. Just beyond the entrance gate stands the **Chan Chaya Pavilion**, formerly used by Cambodian monarchs to review parades and for performances of classical Khmer dancing. Nowadays dance performances are regularly presented at the nearby Cambodiana Hotel.

Dominating the centre of the larger, northern section of the royal compound is the **Royal Throne Hall**. This was built as recently as 1917 in the Khmer style, the architect self-consciously borrowing extensively from the Bayon at Angkor. Inside the Throne Hall, the walls are painted with murals from the *Reamker*, the

Khmer version of the *Ramayana*. As well as coronations, the Throne Hall is used for important constitutional events and, on occasion, for the acceptance of ambassadorial credentials.

To the right (northwest) of the Throne Hall stands the restricted **Royal Residence Compound** of the king, while to the left are several structures of interest. These include the **Royal Treasury**, the **Royal Banqueting Hall** and the **Napoleon III Pavilion**. The pavilion, which was renovated by French volunteers using French money, was originally given by Emperor Napoleon III to his wife, Empress Eugénie. In the 1870s, she had it dismantled and sent across the seas to Phnom Penh as a gift for King Norodom.

The Silver Pagoda

Leaving the main northern compound of the palace by a clearly marked gateway in the southeastern corner, proceed along a narrow southwesterly route that leads to the North Gate of the celebrated **Silver Pagoda** compound. Commissioned by King Norodom in 1892, and then extensively

Stained-glass window in the Napoleon III Pavilion of the Royal Palace, Phnom Penh.

National Museum of Cambodia.

TIP

The riverside serves as a home base for most visitors to Phnom Penh – especially backpackers. Here you'll find a surplus of great restaurants, bars, shops, affordable guesthouses and tuk-tuk drivers ready to take you to all the sights. Unfortunately the presence of tourists also attracts Cambodia's social evils – prostitutes, drug dealers, pickpockets and professional beggars are all very well represented here.

rebuilt by Sihanouk in 1962, the floor of the pagoda is lined with more than 5,000 silver tiles weighing more than 1kg each, or 5 tonnes in total. Rather disappointingly, almost the entire floor, except for a small area, is protected by a thick carpet, so the scale of the grandeur is not so obvious.

The pagoda is also known as **Wat Preah Keo**, or "Temple of the Emerald Buddha". It houses the sacred symbol of the nation, the Emerald Buddha, which dates from the 17th century and is made of crystal. There is also a much larger Buddha figure here, comprised of a total of 90kg (198lbs) of pure gold, encrusted with 9,584 diamonds, the largest of which is 25 carats. Photography within the building is forbidden.

National Museum of Cambodia

Continuing northwards from the Royal Palace on Sothearos Boulevard you will soon come to a public green, behind which is the **National Museum of Cambodia** Ⓑ (227 Kbal Thnal, Preah Norodom Boulevard;

The Royal Palace gate.

tel: 023-217 643; www.cambodiamuseum.info; daily 8am–5pm; no photography allowed, except in the courtyard). The museum, housed in a red pavilion opened in 1917, holds a wonderful collection of Khmer art, including some of the finest pieces in existence. As you enter, buy a copy of the museum guidebook, *Khmer Art in Stone*, which identifies and discusses the most important exhibits, including a 6th-century statue of Vishnu, a 9th-century statue of Shiva and the famous sculpted head of Jayavarman VII in meditative pose. Particularly impressive is a damaged bust of a reclining Vishnu which was once part of a massive bronze statue found at the Occidental Mebon Temple in Angkor.

Wat Ounalom

The headquarters of the Cambodian Buddhist *sangha* and Phnom Penh's most important temple, **Wat Ounalom** Ⓒ stands northwest of the **Foreign Correspondents' Club of Cambodia** (FCCC) and the Royal Palace. Founded in 1443, this extensive temple suffered badly at the hands of the Khmer Rouge

TO GIVE OR NOT TO GIVE

The level of poverty in Cambodia is often shocking to first-time visitors. Conditions are much better than they once were, yet in many tourist areas you will encounter amputees, bedraggled women with malnourished babies, and stray-waif street children, all with their hands out, asking for money. It overwhelms some visitors, leading to the term "beggar burn-out".

Certainly Phnom Penh has a large share of impoverished people in genuine need of assistance. However, some of the people who flock to tourist areas to beg are choosing to do so in spite of other opportunities for assistance that are available to them. Scams abound (most commonly on the riverside) involving women who "borrow" or even rent babies and small children – some of whom they drug and physically abuse – to use them as props to gain sympathy while begging.

If you decide to give money to beggars, small amounts are best, but you should be aware that your gift may do more to placate your own sense of awkwardness than actually help the individual. For longer-lasting results, consider using your money to support one of the many charity shops, restaurants and schools around Phnom Penh, established to train and employ disadvantaged individuals – especially the city's youth.

but is fast recovering. Unfortunately the once-extensive library of the Buddhist Institute, also housed here, will take many years to replace.

To the west of the main temple stands a *stupa* said to contain an eyebrow hair of the Buddha. Within the temple are several archaic Buddha figures, smashed to pieces by the Khmer Rouge but since reassembled. Also on display is a statue of Samdech Huot Tat, head of the *sangha* when Pol Pot came to power and subsequently killed. The statue was recovered from the nearby Mekong and reinstalled after the collapse of Democratic Kampuchea.

On leaving the temple, turn right (south) along Sisowath Quay, the road that runs along the Sap River. This is a delightful area of small riverside cafés and restaurants where it is possible to experience the international affluence of the new Cambodia. It is a good place to stop for Italian coffee and French pastries, or a burrito and gelato. Alternatively, the FCCC is a popular, if somewhat touristy, night spot and offers unsurpassed views across the Sap and Mekong rivers from its well-appointed second-floor restaurant.

North of Wat Ounalom

The *Psar Chaa*, or **Old Market** , located near the riverfront at the junction of Streets 108 and 13, is a densely packed locale offering a wide selection of souvenirs, books, clothing, jewellery, dry goods, street food and fresh produce. Unlike some of the markets, it stays open late into the evening. A tidy, modern night market is held in the square across the street, facing the river, and is now a favourite spot for weekend souvenir shopping.

A short distance to the southwest, at the commercial heart of Phnom Penh, is the extraordinary *Psar Thmay*, literally "New Market", but generally known in English as **Central Market** . Built in 1937 during the French colonial period, it is Art Deco in style and painted bright ochre. The design is cruciform, with four wings dominated by a central dome, and the overall effect has been likened to a Babylonian ziggurat. In and around the four wings almost anything you

Avoid touching people on the head. Cambodians believe that's where one's vital essence resides. Even a hairdresser will ask permission before touching.

The Central Post Office.

TIP

The promenade around the Cambodia-Vietnam Monument, much like the area in front of the Royal Palace, comes alive every evening – especially at weekends. Families and couples lay out mats and recline or eat picnic dinners. Kids come to play games and buy street food from the many sidewalk vendors. The Royal Palace promenade also hosts popular free dance and aerobics classes.

can think of is for sale, including electronic equipment, DVD, clothing, watches, bags and suitcases, and a wide variety of dried and fresh foodstuffs. There are many gold and silver shops beneath the central dome which sell skilfully crafted jewellery as well as Khmer *krama* scarves, antiques, pseudo-antiques and other souvenirs. In 2009, Central Market was renovated. Now with new stalls, wider aisles and fresh paint, it is much cleaner, more orderly and safer than in the past. Within view of the Central Market is **Sorya**, Cambodia's premier shopping centre, and the best place in Cambodia for Western imported cloth, electronics and household items, as well as fast-food chains.

Built on a small mound in the north of the city not far from the banks of the Sap River, **Wat Phnom** Ⓕ (daily) is perhaps the most important temple in Phnom Penh, and from it the capital takes its name. According to legend, around six centuries ago a Cambodian woman called Penh found some Buddha figures washed up on the bank of the Sap. Being both rich and pious,

she had a temple constructed to house them on top of a nearby hill – in fact a mound just 27 metres (88ft) high, but still the highest natural point in the vicinity – hence "Phnom Penh" ("the hill of Penh").

Wat Phnom, the temple built to house the figures, is entered from the east via a short stairway with *naga* balustrades. The main *vihara*, or temple sanctuary, has been rebuilt several times, most recently in 1926. There are some interesting murals from the *Reamker* – the Khmer version of the Indian *Ramayana* – and in a small pavilion to the south is a statue of Penh, the temple's founder.

Wat Phnom is eclectic, to say the least. Although dedicated to Theravada Buddhism, it also houses (to the north of the *vihara*) a shrine to Preah Chau, who is especially revered by the Vietnamese community, while on the table in front are representations of Confucius and two Chinese sages. Finally, to the left of the central altar is an eight-armed statue of the Hindu deity Vishnu. The large *stupa* to the west of the *vihara* contains the ashes of King Ponhea Yat (1405–67).

To the north and east of Wat Phnom, along Street 94 and Street 47 (also known as Vithei France), lie many dilapidated old colonial buildings, increasing numbers of which are being renovated. This is the old **French Quarter**. Should you wish to explore it, leave Wat Phnom by the main eastern stairway and walk due east to the Sap River, noting en route the colonial-style Post Office building, usually resplendent with large portraits of Cambodian royalty. At the river turn left onto Sisowath Quay and then take the next left turn down onto Street 47. Walk north along Street 47 to the roundabout, turn south down Monivong Boulevard, past the French Embassy (on the right) and the British Embassy (on the left), and then turn east by the railway station along Street 106. This route takes you past many examples of French colonial-style architecture.

Wat Phnom.

South of the Royal Palace

As you walk south along Sothearos Boulevard from the palace you will pass an extensive park, in the centre of which stands a statue in heroic Socialist-Realist style depicting two soldiers, one Vietnamese, the other Cambodian, protecting a Cambodian woman and child. This is the **Cambodia-Vietnam Monument**, dedicated to the supposedly unbreakable friendship that links the two peoples: of course the reality is somewhat different (see page 217).

At the southern end of the park, turning west along Sihanouk Boulevard, you will reach the pineapple-shaped **Independence Monument** – in fact, it represents a lotus – built to celebrate Cambodia's independence from France in 1953. Immediately southwest of this monolith is **Wat Lang Ka** (daily; free), the second Phnom Penh temple (after Wat Ounalom) to have been restored after the overthrow of the Khmer Rouge regime. Today it is a flourishing example of the revival of Buddhism in Cambodia. Saffron-robed monks abound, while newly painted murals from the *Jataka* (Buddha life-cycles) fairly gleam from the restored *vihara* walls.

While the Sisowath Quay offers views over the junction of the Sap and Mekong rivers, to understand the unique confluence of waters at Phnom Penh properly you should also see the Bassac River. This is best viewed from the Monivong Bridge, south of the city centre, which marks the start of Route 1 to Ho Chi Minh City. The confluence of the rivers, known in Khmer as **Chatomuk** or "Four Faces", is remarkable for a unique phenomenon: the reversal, from May to October, of the Sap River, which more than doubles the size of the Tonlé Sap. Then, in mid-October, as the level of the Mekong diminishes, the flow of the Sap is again reversed, carrying the surplus waters of the Tonlé Sap southwards to the Mekong and Bassac deltas. The time in October when the waters return to their normal course is celebrated as *Bon Om Tuk*, one of Cambodia's most important festivals.

On national feast days, a ceremonial flame is usually lit on the pedestal of the Independence Monument.

Rough wooden shacks along the Bassac River.

A bureau de change at the Russian Market. Among the many souvenir items on sale here are Khmer Rouge banknotes – unique in that they were never actually issued.

A reminder of the Khmer Rouge regime's brutality.

The Russian Market

The best market for souvenir bargains and discounted, locally manufactured designer clothing is *Psar Tuol Tom Pong*, otherwise known as the **Russian Market** because of the many Russians who shopped here in the 1980s. It is located in the southern part of town, beyond Mao Tse Toung Boulevard (also known as Issarak Street) at the junction of Streets 163 and 432. Despite its unprepossessing appearance from the outside, this is a great place to shop for genuine and imitation antiquities, Buddha figures, silk clothing, silver jewellery and ornaments, gems and old banknotes from previous regimes.

Interestingly, the notes for sale include those of the Khmer Rouge, which had currency printed in China but then had a change of mind; in a radical frenzy, it outlawed money altogether, blew up the central bank and ultimately never issued any notes to the public. The Khmer Rouge money is readily recognised by both its pristine condition – it was never circulated – and the warlike themes on the notes: look for rocket-toting guerrillas, howitzers, machine-guns and fierce-faced Khmer Rouge girl-soldiers.

Head deeper inside to find the full selection and the best bargains. Outdoors, on the rear side, you can also find an ample selection of delicious street food. The market and S21 are often visited together.

S21: Tuol Sleng Genocide Museum

Not for the faint-hearted, just over 1km (0.6 miles) from Tuol Tom Pong Market, to the north of Mao Tse Toung Boulevard, stands the former Tuol Sleng Prison, now **Tuol Sleng Genocide Museum** ❶ (www.tuolslenggenocidemuseum.com; daily 7am–5.30pm). Here, during Pol Pot's years in power, around 20,000 people were interrogated under torture and subsequently murdered, generally together with their families.

The former prison – once a school – is a chilling sight; the pictures of many of those killed stare out at the visitor in black and white from the museum walls, and primitive instruments of torture and execution are on display, as is a bust of Pol Pot. Many of the former

THE SECURITY REGULATIONS

1. YOU MUST ANSWER ACCORDINGLY TO MY QUESTIONS. DON'T TURN THEM AWAY
2. DON'T TRY TO HIDE THE FACTS BY MAKING PRETEXTS THIS AND THAT. YOU ARE STRICTLY PROHIBITED TO CONTEST ME.
3. DON'T BE A FOOL FOR YOU ARE A CHAP WHO DARE TO THWART THE REVOLUTION.
4. YOU MUST IMMEDIATELY ANSWER MY QUESTIONS WITHOUT WASTING TIME TO REFLECT.
5. DON'T TELL ME EITHER ABOUT YOUR IMMORALITIES OR THE ESSENCE OF THE REVOLUTION.
6. WHILE GETTING LASHES OR ELECTRIFICATION YOU MUST NOT CRY AT ALL.
7. DO NOTHING, SIT STILL AND WAIT FOR MY ORDERS. IF THERE IS NO ORDER, KEEP QUIET. WHEN I ASK YOU TO DO SOMETHING, YOU MUST DO IT RIGHT AWAY WITHOUT PROTESTING.
8. DON'T MAKE PRETEXTS ABOUT KAMPUCHEA KROM IN ORDER TO HIDE YOUR JAW OF TRAITOR.
9. IF YOU DON'T FOLLOW ALL THE ABOVE RULES, YOU SHALL GET MANY MANY LASHES OF ELECTRIC WIRE.
10. IF YOU DISOBEY ANY POINT OF MY REGULATIONS YOU SHALL GET EITHER TEN LASHES OR FIVE SHOCKS OF ELECTRIC DISCHARGE.

classrooms were divided up in an incredibly primitive fashion into tiny cells. Everywhere there are crude shackles and cuffs. Initially those executed here were people the Khmer Rouge perceived as "class enemies" and supporters of the former authorities, but soon the Communist regime began to consume itself in a frenzy of paranoia. By the time Tuol Sleng was liberated, in 1979, nearly all those suffering torture and execution were Khmer Rouge officials who had fallen from grace.

Kang Kek Iew, better known as Comrade Duch, was the Chief of Security and Commanding Officer at S21. In February 2009, Duch was the first high-ranking Khmer Rouge officer to be tried for his crimes in a hybrid Cambodian and United Nations Court under the Extraordinary Chambers in the Courts of Cambodia. Duch, now an Evangelical Christian who voluntarily surrendered to authorities, is the only Khmer Rouge official not only to admit his crimes, but also to express remorse and agree to cooperate with the court proceedings (see panel).

The Killing Fields

Finally, for those with the stomach for the experience after visiting Tuol Sleng, about 12km (7.5 miles) southwest of the town are the infamous **Killing Fields of Choeung Ek** (www.cekillingfield.org; daily 8am–5pm). Here victims of the Khmer Rouge, including many from Tuol Sleng, were executed and buried in mass graves. Many of these graves have now been exhumed, and a *stupa*-shaped mausoleum has been erected in the victims' memory. It's a disturbing experience to view row upon row of skulls arranged in tiers in a tall plexi-glass case in the middle of the mausoleum.

In April 2006, Phnom Penh authorities made the very controversial decision to turn over management of the memorial to a private Japanese company, in order to develop the Killing Fields as a visitor attraction. The memorial has been upgraded with a new road and visitor centre, and a higher entrance charge to pay for them. The easiest way to get there is by taxi or tuk-tuk, although moto drivers will also readily make the journey.

FACT

"Land grabs" by developers in new districts around Phnom Penh began receiving international attention in 2008. Neighbourhoods that were once undesirable slums are now hot real estate as the city modernises. Poor families are often squatters with no legal deeds to their property, with little power to negotiate compensation for forced eviction. Some families who receive offers of compensation initially refuse, misguidedly holding out for a "better offer" that never comes.

One of Tuol Sleng's many haunting faces.

BRINGING THE KHMER ROUGE TO TRIAL

Over three decades after the Khmer Rouge regime devastated the nation of Cambodia, some of the most senior perpetrators have finally been brought to justice. Despite overwhelming public desire for them to proceed, the trials have not been without controversy. The original US$60 million budget for three years was increased to $170 million for five years, but international funding was placed on hold when accusations of corruption within the court system surfaced. Many have suggested that the high price tag would be better spent on social programmes in this impoverished country, while others argue that justice and closure for the victims is worth any cost.

Prosecutors would like to bring more than the initial five defendants to trial, but the government has restricted the scope for the time being. So many former Khmer Rouge officers run the present government – including Prime Minister Hun Sen – that the government fears a trial of larger scope would destabilise the country.

The proceedings of the Extraordinary Chambers in the Courts of Cambodia (www.eccc.gov.kh) are open to the public, though attendance has been low, except for key court dates.

Of the major five defendants, Comrade Duch, Nuon Chea and Khieu Samphan have been sentenced to life imprisonment; Ieng Sary and his wife, Ieng Thirith, died in 2013 and 2015 respectively.

PHNOM PENH ENVIRONS

There are many interesting places within easy reach of Phnom Penh. Make a day-trip to see fine examples of classical Khmer temple architecture or gain an introduction to the Cambodian countryside.

Although the most important classical Khmer antiquities are either clustered at Angkor or scattered around the still relatively inaccessible fringes of the country, worthwhile historical sites within a short driving distance of Phnom Penh exist at Tonlé Bati and Angkor Borei to the south of the city, and at Udong, a former capital, to the north.

East to the Mekong

About 18km (11 miles) east of Phnom Penh, off National Highway 1, is **Koki Beach** ❷ (Kien Svay). A low area of mudflats by the west bank of the Mekong, it is a popular picnic spot for locals from Phnom Penh at weekends and holidays. There are also numerous restaurants on stilts specialising in freshwater and seafood delicacies. The best way to get there is to hire a taxi or *moto* from Phnom Penh, as public boats are no longer available. For the truly impecunious, buses depart from Phnom Penh's Central Market.

Also accessible via National Highway 1 is the ferry town of **Neak Luong**, further down the Mekong. It was here that, in August 1973, a USAF B-52 accidentally dropped its entire load of bombs, levelling much of the town and killing or wounding more than 400 civilians – an incident which features prominently at the start of the movie *The Killing Fields*, and which

was instrumental in bringing about a halt to the US bombing of Cambodia. Today there are no visible reminders of the tragedy in this busy little town.

South to Ta Prohm

Takeo province, due south of Phnom Penh and bordering Vietnam, is a very worthwhile destination where you can see some fine examples of classical Khmer temple architecture. Because the province is so close to Phnom Penh, it is relatively simple to visit some of these temples on a day trip from the capital.

Main Attractions
Koki Beach (Kien Svay)
Tonlé Bati
Phnom Tamao Wildlife
    Rescue Centre
Phnom Chisor
Phnom Da
Udong

Apsaras, Ta Prohm temple, Tonlé Bati.

TIP

Cambodians are traditionally modest dressers. Even at the beach, girls will often swim fully clothed. Nude or even topless sun-bathing is not acceptable in Cambodia.

Air-conditioned taxis are available in the vicinity of the Diamond Hotel on Monivong Boulevard in Phnom Penh.

Route 2 from Phnom Penh to **Takeo** is a good road, and the journey should only take 1–1.5 hours. This is a quiet, sleepy country town that makes a pleasant enough place to stop for a meal or – at a pinch – the night. Hotels are adequate, and Khmer, Vietnamese and Chinese food available. Looking around, you would scarcely guess that, during the Khmer Rouge period, Takeo was the headquarters of Ta Mok, the much-feared one-legged general who was arrested in 1999 and imprisoned in Phnom Penh. "Grandfather Mok" and his fanatical southwestern cadre made Takeo just about the most feared zone in the whole country. He died in a military prison in 2006.

You can take two days over this southward route, setting out from Phnom Penh early in the morning and heading directly to **Tonlé Bati** ❸, which is about 32km (20 miles) distant. The chief attraction around the lake is the laterite temple of **Ta Prohm** (open daily), built by King Jayavarman VII on top of an earlier 6th-century Khmer shrine. The result is a well-preserved gem, not unduly large, but with some splendid decorative features. The main sanctuary has five chambers, in each of which is a statue or a Shiva *lingam*. Generally the shrine is favoured by fortune-tellers who will predict your future and read your palm for a few thousand *riel*. At almost any time a traditional orchestra will be playing outside the inner sanctum of the shrine, attracting offerings from pious visitors from Phnom Penh. Clouds of incense waft through the air, and the atmosphere is very much that of a living shrine.

An unusual feature of Ta Prohm may be found on the inner east wall of the sanctuary, about 3 metres (10ft) above the ground. This is a bas-relief which shows a woman carrying a box on her head while a man bows in supplication to another, larger woman. The scene purportedly represents a pregnant woman who gave birth to a child with the assistance of a midwife, but then failed to show the latter appropriate gratitude and respect. As a punishment, the midwife has condemned the woman to carry the afterbirth in a box on her head for the rest of her life. The crouching man is begging the midwife to forgive his wife.

Another small but unusual bas-relief on the inner north wall of the central sanctuary shows, in the upper part, a king sitting with his wife; in the lower part, because the wife was unfaithful, there is a representation of a servant putting her to death by trampling her under his horse's hooves.

Yeay Peau

A short distance from Ta Prohm – about five minutes' walk, on the north side of the approach road in the grounds of a modern temple – is the second of Tonlé Bati's attractions, the small temple of **Yeay Peau**. According to legend, during the early 12th century King Preah Ket Mealea was travelling in the Tonlé Bati area when

Ruins at Ta Prohm.

he met and fell in love with a young girl called Peau. Soon Peau became pregnant, and after a while gave birth to a boy, whom she named Prohm. The king, meanwhile, had returned to Angkor, leaving a ring and a sacred dagger so that the boy could travel to Angkor and identify himself to his father when he had come of age.

In time this came to pass, and Prohm visited Angkor where he lived with his father for several years. On his return to Tonlé Bati, Prohm failed to recognise his mother, seeing instead a woman so beautiful that he asked her to become his wife. Peau objected that she was his mother, but the young man stubbornly refused to believe this. Accordingly, it was decided that a contest should be held to see what should happen. If Prohm, assisted by the local men, could build a temple before Peau, assisted by the local women, could do so, then she would marry him. In the event the wily Peau released an artificial morning star using candles. The men, thinking that it was dawn and the women could not possibly beat them, went to sleep. The women went on to win the contest, and Prohm was obliged to acknowledge Peau as his mother.

That, at least, is the legend. Whatever the real events behind the building of the temples at Tonlé Bati, two classical Khmer temples exist, one named for Prohm and the other for his mother Peau. The latter is much smaller in size and less impressive than Ta Prohm; within it you can see a headless statue of Peau standing beside a seated Buddha.

Around 300 metres northwest of Ta Prohm is a lakeside picnic area, generally tranquil and free of crowds.

Phnom Tamao Wildlife Rescue Centre

About 13km (8 miles) south of Tonlé Bati, turn left at the sign, and head another 6km (4 miles) to reach **Phnom Tamao Wildlife Rescue Centre** ④ (open daily). The centre, part safari and part wildlife rehabilitation facility, is home to numerous wild animals confiscated from poachers, traffickers and people keeping them illegally as pets. Enclosures in the 80-hectare (198-acre)

FACT

The bear sanctuary at Phnom Tamao spreads over several acres and accommodates around 100 rescued sun bears and black bears.

Countryside near Tonle Bati in Takéo Province.

Window with elaborate shutters at Phnom Chisor.

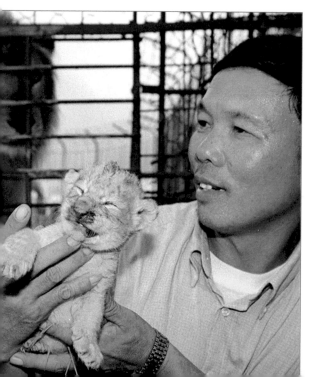

A new arrival at Phnom Tamao Wildlife Rescue Centre.

site include a sizeable population of tigers, and the world's largest captive populations of Malayan sun bears and palliated gibbons. Leopards, Siamese crocodiles, macaques, Asian elephants, and the world's only captive hairy-nosed otter are also present. The centre operates a breeding facility for endangered species, and releases specimens into the wild when feasible. Both **Betelnut Jeep Tours** (tel: 012-619 924; www.betelnut tours.com) and **Free the Bears** (www.freethebears.org) organise enhanced tours of the centre, with special access to the wildlife for their guests.

Chisor Mountain

If zoos are not your thing, then after visiting Tonlé Bati you should continue south on Route 2 for around 23km (14 miles). The intersection for **Phnom Chisor** ❺ (Chisor Mountain) is located close by the two brick towers of **Prasat Neang Khmau** – the "Temple of the Black Virgin", once probably dedicated to the Hindu goddess Kali. A side road heads eastwards at this point, leading to the foot of Phnom Chisor which is about 4km

(2.5 miles) distant. The climb to the top of the hill is 100 metres (330ft) up and involves tackling as many as 750 unevenly spaced concrete steps, but the effort is worth it because of the spectacular views from the top over the surrounding countryside. Snacks and cold drinks are available on the way up and at the top, but it is still a hot and exhausting climb in the heat of the day. Anyone less than superlatively fit should make at least two rest stops on the way up, as there is plenty of time to take in the sights.

The main temple at Phnom Chisor (open daily) stands on the eastern side of the hill. Constructed of brick and laterite, with lintels and doorways of sandstone, the complex dates from the 11th century, when it was known as Suryagiri. The isolation of the site, and the way the temple suddenly appears as you struggle over the crest of the hill, have led some writers to liken the temple's atmosphere to that of a Southeast Asian Stonehenge or Machu Picchu. Views from the far side of the temple, looking east, are spectacular.

The long, straight old road built by the original temple architects is clearly visible, and would make a far more appropriate access point if reclaimed from encroaching nature. Two lesser temples punctuate the progress of this road, and a large natural lake glistens in the distance.

When you have visited Phnom Chisor it is probably best to press on to Takeo for lunch, bypassing nearby Angkor Borei and Phnom Da, which can be visited during the afternoon to view the temples by the warm light of the descending sun.

Angkor Borei

To reach **Angkor Borei** from Takeo, head back northwards along Route 2 until you reach the turn east to Phnom Chisor. Follow this road beyond the hilltop temple, through the town of Sai Waa, until you reach the town of Prey Kabas. Just before you enter this settlement a side road leads away to the southwest and, about 5km (3 miles) along this road, the busy little market town that is your destination. It is believed that, almost 1,500 years ago, **Angkor Borei** was the site of Vyadhapura, the capital of "Water Chen La" before the centre of Khmer civilisation moved northwestwards to Angkor, but unfortunately there is little evidence of this to be seen at present. However, an archaeological museum (tel: 012-201 638; daily) opened in 2008 and displays a modest collection of artefacts from the Chenla and Funan kingdoms, including pottery, jewellery and statuary.

The temple of **Phnom Da** ❻ (open daily) can be reached by crossing the bridge to the south of Angkor Borei and driving – in the dry season – for around 5km (3 miles) to reach the site close to the Vietnamese border. The hilltop temple, which may date from as far back as the 7th or 8th centuries, is of brick and sandstone. Although one of the oldest stone structures in Cambodia, it is in a surprisingly good state of preservation. Nearby on another hilly outcrop is a smaller sandstone temple, thought to have been built about a century after Phnom Da, called **Asram Taa Asey**. This structure was probably dedicated to Hari-Hara, a distinctively Khmer god combining manifestations of Vishnu and Shiva in the same deity.

A word of caution about the whole Phnom Da region: during the hot and dry season it is easy to drive or be driven around, but during the rains the whole area from around Takeo to the Vietnam frontier is flooded, and it is necessary to hire a small boat in Angkor Borei and be taken to the temple sites by water.

North to Udong

Udong, a former capital of Cambodia, can be visited with ease from Phnom Penh on a day trip. Should you have the time and the inclination, however, a more rewarding and informative trip can be made by continuing by road northeastwards to stay overnight in the large Mekong River city-port of Kompong Cham, returning to Phnom Penh the next day. In this way a small tour can be completed, encompassing

Preparing street food in Takéo.

TEA MONEY

Law enforcement officers in Cambodia, much like those in neighbouring countries, have a notorious reputation for corruption. Most of the time foreigners need not interact with police or other government officials, but occasionally tourists find themselves solicited for bribes, often referred to as "tea money" by expats. The most common instances are when foreign drivers are stopped by police, or when tourists have to deal with customs officers and border guards.

Whether someone has committed a legitimate offence and the officer is providing an easy way out, or whether the officer has simply concocted a fake fine out of thin air, paying bribes is still obviously unethical. On the other hand, for some, it can save a lot of unnecessary frustration.

FACT

The Khmers and the Kingdom of Siam (now Thailand) have either been at war or engaged in territorial disputes for hundreds of years. The recent, ongoing skirmishes over Preah Vihear are merely the latest in an endless series of territorial fights.

royal tombs, rubber plantations and an archaic Hindu temple.

The city of Udong is located on low hills about 35km (22 miles) north of Phnom Penh. The road to follow is Route 5, which continues to Kompong Chhnang (not to be confused with the aforementoined Kompong Cham, which is accessed via Route 7), an important port on the Sap River 60km (37 miles) north of Udong. Route 5 winds north out of Phnom Penh on the west bank of the Sap River.

As you drive north, you will notice the **Chruoy Changvar** Peninsula between the Sap and Mekong rivers to the east. If you look closely, small minarets indicate the presence of two or three mosques in the rural villages of the peninsula, so near to and yet so far from Phnom Penh. In fact, the name "Changvar" is said to be derived from the island of Java in Indonesia, and the peninsula is home to one of Cambodia's fascinating but sadly decimated Cham Muslim communities – the Cham people suffered particularly badly under the Khmer Rouge regime.

Cambodian police have a reputation for corruption.

Chruoy Changvar is reached by the **Japanese Bridge** (so named because in 1993 it was rebuilt with Japanese aid) and makes an interesting two-hour side trip from Phnom Penh, being particularly popular with city residents for its dozens of fine riverside restaurants. For Udong, however, ignore the bridge and continue north; you will pass through several prosperous Cham villages with newly restored mosques and silversmiths' workshops. The local Muslims are friendly, and it is quite acceptable to visit the mosques and take photographs of the turbaned Cham men, though – as with Buddhist temples throughout the country and mosques everywhere – shoes should be removed before entering a place of worship, and women should cover their heads. It's polite, too, to stay outside during prayers.

A ruined capital

Udong ❼ – the name means "victorious" – was the capital of Cambodia on several occasions between 1618 and 1866. Today little remains of the former capital's days of glory, but the site (daily; free) is still certainly worth a visit. Two low ridges rise from the surrounding plains; unfortunately both bear the marks of extensive bombing during the years of the Second and Third Indochina Wars, and several of the *stupas* have been destroyed or are in ruins.

The larger of the two hills is called **Phnom Reach Throap**, or "Hill of the Royal Treasury". Here one can see the remains of an enormous Buddha figure – blown up by the Khmer Rouge. The site is also known as **Vihear Preah Ath Roes**. At the northwestern corner of the hill sit four stupas. The first is the tomb of King Monivong (r. 1927–41). The second is said to be the tomb of King Ang Duog (r. 1845–59), though an alternative to this disputed site is next to the Silver Pagoda in Phnom Penh. The third is the tomb of King Soriyopor (r. prior to 1618). The fourth stupa is said to contain a relic of the Buddha.

The smaller ridge has a few stupas and larger structures, including **Ta**

San Mosque. To the south sits **Phnom Vihear Leu**, which is crowned with a shrine, pagoda and a former Khmer Rouge prison.

A short distance northeast of Udong, but only accessible by boat from Prek Kdam, is the former royal city of **Lovek**. Situated on the west bank of the Sap River, Lovek was an interim Cambodian capital, between the times of Angkor and Udong, which flourished in the 16th century. In 1594 it was captured and looted by the burgeoning Kingdom of Ayutthaya, or Siam.

According to legend, the Siamese besieged Lovek in 1593 but were beaten back. Before leaving, however, they used cannons to fire silver shot into the bamboo fortifications surrounding the city. After the Siamese withdrawal the Cambodians tore down these barricades to get at the silver and, as a consequence, when the Siamese returned a year later, they took the city with ease. This legend may not be true, but it is closely associated with the years of Cambodian decay which followed the abandonment of Angkor,

and when you look at Lovek today – or what can be seen from the banks of the Sap River – the former city seems symbolic of that period of decay.

After visiting Udong, retrace your drive down Route 5 for 4km (2.5 miles) to the small town of **Prek Kdam** on the banks of the Sap River. From here it's a short ferry ride across to the east bank of the river, followed by a 42km (26-mile) drive along Route 6 to the junction town of **Skon** (pronounced Skoon), famous for its residents' love of tasty fried tarantulas. The countryside is fertile and verdant (especially during the rainy season), with bright green rice paddies and thousands of spindly sugar palms stretching in every direction.

From Skon follow Route 7 for 47km (30 miles) to Cambodia's fourth-largest city, Kompong Cham (see page 302). The journey, along an excellent road, takes you through countryside rich in rubber plantations. Just outside the town – about 2km (1.2 miles) to the northwest – is the **Wat Nokor Bayon** (see page 302) temple complex, a modern temple set amid ancient ruins, which is best visited at sunset.

A naga balustrade at Udong: the hooded serpent represents Muchalinda, who sheltered the Buddha from a rainstorm.

Udong's stupas against the evening sky.

SIEM REAP AND BATTAMBANG

Ancient temples, some of the country's finest French colonial buildings, and memorials of genocide characterise Cambodia's principal western cities.

Siem Reap waitress.

The west-central towns of Siem Reap and Battambang are very different from each other, but both have a lot to offer. Until a decade ago a dusty wild-west town, Siem Reap's proximity to Angkor has seen it undergo extensive development, with new luxury hotels, bars, restaurants and boutiques catering to the lucrative tourist trade. In contrast, Battambang remains a quiet backwater, noted for its fine French colonial architecture, sparsely visited Angkor-era temples and memorial to Khmer Rouge atrocities. It is possible to travel between the two towns by boat across Tonlé Sap lake in rainy season.

Siem Reap

Siem Reap **❽**, the base town for people visiting the nearby temples of Angkor (just 5km/3 miles away), is a relaxing and pleasant place located by the shady banks of the eponymous river. The town itself has few sights, though with Angkor so close at hand this is perhaps a good thing – the visitor will certainly feel the need to relax after a long day's sightseeing. From Phnom Penh Siem Reap can be reached by bus (around six hours) or express boat (5–6 hours), as well as by plane.

At the northern end of town is the celebrated Victoria Angkor Resort, and next door the **Raffles Grand Hotel d'Angkor ❶**, which has been sensitively restored by the Singapore-based Raffles Group. Over the years many well-known visitors to Angkor have stayed here, including such luminaries as W. Somerset Maugham, Noël Coward, Charlie Chaplin, Jacqueline Kennedy Onassis and Angelina Jolie. Directly opposite and south of the Grand Hotel are the **Royal Independence Gardens** (home to a horde of flying foxes) and the Amansara Resort, a former villa of King Sihanouk.

Southwards, along the bank of the river, lies the delightful old **French Quarter**, which could as well be in Djibouti or Algiers were it not for the Khmer sights and sounds which pervade the area. Just south of the French Quarter is the **Old Market** ❸, or *Psar Chaa*, a popular traditional market with a very wide selection of souvenirs that is open until early evening. Look out for wonderful "temple-rubbings" on rice paper, which are reasonably priced and very attractive when framed. The south side of the market near the river is lined with vendors selling silk *krama* scarves and *sampots* (sarongs), woodcarvings, silverware, T-shirts, traditional toys and other souvenirs, while the northern half is mostly fruit, vegetable, meat, clothing and appliance stalls.

Souvenirs that are superior in quality, such as carved sandstone replicas of Angkor pieces, leather puppets and woodcarvings, can be found at the many shops, boutiques and galleries in the area around the market – especially **Pithnou Street** ❸. Most of these places have fixed prices for their offerings that are several times higher than those at the market.

In the evenings, the tourist crowd congregates on the street that has been nicknamed **Pub Street** ❸ for its exhilarating variety of restaurants, pubs and cafés. Other hot spots include "**The Passage**" (a parallel alley to the south) and Pithnou Street. Another good early evening option is to stroll southwards along the river bank into the southern suburbs of the town.

Not to be missed are the two sites run by **Le Chantiers Écoles** (tel: 063-963 330; www.artisansdangkor.com; daily 7.30am–5.30pm), schools devoted to teaching fine silk weaving, stone and woodcarving techniques to disadvantaged youth. **Artisans d'Angkor** ❸ is located a few hundred metres west off of Sivatha Street, and offers free tours of the carving workshop, where Angkor reproductions, furniture and small souvenirs are made. The **silk farm** also offers free tours where visitors can see every part of farming, harvesting and production of silk, and purchase some of the finest silk products in the country. A free shuttle service at 9.30am and 1.30pm makes the 16km (10-mile) trip from Siem Reap daily.

Tonlé Sap

A particularly worthwhile excursion from Siem Reap lies south on the

Street in the French Quarter, Siem Reap.

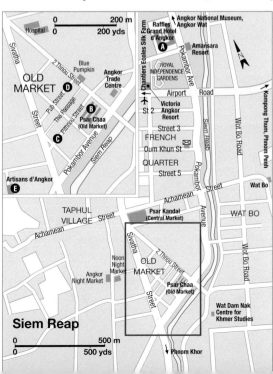

Siem Reap

Emerald green rice fields in the countryside outside Battambang.

Seafood for sale in Siem Reap.

nearby **Tonlé Sap**, Cambodia's Great Lake. The road from the town leads towards **Phnom Krom**, the only hill in an otherwise completely flat landscape. Phnom Krom – which is gradually being quarried away – is surmounted by a 10th-century sandstone temple of the same name which may be reached by a long flight of steps. The climb, while tiring, is well worth it for the view over the nearby lake and north towards Angkor. The scenery varies greatly from season to season, as during the rains the Tonlé Sap expands considerably (see page 195).

During the wet season, Tonlé Sap laps at the base of Phnom Krom, and you can practically walk out to one of the **floating villages**, which move right up by the hill. Many of the houses are built on tall stilts, especially those nearer to the shore. In the dry season, you will have to travel about 5km (3 miles) further on, to **Chong Khneas**, where the "port" for Battambang and Phnom Penh is located. From here you can hire a boat with a driver to get out to the lake. Choose a boat with a good roof as a sun shield.

The "village" consists of a fairly wide main thoroughfare, with narrow passages between houseboats, stilt houses and extensive fish traps. The water isn't deep – in the dry season it would be possible to stand in some places – but it is immensely rich in silt and sediment, so the propellers of the boats look almost as though they are churning warm chocolate. The people are not rich, but there are all kinds of unexpected amenities in their unusual community. There are a couple of floating petrol stations, a police station, fish farms, floating restaurants and even pigsties. Men fish and repair vessels or work on their houses, women cook and wash up in kitchens at the stern of the boats, and children play on the wooden decks and landings, or swim in the muddy waters of the lake.

Also moving with the seasonal rise and fall of the lake is the **Greater Environment Chong Khneas Office**, popularly known as the Gecko Environment Centre (tel: 063-963 525). This centre's focus is to promote environmental awareness among the local community, and is worth visiting for its displays on the flora and fauna found in the area.

Battambang

Battambang ❾, Cambodia's second-largest city, is located 5–6 hours southwest of Siem Reap by bus, or 4–9 hours by boat (the trip is faster in the rainy season). The town has some of the country's finest examples of colonial architecture, especially around the riverfront and market, where old merchant shops exhibit the typical blue wooden shutters, rounded archways, second-floor balconies and triangular roof braces in the French style.

The **Provincial Museum** (Street 1; Mon–Fri 8–11am and 2–5pm) is a pleasant little museum along the river between the **Old Iron** and **Old Stone** bridges. Within the single showroom are statuary and a few ceramics from the Angkor period, as well as a sizeable Buddha collection and some examples of metalwork from archaeological finds. If you visit Wat Banan or Wat Ek Phnom, a visit to the museum helps round out the experience by showing you the sorts of items once housed in the temples when they were in use.

Further south along the river, Battambang's nightlife epicentre is in front of the **central post office**. A **night market** with food stalls is set up here every evening, along with live entertainment on the busy weekends.

Around Battambang

Battambang's most interesting sights are located outside the city. Heading 2km (1.2 miles) out of town, stop at **Wat Kor Village** to see the **21 Khmer heritage houses**. Only two of these old wooden stilt-houses are actually open for visitors, of which **Khor Sang** (daylight hours; donation) is the more popular. The owner proudly gives a guided tour of the "new house", built in 1907, and the original home connected at the back, built in 1890.

Heading 28km (17 miles) south along Stung Sangker through the countryside, **Banan Mountain** rises 71 metres (233ft) out of rice paddies and coconut groves. After climbing 358 steps, you will come to **Wat Banan** (open daylight hours). It was built by Udayadityavarman II in the 11th century, but was badly damaged in fighting between the Vietnamese and Khmer Rouge. Ladies at the bottom will offer to carry your things up the mountain, show you around, and massage you at the halfway rest stop, all for a meagre US$5.

Looping back to Phnom Penh, about 12km (8 miles) from the city, the **Killing Caves of Phnom Sampeau** (open daylight hours) tunnel into the peak of the mountain, accessible by a steep road from the parking area below. Here the Khmer Rouge pushed people through the roof of the caverns to their death on the rocks below. A stairway leads down into the main cavern where a new glass monument holds the skulls and bones of victims next to a large reclining Buddha. Visitors will constantly be solicited for donations to build one of several wats under construction on the mountain's summit. A steep staircase leads down the mountain from the wats on the highest peak – this is best only for descents.

Stilt house on Tonlé Sap.

GROWING THROUGH ART

Phare Ponleu Selpak (The Brightness of Art) originated in the refugee camps along the Thai border in 1986. The central idea was to use artistic expression to help refugee children overcome the trauma of war. This concept was brought back to Battambang by these child refugees, who then formally founded PPS in 1994. Thirty children live on site who are supported entirely by PPS, with another 50 supported children living with their families. PPS provides 1,250 disadvantaged students with a formal education, in conjunction with enrolment in either their music school, visual arts school or, most famously, **circus school**. Check the show schedule at www.phareps.org. To visit PPS, head almost 1km (0.5 miles) west from the Vishnu roundabout on NH5, then take a right turn, continuing for about half a kilometre (0.3 miles).

Ta Prohm covered with the roots
of a banyan tree.

ANGKOR

This ancient capital of the Khmer kingdom is the cultural and spiritual heart of Cambodia. Although monumental in scale, it offers intimate glimpses into lives lived in a distant past.

Angkor is one of the wonders of the world. Perhaps nowhere else on earth, except in the Valley of the Nile in Egypt, are the relics of antiquity found in such overwhelming grandeur. Dating from the golden years of the Khmer civilisation between around AD 800 and 1300, Angkor is a unique repository of incredible craftsmanship on a staggering scale. The sense of a mysterious "lost world" is heightened by the jungle setting, with some of the temples (notably Ta Prohm and Preah Khan) surrounded by writhing roots, lianas and giant forest trees.

When the French first opened this remarkable site to tourism it was usual to distinguish between the "Small Circuit" comprising the central temples of the complex, and the "Great Circuit", taking in the outer temples. Today, when air-conditioned taxis have replaced elephants and horses as the most popular means of transportation here, it still makes a great deal of sense to follow – at least approximately – these designated routes. Therefore in this chapter the two circuits are described in turn; the Small Circuit starts on page 286, the Great Circuit on page 292 and descriptions of sites beyond the circuits on page 295.

Angkor Wat itself refers to just one part of the rambling complex. Angkor Thom, to the north of Angkor Wat, encompasses many fine temples and palaces, including the Bayon, Preah Khan and Ta Prohm. At Roluos, to the southeast of both Angkor Wat and Angkor Thom, are the earliest surviving Khmer relics in the entire Angkor area, predating Angkor Wat by about 200 years. Most visitors generally take either two or three days to explore the site, but one could easily spend longer.

The entrance to the site is just 5km (3 miles) north of Siem Reap. The road to Angkor leads past the **Angkor National Museum** (see page 293), to a tollbooth. Buy your visitor's pass or

Main Attractions
Angkor Thom and the Bayon
Angkor Wat
Preah Khan
Ta Prohm
Roluos
Banteay Srei

Gate at Angkor Thom.

TIP

The Angkor complex (all areas) is open daily from 5am until 6pm between September and May, and until 6.30pm between June and August. A one-day ticket costs US$37. Multiple-entry tickets, which require one passport photograph, are available for 3 days ($62) or 7 days ($72). Access to Phnom Kulen (see page 296) costs extra. As might be expected, the boom in tourist arrivals since the turn of the millennium is having a negative impact on the old stones and pathways. An elaborate system of ironwood walkways and staircases is being built, but it will take years to complete. Buses are banned from entering Angkor Thom.

have your pass inspected here before you proceed on your tour. The passes come in one-day (US$37), three-day (US$62) or seven-day (US$72) form (see also margin tip on the Angkor complex). It cannot be extended and the days must run consecutively. About 1km (0.6 miles) beyond the tollbooth the road reaches the south side of Angkor Wat, and you will catch your first sight of the famous monument. For the moment, however, it is probably better to visit the city of Angkor Thom; Angkor Wat should be visited in the late afternoon when the complex is best illuminated by the sun.

The Small Circuit

Angkor Thom

Angkor Thom Ⓐ, or "Great City", encompasses a huge, square area of land enclosed within an 8-metre (26ft) -high defensive wall and outer moats approximately 100 metres (330ft) wide. Each side of the wall is about 3km (2 miles) long, and it has been suggested that, at the height of its wealth and power, the city may have supported as many as 1 million people. The founder and architect was the Buddhist King Jayavarman VII (1181–1220), probably the most prolific builder the Khmer Empire ever produced.

There are five gateways into Angkor Thom, each approached by a causeway built across the moat. As you approach from the south the view of the fortifications is impressive. The causeway is flanked by 108 large stone figures, 54 gods on the left and an equivalent number of demons on the right. In the distance, at the far end of the causeway, the southern gateway bears four huge enigmatic faces facing in the cardinal directions.

The Bayon

Passing through this prodigious gateway, the road continues northwards for around 1.5km (1 mile) to reach the **Bayon** Ⓘ, at the centre of Angkor Thom. This temple, which should be entered from the east, was built in the late 12th century by Jayavarman VII. Always a favourite with visitors, the

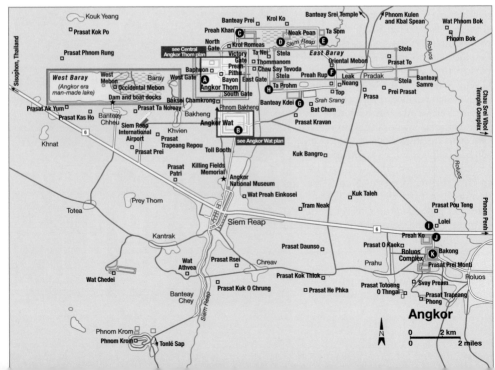

Angkor

Bayon is possibly the most celebrated structure at Angkor after Angkor Wat itself, and justly so.

It is thought to represent a symbolic temple-mountain and rises on three levels, the first of which bears eight cruciform gateways. These are linked by galleries that contain some of the most remarkable bas-reliefs at Angkor; they combine numerous domestic and everyday scenes with historical details of battles won and lost by the Khmers. The domestic scenes, many of which are in smaller bas-reliefs below the main war scenes, show details of fishermen, market scenes, festivals, cockfights, removing lice, hunting, women giving birth, and so on. It is unusual to find such graphic depictions of everyday, mundane life at Angkor, as most bas-reliefs are of a religious nature. There are also everyday scenes from the royal court, including nobles, wrestlers, sword fighters and dancing girls.

To view the bas-reliefs, which are well worth an hour or two of your time, it is best to start near the east entrance to the Bayon and proceed clockwise, via the south wall, keeping the carvings to your right. The **East Gallery**, which is in an excellent state of preservation, features a military procession of Khmer troops, elephants, ox-carts, horsemen and musicians. Parasols shield the commanders of the troops, who include Jayavarman VII. The **South Gallery** is spectacular and contains some of the finest bas-reliefs of all. The early panels depict the great naval battle that took place on the Tonlé Sap in 1177. The Khmers have no head coverings and short hair, while the Cham invaders wear strange hats which resemble long hair. The fighting is intense, with bodies falling from the boats and sometimes being taken by crocodiles. The **North Gallery** depicts entertainers such as acrobats, jugglers and wrestlers, as well as local wildlife.

After viewing the galleries, spend some time at the third level examining the vast, mysterious faces with their sublime smiles. The central shrine, which is circular, is also at the third level, and features the faces of the *bodhisattva* Avalokitesvara.

The Elephant Terrace at Angkor Thom.

Stone carving on the Bayon depicting daily life.

Kings' terraces

Next is the mighty **Baphuon** – now open to the public after years of restoration (see panel) – and the former royal palace of Phimeanakas, where you reach the celebrated **Elephant Terrace** . Also built by Jayavarman VII, this structure is over 300 metres (970ft) long, and has three main platforms and two lesser ones. The terrace was probably used by the king, the royal family, ministers and generals to review their forces, and perhaps to watch other entertainments. The whole terrace is elaborately decorated not only with the sandstone elephants which give it its name, but also with detailed tigers, lions, geese and lotus flowers.

Immediately to the north stands the **Leper King Terrace** . Like the Elephant Terrace, this much smaller structure dates from the late 12th century and is chiefly remarkable for its many bas-reliefs. After seeing this, you should head southwards back to the Bayon and leave Angkor Thom by the South Gate. A few hundred metres beyond the South Gate,

Sunrise at Angkor Wat.

to the west side of the road, the hill of **Phnom Bakheng** rises 67 metres (218ft) above the surrounding plains. This is an ideal spot from which to view the distant spires of Angkor Wat at sunset (although it does get horribly crowded), but it is worth climbing at any time of the day. On the east side a steep and treacherous stairway provides a swift but difficult means of ascent. Alternatively, and much more easily, a winding path leads to the summit via the south side of the hill.

Angkor Wat

From Phnom Bakheng hill continue south to **Angkor Wat** . By any standards this must be the highlight of any visit to the Angkor region – the great temple is simply unsurpassed by any other monument. Construction of this masterpiece is thought to have begun during the reign of Surayavarman II (1112–52), and to have been completed sometime after his death. Authorities claim that the amount of stone used in creating this massive edifice is about the same as that used in building the Great Pyramid of Cheops

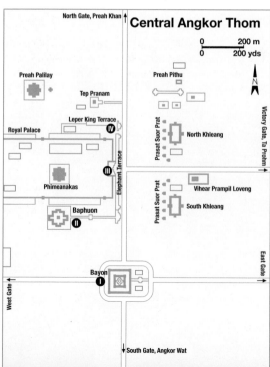
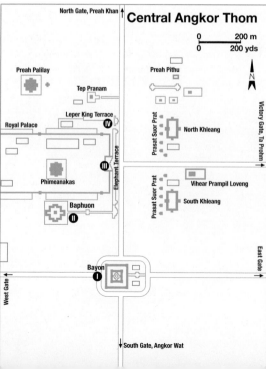

Central Angkor Thom

North Gate, Preah Khan

0 — 200 m
0 — 200 yds

N

Preah Palilay

Preah Pithu

Tep Pranam

Leper King Terrace

Royal Palace

Prasat Suor Prat

North Khleang

Elephant Terrace

Victory Gate, Ta Prohm

Phimeanakas

Prasat Suor Prat

Vihear Prampil Loveng

Baphuon

South Khleang

East Gate

West Gate

Bayon

South Gate, Angkor Wat

in Egypt, though Angkor Wat has many more exposed surfaces, nearly all of which are elaborately carved to a remarkable standard.

Angkor Wat was established as a Hindu temple dedicated to the god Shiva, but it is also thought to have been envisaged as a mausoleum for Surayavarman II. Its orientation is different from that of most temples at Angkor, as the main entrance is from the west rather than the east: this is thought to be related to the association between the setting sun and death. The bas-reliefs – one of the most important elements of the temple – are intended to be viewed from left to right, conforming to Hindu practice.

The sheer scale of Angkor Wat is difficult to grasp in a single visit. The area of land covered by the complex is around 210 hectares (500 acres) and it is surrounded by a moat which is 200 metres (650ft) wide. Just walking to the central shrine across the moat and along the main causeway is a humbling experience. At the end, the main towers of the temple rise to an astonishing 65 metres (210ft) through three separate levels. At the third level there are five great towers – one at each corner, and the great central spire. These towers are conical, tapering to a lotus-shaped point.

Yet, despite these overwhelming statistics, Angkor is a very human place. Vendors of all kinds of goods, from cold drinks and snacks to the ubiquitous sarongs and *krama* (Khmer scarves), are everywhere. Cattle wander across the main temple enclosure, while buffalo laze and flick their tails in the broad moats surrounding the complex.

A monk praying at Angkor Wat.

Angkor Wat: first level

Proceeding along the central causeway, you should enter the central sanctuary at the first level and turn right to walk round the entire gallery of bas-reliefs – no small feat, as there is much to see. Near the entrance to the first gallery there is a huge stone standing figure with eight arms bearing symbols which indicate that the statue was of Vishnu. In recent times, however, a Buddha head has replaced

Monks passing through the gate into Phimeanakas Temple, the Baphuon.

RESTORING BAPHUON

Baphuon is a massive three-tiered temple-mountain built in the 11th century by King Udayaditavarman II (1050–66). It represents Mount Meru, and was dedicated to the Hindu god Shiva. A central tower with four entrances once stood at the summit. In its days of glory it would have been 50 metres (164ft) high, and it certainly made an impression on the Chinese visitor Chou Ta-kuan, who described it in 1297 as "a tower of bronze… a truly astonishing spectacle, with more than ten chambers at its base". It is sufficiently important to have given its name to an 11th-century style of Khmer architecture. In the 15th century Baphuon was rededicated to Buddhism, and a 9 metre by 70 metre (30 by 230ft) reclining Buddha was added to the temple's second level on the west side. Baphuon had long since collapsed, probably because the massive central tower rested on sandy ground. The École Française d'Extrême-Orient began the process of carrying out restoration as long ago as 1960, but had to abandon the work when the Second Indochina War spilt over into Cambodia and made the war effort too risky. Restoration started again in 1995, again under the guidance of French archaeologists, and until recently, visitor access was restricted. It is now possible to visit Baphuon and climb to the very top for views of much of Angkor Thom.

TIP

The monuments at Angkor are on a truly monumental scale and require both time and motorised transport to visit. It's possible to visit all the main sites over a period of days by bike, or better yet by motorbike, but by far the best way is in an air-conditioned car with a driver who may double as a guide. Angkor is very hot, and the risk of sunstroke should not be underestimated. After an hour exploring ancient ruins under a blazing sun, it is not just a relief to climb into an air-conditioned car to reach the next site – it is sensible too.

that of Vishnu, and the statue is now much venerated by local Buddhists.

The bas-reliefs of Angkor's first-level galleries are all truly remarkable, but even so some stand out. Look for the following highlights:

In the West Gallery ❶
The Battle of Kurukshetra: The southern part of the west gallery depicts a scene from the great Hindu epic, the *Mahabharata*, in which the opposing Kauravas and Pandavas clash with each other.

The Battle of Lanka: This panel depicts a well-known scene from the *Ramayana* and must be considered one of the finest bas-reliefs at Angkor Wat. It depicts a long struggle between Rama and the demon-king of the island of Lanka, Ravana.

In the South Gallery ❷
The Army of King Surayavarman II: This splendid panel shows the victorious army in triumphal march. Suraya-varman rides a great war elephant and carries a battleaxe. He is shaded by 15 umbrellas and fanned by numerous servants. The main ranks of Khmer soldiers march in close order. To the west

is one of the earliest representations of Thais, at this time fighting as mercenary troops for the Khmer Empire. Contrasting with the serried ranks of the Khmers, the Thais march out of step and wear long, dress-like sarongs.

The Scenes of Heaven and Hell: The scenes on this panel, depicting the various rewards and punishments of heaven and hell, are truly terrifying. Those who have done well and accumulated merit in this life seem to be fine – they approach Yama, the judge of the dead, apparently confident of passage to heaven – but, beneath them, sinners are being dragged to hell by hideous devils wielding heavy clubs.

In the East Gallery ❸
The Churning of the Ocean of Milk: This is probably the best executed and most spectacular of all the bas-reliefs at Angkor. In one huge, brilliantly carved panel, 88 *asura* (devils) on the left (south side) and 92 *deva* (gods) on the right (north side) churn the ocean of milk with a giant serpent for 1,000 years. Their purpose is to extract the elixir of immortality, which both covet. Overhead finely carved *apsara*

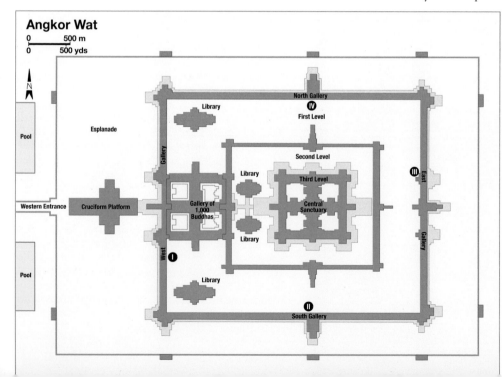

sing and dance to encourage the gods and devils in their endeavour.

The Victory of Vishnu over the Demons: Vishnu, riding on a *garuda*, is engaged in mortal combat with legions of devils. Perhaps predictably, the powerful god takes on all comers and, despite the odds, emerges victorious.

In the North Gallery ⓸

The Victory of Krishna over Bana: In this panel Vishnu, as Krishna, rides a *garuda*. A burning walled city is the residence of Bana, the demon-king. The *garuda* puts out the fire and captures Bana; then, in a spirit of mercy, Krishna kneels before Shiva and asks that the life of the demon-king be spared.

The Battle between the Gods and the Demons: This finely carved panel features yet another battle scene. Here gods of the Brahmanic pantheon struggle with various devils. The gods are distinguishable by their traditional mounts and aspects: Shiva, for example, rides a sacred goose, while Vishnu has four arms and is seated on a *garuda*.

Angkor Wat: upper levels

After examining the galleries of bas-reliefs, you should enter the central complex and climb up to the second level by the usual steep flights of steps. The exterior of this level is rather plain, but within more than 1,500 *apsara* – celestial dancers – grace the walls.

In times past, only the king and the high priest were allowed on the top (third) gallery of Angkor Wat. The central sanctuary rises 42 metres (137ft) above the top level, bringing the overall height of the central tower to the same height as that of the cathedral of Notre-Dame in Paris.

The central sanctuary and the third level of Angkor Wat are ideal places to visit at sunset. Superb views are available across the entire temple, and – perhaps for the first time – it is possible to grasp clearly the stupendous size of the entire complex. As the sun sinks, warm, golden or red rays of sunshine pierce the elaborately carved sandstone window buttresses, illuminating the very finest and best-preserved *apsara* to be found anywhere

A primate inhabitant of Angkor Wat.

The view of Angkor Wat from Phnom Bakheng.

Stone carving showing sinners being taken to hell at the South Gallery, Angkor Wat.

at Angkor. It is truly an unforgettable experience. The uppermost level is once again open to visitors, with the installation of safer wooden stairways. This follows the death of a Japanese tourist who slipped and fell down the treacherous, narrow stone steps.

The Great Circuit

Preah Khan

From Siem Reap head north past Angkor Wat, through Angkor Thom, to the North Gate. Next, turning due east, stop opposite the row of cold-drink stalls directly in front of the west entrance to **Preah Khan ○**, the temple of the "Sacred Sword", also founded by the Buddhist King Jaya-varman VII. Built in the style of the Bayon and dedicated to Buddhism, the temple served as both a monas-tery and the centre of the former royal city. There is a magical quality which comes from the feeling of proximity to nature; this is because the temple still awaits full restoration, and great trees with smothering roots still cling to the sandstone and laterite walls.

An inscribed stone stele, found at Preah Khan in 1939 and removed for safekeeping to the Angkor National Museum, indicates that the temple was once the heart of the ancient city of Nagarajayacri. The central sanctuary was dedicated in 1191, during Jayavar-man VII's reign. However, Jayavarman was followed by a series of Hindu-oriented kings who did their best to Hinduise the great Buddhist sanctuary. Accordingly, images of the Buddha were chipped out of their niches, and elsewhere in the interior of the shrines Buddha images were transformed into *rishi*, or ascetics, by the simple addi-tion of beards.

The central sanctuary of Preah Khan is cruciform, with four entrances. Look for the "Hall of Dancers", with its finely carved rows of *apsara* which decorate the walls. If you are agile enough to clamber over (and sometimes under) the great piles of fallen stone in the northeastern sec-tion of the main sanctuary, you can visit the "Shrine of the White Lady" – an elegant figure, supposedly not an *apsara* but the wife of Jayavarman VII, tucked away in a hidden room. The shrine is still venerated, and sup-plicants light incense and leave offer-ings of money. You will need a guide to find this out-of-the-way spot, but the effort is worth it.

Neak Pean

After leaving Preah Khan, head east-wards along the road leading to the East Baray. About 2.5km (1.5 miles) from Preah Khan a track leads south-wards for around 300 metres (975ft) to the temple of **Neak Pean ○**, or "The Coiled Serpents". This structure, which dates from the second half of the 12th century, was built by Jaya-varman VII and dedicated to Bud-dhism. Located in the midst of the Jayatataka on the North Baray, Neak Pean now remains dry for most of the year, but it was once an island, and its whole purpose is closely con-nected with water.

The temple, which is quite small by Angkorean standards, is set in an artificial pond 70 metres (230ft) square. This central pool is surrounded at the cardinal points by four smaller square pools set somewhat more deeply into the earth. In the centre of the main pool is a circular island bearing a stepped laterite shrine dedicated to the *bodhisattva* Avalokitesvara. Two intertwined serpents circle the base of the island and give the complex its name. The central pool is said to represent the Himalayan Lake Anavatapta, located at the summit of the universe, which was believed to give birth to the four great rivers of the world. These four rivers are represented at Neak Pean by four gargoyle-like heads which, when opened, would permit water to flow from the main pool to the four smaller pools. In times past, pilgrims to Neak Pean would consult with resident priests and then repair to the appropriate pool, where servants of the shrine would release a plug and allow the magical waters of the central pool to pour out over the supplicant.

About 2km (1.2 miles) east of Neak Pean stands the tranquil and charming temple of **Ta Som** **E**. Built in the late 12th century by the indefatigable Jayavarman VII, and inevitably dedicated by him to Buddhism, the Bayon-style temple was also built to honour Jayavarman's father. Ta Som is not one of the "great" temples of Angkor in that it is not monumental in size. What makes it special, however, is its setting on the northeastern limits of the great Angkorean complex. It is off the beaten track, sees relatively few visitors, and as a consequence is filled with birdsong and the sound of cicadas.

In the East Baray

Located in the midst of the East Baray, the 10th-century **Oriental Mebon** is another example of an artificial temple-mountain representing Mount Meru – one of the enduring themes of classical Khmer architecture. Surrounded by three laterite enclosure walls, the "mountain" rises through three levels before culminating in a central platform bearing four smaller

TIP

The **Angkor National Museum** (www.angkor nationalmuseum.com; daily Apr–Sept 8.30am–6pm, Oct–Mar until 6.30pm), formerly known as the Angkor Conservatory, is situated on the road between Siem Reap and the main entrance. The well-equipped galleries provide an excellent introduction to Angkor and the civilisation that built it. Many visitors, however, give it a miss – being either impatient to see the real thing in situ, or baulking at the relatively expensive entrance fee.

The temple of Neak Pean.

outer towers and one larger central tower. The stairways at the foot of the artificial mound are flanked by carved sandstone lions, while elephants stand astride the corners of the second and third levels.

Close by is **Preah Rup** , a Hindu temple dedicated to the god Shiva, which also dates from the 10th century. Visitors to Preah Rup should climb to the top of the monument for excellent views north across the East Baray, as well as southwest, where the distant spires of Angkor Wat can be distinguished in clear weather.

As you leave Preah Rup heading west, the road passes the great reservoir of **Srah Srang**, or "Royal Bath". This large body of water, 300 metres (970ft) by 700 metres (2,270ft), was built on the orders of Jayavarman VII and, especially in the late afternoon and evening, makes a delightful sight as buffaloes bathe in its tranquil waters. At the western side of the lake is a sandstone landing stage flanked by lions and bearing a large *garuda* on the back of a three-headed serpent.

Immediately west of the landing stage a gateway in a high laterite wall gives access to **Banteay Kdei**, the "Citadel of the Cells". The temple was used as a Buddhist monastic complex until the mid-20th century. As a consequence it is less overgrown than some of the other outer temples, and very pleasant to stroll through. Visitors are advised to follow the central corridor through the "Hall of the Dancing Girls" – so called from a bas-relief of dancers cut into the wall – and on to the central sanctuary, which contains a recent Buddha image, still much venerated by the local people.

Ta Prohm

Finally, and ideally towards the end of the day, the route leads past Banteay Kdei for a distance of about 1km (0.6 miles) to reach the spectacular temple of **Ta Prohm**, or "Ancestor of Brahma". This very large complex was, yet again, the work of Jayavarman VII and dedicated to Buddhism. A stone stele, now removed to the Angkor National Museum, tells us

quite a lot about it: for example, in its prime the temple owned 3,140 villages and was maintained by some 79,365 people, including 18 high priests, 2,740 officials, 2,202 assistants and 615 dancers.

Ta Prohm is a long, low complex of buildings all on the same level, with a series of concentric galleries connected by passages that provide shade in the heat of the day. The entire complex is surrounded by a rectangular laterite wall of around 700 metres (2,270ft) in width by 1,000 metres (3,300ft) in length. What makes Ta Prohm so special is that, following an unusual archaeological decision, the jungle has been only partly cut back, so that the buildings are covered with the roots of huge banyan and kapok trees which rise high above the temple. In an otherworldly scene, spectacular writhing limbs bind lintels and crack vaulted passageways, while parrots fly in the upper canopy and break the stillness with their sharp cries. Rather breaking the spell, local children often follow tourists around this part of Angkor, which can be somewhat trying – best advice is to politely appeal to them to leave you in peace.

Ta Prohm was used in the filming of *Tomb Raider* in 2000. The central courtyard features in the scene where Angelina Jolie picks a jasmine flower and is promptly dropped into a deep vault.

Beyond the Circuits

The Roluos complex

Some 11 centuries ago King Jayavarman II (802–50), remembered as the founder of the first unified Khmer state, made his capital at Hariharalaya ("The Dwelling Place of Hari-Hara", a deity combining the attributes of both Vishnu and Shiva). Today the Roluos complex of temples, which are the oldest in Angkor, marks the site of this first Angkorean capital.

Roluos is located to the southeast of the other temples.

Founded by King Yasovarman I (889–908), **Lolei** ❶ was dedicated to the Hindu deity Shiva. Most people come here to see the magnificent carvings and well-preserved stone inscriptions, though the four central brick towers are somewhat tumbledown and covered with shrubbery. Just to the south stands **Preah Ko** ❿, the "Sacred Bull". Built by King Indravarman I (877–89), it is set amid attractive rural scenery and, being somewhat off the beaten track, is usually tranquil and rarely visited. The main sanctuary consists of six brick towers set on a low laterite platform. A short distance beyond Preah Ko rises the solid mass of **Bakong** ❶, a late 9th-century Hindu temple dedicated to Shiva. A thousand years ago Bakong was the central feature of Hariharalaya. It is built as a temple-mountain on an artificial mound surrounded by a moat and outer enclosure walls. Bakong, which is easily the largest monument of the Roluos group, is

FACT

Since the final collapse of the Khmer Rouge in the late 1990s, Angkor has gradually reopened to the world. Miracu-lously, in a country so devastated by war, the great temple complexes survived remarkably unscathed, and today, after pain-staking clearance of unexploded ordnance and dense vegetation, restoration and conservation are once again well under way.

Roots over Ta Prohm temple.

At Kbal Spean, images of Hindu deities are carved onto the river-bed.

Library buildings at Banteay Srei.

best entered from the east by a processional way decorated with seven-headed *naga* serpents.

Banteay Srei

The justly famed temple of **Banteay Srei** lies about 30km (20 miles) northeast of Siem Reap. While Angkor Wat, Angkor Thom and the Bayon impress by their sheer size, Banteay Srei inspires through meticulous detail. It is, indeed, a scrupulously executed miniature temple complex carved in fine pink sandstone – and in the quality of the stone and the soft, almost mellifluous charm of the colour lies much of the temple's appeal. Founded in the second half of the 10th century, Banteay Srei is of rectangular design, enclosed by three walls and the remains of a moat. The central complex consists of a number of structures including, most importantly, shrines dedicated to Shiva (the central and southern buildings) and to Vishnu (the northern building). The main themes represented in the many elaborately carved lintels and frontons are derived from the Hindu epic, the *Ramayana*. Also worthy of note are the finely carved figures of male and female divinities set in recessed niches of the central towers.

Mountain pilgrimage sites

Phnom Kulen is considered sacred by the Khmers and has been a pilgrimage site for many centuries. Legend has it that it was here King Jayavarman II proclaimed himself as god-king in AD 802, giving rise to an independent Cambodian state. Although it has been open to tourism for several years now, reaching the mountain is still a fairly arduous undertaking. Phnom Kulen is about 40km (25 miles) northeast of Siem Reap and about 15km (9 miles) beyond Banteay Srei in the direction of the former Khmer Rouge stronghold of Anglong Veng. It's a strenuous 90-minute climb to the top of the mountain, where there is a small pagoda called **Wat Chuop**. There are fine views from the summit at 487 metres (1,598ft) across the surrounding forested uplands, and a walk of a further 30 or so minutes will bring you to a small river – leading ultimately to the Tonlé Sap – in which numerous *linga* have been carved to sanctify the holy water as it makes its way down to the plains.

Much quieter and more isolated is **Kbal Spean**, established as a hill retreat by Khmers in the mid-11th century. Located about 10km (6 miles) beyond Banteay Srei on the same rough dirt road, it's quite a climb up to the densely forested hill, and in places you have to pull yourself up fairly steep paths with jungle vines. It's well worth the effort, though – the river flows under a natural sandstone bridge and over dozens of carvings of *linga*, as well as representations of Rama, Lakshmi, Hanuman and Vishnu. In recent years some of the carvings have been hacked from the rock by art thieves, but there is still enough here to make Kbal Spean impressive indeed.

A Portrait of Angkor

A unique 13th-century Chinese manuscript sheds light on the workings of the great city of Angkor, and its Indic traditions.

A Chinese envoy, Chou Ta-kuan, visited Angkor during the reign of Indravarman III (1296–1308) and left a detailed manuscript describing his experiences. This unique document provides a window on all aspects of 13th-century Angkorean life – as it is unconstrained by the Indic tradition of excluding ordinary people from literature.

Chou Ta-kuan tells us that the Khmer Empire, known to its inhabitants as Kan-po-chih (Cambodia), began at present-day Vung Tau (Vietnam); all of the southern Mekong region lay within its boundaries. Chou recognised three religious traditions established at Angkor: Brahmanism, Buddhism and Shivaism. Most familiar, both to him and to the present-day visitor, were the Theravadan Buddhists, known by a Tai term, Chao Ku. The Shivaists were already a declining influence at this time; Chou found their temples poorer than those of the Buddhists, housing a Shiva *lingam*.

Chou records: "The walled city of Angkor was some five miles in circumference. It had five gates, with five portals. Outside the wall stretched a great moat across which massive causeways gave access to the city. The Palace stands to the north of the Golden Tower and the Bridge of Gold; starting from the gate its circumference is nearly one-and-a-half miles. The tiles of the central dwelling are of lead; other parts of the palace are covered with pottery tiles, yellow in colour... Out of the Palace rises a golden tower, to the top of which the ruler ascends nightly to sleep. By contrast, the houses of the ordinary folk were thatched with straw, for 'no one would venture to vie with the nobility'."

Class system

In fact, as Chou makes clear, late 13th-century Khmer society was rigidly stratified by class. At the base of the pyramid were slaves, many of whom were reportedly captured "mountain tribes". They were set apart from free people by various prohibitions: they could not sleep in houses, though they could lie beneath them; on entering a house they had to prostrate themselves before beginning work; they had no civil rights; their marriages were not recognised by the state; and they were obliged to call their owners "father" and "mother". Slaves often tried to run away, and when caught would be tattooed, mutilated and shackled.

Above the slaves were a number of classes who were free but not part of the nobility. These included slave-owners, landholders, resident and visiting traders and, most probably, market traders, who according to Chou were mainly women. The position of other "free" people outside the elite is a matter for speculation, but it is clear that a considerable number of ethnic Chinese had already settled in the city by this early date. Chou, naturally enough, remarks on this, explaining that his compatriots liked Angkor as it was so warm that there was no need to spend much money on clothes, while food was plentiful and women "easily persuaded".

The king and his immediate entourage, the high elite, topped the pyramid. Chou was perplexed by the king's relative accessibility, which was so unlike the Emperor of China's court. In fact, his approach to royal audiences seems closer to the Sukhothai system of Siam than to the Chinese (or Viet).

Chou may not have known it but, by the end of the 13th century, the Khmers, influenced by both the rising power of their Thai neighbours and the growing strength of Theravada Buddhism, were reaffirming their Indic identity even as they paid tribute to China.

The Leper King Terrace, Angkor Thom.

ANGKOR ARCHITECTURAL STYLES

Cambodia's top tourist attraction is one of the greatest architectural ensembles on earth, with a sumptuous range of exquisite styles and details.

Angkor Period architecture is generally dated from Jayavarman II's establishment of Hariharalaya as Khmer capital near the site of present-day Roluos at the beginning of the 9th century. From this time until the eventual 15th-century abandonment of Angkor, art historians identify 10 distinct architectural styles, each named after its most famous example:

875–90 Preah Ko: this style is characterised by the use of brick towers and stone lintels. Sculptured figures are larger and heavier than in pre-Angkorean traditions.

890–925 Bakheng: the use of Mount Meru as a model for temple-mountains evolved, often with five towers arranged in a quincunx (one at each corner of a rectangle with the fifth in the middle).

921–41 Koh Ker: this short-lived style was developed during the reign of Jayavarman IV. The finest surviving examples are Sugriva and Valin, two monkey-headed brothers from the Ramayana, at the National Museum in Phnom Penh.

945–65 Pre Rup: this style, developed during the reign of Rajendravarman, expands on the Bakheng style with five towers arranged in a quincunx, but higher, steeper and with more tiers.

967–1000 Banteay Srei: characterised by exquisitely ornate carvings and distinctly sensuous apsara and devata female figures.

965–1025 Khleang: marked by the increasing use of massive stone blocks and limited decoration, cruciform gopura gateways and long galleries.

1025–1080 Baphuon: Khmer architecture close to its majestic apogee. Vast proportions and long, vaulted galleries. Sculpture combines increasing realism and narrative sequence in bas-reliefs.

1080–1175 Angkor Wat: the apex of Khmer architectural and sculptural genius.

1180–1240 Bayon: considered a synthesis of previous styles.

Detail from the Elephant Terrace, dating from the Bayon period (1180–1240). This time is characterised by a noticeable decline in quality of materials (laterite rather than sandstone), and increasing use of Buddhist – as opposed to Hindu – imagery.

One of the five towers at Angkor Wat, the greatest of all Khmer temple-mountains. Construction began in the early 1100s. It has the finest bas-relief narratives, and the art of lintel carving, too, reached its zenith during this period (1080–1175).

Angkor is still venerated by Cambodian Buddhists today, with some of the ancient temples functioning as shrines.

CLASSICAL KHMER TEMPLE LAYOUT AND IMAGERY

The central feature of the classical Khmer temple is a stylised representation of Mount Meru of Hindu mythology, with the mountain symbolised by the tiered base and central tower. The concept was extended through the Bakheng period (see page 298) with the addition of more towers and a causeway leading across the surrounding moat. Angkor Wat marks the final, spectacular, evolution of the style.

Main entranceways – with a few exceptions, notably at Angkor Wat itself – are from the east, marked by decorated gateways or gopura. The central temple complex, generally set within several concentric enclosure walls, is usually characterised by the presence of linga (male phalli) and their counterpart, the female yoni. In times past, lustral water was poured over linga and yoni, often conjoined, before being used as a source of blessing and purification.

Statues of the major Hindu deities Shiva, Vishnu and Brahma are often present, often joined by other figures from Hinduism including Nandi, the bull mount of Shiva, naga serpents, and the garuda, the half-bird, half-human mount of Vishnu.

As Buddhism gradually replaced Hinduism from around the 11th century onwards, images of the Buddha and scenes from the Ramayana were used in temple consecration and decoration.

Images of apsaras, heavenly dancers, adorn many of the temple walls around Angkor. The most sensuous examples of this Hindu style date from the Banteay Srei period (967–1000).

Angkor is still venerated by Cambodian Buddhists today, with some of the ancient temples functioning as shrines.

Girl at Wat Nokor Bayon.

CENTRAL AND NORTHEAST CAMBODIA

The Mekong River is essential to life in Cambodia. This chapter explores the riverine towns and countryside upstream from Phnom Penh, and the remote northeastern provinces – Ratanakiri and Mondulkiri.

It is difficult to overstate the importance of the Mekong to Cambodia. Rising in Tibet, it flows for more than 4,000km (2,500 miles) through six different countries before reaching the sea, but it is in Cambodia that the river is at its most complex. After passing through the Si Phan Don or "Four Thousand Islands" region of southernmost Laos and roaring over the Khon Phapheng Falls, the Mekong enters Cambodia and flows south through Stung Treng, Kratie and Kompong Cham provinces. Up to this point it is still just a large river. When the waters reach Phnom Penh, however, they are joined by the Sap River from the northwest, while the Bassac River breaks away towards the southeast.

Around 1,500 years ago, when an independent kingdom centred on the Phnom Penh region first emerged, it was dubbed "Water Chen La" by the Chinese annalists because of its dependence on the Mekong. Over the intervening centuries little has occurred to change the Cambodian people's reliance on the Mekong for their fundamental existence. If it has aptly been said that "Egypt is the gift of the Nile", then the Mekong – together with its related rivers the Sap and the Bassac – remains Cambodia's lifeline.

Mekong river traffic.

North to Kompong Cham

The easiest and most convenient way to explore the Cambodian Mekong used to be to set out by boat from Phnom Penh. Unfortunately, public boats leaving from Phnom Penh or Kompong Cham have stopped running now that road improvements have led to cheaper and quicker bus rides. These days the only way to get to Kompong Cham and Kratie from the capital is by road. National Highway 7 has been improved though remains under frequent construction, making

Main Attractions

Wat Nokor Bayon
Kratie
Dolphin-Spotting at Sambor
Stung Treng
Lumphat Wildlife Sanctuary and Virachey National Park

Detail at Wat Nokor Bayon.

Guardian at the entrance of Wat Nokor Bayon.

Meet the locals – Khmer family from a village near Kompong Cham.

the journey to Kompong Cham under four hours. There are regular connections to the towns by taxi and bus. The latter leave from Psar Thmay (Central Market) in Phnom Penh.

The 120km (75-mile) journey from the capital northeast to **Kompong Cham** ⑩, Cambodia's fourth-largest city, is straightforward, on good roads. There are no major attractions in the prosperous city itself, though there are some attractive old buildings, and the Mekong Hotel, located right on the waterfront, provides a pleasant location to have a drink or something to eat while watching life on the great river which sweeps by endlessly. Small boats with one or two fishermen cast their nets and drift slowly downstream. Occasional ferryboats still ply the river, and large cargo ships push their way upstream against the muddy waters, to take on or offload goods, especially rubber from the extensive plantations in the region. If you have time only for lunch, a couple of good restaurants near the junction of Monivong Boulevard and Vithei Pasteur Road serve Khmer and Chinese food.

The entrancing ruins of **Wat Nokor Bayon**, an 11th-century sandstone and laterite temple, are located some 2km (1.2 miles) to the northwest of the town. The complex is a fascinating blend of the contemporary and the archaic. It was originally dedicated to Mahayana Buddhism, but at some point, probably during the 15th century, the temple was rededicated to Theravada Buddhism, and a modern temple set amid the ancient ruins still functions as a Buddhist centre today. There are numerous niches and hidden shrines, and a large reclining Buddha within.

Kratie

Leave Kompong Cham by way of the Japanese-built bridge across the Mekong, which opened in 2002 and provides direct road access between Phnom Penh and Ho Chi Minh City. From here, it is approximately another 2.5–3 hours to **Kratie** ⑪, pronounced "kra-chey" (and sometimes spelt "Krâcheh").

There is an unexpected charm to this isolated riverside port, which

still retains some fine, if inevitably decaying, examples of French colonial architecture. One reason for Kratie's relatively good state of preservation is that it fell under Khmer Rouge control at an early stage in the civil war, and was not subjected to either fierce fighting or subsequent bombing. There are three or four hotels along the waterfront by the boat dock, and several restaurants serving variations on Cambodian, Chinese and Vietnamese cuisine. The waterfront also has several small establishments selling beer and soft drinks which make an excellent place to sit and watch the sunset over the Mekong. The administrative section of the town lies to the south of the dock beyond the hotels, while a large market beside the dilapidated road leading east to Phumi Samraong and Snuol, towards the Vietnamese frontier, serves most of Kratie province.

The Mekong dolphin

It's possible to charter a boat or take a taxi to travel the 30km (20 miles) north of Kratie to the peaceful riverside village of **Sambor** ⑫, with its attractive temple. If you travel on the river there is a chance of seeing the rare Mekong dolphin, an endangered species which is making something of a comeback in the waters near Kratie, and which has become a major attraction. More correctly known as the Irrawaddy dolphin, this is a delightful and sociable mammal which has been driven to the verge of extinction by fishermen using explosives and nets, collisions with rafts of teak logs, and fatal encounters with the sharp propellers of speeding long-tail boats.

In Cambodia nowadays it is common to blame the Khmer Rouge for all manner of ills, from the looting of ancient temples to the destruction of the country's natural habitat. In line with this, Cambodian fisheries experts assert that Mekong dolphins were slaughtered wholesale by the Khmer Rouge for their meat and oil, claiming that "five dolphins a day were killed in the Tonlé Sap alone". It was recently estimated that there are no more than 150 of these rare creatures surviving in the waters of the Middle Mekong, about half in Laos and the remainder in the Cambodian provinces of Kratie and Stung Treng.

> **QUOTE**
>
> "Chinese sailors coming to the country note with pleasure that it is not necessary to wear clothes and, since rice is easily available, women easily married, houses easily run and trade easily carried on, a great many sailors desert to take up permanent residence."
>
> Chou Ta-kuan, 13th century

Dolphin-spotting on the Mekong near Kampi.

Irrawaddy (a.k.a. Mekong) dolphins can be seen in the river north and south of Kratie.

There are still some wild elephants in the northeastern forests.

Fortunately tourism may provide an economic stimulus for the protection and preservation of this unique species; certainly the Cambodian Ministry of Tourism is conscious of the potential attraction of dolphin-watching, and announced its intention of promoting the natural environment of the Middle Mekong as "an alternative destination to Angkor". The boatmen of Kratie know where the dolphins are to be found and will take visitors to see them for a small fee.

One such destination is the village of **Kampi**, about 17km (11 miles) north of Kratie, where a group of around 25 dolphins is said to be found. Visitors report that it is generally possible to see several of these large mammals, which grow to 2–3 metres (6–10ft) in length, hunting and playing offshore. The dry season, when water levels are lower, is the best time for spotting them. It is also easier to find them early in the morning or during the late afternoon when they are feeding.

Beyond Kratie, the Mekong continues due north for 140km (88 miles) to the riverside town of Stung Treng. The road from Kratie to Stung Treng runs inland, well away from the river, while the latter attains widths of several kilometres in these remote reaches. It takes between three and four hours to reach Stung Treng by express boat from Kratie, and services are far from regular. Until around 2002 there was a risk of banditry along this stretch of river, but these days the journey is considered perfectly safe.

Stung Treng

The town of **Stung Treng** (Stoĕng Trêng) ⓭ nestles on the banks of the Tonlé Sekong lake a short distance from the east bank of the Mekong. It is a small place, surprisingly clean, with a well-maintained park beside the waterfront. Passable accommodation is available, and the usual selection of Khmer and Chinese dishes is served in a couple of small restaurants located to the west of the covered market – the latter has a dubious reputation as an important centre for trading in endangered species, including tiger and bear parts. There's nothing much to do or see in this sleepy backwater (less sleepy than it was, however, due to a new Chinese-built road to

the Lao border), but Stung Treng does make a suitable base for trips upriver. It is now possible to charter a boat for a day trip to the Lao frontier about 50km (30 miles) north of the town.

The Cambodian border post at the hamlet of Phumi Kompong Sralau is marked by a small border station flying the Cambodian flag, while a little upstream at the Lao settlement of Thai Boei another building flying the Lao flag marks the frontier of the Lao province of Champasak (see page 174). Foreigners can now cross into Laos at this point, provided they have a valid Lao visa (obtained in Phnom Penh), and vice versa from Laos to Cambodia. It is now also possible to proceed upriver to the Lao town of Hat Xai Khun and thence to Pakse and Champasak. Make enquiries in Stung Treng before setting out.

It is also possible to cross the Mekong by boat from Stung Treng to the small settlement of Thalabarivat, where the ruins of a pre-Angkorean temple may be seen. Similarly, a weekly boat runs from Stung Treng up the Tonlé Kong to Siempang.

The Northeast: Ratanakiri and Mondulkiri provinces

To the east of Stung Treng and away from the river lies the beautiful and undeveloped upland province of **Rattanakiri**, home to some of Cambodia's least-known tribal peoples. It is possible to reach Ban Lung, the provincial capital, by road from Stung Treng, but the journey is arduous and takes at least 10 hours – far longer in the rainy season, when the road becomes impassable. There is an airport in Ban Lung, but it is only open to private and chartered flights. The Ministry of Tourism is keen to promote both Rattanakiri and the adjoining province of **Mondolkiri** as destinations for eco-tourism and trekking, but this project remains in its infancy.

As a part of this drive, and to protect threatened wildlife, almost half of Rattanakiri has been designated a protected area, including **Lumphat Wildlife Sanctuary** and **Virachey National Park**. Lying along the southern frontier of Laos and the western frontier of Vietnam, Virachey is very remote. Fauna which may be seen includes the slow loris, pig-tailed macaque, gibbon and douc langur, as well as wild elephant, gaur, bintang and sometimes even tiger. The area is also home to some of Cambodia's smallest and least assimilated minorities, including the Kavet, Brao, Kreung, Krachok and Jarai peoples. Despite its remoteness, Virachey is among Cambodia's best-administered national parks, offering organised tours from the park headquarters at Ban Lung. Roads within the province, as in neighbouring Mondolkiri, remain poor – though they are constantly being upgraded – but access by air (when it becomes available again) between Phnom Penh and Ban Lung is easy, and most of both provinces are readily accessible by four-wheel-drive vehicle except during the rainy season, approximately between June and October.

FACT

Just to the south of Kompong Cham, the river island of Koh Pbain is a popular picnic spot. In the dry season it is reached by a rickety bamboo bridge that is taken down and reassembled on an annual basis as the waters rise. The inhabitants are mainly Cham Muslims, whose men fish the river while the women weave cotton karma (see page 228) on looms set up in the shade beneath their houses.

Cheerful face at Wat Roka Kandal.

LAO AND CAMBODIAN FESTIVALS

Visiting either of the two countries when they are energised by one of their exuberant festivals makes a special trip even more memorable.

The vast majority of festivals in Laos and Cambodia are derived from Buddhism and are tied to the lunar calendar. Buddhist festivals celebrated in both countries include the **Magha Puja** or "Day of the Four Auspicious Occasions" (January/February); the **New Year Festival** (April); **Vesak** or "Buddha's Birthday" (May or June); and **Boun Haw Khao Padap Dinh** (Laos, August) or **Bon Pchum Ben** (Cambodia, September/October), both of which worship deceased friends and family members.

Travellers often confuse the Khmer Water Festival, known as **Bon Om Tuk**, with Khmer New Year, due to the spirited nature of both celebrations, and the fact that Cambodians throw water in the New Year. However, Bon Om Tuk, which occurs in October or November, commemorates the victory of King Jayavarman VII over the Chams at Angkor in 1177. It also marks the time each year when the current of the Tonlé Sap River reverses its course. The three-day event, which rivals the Khmer New Year in its riotous exuberance, is celebrated in both Phnom Penh and Angkor with highly competitive boat races. The longboats are colourfully decorated and rowed by up to forty participants. It's a very busy time, so book accommodation well in advance. A month later, a similar festival, known as **Boun Awk Phansa**, is celebrated in Laos.

Other notable events include an ancient fertility festival in Laos known as the **Boun Bang Fai** or "Rocket Festival", and **Bon Choat Preah Nengkal** ("Ploughing of the Holy Furrow") in Cambodia. Both usually occur in May.

Cambodia's Bon Om Tuk festival takes place in October or November to mark the reversal of the current of the Tonlé Sap River. Also known as the Khmer Water Festival, it is celebrated with boat races and a great deal of water-based high jinks.

The Buddhist Magha Puja festival is marked at Wat Phu near Champasak. In Laos it is usually called the Boun Makha Busa.

At the Bon Pchum Ben festival in September or October, the villagers of Vihear Sour village, 50km (30 miles) northeast of Phnom Penh, organise buffalo-racing and Khmer wrestling during the 15-day event, held in memory of the spirits of the dead.

A New Year parade at Luang Prabang. The former royal capital of Laos is the best place to experience this joyful occasion, with various events lasting for a full three weeks.

THE NEW YEAR

Both Cambodia and Laos celebrate the New Year with festivities during the same week in April. The Khmer New Year is celebrated on 14–16 April and known as Chol Chnam Thmey. The Laos New Year, likely derived from the former, is celebrated on 13–15 April, and known as Boun Pi Mai. New Year's Eve is marked by fireworks at the stroke of midnight (apparently 1.36am in Cambodian reckoning). The eve and morning of the first day are times when families worship their ancestors at special holiday altars, and then visit the local pagoda to make prayers and offerings to Buddha. In temples people erect sand mounds representing Culamuni Catiya, the stupa at Tavatimsa, where Buddha's hair and diadem are said to be buried. Afternoon activities for young people during the holiday focus on traditional games – which include dousing each other with water and smearing talcum powder on each other's faces. The second day of the festival is a time to donate to charity and do symbolic works of merit. On the third day people visit local temples to bathe Buddha statues and receive baptisms from monks.

...w Year festivities in ...s often involve ...des of masked ...acters.

...er-splashing at the New Year. Foreigners are not exempt, so ... care of valuables.

New Year festivities in Laos often involve parades of masked characters.

PREAH VIHEAR

The temple of Preah Vihear is one of the most impressive Khmer historical sites. Closed by war for more than 20 years and in a sensitive border area, it is only intermittently accessible.

Main Attractions
Views down to the plains
Gopura carvings
Main sanctuary

Preah Vihear temple.

S et high on a cliff on the edge of the Dangrek Mountains overlooking Cambodia, **Preah Vihear** ⓮ (known to the Thais as Khao Phra Viharn) is remarkable both for its interesting Khmer architecture and for its stunning location. Long claimed by both Thailand and Cambodia, the temple complex was finally awarded to the latter by the World Court in 1963, though the question of ownership still rankles with many Thais. This has led to periodic military skirmishes, resulting in the occasional temporary closure of the site to visitors. At the time of going to press, the dispute has cooled down and the site is once again open to the public with free admission to encourage Cambodia-based tourism there. In 2013, the International Court of Justice ruled that the area on the east and west of the temple belongs to Cambodia and that Thailand should withdraw all troops immediately. In mid-2015, the British Foreign Office officially lifted its travel ban on the Preah Vihear temple area. However, always check the Foreign Office's website before travelling, as tensions between the two countries are high and the conflict could reignite at any moment.

Since 2015, the site has been accessible only from the Cambodian side, via Anlong Veng. Although the road has improved recently, it remains dangerously steep at the top and unpaved along the bottom half. Visitors are required to purchase a ticket and use local transport (jeep or motorbike), and are not allowed to walk or use their own transportation. The temple itself is best visited as a day trip. Be sure to leave early in the morning to allow enough time to explore it properly, for the site is large and it closes early.

Temple on a peak

Preah Vihear is an extraordinary place, possibly the most impressive

Khmer historical site after Angkor. Although in need of extensive restoration, the temple is quite magnificent, and one is left wondering how the original builders transported such massive blocks of stone to the peak of the Dangrek escarpment – a height of 550 metres (1,800ft). In fact, Preah Vihear took around 200 years to build, starting during the reign of Rajendravarman II in the mid-10th century and only reaching completion in the early 12th century during the reign of Surayavarman II. It was the latter monarch, beyond doubt a visionary builder, who also began the construction of Angkor Wat. It is thought that the Khmers held the locality in reverence for at least 500 years before the building of the temple.

Constructed in the Baphuon and early Angkor styles, Preah Vihear was originally Hindu and dedicated to Shiva. Of the four main *gopura*, or elaborately decorated gateways, the first two are in serious disrepair, though fine examples of carving – *apsara* and divinities – are still visible. The third and fourth *gopura* are comparatively well preserved, with a finely carved lintel depicting Shiva and his consort Uma sitting on Nandi, the bull, Shiva's traditional mount.

The temple comprises five separate stages, with the massive bulk of the fourth, main sanctuary perched high on the clifftop. Here the great *prasat* or central spire has been thrown to the ground, and mighty blocks of carved stone lie in a tumbled heap, awaiting restoration. Everywhere there are army bunkers along the temple, ready to return fire, should Thailand decide to provoke yet another fight.

The temple is now firmly under the control of the Cambodian army, and young soldiers watch silently as a regular stream of visitors explores the ancient site. Once through the main temple complex, head for the clifftop behind for breathtaking views across the plains below.

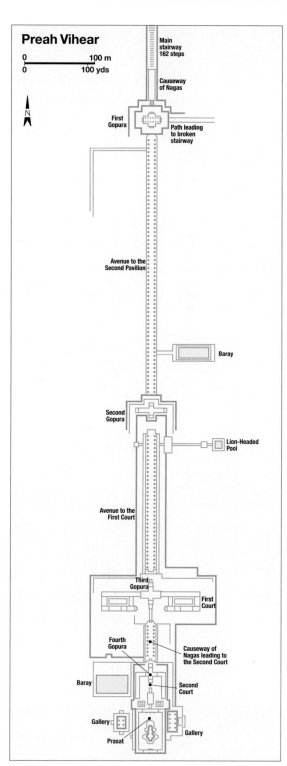

Preah Vihear

0 ___ 100 m
0 ___ 100 yds

N

Main stairway 162 steps

Causeway of Nagas

First Gopura

Path leading to broken stairway

Avenue to the Second Pavilion

Baray

Second Gopura

Lion-Headed Pool

Avenue to the First Court

Third Gopura

First Court

Fourth Gopura

Causeway of Nagas leading to the Second Court

Baray

Second Court

Gallery

Gallery

Prasat

Sunset at Serendipity Beach in Sihanoukville.

THE CAMBODIAN COAST

Old French beach resorts are reawakening as foreign tourists and Phnom Penh's wealthiest head back to sand and surf. All the while, the country's greatest ecological treasures are only just being discovered.

In times past, before the war years, the Cambodian coast enjoyed an idyllic reputation among middle-class Cambodians, French colonialists and wealthy foreign visitors alike. Perhaps because of this historical association with domestic and foreign elites, the palm-fringed southern coast – a region studded with the elaborate villas of the wealthy, including that of King Sihanouk at Kep – fared particularly badly under the harsh rule of the obsessively anti-urban Khmer Rouge. Kep, in particular, was systematically razed to the ground, while ordinary people (except fishermen) were moved away from the coast to prevent the possibility of flight from the DK "people's paradise" by way of the sea. Even the movements of those permitted to fish were tightly monitored by Khmer Rouge cadres, while traffic through the port of Sihanoukville was limited to the occasional exchange of Cambodian raw materials for Chinese and North Korean armaments and other aid.

Today all this has changed, and relatively fast. The coast is being developed as a tourist destination, and foreign investors have joined local businessmen in developing hotels, resorts and better-quality restaurants. To be sure, there is some way to go – but for the people of Phnom Penh and for foreign travellers, trips to the coast

and long hours of swimming and sun-bathing by the Gulf of Thailand are back in vogue.

There are two main routes south from Phnom Penh to the coast: National Highway 3 via Angk Tasaom to Kampot, and National Highway 4 via Kampong Speu to Sihanoukville. The 148km (95-mile) drive from Phnom Penh to Kampot takes 2.5–3 hours by taxi, while the well-surfaced road from the capital to Sihanoukville is 230km (143 miles) long and takes approximately 3–3.5 hours to

Mermaid statue on Kep Beach.

cover. The railway service south was discontinued; however, a new renovation is under way to revive Cambodia's rail lines.

Kampot

Kampot ⓕ, the capital of the eponymous province, is a small, relaxed town of around 39,000 people. Just 5km (3 miles) inland, by the banks of the Sanke River, there is a coastal feel to the place which adds to its rather languid appeal. "Downtown" Kampot centres on a large roundabout space about 400 metres (1,300ft) east of the river. This area is the main commercial hub and also the location of the two best hotels. The road north from the roundabout leads out past a large covered market – a favourite with visitors from Phnom Penh, who stop off here to buy the fresh seafood for which Kampot is renowned. Of more interest to the foreign visitor, however, is the series of narrow, colonnaded streets leading west from the roundabout to the riverfront. Although in need of restoration, there are some fine examples of French architecture to be seen

in this warren, as well as the best of Kampot's restaurants.

Travellers staying overnight in Kampot should check into one of the hotels at the roundabout, head east towards the river for a bite to eat, then walk the length of the delightful riverfront which, shaded by casuarina trees, offers views of the nearby Chuor Phnom Damrei (Elephant Mountains). There are some particularly handsome colonial buildings in this area, notably the **Governor's Residence** and the main post office at the southern end of the riverfront. Fishing boats cluster on the far side of the Sanke River.

There are just a few popular sites to see outside Kampot itself. One is Phnom Chhnork, a Funan-era cave temple about halfway between Kampot and Kep, reachable by tuk-tuk and located behind an unmarked wat.

Bokor National Park

Kampot shelters in the lee of the Chuor Phnom Damrei, a wild region of wildlife-rich forests and sheer rock outcrops. About 37km (23 miles)

A backstreet in Kampot city.

northwest of town and located within **Bokor National Park** is the 1,079-metre (3,506ft) -high former hill station of **Bokor** . Often shrouded in mist, the hill resort was built by the French in the early 1920s, but later fell on hard times under the Communist guerrillas and the Khmer Rouge. The hillsides still harbour the danger of landmines, so visitors should keep to the tracks.

The ruins of the old hill station include the **Black Palace** complex, King Sihanouk's former retreat, the old **Bokor Palace Hotel** and a small, abandoned church. The area went under extensive redevelopment by a Korean investor for several years, and was closed to the public. A new resort, the Thansur Bokor Highland Resort and Casino, has now opened. Thankfully too, the national park road leading up the mountain has re-opened and visitors can once again explore the area. Undoubtedly, however, the casino will affect the previously peaceful atmosphere.

The journey up to Bokor Mountain requires a long and winding ride along a new road with hairpin turns. Visitors will be rewarded for their efforts, with absolutely spectacular views of the coast and cool (sometimes distinctly chilly) mountain air. If you wish to spend a night at the hill station, hostel-style accommodation is available, but do bring your own food, as there are no shops or restaurants (apart from the casino) at the top. Enquire at the ranger station (tel: 015-832 517).

Kep

Another old, celebrated resort town is **Kep** (Kipe) , known to the French as Kep-sur-Mer. The 30km (20-mile) drive from Kampot can be covered by *moto*. In prewar times the 7km (4-mile) stretch of palm-fringed beach was lined with the villas of rich Cambodians and French settlers, but then the Khmer Rouge arrived and destroyed virtually every building in town.

Today Kep is back on the tourist circuit, though much rebuilding remains to be done. Ruined villas and mansions, purchased (speculatively) by Cambodia's powerful elite for a pittance in the 1990s, dot the countryside. Some are currently occupied by squatters, but will eventually be redeveloped. For now the ruins add to the atmosphere. Although there are good hotels and restaurants here, many visitors choose to stay in Kampot, driving out to Kep for a day of sunbathing, fishing, swimming and indulging in the excellent local seafood – particularly crab.

Kep has two beaches: **Coconut Beach** is just south of a giant crab statue, and **Kep Beach** is overlooked by a statue of a nude fisherman's wife. Despite their popularity, however, the beaches are not the country's finest, and white sand has been trucked in from Sihanoukville to rejuvenate them in the past.

A short distance off the Kep shore lies **Koh Tunsai**, also known as "Rabbit Island", which can easily be reached by boat and makes a popular

Bamboo pipes are used for carrying palm toddy (made from the juice of coconut palms). Toddy is widely collected in Cambodia and used for making sugar or alcoholic drinks.

The beachfront at Kep.

TIP

Within Ream National Park, ranger-led boat trips on the Prek Tuk River last about 6 hours. Trips to the nearby islands of Koh Ses and Koh Thmei can last all day. Stops can include beaches, fishing villages and snorkelling (bring your own equipment). Freshwater dolphins, dugongs and spot-billed pelicans are among the wildlife that can be seen in the estuary.

A vendor tucks into one of her cooked tarantulas, with a live one going spare.

excursion. The island has four small but beautiful beaches with good swimming and snorkelling. The large island clearly visible to the south is Phu Quoc and belongs to Vietnam, as does the smaller Hai Tac Archipelago scattered to the southeast. The sea frontier in this region is still in dispute between Cambodia and Vietnam, and ownership of Phu Quoc in particular remains a serious bone of contention between the two countries. As of March 2014, Vietnam allows foreign tourists arriving by sea to visit Phu Quoc, without a visa, for up to 30 days). The land frontier with Vietnam is only about 50km (30 miles) east of Kep, and the border crossing to the Mekong Delta town of Ha Tien is open to international travellers.

Kirirom and Ream national parks

It is possible to travel directly from Kampot to Sihanoukville using National Highway 3, paralleling the run-down railway line, but most people will prefer to use National Highway 4 from Phnom Penh. This 230km (144-mile) journey takes between two and three hours by bus or taxi. Sihanoukville International Airport is 18km (12 miles) east of town. Flights were suspended in 2007 when a flight went down near Bokor hill station but have resumed from Siem Reap on a limited basis.

The road passes through the small provincial capital of Kampong Speu before rising over a forested spur of the Chuor Phnom Damrei. Just before the small settlement of Sre Khlong, a dusty road rising into the mountains leads to the former hill station of **Kirirom** ⑱ – a sign to the right of the road announces Preah Sumarit Kossomak National Park in Roman script. Once the hot-season retreat of wealthy Phnom Penh residents, Kirirom was – like Kep – deliberately blown up by the Khmer Rouge. At present it is still seldom visited, but as the site of Cambodia's first officially designated national park it is beginning to flourish again.

After crossing the Chuor Phnom Damrei, Route 4 forks as it drops

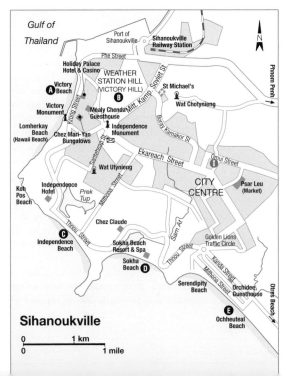

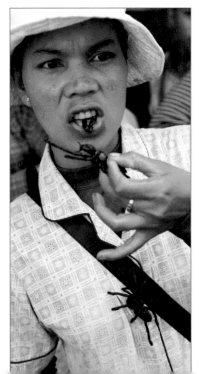

down to the coast; the southern fork leads to **Ream National Park** ⑲ (tel: 012-875 096; daily 9am–5pm), while the western route continues to Sihanoukville. Just 18km (12 miles) from town near the airport, Ream includes 210 sq km (81 sq miles) of coastal forests, including the Prek Tuk Sap estuary, mangrove forests, isolated beaches and two islands, as well as coral reefs. English-speaking rangers lead guided hikes and boat trips around the park, though the resident macaques, pangolins, sun bears and muntjac (mouse deer) are most likely to be seen after dark when the park is closed.

Sihanoukville

For the foreseeable future, Sihanoukville ⑳, also known as Kompong Som, will remain the heart of Cambodia's "Riviera". Like Kep, this town was once a holiday haven for the rich, and fortunately the Khmer Rouge wrought less thorough destruction here, probably because the deep-water port and railway terminus provided a key communications link with Phnom Penh.

Nowadays, the resort town is packed at weekends with visitors from the capital. As the country's third-most-visited tourist destination, Sihanoukville is seeing a steadily increasing number of foreign visitors, and can be crowded during the dry season. There are numerous hotels and guesthouses of all classes, with many run by expat Westerners. Sihanoukville's restaurants offer a wide choice of cuisines, and seafood is fresh and plentiful. The city also has a healthy nightlife, with countless beach bars, several discos and nightclubs, numerous examples of the increasingly common karaoke bar, and even a casino.

The main activities are, as one might expect, sunbathing and swimming. There's also good snorkelling and fishing, while diving trips are available with experienced dive instructors. In all, Sihanoukville has about 10km (6 miles) of beachfront, divided into four main beaches.

Starting in the north, the first stretch of sand is **Victory Beach** ⓐ, between the harbour and Koh Pos Island – really two beaches divided

Occheuteal Beach, Sihanoukville.

The Indochinese tiger or Corbett's tiger (panthera tigris corbetti).

CAMBODIA'S NATIONAL PARKS

Nearly 25 percent of Cambodia (43,000 sq km/16,602 sq miles) has been designated as wildlife sanctuaries, national parks or some other form of protected land reserve. Unfortunately, though, the government lacks the resources, and, in some cases, the desire to protect the parks adequately. As such, illegal logging and poaching are serious problems. Even with the help of several prominent NGOs, it's a battle that won't be won in the near future.

Protected areas of interest to travellers include Peam Krasaop Wildlife Sanctuary, the Southern and Central Cardamoms Protected Forests, and the national parks of Botum Sakor, Ream, Bokor, Kep and Kirirom. Most of these areas have had little encroachment by development and are a treasure trove of endangered species. Undoubtedly they also hide many "new" species, unknown to science. Tigers, elephants, gaur, leopards and langurs are found in the jungles, while aquatic species include the Irrawaddy dolphin, humpback dolphin, dugong and sea turtles.

Park rangers are paid precious little for their jobs, and confront many dangers in their work – including poachers armed with assault rifles. Please consider tipping generously when taking a guided tour. It not only encourages their conservation efforts but also discourages them from joining in illegal activities themselves.

Many Sihanoukville addresses are quoted from the Golden Lions traffic circle.

by a rocky point and a small hillock – about 2km (1.2 miles) long. The north end is more developed, with several restaurants and budget-priced bungalows. Right above the beach here is **Weather Station Hill** (also known as Victory Hill), once the main backpackers' area, comprising a plethora of guesthouses, restaurants and bars, travel agencies, CD shops and internet cafés. Lately it's become known as one of Sihanoukville's red-light districts, though some of the legitimate venues here adamantly oppose the trend. The southern stretch of Victory Beach is popular among Cambodians. Also known as Lomherkay Beach, it is lined with beach shelters and shack-style stalls.

Further south is a tiny stretch known as Koh Pos Beach, where the waves are rougher. **Independence Beach** ❻, between the renovated Independence Hotel and the south-western peninsula, is popular with weekenders from the capital but is often deserted midweek. It has few facilities. **Sokha Beach** ❼, between the peninsula and a Cambodian army

base, offers a beautiful stretch of white sand, shady palm trees and adequate facilities. It is dominated by the lovely Sokha Beach Resort and Spa, but access to the beach is available to non-guests, including use of the resort pool, for a small fee.

Finally, **Ochheuteal Beach** ❺, stretching away to the south of the town, is around 4km (2.5 miles) long, and relatively tranquil. Of all the beaches, this is by far the most popular, with numerous bars, restaurants and hotels recently opened or under development. It offers the widest variety of food and accommodation. The area at its extreme northern end is nicknamed Serendipity Beach, and here you will find bungalows, guesthouses and restaurants situated right on the sand. The far southern end of the beach is known as Otres Beach, though much of this section is being developed, and includes an enormous mansion owned by Prime Minister Hun Sen.

Visitors should note that Sihanoukville is a surprisingly spread-out place. The rather shabby and characterless

SEX TOURISM

Human trafficking, particularly in the form of sex tourism, is an epidemic in Cambodia. Most of the effort in combating the problem has been directed toward Western paedophiles seeking child prostitutes – much of which is happening in Sihanoukville. Unfortunately half of the perpetrators – Asian and, particularly, Cambodian paedophiles – are largely overlooked. Visitors should be aware that all forms of prostitution are illegal in Cambodia. Thankfully a number of Western countries, including Australia, the USA and the UK, have adopted strict new laws allowing prosecution of its citizens for under-aged sex abroad. Report suspicious behaviour to the Child Helpline Cambodia (www.childhelpline.org.kh; tel: 023-720 555) or ChildSafe Hotline (www.think childsafe.org; tel: 012-478 100).

town centre, with its busy markets and torn-up asphalt-and-rubble streets, is about 2km (1.2 miles) away from the port and railway station. Most visitors prefer to stay out at one of the beaches.

Diving off the Gulf islands

There are a number of offshore islands which can be visited by arrangement with one of several companies offering boat charters. Locals divide these islands into three groups: the **Kompong Som Islands**, lying close to the west of the port within an easy half-day's trip; the **Ream Islands**, which are scattered to the east towards the fishing village of Phsar Ream; and, finally and more distantly, the **Koh Tang Islands**, which lie further out to sea, between four and eight hours' journey from Sihanoukville.

Local diving companies recommend the Kompong Som group, and more especially Koh Koang Kang together with Koh Rung Samloem, for swimming and snorkelling when the prevailing winds are from the southwest (March to October). Koh Rong is home to the new,

ultra-exclusive Song Saa Resort. The Ream group, more protected by the bulk of the mainland, is reportedly a better bet during the cool season (November to February), when the winds blow from the north. For snorkelling, the waters around Koh Chraloh, Koh Ta Kiev and Koh Khteah are highly recommended, though the proximity of the mainland and related high levels of silt can reduce visibility, especially in choppy weather. Finally, Koh Tang, Koh Prins and the nearby islands are recommended for more serious divers who may wish to spend a night or two away from Sihanoukville, either moored in the lee of one of the islands or camping on shore. This whole area is rich in a diverse marine life, with large fish, excellent visibility and sunken wrecks that can be explored with appropriate supervision. The most experienced and knowledgeable diving operator in Sihanoukville is **Chez Claude** (hilltop near Sokha Resort; tel: 012-824 870), which has been managing a diving resort since 1992.

Portable street vendor's wagon selling baguettes and snacks.

Serendipity Beach, Sihanoukville, along from Ochheuteal Beach.

TIP

Koh Kong was once a
popular spot for
Thailand's expats to
make "visa-runs", until
new Thai laws made this
less practical. Like all
border crossings in
Cambodia, both sides of
the line inspire complaints
about corruption and
questionable fees.

The coastal "Wild West"

The coast to the west of Sihanoukville is almost completely undeveloped. There are no roads hugging
the coastline around Kompong Som
Gulf, and a journey overland to the
isolated but beautiful province of
Koh Kong requires a long drive
on the newly developed National
Highway 48. There is also an alternative route by sea, but at the time
of writing it was suspended. **Tunlop
Rolork**, a small fishing port about
2km (1.2 miles) north of Sihanoukville's main harbour, maintains a
small fleet of fast boats which provide a passenger service to Koh Kong.
These vessels are really intended to
serve as river ferries and are ill-suited
to rough weather in open seas, so
are certainly best avoided during
the southwest monsoons which
blow between June and October.
During the cool season, however,
they provide a fast and convenient
way of travelling along the coast to
Thailand. The journey from Sihanoukville to Koh Kong takes between
three and four hours, with boats

leaving daily at noon. Check with
local tour companies for the status,
well in advance.

The alternative is to travel back
up Route 4 toward Phnom Penh, as
far as the small junction village of
Kaong – a distance of about 60km (37
miles) – and then turn left for 15km
(9 miles) to reach the small port of
Sre Ambei. This is really the start of
the Cambodian coast's "Wild West". It
soon becomes apparent from the wide
range of Thai goods available in town
that Sre Ambei, although notionally
a fishing port, is a smugglers' haven
which flourishes on illicit trade with
nearby Trat and Koh Kong. Goods
are brought in by sea from Thailand
and discreetly despatched to Phnom
Penh and all points north via Route
4, thereby avoiding the docks and customs officials of Sihanoukville.

There are a couple of dubious
guesthouses, but Sre Ambei really is
not a nice place to stay overnight. It
does, however, provide a good base
to visit **Stung Phong Roul Waterfall**, one of the most scenic in the
country. The falls are 20km (12 miles)
northeast of town, halfway to Kirirom
National Park, via a rather treacherous
road. Sre Ambei also has an attractive
Buddhist temple, located on the hill
behind the main market. Shared taxis
from Sihanoukville do the journey in
around 1.5 hours.

Koh Kong

The route that the fast boats take to
Koh Kong cuts west across Kompong
Som Gulf before turning into the
open waters of the Gulf of Thailand
and heading north along the coast.
Most boats take the opportunity to
stop briefly at Koh Sdach, the most
important of the tiny and remote
Samit Islands, where the really adventurous traveller may choose to stop
overnight and take another boat in the
morning. There is basic accommodation (try Mean Chey Guesthouse; tel:
011-788 852), as well as a number of
fishermen's restaurants – though, as

*The harbour at Krong
Koh Kong.*

with Sre Ambei, smuggling is clearly a lucrative pastime in these waters and Koh Sdach is, by any standards, a smugglers' den. There is not a great deal to do or to see here other than snorkelling, though, and most travellers will prefer to head straight on towards Koh Kong.

About two hours' drive from Koh Sdech, **Koh Kong ㉑** – confusingly the name of the province, the provincial capital *and* an offshore island – is a fast-developing coastal resort designed especially to appeal to visitors from neighbouring Thailand (particularly those renewing visas). It is also a convenient point for entering or leaving Cambodia by land. When Thailand shortened the length of visas available at land borders a few years ago this stunted the growth of Koh Kong as a visa-run destination. Nonetheless, the place has something of a Thai feel to it, being a clearing point for imported Thai goods, both legal and illegal, where the Thai *baht* is as welcome as the Cambodian *riel*. Before the "Zero Years" of the Khmer Rouge, Koh Kong was largely settled by ethnic Thais who had lived there for generations. After the Khmer Rouge victory most of them fled across the nearby border to Thailand. In the years since the Khmer Rouge were toppled from power, local Thais have moved back to Koh Kong in significant numbers, and Thai is widely spoken and understood here.

Koh Kong's most exciting development, however, is as a base for ecotourism. The nearby **Koh Kong Conservation Corridor** encompasses the **Cardamom Mountains**, **Peam Krasaop Wildlife Sanctuary**, **Koh Por** and **Tatai waterfalls**, **Koh Kong Island**, **Southern and Central Cardamoms Protected Forests**, and a portion of **Botum Sakor National Park**. All of these sights present endless outdoor activities and opportunities to see endangered species.

Koh Kong is just 10km (6 miles) by taxi from the border post of Ban Hat Lek, and the presence of Cambodia's larger neighbour is everywhere to be felt. Nearly all the consumer goods on sale in town are brought in by road or ferried in from Thailand. A casino on Cambodian territory just opposite Ban Hat Lek attracts many Thais keen to enjoy the gambling denied them by law at home. Should you decide to leave Cambodia here, take a taxi to the border post of Ban Hat Lek on the Thai side; from there, minibuses leave at regular intervals throughout the day for Trat, whereupon you can transfer to a fast, air-conditioned bus to Bangkok. Depending on the traffic and the time of day, it will take around five hours to reach Bangkok's eastern bus terminal at Ekamai from Trat.

Thanks to the newly engineered Highway 48 that passes through wetlands, forests and the Chuor Phnom Kravanh (Cardamom Mountains), Koh Kong is now more firmly connected to Phnom Penh and the rest of Cambodia. There is also an airport, with direct flights to and from Phnom Penh several times a week.

Cambodia's forests harbour an immense quantity and variety of insect life, including numerous colourful butterfly species.

Maybe one to avoid…

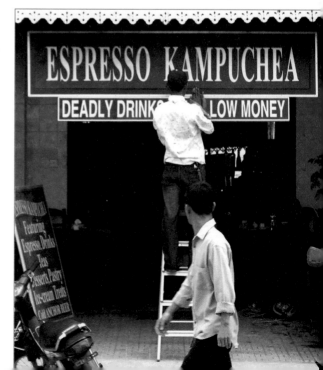

A local fisherman at work.

TRAVEL TIPS
LAOS & CAMBODIA

LAOS

Transport

A – Z

Language

Further Reading

CAMBODIA

Transport

A – Z

Language

Further Reading

TRANSPORT

GETTING THERE AND GETTING AROUND

GETTING THERE

By Air

There are three international airports in Laos: **Wattay International Airport** in Vientiane, **Luang Prabang International Airport** in the old capital, and **Pakse International Airport** in Champasak province. Vientiane is served by international flights from Thailand (Bangkok and Chiang Mai), Vietnam (Ho Chi Minh City and Hanoi), Cambodia (Phnom Penh and Siem Reap), China (Kunming), Malaysia (Kuala Lumpur) and South Korea (Seoul). Most visitors travel via Bangkok, from which there are daily connections to Vientiane as well as to Luang Prabang. It is also possible to fly to Luang Prabang from Chiang Mai.

To save money on flying into Laos, one option is to fly from Bangkok to the northeastern Thai town of Udon Thani (for onward travel by road to Vientiane) or to Ubon Ratchathani (for onward travel by road to Pakse in

A tuk-tuk speeds through Vientiane.

southern Laos). From Udon Thani, the **Thai-Lao International Bus** takes visitors across the Friendship Bridge to Talaat Sao in Vientiane eight times daily (8am, 9am, 10.30am, 11.30am, 2pm, 3pm, 4.30pm, 6pm); from Nong Khai, the bus leaves six times daily (7.30am, 9.30am, 12.40pm, 2.30pm, 3.30pm, 6pm); alternatively, public buses (No. 14), tuk-tuks, songthaew (trucks converted into passenger vehicles) and taxis are also available. From Ubon Ratchathani, the Thai-Lao International Bus takes visitors to Pakse two times daily (9.30am and 3.30pm) and takes 3 hours.

Lao Airlines (tel: 021-211 050; www.laoairlines.com) is the national carrier and provides regular services between Vientiane and the following regional destinations: Bangkok, Chiang Mai, Hanoi, Ho Chi Minh City, Phnom Penh, Siem Reap, Singapore and Kunming. There are also connections between Luang Prabang, Bangkok, Chiang Mai, Hanoi and Siem Reap. There are flights between Pakse and Bangkok, Ho Chi Minh City and Siem Reap.

Bangkok Airways (www.bangkokair. com), Thai (www.thaiairways. com), Vietnam Airlines (www. vietnamairlines.com), China Eastern (www.flychinaeastern.com) and Jin Air (www.jinair.com) provide regular flight services to Laos. Check with the individual airlines for flight schedules and fares. Budget carrier Air Asia (www.airasia.com) offers cheap flights from Bangkok to Udon Thani as well as to Ubon Ratchathani, and operates direct flights between Luang Prabang, Kuala Lumpur and Bangkok. Departure tax is included in ticket prices.

By Land

At present, there are 24 international border checkpoints. You can obtain a 30-day tourist visa-on-arrival (VOA) at these checkpoints, unless otherwise indicated (see list). As visa regulations may change without notice, check with a Lao Embassy or Consulate before travelling.

From China, you can enter via two checkpoints, including the Mengla-Boten checkpoint in Luang Nam Tha province. From Thailand, enter via one of eleven checkpoints including Chiang Khong/Huay Xai (Lao–Thai Friendship Bridge) in Bokeo province; Huay Kon/Muang Ngeun and Nakasing/Nam Hong, both in Sainyabuli province; Beung Kan/Paksan in Bolikhamsai province (no VOA); Nakhon Phanom/Tha Kaek in Khammuan province; Mukdahan/Savannakhet in Savannakhet province; Chong Mek/Vang Tao in Champasak province (near Pakse); or Nong Khai/Vientiane via the Lao–Thai Friendship Bridge. The last checkpoint is the most popular among foreign visitors. If

Loading provisions onto a Nam Ou riverboat.

LAOS

is widely available, which makes it possible to visit at least part of every province in Laos.

Regular buses, many air-conditioned, supply the main national highways. There are also an increasing number of minivan operations springing up to take passengers in more comfort and slightly quicker than the regular buses. For more remote routes, large flat-bed trucks fitted with wooden seats, pick-ups, or trucks converted into passenger vehicles by the addition of two long wooden benches in the back (all of which are known as songthaew) are the most common forms of road transport.

you are entering Laos at Tha Kaek (Khammuan) or Savannakhet, there is a short ferry crossing across the Mekong River.

From Vietnam, you can cross at eight checkpoints including Sop Houn/Tay Trang in Phongsali province; Nam Xoi/Na Maew in Hua Phan province; Nam Can/Nam Khan in Xieng Khuang province; Cau Treo/Nam Phao in Bolikhamsai province; Na Phao/Chalo in Khammuan province; Lao Bao/Dansavanh in Savannakhet province; and Bo Y/Ngoc Hoi in Attapeu province.

From Cambodia, you can enter by the Voen Kham/Si Phan Don crossing.

GETTING AROUND

On Arrival

From Vientiane's Wattay International Airport the journey into the centre of town (about 4km/2.5 miles) is a painless 15-minute drive by taxi or tuk-tuk. Large hotels often provide limousine service from the airport if arranged prior to check-in. There is no airport bus service or public transport.

From the Luang Prabang International Airport the journey into the centre of the city (about 4km/2.5 miles) takes about 15 minutes by taxi, tuk-tuk or minitruck. Again, large hotels often provide limousine service from the airport if arranged prior to check-in. No public transport is available.

The journey by public bus or the Thai-Lao International Bus from the Lao–Thai Friendship Bridge to Talaat Sao (Morning Market) in the centre of Vientiane takes about 30 minutes. The journey can also be made by tuk-tuk, taxi or private car. The larger hotels can provide limousine pick-up service from the bridge if the arrangement is made prior to arrival at the border.

By Air

Lao Airlines (www.laoairlines.com; tel: 021-211 050) flies to several domestic destinations, and its service has improved in recent years, though schedules still tend to be irregular and dependent on demand and on the weather. It is not uncommon for flights to be cancelled or delayed. Visitors are advised to confirm their flight reservation prior to travelling even if they have a confirmed ticket, and to arrive at the airport early, especially during peak seasons and around holidays.

The main routes are Vientiane–Luang Prabang, Vientiane–Pakse and Vientiane–Xieng Khuang. Less frequent domestic destinations include Udomxai, Huay Xai, Luang Nam Tha and Savannakhet.

The airport departure tax is included in ticket prices.

If you have the budget, it is possible to charter a helicopter with a foreign pilot through **Westcoast Helicopter** in Vientiane. **Lao Skyway** also provides charter services on its helicopters and fixed-wing planes. A number of regional airlines also have offices in Vientiane (see box).

Lao Skyway
Wattay International Airport, Vientiane
Tel: 021-513 022
www.laoskyway.com

Lao Westcoast Helicopter
Wattay Airport, Vientiane
Tel: 021-512 023
www.laowestcoast.laopdr.com

By Road

The road system in Laos has improved tremendously. An array of foreign governments and international aid organisations is currently funding road-improvement projects. However, many roads remain in poor condition. Inter-provincial transport by bus and truck

Tuk-tuks, Jumbos and Taxis

For short trips in the centres of town, stick to tuk-tuks and jumbos (a larger version of the tuk-tuk); the pedicab *(samlo)* has virtually disappeared with the increase in motorcycle and car traffic. In Vientiane the city bus system is of little use to tourists, as it only runs between the centre of the city and outlying villages. Car taxis in Vientiane can be found in front of major hotels, the morning market and the airport – always negotiate the price before you set out.

By Boat

Not so long ago the 7,400km (4,600 miles) of navigable waterways in Laos constituted the country's only transport network. Today, they remain,

Airline Offices

Bangkok Airways
57/6 Srisawangwong Road, Luang Prabang
Tel: 071-253 334
www.bangkokair.com

China Eastern
Souphanouvong Road, Vientiane
Tel: 021-212 300
www.flychinaeastern.com

Lao Airlines
2 Pangkham Road, Vientiane
Tel: 021-212 051-4
www.laoairlines.com

Thai Airways
70/101–103 Luang Prabang Road, Vientiane
Tel: 021-222 527-9
www.thaiairways.com

Vietnam Airlines
1st Floor, Lao Plaza Hotel, 63 Samsenthai Road, Vientiane
Tel: 021-217 562/618
www.vietnamairlines.com

CAMBODIA

Mekong riverboats.

by and large, a great way to get around the country. Services grind to a halt on some of the shallower stretches of water during the dry season.

The main long-distance river trip for tourists runs from Huay Xai in the northwest down to Luang Prabang. Boats take two days to reach Luang Prabang, overnighting in the riverside village of Pakbeng; alternatively, there are speedboats, which reach Luang Prabang in 6 to 8 hours. These vessels use a powerful engine mounted on a wooden boat and reach speeds of 80km (50 miles) per hour. Safety is a concern (also, bring earplugs). The beautiful Nam Ou River, which flows into the Mekong near Luang Prabang, is navigable most of the year as far north as Hat Sa near Phongsali and is considered one of the best river cruises in Laos.

These days, the route from Vientiane to Pakse in the south is mainly used for cargo traffic, but smaller passenger ferries from Pakse to Champasak and Don Khong still run.

A luxury alternative for river enthusiasts is now available on two routes. In the north, the vessel *Luang Say* (www.luangsay.com) travels from Huay Xai to Luang Prabang with an overnight stop at an attractive lodge near Pakbeng. The boat carries 40 passengers in comfort, and makes stops at points of interest along the way. In Southern Laos, the *Vat Phou* (www.vatphou.com), a steel-hulled vessel with 10 staterooms, makes a

four-day round-trip cruise from Pakse to the Si Phan Don area, visiting the famous Khmer temple site of Wat Phou as well.

Throughout the country, river taxis are available for short trips to sites such as temples and caves that are inaccessible by road.

Asian Oasis
Bangkok, tel: 66 2-655 6245
www.asian-oasis.com

Bicycle and Vehicle Hire

Perhaps the best way to get around any town in Laos is to hire a bicycle, or, for more ambitious day trips, a motorcycle. Bicycles can be hired for the day from restaurants and guesthouses in towns throughout Laos, and small motorcycles can be hired from dealers in Vientiane, Luang Prabang and Savannakhet. Cars, pick-ups and 4WD vehicles are available for hire from private operators in Vientiane.

Asia Vehicle Rental
Setthathirath Road, Vientiane
Tel: 021-223 867
www.avrlaos.com

Cycle Touring

Increasingly Laos is becoming a destination for long-distance cycle touring. Most cyclists bring their own bicycles with them; however, there are bicycle shops in the main tourist hotspots that sell bikes that may be used for touring. There are currently no hire options for long-distance cycling in Laos.

There are a few practical steps to enhance the cycle touring experience in Laos, the major one being what to take. The most important fact is that Laos, even in the rainy and cool seasons, is a hot place. It is important to pack light. With this in mind, cycling with backpacks, or camel packs for water, is not recommended.

Accommodation is plentiful and, therefore, there is no need to camp or take camping equipment. Likewise, most guesthouses will supply a towel and toiletries, even in the more remote areas of the country.

Another major piece of advice is spares – take spares for your bike. Whilst most towns and villages will have a local bike mechanic, there are always sections between that may need spares to be utilised. Take a spare inner tube, a puncture repair kit and a pump as a minimum. However, it is also prudent to take a spare spoke and a multi-tool to allow roadside repairs.

Maps and directional equipment are not essential, mainly due to the small number of roads and the reasonable signage in the country.

Finally, sunscreen, hats and sunglasses are all vital pieces of equipment. The average cyclist will spend 8–10 hours a day cycling in the sun. The choice of clothing needs to fit the conditions: usually loose-fitting tops and sportswear bottoms, with sandals or specific cycling shoes on the feet. Comfort in the warm, humid environment is crucial.

A – Z

A HANDY SUMMARY
OF PRACTICAL INFORMATION

A

Accommodation

Hotel and guesthouse standards in Laos, especially in the larger towns, have improved tremendously in recent years, though there are still relatively few luxury hotels, and these are mainly located in Vientiane and, increasingly, Luang Prabang. There are smaller, "boutique" hotels and spas in many locations, especially in Luang Prabang, where the old town's Unesco-protected status prohibits the building of multistorey structures that would change the former royal capital's character. Some of the most interesting places to stay include

former royal palaces or villas, such as Villa Santi in Luang Prabang and the Champasak Palace Hotel in Pakse. Elsewhere, in the Mekong Valley towns like Savannakhet and Tha Khaek, as well as in Luang Prabang and Vientiane, former French colonial buildings are being similarly restored to function as boutique hotels or superior-quality guesthouses. Hotels are springing up at a pace in locations with tourist attractions – Phonsavan is one such place. The Laos tourist industry is driving a hotel-building frenzy in places previously reserved for backpacker-style guesthouses.

Away from the few main tourist areas, however, it's a different matter. Most accommodation is

adequate – and improving – but aimed at a backpacker clientele, since wealthy businesspeople have little need to visit or stay in places like Attapeu, Luang Namtha or Udomxai. Therefore accommodation tends to be very reasonably priced, whether at mid-range or cheaper budget establishments.

Except in large, first-class hotels in Vientiane and at a few other locations, service can be slow, but is almost always friendly. Booking ahead by internet is easier than by telephone if you don't speak Lao (or Thai). Cable television has become increasingly common in recent years, with unlimited access to international news programmes – the Lao authorities, despite being

Prayer flags at Wat Phuang Kaew, Don Khong.

at least notionally Communist, make no attempt to restrict access to services such as the BBC, CNN or Al-Jazeera. Most quality hotels have gone wireless over the past five years, and even if there is no internet access in your room, the chances are that you can get online in the hotel lobby. Upcountry or in backpacker guesthouses it's still rare to find wireless internet access, but the chances are there will be an internet café just around the corner.

There are no truly outstanding websites for accommodation in Laos, and those that do exist are often out of date. Perhaps the best are www.visit-laos.com/hotels and www.asiawebdirect.com/laos.

Admission Charges

Admission charges remain something of an inexact science in Laos. As a basic rule, the further away from Vientiane and Luang Prabang, the less likelihood there is of having to pay admission charges. National museums and some of the more celebrated temples in Luang Prabang and Vientiane now impose a small charge, usually of US$1–2.

B

Budgeting for Your Trip

Laos remains a relatively inexpensive country, though of course it is possible to spend more if you stay in the most expensive hotels and dine in the most expensive restaurants. Essentially, budget travellers should allow US$30 a day, but even less than that away from Vientiane and the other main towns. Mid-range costs are around US$50–80 a day, while top end, including a self-

drive car, will cost in the region of US$100–200 per day.

C

Children

The family is the centre of Lao life and locals will take great pleasure in seeing a travelling family. Companionship and assistance will be abundant. Parents, however, should prepare their children for all the minor inconveniences and delays common when travelling in a developing country and, of course, take extra care with hygiene matters.

Children should never approach dogs, monkeys or other small animals anywhere without proper adult supervision; the risk of rabies is much higher here than at home.

For children from more temperate climes the tropical sun can be fierce, so high SPF sun-block lotion and hats are important.

Climate

Laos, like most of mainland Southeast Asia, has three main seasons. The rainy season, marked by the arrival of the monsoon between May and July, can last until as late as November. During this season, the weather is as hot and sticky as a bowl of sticky rice and – as one would expect – often wet; temperatures during the day average around 30°C (86°F) in the lowlands and 25°C (77°F) in the mountain valleys.

The monsoon is followed by a dry, cool season, from November until mid-February, which is overall the best time to visit. Days are still warm to hot, but overnight temperatures in the Mekong River Valley can drop as low as 14°C (57°F). It is notably colder in the north during these months: Luang Prabang averages around 28°C (82°F) in the day but just 13°C (55°F) at night in December and January, and often lower than that.

The third season, dry, increasingly hot and dusty, begins in late February and lasts until May; temperatures in the Mekong River Valley reach 38°C (100°F) in March and April. Again the temperatures are somewhat lower in the northern hills, particularly at night.

What to Wear

In general, the Lao seem quite happy with the recent influx of tourists to

Electricity

The electric system in Laos runs on a 220V AC circuit, and most outlets use two-prong flat or round sockets. Even in Vientiane, blackouts do happen, most often when the rains are heaviest in July and August. Some rural areas receive electricity only at certain times, while many villages manage to survive without any power at all.

their country. One aspect of this trend they tend to dislike, however, is the way many travellers dress while in Laos. The Lao are very conservative when it comes to dress, and expect foreign visitors to respect this custom.

Women should avoid clothing that bares the thighs, shoulders or breasts; long trousers, walking shorts and skirts are acceptable, while tank tops, short skirts and running shorts are not. Both men and women should dress conservatively, especially when making a visit to a temple or government office.

Sandals or shoes that can be taken off and on easily are a sensible idea, as shoes must always be removed before entering a Lao house or temple. See also Etiquette.

Whatever the season, bring lightweight cotton clothing and a light jacket or pullover for those rare, welcome, cool nights during December and January.

Crime and Safety

Petty crime as far as the visitor is concerned is almost non-existent in Laos, although over the last few years the number of tourists reporting thefts has certainly risen. By following a few simple rules most crimes are easily avoided. It is best not to flaunt your money and other valuables and always keep a lock on your packs and suitcases. The usual rules apply when travelling on buses and boats: keep a watch on your belongings and don't carry too much money in trouser pockets. Drugging and robbing tourists on long-distance buses and in restaurants has occurred recently, so the rule must always be to politely refuse food or drink from strangers and never leave food or drink unattended. When riding on buses try to get a seat near the middle of the vehicle. One danger is that presented by unexploded ordnance (UXO): the golden rule is

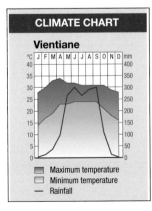

CLIMATE CHART

Vientiane

- Maximum temperature
- Minimum temperature
- Rainfall

to avoid straying off paths in remote areas, particularly in the east of the country,
Be aware that though drugs such as marijuana are readily available in Laos, they are illegal and police will come down hard on offenders. It is not unusual for a local to sell to a foreigner and then turn them into the police later.

Customs

There is little security at Laos's border checkpoints. Restrictions on drugs, weapons and pornography apply, but there is no limit on the amount of Lao and foreign currency you can bring into the country.

The duty-free allowance for each visitor is 1 litre of spirits, 2 litres of wine and 200 cigarettes, 50 cigars or 250g of tobacco, 250ml of cologne and 50ml of perfume. One regulation worth keeping in mind is the restriction on Buddha images and antiquities; travellers have been stopped on exit and detained while authorities examine a purchase to ensure that it is not a national treasure.

See also the Laos Customs website www.laocustoms.laopdr.net.

D

Disabled Travellers

Facilities for disabled travellers scarcely exist in Laos, and this is a difficult country for the disabled to travel in – at least beyond Vientiane and Luang Prabang. Relatively few hotels or guesthouses have elevators, and there are no special ramps for wheelchairs.

E

Embassies and Consulates

Lao Embassies and Consulates Overseas

Australia and New Zealand
1 Dalman Crescent, O'Malley, Canberra, ACT 2606
Tel: 61 2-6286 4595
www.laosembassy.net
United Kingdom
49 Porchester Terrace, London W2 3TS
Tel: 030-20 7402 3770
United States
2222 S Street NW, Washington DC 20008

A monsoon storm closes in.

Tel: 1 202-332 6416
www.laoembassy.com

Foreign Embassies in Vientiane
Australia
Km 4, Thadeua Road, Ban Wat Nak
Tel: 021-353 800
www.laos.embassy.gov.au
United Kingdom
Yokkabat Street, Phonexay
Tel: 030-770 0000
www.gov.uk/government/world/laos
United States
Km 9, Thadeua Road, Ban Somvang Thai
Tel: 021-487 000
www.usembassy.gov

Etiquette

The best thing any visitor to Laos can do is smile, smile and smile again. As in other Buddhist countries, remember to dress neatly (see also What to Wear), and always remove your shoes when entering a private house or a temple. Women should avoid touching monks – to give a monk anything, first pass it to a male to hand to the monk. Keeping calm in tense situations is most important; the Lao do not take kindly to someone losing their temper. The only thing anger achieves is more frustration. Beware of touching someone on the head: it is believed that one's vital essence resides in the head and therefore even a hairdresser will always ask permission before touching.

Emergencies

Police Tel: 191
Fire Tel: 190
Ambulance Tel: 195

G

Gay and Lesbian Travellers

As with the attitude towards women, there exists in Laos a dichotomy between the political (Communist) and social (Buddhist) perceptions of gays. While the traditional attitudes towards homosexuality are relaxed, the government takes a dim view. While travelling gay couples are not affected by this, the law prohibits "cohabitation" between Laos and foreigners, regardless of their sexual orientation.

H

Health and Medical Care

Laos is still a developing country, and it is a good idea to take the necessary health precautions before arriving. The following immunisations, some of which require multiple injections, are recommended: hepatitis A, typhoid, diptheria, tetanus, hepatitis B, polio and tuberculosis. Optional vaccinations include rabies and Japanese B encephalitis, a mosquito-borne disease that is very rare. Medicine to combat malaria – common in Laos outside Vientiane – is available, but consult a doctor before beginning any medication.

While in the country, be particularly careful of water and ice; only consume water that comes from carefully sealed containers or has been boiled thoroughly. Heat exhaustion and prickly heat can result from dehydration and salt

LAOS

CAMBODIA

deficiency, so drink lots of fluids, avoid intense activity when the sun is strongest, and rest frequently during the day. Travellers' diarrhoea is quite common, though usually not serious; be sure to avoid dehydration problems by replacing the fluids your body will lose.

Medical Services

Medical services in Laos are limited; the most extensive are in Vientiane, where even the two state hospitals, **Mahosot** and **Clinique Setthathirat**, are not up to international standards. Even the **International Clinic** at Mahosot is best reserved for only minor injuries. The **Friendship Hospital** is a specialised medical centre for trauma and orthopaedics. Most foreign residents requiring minor medical attention choose to visit the **Australian Embassy's** clinic, but pay US$50 per consultation. All numbers are for Vientiane.

Australian Clinic
Australian Embassy,
Thadeua Road
Tel: 021-353 840
http://laos.embassy.gov.au
Setthathirat Hospital
Thadeua Road, Ban Thaphalansa
Tel: 021-314 944
Friendship Hospital
Phontong Road,
Ban Phonsavang
Tel: 021-710 004
International Clinic, Mahosot Hospital
Fa Ngum, Ban KaoNyot
Tel: 021-214 022
Many Vientiane residents and expats opt for facilities just across the river in Thailand.
AEK Udon International Hospital
555/5 Posri Road, Udon Thani, Thailand
Tel: 66 42-342 555
www.aekudon.com

Nong Khai Wattana Hospital
1159/4 Moo 2, Prachak Road,
Nong Khai, Thailand
Tel: 66 42-465 201/8
www.wattanahospital.net

Internet

Internet cafés are found all over town in Vientiane, Luang Prabang and Vang Vieng, which receive the highest numbers of travellers, and connections are very good. Costs are also low in these major towns because of stiff competition, and can be as cheap as 100 kip per minute (about US$0.10). In many of the other provinces, internet facilities are becoming increasingly available and reliable, but costs are higher in places in which only one or two shops offer internet-based services. Visual internet telephony and PC-to-phone services are also well supported. In addition, stored-value pay-as-you-use internet cards, for use with land lines, can be purchased from Lao Telecom branches and at some internet cafés and retail outlets.

M

Media

Newspapers and Magazines

The Lao government produces two newspapers for the expat community in Vientiane: the English-language *Vientiane Times* (www.vientianetimes.org.la) and the French-language *Le Rénovateur* (http://le-renovateur. net). The latter has a far snappier design, and also tends to be more up-to-date on current events in town, so go for that one if you can read French. The state-run *kpl News* (http://kpl.gov.la/En/Default.aspx)

puts out a daily news bulletin in English. The *Bangkok Post* (www.bangkokpost.com) and *The Nation* (www.nationmultimedia.com), the two main English-language dailies from Bangkok, are available in hotels, shops and restaurants in Vientiane.

A good selection of English-language, coffee-table books and other trade titles, maps and postcards can be found at the biggest bookshop in Vientiane, Monument Books. The Book Café specialises in second-hand books.
Monument Books
124/1 Nokeo Khumman Road
www.monument-books.com/laos.php
Tel: 021-243 708
Book Café
Heng Boun Road
Tel: 020-5689 3741

Television and Radio

The Lao government broadcasts on one radio station – Lao National Radio – throughout the country, but most Lao rely on Thai radio for entertainment. Expats often use shortwave to pick up programmes from the BBC, VOA and Australia Broadcasting Corporation.

Lao National Television now has two channels but, again, almost all Lao prefer Thai television; as you make your way around the country, you will probably find most televisions tuned to one of the popular Thai soap operas. Satellite TV is now widely available in Vientiane and Luang Prabang, offering channels like CNN, MTV and BBC World Service.

Money

The unit of currency is the kip, and notes are now issued in the following denominations: 500, 1,000, 2,000, 5,000, 10,000, 20,000, 50,000 and 100,000. There are no coins, and notes smaller than 500 have been rendered obsolete. While stores and services in Laos are officially forbidden to use any other currency, virtually any merchant will (gladly) accept US dollars or Thai baht in lieu of the shaky kip. Nonetheless, one should keep a supply of the local currency on hand for making small purchases.

You can buy kip at foreign exchange banks and other exchange offices. At time of press, US$1 was roughly equivalent to 8,100 kip. The kip is not a convertible currency outside Laos and should therefore be used up before departure. It is possible to change kip into US$

Lao Massage

In addition to the services of major hotels, good massage parlours can be found in major cities around the country. Traditional Lao massage can be quite rigorous, so be prepared to have every part of the body worked.

Vientiane

Champa Spa
Pangkham Road
Tel: 021-251 926
http://champaspa.com
Traditional massage parlour with

a number of different packages to choose from.
Sokpaluang Temple
Sokpaluang Road
Traditional massage, herbal saunas, herbal tea.

Luang Prabang

Lao Red Cross
Wisunalat Road
Housed in a beautifully restored Lao-French building, the Red Cross offers traditional herbal saunas and a combination Swedish-Lao massage.

Public Holidays

The following days are observed as official public holidays. The public holidays associated with the beginning and the end of the Buddhist fasting period are movable lunar dates:

1 January New Year's Day
6 January Pathet Lao Day
20 January Army Day
14 February Chinese and Vietnamese New Year
8 March International Women's Day
22 March People's Party Day
13, 14, 15 April *Pi Mai Lao* (Lao New Year)
28 April *Vesak Day* (Buddha Day)
1 May Labour Day
1 June Children's Day
June/July *Khao Pansa* (Buddhist fasting period begins)
13 August *Lao Issara* (Free Laos Day)
September/October *Bouk Ok Pansa* (End of Buddhist fasting period)
12 October Liberation Day
2 December Lao National Day

at Vientiane airport, sometimes at Luang Prabang airport, and possibly at a private money changer (for a lousy rate). Otherwise it's virtually impossible.

Most major international currencies, as well as travellers' cheques in US dollars, pounds sterling, and often euros, can be exchanged at banks and money changers in major towns. The Lao almost always use cash, but credit cards are accepted at more and more hotels, restaurants and shops in Vientiane and Luang Prabang, where a 5 percent service charge is sometimes added to the bill. Cash advances can also be obtained on a visa/MasterCard in Vientiane. There are some ATMs in Vientiane now, though they may not always be reliable. Banks are usually open Monday to Friday 8.30am–4pm.

Vientiane

ANZ Vientiane Commercial Bank
33 Lane Xang Avenue
Tel: 021-222 700
Banque pour le Commerce Extérieur Lao
1 Pangkham Street
Tel: 021-213 200
www.bcellaos.com
Indochina Bank
Capital Tower, 116, 23 Singha Road
Tel: 021-455 000-2

www.indochinabank.com
Joint Development Bank
82 Lane Xang Avenue
Tel: 021-213 532-6
www.jdbbank.com.la
Lao Development Bank
13 Souphanouvong Road
Tel: 021-213 300-4
www.ldblao.la
Siam Commercial Bank
117 Lane Xang Avenue
Tel: 021-213 500-1
www.scb.co.th
Western Union
Krungsri Ayuthaya Bank, 84/1 Lane Xang Avenue
Tel: 021-214 575-7
www.krungsri.com

Luang Prabang

Lao Development Bank
Wisunalat Road
Tel: 071-212 185
www.ldblao.la

Savannakhet

Lao Development Bank
30 Oudomsin Road
Tel: 041-212 226
www.ldblao.la

Pakse

Lao Development Bank
No. 13 Road South
Tel: 031-212 173
www.ldblao.la

Huay Xai

Lao Development Bank
Ban Konekeo
Tel: 084-211 492
www.ldblao.la

Banknotes of the Lao currency, the kip.

Tipping

Tipping is not expected in Laos, except at a few upmarket restaurants in Vientiane and Luang Prabang, where you might leave 10–15 percent if a service charge has not already been added to your bill. Taxi and tuk-tuk drivers also do not expect to be tipped, unless the trip was unusually difficult or much longer than originally expected.

O

Opening Hours

Government offices are officially open 8am–noon and 1–4.30pm, Monday to Friday. But don't expect to get anything done after 11.30am or before 2pm, during which time most employees are enjoying lunch and a midday rest at home.

Most shops close for an hour during lunch, and are open for a half-day on Saturday. Almost all businesses are closed on Sunday.

P

Photography

Internet cafés and photographic shops are attuned to the needs of the travelling digital photographer, and can transfer images stored on a digital camera memory card to a CD ROM. Shops in the major towns will carry memory cards and batteries.

On the whole Lao people do not object to having their pictures taken,

LAOS

CAMBODIA

Telephone Area Codes

Champasak 031
Huay Xai 084
Luang Nam Tha 086
Luang Prabang 071
Pakse 031
Paksan 054
Phongsali 088
Sainyabuli 074
Sam Neua 064
Savannakhet 041
Sekong 038
Tha Kaek 051
Udomxai 081
Vang Vieng 023
Vientiane 021
Xieng Khuang 061

but it is still polite to ask permission before doing so as some will actively dislike having their pictures taken. Always show restraint when photographing people at prayer, and monks. Avoid photographing anything to do with the military.

Postal Services

The Lao postal service offers reliable service at reasonable prices. There are post offices in every provincial capital, painted in the same colour scheme of mustard yellow. For sending packages abroad, most expats use the **Express Mail Service (EMS)**.

Receiving incoming mail at the main post office in Vientiane is possible, although remember that all packages must be opened and their contents displayed for inspection. Residents check their boxes at the post office daily, as there is no home-delivery service.

A number of international courier agencies offer their services in Vientiane:
DHL Laos
#031 Group 03,
Ban Wattaynoy Thong,
Nongno Street
Tel: 021-214 868
www.dhl.com.la
Express Mail Service (EMS)
Vientiane Post Office
Saylom Road
Tel: 021-216 425
www.ems.post
FedEx
Vientiane Post Office
Saylom Road
Tel: 021-223 278
www.fedex.com/la/
Lao Freight Forwarder
Km 3, Thadeua Road
Tel: 021-313 321
www.laoff.laopdr.com

Overseas Courier Service Laos
8 Luang Prabang Road,
Ban Khountathong
Tel: 021-263 378
www.ocs.co.th/Laos/
TNT Express Laos
Luang Prabang Road, 3rd floor, Thai Airways International Office
Tel: 021-261 918
www.tnt.com

Public Toilets

These scarcely exist, and most people will be obliged to use hotel or restaurant toilets in the towns, or the great outdoors when upcountry. The upside is that toilets are generally clean. Bring your own paper, or learn to use water to wash with like the locals.

R

Religious Services

A number of religious communities in Vientiane offer services to the public:

Christian
Church of the Holy Spirit
ARDA Centre
93 Luang Prabang Road
Tel: 021-217 162
www.the-chs.org
Church of the Sacred Heart
193 Samsenthai Road
Tel: 021-216 219
Lao Evangelical Church
Luang Prabang Road, Ban Nakham
Tel: 021-216 052, 216 222
Seventh Day Adventist
Nong Bone Road
Tel: 021-412 701
www.adventist.la

Baha'i
The Spiritual Assembly of the Bahá'ís of Lao People's Democratic Republic
P.O. Box 189
nsalaos@gmail.com

Muslim
Jamia Masjid
Ban Xengyen, near Namphu Circle
Tel: 020-5561 3302

T

Telephones

Until 1990, Laos was connected with the world, except Thailand and the USSR, by only one phone line – only one incoming or outgoing international call could be placed

at a time. Things have changed a lot since then, with all major towns linked by phone and International Direct Dialling (IDD) widely available, providing a reliable service to more than 150 destinations worldwide.

International calls can be made from Lao Telecom offices (usually operator-assisted), at post offices, or from public phones with IDD facility. For the last you will need to purchase a phone card, which is available at post and telecommunication offices as well as many shops throughout the country. Fax services are also available at most Lao Telecom offices and many post offices. Many other places, such as hotels and guesthouses, also have phone, fax and email facilities.

To call long distance within the country, dial 0 first, then the provincial area code and number. For international calls, dial 00 first, country code, then the area code and number. Mobile phone numbers in Laos normally begin with the prefix 020.

Mobile Telephones
Mobile phone coverage is surprisingly good throughout the country. In addition to Lao Telecom (Laotel; Call Centre tel: 101), a handful of other local service providers also offer mobile phone services, including Enterprise of Telecommunications Lao (ETL). Visitors with GSM-enabled mobile phones can buy a starter kit from ETL (www.etllao.com) for US$5, which consists of a SIM card with a local phone number and about 20,000 kip (about US$2) worth of stored value, from which international and local calls and text messages can be made. The credit can be topped up at any ETL outlet or newsagents.

Tourist Information

Department of Tourism Marketing of the Ministry of Information, Culture and Tourism
Lane Xang Avenue, Ban Hatsady
Tel: 021-212 248/251
www.tourismlaos.org
This government-run tourism office can provide some good information about tours in the country. It is also cooperating with local tour operators

Time Zone

Laos is 7 hours ahead of Greenwich Mean Time (GMT).

Lao postage stamps.

in providing ecotourism tours. See also www.ecotourismlaos.com for more internet resources.

Websites

Ecotourism Laos: Set up by the Lao National Tourism Administration, this site offers information on Lao travel facts and practicalities; advice on the dos and don'ts in the country; suggestions on travel-related activities. There are also online maps and a photo gallery, and listings for accommodation and tour operators. www.ecotourismlaos.com
Lao Embassy in the US: A good place to check for current information on visa regulations, this site includes helpful links to government departments and affiliated organisations. www.laoembassy.com
Vientiane Times: The website of the Ministry of Information, Culture and Tourism's English-language newspaper, offering archived articles and good links to other news sources about Laos. www.vientianetimes.org.la
Travel Lao PDR: A comprehensive site offering detailed travel information and contacts for hotels and transportation. www.travel.laopdr.com
Greater Mekong Subregion: Official tourism website for this region, covering Laos, Cambodia, Myanmar, Thailand, Vietnam and Yunnan province (China). www.visit-mekong.com
Visit Laos: This informative website has general information on Lao language, history and culture, and on each province. www.visit-laos.com
Travelfish: This contains well-written and up-to-date write-ups on Laos and its provinces. Included are travel information, hotel and restaurant reviews, suggested activities, a

travellers' forum and an FAQ section. www.travelfish.org
Tripadvisor: A treasure trove of advice and reviews, (good and bad) from fellow travellers, covering restaurants, accommodation, nightlife and much, much more. www.tripadvisor.com

Travel Agencies

Vientiane
Diethelm Travel Laos, Ltd.
Phonsinuan Village
Tel: 021-262 058
www.diethelmtravel.com
Exo Travel
15 Kaysone Road
Tel: 021-454 640
www.exotravel.com
Green Discovery Laos
Hang Boun Road
Tel: 021-264 680
www.greendiscoverylaos.com
Inter-Lao Tourism
111 Ban Mixay, Setthathirat Road
Tel: 021-214 669
www.interlao.com

Luang Prabang
Diethelm Travel Laos, Ltd
Ban Visoun, No. 94
Tel: 071-261 011-3
www.diethelmtravel.com
Exo Travel
44/3 Ban Wat Nong,
Khem Khong Road
Tel: 071-252 879
www.exotravel.com
Tiger Trail Travel
Ban Phon Peng Road
Tel: 071-252 655
www.laos-adventures.com

Pakse
Diethelm Travel Laos, Ltd.
Ban Thaluang

Tel: 031-212 596
www.diethelmtravel.com

V

Visas and Passports

To enter Laos you must have a valid passport. Citizens of all countries are also required to apply for an entry tourist visa, except as follows: Brunei Darussalam, Cambodia, Malaysia, Philippines, Singapore, Thailand and Vietnam. Thirty-day single-entry tourist visas are issued on arrival at Wattay International Airport in Vientiane, Luang Prabang International Airport, Pakse International Airport, and at the international border checkpoints (see page 322). You will need one passport photo and between US$30 and US$45 (visa fees vary depending on what passport you are holding) for the visa application. There is an "overtime" charge of US$1 for entry after 4pm and at weekends. Alternatively, 30-day tourist visas and 30-day business visas can be obtained in advance of your trip at a Lao embassy or consulate, or at travel agencies in any major city in Asia.

Extension of Stay
Visa extensions can be obtained from the Lao Immigration Office at the Ministry of the Interior in Vientiane, opposite Talaat Sao (Morning Market), tel: 021-212 529. The cost is US$2 per day up to a maximum of 30 days. Tour agencies, guesthouses and some cafés can also arrange visa extensions for a small fee. Overstaying your visa will cost US$10 for each day.

W

Weights and Measures
Metric.

Women Travellers
Attitudes towards women in Laos are somewhat contradictory. While the socialist ethic espouses gender parity, traditional Buddhist beliefs give women a lower status than men. Lao men have little of the conception of foreign women as "easy" and the woman traveller is unlikely to be subjected to unwanted attention. On the other hand, the Lao are very group-oriented, and a woman travelling alone would seem odd to the Lao.

LAOS

CAMBODIA

LANGUAGE

UNDERSTANDING THE LANGUAGE

GENERAL

what? *nyang?*
who? *pai?*
when? *vila?*
where? *sai?*
why? *ben nyang?*
how? *nyow dai?*
What is this? *an nee men nyang?*
Do you speak English/French/Lao?
wow dai baw passa ungkit/falang/lao?

GREETINGS

Hello *sabai dee*
Goodbye (person leaving) *la gon*
Goodbye (person staying) *sok dee*
Nice to meet you *nyin dee tee hu chak*
What is your name? *chao seu nyang?*
My name is... *koy seu...*
Where are you from? *Chao ma tae sai?*
**I come from the USA/England/
Canada/France** *koy ma tae
amelikaa/ungkit/kanada/falang*
How are you? *sabai dee baw?*
I'm fine *sabai dee*
Excuse me *kho thoht*
Thank you *kop chai*
You're welcome *baw pen nyang*

DIRECTIONS/
TRANSPORT

Where is...? *you sai...?*
toilet *hong nam*
restaurant *han ahan*
hotel *hong haem*
bank *tanakan*
hospital *hong maw*
police station *satanee tamluat*
left *sai*
right *kua*
car *lot nyai*
bus *lot meh*

bus station *satanee lotmeh*
bicycle *lot teep*
aeroplane *nyon*
motorcycle *lot chak*
pedicab *sam law*
post office *bai sanee*
tourist office *hong kan tong teeow*
embassy *satantut*

SHOPPING

How much is...? *tow dai...?*
this one *toh nee*
that one *toh nan*
money *ngeun*
change *ngeun noi*
price *lakaa*
cheap *teuk*
expensive *peng*

RESTAURANTS

eat *gin khao*
drink *deum*
drinking water *nam deum*
cold water *nam yen*
ice *nam kon*
tea *nam saa*
coffee *ka fei*
milk *nom*

Language Schools

A number of language schools
in Vientiane offer short-term Lao
language classes:
Lao-American College (LAC)
Phonkheng Village
Tel: 021-900 454
Vientiane College
23 Singha Road
Tel: 021-414 873
www.vientianecollege.com

sugar *nam tan*
rice *khao*
fish *bpa*
beef *sin ngua*
pork *moo*
chicken *gai*
plate *chan*

DAYS AND TIME

Monday *wan chan*
Tuesday *wan angkan*
Wednesday *wan put*
Thursday *wan pahad*
Friday *wan souk*
Saturday *wan sao*
Sunday *wan ateet*
today *meu nee*
this morning *sao nee*
this evening *meu leng*
tomorrow *meu eun*
yesterday *meu wan nee*
What time is it? *chak mong laeoh?*

NUMBERS

zero *soun*
one *neung*
two *song*
three *sam*
four *see*
five *ha*
six *hok*
seven *jet*
eight *baet*
nine *gao*
ten *sip*
eleven *sip-et*
twenty *sao*
twenty-one *sao-et*
twenty-two *sao-song*
thirty *sam-sip*
hundred *loi*
thousand *pan*
million *lan*

FURTHER READING

CULTURE AND RELIGION

Lao Textiles and Traditions by Mary Connors. The authoritative text on Lao textiles, this widely quoted volume offers a clear introduction to history, style and technique.
Traditional Recipes of Laos by Phia Sing. This book, written by the former chef and Social Director at the Royal Palace in Luang Prabang, contains recipes for traditional Lao dishes and Luang Prabang specialities.
Treasure from Laos. A beautifully produced cultural history of Laos featuring old black-and-white images.

HISTORY AND POLITICS

Lao Peasants Under Socialism by Grant Evans. A harsh analysis of the Communist programme in Laos and the failure of socialism to better the lives of rural Lao citizens.
Politics of Ritual and Remembrance: Laos since 1975 by Grant Evans. An engaging work full of provocative observations about the period between the pre- and post-war regimes, the exploitation by the Party of religious symbols and traditions, and the challenges facing the current Communist regime.
Tragic Mountains: The Hmong, the Americans and the Secret Wars for Laos, 1942–92 by Jane Hamilton-Merritt. A former foreign correspondent in Laos, Hamilton-Merritt documents the Hmong struggle for freedom.
The Politics of Heroin in Southeast Asia by Alfred W. McCoy. The classic work on the politics and economics of opium production in the region.
The Ravens: Pilots of the Secret War of Laos by Christopher Robbins. This entertaining book relates the story of the American air war in Laos with an emphasis on tactical details.

In Search of Southeast Asia: A Modern History edited by David J. Steinberg. One of the most highly regarded introductions to the history of the region, this text includes limited material on Laos, but offers a discussion of the larger historical context from which the country has never been separate.
Buddhist Kingdom, Marxist State: The Making of Modern Laos by Martin Stuart-Fox. In this work on post-1975 Lao politics and history, the author provides one of the clearest discussions of the emergence, victory and rule of the Pathet Lao.
A History of Laos by Martin Stuart-Fox. The best English-language general history of Laos in print, this volume offers a clear and comprehensive narrative that focuses on the development of Lao nationalism in the years since World War II.
Shooting at the Moon: The Story of America's Clandestine War in Laos by Roger Warner. An enjoyable, though profoundly disturbing, history of the secret American war in Laos, using material gleaned from declassified US government material and extensive interviews.

TRAVEL

A Dragon Apparent: Travels in Cambodia, Laos and Vietnam by Norman Lewis. A first-class travel narrative of the 1950s that gives you a sense of just how much – and how little – has changed in Indochina since the early post-war days.
The Lands of Charm and Cruelty: Travels in Southeast Asia by Stan Stesser. Originally published in The New Yorker, Stesser's section on Laos provides an entertaining and insightful look at Lao politics and society in the early 1990s.
Another Quiet American: Stories of Life in Laos by Brett Dakin. An amusing and informed account of

life in contemporary Laos by a former American resident of Vientiane.

CONTEMPORARY FICTION

Mother's Beloved: Stories from Laos by Bounyavong Outhine. A collection of 14 short stories by a Vientiane-based novelist, these contemporary and near-contemporary tales reflect compassion and tradition, often in the face of adversity.
The Coroner's Lunch by Colin Cotterill. The first of a series of six books by English writer Colin Cotterill, all set in Laos and featuring an unlikely but endearing Lao detective, Dr Siri.

NATURAL HISTORY

A Photographic Guide to Birds of Vietnam, Cambodia and Laos by Peter Davidson. A handy guide to the colourful birdlife of Indochina.
The Birds of South-East Asia, a Field Guide by Craig Robson. The definitive comprehensive guide for birdwatchers.
A Field Guide to the Mammals of South-East Asia by Charles Francis. The first detailed guide to the wildlife of mainland Southeast Asia from Indochina south to Malaysia.

OTHER INSIGHT GUIDES

Insight Guide Southeast Asia is a superbly illustrated guide covering the region. Individual titles to this region include Insight Guides to Bali and Lombok, Indonesia, Malaysia, Myanmar (Burma), Philippines, Thailand and Vietnam, as well as City Guides to Kuala Lumpur and Singapore.
Insight Guide: Explore feature self-guided walks and tours and include a useful full-size fold-out map. Southeast Asian titles include Bali, Bangkok and Kuala Lumpur.

LAOS

CAMBODIA

TRANSPORT

GETTING THERE AND GETTING AROUND

GETTING THERE

By Air

Most international visitors to Cambodia arrive by air at either **Phnom Penh International Airport** or **Siem Reap-Angkor International Airport**. In response to the Cambodian government's open skies policy, an increasing number of airlines are flying into Cambodia via a number of regional airports in Asia, including Bangkok, Ho Chi Minh City, Hanoi, Kuala Lumpur, Singapore, Taipei, Kunming, Hong Kong, Seoul, Vientiane and Luang Prabang.

The airlines serving Cambodia include Bangkok Airways, Cambodia Angkor Air, China Southern Airlines, Dragonair, Emirates Airlines, EVA Air, Lao Airlines, Malaysia Airlines, Shanghai Airlines, Silk Air, Thai Airways and Vietnam Airlines. Budget carriers Jetstar Asia, operating from Singapore, and Air Asia operating from Kuala Lumpur, now offer flights to Phnom Penh and Siem Reap. Air Asia also flies from Bangkok to Phnom Penh.

A departure tax of US$25 is included in the price of all international flights. For a comprehensive list of airlines flying to and from Cambodia, as well as for flight details and schedules, call the airport information hotline (tel: 023-890 890), or visit www.cambodia-airports.com.

By Land

For foreign visitors, there are several points of entry into Cambodia by road.

From Thailand, the most popular points of entry are at Poipet/Banteay Meanchey, Cham Yeam/Koh Kong and O'Smach/Ordor Meanchey. There are also entry points at Choam and Pruhm, but these crossings are located in the more remote areas of the country.

From Vietnam, you can enter at Bavet/Svay Rieng, Prek Chak/Xa Xia, Phnom Den/Tinh Bien, O Yadaw/Le Tanh, Trapaeng Thlong/Xa Mat, Trapaeng Sre/Loc Ninh, Banteay Chakrey/Khanh Binh and Kham Sam Nor/Kandal. From Laos, cross at Dom Kralor/Stung Treng, but the situation sometimes changes, so check with your consulate or travel agent before travelling.

Cambodian border guards are notorious for running scams and overcharging. Their efforts usually only amount to the loss of a few dollars, but it's a good idea to bring yourself up-to-date on the most recent border regulations before you cross, as a precaution.

By Sea

It is possible to travel between Kep or Sihanoukville and Phu Quoc, a large island resort controlled by Vietnam. Ferries and private charters run between the destinations but transportation must be confirmed in advance and likewise visas should be secured at embassies prior to departure.

GETTING AROUND

On Arrival

Phnom Penh International Airport

The airport is 10km (6 miles) from the centre of Phnom Penh, and the journey into town takes around 20 minutes. The average fare to Phnom Penh centre is about US$12 by taxi or US$7 by tuk-tuk.

Siem Reap-Angkor International Airport

The airport is located about 8km (5 miles) from town. The journey by taxi or moto will take 10–15 minutes. Most hotels, as well as some of the better guesthouses, provide airport transfers for guests who have confirmed reservations.

By Air

Cambodian Angkor Air and Cambodian Bayon Airlines serve Siem Reap, Sihanoukville, and Phnom Penh. Bassaka Air serves Phnom Penh and Siem Reap. Routes and timetables change frequently. Consult the airlines or your travel agent, or check flight schedules on www.cambodia-airports.com. A domestic airport tax of US$6 is levied and included in the ticket price.

By Bus

Several air-conditioned bus services offer comfortable and affordable trips between Phnom Penh and various destinations, including Siem Reap, Sihanoukville, Kampot/Kep, Battambang, Kompong Cham, Kratie and Poipet. The road to Sihanoukville is one of the best in the country.

Shorter trips to places such as Udong or Kompong Chhnang can also easily be made by air-conditioned buses. Many bus services depart from the bus terminal near *Psar Thmay* (Central

Market). You can also check with your guesthouse or a travel agent.

By Boat

Air-conditioned boats ply the route between Phnom Penh and Siem Reap, departing just beyond the Japanese Bridge at the northern end of Phnom Penh. Travelling up the Sap River, you will pass Cham fishing communities and, as the boat enters Tonlé Sap, large Vietnamese and Khmer boat communities can be seen. The journey takes around 6 hours and usually begins at 7am. Chances are that the boats are overcrowded and you will have to ride on the roof. With the improvement of the roads between the two cities, however, this mode of transport is fast losing its popularity to air-conditioned buses, which are cheaper, more comfortable and far quicker. Boat services to Kompong Cham or Kratie from Phnom Penh have been discontinued due to declining demand.

By Train

Passenger rail services are being renovated but their future schedules and development remains uncertain and precarious. Traditionally train travel in Cambodia was neither comfortable nor convenient though new projects may change this.

Taxis, Tuk-Tuks and Pedicabs

Motorcycle taxis, or "motos", as they are known, can be found all over the country. The drivers are usually recognisable by the fact that they wear hats of some sort (helmets are now required for the driver, but not the passenger). Because taxis are usually hard to find in Phnom Penh, the moto is the best way to get somewhere quickly. Many moto drivers speak some English. Expect to pay US$1 for a short journey, and US$2 for longer ones. Always agree the fare beforehand. Motos normally wait at the airport, and this can be

a viable way into town if you arrive alone. The fare is less than US$5.

In Phnom Penh and Angkor the "cyclo" or pedicab was once popular but has gradually fallen out of favour, as the tuk-tuk has risen to take its place. Tuk-tuks are large, four-wheel covered wagons that are pulled by motorbikes. Tuk-tuks can carry up to four passengers, though they are more comfortable for two. Among tourists, they are more popular than motos, though they can be up to double the price; and are not necessarily a safer mode of transport. Air-conditioned taxis are readily available at the airports. Within Phnom Penh city, they may be difficult to locate quickly. In Siem Reap, there are plenty of taxis ready and willing to take you around the temples at Angkor. At the time of writing they charge at least US$60 for a full day in and around Angkor and Siem Reap. You may have to pay up to US$100 to visit the temples further afield.

An option for long-distance travel is the share-taxi. These vehicles ply between Phnom Penh and all the major towns. The drivers may wait until they have filled the vehicle to overflowing, sometimes taking up to six or seven passengers, so this is not always a comfortable form of transport, although it is certainly a cheap way to get around.

Alternatively, freelance taxi drivers can be arranged via your hotel, guesthouse, or contact a taxi firm such as Global Taxi (tel: 011 311 888) in Phnom Penh.

Bicycle and Vehicle Hire

In many parts of Cambodia, bicycles are offered to rent. These bicycles are often older-style road bicycles but are usually well maintained and the rental charges are small. Cycling around the smaller towns and cities of Cambodia can be a great way to see the sights. Never leave your passport as a guarantee for the bicycle you rent.

Tourists are not allowed to drive their own cars in Phnom Penh and Siem Reap, and must hire a driver. Motorcycle rental is allowed in most of Cambodia, but not in Siem Reap and Angkor. In Sihanoukville, car and motorcycle rentals are occasionally problematic due to the daily whims of local police. The car and motorcycle rental regulations change from time to time, so it is necessary to plan ahead of travel.

Airline Offices

Air Asia
179 Street Sisowath,
Phnom Penh
Tel: 023-983 777
www.airasia.com
Air France
Tel: 023-965 500
www.airfrance.com
Asiana Airlines
A16 Domestic Terminal Office Building,
Phnom Penh
Tel: 023-890 441-2
http://ea.flyasiana.com
Bangkok Airways
61A Street 214,
Phnom Penh
Tel: 023-971 771
www.bangkokair.com
Cambodia Angkor Air
206A Norodom Boulevard,
Phnom Penh
Tel: 023-666 6786
www.cambodiaangkorair.com
China Southern Airlines Co., Ltd.
Hotline: 4006695539-1-1,
4006695539-1-2
www.csair.com
Dragonair
Suite 12–14C, Regency Complex C,
168 Monireth Boulevard,
Phnom Penh
Hotline: 1800 209783
www.dragonair.com
EVA Air
Suite 11-14B/79, Street 205,

Phnom Penh
Tel: 023-210 303
www.evaair.com
Jetstar Airways
Tel: 023-220 909
www.jetstar.com
Korean Air
Tel: 023-224-047
www.koreanair.com
Lao Airlines
58B Sihanouk Blvd,
Phnom Penh
Tel: 023-216 563
www.laoairlines.com
Malaysia Airlines
35-37 Street 214,
Phnom Penh
Tel: 023-962 508
www.malaysiaairlines.com
Silk Air
2-4A, Regency C, Samdech Monireth,
Phnom Penh
Tel: 023-988 629
www.silkair.com
Singapore Airlines
www.singaporeair.com
Thai Airways International
298 Mao Tse Toung Boulevard,
Phnom Penh
Tel: 023-214 359
www.thaiairways.com
Vietnam Airlines
41 Street 214, Phnom Penh
Tel: 023-990 840
www.vietnamairlines.com

A – Z

A HANDY SUMMARY
OF PRACTICAL INFORMATION

A

Accommodation

Luxury accommodation in Cambodia is limited to a few major centres: Phnom Penh, Siem Reap and Sihanoukville. Phnom Penh offers a fine choice of luxury accommodation at very reasonable prices, considering the amenities on offer. Mid-level accommodation can be found in abundance and is usually quite comfortable. At the lower end, guesthouses are common, and some of them are excellent. Compared with what was available a few years ago, the general situation in Cambodia has improved tremendously. Above the US$15 or $20 level all rooms will be air-conditioned and normally have satellite television and a refrigerator. Hot water is usually available in mid-level and luxury accommodation. Under US$15 usually gets you a cold shower and ceiling fan. You may or may not have windows and a TV with international cable stations.

Booking ahead is a good idea, particularly in Phnom Penh and Siem Reap, as well as Sihanoukville during high season (roughly October to March). It's best to book directly through the hotel or through an online service rather than a tour office. Tour offices will mark up the price considerably. Moto and tuk-tuk drivers can drive you around and help you find accommodation when you first arrive. However, be aware that they receive a commission from the hotel, which may be added to the price of the room. Beware of taxi drivers at the airport who try to tell you that your chosen hotel is already full, under renovation or full of prostitutes. This will rarely, if ever, be true. It's common for taxi drivers to pull a bait-and-switch, taking you to the wrong hotel (one where they collect a commission). If this happens, hold your ground (unless the other hotel looks like a better deal), and don't pay the difference in the fare to take you to the correct hotel.

Bed bugs can be a problem in Cambodia's budget hotels. Check for grey stains on sheets, tiny exoskeletons on the floor (particularly behind and under the bed), blood smears on walls, and tiny bugs (or black deposits of faeces in nests) in the folds of the mattress. Where signs are found, do not simply change rooms – it's best to find another hotel entirely.

Unlike in Vietnam or Laos, Cambodian hotels do not need to retain passports to present to police. Receptionists will copy basic information and then immediately return them to guests.

Useful hotel booking services include www.cambodia-hotels.com and www.agoda.com.

Admission Charges

Admission charges vary widely. Sights off the beaten track generally have cheap admission charges, while places that receive lots of foreign tourists, notably Angkor Wat, can be relatively expensive. Many sights have free admission for Khmers or children.

B

Budgeting for Your Trip

Cambodia is the most expensive country in Indochina. The price difference between Cambodia and both Laos and Vietnam is partly due to Cambodia's reliance on the US dollar, and because so many products are imported. Also, the substantial numbers of foreign NGO workers living in Cambodia for the past two decades have contributed to inflation. Food and drink, transport, internet access, medications and supplies are more expensive here, but accommodation tends to be cheap.

C

Children

Phnom Penh and Angkor Wat have enough diversions and creature comforts to keep the young ones in a good mood, but more remote destinations are certain to be taxing. Cambodians love children, but sometimes express this affection by a firm pinch, which can be a surprise for the child not used to this cultural trait. The beach at Sihanoukville and the temples of Angkor present spectacular "playgrounds" for children, while Phnom Penh can be a bit problematic. Beware of wild monkeys at Angkor and Wat Phnom in Phnom Penh. They are often attracted to children and do bite – and can carry dangerous diseases. Better

Electricity

The electric system runs on a 220V AC circuit, and most outlets use two-prong flat or round sockets. It is a good idea to bring along a torch with you, as temporary power outages are quite common.

hotels normally have swimming pools. Monument Toys in Phnom Penh and Siem Reap carry toys. A large Lego retailer is located beside the Cambodia–Vietnam Friendship Monument in Phnom Penh.

Climate

Cambodia's climate is dictated by the annual monsoon cycle. Between May and October the southwest monsoon brings heavy rainfall, usually for a few hours in the late afternoon on most days. The northwest monsoon, between November and early March, brings somewhat cooler temperatures and lower rainfall. The coolest months are between November and January, and this is generally the optimum time to visit, though even then minimum night-time temperatures seldom fall below 20°C (68°F). March and April see rising temperatures – the latter, which can be furnace-like, is best avoided. The driest months are January and February, when there is little or no rainfall, and the wettest months are usually September and October.

What to Wear

Cambodia is hot all year round, so it is unnecessary to bring a lot of heavy clothes. Even in the cooler months, the temperature does not usually drop below 20°C (68°F) so a light jacket or wind-breaker for chilly early mornings and evenings should suffice. If visiting higher elevations such as Bokor hill station (near Kampot town), however, warmer clothing is necessary, especially if you are staying overnight on the hill. During the monsoon season things get pretty wet, so do remember to bring along some lightweight protection against the rain.

A strong pair of shoes is essential if you are visiting the temples at Angkor. A hat is also recommended when visiting Angkor: much of the site is exposed, and it is amazing how quickly you can feel debilitated without something covering your head.

When visiting temples and mosques, men and women should dress appropriately: no skimpy clothing. Knee-length shorts are just about acceptable, but running shorts are not. To visit one of Phnom Penh or Siem Reap's more exclusive restaurants you will require reasonably smart clothes. If you do forget anything you believe is essential you will almost certainly be able to pick it up in Phnom Penh at

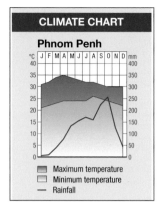

CLIMATE CHART

Phnom Penh

- Maximum temperature
- Minimum temperature
- Rainfall

one of the many very good markets, malls or shops.

Crime and Safety

Cambodia has become a lot safer for travellers in recent years. However, parts of Phnom Penh and Sihanoukville are a little risky after dark, and at any time of day basic precautions should be taken to avoid falling victim to the many pickpockets found in markets and tourist areas. Always use a money belt, lock valuables in your hotel safe, and don't flaunt electronics and jewellery. Most travellers – especially men – will be confronted by tuk-tuk and moto drivers selling drugs and prostitutes. Hard drugs are readily available, including cocaine, heroin and opium – and all very much illegal.

Cambodia has long received attention as a source for human trafficking and haven for paedophiles. Recent laws both in Cambodia and abroad are serving to deter these heinous crimes.

Sihanoukville is one of the few places in Cambodia to have a growing reputation for serious crime. Armed robbery is reported often, and there have been some cases of rape, all on the beach. It is not safe to visit empty sections of the beach alone, nor go to the beach after dark without several people to accompany you.

The threat from bandits is diminished but still relevant in remote parts of the country such as the northeast and southwest. Another danger is unexploded ordnance (UXO): do not stray off paths in remote areas of the country,

Beware of strangers offering free drinks in bars. Druggings and robberies, as well as overdose, have been reported. Likewise beware of

invitations from the Filipino mafia in tourist areas around Phnom Penh (particularly Sorya Shopping Centre and the river front). The mafia approach tourists and act out an elaborate scam in which they lure tourists to secluded locations and pressure them into rigged card games.

Customs

Travelling to and from the country is reasonably trouble-free. As elsewhere, weapons, explosives and narcotics are prohibited. Regulations otherwise are relaxed and simple formalities observed. Any amount of foreign currency can be brought into Cambodia, but the amount of Cambodian currency must not exceed 100,000 riel per person. It is illegal to take antiquities out of the country. The duty-free allowance for each visitor is one bottle of spirits, 200 cigarettes and a reasonable amount of perfume.

D

Disabled Travellers

Despite having so many disabled citizens, little is done in Cambodia to accommodate them. Fortunately most shops and restaurants have ground-floor entrances and seating. Some of the better hotels may have elevators and entry ramps, but budget accommodations rarely do.

E

Embassies and Consulates

Cambodian Embassies and Consulates Overseas

Australia and New Zealand
5 Canterbury Crescent, Deakin ACT 2600, Canberra
Tel: 026-273 5867
www.embassyofcambodia.org.nz/au.htm

South Africa
800 Duncan Street,
Hartfield, 0028 Pretoria
Tel: 27 12-362 4731

United Kingdom and Ireland
64 Brondesbury Park, London, NW6 7AT
Tel: 44 20-8451 7997
www.cambodianembassy.org.uk

United States
4530 16th Street, NW
20011 Washington DC

LAOS

CAMBODIA

Tel: 1 202-726 7742
www.embassyofcambodia.org

Foreign Embassies in Phnom Penh

Australia: 16B National Assembly Street
Tel: 023-213 470
www.cambodia.embassy.gov.au
United Kingdom: 27–29 Street 75
Tel: 023-427 124
http://ukincambodia.fco.gov.uk
United States: 1 Street 96
Tel: 023-728 000
http://cambodia.usembassy.gov

Etiquette

The traditional Cambodian greeting is the sampiah, with hands brought together in front of the face, as if to pray. The higher one raises one's hands and the lower one makes an accompanying bow, the more respect is shown.

Always smile and never lose your temper, otherwise you will lose face and embarrass those around you.

G

Gay and Lesbian Travellers

Cambodians are not hostile towards homosexuals, but any display of public affection, regardless of sexual orientation, is frowned upon. There is no gay "scene" as found in Thailand.

H

Health and Medical Care

Unfortunately Cambodia's health infrastructure is still rather rudimentary, so it is advisable to take all the necessary precautions for a safe trip before you arrive. Immunisation is recommended for cholera, typhoid, tetanus, hepatitis A and B, polio and tuberculosis.

Mosquitoes carrying malaria and dengue fever are widespread in the countryside, but as long as you are staying close to the tourist areas there should be no real problems. Nevertheless, it is advisable to bring along some good mosquito repellent for use on exposed skin

Emergencies

Police Tel: 117 or 023-924 484
Fire Tel: 118 or 023-786 693
Ambulance Tel: 119 or 023-724 891

at night. After dark it is advisable to wear long-sleeved shirts and long trousers.

Avoid drinking water offered to you that has not come directly from a bottle. Bottled water is widely available. Ice is also best avoided. When travelling around the country, and especially walking, carry your own water bottle. Apart from being guaranteed clean, it will also help prevent dehydration. Heat exhaustion, salt deficiency and dehydration cause more problems than anything else, so don't forget sun block and keep drinking liquids.

It is recommended that visitors arrange a comprehensive overseas travel sickness insurance before leaving, including transport home if necessary. If you were to have a major health problem or an accident, it would be wise to consider evacuation to Bangkok or Singapore, where emergency health facilities are better.

Medical Services

Good hospitals in Cambodia are few and far between, although there are decent pharmacies in Phnom Penh and Siem Reap, such as UCare (www.ucarepharma.com). Minor ailments can be treated effectively, but for anything major it would be best to go to Bangkok or Singapore.
Calmette Hospital
3 Monivong Boulevard, Phnom Penh
Tel: 023-426 948
www.calmette.gov.kh
The Calmette is the largest hospital in Phnom Penh and has some French staff.
IMI Dental Clinic
193 Street 208
Tel: 023-212 909
http://imiclinic.com
International SOS Medical and Dental Clinic
161 Street 51
Tel: 023-216 911
www.internationalsos.com
MW Medical Cambodia Clinic
Wimawari Hotel
313 Sisowath Quay, Office No. 3, Ground Floor, Phnom Penh
Hotline: 625 00 625
Sen Sok International University Hospital
91-96 Street 1986, Phnom Penh
Tel: 023-883 712
www.sensokiuh.com
Tropical and Travellers Medical Clinic
88 Street 108, Phnom Penh
Tel: 023-306 802
www.travellersmedicalclinic.com
The best pharmacy in Phnom Penh is the **Pharmacie de la Gare**, tel: 023-

430 205, near the railway station, recommended for all medicines.
U-Care, a pharmacy, is at the corner of Sothearos Boulevard and Street 178, tel: 023-222 499. For optical needs, go to **EyeCare**, 166 Norodom Boulevard, tel: 016-556 601, and five other branches in Phnom Penh.

I

Internet

There are now several internet providers in Cambodia, including most mobile phone service providers, such as Metfone, Cellcard, Mfone, Beeline and Smart. Most restaurants, bars and cafés now offer free Wi-fi, but the speeds are much slower than in neighbouring Vietnam. Internet access at internet cafés is relatively slow and more expensive than in surrounding countries. While internet cafés still exist, they are becoming hard to find as most have been converted to dingy internet gaming rooms for students and the computer terminals have questionable security. Instead bring a Wi-fi-compatible device and surf the web at one of the many conventional, air-conditioned cafés with menus.

M

Media

Newspapers and Magazines

There is a variety of English- and French-language publications available in Cambodia. The *Phnom Penh Post* (www.phnompenhpost.com) is a tabloid newspaper, printed daily, which sticks fairly solidly with events within the country. The *Cambodia Daily* (www.cambodiadaily.com) is available every day and will keep you up-to-date with world events, but in a rather limited format. The *Bangkok Post* and the *International Herald Tribune* are flown in daily from Thailand, and provide a far more comprehensive view of regional and world events.

There is a series of free monthly English-language magazines by *Canby Publications* (www.canbypublications.com) that contain thorough listings of most of the hotels, restaurants and all the local events that might interest a visitor. There are numerous expat magazines as well, of which *Asia Life: Phnom Penh* (www.asialifemagazine.com/

The Cambodian currency – the riel.

cambodia), like its Ho Chi Minh City version, is perhaps the best known.

The following shops sell English-language publications. Bohr's and D's sell second-hand books. D's also has as a lot of photocopies. Monument Books stores are the best (and perhaps only) source for new English-language books in Cambodia, Laos and Myanmar. As neighbouring Vietnam meticulously censors all publications, many expats come to Phnom Penh to buy books. Monument is also one of the only outlets for quality foreign toys.

Bohr's Books
5 Sotheros Boulevard, Phnom Penh
Also Street 172, Phnom Penh
Tel: 012-929 148
D's Books
79 Street 240, Phnom Penh
Also Street 178 Behind FCC, Phnom Penh
Tel: 012-726 355
Monument Books
111 Norodom Boulevard, Phnom Penh
Also Taprohm Hotel, Siem Reap
Tel: 023-223 622
www.monument-books.com/cambodia.php

Money

The Cambodian currency is called the riel, although the Cambodian economy is really based on the US dollar. Transactions of more than 4,000 riel usually involve American currency. Cambodian riel comes in denominations of 100,000, 50,000, 20,000, 10,000, 5,000, 2,000, 1,000, 500 and 100. The import and export of riel is prohibited.

At the time of writing, US$1 is approximately equivalent to 4,000 riel. For the sake of practicality, most locals are accustomed to rounding the rate down to 4,000 riel during transactions. It is a good idea to have plenty of small-denomination

US dollars, as they are far easier to change than larger notes. It is also useful to carry some small riel notes (500 and 1,000) for minor purchases. One way of collecting small change in riel is to buy small items, such as mineral water and canned drinks, at the local shops – using small US dollar notes. All major currencies can be changed at the airports in Phnom Penh and Siem Reap, and also at upmarket hotels, although the latter usually reserve the service for their guests.

Gold shops also act as money-changers (for cash exchange only) and are found around the markets in town. Their rates are better than the banks' and hotels'. Note that while damaged riel notes are acceptable to the locals, even the slightest tear in a large US note renders it unusable in Cambodia.

Travellers' Cheques and Credit Cards

Travellers' cheques have become easier to cash in well-touristed areas such as Phnom Penh, Siem Reap and Sihanoukville, but they remain difficult to change upcountry. Again, it is preferable to have US dollar cheques.

Credit cards have also become more widely accepted. Most good hotels, restaurants and boutiques will accept Visa, JCB, MasterCard and sometimes Amex. Cash advances on cards are possible in some banks in Phnom Penh, Siem Reap, Battambang and Sihanoukville. Most businesses charge a 3 percent fee for credit card usage. ATMs are widely available in Phnom Penh, Siem Reap and large towns.

Tipping

Tipping is not a traditional part of Khmer culture, but it is becoming expected in tourist venues, and with wages being so low it is certainly appreciated. If you feel you have been

well treated, a small token of your gratitude (suggested 10 percent) would not be out of place. Hotels and top restaurants will have already added a service charge to your bill.

Phnom Penh
Acleda Bank
28 Mao Tse Toung Boulevard
Tel: 023-214 634
www.acledabank.com.kh
ANZ Royal Bank
265 Sisowath Quay
Tel: 023-999 000
www.anzroyal.com
Cambodian Post Bank Plc.
265-269 Ang Doung Street
Tel: 023-226 888
wwww.cambodiapostbank.com
Cambodian Commercial Bank
26 Monivong Boulevard
Tel: 023-426 145
www.ccb.com.kh
Canadia Bank Plc.
315 Ang Doung Street
Tel: 023-868 222
www.canadiabank.com.kh
Ernst & Young Cambodia
64 Norodom Boulevard
Tel: 023-860 450
www.ey.com/kh
Foreign Trade Bank of Cambodia
33CD Street 169
Tel: 023-862 111
www.ftbbank.com
PricewaterhouseCoopers
58C Sihanouk Boulevard
Tel: 023-218 086
www.pwc.com/kh
Standard Chartered Bank
Unit G-02, Himawari Hotel Apartments, PO Box 46
Tel: 023-216 685
www.sc.com/kh
Union Commercial Bank Ltd
UCB Building, 61 Street 130
Tel: 023-427 995
www.ucb.com.kh

Sihanoukville
Canadia Bank Plc.
197 Independent Boulevard
Tel: 034-933 490
www.canadiabank.com.kh
Union Commercial Bank Ltd
195 Ekareach Street
Tel: 034-933 833
www.ucb.com.kh

O

Opening Hours

Banks are normally open Monday to Friday 8.30am–3.30pm and sometimes Saturday mornings. Government offices and official bodies

LAOS

CAMBODIA

open Monday to Saturday 7.30–11.30am and 2–5.30pm. Post offices open Monday to Saturday 7am–7pm. Banks, administrative offices and museums are closed on all public holidays and occasionally on religious festivals. Shops and supermarkets are usually open for longer hours. However, Cambodians tend to go home early. It's always safest to assume shops and offices (even very busy ones) will close 30 minutes to 1 hour earlier than posted.

P

Photography

Most shops provide digital camera-to-CD and print services. Memory cards or sticks are also widely available and very cheap. Print, slide and video film are increasingly difficult to find in Phnom Penh and Siem Reap.

Cambodians, on the whole, do not mind being photographed, although it is always advisable to ask first. Show restraint when photographing people at prayer, and monks. Also, be careful when photographing soldiers or anything military. Government, police and military buildings generally should not be photographed.

Postal Services

The postal service, like many other services, has improved over the last few years, though it is still not entirely reliable. Mail is forwarded via Bangkok and therefore arrives much more quickly than ever before. Costs are very reasonable: a 10g airmail letter costs between 2,000 and 6,000 riel. Postcards are anything from 2,000 to 4,000 riel to anywhere in the world.

Ministry of Posts and Telecommunication
East of Wat Phnom on Street 13, Phnom Penh
Tel: 023-426 832

Courier Services

A number of international courier agencies offer their services in Phnom Penh:
DHL Express Cambodia
Plot 174-175, Russian Boulevard
Tel: 023-970 999
www.dhl.com.kh
TSP EXPRESS (Cambodia) Co. (FedEx)
71 Street 242
Tel: 023-216 708
www.fedex.com/kh

Public Toilets

Western sit-down toilets are a standard feature in hotels, restaurants and most other venues frequented by tourists. They will have toilet paper most of the time – if not, ask the staff.

What few public toilets exist are often dirty "squatty potties", and will always charge a small fee (usually 1,000 riel or less). Toilet paper will cost extra.

R

Religious Services

Christian
International Christian Assembly
37M Street 16
Tel: 092-987 714
www.ica-cambodia.org
Catholic Church – Residence of the Bishop
787 Monivong Boulevard
Email: apostolicvicariate.phnompenh@gmail.com

Buddhist
Buddhist Institute
Sisowath Quay
Tel: 023-212 046

T

Telephones

Telephone costs in Cambodia are high – international calls vary between US\$1.60 and \$3 per minute, domestic calls between 300 riel and 700 riel per minute. Telephone booths are installed around Phnom Penh and other major tourist destinations. Many of these booths take phone cards, and it is possible to telephone most countries directly. Cards for US\$5, \$20 and \$50 can be purchased at post offices and many good hotels. To call abroad from Cambodia, dial the international access code 001 (or 007 from mobiles for a cheaper rate), followed by the country code, area code and telephone number. Mobile phone numbers begin with 01 or 09.

Mobile Phones
If you wish your mobile to function with the same number while you are in Cambodia, this is possible, although depending on your provider's system, you may be charged a very high rate to receive calls from callers who do not know you are abroad.

Public Holidays

There are numerous official public Cambodian holidays, but keep in mind that many things will also close for major festivals and internationally celebrated holidays like Christmas.
1 January International New Year's Day
7 January Victory Over the Genocide
8 March International Women's Day
13–16 April Khmer New Year
1 May International Workers' Day
8 May International Children's Day
13–15 May The King's Birthday
18 June The Queen Mother's Birthday
24 September Constitution Day
29 October Coronation Day
31 October The King Father's Birthday
9 November Independence Day
10 December International Human Rights Day

Alternatively, purchase a local SIM card to install in the telephone. Metfone, Cellcard, Mfone, Beeline and Smart are four of the most popular mobile phone service providers based in Cambodia. Coverage is good in Phnom Penh, reasonable in Siem Reap, Battambang, Sihanoukville and Kampong Cham, but out in the countryside it is often nonexistent. Most offer 3G internet service plans as well. It is much cheaper and more convenient to pre-pay using phone cards, which are available at branded shops and kerbside vendors.

Another solution is to rent a mobile phone locally and use the local number assigned to the handset. Mobile telephones are offered for rent at the airport. Countless shops selling new and inexpensive used phones are in every town.

Telephone Area Codes by Province
Banteay Meanchey 54
Battambang 53
Kampot 33
Kandal 24
Kep 36
Koh Kong 35
Kompong Cham 42
Kompong Chhnang 26
Kompong Speu 25
Kompong Thom 62
Kratie 72
Mondolkiri 73
Oddar Meanchey 65
Phnom Penh 23
Preah Vihear 64
Prey Veng 43
Pursat 52

Rattanakiri 75
Siem Reap 63
Sihanoukville (Kompong Som) 34
Stung Treng 74
Svay Rieng 44
Takeo 32
Note: When dialling to a different area code within Cambodia or to a mobile telephone, dial 0 before the area code.

Tourist Information

Cambodia's tourist office is at 262 Monivong Boulevard in Phnom Penh. Tel: 023-218 585; info@ tourismcambodia.com; www.tourism cambodia.com

Websites

Tourism of Cambodia: www. tourismcambodia.com. The official website for information on visiting Cambodia.
General Information on Cambodia: With a comprehensive business directory. www.gocambodia.com
The Phnom Penh Post: The latest English-language news on events inside the country. www.phnompenhpost.com
Beauty and Darkness: Cambodia in Modern History: Documents, essays, oral histories and photos relating to the recent history of Cambodia, with an emphasis on the Khmer Rouge period. www.mekong.net
Extraordinary Chambers in the Courts of Cambodia: a UN-backed court website prosecuting five of the top Khmer Rouge leaders. www.eccc.gov.kh

Sex Tourism

Cambodia has garnered an unfortunate reputation as a destination for sex tourists, particularly those who exploit young children. The Cambodian government and foreign NGOs like the ChildSafe Movement (www.thinkchildsafe.org) have initiated a campaign to end these activities, and several foreign paedophiles are serving sentences in Cambodian prisons. Recently volunteerism which includes brief visits or stints "helping out" in local orphanages has come under fire for putting children at risk in the presence of strangers. Numerous fake orphanages have sprung up across the countries seeking to profit from well-meaning tourists and exploit street children in the process.

Time Zone

Cambodia is 7 hours ahead of Greenwich Mean Time (GMT).

Specialist books on Cambodia: White Lotus Press based in Bangkok carries new and out-of-print books about Cambodia. www.whitelotuspress.com
Cambodian Genocide Programme: A regularly updated site on the political and criminal history of the Khmer Rouge in Democratic Kampuchea and afterwards. www.yale.edu/cgp
Andy Brouwer's Cambodia Tales: This site is by Andy Brouwer, a very keen Cambodia enthusiast. Personal experiences with interviews and the latest news. www.andybrouwer.co.uk
LTO Cambodia: The blog of a long-time expat living in Phnom Penh. ltocambodia.blogspot.com
Fish Egg Tree: an author's blog, highlighting adventures and current events in Vietnam and Cambodia. www.fisheggtree.blogspot.com
Canby Publications Cambodia Guides: The online edition of the city guides for Phnom Penh, Siem Reap, Sihanoukville and the rest of Cambodia. www.canbypublications.com
Bayon Pearnik: A free monthly tourist magazine. www.bayonpearnik.com
Maurice Glaize's Guide to Angkor: Glaize's definitive 1944 guide in English. www.theangkorguide.com
Apsara Authority: website of the authority responsible for the conservation of Angkor Wat and other heritage sites in Siem Reap. www.apsaraauthority.gov.kh
Travelfish: a comprehensive and up-to-date guide on travel in Cambodia and Southeast Asia. www.travelfish.org/country/cambodia
Khmer440: The expat guide to Cambodia with the inside scoop, and a notoriously edgy forum. www.khmer440.com
ThingsAsian: Publishers of the popular To Asia with Love series, the site features submitted stories about Cambodia from both widely published authors and amateurs. www.thingsasianpress.com
Bong Thom: an English-Khmer audio phrasebook with hundreds of free mp3 downloads. www.bongthom.com/ akonline

Travel Agencies

Phnom Penh

5 Oceans
139E0 Street 136

Tel: 023-221 537
Email: 5oceans@online.com.kh
www.5oceanscambodia.com
Apsara Tours
8 Street 254
Tel: 023-216 562/212 019
Email: apsaratours@online.com.kh
www.apsaratours.com.kh
Asian Trails
22 Street 294
Tel: 023-216 555
Email: res@asiantrails.com.kh
www.asiantrails.travel
Diethelm Travel
65 Street 240
Tel: 023-219 151
Email: dt cambodia@kh.diethelmtravel.com
www.diethelmtravel.com
East-West Travel (Cambodia) Ltd
16bis Street 57
Tel: 023-216 065
Email: info@eastwest-travel.com
www.eastwest-travel.com
Eurasie Travel
AC04 Street 55
Tel: 023-426 456
Email: sales@eurasietravel.com.kh
www.eurasietravel.com.kh
KK International Travel & Tours Co.
203E Street 13
Tel: 023-724 349
Email: info@kktravel.com.kh
www.kktravel.com.kh
K.U. Travel & Tours
77 Street 240
Tel: 023-723 456
Email: info@kucambodia.com
www.kucambodia.com
Plus Holiday. Travel
333B Monivong Blvd
Tel: 023-219 161
Email: customerservice@plusholiday.travel
www.plusholiday.travel

Siem Reap

AAA Travel & Tours
Tel: 063-967 001
Email: sale@angkorasiaadventures.com
www.angkorasiaadventures.com
Angkor Destination Travel
629 Phum Mondul I
Tel: 063-767 868
www.angkordestination.com
Apsara Tours
Thnal Village
Tel: 063-380 198
Email: apsaratours@online.com.kh
www.apsaratours.com.kh
Diethelm Travel
121 National Road 6
Tel: 063-963 524
dt cambodia@kh.diethelmtravel.com
www.diethelmtravel.com
Eurasie Travel
28 National Road 6
Tel: 063-963 449

LAOS

CAMBODIA

Email: info@eurasietravel.com.kh
www.eurasietravel.com.kh

V

Visas and Passports

Your passport should be valid for at least 6 months. An entry visa is also required for citizens of all countries except Malaysia, the Philippines, Singapore, Vietnam and Laos. Single-entry Cambodian tourist visas, valid for 30 days, are issued on arrival at Phnom Penh International Airport and Siem Reap-Angkor International Airport. Cambodian visas are also issued at nine Cambodia–Vietnam border checkpoints including Bavet and Kham Sam Nor, at eight Cambodia–Thailand border checkpoints including Cham Yeam/Koh Kong, Poipet/Banteay Meanchey and O'Smach/Ordor Meanchey and two Cambodia–Laos border crossings including Veun Kham/Dom Kralor.

As visa requirements change from time to time, check the situation with your consulate or a reliable travel agent, or look up the Cambodian Immigration Department website (www.immigration.gov.kh) before you travel. You will need one passport-size photograph (10.2 x 15.2cm, or 4 x 6 inches) and US$30 in cash for the visa (US$5 extra if you enter by land and your bus driver processes it, sparing you the line through customs and immigration).

A backstreet pharmacy in Phnom Penh.

Visas can also be obtained through the Cambodian Embassy or Consulate in your own country. A list of embassies located outside of Cambodia can be found at www.embassyofcambodia.org/other_embassies.html

To apply for an e-visa online, simply access the Ministry of Foreign Affairs and International Cooperation website at www.evisa.gov.kh. You will need to have your passport and credit card information ready, as well as a recent passport-size digital photograph. The e-visa will be sent to the email address you have provided. In addition to the usual visa fee, there is an extra processing charge of US$7. At present, e-visas are available for entry to Cambodia via Phnom Penh International Airport, Siem Reap International Airport and three border crossings with Thailand, and departure from the country via all points. Only tourist visas can be applied for online at the time of writing. For e-visa related questions, visit the website or email: cambodiaevisa@evisa.gov.kh.

Extension of Stay

Tourist visas can be extended only once at the Department for Foreigners (Mon–Fri 8–11am and 2–4pm; tel: 012-581 558; email: visa.info@immigration.gov.kh). The office is located on Pochentong Road (332 Confédération de Russie) opposite Phnom Penh International Airport. A 30-day extension costs

Cambodia uses the metric system. Items in the market are sold by the kilogram. Petrol is sold by the litre. Hours are counted from 1–24.

US$45 (28-day service). Some guesthouses and travel agencies in Phnom Penh (try Lucky!Lucky! at 413Eo Monivong Boulevard) will also handle visa extensions for a nominal fee – a far more convenient option. "Ordinary" (former business) visas (US$35 for the first month) can be extended indefinitely through guesthouses and travel agencies. Overstaying your visa will set you back by US$6 per day.

W

Women Travellers

Women are unlikely to experience any unwelcome advances from Khmer men, but the usual common-sense caveats regarding conservative dress apply. Cambodian men are polite and respectful by nature, but excessive consumption of alcohol can obscure this, so pay attention in discos and the like. More serious is the danger of late-night muggings; women travelling alone are likely to be seen as an easy target, particularly in Sihanoukville and Phnom Penh. Only the foolhardy would resist an armed demand for money of this nature.

LANGUAGE

UNDERSTANDING THE LANGUAGE

THE KHMER LANGUAGE

The Khmer language, also called Cambodian, is a Mon-Khmer language spoken by most of the people of Cambodia, as well as in parts of northeastern Thailand and southern Vietnam. Khmer belongs to the Austroasiatic group of languages, which is widely spread throughout mainland Southeast Asia. Other languages in this group, which is generally considered to have been one of the earliest in the region, include Mon, Vietnamese and Wa. Cambodian is a non-tonal language that has borrowed heavily from Sanskrit, Pali, Thai, Chinese and Vietnamese. It has been written since at least the 7th century AD, using a script derived from India. It is widely accepted that Thai script was derived from Khmer in the 12th century.

Because of the difficulty of learning Cambodian script, short-time visitors to the country are unlikely to achieve any great fluency in Khmer – though the lack of tones makes it easier for Westerners than, say, Vietnamese or Thai. It is relatively easy to acquire some basic vocabulary, however, and any such effort will be greatly appreciated by the Cambodians. English is rapidly becoming the second language, especially in Phnom Penh, Siem Reap and Kompong Som. Older people, particularly among the elite, may speak French. Some members of the Sino-Cambodian community speak Guoyu, or Mandarin Chinese. Thai is widely understood in Battambang and the west of the country; similarly Vietnamese is widely understood in the east of the country. Cham, the language of Cambodia's Muslims, is an Austronesian language related to Malay – but virtually all Cambodia's Chams are fluent in Khmer.

Language School

Offering Khmer language classes:
Khmer School of Language
52G Street 454, Phnom Penh
Tel: 23-213 047
www.kslkhmerlanguage.com

GENERAL

what *ey*
who *niak nah*
when *bpehl*
where *eah nah*
why *haeht ey*
What is this? *nih ch'muah ey?*
Does anyone speak English? *tii nih mian niak jeh piasah ohngkleh teh?*
I don't understand *k'nyom men yooul teh*

GREETINGS

Hello *jumreap sooa*

Shopping and Restaurants

How much is...? *t'lay pohnmaan...?*
money *loey*
change *dow*
cheap *towk*
expensive *t'lay*
market *p'sah*
bank *tho neea kear*
restaurant *haang bai*
eat *bpisah*
I want a ... *k'nyom jang baan ...*
drinking water *dteuk soht*
ice *dteuk kok*

How are you? *tau neak sok sapbaiy jea the?*
I'm fine *k'nyom sok sapbaiy*
Good morning *arun suor sdei*
Good afternoon *tiveah suor sdei*
Good evening *sayoanh suor sdei*
Goodnight *reahtrey suor sdei*
My name is... *k'nyom tch muoh...*
What is your name? *lok tch muoh ey?*
Yes *baat*
No *dteh*
Please *sohm mehta*
Thank you *orgoon*
Excuse me *sohm dtoh*
Goodbye *leah suhn heuy*
Where are you from? *niak mao pi patet nah?*
I come from... *k'nyom mao pi...*

DIRECTIONS/ TRANSPORT

Where is...? *noev eah nah...?*
toilet *bawngkohn*
hotel *sohnthakia*
hospital *mon dtee bpeth*
police station *s'thaanii bpohlis*
turn left *bawt ch'weng*
turn right *bawt s'dum*

tea *dtae*
coffee *kahfeh*
milk *dteuk daco*
sugar *sko*
rice *bai*
fish *dt'ray*
beef *saich koh*
pork *saich jruk*
chicken *moan*
plate *jahndtiap*
glass *kaehu*
beer *bia*

Heed the warning signs in Cambodia.

go straight on *teuv trawng*
car *laan*
bus *laan ch'noul*
bus station *kuhnlaing laan ch'noul*
boat *dtook*
train *roht plerng*
aeroplane *yohn hawh*
bicycle *kohng*
cyclo *see kloa*
post office *bprai sa nee*
embassy *s'thaantuut*

DAYS AND TIME

today *t'ngai nih*
tomorrow *t'ngai saaik*
yesterday *m'serl menh*
morning *bpreuk*
afternoon *r'sial*
evening *l'ngiat*
month *khaeh*
year *ch'nam*
last year *ch'nam moon*
new year *ch'nam thmey*

next year *ch'nam groy*
Sunday *t'ngai aadteut*
Monday *t'ngai jan*
Tuesday *t'ngai onggeea*
Wednesday *t'ngai bpoot*
Thursday *t'ngai bprahoaa*
Friday *t'ngai sok*
Saturday *t'ngai sao*
January *ma ga raa*
February *kompheak*
March *mee nah*
April *meh sah*
May *oo sa phea*
June *mi thok nah*
July *ka kada*
August *say haa*
September *kan'ya*
October *dto laa*
November *wech a gaa*
December *t'noo*

NUMBERS

one *moo ay*

two *bpee*
three *bey*
four *buon*
five *bpram*
six *bpram moo ay*
seven *bpram bpee*
eight *bpram bey*
nine *bpram buon*
ten *dahp*
eleven *dahp moo ay*
twelve *dahp bpee*
sixteen *dahp bpram moo ay*
twenty *m'phey*
twenty-one *m'phey moo ay*
thirty *saam seup*
forty *seah seup*
fifty *haa seup*
sixty *hok seup*
seventy *jeht seup*
eighty *bpait seup*
ninety *gao seup*
hundred *mooay roy*
thousand *mooay bpoan*
ten thousand *mooay meun*
one million *mooay leeun*

FURTHER READING

GENERAL INTEREST

The Land and People of Cambodia by David P. Chandler (1991). An excellent introduction to Cambodia by the foremost expert.
The Making of Southeast Asia by G. Coedes (London: 1966). A seminal account of the development of Indian cultural influence in Cambodia and elsewhere in Southeast Asia.
Swimming to Cambodia by Spalding Gray (1988). Strange, humorous and sometimes moving monologue by an actor and writer involved in the making of the film *The Killing Fields*.
Phnom Penh Then and Now by Michel Igout (1993). As the name implies, photographic record of the Cambodian capital before and after Democratic Kampuchea.
Eternal Phnom Penh by R. Werly and T. Renaut (Hong Kong: Editions d'Indochine, 1995). Well illustrated, with introduction by Jean Lacouture.

PRE-ANGKOR AND ANGKOR HISTORY

Reporting Angkor: Chou Ta-Kuan in Cambodia 1296–97 by Robert Philpotts (1996). The account of the celebrated 13th-century Chinese ambassador seen through contemporary eyes.
The Customs of Cambodia by Chou Ta-kuan (Zhou Daguan) (Bangkok: The Siam Society, 1987). A must – beautifully illustrated with photographs of contemporary scenes from the Bayon as well as 19th-century French engravings.
Society, Economics and Politics in Pre-Angkor Cambodia by Michael Vickery (Tokyo: Toyo Bunko, 1998). The definitive study of the period.

POST-ANGKOR AND COLONIAL PERIOD

Facing the Cambodian Past by David P. Chandler (Chiang Mai: Silkworm Books, 1996). Invaluable collection of essays and articles covering a period of Cambodian history which is usually ignored.
A History of Cambodia by David P. Chandler (Chiang Mai: Silkworm Books, 1998). The best introduction to Cambodian history available.
Travels in Siam: Cambodia and Laos 1858–60 by Henri Mouhot (1986). Fascinating 19th-century account by the Frenchman who "discovered" Angkor before going on to die tragically at Luang Prabang in Laos.
Cambodia After Angkor: The Chronicular Evidence for the 14th to 16th Centuries by Michael Vickery (Michigan: 1977). Serious study for the specialist.

INDEPENDENCE AND THE VIETNAM WAR

Politics and Power in Cambodia: The Sihanouk Years by Milton Osborne (1973). Perceptive account of the mercurial King Sihanouk's role in the making and breaking of independent Cambodia.
Sideshow: Kissinger, Nixon and the Destruction of Cambodia by William Shawcross (London: André Deutsch, 1979). Seminal – cannot really be beaten. This book deeply infuriated Kissinger.
River of Time by Jon Swain (London: William Heinemann, 1996). Magical account of this foreign correspondent's love affair with Vietnam and Cambodia. He was one of the journalists menaced by the victorious Khmer Rouge when they entered Phnom Penh – a chilling scene represented in the film *The Killing Fields* which, once seen, can never be forgotten.

THE KHMER ROUGE YEARS

When the War Was Over: The Voices of Cambodia's Revolution and Its People by Elizabeth Becker (New York: Simon and Schuster, 1986). Becker was one of only three Westerners in Phnom Penh as the Vietnamese invasion of Democratic Kampuchea began. Contains memorable accounts of her interview with Pol Pot and of the murder of Scottish academic Malcolm Caldwell by unknown assassins.
Brother Enemy: The War after the War, a History of Indochina since the Fall of Saigon by Nayan Chanda (New York: Collier Books, 1986). The best book written about the Third Indochina War by the experienced and knowledgeable editor of *Far Eastern Economic Review*.
Pol Pot Plans the Future: Confidential Leadership Documents from Democratic Kampuchea, 1976–1977 by David P. Chandler, Ben Kiernan and Chanthou Boua (New Haven: Yale University Southeast Asia Studies, 1988). An amazing book – check out the extraordinary Khmer Rouge "plans" to develop tourism ("must build hotels"), and the records of its illicit trade in endangered wildlife.
Brother Number One: A Political Biography of Pol Pot by David P. Chandler (Chiang Mai: Silkworm Books, 1992). Comprehensive biography of the Khmer Rouge leader.
The Rise and Demise of Democratic Kampuchea by Craig Etcheson (Boulder: Westview Press, 1984). Excellent, balanced account.
Genocide and Democracy in Cambodia: The Khmer Rouge, the UN and the International Community edited by Ben Kiernan (1993). Probably the best book on the DK regime.
Cambodia: Year Zero by F. Ponchaud (New York: Holt, Rinehart and Winston, 1978). By the French priest who first opened the world's eyes to the hideous excesses of the Khmer Rouge regime.

PERSONAL ACCOUNTS

A Cambodian Prison Portrait: One Year in the Khmer Rouge's S-21 by Vann Nath (Bangkok: White Lotus, 1998). The author was one of the

LAOS

CAMBODIA

very few prisoners who survived incarceration in Tuol Sleng – saved because he was an artist who could paint and sculpt busts of Pol Pot.
Children of Cambodia's Killing Fields: Memoirs by Survivors by Dith Pran (1997).
The Death and Life of Dith Pran by Sydney Schanberg (1985). The basis for the film *The Killing Fields*.
Voices from S-21: Terror and History in Pol Pot's Secret Prison by David P. Chandler (2000). Accounts from the horrific prison of Tuol Sleng.

THE VIETNAMESE PERIOD AND UNTAC

The China–Cambodia–Vietnam Triangle by Wilfred Burchett (1981). Political analysis by a veteran Australian Communist.
War of the Mines: Cambodia, Landmines and the Impoverishment of a Nation by Paul Davies and Nic Dunlop (1994). Excellent black-and-white photography.
Heroes by John Pilger (1986).
The Quality of Mercy: Cambodia, Holocaust and Modern Conscience by William Shawcross (André Deutsch, 1984). Critically examines collusion between the defeated Khmer Rouge, China and the West at the expense of Cambodia (and Vietnam).
War and Hope: The Case for Cambodia by Norodom Sihanouk (1980).

CONTEMPORARY CAMBODIA

The Tragedy of Cambodian History by David P. Chandler (Chiang Mai: Silkworm Books, 1994). A perceptive and highly readable history seen from the perspective of the late 20th century.
Off the Rails in Phnom Penh: Into the Dark Heart of Guns, Girls and Ganja by Amit Gilboa (Bangkok: Asia Books, 1998). The title says it all – but there is more to Phnom Penh than brothels and marijuana.
Sihanouk: Prince of Light, Prince of Darkness by Milton Osborne (Chiang Mai: Silkworm Books, 1994). A dark portrait of the ruler.

MINORITIES AND RELIGION

Islam in Kampuchea (Phnom Penh: NCUFK, 1987). Cambodia's Cham

Muslim minority suffered horribly under the Democratic Kampuchean regime, as this book makes clear.

PEOPLE AND SOCIETY

The Warrior Heritage: A Psychological Perspective of Cambodian Trauma by Seanglim Bit (El Cerrito: Seanglim Bit, 1991). A fascinating interpretation of the various cultural and historical factors making up the Cambodian psyche from a Khmer scholar.
Cambodian Culture since 1975: Homeland and Exile edited by May Ebihara, Carol Mortland and Judy Ledgerwood (1994). Useful for its insights into overseas Cambodian communities.

ARTS AND CULTURE

Angkor: An Introduction by G. Coedes (1963). Essential reading – insightful, informed and readable.
Angkor Cities and Temples by Claude Jacques and Michael Freeman (1998). Large-format picture book of great beauty and detail.

Send Us Your Thoughts

We do our best to ensure the information in our books is as accurate and up-to-date as possible. The books are updated on a regular basis using local contacts, who painstakingly add, amend and correct as required. However, some details (such as telephone numbers and opening times) are liable to change, and we are ultimately reliant on our readers to put us in the picture.
We welcome your feedback, especially your experience of using the book "on the road". Maybe we recommended a hotel that you liked (or another that you didn't), or you came across a great bar or new attraction we missed.
We will acknowledge all contributions, and we'll offer an Insight Guide to the best letters received.

Please write to us at:
Insight Guides
PO Box 7910
London SE1 1WE
Or email us at:
hello@insightguides.com

The Royal Palace of Phnom Penh and Cambodian Royal Life by Julio A. Jeldres (1999). The author is a long-time friend and confidant of King Sihanouk, and so well placed to write this book.

KHMER CULTURE ABROAD

Khmer Heritage in Thailand by Etienne Aymonier (1999).
Northeast Thailand from Prehistoric to Modern Times by Peter Rogers (Bangkok: DK Books, 1996). Information on the Suai or ethnic Khmers of the Thai provinces of Surin, Buriram and Sisaket.

TRAVEL

A Dragon Apparent: Travels in Cambodia, Laos and Vietnam by Norman Lewis (London: Eland, 1982). Classic travel writing.
A Pilgrimage to Angkor by Pierre Loti (Chiang Mai: Silkworm, 1996). Reprint of the 19th-century classic.
Derailed in Uncle Ho's Victory Garden by Tim Page (1995). Return to Vietnam and Cambodia by the renowned British war photographer, now recording his impressions of Indochina at peace.

FILMOGRAPHY

Apocalypse Now (1979). Director: Francis Ford Coppola. Starring: Marlon Brando, Martin Sheen, Robert Duvall. Based on the novel *Heart of Darkness* by Joseph Conrad. During the Vietnam War, Captain Willard (Martin Sheen) is sent upriver into Cambodia with orders to find and kill Colonel Kurtz (Marlon Brando). Before reaching Kurtz, Willard embarks on an odyssey of epic and surreal proportions. There are many memorable scenes, not least the helicopter attack on a Vietnamese village to the accompaniment of Wagner's *Ride of the Valkyries*.
The Killing Fields (1984). Director: Roland Joffe. A *New York Times* journalist and his Cambodian assistant are caught up in the Khmer Rouge revolution of 1975. The film portrays the horrors of the Khmer Rouge period with Dith Pran, played by Haing Ngor, trying to escape the country.

CREDITS

Insight Guide Credits

Distribution
UK, Ireland and Europe
Apa Publications (UK) Ltd;
sales@insightguides.com
United States and Canada
Ingram Publisher Services;
ips@ingramcontent.com
Australia and New Zealand
Woodslane; info@woodslane.com.au
Southeast Asia
Apa Publications (SN) Pte;
singaporeoffice@insightguides.com
Hong Kong, Taiwan and China
Apa Publications (HK) Ltd;
hongkongoffice@insightguides.com
Worldwide
Apa Publications (UK) Ltd;
sales@insightguides.com
**Special Sales, Content Licensing
and CoPublishing**
Insight Guides can be purchased in
bulk quantities at discounted prices.
We can create special editions,
personalised jackets and corporate
imprints tailored to your needs.
sales@insightguides.com
www.insightguides.biz

Printed in China by CTPS

All Rights Reserved
© 2017 Apa Digital (CH) AG and
Apa Publications (UK) Ltd

First Edition 2000
Fourth Edition 2017

www.insightguides.com

Editor: Tom Fleming
Author: Andrew Forbes
Head of Production: Rebeka Davies
Update Production: AM Services
Picture Editor: Tom Smyth
Cartography: original cartography
Cosmographics, updated by Carte

Contributors

This fully revised and updated edition
was managed and edited by Tom
Fleming at Insight Guides' London
office, and updated by Magdalena
Helsztyńska-Stadnik.
    This new incarnation of Insight
Guide Laos & Cambodia builds on the
content of earlier editions, largely
written by Andrew Forbes. Other major
contributors include David Henley.
Peter Holmshaw, Brett Dakin and
Simon Robson.
    Andrew Forbes has been based in

Chiang Mai for more than twenty
years, where he runs the CPA Media
agency and has been involved in
Southeast Asian studies for over a
quarter of a century.
    Bringing both countries to life was
the principal photographer, Peter
Stuckings, who calls Ho Chi Minh City
his home and spends most of his time
exploring the Indochina region with his
trusty camera and motorbike.
    The book was proofread by Jan
McCann and indexed by Penny Phenix.

About Insight Guides

Insight Guides have more than
45 years' experience of publishing
high-quality, visual travel guides. We
produce 400 full-colour titles, in both
print and digital form, covering more
than 200 destinations across the
globe, in a variety of formats to meet
your different needs.
    Insight Guides are written by
local authors who use their on-the-
ground experience to provide the

very latest information; their local
expertise is evident in the extensive
historical and cultural background
features. All the reviews in **Insight
Guides** are independent; we strive
to maintain an impartial view. Our
reviews are carefully selected to
guide you to the best places to eat,
go out and shop, so you can be
confident that when we say a place
is special, we really mean it.

Legend

City maps

	Freeway/Highway/Motorway
	Divided Highway
	Main Roads
	Minor Roads
	Pedestrian Roads
	Steps
	Footpath
	Railway
	Funicular Railway
	Cable Car
	Tunnel
	City Wall
	Important Building
	Built Up Area
	Other Land
	Transport Hub
	Park
	Pedestrian Area
🚌	Bus Station
ℹ	Tourist Information
✉	Main Post Office
✚	Cathedral/Church
☾	Mosque
✡	Synagogue
⚥	Statue/Monument
⚑	Beach
✈	Airport

Regional maps

	Freeway/Highway/Motorway (with junction)
	Freeway/Highway/Motorway (under construction)
	Divided Highway
	Main Road
	Secondary Road
	Minor Road
	Track
	Footpath
	International Boundary
	State/Province Boundary
	National Park/Reserve
	Marine Park
	Ferry Route
	Marshland/Swamp
	Glacier Salt Lake
✈ ✈	Airport/Airfield
∴	Ancient Site
⊖	Border Control
	Cable Car
	Castle/Castle Ruins
⋒	Cave
⌂	Chateau/Stately Home
† ✝	Church/Church Ruins
⌁	Crater
⸙	Lighthouse
▲	Mountain Peak
★	Place of Interest
※	Viewpoint

INDEX

Main references are in bold type

INSIGHT ● GUIDES

OFF THE SHELF

Since 1970, INSIGHT GUIDES has provided a unique perspective on the world's best travel destinations by using specially commissioned photography and illuminating text written by local authors.

Whether you're planning a city break, a walking tour or the journey of a lifetime, our superb range of guidebooks and phrasebooks will inspire you to discover more about your chosen destination.

INSIGHT GUIDES

offer a unique combination of stunning photos, absorbing narrative and detailed maps, providing all the inspiration and information you need.

PHRASEBOOKS & DICTIONARIES

help users to feel at home, when away. Pocket-sized with a free app to download, they go where you do.

CITY GUIDES

pack hundreds of great photos into a smaller format with detailed practical information, so you can navigate the world's top cities with confidence.

EXPLORE GUIDES

feature easy-to-follow walks and itineraries in the world's most exciting destinations, with our choice of the best places to eat and drink along the way.

POCKET GUIDES

combine concise information on where to go and what to do in a handy compact format, ideal on the ground. Includes a full-colour, fold-out map.

EXPERIENCE GUIDES

feature offbeat perspectives and secret gems for experienced travellers, with a collection of over 100 ideas for a memorable stay in a city.

www.insightguides.com

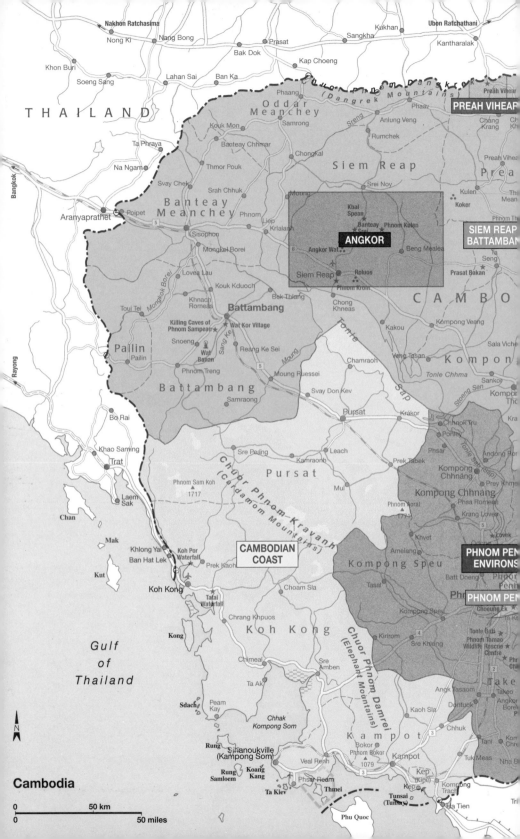